IMPORTANT

HERE IS YOUR REGISTRATION CODE TO ACCESS MCGRAW-HILL
PREMIUM CONTENT AND MCGRAW-HILL ONLINE RESOURCES

For key premium online resources you need THIS CODE to
gain access. Once the code is entered, you will be able to
use the web resources for the length of your course.

Access is provided only if you have purchased a new book.

If the registration code is missing from this book, the registration
screen on our website, and within your WebCT or Blackboard course
will tell you how to obtain your new code. Your registration code can
be used only once to establish access. It is not transferable.

To gain access to these online resources

1. **USE** your web browser to go to: **www.mhhe.com/palmer10**

2. **CLICK** on "First Time User"

3. **ENTER** the Registration Code printed on the tear-off bookmark on the right

4. After you have entered your registration code, click on "Register"

5. **FOLLOW** the instructions to setup your personal UserID and Password

6. **WRITE** your UserID and Password down for future reference. Keep it in a safe place.

If your course is using WebCT or Blackboard, you'll be able to use this code to
access the McGraw-Hill content within your instructor's online course.

To gain access to the McGraw-Hill content in your instructor's WebCT or
Blackboard course simply log into the course with the user ID and Password
provided by your instructor. Enter the registration code exactly as it appears to
the right when prompted by the system. You will only need to use this code the
first time you click on McGraw-Hill content.

These instructions are specifically for student access. Instructors are not
required to register via the above instructions.

The McGraw-Hill Companies

 Higher Education

Thank you, and welcome to your
McGraw-Hill Online Resources.

ISBN 13: 978-0-07-325090-8
ISBN 10: 0-07-325090-2 T/A A HISTORY OF THE MODERN WORLD

34FB–EQHB–AFUX–KGD7–KXMW

REGISTRATION CODE
REGISTRATION CODE

The McGraw-Hill Companies

Mc Graw Hill **Higher Education**

A HISTORY OF THE MODERN WORLD

TENTH EDITION

A HISTORY OF THE
MODERN WORLD

 R.R. Palmer   Joel Colton   Lloyd Kramer

McGraw
Hill

Boston   Burr Ridge, IL   Dubuque, IA   Madison, WI   New York
San Francisco   St. Louis   Bangkok   Bogotá   Caracas   Kuala Lumpur
Lisbon   London   Madrid   Mexico City   Milan   Montreal   New Delhi
Santiago   Seoul   Singapore   Sydney   Taipei   Toronto

The McGraw·Hill Companies

 Higher Education

A HISTORY OF THE MODERN WORLD
Published by McGraw-Hill, a business unit of The McGraw-Hill Companies, Inc., 1221
Avenue of the Americas, New York, NY, 10020.

This book is printed on acid-free paper.

1 2 3 4 5 6 7 8 9 0 DOW/DOW 0 9 8 7 6

ISBN-13: 978-0-07-310692-2
ISBN-10:   0-07-310692-5

Vice President and Editor-in-Chief: *Emily Barrosse*
Publisher: *Lyn Uhl*
Senior Sponsoring Editor: *Monica Eckman*
Developmental Editor: *Larry Goldberg*
Marketing Manager: *Katherine Bates*
Managing Editor: *Jean Dal Porto*
Lead Project Manager: *Susan Trentacosti*
Manuscript Editor: *Maxine Barber*
Art Director: *Jeanne Schreiber*
Art Editor: *Ayelet Arbel*
Illustrators: *Mapping Specialists and Ayelet Arbel*
Designer: *Marianna Kinigakis*
Photo Research Coordinators: *Nora Agbayani and Sonia Brown*
Photo Researcher: *PhotoSearch, Inc., NY*
Cover Credit: *Erich Lessing/Art Resource, NY © 2006 Artist Rights Society (ARS), New
York, ADAGP, Paris.*
Senior Supplement Producer: *Louis Swaim*
Lead Media Producer: *Sean Crowley*
Media Project Manager: *Wendy Constantine*
Production Supervisor: *Janean A. Utley*
Composition: *10/12 Times Roman, by TBH Typecast, Inc.*
Printing: *45# New Era Matte, R.R. Donnelley & Sons*

Library of Congress Catalog Number: 2006921641

www.mhhe.com

R.R. PALMER was born in Chicago in 1909. After graduating from the University of Chicago he received his Ph.D. from Cornell University in 1934. From 1936 to 1963 he taught at Princeton University, taking leave during World War II to work on historical projects in Washington, D.C. In 1963 he moved to Washington University in St. Louis to serve as dean of arts and sciences but in 1969 resumed his career in teaching and research, this time at Yale. After his retirement in 1977 he lived in Princeton, where he was affiliated with the Institute for Advanced Study, and then in a retirement community in Newtown Pennsylvania. Of the numerous books he wrote, translated, and edited, three of the most important have been his *Catholics and Unbelievers in Eighteenth-Century France* (1939); *Twelve Who Ruled: The Year of the Terror in the French Revolution* (1941, 1989); and his two-volume *Age of the Democratic Revolution* (1959, 1964), the first volume of which won the Bancroft Prize. He served as president of the American Historical Association in 1970, received honorary degrees from universities in the United States and abroad, and was awarded the Antonio Feltrinelli International Prize for History in Rome in 1990. He was a long-time fellow of the American Philosophical Society and of the American Academy of Arts and Sciences. He died in 2002, widely recognized as one of the preeminent historians of his generation.

JOEL COLTON was born in New York City. A graduate of the City College of New York, he served as a military intelligence officer in Europe in World War II, and received his Ph.D. from Columbia University in 1950. Until his retirement in 1989 he served on the faculty of Duke University, chairing the department of history from 1967 to 1974 and chairing the university's academic council from 1971 to 1973. On leave from Duke, he served from 1974 to 1981 with the Rockefeller Foundation in New York as director of its research and fellowship program in the humanities. In 1986 Duke voted him a Distinguished Teaching Award. He has received Guggenheim, Rockefeller Foundation, and National Endowment for the Humanities fellowships. He has served on the editorial boards of the *Journal of Modern History, French Historical Studies* and *Historical Abstracts,* and has been co-president of the International Commission on the History of Social Movements and Social Structures. In 1979 he was elected a fellow of the American Academy of Arts and Sciences. His writings include *Compulsory Labor Arbitration in France, 1936–1939* (1951); *Léon Blum: Humanist in Politics* (1966, 1987), for which he received a Mayflower Award; *Twentieth Century* (1968,1980) in *The Time-Life Great Ages of Man Series;* and numerous contributions to journals, encyclopedias, and collaborative volumes. He served as co-author with Professor Palmer of the second to eighth editions of *A History of the Modern World* and with Professor Kramer of the ninth and the current editions.

LLOYD KRAMER was born in Maryville, Tennessee, and graduated from Maryville College. He received his Ph.D. from Cornell University in 1983. Before entering Cornell, he was a teacher in Hong Kong and he traveled widely in Asia. After completing his graduate studies, he taught at Stanford University and Northwestern University. Since 1986 he has been a member of the faculty at the University of North Carolina, Chapel Hill, where he is currently Dean Smith Distinguished Term Professor and Chair of the History Department. He has received two awards for distinguished undergraduate teaching. His writings include *Threshold of a New World: Intellectuals and the Exile Experience in Paris, 1830–1848* (1988); *Lafayette in Two Worlds: Public Cultures and Personal Identities in an Age of Revolutions* (1996), which won the Gilbert Chinard Prize from the Society for French Historical Studies and the Annibel Jenkins Biography Prize from the American Society for Eighteenth-Century Studies; and *Nationalism: Political Cultures in Europe and America* (1998). He has also co-edited several books, including a collection of essays on historical education in America and *A Companion to Western Historical Thought* (2002). He has been a member of the School of Historical Studies at the Institute for Advanced Study and a Fellow at the National Humanities Center; and he served as president of the Society for French Historical Studies.

Brief Contents

Contents

List of Illustrations

List of Chronologies, Maps, Charts, and Tables

Preface

Dramatic events in the contemporary world—wars, revolutions, terrorist attacks, catastrophic natural disasters, economic crises and the endless stream of daily news—often obscure the long historical processes that have created the societies in which we live and the problems with which we cope. The mass media pay little attention to the broader historical patterns and contexts that give deeper meaning to the swiftly moving events of our era. This new edition of *A History of the Modern World* may be seen as the most recent version of a continuing search for historical perspectives on the complex, often bewildering, events of our age. It thus carries a guiding assumption that the events, cultures, and conflicts of the contemporary world are always evolving out of the long, complex histories of diverse peoples, ideas, institutions, social mores, economic exchanges, and struggles for political power.

These multiple levels of human history have created modern societies and exerted wide influence on people and cultures around the world. This book therefore describes the histories of specific nations and people and emphasizes landmark events such as wars and revolutions, but it also stresses broad historical trends that have developed deep below the most prominent historical events and created what we now call "the modern world." Our narrative explores the rise of nation-states and the conflicts that have shaped the world over the last several centuries, yet it links such transitions and events to the wider historical influence of the evolving global economy, the development of science and technology, the rise of industry, the significance of religious traditions, the origin and diffusion of new ideas, the changing mores of family and social life, and the complex relations between Western cultures and other cultures around the world.

The term *modern,* as we use it in this book, refers to the historical evolution of societies and cultures that may be said to have had the greatest influence in shaping the modern world—a phase of human history that began to develop about five or six centuries ago and is now evolving more rapidly in more places than ever before. This book makes no claim to be a world history, valuable as such histories may be. By design it focuses primarily on developments in the West until the spread of distinctively modern economic, social, and political institutions in the recent past leads to an increasing global emphasis in the book's later chapters. Although the narrative stresses the influence of European societies (that is, societies shaped by Europeans or the descendants of Europeans) in the emergence of "modern" institutions and social practices, it also emphasizes the worldwide exchanges, conflicts, and interactions that have contributed to the increasingly global culture of the contemporary era.

ORGANIZATION OF THE BOOK: CHANGES AND CONTINUITIES

As in the past, the book is organized in chapters that carry the narrative across specific chronological eras, moving steadily toward the present. Yet the clearly defined and numbered sections within each chapter often deal with themes, events, or issues that do not develop in simple chronological order. Each chapter focuses on a specific time frame but also on themes and problems of continuing historical importance. The chronological organization gives readers a broad historical framework and also provides opportunities for further analysis and discussion of specific historical themes or problems—discussions that can draw, for example, on other materials which can be found on the companion Online Learning Center Web site (www.mhhe.com/palmer10), which now includes an Interactive Glossary.

Although the history of political institutions, revolutions, and international conflicts remains important in this new edition, some details of national and political history have been reduced to expand the discussion of social, cultural, and intellectual history—all of which have been influential in recent historical scholarship. There are sections on the role of women in various historical contexts and eras; descriptions of cultural and intellectual movements from the early modern to the contemporary period; and new analyses of the political, economic, and cultural interactions that have shaped modern global history. Chapters on the Scientific Revolution and the early global economy have been moved in order to show more clearly the chronological relation of notable cultural and economic developments.

In the earlier chapters readers will find discussions of family life during the Renaissance and Reformation; descriptions of literary debates, salon culture, and the evolving public sphere in the Enlightenment; and insights into the cultural dimensions of the French Revolution. Later chapters of the book (in the second volume of the paperback edition) include sections on the emergence of feminism, cultural debates about science and the idea of progress, and discussions of modernist and postmodernist cultural movements.

The chapters on the world since 1945 have been reorganized and divided into new thematic sections. The two longest chapters in the previous edition's narrative of recent historical events have been divided into four new, more concise chapters that will be easier for students and others to read. The new, shorter chapters have a clearer thematic organization, and they convey key patterns in the development of postcolonial societies in Asia, Africa, and the Middle East, as well as the demise of communism in Europe. These reorganized chapters also include new information on recent international confrontations and on the growing globalization of contemporary economic and cultural life. We believe that specific historical information about such developments is the essential starting point for historical analysis, balanced historical insights, and the comprehension of historical change.

Our intention is to help students and other readers understand the complexities of great events such as the religious wars of earlier centuries, the American, French, and Russian Revolutions, the twentieth-century world wars, the spread of democracy and the challenges it has faced, the creation and collapse of the Western-dominated colonial empires, the emergence of new, postcolonial nation-states, and the continuing search for an international order. Readers will also find updated information on current issues such as terrorism, recent upheavals in the Middle East, and the continuing struggle for economic development in the world's poorest countries.

Other revisions have been introduced to make the book even more accessible for a new generation of readers. The visual component has again been extended through the addition of new illustrations, including new images of important works by modern artists such as Pablo Picasso, Berthe Morisot, Jackson Pollock, and Henry Moore. Like other kinds of documents and sources, the images and artwork from past cultures provide important historical information. Knowing how to read and critically evaluate an illustration, painting, or photograph is an essential form of analytical thought and is invaluable for cross-cultural comparisons. In addition to the many illustrations in each chapter, four-color inserts convey both the artistic creativity and the cultural or social preoccupations of different historical eras. The brief captions that accompany all of the illustrations connect events or issues to the book's narrative.

Other key features of this new edition include newly drawn, easier-to-read maps, presented in sharper color. The wide range of maps and charts shows the changing boundaries, populations, and economies of nations and regions over the years. In addition to the revised maps, new chronological timelines—as suggested by reviewers—have been incorporated into each chapter to give a convenient summary of the notable events and dates in each historical era. The revised, up-to-date entries for the comprehensive Suggestions for Further Reading, long a valued feature of the book, include new listings of useful Web sites as well as the titles of significant new scholarly publications.

The changes in this latest version of *A History of the Modern World* have been introduced to enhance the book's accessibility, but not to replace or weaken the style, content, narrative, and analytical qualities that have appealed to teachers and students over the years. More generally, readers will find that the book in its newest edition expresses again a strong belief in the value of historical knowledge and historical perspectives for anyone who wishes to understand as well as to live in the evolving modern world. It achieves its purpose whenever it helps readers of any age or background gain new perspectives on themselves and their world through the new knowledge or new insights that it may offer.

SUPPLEMENTS FOR THE INSTRUCTOR

Instructor's Manual/Test Bank   The first half of this unique manual offers a chapter-by-chapter guide to some of the best documentaries, educational and feature films, videos, and audio recordings to enhance classroom discussion. Brief overviews help instructors select the films best suited to each course topic. The manual also provides instructors with chapter objectives and points for discussion for each chapter, followed by a test bank containing multiple-choice, essay, and identification test questions.

Computerized Test Bank   This CD-ROM version of the test bank is available for both Macintosh and IBM-compatible computers to allow instructors to customize each test.

Overhead Transparencies   This set of over 150 overhead color transparencies of maps from the text can be used to illuminate classroom lectures.

Slide Set   Available through your local McGraw-Hill sales representative, instructors can choose from a list of hundreds of fine art slides to create a customized slide set that will complement the text and enhance classroom lectures.

Instructor Online Learning Center Web Site (www.mhhe.com/palmer10)   At the home page for this text-specific Web site, instructors will find a downloadable version of the Instructor's Manual. Instructors can also create Web-based homework assignments or classroom activities by linking to the Student Online Learning Center and can create an interactive course syllabus using McGraw-Hill's PageOut site.

PageOut (www.mhhe.com/pageout)   On the PageOut Web site instructors can create their own course Web sites. PageOut requires no prior knowledge of HTML, no long hours of coding, and no design skills on the instructor's part. Instructors need simply to plug the course information into a template and click on one of the 16 designs. The process takes little time and creates a professionally designed Web site. Powerful features include an interactive course syllabus that lets instructors post content and links, an online gradebook, lecture notes, bookmarks, and a discussion board where instructors and students can discuss course-related topics.

Videos   A wide range of videos on classic and contemporary topics in history is available through the Films for the Humanities and Sciences collection. Instructors can illustrate and enhance lectures by selecting from a series of videos correlated to the course. Contact your local McGraw-Hill sales representative for further information.

 ## SUPPLEMENTS FOR THE STUDENT

Student Study Guide   Prepared by Joel Colton and Megan McLean, this user-friendly Study Guide helps students process and master important concepts in the text not through rote memorization but by stimulating reflection and interpretation. For each of the 133 sections of the textbook, the Study Guide provides study questions, key discussion sentences, and identification test questions. Each chapter includes general essay questions and general discussion passages. Selected map exercises are also provided. In addition, questions on the numerous illustrations in the text are included in the sections to which they most closely relate and are designed to encourage interpretation and analysis, specifically on the ways in which the illustrations supplement the discussions in the text.

Student Online Learning Center Web Site (www.mhhe.com/palmer10)   New to this Web site and requested by reviewers is an Interactive Glossary, an important learning tool for students that complements the terms and topics highlighted in the margins of the textbook. At this text-specific Web site, students can link to an interactive study guide, including online essay questions, interactive mapping exercises, Internet exercises, interactive chronologies, and links to online primary source documents. Links to trusted history search engines also make the Online Learning Center an ideal place to begin Web-based research.

PowerWeb   PowerWeb for World History gives students password-protected, course-specific articles with assessments from current research journals and popular press articles, refereed and selected by World History instructors, and especially useful for materials that go beyond the scope of this book.

 ## ACKNOWLEDGMENTS

We again gratefully acknowledge the help of the many people who have assisted with the production of this book. We owe a special debt to the editors and staff of McGraw-Hill, Inc., which has published this book since its seventh edition. We are grateful also to Alfred A. Knopf, Inc., the earlier publisher of the book, and to Ashbel Green and the Knopf staff for continuing to make it available in a trade edition for the general public. The support and assistance of Lyn Uhl, Monica Eckman, Larry Goldberg, Susan Trentacosti, Marianna Kinigakis, Ayelet Arbel, Nora Agbayani, Janean Utley, Sonia Brown, Louis Swaim, Sean Crowley, and Katherine Bates at McGraw-Hill have been invaluable and essential. We also thank Christine Buese and Deborah Bull for their expert assistance on illustrations and Bethany Keenan for her help in identifying useful Web sites.

We have benefited from the expert advice of reviewers who have offered suggestions for the ways in which a new edition of this book might be revised; and we have absorbed many additional ideas from other colleagues who have used earlier editions of the book in their courses. We mention specifically the following reviewers: Marc Baer, Hope College; Robert Brown, University of North Carolina at Pembroke; Nathanael Greene, Wesleyan

University; L. Edward Hicks, Faulkner University; George Marcopoulos, Tufts University; James McSwain, Tuskegee University; Florene Memegalos, Hunter College; Jenny Nicholas, West High School; David J. Proctor, Tufts University; Sarah Rudell, Wayzata High School; Tamas Ungvari, California State University, Northridge; and Michael Zirinsky, Boise State University. Other colleagues who provided feedback also deserve mention: Joseph J. Colistra, LaSalle College High School; Michael Corey, Lincoln Way High School; Virginia Mancini, Pleasantville High School; Henry A. Ploegstra, St. Mark's School of Texas; and Michael Stoll, Hinsdale South High School. None of these individuals are in any way responsible for the book's shortcomings, but all have contributed to its strengths. We wish also to acknowledge the exceptional support and contributions of our colleagues and our families.

Finally, we note with a sense of deep loss that our colleague and co-author Robert R. Palmer (who always published as R. R. Palmer) died in 2002 after a long career of outstanding accomplishments. His superb contributions to the study of the French Revolution and of eighteenth- and early nineteenth-century history on both sides of the Atlantic have deservedly received wide recognition. His far-reaching intellect, searching acuity, historical insights, and broad-gauged interests marked this work from its beginning, and he remains the guiding influence and inspiration behind this book. The scholarly collaboration that has long characterized *A History of the Modern World* meanwhile continues and takes on new forms in this new edition, for which the most recent co-author has assumed the major responsibility.

Joel Colton
Lloyd Kramer

Geography and History

History is the experience of human beings in time, but that experience takes place also in geographic space. Geography describes and maps the earth, but it also studies the changing interactions between human beings and the environments in which they live.

The universe, of which our planet earth and our solar system form but a small part, is now thought to be at least 12 billion years old. Most scientists believe the earth is about 4.6 billion years old. Yet the entire history (and prehistory) of humankind goes back only 3.5 to 5 million years, or perhaps only 2 million years, depending on how humans are defined. What we call history—the recorded cultures and actions of human beings—began with the invention of early forms of writing only about 5,500 years ago.

Oceans and continents have moved about over time, changing in size, shape, and location. The continents as we know them took on their distinctive forms less than 100 million years ago. Dinosaurs, which became extinct some 60 million years before the first humans even emerged, could walk from North America to Europe (as we now call these continents) on solid land in a warm climate. It is only a few thousand years since the end of the most recent glacial age. That Ice Age, which *Ice Age* began about 2 million years ago and reached its coldest point only 20,000 years ago, was caused by a slight shift in the earth's orbit around the sun. Water froze into ice 1–2 inches thick and covered the northern parts of the planet (in North America as far south as present-day Chicago and in Europe across large parts of the British Isles and the nearby mainland). The melting of this ice produced the coastlines, offshore islands, inland seas, straits, bays, and harbors that we know today, as well as some of the large river systems and lakes. The process of change in the earth's surface continues. Niagara Falls, on the border between the United States and Canada, has been receding because the ongoing cascade of water erodes the underlying rock. The ocean's tides and human construction erode our shorelines as well, and many scientists believe current patterns of global warming may eventually change the oceans and coasts in much of the world.

Oceans presently cover more than two-thirds of the earth's surface, and many large land areas in the remaining third are poorly suited for habitation by human beings or most other animal and plant organisms. One-tenth of the land remains under ice, as in Antarctica and Greenland; much is tundra; much is desert, as in the Sahara; and much land lies along the windswept ridges of high mountains. Like the oceans, these regions have been important in human history, often acting as barriers to movement and settlement. Human history has therefore evolved in relatively small, scattered sections of the earth's total surface.

Researchers have found persuasive material evidence to show that *Origins of human* human beings originated in Africa. Humans belonging to the species *Homo* *beings* *erectus,* the Latin term used by anthropologists and others to denote the upright, walking predecessors of modern humans, seem to have migrated from Africa about 1.8 million years ago, perhaps because of environmental pressures or perhaps because of simple curiosity. Our own species *Homo sapiens,* the Latin term connoting increased cognitive and judgmental abilities, emerged no more than about 100,000 years ago. When humans went beyond merely utilitarian accomplishments and demonstrated aesthetic and artistic interests as well as advanced toolmaking (about 35,000 years ago), we refer to them as the subspecies *Homo sapiens sapiens*. They were the remaining survivors of a very complex human family tree.

The great Ice Age lowered the seas by hundreds of feet and froze huge quantities of water. The English Channel became dry. Land bridges opened up between Siberia and North America over what we now call the Bering Strait. Hunters seeking game walked from one continent to the other. When the glaciers melted, forests sprang up, and many of the open areas in which humans had hunted disappeared, providing added motivation for movement.

Our human ancestors spread eventually to every continent except Antarctica. In doing so, human groups became isolated from each other for millennia, separated by oceans, deserts, or mountains. Wherever they wandered, they evolved slightly over time, developing superficial physical differences that modern cultures have defined as the characteristics of various racial groups. But "race" is a cultural idea rather than a mark of biologically significant differences. All human beings belong to the *Homo sapiens* species, all derive from the same biological ancestry, and all are mutually fertile. Only a very few human genes are responsible for physical differences such as skin pigmentation, in comparison to the vast number of genes that are shared by all members of the human species.

Race: a cultural concept

The basic anatomy and genetic makeup of modern humans has not changed over the last 100,000 years. Geographic separation accounts for the emergence over shorter time periods of distinctive cultures, which can be seen, for example, in the different historical and cultural development of the pre-Columbian Americas, Africa, China, India, the Middle East, and Europe. On a still smaller time scale, geographic separation also explains differences in languages and dialects.

Geography and culture

Geographic distances and diversity of climate have also produced differences in flora and fauna, and hence in the plants and animals upon which humans are dependent. Wheat became the most usual cereal in the Middle East and Europe, millet and rice in East Asia, sorghum in tropical Africa, maize in pre-Columbian America. The horse, first domesticated in north-central Asia about 4,500 years ago, was for centuries a mainstay of Europe and Asia for muscle power, transportation, and fighting. The somewhat less versatile camel was adopted later and more slowly in the Middle East, and the Americans long had no beasts of burden except the llama. Such differences did not begin to diminish until early modern travelers crossed the oceans, taking plants and animals with them and bringing others back to environments where they had never lived before.

Although much remains obscure about the origins of life, and new discoveries and calculations are always displacing older hypotheses, paleontologists studying plant and animal fossils (including human ones) have used techniques such as radiocarbon dating to transform our knowledge of the earth and of the earliest human beings. In geography, aerial and satellite photography and computer technology have enabled us to refine older conceptions of continents and oceans. And astrophysicists are now studying vast amounts of new data about the universe, which have been sent to them from powerful telescopes mounted on unmanned spaceships.

Cartography, the art and science of mapmaking, has evolved rapidly, but we tend to forget how our maps often remain conventional and even parochial. It was Europeans and descendants of Europeans who designed our most commonly used maps, which are oriented North-South and West-East from fixed points in their horizons, and which therefore reflect their own European cultural assumptions. Similar biases can be found in the maps of other cultures too. The Chinese for centuries defined and visualized their country as the "Middle Kingdom." In the early modern centuries maps drawn in India typically represented South Asia as forming the major part of the world. One such map depicted the European continent as a few marginal areas labeled England, France, and "other hat-wearing islands."

Changing conceptualizations of the globe continue in our day. A map drawn and published in contemporary Australia, demonstrating the Australian perspective from "down under," shows South Africa at the top of the map and Capetown at the very tip, the large expanse of contemporary African nations in the middle, and the various European countries crowded at the bottom, the latter appearing quite insignificant. The European-invented term "Middle East" has been called into question, and this region of the world is perhaps better designated as Western Asia. Even our traditional concept of Europe as one of the seven continents (Africa, Asia, Europe, North America, South America, Australia, and Antarctica) is now questioned. Why, for example, should the Indian peninsula be a "subcontinent" when it roughly matches the size and exceeds the population and diversity of the European "continent" (at least that part of the "continent" that lies west of the former Soviet Union)? Europe itself is, of course, actually a peninsula, in a way that the other continents are not. Some geographers ask us to consider it more properly as part of Asia, the western part of a great "Eurasian landmass." Defined in these terms, Europe becomes more of a cultural conception, arising out of perceived differences from Asia and Africa, than a continent in a strictly geographical sense.

Europe's Influence on Modern History

However we define its place on the globe, Europe has undoubtedly shaped much of modern world history—partly because of its overseas expansion, partly because of what it borrowed from other parts of the world, and partly because of its decisive economic and cultural influence on the emergence of an increasingly global civilization. Europe is of course only one of many important cultural spheres in human history. Its economy, political systems, religious traditions, and social institutions are not the sole historical path to modernity; indeed, people in other regions of the world have often challenged or rejected European forms of "modernization" as they have built their own modern societies. Yet even the critique or rejection of European institutions has usually required historical analysis of Europe's development and role in the world. Much of the modern global economy, for example, emerged in the international trade that Europe's imperial powers controlled and expanded after the sixteenth century. European political ideas, science, philosophy, cultural mores, and people also spread widely across the world, contributing to both the constructive and destructive patterns of modern political, social, and cultural life. Ideas and people have meanwhile flowed constantly into Europe from other parts of the world, so that European societies remain a vital center for cross-cultural exchanges and conflicts.

Europe and history

It is possible to narrate a "history of the modern world" from widely diverging perspectives and with an emphasis on quite different historical themes. This book, however, begins with the recognition that Europe developed and promoted many of the distinctive "modern" ideas and institutions that have now evolved in various forms throughout the contemporary world. Historical understanding of modernity must therefore include a comprehensive analysis of Europe—though an accurate history of the modern world must also insist that Europe represents only one of the diverse, complex cultures that continue to shape modern global history.

Europe exemplifies the perennial interactions between human activity and the natural environment, and the study of its historical evolution should begin with some attention to its geography. The accompanying topographical map shows the main physical features of Europe and its surrounding geographical space. This topography has remained virtually unchanged over historic time, despite the constant political and cultural transformations in European societies. Europe is not large. Even with European Russia, it contains hardly more than 6 percent of the earth's land surface, occupying about the same area as the United States mainland plus Alaska. It is only a little larger than Australia. It is physically separated from Africa by the Mediterranean Sea, although the Mediterranean historically has been as much a passageway as a barrier. A truer barrier emerged when the Sahara Desert dried up only a few thousand years ago, which suggests why northern Africa has often been as connected to southern Europe, or culturally to the Middle East, as to sub-Saharan Africa. The physical separation of Europe from Asia is even less clear. The conventional boundary has been the Ural Mountains in Russia, but they are a low and wide chain that does not stretch far enough to make an adequate boundary. The Russians themselves do not recognize any official distinction between European and Asian Russia.

The Mediterranean Sea

Europe is indeed one of several peninsulas jutting off from Asia, like the Arabian and Indian peninsulas. But there are differences. For one thing, the Mediterranean Sea is unique among the world's bodies of water. Closed in by the Strait of Gibraltar, which is only 8 miles wide, it is more shielded than other seas from the open ocean and is protected from the most violent ocean storms. Though over 2,000 miles long, it is subdivided by islands and peninsulas into lesser seas with identities of their own, such as the Aegean and the Adriatic, and it provides access also to the Black Sea. Because it is possible to travel great distances without being far from land, navigation developed on the Mediterranean from early times and one of the first civilizations appeared on the island of Crete. It is possible also to cross between Europe and Asia at the Bosporus and between Europe and Africa at Gibraltar. Populations became mixed by migration, and various historic empires—the Carthaginian, Roman, Byzantine, Arabic, Spanish, Venetian, and Ottoman—have effectively used the Mediterranean to govern their component parts. After the Suez Canal was built in the nineteenth century, the Mediterranean became an important segment in the "lifeline of empire" for the British Empire in its heyday.

Mountains

In southern Europe, north of the Mediterranean and running for its whole length, is a series of mountains, produced over the geological ages by the pushing of the gigantic mass of Africa against the small Eurasian peninsula. The Pyrenees close off Spain from the north, as the Alps do Italy; the Balkan Mountains are difficult to penetrate. The only place where one can travel at water level from the Mediterranean to the north is by the valley of the Rhone River, so that France is the only country that belongs both to the Mediterranean and northern Europe. North of the mountains is a great plain extending from western France all the way into Russia and on into Asia, passing south of the Urals. If one were to draw a straight line from Amsterdam east through what is called the Caspian Gate, north of the Caspian Sea, as far as western China, one would never in traveling these 3,500 miles be higher than 2,000 feet above sea level. This plain has at various times opened Europe to Mongol and other invasions, enabled the Russians to move east and create a huge empire, and made Poland a troubled battleground.

Rivers

The European rivers are worth particular attention. Most are navigable, and they also give access to the sea. With their valleys, they provided areas where intensive local development could take place. Thus the most important older cities of Europe are on rivers—London on the Thames, Paris on the Seine, Vienna and Budapest on the Danube, Warsaw on the Vistula. In northern Europe it was often possible to move goods from one river to another, and then in the eighteenth century to connect them by canals. The importance of water is shown again by the location of Copenhagen, Stockholm, and St. Petersburg on the Baltic and of Amsterdam and Lisbon, which grew rapidly after Europeans began traversing the Atlantic Ocean.

There are important geographical conditions such as climate that a topographical map cannot show. Climate depends on latitude, ocean currents, and winds that bring or withhold rainfall. Europe lies as far north as the *Climate* northern United States and southern Canada, but the parts of Europe near the sea have less extreme temperatures than the corresponding northerly regions of North America. The Mediterranean countries have more sunshine and less severe winters than either northern Europe or the northern United States. Everywhere the winters are cold enough to suppress infectious pathogens and pests and keep out certain diseases that afflict warmer countries. The warm summers with their growing seasons have produced an annual cycle of agriculture, and rainfall has been adequate but not excessive. Europe is the only continent that has no actual desert. It is also for the most part a region of fertile soil. In short, since the end of the Ice Age, or since humans learned to survive winters, Europe has been one of the most favored places on the globe for human habitation.

If we say that climate and the environment not only set limits but also provide opportunities for what human beings can do, then there is no such thing as geographical determinism. Geography is not destiny. What happens depends *Geographical* on the application of knowledge and abilities in any particular time and *determinism* place and in any particular culture. What constitutes a natural resource varies with the state of technology and the possibilities of economic exchange. Even the disadvantages of distance can be overcome by developing new means of transportation. The oceans that long divided human beings became a highway for the Portuguese, Spanish, Dutch, French, and English, and later for others. Chinese and Arab sailors also used the oceans for trade across Asia and East Africa. For most of human history, however, neither persons, information, nor commands could travel much more than 30 miles a day. Localism prevailed, and large-scale commercial or governmental organizations were hard to create and maintain. Like most other regions of the world, therefore, Europe was long made up of small local units, pockets of territory each with its own customs, way of life, and manner of speech, largely unknown to or ignorant of others, and looking inward upon itself. A "foreigner" might come from a thousand miles away, or from only ten.

Agriculture, like commerce and industry, depends on human invention *Agriculture* and decision making. The state of agriculture obviously depends on natural conditions, but it has also depended historically on the invention of the plow, the planting of appropriate crops, the rotation of fields to prevent soil exhaustion, and the availability of livestock from which manure could be obtained as fertilizer. It benefits from stability and is affected by demographic changes. If population grows, new and less fertile or more distant areas must be brought under cultivation. Nor can agriculture be improved without the building of roads and a division of labor between town and country, in which agrarian workers produce surpluses for those not engaged in agriculture. And for agriculture, as for other productive enterprises, elementary security is essential. Farming cannot proceed, nor food be stored over the winter, unless the men and women who work the fields can be protected from attack.

The maps in the present volume cannot show in detail all of the waterways, mountains, and geographical barriers that have helped to shape the course of human history, but they do point to the role of geography in the evolution of political and economic power, or what has become known as geopolitics. Human beings have always developed their institutions and cultures through a complex relation with the natural world, and maps remind us that all human activities take place in geographical space. Readers can also use their imaginations and the scale of maps to convert space into time, remembering that until the invention of the railroad both people and news traveled far more slowly than today. At a rate of 30 miles a day it would take three weeks to travel from London to Venice, and at least six weeks for an exchange of letters. Communication to places outside Europe took even longer. In our own day, when we travel at supersonic speeds and measure electronic communication in nanoseconds, or one-billionth of a second, the barriers of geographic space have virtually disappeared. Yet human beings remain profoundly dependent on their natural environments, and human history remains firmly embedded in the geography of the planet earth.

C h a p t e r **1**

THE RISE OF EUROPE

It may seem strange for a history of the modern world to begin with the European Middle Ages, for Europe is not the world and the Middle Ages were not modern. But much of what is now meant by "modern" made its first appearance in Europe, and to understand both modern Europe and the wider modern world it is necessary to reach fairly far back in time.

Over the centuries between roughly 1500 and 1900, Europe created the most powerful combination of political, military, economic, technological, and scientific apparatus that the world had ever seen. In doing so, Europe radically transformed itself, and also profoundly affected other societies and cultures in America, Africa, and Asia—sometimes destroying them, sometimes stimulating or enlivening them, and always presenting them with problems of resistance or adaptation. This European ascendancy became apparent about 300 years ago. It reached its zenith with the European colonial empires at the beginning of the twentieth century. Since then, the position of Europe has relatively declined, partly because of conflicts within Europe itself, but mainly because the apparatus which had made Europe so dominant can now be found in other countries. Some, like the United States, are in many ways cultural and political offshoots of Europe. Others have very different and ancient backgrounds. But whatever their backgrounds, and willingly or not, all peoples in the contemporary world have been caught up in processes of "modernization" or "development," which usually turns out to mean acquiring or adapting some of the technical skills and powers first exhibited by Europeans.

There is thus in our time a kind of global modern civilization which overlies or penetrates the diverse, regional cultures of the world. This civilization is an interlocking global system, in that conditions on one side of the globe have repercussions on the other. Communications are almost instantaneous and news travels everywhere. If the air is polluted in one country, neighboring countries are affected; if oil ceases to flow from the Middle East, the life of Europe, North America, and Japan may become very difficult. The modern world depends on elaborate means of transportation; on science, industry, and machines;

Chapter emblem: A medieval representation of Saint Augustine. (Scala/Art Resource, NY) on new sources of energy to meet insatiable demands; on scientific medicine, public hygiene, and methods of raising food. States and nations fight wars by advanced methods, and negotiate or maintain peace by diplomacy. There is an earth-encompassing network of finance and trade, loans and debts, investments and bank accounts, with resulting fluctuations in monetary exchanges and balances of payments. Some 190 very unequal and disunited members compose the United Nations and represent every region of the world, but the very concept of the nation, as represented in that body, is derived largely from Europe.

In most modern countries there have been pressures for increased democracy, and all modern governments, democratic or not, seek to arouse the energies and support of their populations. In a modern society old customs loosen, and ancestral religions are often questioned or transformed. There are usually demands for individual liberation, and an expectation of a higher standard of living. Modern societies typically move toward more equality between sexes and races, between adherents of different religions, or between different parts of the same country; and most modern governments try to reduce the gap between very high and low incomes. Movements for social change may be slow and gradual, or revolutionary and catastrophic, but movement of some kind is universal.

Such are a few of the historical trends of modernity. New "modernizing" forms of technology, culture, or economic organization now emerge in many different regions of the world, but most of the early patterns of modernity appeared first in Europe or in the extension of European societies (including the United States). The present book thus deals mainly with the historical growth of European societies and civilization, with increasing attention in later chapters to the earth as a whole. Antimodern movements and protests have also been part of modern world history. When they occur in Asia or Africa, they are often called anti-Western, as if to show that Europe and the "West" have been at the heart of the problem. Even those movements that most vigorously challenge Western social and cultural systems must confront the institutions, ideas, and legacies of modern European history.

If "modern" refers especially to a certain complicated way of living, it has also another sense, meaning merely what is recent or current. As a time span the word "modern" is purely relative. It depends on what we are talking about. A modern kitchen may be as much as 5 years old, modern physics is about 100 years old, modern science over 300, the modern European languages about 1,000. Modern civilization, the current civilization in which we are living, and which is always changing, is in one sense a product of the last two centuries, but in other senses it is much older. Roughly speaking, it may be said that modern times began in Europe about 1500. Modern times were preceded by a period of 1,000 years called the Middle Ages, which set in about A.D. 500, and which were in turn preceded by about another 1,000 years of classical Greek and Roman civilization. Before that reached the long histories of Egypt and Mesopotamia, and, further east, of the Indus Valley and China. All times prior to the European Middle Ages are commonly called "ancient." But the whole framework—ancient, medieval, and modern—is largely a matter of words and convention, whose meaning developed mainly with reference to Europe. We shall begin our history with a running start, and slow down the pace, surveying the scene more fully in proportion as the times grow more "modern."

1. ANCIENT TIMES: GREECE, ROME, AND CHRISTIANITY

Europeans were by no means the pioneers of human civilization. Half of recorded history had passed before anyone in Europe could read or write. The priests of Egypt began to keep written records between 4000 and 3000 B.C., but 2,000 years later the poems of Homer were still being circulated in the Greek city-states by word of mouth. Shortly after 3000 B.C., while the pharaohs were building the pyramids, Europeans were laboriously setting up the huge, unwrought stones called megaliths, of which Stonehenge is the best-known example. In a word, until after 2000 B.C., Europe was in the Neolithic or New Stone Age. This was in truth a great age in human history, the age in which human beings learned to make and use sharp tools, weave cloth, build living quarters, domesticate animals, plant seeds, harvest crops, and sense the returning cycles of the months and years. But the Middle East—Egypt, the Euphrates and Tigris valley, the island of Crete, and the shores of the Aegean Sea (which belonged more to Asia than to Europe)—had reached its Neolithic Age 2,000 years before Europe. By about 4000 B.C. the Middle East was already moving into the Bronze Age.

After about 2000 B.C., in the dim, dark continent that Europe then was, great changes began that are now difficult to trace. Europeans, too, learned how to smelt and forge metals, with the Bronze Age setting in about 2000 B.C. and the Iron Age about 1000 B.C. There was also a steady infusion of new peoples into Europe. They spoke languages related to languages now spoken in India and Iran, to which similar peoples migrated at about the same time. All these languages (whose interconnection was not known until the nineteenth century) are now referred to as Indo-European, and the people who spoke them became the ancestors both of the classical Greeks and Romans and of the Europeans of modern times. All European languages today are Indo-European with the exceptions of Basque, which is thought to be a survival from before the Indo-European invasion, and of Finnish and Hungarian, which were brought into Europe from Asia some centuries later. It was these invading Indo-Europeans who diffused over Europe the kind of speech from which the Latin, Greek, Germanic, Slavic, Celtic, and Baltic languages were later derived.

Indo-Europeans

The Greek World

The first Indo-Europeans to emerge into the clear light of history, in what is now Europe, were the Greeks. They filtered down through the Balkan peninsula to the shores of the Aegean Sea about 1900 B.C., undermining the older Cretan civilization and occupying most of what has since been called Greece by 1300 B.C. Beginning about 1150 B.C., other Greek-speaking tribes invaded from the north in successive waves. The newcomers included many restless, rough, and warlike tribes, and their coming ushered in several centuries of chaos and unrest before a gradual stabilization and revival began in the ninth century. The *Iliad* and the *Odyssey,* written down about 800 B.C., but composed and recited much earlier, probably refer to wars between the Greeks and other centers of civilization, of which one was at Troy in Asia Minor. The siege of Troy is thought to have occurred about 1200 B.C.

Greek accomplishments

The ancient Greeks proved to be an exceptionally gifted people, achieving supreme heights in thought and letters. They absorbed the knowledge of earlier eastern cultures, the mathematical lore of the ancient Chaldeans, and the arts and crafts that they found in Asia Minor and on voyages to Egypt. They added immediately to everything that they learned. It was the Greeks of the fifth and fourth centuries B.C. who formulated what the Western world long meant by the beautiful, and who first speculated on political freedom.

The Parthenon, constructed in ancient Athens during the fifth century B.C. to honor the goddess Athena, gave architectural form to the Greek respect for balance, order, and symmetry. (Scala/Art Resource, NY)

As they settled down, the Greeks formed tiny city-states, all independent and often at war with one another, each only a few miles across, and typically including a coastal city and its adjoining farmlands. Athens, Corinth, and Sparta were such city-states. Many were democratic, which meant that all male citizens could congregate in the marketplace to elect officials and discuss their public business. They were not democratic in a modern sense in that slaves, resident noncitizens (called "metics"), and women were excluded from political life.

Politics was turbulent in the small Greek states. Democracy alternated with aristocracy, oligarchy, despotism, and tyranny. From this rich fund of experience was born systematic political science as set forth in the unwritten speculations of Socrates and in the *Republic* of Plato and the *Politics* of Aristotle in the fourth century B.C. The Greeks also were the first to write history as a subject distinct from myth and legend. Herodotus, "the Father of History," traveled throughout the Greek world and far beyond, ferreting out all he could learn of the past; and Thucydides, in his account of the wars between Athens and Sparta, presented history as a guide to enlightened citizenship and constructive statecraft.

The classical virtues

Perhaps because they were a restless and vehement people, the Greeks came to prize the "classical" virtues, which they were the first to define and which would have great influence in the subsequent history of European societies. For them, the ideal lay in moderation, or a golden mean. They valued order, balance, symmetry, clarity, and control. Their statues of idealized males revealed their conception of what humans ought to be—noble creatures, dignified, poised, unterrified by life or death, masters of themselves and their feelings. Their architecture, as in the Parthenon, made use of exactly measured angles and rows of columns. The classical "order," or set of carefully wrought pillars placed in a straight line at specified intervals, represented the firm impress of human reason on the brute materials of nature. The same sense of form was thrown over the torrent of human words. Written language became contrived, carefully planned, organized for effect. The epic poem, the lyric, the drama, the oration, along with history and the philosophical dialogue, each with its own rules and principles of composition, became the "forms" within which, in Western civilization, writers long expressed their thoughts.

Reflecting on the world about them, Greek philosophers concluded that something more fundamental existed beyond the world of appearances, that true reality was not what met the eye. With other peoples, and with the Greeks themselves in earlier times, this same realization had led to the formation of myths, dealing with invisible but mighty beings known as gods and with faraway places on the tops of mountains, beneath the earth, or in a world that followed death. Greek thinkers set to criticizing the web of myth. They looked for rational or natural explanations behind the variety and confusion that they saw. Some, observing human sickness, said that disease was not a demonic possession, but a natural sequence of conditions in the body, which could be identified, understood, and even treated in a natural way. Others, turning to physical nature, said that all matter was in reality composed of a very few things—made up of atoms or elements—which they usually designated as fire, water, earth, and air. Some said that change was a kind of illusion, all basic reality being uniform; some, that only change was real, and that the world was in flux. Some, like Pythagoras, found the enduring reality in "number," or mathematics. The Greeks, in short, laid the foundations for science. Studying also the way in which the mind worked, or ought to work, if it was to reach truthful conclusions, they developed the science of logic. The great codifier of Greek thought on almost all subjects in the classical period was Aristotle, who lived in Athens from 384 to 322 B.C.

Spread of Greek civilization

Greek influence spread widely and rapidly. Hardly were some of the city-states founded when their people, crowded within their narrow bounds, sent off some of their number with equipment and provisions to establish colonies. In this way Greek cities were very early established in south Italy, in Sicily, and even in the western Mediterranean, where Marseilles was founded about 600 B.C. Later the Greek city-states, unable to unite, succumbed to conquest by Philip of Macedon, who came from the relatively crude northern part of the Greek world, and whose son, Alexander the Great (356–323 B.C.), led a phenomenal, conquering march into Asia, across Persia, and on as far as India itself. Alexander's empire did not hold together, but Greek civilization, after having penetrated the western Mediterranean, now began to influence the ancient peoples of Egypt and the Middle East. Greek thought, Greek art, and the Greek language spread far and wide, drawing at the same time on the knowledge and creativity of other ancient cultures. The most famous "Greeks" after the fourth century B.C. and on into the early centuries of the Christian era usually did not come from Greece but from the Hellenized Middle East, and especially from Alexandria in Egypt. Among these later Greeks were the great summarizers or writers of encyclopedias in which ancient science was passed on to later generations—Strabo in geography, Galen in medicine, Ptolemy in astronomy. All three lived in the first and second centuries A.D.

The Roman World

In 146 B.C. the Greeks of Greece were conquered by a new people, the Romans, who kept their own Latin language but rapidly absorbed what they could of the intellectual and artistic culture of the Greeks. Over a period of two or three centuries they assembled an empire

The Forum was the vital center of Roman public life and a symbol of imperial power. Rome's distinctive sense of grandeur and social order can still be discerned in the Forum's ruins, which are pictured here with the famous coliseum in the background.
(Royalty-Free/CORBIS)

in which the whole world of ancient civilization (west of Persia) was included. Egypt, Greece, Asia Minor, Syria all became Roman provinces, but in them the Romans had hardly any deep influence except in a political sense. In the West—in what are now Tunisia, Algeria, Morocco, Spain, Portugal, France, Switzerland, Belgium, and England—the Romans, though ruthless in their methods of conquest, in the long run acted as civilizing agents, transmitting to these hitherto isolated countries the age-old achievements of the East and the more recent culture of Greece and of Rome itself. So thorough was the Romanization that in the West Latin even became the commonly spoken language. It was later displaced by Arabic in Africa but survives to this day, transformed by time, in the Romance languages of France, Italy, Spain, Portugal, and Romania.

The Roman Empire

In the Roman Empire, which lasted with many vicissitudes from about 31 B.C. to the latter part of the fifth century A.D., virtually the entire civilized world of the ancient West was politically united and enjoyed generations of internal peace. Rome was the center, around which in all directions lay the "circle of lands," the *orbis terrarum,* the known world—that is, as known in the West, for the Han Empire at the same time in China (202 B.C. to A.D. 220) was also a highly organized cultural and political entity. The Roman Empire consisted essentially of the coasts of the Mediterranean Sea, which provided the great artery of transport and communication, and from which no part of the empire, except northern Gaul (France), Britain, and the Rhineland, was more than a couple of hundred miles away. Civilization among the elites in this vast empire was remarkably uniform; there were no distinct nationalities, and the most significant cultural difference was that east of Italy the predominant language was Greek;

in Italy and west of it, Latin. Cities grew up everywhere, engaged in a busy commercial life, exchanged ideas with one another, and, like the cities in other ancient cultures, relied on the labor of slaves. There were always more cities in the East, where most of the manufacturing crafts and the densest population were still concentrated, but they sprang up now in the West—indeed, most of the older cities of France, Spain, England, and western and southern Germany boast of some kind of origin under the Romans.

The distinctive aptitude of the Romans lay in organization, administration, government, and law. Never before had armies been so systematically formed, maintained over such long periods, dispatched at a word of command over such distances, or maneuvered so effectively on the field of battle. Never had so many peoples been governed from a single center. The Romans had at first possessed self-governing and republican institutions, but they lost them in the process of conquest, and the governing talents which they displayed in the days of the empire were of an authoritarian character—talents, not for self-government, but for managing, coordinating, and ruling the manifold and scattered parts of one enormous system. Locally, cities and city-states enjoyed a good deal of autonomy. But above them all rose a pyramid of imperial officials and provincial governors, culminating in the emperor at the top. The empire kept peace, the *pax Romana,* and even provided a certain justice for its many peoples. Lawyers worked on the body of principles known ever afterward as Roman law.

The pax Romana

Roman judges had somehow to settle disputes between persons of different regions, with conflicting local customs, for example, two merchants of Spain and Egypt. The Roman law came therefore to hold that no custom is necessarily right, that there is a higher or universal law by which fair decisions may be made, and that this higher, universal, or "natural" law, or "law of nature," will be understandable or acceptable to everyone, since it arises from human nature and reason. Here the lawyers drew on Greek philosophy for support. They held also that law derives its force from being enacted by a proper authority (not merely from custom, usage, or former legal cases); this authority to make law they called *majestas,* or sovereign power, and they attributed it to the emperor. Thus the Romans emancipated the idea of law from mere custom on the one hand and mere caprice on the other; they regarded it as something to be formed by enlightened intelligence, consistent with reason and the nature of things; and they associated it with the solemn action of official power. It must be added that Roman law favored the state, or the public interest as seen by the government, rather than the interests or liberties of individual persons, and it generally provided men with more legal privileges than women. These principles, together with more specific ideas on such matters as property, debt, marriage, and wills were in later centuries to have a great effect in Europe.

The Coming of Christianity

The thousand years during which Greco-Roman civilization arose and flourished were notable in another way even more momentous for all later human history. It was in this period that the great world religions came into being. Within the time bracket 800 B.C.–A.D. 700 the lives of Confucius and Buddha, of the major Jewish prophets, and of Muhammad are all included. At the very midpoint (probably about 4 B.C.), in Palestine in the Roman Empire, a man named Jesus was born, believed by his followers to be the Son of God. Like Jesus, the first Christians were Jews; but both under the impulse of its own doctrine, which held that all people were alike in spirit, and under the strong leadership of Paul, a man of Jewish birth, Roman citizenship, and Greek culture, Christianity began to

make converts. The new religion gradually fused the monotheism of Judaism and its ethical teachings with various themes in Greek philosophy, creating a new synthesis of Judeo-
Greek thought that would shape much of the later history of ideas in Western cultures.
Christianity gained adherents across most of the Roman Empire, and there were certainly
a few Christians in Rome by the middle of the first century. Both Paul and the elder apostle, Peter, according to church tradition, died as martyrs at Rome in the time of the
Emperor Nero about A.D. 67.[1]

*Emergence and spread
of Christianity*

The Christian teaching spread at first among the poor, the people at the
bottom of society, those whom Greek glories and Roman splendors had
passed over or enslaved, and who had the least to delight in or to hope for
in the existing world. Women were also drawn to the new religion, perhaps
in part because early Christianity offered them more autonomy and more opportunities for
leadership than they found in the traditional patriarchal order of Roman law and families.
Gradually Christian ideas reached the upper classes; a few classically educated and well-
to-do people became Christians; in the second century Christian bishops and writers were
at work publicly in various parts of the empire. In the third century the Roman government, with the empire falling into turmoil, and blaming the social troubles on the Christians, subjected them to wholesale persecution. In the fourth century (possibly in A.D. 312)
the Emperor Constantine accepted Christianity. By the fifth century the entire Roman
world was formally Christian; no other religion was officially tolerated; and the deepest
thinkers were Christians who combined Christian beliefs with the now thousand-year-old
tradition of Greco-Roman thought, philosophy, and social institutions.

It is impossible to exaggerate the importance of the coming of Christianity. It brought
with it, for one thing, an altogether new sense of human life. Where the Greeks had
demonstrated the powers of the mind, the Christians explored the soul, and they taught that
in the sight of God all souls were equal, that every human life was sacrosanct and invio-

Christian beliefs

late, and that all worldly distinctions of greatness, beauty, and brilliancy
were in the last analysis superficial. Where the Greeks had identified the
beautiful and the good, had thought ugliness to be bad, and had shrunk
from disease as an imperfection and from everything misshapen as horrible
and repulsive, the Christians resolutely saw a spiritual beauty even in the plainest or most
unpleasant exterior and sought out the diseased, the crippled, and the mutilated to give
them help. Love, for the ancients, was never quite distinguished from Venus; for the Christians, who held that God was love, it took on deep overtones of sacrifice and compassion.
Suffering itself was in a way divine, since God had also suffered on the Cross in human
form. A new dignity was thus found for suffering that the world could not cure. At the
same time the Christians worked to relieve suffering as none had worked before. They
protested against the massacre of prisoners of war, against the mistreatment and degradation of slaves, against the sending of gladiators to kill each other in the arena for another's
pleasure. In place of the Greek and pagan self-satisfaction with human accomplishments
they taught humility in the face of an almighty Providence, and in place of proud distinctions between high and low, slave and free, civilized and barbarian, they held that all men
and women were alike because all were children of the same God.

---

[1]The terms B.C. (Before Christ) and A.D. (Annõ Domini) are generally used now with little attention to their religious origin. With so many creeds and faiths in the modern world employing this system of calculating dates,
readers will increasingly encounter the substitute usage B.C.E. (Before the Common Era) and C.E. (Common Era).

On an intellectual level Christianity also marked a revolution. It was Christianity, not rational philosophy, that dispelled the swarm of greater and lesser gods and goddesses; the blood sacrifices and self-immolation; or the frantic resort to magic, fortune-telling, and divination. The Christians taught that there was only one God. The pagan conception of local, tribal, or national gods disappeared. For all the world there was only one plan of Salvation and one Providence, and all human beings took their origin from one source. The idea of the world as one thing, a "universe," was thus affirmed with a new depth of meaning. The very intolerance of Christianity (which was new to the ancient world) came from this sense of human unity, in which it was thought that all people should have, and deserved to have, the one true and saving religion.

The Christians were often denounced and persecuted for their political ideas. The Roman Empire was a world state; there was no other state but it; no living human being except the emperor was sovereign; no one anywhere

Persecution

on earth was his equal. Between gods and human beings, in the pagan view, there was moreover no clear distinction. Some gods behaved very humanly, and some human creatures were more like gods than others. The emperor was held to be veritably a god. A cult of Caesar was established, regarded as necessary to maintain the state, which was the world itself. All this the Christians firmly refused to accept. It was because they would not worship Caesar that the Roman officials regarded them as social incendiaries who must be persecuted and stamped out.

The Christian doctrine on this point went back to the saying gathered from Jesus, that one should render to Caesar the things that were Caesar's, and to God those that were God's. The same dualism was presented more systematically by St. Augustine about A.D. 420 in his *City of God*. Few books have been more influential in shaping the later development of Western civilization.

St. Augustine

The "world," the world of Caesar, in the time of St. Augustine, was going to ruin. Rome itself was plundered in 410 by heathen barbarians. Augustine wrote the *City of God* with this event obsessing his imagination. He wrote to show that though the material world could perish there was yet another world that was more enduring and more important.

There were, he said, really two "cities," the earthly and the heavenly, the temporal and the eternal, the city of man and the City of God. The earthly city was the domain of state and empire, of political authority and political obedience. It was a good thing, as part of God's providential scheme for human life, but it had no inherently divine character of its own. The emperor was human. The state was not absolute; it could be judged, criticized, or corrected from sources outside itself. It was, for all its majesty and splendor, really subordinate in some way to a higher and spiritual power. This power lay in the City of God. By the City of God Augustine meant many things, and readers found all sorts of meanings in later ages. The heavenly city might mean heaven itself, the abode of God and of blessed spirits enjoying life after death. It might mean certain elect spirits of this world, the good people as opposed to the bad. It might, more theoretically, be a system of ideal values or ideal justice, as opposed to the crude approximations of the actual world.

In any case, with this Christian dualism the Western world escaped from what is called Caesaropapism, a political system in which one person holds the powers of ruler and of pontiff. Instead, the spiritual power and the political power were held to be separate and independent. In later times

Caesaropapism

popes and kings often quarreled with each other; the clergy often struggled for political power, and governments have often attempted to dictate what people should believe, or

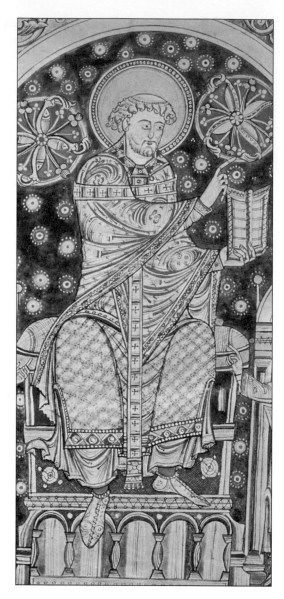

St. Augustine's wisdom and influence on Christian theology were honored throughout the Middle Ages; he appears here in a medieval illustration, dispensing truths from a celestial throne.
(Scala/Art Resource, NY)

love, or hope for. But speaking in general of European history neither side has ever won out, and in the sharp distinction between the spiritual and the temporal has lain the germ of many liberties in later societies. At the same time the idea that no ruler, no government, and no institution is too mighty to rise above moral criticism eventually opened the way to a dynamic and progressive way of living in the West.

2. THE EARLY MIDDLE AGES: THE FORMATION OF EUROPE

There was really no Europe in ancient times. In the Roman Empire we may see a Mediterranean world, or even a West and an East in the Latin- and Greek-speaking portions. But the West included parts of Africa as well as of Europe, and Europe as we know it was divided by the Rhine-Danube frontier, south and west of which lay the civilized provinces of the empire, and north and east the "barbarians" of whom the Roman world knew almost nothing. To the Romans "Africa" meant Tunisia-Algeria; "Asia" meant the Asia Minor peninsula; and the word "Europe," since it meant little, was scarcely used by them at all. It was in the half-millennium from the fifth to the tenth centuries that Europe as such for the first time emerged with its peoples brought together in a life of their own, clearly set off from Asia or Africa and beginning to create a culture that would become "Western."

The Disintegration of the Roman Empire

The Roman Empire began to fall apart, especially in the West, and the Christianizing of the empire did nothing to impede its decline. The Emperor Constantine, who in embracing Christianity undoubtedly hoped to strengthen the imperial system, also took one other significant step. In A.D. 330 he founded a new capital at the old Greek city of Byzantium, which he renamed Constantinople. (It is now Istanbul.) Thereafter the Roman Empire had two capitals, Rome and Constantinople, and was administered in two halves. Increasingly the center of gravity moved eastward, as if returning to the more ancient centers in the Middle East, as if the experiment of civilizing the West were to be given up as a failure.

Founding of Constantinople

Throughout its long life the empire had been surrounded on almost all sides by people whom the Romans called "barbarians"—wild Celts in Wales and Scotland, Germans in the heart of Europe, Persians or Parthians in the East ("barbarian" only in the ancient sense of speaking neither Greek nor Latin), and, in the southeast, the Arabs. These barbarians, always with the exception of Persia, had never been brought within the pale of ancient Greek or Roman civilization. Somewhat like the Chinese, who about 200 B.C. built several walls to solve the same problem, the Romans simply drew a line beyond which they themselves rarely ventured and would not allow the barbarians to pass. Nevertheless outsiders filtered into the empire. As early as the third century A.D. emperors and generals recruited bands of them to serve in the Roman armies. Their service over, they would receive farmlands, settle down, marry, and mingle with the population. By the fourth and fifth centuries a good many such individuals were even reaching high positions of state.

At the same time, in the West, for reasons that are not fully understood, the activity of the Roman cities began to falter, commerce began to decay, local governments became paralyzed, taxes became more ruinous, and free farmers were bound to the soil. The army seated and unseated emperors. Rival generals fought with each other. Gradually the West fell into decrepitude, and the old line between the Roman provinces and the barbarian world made less and less difference.

Decline in the West

After some centuries of relative stability, the barbarians themselves, pressed by more distant peoples from Asia, rather suddenly began to move. Sometimes they first sought peaceable access to the empire, attracted by the warmer Mediterranean climate, or desiring to share in the advantages of Roman civilization. More often, Germanic tribes moved swiftly and by force, plundering, fighting, and killing as they went. In 476 a barbarian chieftain deposed the last Roman emperor in the West. Sometimes in the general upheaval peoples from Asia rapidly intermixed with other populations in the old Roman Empire. The most famous of these invaders were the Huns, who cut through central Europe and France about 450 under their

Barbarian invasions

leader Attila, the "scourge of God"—and then disappeared. Nor were these invasions all. Two centuries later new irruptions burst upon the Greco-Roman world from the southeast, where hitherto outlying peoples poured in from the Arabian deserts. The Arabs, aroused by the new faith of Islam (Muhammad died in 632), fell as conquerors upon Syria, Mesopotamia, and Persia; occupied Egypt about 640 and the old Roman Africa about 700; and in 711 reached Spain.

Beneath these blows the old unity of the Greco-Roman or Mediterranean world was broken. The "circle of lands" divided into three segments. Three types of civilization now confronted each other across the inland sea.

The Byzantine World, the Arabic World, and the West about 700

Byzantine Empire

The Eastern Roman, Later Roman, Greek, or Byzantine Empire (all names for the same empire) with its capital at Constantinople, and now including only the Asia Minor peninsula, the Balkan peninsula, and parts of Italy, made up one segment of the circle of lands. It represented the most direct continuation of the ancient civilizations of the Middle East. It was Christian in religion and Greek in culture and language. Its people felt themselves to be the truest heirs both of early Christianity and of earlier cultures in Greece. Art and architecture, trades and crafts, commerce and navigation, thought and writing, government and law, while not so creative or flexible as in the classical age, were still carried on actively in the eastern empire, on much the same level as in the closing centuries of ancient times. For all Christians, and for heathen barbarians in Europe, the emperor of the East stood out as the world's supreme ruler, and Constantinople as the world's preeminent and almost fabulous city.

Arabic world

The second segment of the Mediterranean world was the Arabic and Islamic. It became the most dynamic culture in the lands of the old Roman Empire, reaching from the neighborhood of the Pyrenees through Spain and all North Africa into Arabia, Syria, and the East. Arabic was its language; it became, and still remains, the common speech from Morocco to the Persian Gulf. Islam was its religion, and it looked to the prophet Muhammad (c. 570–632) and the Qur'an (or Koran) for its religious truths. Muhammad had spent his early adult years as a merchant in Mecca on the Arabian peninsula, but he began to have a series of intense religious revelations when he was about 40 years old. These revelations led Muhammad to a devout and uncompromising monotheism, which stressed the great power of God—or Allah in Arabic—and the human duty to adhere to God's will. Muhammad saw himself as a prophet in the Jewish and Christian tradition, but he soon came to define his revelations and teachings as the beginning of a new religion. The messages that came to Muhammad through revelation were written down in the sacred book of Islam, the Qur'an, which was organized into 114 chapters (called *suras*). Emphasizing submission to God, the importance of prayer, and an ethical obligation to help others, the Qur'an provided directions for the affairs of daily life as well as a powerful, poetic vision of the grandeur of God.

Muhammad's revelations attracted little early support in Mecca. Indeed, the hostility there forced him to move north in 622 to the city of Medina. This famous flight (the *Hegira*) brought him to a more receptive community, where his teachings quickly gained numerous adherents and from where the first Muslims set out to spread the new faith across all of Arabia, including Mecca. Muhammad died in 632, but the new religion con-

The sixth-century emperor Justinian built the great Hagia Sophia to display his commitment to the Christian religion and the power of his capital city, Constantinople. The church became a mosque after the Byzantine Empire fell to Muslim invaders in the fifteenth century, but it remains the most famous achievement of Byzantine architecture.
(Hirmer Fotoarchiv)

tinued to expand rapidly in all directions. Leadership passed to a series of caliphs who were initially relatives of Muhammad himself. As Muslims conquered new territories and won new converts throughout the Middle East and North Africa, the lands of Islam came under the control of these caliphs. All Muslims were included in the caliphate. The ruling caliph exercised both spiritual and political authority, and he was regarded as the true religious and military successor of Muhammad himself.

Conflicts and lasting divisions nevertheless developed during the era of the third Caliph, Uthman—one of the sons-in-law of Muhammad and a leader of the Umayyad family. Supporters of Ali, a rival leader and also a son-in-law of Muhammad, killed Uthman in 656, and Ali came to power as the fourth caliph. This violence did not resolve the conflict, however, and Ali himself was soon murdered. Ali's followers refused to accept the legitimacy of the Umayyad family, which now regained control of the caliphate. A minority faction, called Shiites, continued to honor Ali and to claim that all true leaders of Islam must descend from him. Although most Muslims supported the Umayyad caliphs, the Shiite minority remained a permanent presence within Islam, sustaining the memory of Ali and challenging the religious legitimacy of the dominant Sunnis (a term that emerged later). Meanwhile, the Umayyad dynasty set up its capital in Damascus, and some members of the family eventually extended their power as far west as Spain.

The Arabic world, like the Byzantine, built upon the heritage of the Greco-Romans. In religion, the early Muslims regarded themselves as successors to the Jewish and Christian traditions. They considered the line of Jewish prophets since Abraham to be spokesmen of the true God, and they put Jesus in this line. But they added that Muhammad was the last and greatest of the prophets, that the Qur'an set forth a revelation replacing that of the Jewish Bible, that the Christian New Testament was mistaken because Christ was not divine, and that the Christian belief in a Trinity was erroneous because there was in the strictest sense only One True God. To the Muslim Arabs, therefore, all Christians were dangerous or misguided infidels.

In mundane matters, the Arabs speedily took over the civilization of the lands they conquered. In the caliphate, as in the Byzantine Empire, the civilization of the ancient world went its way without serious interruption. Huge buildings and magnificent palaces were constructed; ships plied the Mediterranean; Arab merchants ventured over the deserts and traversed the Indian Ocean; holy or learned men corresponded over thousands of miles. The government developed efficient systems to collect taxes, enforce the laws, and keep the provinces in order. In the sciences the Arabs not only learned from but also went beyond the Greeks. They translated Greek scientific literature: we know some of it today only through these medieval Arabic versions. Arab geographers had a wider knowledge of the world than anyone had possessed up to their time. Arab mathematicians developed algebra so far beyond the Greeks as almost to be its creator ("algebra" is an Arabic word), and in introducing the "Arabic" numerals (through their contacts with India) they made arithmetic, which in Roman numerals had been formidably difficult into something that every schoolchild can be taught.

The third segment of the ancient Greco-Roman world was Latin Christendom, which about A.D. 700 did not look very promising. It was what was left over from the other two—what the Byzantines were unable to hold and the Arabs were unable to conquer. It included only Italy (shared in part with the Byzantines), France, Belgium, the Rhineland, and Britain. Barbarian kings were doing their best to rule small kingdoms, but in truth all government had fallen to pieces. Usually the invading barbarians remained a minority, eventually to be absorbed. Only in England, and in the region immediately west of the Rhine, did the Germanic element supersede the older Celtic and Latin. But the presence of violent invaders, armed and fierce amid peasants and city dwellers reduced to passivity by Roman rule, together with the disintegration of Roman institutions that had gone on even before the invasions, left this region in chaos.

Latin Christendom

The Western barbarians, as noted, were Germanic; and the Germanic influence became a distinctive contribution to the making of Europe. Some Germans were Christian by the fourth century, but most were still heathen when they burst into the Roman Empire. Their languages had not been written down, but they possessed an intricate folklore and religion in which fighting and heroic valor were much esteemed. Though now in a migratory phase, they were an agricultural people who knew how to work iron, and they had a rudimentary knowledge of the crafts of the Romans. They were organized in small tribes and had a strong sense of tribal kinship, which (as with many similar peoples) dominated their ideas of leadership and law. They enjoyed more freedom in their affairs than did the citizens of the Roman Empire. Many of the tribes were roughly self-governing in that all free men, those entitled to bear arms, met in open fields to hold council; and often the tribe itself elected its leader or king. They had a strong sense of loyalty to persons, of fealty to the acknowledged king or chief; but they had no sense of loyalty to large or general institutions. They had no sense of the state—of any distant, impersonal, and continuing source of law and rule. Law they regarded as the inflexible custom of each tribe. In the absence of abstract jurisprudence or trained judges, they settled disputes by rough and ready methods. In the ordeal, for example, a person who obstinately floated when thrown into water was adjudged guilty. In trial by battle, the winner of a kind of ritualistic duel was regarded as innocent. The gods, it was thought, would not allow wrong to prevail.

Germanic customs

The Germans who overran the old Roman provinces found it difficult to maintain any political organization at more than a local level. Security and civil order all but disappeared. Peasant communities were at the mercy of wandering bands of habitual fighters. Fighters often captured peasant villages, took them under their protection, guarded them from further marauders, and lived off their produce. Sometimes the same great fighting man came to possess many such villages, moving with his retinue of horsemen from one village to another to support himself throughout the year. Thus originated a new distinction between lord and servant, noble and commoner, martial and menial class. Life became local and self-sufficient. People ate, wore, used, and dwelled in only what they themselves and their neighbors could produce. In contrast to the economies of the Byzantine and Islamic worlds, Western trade died down, the cities became depopulated, money went out of circulation, and almost nothing was bought or sold. The Roman roads fell into neglect; people often used them as quarries for ready-cut building blocks for their own crude purposes. The West not only broke up into localized villages but also ceased to have habitual exchanges across the Mediterranean. It lost contact with the eastern centers from which its former civilization had always been drawn. From roughly A.D. 500 on, Europe fell into what some later historians would call the "Dark Ages."

The Church and the Rise of the Papacy

Only one organized institution maintained a tie with ancient civilization. Only one institution, reaching over the whole West, could receive news or dispatch its agents over the whole area. This institution was the Christian church. Its framework still stood; its network of bishoprics, as built up in late Roman times, remained intact except in places such as England, where the barbarian conquest was complete.

In addition, a new type of religious institution spread rapidly with the growth of monasteries. The serious and the sensitive, both men and women (though not together, to be sure), rejected the savagery about them and retired into communities of their own. Usually they were left unmolested by rough neighbors who held them in religious awe. In a world of violence they formed islands of quiet, peace, and contemplation. Their prayers, it was believed, were of use to all the world, and their example might at the least arouse pangs of shame in more worldly people. The monastic houses generally adopted the rule of St. Benedict (c. 480–543) and were governed by an abbot. Dedicated to the same ideals, they formed unifying filaments throughout the chaos of the Latin West.

Growth of monasteries

Bishops, abbots, and monks looked with veneration to Rome as the spot where St. Peter, the first apostle, had been martyred. The bishop of Rome corresponded with other bishops, sent out missionaries, gave advice on doctrine when he could, and attempted to keep in mind the situation throughout the Latin world as a whole. Moreover, with no emperor any longer in Rome, the bishop took over the government and public affairs of the city. Thus the bishop of Rome, while claiming a primacy over all Christians, was not dominated by any secular power. In the East the great church functionaries, the patriarchs, fell under the influence of the emperor who continued to rule at Constantinople. A tradition of Caesaropapism grew up in the East; but in the West the independence of the bishop of Rome now confirmed in practice a principle always maintained by the great churchmen of the West—the independence of the spiritual power from the political or temporal.

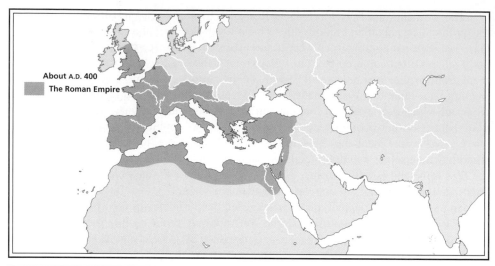

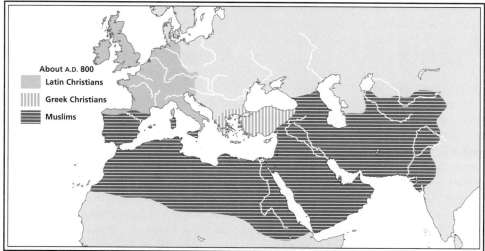

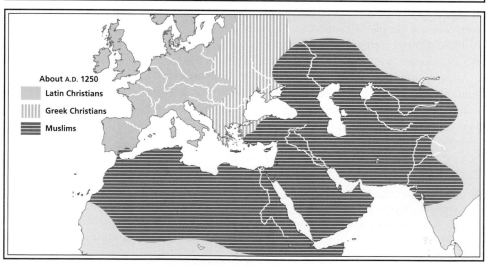

The growing authority of the popes was fortified by various arguments. St. Peter, it was held, had imparted the spiritual authority given to him by Christ himself to the Roman bishops who were his successors. This doctrine of the "Petrine supremacy" was based on two verses in the Bible (Matthew xvi, 18–19), according to which Christ designated Peter as the head of the church, giving him the "power of the keys" to open and close the doors of eternal salvation. As for the pope's temporal rule in Rome, it was affirmed that the Emperor Constantine had endowed the bishop with the government of the city. This "Donation of Constantine" was accepted as historical fact from the eighth century to the fifteenth, when it was proved to be a forgery.

Papal authority

It was the church that incorporated the barbarians into a higher way of life, and when barbarians embraced a more civilized way of living, it was the church that they entered. As early as about A.D. 340, the church sent out Ulfilas to convert the Goths; his translation of the Bible represents the first writing down of any Germanic language. About 496 the king of the Franks, Clovis, was converted to Christianity. A hundred years later, in 597, the king of Kent in southeast England yielded to the persuasions of Augustine of Canterbury, a missionary dispatched from Rome, and the Christianization of the Anglo-Saxons gradually followed. Missionaries from Ireland also, to which Christians of the Roman Empire had fled before the heathen barbarians, now returned to both Britain and the Continent to spread the gospel. By A.D. 700, after three centuries of turmoil, the borders of Christianity in the West were again roughly what they had been in late Roman times. Then in 711, as we have seen, the Arabs entered Spain. They crossed the Pyrenees and raced toward central Europe, but were stopped by a Christian and Frankish army in 732 at Tours on the river Loire. Islam was turned back into Spain, thereby allowing the people of Western Europe to expand their emerging Latin Christian culture.

Conversion of the barbarians

The Empire of Charlemagne, 800–814

Among the Franks, in what is now northern France and the German Rhineland, there had arisen a line of capable rulers of whom the greatest was Charlemagne. The Frankish kings made it their policy to cooperate with the pope. The pope needed a protector against depredations by his barbarian neighbors and against the political claims of the Byzantine Empire upon the city of Rome. The Frankish kings, in return for protection thus offered, won papal support to their side. This made it easier for them to control their own bishops, who were more often seen on horseback than in the episcopal chair, and was of use in pacifying their own domains and in wars of conquest against the heathen. In the year 800, in Rome, the pope crowned Charlemagne as emperor of the West. Frankish king and Roman

THE MEDITERRANEAN WORLD about A.D. 400, 800, and 1250

Greco-Roman civilization, centered about the Mediterranean, was officially Christian and politically unified under the Roman Empire in A.D. 400 but broke apart into three segments in the early Middle Ages. Each segment developed its own type of life. Each segment also expanded beyond the limits of the ancient Mediterranean culture. By 1250 Latin Christendom reached to the Baltic and beyond. Greek Christendom penetrated north of the Black Sea to include the Russians. The Muslim world spread into inner Asia and Africa. In 1250, and until 1492, the Muslims, or Moors, still held the southern tip of Spain. Jews lived in varying numbers in each of the three segments.

This image of a monastery in a medieval Spanish manuscript shows how the early monks became known for their learning as well as their religious contemplation and disciplined labor.
(Pierpont Morgan Library/Art Resource, NY)

bishop both believed that if only the Roman Empire could be restored peace and order might once more reign. Church and empire, religion and the state, were to be as two mighty swords employed in the same holy cause.

Charlemagne

Charlemagne crossed the Pyrenees and won back the northeastern corner of Spain to Christian rule. He overthrew and subordinated the barbarian kings who had set themselves up in northern Italy. He sent forces down the Danube, penetrated into Bohemia, and proceeded against some of the still heathen Germans (the Saxons) who lived along the river Elbe, and whom he either massacred or converted to Christianity. All these regions he brought within his new empire. Except for England and Ireland, which remained outside, the borders of his empire were coextensive with those of the Latin Christian world.

Once more, to a degree, the peoples of Western Europe were united under an empire. But a momentous change had occurred. Its capital did not lie in the ancient world of the Mediterranean. Its capital was now in northern Europe at Aix-la-Chapelle, or Aachen, near the mouth of the Rhine. Its ruler, Charlemagne, was a German of an ethnic group which had remained outside ancient civilization. Its people were Germans, French, and Italians, or, more precisely, the ancestors from whom these nationalities were to emerge. In the Greco-Roman world the north had always been at best provincial. Now the north became a center in its own right. Charlemagne dispatched embassies to the Byzantine emperor at Constantinople and to Harun al-Rashid, the great Muslim caliph at Baghdad. In intellec-

Revival of learning

tual matters, too, the north now became a capital. Centuries of violence and confusion had virtually destroyed education and systematic learning, even for the most powerful families in Europe. Charlemagne himself, though he understood Latin, could barely read and never learned to write. He used his authority, however, to revive the all but forgotten ancient learning and to spread education at least among the clergy. To his palace school came scholars from England, Germany, France, Italy, Spain. They wrote and spoke in Latin, the only Western language in which complicated ideas could at the time be expressed. Disintegrating ancient manuscripts were copied and recopied to assure a more abundant supply for study—always by hand, but in a more rapid script than had before been used. This so-called "Carolingian minuscule," evolved into the small letters of the modern Western alphabet, only the capital letters being Roman. Meanwhile, Charlemagne sought to foster commerce by creating a new and more reliable coinage, which was based on silver, the gold coins of the Roman Empire having long since vanished.

Ninth-Century Invasions; Europe by 1000

In Charlemagne's empire we first see the shape of Europe as a unit of society and culture distinct from the Mediterranean world of antiquity. The empire did not last. New waves of invaders assailed Western Christendom in the ninth century. The Magyars (called in Latin "Hungarians") terrified various parts of Europe until they settled down on the middle Danube about the year 900. New Germanic tribes uprooted themselves, coming this time *Second wave of invaders* from Scandinavia, and variously known as Norse, Vikings, or Danes. Bursting out in all directions, they reached Kiev in Russia in 864, discovered Iceland in 874, and even touched America in 1000. In the Christian world they assaulted the coasts and pushed up the rivers but settled in considerable numbers only in the Danelaw in England and in Normandy in France. Meanwhile the Arabs raided the shores of France and Italy and occupied Sicily. Nowhere was the power of government strong enough to ward off such attacks. Everywhere the harassed local population found its own means of defense or, that failing, was slaughtered, robbed, or carried off into slavery.

Gradually the second wave of invaders was incorporated as the first had been, by the same process of conversion to Christianity. By the year 1000 this process was nearly complete. In 1001 the pope sent a golden crown to the Magyars to crown St. Stephen as their first king, thus bringing Hungary within the orbit of the Latin West. Poland, Bohemia, and the Scandinavian homelands of the Norse were Christianized during the same era. In older Christian countries, such as France, the last remote and isolated rustics—the "heathen" who lived in the "heath"—were finally ferreted out by missionaries and brought within the Christian fold. In Christian countries Christianity now permeated every corner, and the historic peoples of western Europe had come together within the spreading religious and cultural system of the Latin church.

Meanwhile West and East continued to drift apart. The refusal of *"Great Schism of East* Greek patriarchs at Constantinople to recognize the claims to primacy of *and West"* the bishop of Rome, whom they regarded as a kind of Western barbarian, and the refusal of the Roman pontiff to acknowledge the political pretensions of the Byzantine Empire, led to the Great Schism of East and West. This schism, after developing for three centuries, became definite in 1054. It divided the Christian world into the Latin or Roman Catholic and the Greek Orthodox churches. It was from Constantinople that Christianity reached the peoples of Russia. The Russians, like the Balkan peoples, remained out of contact with most of Europe during the centuries when spiritual and intellectual contacts were carried through the clergy. They believed, indeed, that the Latin West was evil, heretical, and unholy. The Latin West, at the same time, by the schism, cut one more of its ties with antiquity and emerged more clearly as an independent center of its own civilization.

Emerging Europe

By the year 1000, or soon thereafter, the entity that we call Europe had come into existence. From the turbulence that followed the collapse of the Greco-Roman civilization had issued the peoples and the countries that would evolve into modern Europe. A kingdom of France had emerged, adjoining the great ill-defined bulk of Germany to the east. There were small Christian kingdoms in northern Spain and a number of city-states in the Italian peninsula. In the north there were now a kingdom of England and a kingdom of Scotland; Denmark, Norway, and Sweden had also taken form. In the east rose the three great kingdoms of Poland, Bohemia, and Hungary, the first two predominantly Slavic, Hungary predominantly Magyar, but all were Latin and Catholic in culture and religion, and Western in orientation. The east Slavs, or Russians, and the Slavs and other peoples of the Balkan peninsula also formed kingdoms of their own. Their languages and religion were diverging from the cultures of Western Europe. Christianized by Byzantine missionaries, they were Greek and Orthodox in culture and religion, and oriented toward Constantinople.

The civilization of Western Europeans in the year 1000 was still not much to boast of in the more polished circles of Byzantium or Baghdad. It might still seem that the West would suffer more than the East from their separation. But the West began at this time to experience new social and economic activity, ushering in the European civilization of the High Middle Ages.

༻ 3.   THE HIGH MIDDLE AGES: SECULAR CIVILIZATION

Agriculture and the Feudal System after 1000

Some historical periods are so dynamic that a person who lives to a mature age can remember sweeping changes that have come in one's own lifetime. Such a time began in Europe in the eleventh century. People could see new towns rise and grow before their eyes. They could observe new undertakings in commerce or government. Most of the cities that Europe was to know before the modern industrial era sprang up between about 1050 and 1200. The population of western Europe, which had been sparse even in Roman days, and which was even sparser after 500, suddenly began to grow denser about the year 1000, and it expanded steadily for two or three hundred years. The people of the High Middle Ages did not develop the conception of progress because their minds were set upon timeless values and personal salvation in another world, but the period was nevertheless one of rapid progress in nonreligious or "secular" matters. Much was created that remained fundamental far into modern times.

Agriculture and population growth

The new era was made possible by the process of growth in population which went along with agricultural changes. After the Norse and Magyar inroads had stopped, Europe was spared the assaults of other invaders. There came to be more security of life and limb. Farmers could plant with more confidence that they would reap, and people could build houses with the expectation of passing them on to their children. Hence there was more planting and building. Sometime before the year 1000 a heavier plow was invented, which cut a deeper furrow. Better methods of harnessing horses had been found than the ancients had ever known. The Romans had continued simply to throw a yoke over a horse's neck, so that the animal in pulling a weight easily choked. Europeans, before the year 1000, began to use a horse collar that rested on the animal's shoulders. The single horse could pull a greater load, or several horses could now for the first time be hitched in tandem. The amount of available animal power was thus multiplied, at a time when animals were the main source of power other than human muscle. Windmills, unknown to the ancients, were developed in the Low Countries about this time. They too offered a new source of power. Thus at the very beginning of a specifically "European" history, one may detect characteristics of sub-sequent European civilization—a search for technological invention, a quest for new sources of energy.

With such labor-saving devices people continued to work very hard, but they obtained more results by their efforts. Probably the use of such inventions, together with the influence of the Christian clergy, accounts for the gradual disappearance of slavery from Europe and its replacement by the less-abject and less-degrading status of serfdom. It is true that medieval Christians, when they could, continued to enslave whites as they were later to do with blacks. Usually such slaves were captives in war, taken from tribes not yet converted to Christianity, and sometimes exported as a form of merchandise to the Byzantine and Muslim worlds. As the successive European peoples became Christianized, the supply of slaves dried up. Medieval Christians did not enslave each other, nor was slavery essential to any important form of production.

Not only did population increase, and work become more productive, but also groups of people became less isolated from one another. Communications improved. The roads remained poor or nonexistent, but bridges were built across European rivers, and settlers filled in the wildernesses that had formerly separated the inhabited areas. Trees were felled, land was cleared, and the rural population clustered in village communities. The "nucleated" village gave more security, more contact between families, and readier access to the blacksmith or the priest. It also made possible a communally orga-nized agriculture.

Better ways of using land were introduced in the "three-field" system, *Three-field system* which spread to almost every region where cereal crops were the staple. In this "system" the peasant village divided its arable fields into three parts. In a given year one part was sown with one crop, such as wheat; a second part with another, such as barley; and the third was left to lie fallow. The three parts were rotated from year to year. Thus soil exhaustion was avoided at a time when fertilizers were unknown. For-merly, half or less of the available fields had been cultivated at any one time. With the three-field system two-thirds of the land came into annual use. This change, reinforced by better plowing and more effective employment of animals, led to a huge increase in the supply of food.

The peace and personal security necessary to agriculture were also advanced, in the absence of effective public authority, by the growth of *Feudalism* institutions that we know as "feudalism." Feudalism was intricate and diverse, but in essence it was a means of carrying on some kind of govern-ment on a local basis where no organized state existed. After the collapse of Charle-magne's empire the real authority fell into the hands of persons who were most often called "counts." The count was the most important man of a region covering a few hun-dred square miles. To build up his own position, and strengthen himself for war against other counts, he tried to keep the peace and maintain control over the lesser lords in his county, those whose possessions extended over a few hundred or a few thousand acres. These lesser lords accepted or were forced to accept his protection. They became his vas-sals, and he became their "lord." The lord and vassal relation was one of reciprocal duties.

Most people in the Middle Ages worked in the fields, coping like the peasant in this late medieval illustration with the seasons, soil, seeds, and animals that shaped agricultural life. (The British Library)

The lord protected the vassal and assured him justice and firm tenure of his land. If two vassals of the same lord disputed the possession of the same village, the lord decided the case, sitting in council (or "court") with all his vassals assembled and judging according to the common memory or customary law of the district. If a vassal died young, leaving only small children, the lord took the family under his "wardship" or guardianship, guaranteeing that the rightful heirs would inherit in due time. Correspondingly the vassal agreed to serve the lord as a fighting man for a certain number of days in the year. The vassal also owed it to the lord to attend and advise him, to sit in his court in the judging of disputes. Usually he owed no money or material payment; but if the lord had to be ransomed from captivity, or when his children married, the vassal paid a fee. The vassal also paid a fee on inheriting an estate, and the income of estates under wardship went to the lord. Thus the lord collected sporadic revenues with which to finance his somewhat primitive government.

This feudal scheme gradually spread across northern Europe. Lords at the level of counts became in turn the vassals of dukes. In the year 987 the great lords of France chose Hugh Capet as their king and became his vassals. The kings of France enjoyed little real power for another 200 years, but the descendants of Hugh occupied their throne for eight centuries, until the French Revolution. Similarly the magnates of Germany elected a king in 911; in 962 the German king was crowned emperor, as Charlemagne had been before him;

Capetian kings

thus originated the Holy Roman Empire, of which much will be heard in the following chapters.

England in these formative centuries did not choose a king by election. England was conquered in 1066 by the Duke of Normandy, William. The Normans (the Norse reshaped by a century of Christian and French influences) imposed upon England a centralized and efficient type of feudalism which they had developed in Normandy. In England, from an early date, the king and his officials therefore had considerable power, which led to more civil peace and personal security than on the Continent. Within the framework of a strong monarchy self-governing institutions could eventually develop with a minimum of disorder.

The Normans in England

The notable feature of feudalism was its mutual or reciprocal character. In this it differed from the old Roman imperial principle, by which the emperor had been a majestic and all-powerful sovereign. Under feudalism no one was sovereign. King and people, lord and vassal, were joined in a kind of contract. Each owed something to the other. If one defaulted, the obligation ceased. If a vassal refused his due services, the king had the right to enforce compliance. If the king violated the rights of the vassal, the vassals could join together against him. The king was supposed to act with the advice of the vassals, who formed his council or court. If the vassals believed the king to be exceeding his lawful powers, they could impose terms upon him. Although feudalism was always a hierarchical system of lords and vassals, its mutual or contractual character contributed to later European ideas of constitutional government.

Feudalism applied in the strict sense only to the military or noble class. Below the feudal world lay the vast mass of the peasantry. In the village, the lowliest vassal of a higher noble was lord over his own subjects. The village, with its people and surrounding farmlands, constituted a "manor," the estate of a lord. In the eleventh century most people of the manor were serfs. They were "bound to the soil" in that they could not leave the manor without the lord's permission. Few wanted to leave anyway, at a time when the world beyond the village was unknown and dangerous, and filled at best only with other similar manors. The lord, for his part, could not expropriate the villagers or drive them away. He owed them protection and the administration of justice. They in turn worked his fields and gave him part of the produce of their own. No money changed hands, because there was virtually no money in circulation. The manorial system was the agricultural base on which a ruling class was supported. It supported also the clergy, for the church held much land in the form of manors. It gave the protection from physical violence and the framework of communal living without which the peasants could not grow crops or tend livestock.

The manor and serfs

With the rise of agricultural productivity, lords and even a few peasants could produce a surplus, which they might sell if only they could find a market. The country was able to produce enough food for a town population to live on. And since population grew with the increase of the food supply, a surplus of population also began to exist. Restless spirits among the peasants now wanted to get away from the manor. And many went off to the new towns.

The Rise of Towns and Commerce

We have seen how the ancient cities had decayed. In the ninth and tenth centuries, with few exceptions, there were none left in western Europe. Here and there one would find a cluster of population around the headquarters of a bishop, a great count, or a king. But there were no commercial centers. There was no merchant class. The simple crafts—weaving, metalworking, harness making—were carried on locally on the manors. Rarely, an itinerant trader might appear with such semiprecious goods as he could carry for long distances on donkeys—Eastern silks, or a few spices for the wealthy. Among these early traders Jews were often important, because Judaism, part of the Byzantine and Arabic worlds as well as the Western, offered one of the few channels of communication among the different Mediterranean cultures.

Long-distance trade

Long-distance trading was the first to develop. The city of Venice was founded about 570 when refugees fled from invaders and settled in its islands. The Venetians, as time went on, brought Eastern goods up the Adriatic and sold them to traders coming down from central Europe. In Flanders in the north, in what is now Belgium, manufacturers of woolen cloth emerged. Flemish woolens were of a unique quality, owing to peculiarities of the atmosphere and the skill of the weavers. They could not be duplicated elsewhere. Nor could Eastern goods be procured except through the Venetians—or the Genoese or Pisans. Such goods could not possibly be produced locally, yet they were in demand wherever they became known. Merchants traveled in increasing numbers to sell them. Money came back into more general circulation; where it came from is not quite clear, since there was little mining of gold or silver until the end of the Middle Ages. Merchants began to establish permanent headquarters, settling within the deserted walls of ghostly Roman towns or near the seat of a lord or ecclesiastic, whose numerous retainers might become customers. Craftsmen moved from the overpopulated manors to these same growing centers, where they might produce wares that the lords or merchants would wish to buy. The process, once started, tended to snowball: the more people settled in such an agglomeration, the more they needed food brought to them from the country; and the more craftsmen left the villages, the more the country people, lords and serfs, had to obtain clothing and simple tools and utensils from the towns. Hence a busy local trade developed also.

Growth of towns

By 1100, or not long thereafter, such centers existed all over Europe, from the Baltic to Italy, from England as far east as Bohemia. Usually there was one about every 20 or 30 miles. The smallest towns had only a few hundred inhabitants; the larger ones had two or three thousand, or sometimes more. Each carried on a local exchange with its immediate countryside and purveyed goods of more distant origin to local consumers. But their importance was by no means merely economic. What made them "towns" in the full sense of the word was their acquisition of political rights.

The merchants and craftsmen who lived in the towns did not wish to remain, like the country people, subject to neighboring feudal lords. At worst, the feudal lords regarded merchants as a convenient source of ready money; they might hold them up on the road, plunder their mule trains, collect tolls at river crossings, or extort cash by offering "protection." At best, the most well-meaning feudal lord could not supervise the affairs of merchants, for the feudal and customary law knew nothing of commercial problems. The traders in the course of their business developed a "law merchant" of their own, having to do with money and moneychanging, debt and bankruptcy, contracts, invoices, and bills of lading. They wished to have their own means of apprehending thieves, runaway debtors, or sellers of fraudulent goods. They strove, therefore, to get recognition for their own law, their own courts, their own judges and magistrates. They wished, too, to govern their towns themselves and to avoid payment of fees or taxes to nearby nobles.

Everywhere in Latin Christendom, along about 1100, the new towns struggled to free themselves from the encircling feudalism and to set themselves up as self-governing little republics. Where the towns were largest and closest together—along the highly urbanized arteries of the trade routes, in north Italy, on the upper Danube and Rhine rivers, in Flanders, or on the Baltic coast—they emancipated themselves the most fully. Venice, Genoa, Pisa, Florence, Milan became virtually independent city-states, each governing a substantial tract of its surrounding country. In Flanders also, towns like Bruges and Ghent dominated their localities. Along the upper Danube, the Rhine, the North Sea, the Baltic, many towns became imperial free cities within the Holy Roman Empire, each a kind of small republic owing allegiance to no one except the distant and usually ineffectual emperor. Nuremberg, Frankfurt, Augsburg, Strasbourg, Hamburg, and Lübeck were free cities of this kind. In France and England, where the towns in the twelfth century were somewhat less powerful, they obtained less independence but received charters of liberties from the king. By these charters they were assured the right to have their own town governments and officials, their own courts and law, and to pay their own kind of taxes to the king in lieu of ordinary feudal obligations.

Often towns formed leagues or urban federations, joining forces to repress banditry or piracy or to deal with ambitious monarchs or predatory nobles. The most famous such league was the Hanse; it was formed mainly of German towns, fought wars under its own banner, and dominated the commerce of the North Sea and the Baltic until after 1300. Similar tendencies of the towns to form political leagues, or to act independently in war and diplomacy, were suppressed by the kings in England, France, and Spain.

The fact that Italy, Germany, and the Netherlands were commercially more advanced than the Atlantic countries in the Middle Ages, and so had a more intensive town life, was to be one cause (out of many) preventing political unification in the early modern era. Not until 1860 or 1870 were nationwide states created in this region. In the west, where more of a balance was kept between town and country, the towns were absorbed into nationwide monarchies that were arising under the kings. This early difference between central and western Europe would later shape much of Europe's history in modern times.

The liberties won by the towns were corporate liberties. Each town *Corporate liberties* was a collective entity. The people in towns did not possess individual rights, but only the rights which followed from being a resident of a particular town. Among these were personal liberty; no townsman could be a serf, and fugitive serfs who lived over a year in a town were generally deemed to be free. But townspeople did not seek individual liberty in the modern sense. The world was still too unsettled for the individual to act alone. The citizens wanted to join together in a compact body and to protect themselves by all sorts of regulations and controls. The most obvious evidence of this communal solidarity was the wall within which most towns were enclosed. The citizens in time of trouble looked to their own defense. As the towns grew, they built new walls farther out. Today, in Paris or Cologne, one may still see remains of different walls in use from the tenth to the thirteenth centuries.

Economic solidarity was of more day-to-day importance. The towns required neighboring peasants to sell foodstuffs only in the town marketplace. They thus protected their food supply against competition from other towns. Or they forbade the practice of certain trades in the country; this was to oblige peasants to make purchases in town and to protect the jobs and livelihood of the town craftsmen. They put up tariffs and tolls on the goods of other towns brought within their own walls. Or they levied special fees on merchants from outside who did business in the town. In Italy and Germany they often coined their own money; and the typical town fixed the rates at which various moneys should be exchanged. The medieval towns, in short, at the time of their greatest liberty, followed in a local way

The crafts and trade in medieval towns were dominated by the guilds, whose symbols conveyed the meaning of their work. The sheep on this emblem represents the wool guild in Florence.
(Alinari/Art Resource, NY)

the same policies of protectionism and exclusiveness which national governments were often to follow in modern times.

Guilds

Within each town merchants and craftsmen formed associations called "guilds," whose "masters" supervised the affairs of a specific trade or craft. Merchants formed a merchant guild. Stonemasons, carpenters, barbers, dyers, goldsmiths, coppersmiths, weavers, hatters, tailors, shoemakers, grocers, and apothecaries formed craft guilds of their own. The guilds served a public purpose. They provided that work should be done by reliable and experienced persons, thereby protecting people from the pitfalls of shoddy garments, clumsy barbers, poisonous drugs, or defective and poorly built houses. They also provided a means of vocational education and marked out a career for young men. Women also worked in many trades and could belong to guilds; they were particularly numerous in certain guilds of the clothing trades. Women were nevertheless excluded from some of the guilds' social activities, and they were not granted the political privileges that men received as they moved up through the ranks of the guild hierarchy. Typically a boy became an apprentice to some master, learned the trade, and lived with and was supported by the master's family for a term of years, such as seven. Then he became a journeyman, a qualified and recognized worker, who might work for any master at a stated wage. Most workers remained journeymen throughout their lives, especially in the later Middle Ages. The guild system enabled some workers to improve their social position, however; and a lucky young man might eventually become a master, open his own shop, hire journeymen, and take apprentices. So long as the towns were growing, a boy had some chance to become a master; but as early as 1300 many guilds were becoming frozen, and the masters were increasingly chary of admitting new persons to their own status. Although widows often continued to work in the trades or artisanal crafts of their husbands, women almost never became masters. From the beginning, in any case, it was an important function of the guilds to protect their own members. The masters, assembled together, preserved their reputation by regulating the quality of their product. They divided work among themselves and fixed the terms of apprenticeship, the wages to be paid to journeymen, and the prices at which their goods must be sold. Or they took collective steps to meet or keep out the competition of the same trade in nearby towns.

Whether among individuals within the town itself, or as between town and country, or between town and town, the spirit of the medieval economy was to prevent competition. Risk, adventure, and speculation were not wanted. Almost no one thought it proper to work for monetary profit. The few who did, big merchants trading over large areas, met with suspicion and disapproval wherever they went.

The towns tried in many ways to subject the peasants' interests to their own but nevertheless had an emancipating influence on the country. A rustic by settling in town might escape from serfdom. But the town influence was more widespread and far out of proportion to the relatively small number of people who could become town dwellers. The growth of towns increased the demand for food. Lords began to clear new lands. All western

Towns and the decline of serfdom

Europe set about developing a kind of internal frontier. Formerly villages had been separated by dark tracts of roadless woods, in which wolves roamed freely, shadowed by the gnomes, elves, and fairies of popular folklore. Now pioneers with axes cleared farmlands and built villages. The lords who usually supervised such operations (since their serfs were not slaves, and could not be moved at will) offered freer terms to entice peasants to settle on the new lands. It was less easy for the lord of an old village to hold his people in serfdom when in an adjacent village, within a few hours' walk, the people were free.

The peasants, moreover, were now able to obtain a little money by selling produce in town. The lords wanted money because the towns were producing more articles which money could buy. It became common for peasants to obtain personal freedom, holding their own lands, in return for an annual money payment to the lord for an indefinite period into the future. As early as the twelfth century serfdom began to disappear in northern France and southern England, and by the fifteenth century it had disappeared from most of western Europe. The peasant could now, in law, move freely about. But the manorial organization remained; the peasant owed dues and fees to the lord and was still under his legal jurisdiction.

The Growth of Monarchies and Government Institutions

Meanwhile the kings were busy, each trying to build his kingdom into an organized monarchy that would outlast his life. Monarchy became hereditary; the king inherited his position like any other feudal lord or possessor of an estate. Inheritance of the crown made for peace and order, for elections under conditions of the time were usually turbulent and disputed, and where the older Germanic principle of elective monarchy remained alive,

Changes in monarchical rule

as in the Holy Roman Empire, there was periodic commotion. The kings sent out executive officers to supervise their interests throughout their kingdoms. The kings of England, adopting an old Anglo-Saxon practice, had a sheriff in each of the 40 shires; the kings of France created similar officers who were called bailiffs. The kings likewise instituted royal courts, under royal justices, to decide property disputes and repress crime. This assertion of legal jurisdiction, together with the military might necessary to enforce judgments upon obstinate nobles, became a main pillar of the royal power. In England especially, and in lesser degree elsewhere, the kings required local inhabitants to assist royal judges in the discovery of relevant facts in particular cases. They put them on oath to declare what they knew of events in their own neighborhood. It is from this enforced association of private persons with royal officers that the jury developed.

Taxation
The kings needed money to pay for their governmental machinery or to carry on war with other kings. Taxation, as known in the Roman Empire, was quite unknown to the Germanic and feudal tradition. In the feudal scheme each person was responsible only for the customary fees which arose on stated occasions. The king, like other lords, was supposed to live on his own income—on the revenue of manors that he owned himself, the proceeds of estates temporarily under his wardship, or the occasional fees paid to him by his vassals. No king, even for the best of reasons, could simply decree a new tax and collect it. At the same time, as the use of money became more common, the kings had to assure themselves of a money income. As the towns grew up, with a new kind of wealth and a new source of money income, they agreed to make stipulated payments in return for their royal charters.

The royal demands for money and the claims to exercise legal jurisdiction were regarded as innovations. They were constantly growing and sometimes were a source of abuse. They met with frequent resistance in all countries. A famous case historically (though somewhat commonplace in its own day) was that of Magna Carta in England in 1215, when a group of English lords and high churchmen, joined by representatives of the city of London, required King John to confirm and guarantee their historic liberties.

The king, as has been said, like any lord, was supposed to act in council or "court" with his vassals. The royal council became the egg out of which departments of government were hatched—such as the royal judiciary, exchequer, and military command. From it also was hatched the institution of parliaments. The kings had always, in a way, held great parleys or "talks" (the Latin *parliamentum* meant simply a "talking") with their chief retainers. In the twelfth and thirteenth centuries the growth of towns added a new element to European life. To the lords and bishops was now added a burgher class, which, if of far inferior dignity, was too stubborn, free-spirited, and well furnished with money to be overlooked. When representatives of the towns began to be summoned to the king's great "talks," along with lords and clergy, parliaments may be said to have come into being.

Origins of parliaments

Parliaments, in this sense, sprouted all over Europe in the thirteenth century. Nothing shows better the similarity of institutions in Latin Christendom, or the inadequacy of tracing the history of any one country by itself. The new assemblies were called *cortes* in Spain, diets in Germany, Estates General or provincial estates in France, parliaments in the British Isles. Usually they are referred to generically as "estates," the word "parliament" being reserved for Britain, but in origin they were all essentially the same.

The kings called these assemblies as a means of publicizing and strengthening the royal rule. They found it more convenient to explain their policies, or to ask for money, to a large gathering brought together for that purpose than to have a hundred officials make local explanations and strike local bargains in a hundred different places. The kings did not recognize, nor did the assemblies claim, any right of the parliament to dictate to the king and his government. But usually the king invited the parliament to state grievances; his action upon them was the beginning of parliamentary legislation.

The three estates
The parliaments were considered to represent not the "nation" nor "people" nor yet the individual citizen, but the "estates of the realm," the great collective interests of the country. The first and highest estate was the clergy; the second was the landed or noble class; to these older ruling groups were added, as a "third estate," the burghers of the chartered towns. Quite commonly these three types of people sat separately as three distinct chambers. But the pattern varied from country to country. In England, Poland, and Hungary the clergy as a whole

ceased to be represented; only the bishops came, sitting with lay magnates in an upper house. Eventually the burghers dropped out in Poland, Bohemia, and Hungary, leaving the landed aristocracy in triumph in eastern Europe. In Castile and Württemberg, on the other hand, the noble estate eventually refused to attend parliament, leaving the townspeople and clergy in the assemblies. In some countries—in Scandinavia, Switzerland, and in the French Estates General—even peasants were allowed to have delegates.

In England the Parliament developed eventually in a distinctive way. *England's Parliament* After a long period of uncertainty there came to be two houses, known as the Lords and the Commons. The Lords, as in Hungary or Poland, included both great prelates and lay magnates. The House of Commons developed features not found on the Continent. Lesser landholders, the people who elsewhere counted as small nobles, sat in the same House of Commons with representatives of the towns. The Commons was made up of "knights and burgesses," or gentry and townsmen together, a fact which greatly added to its strength, for the middle class of the towns long remained too weak to act alone. The mingling of classes in England, the willingness of townsmen to follow the leadership of the gentry, and of the gentry to respect the interests of townsmen, helped to root representative institutions in England more deeply than in other countries during the medieval era. Moreover, England was a small country in the Middle Ages. There were no provincial or local parliamentary bodies (as in France, the Holy Roman Empire, or Poland) which might jealously cut into the powers of the central body or with which the king could make local arrangements without violating the principle of representative government. And finally, as a reason for the strength of Parliament in England, the elected members of the House of Commons very early obtained the power to *commit* their constituents. If they voted a tax, those who elected them had to pay it. The king, in order to get matters decided, insisted that the votes be binding. Constituents were not allowed to repudiate the vote of their deputies, nor to punish or harass them when they came home, as often happened in other countries. Parliament thus exercised power as well as rights.

In summary, the three centuries of the High Middle Ages laid foundations both for order and for freedom. Slavery was defunct and serfdom was expiring. Politically, the multitude of free chartered towns, the growth of juries in some places, and the rise of parliaments everywhere provided means by which peoples could take some part in their governments. The ancient civilizations had never created a free political unit larger than the city-state. The Greeks had never carried democracy beyond the confines within which people could meet in person, nor had the Romans devised means by which, in a large state, the governed could share any responsibilities with an official bureaucracy. The ancients had never developed the idea of representative government, or of government by duly elected and authorized representatives acting at a distance from home. The idea is by no means as obvious or simple as it looks. It first appeared in the medieval monarchies of the West, and, after much subsequent development, it would become a fundamental principle for political systems in most of the modern world.

4. THE HIGH MIDDLE AGES: THE CHURCH

So far in our account of the High Middle Ages we have told the story of Hamlet without speaking of the Prince of Denmark, for we have left aside the church, except, indeed, when some mention of it could not be avoided. In the real life of the time the church was omnipresent. Religion permeated political and social life. In feudalism the mutual duties of lord and vassal were confirmed by religious oaths, and bishops and abbots, as holders of lands, became feudal personages themselves. In the monarchies, the king was crowned by the chief churchman of his kingdom, adjured to rule with justice and piety, and anointed with holy oils. In the towns, guilds served as lay religious brotherhoods; each guild chose a patron saint and marched in the streets on holy days. For amusement the townspeople watched religious dramas, the morality and miracle plays in which religious themes were enacted. The rising town, if it harbored a bishop, took especial care to erect a new cathedral. Years of effort and of religious fervor produced the Gothic cathedrals which still stand as the best-known memorials of medieval civilization.

The Development of the Medieval Church and Papacy

If, however, we turn back to the tenth century, the troubled years before 1000, we find the church in as dubious a condition as everything else. It was fragmented and localized. Every bishop went his own way. Though the clergy was the only literate class, many of the clergy themselves could not read and write. Christian belief was mixed with the old pagan magic and superstition, and most Christians knew nothing about the theology that had shaped the traditions of the Catholic church. The monasteries were in decay. Priests often lived in a concubinage that was generally condoned. It was customary for them to marry, so that they had recognized children, to whom they intrigued to pass on their churchly position. Powerful laymen often dominated their ecclesiastical neighbors, with the big lords appointing the bishops and the little ones appointing the parish priests. When people thought about Rome at all, they sensed a vague respect for something legendary and far away; but the bishop of Rome, or pope, had no influence and was treated in unseemly fashion by nobles in his own city.

The church in crisis

The Roman Catholic church is in fact unrecognizable in the jumble of the tenth century. So far at least as human effort was concerned, it was virtually created in the eleventh century along with the other institutions of the High Middle Ages.

The impulse to reform came from many quarters. Sometimes a secular ruler undertook to correct conditions in his own domains. For this purpose he asserted a strict control over his clergy. In 962 the Holy Roman Empire was proclaimed. This Empire, like the Carolingian and Roman empires which it was supposed to continue, was in theory coterminous with Latin Christendom itself and endowed with a special mission to preserve and extend the Christian faith. Neither in France nor in England (nor, when they became Christian states, in Spain, Hungary, Poland, or Scandinavia) was this claim of the Holy Roman Empire ever acknowledged. But the Empire did for a time embrace Italy as well as Germany. The first emperors, in the tenth and eleventh centuries, denouncing the conditions of the church in Rome, strove to make the pope their appointee.

Reform efforts

At the same time a reform movement arose from spiritual sources. Serious Christians took matters into their own hands. They founded a new monastery at Cluny in France, which soon had many affiliated houses. It was their purpose to purify monastic life and to set a higher Christian ideal to which all clergy and laity might aspire. To rid themselves of immediate local pressures, the greed, narrowness, ignorance, family ambition, and self-satisfied inertia that were the main causes of corruption, the Cluniacs refused to recognize any authority except that of Rome itself. Thus, at the very time when conditions in Rome were at their worst, Christians throughout Europe built up the prestige of Rome, of the idea of Rome, as a means to raise all Latin Christendom from its depths.

CHRONOLOGY OF NOTABLE EVENTS, 500 B.C.–A.D. 1300

500–300 B.C.	Creative era of Classical Greek Civilization: Plato, Aristotle
46 B.C.	Roman Republic conquers Greece
45–31 B.C.	Roman Republic evolves into the Roman Empire
c. A.D. 26–29	Jesus is active in Palestine; beginnings of Christianity
306–337	Roman Emperor Constantine: toleration of Christianity
c. 420	St. Augustine writes *City of God*
476	End of Roman Empire in the West
450–750	Roman Catholic Church gains converts and influence in Western Europe
610–632	Prophet Muhammad teaches the new religion of Islam
635–750	Islam spreads across Middle East, North Africa, and Spain
800	Coronation of Emperor Charlemagne; the Carolingian Empire
1000–1200	Improvements in European agriculture and rise of towns
1054	Schism of Roman Catholic Church and Orthodox Eastern Church
1095–1099	First Christian Crusade in Palestine
1100–1200	Arabic and Greek science enters European Culture
1147–1221	Second-Fifth Christian Crusades
1198–1216	Pope Innocent III: height of Medieval Papacy
1100–1300	Development of Universities and Scholasticism
1267–1273	Thomas Aquinas writes the *Summa Theologica*

As for the popes in Rome, those who preserved any independence of judgment or respect for their own office, it was their general plan to free themselves from the Roman mobs and aristocrats without falling into dependence upon the Holy Roman Emperor. In 1059 Pope Nicholas II issued a decree providing that future popes should be elected by the cardinals. The cardinals, at that time, were the priests of churches in the city of Rome or bishops of neighboring dioceses. By entrusting the choice of future popes to them, Pope Nicholas hoped to exclude all influence from outside the clergy itself. Popes have been elected by cardinals ever since, though not always without influence from outside.

One of the first popes so elected was Gregory VII, known also as Hildebrand, a dynamic and strong-willed man who was pope from 1073 to 1085. He had been in touch with the Cluniac reformers, and dreamed of a reformed and reinvigorated Europe under the universal guidance of the Roman pontiff. Gregory believed that the church should stand apart from worldly society, that it should judge and guide all human actions, and that a pope had the supreme power to judge and punish kings and emperors if he deemed them sinful. His ideal was not a "world state," but its spiritual counterpart, a world church officered by a single-minded and disciplined clergy, centralized under a single authority. He began by insisting that the clergy free itself of worldly involvements. He required married priests to put aside their wives and families.

Gregory VII

Celibacy of the clergy, never generally established in the Greek Orthodox church, and later rejected by Protestants in the West, became the rule for the Roman Catholic priesthood. Gregory insisted also that no ecclesiastic might receive office through appointment by a layman. In his view only clergy might institute or influence clergy, for the clergy must be independent and self-contained.

Gregory soon faced a battle with that other aspirant to universal supremacy and a sacred mission, the Holy Roman Emperor, who at this time was Henry IV. In Germany the bishops and abbots possessed a great deal of the land, which they held and governed under the emperor as feudal magnates in their own right. To the emperor it was vitally important to have his own men, as reliable vassals, in these great

Lay investiture

positions. Hence in Germany "lay investiture" had become very common. "Lay investiture" meant the practice by which a layman, the emperor, conferred upon the new bishop the signs of his spiritual authority, the ring and the staff. Gregory prohibited lay investiture. He supported the German bishops and nobles when they rebelled against Henry, but the emperor remained obstinate. Gregory then excommunicated him, that is, outlawed him from Christian society by forbidding any priest to give him the sacraments. Henry, baffled, sought out the pope at Canossa in Italy to do penance. "To go to Canossa" in later times became a byword for submission to the will of Rome.

In 1122, after both original contenders had died, a compromise on the matter of lay investiture was effected by which bishops recognized the emperor as their feudal head but looked to Rome for spiritual authority. But the struggle between popes and emperors went on unabated. The magnates of Germany, lay lords as well as bishops, often allied with the pope to preserve their own feudal liberties from the emperor. The emperor in Germany was never able to consolidate his domains as did the kings in England and France. The unwillingness of lords and churchmen (and of towns also, as we have seen) to let the emperors build up an effective government left its mark permanently upon Europe in two ways. It contributed to the centralization of Latin Christendom under Rome, while it blocked the development of a more unified monarchical state in central Europe.

Innocent III

The height of the medieval papacy came with Innocent III, whose pontificate lasted from 1198 to 1216. Innocent virtually realized Gregory's dream of a unified Christian world. He intervened in politics everywhere. He was recognized as a supreme arbiter. At his word, a king of France took a wife, a king of England accepted an unwanted archbishop, a king of León put aside the cousin whom he had married, and a claimant to the crown of Hungary deferred to his rival. The kings of England, Aragon, and Portugal acknowledged him as feudal overlord within their realms. Huge revenues now flowed to Rome from all over Latin Christendom, and an enormous bureaucracy worked there to dispatch the voluminous business of the papal court. As kings struggled to repress civil rebellion, so Innocent and his successors struggled to repress heresy, which, defined as doctrine at variance with that of the church at large, was becoming alarmingly common among the Albigensians of southern France.

In 1215 Innocent called a great church council, the greatest since antiquity, attended by 500 bishops and even by the patriarchs of Constantinople and Jerusalem. The council labored at the perplexing task of keeping the clergy from worldly temptations. By forbidding priests to officiate at ordeals or trials by battle, it virtually ended these survivals of barbarism. It attempted to regularize belief in the supernatural by controlling the superstitious traffic in relics. It declared the sacraments to be the channel of God's saving grace and defined them authoritatively.[2] In the chief sacrament, the Eucharist or Mass, it promulgated the dogma of transubstantiation, which held that, in the Mass, the priest converts the substance of bread and wine into the substance of Christ's body and blood. Except for heretics, who were suppressed, the reforms and doctrines of Innocent's council were accepted with satisfaction throughout Latin Europe.

Intellectual Life: The Universities, Scholasticism

Under the auspices of the church, as rising governments gave more civil security, and as the economy of town and country became able to support people devoted to a life of thought, the intellectual horizon of Europeans began to open. The twelfth and thirteenth centuries saw the founding of the first universities. These originated in the natural and spontaneous coming together of teachers and students which had never wholly disappeared even in the most chaotic era of the early Middle Ages. By 1200 there was a center of medical studies at Salerno in south Italy, of legal studies at Bologna in north Italy, of theological studies at Paris. Oxford was founded about 1200 by a secession of disgruntled students and professors from Paris; Cambridge, shortly thereafter. By 1300 there were a dozen such universities in Latin Europe; by 1500 there were almost a hundred.

The founding of universities

As the early agglomerations of traders developed into organized towns and guilds, so the informal concourses of students and teachers developed into organized institutions of learning, receiving the sharp corporate stamp that was characteristic of the High Middle Ages. It was in having this corporate identity that medieval universities resemble our own and differed from the schools of Athens or Alexandria in ancient times. A university, the University of Paris, for example, was a body of individuals, young and old, interested in learning and endowed by law with a communal name and existence. It possessed definite liberties under some kind of charter, regulated its own affairs through its own officials, and kept its own order among its often boisterous population. It gave, and even advertised, courses and lectures, and it decided collectively which professors were the best qualified to teach. It might consist of distinct schools or "faculties"—the combination of theology, law, and medicine, as at Paris, was the most usual. It held examinations and awarded degrees, whose meaning and value were recognized throughout the Latin West. The degree, which originated as a license to teach, admitted its holder to certain honors or privileges in the same way that members of other guilds were authorized to practice a specific craft. With such degrees, professors might readily move from one university to another. Students moved easily also because all universities used the Latin language and offered a similar curriculum. The university, moreover, though typically beginning in poverty, was a corporate body capable of holding property; and the benefactions of pious donors often built up substantial endowments in lands and manors. So organized, free from outside control, and enjoying an income from property, the university lived on as a permanent institution, through good times and bad.

---

[2]A sacrament is understood to be the outward sign of an inward grace. In Catholic doctrine the sacraments were and are seven in number: baptism, confirmation, penance, the Eucharist, extreme unction, marriage, and holy orders. Except for baptism, a sacrament may be administered only by a priest. A dogma is the common belief of the church, in which all the faithful share and must share so long as they are members of the church. Dogmas are regarded as implicitly the same in all ages; they cannot be invented or developed, but may from time to time be clarified, defined, promulgated, or proclaimed.

Theology

The queen of the sciences was theology, the intellectual study of religion. Many in Europe, by the eleventh century, were beginning to reflect upon their beliefs. They continued to believe in God but could no longer believe with unthinking acceptance. It was accepted as a fact, for example, that the Son of God had been incarnated as a man in Jesus Christ. But in the eleventh century an Italian named Anselm, who became archbishop of Canterbury, wrote a treatise called *Cur Deus Homo?*—"Why Did God Become Man?"—giving reasoned explanations to show why God had taken human form to save sinful human beings. Anselm argued that reason strongly supported the Christian faith in God. Soon afterward Abelard, who taught at Paris, wrote his *Sic et Non*—"Yes and No" or "Pro and Con"—a collection of inconsistent statements made by St. Augustine and other Fathers of the Church. Abelard's purpose was to apply logic to the inherited mass of patristic writings, show wherein the truth of Christian doctrine really lay, and so make the faith consistent with reason and reflection.

Meanwhile, in the twelfth century a great stream of new knowledge poured into Europe, bringing about a veritable intellectual revolution. It was derived from the Arabs, with whom Christians were in contact in Sicily and Spain. The Arabs, as has been seen, had taken over the ancient Greek science, translated Greek writings into Arabic, and in many ways added further refinements of their own. Bilingual Christians (assisted by numerous learned Jews who traveled readily between the Christian and Muslim worlds) translated these works into Latin. Above all, they translated Aristotle, the great codifier of Greek knowledge who had lived and written in the fourth century B.C. The Europeans, drawing on the commentaries of Muslim scholars such as Averroës (1126–1198), were overwhelmed by this sudden disclosure of an undreamed universe of knowledge. Aristotle became The Philosopher, the unparalleled authority on all branches of knowledge other than religious.

Arabic and Greek learning

The great problem for Europeans was how to digest the gigantic bulk of Aristotle, or, in more general terms, how to assimilate or reconcile the body of Greek and Arabic learning to the Christian faith. The universities, with their "scholastic" philosophers or "schoolmen," performed this function. Most eminent of scholastics was Thomas Aquinas (1225–1274), the Angelic Doctor, known also to his own contemporaries as the Dumb Ox from the slow deliberation of his speech. His chief work, appropriately called the *Summa Theologica,* was a survey of all knowledge.

Thomas Aquinas

The chief accomplishment of Thomas Aquinas was his demonstration that faith and reason could not be in conflict. By reason he meant a severely logical method, with exact definition of words and concepts, deducing step by step what follows and must follow if certain premises are accepted. His philosophy is classified as a form of moderate "realism," a term whose medieval meaning differed from its common usage today. For medieval philosophers "realism" meant that the general idea is more "real" than the particular—that "man" or "woman" is more real than this or that man or woman, that "law" as such is more real and binding than this or that particular law. He derived his philosophy from what he took to be the nature of God, of law, of reason, of human life, and of beings in general. Thomas taught a hierarchic view of the universe and of society, of which God was the apex. All things and all people were subordinated to God in a descending order, each bound to fulfill the role set by its own place and nature. It was the emphasis on the superior reality of abstractions that enabled people in the Middle Ages to believe steadfastly in the church while freely

THE MEETING OF ST. ANTHONY AND ST. PAUL
by Sassetta (Italian, 1392–1450)

This picture conveys the abstractness of medieval thought. There is no attempt to portray the figures as unique individuals; they are typical saints with the halos designating sacred persons. St. Anthony appears in three places—walking alone, converting a centaur, and embracing St. Paul. The forest and hills represent the idea of trees or mounds of earth, but there is no physical specificity in these representations of nature.

THOMAS AQUINAS
by Fra Bartelemo (Italian, 1472–1517)
Thomas Aquinas combined Aristotelian knowledge with Christian faith in his scholastic theology, thus gaining permanent respect (and sainthood) from the Catholic Church and artistic recognition from painters such as Fra Bartelemo.
(Nicolo Orsi Battaglini/Art Resource, NY)

attacking individual churchmen, to have faith in the papacy while denouncing the popes as scoundrels—or to accept without difficulty the mystery of transubstantiation, which declared that what admittedly looked and tasted like bread and wine was, in real inner substance, the body of Christ.

Scholasticism

The scholastic philosophy, as perfected by Thomas Aquinas, was not very favorable to the growth of natural science, because its emphasis on an inner reality drew attention away from the actual details and behavior of concrete things. On the other hand, the scholastic philosophy laid foundations on which later European thought was to be reared. It habituated Europeans to great exactness, to careful distinctions, even to the splitting of hairs. It called for disciplined thinking. And it made the world safe for reason. If any historical generalization may be made safely, it may be said that any society that believes reason to threaten its foundations will suppress reason. In Thomas's time, there were some who said that Aristotle and the Arabs were infidels, dangerous influences that must be silenced. Any reasoning about the faith, they warned, was a form of weakness. Thomas's doctrine that faith could not be endangered by reason gave a freedom to thinkers to go on thinking.

The Crusades; New Invasions; Europe by 1300

Meanwhile, the West was beginning to expand. Europe in the eleventh century launched a military offensive against Islam. All Latin Christendom went on the Crusades. War itself was subordinated to the purposes of religion.

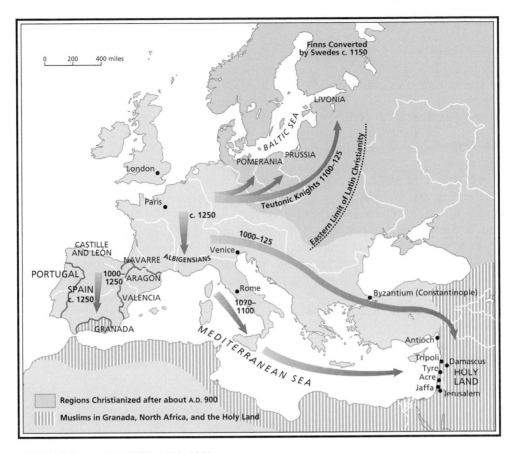

CRUSADING ACTIVITY, 1100–1250

Medieval Christendom expanded geographically until about 1250. Darker regions are those christianized shortly before and after 1000. Arrows indicate organized military-religious expeditions, which by 1250 had recovered most of Spain from Muslim control, but had failed to do so in the Holy Land. Dates are rounded and very rough.

The most ambitious, best remembered, and least successful of such expeditions were the Crusades to win back the Holy Land. The First Crusade was preached in 1095 by Pope Urban II, who hoped thereby to advance the peace of God by draining off bellicose nobles to fight the infidels and to build up the pope's leadership in Europe. Crusades to the Holy Land, with varying success, and sometimes departing woefully from their religious aims, went on

Crusades to the Holy Land

intermittently for 200 years. It was the growth of Italian shipping in the Mediterranean, the rise of more orderly feudal monarchies, the increasing sense of a Europe-wide common purpose that made possible the assembly and transport of considerable forces over a great distance. But the motivation for such Crusades, especially in the beginning, came mostly from a wave of religious fervor that brought nobles and commoners alike into the Crusader armies. This fervor contributed to brutal, deadly attacks on Jewish communities within Europe as well as to the extraordinary violence against entire Muslim populations in cities such as Antioch and Jerusalem. At the same time, however, the Crusades gave Europeans a new awareness of the world beyond their own local realms of religion and small-town economies. Historians have argued that the Crusaders' contacts with Arab societies in the Middle East stimulated subsequent European economic development and a new cultural identity among "Western" peoples. Although this argument points to important consequences of the Crusades, it is also true that the campaigns against Islam grew out of Europe's own growing political and military strength. For a century the Latin Christians occupied parts of Palestine and Syria. But military defeats forced them to withdraw in the thirteenth century, and the Muslims remained in possession.

Other crusades

Other crusades (for such they were) had more lasting results. A party of Normans won Sicily from the Arabs about 1100. Iberian Christians, descending from the mountains of northern Spain, carried on a *reconquista* of two centuries against the Moors. By 1250 they had staked out the Christian kingdoms of Portugal, León, Castile, Aragon, and Valencia, leaving the Muslims only Granada in the extreme south, which was conquered much later, in 1492. In southern France, an Albigensian crusade in the thirteenth century put down the heretics, those born in the Christian faith but erring from the reigning interpretations of it. Crusading expeditions were also launched against a few remaining "heathen" populations in northeastern Europe. The Teutonic Order, a military-religious society of knights founded originally to fight in the Holy Land, transferred its operations to the north. Christianity was brought by the sword to primitive Prussia and the east Baltic regions.

About the year 1250 there developed a new threat of invasion from Asia. As the Huns had burst out of Asia in the fifth century, and the Magyars in the ninth, so now the Tartars appeared in the thirteenth century, to be followed in the fourteenth by the Ottoman Turks. We shall see how the Turks long continued to press upon central Europe. But, on the whole, by the thirteenth century, Europe was capable of resistance. Always until then it had been vulnerable as an outlying, backward, thinly populated protuberance from the Eurasian land mass. It had lain open in the remote past to wandering Indo-Europeans, then to Roman imperial conquerors, to Germanic barbarians, to Huns, Magyars, and, in part, the Arabs. All these were gradually assimilated by the Roman church, the Latin language, the common institutions of feudalism, monarchy, a free town life, parliamentary assemblies, and scholastic learning. An increasingly connected and coherent culture ran from England to Sicily and from Portugal to Poland.

The "rise of Europe"

By 1300 the "rise of Europe" was an accomplished fact. The third of the three segments into which the Greco-Roman world had divided, the one which in A.D. 700 had been the most isolated and fragmented, now some 600 years later had a civilization of its own. It was still only one among the several great cultures of the world, such as the Islamic, Byzantine, Indian, and Chinese. It enjoyed no preeminence. The Chinese empire, for example, in the thirteenth century, had cities whose population reached into millions. It had an affluent merchant class, great textile manufacturers, and an iron industry that produced over 100,000 tons a year. The arts and sciences were assiduously pursued. Government was centralized and complex; it issued paper money and employed a civil service recruited by competitive examinations. Books on religious, technical, and agricultural subjects, including whole multivolume encyclopedias, were printed in enormous numbers, even though the lack of an alphabet and the thousands of Chinese characters made it difficult for literacy to become widely spread. The Venetian Marco Polo was dazzled by the China that he lived in from 1275 to 1292.

Europeans took pride in their crusading armies, represented here in a medieval image of the conquest of Antioch in 1098 during the First Crusade.
(Art Resource, NY)

Many have asked why China did not generate, as Europe did in these centuries, the forces that ultimately led to the modern scientific and industrial world. One answer is suggested by the fact that it was Europeans such as Marco Polo who went to China, not Chinese who went to Europe. It was the Chinese who invented printing, but it was Europe that was revolutionized by printed books. The Chinese knew of gunpowder, but the Europeans developed more effective guns. Chinese merchant vessels also traded with India but did not pursue the advantage. In the fifteenth century, over the years 1405 to 1433, a Ming emperor launched a large-scale series of long-range naval expeditions, seven in all, headed by his admiral Cheng Ho. The expeditions sailed to ports in Southeast Asia, India, the Persian Gulf, and East Africa, exchanging gifts in transactions that recognized the emperor's power and prestige. But the emperor and his advisers ultimately terminated the entire venture. China turned its back on overseas commercial opportunities and turned inward to the protection and expansion of its land frontiers. Never again (until the recent past) did it embark on similar expeditions or send its ships to distant, unknown seas. It was the Europeans who pursued the development of trade in India and also crossed the Atlantic to discover America. Somehow Europe became more enterprising and restless, perhaps because in Europe there was no all-embracing empire as in China, but kings, lords, and towns that competed with each other. With religion and the church kept distinct from the state, the questions of what one should do with one's life were less dependent on the political powers than in China. Europe was disorderly and full of conflict—rivalries and wars between kings, quarrels between kings and their barons, disputes between church and state, clashes between lords and their peasant workers. Much of this conflict was destructive, yet there was also a kind of freedom in such disorder and a dynamism which promoted change.

European civilization in 1300

European civilization in 1300 was by no means a "modern" society, yet the ancient and medieval cultures on European lands had created institutions and traditions that remained influential even in the most recent eras of modern world history. By 1300 people in Europe had developed separate (at times contending) institutions of church and state to control a growing population, economic institutions to promote urban commerce and long-distance trade, judicial and parliamentary councils to codify or revise the law, and universities to teach or redefine their intellectual traditions. These traditions included a pervasive, enduring faith in Christianity, but the ancient Christian beliefs were challenged, revised, and extended by other ancient traditions of rhetoric, philosophy, and rational inquiry—all of which contributed to the emergence of what is now called early modern history.

For interactive exercises, glossary, chronologies, and more, go to the *Online Learning Center* at **www.mhhe.com/palmer10.**

Chapter 2

THE UPHEAVAL IN WESTERN CHRISTENDOM, 1300–1560

In the transition from traditional to more modern forms of society all the old civilizations have had to reexamine their religious base. Today we can observe this process at work everywhere: the Chinese reconsider the age-old teachings of Confucius, the Muslims enter into wider activities than those known to the Qur'an, and the peoples of India are rapidly expanding an economy in which historic Hindu practices no longer form the dominant pattern. People in modern societies do not necessarily reject their ancestral religion. In fact, they may strongly reaffirm it, but they usually try also to adapt it to modern economic and political conditions and to make room for new and non-religious interests. The process of developing a variety of activities outside the sphere of religion is called "secularization."

Latin Christendom was the first of the world's major religious cultures to become "secularized." In the very long run it was those aspects of European civilization that were least associated with Christianity, such as natural science and industrial technology, or military and economic power, that the non-European world proved to be most willing to adopt. If in our own time there has come to be such a thing as a global civilization, it is because all the world's great traditional cultures have been increasingly secularized. This secularization of human cultures, although often challenged by popular religious movements in the contemporary world, remains one of the decisive trends in modern world history, and it is a trend that began to appear in Europe at the end of the Middle Ages.

The Europe which had become both expansive and more prosperous by the thirteenth century soon entered upon a series of disasters. The Mongols after about 1240 held Russia in subjugation for 200 years. The Ottoman Turks, who had originated in central Asia, penetrated the Byzantine Empire, crushed the medieval Serbian kingdom at the battle of Kosovo in 1389, and spread over the Balkans. They took Constantinople itself in 1453. Eastern Christianity continued to exist, but under alien political domination. Latin Christianity,

Chapter emblem: Detail from *A Portrait of a Family* by Lavinia Fontana (1552–1614). (Scala/Art Resource, NY)

reaching from Poland and Hungary to the Atlantic, remained independent but was beset with troubles. The authority of the papacy and of the Roman Catholic church was called into question. Eventually the Protestant churches emerged, and the religious unity of medieval civilization disappeared. Yet new forces also asserted themselves alongside or outside the religious tradition. Government, law, philosophy, science, the arts, material and economic activities were pursued with less regard for Christian values. Power, order, beauty, wealth, knowledge, and control of nature were regarded as desirable in themselves.

In this mixture of decline and revival, of religious revolution and secularization, medieval Christendom evolved into the social, political, and cultural world of early modern Europe.

✒ 5.   DISASTERS OF THE FOURTEENTH CENTURY

The Black Death and Its Consequences

During the fourteenth century, and quite abruptly, almost half the population of Europe was wiped out. Although it is impossible to know exactly how many people lived in medieval Europe, the total population probably fell from roughly 70 million in 1300 to about 45 million in 1400. Some died in sporadic local famines that began to appear after 1300. The great killer, however, was the plague, or Black Death, which first struck Europe in 1348. The precise medical cause of the plague is still debated. Most modern historians believe that the disease was carried by rats, but this theory may not explain how the contagion moved so quickly across Europe or why so many humans became vulnerable to a bacillus that normally lives in rodents. Despite the uncertainty about its physiological origins, historians agree that the plague had decisive effects on European social life. Since the plague returned at irregular and unpredictable intervals, and killed off the young as well as the old, it disrupted marriage and family life and made it impossible for many years for Europe to regain the former level of population. In some places whole villages disappeared. Cultivated fields were abandoned for want of able-bodied men and women to work them. The towns were especially vulnerable, because the contagion spread quickly through populations crowded within town walls. Trade and exchange were obstructed; prices, wages, and incomes moved erratically; famine made its victims more susceptible to disease; and deaths from the plague contributed to famine. The living were preoccupied with the burial of the dead and with fears for their own future.

The Black Death

There were immediate social and political repercussions. In some cases, survivors benefited because the scarcity of labor led to higher wages. On the other hand, in the general disorganization, and with landowners and urban employers decimated also, many of the poor could find no work or took to vagabondage and begging. The upper classes, acting through governments, attempted to control wages and prices. Rebellions of workers broke out in various towns, especially in Flanders, and there were massive insurrections of peasants in many parts of Europe. In France these were called "jacqueries" (from "Jacques," a nickname for a peasant), of which the first was in 1358. In England a similar large-scale uprising in 1381 came to be known as Wat Tyler's rebellion. Sometimes the spokesmen for these movements went beyond their immediate grievances to raise broader social questions about why some should be rich and others poor. Governments and the upper classes replied to this menace with ferocious repression. The peasants generally returned to their

Revolts and repression

usual labors. Yet something was gained for the rural workers, at least in the long run, as underlying economic and demographic forces continued to assert themselves. The landowners, or feudal class, in order to get the work done on their manors and assure their own incomes, had to offer more favorable terms. These included, for example, the giving of lifetime tenures to peasant families, in return for fixed payment of sums of money. Over the years many of these peasant holdings became hereditary and the value of money decreased, so that payment of a shilling, for example, which in 1400 represented a significant amount, became much less burdensome for the rural worker by 1600. In effect, a class of small peasant property owners began to emerge in much of Europe.

The kings also, who had been building up their position against the church and the feudal lords since the eleventh century, found their problems complicated by the disasters of the fourteenth. They still had their governments to maintain, and their ambitions to satisfy, even if death removed large fractions of their subjects. They even had to increase their incomes, as it became usual for kings to employ royal armies of foot soldiers against the recurring possibility of feudal resistance. Various means of increasing the royal spending power were devised. Currency was debased; that is, the king ordered a given weight of gold or silver to represent a larger number of monetary units. Thus he temporarily had more money, but the result was inflation and higher prices, that is, the declining value of money already mentioned. New taxes were introduced. About 1300 the kings of both England and France undertook to tax the clergy of their respective kingdoms, in both of which the clergy were substantial owners of land. The kings made increasing demands as well on great noble landholders and urban merchants. These demands were resisted, or made subject to bargains by the representative bodies whose origin was described in the last chapter, so that the fourteenth century, and still more the fifteenth, has been called the "golden age" of the medieval parliaments.

In 1337 the Hundred Years' War began between England and France. The battles all took place in France, which was internally divided, some parts, like Aquitaine, having long belonged to the English crown. France was ravaged by marauding bands of English soldiers and their French *The Hundred Years' War*

adherents, until French forces began to achieve military victories under the inspired leadership of Joan of Arc, the young woman whom the English burned at the stake in Rouen in 1431 after she was convicted by the church of heresy and witchcraft. In England the effects of the long and intermittent war were less divisive. As English soldiers with their longbows defeated the mounted French knights, a kind of early patriotism arose in England. Parliament widened its powers as the kings needed money for their campaigns. But the great English barons also became more unruly. They deposed Richard II in 1399, then quarreled among themselves, in a confusion punctuated by invasion from Scotland and revolt in Wales. Disorder became worse in the fifteenth century. Dukes and earls and their followers formed private armies and fought with each other; they defied the royal law courts and intimidated juries, used Parliament and government for their own purposes, and exploited their peasants. From about 1450 until 1485 England was beset by upper-class turmoil that came to be called the Wars of the Roses, because the opposing noble factions adopted red and white roses as their symbols.

Troubles of the Medieval Church

Meanwhile similar calamities afflicted the church. In 1300, the church of the High Middle Ages, centralized in the papacy, stood at its zenith. But the church was weakened by its

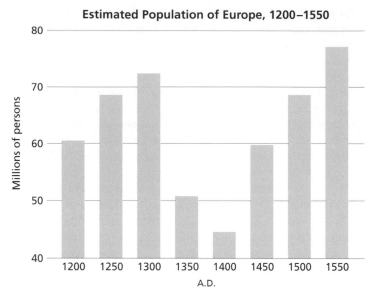

Estimated Population of Europe, 1200–1550

Source: M. K. Bennett, *The World's Food* (New York: Harper, 1954).

This graph shows the growth of Europe's population after 1200, the catastrophic impact of the Black Death in the fourteenth century, and the revival of the European population after the early 1400s.

very successes. It faced the danger that besets every successful institution—a form of government or a university, to choose modern examples—the danger of believing that the institution exists for the benefit of those who conduct its affairs. The papacy, being at the top, was the most liable to this danger. It became "corrupt," set in its ways, out of touch with public opinion, and controlled by a self-perpetuating bureaucracy. It was unable to reform itself, and unwilling to let anyone else reform it.

Both Edward I of England and Philip the Fair of France, in the 1290s, assessed taxes on the landed estates belonging to the great abbeys, bishoprics, and other components of the church. The pope, Boniface VIII, prohibited the taxation of clergy by the civil ruler. In the ensuing altercation, in 1302, he issued the famous bull, *Unam Sanctam,* the most extreme of all assertions of papal supremacy, which declared that outside the Roman church there was no salvation, and that "every human creature" was "subject to the Roman pontiff."[1] The French king sent soldiers to arrest Boniface, who soon died. French influence in the College of Cardinals brought about the election of a pope who was expected to be subservient to

The "Babylonian Captivity"

Philip, and who took up his residence, with his court and officials, at Avignon on the lower Rhone river, on what were then the borders of France. Thus began the "Babylonian Captivity" of the church. The rest of Europe regarded the popes at Avignon throughout the century as tools of France. The papacy lost much of its prestige as a universal institution.

---

[1]Bulls, so-called from the Latin word for their seal, are known by their first one or two Latin words, which in this case mean "one holy (church)"; a "bull," while the most solemn form of papal edict, does not as such embody a dogma; and it is not Catholic practice today to affirm this policy of Boniface VIII.

Attempts to correct the situation made matters worse. In 1378 the College of Cardinals, torn by French and anti-French factions within it, elected two popes. Both were equally legitimate, being chosen by cardinals, but one lived at Rome, one at Avignon, and neither would resign. The French and their supporters recognized the Avignon pope; England and most of Germany, the Roman. For forty years both lines were perpetuated. There were now two papacies, estranged by the Great Schism of the West.

The Great Schism

Never had the papacy been so externally magnificent as in the days of the Captivity and the Schism. The papal court at Avignon surpassed the courts of kings in splendor. The papal officialdom grew in numbers, ignoring the deeper problems while busily transacting each day's business. Papal revenues mounted, and new papal taxes were devised, for example, the "annates," by which every bishop or abbot in Christendom had to transmit to Rome most of the first year's income of his office. In the continuing movement of funds from all over Europe to the papal court, from the thirteenth century on, a new class of international bankers rose and prospered.

But the papacy, never so sumptuous, had never since the tenth century rested on such shaky foundations. People pay willingly for institutions in which they believe, and admire magnificence in leaders whom they respect. But before 1378, with the pope submissive to France, and after 1378, with two popes and two papacies to support, there was growing complaint at the extravagance and worldliness of papal rule. It must be remembered that all this happened in a Europe traumatized by the plague, and with a declining number of people expected to bear increasing financial burdens. The most pious Christians were the most shocked. They recognized the vital necessity of obtaining God's grace, but with two churches under two popes, each claiming to hold the keys of Peter, how could they be certain that their church gave true salvation? In a society that was still primarily a religious community, this sense of religious insecurity was a source of uneasiness and dread.

The old moorings were weakened, the wrath of God seemed to be raining upon the earth, and no one had the slightest notion of how the world was going to turn out. Symptoms of mass neurosis appeared. Some people sought refuge in a hectic merriment or luxury and self-indulgence. Others became preoccupied with grisly subjects. Some frantically performed the Dance of Death in the cemeteries, while others furtively celebrated the Black Mass, parodying religion in a mad desire to appease the devil. The Order of Flagellants grew up; its members went through the streets, two by two, beating each other with chains and whips. Religious anxieties and fearful religious rumors contributed also to waves of anti-Jewish violence, murder, and expulsion that spread across parts of France and Germany in the fourteenth century. And it was at this time that people first became obsessed with the fear of witches, a delusion that would ultimately cause thousands of persons (often older women) to be tortured and executed over the following three centuries.

Responses to crisis

Disaffection with the church, or the thought that it might not be the true or the only way to salvation, spread in all ranks of society. It was not only kings who disputed the claims of the clergy but also obscure parish priests, close to the distress of ordinary people, who began to doubt the powers of their ecclesiastical superiors. One of these humble clerics was William Langland, who in his *Piers Plowman,* in the 1360s, contrasted the sufferings of the honest poor with the hypocrisy and corruption in high places. Such unsettling ideas spread very widely; in England those who held them were known as Lollards. Since the actual poor left no records, it is hard to say exactly what they thought, but some of their ideas were probably

Lollards and Hussites

Extreme expressions of religious anxiety appeared in the later Middle Ages among the flagellants who wandered through towns beating themselves to appease the wrath of God. They are portrayed here in a later sixteenth-century engraving of their processions.
(Giraudon/Art Resource, NY)

expressed by John Wyclif, who taught at Oxford. About 1380, Wyclif was saying that the true church could do without elaborate possessions, and even that an organized church might not be necessary for salvation, since ordinary, devout persons could do without priests and obtain salvation by reading the Bible, which he translated into English. Similar ideas appeared in Bohemia in central Europe, with John Huss as their spokesman. Here they became a national movement, for the Hussites were both a religious party and at the same time a Slavic or Czech party protesting against the supremacy of the Germans who lived in Bohemia. The Hussite wars ravaged central Europe for decades in the fifteenth century. The ideas of the Lollards and of Huss and Wyclif were branded as heresy, or unacceptable deviations from the true doctrine of the church.

Influential and established persons did not yet turn to heresy, and still less to witchcraft or flagellation. Their answer to the needs of the day was to assemble a great Europewide or general council of the church, in which reforms could be pressed by the whole body of Christians upon the reluctant and rival popes.

The Conciliar Movement

In 1409 such a church council met at Pisa. All parts of the Latin West were represented. The council declared both reigning popes deposed and obtained the due election of another, but since the first two refused to resign there were now three. In 1414 an even greater and more fully attended council met at Constance. Its aims were three: to end the now threefold schism, to extirpate heresy, and to reform the church "in head and members," or from top to bottom. Not much was accomplished in reform. To discourage heresy, John Huss was interrogated, condemned, and burned at the stake. The schism was ended. All three popes were at last persuaded or compelled to withdraw, and another, Martin V, was elected. The unity of the church, under the papacy, was at last restored.

The majority of the Council of Constance wished to make general councils part of the permanent apparatus of the church for all time in the future. Martin V, however, soon reaffirmed the prerogatives of the papal office, dissolved the Council of Constance, and repudiated its decrees. The next 30 years saw a continuing contest of wills between successive popes and successive councils.

General councils

In this battle for jurisdiction few reforms could be adopted, and fewer still could be enforced. Increasingly the life of the church was corrupted by money. No one believed in bribery, but everyone knew that many high churchmen (like many high civil officials of the day) could be bribed. To buy or sell a church office was a crime in the canon law known as "simony," but it was a crime which in the fifteenth century could not be suppressed. For churchmen to live with mistresses was considered understandable, if unseemly; the standards of laymen in such matters were not high; but for a bishop or other ecclesiastic to give lucrative church positions to his own children (or other relatives) was the abuse known as nepotism, and it, too, could not be eradicated. To sell divine grace for money, all agreed, was not only wrong but also impossible. But in 1300 Boniface VIII had given encouragement to the practice of "indulgences." A person, if properly confessed, absolved, and truly repentant, might, by obtaining an indulgence, be spared certain of the temporal punishments of purgatory. One usually obtained such an indulgence in return for a donation of money. The practice proved to be a fatally easy method of fund raising, despite complaints against the sale of indulgences simply for money.

Church corruption and indulgences

Gradually the popes prevailed over the councils. The conciliar movement was greatly weakened for Christendom as a whole when the powerful French element secured its aims by a local national arrangement. In the Pragmatic Sanction of Bourges, in 1438, the Gallican (or French) church affirmed the supremacy of councils over popes, declared its administrative independence from the Holy See, suppressed the payment of annates to Rome, and forbade papal intervention in the appointment of French prelates. The papacy thus lost influence in France, but the popes remained preeminent in Europe as a whole. In 1449, with the dissolution of the Council of Basel, the conciliar movement came to an end. In 1450 a great Jubilee was held to celebrate the papal triumph.

The papacy, its prestige and freedom of action thus secured, now passed into the hands of a series of cultivated gentlemen, men of the world, men of "modern" outlook in tune with their times—the famous popes of the Renaissance. Some, like Nicholas V (1447–1455) or Pius II (1458–1464), were accomplished scholars and connoisseurs of books. Some were like Innocent VIII (1484–1492), a pleasant man who was the first pope to dine in public with ladies. Alexander VI (1492–1503), of the Spanish Borgia family, exploited his office for the benefit of his relatives, trying to make his son Cesare Borgia the ruler of all Italy, while his daughter, Lucretia Borgia, became duchess of Ferrara and gathered literary men and artists at her famous Renaissance court. Alexander VI's successor, Julius II (1503–1513), was a capable general, and Leo X (1513–1521) was a superb patron of architects and painters. But we must now describe the Italian Renaissance, in which worthies of this kind were elevated to the Holy See.

The Renaissance popes

✵ 6.   THE RENAISSANCE IN ITALY

In Italy in the fifteenth century, and especially at Florence, we observe not merely a decay of medieval certainties but the appearance of a new and invigorating attitude toward the world. The Renaissance, a French word meaning "rebirth," first received its name from those who thought of the Middle Ages as a dark time from which the human spirit had to be awakened. It was called a *re*birth in the belief that people now, after a long interruption, had taken up and resumed a civilization like that of the Greco-Romans. Medieval people had thought of the times of Aristotle or Cicero as not sharply distinct from their own. In the Renaissance, with a new historical sense, arose the conception of "modern" and "ancient" times, separated by a long period with a different lifestyle and appropriately called the Middle Ages.

The basic institutions of Europe, the distinctive languages and national cultures, the great frameworks of collective action in law, government, and economic production—all originated in the Middle Ages. But the Renaissance marked a new era in thought and feeling, by which Europe and its institutions were in the long run to be transformed. The origins of modern natural science can be traced more to the medieval universities than to the Renaissance thinkers. But it was in the Italy of the Quattrocento (as Italians call the fifteenth century) that other fields of thought and expression were first culti-

The Italian influence

vated. The Italian influence in other countries, in these respects, remained very strong for at least 200 years. It pertained to high culture, and hence to a limited number of persons, but extended over the whole area represented by literature and the arts—literature meaning all kinds of writing and the arts including all products of human skill. The effects of the Italian Renaissance, though much modified with the passage of time, were evident in the books and art galleries of Europe and America, and in the architecture of their cities, even after the revolution of "modern" art in the early twentieth century. They involved the whole area of culture which was neither theological nor scientific but concerned with moral and civic questions about what human beings ought to be or ought to do, with the answers reflected in matters of taste, style, propriety, decorum, personal character, and education. In particular, it was in Renaissance Italy that an almost purely secular attitude first appeared, in which life was no longer seen by leading thinkers as a brief preparation for the hereafter.

The Italian Cities and the New Conception of Life

The towns of Italy, so long as trade converged in the Mediterranean, were the biggest and most bustling of all the towns that rose in Europe in the Middle Ages. The crafts of Italy included many refined trades such as those of the goldsmith or stonecarver, which were so zealously pursued that artisanship turned into art, and a delight in the beautiful became common among all classes. Merchants made fortunes in commerce: they lent their money to popes or princes and so made further fortunes as bankers. They bought the wares of the craftsmen-artists. They rejoiced, not so much in money or the making of money, as in the beautiful things and psychological satisfactions that money could buy; and if they forgot the things that money could not buy, this is only to say again that their outlook was becoming more "secular."

The Italian city-states

The towns were independent city-states. There was no king to build up a government for Italy as a whole, and for several generations the popes were either absent at Avignon or engaged in disputes arising from the Great Schism, so that the influence of Rome was unimportant. The merchant oli-

The wealthiest persons in Italian towns were often bankers who made money from the kind of financial exchange that appears in this fifteenth-century illustration.
(Scala/Art Resource, NY)

garchies, each in its own city, enjoyed an unhampered stage on which to pursue interests other than those of business. In some, as at Milan, they succumbed to or worked with a local prince or despot. In others, as at Florence, Venice, and Genoa, they continued to govern themselves as republics. They had the experience of contending for public office, of suppressing popular revolt or winning popular favor, of producing works of public munificence, of making alliances, hiring armies, outwitting rivals, and conducting affairs of state. In short, Italy offered an environment in which many facets of human personality could be developed.

All this was most especially true in Florence, the chief city of Tuscany, which had grown wealthy in the later Middle Ages from the production of woolens. In the fifteenth century it had a population of about 60,000, which made it only moderately large as Italian cities went. Yet, like ancient Athens, Florence produced an extraordinary sequence of gifted individuals. From the years of Dante, Petrarch, and Boccaccio, who all died before 1375, to those of Machiavelli, who lived until 1527, an amazing number of the leading figures of the Italian Renaissance were Florentines. Like Athens also, Florence lost its republican liberty as well as its creative powers. Its history can be summarized in that of the Medici family. The founder of the family fortunes was Giovanni (1360–1429), a merchant and banker of Florence. His son, Cosimo de' Medici (1389–1464), allying himself with the popular element against some of the leading families of the republic, soon became unofficial ruler himself.

The Medici family

Two wool merchants display their goods and bags of wool. This illustration, which is from a 1492 book on arithmetic, shows the use of both Arabic and Roman numerals.
(Biblioteca Riccardiana, Florence)

Cosimo's grandson, Lorenzo the Magnificent (1449–1492), also used his great wealth to govern but is chiefly remembered as a poet, connoisseur, and lavish benefactor of art and learning. In the next century Tuscany became a grand duchy, of which the Medici were hereditary grand dukes until the family died out in 1737. Thus established, they furnished numerous cardinals and two popes to the church, and two Medici women became queens of France.

A secular conception of life

What arose in Italy, in these surroundings, was no less than a new secular conception of life. It seemed very doubtful whether a quiet, cloistered, or celibate life was on a higher plane than an active gregarious life, or family life, or even a life of promiscuity and adventure. It was hard to believe that clergy were any better than laity or that life led to a stern divine judgment in the end. That human will and intelligence might prove misleading seemed a gloomy doctrine. The belief that human beings were frail creatures, in need of God's grace and salvation, though perhaps said with the lips, seemed to evoke less feeling in the heart. Instead, what captivated the Italians of the Renaissance was a sense of the vast range of human powers.

Formerly, the ideal behavior had been seen in renunciation, in a certain disdain for the concerns of this world. Now a life of involvement was also prized. Formerly, poverty had been greatly respected, at least in Christian doctrine. Now there was more praise for a proper enjoyment of wealth. Medieval Europeans had admired a life of contemplation, or meditative withdrawal. Now the humanist Leonardo Bruni could write, in 1433, "The whole glory of man lies in activity." Often, to be sure, the two attitudes existed in the same person. Sometimes they divided different groups within the same city. As always, the old persisted along with the new. The result might be psychological stress and civil conflict.

Individualism

The new esteem for human activity took both a social and an individualistic turn. In cities maintaining their republican forms, as at Florence in the early fifteenth century, a new civic consciousness or sense of public duty was expressed. For this purpose the writings of Cicero and other

This procession is part of a fresco that Benozzo Gozzoli executed in 1469 for a Medici chapel. Although its title refers to the three kings on their way to Bethlehem, it actually represents important personages in fifteenth-century Florence. Cosimo de' Medici is on a white horse, followed by a throng of supporters.
(Scala/Art Resource, NY)

ancients were found to be highly relevant, since they provided an ethics independent of the Christian and medieval tradition. There was also a kind of cult of the great individual, hardly known to the ancients, and one which gave little attention to collective responsibility. Renaissance individualism emphasized the outstanding attainments of extraordinary men (women, by contrast, were usually expected to pursue the ordinary tasks of domestic life). The great man shaped his own destiny in a world governed by fortune. He had *virtù,* the quality of being a man (*vir,* "man"), and although a few women might also exhibit *virtù,* it was a quality which in the society of the day was more to be expected in the most aggressive adult males. It meant the successful demonstration of human powers. A man of *virtù,* in the arts, in war, or in statecraft, was a man who knew what he was doing, who, from resources within himself, made the best use of his opportunities, hewing his way through the world and excelling in all that he did. For the arts, such a spirit is preserved in the autobiography of Benvenuto Cellini.

The growing preoccupation with things human can be traced in new forms of painting, sculpture, and architecture that arose in Italy at this time. These arts likewise reflected

Lorenzo de' Medici, known as the Magnificent, examines a model for a villa that was built for him about 1480 on the outskirts of Florence.
(Scala/Art Resource, NY)

an increasing this-worldliness, a new sense of reality and a new sense of space, of a kind different from that of the Middle Ages, and which was to underlie much European thought until the early twentieth century. Space was no longer indeterminate, unknowable, or divine; it was a zone occupied by physical human beings, or one in which human beings might at least imagine themselves moving about. Reality meant visible and tangible persons or objects in this space, "objective" in the sense that they looked or felt the same to all normal persons who perceived them. It was a function of the arts to convey this reality, however idealized or suffused by the artist's individual feeling, in such a way that observers could recognize in the image the identity of the subject portrayed.

Architecture reflected the new tendencies. Though the Gothic cathedral at Milan was built as late as 1386, at Florence and elsewhere architects preferred to adapt Greco-Roman principles of design, such as symmetrical arrangements of doors and windows, the classical column, the arch and the dome. More public buildings of a nonreligious character were built, and more substantial town houses were put up by wealthy merchants, in styles meant to represent grandeur, or civic importance, or availability and convenience for human use. Gardens and terraces were added to many such buildings.

Realism in sculpture and painting

Sculpture, confined in the Middle Ages to the niches and portals of cathedrals, now emerged as an independent and free-standing art. Its favored subjects were human beings, now presented so that the viewer could walk around the object and see it from all directions. The difference from the religious figures carved on medieval churches was very great. Like the architects, the sculptors in parting from the immediate past found much in the Greek and Roman tradition that was modern and useful to their purpose. They produced portrait busts of eminent contemporaries, or figures of great leaders, sometimes on horseback, or statues depicting characters from Greco-Roman history and mythology. The use of the nude, in mythological or allegorical subjects, likewise showed a conception of humanity that was more in keeping with the Greek than with the Christian tradition.

Painting was less influenced by the ancients, since the little of ancient painting that had survived was unknown during the Renaissance. The invention of painting in oils opened new pathways for the art. Merchants, ecclesiastics, and princes provided a mounting demand. In subject matter painting remained conservative, dealing most often with religious themes. It was the conception and presentation that were new. The new feeling for space became evident. With the discovery of the mathematics of perspective, space was presented in exact relation to the beholder's eye. The viewer, in a sense, entered into the world of the painting. A three-dimensional effect was achieved, with careful representation of distance through variation of size, and techniques of shading or chiaroscuro added to the illusion of physical volume. Human figures were often placed in a setting of painted architecture, or against a background of landscape or scenery, showing castles or hills, which though supposedly far away yet framed the composition with a knowable boundary. In such a painting everything was localized in place and time; a part of the real world was caught and put in the picture. The idea was not to suggest eternity, as in earlier religious painting, nor yet to express private fantasy or the workings of the unconscious, as in much "modern" art, but to present a familiar theme in an understandable setting, often with a narrative content, that is, by the telling of a story.

Painters were able also, like the sculptors, by a close study of human anatomy, to show people in distinctive and living attitudes. Faces took on more expression as artists sought to depict individual personalities. Painting became less symbolic, less an intimation of general or abstract truths, more a portrayal of concrete realities as they met the eye. In the portrait by Bellini of a *condottiere* the reader can see how a strong, real, and vivid personality looks out from the canvas. Similarly, the great religious paintings were peopled with human beings. In Leonardo da Vinci's *Last Supper* Christ and his disciples are seen as a group of men each with his own characteristics. Raphael's Madonnas seem to be young Italian women, and in the mighty figures of Michelangelo the attributes of humanity invade heaven itself.

Humanism: The Birth of "Literature"

The literary movement in Renaissance Italy is called humanism because of the rising interest in humane letters, *litterae humaniores*. There had indeed been much writing in the later Middle Ages. Much of it had been of a technical character, as in theology, philosophy, or law; some of it had been meant to convey information, as in chronicles, histories, and descriptions of the physical world. Great hymns had been composed, lively student songs had been sung at the universities, plays had been performed in cathedrals, the old legends of King Arthur and Roland had been written down, and occasionally a monk would try his hand at a long narrative poem. Yet a new kind of literature and literary culture began to appear in the fourteenth and fifteenth centuries in Italy. A new class of writers looked upon literature as their main life's work, wrote for each other and for a somewhat larger public, and used writing to deal with general questions, or to examine their own states of mind, or resolve their own difficulties, or used words to achieve artistic effects, or simply to please and amuse their readers. Almost all of the writers were men, but a few women also entered the new literary culture of the era. The writings of Christine de Pisan, for example, helped

**PORTRAIT
OF A CONDOTTIERE
by Giovanni Bellini (Italian,
1430–1516)**

**This portrait provides an em-
phatic statement of Renaissance individualism. The artist
represents here a concrete,
strong-willed human being
rather than an abstract type,
stressing his subject's independence and self-sufficiency by
placing him against a dark and
entirely vacant background.**
(Giovanni Bellini, *Giovanni Emo,*
Samuel H. Kress Collection, © 2000
Board of Trustees, National Gallery
of Art, Washington, D.C.)

to spread humanist themes in France during the early fifteenth century (her family had
moved to France from Italy) and also demonstrated that women could participate in the
debates of European intellectual life.

Humanists and Latin

The Italian humanists, like their predecessors, wrote a good deal in
Latin. They differed from earlier literate persons in that they were not, for
the most part, members of the clergy. They complained that Latin had
become monkish, barbaric, and "scholastic," a jargon of the schools and universities, and
they greatly preferred the classic style of a Cicero or a Livy. Medieval Latin was a vigorous living language that used words in new senses, many of which have passed into
English and the Romance languages as perfectly normal expressions. Yet in the ancient
writers the humanists found qualities that medieval writing did not have. They discovered
a new range of interests, a new sensibility, discussion of political and civic questions, a
world presented without the overarching framework of religious belief. In addition, the
Greeks and Romans unquestionably had style—a sense of form, a taste for the elegant and
the epigrammatic. They had often also written for practical ends, in dialogues, orations, or
treatises that were designed for purposes of persuasion.

If the humanists therefore made a cult of antiquity, it was because they saw kindred
spirits in ancient cultures. They sensed a relevancy for their own time. The classical influence, never wholly absent in the Middle Ages, now reentered as a main force in the higher
civilization of Europe. The humanists polished their Latin, and increasingly they learned

Greek. They searched assiduously for classical texts hitherto unknown. Many were found; they had of course been copied and preserved by the monks of preceding times.

But while a special dignity attached to writing in Latin, known throughout Europe, most of the humanists wrote in Italian also. Or rather, they used the mode of speech current in Florence. This had also been the language of Dante in the *Divine Comedy*. To this vast poem the humanists now added many writings in Florentine or Tuscan prose. The result was that Florentine became the standard form of modern Italian. It was the first time that a European vernacular—that is, the common spoken tongue as opposed to Latin—became thus standardized amid the variety of its dialects and adapted in structure and vocabulary to the more complex requirements of a written language. French and English soon followed, and most of the other European languages somewhat later.

The vernacular

The Florentine exile, Francesco Petrarca, or Petrarch, has been called the first man of letters. The son of a merchant, he spent his life in travel throughout France and Italy. Trained for the law, and an ordained clergyman, he became a somewhat rootless critic of these two esteemed professions, which he denounced for their "scholasticism." He lived in the generation after Dante, dying in 1374, and he anticipated the more fully developed humanism that was to come. His voluminous writings show the complex, contradictory attitudes of early Renaissance thought. Attracted by life, love, beauty, travel, and connections with people of importance in church and state, he could also spurn all these things as ephemeral and deceptive. He loved Cicero for his common sense and his commitment to political liberty; indeed, he discovered a manuscript of Cicero's letters in 1345. He loved St. Augustine for his otherworldly vision of the City of God. But in Cicero's writings he also found a deep religious concern, and in St. Augustine he esteemed the active man who had been a bishop, a writer heavily engaged in the controversies of his time, and one who taught that for true Christians the world is not evil.

Petrarch

Petrarch wrote sonnets in Italian, an epic in Latin, an introspective study of himself, and a great many letters which he clearly meant to be literary productions. He aspired to literary fame. In all this we see a new kind of writer, who uses language not merely as a practical tool but as a medium of more subtle expression, to commune with himself, to convey moods of discouragement or satisfaction, to clarify doubts, to improve his own understanding of the choices and options that life affords. With Petrarch, in short, literature became a kind of calling, and also a consideration of moral philosophy, still related but no longer subordinate to religion. It was moral philosophy in the widest sense, raising questions of how human beings should adjust to the world, what a good life could be or ought to be, or where the genuine and ultimate rewards of living were to be found.

Petrarch was an indication of things to come. Boccaccio, his contemporary and also a Florentine, wrote the *Decameron* in Italian, a series of tales designed both to entertain and to impart a certain wisdom about human character and behavior. They were followed by the main group of humanists, far more numerous but less well remembered. Men of letters began to take part in public life, to gather students and found schools, to serve as secretaries to governing bodies or princes, and even to occupy office themselves. Thus the humanist Coluccio Salutati became chancellor of Florence in 1375. During the following decades Florence was threatened by the expansive ambitions of Milan, where the princely despotism of the Visconti family had established itself. Against such dangers a new and intense civic consciousness asserted itself. Salutati, in addition to the usual duties of chancellor, served the state with his pen, glorifying Florentine liberty and identifying it with the liberties of ancient republican Rome before they were undermined by the Caesars. He was succeeded as chancellor

The humanists

The three men in this painting were Florentine humanists around 1490. They appear in a larger work that the artist Domenico Ghirlandaio painted for a chapel. Ghirlandaio followed the typical Renaissance practice of using religious stories or events to convey secular subjects and ideas.
(Alinari/Art Resource, NY)

by two other humanists, Bruni and Poggio. Bruni wrote a history of Florence which marked a new achievement in historical writing, when compared with the annals and chronicles of the Middle Ages. He saw the past as clearly past, different from but relevant to the present; and he introduced a new division of historical periods. On the model of such ancient writers as Livy, he adopted a flowing narrative form. And he used history for a practical political purpose, to show that Florence had a long tradition of liberty and possessed values and attainments worth fighting for against menacing neighbors. History took on a utility that it had had for the Greeks and Romans and was to retain in the future in Europe and eventually in other parts of the world: the function of heightening a sentiment, not yet of nationalism, but of collective civic consciousness or group identity. It was meant to arouse its readers to a life of commitment and participation.

All this literary activity was of a scholarly type, in which authors broadened their understanding as much by reading as by personal experience of the world. And scholarly activity, the habit of attending closely to what a page really said, had consequences that went beyond either pure literature or local patriotism. A new critical attitude developed. Bruni, in his history, showed a new sense of the need for authentic sources. Lorenzo Valla became one of the founders of textual criticism. Studying the Latin language historically, he observed that its characteristic words and expressions varied from one time to another. He put this knowledge to the service of the king of Naples in a dispute with the pope. Valla showed, by analysis of the language used in the document, that the Donation of Constantine, on which the papacy then based its temporal claims, could not have been written in Constantine's time in the fourth century, and so was a forgery. Such scholarship helped establish modern methods for assessing the truth of written texts, and it contributed also to humanist optimism about the range and utility of human knowledge. Pico della Mirandola

Modern critical methods

and others looked for aspects of truth not revealed in the Christian scriptures. In 1486, the enthusiastic and very learned Pico, for example, claimed at the age of 23 that he could summarize all human knowledge in 900 theses, which he had drawn from "the Chaldaic, Arabic, Hebrew, Grecian, Egyptian, and Latin sages."

Schooling, Manners, and Family Life

While Italian humanism thus contributed much to literature and scholarship, to classical learning, and to the formation of modern national languages, it also had tangible and lasting effects in education. Here its impact persisted in all regions of European civilization down to the present. The medieval universities were essentially places for professional training in theology, medicine, and law. Except in England this continued to be their primary function. What came to be known as secondary education, the preparation of young men either for the universities or for "life," owes more to the Renaissance. The organized education of women came much later; some girls learned to read at home or in one of the few female primary schools, but young women were excluded from humanist academies and Renaissance universities.

Medieval schooling had been chaotic and repetitious. Youngsters of all ages sat together with a teacher, each absorbing from the confusion whatever could be understood of Latin rules and vocabulary. The Renaissance launched the idea of putting different age groups or levels of accomplishment into separate classes, in separate rooms, each with its own teacher, with periodic promotion of the pupil from one level to the next. Latin remained the principal subject, with Greek now added. But many new purposes were seen in the study of Latin.

Renaissance education

It was intended to give skill in the use of language, including the pupil's native tongue. Rhetoric was the art of using language to influence others. It heightened communication. Knowledge alone was not enough, said the historian and chancellor Bruni, who also wrote a short work on education—"to make effectual use of what we know we must add the power of expression." Nor was Latin merely the necessary professional tool for the priest, the physician, the lawyer, or the government servant. The student learned Latin (and Greek) in order to read the ancient writings—epics, lyrics, orations, letters, histories, dialogues, and philosophical treatises—and it was assumed that such writings offered practical lessons for the educated elites of every generation. Readers therefore learned how to find relevant historical models or failures in the rise and decline of the Roman republic and the troubles of the Greek city-states. The classics were meant also to have a moral impact, to produce a balanced personality, and to form character. Not everyone could be important or gifted, said the humanist Vittorino, but we all face a life of "social duty" and are responsible for our "personal influence" on others. These aims became permanent themes in the educational systems that trained the young men of early modern Europe.

Young people were trained also for a more civilized deportment in everyday social living. Personal style in the upper classes became somewhat more studied. Hitherto Europeans had generally acted like big children; they spat, belched, and blew their noses without inhibition, snatched at food with their fingers, bawled at each other when aroused, or sulked when their feelings were offended. It was Italians of the Renaissance who first taught more polite habits. Books of etiquette began to appear, of which the most successful was Castiglione's *Book of the Courtier* (1528). The "courtier" was ancestor to the "gentleman"; "courtesy" was originally the kind of behavior suited to princely courts.

This painting by the Italian artist Lavinia Fontana (1552–1614) portrays an appreciation for the generations and social roles that constituted late Renaissance family life. The people are arranged by age and gender, thus suggesting a different identity and destiny for each person and each group.

(Scala/Art Resource, NY)

The "courtier"

The "courtier," according to Castiglione, should be a man of good birth but is chiefly the product of training. His education in youth, and his efforts in mature years, should be directed toward mixing agreeably in the company of his equals. His clothes should be neat, his movements graceful, his approach to other people perfectly poised. He must converse with facility, be proficient in sports and arms, and know how to dance and appreciate music. He should know Latin and Greek. With literary and other subjects he should show a certain familiarity but never become too engrossed. For the well-bred man speaks with "a certain carelessness, to hide his art, and show that what he says or does comes from him without effort or deliberation." Pedantry and heaviness must yield to an air of effortless superiority, so that even if the "courtier" knows or does something seriously, he must treat it lightly as one of many accomplishments. At its best, the code taught a consideration for the feelings of others and incorporated some of the moral ideas of the humanists, aiming at a creditable life in active society. Castiglione's book was translated into numerous languages, and a hundred editions were printed before 1600.

Castiglione's ideal court also included women, whose civilizing influence was supposed to encourage the good manners, polite conversation, and cultural graces that rough-edged men might otherwise ignore. Expressing views of men and women that shaped much of Renaissance culture, Castiglione expected men to cultivate a "robust and sturdy manliness," which would be balanced in court society by the "soft and delicate tenderness" of women. Such distinctions suggested also the gender divisions in Renaissance families and households, including those that were far removed from the courts of princes.

The marriages that created Renaissance households grew out of careful negotiations in which the families of prospective brides and grooms sought to enhance their respective social positions. In Florence, for example, par- *Renaissance marriages* ents typically arranged for their daughters to be married by age 18 to older men whose economic or political connections would be advantageous to the young woman's own family. Florentine husbands, who had usually reached age 30 before their first marriage, were well advanced in trades or professions before they established their new households, which depended also on the dowries that they received through their marriage contracts. The different ages of husbands and wives reinforced the gender divisions in Renaissance families; men pursued their public careers with their professional peers while their much younger wives raised children in the home. The high mortality rates in Renaissance cities, however, meant that women often outlived their older husbands, and, as young widows were forced to raise the children and manage the household. The young men who attended the new Renaissance schools therefore came from families in which mothers usually provided the most important training during their early years. Renaissance education and manners, as taught in the new schools and academies of the era, thus developed within the distinctive patterns of family life in the Italian cities.

Politics and the Italian Renaissance

The Italian Renaissance, for all its accomplishments, produced no institution or great idea by which masses of people living in society could be held together. Indeed, the greatest of Europe's institutions, the Roman church, in which Europeans had lived for centuries, and without which they did not see how they could live at all, fell into neglect under the Renaissance popes. Nor did Italy develop any effective political institutions. Florence during the fifteenth century passed from a high-spirited republicanism to acceptance of one-man rule. Throughout the peninsula the merchants, bankers, connoisseurs, and courtly classes who controlled the city-states could not fight for themselves, nor arouse their citizens to fight for them. They therefore hired professional fighting men, *condottieri,* private leaders of armed bands, who contracted with the various city-states to carry on warfare and often raised their price or changed sides during hostilities. Italian politics became a tangled web, a labyrinth of subterfuge and conspiracy, a platform on which powerful individuals might exhibit their *virtù.* "Italian cunning" became a byword throughout Europe. Dictators rose and fell. The Medici became dukes in Florence, the Sforza in Milan, while in Venice and Genoa, where the republics survived, narrow oligarchies held tight control. These states, along with the states of the church, jockeyed about like pugilists in a ring, held within an intricate, shifting, and purely local balance of power.

Italy was the despair of its patriots, or of such few as remained. One of these was Niccolò Machiavelli, who, in *The Prince* (1513), wrote the most *Machiavelli* lasting work of the Italian Renaissance. He dreamed of the day when the citizens of his native Florence, or indeed of all Italy, should behave like early Romans — show virility in their politics, fight in citizen armies for patriotic causes, and uphold their

The governing council in Florence deliberates on going to war against Pisa during a brief period of republican revival after the Medici were expelled in 1494. A nemesis, or omen of failure and retribution, floats over the councilors' heads and represents the challenge of making political decisions in a Renaissance Italian state.

(Alinari/Art Resource, NY)

dignity before Europe. It was outside Italy, in kings Ferdinand of Aragon, Louis XI of France, and Henry VII of England, that Machiavelli was obliged to find his heroes. He admired them because they knew how to exercise power and how to build strong states. In *The Prince* he produced a handbook of statecraft which he hoped Italy might find useful. He produced also the first purely secular treatise on politics.

Medieval writings on politics, those of Thomas Aquinas or Marsiglio of Padua, for example, had always talked of God's will for the government of people, with such accompanying matters as justice and right, or divine and natural law. All this Machiavelli put aside. He "emancipated" politics from theology and moral philosophy. He undertook to describe simply what rulers actually did. What really happens, said Machiavelli, is that effective rulers and governments act only in their own political interest. They keep faith or break it, observe treaties or repudiate them, are merciful or ruthless, forthright or sly, peaceable or aggressive, according to their estimates of their political needs. Machiavelli was prepared to admit that such behavior was bad; he only insisted that it was in this way, however regrettably, that successful rulers behaved. He was thought unduly cynical even in an age that lacked political delicacy. He had nevertheless diagnosed the new era with considerable insight. It was an age when politics was in fact breaking off from religion, with the building up of states and state authority emerging as goals that required no other justification.

But the most successful states of the time, as Machiavelli saw, were not in Italy. They were what history knows as the New Monarchies, and they owed their strength to something more than princely craft, for they enjoyed a measure of loyalty from the people they governed. The city-states in Renaissance Italy failed to sustain even this limited sense of loyalty between governments and their people. Italian politics became an affair of individual or elite *virtù;* and, as outsiders began to realize, the people of Italy lost interest in both the politics and the wars of their own city-states.

So Italy, the sunny land of balmy Mediterranean skies, rich in the busy life of its cities, its moneyed wealth, its gorgeous works of art, became vulnerable to the depredations of less easygoing peoples, from Spain and the *Italian vulnerability* north, who possessed institutions in which men could act together in large numbers. In a new age of rising national monarchies the city-states of Italy were too small to compete. In 1494 a French army crossed the Alps. Italy became a bone of contention between France and Spain. In 1527 a horde of undisciplined Spanish and German mercenaries, joined by footloose Italians, fell upon Rome itself. Never, not even from the barbarian Goths of the fifth century, had Rome experienced anything so horrible and degrading. The city was sacked, thousands were killed, soldiers milled about in an orgy of rape and loot, the pope was imprisoned, and cardinals were mockingly paraded through the streets facing backward on the backs of mules.

After the sack of Rome the Italian Renaissance faded away. Politically, for over three hundred years, Italy remained divided, the passive object of the ambitions of outside powers. Meanwhile its culture permeated the rest of Europe.

7.   THE RENAISSANCE OUTSIDE ITALY

Outside Italy people were much less conscious of any sudden break with the Middle Ages. Developments north of the Alps, and in Spain, were more an outgrowth of what had gone before. There was indeed a Renaissance in the Italian sense. In some of the innovations in painting the Flemish masters preceded those of Italy. In the north also, as in Italy, writers favored a revival of classical Latin, but the modern written languages also began to develop.

The northern Renaissance was more a blend of the old and the new. In it, above all, the religious element was stronger than in Italy. The most important northern humanists were writers like Thomas More in England and Erasmus in Holland. The French humanism that produced the earthy François Rabelais also produced the austere John Calvin.

Religious Scholarship and Science

Christian humanists

Historians like to distinguish between the "pagan" humanism of Italy and the Christian humanism of the north. In the north, Christian humanists studied the Hebrew and Greek texts of the Bible and read the Church Fathers, both Latin and Greek, in order to deepen their understanding of Christianity and to restore its moral vitality. Among people without pretense to humanistic learning, religion also remained a force. Medieval intellectual interests persisted. This is apparent from the continuing foundation of universities. The humanists generally regarded universities as centers of a pedantic, monkish, and "scholastic" learning. Concentrating upon theology, or upon medicine and law, the universities gave little encouragement to experimental science and still less to purely literary studies. In Italy in the fifteenth century no new universities were established. But in Spain, in France, in Scotland, in Scandinavia, and above all in Germany, new universities continued to develop. Between 1386 and 1506 no less than 14 universities were established in Germany. At one of the newest, Wittenberg, founded in 1502, Martin Luther was to launch the Protestant Reformation.

Germany at this time, on the eve of the great religious upheaval, and before the shift of the principal commercial arteries from central Europe to the Atlantic seaboard, was a main center of European life. Politically, the German-speaking world was an ill-defined and ill-organized region, composed of many diverse parts, from which the Netherlands and Switzerland were not yet differentiated. Economically, nevertheless, western and southern Germany enjoyed a lead over most of Western Europe; the towns traded busily, and German banking families, like the famous Fugger, controlled more capital than any others in Europe. Technical inventiveness was alive; mining was developing; and it was in the Rhineland, at Mainz, that Gutenberg, about 1450, produced the first European books printed with movable type. In painting, the western fringe of the Germanic world produced the Flemish masters, and south Germany gave birth to Albrecht Dürer and the Holbeins.

Intellectually, Germany shared in the Latin culture of Europe, a fact often obscured by the Latin names that German authors used in the early modern era. Regiomontanus (the Latin name of Johann Müller) laid the foundations during his short lifetime (1436–1476)

German contributions to early modern science

for a mathematical conception of the universe. He was probably the most influential scientific worker of the fifteenth century, especially since Leonardo da Vinci's scientific labors remained unknown. Nicholas of Cusa (1401?–1464), a Rhinelander, was a churchman whose mystical philosophy entered into the later development of mathematics and science. From such a background of mathematical interests came Copernicus (Niklas Koppernigk, 1473–1543), who believed that the earth moved about the sun; he was indeed a Pole, but he originated in the mixed German-Polish region of East Prussia. Fortified by the same mathematical interests, Europe's best-known cartographers were also Germans, such as Behaim and Schöner, whose world maps represented the most advanced geographical knowledge of the time. Paracelsus (Latin for Hohenheim) undertook to revolutionize medicine at the University of Basel. His wild prophecies made him a mixture of scientist and charlatan; but, in truth, science was not yet clearly distinguished from the occult, with which it shared the idea of control over natural forces. A similar figure, remembered in literature and the arts, was the celebrated Dr. Faustus. In real life, Faust, or Faustus, was perhaps a learned German of the first part of the sixteenth century. He was rumored to have sold his soul to the devil in return for knowledge and power, The Faust story was dramatized in England as early as 1593 by Christopher Marlowe, and, much later, by Goethe in German poetry. In the legend of Faust later generations were to see a symbol of the inordinate ambitions of modern people.

The idea of human powers to understand and control physical nature, as developed most especially north of the Alps, corresponded in many ways to the more purely Italian and humanistic idea of the infinite richness of human personality. Together, they constituted the new Renaissance spirit, for both emphasized the emancipation of humanity's limitless potentialities. The two ideas constantly interacted; in fact, most of the scientific workers just mentioned—Regiomontanus, Nicholas of Cusa, Copernicus—spent many years in Italy, receiving the stimulus of Italian thought.

Mysticism and Lay Religion

In the north a genuine religious impulse, in addition to religious humanistic scholarship, also remained alive. Where in Italy the religious sense, if not extinct, seemed to pass into a joyous and public cult in which God was glorified by works of art, in the north it took on a more mystical and soberly moral tone. Germany in the fourteenth century produced a series of mystics. The mystic tendencies of Nicholas of Cusa have been mentioned. More typical mystics were Meister Eckhart (d. 1327) and Thomas à Kempis (d. 1471), author of the *Imitation of Christ*. The essence of mysticism lay in the belief, or experience, that the individual soul could in perfect solitude commune directly with God. The mystic had no need of reason, nor of words, nor of joining with other people in open worship, nor of the sacraments administered by the priests—nor even of the church. The mystics did not rebel against the church; they accepted its pattern of salvation; but at bottom they offered, to those who could follow, a deeper religion in which the church as a social institution had no place. All social institutions, in fact, were transcended in mysticism by the individual soul; and on this doctrine, both profound and socially disruptive, Martin Luther was later to draw.

Mysticism and the individual soul

For the church, it was significant also that religion was felt deeply outside the clergy. Persons stirred by religion, who in the Middle Ages would have taken holy orders, now frequently remained laymen. In the past the church had often needed reform. But in the past, in the bad times of the tenth century, for example, the clergy had found reformers within their own ranks. The church had thus been repeatedly reformed and renewed without revolution. Now, in the fifteenth and early sixteenth centuries an ominous line seemed to be increasingly drawn: between the clergy as an established interest, inert and set in its ways, merely living, and living well, off the church; and groups of people outside the clergy—religious laypersons, religiously inclined humanists and writers, impatient and headstrong rulers—who were more influential than ever before and more critical of ecclesiastical abuses.

Lay religion was especially active in the Netherlands. A lay preacher, Gerard Groote, attracted followers by his sermons on spiritual regeneration. In 1374 he founded a religious sisterhood, which was followed by establishments for religiously minded men. They

The Sisters and Brothers of the Common Life

called themselves, respectively, the Sisters and the Brothers of the Common Life, and they eventually received papal approval. They lived communally, but not as monks and nuns, for they took no vows, wore ordinary clothing, and were free to leave at will. They worked at relieving the poor and in teaching. The schools of the Brothers, since some of them came to have as many as a thousand boys, were the first to be organized in separate classes, each with its own room and its own teacher, according to the pupil's age or level of advancement. The Sisters maintained similar though less elaborate schools for girls. Reading and writing were of course taught, but the emphasis was on a Christian ideal of character and conduct, to instill such qualities as humility, tolerance, reverence, love of one's neighbor, and the conscientious performance of duty. This Modern Devotion, as it was called, spread widely in the Netherlands and adjoining parts of Germany.

Erasmus of Rotterdam

Erasmus of Rotterdam

In this atmosphere grew up the greatest of all the northern humanists, and indeed the most notable figure of the entire humanist movement, Erasmus of Rotterdam (1466–1536). Like all the humanists, Erasmus chose to write in a "purified" and usually intricate Latin style. He regarded the Middle Ages as benighted, ridiculed the scholastic philosophers, and studied deeply the classical writers of antiquity. He had the strength and the limitations of the pure man of letters. To the hard questions of serious philosophy he was largely indifferent; he feared the unenlightened excitability of the common people, and he was almost wholly unpolitical in his outlook. He rarely thought in terms of worldly power or advantage and made too little allowance for those who did. An exact contemporary to the most worldly Renaissance popes, Erasmus was keenly aware of the need for reform of the clergy. He put his faith in education, enlightened discussion, and gradual moral improvement. He led no burning crusade and counseled against all violence or fanaticism. He prepared new Greek and Latin editions of the New Testament. Urging people to read the New Testament in the vernacular languages, he hoped that a better understanding of Christ's teaching might turn them from their evil ways. In his *Praise of Folly* he satirized all worldly pretensions and ambitions, those of the clergy most emphatically. In his *Handbook of a Christian Knight* he showed how a man might take part in the affairs of the world while remaining a devout Christian, and in his influential treatise *On Civility in Children* he offered guidance for proper behavior in the social situations of daily life. Tolerance, restraint, good manners, scholarly understanding, a love of peace, a critical and reforming zeal, and a reasonable tone from which shouting and bad temper were always excluded—such were the Erasmian virtues.

Erasmus achieved an international eminence such as no one of purely intellectual attainments had ever enjoyed. He corresponded with the great of Europe. He lectured at Cambridge and edited books for a publisher at Basel. The king of Spain named him a councilor, the king of France called him to Paris, and Pope Leo X assisted him when he was in trouble. Theologians found fault with Erasmus's ideas (in which, indeed, the supernatural had little importance), but among the leaders of the church, the popes and prelates, he had many admirers. Erasmus, it must be noted, attacked only the abuses in the church, the ignorance or sloth of the clergy, and the moral or financial corruption of their lives. The essence and principle of the Roman Catholic church he never called into question. Whether the Erasmian spirit, so widely diffused about 1520, would have sufficed to restore the church without the revolutionary impact of Protestantism is one of the many unanswerable questions of history.

8.   THE NEW MONARCHIES

Meanwhile, in Europe outside Italy, kings were actively building the institutions of the modern state. It was these states, more than any other single factor, that were to determine the course of the religious revolution. Whether a country turned Protestant, remained Catholic, or divided into separate religious communities was to depend very largely upon political considerations.

War, civil war, class war, feudal rebellion, and plain banditry afflicted a good deal of Europe in the middle of the fifteenth century. In this formless violence central governments had become very weak. Various rulers now tried to impose a kind of civil peace. They have been conveniently called the New Monarchs, but they were not really very new because they resumed the interrupted labors of kings in the High Middle Ages. They thus laid foundations for later national, or at least territorial, states.

The New Monarchs offered the institution of monarchy as a guarantee of law and order. Arousing latent sentiments of loyalty to the reigning dynasty, they proclaimed that hereditary monarchy was the legitimate form of public power, which all should accept without turmoil or resistance. They especially enlisted the support of middle-class people in the towns, who were tired of the private wars and marauding habits of the feudal nobles. Townspeople were willing to let parliaments be dominated or even ignored by the king, for parliaments had proved too often to be strongholds of unruly barons, or had merely accentuated class conflict. The king, receiving money in taxes, was able to organize armies with which to control the nobles. The use of the pike and the longbow, which enabled the foot soldier to stand against the horseman, was here of great potential value. The king, if only he could get his monarchy sufficiently organized and his finances into reliable order, could hire large numbers of foot soldiers, who generally came from the growing population of commoners, unlike the knightly horsemen. But to organize his monarchy, the king had to break down the mass of feudal, inherited, customary, or "common" law in which the rights of the feudal classes were entrenched. For this purpose, at least on the Continent, the New Monarch made use of Roman law, which was now actively studied in the universities. He called himself a "sovereign"—it was at this time that kings began to be addressed as "majesty." The king, said the experts in Roman law, incorporated the will and welfare of the people in his own person. He could therefore *make* law by his own authority, regardless of previous custom or even of historic liberties—and they quoted Latin phrases to argue that "what pleases the prince has the force of law."

The New Monarchy in England, France, and Spain

The New Monarchy came to England with the dynasty of the Tudors (1485–1603), whose first king, Henry VII (1485–1509), after gaining the throne by force, put an end to the civil turbulence of the Wars of the Roses.

The Tudors

In these wars the great English baronial families had seriously weakened each other, to the great convenience of the king and the bulk of the citizenry. Henry VII passed laws against "livery and maintenance," the practice by which great lords maintained private armies wearing their own livery or insignia, and he used his royal council as a new court to deal with property disputes and infractions of the public peace. It met in a room decorated with stars, whence its name, the Star Chamber. It represented the authority of the king and his council, and it operated without a jury. Later denounced as an instrument of despotism, it was popular enough at first, because it preserved order and rendered substantial justice.

ERASMUS OF ROTTERDAM
by Hans Holbein, the Younger (German,
1497–1543)

**This portrait was painted in 1523, when
Erasmus was 56, and the Lutheran
Reformation had begun in Germany. A
classic portrayal of humanism at its best,
the painting captures the life of thought
and emphasizes the only weapon that
Erasmus could use—the pen.**
(Alinari/Art Resource, NY)

Henry VII, though miserly and unpleasant in person, was accepted as a good ruler. National feeling in England consolidated around the house of Tudor.

The Valois

In France the New Monarchy was represented by Louis XI (1461–1483), of the Valois line, and his successors. In the five centuries since the first French king had been crowned, the royal domain had steadily expanded from its original small nucleus around Paris through a combination of inheritance, marriage, war, intrigue, and conquest. Louis XI continued to round out the French borders. Internally, he built up a royal army, suppressed brigands, and subdued rebellious nobles. He acquired far greater powers than the English Tudors to raise taxation without parliamentary consent. The French monarchy also enlarged its powers over the clergy. We have seen how, by the Pragmatic Sanction of 1438, the Gallican church had won considerable independence to manage its own administrative affairs. In 1516 King Francis I reached an agreement with Pope Leo X in the Concordat of Bologna, which rescinded the Pragmatic Sanction. The pope henceforth received his "annates," or money income, from French ecclesiastics, but the king appointed the French bishops and abbots. The fact that, after 1516, the kings of France already controlled their own national clergy was one reason why, in later years, they were never tempted to turn Protestant.

Aragon and Castile

Strictly speaking, there was no kingdom of Spain. Various Spanish kingdoms had combined into two, Aragon and Castile. To Aragon, which lay along the Mediterranean side of the peninsula, belonged the Balearic Islands, Sardinia, Sicily, and the south Italian kingdom of Naples. To Castile, after 1492, belonged the newly discovered Americas. The two were joined in a personal union by the marriage of Ferdinand of Aragon and Isabella of Castile in 1469. The union was personal only; that is, both kingdoms recognized the two monarchs, but they had no common political, judicial, or administrative institutions. There was little or no Spanish national feeling; indeed, the Catalans in northern Aragon spoke a language quite different from Castilian Spanish. The most significant common feeling throughout

Spain came from the sense of belonging to the Spanish Catholic church. The common memory was that of the Christian crusade against the Moors. The one common institution, whose officials had equal authority and equal access to all the kingdoms, was a church court, the Inquisition. Meanwhile, the *reconquista* was at last completed when the southern tip of Spain, Granada, was conquered from the Moors in 1492. Its annexation added to the heterogeneous character of the Spanish dominions.

In these circumstances the New Monarchy in Spain followed a religious bent. Unification took place around the church. The rulers, though they made efforts at political centralization, worked largely through facilities offered by the church, and the early sense of "Spanishness" was linked to a sense of Catholicity. Formerly the Spanish had been among the most tolerant of Europeans; Christians, Muslims, and Jews had managed to live together. But in the wave of religious excitement that accompanied the conquest of Granada both the Jews and the Moors were expelled. The expulsion of the Jews by a decree of 1492 was actually a sign of former toleration in Spain, for the Jews had been earlier expelled from England in 1290 and from France in 1306. They were not again legally allowed in England until the mid-seventeenth century, nor in France (with great exceptions) until the French Revolution. In Spain, as in the history of many European peoples, the emergence of an early "national" consciousness seemed to produce a feeling against Jews as "outsiders."[2]

All persons in Spain were now supposed to be Christians. In fact, however, Spain was one of the places in Europe where a person's Christianity could not be taken for granted, because many Spanish families had been Jewish or Muslim for centuries and had only accepted Christianity to avoid expulsion. Hence arose a fear of false Christians, of an unassimilated element secretly hostile to the foundations of Spanish life. It was feared that Moriscos (Christians of Moorish background) and Marranos (Christians of Jewish background) retained a clandestine sympathy for the religion of their forebears. Thousands of such persons were brought before the Inquisition, where, as in the civil courts under Roman procedure, torture could be employed to extort confessions. It was thus safest to be profuse in one's external religious devotions because adherence to the Catholic Church became the way of proving oneself to be a good Spaniard.

Fusing the national and the Catholic

The life of Spain carried forward some of the long-existing commitment to a crusade—which had now evolved into a campaign within Spain against Moriscos and Marranos, and a new campaign against the Moors in Africa itself, which the Spanish invaded immediately after the conquest of Granada. The Spanish also extended their religious energies into the Americas, where the Spanish church set about gathering the Indians into the Christian fold. And Spain's strong religious identity would soon contribute to its growing role in the wider political and religious conflicts of sixteenth-century Europe. Spanish history had prepared the country (before Protestantism ever appeared) to become a leading defender of Roman Catholic traditions as well as an advocate for Catholic renewal and internal reforms.

---

[2]The Jews who left Spain (the Sephardic Jews) went to North Africa and the Middle East, and in smaller numbers to the Dutch Netherlands and even to southwestern France (one of the exceptions noted above). Those who left England two centuries earlier generally went to Germany, the great center of Ashkenazic Jewry in the Middle Ages. Driven from Germany in the fourteenth century they concentrated in Poland, which remained the great center of European Jews until the Nazi massacres of the 1940s.

The Holy Roman Empire and the Habsburg Supremacy

Ideas of the New Monarchy were at work even in Germany, which is to say, in the Holy Roman Empire. There were three kinds of states in the Empire. There were the princely states—duchies, margraviates, etc.—each a little hereditary dynastic monarchy in itself, such as Saxony, Brandenburg, or Bavaria. There were ecclesiastical states—bishoprics, abbacies, etc.—in which the bishop or abbot, whose rule was of course not hereditary, conducted the government. A large portion of the area of the Empire consisted of these church-states. Third, there were the imperial free cities, some 50 in number; their collective area was not large, but they dominated the commercial and financial life of the country.

The German states, over the centuries, had prevented the emperor from infringing upon their local liberties. They had taken care to keep the emperorship an elective office, so that with each election local liberties could be reaffirmed. After 1356 the right of electing an emperor was vested in seven electors—namely, four of the princely lords, the Count Palatine, Duke of Saxony, Margrave of Brandenburg, and King of Bohemia (the one king in the Empire), and in three ecclesiastical lords, the archbishops of Mainz, Trier, and Cologne. In 1452 the electors chose the Archduke of Austria to be emperor.

The Habsburgs

His family name was Habsburg. The Habsburgs, by using the resources of their hereditary possessions in Austria (and later elsewhere) and by delicately balancing and bribing the numerous political forces within Germany, managed to get themselves consistently reelected to the Holy Roman emperorship in every generation, with one exception, from 1452 until 1806. The Habsburg emperors also tried to introduce the centralizing principles of the New Monarchy into an empire that lacked institutions for the exercise of centralized power.

Under Maximilian I (1493–1519) there seemed to be progress in that direction: the Empire was divided into administrative "circles," and an Imperial Chamber and Council were created, but they were all doomed to failure before the immovable obstacle of states' rights. Maximilian was also the author of the Habsburg family fortunes through his strategic use of royal marriages, which brought the Habsburgs into control of a vast empire. Maximilian's grandson, Charles, thus inherited from his four grandparents the lands of Austria, the Netherlands, and part of Burgundy; Castile and Aragon in Spain; the whole of Spanish America; and scattered possessions in Italy and the Mediterranean. In addition, in 1519, Charles was elected Holy Roman Emperor and so became the symbolic head of all Germany.

Charles V

Charles V of the Empire (he was known as Charles I in Spain) was thus beyond all comparison the most powerful ruler of his day. But still other fortunes awaited the house of Habsburg. The Turks, who had occupied Constantinople in 1453, were at this time pushing through Hungary and menacing central Europe. In 1526 they defeated the Hungarians at the battle of Mohacs. The parliaments of Hungary, and of the adjoining kingdom of Bohemia, hoping to gain allies in the face of the Turkish threat, thereupon elected Charles V's brother Ferdinand as their king. Ferdinand soon lost much of Hungary to the Turkish Sultan, Sulayman I, but he retained his royal crown and gradually expanded Habsburg influence in central Europe. No royal family since Charlemagne had stood so far above all rivals. Contemporaries cried that Europe was threatened with "universal monarchy," with a kind of imperial system in which no people could preserve its independence from the Habsburgs.

The reader who wishes to understand the religious revolution, and the consequent emergence of Protestantism must bear in mind the intricate interplay of the factors that have now been outlined: the decline of the church; the growth of secular and humanistic feeling; the spread of lay religion outside the official clergy; the rise of monarchs who

This painting entitled *Interrogation of the Jews*, by an unknown artist in the 1480s, suggests the dangers that non-Christian people faced in late fifteenth-century Spain. Influential, wealthy interrogators questioned the beliefs or behavior of persons whose religion made them "suspicious" and vulnerable to the powerful people who distrusted them.
(Museo de Bellas Artes, Zaragoza, Spain)

wished to control everything in their kingdoms, including the church; the resistance of feudal elements to these same monarchs; the lassitude of the popes and their fear of church councils; the division of Germany; the Turkish entry into central Europe; the zeal of Spain; the preeminence of Charles V; and the fears felt in other countries, especially in France, of absorption by the amazing empire of the Habsburgs.

9. THE PROTESTANT REFORMATION

Three streams contributed to the religious upheaval in sixteenth-century Europe. First, among common people, or the laboring poor, who might find their spokesmen among local priests, there was an endemic dissatisfaction with all the grand apparatus of the church, or a belief that its bishops and abbots were part of a wealthy and oppressive ruling class. For such people, religious ideas were mixed with protest against the whole social order. They found expression in the great peasant rebellion in Germany in the 1520s. The sects which emerged from these social groups are known historically as Anabaptists, and the modern Baptists, Mennonites, and Moravian Brothers are among their descendants. Second, and forming a

Political and social discontents

EUROPE, 1526

The main feature of the political map of Europe about 1526 is the predominance of the house of Habsburg. Much of Europe was ruled by the Habsburg Emperor Charles V, who was at the same time King Charles I of Spain. Charles left his possessions in Austria, Hungary, and Bohemia to his brother and those in Spain, the Netherlands, Italy, and America to his son, thereby establishing the Austrian and Spanish branches of the Habsburg dynasty. France was nearly encircled by Habsburg dominions and habitually formed alliances to oppose the Habsburg kings.

group generally more educated and with broader views of the world, were the middle classes of various European cities, especially of cities that were almost autonomous little republics, as in Germany, Switzerland, and the Netherlands. They might wish to manage their own religious affairs as they did their other business, believing that the church hierarchy was too much embedded in a feudal, baronial, and monarchical system with which they had little in common. The modern churches of Calvinist origin came in large part from this stream. Third, there were the ruling sovereigns and princes, who had long disputed with the church on matters of property, taxes, legal jurisdiction, and political influence. All such rulers wanted to be masters in their own territory. In the end it was the power of such rulers that determined which form of religion should officially prevail. The Lutheran and Anglican churches were in this tradition, and to some extent the Gallican church, as the French branch of the Roman Catholic church was called. As it turned out, by 1600, the second and third streams had won many successes, but the first was suppressed. Socio-religious radicalism was reduced to an undercurrent in countries where Anglican, Lutheran, Calvinist, or Roman Catholic churches were established during the sixteenth century.

Since northern Europe became Protestant while the south remained Catholic, it may look as if the north had broken off in a body from a once solid Roman church. The reality was not so simple. Let us for a moment put aside the term "Protestant," and think of the adherents of the new religion as religious revolutionaries.[3] Their ideas were revolutionary because they held, not merely that "abuses" in the church must be corrected, but also that the Roman church itself was wrong in principle. Even so, there were many who hoped, for years, that old and new ideas of the church might be combined. Many deplored the extremes but gradually in the heat of struggle had to choose one side or the other. The issues became drawn, and each side aspired to destroy its adversary. For over a century the revolutionaries maintained the hope that "popery" would everywhere fall. For over a century the upholders of the old order worked to annihilate or reconvert "heretics." Only slowly did Catholics and Protestants come to accept each other's existence as an established fact of European society. Though the religious frontier that was to prove permanent appeared as early as 1560, it was not generally accepted until after the Thirty Years' War, which ended in 1648.

Luther and Lutheranism

The first who successfully defied the older church authorities was Martin Luther. He was a monk, and an earnest one, until he was almost 40 years old. A vehement and spiritually uneasy man, with many dark and introspective recesses in his personality, Luther was terrified by the thought of the awful omnipotence of God, distressed by his own littleness, apprehensive of the devil, and suffering from the chronic conviction that he was damned. The means offered by the church to allay such spiritual anguish—the sacraments, prayer, attendance at Mass—gave him no satisfaction. From a reading and pondering of St. Paul (Romans i, 17)—"the just shall live by faith"—there dawned upon him a new realization and sense of peace. He developed the doctrine of justification by faith alone. This held that what "justifies" a person is not what the church knew as "works" (prayer, alms, the sacraments, holy living) but "faith alone," an inward bent of spirit given to each soul directly by God. Good works, Luther thought, were the consequence and external evidence of this inner

Luther's "justification by faith"

---

[3]The word "Protestant" arose as an incident in the struggle, at first denoting certain Lutherans who drew up a formal protest against an action of the diet of the Empire in 1529. Only very gradually did the various groups of anti-Roman reformers think of themselves as collectively Protestant.

Martin Luther and his wife Catherine, portrayed here by the artist Lucas Cranach the Elder, represent the acceptance of marriage among the clergy and religious leaders of the new Protestant churches. Catherine had lived in a convent before she married Luther and took on the new tasks of a religious wife in a Protestant minister's household.
(Scala/Art Resource, NY)

grace, but in no way its cause. People did not "earn" grace by doing good; they did the good because they possessed the grace of God. With this idea Luther for some years lived content. Even years later some high-placed churchmen believed that in Luther's doctrine of justification by faith there was nothing contrary to the teachings of the Catholic church.

Luther, now a professor at Wittenberg, was brought out of seclusion by an incident of 1517. A friar named Tetzel was traveling through Germany distributing indulgences, authorized by the pope to finance the building of St. Peter's in Rome. Tetzel claimed that indulgences would free people from some of the punishments of purgatory, and in return for the indulgences the faithful paid certain stipulated sums of money. Luther thought that people were being deluded, that no one could obtain grace in this way, or ease the pains of relatives in purgatory, as was officially claimed. In the usual academic manner of the day, he posted 95 theses on the door of the castle church at Wittenberg. Reviewing the Catholic sacrament of penance, Luther held in these theses that, after confession, the sinner is freed of sinful burdens not by the priest's absolution but by inner grace and faith alone. Increasingly, it seemed that the priesthood performed no necessary function in the spiritual relation between human beings and God.

Luther at first appealed to the pope, Leo X, to correct the abuse of indulgences in Germany. When the pope refused action Luther (like many before him) urged the assembly of a general church council as an authority higher even than the pope. He was obliged, however, to admit in public debate that even the decision of a general council might be mistaken. The Council of Constance, he said, had in fact erred in its condemnation of John Huss. But if neither the pope, nor yet a council, had authority to define true Christian belief, where was such authority to be found? Luther's answer was, in effect: there is no such authority. He held that individuals might read the Bible and freely make their own interpretations according to their own conscience. This idea was as revolutionary for the church as would be the assertion today that neither the Supreme Court nor any other body may authoritatively interpret or enforce the Constitution of the United States, since each citizen may interpret the Constitution in his or her own way.

From his first public appearance Luther won ardent supporters, for there was a good deal of resentment in Germany against Rome. In 1519 and 1520 he rallied public opinion in a series of tracts, setting forth his main beliefs. He declared that the claim of the clergy to be different from the laity was an imposture. He urged people to find Christian truth in the Bible for themselves, and in the Bible only. He denounced the reliance on fasts, pilgrimages, saints, and Masses. He rejected the belief in purgatory. He reduced the seven sacraments to two—baptism and the communion, as he called the Mass. In the latter he repudiated the new and "modern" doctrine of transubstantiation, while affirming that God was still somehow mysteriously present in the bread and wine. He declared that the clergy should marry, upbraided the prelates for their luxury, and demanded that monasticism be eliminated. To drive through such reforms, while depriving the clergy of their pretensions, he called upon the temporal power, the princes of Germany. He thus issued an invitation to the state to assume control over religion, an invitation which, in the days of the New Monarchy, a good many rulers were enthusiastically willing to accept.

Luther's criticisms of the Church

Threatened by a papal bull with excommunication unless he recanted, Luther solemnly and publicly burned the bull. Excommunication followed. To the emperor, Charles V, now fell the duty of apprehending the heretic and repressing the heresy. Luther was summoned to appear before a diet of the Empire, held at Worms in the Rhineland. He declared that he could be convinced only by Scripture or right reason; otherwise "I neither can nor will recant anything, since it is neither right nor safe to act against conscience. God help me! Amen." He was placed under the ban of the Empire. But the Elector of Saxony and other north German princes took him under their protection. In safe seclusion, he began to translate the Bible into German.

Lutheranism, or at least anti-Romanism, quickly swept over Germany, assuming the proportions of a national upheaval. It became mixed with all sorts of political and social revolution. A league of imperial knights, adopting Lutheranism, attacked their neighbors, the church-states of the Rhineland, hoping by annexations to enlarge their own meager territories. In 1524 the peasants of a large part of Germany revolted. They were stirred by new religious ideas, worked upon by preachers who went beyond Luther in asserting that each individual could readily understand what was right or wrong. Their aims, however, were social and economic; they demanded a regulation of rents and security of common village rights and complained of exorbitant exactions and oppressive rule by their manorial overlords. Luther repudiated all connection with the peasants, called them filthy swine, and urged the princes to suppress them by the sword. The peasants were unmercifully put down, but popular unrest continued to stir the country, expressing itself, in a religious age, in various forms of extreme religious frenzy.

Social revolution

The radical Anabaptist movement in Münster was severely repressed after the city's former rulers regained control in early 1536. This illustration depicts the public torture and death of John of Leyden, whose punishment served as a vivid warning to other revolutionary Protestants throughout Germany.
(akg-images)

Various religious leaders attracted devout followers, who came to be known collectively as Anabaptists. Some said that all the world needed was love, some that Christ would soon come again, some that they were saints and could do no wrong, and some that infant baptism was useless, immersion of full-grown adults being required, as described in the Bible. The roads of Germany were alive with religious radicals, of whom some tens of thousands converged in 1534 on the city of Münster. There they proclaimed the reign of the saints, abolished property, and introduced polygamy as sanctioned in the Old Testament. A Dutch tailor, John of Leyden, claimed that authority came to him directly from God. Hemmed in by besieging armies, he ruled Münster by a revolutionary terror. Luther advised his followers to join even with Catholics to repress such a dangerous religious and social menace. After a full year Münster fell to the forces of its former rulers. The "saints" were pitilessly rooted out; John of Leyden died in torture.

Luther's reaction

Luther, horrified at the way in which religious revolution became confused with social revolution, defined his own position more conservatively. He restricted, while never denying, the right of private judgment in matters of conscience, and he made a larger place for an established clergy, Lutheranized, to be sure, but still established as teachers over the laity. Always well disposed to temporal rulers, having called upon the princes to act as religious reformers, he was thrown by the peasant and Anabaptist uprisings into an even closer alliance with them.

Lutheranism became more submissive to the state. Christian liberty, Luther insisted, was an internal freedom, purely spiritual, known only to God. In worldly matters, he said, the good Christian owed obedience to established authority. Lutheranism thus came to view the state with more deference and respect than governments usually received from either Roman Catholicism or the Calvinism which soon arose.

In the revolution that was rocking Germany it was not the uprising of imperial knights, nor that of peasants or tailors and journeymen, that was successful, but the rebellion of the higher orders of the Empire against the emperor. Charles V, as Holy Roman Emperor, was bound to uphold Catholicism because only in a Catholic world did the Holy Empire have any meaning. The states of the *Political rebellion* Empire, always fearing the loss of local liberty, saw in Charles's efforts to repress Luther a threat to their own freedom. Many imperial free cities, and most of the dynastic states of north Germany, now insisted on adding to their other rights and liberties the right, or liberty, to determine their own religion. The right or power to reform, they said, belonged to member states, not to the Empire itself. They became Lutheran, locally, introducing Lutheran bishops, doctrines, and forms of worship. Where a state turned Lutheran it usually confiscated the church properties within its borders, a process which considerably enriched some of the Lutheran princes and gave them a strong material interest in the success of the Lutheran movement. In most of the church-states, since the Catholic archbishop or bishop was himself the government, Catholicism prevailed. But a few church-states turned Lutheran. A good example of the secularization of a church-state was afforded in East Prussia, just outside the Empire. This territory belonged to the Teutonic Order, a Catholic organization of which the grand commander, an elective official, was at this time Albert of Brandenburg. In 1525 Albert declared for Luther and converted East Prussia into a secular duchy, of which he and his descendants became hereditary dukes.

Against the emperor, a group of Lutheran princes and free cities formed the League of Schmalkald. The king of France, Francis I, though a Catholic in good standing, allied with and supported the League. Political interests overrode religious ones. Against the "universal monarchy" of the swollen Habsburgs the French found alliances where they could, allying with the Turks as with the Lutherans, building up a balance of power against their mighty foe. It became the studied policy of Catholic France to maintain the religious division of Germany.

Threatened by French and Turkish armies and challenged by the resistance of German princes within his own empire, Charles appealed to the pope, urging him to assemble a Europe-wide council in which all disputed *Charles's appeals to* matters could be considered, the Protestants could be heard, compromises *the papacy* could be effected, and church unity and German unity (such as it was) could be restored. The king of France schemed at Rome to prevent the pope from calling any such council. The kings of both France and England urged national councils instead, in which religious questions could be settled on a national basis. Pope after pope delayed. The papacy feared that a council of all Latin Christendom might get out of control, since Catholics as much as Protestants demanded reform. To the papacy, remembering the Council of Constance, nothing was more upsetting than the thought of a council, not even the Protestants, not even the Turks. So the popes procrastinated, no council met, years passed, and a new generation grew up in Lutheranism. Meanwhile the Schmalkaldic League, allied with France, actually went to war with the emperor in 1546. Germany fell into an anarchy of civil struggle between Catholic and Protestant states, the latter aided by France. The war was ended by the Peace of Augsburg of 1555.

CHRONOLOGY OF NOTABLE EVENTS, 1309–1555

1309–1378	"Babylonian Captivity": Papacy in Avignon
1337–1453	Hundred Years' War between England and France
1348–1350	Black Death decimates European population
c. 1350–1500	Renaissance Humanism and Art
1378–1417	Schism of Roman Catholic Church: Popes in Avignon and Rome
1454	Johann Gutenberg begins printing books with movable type
1494	French invasion of Italy destroys independence of city-states
1513	Niccolò Machiavelli writes *The Prince*
1517	Martin Luther posts his "95 theses"; beginning of Protestant Reformation
1545–1563	Roman Catholic Council meets at Trent; promotes Catholic reforms
1555	Peace of Augsburg recognizes Protestant and Catholic states in Germany

The terms set at Augsburg signified a complete victory for the cause of Lutheranism and states' rights. Each state of the Empire received the liberty to be either Lutheran or Catholic as it chose. No individual freedom of religion was permitted; if a ruler or a free city decided for Lutheranism, then all persons had to be Lutheran. Similarly in Catholic states all had to be Catholic. The Peace of Augsburg provided also, by the so-called Ecclesiastical Reservation, that any Catholic bishop or other churchman who turned Lutheran in the future (or who had turned Lutheran as recently as 1552) should not carry his territory with him, but should turn Lutheran as an individual and move away, leaving his land and its inhabitants Catholic. Since the issues in Germany were still far from stabilized, this proviso was often disregarded in later years.

The Peace of Augsburg

The Peace of Augsburg was thus, in religion, a great victory for Protestantism, and at the same time, in German politics and constitutional matters, a step in the disintegration of Germany into a mosaic of increasingly separate states. Lutheranism prevailed in the north and in the south in the duchy of Württemberg and various detached islands formed by Lutheranized free cities. Catholicism prevailed in the south (except in Württemberg and certain cities), in the Rhine valley, and in the direct possessions of the house of Habsburg, which in 1555 reached as far north as the Netherlands. The Germans, because of conditions in the Holy Roman Empire, were the one large European people to emerge from the religious conflict almost evenly divided between Catholic and Protestant.

No rights were granted by the Peace of Augsburg to another group of religious revolutionaries which neither Lutherans nor Catholics were willing to tolerate, namely, the followers of John Calvin.

Lutheranism, it must be pointed out, was adopted by the kings of Denmark and Sweden as early as the 1520s. Since Denmark controlled Norway, and Sweden ruled Finland and the eastern Baltic, all Scandinavia and the Baltic regions became, like north Germany, Lutheran. Beyond this area Lutheranism failed to take root. Like Anglicanism in England (to be described shortly), Lutheranism was too closely associated with established states to spread easily as an international movement. The most successful international form of the Protestant movement was Calvinism.

Calvin and Calvinism

John Calvin was a Frenchman, born Jean Cauvin, who called himself Calvinus in Latin. Born in 1509, he was a full generation younger than Luther. He was trained both as a priest and as a lawyer and had a humanist's knowledge of Latin and Greek, as well as Hebrew. At the age of 24, experiencing a sudden conversion, or fresh insight into the meaning of Christianity, he joined forces with the religious revolutionaries of whom the best known was then Luther. Three years later, in 1536, he published, in the international language, Latin, his *Institutes of the Christian Religion.* *Calvin's Doctrines* Where Luther had aimed much of his writing either at the existing rulers of Germany, or at the German national feeling against Rome, Calvin addressed his *Institutes* to all the world. He seemed to appeal to human reason itself; he wrote in the severe, logical style of the trained lawyer; he dealt firmly, lucidly, and convincingly with the most basic theological issues. In the *Institutes* people in all countries, if dissatisfied with the existing Roman church, could find cogent expression of universal propositions, which they could apply to their own local circumstances as they required.

With Luther's criticisms of the Roman church, and with most of Luther's fundamental religious ideas, such as justification by faith and not by works, Calvin agreed. In what they retained of the Catholic Mass, the communion or Lord's Supper as they called it, Luther and Calvin developed certain doctrinal differences. Both rejected transubstantiation, but where Luther insisted that God was somehow actually present in the bread and wine used in the service ("consubstantiation"), Calvin and his followers tended more to regard it as a pious act of symbolic or commemorative character.

The chief differences between Calvin and Luther were two. Calvin made far more of the idea of predestination. Both, drawing heavily on St. *Predestination* Augustine, held that human beings could never earn salvation by their own actions, that any grace which anyone possessed came from the free action of God alone. God, being Almighty, knew and willed in advance all things that happened, including the way in which every life would turn out. God thus knew and willed, from all eternity, that some were saved and some were damned. Calvin, a severe critic of human nature, felt that those who had grace were relatively few. They were the "elect," the "godly," the small group chosen without merit of their own, from all eternity, for salvation. People could feel in their own minds that they were among the saved, God's chosen few, if throughout all trials and temptations they persisted in pursuing a saintly life. Thus the idea of predestination, of God's omnipotence, instead of turning to fatalism and resignation, became a challenge to unrelenting effort, a sense of burning conviction, a conviction of being on the side of that Almighty Power which must in the end be everlastingly triumphant. It was the most resolute spirits that were attracted to Calvinism. Calvinists, in all countries, were militant, uncompromising, perfectionist—or Puritan, as they were called first in England and later in America.

The second way in which Calvinism differed from Lutheranism was in its attitude to society and to the state. Calvinists refused to recognize the subordination of church to state, or the right of any government—king, parliament, or civic magistracy—to lay down laws for religion. On the contrary, they insisted that true Christians, the elect or godly, should Christianize the state. They wished to remake society itself into the image of a religious community. They rejected the institution of bishops (which both the Lutheran and Anglican churches retained) and provided instead that the church should be governed by presbyteries, elected bodies made up of ministers and devout laymen. By thus bringing an element of lay control into church affairs, they broke the monopoly of priestly power and so promoted secularization. On the other hand, they were the reverse of secular, for they wished to Christianize all society.

Calvin's Geneva

Calvin, called in by earlier reformers who had driven out their bishop, was able to set up his model Christian community at Geneva in Switzerland. A body of ministers ruled the church; a consistory of ministers and elders ruled the town. The rule was strict; all loose, light, or frivolous living was suppressed; disaffected persons were driven into exile. The form of worship was severe and favored the intellectual rather than the emotional or the aesthetic. The service was devoted largely to long sermons elucidating Christian doctrine, and all appeals to the senses—color, music, incense—were rigidly subdued. The black gown of Geneva replaced brighter clerical vestments. Images, representing the saints, Mary, or Christ, were taken down and destroyed. Candles went the way of incense. Chanting was replaced by the singing of hymns. Instrumental music was frowned upon, and many Calvinists thought even bells to be a survival of "popery." In all things Calvin undertook to regulate his church by the Bible. Nor was he more willing than Luther to countenance any doctrine more radical than his own. When a Spanish refugee, Michael Servetus, who denied the Trinity, that is, the divinity of Christ, sought asylum at Geneva, Calvin pronounced him a heretic and had him burned at the stake.

The spread of Calvinism

Reformers of all nationalities flocked to Geneva to see and study a true scriptural community so that they might reproduce it in their own countries. Geneva became the Protestant Rome, the one great international center of Reformed doctrine. Everywhere Calvinists made their teachings heard (even in Spain and Italy in isolated cases), and everywhere, or almost everywhere, little groups which had locally and spontaneously broken with the old church found in Calvin's *Institutes* a reasoned statement of doctrine and a suggested method of organization. Thus Calvinism spread very widely. In Hungary and Bohemia large elements turned Protestant, and usually Calvinist, partly as a way of opposing the Habsburg rule. In Poland there were many Calvinists, along with less-organized Anabaptists and Unitarians, or Socinians, as those who denied the Trinity were then called. Calvinists spread in Germany, where, opposing both Lutheran and Catholic churches as ungodly impositions of worldly power, they were disliked equally by both. In France the Huguenots were Calvinist, as were the Protestants of the Netherlands. John Knox in the 1550s brought Calvinism to Scotland, where Presbyterianism became and remained the established religion. At the same time Calvinism began to penetrate England, from which it was later to reach British America, giving birth to the Presbyterian and Congregationalist churches of the United States.

Calvinism and democracy

Calvinism was far from democratic in any modern sense. It carried an almost aristocratic outlook, in that those who sensed themselves to be God's chosen few felt free to dictate to the wider population of lost souls. Yet in many ways Calvinism entered into the development of what became democracy. For one thing, Calvinists never venerated the state; they always held that the sphere of the state and of public life was subject to moral judgment. For another, the Calvinist doctrine of the "calling" taught that a person's labor had a religious dignity and that any form of honest work was pleasing in the sight of God. In the conduct of their own affairs Calvinists developed a type of self-government. They formed "covenants" with one another and devised machinery for the election of presbyteries. They refused to believe that authority was transmitted downward through bishops or through kings. They were inclined also to a democratic outlook by the circumstance that in most countries they remained an unofficial minority. Only at Geneva, in the Dutch Netherlands, in Scotland,

This image of John Calvin suggests that his influence among Protestants came from his intellectual rigor as well as his disciplined leadership of the religious reformers in Geneva.
(Snark/Art Resource, NY)

and in New England (and for a few years in England in the seventeenth century) were Calvinists ever able to prescribe the mode of life and religion of a whole country. In England, France, and Germany, Calvinists remained in opposition to the established authorities of church and state and hence were disposed to favor limitations upon established power. In Poland and Hungary many Calvinists were nobles who disliked royal authority.

The Reformation in England

England was peculiar in that its government broke with the Roman church before adopting any Protestant principles. Henry VIII (1509–1547) in fact prided himself on his orthodoxy. When a few obscure persons, about 1520, began to whisper Luther's ideas in England, Henry himself wrote a *Defense of the Seven Sacraments* in refutation, for which a grateful pope conferred

Henry VIII

upon him the title "Defender of the Faith." But the king had no male heir. Recalling the violent anarchy from which the Tudor dynasty had extricated England, and determined as a New Monarch to build up a durable monarchy, he decided that he must remarry in order to have a son. He therefore requested the pope, Clement VII, to annul his existing marriage to Catherine of Aragon. Popes in the past had obliged monarchs in similar situations. The pope now, however, was embarrassed by the fact that Catherine, who objected, was the aunt of the Emperor Charles V, whom the pope was in no position to offend. Henry, not a patient man, drove matters forward. He appointed a new archbishop of Canterbury, repudiated the Roman connection, secured the annulment of his earlier marriage, and married the youthful Anne Boleyn. The fact that only three years later he put to death the unfortunate Anne, and thereafter in quick succession married four more wives, for a total of six, threw considerable doubt on the original character of his motives.

Henry acted through Parliament, believing, as he said, that a king was never stronger than when united with representatives of his kingdom. In 1534 Parliament passed the Act of Supremacy, which declared the English king to be the "Protector and Only Supreme Head of the Church and Clergy of England." All subjects were required, if asked, to take the oath of supremacy acknowledging the religious headship of Henry and rejecting that of the pope. For refusing this oath Sir Thomas More, a statesman and humanist best known as the author of *Utopia,* was executed for treason. He received a somewhat delayed reward four centuries later when the Roman church pronounced him to be a saint. Henry, in the next few years, closed all the monasteries in England, seized the extensive monastic lands, and passed them out to numerous followers. He thus strengthened and reconstituted a landed aristocracy which had been seriously weakened in the Wars of the Roses. The new landed gentry remained firm supporters of the house of Tudor and the English national church, whatever its doctrines.

The Act of Supremacy

It was Henry's intent not to change the doctrines at all. He simply wished to be the supreme head of an English Catholic church. On the one hand, in 1536, he forcibly suppressed a predominantly Catholic rebellion, and, on the other, in 1539, through the Six Articles, required everybody to believe in transubstantiation, the celibacy of the clergy, the need of confession, and a few other test items of Catholic faith and practice. But it proved impossible to maintain this position, for a great many people in England began to favor one or another of the ideas of Continental Reformers, and a small minority were willing to accept the entire Protestant position.

For three decades the government veered about. Henry died in 1547 and was succeeded by his 10-year-old son, Edward VI, the child of his third wife, Jane Seymour. The Protestant party now came to the fore. But Edward died in 1553 and was succeeded by his much older half-sister, Mary, the daughter of Catherine of Aragon and a devout Roman Catholic whose whole life had been embittered by the break with Rome. Mary tried to re-Catholicize England, but she actually made Catholicism more unpopular with the English. In 1554 she married Philip of Spain, who became king of England, though only in name. The English did not like Philip, nor the Spanish, nor the intense Spanish Catholicism that Philip represented. Under Mary, moreover, some three hundred persons were burned at the stake, as heretics, in public mass executions. It was the first (and last) time that such a thing had happened in England, and it set up a wave of horror. In any event, Mary did not live long. She was succeeded in 1558 by Henry's younger daughter, Elizabeth, the child of Anne Boleyn. Whatever Elizabeth's real views in religion might be (she concealed them successfully and was rumored to have none), she could not be a Roman Catholic. For Catholics she was illegitimate and so unable to be queen.

The Church of England

Under Elizabeth the English became Protestant, gradually and in their own way. The Church of England took on a form of its own. Organizationally, it resembled a Lutheran church. It was a state church, for its existence and doctrines were determined by the temporal power, in this case the monarch acting through Parliament. All English subjects were obliged to belong to it, and laws were passed against "recusants," a term used to cover both the Roman Catholics and the more advanced Calvinists who refused to acknowledge it. With the exception of monasteries and certain other church foundations, the Church of England retained the physical possessions, buildings, and internal organization of the medieval church—the bishops and the archbishops, who continued to sit in the House of Lords, the episcopal

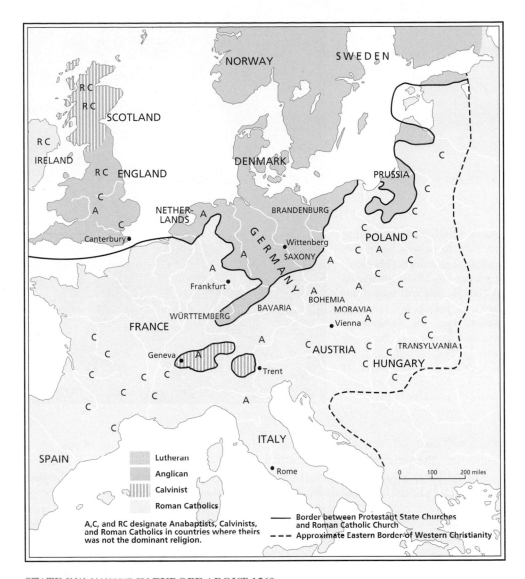

STATE RELIGIONS IN EUROPE ABOUT 1560

This map shows the legally authorized, established churches about 1560, but it does not show the precise distributions of religious communities. Many Catholics lived north of the heavy line, and many Protestants south of it. Most widely dispersed were the Calvinists and the more radical Protestants or Anabaptists. In Germany, under the Holy Roman Empire, each principality and free city chose its own religion; hence, the Germans were the only large European nationality to emerge from the Reformation almost evenly divided between Catholics and Protestants.

Queen Elizabeth I wanted her portraits to convey her power and royal grandeur. This painting from the 1580s, attributed to Nathan Hilliard, uses clothing and jewels to show her wealth and an ornamental ermine to symbolize her royal rank.
(By permission of the Marquess of Salisbury. Photograph: Photographic Survey, Courtauld Institute of Art)

courts with their jurisdiction over marriage and wills, the tithes or church taxes paid by all landowners, the parish structure, the universities of Oxford and Cambridge.

In religious practice, the Church of England was definitely Protestant: English replaced Latin as the language of the liturgy, there was no cult of the saints, and the clergy married, though Elizabeth confessed to some embarrassment at the thought of an archbishop having a wife. In doctrine, it was Elizabeth's policy to make the dogmas broad and ambiguous, so that persons of all shades of belief could be more readily accommodated. The Thirty-nine Articles (1563), composed by a committee of bishops, defined the creed of the Anglican church. In the light of the burning issues of the day many of the articles were evasive, though Protestant in tone. All but one of the Anglican bishops had been newly appointed by Elizabeth at her accession; many had lived in exile among Continental Protestants in the reign of Mary Tudor; and except on the matter of church government through bishops (known as episcopacy) a strong Calvinist impress was set upon Anglican belief in the time of Elizabeth.

The same ecclesiastical settlement was prescribed for Ireland, where English or rather Anglo-Norman conquerors had settled since the twelfth century, shortly after the Norman conquest of England. A replica of the Church of England was now established, called the Church of Ireland, which took over the properties and position of the Roman church. The native Irish, however, remained almost solidly Roman Catholic. As in Hungary or Bohemia people who resented the Habsburgs were likely to turn Protestant rather than share in the ruler's religion, so in Ireland the fact that the ruling English were Protestant only confirmed the Irish in their attachment to the Roman church. The Catholic priests, deprived of status, income, and church buildings, and often in hiding, became national leaders of a discontented people.

The Consolidation of Protestantism by 1560

Neither in England, nor in Germany, nor in international Calvinism were the religious issues regarded as settled in 1560. Nor had the Roman church accepted the new situation. But by 1560 the chief Protestant doctrines had been affirmed, and geographically Protestantism had made many conquests. The institutional unity of Latin Christendom had been broken. A world of separate churches, states, and nations was taking its place.

Protestants differed with one another, yet there was much that all had in common. All rejected the papal authority. None participated in any effective international organization; the ascendancy of Geneva was spiritual only and proved to be temporary. All Protestants rejected the special, sacerdotal, or supernatural character of the priesthood; indeed, the movement was perhaps most fundamentally a revolt against the medieval position of the clergy. Protestants generally called their clergy ministers, not priests. All Protestant clergy could marry. There were no Protestant monks, nuns, or friars. All Protestant churches replaced Latin with the vernacular in religious services—English, French, German, Czech, as the case might be. All Protestants reduced the number of sacraments, usually to two or three; such sacraments as they retained they regarded more as symbols than as actual carriers of divine grace; all believed, in one way or another, in justification by faith. All denied transubstantiation, or the miracle of the Mass. All gave up the obligatory confessional, and with it priestly absolution. All gave up the idea of purgatory as a kind of temporal zone between heaven and hell and hence abandoned the practice of saying prayers and Masses for the dead. It need hardly be added that nothing like indulgences remained. All gave up the cult of the saints and of the Virgin Mary, whose intercession in heaven was no longer expected. All declared that the one true source of Christian belief was the Holy Scripture. And while all established Protestant churches in the sixteenth century insisted on conformity to their own doctrines, allowing no individual freedom, all Protestants still had some small spark of the spirit first ignited by Luther, so that none flatly repudiated the right of private judgment in matters of conscience.

What Protestants held in common

It has sometimes been maintained that one of the motivations in Protestantism was economic—that a new acquisitive, dynamic, capitalistic impulse shook off the restrictions imposed by medieval religion. The fact that Protestant England and Holland soon underwent a rapid capitalistic development gives added credibility to this idea. The alacrity with which Protestant governments confiscated church lands shows a keen material interest; but in truth, both before and after the Reformation, governments confiscated church properties without breaking with the Roman church. That profound economic changes were occurring at the time will become apparent in the following chapter. Yet it seems that economic conditions were far less decisive than religious convictions and political circumstances. Calvinism won followers not only in cities but also in agrarian countries such as Scotland, Poland, and Hungary. Lutheranism spread more successfully in the economically retarded north Germany than in the busy south. The English were for years no more inclined to Protestantism than the French, and in France, while many lords and peasants turned Protestant, Paris and many other towns remained as steadfastly Catholic. It is possible that Protestantism, by casting a glow of religious righteousness over a person's daily business and material prosperity, later contributed to

The ideal Protestant household is represented by an unknown artist in this sixteenth-century Dutch painting of the family of a successful merchant. There are clear divisions between the men, women, and children, but everyone expresses the sobriety and wealth of a prosperous Calvinist community.

(© Rijksmuseum Foundation)

the economic success of Protestant peoples, but it does not seem that the Protestant work ethic or any other economic factors were of any distinctive importance in the first stages of Protestantism.

Protestants and family life

The new religious movements had a more immediate influence on attitudes about marriage and the family. In contrast to medieval Catholicism, which had praised sexual abstinence and celibacy as key traits of the most exalted religious persons, Protestantism strongly promoted marriage as the ideal social institution for clergy and lay people alike. Parenthood became honorable for even the most pious Protestant leaders. Although women sometimes wrote hymns or preached in the more radical Protestant churches, the model Protestant woman was the conscientious mother in a devout, religious household. The opportunities, even if limited, that some women had found in medieval convents and religious communities disappeared in Protestant societies, which may explain why nuns in Protestant territories were often among the last persons to accept the new religious ideas.

Apart from the new emphasis on marriage, however, Protestants did little to change the role of women in Christian churches or in the wider social order. The pastors in Protestant communities were all men, and though more women may have become literate in order to read the Bible, they became less visible in Protestant rituals as the long venerated female saints vanished from prayers, religious writings, and charitable institutions. Meanwhile, women in the convents of Catholic countries were more strictly cloistered and controlled as Catholicism developed its own powerful movements for reform and reorganization.

ℰ 10.   CATHOLICISM REFORMED AND REORGANIZED

The Catholic movement corresponding to the rise of Protestantism is known as the Catholic Reformation or the Counter Reformation, the former term being preferred by Catholics; the latter by Protestants. Both are applicable. On the one hand the Catholic church underwent a genuine reform, which might have worked itself out in one way or another even if the stimulus of revolutionary Protestantism had been absent. On the other hand the character of the reform, the decisions made, and the measures adopted were shaped by the need of responding explicitly to the Protestant challenge; and certainly, also, there was a good deal of purely "counter" activity aimed at the elimination of Protestantism as such.

The demand for reform was as old as the abuses against which it was directed. Characteristically, it had expressed itself in the demand for a general or ecumenical church council. The conciliar movement, defeated by the popes about 1450, showed signs of revival after 1500. The Lutheran upheaval thus provoked new calls for a general council of the church, and we have seen how Charles V, in the interests of German unity, sought to persuade the pope to assemble an adequately empowered council, which might remove some of the abuses in the church and take away the grounds upon which many Germans were turning to Lutheranism. But meanwhile the king of France found reason to favor the pope and to oppose the emperor. The French king, Francis I (1515–1547), could support the pope because he had obtained from the papacy what he wanted, namely, control over the Gallican church, as acquired in the Concordat of Bologna of 1516. And he had reason to oppose Charles V, because Charles V ruled not only in Germany but also in the Netherlands, Spain, and much of Italy, thus encircling France and threatening Europe with what contemporaries called "universal monarchy." Francis I therefore actively encouraged the Protestants of Germany, as a means of maintaining dissension there, and used his influence at Rome against the calling of a council by which the troubles of the Catholic world might be relieved.

The call for reform

Gradually, in the curia, there arose a party of reforming cardinals who concluded that the need for reform was so urgent that all dangers of a council must be risked. Pope Paul III summoned a council to meet in 1537, but the wars between France and the Empire forced its abandonment. Finally, in 1545, a council assembled and began deliberations. It met at Trent, on the Alpine borders of Germany and Italy. The Council of Trent, which shaped the destiny of modern Catholicism, sat at irregular intervals for almost 20 years. It was not until the Second Vatican Council in the 1960s that some of the main decisions made at Trent were substantially modified.

The Council of Trent

The council was beset by difficulties of a political nature, which seemed to show that under troubled conditions an international council was no longer a suitable means of regulating Catholic affairs. Significantly, it was not well attended. Whereas earlier councils of the church had assembled as many as 500 prelates, the attendance at Trent was never nearly so great; it sometimes fell as low as 20 or 30, and the important decree on "justification," the prime issue raised by Luther, and one on which some good Catholics had until then believed a compromise to be possible, was passed at a session where only 60 prelates were present. Even with the small attendance, the old conciliar issue was raised. A party of bishops believed that the bishops of the Catholic church, when assembled in council from all parts of the Catholic world, collectively constituted an authority superior to that of the pope. To stave off this "episcopal" movement was one of the chief duties of the cardinal legates deputed by the pope to preside over the sessions.

Preserving papal authority

The popes managed successfully to resist the idea of limiting the papal power. In the end they triumphed, through a final ruling voted by the council, that no act of the council should be valid unless accepted by the Holy See. It is possible that had the conciliar theory won out, the Catholic church might have become as disunited in modern times as the Protestant. It was clear, at Trent, that the various bishops tended to see matters in a national way, in the light of their own problems at home, and to be frequently under strong influence from their respective secular monarchs. In any case, the papal party prevailed, which is to say that the centralizing element, not the national, triumphed. The Council of Trent thus preserved the papacy as a center of unity for the Catholic church and helped prevent the very real threat of its dissolution into state churches. Even so, the council's success was not immediate, for in every important country the secular rulers at first accepted only what they chose of its work, and only gradually did its influence prevail.

Questions of national politics and of church politics apart, the Council of Trent addressed itself to two kinds of labors—to a statement of Catholic doctrine and to a reform of abuses in the church. When the council began to meet in 1545, the Protestant movement had already gone so far that any reconciliation was probably impossible: Protestants, especially Calvinists, simply did not wish to belong to the church of Rome under any conditions. In any case, the Council of Trent made no concessions.

The Council of Trent: defining Catholic doctrine

It declared justification to be by works and faith combined. It enumerated and defined the seven sacraments, which were held to be vehicles of grace independent of the spiritual state of those who received them. The priesthood was declared to be a special estate set apart from the laity by the sacrament of holy orders. The procedures of the confessional and of absolution were clarified. Transubstantiation was reaffirmed. As sources of Catholic faith, the council put Scripture and tradition on an equal footing. It thus rejected the Protestant claim to find true faith in the Bible alone and reasserted the validity of church development since New Testament times. The Vulgate, a translation of the Bible into Latin made by St. Jerome in the fourth century, was declared to be the only version on which authoritative teaching could be based. The right of individuals to believe that their own interpretation of Scripture was more true than that of church authorities (private judgment) was denied. Latin, as against the national languages, was prescribed as the language of religious worship—a requirement abolished by the Second Vatican Council in the 1960s. Celibacy of the clergy was maintained. Monasticism was upheld. The existence of purgatory was reaffirmed. The theory and correct practice of indulgences were restated. The veneration of saints, the cult of the Virgin, and the use of images, relics, and pilgrimages were approved as spiritually useful and pious actions.

It was easier for a council to define doctrines than to reform abuses, since the latter consisted in the rooted habits of people's lives. The council decreed, however, a drastic reform of the monastic orders. It acted against the abuse of indulgences while upholding the principle. It ruled that bishops should reside habitually in their dioceses, attend more carefully to their proper duties, and exercise more administrative control over clergy in their own dioceses. The abuse by which one man had held numerous church offices at the same time (pluralism) was checked, and steps were taken to assure that church officials should be competent. To provide an educated clergy, the council ordered that a seminary should be set up in each diocese for the training of priests.

The Counter Crusade

As laws in general have little force unless sustained by opinion, so the reform decrees of the Council of Trent would have remained ineffectual had not a renewed sense of religious seriousness been growing at the same time. Herein lay the inner force of the Catholic Reform. In Italy, as the Renaissance became more undeniably pagan, and as the sack of Rome in 1527 showed the depths of hatred felt even by many Catholics toward the Roman clergy, the voices of moralists began to be heeded. The line of Renaissance popes was succeeded by a line of reforming popes, of whom the first was Paul III (1534–1549). The reforming popes insisted on the primacy of the papal office, but they regarded this office, unlike their predecessors, as a moral and religious force. In many dioceses the bishops began on their own initiative to be stricter. The new Catholic religious sense, more than the Protestant, centered in a reverence for the sacraments and a mystical awe for the church itself as a divine institution. Both men and women founded many new religious orders, of which the Jesuits became the most famous. Others were the Oratorians for men and the Ursulines for women. The new orders dedicated themselves to a variety of educational and philanthropic activities. Missionary fervor for a long time was more characteristic of Catholics than of Protestants. It reached into Asia and the Americas, and in Europe expressed itself as an intense desire for the reconversion of Protestants. It showed itself, too, in missions among the poor, as in the work of St. Vincent de Paul among the human wreckage of Paris, for which the established Protestant churches failed to produce anything comparable. In America, as colonies developed in the sixteenth and seventeenth centuries, the Protestant clergy tended to take the layman's view of the Indians, while Catholic clergy labored to convert and protect them; and the Catholic church generally worked to mitigate the brutal treatment of enslaved Africans, to which the pastors in English and Dutch colonies, perhaps because they were more dependent upon the laity, remained largely indifferent.

Catholic religious renewal

We have seen how in Spain, where the Renaissance had never taken much hold, the very life of the country was connected to a kind of ongoing Christian crusade. It was in Spain that much of the new Catholic feeling first developed, and from Spain that much of the missionary spirit first went out. Spanish writers produced the most influential sixteenth-century accounts of Catholic mysticism, including Teresa of Avila's famous descriptions of her encounters with Christ. It was also Spain that produced St. Ignatius Loyola (1491–1556). A soldier in youth, he too, like Luther and Calvin, had a religious "experience" or "conversion," which occurred in 1521, before he had heard of Luther and while Calvin was still a boy. Loyola resolved to become a soldier of the church, a militant crusader for the pope and the Holy See. On this principle he established the Society of Jesus, commonly known as the Jesuits. Authorized by Pope Paul III in 1540, the Jesuits constituted a monastic order of a new type, less attached to the cloister, more directed toward active participation in the affairs of the world. Only men of proven strength of character and intellectual force were admitted. Each Jesuit had to undergo an arduous and even horrifying mystical training, set forth by Loyola in his *Spiritual Exercises*. The order was ruled by an iron discipline, which required each member to see in his immediate superior the infallibility of the Holy Church.

The Jesuits

St. Ignatius Loyola's religious inspiration is portrayed in this painting by Peter Paul Rubens, whose work often represented the religious and political leaders of Catholic countries.
(Giraudon/Art Resource)

If, said Loyola, the church teaches to be black what the eye sees as white, the mind must believe it to be black.

For two hundred years the Jesuits were the most famous schoolmasters of Catholic Europe, eventually conducting some 500 schools for boys of the upper and middle classes. In them they taught, besides the faith, the principles of gentlemanly deportment (their teaching of dancing and dramatics became a scandal to more puritanical Catholics), and they carried over the Renaissance and humanist idea of the Latin classics as the main substance of adolescent education. The Jesuits made a specialty of work among the ruling classes. They became confessors to kings and hence involved in political intrigue. In an age when Protestants subordinated an organized church either to the state or to an individual conscience, and when even Catholics frequently thought of the church within a national framework, the Jesuits seemed almost to worship the church itself as a divine institution, the Church Militant and the Church Universal, internationally organized and governed by the Roman pontiff. All full-fledged Jesuits took a special vow of obedience to the pope. Jesuits in the later sessions of the Council of Trent fought obstinately, and successfully, to uphold the position of Rome against that of the national bishops.

By 1560 the Catholic church, renewed by a deepening of its religious life and by an uncompromising restatement of its dogmas and discipline, had devised also the practical machinery for a counteroffensive against Protestantism. The Jesuits acted as an international missionary force. They recruited members from all countries, including those in which the governments had turned Protestant. English Catholics, for example, trained as Jesuits on the Continent, returned to England to attempt to overthrow the heretic usurper, Elizabeth, seeing in the universal church a higher cause than national independence in religion. Jesuits poured also into the most hotly disputed regions where the religious issue still swayed in the balance—France, Germany, Bohemia, Poland, Hungary. As after every great revolution, many people after an initial burst of Protestantism were inclined to turn back to the old order, especially as the more crying evils within the Catholic church were corrected. The Jesuits reconverted many who thus hesitated.

For the more recalcitrant other machinery was provided. All countries censored books; Protestant authorities labored to keep "papist" works from the eyes of the faithful, and Catholic authorities took the same pains to suppress all knowledge of "heretics." All bishops, Anglican, Lutheran, and Catholic, regulated reading matter within their dioceses. In the Catholic world, with the trend toward centralization under the pope, a special importance attached to the list published by the bishop of Rome, the papal Index of Prohibited Books. Only with special permission, granted to reliable persons for special study, could Catholics read books listed on the Index, which was not abandoned until the 1960s.

All countries, Protestant and Catholic, also set up judicial and police machinery to enforce conformity to the accepted church. In England, for example, Elizabeth established the High Commission to bring "recusants" into the Church of England. All bishops, Protestant and Catholic, likewise possessed machinery of enforcement in their episcopal courts. But no court made itself so dreaded as the Inquisition. In reality two distinct organizations went under this name, the word itself being simply an old term of the Roman law, signifying a court of inquest or inquiry. One was the Spanish Inquisition, established originally, about 1480, to ferret out Jewish and Muslim survivals in Spain. It was then introduced into all countries ruled by the Spanish crown and employed against Protestantism, particularly in the Spanish Netherlands, which was an important center of Calvinism. The other was the Roman or papal Inquisition, established at Rome in 1542 under a permanent committee of cardinals called the Holy Office; it was in a sense a revival of the famous medieval tribunal established in the thirteenth century for the detection and repression of heresy. Both the Spanish and the Roman Inquisitions employed torture, for heresy was regarded as the supreme crime, and all persons charged with crime could be tortured, in civil as well as ecclesiastical courts, under the existing laws. In the use of torture, as in the imposition of the harshest sentence, burning alive, the Roman Inquisition was less severe than the Spanish. The Roman Inquisition in principle offered a court to protect purity of faith in all parts of the Catholic world. But the national resistance of Catholic countries proved too strong; few Catholics wished the agents of Rome inquiring locally into their opinions; and the Roman Inquisition never functioned for any length of time outside of Italy.

Enforcing religious conformity

In the "machinery" of enforcing religious belief, however, no engine was to be so powerful as the apparatus of state. Where Protestants won control of government, people became Protestant. Where Catholics retained control of governments, Protestants became in time small minorities. And it was in the clash of governments, which is to say in war, for about a century after 1560, that the fate of European religion was worked out. In 1560 the strongest powers of Europe—Spain, France, Austria—were all officially Catholic. The Protestant states were all small or at most middle-sized. The Lutheran states of Germany, like all German states, were individually of little weight. The Scandinavian monarchies were far away. England, the most considerable of Protestant kingdoms, was a country of only four million people, with an independent and hostile Scotland to the north, and with no sign of colonial empire yet in existence. In the precedence of monarchs, as arranged in the earlier part of the century, the king of England ranked just below the king of Portugal, and next above the king of Sicily. Clearly, had a great combined Catholic crusade ever developed, Protestantism could have been wiped out. Yet such a crusade, partially launched on various fronts by the king of Spain, never succeeded. Religious divisions became a permanent reality in European culture, contributing eventually, like Renaissance humanism and the new European monarchies, to a gradual secularization of modern societies.

For interactive exercises, glossary, chronologies, and more, go to the *Online Learning Center* at **www.mhhe.com/palmer10.**

Chapter *3*

ECONOMIC RENEWAL AND WARS OF RELIGION, 1560–1648

It is convenient to think of European history in the period following 1560 as the age of the Wars of Religion, which may be said to have ended with the Peace of Westphalia in 1648. France, England, the Netherlands, and the Holy Roman Empire fell into internal and international struggles in which religion was often the most burning issue, but in which political, constitutional, economic, and social questions were also involved. The time of the long, drawn-out conflicts between Catholics and Protestants was also a time of economic renewal. From the beginning of the sixteenth century European society was transformed by contacts with a newly discovered overseas world, by expanded trade routes, an emergent capitalism, and the formation of new social classes.

This was the era in which the modern global economic system began to develop. The effects of these profound changes, however, were obscured and delayed by the politico-religious struggles. In the present chapter we must first examine the geographical discoveries, then survey the broad new economic and social developments under way, and finally trace the impact of the religious wars on various parts of Europe. The wars, as we shall see, left Spain and Germany very much weakened, and opened the way for the English, Dutch, and French to profit from the economic changes and play leading roles in the drama of early modern times.

11. THE OPENING OF THE ATLANTIC

Always until about 1500 the Atlantic Ocean had been a barrier, an end. About 1500 it became a bridge, a starting place. The consequences were enormous for all concerned. In

Chapter emblem: Detail from Jean Bourdichon (1457–1521), *The Four Estates of Society: Work,* which shows a carpenter working with the tools of his craft. (Giraudon/Art Resource, NY)

general, they were favorable for Europeans but devastating for peoples elsewhere—in America through massive depopulation by diseases such as smallpox brought from Europe, in Africa through the transatlantic slave trade, and ultimately in places as far away as Australia through the destruction of long-existing cultures or languages. Older, celebratory accounts of Europe's "overseas discoveries" have therefore been widely challenged in recent decades by historians who approach the story of European expansion from the perspective of Native Americans or African Americans. Viewed from these perspectives, Columbus's first voyage to America in 1492 launched a history of terrible losses rather than a story of heroic European explorations and conquests.

But few would deny that the new, complex association of the Old and New Worlds, as Europeans called them, became a momentous event in human history. The endless migration of people, the worldwide movement of trade, and the disorienting experiences of cross-cultural encounters marked the true beginning of modern global history. Europeans transformed or even destroyed numerous other cultures, but their own culture was also transformed through steadily expanding contacts with other peoples, social traditions, and religions in every part of the world. A new wealthy commercial class grew up in cities along Europe's Atlantic coast. Naval power became decisive. European populations grew with the adoption of the American potato, and people in Europe became dependent on imported commodities such as sugar and tobacco. European writers took increasing pride in their understanding of the world and in what they regarded as the superiority of their own cultural or religious traditions. There was also much speculation on the diversity of the human races and cultures, which sometimes led to a new kind of race consciousness on the part of Europeans and sometimes to a cultural relativism in which European customs were seen as only one variant of human behavior as a whole. Meanwhile, people in the Americas and Africa struggled to defend their own evolving cultures and institutions as European soldiers, traders, and missionaries entered the various civilizations of an increasingly interconnected transatlantic economic system.

Cultural transformation and destruction

The Portuguese in the East

Europeans had skirted their Atlantic coast since prehistoric times. Vikings had settled in Iceland in the ninth century and had even reached North America soon thereafter. In 1317 Venetians had established the Flanders galleys, commercial flotillas that regularly made the passage between the Adriatic and North seas. In the fifteenth century, improvements in shipbuilding, the rigging of sails, and the adoption of the mariner's compass made it feasible to sail on the open ocean out of sight of land. When the Portuguese about 1450 settled in the Azores Islands, in the mid-Atlantic, they found steady westerly winds to assure a safe return to Europe. It seemed that the ocean might even lead to Asia.

For centuries Asia had been a source for Europe of many highly valued commodities, partly manufactures in which Europe could not compete, such as silk and cotton fabrics, rugs, jewelry, porcelains, and fine steel, and partly raw or semimanufactured drugs and foodstuffs, such as sugar and, above all, spices. Europeans had never themselves gone to the sources of supply of Eastern goods. Somewhere, east of Suez, barely known to Europeans, was another world of other merchants who moved the wares of China, India, and the East Indies Spice Islands by caravan over land and by boat through the Red Sea or Persian Gulf to the markets of the eastern Mediterranean. Traders of the two worlds met and did business at such thriving centers as Alexandria or Beirut or Constantinople.

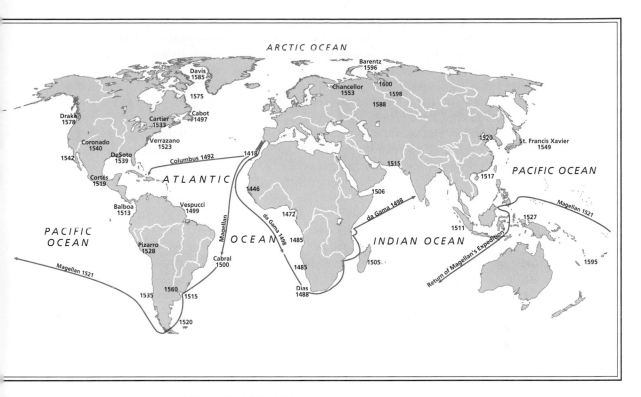

EUROPEAN DISCOVERIES, 1450–1600

Discovery means the bringing of newly found countries within the habitual knowledge or permanent commercial activity of the society from which the discoverer comes. Although sailors and travelers from Asia had long made voyages to distant places and engaged in trade across the Indian Ocean or South Pacific, it was the Europeans who discovered much of the world in the sense indicated here. They did so in the period between 1450 and 1600, using maritime skills and geographical knowledge developed in the Mediterranean and off the Atlantic coast. Dates on the map show the years of first significant European arrival at the points indicated.

In 1498 the Portuguese navigator Vasco da Gama, having rounded Africa in the wake of other intrepid explorers, found himself in the midst of the unknown world of Arab commerce. He landed on the Malabar Coast (the southwest coast of India), where he found a busy commercial population of heterogeneous religious background. These people knew at least as much about Europe as Europeans did about India (one Jew was able to act as da Gama's interpreter), and they realized that the coming of the Portuguese would disturb their established channels of commerce. Da Gama, playing upon local rivalries, was able to load his ships with the coveted wares, but on his second voyage, in 1502, he came better prepared, bringing a fighting fleet of no less than 21 vessels. A ferocious war broke out between the Portuguese and Arab merchants, the latter supported in one way or another by the Egyptians, the Turks, and even the distant Venetians, all of whom had an interest in maintaining the old routes of trade. For the Portuguese, trained like the Spaniards in long wars against the Moors at home, no atrocities were too horrible to commit against the infidel competitors whom they found at the end of their heroic quest. Cities were devastated, ships were burned at their docks, prisoners were butchered, and their dismembered hands, noses, and ears were sent back as derisive trophies. One Brahmin, mutilated in this way, was left alive to bear them to his people. Such, unfortunately, was India's introduction to the West.

In the following years the Portuguese built permanent fortified stations at Goa on the Malabar Coast, at Aden near the mouth of the Red Sea, at Hormuz near the mouth of the Persian Gulf, and in East Africa. In 1509 they reached Malacca, near modern Singapore, from which they passed northward into China itself and eastward to Amboina, the heart of the Spice Islands, just west of New Guinea. Thus an empire was created, the first of Europe's commercial-colonial empires, maintained by superiority of firearms and sea power and with trade alternating with war and plunder. The early European traders were soon followed by bold Jesuits, including St. Francis Xavier, who, by 1550, had baptized thousands of souls in India, Indonesia, and even Japan.

Portuguese trading empire

By the new route the cost of Eastern goods for Europeans was much reduced, for the old route had involved many transshipments, unloadings, and reloadings, movements by sea and by land, through the hands of many merchants. In 1504 spices could be bought in Lisbon for only a fifth of the price demanded in Venice. The Venetians (who in their desperation even talked of digging a Suez canal) were hopelessly undersold: their trade thereafter was confined to products of the Middle East. As for the Portuguese, never was a commercial monopoly built so fast. The lower prices added enormously to European demand and consumption. Beginning in 1504, only five years after da Gama's first return, an average of 12 ships a year left Lisbon for the East.

The Discovery of America

Meanwhile, the same quest for a route to the East had led to the somewhat disappointing discovery of America. Like most such discoveries, this was no chance hit of an isolated genius. Behaim's globe, constructed in 1492, the very year of Columbus's first voyage, suggested that China could be reached by crossing the Atlantic and thus supported the idea of sailing westward to arrive in the East. Nevertheless, it was Christopher Columbus who had the persistence and daring to undertake the unprecedented westward voyage. Before the invention of sufficiently accurate clocks (in the eighteenth century) mariners had no way of determining longitude, that is, their east-west position, and learned geographers greatly underestimated the probable distance from Europe westward to Asia. When Columbus struck land, he naturally supposed it to be an outlying part of the Indies. The people were soon called Indians, and the islands where Columbus landed, the West Indies.

Columbus had sailed with the backing of Queen Isabella of Castile, and the new lands became part of the composite dominions of the crown of Spain. The Spaniards, hoping to beat the Portuguese to the East (which da Gama had not yet reached), received Columbus's first reports with enthusiasm. For his second voyage they gave him 17 ships, filled with 1,500 workmen and artisans. Columbus himself, until his death in 1506, kept probing about in the Caribbean, baffled and frustrated, still believing he had discovered a route to Asia and hoping to find something that looked like the fabulous East. Others were more willing to accept the new land for what it was. Churchmen, powerful in Spain, regarded it as a new field for crusading and conversion. The government saw it as a source of gold and silver for the royal exchequer. Footloose gentry of warlike habits, left

An Episode in the Conquest of America **was painted by the Dutch artist Jan Mostaert about 1545. In this detail from an early European visualization of the New World, the American Indians are seen as naked, helpless, confused, and very different from Europeans.**
(Foto Marburg/Art Resource, NY)

idle by the end of war with the Moors in Iberia, turned to America to make their fortunes. The *conquistadores* fell upon the new lands. Cortés conquered the Aztecs in Mexico; Pizarro, the Incas in Peru. They despoiled the native empires. Mines for precious metals were opened almost immediately. The Indians were put to forced labor, in which many died. The rapid decline in the Indian population, the attempts of the church to protect its Indian converts, and the restrictions set by royal authorities on their exploitation led almost immediately to the importation of African slaves, of whom, it was estimated, 100,000 had been brought to America by 1560. This massive, forced migration of Africans continued for more than two centuries; indeed, the number of enslaved Africans reaching America, including the two continents and the West Indies, was far greater than the number of Europeans who settled there before 1800.

Conquest begins in the Americas

Meanwhile, explorers began to feel their way along the vast American continent that barred them from Asia. A Spanish expedition, led by Magellan, found a southwestern passage in 1520, sailed from the Atlantic into the Pacific, crossed the Pacific, discovered the Philippine Islands, and fought its way through hostile Portuguese across the Indian Ocean back to Spain. The globe was thus

Further explorations

circumnavigated for the first time, and an idea of the true size and interconnection of the oceans was brought back to Europe. Geographical experts immediately incorporated the new knowledge. Europeans still knew little about the vast, newly discovered continents, however, and other explorers sailing for Spain, the Cabots sailing for England, Jacques Cartier for France, began the long and fruitless search for a northwest passage to the Pacific. An English expedition, looking for a northeast passage, discovered the White Sea in 1553. English merchants immediately began to take the ocean route to Russia. Archangel became an ocean port.

For a century it was only the Spanish and Portuguese who followed up the new ocean routes to America and the East. These two peoples, in a treaty of 1494, divided the globe between them by an imaginary north-and-south line that ran from a point in the middle of the North Atlantic Ocean through the north pole and across eastern Asia. Spain claimed all the Americas by this treaty, and Portugal, all rights of trade in Africa, Asia, and the East Indies. But when Brazil was discovered in 1500 by Pedro Cabral, it was found to be far enough east to lie within the Portuguese area, and when the Philippine Islands were discovered by Magellan in 1521, they were claimed to be in the Spanish zone.

In the populous, long-established civilizations of the East the Portuguese were never more than a handful of outsiders who could not impose their language, their religion, or their way of life. It was otherwise in the Americas, where previously unknown diseases such as smallpox decimated the native populations, and where Spanish invaders set about imposing European culture on the weakened and demoralized survivors.

The Spanish Empire in America

In South America, Mexico, and the Caribbean, after the first ferocity of the *conquista,* the Spanish established their own civilization. In Protestant countries, and also in France, as the years went on there arose an extremely unfavorable idea of the Spanish regime in America, where, it was noted, the Inquisition was presently established and the native peoples were reduced to servitude by the conquerors. The Spanish themselves came to dismiss this grim picture as a false legend concocted by their rivals. The true character of the Spanish empire in America is not easy to portray. The Spanish government (like the home governments of all colonial empires) regarded its empire as existing primarily for the benefit of the mother country. The Indians were put into servitude, to work in mines or in agriculture. They also died in large numbers from infections brought by Europeans to which Europeans over past centuries had developed immunities but against which the native American peoples had no such protection. The same was true farther north in what later became the United States. The Spanish government made efforts to moderate the exploitation of Indian labor. It introduced the encomienda, by which Indians were required to work for an owner a certain number of days in the week, while retaining parcels of land on which to work for themselves. How much the royal regulations were enforced on remote encomiendas is another question, to which answers vary. Black African slavery became less important in most of Spanish America than it later became in some of the Dutch, French, and English colonies or in Portuguese Brazil. But the white population remained relatively small. Castilian Spaniards looked down on American-born whites, called Creoles. Since fewer women than men emigrated from Spain, there arose a large class of mestizos, of mixed white and Indian descent.

Spanish colonial rule

The mestizos, along with many pure Indians, adopted to a considerable degree the Spanish language and the faith of the Spanish church. The Indians, while unfree, had

Europeans negotiate with an African chief and his council on the Guinea coast, perhaps for the purchase of slaves. The Europeans have guns while the Africans have only spears, but in contrast to early European images of American Indians the Africans are fully clothed and seated in a dignified manner.
(Photographs and Prints Division, Schomburg Center for Research in Black Culture, The New York Public Library, Astor, Lenox and Tilden Foundations)

Black slaves are stooped over in a diamond-processing operation in Brazil, while white overseers watch with whips.
(Photographs and Prints Division, Schomburg Center for Research in Black Culture, The New York Public Library, Astor, Lenox and Tilden Foundations)

usually lacked freedom under their own tribal chiefs; they were spared from tribal war; and the rigors of the Inquisition were mild compared with the physical cruelty that many faced under the Aztecs or Incas. The printing press was brought to Mexico in 1544. By the middle of the sixteenth century Spanish America consisted of two great viceroyalties, those of Mexico and Peru, with 22 bishoprics, and with a university in each viceroyalty; the University of Lima was established in 1551, that of Mexico in 1553.

When Harvard College was founded in New England (in 1636), there were five universities on the European model in Spanish America.

The Potosí silver mines

In 1545 a great discovery was made, the prodigiously rich silver deposits at Potosí in Peru. (It is now in Bolivia.) Almost simultaneously, better methods of extracting silver from the ore by the use of mercury were developed. American production of precious metals shot up suddenly and portentously. For years, after the mid-century, 500,000 pounds of silver and 10,000 pounds of gold flowed annually from America to Spain. The riches of Potosí financed the European projects of the king of Spain. Peruvian ores, Indian labor, and Spanish management combined to make possible the militant, anti-Protestant phase of the Counter Reformation.

Meanwhile, beginning in 1565, the Spanish also established a lucrative trade route between their colonies in Mexico and the Philippines. Large ships called the "Manila Galleons" carried vast cargoes of silver from Acapulco to Manila, where the silver was traded for Chinese luxury goods—spices, porcelain, silks, and ivory—all of which were transported back to Mexico and on to Europe. This valuable trade continued until the early nineteenth century. It carried perhaps a third of all the silver extracted from Spain's American colonies off to Asia; and it helped to create the first modern global network for commercial exchange, in part because it brought Chinese consumers the only commodity that they wanted to buy from Europeans during this era. Silver from New World mines therefore sustained the whole Asian-American-European trading system and enabled Spain to control much of the burgeoning global market for Chinese products.

The opening of the Atlantic thus reoriented Europe. In an age of oceanic communications Europe became a center from which America, Africa, and Asia could all be reached. In Europe itself, the Atlantic coast enjoyed great advantages over the center. No sooner did the Portuguese begin to bring spices from the East Indies than Antwerp began to flourish as the point of redistribution for northern Europe. But for a century after the Spanish and Portuguese began to build their empires, the northern peoples did not take to the oceans. French corsairs did indeed put out from Bayonne or Saint-Malo, and Dutch prowlers and English "sea dogs" followed at the close of the century, all bent upon plundering the Iberian treasure ships. Still the Spanish and Portuguese kept their monopoly. No organized effort, backed by governments, came from the north until about 1600. For it is by no means geography alone that determines economic development; the English, Dutch, and French could not make use of the opportunities with which the opening of the Atlantic provided them until they had cleared up their domestic troubles and survived the perils and hazards of the Wars of Religion.

12.   THE COMMERCIAL REVOLUTION

Population growth

In the great economic readjustment that was taking place in Europe, the opening of ocean trade routes was important, but it was by no means the only factor. Two others were the growth of population and a long, gradual rise in prices, or a slow inflation.

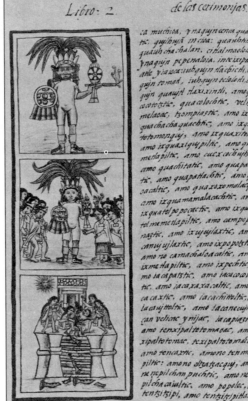

The Spaniards stamped out much of the Indian religion as idolatrous, yet it is to Spanish priests that we owe the preservation of much of our knowledge of the pre-Conquest culture. This page is from a book in which a Spaniard wrote down the Aztec language in the Latin alphabet. A human sacrifice is also depicted.
(Scala/Art Resource, NY)

European population again grew rapidly, as in the High Middle Ages, reaching about 90 million in 1600, of which 20 million represented the growth during the sixteenth century. The increase took place in all countries, though the distribution was quite different from the population increases in more recent times. England in 1600 had no more than five million inhabitants. France had almost four times as many, and the German states altogether about as many as France. Italy and Spain had fewer than France, and distant Russia, within its then boundaries, may have had no more than 10 million people. Some cities grew substantially, with London and Paris approaching 200,000; Antwerp, Lisbon, and Seville, thanks to the ocean trade, jumped to 100,000 by 1600. But smaller towns remained much the same; Europe as a whole was probably no more urbanized than in the later Middle Ages. Most of the population growth represented increasing density in the rural regions.

The steady rise in prices, which is to say the steady decline in value of a given unit of money (such as a shilling), constituted a gradual inflation. It has been called a "price revolution," but it was so slow as to be hardly comparable to the kinds of inflation known in some modern societies. One cause seems to have emerged from the growth of population itself, which set up an increasing demand for food. This meant that new land was brought under cultivation, land that was less fertile, more inaccessible or more difficult to work than the fields that had been cultivated previously. With increasing costs of production, agricultural prices

The price revolution

The silver mines at Potosí, portrayed here in a late sixteenth-century illustration, sent over 500,000 pounds of silver to Spain every year. American precious metals and the labor of American Indians enabled the Spanish government to wage its costly European wars and to maintain a lucrative trade with Chinese merchants in Asia.
(Courtesy of The Hispanic Society of America, New York)

rose; in England, for example, they about quadrupled during the sixteenth century. Prices were also pushed upward by the increase in the volume of money. The royal habit of debasing the currency brought a larger amount of money into circulation, since larger numbers of florins, *reals,* or *livres* were obtained from the same amount of bullion. The flow of gold and silver from America also made money more plentiful, but the impact of Peruvian and Mexican mines can easily be exaggerated. Even before the discovery of America, the development of gold and silver mines had augmented the European money supply. Although the expansion of both population and commerce checked the inflationary forces, the long trend of prices was upward. It affected all prices, including rents and other payments that were set in money values, but the price of hired labor, that is, wages, rose the least. The price changes thus had different effects on the well-being of social classes.

Commercial undertakings were favored by the rising prices and growing population. Merchants could count on increasing numbers of customers, new people could enter trade with hope of success, stocks of goods rose in value with the passage of time, and borrowed money could more easily be repaid. Governments benefited also, so far as kings could count on having more taxpayers and more soldiers.

The economic changes in Europe in the early modern period have been called the "Commercial Revolution," signifying the rise of a capitalistic economy and the transition from a town-centered to a nation-centered economic system. This "revolution" was an exceptionally slow and protracted one; it began at least as early as the fourteenth century and lasted until machine industry began to overshadow commerce in the early nineteenth century.

Changes in Commerce and Production

In the Middle Ages the town and its adjoining country formed an economic unit. Craftsmen, organized in guilds, produced common articles for local use. Peasants and lords sold their agricultural products to the local town, from which they bought what the craftsmen produced. The town protected itself by its own tariffs and regulations. In the workshop the master both owned his "capital"—his house, workbench, tools, and materials—and acted as a workman himself along with half a dozen journeymen and apprentices. The masters owned a modest capital, but they were hardly capitalists. They produced only upon order, or at least for customers whose tastes and number were known in advance. There was little profit, little risk of loss, and not much innovation.

All this changed with the widening of the trading area, or market. Even in the Middle Ages, as we have seen, there was a certain amount of long-distance trading in articles that could not be produced as well in one place as in another. Gradually more articles came within this category. Where goods were produced to be sold at some time in the future, in faraway places, to persons unknown, the local guildmaster could not manage the operation. He lacked the money (or "capital") to tie up in stocks of unsold wares; he lacked the knowledge of what distant customers wanted, or where, in what quantities, and at what price people would buy. In this new type of long-distance business, new kinds of entrepreneurs became prominent in European commercial life. They usually started out as merchants working in an extensive market and ended up as bankers. The Italian Medici family has been mentioned as important in Renaissance banking and culture. Equally typical were the German Fuggers.

New entrepreneurs

The first of this family, Johann Fugger, a small-town weaver, came to Augsburg in 1368. He established a business in a new kind of cloth, called fustian, in which cotton was mixed, and which had certain advantages over the woolens and linens in which people then clothed themselves. He thus enjoyed a more than local market. Gradually the family began to deal also in spices, silks, and other Eastern goods obtained at Venice. They invested their large profits in other enterprises, notably mining. They lent money to the Renaissance popes. They lent Charles V the money which he spent to obtain election as Holy Roman Emperor in 1519. They became bankers to the Habsburgs in both Germany and Spain. Together with other German and Flemish bankers, the Fuggers financed the Portuguese trade with Asia, either by outright loans or by providing in advance, on credit, the cargoes which the Portuguese traded for spices. The wealth of the Fuggers became proverbial and declined only through repeated Habsburg bankruptcies and with the general economic decline that beset Germany in the sixteenth century.

Other dealers in cloth, less spectacular than the first Fugger, broke away from the town-and-guild framework in other ways. England until the fifteenth century was an exporter of raw wool and an importer of finished woolens from Flanders. In the fifteenth century certain English entrepreneurs began to develop the spinning, weaving, and dyeing of wool in England. To avoid the restrictive practices of the towns and guilds they "put out" the work to people in the country, providing them with looms and other equipment for the purpose, of which they generally retained the ownership themselves. This "putting out" or "domestic" system spread very widely outside the guild system, and, by the early modern period, typically depended on a gendered division of labor. Women usually did the work of spinning wool into thread (hence the later English term for an unmarried woman, "spinster"); men usually wove the thread into cloth. In France the cloth dealers of Rouen, feeling the competition of the new silk trade, developed a lighter, cheaper, and more simply made type of woolen cloth. Various guild regulations in Rouen, to protect the workers there, prohibited the manufacture of this cheaper cloth. The Rouen dealers, in 1496, took the industry into the country, installed looms in peasant cottages, and farmed out the work to the peasants.

The "putting out" system

STUDY OF TWO BLACK HEADS
by Rembrandt van Rijn (Dutch, 1606–1669)

One consequence of the new international trade was the transportation of enslaved black Africans to the Americas. Some Africans appeared also in Europe, where their presence contributed to the growing speculation on the diversity of the human races. Rembrandt, though he never traveled more than 20 miles from his native Leyden, painted all types of people who streamed into the Netherlands, including these two men who had to cope with the strange European world into which they had been cast.

(Maurithshuis, The Hague)

Capital and Labor

The system of rural household industry remained typical of production in many lines (cloth, hardware, etc.) in western Europe until the introduction of factories in the late eighteenth century. It signified a new divergence between capital and labor. On the one hand were the workers, men and women who worked as the employer needed them, received wages for what they did, and had little interest in or knowledge of more than their own task. Living both by agriculture and by cottage industry, they formed an expansible labor force, available when labor was needed, left to live by farming or local charity when times were bad. On the other hand was the manager or entrepreneur (almost always a man) who directed the whole affair. He had no personal acquaintance with the workers. Estimating how much of his product, let us say woolens, he could sell in a national or even international market, he purchased the needed raw materials, passed out wool to be spun by one group of peasants, took the yarn to another group for weaving, collected the cloth and took it still elsewhere to be dyed, paying wages on all sides for services rendered, while retaining ownership of the materials and the equipment and keeping the coordination and management of the whole enterprise in his own head. Much larger business enterprises could be established in this way than within the municipal framework of guild and town. Indeed, the very master weavers of the guilds often sank to the status of subcontractors, hardly different from wage employees, of the great "clothiers" and "drapers" by whom the business was dominated. The latter, with the widening market, became personages of national or even international repute. And, of course, the bigger the business the more of a capital investment it represented.

Divergence between capital and labor

Certain other industries, new or virtually new in the fifteenth and sixteenth centuries, could by their nature never fit into a town-centered system and were capitalistic from the start, in that they required a large initial outlay before any income could be received. One such was mining. Another was printing and the book trade. Books had a national and even international market, being mainly in Latin; and no ordinary craftsman could afford the outlay required for a printing press, for fonts of type, supplies of paper, and stocks of books on hand. Printers therefore borrowed from capitalists or shared with them an interest in business. Shipbuilding was so stimulated by the shift to the oceans as almost to be a new industry, and still another was the manufacture of cannons and muskets. For the latter the chief demand came from the state, from the New Monarchies which were organizing national armies. In the rise of capitalism the needs of the military were in fact fundamentally important. Armies, which started out by requiring thousands of weapons, in the seventeenth century required thousands of uniforms, and in the eighteenth century many new barracks and fortifications. These heavy demands were the first to require mass production. Where governments themselves did not take the initiative, private middlemen stepped in as links to the many small handicraft workers and families who before the industrial age still manufactured the actual product.

New industries

The new sea route to the East and the discovery of America brought a vast increase in trade not only of luxury items but of bulk commodities like rice, sugar, tea, and other consumer goods. Older commercial activities were transformed by the widening of markets. Spain increasingly drew cereals from Sicily. The Netherlands were fed from Poland; the French wine districts lived on food brought from northern France. With the growth of shipping, the timber, tar, pitch, and other "naval stores" of Russia and the Baltic entered the commercial scene. There was thus an ever-growing movement of heavy staple commodities, in which again only persons controlling large funds of capital could normally take part.

The growing production of cloth in early modern Europe depended on the labor of families in rural cottage industries. Spinning thread became an important economic activity for many women, as Jean Bourdichon (1457–1521) demonstrates in this illustration of a family at work. The man is apparently a skilled woodworker, and the child is gathering wood chips that can be used for cooking food or heating the house. The solid walls and ceiling show that this is a prosperous, hard-working family.
(Giraudon/Art Resource, NY)

Not all capital was invested; some was simply lent to the church, to governments, to impecunious nobles, or, though perhaps this was the least common type of lending in the sixteenth century, to persons engaged in trade and commerce. Bankers and others who lent money expected to receive back, after a time, a larger sum than that of the loan. They expected "interest"; and they sometimes received as much as 30 percent a year. In the Middle Ages the taking of interest had been frowned upon as usury, denounced as avarice, and forbidden in the canon law. It was still frowned upon in the sixteenth century by almost all but the lenders themselves. The Catholic church maintained its prohibitions. The theologians of the University of Paris also ruled against it in 1530. Luther, who hated bankers like the Fuggers, continued to preach against usury. Calvin made allowances, but as late as 1640, in capitalist Holland itself, the stricter Calvinist ministers still denounced lending at interest.

New banking practices

Nothing could stop the practice. Borrowers compounded with lenders to evade prohibitions, and theologians of all churches began to distinguish between "usury" and a "legitimate return." Gradually, as interest rates fell, as banking became more established, and as loans were made for economically productive uses rather than to sustain ecclesiastics, princes, and nobles in their personal habits, the feeling against a "reasonable" interest died down and interest became an accepted feature of capitalism. The Bank of Amsterdam, for example, attracted depositors because they knew their money was safe, would earn interest, and could be withdrawn at will. Deposits thus flowed into the bank from all countries and enabled it to make low-interest loans that financed new commercial activities.

The net effect of all these developments was a "commercialization of industry." The dynamic, entrepreneurial persons in commercial life were the merchants. Industry, the actual processes of production, still in an essentially handicraft stage, was subordinate to the buyers and sellers. Pro-

Commercial capitalism

ducers—spinners, weavers, hatters, metalworkers, gunsmiths, glassworkers—worked to fill the orders of the merchants, and often with capital which the merchants supplied and owned. The entrepreneur who knew where the article could be sold prevailed over the person who simply knew how to produce it. This commercial capitalism remained the typical form of capitalism until after 1800, when, with the introduction of power machinery, it yielded to industrial capitalism, and merchants became dependent on industrialists who owned, understood, and organized the machines.

Mercantilism

There was still another aspect of the commercial revolution, namely, the various government policies that go historically under the name of "mercantilism." Rulers, as we have seen, were hard pressed for money and needed more of it as it fell in value. The desire of kings and their advisers to force gold and silver to flow into their own kingdoms was one of the first impulses leading to mercantilist regulation. Gradually this "bullionist" idea was replaced by the more general idea of building up a strong and self-sufficient economy. The means adopted, in either case, was to "set the poor on work," as they said in England, to turn the country into a hive of industry, to discourage idleness, begging, vagabondage, and unemployment. New crafts and manufactures were introduced, and favors were given to merchants who provided work for "the poor" and who sold the country's products abroad. It was thought desirable to raise the export of finished goods and reduce the export of unprocessed raw materials, to curtail all imports except of needed raw materials, and thus obtain a "favorable" balance of trade so that other countries would have to pay their debts in bullion. Since all this was done by a royal or nationwide system of regulations, mercantilism became in the economic sphere what the state building of the New Monarchies was in the political, signifying the transition from town to national units of social living.

Mercantilists frowned upon the localistic and conservative outlook of the guilds. In England the guilds ceased to have importance. Parliament, in the time of Elizabeth, did on a national scale what guilds had once done

Opposition to guilds

locally when it enacted the Statute of Artificers of 1563, regulating the admission to apprenticeship and level of wages in various trades. In France the royal government maintained the legal existence of the guilds, because they were convenient bodies to tax, but it deprived them of most of their old independence and used them as organizations through which royal control of industry could be enforced. In both countries the government assisted merchants who wished to set up domestic or cottage industry in the country, against the protests of the town guilds, which in their heyday had forbidden rural people to engage in crafts. Governments generally tried to suppress idleness. The famous English Poor Law of 1601 (which remained in effect, with amendments, until 1834) was designed both to force people to work and to relieve absolute destitution.

Governments likewise took steps to introduce new industries. The silk industry was brought from Italy to France under royal protection, to the dismay of French woolen and linen interests. The English government assisted in turning England from a producer of raw wool into a producer of finished woolens, supervising the immigration of skilled Flemish weavers and even fetching from faraway Turkey, about 1582, two youths who understood the more advanced dyeing arts of the Middle East. Generally, under mercantilism, governments fought to steal skilled workers from each other while prohibiting or discouraging the emigration of their own skilled workers, who might take their trade secrets and "mysteries" to foreign parts.

National markets

By such means governments helped to create a national market and an industrious nationwide labor supply for their great merchants. Without such government support the great merchants, such as the drapers or clothiers, could never have risen and prospered. The same help was given to merchants operating in foreign markets. Henry VII of England in 1496 negotiated a commercial treaty with Flanders; and in the next century the kings of France signed treaties with the Ottoman Empire by which French merchants obtained privileges in the Middle East. A merchant backed by a national monarchy was in a much stronger position than one backed merely by a city, such as Augsburg or Venice. This backing on a national scale was again given when national governments subsidized exports, paying bounties for goods whose production they wished to encourage, or when they erected tariff barriers against imports to protect their own producers from competition. Thus a national tariff system was superimposed on the old network of provincial and municipal tariffs. These latter were now thought of as "internal tariffs," and mercantilists usually wished to abolish them to create an area of free trade within the state as a whole. But local interests were so strong that for centuries they were unable to get rid of local tariffs except in England.

In distant parts of the world, or in less accessible regions nearer home, such as the Muslim lands or Russia, it was not possible for individual European merchants to act by merely private initiative. Merchants trading with such countries needed a good deal of capital, they often had to obtain special privileges and protection from native rulers, and they had to arm their ships against Barbary or Malay pirates or against hostile Europeans. Merchants and their respective governments came together to found official companies for the transocean trade. In England, soon after the English discovery of the White Sea in 1553, a Russia Company was established. A Turkey Company soon followed. Shortly after 1600 a great many such companies were operating out of England, Holland, and France. The most famous of all were the East India Companies, which the English founded in 1600, the Dutch in 1602, the French not until 1664. Each of these companies was a state-supported organization with special rights. Each was a monopoly in that only merchants who belonged to the company could legally engage in trade in the region for which the company had a charter. Each was expected to find markets for the national manufactures, and most of them were expected to bring home gold or silver. With these companies the northern European peoples began to encroach on the Spanish and Portuguese monopoly in America and the East. With them new commercial-colonial empires were to be launched. But, as has been already observed, before this could happen it was necessary for certain domestic and purely European conflicts and controversies to be settled.

13.   CHANGING SOCIAL STRUCTURES

Social structure, for present purposes, refers to the composition, functions, and interrelationships of social classes. Because changes in social structure are slow, they are hard to identify with any particular period of time. In general, however, with the effects of the commercial revolution, population growth, and the falling value of money, the classes of

The headquarters of the Dutch East India Company in Bengal in 1665, long before the British gained predominance there. It is wholly walled off from the Indian life around it, with offices, living quarters, and spacious gardens for employees of the company.
(© Rijksmuseum, Amsterdam)

Europe, broadly defined, took on forms that were to last until the industrial era of the nineteenth and twentieth centuries. These classes were the landed aristocracy, the peasantry or mass of agricultural workers, the miscellaneous middle classes, and the urban poor.

While all prices rose in the sixteenth century, it was agricultural prices that rose the most. Anyone who had agricultural products to sell was likely to benefit. Among such beneficiaries were peasants who held bits of land in return for payments to a manorial lord set in unchangeable sums of money, in the old values of the fourteenth or even thirteenth century. The price inflation of the sixteenth century enabled such peasants in effect to pay much less to the lord than in the past. Other rural workers, however, either held no land of their own or produced only at a subsistence level with nothing to sell in the market. Such peasants, and hired hands dependent on wages, found their situation worsened. Village life became less egalitarian than it had been in the Middle Ages. In England a class of small freeholders (the "yeomanry") developed between the landed gentry and the rural poor. On the Continent, at least in France, western Germany, and the Netherlands, some peasants acquired more secure property rights, resembling those of small freeholders in England. But both in England and on the Continent a large class of unpropertied rural workers remained in poverty.

Small freeholders

Land rents went up as agricultural prices rose, and inflation and population growth drove up rentals for housing in the towns. Owners of real property (that is, land and buildings) were favored by such changes, but within the former class of feudal lords the effects were mixed. If one's great-grandfather had let out land in earlier times in exchange for fixed sums of money, the value of the income received had actually declined. But those who received payments in kind from their tenants, for example, in bushels of wheat or barley, or who managed their estates themselves, could sell their actual agricultural products at current prices and so increase their money income.

Social Classes

The former feudal class, or nobles, thus turned into a more modern kind of aristocracy. If income from their estates declined, they sought service in the king's army or government or appointment to the more prestigious offices in the church. If landed income increased, they were more wealthy. In either case they became more concerned with civilian pursuits and were likely to develop more refined tastes and pay more attention to the education of their children. Like the peasants, the landowning class became more heterogeneous, ranging from the small gentry to the great peers of England and from small or impoverished nobles to the *grands seigneurs* of France. Some led a life of leisure; others were eager to work in the higher reaches of organized government. The most impoverished nobles sometimes had the longest pedigrees. As their social functions changed, and as persons of more recent family background competed for education, government employment, and even military service, there came to be an increasing importance set upon ancestry as a badge of status. Among the upper class, there was more insistence on high birth and distinguished forebears in the seventeenth and eighteenth centuries than there had been before. But many nobles also claimed that they deserved special privileges because they contributed meritorious service to kings or the expanding national governments.

The bourgeoisie

Below the aristocracy were the "middle classes," or "bourgeoisie." *Bourgeois* was a French word, which, like the English "burgher," originally meant a person living in a chartered town or borough and enjoying its liberties. The bourgeoisie was the whole social class made up of individual bourgeois. In a much later sense of the word, derived from Karl Marx, the term "bourgeoisie" was applied to the class of owners of capital. This Marxist concept of the bourgeoisie must be kept distinct from the meaning of the word in an earlier era. "Bourgeoisie" referred in preindustrial times to the middle levels of society between the aristocracy, which drew its income from land, and the laboring poor, who depended on wages or charity, or who often went hungry. Class lines tended to blur as aristocratic families formed the habit of living in towns and middle-class burghers began to buy land in the country. Some bourgeois thus came to live on landed rents, while some of the gentry and aristocracy, most notably in England, bought shares in the great overseas trading companies or engaged in other forms of business enterprise. Aristocrats possessing large agricultural estates, timberlands, or mines increasingly brought their products to market to be sold at a profit. But even when aristocrat and bourgeois became economically more alike, a consciousness of social difference between them remained.

Middle class growth and diversity

The middle class became more numerous in the sixteenth century, and increasingly so thereafter. It was an indefinite category, since the countries of Europe were very different in the size and importance of their middle classes, in the kinds of persons who belonged to them, and in the types of occupations pursued. Near the top were the urban elites who governed the towns; they might draw their incomes from rural property, from commerce, or from the emoluments of government itself, and they sometimes intermarried with persons of noble status. Especially where the towns were strong or royal government was weak, as in the Netherlands, the German free cities, or north Italy, such urban patriciates formed virtual aristocracies in themselves. But in a larger perspective the families of merchants, bankers, and shipowners were middle-class, as were those of the traditional learned professions, law and medicine. So in general were judges, tax officials, and other employees of governments, except in the highest ranks. In the professions and in government service the younger sons of the aristocracy might be found alongside the offspring of the middle classes, most commonly in England, less so in France, and even less as one moved into Germany or Spain.

The clergy was drawn from all classes; there were poor parish priests, who might be the sons of peasants, and noblemen among the bishops and abbots; but the bulk of the clergy was recruited from middle-class families. In Protestant countries, where the clergy married, their sons and daughters became an important element in the middle class. Members of trade guilds were middle class, though the guilds differed widely in social status, from those of the great wholesale merchants or the goldsmiths, down through the guilds of such humble occupations as the tanners and barrel makers. At the bottom the middle class faded into the world of small retail shopkeepers, innkeepers, owners of workshops in which ordinary articles were manufactured by hand, the lesser skilled tradespeople, and their employees, journeymen, and apprentices.

The working class poor

The mass of the population in all countries was composed of the working poor. These included not only the unskilled wage laborers but the unemployed, unemployable, and paupers, with a large fringe that turned to vagabondage and begging. They were unable to read or write and were often given to irregular habits which distressed both middle-class persons and government officials. The efforts of mercantilist governments to put the poor to work, or make them contribute to the wealth of the country, have already been mentioned. Charitable relief also developed toward the end of the sixteenth century, as shown in the English Poor Law of 1601 and in similar efforts on the Continent. The idea gained ground that begging was a public nuisance and that the poor should be segregated in workhouses or hospices from the rest of society. Most of the poor were of course not recipients of such relief. They were the people who tilled the fields, tended the livestock, dug in the mines, or went to sea as fishermen and common sailors. They also found work in the towns as casual laborers, porters, water carriers, or removers of excrement; or they entered the domestic service of noble and upper middle-class families, whose rising standard of living required a growing number of chambermaids, cooks, washerwomen, footmen, lackeys, coachmen, and stable boys. Domestic service was in fact the most common job for women during the entire period of early modern history, and the pay for such work remained extremely low. Wages rose less than prices in the sixteenth century. The poor, if not positively worse off than in former times, gained the least from the great commercial developments with which economic history is usually concerned. The very growth of social differentiation, the fact that the middle and upper classes made such advances, left the condition of the poor correspondingly worse.

Social Roles of Education and Government

Education in the latter part of the sixteenth century took on an altogether new importance for the social system. One consequence of the Reformation, in both Protestant and

Catholic countries, was the attempt to put a serious and effective pastor in each parish. This set up a demand for a more educated clergy. The growth of commerce made it necessary to have literate clerks and agents. Governments wanted men from both the noble and middle classes who could cooperate in large organizations, be reliable, understand finance, keep records, and draft proposals. There was also a widespread need for lawyers.

New schools and universities

The new demand for education was met by an outburst of philanthropy, which reached a high point in both England and France between about 1580 and 1640. Many endowed scholarships were established. At what would now be called a secondary level, hundreds of "grammar schools" were founded at this time in England. In France the *collèges* combined the work of the English grammar school with what corresponded to the first year or two of university work at Oxford or Cambridge. Of the 167 most important French colleges still existing at the time of the Revolution in 1789, only 36 had been founded in the centuries before 1560, and 92 were established in the years between 1560 and 1650. Provision for girls' schools was more sporadic, but the Ursuline sisters, for example, founded in Italy in 1535, had established about 350 convents by the year 1700 in Catholic Europe and even in Canada, in most of which the education of girls was a principal occupation of the sisters.

Wider access to education

Dutch and Swiss Protestants founded the universities of Leyden and Geneva. New universities, both Protestant and Catholic, appeared in Germany. In Spain the multiplication of universities was phenomenal. Castile, with only 2 universities dating from the Middle Ages, had 20 by the early seventeenth century; Salamanca was enrolling over 5,000 students a year. Five universities also existed in Spanish America by 1600. In England, new colleges were founded at Oxford and Cambridge, and it was especially in these years that some of the Oxford and Cambridge colleges became very wealthy. Annual freshman admissions at Oxford, barely 100 in 1550, rose to over 500 in the 1630s, a figure not exceeded, or even equaled, during the following two hundred years.

The schools, colleges, and universities drew their students from a wide range of social classes. For girls less organized schooling was offered, but an intelligent and lucky boy of poor family had perhaps a better chance for education than at any time in Europe until very recently. In Spain most of the students seem to have been lesser nobles, or "hidalgos," aspiring to positions in the church or government; but hidalgos were very numerous in Spain, overlapping with what might be called the middle class in other countries. The French colleges, including those operated by the Jesuits, recruited their students very widely, taking in the sons of nobles, merchants, shopkeepers, artisans, and even, more rarely, of peasants. English grammar schools did likewise; it was in later times that a few of them, like Eton and Harrow, became more exclusive Public Schools. As for universities, we have detailed knowledge for Oxford, which recorded the status of its students at matriculation, classifying them as "esquires," "gentlemen," "clergy," and "plebeians." From 1560 to 1660 about half of the Oxford students were "plebeians," which in the language of that time could embrace the whole middle class from big merchants down to quite modest levels. It seems certain that Oxford and Cambridge were more widely representative of the English people in 1660 than in 1900.

Government and social classes

Social classes were formed not only by economic forces, and not only by education, but also by the action of governments. Government could inhibit economic growth, as in Spain, or promote it, as in England. Kings contributed to the rise of capitalism and a business class by granting

A seventeenth-century monk is teaching in Spain at the University of Salamanca, one of the largest European universities of the time and an example of how such institutions expanded in both Catholic and Protestant countries during the century after the Protestant Reformation.
(Index/Bridgeman Art Library)

monopolies, borrowing from bankers, and issuing charters to trading companies. In many countries, and notably in France, many families owed their middle-class position to the holding of government offices, some of which might become a form of inheritable property. It might also be the action of governments, as much as economic conditions, that defined or promoted distinctions between nobles and commoners, or "privileged" and "unprivileged" classes. Where peasants suffered heavily from royal taxes, it was more from political than from economic causes. The king, by "making" nobles—that is, by conferring titles of nobility on persons who did not inherit them—could raise a few in the middle class to higher status. Tax exemption could be a sign of high social standing. The king was also the fountain of honor, at the top of "society." The royal court formed the apex of a pyramid of social rank, in which each class looked up to or down upon the others. Those favored with the royal presence disdained the plain country nobility, who sniffed at the middle classes, who patronized or disparaged the hired servants, day laborers, and the poor. Looking upward, people were expected to show deference for their betters.

Eastern and Western Europe

One other remark may be made on social structure. It was in the sixteenth century that important social differences developed between eastern and western Europe. In the west, the changes brought by the commercial revolution were advantageous to the middle class and to many of the peasantry for whom the old burdens of the manorial system were lightened. In eastern Europe, it was the lords who benefited from rising prices and the growing market for grain and forest products. Here too the institution of the manor existed; but the peasants' land tenures were more precarious than in the west, more dependent on accidents of death or on the wishes of the lord, and the lord worked a larger part of the manor with his own workforce for his own use or profit.

The rise of prices and expansion of Baltic shipping gave the lord the incentive to increase his output. In northeast Germany (where such lords were called Junkers), in Poland, and as time went on in Russia, Bohemia, and Hungary, beginning in the sixteenth century and continuing into the eighteenth, a vast process set in by which the mass of the peasantry sank into serfdom. It was hastened in many regions by the violence and insecurity engendered by the religious wars. Typically, peasants lost their individual parcels of land or received them back on condition that they render unpaid labor services to the lord. Usually peasants owed three or four days a week of such forced labor (called *robot* in Bohemia and adjoining territories), remaining free to work during the remainder of the week on their own parcels. Often the number of days of *robot* exacted by the lord was greater, since in eastern Europe, where central monarchy was weak and centralized legal systems were almost unknown, the lord himself was the final court of appeal for his people. His people were in fact his "subjects."

Serfdom in eastern Europe

Serfdom in Germany was not called serfdom, but "hereditary subjection." By whatever name they were known throughout eastern Europe, serfs, or hereditary subjects of the manorial lord, could not leave the manor, marry, or learn a trade without the lord's express permission. The lord, drawing on this large reserve of compulsory labor, using most of it for agriculture but teaching some quick-minded youths the various handicrafts that were needed on the estate, worked the land as his own venture, sold the produce, and retained the profit.

Thus, in eastern Europe at the beginning of modern times, the rural masses lost personal freedom and lived in a poverty unknown among the peasants to the west, poor as the latter were. In western Europe there were peasants who were already on the way to becoming small proprietors. They were free people under the law. They could migrate, marry, and learn trades as opportunity offered. Those who held land could defend it in the royal courts and raise crops and take part in the market economy on their own account. They owed the lord no forced labor—or virtually none, for the ten days a year of corvée still found in parts of France hardly compared with the almost full-time *robot* of the peasant of eastern Europe.

The landlord in the east, from the sixteenth century onward, was solidly entrenched in his own domain, monarch of all he surveyed, with no troublesome bourgeoisie to annoy him (for towns were few), and with kings and territorial rulers solicitous of his wishes. Travelers from the west were impressed with the wealth of great Polish and Lithuanian magnates, with their palatial homes, private art galleries, well-stocked libraries, collections of jewels, gargantuan dinners, and lavish hospitality. The Junkers of northeast Germany lived more modestly, but enjoyed the same kind of independence and social superiority.

The growing power of wealthy landlords and the weakening position of impoverished peasants would have decisive social and political consequences for the later history of Prussia, Poland, Russia, and the Austrian world. But meanwhile, amidst all the economic growth, social development, and overseas conquests that have been described in the preceding pages, Europe was torn by the destructive ferocity of the Wars of Religion.

14. THE WARS OF CATHOLIC SPAIN: THE NETHERLANDS AND ENGLAND

The Ambitions of Philip II

Charles V, having tried in vain for 35 years to preserve religious unity in Germany, abdicated his many crowns and retired to a monastery in 1556, the year after the Peace of Augsburg had given the ruler of each German state the right to choose its own religion. He left Austria, Bohemia, and Hungary (or the small part of it not occupied by the Turks) to his brother Ferdinand, who was soon elected Holy Roman Emperor (see map, p. 78). All his other possessions Charles left to his son Philip, who became Philip II of Spain. The Habsburg dynasty remained thereafter divided into two branches, the Austrian and the Spanish. The two cooperated in European affairs. The Spanish branch for a century was the more important. Philip II (1556–1598) not only possessed the Spanish kingdoms but in 1580 inherited Portugal, so that the whole Iberian peninsula was brought under his rule. He possessed the 17 provinces of the Netherlands and the Free County of Burgundy, which were member states of the Holy Roman Empire, lying on its western border, adjacent to France. Milan in north Italy and Naples in the south belonged to Philip, and since he also held the chief islands, as well as Tunis, he enjoyed a naval ascendancy in the western Mediterranean which was threatened only by the Turks. For five years, until 1558, he was titular king of England, and in 1589, in the name of his daughter, he laid claim to the throne of France. All America belonged to Philip II, and after 1580 all the Portuguese empire as well, so that except for a few nautical daredevils all ships plying the open ocean were the Spanish king's.

Philip II therefore naturally regarded himself as an international figure, and the more so because he combined the organizing methods of a new monarchy with a profound interest in the political and religious issues that were dividing post-Reformation Europe. He saw Spain as a leader of European Catholicism, and he believed that the advance of Spanish power in Europe served the cause of the universal church as well as the interests of his own monarchy and the people of Spain. Yet his attempts to protect and enhance Spanish power in Italy sometimes led to conflicts with the popes, and much of his foreign policy was directed against the Ottoman Empire in a continuing struggle for control of the Mediterranean Sea. European Protestantism was thus only one of Philip's many international concerns.

Philip's goals

Philip's active participation in Europe's religious wars should therefore be seen as part of his wider military and political campaigns to protect Spanish and Habsburg interests rather than a single-minded crusade for Catholicism. In his personal life, he was serious, devout, and hardworking. He gave the most detailed attention to the management of his far-flung territories. The wealth that flowed to his country from Potosí and other mines in South America enabled Philip to pursue his goals throughout Europe and the Mediterranean. Meanwhile, Spain also entered upon the Golden Age of its early modern culture.

In this period, the *siglo de oro,* running in round dates from 1550 to 1650, Cervantes wrote his *Don Quixote* (in two parts, 1605, 1615) and Lope de Vega wrote his 200 dramas, while El Greco, Murillo, and Velázquez painted their pictures, and the Jesuit Suarez composed works on philosophy and law that were read even in Protestant countries. As Cervantes showed in *Don Quixote,* many Spaniards were highly aware of the enduring tensions between high ideals and the difficult realities of social, political, and religious life. But Catholic traditions and the Catholic Church remained a powerful force in Spanish culture. The church was vitally present at every social level, from the archbishop of Toledo, who ranked above grandees and could address the king as an equal, down to a host of penniless and mendicant friars, who mixed with the poorest and most disinherited of the people.

The Escorial

Philip II built himself a new royal residence, the Escorial, which well expressed in solid stone its creator's political and religious determination. Madrid itself was a new town, merely a government center, far from the worldly distractions of Toledo or Valladolid. But it was 30 miles from Madrid, on the bleak arid plateau of central Castile, overlooked by the jagged Sierra, that Philip chose to erect the Escorial. He built it in honor of St. Lawrence, on whose feast day he had won a battle against the French. The connecting buildings were laid out in the shape of a grill, since, according to martyrologists, St. Lawrence, in the year 258, had been burned alive on a grill over burning coals. Somber and vast, made of blocks of granite meant to last forever, and with its highest spire rising three hundred feet from the ground, the Escorial was designed not only as a palace but as a center for religious life and the efficient management of a vast empire. Working constantly in this somber setting, Philip II dispatched his couriers to Mexico, to Manila, to Vienna, and to Milan. He sent his troops off to Italy and the Netherlands, his diplomats to all the royal courts of Europe, and his spies wherever they were needed—seeking to extend the influence of his powerful state and (when possible) to promote the Catholicism in which he devoutly believed.

The first years of Philip's reign were also the first years of Elizabeth's reign in England, where the religious issue was still in flux; they were years in which Calvinism agitated the Netherlands, and when France, ruled by teenaged boys, fell apart into implacable civil war. Religious loyalties that knew no frontiers overlapped all political boundaries. Everywhere there were people who looked for guidance outside their own countries. Fervent Calvinists in England, France, and the Netherlands felt closer to one another than to their own monarchs or their own neighbors. Fervent Catholics, in all three countries, welcomed the support of international Catholic forces—the Jesuits, the king of Spain, the pope. National unity threatened to dissolve or was not yet formed. The sense of mutual trust between people who lived side by side was eaten away; and people who lived not only in the same country, but in the same town, on the same street, or even in the same house, turned against each other in the name of a higher cause.

The Catholic offensive

For about five years, beginning in 1567, it seemed that a resurgent Catholicism might prevail. Catholic forces took the offensive on all fronts. In 1567 Philip sent a new and firmer governor general to the Netherlands, the Duke of Alva, with 20,000 Spanish soldiers; the duke proceeded to suppress religious and political dissidents by establishing a Council of Troubles. In 1569 Philip, who was preparing for a new war with the Ottoman Turks, put down a revolt of the Moriscos (converted Muslims) in Spain. In the same year the Catholics of northern England, led by the Duke of Norfolk and sewing the cross of crusaders on their garments, rose in armed rebellion against their heretic queen. In the next year, 1570, the pope excommunicated Elizabeth and absolved her subjects from allegiance to her, so that English Catholics, if they wished, could henceforth in good conscience conspire to overthrow her. In 1571 the Spanish joined with the Venetians and others to win a great naval battle against the Turks, at Lepanto off the coast of Greece. Although this battle was part of the ongoing military struggle for political and economic control of the Mediterranean, some Spanish sailors wove a cross on their sails and portrayed their war with the Ottomans as a new Christian resistance to Islam. In the next year, 1572, the Catholic leaders of France, with the advice of the pope and of Philip II, decided to make an end of the Huguenots, or French Protestants. Over 3,000 were seized and put to death on the eve of

KING PHILIP II
By Titian (Italian, 1488–1576)
This portrait of the Spanish king suggests the highly focused political, religious, and military purpose in this devout Catholic monarch.
(Alinari/Art Resource, NY)

St. Bartholomew's Day in Paris alone; and this massacre was followed by lesser liquidations throughout the provinces.

But none of these victories proved enduring. The Turks soon recovered from their defeat at Lepanto and built a new fleet. In fact, they took Tunis from Philip two years later. The Moriscos were not assimilated (they would be expelled from Spain in 1609). The English Catholic rebellion was stamped out; 800 persons were put to death by Elizabeth's government. The revolt in the Netherlands remained very much alive, as did the French Huguenots. Twenty years later England was Protestant, the Dutch were winning independence, a Huguenot had become king of France, and the Spanish fleet had gone to ruin in northern waters.

The Revolt of the Netherlands

The Netherlands, or Low Countries, roughly comprised the area of the modern kingdoms of the Netherlands and Belgium and the grand duchy of Luxembourg. They consisted of 17 provinces, which in the fifteenth century, one by one, had been inherited, purchased, or conquered by the dukes of Burgundy, from whom they were inherited by Charles V and his son,

The Netherlands provinces

Philip II. In the mid-sixteenth century neither a Dutch nor a Belgian nationality yet existed. In the northern provinces the people spoke German dialects; in the southern provinces they spoke dialects of French; but neither here, nor elsewhere in Europe, was it felt that language boundaries had anything to do with political borders. The southern provinces had for centuries been busy commercial centers, and we have seen how Antwerp, having once flourished in trade with Venice, now flourished in trade with Lisbon. The northern provinces that were most open to the sea, the counties of Holland and Zeeland, had developed rapidly in the fifteenth century. They had a popular literature of their own, written in their own kind of German, which came to be called Dutch. The wealth of the northern provinces was drawn from deep-sea fishing. Amsterdam was said to be built on herring bones, and the Dutch, when they added trading to fishing, still lived by the sea.

The northern provinces felt no tie with each other and no sense of difference from the southern provinces. Each of the 17 provinces was a small state or country in itself, and each enjoyed typical medieval liberties and privileges. The only common bond of all 17 provinces was simply that beginning with the dukes of Burgundy they had the same ruler; but since they had the same ruler, they were called upon from time to time to send delegates to an estates general, and so developed an embryonic sense of federal collaboration. The feeling of Netherlandish identity was heightened with the accession of Philip II, for Philip, unlike his father, was thought of as foreign, a Spaniard who lived in Spain; and after 1560 Spanish governors general, Spanish officials, and Spanish troops were seen more frequently in the Netherlands. Moreover, since the Netherlands was the crossroads of Europe, with a tradition of earnestness in religion, Protestant ideas took root very early, and after 1560, when the religious wars began in France, a great many French Calvinists fled across the borders. At first, there were probably more Calvinists in the southern provinces than in the northern, more among the people whom we now call Belgians than among those whom we now call Dutch.

The revolt against Philip II was inextricably political and religious at the same time, and it became increasingly an economic struggle as the years went by. It began in 1566, when some 200 nobles of the various provinces founded a league to check the "foreign" or Spanish influence in the Netherlands. The league, to which both Catholic and Protestant nobles belonged, petitioned Philip II not to employ the Spanish Inquisition in the Netherlands. They feared the trouble it would stir up; they feared it as a foreign court; they feared that in the enforcement of its rulings the liberties of their provinces would be crushed. Philip's agents in the Netherlands refused the petition. A mass revolt now broke out. Within a week fanatical Calvinists pillaged 400 churches, pulling down images, breaking stained-glass windows, defacing paintings and tapestries, making off with gold chalices, destroying with a fierce contempt the symbols of "popery"— and "idolatry." The rank and file for these anti-Catholic and anti-Spanish demonstrations consisted chiefly of journeymen wage earners, whose fury was driven by social and economic grievances as well as religious belief. Before such vandalism many of the petitioning nobles recoiled; the Catholics among them, as well as less militant Protestants, unable to control their revolutionary followers, began to look upon the Spanish authorities with less disfavor.

Revolt of the Netherlands

Philip II, appalled at the sacrilege, forthwith sent in the Inquisition, the Duke of Alva, and reinforcements of Spanish troops. Alva's Council of Troubles, nicknamed the Council of Blood, sentenced some thousands to death, levied new taxes, and confiscated the estates of a number of important nobles. These measures united people of all classes in opposition. What might have been primarily a class conflict now took on the character of a national opposition. At its head emerged one of the noblemen whose estates had been confiscated, William of Orange (called William the Silent), Philip II's "stadholder" or lieutenant in the County of Holland. Beginning to claim the authority of a sovereign, he authorized ship captains to make war at sea. Fishing crews, "sea dogs," and downright pirates began to raid the small port towns of the Netherlands and France, descending upon them without warning, desecrating the churches, looting, torturing, and killing, in a wild combination of religious rage, political hatred, and lust for booty. The Spanish reciprocated by renewing their confiscations, their inquisitorial tortures, and their burnings and hangings. The Netherlands was torn by anarchy, revolution, and civil war. No lines were clear, either political or religious. But in 1576 the anti-Spanish feeling prevailed over religious difference. Representatives of all 17 provinces, putting aside the religious question, formed a union to drive out the Spanish at any cost.

The Involvement of England

But the Netherlands revolution, though it was a national revolution with political independence as its first aim, was only part of the international politico-religious struggle. All sorts of other interests became involved in it. Queen Elizabeth of England lent aid to the Netherlands, though for many years surreptitiously, not wishing to provoke a war with Spain, in which it was feared that English Catholics might side with the Spaniards. Elizabeth was troubled by having on her hands an unwanted guest, Mary Queen of Scots. Mary had remained a Catholic and had been queen of France until her husband's premature death, and queen of Scotland until driven out by irate Calvinist lords, and who—if the pope, the king of Spain, the Society of Jesus, and many English Catholics were to have their way—would also be queen of England instead of the usurper Elizabeth.[1] Elizabeth under these circumstances kept Mary Stuart imprisoned. Many intrigues were afoot to put Mary on the English throne, some with and some without Mary's knowledge.

England lends support to the Dutch

In 1576 Don Juan, hero of the Spanish naval victory at Lepanto and half-brother of Philip II, became governor general of the embattled Netherlands. He developed a grandiose plan to subdue the Netherlands and then to use that country as a base for an invasion of England. After overthrowing Elizabeth with Spanish troops, he would put Mary Stuart on the throne, marry her himself, and so become king of a re-Catholicized England. Thus the security of Elizabethan and Protestant England was coming to depend on the outcome of fighting in the Netherlands. Elizabeth signed an alliance with the Netherlands patriots.

Don Juan died in 1578 and was succeeded as governor general of the Netherlands by the prince of Parma. A diplomat as well as a soldier, Parma broke the solid front of the 17 provinces by a mixture of force and persuasion. He promised that the historic liberties of the provinces would be respected, and he appealed not only to the more zealous Catholics but also to moderates who were wearying of the struggle and repelled by mob violence and religious vandalism. On this basis he rallied the southernmost provinces to his side. The seven northern provinces, led by Holland and Zeeland, responded by forming the Union of

---

[1]Mary Stuart, a great-granddaughter of Henry VII, was the next lawful heir to the English throne after Elizabeth, since Elizabeth had no children.

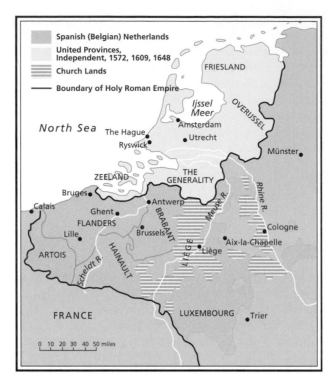

THE LOW COUNTRIES, 1648

This group of towns and provinces, along the lower reaches of the Rhine, Meuse, and Scheldt rivers, originated in the Middle Ages as part of the Holy Roman Empire. The northern or Dutch provinces were recognized as independent of the Empire in 1648. Early in the seventeenth century a political frontier emerged between the "Dutch" and "Belgian" parts, but the word "Belgium" was not used until much later, the southern or Habsburg provinces being called the Spanish Netherlands in the seventeenth century and the Austrian Netherlands in the eighteenth. The large bishopric of Liège remained a separate church-state until the French Revolution. The language frontier, then as now, ran roughly east and west somewhat south of Brussels, with French to the south and Flemish (a form of Dutch, and hence Germanic) to the north of the line.

The Union of Utrecht

Utrecht in 1579. In 1581 they formally declared their independence from the king of Spain, calling themselves the United Provinces of the Netherlands. Thus originated what was more commonly called the Dutch Republic, or simply "Holland" in view of the predominance of that county among the seven. The great Flemish towns—Antwerp, Ghent, and Bruges—at first sided with the Union.

Where formerly all had been turmoil, a geographical line was now drawn. The south rallying to Philip II now faced a still rebellious north. But neither side accepted any such partition. Parma still fought to reconquer the north, and the Dutch, led by William the Silent, still struggled to clear the Spanish out of all 17 provinces. Meanwhile the two sides fought to capture the intermediate Flemish cities. When Parma moved upon Antwerp, still the leading port of the North Sea, and one from which an invasion of England could best be mounted, Elizabeth at last openly entered the war on the side of the rebels, sending 6,000 English troops to the Netherlands under the Earl of Leicester in 1585.

The vast size of the Spanish naval armada and the English opposition to it are suggested in this illustration by an unknown artist. Both navies had crosses on the flags of their ships, thereby claiming divine support for their cause and indicating the religious and national stakes in this epic conflict.
(National Maritime Museum, London)

England was now clearly emerging as the chief bulwark of Protestantism and of anti-Spanish feeling in northwestern Europe. In England itself, the popular fears of Spain, the popular resentment against Catholic plots revolving about Mary Stuart, and the popular indignation at "foreign" *England as bulwark of Protestantism* and "outside" meddling in English matters produced an unprecedented sense of national solidarity. The country rallied to Protestantism and to Elizabeth, and even the Catholic minority for the most part disowned the conspiracies against her. The English were now openly and defiantly allied with the Protestant Dutch. Not only were they fighting together in the Netherlands, but both English and Dutch sea raiders also fell upon Spanish shipping, captured the treasure ships, and even pillaged the mainland coast of northern South America. The Dutch were beginning to penetrate East Indian waters. Elizabeth was negotiating with Scotland, with German Calvinists, and with French Huguenots. At the Escorial it was said that the Netherlands could only be rewon by an invasion of England, that the queen of the heretics must be dethroned, that it was cheaper to launch a gigantic attack upon England than to pay the cost of protecting Spanish galleons year after year against the depredations of piratical sea dogs.

Philip II therefore prepared to invade England. The English retorted with vigor. Mary Stuart, after almost 20 years of imprisonment, was executed in 1587; an aroused Parliament, more than Elizabeth herself, demanded her life on the eve of foreign attack. Sir Francis Drake, most spectacular of the sea dogs, sailed into the port of Cádiz and burnt the very ships assembling there to join the Armada. This was jocosely described as singeing the beard of the king of Spain.

The great Armada, the *armada católica,* was ready early in 1588. With crosses on the sails and banners bearing the image of the Holy Virgin, it *The Spanish Armada* went forth as to a new Lepanto against the Turks of the north. It consisted of 130 ships, weighing 58,000 tons, carrying 30,000 men and 2,400 pieces of artillery—the most prodigious assemblage of naval power that the world had ever seen. The plan was for the fleet to sail to the Netherlands, from which it was to escort the prince of Parma's army across the straits to the English coast.

But the Armada never reached the Spanish army. It was met in the English Channel by some 200 English vessels, which encircled the Spanish fleet near Calais. The English

CHRONOLOGY OF NOTABLE EVENTS, 1492–1648

1492	Christopher Columbus reaches America
1519–1522	Ferdinand Magellan circumnavigates the globe
1519–1533	Spanish conquests of Native American empires in the Americas
1556–1598	Reign of King Philip II in Spain
1562–1598	Religious and civil wars in France
1565	"Manila Galleons" open Spanish trade route between Asia and America
1566	Revolt against Spanish control begins in the Netherlands
1588	Spanish Armada is destroyed off the coast of England and Scotland
1598	King Henry IV issues Edict of Nantes; grants religious rights to French Protestants
1618–1648	The Thirty Years' War in Germany
1648	Peace of Westphalia recognizes system of sovereign European states

craft—lighter, smaller, and faster, though well furnished with guns—harried the lumbering mass of the Armada, broke up its formations, and attacked its great vessels one by one. It found no refuge at Calais, and English fireships drove it out again to sea. Then arose a great storm, which the English would later call the "Protestant wind." The storm blew the broken Armada northward around the tip of Scotland, the Orkneys, the Hebrides, and northern Ireland—forbidding coasts which the Spaniards had to skirt without charts or pilots or adequate provisions, and which they strewed with their wreckage and their bones.

The Results of the Struggle

The war for control of the Netherlands went on for several years, even after Philip died in 1598. In the wars with Spain the English had, above all else, assured their national independence. They had acquired an intense national spirit, a love of "this other Eden, demi-paradise," "this precious stone set in the silver sea," as Shakespeare wrote; and they had become more solidly Protestant, almost unanimously set against "popery." With the ruin of the Armada, they were more free to take to the sea; we have seen how the English East India Company was founded in 1600.

Partition of the Netherlands

In the Netherlands, the battle lines swayed back and forth until 1609. In that year a Twelve Years' Truce was agreed to. By this truce the Netherlands were partitioned. The line of partition ran somewhat farther north than it had in Parma's time, for the Spaniards had retaken Antwerp and other cities in the middle zone. The seven provinces north of the line, those that had formed the Union of Utrecht in 1579, were henceforth known as Dutch. The ten provinces south of the line were known as the Spanish Netherlands. Protestants in the south either became Catholics or fled to the north, so that the south (the modern Belgium) became solidly Catholic, while the number of Protestants in the north was increased. Even so, the Dutch were not a completely Protestant people, for probably as many as a third of them remained Catholic. Calvinism was the religion of most Dutch burghers and the religion favored by the state; but in the face of an exceptionally large religious minority the Dutch Netherlands adopted a policy of toleration.

The southern Netherlands were ruined by almost 40 years of war. The Dutch, more-over, occupied the mouth of the Scheldt River and refused to allow oceangoing vessels to proceed upstream to Antwerp or to Ghent. The Scheldt remained "closed" for two centuries, and the Flemish cities never recovered their old position. Amsterdam became the commercial and financial center of northern Europe; it retained its commercial supremacy for a century and its financial supremacy for two centuries. For the Dutch, as for the English, the weakening of Spanish naval power opened the way to the sea. The Dutch East India Company was organized in 1602. Both Dutch and English began to found overseas colonies. The English settled in Virginia in 1607, the Dutch at New York in 1612.

As for Spain, while it remained the most formidable military power of Europe for another half-century, its political and economic decline had already begun. At the death of Philip II the monarchy was living from hand to mouth, habitually depending on the next arrival of treasure from the Indies. The productive forces of the country were weakened by inflation, by taxation, by emigration, by depopulation. At Seville, for example, only 400 looms *The beginnings of Spanish decline* were in operation in 1621, where there had been 16,000 a century earlier. Spain suffered from the very circumstances that made it great. Qualities that developed in the centuries of religious war and in the reliance upon imported gold or silver from America were not those on which a more modern economy and society could easily be built. The long history of campaigns against infidels and heretics had produced an exceptionally large number of minor aristocrats who often saw their class status as a reason to avoid various forms of mundane work. Their relative indifference to the newer, expanding institutions of European commercial activity may have influenced the country as a whole. In any case, many of the ablest Spaniards continued to enter the church, and there were few innovations in Spain's political and economic life.

The very unity accomplished under Ferdinand and Isabella threatened to dissolve. After more than a century of the Inquisition people were still afraid of false Christians and crypto-Muslims. The question of the Moriscos rose again in 1608. The Moriscos included some of the best farmers and most skilled artisans in the country. They lived in almost all parts of Spain and were in no sense a "for- *The Moriscos* eign" element, since they were simply the descendants of those Spaniards who, in the Muslim period, which had begun 900 years before, had adopted the Muslim religion and Arabic language and culture. They were now supposedly Christian, but the true and pure Christians accused them of preserving in secret the rites of Islam and of sympathy for the Barbary pirates. They were thought to be clannish, marrying among themselves; and they were so efficient, sober, and hardworking that they outdistanced other Spaniards in competition. In 1609 some 150,000 Moriscos were driven out of Valencia; in 1610 some 64,000 were driven from Aragon; in 1611 an unknown number were expelled from Castile. All were simply put on boats and sent off with what they could carry. Spain, whose total population was rapidly falling in any case, thus lost one of the most socially valuable, if not religiously orthodox, of all its minorities.

Nor could the Christian kingdoms hold peaceably together, despite the centralizing projects of the main government minister, the Count of Olivares. Coming to power under King Philip IV in 1621, Olivares sought to curb the independence of the church, increase the king's revenues, control the aristocracy, and send the Spanish army into both the Netherlands and the religious wars in Germany. His policies provoked strong opposition throughout Spain. In 1640 Portugal, which had been joined to the Spanish crown since 1580 when its own ruling line had run out, reestablished its independence. That same year Catalonia rose in open rebellion. The Catalan war, in which the French streamed across the

Pyrenees to aid the rebels, lasted for almost 20 years. Catalonia was at last reconquered, but it managed to preserve its old privileges and separate identity. Catalan and Castilian viewed each other with increased repugnance. The Spanish kingdoms were almost as disunited, in spirit and in institutions, as in the days of Isabella and Ferdinand. They suffered, too, during the seventeenth century from a line of kings whose mental peculiarities reached the point of positive imbecility. Meanwhile, however, the might of Spain was still to be felt in both Germany and France.

✑ 15. THE DISINTEGRATION AND RECONSTRUCTION OF FRANCE

Both France and Germany, in the so-called Wars of Religion, fell into an advanced state of decomposition. France was torn apart by almost 40 years of civil war between 1562 and 1598, while Germany entered a long period of civil troubles that culminated in the Thirty Years' War between 1618 and 1648. From this decomposition France recovered in the seventeenth century, but Germany did not.

Political and Religious Disunity

The Wars of Religion in France, despite the religious savagery shown by partisans of both sides, were no more religious than they were political. They were essentially a new form of the old phenomenon of feudal rebellion against a higher central authority. "Feudal," in this postmedieval sense, generally refers not to nobles only, but to all sorts of groups having rights within the state, and so includes towns and provinces, and even craft guilds and courts of law, in addition to the church and the noble class. It remained to be seen whether all these elements could be welded into one body politic.

In France the New Monarchy, resuming the work of medieval kings, had imposed a certain unity on the country. Normally the country acted as a unit in foreign affairs. The king alone made treaties, and in war his subjects all fought on his side, if they fought at all. Internally, the royal centralization was largely administrative; that is, the king and those who worked for him dealt with subordinate bodies of all kinds, while these subordinate bodies remained in existence with their own functions and personnel. France by the ideas of the time was a very large country. It was three times as large as England and five times as populous—roughly 18 million in the sixteenth century. At a time when the traveler could move hardly 30 miles a day, it took three weeks of steady plodding to cross the kingdom. Local influence was therefore very strong. Beneath the platform of royalty there was almost as little substantial unity in France as in the Holy Roman Empire. When the Empire had 300 "states," France had some 300 areas with their own legal systems. Where the Empire had free cities, France had *bonnes villes,* the king's "good towns," each with its stubbornly defended corporate rights. Where the Empire had middle-sized states like Bavaria, France had provinces as great as some European kingdoms—Brittany, Burgundy, Provence, Languedoc—each ruled by the French king, to be sure, but each with its own identity, autonomy, laws, courts, tariffs, taxes, and parliament or provincial estates. To all this diversity, in France as in Germany, was now added diversity of religion. Calvin himself was by birth and upbringing a Frenchman. Calvinism spread in France very rapidly.

Nor was France much attached to a papal or international Catholicism. The French clergy had long struggled for its national or Gallican liberties; the French kings had dealt

Centralization vs. localism

rudely with popes, ignored the Council of Trent, and allied for political reasons with both the Lutherans and the Turks. Since 1516 the king of France had the right to nominate the French bishops. The fact that both the monarchy and the clergy already felt independent of Rome held them back from the revolutionary solutions of Protestantism. The Protestantism which did spread in France therefore developed without government support and embraced the most radical theological wing of the Reformation, namely Calvinism, which preached at kings, attacked bishops, smashed religious images, and desecrated the churches. Within the main countries that became Protestant—England, north Germany, even the Netherlands—this extreme Protestantism was the doctrine of a minority. In France there was no middle-of-the-road Protestantism, no broad and comfortable Anglicanism, no halfway Lutheranism inspired by governments; and in the long run, as will be seen, the middle of the road was occupied by Catholics.

At first, however, the Huguenots, as the French Calvinists were called, though always a minority, were neither a small group nor modest in their demands. In a class analysis, it is clear that it was chiefly the nobility that *The Huguenots* was attracted to Protestantism, though of course it does not follow that most French Protestants were nobles, since the nobility was a small class. More than a third, and possibly almost a half, of the French nobility was Protestant in the 1560s or 1570s. Frequently the seigneur, or lord of one or more manors, believed that he should have the right to regulate religion on his own estates, as the princes of Germany decided the religion of their own territories. It thus happened that a lord might defy the local bishop, put a Calvinist minister in his village church, throw out the images, simplify the sacraments, and have the service conducted in French. In this way peasants also became Huguenots. Occasionally peasants turned Huguenot without encouragement by the lord. It was chiefly in southwestern France that Protestantism spread as a general movement affecting whole areas. But in all parts of the country, north as well as south, many towns converted to Protestantism. Usually this meant that the bourgeois oligarchy, into whose hands town government had generally fallen, went over to Calvinism and thereupon banned Catholic services. The journeymen wage earners might follow along; or estranged by class differences arising from within the local economy, they might remain attached to their old priests. In general, the unskilled laboring population probably remained the least touched of all classes by Calvinist doctrine.

Both Francis I and Henry II opposed the spread of Calvinism—as did Lutheran and Anglican rulers—for Calvinism, a kind of grassroots move- *Opposition to* ment in religion, rising spontaneously among laity and reforming ministers, *Calvinism* seemed to threaten not only the powers of monarchy but also the very idea of a nationally established church. The fact that in France the nobility, a traditionally ungovernable class, figured prominently in the movement only made it look the more like political or feudal rebellion. Persecution of Huguenots, with burnings at the stake, began in the 1550s.

Then in 1559 King Henry II was accidentally killed in a tournament. He left three sons, of whom the eldest in 1559 was only 15. Their mother, Henry's widow, was Catherine de' Medici, an Italian woman who brought to France some of the polish of Renaissance Italy, along with some of its taste for political intrigue, with which she attempted to govern the country for her royal sons. (Their names were Francis II, who died in 1560, Charles IX, who died in 1574, and Henry III, who lasted until 1589.) With no firm hand in control of the monarchy, the country fell apart; and in the ensuing chaos various powerful factions tried to get control of the youthful monarchs for their own purposes. Among these factions were both Huguenots and Catholics. The Huguenots, under persecution, were too strong a minority to go into hiding. Counting among their number a third or more of the professional warrior class, the nobles, they took naturally and aggressively to arms.

The Civil and Religious Wars

The civil wars in sixteenth-century France were not wars in which one region of a country takes up arms against another, each retaining some apparatus of government, as in the American Civil War or the civil wars of the seventeenth century in England. They were civil wars of the kind fought in the absence of government. Roving bands of armed men, without territorial base or regular means of subsistence, wandered about the country, fighting and plundering, joining or separating from other similar bands, in shifting hosts that were quickly formed or quickly dissolved. The changing economic and social conditions of the era detached many people from their old routines and threw them into a life of adventure. The more prominent leaders could thus easily obtain followers, and at the coming of such cohorts the peasants usually took to the woods, while bourgeois would lock the gates of their cities. Peasants would form protective leagues, like vigilantes; and even small towns maintained diminutive armies.

The Huguenots were led by various personages of rank, such as Admiral de Coligny and Henry of Bourbon, king of Navarre, a small independent kingdom at the foot of the Pyrenees between Spain and France. A pronounced Catholic party arose under the Guise family, headed by the Duke of Guise and the Cardinal of Lorraine. Catherine de' Medici was left in the middle, opposed like all monarchs to Calvinism but unwilling to fall under the domination of the Guises. While the Guises wished to extirpate heresy, they wished even more to govern France. Among the Huguenots some fought for local liberties in religion, while the more ardent spirits hoped to drive "idolatry" and "popery" out of all France, and indeed out of the world itself. Catherine de' Medici for a time tried to play the two parties against each other. But in 1572, fearing the growing influence of Coligny over the king, and taking advantage of a great concourse of leading Huguenots in Paris to celebrate the marriage of Henry of Navarre, she decided to rid herself of the heads of the Huguenot party at a single blow. In the resulting massacre of St. Bartholomew's Day some thousands of Huguenots were dragged from their beds after midnight and unceremoniously murdered. Coligny was killed; Henry of Navarre escaped by temporarily changing his religion.

St. Bartholomew's Day massacre

This outrage only aroused Huguenot fury and led to a renewal of civil war, with mounting atrocities committed by both sides. The armed bands slaughtered each other and terrorized noncombatants. Both parties hired companies of mercenary soldiers, mainly from Germany. Spanish troops invaded France at the invitation of the Guises. Protestant towns, such as Rouen and La Rochelle, appealed for armed support from Elizabeth of England, reminding her that kings of England had once reigned over their parts of France; but Elizabeth was too preoccupied with her own problems to give more than very sporadic and insignificant assistance. Neither side could subdue the other, and hence there were numerous truces, during which fighting still flared up, since no one had the power to impose peace.

The Politiques

Gradually, mainly among the more perfunctory Catholics, but also among moderate Protestants, there developed still another group who thought of themselves as the "politicals" or *politiques*. The *politiques* concluded that too much was being made of religion, that no doctrine was important enough to justify everlasting war, that perhaps after all there might be room for

The St. Bartholomew's Day Massacre, in which thousands of Protestants were massacred in Paris in 1572, sparked waves of further atrocities by both sides in France's religious wars. As this image of the massacre suggests, it also became an enduring symbol of the brutal conflicts that divided the nation throughout the late sixteenth century.
(Musée Cantonal de Beaux Arts, Lausanne)

two churches, and that what the country needed above all else was civil order. Theirs was a secular rather than a religious view. They believed that people lived primarily in the state, not in the church. They were willing to overlook the religious ideas of people in different churches if such persons would simply obey the king and go peaceably about their business. To escape anarchy they put their hopes in the institution of monarchy. Henry of Navarre, now again a Protestant, was at heart a *politique*. Another was the political philosopher Jean Bodin (1530–1596), the first thinker to develop the modern theory of sovereignty. He held that in every society there must be one power strong enough to give law to all others, with their consent if possible, without their consent if necessary. Thus from the disorders of the religious wars in France was germinated the idea of royal absolutism and of the sovereign state.

The End of the Wars: Reconstruction under Henry IV

In 1589 both Henry III, the reigning king, and Henry of Guise, the Catholic party chief who was trying to depose him, were assassinated, each by a partisan of the other. The throne now came by legal inheritance to the third of the three Henrys, Henry of Navarre, the Huguenot chieftain. He reigned as Henry IV. Most popular and most amiably remembered of all French kings, except for medieval St. Louis, he was the first of the Bourbon dynasty, which was to last until the French Revolution.

The civil wars did not end with the accession of Henry IV. The Catholic party refused to recognize him, set up a pretender against him, and called in the Spaniards. Henry, the *politique,* sensed that the majority of the French people were still Catholic and that the Huguenots were not only a minority but, after 30 years of civil strife, an increasingly

Henry IV accepts Catholicism

unpopular minority. Paris especially, Catholic throughout the wars, refused to admit the heretic king within its gates. Supposedly remarking that "Paris is well worth a Mass," Henry IV in 1593 abjured the Calvinist faith, and subjected himself to the elaborate processes of papal absolution. Thereupon the *politiques* and less excitable Catholics consented to work with him. The Huguenots, at first elated that their leader should become king, were now not only outraged by Henry's abjuration but also alarmed for their own safety. They demanded positive guarantees for their personal security as well as protection of their religious liberty.

The Edict of Nantes

Henry IV in 1598 responded by issuing the Edict of Nantes. The Edict granted to every seigneur, or noble who was also a manorial lord, the right to hold Protestant services in his own household. It allowed Protestantism in towns where it was in fact the prevailing form of worship, and in any case in one town of each *bailliage* (a unit corresponding somewhat to the English shire) throughout the country; but it barred Protestant churches from Catholic episcopal towns and from a zone surrounding and including the city of Paris. It promised that Protestants should enjoy the same civil rights as Catholics, the same chance for public office, and access to the Catholic universities. In certain of the superior law courts it created "mixed chambers" of both Protestants and Catholics—somewhat as if a stated minority representation were to be legally required in United States federal courts today. The Edict also gave Protestants their own means of defense, granting them about 100 fortified towns to be held by Protestant garrisons under Protestant command.

The Huguenot minority, reassured by the Edict of Nantes, became less of a rebellious element within the state. The majority of the French people viewed the Edict with suspicion. The parlements, or supreme law courts, of Paris, Bordeaux, Toulouse, Aix, and Rennes all refused to recognize it as the law of the land. It was the king who forced toleration upon the country. He silenced the parlements and subdued Catholic opposition by doing favors for the Jesuits. France's chief minority was thus protected by the central government, not by popular wishes. Where in England the Catholic minority had no rights at all, and in Germany the religious question was settled only by cutting the country into small and hostile fragments, in France a compromise was effected, by which the Protestant minority had both individual and territorial rights. A considerable number of French statesmen, generals, and other important persons in the seventeenth century were Protestants.

Henry IV, having appeased the religious controversy, did everything that he could to let the country gradually recover from its decades of civil war. His ideal, as he breezily put it, was a "chicken in the pot" for every Frenchman. He worked also to restore the ruined government, to collect taxes, pay officials, discipline the army, and supervise the administration of justice. Roads and bridges were repaired and new manufactures were introduced under mercantilist principles. Never throughout his reign of 21 years did he summon the Estates General. A country that had just hacked itself to pieces in civil war was scarcely able to govern itself, and so, under Henry IV, the foundations of the later royal absolutism of the Bourbons were laid down.

The foundations of absolutism

Henry IV was assassinated in 1610 by a crazed fanatic who believed him a menace to the Catholic church. Under his widow, Marie de' Medici, the nobility and upper Catholic clergy again grew restless and forced the summoning of the Estates General, in which so many conflicting and mutually distrustful interests were represented that no program could be adopted. Marie dismissed them in 1615 to the general relief of all concerned. No Estates General of the kingdom as a whole thereafter met until the French Revolution. National government was to be conducted by and through the king.

Cardinal Richelieu

In the name of Marie de' Medici and her young son, Louis XIII, the control of affairs gradually came into the hands of an ecclesiastic, Cardinal Richelieu. In the preceding generation Richelieu might have been called a *politique*. It was the state, not the church, whose interests he worked to further. He tried to strengthen the state economically by mercantilist edicts. He attempted to draw impoverished gentlemen into trade by allowing them to engage in maritime commerce without loss of noble status. For wholesale merchants, as an incentive, he made it possible to become nobles, in return for payments into the royal exchequer. He founded and supported many commercial companies on the Anglo-Dutch model.

For a time it seemed that civil war might break out again. Nobles still feuded with each other and evaded the royal jurisdiction. Richelieu pro-hibited private warfare and ordered the destruction of all fortified castles not manned and needed by the king himself. He even prohibited dueling, a custom much favored by the nobles of the day, but regarded by Richelieu as a mere remnant of private war. The Huguenots, too, with their own towns and their own armed forces under the Edict of Nantes, had become something of a state within the state. In 1627 the Duke of Rohan led a Huguenot rebellion, based in the city of La Rochelle, which received military support from the English. Richelieu after a year suppressed the rebellion and in 1629, by the Peace of Alais, amended the Edict of Nantes. For this highly secularized cardinal of the Catholic church it was agreeable for the Protestants to keep their religion but not for them to share in the instruments of political power. The Huguenots lost, in 1629, their fortified cities, their Protestant armies, and all their military and territorial rights, but in their religious and civil rights they were not officially disturbed for another 50 years.

Renewed threat of civil war

The French monarchy no sooner reestablished itself after the civil wars than it began to return to the old foreign policy of Francis I, who had opposed on every front the European supremacy of the house of Habsburg. The Spanish power still encircled France at the Pyrenees, in the Mediterranean, in the Free County of Burgundy (the Franche-Comté), and in Belgium. The Austrian branch had pretensions to supremacy in Germany and all central Europe. Richelieu found his opportunity to assail the Habsburgs in the civil and religious struggles which now began to afflict Germany.

16. THE THIRTY YEARS' WAR, 1618–1648: THE DISINTEGRATION OF GERMANY

The Holy Roman Empire extended from France on the west to Poland and Hungary on the east. It included the Czechs of Bohemia and sizable French-speaking populations in what are now Belgium, Lorraine, eastern Burgundy, and western Switzerland; but with these exceptions the Empire was made up of Germans (see maps, pp. 78, 142–143). Language, however, was far less important than religion as the tie which people felt to be basic to a community; and in religion the Empire was almost evenly divided. Where in England, after stabilization set in, Roman Catholics sank to a minority of some 3 percent, and in France the Huguenots fell to not much over 5 percent, in Germany there was no true minority, and hence no majority, and religion gave no ground for national concentration. Possibly there were more Protestants than Catholics in the Empire in 1600, for not only was Protestantism the state religion in many of the 300 states, but individual Protestants were also numerous in the legally Catholic states of the Austrian Habsburgs. Bohemia had a Protestant majority, rooted in the Czech people. Farther east, outside the Holy Roman Empire, the Hungarian nobles were mainly Protestant, and Transylvania, in the elbow of the Carpathian Mountains, was an active center of Calvinism.

German decline

In 1500 Germany had led in the life of Europe, but by 1600 it had lost much of its former cultural creativity and leadership. Where both Catholics and Calvinists recognized international affiliations, Lutherans were suspicious of the world outside the Lutheran states of Germany and Scandinavia, and hence suffered from a cultural isolation. The German universities, both Lutheran and Catholic, attracted fewer students than formerly, and their intellectual effort was consumed in combative dogmatics, each side demonstrating the truth of its own ideas. Many of the most deadly, large-scale campaigns against witchcraft took place in the small German states, and more women were burned as witches in Germany than in other countries in Western Europe. The commerce of south Germany and the Rhineland was in decay, both because of the shift of trade to the Atlantic and because the Dutch controlled the mouth of the Rhine in their own interests. German bankers, such as the Fuggers, were of slight importance after 1600. Capital was now being formed in the centers of maritime trade.

Background of the Thirty Years' War

The Peace of Augsburg in 1555 had provided that in each state the government could prescribe the religion of its subjects. In general, in the decades following the Peace of Augsburg, the Lutherans made considerable gains, putting Lutheran administrators into the church states, or "secularizing" them and converting them into lay principalities. In addition, Calvinism spread into Germany. Though Calvinists had no rights under the Peace of Augsburg, a number of states became Calvinist. One of these was the Palatinate, important because it was strategically placed across the middle Rhine, and because its ruler, the Elector Palatine, was one of the seven persons who elected the Holy Roman Emperor. In 1608 the Protestant states, urged on by the Elector Palatine, formed a Protestant union to defend their gains. To obtain support, they negotiated with the Dutch, with the English, and with Henry IV of France. In 1609 a league of Catholic German states was organized by Bavaria. It looked for help from Spain.

Lutheran gains

The Germans were thus falling apart, or rather coming together, into two parties in anticipation of a religious war, and each party solicited foreign assistance against the other. Other issues were also maturing. The Twelve Years' Truce between Spain and the Dutch, signed in 1609, was due to expire in 1621. The Spanish (whose military power was still unaffected by internal decline) were again preparing to crush the Dutch Republic. Since the Dutch insisted on independence, a renewal of the Dutch-Spanish war appeared to be inevitable. The Spanish also wished to consolidate the Habsburg position in central Europe and enhance their access to the Netherlands by gaining control of new territories along the Rhine River and in various Swiss cantons (see map, pp. 142–143).

These Spanish designs in the Rhineland and Switzerland naturally aroused the opposition of France. Moreover, the Austrian branch of the Habsburg family was slowly bestirring itself to eradicate Protestantism in its own domains and to turn the Holy Roman Empire into a more modern type of state. The idea of a strong power in Germany was abhorrent to the French. Through opposition to the Habsburgs, France was again put in the position of chief protector of Protestantism. France was a giant of Europe, five times as populous as England, over ten times as populous as Sweden or the Dutch Republic, incomparably more populous than any single German state. And France after 1600 was at last unified within—at least relatively. As a French writer has observed, speaking of these years, the appearance of the fleur-de-lis upon the Rhine would tumble to the ground the vast projects of the Counter Reformation.

The Thirty Years' War, resulting from all these pressures, was therefore exceedingly complex. It was a German civil war fought over the Catholic-Protestant issue. It was also a German civil war fought over constitutional issues, between the emperor striving to build up the central *The complexity of the Thirty Years' War*

power of the Empire and the member states struggling to maintain independence. These two civil wars by no means coincided, for Catholic and Protestant states were alike in objecting to imperial control. It was also an international war, between France and the Habsburgs, between Spain and the Dutch, with the kings of Denmark and Sweden and the prince of Transylvania becoming involved, and with all these outsiders finding allies within Germany, on whose soil most of the battles were fought. The wars were further complicated by the fact that many of the generals were soldiers of fortune who aspired to create principalities of their own and who fought or refused to fight to suit their own convenience.

The Four Phases of the War

The fighting began in Bohemia. It is in fact customary to divide the war into four phases, the Bohemian (1618–1625), the Danish (1625–1629), the Swedish (1630–1635), and the Swedish-French (1635–1648). *The Bohemian war*

In 1618 the Bohemians, or Czechs, fearing the loss of their Protestant liberties, dealt with two emissaries from the Habsburg Holy Roman Emperor, Matthias (who was also their king), by a method occasionally used in that country—throwing them out of the window. After this "defenestration of Prague" the king-emperor sent troops to restore his authority, whereupon the Bohemians deposed him and elected a new king. In order to obtain Protestant assistance, they chose the Calvinist Elector Palatine, the head of the Protestant Union, who assumed the title of Frederick V. He brought aid to the Bohemians from the Protestant Union, the Dutch, and the prince of Transylvania. The Emperor Ferdinand, Matthias's successor, assisted by money from the pope, by Spanish troops sent from Milan, and by the forces of Catholic Bavaria, managed to overwhelm the Bohemians at the battle of the White Mountain in 1620. Frederick fled, jeered or pitied as the "winter king." His ancestral domains in the Palatinate were overrun by the Spaniards.

The Habsburgs now set out to reconquer and revolutionize Bohemia. The Emperor Ferdinand got himself elected as king and soon confiscated the estates of almost half the Bohemian nobles. He granted these lands as endowments for Catholic churches and monasteries or as gifts to adventurers of all nationalities who had entered his service and who became the new landed aristocracy of Bohemia.

With Protestant fortunes at a low ebb, and the Protestant Union itself dissolved in 1621, the lead in Protestant affairs was now taken by the king of Denmark, who was also

Ifrael ex. Cum Priul. Reg.

A la fin ces Voleurs infames et perdus ,
Comme fruits malheureux a cet arbre pendus

Monftrent bien que le crime (horrible et noire engeance)
Eft luy mefme inftrument de honte et de vengeance ,

Et que ceft le Deftin des hommes vicieux
Defprouuer toft ou tard la iuftice des Cieux

The violence of the Thirty Years' War in Germany, depicted here in a vivid illustration by Jacques Callot entitled simply *The Hanging Tree* (1633), produced terror, bitter memories, and political divisions in central Europe that lasted long after the fighting finally ended in 1648.
(Anne S.K. Brown Military Collection, Brown University Library)

Duke of Holstein, a state of the Holy Roman Empire. With a little aid from the Dutch and English, and with promises from Richelieu, he entered the fray. Against him the Emperor Ferdinand raised another army, or, rather, commissioned Albert of Wallenstein to raise one on his own private initiative. Wallenstein assembled a force of professional fighters, of all nationalities, who lived by pillage rather than by pay. His army was his personal instrument, not the emperor's, and he therefore followed a policy of his own, which was so tortuous and well concealed that the name of Wallenstein has always remained an enigma. Wallenstein and other imperial generals soon defeated the king of Denmark, reached the Baltic coast, and even invaded the Danish peninsula.

The full tide of the Counter Reformation now flowed over Germany. Not only was Catholicism again seeping into the Palatinate, and again flooding Bohemia, but it also rolled northward into the inner recesses of the Lutheran states. By the Edict of Restitution, in 1629, the emperor declared all church territories secularized since 1552 automatically restored to the Catholic church. Some of these territories had been Protestant since the oldest person could remember. Terror swept over Protestant Germany. It seemed that the whole Protestant Reformation, now a century old, might be undone.

French and Swedish alarm

Among those to be alarmed were the French and the Swedes. Richelieu, however, was still putting down fractious nobles and Huguenots. He had not yet consolidated France to his satisfaction and believed that France, without fighting itself, could counter the Habsburg ambitions through the use of allies. He sent diplomats to help extricate the king of Sweden from a war with Poland, and he promised him financial assistance, which soon rose to a million livres a year in return for the maintenance in Germany of 40,000 Swedish troops. The Dutch subsidized the Swedes with some 50,000 florins a month.

The king of Sweden was Gustavus Adolphus, a ruler of superlative ability, who had conciliated all parties in Sweden and had extended Swedish holdings on the east shore of the Baltic. Using Dutch and other military experts, he had created the most modern army of the time, noted for its firm discipline, high courage, and mobile cannon. Himself a religious man, he had his troops march to battle singing Lutheran hymns. He was ideally suited to be the Protestant champion, a role he now willingly took up, landing in Germany in 1630. Richelieu, besides giving financial help, negotiated with the Catholic states of Germany, playing on their fears of imperial centralization and seeking to isolate the emperor, against whom the Swedish war machine was now hurled.

Gustavus Adolphus

The Swedes, with military aid from Saxony, won a number of spectacular victories, at Breitenfeld in 1631 and Lützen in 1632, where, however, Gustavus Adolphus was killed. His chancellor, Oxenstierna, carried on. The Swedish army penetrated into Bohemia and as far south as the Danube. What those in the higher counsels of Sweden were aiming at is not clear. Perhaps they dreamed of a great federal Protestant empire, to include Scandinavia and north Germany, a Lutheran empire confronting a Catholic and Habsburg empire in the south. But the brilliant Swedish victories came to little. Both sides were weakened by disagreement. Wallenstein, who disliked the Spanish influence in Germany, virtually ceased to fight the Swedes and Saxons, with whom he even entered into private talks hoping to create an independent position for himself. He was finally disgraced by the emperor and assassinated by one of his own staff. On the Swedish-Saxon side, the Saxons decided to make a separate peace. Saxony therefore signed with the emperor the Peace of Prague of 1635. The other German Protestant states concurred in it and withdrew their support from the Swedes. The emperor, by largely annulling the Edict of Restitution, allayed Protestant apprehensions. The Swedes were left isolated in Germany. It seemed that the German states were coming together, that the religious wars might be nearing an end. But, in fact, in 1635, the Thirty Years' War was only well begun. Neither France nor Spain wished peace or reconciliation in Germany.

Richelieu renewed his assurances to the Swedes, paid subsidies even to the wealthy Dutch, hired a German princeling, Bernard of Saxe-Weimar, to maintain an army of Germans in the French service, and at last brought Catholic France into open support of the German Protestants.

So the fleur-de-lis finally moved toward the Rhine, though not at first with the success for which the French or Protestants might hope. The Spanish, from their bases in Belgium and Franche-Comté, drove instead deep into France. Champagne and Burgundy were ravaged, and Paris itself was seized with panic. The Spanish also raided the south. The French had a taste of the plunder, murder, burnings, and stealing of cattle by which Germany had been afflicted. But the French soon turned the tables. When Portugal and Catalonia rebelled against Philip IV, France immediately recognized the independence of Portugal under the new royal house of Braganza—as did England, Holland, and Sweden with equal alacrity. French troops streamed over the Pyrenees into Catalonia, spreading the usual devastation. Richelieu even recognized a Catalan republic.

European involvement

In Germany the last or Swedish-French phase of the war was not so much a civil war among Germans as an international struggle on German soil. Few German states now sided with the French and Swedes. A feeling of national resentment against foreign invasion even seemed to develop.

The Peace of Westphalia, 1648

Peace talks began in 1644 in Westphalia, at the two towns of Münster and Osnabrück. The German states were crying for peace, for a final religious settlement, and for "reform" of the Holy Roman Empire. France and Sweden insisted that the German states should individually take part in the negotiations, a disintegrating principle that the German princes eagerly welcomed and which the emperor vainly resisted. To Westphalia, therefore, hundreds of diplomats and negotiators now repaired, representing the Empire, its member states, Spain, France, Sweden, the Dutch, the Swiss, the Portuguese, the Venetians, many other Italians, and the pope. There had been no such European congress since the Council of Constance, and the fact that a European assemblage had in 1415 dealt with affairs of the church, and now in the 1640s dealt with affairs of the state, war, and power, was a measure of the secularization that had come over Europe.

Lengthy peace negotiations

The negotiations dragged on, because the armies were still fighting, and after each battle one side or the other raised its terms. France and Spain refused to make peace with each other at all and in fact remained at war until 1659. But for the Holy Roman Empire a settlement was agreed to, incorporated in 1648 in the two treaties of Münster and Osnabrück, and commonly known as the Peace of Westphalia.

The Peace of Westphalia represented a general checkmate to the Counter Reformation in Germany. It not only renewed the terms of the Peace of Augsburg, granting each German state the right to determine its own religion, but it also added Calvinism to Lutheranism and Catholicism as an acceptable faith. On the controversial issue of church territories secularized after 1552 the Protestants won a complete victory; Catholic claims to the territories were abandoned.

Dissolution of the Holy Roman Empire

The dissolution of the Holy Roman Empire, which had been advanced by the drawing of internal religious frontiers in the days of Luther, was now confirmed in politics and international law. Borderlands of the Empire fell away. The Dutch and Swiss ceased to belong to it, and both the United Provinces and Swiss cantons (or Helvetic Body) were recognized as sovereign and independent. From the disintegrating western frontier of the Holy Roman Empire the French cut off small pieces, receiving sovereignty over three Lorraine bishoprics, which they had occupied for a century, and certain rights in Alsace which were so confused that they later led to trouble. The king of Sweden received new territories in northern Germany, thus adding to Sweden's trans-Baltic possessions.

It was in the new constitution of the Empire itself, not in territorial changes, that the greatest victory of the French and their Swedish and Dutch allies was to be found. The German states, over 300 in number, became virtually sovereign.

Germany fragmented

Each received the right to conduct diplomacy and make treaties with foreign powers. The Peace of Westphalia further stipulated that no laws could be made by the Empire, no taxes could be raised, no soldiers could be recruited, no war could be declared or peace terms ratified except with the consent of the imperial estates—the 300-odd princes, ecclesiastics, and free cities in the Reichstag assembled. Since it was well known that agreement on any such matters was impossible, the principle of self-government, or of medieval constitutional liberties, was used to destroy the Empire itself as an effective political entity. While most other European countries were consolidating under royal absolutism, Germany sank back into fragmentation and localism.

The Peace of Westphalia blocked the Counter Reformation, frustrated the Austrian Habsburgs, and forestalled for almost two centuries any movement toward German national unification. Within Europe as a whole, however, it marked the advent in international law of the modern system of sovereign states. The diplomats who assembled at Westphalia represented independent powers which recognized no superior or common tie. No one any longer pretended that Europe had any significant religious or political unity. Statesmen delighted in the absence of any such unity, in which they sensed the menace of "universal monarchy." Europe was understood to consist of a large number of unconnected sovereignties, free and detached atoms, or states, which acted according to their own laws, following their own political interests, forming and dissolving alliances, exchanging embassies and legations, alternating between war and peace, shifting position with a shifting balance of power.

System of sovereign states

Physically Germany was wrecked by the Thirty Years' War. Cities were sacked by mercenary soldiers with a rapacity that their commanders could not control; or the commanders themselves, drawing no supplies from their home governments, systematically looted whole areas to maintain their armies. Magdeburg was besieged ten times; Leipzig, five. In one woolen town of Bohemia, with a population of 6,000 before the wars, the citizens fled and disappeared, the houses collapsed, and eight years after the peace only 850 persons were found there. The peasants, murdered, put to flight, or tortured by soldiers to reveal their few valuables, ceased to farm; agriculture was ruined; starvation followed, and with it came pestilence. Even revised modern estimates allow that in many extensive parts of Germany as much as a third of the population may have perished. The effects of fire, disease, undernourishment, homelessness, and exposure in the seventeenth century were the more terrible because of the lack of means to combat them. The horrors of modern war for civilians are not wholly different from horrors that men and women have experienced in the past.

Germany as such, physically wrecked and politically cut into small pieces, ceased for a long time to play any significant part in European affairs. A kind of political and cultural vacuum existed in central Europe. On the one hand, the western or Atlantic peoples— French, English, Dutch—began in the seventeenth century to take the lead in European politics, trade, and culture. On the other hand, in eastern Germany, around Berlin and Vienna, new and only half-German centers of power began to form. These themes will be traced in the two following chapters.

With the close of the Thirty Years' War the Wars of Religion came to an end. While religion remained an issue in some later conflicts, it was never again an important cause of conflicts in the political affairs of Europe as a whole. In general, by the close of the seventeenth century, the division between Protestant and Catholic had become stabilized. Neither side any longer expected to make territorial gains at the expense of the other. Both the Protestant and the Catholic reformations were accomplished facts. The political struggle for territory, wealth, and strategic alliances had become secularized in that "reasons of state" now prevailed over religious allegiances in shaping both the foreign policies of governments and the military conflicts of sovereign powers.

Austrian Habsburgs

Spanish Habsburgs

Swedish Dominions

Brandenburg-Prussia

Church Lands

Ottoman Empire controlled lands

Boundary of the Holy Roman Empire

0   100   200   300 miles

SHETLAND I.

ORKNEY I.

SCOTLAND

Edinburgh

North Sea

Belfast

IRELAND

Dublin

Liverpool

ENGLAND
(COMMONWEALTH 1649–1660
UNITED KINGDOM 1707)

Bristol

London

ENGLISH CHANNEL

ATLANTIC OCEAN

NORWAY

Bergen

KINGDOM OF
DENMARK AND NORWAY

SWEDEN

Stockholm

Baltic Sea

DENMARK
(TO SWEDEN, 1658)

Copenhagen

SCHLESWIG

HOLSTEIN

SWEDISH
POMERANIA

Stralsund

BRANDENBURG-PRUSSIA

Danzig

UNITED
PROVINCES

Amsterdam

Ryswick

Utrecht

Hamburg

Lübeck

Stettin

POMERANIA

Vistula

Bremen

Verden

HANOVER

Osnabrück

Berlin

Magdeburg

BRANDENBURG

GREAT
POLAND

Warsaw

Brussels

Münster

MINOR

SPANISH
NETH.

Cologne

GERMAN STATES

Leipzig

SAXONY

Breslau

SILESIA

Rouen

Paris

Trier

Manz

Metz

PALATINATE

Dresden

Prague

BOHEMIA

MORAVIA

Rennes

Nantes

Orléans

LORRAINE

ALSACE

Strasbourg

BAVARIA

Augsburg

AUSTRIA

Vienna

HUNGARY

FRANCE

La Coruña

León

Oporto

Valladolid

PORTUGAL
(TO SPAIN
1580–1640)

Lisbon

Mérida

SPAIN

Escorial

Madrid

CASTILE

Toledo

Bordeaux

Lyon

Montauban

Avignon

Marseille

NAVARRE

PYRENEES

Saragossa

ARAGON

CATALONIA

Barcelona

Valencia

BALEARIC I.

MINORCA

MAJORCA

FRANCHE
COMTÉ

SWISS CANTONS

SAVOY

PIEDMONT

Milan

Parma

Genoa

Venice

REPUBLIC OF VENICE

SLAVONIA

BOSNIA

Belgrade

Zara

Adriatic Sea

Florence

TUSCANY

PAPAL
STATES

Rome

Aquila

Bari

CORSICA
(Genoa)

SARDINIA

Naples

NAPLES

KINGDOM OF THE
TWO SICILIES

Seville

Cadiz

Murcia

Malaga

Tangier
(Spain)

Ceuta

Algiers

Oran (Spain)

Tunis

Palermo

SICILY

MALTA
(Knights of St. John)

FEZ AND MOROCCO

ALGERIA

TUNISIA

Mediterranean Sea

B A R B A R Y   S T A T E S

EUROPE, 1648

This map shows the European states at the time of the Peace of Westphalia. A plurality of independent sovereign states was henceforth considered normal. The plurality of religions was also henceforth taken for granted within Europe as a whole, though each state continued to require or favor religious uniformity within its borders. By weakening the Habsburgs and furthering the disintegration of Germany, the Peace of Westphalia opened the way for the political ascendancy of France.

THE GROWING POWER OF WESTERN EUROPE, 1640–1715

If the reader were to take a map of Europe, set a compass on the city of Paris, and draw a circle with a radius of 500 miles, a zone would be marked out from which much of modern "Western" civilization radiated after about 1640. It was within this zone that a secular society, modern natural science, a developed capitalism, the modern state, parliamentary government, democratic ideas, machine industry, and much else either originated or received their first full expression. The extreme western parts of Europe—Ireland, Portugal, and Spain—were somewhat outside the zone in which the most rapid changes occurred. But within it were England, southern Scotland, France, the Low Countries, Switzerland, western and central Germany, and northern Italy. This area, for over two hundred years beginning in the seventeenth century, was the earth's principal center of what anthropologists might call cultural diffusion. Although the economy and culture of Western Europe were deeply influenced by the expanding trade and contacts with people outside Europe, the growing power of western European states, trading companies, science, and cultural institutions had a profound and spreading impact on the rest of Europe, the Americas, and ultimately the whole world.

This western European influence grew steadily in the half-century following the Peace of Westphalia. The fading out of the Italian Renaissance, the subsiding of religious wars, the ruin of the Holy Roman Empire, and the decline of Spain all cleared the stage on which the Dutch, English, and French were to be the principal actors. But the Dutch were few in number, and the English during most of the seventeenth century were weakened by domestic discord. It was France that for a time played the most imposing

Chapter emblem: Detail from a portrait of King Louis XIV by Hyacinthe Rigaud (1659–1743). (Giraudon/Art Resource, NY)

role. The whole half-century following the Peace of Westphalia is in fact often called the Age of Louis XIV.

17. THE *GRAND MONARQUE* AND THE BALANCE OF POWER

This king of France inherited his throne in 1643 at the age of 5, assumed the personal direction of affairs in 1661 at the age of 23, and reigned for 72 years until his death in 1715. No one else in modern history has held so powerful a position for so long a time. Louis XIV was more than a figurehead. For over half a century, during his whole adult life, he was the actual and working head of the French government. Inheriting the state institutions that Richelieu had developed earlier in the seventeenth century, he made France the strongest country in Europe. Using French money, by bribes or other inducements, he built up a pro-French interest in virtually every country from England to Turkey. His policies and the counterpolicies that others adopted against him set the pace of public events, and his methods of government and administration, war and diplomacy, became a model for other rulers to copy. During this time the French language, French thought and literature, French architecture and landscape gardens, and French styles in clothes, cooking, and etiquette became the accepted standard for Europe. Louis XIV was called by his fascinated admirers Louis the Great, the *Grand Monarque,* and the Sun King.

Internationally, the consuming political question of the last decades of the seventeenth century (at least in western Europe—eastern Europe we reserve for the next chapter) was the fate of the still vast possessions of the Spanish crown. Spain was what Turkey was later called, "the sick man of Europe." To its social and economic decline was added hereditary physical deterioration of its rulers. In 1665 the Spanish throne was inherited by Charles II, an unfortunate afflicted by many ills of mind and body, impotent, even imbecile, the pitiable product of generations of inbreeding in the Habsburg house. His rule was irresolute and feeble. It was known from the moment of his accession that he could have no children and that the Spanish branch of the Habsburg family would die out with his death. The whole future not only of Spain but also of the Spanish Netherlands, the Spanish holdings in Italy, and all Spanish America was therefore in question. Charles II dragged out his miserable days until 1700, the object of jealousy and outright assault during his lifetime, and precipitating a new European war by his death.

The weakness of Spain

Louis XIV, who in his youth married a sister of Charles II, intended to benefit from the debility of his royal brother-in-law. His expansionist policies followed two main lines. One was to push the French borders eastward to the Rhine, annexing the Spanish Netherlands (or Belgium) and the Franche-Comté or Free County of Burgundy, a French-speaking region lying between ducal Burgundy and Switzerland (see maps, pp. 142–143, 147). Such a policy involved the further dismemberment of the Holy Roman Empire. The other line of Louis XIV's ambitions, increasingly clear as time went on, was his hope of obtaining the entire Spanish inheritance for himself. By combining the resources of France and Spain he would make France supreme in Europe, in America, and on the sea. To promote these ends Louis XIV intrigued with the smaller and middle-sized powers of Europe and also contacted dissidents (i.e., potential allies) in all the countries whose governments opposed him.

The ambitions of Louis XIV

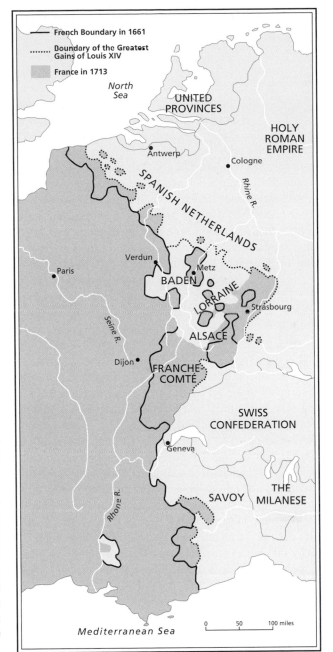

THE EXPANSION OF FRANCE, 1661–1713

The map shows how the foreign policy and wars of King Louis XIV gradually extended France's borders toward the east and northeast, bringing the Franche-Comté and new lands in both Alsace and Lorraine under French control. Louis also gained other territories in the Spanish Netherlands and expanded French holdings in the south along the frontier with Savoy. In addition to the expansion shown here, Louis XIV's other great ambition was to obtain control of Spain and the Spanish Empire in the Americas.

Were Louis XIV to succeed in his aims, he would create the "universal monarchy" dreaded by diplomats, that is to say, a political situation in which one state might subordinate all others to its will. The technique used against universal monarchy was the balance of power. Universal monarchy had formerly been almost achieved by the Austro-Spanish Habsburgs. The Habsburg supremacy had been blocked mainly by a balance of power headed by France, of which the Thirty Years' War and the Peace of Westphalia were the outstanding triumphs. Now the danger of universal monarchy came from France, and it was against France that the balance of power was directed.

The Idea of the Balance of Power

Motives for alliances

The aim of statesmen pursuing policies of balance of power in the seventeenth and eighteenth centuries was generally to preserve their own independence of action to the utmost. Hence the basic rule was to ally against any state threatening domination. If one state seemed to dictate too much, others would shun alliance with it unless they were willing (from ideological sympathy or other reasons) to become its puppets. They would seek alliance with the other weaker states instead. They would thus create a balance or counterweight, or "restore the balance," against the state whose ascendancy they feared. Another more subtle reason for preferring alliance with the weak rather than with the strong was that in such an alliance the leaders of each state could believe their own contribution to be necessary and valued, and by threatening to withdraw their support could win consideration of their own policies. Indeed, the balance of power may be defined as a system in which each state tends to throw its weight where it is most needed, so that its own importance may be enhanced.

Balance-of-power politics

The purpose of balance-of-power politics was not to preserve peace but to preserve the sovereignty and independence of the states of Europe, or the "liberties of Europe," as they were called, against potential aggressors. The system was effective as a means to this end in the seventeenth and eighteenth centuries. Combinations were intricate, and alliances were readily made and unmade to deal with emerging situations. One reason for the effectiveness of the system lay in the great number of states capable of pursuing an independent foreign policy. These included not only the greater and middle-sized states of Austria, Spain, France, England, Holland, Sweden, and Bavaria, but a great number of small independent states, such as Denmark, the German principalities, Portugal after 1640, and Savoy, Venice, Genoa, and Tuscany. States moved easily from one alliance to another or from one side of the balance to another. They were held back by no ideologies or sympathies, especially after the religious wars subsided, but could freely choose or reject allies, aiming only to protect their own independence or enlarge their own interests. Moreover, owing to the military technology of the day, small states might count as important military partners in an alliance. By controlling a strategic location, like the king of Denmark, or by making a contribution of ships or money, like the Dutch Republic, they might add just enough strength to an alliance to balance and overbalance the opposing great power and its allies.

As the ambitions of Louis XIV became bolder, and as the capacity of Spain to resist them withered away, the prevention of universal monarchy under France depended increasingly on combining the states of Europe into a balance of power against him. The balance against Louis XIV was engineered mainly by the Dutch. The most tireless of his enemies, and the one who did more than any other to checkmate him, was the Dutchman William III, the prince of Orange, who in his later years was king of England and Scotland as well.

Let us, after first surveying the Dutch in the seventeenth century, turn to the British Isles, where a momentous conflict occurred between Parliament and king. We shall then examine the French absolute monarchy under Louis XIV and conclude the present chapter with the wars of Louis XIV, particularly the War of the Spanish Succession, in which the resistance to French ambitions ultimately restored the European balance of power.

18. THE DUTCH REPUBLIC

Dutch Civilization and Government

The ambassadors of kings, strolling beside a canal at The Hague, might on occasion observe a number of burghers in plain black garments step out of a boat and proceed to make a meal of cheese and herring on the lawn, and they would recognize in these portly figures the provincial delegates of the Estates General of the United Provinces, as the Dutch government was known in the diplomatic language of the day. Though noblemen lived in the country, the Dutch were the most bourgeois of all peoples. They were not the only republicans in Europe, since the Swiss cantons, Venice, Genoa, and even England for a few years were republics, but of all republics the United Provinces was by far the most wealthy, the most flourishing, and the most important in international diplomacy and culture.

The Dutch acquired a nationality of their own in the long struggle against Spain, and with it a pride in their own freedom and independence. In the later phases of the war with Spain, notably during the Thirty Years' War, they were able to rely more on their wealth and diplomacy than on actual fighting, so that during the whole seventeenth century they enjoyed a degree of comfort, and of intellectual, artistic, and commercial achievement unexcelled in Europe. The classic Dutch poets and dramatists *Dutch achievements* wrote at this time, making a literary language of what had formerly been a dialect of Low German. Hugo Grotius produced, in his *Law of War and Peace,* a pioneering treatise on international law. Baruch Spinoza, of a family of refugee Portuguese Jews, quietly turned out works of philosophy, examining the nature of reality, of human conduct, and of church and state. Spinoza made his living by grinding lenses; there were many other lens grinders in Holland; some of them developed the microscope, and some of these, in turn—Leeuwenhoek, Swammerdam, and others—peering through their microscopes and beholding for the first time the world of microscopic life, became founders of modern biological science. The greatest Dutch scientist was Christian Huyghens (1629–1695), who worked mainly in physics and mathematics; he improved the telescope (a Dutch invention), made clocks move with pendulums, discovered the rings of Saturn, and launched the wave theory of light. A less famous writer, Balthasar Bekker, in his *World Bewitched* (1691) delivered a decisive blow against the expiring superstition of witchcraft. Meanwhile, the extraordinarily learned scholar and artist Anna Maria van Schurman (1607–1678) developed an important seventeenth-century argument for the education of women in her influential treatise *The Learned Maid or Whether a Maid May Be Called a Scholar* (1638).

But the most eternally fresh of the Dutch creations, suffering from no barrier of time or language, were the superb canvases of the painters. Frans Hals produced bluff portraits of the common people. Jan Vermeer threw a spell of magic and quiet dignity over men, and especially women, of the burgher class, many of whom he portrayed in typical domestic scenes. Rembrandt conveyed the mystery of human consciousness itself. In Rembrandt's *Masters of the Cloth Guild* (see color illustrations following p. 288) we face a group of six men who seem about to speak from the canvas, inclined slightly forward, as intent on their business as judges on the proceedings in a courtroom. Such men conducted the affairs of Holland, in both commerce and government; intelligent and calculating but not cunning, honest but determined to drive a hard bargain; the sober black cloaks, with the clean white collars, set against the carved woodwork and rich table covering of the Cloth Hall, seem to suggest that personal vanity must yield to collective undertakings and that personal simplicity must be maintained in the midst of material opulence. And in

Vermeer's *Geographer* (see p. 153), painted in 1669, there appears not only an immaculately scrubbed and dusted Dutch interior, but something of a symbol of the modern world in its youth—the pale northern sunlight streaming through the window, the globe and the map, the dividers in the scholar's right hand, instrument of science and mathematics, the tapestry flung over the table (or is it an Oriental rug brought from the East?), the head lifted in thought, and eyes resting on an invisible world of fresh discoveries and opening horizons. The same interest in the complexities of human character and the details of household objects appears in Vermeer's *Girl Reading a Letter at an Open Window,* which he painted in the late 1650s (see p. 151), and *The Artist's Studio,* which dates from about 1665 (see color illustrations following p. 288).

Dutch paintings in this era showed certain characteristics of the wider seventeenth-century artistic style that came to be known as Baroque. The fascination with lighting, the representation of interior spaces, the use of distinctive colors or subtle hues, and a more naturalistic image of human beings often shaped the distinctive appearance of Baroque paintings. In contrast to most Dutch artists, however, many of the best-known Baroque painters identified with the Catholic Church or the Counter Reformation. The Flemish painter Peter Paul Rubens was one prominent example of this identification with Catholicism in the Low Countries (see his *Portrait of the Artist with Isabelle Brant,* c. 1610, in the color illustrations following p. 000); but art in the Netherlands tended to portray scenes of everyday life rather than the passion of religious ecstasy.

In religion, after initial disputes, the Dutch Republic adopted toleration. Early in the seventeenth century the Dutch Calvinists divided. One group favored a modification of Calvinism, with a toning down of the doctrine of absolute and unconditional predestination. This more moderate Calvinism drew its main support from the comfortable burghers and its doctrines from a theologian of Leyden named Arminius, whose ideas were condemned at an international Calvinist synod in 1618. But beginning in 1632 the Arminians were tolerated. Rights were granted to the large Catholic minority. Jews had long been welcomed in the republic; and Christian sects despised everywhere else, such as the Mennonites, found a refuge in it. Although none of these people had as many political or economic rights as the Calvinists, the resulting mixture stimulated both the intellectual life and the commercial enterprise of the country.

Religious toleration

The Dutch as early as 1600 had 10,000 ships, and throughout the seventeenth century they owned most of the shipping of northern Europe. They were the carriers between Spain, France, England, and the Baltic. They also settled in Bordeaux to buy wines, lent money to vintners, and soon owned many vineyards in France itself. They sailed on every sea. They entered the Pacific by way of South America, where they rounded Cape Horn and named it after Hoorn in Holland. Organized in the East India Company of 1602, their merchants increasingly replaced the Portuguese in India and the Far East. In Java, in 1619, they founded the city of Batavia—the Latin name for Holland. (The city is now called Jakarta.)

Dutch explorations and settlements

Not long after 1600 the Dutch reached Japan. But the Japanese, fearing the political consequences of Christian penetration, in 1641 expelled all other Europeans and confined the Dutch to limited operations on an island near Nagasaki. The Dutch remained for over two centuries the sole link of the West with Japan. In 1612 the Dutch founded their first settlement on Manhattan Island, and in 1621 they established a Dutch West India Company to exploit the loosely held riches of Spanish and Portuguese America. They founded colonies at Pernambuco and Bahia in Brazil (lost soon thereafter) and at Caracas, Curaçao, and in Guiana in the Caribbean. In 1652 the Dutch captured the Cape of Good Hope in

GIRL READING A LETTER AT AN OPEN WINDOW
by Jan Vermeer (Dutch, 1632–1675)

Vermeer's characteristic interest in the mysteries of human character, the subtle shades of light, and the complex folds of a curtain appear in this painting of a young woman who seems to have received a disconcerting message or perhaps long anticipated news from afar.

(Erich Lessing/Art Resource, NY)

South Africa from the Portuguese. Dutch settlers soon appeared. Moving inland, they occupied the territory of the Khoikhoi and displaced or enslaved the people whose ancestors had lived there for centuries. From these Dutch settlers and from French Huguenots and others have come the modern Afrikaner people, whose language and religion still reflect their mainly Dutch origins.

The Bank of Amsterdam

In 1609 the Dutch founded the Bank of Amsterdam. European money was a chaos; coins were minted not only by great monarchs but also by small states and cities in Germany and Italy, and even by private persons. In addition, under inflationary pressures, kings and others habitually debased their coins by adding more alloy, while leaving the old coins in circulation along with the new. Anyone handling money thus accumulated a miscellany of uncertain value. The Bank of Amsterdam accepted deposits of such mixed money from all persons and from all countries, assessed the gold and silver content, and, at rates of exchange fixed by itself, allowed depositors to withdraw equivalent values in gold florins minted by the Bank of Amsterdam. These were of known and unchanging weight and purity. They thus became an internationally sought money, an international measure of value, acceptable everywhere. Depositors were also allowed to draw checks against their accounts. These conveniences, plus a safety of deposits guaranteed by the Dutch government, attracted capital from all quarters and made possible loans for a wide range of purposes. Amsterdam remained the financial center of Europe until the French Revolution.

Under their republican government the Dutch enjoyed great freedom, but it can hardly be said that their form of government met all the requirements of a state. The seven provinces that sent representatives to the Estates General of the United Provinces were all jealous of their own independence. Each province had, as its executive, an elected stadholder, but there was no stadholder for the United Provinces as a whole. This difficulty was overcome by the fact that most of the various provinces usually elected the head of the house of Orange as stadholder. This family had enjoyed exceptional prestige in the republic since the days of William the Silent and the wars for independence, but the prince of Orange, apart from being stadholder, was simply one of the feudal noblemen of the country. In general, however, the commercial class had more wealth than the older noble families, and affairs were usually managed by the burghers.

Politics in the Dutch Republic was a seesaw between the burghers, pacifistic and absorbed with business, and the princes of Orange, to whom the country owed most of its military security. When foreigners threatened invasion, the power of the stadholder increased. When all was calm, the stadholder could do little. The Peace of Westphalia produced a mood of confidence in the burghers, followed by a constitutional crisis, in the course of which the stadholder William II died, in 1650. No new stadholder was elected for 22 years. The burgher, civilian, and decentralizing tendencies prevailed.

William of Orange

In 1650, eight days after his father's death, the third William was born in the house of Orange, seemingly fated never to be stadholder and to pass his life as a private nobleman on his own estates. William III grew up to be a grave and reserved young man, small and rather stocky, with thin, compressed lips and a determined spirit. He learned to speak Dutch, German, English, and French with equal facility and to understand Italian, Spanish, and Latin. He observed the requirements of his religion, which was Dutch Calvinism, with sober regularity. He had a strong dislike for everything magnificent or pompous; he lived plainly, hated flattery, and took no pleasure in social conversation. In these respects he was the opposite of his lifelong enemy the Sun King, whom he resembled only in his diligent preoccupation with affairs. In 1677 he married the king of England's niece, Mary Stuart.

THE GEOGRAPHER
by Jan Vermeer (Dutch, 1632–1675)

The impact on Europe of the opening of the Atlantic may be seen in this painting. For the first time in human history it had become possible to understand with some accuracy the relationships of the oceans and continents throughout the globe. The Dutch built up a large ocean-growing trade, and many of the leading cartographers lived in the Netherlands.

(Städelsches Kunstinstitut, Frankfurt)

Foreign Affairs: Conflict with the English and French

Meanwhile matters were not going favorably for the Dutch Republic. In 1651 the revolutionary government then ruling England passed a Navigation Act. This act may be considered the first of a long series of political measures by which the British colonial empire was built up. It was aimed against the Dutch carrying trade. It provided that goods imported into England and its dependencies must be transported on English ships or on ships belonging to the country exporting the goods. Since the Dutch were too small a people to be great producers and exporters themselves, and lived largely by carrying the goods of others, they saw in the new English policy a threat to their economic existence. The Dutch and English soon entered into a series of three wars, running with interruptions from 1652 to 1674 and generally indecisive, though in 1664 the English annexed New Amsterdam and renamed it New York.

Threats by sea and land

While thus assaulted at sea by the English, the Dutch were menaced on land by the French. Louis XIV made his first aggressive move in 1667, claiming the Spanish Netherlands and Franche-Comté by alleging certain rights of his Spanish wife, and overrunning the Spanish Netherlands with his army. The Dutch, to whom the Spanish Netherlands were a buffer against France, set into motion the mechanism of the balance of power. Dropping temporarily their disputes with the English, they allied with them instead; and since they were able also to secure the adherence of Sweden, the resulting Triple Alliance was sufficient to give pause to Louis XIV, who withdrew from the Spanish Netherlands. But in 1672 Louis XIV again rapidly crossed the Spanish Netherlands, attacked with forces five times as large as the Dutch, and occupied three of the seven Dutch provinces.

The election of William as stadholder

A popular clamor now arose among the Dutch for William of Orange, demanding that the young prince, who was 22 years of age, be installed in the old office of stadholder, in which his ancestors had defended them against Spain. He was duly elected stadholder in six provinces. In 1673 these six provinces voted to make the stadholderate hereditary in the house of Orange. William, during his whole "reign" in the Netherlands, attempted to centralize and consolidate his government, put down the feudal liberties of the provinces, and free himself from constitutional checks, moving generally in the direction of absolute monarchy. He was unable, however, to go far in this course, and the United Provinces remained a decentralized patrician republic until 1795.

Meanwhile, to stave off the immediate menace of Louis XIV, William resorted to a new manipulation of the balance of power. He formed an alliance this time with the minor powers of Denmark and Brandenburg (the small German state around Berlin) and with the Austrian and Spanish Habsburgs. Nothing could indicate more clearly the new balance of power precipitated by the rise of France than this coming over of the Dutch to the Habsburg side. This alliance presented a forceful new challenge to Louis XIV and pushed him into negotiations that ended this phase of his expansionist wars. Peace was signed in 1678 (by the treaty of Nimwegen), but only at the expense of Spain and the Holy Roman Empire, from which Louis XIV took the long coveted Franche-Comté, together with another batch of towns in Flanders (see map, p. 147). The Dutch preserved their territory intact.

William comes to the English throne

In the next ten years came the great windfall of William's life. In 1689 he became king of England. He was now able to bring the British Isles into his perpetual combinations against France. Since the real impact of France was yet to be felt, and the real bid of Louis XIV for universal monarchy was yet to be made, and since the English at this time were rapidly gaining in strength, the entrance of England was a decisive addition to the balance formed against French expansion. In this way the constitutional troubles of England, by bringing a determined Dutchman to the English throne, entered into the general stream of European affairs and helped to assure that western Europe and its overseas offshoots should not be dominated totally by France.

19.   BRITAIN: THE CIVIL WAR

After the defeat of the Spanish Armada and recession of the Spanish threat the English were for a time less closely involved with the affairs of the Continent. They played no significant part in the Thirty Years' War and were almost the only European people west of Poland who were not represented at the Congress of Westphalia. At the time of the Westphalia negotiations in the 1640s they were in fact engaged in a civil war of their own. This English civil war was a milder variant of the Wars of Religion which desolated France, Germany, and the Netherlands. It was fought not between Protestants and Catholics as on the Continent, but between the more extreme or Calvinistic Protestants called Puritans and the more moderate Protestants, who adhered to the established Church of England. As in the wars on the Continent, religious differences were mixed indistinguishably with political and constitutional issues. As the Huguenots represented to some extent feudal rebelliousness against the French monarchy, as German Protestants fought for states' rights against imperial centralization, and the Calvinists of the Netherlands for provincial liberties against the king of Spain, so the Puritans asserted the rights of Parliament against the mounting claims of royalty in England.

The civil war in England took many lives, but was less destructive than most such wars on the Continent; and England escaped the worst horrors of the Wars of Religion. The same was not true of the British Isles as a whole. After 1603 the kingdoms of England and Scotland, while otherwise separate, were ruled by the same king; the kingdom of Ireland remained, as before, a dependency of the English crown. Between England and Presbyterian Scotland there was constant friction, but the worst trouble was between England and Catholic Ireland, which was the scene of religious warfare as savage as that on the Continent.

England in the Seventeenth Century

For the English the seventeenth century was an age of great achievement, during which they made their debut as one of the chief peoples of modern Europe. In 1600 only four or five million persons, in England and Lowland Scotland, spoke the English language. The number did not rise rapidly for another century and a half. But the population began to spread. Religious discontents, reinforced by economic pressures, led to considerable emigration. Twenty thousand Puritans settled in New England between 1630 and 1640, and about the same number went to Barbados and other West India islands during the same years. A third stream, again roughly of the same size, but made up mainly of Scottish Presbyterians, settled in northern Ireland under government auspices, driving away or expropriating the native Celts. English Catholics were allowed by the home government to settle in Maryland. A great many members of the Church of England went to Virginia during and after the mid-century civil war, adding to the small settlement made at Jamestown in 1607. Except for the movement to northern Ireland, called the "plantation of Ulster," these

English emigration to North America

The English playwright William Shakespeare helped to shape the modern English language as well as much of the later history of English theater and literature. This image of the famous author appeared on an early seventeenth-century edition of his collected works.
(Getty Images)

migrations took place without much attention on the part of the government, through private initiative organized in commercial companies. After the middle of the century the government began deliberately to build an empire. New York was conquered from the Dutch, Jamaica from the Spanish, and Pennsylvania and the Carolinas were established. All the thirteen colonies except Georgia were founded before 1700, but there were at that time still less than half a million people in British North America.

The English also, like the Dutch, French, and Spanish at the time, were creating their national culture. Throughout western Europe the national languages, encroaching upon international Latin on the one hand and local dialects on the other, were becoming adequate vehicles for the expression of thought and feeling. William Shakespeare helped to shape the evolving English language through the enduring influence of his great plays, including the famous tragedies *Hamlet, Macbeth,* and *King Lear*—all of which were first performed and published in the early years of the seventeenth century. John Milton published his influential epic poems *Paradise Lost* and *Paradise Regained* later in this same century, after the bitter conflicts of the English Civil War. Shakespeare and Milton projected their mighty conceptions of human experience, aspirations, and tragedy with the imaginative power of both new and old words. The English classical literature, rugged in form but deep in content, vigorous yet subtle in insight, majestic, abundant, and sonorous in expression, was almost the reverse of French classical writing, with its virtues of order, economy, propriety, and graceful precision. Proud of their literary culture and their own great writers, the English could never thereafter quite yield to French standards, nor be dazzled or dumbfounded, as some peoples were, by the cultural glories of the Age of Louis XIV. There were no seventeenth-century painters comparable to those on the Continent, but in music it was the age of Thomas Campion and Henry Purcell, and in architecture the century closed with the great buildings of Christopher Wren.

Economic activity

Economically the English were enterprising and affluent, though in 1600 far outdistanced by the Dutch. They had a larger and more productive country than the Dutch, and were therefore not as limited to purely mercantile and seafaring occupations. Coal was mined around Newcastle and was increasingly used, but was not yet a leading source of English wealth. The great industry was the growing of sheep and manufacture of woolens, which were the main export. Spinning and weaving were done mostly by workers in the country, under the putting-out system, and organized by merchants according to the methods of commercial capitalism. Since 1553 the English had traded with Russia by way of the White Sea; they were increasingly active in the Baltic and eastern Mediterranean; and with the founding of the East India Company, in 1600, they competed with the Dutch in assaulting the old Portuguese monopoly in India and East Asia. But profitable as such overseas operations were, the main wealth of England was still in the land. The richest men were not merchants but landlords, and the landed aristocracy formed the richest class.

Background to the Civil War: Parliament and the Stuart Kings

In England, as elsewhere in the seventeenth century, the kings clashed with their old medieval representative institutions. In England the old institution, Parliament, won out against the king. But this was not the unique feature in the English development. In Germany the estates of the Holy Roman Empire triumphed against the emperor, and much the same thing, as will be seen, occurred in Poland. But on the Continent the triumph of the old representative institutions generally meant political dissolution or even anarchy. Successful governments were generally those in which kingly powers increased; this was the strong tendency of the time, evident even in the Dutch Republic after 1672 under William of Orange. The unique thing about England was that Parliament, in defeating the king, arrived at a workable form of government. Government remained strong but came under parliamentary control. This determined the character of modern England and launched into the history of Europe and of the world the great movement of liberalism and representative institutions.

The violent struggles that ultimately produced England's new political order emerged from the conflicting ambitions of the Stuart kings and the most powerful social groups in the English Parliament. In 1603, on the death of Queen Elizabeth, the English crown was inherited by the son of Mary Stuart, James VI of Scotland. As a descendant of Henry VII he became king of England also, taking there the title of James I. James was a philosopher of royal absolutism. He had even written a book on the subject, *The True Law of Free Monarchy.* By a "free" monarchy James meant a monarchy free from control by Parliament, churchmen, or laws and customs of the past. It was a monarchy in which the king, as father to his people, looked after their welfare as he saw fit, standing above all parties, private interests, and pressure groups. He even declared that kings drew their authority from God and were responsible to God alone, a doctrine known as the divine right of kings.

The Stuarts and Parliament

Probably any ruler succeeding Elizabeth would have had trouble with Parliament, which had shown signs of restlessness in the last years of her reign but had deferred to her as an aging woman and a national symbol. She had maintained peace within the country and fought off the Spaniards, but these very accomplishments persuaded many people that they could safely bring their grievances into the open. James I was a foreigner, a Scot, who lacked the touch for dealing with the English and who was moreover a royal pedant, the "wisest fool in Christendom," as he was uncharitably called. Not content with the actualities of control, as Elizabeth had been, he read the Parliament tiresome lectures on the royal rights. He also was in constant need of money. The wars against Spain had left a considerable debt. James was far from economical, and, in any case, in an age of rising prices, he could not live within the fixed and customary revenues of the English crown. These were of medieval character, increasingly quaint under the new national and international conditions.

Neither to James I nor to his son Charles I, who succeeded him in 1625, would Parliament grant adequate revenue, because it distrusted them both. Many members of Parliament were Puritans, whose Calvinist beliefs made them dissatisfied with the organization and doctrine of the Church of England. Elizabeth had tried to hush up religious troubles, but James threatened to "harry the Puritans out of the land," and Charles supported the Church hierarchy which, under Archbishop Laud, sought to enforce religious conformity. Many members of Parliament were also lawyers, who feared that the common law of England, the historic or customary law, was in danger. They disliked the prerogative courts—the Star Chamber set up by Henry VII to settle disputes without the deliberations of a jury and the High Commission set up by Elizabeth to ensure conformity to the theology of the Church of England. They heard with trepidation the new doctrine that the sovereign king could make laws and decide cases at his own discretion. Last but not least, practically all members of Parliament were property owners. Landowners, supported by the merchants, feared that if the king succeeded in raising taxes on his own authority, their wealth would be insecure. Hence there were strong grounds for resistance.

Parliamentary resistance

In England the Parliament was so organized as to make resistance effective. There was only one Parliament for the whole country. There were no provincial or local estates, as in the Dutch Republic, Spain, France, Germany, and Poland. Hence all parliamentary opposition was concentrated in one place. In this one and only Parliament, there were only two houses, the House of Lords and the House of Commons. The landed interest dominated in both houses, the noblemen in the Lords and the gentry in the Commons. In the Commons the gentry, who formed the bulk of the aristocracy, mixed with representatives of the merchants and the towns. Indeed the towns frequently chose country gentlemen to represent them. Hence the houses of Parliament did not accentuate, as did the estates on the Continent, the class division within the country.

Nor was the church present in Parliament as a separate force. Before Henry VIII's break with Rome the bishops and abbots together had formed a large majority in the House of Lords. Now there were no abbots left, for there were no monasteries. The House of Lords was now predominantly secular; in the first Parliament of James I there were 82 lay peers and 26 bishops. The great landowners had captured the House of Lords. The smaller landowners of the Commons had been enriched by receiving former monastic lands and had prospered by raising wool. The merchants had likewise grown up under mercantilistic protection. Parliament was strong not only in organization but also in the social interests and wealth that it represented. No king could long govern against its will.

In 1629 king and Parliament came to a deadlock. Charles I attempted to rule without Parliament, which could legally meet only at the royal summons. He intended to give England a good and efficient government. Had he succeeded, the course of English constitutional development would have paralleled that of France. But by certain reforms in Ireland he antagonized the English landlords who had interests in that country. By supporting the leadership and theology of the Church of England he made enemies of the Puritans. By attempting to modernize the navy with funds raised without parliamentary consent (called "ship money") he alarmed all property owners, who feared that they would be forced to pay for policies they opposed.

The ship-money dispute illustrates the best arguments of both sides. It was the old custom in England for coastal towns to provide ships for the king's service in time of war. More recently, these coastal towns had provided money instead. Charles I wished to maintain a navy in time of peace and to have ship money paid by the country as a whole, including the inland counties. In the old or medieval view it was the function of the towns which were directly affected to maintain a fleet. In the new view, sponsored by the king, the whole nation was the unit on which a navy should be based. The country gentlemen whom Parliament mainly represented, and most of whom lived in inland counties, had less interest in the navy, and in any case were unwilling to pay for it unless they could control the foreign policies for which a navy might be used. The parliamentary class represented the idea, derived from the Middle Ages, that taxes should be authorized by Parliament. The king represented the newer ideas of monarchy that were developing on the Continent, which included a belief in the king's right to collect revenues that were needed by the state. The politically significant classes in England would not accept such ideas. Until the king could govern with the confidence of Parliament, or until Parliament itself was willing, not merely to keep down taxes but to assume the financial responsibilities of government under modern conditions, neither a navy nor any effectual government could be maintained.

The ship-money dispute

The Scots were the first to rebel. In 1637 they rioted in Edinburgh against attempts to impose the Church of England's prayer book and episcopal organization in Scotland. Charles, to raise funds to put down the Scottish rebellion, convoked the English Parliament in 1640, for the first time in 11 years. When it proved hostile to him, he dissolved it and called for new elections. The same men were returned. The resulting body, since it sat theoretically for 20 years without new elections, from 1640 to 1660, is known historically as the Long Parliament. Its principal leaders were small or moderately well-to-do landowning gentry. The merchant class, while furnishing no leaders, lent its support.

The Long Parliament

The Long Parliament, far from assisting the king against the Scots, used the Scottish rebellion as a means of pressing its own demands. These were revolutionary from the outset. Parliament insisted that the chief royal advisers be not merely removed but impeached and put to death. It abolished the Star Chamber and the High Commission. The most extreme Calvinist element, the "root and branch" men or "radicals," drove through a bill for the abolition of bishops, revolutionizing the Church of England. In 1642 Parliament and king came to open war: the king drawing followers mainly from the north and west; the Parliament, from the commercially and agriculturally more advanced counties of the south and east (see map, p. 166). A series of bloody battles steadily weakened the king's position, and his army dissolved in 1646. During the war, as the price of support from the Scottish army, Parliament adopted the Solemn League and Covenant. This prescribed that religion in England, Scotland, and Ireland should be made uniform "according to the word of God and the example of the best reformed churches." Thus Presbyterianism became the established legal religion of the three kingdoms.

The Emergence of Cromwell

The parliamentary forces, called Roundheads from the close haircuts favored by Puritans, gained their major military victories with an efficient new army, the New Model Army, and a highly competent commander, Thomas Fairfax. The wars also brought a hitherto unknown gentleman named Oliver Cromwell to the foreground. A devout Protestant, he organized a new and especially effective regiment in the New Model Army, the Ironsides, in which extreme Protestant exaltation provided the basis for morale, discipline, and the will to fight. By the late 1640s Cromwell had become the most powerful political and military leader of the parliamentary forces. The army, in which a more popular class was represented than in the Parliament, became the center of advanced democratic ideas. Many of the soldiers objected to Presbyterianism as much as to the Church of England. They favored a free toleration for all "godly" forms of religion, with no superior church organization above local groups of like-minded spirits.

Cromwell concluded that the defeated king, Charles I, could not be trusted, that "ungodly" persons of all kinds put their hopes in him (what later ages would call counterrevolution), and that he must be put to death. Since Parliament hesitated, Cromwell with the support of the army moved against Parliament. The Long Parliament, having started in 1640 with some 500 members, had sunk by 1649 to about 150 (for this revolution, like others, was pushed through by a minority); of these Cromwell now drove out almost 100, leaving a Rump of 50 or 60. This operation was called Pride's Purge, after Colonel Pride who commanded the soldiers by whom Parliament was intimidated; and in subsequent revolutions such excisions have been commonly known as purges, and the residues, sometimes, as rumps. The Rump condemned King Charles for "treason" and sent him to death on the scaffold in 1649.

Pride's Purge

England, or rather the whole British Isles, was now declared a republic. It was named the Commonwealth. Cromwell tried to govern as best he could. Religious toleration was decreed except for Unitarians and atheists on the one hand, and except for Roman Catholics and the most obstinate supporters of the Church of England on the other. Cromwell had to subdue both Scotland and Ireland by force. In Scotland the execution of the king, violating the ancient national Scottish monarchy of the Stuarts, had swung the country back into the royalist camp. Cromwell crushed the Scots in 1650.

Religious violence in the Commonwealth

Meanwhile the Protestant and Calvinist fury swept over Ireland. A massacre of newly settled Protestants in Ulster in 1641 had left bitter memories which were now avenged. The Irish garrisons of Drogheda and Wexford were defeated and massacred. Thousands of Catholics were killed; priests were put to the sword, and women and small children were dispatched in cold blood. Where formerly, in the "plantation" of Ulster, a whole Protestant population had been settled in northern Ireland, bodily replacing the native Irish, now Protestant landlords were scattered over the country as a whole, replacing the Catholic landlords and retaining the Catholic peasantry as their tenants. Ireland's native religion and clergy were driven underground, a foreign and detested church was established, and a new and foreign landed aristocracy, originally recruited in large measure from military adventurers, was settled upon the country, in which it ceased to reside as soon as it assured the payment of its rents.

In England itself Cromwell ruled with great difficulty. His regime was more successful in pursuing English interests abroad, for he not only completed the subjugation of Ireland, but in the Navigation Act of 1651, which barred Dutch ships from carrying goods between other countries and England or its colonies, he also opened the English attack on the Dutch maritime supremacy. He further waged a war with Spain in which England acquired Jamaica, thereby enhancing the English commercial position in the Caribbean and launching an English campaign for some of the vast inheritance of the Spanish Habsburgs. But he failed to gain the support of a majority of the English. The Puritan Revolu-

The execution of King Charles I marked the dramatic triumph of the radical, parliamentary forces in 1649, but the king's death—portrayed here in a seventeenth-century engraving—raised unprecedented questions about the proper limits for political authority and religious radicalism in English society.
(The Granger Collection, NY)

tion, like others, produced its extremists. It failed to satisfy the most ardent and could not win over the truly conservative, so that Cromwell found himself reluctantly more autocratic, and more alone.

A party arose called the Levellers, who were in fact what later times would call radical political democrats. They were numerous in the Puritan army, though their chief spokesman, John Lilburne, was a civilian. Appealing to natural rights and to the rights of Englishmen, they asked for a nearly universal manhood suffrage, equality of representation, a written constitution, and subordination of Parliament to a reformed body of voters. They thus anticipated many ideas of the American and French revolutions over a century later. There were others in whom religious and social radicalism were indistinguishably mixed. George Fox, going beyond Calvinism or Presbyterianism, founded the Society of Friends, or "Quakers." The Quakers caused much consternation by insisting that all believers could have new revelations of spiritual truth, by rejecting various social and religious hierarchies, and by allowing or even encouraging women to preach at their meetings. A more ephemeral group, the "Diggers," proceeded to occupy and cultivate common lands, or lands privately owned, in a general repudiation of property. The Fifth Monarchy Men were a millennial group who felt that the end of the world was at hand. They were so called from their belief, as they read the Bible, that history has seen four empires, those of Assyria, Persia, Alexander, and Caesar; and that the existing world was still "Caesar's" but would soon give way to the fifth monarchy, of Christ, in which justice would at last rule.

Religious and social radicalism

Cromwell opposed such movements by which all established persons in society felt threatened. As a regicide and a Puritan, however, he could not turn to the royalists or the former leaders of the Church of England. Unable to agree even with the Rump, he abolished it also in 1653, and thereafter vainly attempted to govern, as Lord Protector, through representative bodies devised by himself and his followers, under a written constitution, the Instrument of Government. Actually, he was driven to place England under military rule, the regime of the "major generals." These officials, each in his district, repressed malcontents, vagabonds, and "bandits," closed ale houses, and prohibited cockfighting, in a mixture of moral puritanism and political dictatorship. Cromwell died in 1658; and his son was unable to maintain the Protectorate. Two years later, with all but universal assent, royalty was restored. Charles II, son of the dead Charles I, became king of England and of Scotland.

Cromwell, by beheading a king and keeping his successor off the throne for eleven years, had left a lesson which was not forgotten. Though he favored constitutional and parliamentary government and had granted a measure of religious toleration, he had in fact ruled as a dictator in behalf of a stern Puritan minority. The English people now began to blot from their memories the fact that they had ever had a real revolution. The fervid dream of a "godly" England was dissipated forever. What was remembered was a nightmare of standing armies and major generals, of grim Puritans and overwrought religious enthusiasts. The English lower classes ceased to have any political role or consciousness for over a century, except in sporadic rioting over food shortages or outbursts against the dangers of "popery." Democratic ideas were rejected as "levelling." They were generally abandoned in England after 1660 or were cherished by obscure individuals and religious radicals who could not make themselves heard. Such ideas, indeed, had a more continuous history in the English colonies in America, where some leaders of the discredited revolution took refuge.

Legacy of the revolution

20.   BRITAIN: THE TRIUMPH OF PARLIAMENT

The Restoration, 1660–1688: The Later Stuarts

What was restored in 1660 was not only the monarchy, in the person of Charles II, but also the Church of England and the Parliament. Everything, legally, was supposed to be as it had been in 1640. The difference was that Charles II, knowing the fate of his father, was careful not to provoke Parliament to extremes and that the classes represented in Parliament, frightened by the disturbances of the past 20 years, were more warmly loyal to the king than they had been before 1640 and more willing to uphold the established church.

Parliament during the Restoration enacted some far-reaching legislation. It changed the legal basis of land tenure, abolishing certain old feudal payments owed by landholders to the king. The possession of land thus came to resemble private property of modern type, and the landowning class became more definitely a propertied aristocracy. In place of the feudal dues to the king, which had been automatically payable, Parliament arranged for the king to receive income in the form of taxation, which Parliament could raise or reduce in amount. This gave a new power to Parliament and a new flexibility to government. The aristocracy thus cleared their property of customary restrictions and obligations, and at the same time undertook to support the state by imposing taxes on themselves. The English aristocracy proved more willing than the corresponding classes on the Continent to pay a large share

New legislation

of the expenses of government. Its reward was that, for a century and a half, it virtually ran the government to the exclusion of everyone else. Landowners in this period directed not only national affairs through Parliament but also local affairs as justices of the peace. The justices, drawn from the gentry of each county, decided small lawsuits, punished misdemeanors, and supervised the parish officials charged with poor relief and care of the roads. The regime of the landlord-justices came to be called the "squirearchy."

Other classes drew less immediate advantage from the Restoration. The Navigation Act of 1651 was renewed and even added to, so that commercial, shipping, and manufacturing interests were well protected. But in other ways the landed classes now in power showed themselves unsympathetic to the business classes of the towns. Many people in the towns were Dissenters, of the element formerly called Puritan and now refusing to accept the restored Church of England. Parliament excluded Dissenters from the town "corporations," or governing bodies, forbade any dissenting clergymen to teach school or come within five miles of an incorporated town, and prohibited all religious meetings, called "conventicles," not held according to the forms and by the authority of the Church of England. The effect was that many middle-class townspeople found it difficult or impossible to follow their preferred religion, to obtain an education for their children, either elementary or advanced (for Oxford and Cambridge were a part of the established church), to take part in local affairs through the town corporations, or to sit in the House of Commons, since the corporations in many cases chose the burgesses who represented the towns. The lowest classes, the very poor, were discouraged by the same laws from following sectarian and visionary preachers. Another enactment fell upon them alone, the Act of Settlement of 1662, which decentralized the administration of the Poor Law, making each parish responsible only for its own paupers. Poor people, who were very numerous, were condemned to remain in the parishes where they lived. A large section of the English population was immobilized.

Exclusion of Dissenters

But it was not long after the Restoration that Parliament and king were again at odds. The main issue was again religion. Many Protestants throughout Europe at this time were returning voluntarily to Roman Catholicism, a tendency naturally dreaded by the Protestant churches. It was most conspicuously illustrated when the daughter of Gustavus Adolphus himself, Queen Christina of Sweden, to the consternation of the Protestant world, abdicated her throne and was received into the Roman church. In England the national feeling was excitedly anti-Catholic. No measures were more popular than those against "popery"; and the squires in Parliament, stiffly loyal to the Church of England, dreaded papists even more than Dissenters. The king, Charles II, was personally inclined to Catholicism. He admired the magnificent monarchy of Louis XIV, which he would have liked to duplicate, so far as possible, in England. At odds with his Parliament, Charles II made overtures to Louis XIV. The secret treaty of Dover of 1670 was the outcome. Charles thereby agreed to join Louis XIV in his expected war against the Dutch; and Louis agreed to pay the king of England three million livres a year during the war. He hoped also that Charles II would soon find it opportune to rejoin the Roman church.

While these arrangements were unknown in detail in England, it was known that Charles II was well disposed to the French and to Roman Catholicism. England went to war again with the Dutch. The king's brother and heir, James, Duke of York, publicly announced his conversion to Rome. Charles II, in a "declaration of indulgence," announced the nonenforcement of laws against Dissenters. The king declared that he

Among the many religious groups that rose to prominence during the English Revolution, the Quakers became especially notorious for their critique of religious hierarchies and their willingness to let women speak at their meetings. The novelty of the group is suggested in this seventeenth-century French illustration of a woman addressing a Quaker assembly.
(Fotomas Index/Bridgeman Art Library)

Charles II and the Test Act

favored general toleration, but it was rightly feared that his real aim was to promote Roman Catholicism in England. Parliament retorted in 1673 by passing the Test Act, which required all officeholders to take communion in the Church of England. The Test Act renewed the legislation against Dissenters and also made it impossible for Catholics to serve in the government or in the army and navy. The Test Act remained on the statute books until 1828.

While Charles's pro-French and pro-Catholic policies were extremely unpopular, both among the country gentry who disliked the French from prejudice and the merchants who found them increasingly pressing competitors, the situation might not have come to a head except for the avowed Catholicism and French orientation of Charles's brother James, due to be the next king since Charles had no legitimate children. A strong movement developed in Parliament to exclude James by law from the throne. The exclusionists—and those generally who were most suspicious of the king, Catholics, and the French—received the nickname of Whigs. The king's supporters were popularly called Tories. The Whigs, while backed by the middle class and merchants of London, drew their main strength from the upper aristocracy, especially certain great noblemen who might expect, if the king's power were weakened, to play a prominent part in ruling the country themselves. The Tories were the party of the lesser aristocracy and gentry, those who were suspicious of the "moneyed interest" of London, and felt a strong loyalty to church and king. These two parties, or at least their names, became permanently established in English public life. But all the Whigs and Tories together, at this time, did not number more than a few thousand persons.

The Revolution of 1688

James II, despite Whig vexation, became king in 1685. He soon antagonized even the Tories, who strongly supported the Church of England. As landowners they appointed most of the parish clergy, who imparted Tory sentiments to the rural population, and from their ranks were drawn the bishops, archdeacons, university functionaries, and other high personnel of the church. The laws keeping Dissenters and Catholics from office had given Anglicans (i.e., members of the Church of England) a monopoly in local and national government and in the army and navy. James II acted as if there were no Test Act, claiming the right to suspend its operation in individual cases, and appointed a good many Catholics to influential and lucrative positions. He offered a program, as his brother had done, of general religious toleration, to allow Protestant Dissenters as well as Roman Catholics to participate in public life.

Such a program, whether frankly meant as a secularizing of politics or indirectly intended as favoritism to Catholics, was repugnant to the Church of England. Seven bishops refused to endorse it. They were prosecuted for disobedience to the king but were acquitted by the jury. James, by these actions, violated the liberties of the established church, threatened the Anglican monopoly of church and state, and aroused the popular terrors of "popery." He was also forced to take the position philosophically set forth by his grandfather James I, that a king of England could make and unmake the law by his own will. The Tories joined the Whigs in opposition. In 1688, a son was born to James II and baptized into the Catholic faith. The prospect now opened up of an indefinite line of Catholic rulers in England. Leading men of both parties thereupon abandoned James II. They offered the throne to his grown daughter Mary, born and brought up a Protestant before her father's conversion to Rome.

Whigs and Tories in opposition to the crown

Mary was the wife of William of Orange. William, it will be recalled, had spent his adult life blocking the ambitions of the king of France, who likewise had threatened Europe with a "universal monarchy" by absorbing or inheriting the world of Spain. To William III it would be a mere distraction to be husband to a queen of England, or even to be king in his own name, unless England could be brought to serve his own purposes. He was immutably Dutch; his purpose was to save Holland and hence to ruin Louis XIV. His chief interest in England was to bring the English into his balance of power against France. Since the English were generally anti-French, and had chafed under the pro-French tendencies of their kings, William without difficulty reached an understanding with the discontented Whigs and Tories. Protected by a written invitation from prominent Englishmen, he invaded England with a considerable army. James II fled, and William was proclaimed co-ruler with Mary over

William invades England

ENGLAND IN THE SEVENTEENTH CENTURY

The maps show the principal seventeenth-century English towns and the rough division of the country into royalist and parliamentary regions during the English Civil War. King Charles I drew his strongest support from the north and west; Parliament drew its strongest support from the southeast and from London. Similar regional political patterns emerged in later conflicts between the Royalist "Tories" and the Parliamentary "Whigs." The Whigs were generally supported by the upper aristocracy and the commercial classes of London, who opposed the pro-French, pro-Catholic policies of the Stuart kings Charles II and James II.

England and Scotland. In the next year, 1690, at the Boyne River in Ireland, a motley army of Dutchmen, Germans, Scots, and French Huguenots under William III defeated a French and Irish force led by James II. Thus the constitutional liberties of England were saved and Anglican Protestantism remained the official religion of the English nation. James II fled to France.

Louis XIV of course refused to recognize his inveterate enemy as ruler of England. He maintained James at the French court with all the honors due the English king. It was thereafter one of his principal war aims to restore the Catholic and Stuart dynasty across the Channel. The English, contrariwise, had added reason to fight the French. A French victory would mean counterrevolution and royal absolutism in England. The whole Revolution of 1688 was at stake in the French wars.

In 1689, Parliament enacted a Bill of Rights, stipulating that no law could be suspended by the king (as the Test Act had been), no taxes could be raised or army maintained except by parliamentary consent, and no subject (however poor) could be arrested and detained without legal process.

Bill of Rights and the Toleration Act

William III accepted these articles as conditions to receiving the crown. Thereafter the relation between king and people was a kind of contract. It was further provided, by the Act of Settlement of 1701, that no Catholic could be king of England; this excluded the descendants of James II, known in the following century as the Pretenders. Parliament also passed the Toleration Act of 1689, which allowed Protestant Dissenters to practice their religion but still excluded them from political life and public service. Since ways of evading these restrictions were soon found, and since even Catholics were not molested unless they supported the Pretenders, there was thereafter no serious trouble over religion in England and Lowland Scotland.

The English Parliament could make no laws for Scotland, and it was to be feared that James II might someday be restored in his northern kingdom. The securing of the parliamentary revolution in England, and of the island's defenses against France, required that the two kingdoms be organically joined. There was little sentiment in Scotland, however, for a merger with the English. The English tempted the Scots with economic advantages. The Scots still had no rights in the English East India Company, nor in the English colonies, nor within the English system of mercantilism and Navigation Acts. They obtained such rights by consenting to a union. In 1707 the United Kingdom of Great Britain was created. The Scots retained their own legal system and established Presbyterian church, but their government and parliament were merged with those of England. The term "British" came into use to refer to both English and Scots.

As for Ireland, it was now feared as a center of Stuart and French intrigue. The Revolution of 1688 marked the climax of a long record of trouble. Ireland had never been simply "conquered" by England, though certain English or rather Anglo-Norman families had carved out estates there since the twelfth century. By the end of the Middle Ages Ireland was organized as a separate kingdom with its own parliament, subordinate to the English crown. During the Reformation the Irish remained Catholic while England turned Protes-

The Irish threat to the Revolution of 1688

tant, but the monasteries were dissolved in Ireland as in England; and the organized church as such, the established Church of Ireland, with its apparatus of bishoprics, parishes, and tithes, became an Anglican communion in which the mass of native Irish had no interest. Next came the plantation of Ulster, already mentioned, in which a mass of newcomers, mainly Scottish and Presbyterian, settled in the northern part of the island. Then in Cromwell's time, as just seen, English landlords spread through the rest of the country; or rather, a new Anglo-Irish upper class developed, in which English landowning families, residing most often in England, added the income from Irish estates to their miscellaneous revenues.

Ireland therefore by the close of the seventeenth century was a very mixed country. Probably two-thirds of its population was Catholic, of generally Celtic ethnic background; perhaps a fifth was Presbyterian, with recent Scottish connections; the small remainder was made up of Anglicans, largely Anglo-Irish of recent or distant origin in England, who controlled most of the land, manned the official church, and were influential in the Irish

CHRONOLOGY OF NOTABLE EVENTS, 1642–1713

1642–1648	Civil War in England
1649	Execution of King Charles I in London
1649–1658	Oliver Cromwell leads the English "Commonwealth" and "Protectorate"
1660	Restoration of English Monarchy, King Charles II
1661	King Louis XIV takes personal control of French government; reign continues to 1715
1685	Revocation of Edict of Nantes; persecution of French Protestants
1688	"Glorious Revolution" brings William and Mary to English throne and strengthens power of Parliament
1702–1713	War of Spanish Succession; "balance of power" limits French expansion
1713	Peace of Utrecht

parliament. It was essentially a landlord and peasant society, in which the Presbyterian as well as the Catholic mass was overwhelmingly agricultural; towns were small, and the middle class scarcely developed.

After the Revolution of 1688, in which the final overthrow of James II took place at the Boyne River, the English feared Ireland as a source of danger to the postrevolutionary arrangements in England. Resistance of the subjugated Catholics had also to be prevented. English elites who were defending their own liberties at home thus set about destroying the religious, political, and social liberties of Irish Catholics. In addition to the burden of an alien church and absentee landlordism, the Irish were now subjected to a new "penal code." Catholic clergy were banished, and Catholics were forbidden to vote or to sit in the Irish parliament. Catholic teachers were forbidden to teach, and Catholic parents were forbidden to send children overseas to be educated in Catholic schools. No Catholic could take a degree at Trinity College (Dublin University), an Anglican institution. Catholic Irishmen were forbidden to purchase land, to lease it for more than 31 years, to inherit it from a Protestant, or to own a horse worth more than £5. A Catholic whose son turned Protestant found his own property rights limited in his son's favor. Catholics were forbidden to be attorneys, to serve as constables, or, in most trades, to have more than two apprentices. Some disabilities fell on the Protestant Irish also. Thus Irish shipping was excluded from the British colonies, nor could the Irish import colonial goods except through England. Export of Irish woolens and glass manufactures was prohibited. No import tariff on English manufactures could be levied by the Irish parliament. About all that was left to the Irish, in international trade, was the export of agricultural produce; and the foreign exchange acquired in this way went very largely to pay the rents to absentee landlords.

The purpose of the penal code was in part strategic, to weaken Ireland as a potentially hostile country during a long period of English wars with France. In part it was commercial, to favor English manufactures by removing Irish competition. And in part it was social, to confirm the position of the Anglican interest, or "ascendancy" as it came to be called. Parts of the code were removed piecemeal in the following decades, and a Catholic merchant class grew up in the eighteenth century; but much remained in effect for a long

Restrictions for Catholics

time, so that, for example, a Catholic could not vote for members of the Irish parliament until 1793, and even then could not be elected to it. In general, the Irish emerged from the seventeenth century as the most repressed people of western Europe.

England, immediately after the expulsion of James II, joined William III's coalition against France. To the alliance England brought a highly competent naval force, together with very considerable wealth. William's government, to finance the war, borrowed £1,200,000 from a syndicate of private lenders, who in return for holding government bonds were given the privilege of operating a bank. Thus originated, in 1694, both the Bank of England and the British national debt. Owners of liquid assets, merchants of London and Whig aristocrats with fat rent rolls, having lent their money to the new regime, had a compelling reason to defend it against the French and James II. And having at last a government whose policies they could control, they were willing to entrust it with money in large amounts. The national debt rapidly rose, while the credit of the government held consistently good; and for many years the Continent was astonished at the wealth that the British government could tap at will and the quantities of money that it could pour into the wars of Europe.

Coalition against France

The events of 1688 came to be known to the English as the Glorious Revolution. The Revolution was portrayed as vindicating the principles of parliamentary government, the rule of law, and even the right of rebellion against tyranny (though, as noted above, England's governing classes denied all such rights in Ireland). The overthrow of James II and the enactment of new parliamentary restrictions on the power of English kings have often been depicted as the climax in the growth of English constitutional self-government. Political writers like John Locke, shortly after the events, helped to give wide currency to these ideas. There was in truth some justification for these views even though in more recent times some writers have "deglorified" the Revolution of 1688. They point out that it was a class movement, promoted and maintained by the landed aristocracy. The Parliament which boldly asserted itself against the king was at the same time closing itself to large segments of the people. Where in the Middle Ages members of the House of Commons had usually received pay for their services, this custom disappeared in the seventeenth century, so that thereafter only men with independent incomes could sit. After the parliamentary triumph of 1688 this tendency became a matter of law. An act of 1710 required members of the House of Commons to possess private incomes at such a level that only a few thousand persons could legally qualify. This income had to come from the ownership of land. England from 1688 to 1832 was the best example in modern times of a true aristocracy, that is, of a country in which the men of the aristocratic landowning class not only enjoyed privileges but also conducted the government. But the landowning interest was then the only class sufficiently wealthy, numerous, educated, and self-conscious to stand on its own feet. The rule of the "gentlemen of England" was within its strict social limits a regime of political liberty.

The Glorious Revolution

21.   THE FRANCE OF LOUIS XIV, 1643–1715: THE TRIUMPH OF ABSOLUTISM

French Civilization in the Seventeenth Century

Having traveled in the outer orbits of the European political system, we come now to its radiant and mighty center, the domain of the Sun King himself, the France against which the rest of Europe felt obliged to combine because its power threatened the interests of so many other countries—the future of the Spanish possessions, the independence of Holland, the maintenance in England of the parliamentary revolution. The France of Louis XIV owed much of its ascendancy to the quantity and quality of its people. Population was stabilized or possibly even falling in the seventeenth century, the last century in which France was seriously disturbed by famine, pestilence, and peasant rebellion. With 19 million inhabitants in 1700 France was still over three times as populous as England and twice as populous as Spain. Its fertile soil, in an agricultural age, made it a wealthy country, though the wealth was very unevenly distributed.

The contradictions of French society

France was big enough to harbor many contradictions. Millions of its people lived in poverty, yet the number in comfortable or even luxurious circumstances was very large. There were both modest country nobles and cosmopolitan *grands seigneurs*. The middle class included an inordinate number of lawyers, officeholders, and bureaucrats. The country was less commercial than Holland or England, yet in sheer numbers there may have been more merchants in France than in either of the other two countries. Protestants were a declining minority, yet in the mid-seventeenth century there were still more French Huguenots than Dutch Calvinists. It was a self-sufficient country, yet the French in this century began trading in India and Madagascar, founded colonial settlements in Canada, penetrated the Great Lakes and the Mississippi valley, set up plantations in the West Indies, expanded their ancient commerce with the Levant, enlarged their mercantile marine, and for a time had the leading navy of Europe.

The dominance of France meant the dominance not merely of power but of a people whom most Europeans viewed as the forefront of seventeenth-century civilization. They carried over the versatility of the Italy of the Renaissance. In Nicholas Poussin and Claude Lorrain they produced a notable school of painters, their architecture was emulated throughout Europe, and they excelled in military fortification and engineering. Much of their literature, though often written by bourgeois writers, was designed for an aristocratic and courtly audience, which had put aside the uncouth manners of an earlier day and prided itself on the refinement of its tastes and perceptions. Corneille and Racine wrote austere tragedies on the personal conflicts and social relations of human life. Molière, in his comedies, ridiculed bumbling doctors, new-rich bourgeois, and foppish aristocrats, making the word "marquis" almost a joke in the French language. La Fontaine gave the world his animal fables, and La Rochefoucauld, in his witty and sardonic maxims, a nobleman's candid judgment on human nature. In Descartes the French produced a great mathematician and scientific thinker; in Pascal, a scientist who was also a profound spokesman for Christianity; in Bayle, the father of modern skeptics. It was French thought and the French language, not merely the armies of Louis XIV, which in the seventeenth century were sweeping the European world.

Patronage of the arts by Louis XIV

Louis XIV understood that France's dominant position in Europe required more than large armies and that a flourishing cultural life greatly enhanced the international prestige of even the wealthiest or most powerful sovereign state. He therefore gave generous financial support to his favorite writers and artists, especially those who produced works for his new palace at Versailles. He also brought the arts and sciences into the state's administrative system by establishing royal academies in which various theorists taught the correct principles for art, literature, music, dance, and scientific knowledge. The favored or official aesthetic theory in these academies was called classicism, a theory that emphasized order, harmony, and the artistic achievements of antiquity. Following the example of painters

MOLIERE.

dans le rôle d'Arnolphe, de l'École des femmes

(Comedⁱᵉ Française.)   (Année 1670.)

The French playwright Molière often performed in his own plays, including some that were staged at the court of Louis XIV. He is portrayed here as a character in *The School for Wives,* **a popular comedy about conflicts and deceptions in the relations between women and men.**

(Giraudon/Art Resource, NY)

such as Poussin, young artists learned to portray scenes from classical Roman history or mythology with harmonious and almost geometric precision. The great literary theorist of the day, Nicolas Boileau, urged writers to emulate the poetic works of ancient writers who had shown how literature addresses the timeless themes of human knowledge rather than the frivolities of daily life. The classicism of French artists and writers thus fit comfortably with the Sun King's appreciation for order, harmony, and hierarchy in every sphere of social, political, and cultural life.

Yet neither the king nor his official academies could control all of France's artistic and intellectual activity. Some literary critics, soon known as the "Moderns," began to argue that modern literature and knowledge had in fact surpassed the achievements of antiquity and that Boileau's academic writers, soon called the "Ancients," deferred much too rigidly to ancient authorities. Meanwhile, other centers of intellectual life emerged outside the royal academies in the new salons of Paris. Developing rapidly in the second half of the seventeenth century, the salons became the unofficial gathering places for Parisian nobles, wealthy professional persons, and creative writers or artists. They were organized by upper-class women who invited people into their homes to discuss philosophy, literature, and art—all of which could be debated without the formal constraints and solemnity of the academies. The salons attracted criticism and even ridicule from some people in the government and academies, partly because

Salons

they were created by energetic women and partly because they flourished outside the official cultural institutions of the state. But the Parisian salons, like the royal academies, became an enduring, distinctive institution in French cultural life. They also welcomed distinguished foreign visitors, thus contributing to the spread of French ideas and social mores throughout Europe. Parisian-style salons eventually appeared in other European cities, along with French fashion, French manners, and the French language.

The Development of Absolutism in France

This ascendancy of French culture went along with a regime in which political liberties were at a discount. The culture embellished what historians have often called the "absolute monarchy" of Louis XIV, though the king's power was never as far-reaching as the term "absolutism" suggests. The Sun King had to secure the cooperation of the nobility and other social classes; and his power was constrained in various ways by regional institutions, French legal traditions, and a fragmented system of local economies. France had a tradition of political freedom in the feudal sense. It had the same kind of background of feudal liberties as did the other countries of Europe. It had an Estates General, which had not met since 1615 but was not legally abolished. In some regions Provincial Estates, still meeting frequently, retained a measure of self-government and of power over taxation. There were about a dozen bodies known as parlements,[1] which, unlike the English Parliament, had developed as courts of law, each being the supreme court for a certain area of the country. The parlements upheld certain "fundamental laws" which they said the king could not overstep, and they often refused to enforce royal edicts that they declared to be unconstitutional. France, beneath the surface, was almost as diverse as Germany (see map, p. 180). French towns had won charters of acknowledged rights, and many of the great provinces enjoyed liberties written into old agreements with the crown. These local liberties were the main reason for a good deal of institutional complication. There were some 300 "customs" or regional systems of law; it was observed that travelers sometimes changed laws more often than they changed horses. Internal tariffs ran along the old provincial borders. Tolls were levied by manorial lords. The king's taxes fell less heavily on some regions than on others. Neither coinage nor weights and measures were uniform throughout the country. France was a bundle of territories held together by allegiance to the king.

The "parlements"

This older kind of feudal freedom discredited itself in France at the very time when by triumphing in Germany it pulled the Holy Roman Empire to pieces, and when in England it successfully made the transition to a more modern form of political liberty, embodied in the parliamentary though aristocratic state. In France the old medieval or local type of liberty became associated with disorder. It has already been related how after the disorders of the sixteenth-century religious wars people had turned with relief to the monarchy and how Henry IV and then Richelieu had begun to make the monarchy strong. The troubles of the Fronde provided additional incentive for the centralization of political power in France.

The Fronde

The Fronde broke out immediately after the Peace of Westphalia, while Louis XIV was still a child, and was directed against Cardinal Mazarin, who was governing in his name. It was an abortive revolution, led by the same elements, the parlements and the nobility, which were to initiate the great French Revolution in 1789. The parlements, especially the Parlement of Paris, insisted in 1648 on their

---

[1]Spelled *parlements* in French, to distinguish from the English Parliament.

INSPIRATION OF THE EPIC POET
by Nicolas Poussin (French, 1594–1665)
Poussin's interest in both the themes and forms of classicism appear in this image of a poet who yearns for the honor of a laurel crown as he meditates on the Greek god Apollo (with his lyre) and Calliope, the muse of epic poetry. The painting shows the careful symmetry and balance of much seventeenth-century French art.
(Scala/Art Resource, NY)

right to pronounce certain edicts unconstitutional. Barricades were thrown up and street fighting broke out in Paris. The nobility rebelled, as it had often in the past. Leadership was assumed by certain prominent noblemen who had enough wealth and influence to believe that, if the king's power were contained, they might govern the country themselves. The nobility demanded a calling of the Estates General, expecting to dominate over the bourgeoisie and the clergy in that body. Armed bands of soldiers, unemployed since the Peace of Westphalia and led by nobles, roamed about the country terrorizing the peasants. If the nobles had their way, it was probable that the manorial system would fall on the peasants more heavily, as in eastern Europe, where triumphant lords were at this very time exacting increased labor services from the peasants. Finally the rebellious nobles called in Spanish troops, though France was at war with Spain. By this time the bourgeoisie, together with the parlements, had withdrawn support from the rebellious nobles. The agitation subsided in total failure. Bourgeoisie and aristocracy could not work together; the nobles outraged people throughout France by bringing Spanish soldiers into their rebellion; and the *frondeurs,* especially after the parlements deserted them, had no systematic or constructive program, aiming only at the overthrow of the unpopular Cardinal Mazarin and at obtaining offices and favors for themselves.

After the Fronde, as after the religious wars, the bourgeoisie and peasantry of France, to protect themselves against the claims of the aristocracy, were in a mood to welcome the exercise of strong power by the kings. And in the young Louis XIV they had a man more than willing to grasp all the power he could get. Louis, at age 23, on Mazarin's death in 1661, announced that he would govern the country himself. He was the third king of the Bourbon line. It was the Bourbon tradition, established by Henry IV and by Richelieu, to draw the teeth from independent aristocrats, and this tradition Louis XIV followed. He was not a man of any transcendent abilities, though he had the capacity, often found among successful executives, of learning a good deal from conversation with experts. His education was not very good, having been made purposely easy; but he had the ability to see and stick to definite lines of policy, and he was extremely methodical and industrious in his daily habits, scrupulously loading himself with administrative business throughout his reign. He was extremely fond of himself and his position of kingship, with an insatiable appetite for admiration and flattery; he loved magnificent display and elaborate etiquette, though to some extent he simply adopted them as instruments of policy rather than as a personal whim.

With the reign of Louis XIV the "state" in its modern form took a long step forward. The state in the abstract has always seemed somewhat theoretical to the English-speaking world. Let us say, for simplicity, that the state represents a fusion of justice and power. A sovereign state possesses, within its territory, a monopoly over the administration of justice and the use of force. Private persons neither pass legal judgments on others nor control private armies of their own. For private and unauthorized persons to do so, in an orderly state, constitutes rebellion. This was in contrast to the older feudal practice, by which feudal lords maintained manorial courts and led their own followers into battle. Against these feudal practices Louis XIV energetically worked, though not with complete success, claiming to possess in his own person, a sovereign ruler, a monopoly over the lawmaking processes and the armed forces of the kingdom. This is the deeper meaning of his reputed boast, *L'état, c'est moi*—"the state is myself." In the France of the seventeenth century, divided by classes and by regions, there was in fact no practical means of consolidating the powers of state except in the shared deference to one individual.

"L'etat, c'est moi"

The state, however, while representing law and order within its borders, has generally stood in a lawless and disorderly relation to other states, since no higher monopoly of law and force has existed. Louis XIV, personifying the French state, had no particular regard for the claims of other states or rulers. He was constantly either at war or prepared for war with his neighbors. The modern state, indeed, was created by the needs of peace at home and war abroad. Machinery of government, as devised by Louis XIV and others, was a means of giving order and security within the territory of the state, and of raising, supporting, and controlling armies for use against other states.

The idea that law and force within a country should be monopolized by the lawful king was the essence of the seventeenth-century doctrine of absolutism. Its principal theorist in the time of Louis XIV was Bishop Bossuet. Bossuet advanced the old Christian teaching that all power comes from God and that all who hold power are responsible to God for the way they use it. He held that kings were God's representatives in the political affairs of earth. Royal power, according to Bossuet, was absolute but not arbitrary: not arbitrary because it must be reasonable and just, like the will of God which it reflected; absolute in that it was free from dictation by parlements, estates, or other subordinate elements within the country. Law, therefore, was the will of the sovereign king, so long as it conformed to the higher law which was the will of God.

This doctrine, affirming the divine right of kings, was popularly held in France at the time and was taught in the churches. "Absolutism" and "absolute monarchy" became the prevailing concepts of government on much of the European continent in the seventeenth and eighteenth centuries. It must be remembered, however, that these terms referred more to legal theories than to facts. A ruler was "absolute" because he was not legally bound by any other persons or institutions in the country. In reality he became dependent upon a host of advisers and bureaucrats; he often had to compromise with vested interests; and he could be thwarted by the sheer weight of local custom or meet resistance from lawyers, ecclesiastics, nobles, grandees, hereditary officeholders, and miscellaneous dignitaries. And the slow pace of both transportation and communication prevented early modern "absolutist" rulers from controlling their subjects as quickly or as efficiently as governments have controlled their people in modern nation-states.

Absolutism

Government and Administration

Possibly the most fundamental step taken by Louis XIV was to assure himself of control of the army. Armed forces had formerly been almost a private enterprise. Specialists in fighting, leading their own troops, worked for governments more or less as they chose, either in return for money or to pursue political aims of their own. This was especially common in central Europe, but even in France great noblemen had strong private influence over the troops, and in times of disorder nobles led armed retainers about the country. Colonels were virtually on their own. Provided with a general commission and with funds by some government, they recruited, trained, and equipped their own regiments, and likewise fed and supplied them, often by preying upon bourgeois and peasants in the vicinity. In these circumstances it was often difficult to say on whose side soldiers were fighting. It was hard for governments to set armies into motion and equally hard to make them stop fighting, for commanders fought for their own interests and on their own momentum. War was not a "continuation of policy"; it was not an act of the state; it easily degenerated, as in the Thirty Years' War, into a kind of aimless and perpetual violence.

War: a state activity

Louis XIV made war an activity of state. He saw to it that all armed persons in France fought only for him. This produced peace and order in France, while strengthening the fighting power of France against other states. Under the older conditions there was also little integration among different units and arms of the army. Infantry regiments and cavalry went largely their own way, and the artillery was supplied by civilian technicians under contract. Louis XIV created a stronger unity of control, put the artillery organically into the army, systematized the military ranks and grades, and clarified the chain of command, placing himself at the top. The government supervised recruiting, required colonels to prove that they were maintaining the proper number of soldiers, and assumed most of the responsibility for equipping, provisioning, clothing, and housing the troops. Higher officers, thus becoming dependent on the government, could be subjected to discipline. The soldiers were put into uniforms, taught to march in step, and housed in barracks; thus they too became more susceptible to discipline and control.

**LOUIS XIV
by Hyacinthe Rigaud
(French, 1659–1743)**

The grandeur of the Sun King is conveyed in this portrait by Rigaud. He uses the king's clothing, stance, and royal emblems to express the power of the French monarchy.
(Giraudon/Art Resource, NY)

Armed forces became less of a terror to their own people and a more effective weapon in the hands of government. They were employed usually against other governments but sometimes to suppress rebellion at home. Louis XIV also increased the French army in size, raising it from about 100,000 to about 400,000. These changes, both in size and in degree of government control, were made possible by the growth of a large civilian administration, the heads of which under Louis XIV were civilians. They were in effect the first ministers of war, and their assistants, officials, inspectors, and clerks constituted the first organized war ministry.

Louis XIV was not only a vain man, but made it a political principle to overawe the country with his own grandeur. He built himself a whole new city at the old village of Versailles about ten miles from Paris. Where the Escorial in Spain had the atmosphere of a monastery, Versailles was a monument to worldly splendor. Tremendous in size, fitted out with polished mirrors, gleaming chandeliers, and magnificent tapestries, opening on to a formal park with fountains and shaded walks, the palace of Versailles became the marvel of Europe and the envy of lesser kings. It was virtually a public building, much of it used for government offices, with nobles, churchmen, notable bourgeois, and servants milling about on the king's affairs. The more exclusive honors of the château were reserved for the higher aristocrats. The king surrounded his daily routine of rising, eating, and going to bed (known as the *lever, dîner,* and *coucher*) with an infinite series of ceremonial acts, so minute and so formalized that there were, for example, six different entries of persons at the *lever,* and a certain gentleman at a specified moment held the right sleeve of the king's nightshirt as he took it off. The most exalted persons thought themselves the greater for thus waiting on so august a being. With such honors, and by more material favors, many great lords were induced to live habitually at court. Here, under the royal eye, they might

The splendor of Versailles

engage in palace intrigue but were kept away from real political mischief. Versailles had a debilitating effect on the French aristocracy.

For most positions in the government, as distinguished from his personal entourage, Louis XIV preferred to use men whose upper-class status was recent. Such men, unlike hereditary nobles, could aspire to no independent political influence of their own. He never called the Estates General, which in any case no one except some of the nobility wanted. Some of the Provincial Estates, because of local and aristocratic pressures, he allowed to remain functioning. He temporarily destroyed the independence of the parlements, commanding them to accept his orders, as Henry IV had commanded them to accept the Edict of Nantes. He developed a strong system of administrative coordination, centering in a number of councils of state, which he attended in person, and in "intendants" who represented these councils throughout the country. Councilors of state and intendants were generally of bourgeois origin or newly ennobled. Each intendant, within his district, embodied all aspects of the royal government—supervising the flow of taxes and recruiting of soldiers, keeping an eye on the local nobility, dealing with towns and guilds, controlling the more or less hereditary officeholders, policing the marketplaces, relieving famine, watching and often participating in the local law courts. A firm and uniform administration was superimposed upon the heterogeneous mass of the old France. In contrast to England, many local questions were handled by agents of the central government, usually honest and often efficient, but essentially bureaucrats constantly instructed by, and referring back to, their superiors at Versailles.

Administrative tactics of Louis XIV

Economic and Financial Policies: Colbert

To support the reorganized and enlarged army, the panoply of Versailles, and the growing civil administration, the king needed a good deal of money. Finance was always the weak spot in the French monarchy. Methods of collecting taxes were costly and inefficient. Direct taxes passed through the hands of many intermediate officials; indirect taxes were collected by private concessionaries called tax farmers, who made a substantial profit. The state always received far less than what the taxpayers actually paid. But the main weakness arose from an old bargain between the French crown and nobility; the king might raise taxes without consent only if he refrained from taxing the nobles. Only the "unprivileged" classes paid direct taxes, and these came almost to mean the peasants only, since many bourgeois in one way or another obtained exemptions. The system was outrageously unjust in throwing a heavy tax burden on the poor and helpless. Louis XIV was willing enough to tax the nobles but was unwilling to fall under their control, and only toward the close of his reign, under extreme stress of war, was he able, for the first time in French history, to impose direct taxes on the aristocratic elements of the population. This was a step toward equality before the law and toward sound public finance, but so many concessions and exemptions were won by nobles and bourgeois that the reform lost much of its value.

Taxation

Like his predecessors, Louis resorted to all manner of expedients to increase his revenues. He raised the tax rates, always with disappointing results. He devalued the currency. He sold patents of nobility to ambitious bourgeois. He sold government offices, judgeships, and commissions in the army and navy. For both financial and political reasons the king used his sovereign authority to annul the town charters, then sold back reduced rights at a price; this produced a little income but demoralized local government and civic spirit. The need for money arose from the fundamental inability to tax the wealthy. This problem reflected the weakness and limitations of absolutism because the government's

refusal to share its rule with the propertied classes corrupted much of French public life and undermined the political aptitude of the French people.

Louis XIV wished, if only for his own purposes, to make France economically powerful. His great minister Colbert worked for 20 years to do so. Colbert went beyond Richelieu in the application of mercantilism, aiming to make France a self-sufficing economic unit, to expand the export of French goods, and to increase the wealth from which government income was drawn. There was not much that he could do for agriculture, the principal industry of the kingdom, which remained less developed than in England and the Netherlands. But he managed to reduce internal tariffs in a large part of central France, where he set up a tariff union oddly entitled the Five Great Farms (since the remaining tolls were collected by tax farmers); and although vested interests and provincial liberties remained too strong for him to do away with all internal tariffs, the area of the Five Great Farms was in itself one of the largest free-trade areas in Europe, being about the size of England.

The Five Great Farms

For the convenience of business Colbert promulgated a Commercial Code, replacing much of the local customary law with a new model of business practice and regulation. He improved communications by building roads and canals. Working through the guilds, he required the handicraft manufacturers to produce goods of specified kind and quality, believing that foreigners, if assured of quality by the government, would purchase French products. He gave subsidies, tax exemptions, and monopolies to expand the manufacture of silks, tapestries, glassware, and woolens. He helped to found colonies, built up the navy, and established the French East India Company. Export of some goods, notably foodstuffs, was forbidden, for the government wished to keep the populace quiet by holding down the price of bread. Export of other goods, mainly manufactures, was encouraged, partly as a means of bringing money into the country, where it could be funneled into the royal treasury. The growth of the army, and the fact that under Louis XIV the government clothed and equipped the soldiers and hence placed unprecedentedly large orders for uniforms, overcoats, weapons, and ammunition, greatly stimulated the employment of weavers, tailors, and gunsmiths and advanced the commercial capitalism by which such labors were organized. Trade and manufacture thus developed in France under more direct government guidance than in England. They long gave the English an extremely brisk competition. Not until the age of iron and coal did France begin economically to lag.

Colbert's Commercial Code

In general, the system elaborated in the two centuries of Bourbon rule, known in retrospect as the Old Regime, was a society in which groups of many kinds could identify their own special interests with those of the "absolute" monarchy. But it rested on a precarious inconsistency. On the one hand, the royal government, through its intendants and bureaucracy, worked to restrict the privileges of provinces, nobles, and others. On the other hand, it multiplied and protected these and other privileges in its perpetual need for money. The inconsistency was not resolved until the Revolution of 1789, when the principle of equality of rights replaced the regime of privilege.

Thirty thousand workers were employed at one time in the building of the great royal château at Versailles. The seventeenth-century painting (upper) illustrates the complex labor and planning that were required during the process of construction; the lower painting dates from the early eighteenth century, and it shows the activity that surrounded Versailles when the king, government ministers, and nobles were assembled in the vast buildings and gardens. The grandeur and scale of these buildings were designed to symbolize the king's power and to create a sense of awe in the foreign visitors who came to meet Louis XIV or his advisers.

(Réunion des Musées Nationaux/Art Resource, NY; and The Royal Collection © 2000, Her Majesty Queen Elizabeth II)

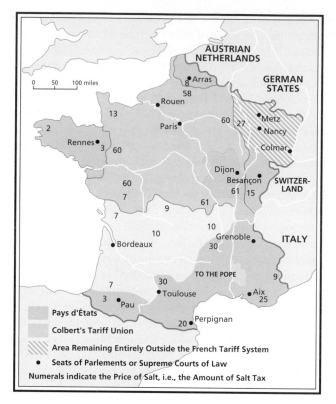

FRANCE FROM THE LAST YEARS OF LOUIS XIV TO THE REVOLUTION OF 1789

The map gives an idea of the diversity of law and administration before the Revolution. Dark areas are "pays d'etats," provinces in which representative bodies ("estates") continued to meet. Cities named are the seats of what the French called parlements (see p. 172). The key indicates Colbert's tariff union, the Five Great Farms. The area marked with hatching remained outside the French tariff system entirely; it continued to trade with the states of the Holy Roman Empire (from which it had been annexed) without interference by the French government. Numerals indicate the price of salt, i.e., the varying burden of the salt tax, in various regions. In general, it will be seen that regions farthest from Paris enjoyed the most "privileges" or "liberties," preserving their legal and judicial identity, Provincial Estates, local tariffs, and a favored position in national taxation.

Religion: The Revocation of the Edict of Nantes, 1685

The consolidation of France under Louis XIV reached its high point in his policies toward religion. For the Catholics, Louis backed the old claims of the Gallican church to enjoy a certain national independence from Rome. He repressed the movement known as Jansenism, a kind of Calvinism within the Catholic church, which persisted for almost two centuries. Jansenists criticized moral laxity in high places as well as the religious influence of the Jesuits, so there was wide support at Versailles when the king moved against all the main centers of Jansenist theology. But it was the Protestants who suffered most in a new wave of religious persecutions.

France, in the early years of Louis XIV's reign, still allowed more religious toleration than any other large state in Europe. The Huguenots had lost their separate political status under Richelieu, but they continued to live in relative security, protected by the Edict of Nantes of 1598. From the beginning, however, toleration had been a royal rather than a popular policy, and under Louis XIV the royal policy changed. The fate of Catholics at the hands of a triumphant Parliament in England suggests that the Protestants in France would have been no better off under more popular institutions.

Bending all else to his will, Louis XIV resented the presence of heretics among his subjects. He considered religious unity necessary to the strength and dignity of his rule. He fell under the influence of certain Catholic advisers, who, not content with the attrition by which some

Louis XIV seeks religious unity

Protestants were turning back to Catholicism in any case, wished to hasten the process to the greater glory of themselves. Systematic conversion of Huguenots was begun. Life for Protestant families was gradually made unbearable. Finally they were literally "dragooned," mounted infantrymen being quartered in Huguenot homes to reinforce the persuasions of missionaries. In 1685 Louis revoked the Edict of Nantes. During the persecutions hundreds of thousands of Protestants left France, migrating to Holland, Germany, and America. Their loss was a severe blow to French economic life, for although Protestants were found in all levels of French society, those of the commercial and industrial classes were the most mobile. With the revocation of the Edict of Nantes France embarked on a century of official intolerance (slowly mitigated in practice), under which Protestants in France were in much the same position as Catholics in the British Isles. The fact that 100 years later, when Protestants were again tolerated, many of them were found to be both commercially prosperous and politically loyal indicates that they fared far better than the Catholic Irish.

All things considered, the reign of Louis XIV brought considerable advantages to the French middle and lower classes. His most bitter critics, with the natural exception of Protestants, were disgruntled nobles such as

Accomplishments of Louis XIV

the duke of Saint-Simon, who thought that he showed too many favors to persons of inferior social rank. Since Protestants were an unpopular minority, his repression of them won much approval. Colbert's system of economic regulation, and perpetuation of the guilds, meant that innovation and private enterprise developed less fully than in England, but France was economically stronger in 1700 than in 1650. Peasants were heavily taxed to pay for Louis XIV's wars, and they suffered through devastating famines after 1690 (also caused partly by the wars). But they did not sink into the serfdom that was rising in eastern Europe. Compared to later times, France was still a hodgepodge of competing jurisdictions, special privilege, and bureaucratic ineptitude. The king was in truth far from "absolute" but France was nevertheless the best organized of the large monarchies on the Continent. Louis XIV, in turning both high and low into dutiful subjects, ended civil war and even advanced the cause of civil equality. For a long time he was generally popular. What finally turned his people against him in his last years was the strain of his incessant wars.

22. THE WARS OF LOUIS XIV: THE PEACE OF UTRECHT, 1713

Before 1700

From the outset of his reign Louis pursued a vigorous foreign policy. The quarrel between the house of France and the house of Habsburg had gone on for more than a century. When

Louis XIV assumed his personal rule in 1661, Spanish territories still faced France on three sides (northeast, east, and south), but so weakened was Spain that this fact was no longer a menace to France so much as a temptation to French expansion. Louis XIV could count on popular support in France, for the dream of a frontier on the Rhine and the Alps was captivating to Frenchmen. He struck first in 1667 by sending a large army into the Spanish Netherlands. He was blocked, as noted earlier, by the Triple Alliance of the Dutch, the English, and the Swedes. With strength renewed by reforms at home, and in alliance now with Charles II of England, he struck again in 1672 (the "Dutch War"), invading the Dutch provinces on the lower Rhine, and this time raising up against him his great adversary and inveterate enemy, the prince of Orange. William III, bringing the Austrian and Spanish Habsburgs, Brandenburg, and Denmark into alliance with the Dutch Republic, forced Louis to sign the treaty of Nimwegen in 1678. The French gave up their ambitions against Holland but took from Spain the rich province of Franche-Comté, which outflanked Alsace on the south and brought French power to the borders of Switzerland (see map, p. 147).

French incursions into the Holy Roman Empire

In the very next year, Louis further infiltrated the dissolving frontier of the Holy Roman Empire, this time in Lorraine and Alsace. By the Peace of Westphalia the French king had rights in this region, but the terms of that treaty were so ambiguous, and the local feudal law so confusing, that claims could be made in contrary directions. French troops thereupon moved in. In 1681 French troops occupied the city of Strasbourg, which, as a free city of the Holy Roman Empire, regarded itself as an independent little republic. A protest went up throughout Germany against this undeclared invasion. But Germany was not a political unity. Since 1648 each German state conducted its own foreign policy, and at this very moment, in 1681, Louis XIV had an ally in the Elector of Brandenburg (forerunner of the kings of Prussia). The diet of the Holy Roman Empire was divided between an anti-French and a pro-French party. The emperor, Leopold I, was distracted by developments in the East. The Hungarians, incited and financed by Louis XIV, were again rebelling against the Habsburgs. They appealed to the Turks, and the Turks in 1683 moved up the Danube and besieged Vienna. Louis XIV, if he did not on this occasion positively assist the Turks, ostentatiously declined to join the proposed crusade against them.

The emperor, with Polish assistance, succeeded in getting the Turkish army out of Austria. Returning to western problems and observing the western border of the Empire crumbling, Franche-Comté already lost, the Spanish Netherlands threatened, and Lorraine and Alsace absorbed bit by bit, the Emperor Leopold gathered the Catholic powers into a combination against the French. The Protestant states at the same time, aroused by the French revocation of the Edict of Nantes in 1685 and by Huguenot émigrés who called down the wrath of God on the perfidious Sun King, began to ally the more readily with William of Orange. Catholic and Protestant enemies of Louis XIV came together in 1686 in the League of Augsburg, which comprised the Holy Roman Emperor, the kings of Spain and of Sweden, the electors of Bavaria, Saxony, and the Palatinate, and the Dutch Republic. In 1686 the king of England was still a protégé of France, but three years later, when William became king in England, that country too joined the League.

The War of the League of Augsburg

The War of the League of Augsburg broke out in 1688. The French armies won battles but could not drive so many enemies from the field. The French navy could not overpower the combined fleets of the Dutch and English. Louis XIV found himself badly strained (it was at this time that he first imposed direct taxes on the French nobles) and finally made peace at Ryswick in the Netherlands in 1697, leaving matters about where they had been when the war began.

In all the warring and negotiating the question had not been merely the fate of this or that piece of territory, nor even the French thrust to the east, but the eventual disposition of the whole empire of Spain. The Spanish king, Charles II, prematurely senile, momentarily expected to die, yet lived on year after year. He was still alive at the time of the Peace of Ryswick. The greatest diplomatic issue of the day was still unsettled.

The War of the Spanish Succession

The War of the Spanish Succession lasted 11 years, from 1702 to 1713. It was less destructive than the Thirty Years' War, for armies were now supplied in more orderly fashion, subject to more orderly discipline and command, and could be stopped from fighting at the will of their governments. Except for the effects of civil war in Spain and of deadly famines in France, the civilian populations were generally spared from violence and destruction. In this respect the war foreshadowed the typical warfare of the eighteenth century, fought by professional armies rather than by whole peoples. Among wars of the largest scale, the War of the Spanish Succession was the first in which religion counted for little, the first in which commerce and sea power were the principal stakes, and the first in which English money was liberally used in Continental politics. It was also the first that can be called a "world war," because it involved the overseas world together with the leading powers of Europe. Wars within Europe were becoming linked to the global competition for colonies and trade.

The struggle had long been foreseen. The two main aspirants to the Spanish inheritance were the king of France and the Holy Roman Emperor. Each had married a sister of the perpetually moribund Charles II, and each could hope to place a younger member of his family on the throne of Spain. During the last decades of the seventeenth century the powers had made various treaties agreeing to "partition" the Spanish possessions. The idea was, by dividing the Spanish heritage between the two claimants, to preserve the balance of power in Europe. But when Charles II finally died in 1700, it was found that he had made a will, which stipulated that the empire of Spain should be kept intact, that all Spanish territories throughout the world should go to the grandson of Louis XIV, and that if Louis XIV refused to accept in the name of his 17-year-old grandson, the entire inheritance should pass to the son of the Habsburg emperor in Vienna. Louis XIV decided to accept. With Bourbons reigning in Versailles and Madrid, even if the two thrones were never united, French influence would run from Belgium to the Straits of Gibraltar, and from Milan to Mexico and Manila. At Versailles the word went out: "The Pyrenees exist no longer."

"The Pyrenees exist no longer"

Never, at least in almost two centuries, had the political balance within Europe been so threatened. Never had the other states faced such a prospect of relegation to the sidelines. William III acted at once; he gathered the stunned or hesitant diplomats into the last of his coalitions, the Grand Alliance of 1701. He died the next year, before hostilities began, and with Louis XIV at the seeming apex of his grandeur, but he had in fact launched the engine that was to crush the Sun King. The Grand Alliance included England, Holland, and the Austrian emperor, supported by Brandenburg and eventually by Portugal and the Italian duchy of Savoy. Louis XIV could count on Spain, which was generally loyal to the late king's will. Otherwise his only ally was Bavaria, whose rivalry with Austria made it a habitual satellite of France. The Bavarian alliance gave the French armies an advanced position toward Vienna and

Threats to political balance

maintained that internal division within Germany which was fundamental to the politics of the time, and of a long time to come.

The war was long, mainly because each side no sooner gained a temporary advantage than it raised its demands on the other. The English, though they sent relatively few troops to the Continent, produced in John Churchill, Duke of Marlborough, a preeminent military commander for the Allied forces. The Austrians were led by Prince Eugene of Savoy. The Allies won notable battles at Blenheim in Bavaria (1704), and at Ramillies (1706), Oudenarde (1708), and Malplaquet (1709) in the Spanish Netherlands. The French were routed; Louis XIV asked for peace but would not agree to it because the Allied terms were so enormous. Louis fought to hold the two crowns, to conquer Belgium, to get French merchants into Spanish America, and at the worst in self-defense. After minor successes in 1710 he again insisted on controlling the crown of Spain. The Spanish fought to uphold the will of the deceased king, the unity of the Spanish possessions, and even the integrity of Spain itself—for the English moved in at Gibraltar and made a menacing treaty with Portugal. Meanwhile, the Austrians landed at Barcelona and invaded Catalonia, which (as in 1640) again rose in rebellion, recognizing the Austrian claimant, so that all Spain fell into civil war.

Motives of the warring states

The Austrians fought to keep Spain in the Habsburg family, to crush Bavaria, and to carry Austrian influence across the Alps into Italy. The Dutch fought as always for their security, to keep the French out of Belgium, and to control access to the river Scheldt. The English fought for these same reasons and also to keep the French-supported Catholic Stuarts out of England and preserve the Revolution of 1688. It was to be expected that the Stuarts, if they returned, would ruin the Bank of England and repudiate the national debt. Both maritime powers, England and Holland, fought to keep French merchants out of Spanish America and to advance their own commercial position in America and the Mediterranean. These being the war aims, the Whigs were the implacable war party in England, the vaguely pro-Stuart and anticommercial Tories being quite willing to make peace at an early date. As for the minor allies, Brandenburg and Savoy, their rulers had simply entered the alliance to gain such advantages as might turn up.

The Peace of Utrecht

The partition of Spain's holdings

Peace was finally made at the treaties of Utrecht and Rastadt of 1713 and 1714. The treaty of Utrecht, with its allied instruments, in fact partitioned the world of Spain. But it did not divide it between the two legal claimants only. The British remained at Gibraltar, to the great irritation of the Spaniards, and likewise annexed the island of Minorca. The Duke of Savoy eventually gained the former Spanish island of Sardinia in return for his contribution to the Allied cause. The rest of the Spanish Mediterranean holdings—Milan, Naples, and Sicily —passed to the Austrian Habsburgs, as did the Spanish Netherlands (or Belgium), subsequently referred to as the Austrian Netherlands. In Spain itself, shorn of its European possessions but retaining America, the grandson of Louis XIV was confirmed as king (Philip V of Spain), on the understanding that the French and Spanish thrones should never be inherited by the same person. The Bourbons reigned in Spain, with interruptions, from Philip V to the republican revolution of 1931. French influence was strong in the eighteenth century, for a good many French courtiers, advisers, administrators, and businessmen crossed the Pyrenees with Philip V. They helped somewhat to revive the Spanish

The battle of Blenheim, fought in Bavaria in 1704, was a great victory for the English and the Allied forces that joined to oppose the French in the War of the Spanish Succession. Blenheim brought fame and honors to the British commander, John Churchill, Duke of Marlborough; for the French, it was the first in a series of devastating military defeats that steadily weakened the power of Louis XIV.
(Fotomas Index/Bridgeman Art Library)

monarchy by applying the methods of Louis XIV, and they passed a swelling volume of French manufactures through Seville into Spanish America.

The old objective of William III, to prevent domination by France, was realized at last. The war itself was the main cause of French loss of strength. It produced poverty, misery, and depopulation, and it exposed Louis XIV to severe criticism at home. Recurring famines and tax increases provoked peasant uprisings, which were brutally repressed. Dissatisfaction with the war led also to a revival of aristocratic and parliamentary opposition. By the peace treaties the French abandoned, for the time being, their efforts to conquer Belgium. They ceased to recognize the Stuart pretender as king of Great Britain. They surrendered to the British two of their colonies, Newfoundland and Nova Scotia (called Acadia), and recognized British sovereignty in the disputed American Northwest, known as the Hudson Bay territory. But the French were only checked, not downed. They retained the conquests of Louis XIV in

Consequences of the war for France

PEASANT FAMILY IN A ROOM
by Louis Le Nain (French, 1593–1648)
Although Le Nain portrayed a family in the early half of the seventeenth century, the people in this painting do not differ much from the peasants who later suffered through wars, famines, and tax increases in the last decades of the long reign of Louis XIV.
(Erich Lessing/Art Resource, NY)

Alsace and the Franche-Comté. Their influence was strong in Spain. Their deeper strength and capacity for recovery were soon evident in renewed economic expansion. Their language and civilization continued to spread throughout Europe.

The Dutch received guarantees of their security. They were granted the right to garrison the "Dutch Barrier," a string of forts in Belgium on the side toward France. But the Dutch, strained by the war and outdistanced by England, never again played a primary role in European political affairs. Two other small states ascended over the diplomatic horizon, Savoy (or Piedmont) and Brandenburg. The rulers of both, for having sided with the victors, were recognized as "kings" by the treaty of Utrecht. Savoy came to be known as "Sardinia," and Brandenburg as "Prussia." More is said of Prussia in the next chapter.

Britain becomes a great power

The greatest winners were the British. Great Britain made its appearance as a great power. Union of England and Scotland had taken place during the war. Based at Gibraltar and Minorca, Britain was now a power in the Mediterranean. Belgium, the "pistol pointed at the heart of England," was in the innocuous hands of the Austrians. The British added to their American holdings, but far more valuable than Newfoundland and Nova Scotia was the *asiento* extorted from Spain. The *asiento* granted the lucrative privilege (which the French had sought) of providing Spanish America with African slaves. Much of the wealth of Bristol and Liverpool

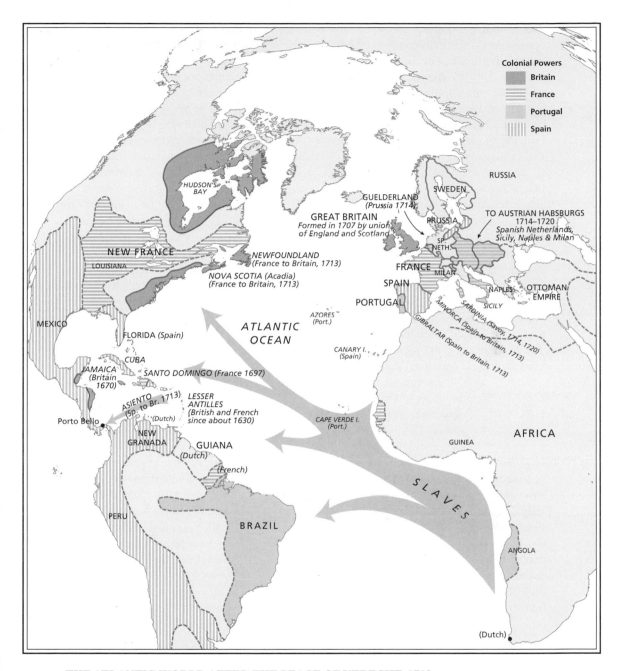

THE ATLANTIC WORLD AFTER THE PEACE OF UTRECHT, 1713

The map shows the partitioning of the Spanish empire and the rise of the British. Spain and its American possessions went to the Bourbon Philip V; the European possessions of Spain—the Netherlands, Milan, Naples and Sicily—went to the Austrian Habsburgs. Britain meanwhile was strengthened by the union of England and Scotland, the acquisition of Minorca, Gibraltar, and the commercial privilege of the "asiento" from Spain, and of Newfoundland and Nova Scotia from France.

in the following decades was to be built upon the slave trade. The *asiento,* by permitting one shipload of British goods to be brought each year to Porto Bello in Panama, also provided opportunities for illicit trade in nonhuman cargoes.

The Spanish empire was pried open, and British merchants entered on an era of wholesale smuggling into Spanish America, competing strenuously with the French, who because of their favored position in Spain were usually able to go through more legal channels. Moreover, the British, by defeating France, assured themselves of a line of Protestant kings and of the maintenance of constitutional and parliamentary government. The ratification of the Peace of Utrecht actually marked a further step in the evolution of English constitutional history. The Whigs, who were the main supporters of the war with France, thought the treaty insufficiently favorable to England. The Tories, pledged to peace, had won the House of Commons in 1710, but the Whigs continued to control the House of Lords. Queen Anne, at the request of Tory leaders and in the interests of peace, raised 12 Tory commoners to the peerage in order to create a Tory majority in the Lords and hence to obtain ratification of the treaty. This established itself as a precedent; it became an unwritten article of the British constitution that when the Lords blocked the Commons on an important issue, the monarch could create enough new lords to make a new majority in that House. After 1713, the Lords never again allowed themselves to be swamped by newcomers and thus acceded in all future disputes to the will of the Commons. The landed aristocracy and their merchant allies could now govern as they saw fit. The result was a rapid increase of wealth in England, precipitating within a few generations a veritable Industrial Revolution.

Confirmation of the European system

Except for the addition of England, the same powers were parties to the treaty of Utrecht in 1713 as to the Peace of Westphalia in 1648, and they now confirmed the system of international relations established by Westphalia. The powers accepted each other as members of the European system; recognized each other as sovereign states connected only by free negotiation, war, and treaty; and adjusted their differences through rather facile exchanges of territory, made in the interests of a balance of power, and without regard to the nationality or presumed wishes of the peoples affected. With Germany still in its "feudal chaos," Italy divided into minor states or controlled by foreign kings, and Spain subordinated to France, the treaty of Utrecht left France and Great Britain as the two most vigorous imperial powers of Europe. These countries soon became the two principal carriers and exporters of the European civilization that would spread its institutions and ideas throughout the modern world. In the next chapter we look at how the societies of central and eastern Europe, developed along lines of their own, even when they were strongly influenced by the growing power and wealth of the western European states.

For interactive exercises, glossary, chronologies, and more, go to the *Online Learning Center* at **www.mhhe.com/palmer10.**

Chapter 5

THE TRANSFORMATION OF EASTERN EUROPE, 1648–1740

In Eastern Europe, in the century after the Peace of Westphalia of 1648, it became apparent that political systems that failed to become more "modern" might be in danger of going out of existence. In the mid–seventeenth century most parts of Eastern Europe belonged to one or another of three old-fashioned political organizations—the Holy Roman Empire, the Republic of Poland, and the empire of the Ottoman Turks (see maps, pp. 193, 194). All three were loose, decentralized, and increasingly ineffective. They were superseded by three new and stronger powers—Prussia, Austria, and Russia. These three, by overrunning the intermediate ground of Poland, came to adjoin one another and cover all Eastern Europe except the Balkans. It was in this same period that Russia expanded territorially, adopted some of the technical and administrative apparatus of western Europe, and became an active participant in European affairs.

East and West are of course relative terms. For the Russians Germany and even Poland were "western." But for Europe as a whole a significant though indefinite social and economic line ran along the Elbe and the Bohemian Mountains to the head of the Adriatic Sea. East of this line towns were fewer than in the West, human labor was less productive, and the middle classes were less strong. Above all, the peasants were governed by their landlords. From the sixteenth to the eighteenth century, in eastern Europe in contrast to what happened in the West, the peasant mass increasingly lost its freedom. The commercial revolution and widening of the market created a strong merchant class in western Europe and tended to turn working people into a legally free and mobile labor force. In eastern Europe these changes strengthened the great landlords who produced for export and who secured their labor force by the institutions of serfdom and "hereditary subjection." The main social unit was the agricultural estate, which the lord exploited with uncompensated compulsory labor (or *robot*) furnished by his people, who could neither migrate, marry, nor learn a trade except as he permitted, and who, until the eighteenth

Chapter emblem: Russian workers building the new city of St. Petersburg during the reign of Tsar Peter I (1689–1725). (Tass/Sovfoto)

century, had no legal protector or court of appeal other than himself. In the East, therefore, the landlords were exceedingly powerful. They were the only significant political class. And the three new states that grew up—Prussia, Austria, Russia—were alike in being landlord states.

✣ 23.   THREE AGING EMPIRES

In 1648 the whole mainland of Europe from the French border almost to Moscow was occupied by the three large and loosely built structures that have been mentioned—the Holy Roman Empire, the Republic of Poland, and the empire of the Ottoman Turks. The Turkish power reached to about 50 miles from Vienna, and it extended over what is now Romania and over the Tartars on the north shore of the Black Sea. Even so, its European holdings were but a projection from the main mass of the Ottoman Empire in Asia and Africa. Poland extended from roughly 100 miles east of Berlin to a hundred miles west of Moscow and virtually from "sea to sea" in the old phrase of its patriots, from the Baltic around Riga almost to the Black Sea coast. The Holy Roman Empire extended from Poland and Hungary to the North Sea.

  These three empires were by no means alike. The Holy Roman Empire bore some of the oldest traditions of Christendom. Poland too had old connections with western Europe and Christian religious institutions. Turkey was a Muslim power, closely connected to the Islamic civilization of the Middle East and filled with peoples who generally lived outside European cultural traditions (despite a long history of Mediterranean trade and commerce). Yet in some ways the three resembled each other. In all of them central authority had become weak, consisting largely of understandings between a nominal head and outlying dignitaries or potentates. All lacked efficient systems of administration and government. All were being made obsolete by newer centralizing states of which France was the leading example. All, but especially Poland and Turkey, were made up of diverse ethnic or language groups. The whole immense area was therefore politically weak. It was malleable in the hands of kings or ruling elites who might become a little stronger than their neighbors. We must try to see in what this weakness consisted, and how newer, stronger state forms were created.

Weaknesses of the empires

The Holy Roman Empire after 1648

With the Holy Roman Empire the reader is already familiar. It was an empire, especially after the Peace of Westphalia, with next to no army, revenues, or working organs of a central government. Voltaire called it neither holy, Roman, nor an empire. Created in the Middle Ages, it was Roman in that it was believed to continue the imperial sway of the Rome of antiquity, and it was holy in being the secular counterpart to the spiritual empire of the pope. It had been ruined by the Reformation, which left the Germans divided almost evenly between Protestant and Catholic, with each side thereafter demanding special safeguards against the other. The Empire continued, however, to be universal in principle, having no relation to nationality and theoretically being a form of government suitable to all peoples, although it had never lived up to this theoretical claim and had shown no expansionist tendency since the Middle Ages. In actuality, the Empire was roughly coterminous with the German states and the region of the German language, except that it excluded after 1648 the Dutch and Swiss, who no longer considered themselves German; and it likewise excluded those Germans who since the fourteenth century had settled along the eastern shores of the Baltic.

Large parts of the Empire had suffered repeatedly from the Thirty Years' War. Yet the war, and the peace terms that followed it, only accentuated a situation that had long been unfavorable. Postwar revival was difficult; the breakup of commercial connections and the wartime losses of savings and capital were hard to overcome. Germany fell increasingly out

Effects of the Thirty Years' War

of step with the economic expansion and cultural changes in western Europe. The burgher class, its ambitions blocked, lost much of its old vitality. No overseas colonies could be founded, for want of strong enough government backing, as was shown when a colonial venture of Brandenburg came to nothing. There was no stock exchange in Germany until one was established at Vienna in 1771, half a century after those of London, Paris, and Amsterdam. Laws, tariffs, tolls, and coinage were more diverse than in France. Even the calendar varied. It varied, indeed, throughout Europe as a whole, since Protestant states long declined to accept the corrected calendar issued by Pope Gregory XIII in 1582; in parts of divided Germany the holidays, the date of the month, and the day of the week changed every few miles. The arts and letters, flourishing in western Europe as never before, were at a low ebb in Germany in the seventeenth century. In science the Germans during and after the Thirty Years' War accomplished less than the English, Dutch, French, or Italians, despite the great mathematician and philosopher Leibniz, one of the great minds of the age. Only in music, as in the work of the Bach family, did the Germans at this time excel. But music was not then much heard beyond the place of its origin. Germany for the rest of the world was a byway in the higher civilization of Europe.

After the Thirty Years' War each German state had sovereign rights. These "states" numbered some 300 or 2,000, depending on how they were counted. The higher figure included the "knights of the Empire," found in south Germany and the Rhineland. They were persons who acknowledged no overlordship except that of the emperor himself. The knights had tiny estates of their own, averaging not over 100 acres apiece, consisting of a castle and a manor or two, enclosed by the territory of a larger state but not forming a part of it. But even without the knights there were about 300 states capable of some independence of action—free cities, abbots without subjects, archbishops and bishops ruling with temporal power, landgraves, margraves and dukes, and one king, the king of Bohemia.

All these states were intent on preserving what were called the "Germanic liberties." They were gladly assisted by outside powers, notably but not exclusively France. The Germanic liberties meant freedom of the member

The "Germanic liberties"

states from control by emperor or Empire. The rulers of the most important states within the empire elected the emperor (there were nine electors by the end of the seventeenth century), and they always required the successful candidate to accept certain "capitulations," in which he promised to safeguard all the privileges and immunities of the states. The Habsburgs, though consistently elected after 1438, had none of the advantages of hereditary rulers, each having to bargain away in turn any gains made by his predecessor. The elective principle meant that imperial power could not be accumulated and transmitted from one generation to the next. It opened the doors to foreign intrigue, since the electors were willing to consider whichever candidate would promise them most. The French repeatedly supported a rival candidate to the Habsburgs. After 1648 they had supporters in the electoral college, Bavaria and Cologne being the most consistently pro-French. In 1742 the French obtained the elevation of their Bavarian ally to the imperial throne. The office of emperor became a political football for Germans and non-Germans.

Nor would the German states, after the Thirty Years' War, allow any authority to the imperial diet. The diet possessed the power to raise troops and taxes for the whole Empire, but the power remained unused because the various states feared that any such action would diminish their own authority and independence. Meanwhile, the states which insisted with such obstinacy on their liberties from the Empire gave few liberties to their subjects. The free cities were closed oligarchies, as indeed were most cities in other countries, but in Germany the burgher oligarchs of the free cities were virtually sovereign also. Most of the other states, large or small, developed in the direction of absolutism. Absolutism was checked for Germany as a whole, only to reappear in miniature in hundreds of different places. Each ruler thought himself a little Louis XIV, each court a small Versailles. Subjects became attached by ties of sentiment to their rulers, who almost always lived in the neighborhood and could be readily seen by passers-by. People liked the little courts, the little armies, the gossipy politics, and the familiar officials of their tiny states; and despite all its flaws, the Empire had the merit of holding this conglomeration of states in a lawful relation to one another. It was a kind of miniature league of nations. For a century and a half after the Peace of Westphalia small states existed alongside larger ones, or often totally enclosed within them, without serious fear for their security and without losing their independence.

Yet there were many ambitious rulers in Germany after the Peace of Westphalia. They had won recognition of their sovereignty in 1648. They were busily building absolutist monarchies. They aspired also to extend their dominions and cut a greater figure in the world. There were other ways of doing this than by devouring their smaller neighbors outright. One was by marriage and inheritance. The Empire in this respect was a paradise for fortune hunters; the variety of possible marriages was enormous because of the great number of ruling families. Another outlet for ambition lay in the high politics of the Empire. The Wittelsbach family, which ruled in Bavaria, managed to win an electorate in the Thirty Years' War; they consistently placed members of the family as archbishop of Cologne, and in ecclesiastical posts elsewhere in the Rhineland. With the interest thus built up, they were able to sell their influence to France, which in turn backed them against the Habsburgs. The Guelph family, ruling in Hanover, schemed for years to obtain an electorate, which they finally extorted from the emperor in 1692; in 1714 they inherited the throne of Great Britain with King George I, preferred by the British as Protestants to their Catholic Stuart cousins. The Hohenzollerns, electors of Brandenburg, inherited territories as far apart as the Rhine and the Vistula.

The half-century after the Peace of Westphalia was thus a highly critical period in central Europe. The situation in Germany was fluid. No one could tell which, if any, of the half-dozen chief German states would emerge in the lead. Nothing was crystallized; anything

CENTRAL AND EASTERN EUROPE, 1660–1795

This complex area is shown in simplified form on p. 194. The upper panel of the map indicates boundaries as of 1660; the lower panel those of 1795. Both panels show the border between the eastern and western agrarian zones, running from the mouth of the Elbe River into central Germany and down to Trieste. East of this line, from the sixteenth to the eighteenth centuries, the mass of people sank into a kind of serfdom in which they rendered forced labor to their lords on large farms. West of the line the peasants owed little or no forced labor and tilled small farms which they owned or rented. This line marks a somewhat imprecise but significant social boundary that would also have an important influence on the political and economic history of modern Europe.

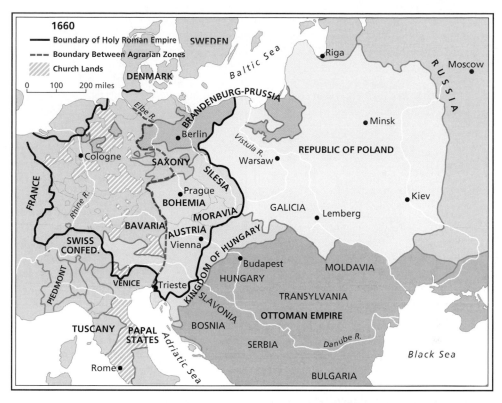

1660
— Boundary of Holy Roman Empire
--- Boundary Between Agrarian Zones
▨ Church Lands
0   100   200 miles

SWEDEN
Baltic Sea
DENMARK
Riga
RUSSIA
Moscow
BRANDENBURG-PRUSSIA
Elbe R.
Berlin
Minsk
Vistula R.
REPUBLIC OF POLAND
Cologne
SAXONY
SILESIA
Warsaw
FRANCE
Rhine R.
Prague
BOHEMIA
MORAVIA
GALICIA
Kiev
Lemberg
BAVARIA
AUSTRIA
Vienna
KINGDOM OF HUNGARY
SWISS CONFED.
VENICE
Trieste
SLAVONIA
Budapest
HUNGARY
MOLDAVIA
TUSCANY
PAPAL STATES
Adriatic Sea
BOSNIA
TRANSYLVANIA
OTTOMAN EMPIRE
Rome
SERBIA
Danube R.
Black Sea
BULGARIA

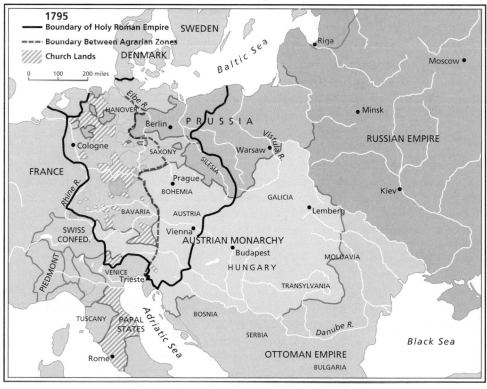

1795
— Boundary of Holy Roman Empire
--- Boundary Between Agrarian Zones
▨ Church Lands
0   100   200 miles

SWEDEN
DENMARK
Baltic Sea
Riga
Moscow
HANOVER
Elbe R.
Berlin
PRUSSIA
Minsk
Cologne
SAXONY
Vistula R.
RUSSIAN EMPIRE
FRANCE
Warsaw
SILESIA
Rhine R.
Prague
BOHEMIA
GALICIA
Kiev
Lemberg
BAVARIA
AUSTRIA
SWISS CONFED.
Vienna
AUSTRIAN MONARCHY
VENICE
Budapest
Trieste
HUNGARY
MOLDAVIA
PIEDMONT
TRANSYLVANIA
TUSCANY
PAPAL STATES
Adriatic Sea
BOSNIA
SERBIA
Danube R.
Black Sea
Rome
OTTOMAN EMPIRE
BULGARIA

AGING EMPIRES AND NEW POWERS

The left panel shows the "three aging empires" which occupied much of central and eastern Europe in the seventeenth century. Though maintaining themselves with growing difficulty under modern conditions, the Polish Republic lasted until 1795, the Holy Roman Empire until 1806, the Ottoman Empire until 1923. Meanwhile, beginning in the seventeenth century, the political leadership in this area was assumed by three states of more modern type, organized around the institutions of monarchy, the standing army, and the professional bureaucracy or civil service—the reorganized Austrian Empire of the Habsburgs, the Hohenzollern kingdom of Prussia, and the Russian Empire of the Romanovs. These are shown in the right panel. All three figured prominently in the affairs of Europe for over 200 years; all perished in the First World War, 1914–1918.

Austria and Prussia

might happen. Two states definitely came forward after 1700, built by the skill and persistence of their rulers—Austria and Prussia. It is a curious and revealing fact that neither really had a name of its own. They were for a long time known most commonly as "houses"—the house of Austria or Habsburg and the house of Brandenburg or Hohenzollern. Each house put together a certain combination of territories. Each would have been as willing to possess any other combination had the course of events been different. By extension of meaning, one came to be called "Austria," which for centuries had been simply an archduchy on the upper Danube. The other, "Prussia," for centuries had meant only a certain stretch of the Baltic coast. To these two states we shall shortly turn.

The Republic of Poland about 1650

Running almost 1,000 miles eastward from the Holy Roman Empire in the middle of the seventeenth century lay the vast tract of the Republic of Poland, called a republic because its king was elected and because the political classes took pride in their constitutional liberties. Its vast size was one cause of its internal peculiarities. No administrative system could have kept up with the expansion of its frontiers, so that a large degree of freedom had always been left to outlying lords. In addition, the population was heterogeneous.

The Polish state was a far more recent and less substantial creation than the Holy Roman Empire. It was made up of two main parts, Poland proper (the Kingdom of Poland) in the west and the Grand Duchy of Lithuania in the east. They had been joined by a union of their crowns (see maps, pp. 193, 194). Only in the west was there a mass of Polish population. The Duchy of Prussia, a fief of the Polish crown, was peopled mainly by Germans. Further east a Byelorussian and Ukrainian peasantry was subject to a scattering of Polish and Lithuanian landlords. Even in Poland itself the town population was not generally Polish, being largely Germans and Jews. The latter spoke Yiddish, derived from German, and were very numerous because a king of Poland in the later Middle Ages had welcomed Jewish refugees fleeing from anti-Jewish violence in Germany. They lived in separate communities with their own law, language, and religion, forming large islands of Orthodox Jewish life in the Gentile ocean. The Germans too held aloof, resisting assimilation to their less-advanced surroundings. An unsurpassable barrier thus existed between town and country. There was no national middle class. The official and political language was Latin. Roman Catholicism was the leading religion.

Poland and Lithuania

Poland is interesting as the region in which the landed aristocracy won over all other groups in the country, neither allowing the consolidation of the state on absolutist lines, nor yet creating an effective constitutional or parliamentary government. The Polish aristocracy, or *szlachta,* made up some eight percent of the population, a far higher proportion than the aristocracy of any country of western Europe. On this ground the old Polish kingdom has sometimes been considered, especially by later Polish nationalists, as the possessor of an early form of democracy. The aristocracy were sticklers for their liberties, called the "Polish liberties," which resembled the German liberties in that they consisted largely of a fierce suspicion of central authority and were a perpetual invitation to foreign interference. As in the Holy Roman Empire, the monarchy was elective, and the king upon election had to accept certain contractual agreements, which, like the German "capitulations," prevented the accumulation of authority by the crown. The Poles were too politically divided to accept one of their own number as king, so from 1572 to the extinction of Poland over two centuries later there were only two native Polish kings who reigned for any length of time. One of these kings was the national hero John Sobieski, who led a decisive campaign against the Turks in the 1680s.

As in Germany, the central diet was ineffective and the centers of political action were local. The aristocracy met in 50 or 60 regional diets, turbulent assemblages of warlike gentry, in which the great lords used the lesser lords for their own purposes. The central diet, from which the towns were excluded, was a periodic meeting of emissaries, under binding instructions from the regional diets. It came to be recognized, as one of the liberties of the country, that the central diet could take no action to which any member objected. Any member, by stating his unalterable opposition, could oblige a diet to disband. This was the famous *liberum veto,* the free veto, and to use it to break up a diet was called "exploding" the diet. The first diet was exploded in 1652. Of 55 diets held from that year to 1764, 48 were exploded.

Weakness of central government

Government became a fiasco. The monopoly of law and force, characteristic of the modern state, failed to develop in Poland. The king of Poland had practically no army, no law courts, no officials, and no income. The nobility paid no taxes. By 1750 the revenues of the king of Poland were about one-thirteenth those of the tsar of Russia and one seventy-fifth those of the king of France. Armed force was in the hands of a dozen or so aristocratic leaders, who also conducted their individual foreign policies, pursuing their own adventures against the Turks, or bringing in Russians, French, or Swedes to help them against other Poles. The landlords became local monarchs on their manorial estates. The mass of the rural population fell deeper into a serfdom scarcely different from slavery, bound to compulsory labor on estates resembling plantations, with police and disciplinary powers in the hands of the lords and with no outside legal or administrative system to set the limits of exploitation.

The huge expanse comprised under the name of Poland was, in short, a power vacuum; and as more powerful centers developed, notably around Berlin and

Pressures on Poland

Moscow, the push against the Polish frontiers became steadily stronger. It was facilitated by the Poles themselves. As early as 1660 the East Prussian fief became independent of the Polish crown. As early as 1667 the Muscovites reconquered Smolensk and Kiev. Already there was confidential talk of partitioning Poland, which, however, was deferred for a century. Much of the history of the modern world would have been different had the Poland of the seventeenth century held together. There would have been no kingdom of Prussia and no Prussian influence in Germany; nor would Russia have become the chief Slavic power or reached so far into central Europe.

The Ottoman Empire about 1650

The Ottoman state, the third of the three empires which together spread over so much of Europe, was larger than either of the others, and in the seventeenth century it was more solidly organized and powerful. In 1529 the Turks had attacked Vienna and seemed about to burst into Germany. To most people in the Christian world the Turks were a mystery as well as a terror. They had formerly been among the rougher of the Muslim peoples, who had migrated from central Asia only a few centuries before and owed most of their higher civilization to the Arabs and the Persians. Their dominions extended, about 1650, from the Hungarian plain and the south Russian steppes as far as Algeria, the upper Nile, and the Persian Gulf. The empire was based to a large degree on military proficiency.

Long before Europe the Turks had a standing army, of which the janissaries were the main striking force. The janissaries were originally recruited from Christian children taken from their families in early childhood, brought up as Muslims, reared in military surroundings, and forbidden to marry; without background or ties, interests, or ambition outside the military organization to which they belonged, they were ideal fighting material in the hands of political leaders. The Turkish forces were long as well equipped as the Christian, being especially strong in heavy artillery. But by the mid-seventeenth century they were falling behind. They had changed little, or for the worse, since the days of Suleiman the Magnificent a century before, whereas in the better-organized Christian states discipline and military administration had been improved, and firearms, land mines, and siegecraft had become more effective.

The Turks cared little about assimilating subject peoples to their language or institutions. Local populations within the empire thus retained most of their cultural traditions and autonomy. Law was religious law derived from the Qur'an. Law courts and judges were hard to distinguish from religious authorities, for there was no separation between religious and secular spheres. The sultan was also the caliph, the commander of the faithful; while on the one hand there was no clergy in the European sense, on the other hand religious influences affected all aspects of life. The Turks, for the most part, applied the Muslim law only to Muslims; and the overall administration of imperial policies was controlled by a powerful government official called the grand vizier.

COUNT STANISLAS POTOCKI
by Jacques-Louis David (French, 1748–1825)

This portrait of a well-known eighteenth-century Polish nobleman—painted by David in 1781—expresses the sense of independent grandeur that characterized the Polish aristocracy for several centuries in the early modern era.

(Erich Lessing/Art Resource, NY)

Tolerance of non-Muslim subjects
The Ottoman government left its non-Muslim subjects to settle their own affairs in their own way, not according to nationality, which was generally indistinguishable, but according to religious groupings. The Greek Orthodox church, to which most Christians in the empire belonged, thus became an almost autonomous intermediary between the sultan and a large fraction of its subjects. Armenian Christians and Jews formed other separate bodies. Except in the western Balkans (Albania and Bosnia) there was no general conversion of Christians to Islam during the Turkish rule, although there were many individual cases of Christians turning Muslim to obtain the privileges of the ruling faith. North of the Danube the Christian princes of Transylvania, Wallachia, and Moldavia (later combined into modern Romania) continued to rule over Christian subjects. They were kept in office for that purpose by the sultan, to whom they paid tribute. In general, since their subjects were more profitable to them as Christians, the Turks were not eager to proselytize for Islam.

The Ottoman Empire was therefore a relatively tolerant empire, far more so than the states of Europe. Christians in the Turkish empire fared better than Muslims would have fared in Christendom or than the Moors had in fact fared in Spain. Christians were less disturbed in Turkey than were Protestants in France, after 1685, or Catholics in Ireland. The empire was tolerant because it was composite, an aggregation of peoples, religions, and laws, having no drive, as did the Western states, toward internal unity and complete legal sovereignty. The same tolerance was evident in the attitude toward foreign merchants, who were active throughout most of the empire.

The king of France had had treaty arrangements with Turkey since 1535, and many traders from Marseilles had spread over the port towns of the Middle East. They were exempted by treaty from the laws of the Ottoman Empire and were liable to trial only by their own judges, who though residing in Turkey were appointed by the king of France. They were free to exercise their Roman Catholic religion, and if disputes with Muslims arose, they appeared in special courts where the word of an infidel received equal/weight with that of a follower of the prophet. Similar rights in Turkey were obtained by other European states. Thus began "extraterritorial" privileges of the kind obtained by Europeans in later centuries in China and elsewhere, wherever the local laws were regarded as "backward," or hostile to Europeans. To the Turks of the seventeenth century there was nothing exceptional about such arrangements. Only much later, under Western influence, did the Turks come to resent these "capitulations" as impairments of their own sovereignty.

"Extraterritorial" privileges

Yet the Turkish rule was oppressive, and the "terrible Turk" was with reason the nightmare of eastern Europe. Ottoman rule was oppressive to Christians if only because it relegated them to a despised position and because everything they held holy was viewed by the Turks with contempt. But it was oppressive also in that it was often arbitrary and brutal even by the none too sensitive standards of Europeans. It was worse in these respects in the seventeenth century than formerly, for the central authority of the sultans had become corrupt, and the outlying governors, or pashas, had a virtual free hand with their subjects.

Disputed regions

Those parts of the Ottoman Empire which adjoined the Christian states were among the least firmly attached to Constantinople. The Tartar Khans of south Russia, like the Christian princes of the Danubian principalities, were simply protégés who paid tribute. Hungary was occupied but was more a battlefield than a province. These regions were disputed by Germans, Poles, and

Russians. It seemed in the middle of the seventeenth century as if the grip of the Turks might be relaxing. But a series of capable grand viziers, of the Köprülü family, came to power and retained it contrary to Turkish customs for 50 years. Under them the empire again launched a military campaign to expand into the Habsburg lands in central Europe. By 1663 the janissaries were again mobilizing in Hungary. Tartar horsemen were on the move. Central Europe again felt the old terror. The pope feared that the dreaded enemy might break into Italy. Throughout Germany by the emperor's order special "Turk bells" sounded the alarm. The states of the Empire voted to raise a small imperial army. The Holy Roman Empire thus bestirred itself temporarily against the historic enemy of European Christians. However, it was not under the auspices of the Holy Roman Empire, but by the house of Austria that the Turks were repelled.

24. THE FORMATION OF AN AUSTRIAN MONARCHY

The Recovery and Growth of Habsburg Power, 1648–1740

The Austria which appeared by 1700 was actually a new creation, though not as obviously so as the two other rising states in Prussia and Russia. The Austrian Habsburgs had long enjoyed an eminent role. Formerly their position had rested on their headship of the Holy Roman Empire and on their family connection with the wealthy Habsburgs of Spain. In the seventeenth century these two supports collapsed. The hope for an effective Habsburg empire in Germany disappeared in the Thirty Years' War. The connection with Spain lost its value as Spain declined, and it vanished when in 1700 Spain passed to the house of France. The Austrian family in the latter half of the seventeenth century stood at the great turning point of its fortunes. It successfully made a difficult transition, emerging from the husk of the Holy Roman Empire and building an empire of its own. At the same time the Habsburgs continued to be Holy Roman Emperors and remained active in German affairs, using resources drawn from outside Germany to maintain their influence over the German princes. The relation of Austria to the rest of Germany remained a political conundrum down to the twentieth century.

The dominions considered by the house of Austria to be its direct possessions were in three parts. The oldest were the "hereditary provinces"— Upper and Lower Austria, with the adjoining Tyrol, Styria, Carinthia, and Carniola. Second, there was the kingdom of Bohemia—Bohemia, Moravia, and Silesia joined under the crown of St. Wenceslas. Third, there was the kingdom of Hungary—Hungary, Transylvania, and Croatia joined under the crown of St. Stephen. Nothing held all these regions together except the fact that the Austrian Habsburg dynasty, in the seventeenth century, reaffirmed its grip upon them all. During the Thirty Years' War the dynasty rooted Protestantism and feudal rebelliousness out of Austria and the hereditary provinces and reconquered and re-Catholicized Bohemia. And in the following decades it conquered Hungary also.

Dominions of Austria

Since 1526 most of Hungary had been occupied by the Turks. For generations the Hungarian plain was a theater of intermittent warfare between the armies of Vienna and Constantinople. The struggle flared up again in 1663, when Turkish armies began to move up the Danube. A mixed force, assembled from the Empire and its various European allies, obliged the Turks in 1664 to accept a 20-year truce. But Louis XIV, who in these years was busily dismembering the western frontier of the Empire, stood to profit greatly from a diversion on the Danube. He incited the Turks (old allies of France through common hostility to the Habsburgs) to resume their assaults, which they did as the 20-year truce came to a close.

Vienna besieged by the Turks

In 1683 a vast Turkish army reached the city of Vienna and besieged it. The Turks again, as in 1529, peered into the very inner chambers of Europe. The garrison and people of Vienna, greatly outnumbered, held off the besiegers for two months, enough time for a defending force to arrive. Both sides showed the "international" character of the conflict. The Turkish army included Christians—Romanian and Hungarian—the latter in rebellion against Habsburg rule in Hungary. The anti-Turkish force was composed mainly of Poles, Austrian dynastic troops, and Germans from various states of the Empire. It was financed largely by Pope Innocent XI; it was commanded in the field by the Habsburg general, Duke Charles of Lorraine, who hoped to protect his inheritance from annexation by France; and its higher command was entrusted to John Sobieski, king of Poland. Sobieski contributed greatly to the relief of Vienna, and his bold action represented the last great military effort of the moribund Republic of Poland. When the Turks abandoned the siege, a general anti-Turkish counteroffensive developed. Armed forces of the pope, Poland, Russia, and the republic of Venice joined with the Habsburgs. It was in this war, in fighting between Turks and Venetians, that the Parthenon at Athens, which had survived for 2,000 years but was now used as an ammunition dump by the Turks, was severely damaged.

Prince Eugene of Savoy

The Habsburgs had the good fortune to obtain the services of a man of remarkable talent, Prince Eugene of Savoy. Eugene, like many other servants of the Austrian house, was not Austrian at all; he was in fact French by origin and education but like many aristocrats of the time he was an international personage. More than anyone else he was the founder of the modern Austrian state. Distinguished both as a military administrator and as a commander in the field, he reformed the supply, equipment, training, and command of the Habsburg forces, along lines laid out by Louis XIV; and in 1697 he won the battle of Zenta, driving the Turks out of Hungary. At the Peace of Karlowitz (1699) the Turks yielded most of Hungary, together with Transylvania and Croatia, to the Habsburg house; and the Ottoman Empire was pushed back permanently into Romania and the Balkans.

The Habsburgs were now free to pursue their designs in the west. They entered the War of the Spanish Succession to win the Spanish crown, but they had to content themselves by the treaty of Rastadt in 1714 with the annexation of the old Spanish Netherlands and with Milan and Naples. Prince Eugene, freed now in the west, again turned eastward. Never before or afterward were the Austrians so brilliantly successful. Eugene captured Belgrade and pushed through the Iron Gate into Wallachia. But the Turks were not yet helpless; and by the Peace of Belgrade (1739) a frontier was drawn which on the Austrian side remained unchanged until the twentieth century. The Turks continued to hold Romania and the whole Balkan peninsula except Catholic Croatia, which was incorporated into the Habsburg empire. The Habsburg government, to open a window on the Mediterranean, developed a seaport at Trieste.

The Austrian Monarchy by 1740

Thus the house of Austria, in two or three generations after its humiliation at the Peace of Westphalia, acquired a new empire of considerable proportions. Though installed in Bel-

The Austrian Habsburgs mobilized a large force of military alllies, including Polish troops under King John Sobieski, to repel the Turkish army that besieged Vienna in 1683. This painting by Franz Geffels (1635–c. 1699) portrays the final, decisive clash that forced the Turks to abandon their siege of the city.

(Erich Lessing/Art Resource, NY (*The Relief of Vienna, 1683* by Franz Geffels (1635/6–c. 1699)))

gium and Italy, it was essentially an empire of the middle Danube, with its headquarters at Vienna in Austria proper, but possessing the sizable kingdoms of Hungary and Bohemia. Though German influence was strong, the empire was international—or nonnational. At the Habsburg court, and in the Habsburg government and army, the names of Czech, Hungarian, Croatian, and Italian noblemen were common. When the nationalist movements swept over Europe in the nineteenth century, the empire was denounced as tyrannical by Hungarians, Croats, Serbs, Romanians, Czechs, Poles, Italians, and even by some Germans, whose national ambitions were blocked by its existence. Later, disillusioned by nationalism in central and eastern Europe, some tended to romanticize unduly the old Habsburg monarchy, noting that it had at least the merit of holding many discordant peoples together.

The empire was from the beginning international, based on a cosmopolitan aristocracy of landowners who felt closer to each other, despite differences of language, than to the laboring masses who worked on their estates. Not for many years, until after 1848, did the Habsburg government really touch these rural masses; it dealt with the landed class and with the

An international empire

relatively few cities, but it left the landlords to control the peasants. The old diets, or assemblies, survived in Bohemia, Hungary, and the Austrian provinces. No diet was created for the empire as a whole. The diets were essentially assemblages of landlords; and though they no longer enjoyed their medieval freedom, they retained powers over taxation and administration and a sense of constitutional liberty against the crown. So long as they

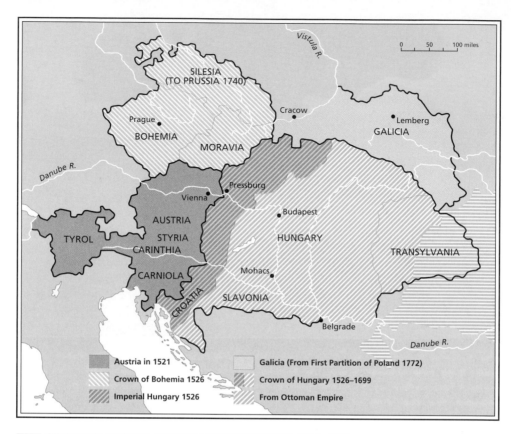

THE GROWTH OF THE AUSTRIAN MONARCHY, 1521–1772

The map shows the main body of the Austrian monarchy as it evolved in the eighteenth century and endured until the collapse of the empire in 1918. There were three main parts: (1) a nucleus, composed of Austria and adjoining duchies, often called the "hereditary provinces"; (2) the lands of the Bohemian crown, which became Habsburg in 1526 and where the Habsburgs reasserted their power during the Thirty Years' War; and (3) the lands of the Hungarian crown, where at first the Habsburgs held only the segment called Imperial Hungary, the rest remaining Turkish until reconquered by the Habsburgs in 1699. In the first partition of Poland (1772) the Habsburgs annexed Galicia. Silesia was lost to Prussia in 1740.

produced taxes and soldiers as needed, and accepted the wars and foreign policy of the ruling house, no questions were asked at Vienna. Religion was a different matter, however, for the Habsburgs forcefully repressed the Protestantism that had spread widely across both Bohemia and Hungary. Many of the estates of Protestant nobles and rebels were confiscated, giving the Habsburgs valuable lands with which to reward soldiers and supporters from all parts of Europe. An increasingly heterogeneous population of Germans, Croats, and Serbs settled in Habsburg territories, especially in Hungary. Meanwhile, the peasants remained in, or reverted to, serfdom.

Despite the concerted political, religious, and military policies of the Habsburg rulers, the Austrian monarchy remained a collection of territories held together by a personal union. Inhabitants of Austria proper considered their ruler as archduke, Bohemians saw in him the king of Bohemia; Magyars, the apostolic king of Hungary. Each country retained its own law, diet, and political life, all of which made it difficult or impossible for the Habsburgs to establish laws and institutions that would be accepted in all the territories they ruled. No feeling in the people held these regions together, and even the several aristocracies were joined only by common service to the Habsburgs. For the empire to exist, all crowns had to be inherited by the same person.

After the reconquest of Hungary the king-archduke, Charles VI (1711–1740), devised a form of insurance to guarantee such an undivided succession. This took the form of a document called the Pragmatic Sanction, first issued in 1713. By it every diet in the empire and the various archdukes of the Habsburg family were to agree to regard the Habsburg territories as indivisible and to recognize only the Habsburg line of heirs. The matter became urgent when it developed that Charles would have no male heir. The direct male line of the Austrian Habsburgs, as of the Spanish a few years before, was about to become extinct. But Charles did have a daughter, Maria Theresa, and he gradually won acceptance of the "Pragmatic Sanction" by all parts of his empire and all members of his family. This agreement recognized Maria Theresa's right to the Habsburg throne and to the inheritance of all Habsburg territories. He then set about having foreign powers guarantee it, knowing that Bavaria, Prussia, or others might well put in claims for this or that part of the inheritance. This process took years, and was accomplished at the cost of many damaging concessions. Charles VI had attempted, for example, to revive Belgium commercially by founding an overseas trading company at Ostend. The British government, before agreeing to guarantee the Pragmatic Sanction, demanded and obtained the renunciation of this commercial project. Finally all powers signed. Charles VI died in 1740, having done all that could be done, by domestic law and international treaty, to assure the continuation of the Austrian empire.

Charles VI and the Pragmatic Sanction

He was scarcely dead when armed "heirs" presented themselves. A great war broke out to partition the Austrian empire, as the Spanish empire had been partitioned shortly before. Bohemia threw off its allegiance. Hungary almost did the same. But these events belong later in the story. At the moment it is enough to know that by 1740 a populous empire of great military strength existed on the Danube.

25. THE FORMATION OF PRUSSIA

It was characteristic of the seventeenth century that very small states were able to play an influential part in European affairs, seemingly out of all proportion to their size. The main reason why small states could act as great powers was that armies were small and weapons were simple. Difficulties of supply and communications, the poor condition of the roads, the lack of maps, the absence of general staffs, together with many other administrative and technical difficulties, reduced the number of soldiers who could be successfully managed in a campaign. The battles of the Thirty Years' War, on the average, were fought by armies of less than 20,000 men. And while Louis XIV, by the last years of his reign, built up a military establishment aggregating some 400,000, the actual field armies in the wars of Louis XIV did not exceed, on the average, 40,000. Armies of this size were well within the reach of smaller powers. If especially well trained, disciplined, and equipped, and if ably commanded, the armies of small powers could defeat those of much larger neighbors. On this fact, fundamentally, the German state of Prussia was to be built.

But Prussia was not the first to exploit the opportunity with spectacular consequences. The first was Sweden.

Sweden's Short-Lived Empire

Sweden almost, but not quite, formed an empire in central and eastern Europe in the seventeenth century. The population of Sweden at the time was not over a million; it was smaller than that of the Dutch Republic. But the Swedes produced a line of extraordinary rulers, ranging from genius in Gustavus Adolphus (1611–1632) through the brilliantly erratic Queen Christina (1632–1654) to the amazing military exploits of Charles XII (1697–1718). The elective Swedish kingship was made hereditary, the royal power freed from control by the estates. Craftsmen and experts were brought from the west, notably Holland; war industries were subsidized by the government; and an army was created with many novel features in weapons, organization, and tactics.

Swedish territorial victories

With this army Gustavus Adolphus crossed the Baltic in the Thirty Years' War, made alliances with Protestant German princes, cut through the Holy Roman Empire, and helped to ward off unification of Germany by the Habsburgs. The Swedish crown, by the Peace of Westphalia, received certain coastal regions of Germany. Subsequently, in a confused series of wars, in which a Polish king claimed to be king of Sweden and a Swedish king claimed to be king of Poland, the Swedes won control of virtually all the shores and cities of the Baltic. Only Denmark at the mouth of that sea and the territories of the house of Brandenburg, which had almost no ports, remained independent. For a time the Baltic was a Swedish lake. The Russians were shut off from it, and the Poles and even the Germans, who lived on its shores, could reach it only on Swedish terms.

Charles XII

The final Swedish campaign for imperial expansion took place during the meteoric reign of Charles XII. As a young man he found his dominions attacked by Denmark, Poland, and Russia; he won remarkable victories over them but would not make peace; he then led an army back and forth across the East European plain, only to be crushed by the Russians. He fled to Turkey and spent long years as a guest and protégé of the Turks. By 1718 the Swedish sphere had contracted to Sweden itself, except that Finland and reduced holdings in northern Germany remained Swedish for a century more. The Swedes in time proved themselves exceptional among European peoples in not harping on their former greatness. They successfully and peaceably made the transition from the role of a great power to that of a small one.

The Territorial Growth of Brandenburg-Prussia

In the long run it was to be Prussia that dominated this part of Europe. Prussia became famous for its "militarism," which may be said to exist when military needs and military values permeate all other spheres of life. Through its influence on Germany over a period of two centuries it played a momentous part in the modern world. The south coast of the Baltic, where Prussia was to arise, was an unpromising site for the creation of a strong political power. It was an uninviting country, thinly populated, with poor soil and without mineral resources, more backward than Saxony or Bohemia, not to mention the busy centers of south Germany and western Europe. It was a flat open plain, merging imperceptibly into Poland, without prominent physical features or natural frontiers (see maps, pp. 4–5,

193, 194, 208–209). The coastal region directly south from Sweden was known as Pomerania. Inland from it, shut off from the sea, was Brandenburg, centering about Berlin. Brandenburg had been founded in the Middle Ages as a border state, a "mark" or "march" of the Holy Roman Empire, to fight the battles of the empire against the then heathen Slavs. Its ruler, the margrave, was one of the seven princes who, after 1356, elected the Holy Roman Emperor. Hence he was commonly called the Elector of Brandenburg. After 1415 the electors were always of the Hohenzollern family.

All Germany east of the Elbe, including Brandenburg, represented a medieval conquest by the German-speaking peoples—the German *Drang nach Osten,* or drive to the East. From the Elbe to Poland, German conquerors and settlers had replaced the Slavs, eliminating them or absorbing them by intermarriage. Eastward from Brandenburg, and outside the Holy Roman Empire, stretched a region inhabited by Slavic peoples. Next to the east came "Prussia," which eventually was to give its name to all territories of the Hohenzollern monarchy. This original Prussia formed part of the lands of the Teutonic Knights, a military crusading order which had conquered and Christianized the native peoples in the thirteenth century. Except for its seacoast along the Baltic, the duchy of Prussia was totally enclosed by the Polish kingdom. To the north, along the Baltic, as far as the Gulf of Finland, German minorities lived among Lithuanians, Latvians (or Letts), and Estonians. The towns were German, founded as German commercial colonies in the Middle Ages, and many of the landlords were German also, descendants of the Teutonic Knights, and later known as the "Baltic barons."

Germans expand eastward

Modern Prussia began to appear in the seventeenth century when a number of territories came into the hands of the Hohenzollerns of Brandenburg, who, we have noted, had ruled in Brandenburg since 1415. In 1618 the Elector of Brandenburg inherited the duchy of Prussia. Another important development occurred when the old ruling line in Pomerania expired during the Thirty Years' War. Although the Swedes succeeded in taking the better part of Pomerania, including the city of Stettin, the Elector of Brandenburg received at the Peace of Westphalia eastern Pomerania. Barren, rural, and harborless though it was, it at least had the advantage of connecting Brandenburg with the Baltic. The Hohenzollerns no sooner obtained it than they began to dream of joining it to the duchy of Prussia, a task which required the absorption of an intermediate and predominantly Slavic area, which was part of Poland, a task not accomplished until 1772.

Territorial acquisitions of the Hohenzollerns

Had the duchy of Prussia and eastern Pomerania been the only acquisitions of the Hohenzollerns, their state would have been oriented almost exclusively toward eastern Europe. But at the Peace of Westphalia they received, in addition to eastern Pomerania, new territories on the west bank of the Elbe. Moreover, through the play of inheritance common in the Holy Roman Empire, the Hohenzollerns had earlier fallen heir, in 1614, to the small state of Cleves on the Rhine at the Dutch border and a few other small territories also in western Germany. These were separated from the main mass around Brandenburg by many intermediate German principalities. But they gave the Hohenzollerns a direct contact with the more advanced regions of western Europe and a base from which larger holdings in the Rhineland were eventually to be built up.

In the seventeenth century, meanwhile, the dominions of the house of Brandenburg were in three disconnected territories. The main one was Brandenburg, with adjoining Pomerania and territories along the Elbe. There was a detached eastern territory in ducal Prussia and another small detached western territory on and near the Rhine. To connect and unify these three territorial possessions became the long-range policy of the Brandenburg house.

In the midst of the Thirty Years' War, in 1640, a young man of 20, named Frederick William, succeeded to these diverse possessions. Known later as the Great Elector, he was the first of the men who shaped modern Prussia. He had grown up under trying conditions. Brandenburg was one of the parts of Germany to suffer most heavily from the war. Its location made it the stamping ground of Swedish and Habsburg armies. In 1640, in the 22 years since the beginning of the war, the population of Berlin had fallen from about 14,000 to about 6,000. Hundreds of villages had been wiped out. Wolves roamed over the countryside.

The Great Elector

Frederick William concluded that in his position, ruling a small and open territory, without natural frontiers or possibility of defense in depth, he must put his main reliance on a competent army. With an effective army, even if small, he could oblige the stronger states to take him into their calculations and so could enter with some hope of advantage into the politics of the balance of power. This long remained the program of the Brandenburgers—to have an army but not to use it, to conserve it with loving and even miserly care, to keep an "army in being," and to gain their ends by diplomatic maneuver. They did so by siding with France against the Habsburgs, or with Sweden against Poland. They aspired also to the title not merely of margrave or elector, but king. The opportunity came in 1701, when the Habsburg emperor was preparing to enter the War of the Spanish Succession. The emperor requested the elector of Brandenburg, who was then Frederick III, to support him with 8,000 troops. The elector named his price: recognition of himself, by the emperor, as king "in Prussia." The emperor yielded; the title, at first explicitly limited to the less honorable king *in* Prussia, soon became king *of* Prussia. The elector Frederick III of Brandenburg became King Frederick I of Prussia. Another rent was made in the old fabric of the Holy Roman Empire. There was now a German king above all the other German princes.

The Prussian Military State

The preoccupation of Prussia with its army was unquestionably defensive in origin, arising from the horrors of the Thirty Years' War. But it outlasted its cause and became the settled habit and character of the country. Prussia was not unique in the attention it paid to its armed forces. The unique thing about Prussia was the disproportion between the size of the army and the size of the resources on which the army was based. The government, to maintain the army, had to direct and plan the life of the country for this purpose. Nor was Prussia the originator of the "standing" army, kept active in time of peace and always preparing for war. Most governments imitated Louis XIV in establishing standing armies, not merely to promote foreign ambitions but to keep armed forces out of the hands of nobles and military adventurers and under control by the state.

The Prussian army

But Prussia was unique in that, more than in any other country, the army developed a life of its own, almost independent of the life of the state. It was older than the Prussian state. In 1657 the Great Elector fought a great battle at Warsaw with soldiers from all parts of his dominions. It was the first time that men from Cleves, Brandenburg, and ducal Prussia had ever done anything together. The army was the first "all Prussian" institution. Institutions of civilian government developed later and largely to meet the needs of the army. And in later generations the army proved more durable than the state. When Prussia collapsed before Napoleon in 1806, the spirit and morale of the Prussian army carried on; and when the Hohenzollern empire finally

Frederick William, who became known as the Great Elector, governed Prussia for almost 50 years (1640–1688) and set his country on a course toward new power and military influence in central Europe.
(Foto Marburg/Art Resource, NY)

crashed in 1918, the army still maintained its life and traditions on into the Weimar Republic, which again it survived. Not until the defeat of Adolf Hitler in the Second World War and the establishment of a new republican regime was the army totally subordinated to civilian authority.

Maintaining the army

In all countries, to some extent, the machinery of the modern state developed as a means of supporting armed forces, but in Prussia the process was exceptionally clear and simple. In Prussia the rulers drew roughly half their income from the crown domain and only about half from taxes. The crown domain, consisting of manors and other productive enterprises owned directly by the ruler as lord, was in effect a kind of government property, for the Prussian rulers used their income almost entirely for state purposes, being personally simple and even Spartan in their habits. The rulers of Prussia, until a century after the accession of the Great Elector, were able to pay the whole cost of their civil government from their own income, the proceeds of the crown domain. But to maintain an army they had to make the domain more productive and also find new income derived from taxes. To develop the domain and account for and transfer the funds, they created a large body of civilian officials. The domain bulked so large that much of the economy of the country was not in private hands but consisted of enterprises owned and administered by the state. For additional income the Great Elector introduced taxes of the kind used in France, such as excise taxes on consumers' goods and a government monopoly on the sale of salt. All taxes, for a century after the accession of the Great Elector, were levied for the use of the army.

Economic life grew up under government sponsorship, rather than through the enterprise of a venturesome business class. This was because, for a rural country to maintain an organized army, productive and technical skills had to be imported, mainly from the West. The Great Elector in his youth spent a number of years in Holland, where he was impressed by the wealth and prosperity that he saw. After becoming elector he settled Swiss and Frisians in Brandenburg (the Frisians were akin to the Dutch); he welcomed Jews from Poland; and when Louis XIV began to persecute the French Protestants, he provided funds and special officials to assist the immigration of 20,000 Huguenots to Brandenburg. French immigrants for a time formed a sixth of the population of Berlin and were

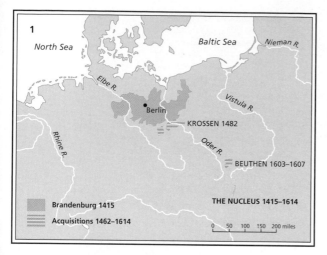

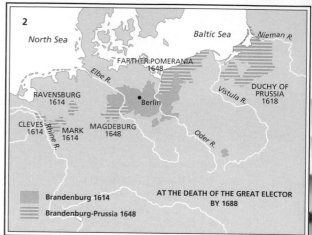

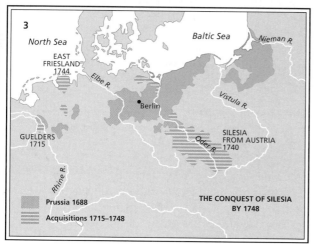

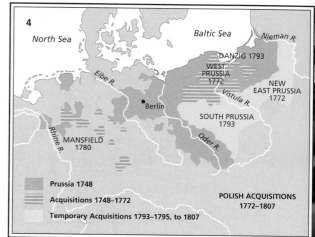

THE GROWTH OF PRUSSIA, 1415–1918

The maps shown here, going well beyond the scope of this chapter, give a conspectus of Prussian history from the time when Brandenburg began to expand in the seventeenth century. One may see, by looking at all the panels together, how Prussia was really an east-European state until 1815; its center of gravity shifted westward, in significant degree, only in the nineteenth century. Panel 2 shows the early formation of three unconnected territories; Panel 3, the huge bulk of Silesia relative to the small kingdom that annexed it; Panel 4, the fruits of the partitions of Poland; Panel 5, Napoleon pared Prussia down. The main crisis at the Congress of Vienna, and its resolution, are shown in Panels 6 and 7. Bismarck's enlargement of Prussia appears in Panel 8. The boundaries established by Bismarck remained unchanged until the fall of the monarchy in 1918.

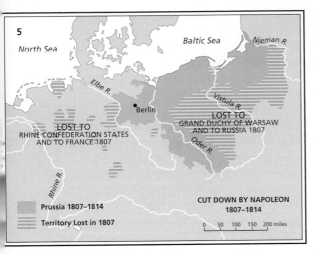

5

North Sea · Baltic Sea · Nieman R. · Elbe R. · Vistula R. · Berlin · LOST TO GRAND DUCHY OF WARSAW AND TO RUSSIA 1807 · LOST TO RHINE CONFEDERATION STATES AND TO FRANCE 1807 · Rhine R. · Oder R.

CUT DOWN BY NAPOLEON 1807–1814

Prussia 1807–1814
Territory Lost in 1807

0   50   100   150   200 miles

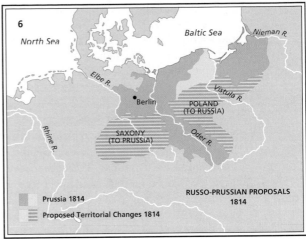

6

North Sea · Baltic Sea · Nieman R. · Elbe R. · Berlin · POLAND (TO RUSSIA) · Vistula R. · Rhine R. · SAXONY (TO PRUSSIA) · Oder R.

RUSSO-PRUSSIAN PROPOSALS 1814

Prussia 1814
Proposed Territorial Changes 1814

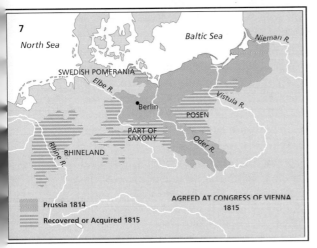

7

North Sea · Baltic Sea · Nieman R. · SWEDISH POMERANIA · Elbe R. · Vistula R. · Berlin · POSEN · PART OF SAXONY · Rhine R. · RHINELAND · Oder R.

AGREED AT CONGRESS OF VIENNA 1815

Prussia 1814
Recovered or Acquired 1815

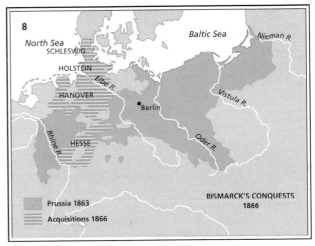

8

North Sea · SCHLESWIG · Baltic Sea · Nieman R. · HOLSTEIN · Elbe R. · HANOVER · Vistula R. · Berlin · Rhine R. · HESSE · Oder R.

BISMARCK'S CONQUESTS 1866

Prussia 1863
Acquisitions 1866

the most advanced commercial element of that comparatively primitive city. The government, as in France under Colbert, initiated and helped to finance various industries; but the importance of such government participation was greater than in France, because the amount of privately owned capital available for investment was incomparably less. Military needs, more than elsewhere, dominated the market for goods, because civilian demand in so poor a country was relatively low; the army, in its requirements for food, uniforms, and weapons became a strong force in shaping the economic growth of the country.

The army had a profound effect also on the social development and class structure of Prussia. The civilian middle class remained submissive, and it became the policy of the rulers to absorb practically the whole landed aristocracy, the Junkers, into military service. They used the army, with conscious purpose, as a means of implementing an "all Prussian" psychology in the landed families of Cleves, Brandenburg, Pomerania, and the former dominions of the Teutonic Knights. The fact that Prussia was a very recent and artificial combination

The army and Prussian society

of territories, so that identification with it was not a natural sentiment, made it all the more necessary to instill loyalty by martial means. Emphasis fell on duty, obedience, service, and sacrifice. That military virtues became characteristic of the whole male Prussian aristocracy was also due, like so much else, to the small size of the population. In France, for example, with perhaps 50,000 male adult nobles, only a small minority served as army officers. In Prussia there were few Junker families that did not have some of their members in uniform.

The Great Elector and his successors, like all absolutist rulers of the era, repressed the estates or parliamentary assemblages in which the landed aristocracy was the main element. To mollify the squires, the rulers promised commissions in the army to men of their class. They promised them also a free hand over their peasants. The Prussian monarchy was largely based on an understanding between the ruler and the landlord gentry—the latter agreed to accept the ruler's government and to serve in his army, in return for holding their own peasants in hereditary subjection. Serfdom spread in Prussia as elsewhere in eastern Europe. In East Prussia the condition of the peasants became as deplorable as in Poland.

The Prussian rulers believed that the Junkers made better army officers because they were brought up in the habit of commanding their own peasants. To preserve the officer class, legislation forbade the sale of "noble" lands, that is, manors, to persons not noble. In France, again by way of contrast, where manorial rights had become simply a form of

Limited social mobility

property, bourgeois and even peasants could legally acquire manors and enjoy a lordly or "seigneurial" income. In Prussia this was not possible; classes were frozen by owning nonexchangeable forms of property. It was thus harder for middle-class persons to enter the aristocracy by setting up as landed gentry. The bourgeois class in any case had little spirit of independence. Few of the old towns of Germany were in Prussia. The Prussian middle class was not wealthy. It was not strong through the possession of private property. The typical middle-class man was an official who worked for the government as an employee of the large crown domain or in an enterprise subsidized by the state. The civil service in Prussia, from the days of the Great Elector, became notable for its honesty and efficiency. But the

Frederick William I

middle class, more than elsewhere, deferred to the nobles, served the state, and stood in awe of the army.

These peculiar features of Prussia developed especially under Frederick William I, who was king from 1713 to 1740. He was an earthy, uncouth man, who disdained whatever savored of "culture," to which his father, his grandfather (the Great Elector), and also his son (Frederick the Great) were all strongly attracted. He begrudged every penny not spent on the army. He cut the expense of the royal household by three-fourths. On his coronation journey to Königsberg he spent 2,547 thalers, where his father had spent five million. He ruled the country in a fatherly German way, supervising it like a private estate, prowling the streets of Berlin in an old seedy uniform, and disciplining negligent citizens with blows of his walking stick. He worked all the time and expected everyone else to do likewise.

He loved the army, which all his policies were designed to serve. He was the first Prussian king to appear always in uniform. He rearranged the order of courtly precedence, moving army officers up and civilians down. His love of tall soldiers is famous; he collected a special unit, men between 6 and 7 feet tall, from all over Europe, and indeed the Russian Tsar Peter the Great sent him some from Asia. He devised new forms of discipline and maneuver, founded a cadet corps to train the sons of the Junkers, and invented a new system of recruiting (the canton system, long the most effective in Europe), by which each regiment had a particular district or canton assigned to it as a source of soldiers. He raised the size of the army from 40,000 at his accession to 83,000 at his death. During his reign Berlin grew to be a city of 100,000, of whom 20,000 were soldiers, a proportion probably matched in no other city of Europe. He likewise left to his successor (for he fought practically no wars himself) a war chest of 7,000,000 thalers.

With this army and war chest Frederick II, later called the Great, who became king in 1740, startled Europe. Charles VI of Austria had just died. His daughter Maria Theresa entered upon her manifold inheritance. All Europe was hedging on its guarantee of the Pragmatic Sanction. While others waited, Frederick struck. Serving no notice, he moved his forces into Silesia, to which the Hohenzollerns had an old though doubtful claim. Silesia was a part of the kingdom of Bohemia on the side toward Poland, lying in the upper valley of the Oder River and adjoining Brandenburg on the north. The addition of Silesia to the kingdom of Prussia almost doubled the population and added valuable industries, so that Prussia now, with 6,000,000 people and an army which Frederick raised to 200,000, at last established itself as a great power. It must be added that, judged simply as a human accomplishment, Prussia was a remarkable creation, a state made on a shoestring, a triumph of work and duty.

The advances of Frederick the Great

২৬ 26.   THE "WESTERNIZING" OF RUSSIA

The affairs of central and eastern Europe, from Sweden to Turkey and from Germany to the Caspian Sea, were profoundly interconnected. The underlying theme of the present chapter, it may be recalled, is that this whole great area was fluid, occupied by the weak political bodies of the Holy Roman Empire, Poland, and Turkey, and that in this fluid area three new powers gradually developed—the modern Austrian monarchy, the kingdom of Prussia, and the Russian empire. All, too, in varying degree, became modern eighteenth-century states by borrowing various ideas and administrative systems from the West, though each of these new eastern states also retained its own distinctive political, social, and cultural characteristics.

In the century after 1650 the old tsardom of Muscovy turned into modern Russia. Moving out from the region around Moscow, the Russians not only established themselves across northern Asia, reaching the Bering Sea about 1700, but also entered into closer relations with Europe, undergoing especially in the time of Tsar Peter the Great (1682–1725) a rapid process of Europeanization. To what extent Russia became truly European has always been an open question, disputed both by western Europeans and by Russians themselves. In some ways the Russians have been European from as far back as Europe itself can be said to have existed, that is, from the early Middle Ages. Ancient Russia had been colonized by Vikings, and the Russians had become Christian long before the Swedes, the Lithuanians, or the Finns.

Europeanization

Yet Russia had not been part of the general development of Europe for a number of reasons. Russia had been converted to the Greek Orthodox branch of Christianity; therefore, the religious and cultural influence of Constantinople, not of Rome, had predominated. Second, the Mongol invasions and conquest about 1240 had kept Russia under Asian domination for about 250 years, until 1480 when a grand duke of Muscovy, Ivan III (1462–1505), was able to throw off the Mongol overlordship and cease payment of tribute. Last, Russian geography, especially the lack of warm-water or ice-free seaports, had made commerce and communication with the West difficult. Russia had therefore not shared in the general European development after about 1100, and the changes that took place in the

The uniforms of these Prussian soldiers in the era of King Frederick II (1740–1786) represent the status and importance of the military class in Prussian society during the eighteenth century.
(akg-images)

seventeenth and eighteenth centuries may accurately be called Europeanization, or at least a wholesale borrowing of the new knowledge and institutions that had developed in the early modern European states. The Europeanizing or westernizing of Russia was by no means a unique thing. It was a step in the expansion of the modern European type of civilization or social organization and hence in the formation of the modern world as we have known it in recent centuries.

Parallels with Prussia

In some ways the new Russian empire resembled the new kingdom of Prussia. Both took form in the great plain which runs uninterruptedly from the North Sea into inner Asia. Both lacked natural frontiers and grew by addition of territories to an original nucleus. In both countries the state arose primarily as a means of supporting a modern army. In both the government developed autocratically, in conjunction with a landlord class which was impressed into state service and which in turn held the peasantry in serfdom. Neither Russia nor Prussia had a native commercial class of any political importance. In neither country could the modern state and army have been created without the importation of new skills from western Europe. Yet Prussia, with its German connections, its Protestant religion, its universities, and its nearness to the busy commercial artery of the Baltic, was far more "European" than

Russia, and the Europeanization of Russia may perhaps better be compared with the later "westernization" of Japan. In the Russia of 1700, as in the Japan of 1870, the main purpose of the westernizers was to obtain scientific, technical, and military knowledge from the West, in part with a view to strengthening their own countries against penetration or conquest by Europeans. Yet here too the parallel must not be pushed too far. In time, the Russian upper classes intermarried with Europeans, and Russian music and literature became part of the culture of Europe. Russia developed a unique blend of European and non-European traits.

Russia before Peter the Great

The Russians in the seventeenth century, as today, were a medley of peoples distinguished by their language, which was of the Slavic family, of the great Indo-European language group. The Great Russians or Muscovites lived around Moscow. Moving out from that area, they had penetrated the northern forests and had also settled in the southern steppes and along the Volga, where they had assimilated various Asian peoples known as Tartars. After two centuries of expansion, from roughly 1450 to 1650, the Russians had almost but not quite reached the Baltic and the Black seas. The Baltic shore was held by Sweden. The Black Sea coast was still held by Tartar Khans under the protection of Turkey. In the rough borderlands between Tartar and Russia lived the semi-independent cowboy-like Cossacks, largely recruited from migratory Russians. West of Muscovy were the White Russians (or Byelorussians) and southwest of Muscovy the Little Russians (Ruthenians or Ukrainians), both in the seventeenth century under the rule of Poland, which was then the leading Slavic power.

The energies of the Great Russians were directed principally eastward. They conquered the Volga Tartars in the sixteenth century and reached the Ural Mountains, which they immediately crossed. Muscovite pioneers, settlers, and townbuilders streamed along the river systems of Siberia, felling timber and trading in furs as they went. In the 1630s, while the English were building Boston and the Dutch New York, the Russians were establishing towns in the vast Asian stretches of Siberia, reaching to the Pacific itself. A whole string of settlements, remote, small, and isolated—Tomsk and Tobolsk, Irkutsk and Yakutsk—extended for 5,000 miles across northern Asia.

It was toward the vast heartland of central Asia that Muscovy really faced, looking out upon Persia and China across the deserts. The bazaars of Moscow and Astrakhan were frequented by Persians, Afghans, Indians, and Chinese. The Caspian Sea, into which flowed the Volga, the greatest of Russian rivers, was better known than was the Baltic. Europe as sensed from Moscow was in the rear. During most of the seventeenth century even Smolensk and Kiev belonged to Poland. Yet the Russians were not totally shut off from Europe. In 1552, when Ivan the Terrible conquered Kazan from the Tartars, he had a German engineer in his army. In the next year, 1553, Richard Chancellor arrived in Moscow from England by the roundabout way of Archangel on the White Sea. Thereafter trade between England and Muscovy was continuous. The tsars valued Archangel as their only inlet from the West through which military materials could be imported. The English valued it as a means of reaching the wares of Persia.

Russia in the seventeenth century reflected its long estrangement from the culture and social mores that had been developing in Europe. Women of the upper classes were secluded and often wore veils. Men wore beards and skirted garments that seemed exotic to Europeans. Customs were crude, wild drunkenness and revelry alternating with spasms of repentance and religious prostration.

Russian estrangement from Europe

CHRONOLOGY OF NOTABLE EVENTS, 1640–1740

1640–1688	Frederick William, the Great Elector, develops state and military power in Prussia
1663	Ottoman Empire begins new phase of expansion in Central Europe
1667–1671	Stephen Razin leads rebellion of rural population in Russia
1683	Ottoman imperial army is forced to abandon siege of Vienna
1698–1725	Tsar Peter the Great introduces "westernizing" reforms in Russia
1711–1740	Habsburg Charles VI builds the Austrian Empire
1713–1740	Frederick William I expands the army and wealth of the Prussian state

Superstition infected the highest classes of church and state. Life counted for little; murder, kidnapping, torture, and elaborate physical cruelty were common. The Russian church supported no such educational or charitable institutions as did the Catholic and Protestant churches of Europe. Churchmen feared the incipient Western influences. "Abhorred of God," declared a Russian bishop, "is any who loves geometry; it is a spiritual sin." Even arithmetic was hardly understood in Russia. Arabic numerals were not used, and merchants computed with the abacus. The calendar was dated from the creation of the world. Ability to predict an eclipse seemed a form of magic. Clocks, brought in by Europeans, seemed as wonderful in Russia as they did in China, where they were brought in by Jesuits at about the same time.

Yet this great, non-European Russia, which fronted on inner Asia, was European in some of its fundamental social institutions. It possessed a variant of the manorial and feudal systems. It felt the same wave of constitutional crises that was sweeping over Europe at the same time. Russia had a duma or council of retainers and advisers to the tsar, and the rudiments of a national assembly corresponding to meetings of the estates in western Europe. In Russia as in Europe the question was whether power should remain in the hands of these bodies or become concentrated in the hands of the ruler. Ivan the Terrible, who ruled from 1533 to 1584 and was the first grand duke of Muscovy to assume the title of tsar,[1] was a shrewd observer of contemporary events in Poland. He saw the dissolution that was overtaking the Polish state and was determined to avoid it in Muscovy. His ferocity toward those who opposed him made him literally terrible, but though his methods differed from the methods commonly used in Europe, his aims were the aims of his European contemporaries. Not long after his death Russia passed into a period known as the Time of Troubles (1604–1613), during which the Russian nobles elected a series of tsars and demanded certain assurances of their own liberties. But the country was racked by contending factions and a civil war in which the violence resembled the religious wars in France or the Thirty Years' War in central Europe.

The Romanovs

In 1613 a national assembly, hoping to settle the troubles, elected a 17-year-old boy as tsar, or emperor, believing him young enough to have no connection with any of the warring factions. The new boy tsar was Michael Romanov, of a gentry family, related by marriage to the old line of Ivan the

---

[1]The Slavic word *tsar*, like the German *Kaiser*, derives from *Caesar*, a title used as a synonym for *emperor* in the Roman, the Holy Roman, and the Byzantine (or Eastern Roman) empires. The spelling *czar*, also common in English, reveals the etymology and the current English-language pronunciation, *zar*.

Terrible. Thus was established, by vote of the political classes of the day, the Romanov dynasty which ruled in Russia until 1917. The early Romanovs, aware of the fate of elective monarchy in Poland and elsewhere, soon began to repress the representative institutions of Russia and set up as absolute monarchs. Here again, though they were more lawless and violent than any European king, they followed the general pattern of contemporary Europe.

Nor can it be said that the main social development of the seventeenth century in Russia, the sinking of the peasantry into an abyss of helpless serfdom, was exclusively a Russian phenomenon. The same process gener-

Serfdom in Russia

ally took place in eastern Europe. Serfdom had long been overtaking the older free peasantry of Russia. In Russia, as in the American colonies, land was abundant and labor was scarce. The natural tendency of labor was to migrate over the great Russian plain. In the Time of Troubles, especially, there was a good deal of movement. The landlords, wishing to assure themselves of their labor force, obtained the support of the Romanov tsars.

The manor, or what corresponded to it in Russia, came to resemble the slave plantation of the New World. Laws against fugitive serfs were strengthened; lords won the right to recover fugitives up to 15 years after their flight, and finally the time limit was abolished altogether. Peasants came to be so little regarded that a law of 1625 authorized anyone killing another man's peasant simply to give him another peasant in return. Lords exercised police and judicial powers. By a law of 1646 landowners were required to enter the names of all their peasants in government registers; peasants once so entered, together with their descendants, were regarded as attached to the estate on which they were registered. Thus the peasants lost the freedom to move at their own will. For a time they were supposed to have secure tenure of their land; but a law of 1675 allowed the lords to sell peasants without the land, and thus to move peasants like chattels at the will of the owner. This sale of serfs without land, which made their condition more like slavery as then practiced in America, became indeed a distinctive feature of serfdom in Russia, since in Poland, Prussia, Bohemia, and other regions of serfdom, the serf was generally regarded as "bound to the soil," inseparable from the land.

Against the loss of their freedom the rural population of Russia protested as best it could, murdering landlords, fleeing to the Cossacks, taking refuge in a vagrant existence, countered by wholesale government-organized manhunts and by renewed and more stringent legislation. A tremendous uprising was led in 1667 by Stephen Razin, who gathered a host of fugitive serfs, Cossacks, and adventurers, outfitted a fleet on the Caspian Sea, plundered Russian vessels, defeated a Persian squadron, and invaded Persia itself. He then turned back, ascended the Volga, killing and burning as he went and proclaiming a war against landlords, nobles, and priests. Cities opened their gates to him; an army sent against him went over to his side. He was finally captured and put to death in 1671. The consequence of the rebellion, for over a century, was that serfdom was clamped on the country more firmly than ever.

Even from the church the increasingly wretched rural people drew little comfort. The Russian Orthodox church at this time went through a great internal crisis, and ended up as hardly more than a department of the tsar-dom, useful to the government in instilling a superstitious reverence for

The Russian Orthodox church

Holy Russia. The Russian church had historically looked to the Patriarch of Constantinople as its head. But the conquest of Constantinople by the Turks made the head of the Greek Orthodox church a merely tolerated inferior to the Muslim sultan-caliph, so that the Russians in 1589 set up an independent Russian patriarch of their own. In the following generations the Russian patriarchate first became dependent on, then was abolished by, the tsarist government.

Stephen Razin became an almost mythic figure in Russian popular memory after leading a vast peasant rebellion in the late 1660s. This painting by Wassili Iwanowitsch Suriow (1848–1916) suggests Razin's later prominence in Russian culture and his symbolic status in modern social and political movements.

(akg-images (*Stepan Rasin,* 1906 by Wassili Iwanowitsch Surikow (1848–1916)))

In the 1650s the Russian patriarch undertook certain church reforms, mainly to correct mistranslations in Russian versions of the Bible and other sacred writings. The changes aroused the horror and indignation of the general body of believers. Superstitiously attached to the mere form of the written word, believing the faith itself to depend on the customary spelling of the name of Jesus, the malcontents saw in the reformers a band of cunning Greek scholars perpetrating the work of Antichrist and the devil. The

Old Believers

patriarch and higher church officials forced through the reforms but only with the help of the government and the army. Those who rejected the reforms came be called Old Believers. More ignorant and fanatical than the established church, agitated by visionary preachers, dividing into innumerable sects, the Old Believers became very numerous, especially among the peasants. Old Believers were active in Stephen Razin's rebellion and in all the sporadic peasant uprisings that followed. The peasants, already placed by serfdom outside the protection of law, were also estranged from the established religion. A distrust of all organized authority settled over the Russian masses, to whom both church and government seemed mere engines of repression.

But while willing enough to modernize to the extent of correcting mistranslations from the Greek, the church officials resisted the kind of modernization that was coming in from western Europe. They therefore opposed Peter the Great at the end of the century. After 1700 no new patriarch was appointed. Peter put the church under a committee of bishops called the Holy Synod, and to the Synod he attached a civil official called the Procurator of the Holy Synod. The Procurator was not a churchman but head of a government bureau whose task was to see that the church did nothing displeasing to the tsar. Peter thus secularized the church, making himself in effect its head. But while the consequences were more extreme in Russia than elsewhere, it must again be noted that this action of Peter's followed the general pattern of Europe. Secular supervision of religion had become the rule almost everywhere, especially in Protestant countries. Indeed an Englishman of the time thought that Peter the Great, in doing away with the patriarchate and putting the church under his own control, was wisely imitating England, which he had visited in his youth.

Peter the Great: Foreign Affairs and Territorial Expansion

The Russia in which Peter the Great became tsar in 1682 was thus already "European" in some ways and had in any case been in contact with Westerners for over a century. Without Peter, Russia would have developed its European connections more gradually. Peter, by his tempo and methods, made the process a social revolution.

Peter obtained his first knowledge of the West in Moscow itself, where a part of the city known as the German quarter was inhabited by Europeans of various nationalities, whom Peter often visited as a boy. Peter also in his early years mixed with Westerners at Archangel, still Russia's only port, for *Exposure to the West* he was fascinated by the sea and took lessons in navigation on the White Sea from Dutch and English ship captains. Like the Great Elector of Brandenburg, Peter as a young man spent over a year in western Europe, especially Holland and England, where he became profoundly aware of the commercial and technical backwardness of his own country. He had considerable talents as a mechanic and organizer. He labored with his own hands as a ship's carpenter in Amsterdam and talked with political and business leaders on means of introducing Western organization and technology into Russia. He visited workshops, mines, commercial offices, art galleries, hospitals, and forts. Europeans saw him as a barbarian of genius, a giant of a man standing a head above most others, bursting with physical vitality and plying all he met with interminable questions on their manner of working and living. He had neither the refinement nor the pretension of Western monarchs; he mixed easily with workmen and technical people, dressed cheaply and carelessly, loved horseplay and crude practical jokes, and dismayed his hosts by the squalid disorder in which he and his companions left the rooms put at their disposal. A man of acute practical mind, he was as little troubled by appearances as by moral scruples.

Peter on his visit to Europe in 1697–1698 recruited almost 1,000 experts for service in Russia, and many more followed later. He cared nothing for the civilization of Europe except as a means to an end, and this end was to create an army and a state which could stand against those of the West. His aim from the beginning was in part defensive, to ward off the Poles, Swedes, and Turks who had long pushed against Russia; and in part expansionist, to obtain warm-water seaports on the Baltic and Black seas, which would offer year-round access to trade with Europe. For all but two years of his long reign Peter was at war.

The Poles were a receding threat to Peter's ambitions. A Polish prince *Polish threat recedes* had indeed been elected tsar of Muscovy during the Time of Troubles, and for a while the Poles aspired to conquer and Catholicize the Great Russians. But in 1667 the Russians had regained Smolensk and Kiev, and the growing anarchy in Poland made that country no longer a menace, except as the Swedes or others might install themselves in it. The Turks and their Tartar dependencies, though no longer expanding, were still obstinate foes. Peter before going to Europe managed in 1696 to capture Azov at the mouth of the Don, but he was unable to hold any of the Black Sea coast; and he came to recognize the inferiority of the Russian army during these campaigns. The Swedes were the main enemy of Russia. Their army, for its size, was still probably the best in Europe.

The aspirations of Peter the Great are suggested in this formal portrait of a monarch whose clothing and appearance resemble the style of Western European elites in the early eighteenth century.
(Scala/Art Resource, NY)

They controlled the whole eastern shore of the Baltic including the Gulf of Finland. In 1697, the Swedish king having died, Peter entered into an alliance with Poland and Denmark to partition the overseas possessions of the Swedish house.

The Swedes

The new king of Sweden, the youthful Charles XII, was in some ways as crude as Peter (as an adolescent he had sheep driven into his rooms in the palace in order to enjoy the warlike pleasure of killing them), but he proved also to have remarkable aptitude as a general. In 1700, at the battle of Narva, with an army of 8,000 men, he routed Peter's 40,000 Russians. The tsar thus learned another lesson on the need of westernizing his state and army. Fortunately for the Russians Charles XII, instead of immediately pressing his advantage in Russia, spent the following years in furthering Swedish interests in Poland, where he forced the Poles to elect the Swedish candidate as their king. Peter meanwhile, with his imported officers and technicians, reformed the training, discipline, and weapons of the Russian army.

Eventually, Charles XII invaded Russia with a large and well-prepared force. Peter used against him the strategy later used by the Russians against Napoleon and Adolf Hitler; he drew the Swedes into the endless plains, exposing them to the Russian winter, which happened to be an exceptionally severe one, and in 1709, at Poltava in south Russia, he met and overwhelmed the demoralized remainder. The entire Swedish army was destroyed at Poltava, only the king and a few hundred fugitives managing to escape across the Turkish frontier. Peter in the next years conquered Livonia and part of eastern Finland. He landed troops near Stockholm itself. He campaigned in Pomerania almost as far west as the Elbe. Never before had Russian influence reached so deeply into Europe.

The imperial day of Sweden was now over, terminated by Russia. Peter had won for Russia a piece of the Baltic shore and with it warm-water outlets. These significant developments ending the great Northern War (1700–1721) were confirmed in the treaty of Nystadt in 1721.

War is surely not the father of all things, as has been sometimes claimed, but these wars did a good deal to shape imperial Russia. The undisciplined, poorly organized Russian army was transformed into a professional force of the kind maintained by Sweden, France, or Prussia. The *War and imperial Russia* elite of the old army had been the *streltsi,* a kind of Moscow guard, composed of nobles and constantly active in politics. A rebellion of the *streltsi* in 1698 had cut short Peter's tour of Europe; he had returned and quelled the mutiny by ferocious use of torture and execution, killing five of the rebels with his own hands. The *streltsi* were liquidated only two years before the great Russian defeat at Narva. Peter then rebuilt the army from the ground up. He employed European officers of many nationalities, paying them half again as much as native Russians of the same grades. He filled his ranks with soldiers supplied by districts on a territorial basis, somewhat as in Prussia. He put the troops into uniforms resembling those of the West and organized them in regiments of standardized composition. He armed them with muskets and artillery of the kind used in Europe and tried to create a service of supply.

With this army he not only drove the Swedes back into Sweden but also dominated Russia itself. At the very time of the Swedish invasion large parts of the country were in rebellion, as in the days of Stephen Razin, for the whole middle and lower Volga, together with the Cossacks of the Don and Dnieper, rose against the tsar and rallied behind slogans of class war and hatred of the tsar's foreign experts. Peter crushed these disturbances with the usual ruthlessness. The Russian empire, loose and heterogeneous, was held together by military might.

While the war was still in progress, even before the decisive battle of Poltava, Peter laid the foundations of a wholly new city in territory conquered from the Swedes and inhabited not by Russians but by various Baltic peoples. Peter named it St. Petersburg after himself and his patron saint. From the beginning it was more truly a city than Louis's spectacular creation at Versailles established at almost the same time. Standing at the head of the Gulf of Finland, it was Peter's chief window on the West. Here he established the offices of government, required noblemen to build town houses, and gave favorable terms to foreign merchants and craftsmen to settle. Peter meant to make St. Petersburg a symbol of the new Russia. It was a new city facing toward Europe and drawing the minds of the Russians westward, replacing the old capital, Moscow, which faced toward Asia and was the stronghold of opposition to his westernizing program. St. Petersburg soon became one of the leading cities of northern Europe. It remained the capital of Russia (renamed Petrograd in 1914) until the Revolution of 1917, when Moscow resumed its old role. After the Revolution Petrograd became Leningrad. Its name reverted to St. Petersburg on the eve of the dissolution of the Soviet Union in 1991.

The founding of St. Petersburg

Internal Changes under Peter the Great

The new army, the new city, the new and expanding government offices all required money, which in Russia was very scarce. Taxes were imposed on an inconceivable variety of objects—on heads, as poll taxes; on land; on inns, mills, hats, leather, cellars, and coffins; on the right to marry, sell meat, wear a beard, or be an Old Believer. The tax burden fell mainly on the peasants; and to assure the payment of taxes the mobility of peasants was further restricted, and borderline individuals were classified as peasants in the government records, so that serfdom became both more onerous and more nearly universal. To raise government revenues and to stimulate production Peter adopted the mercantilist policies exemplified by Colbert in France. He encouraged exports, built a fleet on the Baltic, and developed mining, metallurgy, and textiles, which were indispensable to the army. He organized mixed groups of Russians and foreigners into commercial companies, provided them with capital from government funds (little private capital being available), and gave them a labor supply by assigning them the use of serfs in a given locality.

Mercantilism encouraged

Serfdom, in origin mainly an agricultural institution, began to spread in Russia as an industrial institution also. The fact that serf owners obtained the right to sell serfs without land, or to move them from landed estates into mines or towns, made it easier for industry in Russia to develop on the basis of unfree labor. Nor were the employers of serfs, in these government enterprises, free to modify or abandon their projects at will. They too were simply in the tsar's service. The economic system rested largely on impressment of both management and labor, not on private profit and wages as in the increasingly capitalistic West. In this way Peter's efforts to force Russia to a European level of material productivity widened the social differences between Russia and western Europe.

Serfs in industry

To oversee and operate this system of tax collecting, recruiting, economic controls, serf hunting, and repression of internal rebellion Peter created a new administrative system. The old organs of local self-government wasted away. The duma and the national assembly, decadent anyway in that they could not function without disorder, disappeared. In their place Peter put a "senate" dependent on himself, and 10 territorial areas called "governments," or *gubernii*. The church he ruled through his Procurator of the Holy Synod. At the top of the whole structure was the tsar himself, an absolute ruler and autocrat of all the Russias. Before his death, dissatisfied with his son, he abolished the rule of hereditary succession to the tsardom, claiming the right for each tsar to name his own successor. Transmission of supreme power was thus put outside the domain of law, and in the following century the accession of tsars and tsarinas was marked by strife, conspiracy, and assassination. The whole system of centralized absolutism, while in form resembling that of the West, notably France, was in fact significantly different, for it lacked legal regularity, was handicapped by the poor education of many officials, and was imposed on a turbulent and largely unwilling population. The empire of the Romanovs has been called a state without a people.

New administrative system

Peter sought to assure the success of his reforms by developing what was called "state service," which had been begun by his predecessors. Virtually all landowning and serf-owning aristocrats were required to serve in the army or civil administration. Offices were multiplied to provide places for all. In the state service birth counted for nothing. Peter used men of all classes; Prince Dolgoruky was of the most ancient nobility, Prince Menshikov had been a cook, the tax administrator Kurbatov was an ex-serf, and many others were foreigners of unknown background. Status in Peter's Russia depended not on inherited rank which Peter could not control, but on rank in his state service. "History," wrote a Scot serving in Peter's army, "scarcely affords an example where so many people of low birth have been raised to such dignities as in tsar Peter's reign, or where so many of the highest birth and fortune have been leveled to the lowest ranks of life."

The construction of the city of St. Petersburg became the most important architectural project in Peter the Great's long-term campaign to westernize Russian society. This new city was designed to be a western-looking capital and a new center for commercial contacts with Western Europe; like the construction of the French palace at Versailles, the Russian tsar's architectural goals required the labor of thousands of poor workers and peasants.
(Tass/Sovfoto)

In this respect especially, Peter's program resembled a true social revolution. It created a new governing element in place of the old, almost what in modern terms would be called a party, a body of men working zealously for the new system with a personal interest in its preservation. These men, *Peter's social revolution* during Peter's lifetime and after his death, were the bulwarks against an anti-Western reaction, the main agents in making Peter's revolution stick. In time the new families became hereditary themselves. The priority of state service over personal position was abandoned a generation after Peter's death. Offices in the army and government were filled by men of property and birth. After Peter's revolution, as after some others, the new upper class became merged with the old.

Revolutionary also, suggesting the great French Revolution or the Russian Revolution of 1917, were Peter's unconcealed contempt for everything reminiscent of the old Russia and his zeal to reeducate his people in the new ways. He required all gentry to put their sons in school. He sent many abroad to study. He simplified the Russian alphabet. He edited the first newspaper to appear in Russia. He ordered the preparation of the first Russian book of etiquette, teaching his subjects not to spit on the floor, scratch themselves, or gnaw bones at dinner, to mix socially with women, take off their hats, converse pleasantly, and look at people while talking. The beard he took as a symbol of Muscovite backwardness; he forbade it in Russia, and himself shaved a number of men at his court. He forced people to attend evening parties to teach them manners. He had no respect for hereditary

THE GROWTH OF RUSSIA IN THE WEST

At the accession of Peter the Great in 1682 the Russian empire, expanding from the old grand duchy of Muscovy, had almost reached the Black and Baltic seas. Most of Peter's conquests were in the Baltic region where he pushed back the Swedes and built St. Petersburg. Under Catherine the Great (1762–1796) Russia took part in the three partitions of Poland and also reached the Black Sea. Tsar Alexander I (1801–1825), thanks largely to the Napoleonic wars, was able to acquire still more of Poland and annex Finland and Bessarabia; he also made conquests in the Caucasus. In the nineteenth century the western boundary of Russia remained stabilized, but additional gains were made in the Caucasus. Russia also spread over northern Asia in the seventeenth century, first reaching the Pacific as early as 1630.

aristocracy, torturing or executing the highborn as readily as the peasants. As for religion, we are told that he was a pious man and enjoyed singing in church, but he was contemptuous of ecclesiastical dignity, and in one wild revel paraded publicly with drunken companions clothed in religious vestments and mocking the priests. Like many revolutionists since his time he was aggressively secular.

The Results of Peter's Revolution

Peter's tactics provoked a strong reaction. Some adhered strictly to the old ways; others simply thought that Peter was moving too fast and too indiscriminately toward the new.

Resistance to reforms

Many Russians resented the inescapable presence of foreigners, who often looked down on Russians and who enjoyed special privileges such as the right of free exit from Russia and higher pay for similar employment. One

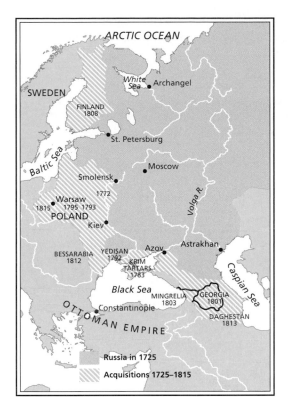

center around which malcontents rallied was the church. Another was Peter's son Alexis, who declared that when he became tsar he would put a stop to the innovations and restore respect for the customs of old Russia. Peter, after some hesitation, finally put his own son to death. He ruled that each tsar should choose his own successor. He would stop at nothing to remake Russia in his own fashion.

Peter died in 1725, proclaimed "the Great" in his own lifetime by his admiring Senate. Few persons in all history have exerted so strong an individual influence, which indirectly became more far-reaching as the stature of Russia itself grew in later centuries. Though the years after Peter's death were years of turmoil and vacillation, his revolutionary changes held firm against those who would undo them. It is not simply that he Europeanized Russia and conquered a place on the Baltic; these developments might have come about in any case. It is by the methods he used, his impatient forcing of a new culture on Russia, that he set the future character of his empire. His methods fastened autocracy, serfdom, and bureaucracy more firmly upon the country. Yet he was able to reach only the upper classes. Many of these became more Europeanized than he could dream, habitually speaking French and living spiritually in France or in Italy. But as time went on many upper-class Russians, because of their very knowledge of Europe, became impatient of the stolid immovability of the peasants around them, sensed themselves as strangers in their own country, or were troubled by a guilty feeling that their position rested on the degradation and enslavement of human beings. Russian psychology, often mysterious to people in the West, could perhaps be explained in part by the violent paradoxes set up by rapid Europeanization. As for the peasant masses, they remained outside the system, egregiously exploited, estranged from their rulers and their social superiors, regarded by them as brutes or children, never sharing in any comparable way in their increasingly Europeanized civilization. Much of this worked itself out in the social conflicts of later times. As for Peter's own time, Russia by his efforts came clearly out of its isolation, its vast bulk was now organized to play a part in international affairs, and its history thenceforward was a part of the history of Europe and increasingly of the world. Russia, like Prussia and the Austrian monarchy, was to be counted among the powers of Europe.

The rising influence of these three monarchies depended in part on their ability to acquire modern weaponry, organize more efficient bureaucracies, and bring new forms of European knowledge into their government institutions. By the beginning of the eighteenth century, European science and technologies often gave European states a comparative advantage in their economic, political, and military encounters with other peoples or governments—as the ruling elites in Austria, Prussia, and Russia had learned from their own struggles for power in central Europe. Indeed, the new science would ultimately become one of the most distinctive and significant forces in modern world history. Science helped to transform economic production, military strategies, and traditional cultures as well as imperial conflicts in Europe and around the world. We must therefore look more closely at the ways in which the development of modern scientific thought increasingly influenced the knowledge and control of both nature and human beings.

For interactive exercises, glossary, chronologies, and more, go to the *Online Learning Center* at **www.mhhe.com/palmer10.**

Chapter 6

THE SCIENTIFIC VIEW
OF THE WORLD

The seventeenth century has been called the century of genius. One reason is that it was the age when science became "modern." It was the great age of Galileo and Sir Isaac Newton, whose combined lifetimes spanned the century, with Galileo dying and Newton being born in the same year, 1642. When Galileo was young, those who probed into the secrets of nature still labored largely in the dark, isolated from one another and from the general public, working oftentimes by methods of trial and error, not altogether clear on what they were trying to do, with their thinking still complicated by ideas not nowadays considered scientific. They had nevertheless accomplished a good deal, without which the intellectual revolution of the seventeenth century would not have occurred. But in a way all scientific investigators before Galileo seem to be precursors, patient workers destined never to enter into the world toward which they labored. In 1727, when Newton died, all was changed. Scientists were in continual touch with one another, and science was recognized as one of the principal enterprises of European society. Scientific methods of inquiry had been defined. The store of factual knowledge had become very large. The first modern scientific synthesis, or coherent theory of the physical universe, had been presented by Newton. Scientific knowledge was applied increasingly to navigation, mining, agriculture, and many branches of manufacture. Science and invention were joining hands. Science was accepted as the main force in the advancement of civilization and progress. And science was becoming popularized; many people who were not themselves scientists "believed" in science and attempted to apply scientific habits of thought to diverse problems of social and political life.

The history of science is too complex a story to be told in this book, but there are a few ideas about it which even a book of this kind must attempt to make clear. First, science, purely as a form of thought, is one of

Science

Chapter emblem: Detail from a portrait of Isaac Newton by an anonymous artist. (Bettmann/Corbis)

the supreme achievements of the human mind, and to have a historical understanding of human intellectual powers one must sense the importance of science, as of philosophy, literature, or the arts. Second, science has increasingly affected practical affairs, entering into the health, wealth, and happiness of humankind. It has changed the size of populations and the use of raw materials, revolutionized methods of production, transport, business, and war, and so helped to relieve some human problems while aggravating others. This is especially true of modern civilization since the seventeenth century. Third, in the modern world ideas have had a way of passing over from science into other domains of thought. Many people today, for example, in their notions of themselves, their neighbors, or the meaning of life, are influenced by ideas which they believe to be those of Freud or Einstein—they talk of repressions or relativity without necessarily knowing much about them. Ideas derived from biology and from Darwin—such as evolution and the struggle for existence—have likewise spread far and wide. Similarly the scientific revolution of the seventeenth century had repercussions far beyond the realm of pure science. It changed ideas of religion and of God and human beings. And it helped to spread certain very deep-seated beliefs, such as that the physical universe is essentially orderly and harmonious, that human reason is capable of understanding and dealing with it, and that human affairs can be conducted by methods of peaceable exchange of ideas and rational discussion. Thus was laid a foundation for belief in free and democratic institutions.

The historical influence of modern science therefore extended far beyond the specific knowledge that transformed the human understanding and use of nature. Scientific methods for establishing truth or defining progress shaped a wide range of modern social institutions, including armies, hospitals, universities, trading companies, government bureaucracies, law courts, and even literary journals. The meaning of the word "modern" became linked to the intellectual prestige of science, and scientific knowledge became the most important intellectual force in the history of the modern world. The purpose of this chapter is to sketch the rise of modern science in the seventeenth century and the emergence of the scientific view of the world and of human affairs. The chapters that follow will describe the increasing application of this new knowledge in the expanding global economy and the influence of scientific thought in eighteenth-century European culture, which is generally known as the Age of Enlightenment.

27.   PROPHETS OF A SCIENTIFIC CIVILIZATION: BACON AND DESCARTES

Science before the Seventeenth Century

The scientific view became characteristic of elite European society about the middle of the seventeenth century. There had, indeed, been a few in earlier times who caught glimpses of a whole civilization reared upon science. To us today the most famous of these is Leonardo da Vinci (1452–1519), the universal genius of the Italian Renaissance, who had been artist, engineer, and scientific thinker all in one. Leonardo, by actual dissection of dead bodies, had obtained an accurate knowledge of human anatomy; he had conceived of the circulation of the blood and the movement of the earth about the sun; and he had drawn designs for submarines and airplanes and speculated on the use of parachutes and poison gases. But Leonardo had not published his scientific ideas. He was known almost exclusively as an artist. His work in science remained outside the stream of scientific thought, without influence on its course.

Leonardo da Vinci

It was not even known until the discovery of his private notebooks in the twentieth century. Leonardo thus figures in the history of science as an isolated genius, a man of brilliant insights and audacious theories, which died with their author's death, whereas science depends on a transmission of ideas in which investigators build upon one another's discoveries, test one another's experiments, and fill in the gaps in one another's knowledge. Modern science evolved as a kind of new cultural system, more dependent on communications and widely shared cultural beliefs than on the brilliance of isolated thinkers. Leonardo's scientific work, remaining unpublished, never entered the cultural institutions in which new scientific knowledge would be produced, challenged, and revised.

A century after the death of Leonardo da Vinci educated Europeans were by no means scientifically minded. Among thoughtful persons many currents were stirring. On the one hand there was a great deal of skepticism, a constantly doubting frame of mind, which held that no certain knowledge is possible for human beings at all, that all beliefs are essentially only customs, that some people believe one thing and some another, and that there is no sound way of choosing between them. This attitude was best expressed by the French essayist Michel de Montaigne (1533–1592), whose thought distilled itself into an eternal question, *Que sais-je?* "What do I know?" with the always implied answer, "Nothing." Montaigne's philosophy led to a tolerant, humane, and broad-minded outlook, but as a system of thought it was not otherwise very constructive. On the other hand, there was also a tendency to over-believe in mysterious, supernatural powers, arising from the same inability to distinguish between true and false. There was no accepted line between chemistry and alchemy or between astronomy and astrology; all alike were regarded as ways of penetrating the "secrets" of nature. The sixteenth century had been a great age of charlatans, such as Nostradamus and Paracelsus, some of whom, notably Paracelsus, mixed magic and valid science in a way hardly understandable to later or modern scientists. As late as the seventeenth century, especially in central Europe where the Thirty Years' War produced chaos and terror, kings and generals kept private astrologers to divine the future.

The two centuries from about 1450 to about 1650 were also the period when fear of witches was at its height. The great campaign against witches thus coincided with Europe's brutal religious wars and with the early development of the new scientific culture among members of Europe's educated elite, but even highly educated persons often believed that witches actually existed. Witches were blamed for all kinds of natural disasters and personal tragedies—bad harvests, epidemics, the mysterious deaths of children. Although most of the persons prosecuted for witchcraft were women, men were also imprisoned or executed for various crimes of "sorcery." The witchcraft panic lasted longest in Germany and central Europe, probably kept alive by the insecurities engendered by the Thirty Years' War. But about 20 persons were hanged as witches in Massachusetts as late as 1692, for the English colonies, as a remote and outlying part of the European world, were among the last to feel some of the intellectual currents originating in Europe. The last known execution for witchcraft took place in 1722 in Scotland.

Witchcraft panic

It was by no means clear, in the early part of the seventeenth century, which way Europe was going to develop. It might conceivably have fallen into a kind of political chaos, as India did at about this time. We have seen how much of Europe was racked by chronic and marauding violence, which was ended by the consolidation of the modern state and the conversion of armed bands into organized and disciplined armies. Similarly, in matters of the mind, there was no settled order. Doubt went with superstition,

Women were executed on charges of witchcraft from the later Middle Ages down through the seventeenth century, when a new fear of witches happened to coincide with the early modern scientific revolution. This mid-seventeenth-century English illustration shows a typical pattern of persecution in which several women were put to death at the same time for the alleged crime of "sorcery" or conspiring with "witches."
(Topham/The Image Works)

indifference with persecution. Science in time provided Europe with a new faith in itself. The rise of science in the seventeenth century possibly saved European civilization from petering out in a long postmedieval afterglow or from wandering off into the diverse paths of a genial skepticism, ineffectual philosophizing, desultory magic, or mad fear of the unknown.

Bacon and Descartes

Two men stand out as prophets of a world reconstructed by science. One was the Englishman Francis Bacon (1561–1626); the other was the Frenchman René Descartes (1596–1650). Both published their most influential books between 1620 and 1640. Both addressed themselves to the problem of knowledge. Both asked themselves how it is possible for human beings to know anything with certainty or to have a reliable, truthful, and usable knowledge of the world of nature. Both shared in the doubts of their day. They branded virtually all beliefs of preceding generations (outside religion) as worthless. Both ridiculed the tendency to put faith in ancient books, to cite the writings of Aristotle or others, on questions having to do with the workings of nature. Both attacked earlier methods of seeking knowledge; they rejected the methods of the "schoolmen" or "scholastics," the thinkers in the academic tradition of the universities founded in the Middle Ages. On the whole, medieval philosophy had been deductive. That is, its characteristic procedure was to start with definitions and general propositions and then discover what further knowledge could be logically deduced from the definitions thus accepted. Or it proceeded by affirming the nature of an object to be such-and-such (e.g., that "man is a political animal") and then described how objects of such a nature do or should behave. These methods, which owed much to Aristotle and other ancient codifiers of human thought, had generally ceased to be fruitful in producing new knowledge of nature. Bacon and Descartes held that the medieval (or Aristotelian) methods were backward. They held that truth is not something that we postulate at the beginning and then explore in all its ramifications, but that it is something which we find at the end, after a long process of investigation, experiment, and intermediate thought.

Bacon and Descartes thus went beyond mere doubt. They offered a constructive program, and though their programs were different, they both became heralds or philosophers of a scientific view. They maintained that there was a true and reliable method of knowledge. And they maintained in addition that once this true method was known and practiced, once the real workings of nature were understood, people would be able to use this knowledge for their own purposes, control nature in their own interests, make undreamed of useful inventions, improve their mechanical arts, and add generally to human wealth and comfort. Bacon and Descartes thus announced the advent of a scientific civilization.

Francis Bacon planned a great work in many volumes, to be known as the *Instauratio Magna* or "Great Renewal," calling for a complete new start in science and civilization. He completed only two parts. One, published in 1620, was the *Novum Organum* or new method of acquiring knowledge. Here he insisted on *inductive* method. In the inductive method we proceed from the particular to the general, from the concrete to the abstract. For example, in the study of leaves, if we examine millions of actual leaves of all sizes and shapes and if we assemble, observe, and compare them with minute scrutiny, we are using an *inductive* method in the sense meant by Bacon; if successful, we may arrive at a knowledge, based on observed facts, of the general nature of a leaf as such. If, on the other hand, we begin with a general idea of what we think all leaves are like, that is, all leaves have stems, and then proceed to describe an individual leaf on that basis, we are following the *deductive* method; we draw logical implications from what we already know, but we learn no more of the nature of a leaf than what we knew or thought we knew at the beginning. Bacon advised his readers to put aside all traditional ideas, to rid themselves of prejudices and preconceptions, to look at the world with fresh eyes, to observe and study the innumerable things that are actually perceived by the senses. Thinkers before Bacon used the inductive method, but he formalized it as a method and became a leading philosopher of empiricism, the founding of knowledge on observation and experience. This philosophy has always proved a useful safeguard against fitting facts into preconceived patterns. It demands that we let the patterns of our thought be shaped by actual facts as we observe them. Scientific knowledge thus links particular facts to general principles and typically combines inductive method with the broader claims of deductive thought.

The other completed part of Bacon's great work, published in 1623, was called in its English translation *The Advancement of Learning*. Here Bacon developed the same ideas and insisted also that true knowledge was useful knowledge. In *The New Atlantis* (1627), he portrayed a scientific utopia whose inhabitants enjoyed a perfect society through their knowledge and command of nature. The usefulness of knowledge became the other main element in the Baconian tradition. In this view there was no sharp difference between pure science and applied science or between the work of the purely scientific investigators and that of the inventors who in their own way probed into nature and devised instruments or machines for putting natural forces to work. The fact that knowledge could be used for

Francis Bacon and empiricism

RENÉ DESCARTES
by Frans Hals (1584–1666)
Descartes worked for many years in Amsterdam, where he developed his work in mathematics, described his philosophical methods of systematic doubt, and sat for this famous portrait by Frans Hals.
(Eric Lessing/Art Resource, NY)

practical purposes became a sign or proof that it was true knowledge. For example, the fact that soldiers could aim their cannon and hit their targets more accurately in the seventeenth century became a proof of the theory of ballistics which had been scientifically worked out. Enthusiastic Baconians believed that knowledge was power. True knowledge could be put to work, if not immediately at least in the long run, after more knowledge was discovered. It was useful to mankind, unlike the "delicate learning" of the misguided scholastics. In this coming together of knowledge and power arose the far-reaching modern idea of progress. And in it arose many modern problems, since the power given by scientific knowledge can be used for either good or evil.

But Bacon, though a force in redirecting the European mind, never had much influence on the development of actual science. Kept busy as Lord Chancellor of England and in other government duties, he was not even fully abreast of the most advanced scientific thought of his day. Bacon's greatest weakness was his failure to understand the role of mathematics. Mathematics, dealing with pure abstractions and proceeding deductively from axioms to theorems, was not an empirical or inductive method of thought such as Bacon demanded. Yet science in the seventeenth century went forward most successfully in subjects where mathematics could be applied. Even today the degree to which a subject is truly scientific depends on the degree to which it can be made mathematical. We have pure science where we have formulas and equations, and the scientific method itself is both inductive and deductive.

René Descartes

Descartes was a great mathematician in his own right. He is considered the inventor of coordinate geometry. He showed that by use of coordinates (or graph paper, in simple language) any algebraic formula could be plotted as a curve in space, and contrariwise that any curve in space, however complex, could be converted into algebraic terms and thus dealt with by methods of calculation. One effect of his general philosophy was to create belief in a vast world of nature that could be reduced to mathematical form.

Descartes set forth his ideas in his *Discourse on Method* in 1637 and in many more technical writings. He advanced the principle of systematic doubt. He began by trying to doubt everything that could reasonably be doubted, thus sweeping away past ideas and clearing the ground for his own "great renewal," to use Bacon's phrase. He held that he could not doubt his own existence as a thinking and doubting being (*cogito ergo sum,* "I think, therefore I exist"); he then deduced, by systematic reasoning, the existence of God and much else. He arrived at a philosophy of dualism, the famous "Cartesian dualism," which held that God has created two kinds of fundamental reality in the universe. One was "thinking substance"— mind, spirit, consciousness, subjective experience. The other was "extended substance"— everything outside the mind and hence objective. Of everything except the mind itself the most fundamental and universal quality was that it occupied a portion of space, minute or vast. Space itself was conceived as infinite and everywhere geometric.

This philosophy had profound and long-lasting effects. For one thing, the seemingly most real elements in human experience, color and sound, joy and grief, seemed somehow to be shadowy and unreal, or at least illusive, with no existence outside the mind itself. But all else was quantitative, measurable, reducible to formulas or equations. Over all else, over the whole universe or half-universe of "extended substance," the most powerful instrument available to the human understanding, namely, mathematics, reigned supreme. "Give me motion and extension," said Descartes, "and I will build you the world."

Descartes also shared Bacon's belief in useful knowledge and human progress. Instead of the "speculative philosophy of the schools," he wrote in the *Discourse on Method,* one might discover a "practical philosophy by which, understanding the forces and action of fire, water, air, the stars and heavens and all other bodies that surround us, as distinctly as we understand the mechanical arts of our craftsmen, we can use these forces in the same way for all purposes for which they are appropriate, and so make ourselves the masters and possessors of nature. And this is desirable not only for the invention of innumerable devices by which we may enjoy without trouble the fruits of the earth and the conveniences it affords, but mainly also for the preservation of health, which is undoubtedly the principal good and foundation of all other good things in this life." Science, in short, opened the way to a better life that philosophy alone could never produce.

28.   THE ROAD TO NEWTON: THE LAW OF UNIVERSAL GRAVITATION

Scientific Advances

Meanwhile actual scientific discovery was advancing on many fronts. It did not advance on all with equal speed. Some of the sciences were, and long remained, dependent mainly on the collection of specimens. Botany was one of these; Europe's knowledge of plants expanded enormously with the explorations overseas, and botanical gardens and herb collections in Europe became far more extensive than ever before, bringing important enlargements in the stock of medicinal drugs. Other sciences drew their impetus from intensive and open-minded observation. The Flemish Vesalius, by a book published in 1543, *The Structure of the Human Body,* renewed and modernized the study of anatomy. Formerly anatomists had generally held

Botany, anatomy, and physiology

that the writings of Galen, dating from the second century A.D., contained an authoritative description of all human muscles and tissues. They had indeed dissected cadavers but had dismissed those not conforming to Galen's description as somehow abnormal or not typical. Vesalius put Galen behind him and based his general description of the human frame on actual bodies as he found them.

In physiology also, dealing with the functioning rather than the structure of living bodies, there was considerable progress. Here the method of laboratory experiment could be profitably used. William Harvey, after years of laboratory work, including the vivisection of animals, published in 1628 a book *On the Movement of the Heart and Blood* which set forth the doctrine of the continual circulation of the blood through arteries and veins. The Italian Malpighi, using the newly invented microscope, confirmed Harvey's findings by the discovery of capillaries in 1661. The Dutch Leeuwenhoek, also by use of the microscope, was the first to see blood corpuscles, spermatozoa, and bacteria, of which he left published drawings. Another seventeenth-century Dutch scientist, Régnier de Graaf, published the first description of the female ovaries, thus challenging Galen's ancient theories of human sexuality and the long-accepted idea that women contributed less than men to the biological processes of reproduction.

Astronomy and physics

These sciences, and also chemistry, although work in them went forward continually, did not come fully into their own until after 1800. They were long overshadowed by astronomy and physics. Here mathematics could be most fully applied, and mathematics underwent a rapid development in the seventeenth century. Decimals came into use to express fractions, the symbols used in algebra were improved and standardized, and in 1614 logarithms were invented by the Scot John Napier. Coordinate geometry was mapped out by Descartes, the theory of probabilities was developed by Pascal, and calculus was invented simultaneously in England by Newton and in Germany by Leibniz. These advances made it more generally possible to think about nature in purely quantitative terms, to measure with greater precision, and to perform complex and laborious computations. Physics and astronomy were remarkably stimulated, and it was in this field that the most astonishing scientific revolution of the seventeenth century took place.

The Scientific Revolution: Copernicus to Galileo

Ever since the Greek Ptolemy had codified ancient astronomy in the second century A.D., educated Europeans had held a conception of the cosmos which we call Ptolemaic. The cosmos in this view was a group of concentric spheres, a series of balls within balls each having the same center. The innermost ball was the earth, made up of hard, solid, earthy substance such as people were familiar with underfoot. The other spheres, encompassing the earth in series, were all transparent. They were the "crystalline spheres" made known to us by the poets; their harmony was the "music of the spheres." These spheres all revolved about the earth, each sphere containing, set in it as a jewel, a luminous heavenly body or orb which moved about the earth with the movement of its transparent sphere. Nearest to the earth was the sphere of the moon; then, in turn, the spheres of Mercury and Venus, then the sphere of the sun, then those of the outer planets. Last came the outermost sphere containing all the fixed stars studded in it, all moving majestically about the earth in daily motion, but motionless with respect to each other because they were held firmly in the same sphere. Beyond the sphere of the fixed stars, in general belief, lay the "empyrean," the home of angels and immortal spirits; but this was not a matter of natural science.

The Ptolemaic system

**A SCHOLAR HOLDING
A THESIS ON BOTANY**
by **Willem Moreelse (Dutch,
before 1630–1666)**

This scholar may be a new doctor of the University of Utrecht, where the little-known painter Willem Moreelse worked in the seventeenth century. Crowned with the laurel, the successful candidate proudly displays his thesis, on which the Latin words announce "any plant shows the presence of God"— an example of the growing scientific interest in hitherto unknown plants that reached Europe from other parts of the world in this era.
(Toledo Museum of Art. Purchased with funds from the Libbey Endowment, Gift of Edward Drumond Libbey. (1962.70))

Persons standing on the earth and looking up into the sky thus felt themselves to be enclosed by a dome of which their own position was the center. In the blue sky of day they could literally see the crystalline spheres; in the stars at night they could behold the orbs which these spheres carried with them. All revolved about the observer, presumably at no very alarming distance. The celestial bodies were commonly supposed to be of different material and quality from the earth. The earth was of heavy dross; the stars and planets and the sun and moon seemed made of pure and gleaming light, or at least of a bright ethereal substance almost as tenuous as the crystal spheres in which they moved. The cosmos was a hierarchy of ascending perfection. The heavens were purer than the earth.

This system corresponded to actual appearances, and except for scientific knowledge would be highly believable today. It was formulated also in rigorous mathematical terms. Ever since the Greeks, and becoming increasingly intricate in the Middle Ages, a complex geometry had grown up to explain the observed motion of the heavenly bodies. The Ptolemaic system was a mathematical system. And it was for purely mathematical reasons that it first came to be reconsidered. There was a marked revival of mathematical interest at the close of the Middle Ages, in the fourteenth and fifteenth centuries, a renewed concentration on the philosophical traditions of Pythagoras and Plato. In these philosophies could be found the doctrine that numbers might be the final key to the mysteries of nature. With them went a metaphysical belief that simplicity was more likely to be a sign of truth than complexity and that a simpler mathematical formulation was better than a more complicated one.

These ideas motivated Nicholas Copernicus (1473–1543), born in Poland of German and Polish background, who, after study in Italy, wrote his epochal work *On the Revolutions of the Heavenly Orbs*. In this book,

Nicholas Copernicus

published in 1543 after his death, he held the sun to be the center of the solar system and of the whole universe; the earth, he argued, was one of the planets revolving in space around it. This view had been entertained by a few isolated thinkers before. Copernicus gave a mathematical demonstration. To him it was a purely mathematical problem. With increasingly detailed knowledge of the actual movement of the heavenly bodies it had become necessary, as the years passed, to make the Ptolemaic system more intricate by the addition of new "cycles" and "epicycles," until, as John Milton expressed it later, the cosmos was

> With Centric and Concentric scribbled o'er,
> Cycle and Epicycle, Orb in Orb.

Copernicus needed fewer such hypothetical constructions to explain the known movements of the heavenly bodies. The heliocentric or sun-centered theory was mathematically simpler than the geocentric or earth-centered theory hitherto held.

The Copernican doctrine long remained a hypothesis known only to experts. Most astronomers for a time hesitated to accept it, seeing no need, from the evidence yet produced, to make such a radical readjustment of current ideas. Tycho Brahe (1546–1601), the greatest authority on the actual positions and movements of the heavenly bodies in the generations immediately after Copernicus, never accepted the Copernican system in full. But his assistant and follower, Johannes Kepler (1571–1630), building on Tycho's exact observations, not only accepted the Copernican theory but carried it further.

Johannes Kepler

Kepler, a German, was a kind of mathematical mystic, part-time astrologer, and scientific genius. Copernicus had believed the orbits of the planets about the sun to be perfect circles. Tycho showed that this belief did not fit the observable facts. It was Kepler who discovered that the orbits of the planets were ellipses. The ellipse, like the circle, is an abstract mathematical figure with knowable properties. Kepler demonstrated that the closer a planet is to the sun in its elliptical orbit, the faster it moves; and he showed that the length of time in which the several planets revolve about the sun varies proportionately with their distance from the sun.

It is not possible for most people to understand the mathematics involved, but it is possible to realize the astounding implications of Kepler's laws of planetary motion. Kepler showed that the actual world of stubborn facts, as observed by Tycho, and the purely rational world of mathematical harmony, as surmised by Copernicus, were not really in any contradiction to each other—that they really corresponded exactly. Why they should he did not know; it was the mystery of numbers. He digested an overwhelming amount of hitherto unexplained information into a few brief statements. He showed a cosmic mathematical relationship between space and time. And he described the movement of the planets in explicit formulas, which any competent person could verify at will.

Galileo

The next scientific step was taken by Galileo (1564–1642). So far the question of what the heavenly bodies were made of had hardly been affected. Indeed, they were not thought of as bodies at all, but rather as orbs. Only the sun and moon had any dimension; stars and planets were only points of light; and the theories of Copernicus and Kepler, like those of Ptolemy, might apply to insubstantial luminous objects in motion. In 1609 Galileo built a telescope. Turning it to the sky, he perceived that the moon had a rough and apparently mountainous surface, as if made of the same kind of material as the earth. Seeing clearly the dark part of the moon in its various phases, and

The Copernican conception of a solar system revolving around the sun was long unknown outside a small circle of experts, and few persons understood the mathematics upon which it was based. But the meaning of the Copernican theories later spread in visual images that depicted the new astronomical view of the sun, earth, and other planets.
(© Trustees of the British Museum)

noting that in every position it only reflected the light of the sun, he concluded that the moon was not itself a luminous object, another indication that it might be made of earth-like substance. He saw spots on the sun, as if the sun were not pure and perfect. He found that the planets had visible breadth when seen in the telescope but that the fixed stars remained only points of light, as if incalculably further away. He discovered also that Jupiter had satellites, moons moving around it like the moon around the earth. These discoveries reassured him of the validity of the Copernican theory, which he had in any case already accepted. They suggested also that the heavenly bodies might be of the same substance as the earth, masses of matter moving in space. Contrariwise, it became easier to think of the earth itself as a kind of heavenly body revolving about the sun. The difference between the earth and the heavens was disappearing. This struck a terrifying blow at all earlier philosophy and theology. Some professors were afraid to look through the telescope, and Galileo was condemned and forced to an ostensible recantation by his church.

Moreover, where Kepler had found mathematical laws describing the movement of planets, Galileo now found mathematical laws describing the movement of bodies on the earth. Formerly it had been thought that some bodies were by nature heavier than others and that heavier bodies fell to the ground faster than light ones. Galileo in 1591, according to the story, dropped a 10-pound and a 1-pound weight simultaneously from the top of the Leaning Tower of Pisa. The truth of this story has been questioned, but in any case Galileo showed that despite all previous speculation on the subject two bodies of different weights, when allowance was made for differences in air resistance due to differences of size or shape, struck the ground at the same time. His further work in dynamics, or the science of motion of bodies, took many years to accomplish. He had to devise more refined means for measuring small intervals of time, find means of estimating the air resistance, friction, and other impediments which always occur in nature, and conceive of pure or absolute motion, and of force and velocity, in abstract mathematical terms. He made use of a new conception of inertia, in which only *change* in motion, not the origination of motion, had to be explained. This dispensed with the need of an Unmoved Mover felt in the older philosophy.

The Achievement of Newton: The Promise of Science

It was the supreme achievement of Isaac Newton (1642–1727) to bring Kepler and Galileo together, that is, to show that Kepler's laws of planetary motion and Galileo's laws of terrestrial motion were two aspects of the same laws. Galileo's discovery that moving bodies move uniformly in a straight line unless deflected by a definite force made it necessary to explain why the planets, instead of flying off in straight lines, tend to fall toward the sun, the result being their elliptical orbits—and why the moon, similarly, tends to fall toward the earth. Newton seems early to have suspected that the answer would be related to Galileo's laws of falling bodies—that is, that gravity, or the pull of the earth upon objects on earth, might be a form of a universal gravitation, or a similar pull characterizing all bodies in the solar system. Great technical difficulties stood in the way, but finally, after inventing calculus, and using a new measurement of the size of the earth made by a Frenchman and experiments with circular motion made by the Dutch Huyghens on the pendulum, Newton was able to bring his calculations to fruition, and to publish, in 1687, his *Mathematical Principles of Natural Philosophy*.

Universal gravitation

This stupendous book showed that all motion that could be timed and measured, whether on the earth or in the solar system, could be described by the same mathematical formulas. All matter moved as if every particle attracted every other particle with a force proportionate to the product of the two masses and inversely proportionate to the square of the distance between them. This "force" was universal gravitation. What it was Newton did not pretend to explain. For 200 years the law stood unshaken, always verified by every new relevant discovery. Only in the past century were its limitations found; it does not hold good in the infinitesimal world of subatomic structure or in the macrocosm of the whole physical universe as now conceived.

It was in Newton's time that the pursuit of natural knowledge became institutionalized. Organized institutions, possessing equipment and funds, were engaged in scientific study, most notably the Royal Society of London, founded in 1662, and the Royal Academy of Sciences in France, founded in 1666. Both originated when earlier and informal groups, usually gentlemen of the landed class, received charters from their governments to pursue scientific interests. Scientific periodicals began to be published. Scientific societies provided the medium for prompt interchange of ideas indispensable to the growth of scientific knowledge. They held meetings, proposed projects for research, and published articles not only on the natural sciences and mathematics, but also on paleography, numismatics, chronology, legal history, and natural law. The work of the learned had not yet yielded to specialization.

In all these activities the promise of science seemed fulfilled. Even in practical affairs conveniences followed, as anticipated by the Baconians. The tides could now be understood and predicted by the gravitational interplay of earth, moon, and sun. Exact mathematical knowledge of the celestial bodies, together with the invention of more accurate timepieces, was of great help to navigation and mapmaking. Measures of latitude, or of north-south distances on the spherical earth, had been known to the ancient Greeks. But longitude, or east-west distances, could not be measured until the eighteenth century, when it became possible to determine it by use of a chronometer and observation of heavenly bodies at a known time. Merchant ships and naval squadrons could thus operate with more assurance. Places on land could be located and mapped more exactly. Eighteenth-century Europeans were the first human beings to have a fairly accurate idea of the shapes and sizes of all the continents and oceans. Better local and regional maps of places in Europe also became available.

Scientific improvements

Mathematical advance, including the development of calculus, which allowed an exact treatment of curves and trajectories, reinforced by technical discoveries in the working of metals, led to an increased use of artillery. Armies in 1750 used twice as many cannon per soldier as in 1650. Naval ordnance also improved. These items made armed forces more expensive to maintain, requiring governments to increase their taxes, and hence producing constitutional crises. Improved firearms heightened the advantage of armies over insurrectionists or private fighting bands, thus strengthening the sovereignty of the state. They also gave Europeans the military advantage over other peoples, in America, India, or elsewhere, on which the world ascendancy of Europe was built in the eighteenth century.

The instance of the steam engine may also be cited. Steam power was eventually almost literally to move the world. In 1700 it was only in its earliest stages, but it was in sight on the horizon. A Frenchman, Denis Papin, in 1681 invented a device in which steam moved a piston, but it produced so little power that it was used only in cooking. British scientists turned their minds to it. Robert Boyle, discoverer of "Boyle's Law" on the pressure of gases, studied the problem; scientists, mechanics, and instrument makers collaborated. In 1702 Thomas Newcomen, a man without scientific training but associated with scientists, produced the steam engine known thereafter as Newcomen's engine, from which, as will be seen, James Watt developed the steam engine as we know it. Newcomen's engine was primitive according to later ideas. It burned so much fuel that it could be used only in coal mines. But it was used. Not long after 1700 it was widely employed to pump water from the coal pits. It saved labor, cheapened production, and opened hitherto unusable deposits to exploitation. It was the first application of steam to an economic purpose.

No distinction was yet felt between pure and applied science. The modern sense of the word hardly existed; what we call "science" was called natural philosophy or "useful knowledge." Traveling public lecturers, in explaining the laws of force and motion, showed their application in devices such as pulleys, scales, levers, cogwheels, waterwheels, and pumps. Such lectures were attended, especially in England, by a mixed audience of philosophers, experimenters, inventors, artisans, landed gentlemen who wished to develop their estates, and small businessmen wishing to enlarge their markets. The scientific movement thus opened the way to agricultural and industrial improvements in Great Britain and other places where the new knowledge was brought into economic activities.

FOUNDING OF THE ACADEMY OF SCIENCES AND THE OBSERVATORY IN 1666
by Henri Testelin (1616–1695)
Testelin was an instructor at the Royal Academy of Painting and a strong defender of the academic traditions in French art. He portrayed King Louis XIV visiting the new Royal Academy of Sciences in this painting, which expresses his respect for both the king and the new scientific knowledge. But Testelin's life also exemplified another side of life in late seventeenth-century France. He was a Protestant who eventually had to give up his academic position and move to the Netherlands to practice his religion.
(Giraudon/Art Resource, NY)

The Scientific Revolution and the World of Thought

It was perhaps in the world of thought that the revolution accomplished from Copernicus to Newton was most profound. It has been called the greatest spiritual readjustment that human beings have been required to make. The old heavens were exploded. Humans were no longer the center of creation. The luminaries of the sky no longer shone to light their way or to give them beauty. The sky itself was an illusion, its color a thing in the mind only, for anyone looking upward was really looking only into the darkness of endless space. The old cosmos, comfortably enclosed and ranked in an ascending order of purity, gave way to a new cosmos which seemed to consist of an infinite emptiness through which particles of matter were distributed. Humans were the puny denizens of a material object swinging in space along with other very distant material objects of the same kind. About the physical universe there was nothing especially Christian, nothing that the God portrayed in the Hebrew or the Christian Bible would be likely to have made. The gap between religion and natural science, always present yet always bridged in the Middle Ages, now opened wider than ever. It was felt with anguish by some in the seventeenth century, notably by the Frenchman Blaise Pascal, a considerable scientist, preeminent mathematician, and deep and troubled Christian believer. He left a record of his state of mind in his *Pensées,* or *Thoughts,* jottings from which he hoped some day to write a great book on the Christian faith. "I am terrified," he said in one of these jottings, "by the eternal silence of these infinite spaces."

But on the whole the reaction was more optimistic. Man might be merely a reed, as Pascal said, but Pascal added, he was "a thinking reed." Human beings might be no longer the physical center of the world. But it was the human mind that had penetrated the world's laws. The Newtonian system, as it became popularized, a process which took about 50 years, led to a great intellectual complacency. Never had confidence in human powers been so high. As the English poet Alexander Pope put it,

The Newtonian system

> *Nature and nature's laws lay hid in night;*
> *God said, "Let Newton be," and all was light.*

Or, according to another epigram on the subject, there was only one universe to discover, and this universe had been discovered by Newton. Everything seemed possible to human reason. Although Newton and most other scientists continued to believe in the existence of God, the old feeling of dependency on divine powers and judgments lost much of its force or became something to be discussed by clergymen in church on Sunday. Human beings were not really little creatures, wayfarers in a world that was alien, yearning for the reunion with God that would bring peace. They were creatures of great capacity in their own right, living in a world that was understandable and manageable. These ideas contributed greatly to the secularizing of European society, gradually pushing religion and churches to the sidelines of European political power and many of the era's new intellectual debates.

The scientific discoveries also reinforced the old philosophy of natural law. This philosophy, developed by the Greeks and renewed in the Middle Ages, held that the universe is fundamentally orderly and that there is a natural rightness or justice, universally the same for all people and knowable by reason. It was very important in political theory, where it stood out against arbitrariness and the mere claims of power. The laws of nature as discovered by science were somewhat different, but they taught the same lesson, namely, the orderliness and minute regularity of the world. It was reassuring to feel that everywhere throughout an infinite space every particle of matter was quietly attracting every other particle by a force proportionate to the product of the masses and inversely proportionate to the square of the distance. The physical universe laid bare by science—orderly, rational, balanced, smoothly running, without strife or rivalry or contention—became a model on which many thinkers, as time went on, hoped to refashion human society. They hoped to make society also fulfill the rule of law.

In some ways it would be possible to exaggerate the impact of pure science. Scientists themselves did not usually apply their scientific ideas to religion and society. Few suffered the spiritual torment of Pascal. Both Descartes and Newton wrote earnest tracts arguing for the truth of certain religious doctrines. Bacon and Harvey were conservative politically,

Isaac Newton became the famous public symbol of the new scientific knowledge and the new scientific researcher. This portrait by an anonymous artist emphasizes the focused brilliance that made Newton an icon in the expanding institutions of scientific culture and in the wider development of eighteenth-century intellectual life.
(Bettmann/Corbis)

upholders of king against Parliament. The Englishman Joseph Glanvill, in the 1660s, used the Cartesian dualism to demonstrate the probable existence of witches. Descartes, despite his systematic doubt, held that the customs of one's country should usually be accepted without question. Natural science, in the pure sense, was not inherently revolutionary or even upsetting. If Europeans in the seventeenth century began to waver in many old beliefs, it was not only because of the stimulus of pure science but also because of an increasing knowledge and study of humanity itself.

29. NEW KNOWLEDGE OF HUMAN BEINGS AND SOCIETY

The discovery and exploration of the world overseas became a decisive new influence on European views of human cultures and the nature of human beings. Europe was already becoming part of the world as a whole and could henceforth understand itself only by comparison with non-European regions. Great reciprocal influences were at work. The influences of European expansion on other parts of the world are easily seen: the Indian societies of America were modified or extinguished; the indigenous societies of Africa were dislocated and many of their members were enslaved and transported; in the long run even the ancient societies of Asia were to be disrupted or undermined. From the beginning the counterinfluence of the rest of the world upon Europe was equally great. It took the form of new medicines, new diseases, new foods, new and exotic manufactures brought to Europe, and the growth of material wealth in west-European countries, but it also affected European thinking. New questions were raised about the diversity of religious traditions, the history of languages, and the origins of human civilizations. The growing involvement with other cultures undermined the old Europe and its ideas, just as Europe was undermining the old cultures beyond the oceans. Vast new horizons opened before Europeans in the sixteenth and seventeenth centuries. Europeans of this period were the first people to know the globe as a whole, to establish colonial outposts around most of the world, or to realize the variety of the human race and its multifarious manners and customs.

The Current of Skepticism

This realization was very unsettling. The realization of human differences had the effect, in Europe, of breaking what has been called the "cake of custom." A new sense of the relative nature of social institutions developed. It became harder to believe in any absolute rightness of one's own ways. Montaigne, already mentioned, expressed the relativist outlook clearly, and nowhere more clearly than in his famous essay on cannibals. The cannibals, he said humorously, did in fact eat human flesh; that was their custom, and they have their customs as we have ours; they would think some of our ways odd or inhuman; peoples differ, and who are we to judge? Travelers' books spread the same message increasingly through the seventeenth century. As one of them observed (whether or not rightly), in Turkey it was the custom to shave the hair and wear the beard, in Europe to shave the beard and wear the hair; *Travelers' tales* what difference does it really make? That the ways of non-Europeans might be good ways was emphasized by Jesuit missionaries. Writing from the depths of the Mississippi Valley or from China, the Jesuit fathers often dwelt on the natural goodness and mental alertness of the native peoples they encountered, perhaps hoping in this way to gain support in Europe for their missionary labors. People from the American wilderness or from Asia sometimes appeared in Europe itself. In 1684 a delegation of aristocratic Siamese arrived in Paris, followed by another in 1686. The Parisians went through a fad for Siam (now Thailand); they recounted how the king of Siam, when asked by a missionary to turn Christian, replied that divine Providence, had it wished a single religion to prevail in the world, could easily have so arranged it. The philosophical Siamese seemed civilized and wise; they allowed Christians to preach in their own country, whereas it was well known what would happen to a Siamese missionary who undertook to preach in Paris. China also was seen at this time as a civilized center of learning, tolerance, and wise ethical traditions. By 1700 there were even professors of Arabic, at Paris, Oxford, and Utrecht, who said that Islam was a religion to be respected, as good for Muslims as Christianity was for Christians.

Skepticism

Thus was created a strong current of skepticism, holding that all beliefs are relative, varying with time and place. Its greatest spokesman at the end of the century was Pierre Bayle (1647–1706). Bayle was influenced by the scientific discoveries also; not exactly that he understood them, for he was an almost purely literary scholar, but he realized that many popular beliefs were without scientific foundation. Between 1680 and 1682 a number of comets were seen. The one of 1682 was studied by a friend of Newton's, Edmond Halley, the first man to predict the return of a comet. He identified the comet of 1682 with the one observed in 1302, 1456, 1531, and 1607, and predicted its reappearance in 1757 (it appeared in 1759); it was seen again in 1910 and 1986

AMBASSADEURS DE SIAM

The arrival of ambassadors from Siam at Versailles in 1684 made a vivid impression on a French generation that was fascinated by reports on distant lands and peoples. Although the bowing ambassadors show the requisite respect for the Sun King, their presence in France contributed to the growing speculation on cultural differences and the relativism of cultural customs.

(Musées Versailles, Reunion des Musées Nationaux/Art Resource, NY)

and is still called Halley's Comet. In the 1680s people were talking excitedly about the significance of comets. Some said that comets emitted poisonous exhalations; others, that they were supernatural omens of future events.

Bayle, in his *Thoughts on the Comet,* argued at great length that there was no basis for any such beliefs except human credulity. In 1697 he published his *Historical and Critical Dictionary,* a tremendous repository of miscellaneous lore, conveying the message that what is called truth is often mere opinion, that most people are amazingly gullible, that many things firmly believed are really ridiculous, and that it is very foolish to hold too strongly to one's own views. Bayle's *Dictionary* remained a reservoir on which skeptical writers continued to draw for generations. Bayle himself, having no firm basis in his own mind for settled judgment, mixed skepticism with an impulse to faith. Born a Protestant, he was converted to Rome, then returned to his Calvinist background. In any case his views made for toleration in religion. For Bayle, as for Montaigne, no opinion was worth burning your neighbor for.

The New Sense of Evidence

But in the study of humankind, as in the study of physical nature, Europeans of the seventeenth century were not generally content with skepticism. They were not possessed by a mere negative and doubting mood, important and salutary as such an attitude was. In the subjects collectively called the humanities, as in pure science, they were looking not for disbelief but for understanding. They wanted new means of telling the true from the false, a new method for arriving at some degree of certainty of conviction. And here, too, a kind of scientific view of the world arose, if that term is understood in a general sense. It took the form of a new sense of evidence. Evidence is that which allows one to believe a thing to be true, or at least truer than something else for which the evidence is weaker. And if to believe without evidence is the sign of primitive or irrational thinking, to require evidence before believing is in a way to be scientific, or at least to trust and use the power of human intelligence.

The new sense of evidence, and of the need of evidence, revealed itself in many ways. One of the clearest was in the law. The English law of evidence, for example, began to take on its modern form at the close of the seventeenth century. It was long believed that less evidence should be necessary in arriving at a verdict of guilty in trials for the most atrocious crimes; this was thought necessary to protect society from the more hideous offenses. *English law of evidence*
From the end of the seventeenth century, in English law, the judge lost his power of discretion in deciding what should constitute evidence, and the same rules of evidence were applied in all forms of accusation, the essential question being recognized as always the same—did such-and-such a fact (however outrageous) occur or did it not? After 1650 mere hearsay evidence, long vaguely distrusted, was ruled definitely out of court. After 1696 even persons charged with felony were allowed legal counsel.

The new sense of evidence was probably the main force in putting an end to the delusions of witchcraft. What made witchcraft so credible and so fearsome was that many persons confessed themselves to be witches, admitting to supernatural powers and to evil designs upon their neighbors. *Evidence and witchcraft*
Many or most such confessions were extracted under torture. Reformers urged that confessions obtained under torture were not evidence, that people would say anything to escape unbearable pain, so that no such confessions offered the slightest ground for believing in witches. As for the voluntary confessions, and even the boastings of some people of their diabolical powers, it was noted that such statements often came from persons who would today be called hysterical or psychotic. Witches came to be regarded as self-deluded. Their ideas of themselves were no longer accepted as evidence. But it must be added that, except in England, the use of legal torture lasted through most of the eighteenth century in criminal cases in which the judge believed the accused to be guilty.

History and Historical Scholarship

What are called the historical sciences also developed rapidly at this time. History, like the law, depends on the finding and using of evidence. The historian and the judge must answer the same kind of question—did such-and-such a fact really occur? All knowledge of history, so far as it disengages itself from legend and wishful thinking, rests ultimately on pieces of evidence, written records, and other works created in the past and surviving in some form or other in the present. On this mass of material the vast picture of the past is

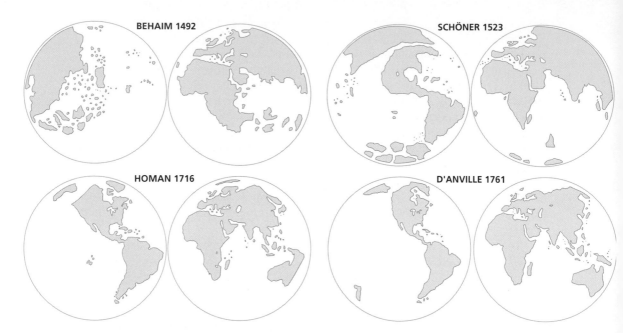

BEHAIM 1492　SCHÖNER 1523

HOMAN 1716　D'ANVILLE 1761

THE GROWTH OF GEOGRAPHICAL KNOWLEDGE

The four maps show the best scientific knowledge at their respective dates. Behaim has no inkling of the existence of America and has filled in the hemisphere opposite to Europe with a mass of islands, representing what he has heard of the East Indies and Japan. He knows pretty well the limits of Africa. Schöner in 1523 fills in America and even distinguishes two American continents. He knows of the Gulf of Mexico but fails to realize the narrowness of the Isthmus of Panama. He knows of the Straits of Magellan (but not Cape Horn) and hopefully fills in a corresponding Northwest Passage in the north. His conception of the Indian Ocean is quite accurate. To Homan, two centuries later, the size and shapes of oceans and continents are well known, but he believes New Guinea joined to Australia and is frankly ignorant of the northwest coast of North America, representing it by a straight line. The Great Lakes and the interior of North America have become known to Europe. D'Anville in 1761 has no island of Tasmania, does not understand that Alaska is a peninsula, and believes the American polar regions to be impassable by sea. Otherwise his map is indistinguishable from one on the same scale today.

built, and without it people would be ignorant of their own antecedents or would have only folktales and oral traditions.

There was much skepticism about history in the seventeenth century. Some said that history was not a form of true knowledge because it was not mathematical. Others said that it was useless because Adam, the perfect man, neither had nor needed any history. Many felt that what passed for history was only a mass of fables. History was distrusted also because historians were often pretentious, claiming to be high-flying men of letters, writing for rhetorical or inspirational appeal or for argumentative reasons, disdaining the hard labor of actual study. History was losing the confidence of thinking people who came to view science as the model for reliable knowledge. How was it possible, they asked, to feel even a modicum of certainty about alleged events that had happened long before any living person had been born?

This doubting attitude itself arose from a stricter sense of evidence, or from a realization that there was really no proof for much of what was said about the past. But scholars set to work to assemble what evidence there was. They hoped to create a new history, one that should contain only reliable statements. Europe was littered with old papers and parchments. Abbeys, manor houses, and royal archives were full of written documents, many of them of unknown age or unknown origin, often written in a handwriting that people could no longer read. Learned and laborious enthusiasts set to work to explore this accumulation. They added so much to the efforts of their predecessors as virtually to create modern critical scholarship and erudition. The French Benedictine monk Jean Mabillon, in 1681, in his book *On Diplomatics* (referring to ancient charters and "diplomas") established the science of paleography, which deals with the deciphering, reading, dating, and authentication of manuscripts. The Frenchman DuCange in 1678 published a dictionary of medieval Latin which is still used. Others, like the Italian Muratori, spent whole lifetimes exploring archives, collecting, editing, or publishing masses of documents, comparing manuscript copies of the same text and trying to discover what the author had really written, rejecting some as fabrications or forgeries, pronouncing others to be genuine pieces of

New historical scholarship

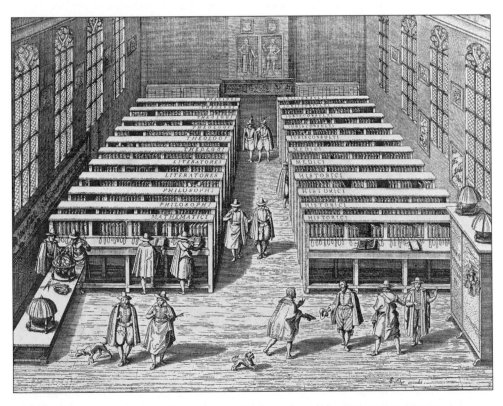

The early modern interest in the preservation and study of historical materials led to a systematic organization of the libraries and sources that careful scholarship would require. This seventeenth-century engraving of a library in Leiden shows the subjects that scholars studied and the tables at which they stood to read the books.
(Corbis)

historical evidence. Others made themselves experts in ancient coins, many of which were far more ancient than the oldest manuscripts; they founded the science of numismatics. Still others, or indeed the same persons, turned to a critical examination of the inscriptions on old buildings and ruins.

Another important but little-known historical "science," namely, chronology, was greatly stimulated also. Chronology deals with the age of the world and with finding a common denominator between the dating systems of various peoples. Probably it is not natural for the human mind to think in terms of dates at all. For simple or nonhistorically minded people it is enough to know that some things happened "long ago." In the seventeenth century the new interest in numbers, evident in physical science, turned also to the human past. Archbishop James Usher, an Anglican prelate of Ireland, after much study of the Bible, announced the date of 4004 B.C. as that of the creation of the world. His chronological system was later printed in the margins of the Authorized Version of the English Bible and is still adhered to by some fundamentalists as if part of the Bible itself. But Usher's system was not accepted by scholars even in his own time. Geographical knowledge was revealing China and its dynasties to Europe; historical knowledge was beginning to discover ancient Egypt. The Chinese and Egyptian records claimed a greater antiquity for their countries than the Old Testament seemed to allow for the human race. There was much erudite conjecture; one scholar about 1700 counted 70 estimates of the age of the world, ranging as high as 170,000 years, a figure which then seemed fantastic and appalling.

The difficulty was not only in the language of the Old Testament. It was in finding the correspondence between the chronological systems of different peoples. A Chinese system of dating by dynasties might be coherent within itself, but how could it be equated with the European system of dating from the birth of Christ, a date as little known to the Chinese as the date of Wu Wang was to Europeans? Even European records presented the same difficulty; the Romans counted by consulships, or from the supposed year of the founding of Rome; many medieval documents told only the year of some obscure ruler's reign. Only infinite patience, interminable research, and endless calculation could reduce such a jumble to the simple system of modern textbooks. This is of more importance than may be at first thought. A common system of dating is a great aid to thinking of human history as an interconnected whole. An overall conception of the human race is made easier by the dating of all events according to the Christian era. This itself, it may be pointed out, is an arbitrary and conventional scale, since Christ is now thought to have been born not in A.D. 1, but in 4 B.C.

A common system of dating

Common dating was of importance in practical affairs as well as in historical knowledge. Europe was disunited even on the Christian calendar. Protestant and some Orthodox countries followed the old or Julian calendar; Catholic countries, the corrected or Gregorian calendar issued in the sixteenth century under authority of Pope Gregory XIII. The two calendars varied in the seventeenth century by 10 days. Only gradually was the Gregorian calendar accepted, by England in 1752, by Russia in 1918. Most other peoples today, in China, India, the Arabic world, and elsewhere, use or recognize the Gregorian calendar. Without a uniform way of specifying days and years it would be difficult to transact international affairs, hold international conferences, make plans, or pay and receive money; a global system for defining time and dates thus became essential for global economic exchanges and communications. This common dating, easily taken for granted, was a consequence of the predominance of Europe in modern times. It is a sign of growing unity in world civilization.

CHRONOLOGY OF NOTABLE EVENTS, 1543–1697

1543	Publication of Copernicus's *On the Revolution of the Heavenly Orbs* and Vesalius's *The Structure of the Human Body*
1609	Galileo builds a telescope
1620–1627	Francis Bacon argues for empirical method to advance knowledge
1637	René Descartes publishes *Discourse on Method*
1651	Thomas Hobbes publishes *Leviathan*
1662	Royal Society is founded in London
1666	Royal Academy of Sciences is founded in Paris
1687	Isaac Newton publishes *Mathematical Principles of Natural Philosophy*
1690	John Locke publishes *Essay Concerning Human Understanding* and *Two Treatises on government*
1697	Pierre Bayle publishes *Historical Critical Dictionary*

The Questioning of Traditional Beliefs

The historical sciences provided a foundation on which a knowledge of human activities in the past could be built, and the growing geographical knowledge spread a panorama of human diversity in the present. This new knowledge shared with natural science the view that many traditional ideas were erroneous but that much could be known by a disciplined use of the human mind. The humanities and the sciences were alike in demanding evidence for belief and in trusting to the power of reason. In their impact on the old certainties of European life, the studies of human cultures exerted possibly a greater direct force than those of nature. Pascal, in his attempt to defend the Christian faith, feared the spirit of Montaigne, the mood of skepticism and denial, which he felt himself, more than he feared the findings of mathematical and physical science. And the movement of historical thought, with its insistence on textual criticism, threw doubt on much of the Christian religion, or at least on the sacred history related in the Bible, which was considered to be part and parcel of religion itself.

Biblical scholarship and criticism

In 1678 a French priest, Richard Simon, published a pioneering work in Biblical criticism, his *Critical History of the Old Testament*. Although his book was condemned both by the church and by the government of Louis XIV, Richard Simon always felt himself to be orthodox; Catholic faith, he insisted, depended more on church tradition than on the literal statements of the Bible. He simply applied to the Old Testament the methods of textual criticism which others were applying to secular documents. He concluded that the Old Testament, as known, rested on medieval manuscripts, many of which were of unknown or doubtful origin, that monkish copyists had introduced errors and corruptions, and that the books thought to have been written by Moses could not have been written by him, since they contained obvious contradictions and matter clearly inserted after his death. Others went further, questioning not merely the evidence of the Biblical text, but the very possibility of some events that it related. From the scientific idea of the absolute regularity of nature on the one hand, and from a strong sense of human credulity on the other, they denied that miracles had ever occurred and looked upon oracles and prophecies among either the Greeks or the Hebrews with a dubious eye.

The most profoundly disturbing of all thinkers of the time was Baruch Spinoza (1632–1677), the lens grinder of Amsterdam, a Jew who was excommunicated by his own synagogue and who refused a professorship at the University of Heidelberg, craving only the quiet to think in peace. Spinoza drew on both the scientific and humanistic thought of his day. He arrived at a philosophy holding that God had no existence apart from the world, that everything was itself an aspect of God—a philosophy technically called pantheism but considered by many to be really atheistic. He denied the inspiration of the Bible, disbelieved in miracles and the supernatural, rejected all revelation and revealed religion, Jewish or Christian, and held that few if any governments of the day were really just. He taught a pure, stern, and intellectual ethical code, and one which had few consolations for the average person. His name became a byword for impiety and horrendous unbelief. People were literally afraid to read his works, even when they could find them, which was not often because of the censorship. His influence spread slowly, through the mediation of other writers, contributing to the later development of rationalist philosophy.

Baruch Spinoza

More widely read, less abstruse, were the writings of the Englishman John Locke (1632–1704), who summarized many of the intellectual trends of his lifetime and exerted a strong influence for the following hundred years. He combined practical experience and theoretical interests in a philosophy that dwelled on the merits of common sense. Educated in medicine, he kept in touch with the sciences and was acquainted with Newton. He was associated with the great Whig noblemen who were the main authors of the English revolution in 1688. For political reasons he spent several years in the 1680s in the Netherlands, where he became familiar with thought on the Continent. He wrote on many subjects—finance, economics, education, religious policy, political theory, general philosophy—always with an engaging directness and sober air of the sensible man of the world. In his *Letter on Toleration* (1689) he advocated an established church but with toleration of all except Roman Catholics and atheists; these he held to be dangerous to society: the former because of a foreign allegiance; the latter because they lacked a basis of moral responsibility. In his *Reasonableness of Christianity* he argued that Christianity, rightly considered, is after all a reasonable form of religion; this softened the friction between religion and natural knowledge but tended to shut out the supernatural and merge religious feeling into an unruffled common sense.

Locke's deepest book was his *Essay Concerning the Human Understanding* (1690). Here he faced the great problem of the day, the problem of knowledge; he asked if it was possible to know anything with certainty, and how certain knowledge was arrived at. His answer was that true or certain knowledge is derived from experience—from perceptions by the sense organs and reflection of the mind on these perceptions. Locke at the end of the century thus echoes Bacon at the beginning; they became the two great pillars of empirical philosophy, insisting on experience and observation as the source of truth. Locke denied Descartes's doctrine of innate ideas, or inevitable disposition of the human mind to think in certain ways. He held that the mind at birth is a blank tablet or *tabula rasa* and that the social environment shapes what people think or believe. Locke's environmentalist philosophy became fundamental to liberal and reforming thought in later years. It seemed that false ideas or superstitions were the result of bad environment and bad education. It seemed that the evil in human actions was due to bad social institutions and that an improvement in human society would improve human behavior. This philosophy, whether or not wholly true in the final analysis, was largely true with respect to many practical conditions. It gave confidence in the possibility of social progress and turned attention to a

The Dutch, Jewish philosopher Baruch Spinoza (1632–1677), portrayed here in a painting by Samuel Van Hoogstraten, developed a materialist or pantheistic philosophy that provoked strong opposition from many of his contemporaries; but Spinoza became an influential thinker for later writers who expressed skepticism about traditional religious beliefs.
(Bettmann/CORBIS)

sphere in which planned and constructive action was possible, namely, the sphere of government, public policy, and legislation. Here we touch on political theory, to which Locke contributed *Two Treatises of Government* (these works are discussed later in this chapter).

30. POLITICAL THEORY: THE SCHOOL OF NATURAL LAW

Political theory can never be strictly scientific. Science deals with what does exist or has existed. It does not tell what ought to exist. To describe what society and government ought to be like, in view of human nature and the capacity to be miserable or contented, is a main purpose of political theory. Political theory is in a sense more practical than science. It is the scientists and scholars who are most content to observe facts as they are. Practical people, and scientists and scholars insofar as they have practical interests, must always ask themselves what ought to be done, what policies ought to be adopted, what measures ought to be taken, what state of affairs ought to be maintained or brought about. Conservatives and radicals, traditionalists and innovators, are alike in this respect. It is impossible in human affairs to escape the word "ought."

But political theory was affected by the scientific view. The Renaissance Italian, Niccolò Machiavelli (1469–1527), whom we have discussed earlier, had opened the way in this direction. Machiavelli too had his "ought"; he preferred a republican form of government in which citizens felt a patriotic attachment to their state. But in his book *The Prince* he disregarded the question of the best form of government, a favorite question of Christian and scholastic philosophers of the Middle Ages. He separated the study of politics from theology and moral philosophy. He undertook to describe how governments and rulers actually behaved. He observed that successful rulers behaved as if holding or increasing power

Niccolò Machiavelli

were their only object, that they regarded all else as means to this end. Princes, said Machiavelli, kept their promises or broke them, told the truth or distorted or colored it, sought popularity or ignored it, advanced public welfare or disrupted it, conciliated their neighbors or destroyed them—depending merely on which course of action seemed the best means of advancing their political interests. All this was bad, said Machiavelli; but that was not the question, for the question was to find out what rulers really did. Drawing his conclusions from the evidence of history, Machiavelli chose to be nonmoral in order to be scientific. To most readers he seemed to be simply immoral. Nor was it possible to draw the line between *The Prince* as a scientific description of fact and *The Prince* as a book of maxims of conduct. In telling how successful rulers obtained their successes, Machiavelli also suggested how rulers *ought* to proceed. And though governments did in fact continue to behave for the most part as Machiavelli said, most people refused to admit that they ought to.

Natural Right and Natural Law

Political theory in the seventeenth century did not embrace the cynicism attributed to Machiavelli. Nor did it fall into the skepticism of those who said that the customs of one's country should be passively accepted or that one form of government was about as good as another. It directly faced the question, What is right? The seventeenth century was the classic age of the philosophy of natural right or of natural law.

"Natural law" and "natural right"

The idea of natural law underlies a good deal of modern democratic development, and its decline in the last century has been closely connected with many of the troubles of recent times. It is not easy to say in what the philosophy of natural law essentially consisted. It held that there is, somehow, in the structure of the world, a law that distinguishes right from wrong. It held that right is "natural," not a mere human invention. This right is not determined, for any country, by its heritage, tradition, or customs, nor yet by its actual laws (called "positive" laws) of the kind that are enforced in the law courts. All these may be unfair or unjust. We detect unfairness or injustice in them by comparing them with natural law as we understand it; thus we have a basis for saying that cannibalism is bad or that a law requiring forced labor from orphan children is unjust. Nor is natural law, or the real rightness of something, determined by the authority of any person or people. No king can make right that which is wrong. No people, by its will as a people, can make just that which is unjust. Right and law, in the ultimate sense, exist outside and above all peoples. They are universal, the same for all. No one can make them up to suit themselves. A good king or a just people is a king or people whose actions correspond to the objective standard. But how, if we cannot trust our own positive laws or customs, or our leaders, or even our collective selves, can we know what is naturally right? How do we discover natural law?

The answer, in the natural law philosophy, is that we discover it by reason. Philosophers of natural law said that human beings are rational animals. And they assumed that all human beings have, at least potentially and when better enlightened, the same powers of reason and understanding—Germans or English, Asians, Africans or Europeans. This view favored a cosmopolitan outlook and made international agreement and general world progress seem realizable goals. As time went on, the premises of this philosophy came to be questioned. By the twentieth century it was widely thought that the human mind was not especially rational but was motivated by unconscious drives or urges or instincts and that human cultural differences were so fundamental that people of different nationalities or classes could never expect to see things in the same way. Challenged by such theories of human irrationality and cultural difference (which could be promoted with much ancient and modern evidence), the older philosophy of a universal natural law lost its hold on many minds.

In the seventeenth and eighteenth centuries, however, it was generally accepted. Some, carrying over the philosophy of the Middle Ages, thought of natural law as an aspect of the law of God. Others, more secular in spirit, held that the natural law stood of itself. These included even some churchmen; a group of theologians, mainly Jesuits, were condemned by the pope in 1690 for holding that universal right and wrong might exist by reason only, whether God existed or not. The idea of natural law and the faith in human reason went side by side, and both were fundamental in the thought of the time. They were to be found everywhere in Europe, in their religious or their secular form.

On the basis of natural law some thinkers tried to create an international law or "law of nations," to bring order into the maze of sovereign territorial states, great and small, that was developing in Europe. Hugo Grotius, in 1625, published the first great book devoted exclusively to this subject, his *Law of War and Peace*. Samuel Pufendorf followed with his *Law of Nature and of Nations* in 1672. Both held that sovereign states, though bound by no positive law or author-

"Law of nations"

ity, should work together for the common good, that there was a community of nations as of individuals, and that in the absence of a higher international sovereignty they were all still subordinate to natural reason and justice. Certain concrete doctrines, such as the freedom of the seas or the immunity of ambassadors, were put forward. The principles of international law remained those of natural law. The content came to include specific agreements between governments, certain kinds of admiralty and maritime law, and the terms of treaties such as the treaties of Westphalia, Utrecht, and others. The means of enforcement, to be sure, remained weak or nonexistent in crises.

Hobbes and Locke

In domestic affairs the philosophy of natural law, though it rather favored constitutional-ism, was used to justify both constitutional and absolutist governments. Right itself was held to be in the nature of things, beyond human power to change. But forms of govern-ment were held to be means to an end. No philosopher at the time thought the state to have an absolute value in itself. The state had to be "justified," made acceptable to the moral consciousness or to reason. There were, indeed, important competing philosophies. On the side of absolutism was the doctrine of the divine right of kings. On the side of constitution-alism were arguments based on heritage or custom, emphasizing the charters, bulls, or compacts of former times and the historic powers of parliaments and estates. But neither the supernatural argument of the divine right of kings nor the historical argument pointing back to liberties of the Middle Ages was entirely satisfactory in the scientific atmosphere of the seventeenth century. Neither carried complete conviction to the reason or moral sense of the most acute thinkers. Both were reinforced by arguments of natural law. Two Englishmen stand out above all others in this connection. Absolutism was philosophically justified by Thomas Hobbes; constitutionalism, by John Locke.

Hobbes (1588–1679) followed the scientific and mathematical discov-eries of his time with more than an amateur interest. In philosophy he held to a materialistic and even atheistic system. In English politics he sided with king against Parliament; he disliked the disorder and violence of the

Absolutism and Thomas Hobbes

civil war of the 1640s and the unstable conditions of the English republic of the 1650s. He concluded that humans have no capacity for self-government. His opinion of human nature was low; he held that people in the "state of nature," or as imagined to exist without government, were quarrelsome and turbulent, forever locked in a war of all against all. In his famous phrase, life in the state of nature was "solitary, poor, nasty, brutish and short." From fear of each other, to obtain order and enjoy the advantages of law and right, people came to a kind of agreement or "contract" by which they surrendered their freedom of action into the hands of a ruler. It was necessary for this ruler to have unrestricted or absolute power. Only thus could he maintain order. It was intolerably dangerous, according to Hobbes, for anyone to question the actions of government, for such questioning might reopen the way to chaos. Government must therefore be a kind of Leviathan (the monster mentioned in the Bible, Job 41); and Hobbes in fact used the word *Leviathan* for the title of his principal book, published in 1651, two years after the execution of King Charles I.

By this book Hobbes became the leading secular exponent of absolutism and one of the principal theorists of the unlimited sovereignty of the state. His influence on later thinkers was very great. He accustomed political theorists to the use of purely natural arguments. He quoted freely from the Bible, but the Bible had no influence on his thought. After Hobbes, all advanced political theorists regarded government as a device created by human purpose. It was no longer considered, except popularly and except by professional theologians, as part of God's divine dispensation to human history. Hobbes also affected later theorists by his arguments for a sovereign authority and, more negatively, by obliging them to refute his idea of an unlimited personal sovereign. But he was never a popular writer. In England the cause which he favored was lost. In those continental countries where royal absolutism prevailed his arguments were received with secret gratification, but his irreligion was too dangerous to make public, and the absolutist argument, on the popular level, remained that of the divine right of kings. In any case Hobbes's arguments were in some ways insufficient for real monarchs. Hobbes abhorred struggle and violence. He believed that absolutism would produce civil peace, individual security, and a rule of law. He also held that absolute power depended on, or had at least originated in, a free and rational agreement by which people accepted it. An absolute monarchy that flagrantly violated these conditions could with difficulty be justified even by the doctrines of Hobbes. It is in these respects that Hobbes differs from totalitarian theorists of more recent times. For Hobbes, in the final analysis, absolute power was an expedient to promote individual welfare. It was a means necessary to the realization of natural law.

John Locke (1632–1704), as has been seen, also stood in the main current of scientific thought and discovery. But in his political philosophy he

John Locke

carried over many ideas of the Middle Ages, as formulated in the thirteenth century by St. Thomas Aquinas and kept alive in England by successive thinkers of the Anglican church. Medieval philosophy had never favored an absolute power. With Hobbes, Locke shared the idea that good government is an expedient of human purpose, neither provided by divine Providence nor inherited by a national tradition. He held, too, like Hobbes and the whole school of natural law, that government was based on a kind of contract, or rational and conscious agreement upon which authority was based. In contrast to Hobbes, he sided with Parliament against king in the practical struggles of politics. About 1680, in the course of these disputes, he wrote *Two Treatises of Government,* which, however, were not published until shortly after the parliamentary revolution of 1688–1689.

Locke took a more genial view of human nature than Hobbes. As he showed in his other books, he believed that a moderate religion was a good thing and above all that people could learn from experience and hence could be educated to an enlightened way of life.

These ideas favored a belief in self-government. Locke declared (in contradiction to Hobbes) that people in the "state of nature" were reasonable and well disposed, willing to get along with one another though handicapped by the absence of public authority. They likewise had a moral sense, quite independently of government; and they also possessed by nature certain rights, quite apart from the state. These rights were the rights to life, liberty, and property.

Locke placed heavy emphasis on the right of property, by which he usually meant the possession of land. His philosophy can in fact be regarded as an expression of the landed classes of England, who challenged the power of kings by defending the political and social rights of private property. Individuals in the state of nature are not altogether able, according to Locke, to win general respect for their individual natural rights. They cannot by their own efforts protect what is "proper" to them, that is, their property. They agree to set up government to enforce observance of the rights of all. Government is thus created by a contract, but the contract is not unconditional, as claimed by Hobbes. It imposes mutual obligations. The people must be reasonable; only rational beings can be politically free. Liberty is not an anarchy of undisciplined will; it is the freedom to act without compulsion by another. Only rational and responsible creatures can exercise true freedom; but adult human beings, according to Locke, are or can be educated to be rational and responsible. They therefore can and should be free. On government, also, certain conditions and obligations are imposed. If a government breaks the contract, if it threatens the natural rights which it is the sole purpose of government to protect, if, for example, it takes away a man's property without his consent, then the governed have a right to reconsider what they have done in creating the government and may even in the last extremity rebel against it. The right to resist government, Locke admits, is very dangerous, but it is less dangerous than its opposite, which would lead to the loss of all liberty; and in any case we are talking about reasonable and responsible people.

If Locke's ideas seem familiar, especially to Americans, it is because of the wide popularizing of his philosophy in the century after his death. Nowhere was his influence greater than in the British colonies. The authors of the American Declaration of Independence and of the Constitution of the United States knew the writings of Locke very thoroughly. Some phrases of the Declaration of Independence echo his very language. In Great Britain also, and in France and elsewhere, in the course of time, Locke's influence was immense. But it should be noted that his ideas did not always mean the same thing for all people or in all places. Locke did not extend his ideas of human liberty to enslaved Africans, apparently because he viewed slavery as a legitimate form of private property. Locke himself invested in the slave-trading Royal African Company and endorsed the development of slavery in the American colonies. The growing influence of Locke's political theories may also have contributed indirectly to the emergence of new racist ideas in the eighteenth century. New justifications for slavery became necessary when the political classes of England and America began to believe that human beings possessed natural rights to life, liberty, and property. How could slavery be reconciled with such beliefs? The answer appeared in new forms of racism, which justified the enslavement of Africans by arguing that the African "race" lacked certain rational human traits of the European "race" and that black people could be denied fundamental human rights because they differed from other human beings.

In general, however, Locke's ideas of natural rights and human liberty were later used to challenge absolutist or repressive institutions, including also the institutions of slavery. What Locke did was to convert an episode in English history into an event of universal

Locke's influence

JOHN LOCKE
by John Greenhill (English, 1642–1676)
Locke's writings on government and natural rights summarized the arguments against royal power in England and also won adherents wherever political theorists challenged monarchical absolutism.
(Snark/Art Resource, NY)

political meaning. In England, in 1688, certain great lords, winning the support of the established church, gentry, and merchants, deposed one king and brought in another. On the new king they imposed certain obligations—specified in the Bill of Rights of 1689 and all dealing with legal or technical interpretations of the English constitution. The Revolution of 1688 was a very English affair. England in 1688 was still little known to the rest of Europe. The proceedings in England, so far as known, might seem no different from a rebellion of the magnates of Hungary. Locke, in arguing that Parliament had been right to eject James II, put the whole affair on a level of reason, natural right, and human nature. It thus came to have meaning for people who had no connection with the specific problems of English political history.

Locke on the English revolution

At the same time, Locke made the English revolution a sign of progress rather than reaction. The new and modern form of government in 1690 was royal absolutism, with its professional bureaucracy and corps of paid officials. Almost everywhere there was resistance to the kings, led by landed interests and harking back to earlier freedoms. Such resistance seemed to many Europeans to be feudal and medieval. Locke made the resistance in England, namely, the Revolution of 1688 against James II, into a modern and forward-looking move. He checked the prestige of absolutism. He gave new prestige to constitutional principles. He carried over, in modified form, many ideas from the scholastic philosophers of the Middle Ages, who had generally maintained that kings had only a relative and restricted power and were responsible to their peoples. To these ideas he added the force of the newer scientific view of the world. He did not rest his case on supernatural or providential arguments. He did not say that constitutional government was the will of God. He said that it rested on experience and observation of human nature, on recognition of certain individual rights and especially the right of property, and on the existence of a purely natural law of reason and justice. He was an almost entirely secular thinker, and, as such, he developed ideas that could be drawn into the political and social conflicts of most modern nations.

One must not claim too much for Locke, or for any writer. England was in fact, in 1688, more modern in many ways than other countries in Europe. The Glorious Revolution was in fact not exactly like uprisings of the landed and propertied classes elsewhere. England in the following century did in fact create a form of parliamentary government that was unique. But facts go together with the theories that give them an understandable meaning. Events in England, as explained by Locke, and as seen in other countries and even in England and its colonies through Locke's eyes, launched into the mainstream of modern history the superb tradition of constitutional government, which has been one of the principal themes in the history of the modern world ever since.

By 1700, at the close of the "century of genius," some beliefs that were to become characteristic of modern times had clearly taken form, notably a faith in science, in human reason, in natural human rights, and in progress. The new scientific knowledge was beginning to transform the global economy, the culture of European elites, and the conflicts within or among European empires. Meanwhile, the cultural institutions of modern science were spreading across Europe, and new scientific theories in physics, astronomy, and physiology were challenging both the theology and thought systems of earlier generations. The following period, generally known as the Age of Enlightenment, was to be a time of clarifying and popularizing ideas which the more creative seventeenth century had produced. These ideas were eventually to revolutionize Europe, America, and the world. They were also in subsequent years to be modified, amended, challenged, and even denied. But they are still very much alive today.

 For interactive exercises, glossary, chronologies, and more, go to the *Online Learning Center* at **www.mhhe.com/palmer10.**

Chapter 7

THE STRUGGLE FOR WEALTH AND EMPIRE

In earlier chapters we have seen how western Europe, and especially England and France, by about the year 1700 came to occupy a position of power and influence in Europe as a whole. We have traced the political history of western Europe through the War of the Spanish Succession, terminated in 1713–1714 by the treaties of Utrecht and Rastadt. Affairs of central Europe and Germany have been carried to 1740. In that year a new kingdom of Prussia and a new or renovated Austrian monarchy, each passing into the hands of a new ruler, stood on the eve of a struggle for ascendancy in central Europe. As for eastern Europe, we have observed the Europeanizing and expansion of the Russian empire.

More important in the long run than these political events, and continuing through the seventeenth and eighteenth centuries, was the cumulative expansion of all forms of knowledge, which we saw in the rapid development of seventeenth-century science and to which we turn again in the next chapter. Equally important was the growing wealth of Europe, or at least of the Atlantic region north of Spain. The new wealth, in the widest sense, meaning conveniences of every kind, resulted partly from the new technical and scientific knowledge, which in turn it helped to produce; and the two together, more wealth and more knowledge, helped to form one of the most far-reaching ideas of modern times, the idea of progress. This idea challenged the traditional deference to ancient authorities and fostered critical inquiry, creative innovations, and remarkable optimism in most spheres of social and intellectual life. Although the world wars and environmental problems of more recent times would eventually provoke widespread anxieties about the historical consequences of new technologies, a belief in progress, even if somewhat chastened, remains a powerful cultural force in all modern societies.

Chapter emblem: Detail from an Indian miniature (c. 1785), showing an Englishwoman and one of her servants in India. (Werner Forman Archive/Art Resource, NY)

The new wealth of Europe was not like the age-old wealth of the great empires in the East, said by Milton to "shower on her kings barbaric pearl and gold." It consisted of gold, to be sure, but even more of bank deposits and facilities for credit, of more and better devices for mining coal, casting iron, and spinning thread, more productive agriculture, better and more comfortable houses, a wider variety of diet on the table, more and improved sailing ships, warehouses, and docks; more books, more newspapers, more medical instruments, more scientific equipment; greater government revenues, larger armies, and more numerous government employees. In the wealthy European countries, and because of the growing wealth, more people were freed from the necessity of toiling for food, clothing, and shelter, and were enabled to devote themselves to all sorts of specialized callings in government, management, finance, war, teaching, writing, inventing, exploring, and researching, and in producing the amenities rather than the barest necessities of life. These new forms of mechanical production, social organization, and specialized knowledge also began to spread to European colonies around the world, thus contributing to the expanding systems of global trade and to the growing belief in human progress.

31.   ELITE AND POPULAR CULTURES

The accumulation of wealth and knowledge was not evenly distributed among the various social classes. There had always been differences between rich and poor, with many gradations between the extremes, but at the time we are now considering, as the seventeenth century turned into the eighteenth, there came to be a more obvious distinction between elite and popular cultures. The terms are hard to define. The elite culture was not exactly the culture of the rich and well-to-do, nor was the popular culture limited to the poor and lower economic classes. The word "elite" suggests a minority within a given range of interests; thus there are elites not only of wealth, but of social position and of power; elites of fashion, of patronage and connoisseurship in the arts, and of artists themselves; elites of education, of special training as in medicine and law, and of discovery and accomplishment in technology and the sciences. In general, persons taking part in an elite culture could share at will in the popular culture by attending public amusements or simply by talking familiarly with their servants. But the relation was asymmetric. Those born in popular culture could not easily share in the intellectual or social culture of the elites, at least not without transforming themselves, through education or marriage, which could occur only in exceptional cases.

A main difference was simply one of language. At the popular level people generally used a local form of speech, varying from one place to another, with a distinctive accent, and with words that had become obsolete elsewhere or that might not be understood even a few miles away. In the Middle Ages this variety had been overcome by the use of Latin. Since the invention of printing and the rise of national literatures, and with the spreading influence of schools, of which we have seen that many were founded between 1550 and 1650, there came to be standard forms of English, French, Italian, and other languages, employed by all educated persons. Grammar and spelling became regularized. Virtually all printing was in a national language when it was not in Latin. Since only a minority were able to get the necessary education, the mass of the people continued to speak as they did before. Their way of talking was now considered a dialect, a peasant language, or what was called *patois* in French

National languages

or *Volkssprache* in German. And while it may be true, as some scientific philologists have said, that no form of speech is "better" than another, it is also true that facility in the national language was a sign of elite culture until the spread of universal elementary schooling in the nineteenth century. It gave access to at least certain segments of the elite culture, as it continues to do today, and it enabled educated persons to participate in the elite institutions of government, commerce, and the professions.

The elite culture was transmitted largely by way of books, although acquired also by word of mouth within favored families and social circles. The popular culture was predominantly oral, although also expressed in cheaply printed almanacs, chapbooks, woodcuts, and broadsides. Since it was so largely *Oral vs. print culture* oral, and left so few written records, popular culture is difficult for historians to reconstruct, although it made up the daily lives, interests, and activities of the great majority in all countries. It must always be remembered that what we read as history, in this as in most other books, is mostly an account of the work of a small minority, either of power-wielders, decision-makers, and innovators whose actions nevertheless affected whole peoples, or of writers and thinkers whose ideas appealed to a limited audience. Persons who were illiterate or barely literate changed their ideas more slowly than the more mobile and more informed members of the elite. Cultural changes initiated by such elites spread slowly, generation after generation, to wider social classes, so that what was characteristic of popular culture at a given moment, such as a belief in magic, had often been common to all classes a century or two before. All people and social classes make history and participate in the processes of historical change, but the new knowledge, education, and wealth in early modern societies also created new forms of social distinctions and new hierarchies of cultural power.

The humanism of the Renaissance, being transmitted so largely through books and the study of Greek and Latin, remained limited to the elite culture. The strength of the Protestant Reformation lay in combining the efforts of highly educated persons, such as Luther and Calvin, with the anger, distress, disillusionment, and hopes of many very ordinary people. The new science and the ensuing eighteenth-century Enlightenment emerged in the work of small numbers of experimenters and writers but slowly reshaped the thinking of others. The process of diffusion might be slow and uncertain. Astrology, for example, was in the Middle Ages a branch of scientific inquiry; in the seventeenth century astrologers were still consulted by emperors and kings; then divination by the stars was denounced by both the clergy and secular thinkers as a superstition, and astrology was expelled from astronomy, but horoscopes still appear in American and European newspapers in our own time.

The differences of wealth, if not wholly decisive, were of great importance. Culture in the broader or anthropologist's sense of the word includes material circumstances of food, drink, and shelter. In some respects the lot of the poor in the seventeenth century was worse than in the Middle Ages. Less meat was eaten in Europe, because as population grew there was less land available for the raising of *Living standards* livestock. With the growth of a market economy many peasants raised wheat, but ate bread made of rye, barley, or oats, or even looked for acorns and roots in times of famine. The consumption of bread by working people in France in the eighteenth century was about a pound per day per person, because little else except cabbages and beans was eaten on ordinary days; after 1750 the use of white bread became more usual. Meanwhile the rich, or the merely affluent, developed more delicate menus prepared by professional cooks, one of whom is said to have committed suicide when his soufflé fell.

In the towns the poor lived in crowded and unwholesome buildings, and in the country they lived in dark and shabby cabins where stoves only gradually replaced holes in the roof for the escape of smoke. The poor had no glass in their windows, the middle classes had some, and the rich had glass windows and mirrors in profusion. In humble homes the dishes were wooden bowls, slowly replaced by pewter, while china plates began to appear on the tables of the more well-to-do. Table forks, with one for each diner, originating in Italy, were brought to France in the sixteenth century by Catherine de Medici along with other items of Italian culture, and soon spread among those able to afford them, though Louis XIV still preferred to use his fingers. Silver bowls and pitchers were ancient but became more elaborate and more often seen in upper-class circles. The poor had no furniture, or only a few benches and a mat to sleep on; the middle classes had chairs and beds; the rich not only had substantial furniture but were becoming more conscious of style. Among persons of adequate income it became usual to have houses with specialized rooms, such as separate bedrooms, and a dining room. The prominent and the fashionable fitted out rooms for social receptions and entertainments, called salons in France, with walls of wood paneling, lighted by chandeliers reflected in mirrors, and provided with sofas and armchairs, which the invention of upholstery made more comfortable. The poor, after dark, huddled on chests or on the floor by a single candle.

Housing conditions

In the use of beverages the seventeenth century saw progress, if that is the right word. Coffee and tea, along with sugar and tobacco, all imported from overseas, were exotic rarities in 1600, more widely enjoyed in 1700, and available to all but the very destitute by the time of the French Revolution. Coffee shops developed and taverns multiplied. Cheap wines became more plentiful in southern Europe, as did beer in the north. The distillation of alcohol had been developed in the Middle Ages, when brandy, a distilled wine, was used as a medicine; by the seventeenth century it was a familiar drink. Whisky and gin also came into use at about this time. The taverns and coffee shops offered a place for neighborly gatherings for the middling and lower social classes. Drunkenness became a more visible problem in European cities, especially among workers who could not drink in domestic privacy and who were therefore often seen in the streets, as shown by Hogarth's pictures of "Gin Lane" in London about 1750. Arising from all this poverty and disorganization, especially in the large cities, was an increase in out-of-wedlock births and abandonment of children. It was calculated that in Paris in 1780 there were 7,000 abandoned children for 30,000 births, but many of these infants were brought from the country to be deposited in the foundling hospitals of the city, which were overwhelmed.

Religion

There was much that persons of all classes and cultures shared. Most important, in principle, was religion. The refined and the rude, the learned and the untutored, heard the same sermons in church, were baptized, married, and buried by the same sacraments, often by the same priest, and were subject to religious and moral obligations that transcended the boundaries of social class. Such was most likely to be the case in small communities of unmixed religion or where the lord and lady of the manor attended the same church as the villagers. Where different churches existed in fact, whether or not officially tolerated, religion played less of a role in social cohesion. In England, for example, the Nonconformists, who succeeded the old Puritans after the Stuart Restoration, developed a kind of middle-class culture that was noticeably different from the culture of the Anglican gentry. Rich families in both Protestant and Catholic countries might have their own private chaplains and build chapels of their own. In towns that were big enough for neighborhood diversification some churches

GIN LANE
by William Hogarth (English, 1697–1764)

Hogarth showed both the popularity and dangers of alcohol in the lives of Britain's working classes, as in this illustration of drunkenness in the streets of London.

(Metropolitan Museum of Art, Harris Brisbane Dick Fund, 1932)

The popularity of coffee and tea in the eighteenth century made the coffeehouse a popular meeting place in large cities such as London and Paris. The establishment portrayed here attracted a fashionable, wealthy clientele, but many coffeehouses also catered to the lower classes.

(The Metropolitan Museum of Art, Harris Brisbane Dick Fund, 1935 (35.100.31))

became fashionable and others merely popular. In any case some people in the seventeenth century were not very religious at all; these would include those in inaccessible rural areas as well as some of the poorest in the larger towns, who were often uprooted and homeless migrants from an overcrowded countryside. Reforming bishops, especially in France, undertook to ameliorate the situation, so that the seventeenth century was a great age of internal missionary work, and it may be that in the following century, as skepticism began to pervade the elite culture, the popular culture became more Christianized than it had been in the past.

Health

Rich and poor were subject to the same diseases, the same dangers of tainted food and polluted water, and the same smells and filth in noisy streets littered with horse droppings, puddles, and garbage. Not of course equally: in the elite culture people called on the service of doctors, who had been trained in the universities, while ordinary sufferers sought out popular healers, who were often women and whose remedies consisted of strange herbs or mysterious potions (women did not become doctors because they could not attend universities); and it made a difference whether one rode through the streets in a coach, as the affluent did, or picked one's way on foot with the common people. Congestion was worst in rapidly growing cities, such as London, Paris, Amsterdam, and Naples, where the differences between wealth and poverty were both more extreme and more shockingly visible. There were recurrent fears of shortage of food, as crop failure or local famine struck this or that region, in which case some starved and some ate less, while those able to do so simply paid higher prices. In some towns charitable organizations developed, often on the initiative of upper-class women, to finance and assist religious sisters in relief of the poor. Hunger and the fear of hunger sometimes produced riots, which however had little political significance except insofar as upper-class people tried to make use of them for their own purposes.

It was also in less material aspects that the elite and popular cultures increasingly diverged. The upper strata set a new importance on polite manners, in which the French now set the tone, with much bowing, doffing of hats, and exchange of compliments, beside which the manners of ordinary people now seemed uncouth. The etiquette of princely courts became more formal, the court fools and jesters disappeared, and royalty surrounded itself not with rough retainers but with ladies and gentlemen. About 1600 the plays of Shakespeare were staged in public theaters where all classes mixed and enjoyed the same performance, but in the following century it became usual for the upper classes to have private theaters. People of higher social position took to stylish dancing, which their children had to learn from dancing teachers, while plain people continued to cavort more spontaneously in country dances and jigs. For evening parties, the polite world met in salons to engage in the art of cultured conversation, while working people, especially in the country, met in a neighbor's house after the day's labors were over, and there, while the men mended their implements and the women mended the clothes, engaged in local gossip, listened to storytellers, or sat by while someone read aloud from one of the cheaply printed books that were now widely circulated.

Politeness, etiquette, entertainment

Enough of these books have survived, along with popular almanacs, to make it possible to form some ideas of the mental horizons of the nonliterate and inarticulate classes. They were often written by printers or their employees or by others who were in effect intermediaries between the elite and popular cultures and who purposely addressed themselves to what they knew of popular interests. The almanacs purveyed astrological observations, advice on the weather, proverbs, and scraps of what had once been science but was now offered as occult wisdom. Other little books undertook to teach the ABCs or told how to behave in church; how to approach persons of the other sex; how to show respect for superiors; or how to compose a proper letter of love, thanks, or condolence, or have such a letter written by the professional letter writers to whose services illiterate persons resorted. Still others put into print the stories that had long circulated in the oral tradition, fairy tales, saints' lives, or accounts of outlaws such as Robin Hood. Miracles, prodigies, witches, ogres, angels, and the devil figured prominently in such narratives.

It is a curious fact that where educated persons were now schooled in Greek mythology and admired the heroes of ancient Rome, the plain people were still engrossed by tales of medieval chivalry, knights errant, and holy hermits that had once been told in baronial halls. Memories of the times of King Arthur and Charlemagne lingered in the popular consciousness. There were many long and complex tales of the exploits of Roland and other paladins who had fought for Christianity against the infidels, all set in a world of faraway adventure without definite location in time or place. Saracens, Moors, Turks, and Muslims, and at times Jews, were generally portrayed in such stories as menacing figures.

Belief in witchcraft and magic was to be found in 1600 in all social classes. The witches in *Macbeth* were perfectly believable to Shakespeare's audience. Learned books were still written on these subjects, and indeed it may be that learned writers and the judges in law courts had stirred up more anxiety about witches and magicians than ordinary people would otherwise have felt. By 1700 a great change was evident: witches, magicians, and miscellaneous enchantments were disappearing from the elite culture, but they still figured in the popular mind. Unaffected as yet by either science or doubt, most ordinary people inclined to think that there was something true about magic, which they distinguished as good and bad. Good magic unlocked the "secrets" of nature; popular writings on alchemy told of famous sages of the past who knew how to turn base metals into gold; there were special formulas that added to the efficacy of prayer. Some old women had a secret knowledge of medicinal herbs, in which indeed there might be some pragmatic value but which was blended with the mysterious and the occult. Bad magic was used to cause harm; it taught the black arts; it gave force to curses; it often involved a compact with the devil; it was what made witches so fearsome. By 1700 such ideas were subsiding. Judges no longer believed that such powers existed, and so would no longer preside at witchcraft trials. The same may be said of belief in prophecies and oracles: in the elite culture only those recorded in the Bible retained any credibility, but there was still a popular acceptance of recent prophecies and foretellings of the future.

Witchcraft and magic

Popular culture continued to express itself also in fairs and carnivals. For men and women who lived limited lives these were exciting events that occurred only at certain times of the year and to which people flocked from miles around. At the fairs one could buy things that local shops and wandering peddlers could not supply. There would be puppet shows, jugglers, and acrobats. There were conjurers who refused to admit like modern magicians that they were using merely natural means. A mountebank was someone who mounted a platform (*banco* in Italian) where he sold questionable remedies for various ills while keeping up a patter of jokes and stories, often accompanied by a clown. Blind singers and traveling musicians entertained the throngs, and for the tougher minded there were cockfights and bear baiting. In such a hubbub itinerant preachers might denounce the vanities of this world or throw doubt on the wisdom of bishops and lawyers.

Carnival went on for several weeks preceding Lent. The word itself, from the Italian *carne vale,* meant "farewell to meat," from which good Christians were to abstain during the 40-day Lenten fast; in France it climaxed in the Mardi Gras ("fat Tuesday"). It persisted in Protestant countries also. It was a time for big eating and heavy drinking and for general merrymaking and foolery. Comical processions marched through the streets. Farces were performed and mock sermons were delivered. Young men showed their strength in tugs-of-war, footraces,

Carnival

A CARNIVAL ON THE FEAST DAY OF SAINT GEORGE
by Pieter Bruegel, the Younger (Flemish, 1564–1638)
Carnivals broke the normal patterns of daily life in towns and villages throughout the early modern era. This painting shows an early seventeenth-century carnival near the Flemish city of Antwerp, but the games, eating, drinking, dancing, and banners were typical of the carnivals in almost every European village during this era.
(Christie's Images/Bridgeman Art Library)

and a rough-and-tumble kind of football. A common theme was what was called in England "the world turned upside down." Men and women put on each other's clothing. Horses were made to move backward with the rider facing the tail. Little street dramas showed the servant giving orders to the master, the judge sitting in the stocks, the pupil beating the teacher, or the husband holding the baby while the wife clutched a gun. In general, the carnival was a time for defying custom and ridiculing authority. It is hard to know how much such outbursts were expressions of genuine resentments and how much they were only a form of play. They could, indeed, be both.

In 1600 people of all classes took part in these festive activities. In the following century, as both the Protestant and the Catholic Reformations extended their influences, the clergy undertook to purge such public events of what they considered excesses, and with the growth of the state the civil authorities began to frown on them as incitements to subversion. By 1700 the people of elite culture, the wealthy, the fashionable, and the educated, were more inclined to stay away or attended only as spectators to be amused at the simple pleasures of the common people. In the eighteenth century, as the various elites took to more formal manners and to neoclassicism in literature and the arts, the gulf between the elite and popular cultures widened. The clergy campaigned against necromancy and tried to restrain the faithful in the matter of pilgrimages and veneration of dubious local saints. As the medical profession developed, the popular healers and venders of nostrums were seen as charlatans and quacks. As scientific and other knowledge increased among educated elites, those who lacked such knowledge appeared to be simply superstitious or ignorant. It may be said both that the elites withdrew from the popular culture and that the people as a whole had not yet been brought into the pale of higher civilization. In any case, class distinctions became sharper than ever. But nothing ever stands still, and before the year 1800 there were persons in the elite culture who were beginning to "rediscover" the people, to collect ballads and fairy tales, and to lay a foundation for what in the nineteenth century was called "folklore."

32. THE GLOBAL ECONOMY OF THE EIGHTEENTH CENTURY

The opening of the Atlantic in the sixteenth century, it will be recalled, had reoriented Europe. In an age of oceanic communications western Europe became a center from which America, Asia, and Africa could all be reached. A global economy had been created. The first to profit from it had been the Portuguese and Spanish, and they retained their monopoly through most of the sixteenth century; but the decline of the Portuguese and Spanish paved the way for the triumph of the British, the French, and the Dutch. In the eighteenth century the outstanding economic development was the expansion of the global economy and the fact that Europe became incomparably wealthier than any other part of the world.

Commerce and Industry in the Eighteenth Century

The increase of wealth was brought about by the methods of commercial capitalism and handicraft industry. Though the Industrial Revolution in England is usually dated from 1760 or 1780, it was not until the nineteenth century that the use of steam engines and power-driven machinery, and the growth of large factories and great manufacturing cities, brought about the conditions of modern industrialism. The economic system of the eighteenth century, while it contained within itself the seeds of later industrialism, represented the flowering of the older merchant capitalism, domestic industry, and mercantilist government policies which had grown up since the sixteenth century.

Most people in the eighteenth century lived in the country. Agriculture was the greatest single industry and source of wealth. Cities remained small. London and Paris, the largest of Europe, each had a population of *Rural industry* 600,000 or 700,000, but the next largest cities did not much exceed 200,000, and in all Europe at the time of the French Revolution in 1789 there were only 50 cities with as many as 50,000 people. Urbanization, however, was no sign of economic advancement. Spain, Italy, and even the Balkan peninsula, according to an estimate made in the 1780s, each had more large cities (over 50,000) than did Great Britain. Urbanization did not equate with industry because most industry was carried on in the country, by peasants and part-time agricultural workers who worked for the merchant capitalists of the towns. Thus, while it is true to say that most people still lived in the country, it would be false to say that their lives and labors were devoted to agriculture exclusively. One English estimate, made

Most people who were "engaged in manufactures" in eighteenth-century Europe still worked in their own rural homes. This engraving from the early 1780s shows three women at work in an Irish cottage, where they are spinning and winding thread while another woman prepares a meal and watches a child.
(SSPL/The Image Works)

in 1739, held that there were 4,250,000 persons "engaged in manufactures" in the British Isles, a figure that included women and children and comprised almost half the entire population. These people worked characteristically in their own cottages, employed as wage earners by merchant capitalists under the "domestic" system. Almost half of them were engaged in the weaving and processing of woolens. Others were in the copper, iron, lead, and tin manufactures; others in leather goods; much smaller were the paper, glass, porcelain, silk, and linen trades; and smallest of all, in 1739, was the manufacture of cotton cloth, which accounted for only about 100,000 workers. The list suggests the importance of nonagricultural occupations in the preindustrial age.

England, even with half its population engaged at least part of the time in manufactures, was not yet the unrivaled manufacturing country that it was to become after 1800. England in the eighteenth century produced no more iron than Russia and no more manufactures than France. The population of England was still small; it began to grow rapidly about 1760, but as late as 1800 France was still twice as populous as England and Scotland together. France, though less intensively developed than England, with probably far less than half its people "engaged in manufactures," nevertheless, because of its greater size, remained the chief industrial center of Europe.

Although foreign and colonial trade grew rapidly in the eighteenth century, it is probable that, in both Great Britain and France, the domestic or internal trade was greater in volume and occupied more people. Great Britain, with no internal tariffs, with an insignificant guild system, and with no monopolies allowed within the country except to inventors, was the largest area of internal free trade in Europe. France, or at least Colbert's Five Great Farms, offered an almost equal-sized free-trading internal market. A great deal of economic activity was therefore domestic, consisting of exchange between town and town or between region and region. The proportions between domestic and international trade cannot be known. But foreign trade was increasingly important for the largest business enterprises. International trade created the greatest commercial fortunes and the main accumulations of new capital. And it was the foreign trade that led to international rivalry and war.

The World Economy: The Dutch, British, and French

On the international economic scene a great part was still played by the Dutch. After the Peace of Utrecht the Dutch ceased to be a great political power; but their role in commerce, shipping, and finance remained undiminished, or diminished only when compared to the continuing commercial growth of France and Great Britain. They were still the middlemen and common carriers for other peoples. Their freight rates remained the lowest of Europe. They continued to grow rich on imports from the East Indies. To a large extent also, in the eighteenth century, the Dutch lived on their investments. The capital they had accumulated over 200 years they now lent out to French or British or other entrepreneurs. Dutch capital was to be found in every large commercial venture of Europe and was lent to governments far and wide. A third of the capital of the Bank of England in the mid–eighteenth century belonged to Dutch shareholders. The Bank of Amsterdam remained the chief clearinghouse and financial center of Europe. Its supremacy ended only with the invasion of Holland by a French Revolutionary army in 1795.

Trade

The Atlantic trade routes, leading to America, to Africa, and to Asia, attracted the merchants of many nationalities in Europe. A great many East India companies were established—usually to do business in America as well as the East, for the "Indies" at the beginning of the eighteenth century was still a general term for the vast regions overseas. Both the English and the French East India companies were reorganized, with an increased investment of capital, shortly after 1700. A number of others were established—by the Scots, the Swedes, the Danes, the imperial free city of Hamburg, the republic of Venice, Prussia, and the Austrian monarchy. But, with the exception of the Danish company that lasted some 60 years, they all failed after only a few years, either for insufficiency of capital or because they lacked strong diplomatic, military, and naval support. Their failure showed that, in the transocean trade, unassisted business enterprise was not enough. Merchants needed strong national backing to succeed in this sphere. Neither free city, nor small kingdom, nor tiny republic, nor the amorphous Austrian empire provided a firm enough base.

East India companies

It was the British and French who won out in the commercial rivalry of the eighteenth century. Britain and France were alike in having, besides a high level of industrial production at home, governments organized on a national scale and able to protect and advance, under mercantilist principles, the interests of their merchants in distant countries. For both peoples the eighteenth century—or the three-quarters of a century between the end of the War of the Spanish Succession in 1713 and the beginning of the French Revolution in 1789—was an age of spectacular enrichment and commercial expansion.

Commercial rivalry

Although the trade figures are difficult to arrive at, French foreign and colonial trade may well have grown even more rapidly than the British in the years between the 1720s and the 1780s. In any event, by the 1780s, the two countries were about equal in their total foreign and colonial trade. The British in the 1780s enjoyed proportionately more of the trade with America and Asia; the French, more of the trade with the rest of Europe and the Middle East. The contest for markets played an important part in the colonial and commercial wars between Britain and France all through the eighteenth century and on into the final and climactic struggle, and British triumph, in the time of Napoleon.

Asia, America, and Africa in the Global Economy

In the expanding global economy of the eighteenth century each continent played its special part. The European trade with Asia was subject to an ancient limitation. Asia was almost useless as a market for European manufactures. There was much that Europeans wanted from Asia but almost nothing that Asians wanted from Europe. The peoples of Chinese, Indian, and Malay culture had elaborate civilizations with which they were content; Asian elites in this era lacked the dynamic restlessness of European entrepreneurs, and the masses were so impoverished (more so even than in Europe) that they could buy nothing anyway. Europeans found that they could send little to Asia except gold. The trade of gold from Europe to Asia had gone on since ancient times, and even more gold and silver flowed to east Asia from European colonies in the Americas after the sixteenth century. Accumulating over time, the wealth from this trade became one source of the fabulous treasures of Eastern princes. To finance the swelling demand for Asian products it was necessary for Europeans constantly to replenish their stocks of gold. The British found an important new supply in Africa along the Gulf of Guinea, where one region (the present Ghana) was long called the Gold Coast. The word "guinea" became the name of a gold coin minted in England from 1663 to 1813 and long remained a fashionable way of saying 21 shillings.

Spices and Eastern manufactures

What Europeans sought from Asia was still in part spices—pepper and ginger, cinnamon and cloves—now brought in mainly by the Dutch from their East India islands. But they wanted manufactured goods also. Asia was still in some lines superior to Europe in technical skill. It is enough to mention rugs, chinaware, and cotton cloth. The very names by which cotton fabrics are known in English and other European languages reveal the places from which they were thought to come. "Madras" and "calico" refer to the Indian cities of Madras and Calicut; "muslin," to the Arabic city of Mosul. "Gingham" comes from a Malay word meaning "striped"; "chintz," from a Hindustani word meaning "spotted." Most of the Eastern manufactures were increasingly imitated in the eighteenth century in Europe. Axminster and Aubusson carpets competed with Oriental rugs. In 1709 a German named Boettcher discovered a formula for making a vitreous and translucent substance comparable to the porcelain of China; this European "china," made at Sèvres, Dresden, and in England, soon competed successfully with the imported original.

Cotton fabrics were never produced in Europe at a price to compete with India until after the introduction of power machinery, which began in England about 1780. Before that date the demand for Indian cotton goods was so heavy that the woolen, linen, and silk interests became alarmed. They could produce nothing like the sheer muslins and bright calico prints which caught the public fancy, and many governments, to protect the jobs and capital involved in the old European textile industries, simply forbade the import of Indian cottons altogether. But it was a time of many laws and little enforcement, the forbidden fabrics continued to come in, and Daniel Defoe observed in 1708 that, despite the laws, cottons were not only sought as clothing by all classes, but "crept into our houses, our closets and bedchambers; curtains, cushions, chairs and at last beds themselves were nothing but calicoes or Indian stuffs." Gradually, in the face of tariff protection for "infant industries" in Europe, and the rapid growth of European cotton manufactures, import of cottons and other manufactures from Asia declined. After about 1770 most of the imports of the British East India Company consisted of tea, which was brought from China.

The Americas, including the West Indies, bulked larger than Asia in the eighteenth-century trade of western Europe. The American trade was based mainly on one commodity—sugar. Sugar had long been known in the East, and in the European Middle Ages little bits of it had trickled through to delight the palates of lords and prelates. About 1650 sugar cane was brought in quantities from the East and planted in the West Indies by Europeans. A whole new economic system arose in a few decades. It was based on the "plantation." A plantation was an economic unit consisting of a considerable tract of land, a sizable investment of capital, often owned by absentees in France or England, and a force of impressed labor, supplied by black workers brought from Africa as slaves. Sugar, produced in quantity with cheap labor at low cost, proved to have an inexhaustible market.

Sugar and the plantation system

The eighteenth century was the golden age, economically speaking, of the West Indies. From its own islands alone, during the 80 years from 1713 to 1792, Great Britain imported a total of £162,000,000 worth of goods, almost all sugar; imports from India and China, in the same 80 years, amounted to only £104,000,000. The little islands of Jamaica, Barbados, St. Kitts, and others, as suppliers of Europe, not only dwarfed the whole mainland of British America but the whole mainland of Asia as well. For France, less well established than Britain on the American mainland and in Asia, the same holds with greater force. The richest of all the sugar colonies, Santo Domingo (now divided between Haiti and the Dominican Republic) belonged to France.

The plantation economy, first established in sugar and later in cotton (after 1800), brought Africa into the foreground. Slaves had been obtained from Black Africa from time immemorial, both by the Roman Empire and by the Muslim world, both of which, however, enslaved blacks and whites indiscriminately. After the European discovery of America, blacks were taken across the Atlantic by the Spanish and Portuguese. Dutch slavetraders also took them to Virginia in 1619, a year before the arrival of the Pilgrim Fathers in Massachusetts. But slavery in the Americas before 1650 may be described as occasional. With the rise of the plantation economy after 1650, and especially after 1700, it became a fundamental economic institution. Slavery now formed the labor supply of a very substantial and heavily capitalized branch of world production. About 610,000 blacks were landed from Africa in the island of Jamaica alone between 1700 and 1786. Total figures are hard to give, but it is certain that, until well after 1800, far more Africans than Europeans made the voyage to the Americas.

Slave trade

The transatlantic slave trade in the eighteenth century was conducted mainly by English-speaking interests, principally in England but also in New England, followed as closely as they could manage it by the French. Yearly export of merchandise from Great Britain to Africa, used chiefly in exchange for slaves, increased tenfold between 1713 and 1792. As for merchandise coming into Britain from the British West Indies, virtually all produced by slaves, in 1790 it constituted almost a fourth of all British imports. If we add British imports from the American mainland, including what after 1776 became the United

States, the importance of black labor to the British economic system will appear still greater, since a great part of exports from the mainland consisted of agricultural products, such as tobacco and indigo, produced partly by slaves. The rapid growth of trade within the British empire and the phenomenal rise of British capitalism in the eighteenth century were therefore based to a considerable extent on the enslavement of Africans. The town of Liverpool, an insignificant place on the Irish Sea in 1700, built itself up by the slave trade and the trade in slave-produced commodities to a busy transatlantic commercial center, which in turn, as will be seen later, stimulated the "industrial revolution" in Manchester and other neighboring towns.

Slavery and British capitalism

The west-European merchants, British, French, and Dutch, sold the products of America and Asia to their own peoples and those of central and eastern Europe. Trade with Germany and Italy was fairly stable. With Russia it enormously increased. To cite the British record only, Britain imported 15 times as much goods from Russia in 1790 as in 1700, and sold the Russians 6 times as much. The Russian landlords, as they became Europeanized, desired Western manufactures and the colonial products such as sugar, tobacco, and tea which could be purchased only from western Europeans. They had grain, timber, and naval stores to offer in return. Similarly, landlords of Poland and north Germany, in the seventeenth and eighteenth centuries, found themselves increasingly able to move their agricultural products out through the Baltic and hence increasingly able to buy the products of western Europe, America, and Asia in return. Landlords of eastern Europe thus had an incentive to make their estates more productive. "Big" agriculture spread, developing in eastern Europe a system not unlike the plantation economy of the New World. It had many effects. It contributed, along with political causes, to reducing the bulk of the east-European population to serfdom. It helped to bring western European culture to the upper classes of eastern Europe. And it helped to enrich the cities and merchants of western Europe.

The Wealth of Western Europe: Social Consequences

The wealth which accumulated along the Atlantic seaboard of Europe was, in short, by no means produced by the efforts of western Europeans only. All the world contributed to its formation. The natural resources of the Americas, the gold and people of Africa, the labor of enslaved workers on Caribbean islands, the resources and manufacturing skills of Asia, all alike went into producing the vastly increased volume of goods moving in world commerce. Europeans directed the movement. They supplied capital; they contributed technical and organizing abilities; and it was the demand of Europeans, at home in Europe and as traders abroad, that set increasing numbers of Indians to spinning cotton, Chinese to raising tea, Malays to gathering spices, and Africans to the tending of sugar cane. A few non-Europeans might benefit in the process—Indian or Chinese merchants "subsidized" by the East Indian companies, African chiefs who captured slaves from neighboring tribes and sold them to Europeans. But the profits of the world economy really went to Europe. The new wealth, over and above what was necessary to keep the far-flung and polyglot labor force in being, and to pay other expenses, piled up in Britain, Holland, and France.

Private property

Here it was owned by private persons. It accumulated within the system of private property and as part of the institutions of private enterprise or private capitalism. Governments were dependent on these private owners of property, for governments, in western Europe, had no important sources of revenue except loans and taxes derived from their peoples. When the owners of

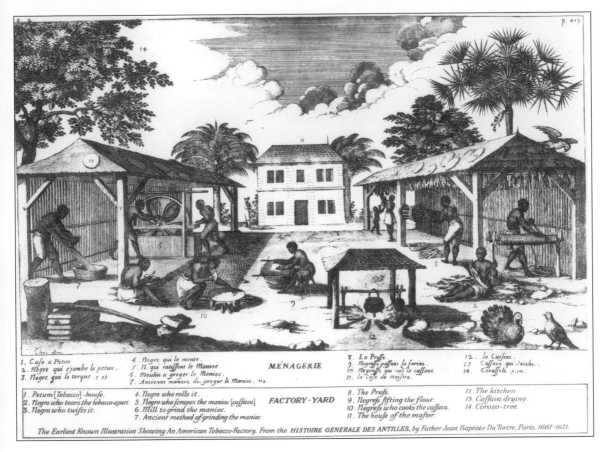

1. Cafe a Petun.	4. Negre qui le monte.		¥. La Preffe.	12. la Cuifine.
2. Negre qui e'jambe le petun.	5. N. qui ratiffent le Manioc.	MÉNAGERIE	9. Negreffe paffans la farina.	13. Caffane qui Seiche.
3. Negre qui le torque. p. 93.	6. Moulin a greger le Manioc.		10. Negreffe qui cuit la caffane	14. Coraffole. p.111.
	7. Ancienne maniere de greger le Manioc. 112.		11. la Cafe du maistre.	

1. Petum [Tobacco]-houfe.	4. Negro who rolls it.		8. The Prefs.	12. The kitchen
2. Negro who tears the tobacco apart.	5. Negro who fcrapes the manioc [caffava]	FACTORY-YARD	9. Negrefs fifting the flour.	13. Caffava drying.
3. Negro who twifts it.	6. Mill to grind the manioc.		10. Negrefs who cooks the caffava.	14. Corozo-tree.
	7. Ancient method of grinding the manioc.		11. The houfe of the mafter.	

The Earliest Known Illustration Showing An American Tobacco-Factory. From the HISTOIRE GENERALE DES ANTILLES, by Father Jean Baptiste Du Tertre, Paris, 1667-1671.

European traders and merchants gained much of their new wealth in the seventeenth and eighteenth centuries from commodities produced on plantations in the Americas and the Caribbean. This plantation economy depended on the labor of enslaved African workers such as the people in this seventeenth century illustration, who are preparing tobacco for export from one of the Caribbean islands.

(Rare Books and Manuscripts Division, New York Public Library, Astor, Lenox and Tilden Foundations)

wealth gave their support, the government was strong and successful, as in England. When they withdrew support, the government collapsed, as it was to collapse in France in the Revolution of 1789.

In a technical sense there were many "capitalists" in western Europe, persons who had a little savings which they used to buy a parcel of land or a loom or entrusted to some other person to invest at interest. And in a general sense the new wealth was widely distributed; the standard of living rose in western Europe in the eighteenth century. Tea, for example, which cost as much as £10 a pound when introduced into England about 1650, was an article of common consumption a hundred years later. But wealth used to produce more wealth, that is, capital, was owned or controlled in significant amounts by relatively few persons. In the eighteenth century some people became unprecedentedly rich (including some who started quite poor, for it was a time of open opportunity); the great intermediate layers of society became noticeably more comfortable; and the people at the bottom, such as the serfs of eastern Europe, the Irish peasantry, the dispossessed farm workers in England, the poorest peasants and workers of France, were worse off than they had been before. The poor continued to live in hovels. The prosperous created for themselves that pleasant, comfortable world of the eighteenth century that connoisseurs still admire, a world of well-ordered Georgian homes, closely cropped lawns and shrubs, furniture by Chippendale or à la Louis XV, coach-and-four, family portraits, high chandeliers, books bound in morocco, and a staff of servants "below stairs."

The merging of bourgeois and aristocratic wealth

Families enriched by commerce, and especially the daughters, mixed and intermarried with the old families who owned land. Women thus played an essential economic role in the carefully arranged marriages that both protected and increased the wealth of upper-class families. Landowners needed the capital that could be acquired through marriages with the daughters of wealthy traders; prosperous entrepreneurs sought the landed properties that might come into their families through marriages with women of the old aristocracy. But marriage was only one of the ways in which the old and new wealth of Europe came together. The merchant in England or France no sooner became prosperous than he bought himself a landed estate. In France he might also purchase a government office or patent of nobility. Contrariwise, the landowning gentleman, especially in England, no sooner increased his landed income than he invested the proceeds in commercial enterprise or government bonds. The two forms of property, bourgeois and aristocratic, tended to merge. Until toward the end of the century the various propertied interests worked harmoniously together, and the unpropertied classes, the vast majority, could influence the government only by riot and tumult. The eighteenth century, though an era of rapid commercial expansion, was on the whole an age of considerable social stability in western Europe. It was the upheavals of the French Revolution that would disrupt and transform much of the social and political order in European societies after 1789.

The foregoing might be illustrated from the lives of thousands of men and women. Two examples are enough, one English and one French. They show the working of the world economic system, the rise of the commercial class in western Europe, and the role of that class in the political life of the Western countries.

Thomas Pitt

Thomas Pitt, called "Diamond" Pitt, was born in 1653, the son of a parish clergyman in the Church of England. He went to India in 1674. Here he operated as an "interloper," trading in defiance of the legal monopoly of the East India Company. Returning to England, he was prosecuted by the company and fined £400 but was rich enough to buy the manor of Stratford and with it the borough of Old Sarum, a rotten borough which gave him a seat in the House of Commons without the trouble of an election. He soon returned to India, again as an interloper, where he competed so successfully with the company that it finally took him into its own employment. He traded on his own account, as well as for the company, sent back some new chintzes to England, and defended Madras against the local ruler of the Carnatic, the coastal area around Madras, buying him off with money. In 1702, though his salary was only £300 a year, he purchased a 410-carat uncut diamond for £20,400. He bought it from an Indian merchant who had himself bought it from an English skipper, who in turn had stolen it from the slave who had found it in the mines and who had concealed it in a wound in his leg. Back in Europe, Pitt had his diamond cut at Amsterdam and sold it in 1717 to the regent of France for £135,000. The regent put it in the French crown; it was appraised at the time of the French Revolution at £480,000. "Diamond" Pitt died in 1726. One of his daughters became the Countess of Stanhope and one of his sons became the Earl of Londonderry. Another son became father to the William Pitt who guided Britain through the

THE DUET
by Arthur Devis (English, 1711–1787)

The prosperity of the upper classes in eighteenth-century England supported the culture and comforts that are represented in this painting. Expanding global trade provided a pleasant, comfortable life for increasingly wealthy European elites and a new market for good furniture, fine art, and talented gardeners.

(Victoria & Albert Museum/Art Resource, NY)

Seven Years' War with France and who was raised to the peerage as the Earl of Chatham. After this Pitt the city of Pittsburgh was named, so that a fortune gained in the East gave its name to a frontier settlement in the interior of America. Chatham's younger son, the second William Pitt, became prime minister at 24. The younger Pitt guided Britain through its wars with revolutionary France and Napoleon, until his death in 1806 during the high tide of the Napoleonic empire.

Jean-Joseph Laborde was born in 1724, of a bourgeois family of southern France. He went to work for an uncle who had a business at Bayonne trading with Spain and the East. From the profits he built up vast planta-

Jean-Joseph Laborde

tions and slaveholdings in Santo Domingo. His ships brought sugar to Europe and returned with prefabricated building materials, each piece carefully numbered, for his plantations and refineries in the West Indies. He became one of the leading bankers in Paris. His daughter became the Countess de Noailles. He himself received the title of marquis, which he did not use. He bought a number of manors and châteaux near Paris. As a real estate operator he developed that part of Paris, then suburban, now called the Chaussée d'Antin. During the Seven Years' War he was sent by the French government to borrow money in Spain, where he was told that Spain would lend nothing to Louis XV but would gladly lend him personally 20,000,000 reals. In the War of American Independence Laborde raised 12,000,000 livres in gold for the government to help pay the French army and navy, thus contributing to the success of the American Revolution. He acted as investment agent for Voltaire, gave 24,000 livres a year to charity, and subscribed 400,000 livres in 1788 toward building new hospitals in Paris. In July 1789 he helped to finance the insurrection which led to the fall of the Bastille and the Revolution. His son, in June 1789, took the Oath of the Tennis Court, swearing to write a constitution for France. He himself was guillotined in 1794. His children turned to scholarship and the arts.

◈ 33.   WESTERN EUROPE AFTER THE PEACE OF UTRECHT, 1713–1740

The Peace of Utrecht registered the defeat of French ambitions in the wars of Louis XIV. The French move toward "universal monarchy" had been blocked. The European state system had been preserved. Europe was to consist of independent and sovereign states, all legally free and equal, continuously entering or leaving alliances along the principles of the balance of power. The peace settlement of 1713–1714 placed the Bourbon Philip V on the Spanish throne but gave most of Spain's European possessions, outside Spain itself, to the Austrian Habsburgs (see maps, pp. 187, 313). Great Britain, which had been consolidated during the wars as a combined kingdom of England and Scotland, took Newfoundland, Nova Scotia, and the Hudson Bay region from France and, taking Gibraltar and Minorca from Spain, became a naval power in the Mediterranean. The British also received trading rights in Spanish America, thus enhancing their position as the most dynamic power in the rapidly developing transatlantic economic system.

Repairing the damages of war

Governments now turned to repairing the damages of war. Spain was somewhat rejuvenated by the French influence under its new Bourbon house. The drift and decadence that had set in under the last Habsburgs were at least halted. The Spanish monarchy was administratively strengthened. Its officials followed the absolutist government of Louis XIV as a model. The estates of the east-Spanish kingdoms, Aragon and Valencia, ceased to meet, going like the Estates General of France into the limbo of obsolete institutions. On the whole the French influence in eighteenth-century Spain was intangible. Nothing was changed in substance, but the old machinery functioned with more precision. Administrators were better trained and took a more constructive attitude toward government work; they became more aware of the world north of the Pyrenees and recovered confidence in their country's future. They tried also to tighten up the administration of their American empire. More revenue officers and coast guards were introduced in the Caribbean, whose zeal led to repeated clashes with smugglers, mainly British. Friction on the Spanish Main, reinforced by Spanish dislike for British occupation of Gibraltar, kept Spain and Britain in a continual ferment of potential hostility.

The Dutch after Utrecht receded from the political stage, though their alliance was always sought because of the huge shipping and financial resources they controlled. The Swiss also became important in banking and financial circles. The Belgians founded an overseas trading company in 1723 on the authority of their new Austrian ruler; this "Ostend Company" sent out six voyages to China, which were highly profitable, but the commercial jealousy of the Dutch and British obliged the Austrian emperor to withdraw his support, so that the enterprise soon came to an end. The Scots began at about this time to play their remarkable role of energizing business affairs in many countries. Union with England gave them access to the British empire and to the numerous commercial advantages won by the English. John Law, the financial wizard of France, was a Scot, as was William Paterson, one of the chief founders of the Bank of England.

France and Britain after 1713

Our main attention falls on Britain and France. Though one was the victor and the other the vanquished in the wars that ended in 1713, and though one stood for absolutism and the other for constitutionalism in government, their development in the years after Utrecht was in some ways surprisingly parallel. In both countries for some years the king was personally ineffective, and in both the various propertied interests therefore gained many advantages. Both enjoyed the commercial expansion described above. Both went through a short period of financial experimentation and frantic speculation in stocks, the bubble bursting in each case in 1720. Each was thereafter governed by a statesman, Cardinal Fleury in France and Robert Walpole in England, whose policy was to keep peace abroad and conciliate all interests at home. Fleury and Walpole held office for about two decades, toward the end of which the two countries again went to war. But the differences are at least as instructive as the parallels.

In France the new king was a child, Louis XV, the great-grandson of Louis XIV, and only five years old when his reign began in 1715. The government was entrusted to a regent, the Duke of Orleans, an elder cousin of the young king. Orleans, lacking the authority of a monarch, had to admit the aristocracy to a greater share of the power that nobles had lost during the long reign of Louis XIV. Most of the nobles had never liked the absolutist policies of Louis XIV, and there was much dissatisfaction with absolutism among all classes, because of the ruin and suffering brought by Louis XIV's wars.

The higher nobles, ousted by Louis XIV, now reappeared in the government. For a time Orleans worked through committees of noblemen, roughly corresponding to ministries, a system lauded by its backers as a revival of political freedom; but the committees proved so incompetent that they were soon abandoned. The old parlements of France, and especially the Parlement of Paris, which Louis XIV had reduced to silence, vigorously reasserted themselves after his death. The parlements were primarily law courts, originally composed of bourgeois judges. But Louis XIV and his predecessors, to raise money, had made the judgeships into offices to be sold; and they attached titles of nobility to increase the price. Hence in the time of the Regency the judges of the parlements had bought or inherited their seats and were almost all nobles. Because they had property rights in their offices, they could not be removed by the king. The Regent conceded much influence to the Parlement of Paris, utilizing it to modify the will of Louis XIV. The parlements broadened their position, claiming the right to assent to legislation and taxes, through refusing to enforce government measures that they considered contrary to the unwritten constitution or fundamental laws of France. They managed to exercise this right, off and on, from the days of the Regency until the great Revolution of 1789. The eighteenth century, for France, was a period of absolutism checked and balanced by organized privileged groups. It was an age of aristocratic resurgence, in which the nobles won back many of the powers that Louis XIV had taken from them.

Aristocratic resurgence

In Great Britain the Parliament was very different from the French parlements, and the British aristocracy was more politically competent than the *noblesse* of France. Parliament proved an effective machine for the conduct of public business. The House of Lords was hereditary, with the large exception of the bishops, who were appointed by the government and made up about a quarter of the active members of the upper house. The House of Commons was not at all representative of the country according to modern ideas. Only the wealthy, or those patronized by the wealthy, could sit in it, and they were chosen by diverse and eccentric methods, in counties and towns, almost without regard to the size or wishes of the population. Some boroughs were owned outright, like the Old Sarum of the Pitt family. But through the machinations of bosses, or purchase of seats, all kinds of interests managed to get representatives into the Commons. Some members spoke for the "landed interest";

The English Parliament

others for the "funded interest" (mainly government creditors); others for the "London interest," the "West India interest," the "East India interest," and others. All politically significant groups could expect to have their desires heeded in Parliament, and all therefore were willing to go through parliamentary channels. Parliament was corrupt, slow, and expensive, but it was effective. For Parliament was not only a roughly representative body; it had also acquired, in practice, the power to legislate.

Queen Anne, the last reigning Stuart, died in 1714. She was succeeded by George I, Elector of Hanover, as provided for by Parliament in the Act of Settlement of 1701. George I was the nearest relative of the Stuarts who was also a Protestant. A heavy middle-aged German who spoke no English, he continued to spend much of his time in Germany, and he brought with him to England a retinue of German ministers and mistresses. He was never popular in England, where he was regarded as at best a political convenience. He was in no position to play a strong hand in English public life, and during his reign Parliament gained considerable independence from the crown.

The main problem was still whether the principles of the Revolution of 1688 should be maintained. The agreement which had made that revolution relatively bloodless proved to be temporary. The Whigs, who considered the revolution as their work, long remained a minority made up of a few great landowning noblemen, wealthy London merchants, lesser businesspeople, and nonconformists in religion. The Whigs generally controlled the House of Lords, but the House of Commons was more uncertain; at the time of the Peace of Utrecht its majority was Tory. We have already noted the significance for English constitutional development of the conflict at that time between the prowar Whig majority in the House of Lords and the Tory majority in Commons and how the conflict was resolved to help establish the primacy of the House of Commons.

Whigs and Tories

After 1714 the two parties tended to dissolve, and the terms "Whig" and "Tory" ceased to have much definite meaning. In general the government, and the Anglican bishops who were close to the government, remained "Whig." Men who were remote from the central government, or suspicious of its activities, formed a kind of country party quite different from the earlier Tories. Gentry and yeomen of the shires and byways were easily aroused against the great noblemen and men of money who led the Whigs. In the established church the lesser clergy were sometimes critical of the Whig bishops. Outside the official church were a group of Anglican clergy who refused the oath of loyalty after 1688 and were called Non-Jurors; they kept alive a shadow church until 1805. In Scotland also, the ancestral home of the Stuarts, many were disaffected with the new regime.

Tories, Non-Jurors, and Scots made up a milieu after 1688 in which what would now be called counterrevolution might develop. Never enthusiastic for the "Whig wars" against France, critical of the mounting national debt which the wars created, distrustful of the business and moneyed interests, they began to look wistfully to the exiled Stuarts. After 1701, when James died in France, the Stuart claims devolved upon his son, who lived until 1766, scheming time and again to make himself king of England. His partisans were known as Jacobites, from *Jacobus,* the Latin for James. They claimed that he had a divine

"James III"

right to the monarchy and regarded him as "James III," whereas others called him the Pretender. The Jacobites felt that if he would give up his Catholic religion, he should be accepted as Britain's rightful king.

The Whigs could not tolerate a return of the Stuarts. The restoration of "James III" and his divine-right partisans would undo the principles of the Glorious Revolution—limited monarchy, constitutionalism, parliamentary supremacy, the rule of law, the toleration of dissenting Protestants, in short all that was summarized and defended in the political writings of John Locke. Moreover, those who held stock in the Bank of England or who had lent their money to the government would be ruined, since "James III" would surely repudiate a debt contracted by his foes. The Whigs were bound to support the Hanoverian George I. And George I was bound to look for support in a strange country among the Whigs.

George lacked personal appeal even for his English friends. To his enemies he was ridiculous and repulsive. The successful establishment of his dynasty would ruin the hopes of Tories and Jacobites. In 1715 the Pretender landed in Scotland, gathered followers from the Highlands, and proclaimed a rebellion against George I. Civil war seemed to threaten. But the Jacobite leaders bungled, and many of their followers proved to be undecided. They were willing enough to toast the "king over the water" in protest against the Whigs but not willing in a showdown to see the Stuarts, with all that went with them, again in possession of the crown of England.

Threats of civil war

The Fifteen, as the revolt came to be called, petered out. But 30 years later came the Forty-five. In 1745, during war with France, the Pretender's son, "Bonnie Prince Charlie" or the "Young Pretender," again landed in Scotland and again proclaimed rebellion. This time, though almost no one in England rallied, the uprising was more successful. A Scottish force penetrated to within 80 miles of London and was driven back and crushed with the help of Hanoverian regiments rushed over from Germany. The government set out to destroy Jacobitism in the Scottish Highlands. The social system of the Highlands was wiped out, the clans were broken up, and their lands were forcibly reorganized according to modern notions of property and of landlord and tenant.

The Jacobite uprisings confirmed the old reputation of England in the eyes of Europe, namely, as Voltaire said, that its government was as stormy as the seas that surrounded it. To partisans of monarchy on the Continent they illustrated the weaknesses of parliamentary government. But their ignominious collapse actually strengthened the parliamentary regime in England. They left little permanent mark and soon passed into romantic legend.

The "Bubbles"

Meanwhile, immediately after the Peace of Utrecht, the problem of dealing with a large postwar government debt had to be faced in both England and France. Organized permanent public debt was new at the time. The possibilities and limitations of large-scale banking, paper money, and credit were not clearly seen. In France there was much amazement at the way in which England and Holland, though smaller and less wealthy than France, had been able to maximize their resources through banking and credit and even to finance the alliance which had eclipsed the Sun King. In addition there was much private demand for both lending and borrowing money. Private persons all over western Europe were looking for enterprises in which to invest their savings. And promoters and organizers, anticipating a profit in this or that line of business, were looking for capital with which to work. Out of this whole situation grew the "South Sea bubble" in England and the "Mississippi bubble" in France. Both bubbles broke in 1720, and both had important long-range effects.

A close tie between government finance and private enterprise was usual at the time, under mercantilist ideas of government guidance of trade. In England, for example, a good deal of the government debt was held by companies organized for that purpose. The government would charter a company, strengthen it with a monopoly in a given line of

Ties between government and private enterprise

business, and then receive from the company, after the stockholders had bought up the shares, a large sum of cash as a loan. Much of the British debt, contracted in the wars from 1689 to 1713, was held in this way by the Bank of England, founded in 1694; by the East India Company, reorganized in 1708 in such a way as to provide funds for the government; and by the South Sea Company, founded in 1711. The Bank enjoyed a legal monopoly over certain banking operations in London, the East India Company over trade with the East, the South Sea Company for exploiting the *asiento* and other commercial privileges extorted from Spain. The companies were owned by private investors. Savings drawn from trade and agriculture, put into shares in these companies, became available both for economic reinvestment and for use of the government in defraying the costs of war.

John Law

In 1716 the Prince Regent of France was attracted to a Scottish financier, John Law, reputedly by Law's remarkable mathematical system in gambling at cards. Law founded a much-needed French central bank. In the next year, 1717, he organized a *Compagnie d'Occident,* popularly called the Mississippi Company, which obtained a monopoly of trade with Louisiana, where it founded New Orleans in 1718. This company, under Law's management, soon absorbed the French East India, China, Senegal, and African companies. It now enjoyed a legal monopoly of all French colonial trade. Seeing this trade as a means to solve France's financial problems, the Regent authorized Law to assume the entire government debt. The Mississippi Company received from individuals their certificates of royal indebtedness or "bonds" and gave them shares of company stock in return. It proposed to pay dividends on these shares and to extinguish the debt from profits in the colonial trade and from a monopoly over the collection of all indirect taxes in France. The project carried with it a plan for drastic reform of the whole taxation system, to make taxes both more fair to the taxpayer and more lucrative to the government. Shares in the Mississippi Company were gobbled up by the public. There was a frenzy of speculation, a wild fear of not buying soon enough. Quotations rose to 18,000 livres a share. But the company rested only on unrealized projects. Shareholders began to fear for their money. They began to unload. The market broke sharply. Many found their life savings gone. Others lost ancestral estates on which they had borrowed in the hope of getting rich. Those, however, who had owned shares in the company before the rise, and who had resisted the speculative fever, lost nothing by the bursting of inflated prices and later enjoyed a gilt-edged commercial investment.

Much the same thing happened in England, where it was thought by many that Law was about to provide a panacea for France. The South Sea Company, outbidding the Bank of England, took over a large fraction of the public debt by receiving government "bonds" from their owners in return for shares of its stock. The size and speed of profits to be made in Spanish America were greatly exaggerated, and the market value of South Sea shares rose rapidly for a time, reaching £1,050 for a share of £100 par value. Other schemes abounded in the passion for easy money. Promoters organized mining and textile companies, as well as others of more fanciful or bolder design—a company to bring live fish to market in tanks, an insurance company to insure female chastity, a company "for an undertaking which shall in due time be revealed." Shares in such enterprises were snatched at mounting prices. But in September 1720 the South Sea stockholders began to sell, doubting whether operations would pay dividends commensurate to £1,000 a share. They dragged down the whole unstable structure. As in France, many people found that their savings or their inheritances had disappeared.

Indignation in both countries was extreme. Both governments were implicated in the scandal. John Law fled to Brussels. The Regent was discredited; he resigned in 1723, and French affairs were afterward conducted by Cardinal Fleury. In England there was a change of ministers. Robert Walpole, a country gentleman of Whig persuasion who had long sat in the Commons and who had warned against the South Sea scheme from the beginning, became the principal minister to George I.

Britain recovered from the crisis more successfully than France. Law's bank, a useful institution, was dissolved in the reaction against him, and France lacked an adequate banking system during the rest of the century. French investors developed a morbid fear of paper securities and a marked preference for putting their savings into land. Commercial capitalism and the growth of credit institutions in France were retarded. In England the same fears were felt. Parliament passed the "Bubble Act," forbidding all companies except those specifically chartered by the government to raise capital by the sale of stock. In both countries the development of joint-stock financing along the lines of the modern corporation was slowed down for over a century. Business enterprises continued to be typically owned by individuals and partnerships, which expanded by reinvestment of their own profits and so had another reason to keep profits up and wages down. But in England Walpole managed to save the South Sea Company, the East India Company, and the Bank, all of which were temporarily discredited in the eyes of the public. England continued to perfect its financial machinery.

The "Bubble Act"

The credit of the two governments was also shaken by the "bubbles." Much of the French war debt was repudiated in one way or another. Repudiation was in many cases morally justifiable, for many government creditors were unscrupulous war profiteers, but financially it was disastrous, for it discouraged honest people from lending their money to the state. Nor was much accomplished toward reform of the taxes. The nobles continued to evade taxes imposed on them by Louis XIV, John Law's plans for taxation evaporated with the rest of his project, and when in 1726 a finance minister tried to levy a two percent tax on all property, the vested interests, led by the Parlement of Paris, demolished this proposal also. Lacking an adequate revenue, and repudiating its debts, the French monarchy had little credit. The conception of the public or national debt hardly developed in France in the eighteenth century. The debt was considered to be the king's debt, for which no one except a few ministers felt any responsibility. The Bourbon government in fact often borrowed through the church, the Provincial Estates, or the city of Paris, which lenders considered to be better financial risks than the king himself. The government was severely handicapped in its foreign policy and its wars. It could not fully tap the wealth of its own subjects.

Credit and the National Debt

In England none of the debt was repudiated. Walpole managed to launch and keep going the system of the sinking fund, by which the government regularly set aside the wherewithal to pay interest and principal on its obligations. The credit of the British government became absolutely firm. The debt was considered a national debt, for which the British people themselves assumed the responsibility. Parliamentary government made this development possible. In France no one could tell what the king or his ministers might do, and hence the French were reluctant to trust them with their money. In England the people who had the money could also, through Parliament, determine the policies of state, decide what the money should be spent for, and levy enough taxes to maintain confidence in the debt. Similarities to France there were; the landowners who controlled the British Parliament, like those who controlled the Parlement of Paris, resisted direct taxation, so that the British government drew two-thirds or more of its revenues from indirect taxes

M. BACHELIER, DIRECTOR OF THE LYONS FARMS
by Jean-Baptiste Oudry (French, 1686–1755)

The "farms" of which M. Bachelier was a director were the semiprivate syndicates to which
the French monarchy delegated or farmed out the collection of its indirect taxes. Tax farmers
were generally hated, and many became very rich. Nothing is known of the man in this picture,
but with his huge wig, his lace cuffs, and his left hand politely extended, he typifies the ruling
elite at the close of the reign of Louis XIV.

(University of Michigan Museum of Art (1968/1.76))

paid by the mass of the population. Yet landowners, even dukes, did pay important amounts of taxes. There were no exemptions by class or rank, as in France. All propertied interests had a stake in the government. The wealth of the country stood behind the national debt. The national credit seemed inexhaustible. This was the supreme trump card of the British in their wars with France from the founding of the Bank of England in 1694 to the fall of Napoleon 120 years later. And it was the political freedom and power of Parliament that gave Britain's government its economic strength.

Fleury in France, Walpole in England

Fleury was 73 years old when he took office in 1726 and 90 when he left it. He was not one to initiate programs for the distant future. Louis XV, as he came of age, proved to be indolent and selfish. Public affairs drifted, while France grew privately more wealthy, especially the commercial and bourgeois classes. Walpole likewise kept out of controversies. His motto was *quieta non movere,* "let sleeping dogs lie." It was to win over the Tory squires to the Hanoverian and Whig regime that Walpole kept down the land taxes; this policy was successful, and Jacobitism quieted down. Walpole supported the Bank, the trading companies, and the financial interests, and they in turn supported him. It was a time of political calm, in which the lower classes were quiet and the upper classes were not quarreling, favorable therefore to the development of parliamentary institutions.

Walpole has been called the first prime minister and the architect of cabinet government, a system in which the prime minister and the ministers who head the cabinet departments are also members of the legislative body. He saw to it, by careful rigging, that a majority in the Commons

Cabinet government

always supported him. He avoided issues on which his majority might be lost. He thus began to acknowledge the principle of cabinet responsibility to a majority in Parliament, which was to become an important characteristic of cabinet government. And by selecting colleagues who agreed with him, and getting rid of those who did not, he advanced the idea of the cabinet as a body of ministers bound to each other and to the prime minister, obligated to follow the same policies and to stand or fall as a group. Thus Parliament was not only a representative or deliberative body, but also one that developed an effective executive organ, without which neither representative government nor any government could survive.

To assure peace and quiet in domestic politics the best means was to avoid raising taxes. And the best way to avoid taxes was to avoid war. Fleury and Walpole both tried to keep at peace. They were not in the long run successful. Fleury was drawn into the War of the Polish Succession in 1733. Walpole kept England out of war until 1739. He always had a war party to contend with, and the most bellicose were those interested in the American trade—the slave trade, the sugar plantations, and the illicit sale of goods in the Spanish empire. The British official figures show that while trade with Europe in the eighteenth century was always less in war than in peace, trade with America always increased during war, except, indeed, during the War of American Independence.

In the 1730s there were constant complaints of indignities suffered by Britons on the Spanish Main. The war party produced a Captain Jenkins, who carried with him a small box containing a withered ear, which he said had been cut from his head by the outrageous Spaniards. Testifying in the House of Commons, where he "commended his soul to God and his cause to his country," he stirred up a commotion which led to war. So in 1739, after 25 years of peace, England plunged with wild enthusiasm into the War of Jenkins's Ear.

"They are ringing the bells now," said Walpole; "they will soon be wringing their hands." The war soon merged into a conflict involving Europeans and others in all parts of the world. European wars could no longer be contained within Europe. The global economic and colonial systems that produced the expanding global trade also produced a series of global wars in which the European powers extended their conflicts across all of the distant territories and seas they sought to control.

34. THE GREAT WAR OF THE MID-EIGHTEENTH CENTURY: THE PEACE OF PARIS, 1763

The fighting lasted until 1763, with an uneasy interlude between 1748 and 1756. It went by many names. The opening hostilities between England and Spain were called, by the English, the War of Jenkins's Ear. The struggle on the Continent in the 1740s over the Habsburg inheritance was often known as the War of the Pragmatic Sanction. The Prussians spoke of the three "Silesian" wars. British colonials in America called the fighting of the 1740s King George's War, or used the term "French and Indian Wars," for the whole sporadic conflict. Disorganized and nameless struggles at the same time shook the peoples of India. Eventually these wars came to be called the War of the Austrian Succession (for hostilities between 1740 and 1748) and the Seven Years' War (for the conflicts between 1756 and 1763). The two wars were really one. They involved the same two principal issues: the global duel of Britain and France for colonies, trade, and sea power, and the European duel of Prussia and Austria for territory and military power in central Europe.

Eighteenth-Century Warfare

Warfare at the time was in a kind of classical phase, which strongly affected the development of events. It was somewhat slow, formal, elaborate, and indecisive. The enlisted ranks of armies and navies were filled with men considered economically useless, picked up by recruiting officers among unwary loungers in taverns or on the wharves. All governments protected their productive population, peasants, mechanics, and bourgeois, preferring to keep them at home, at work, and paying taxes. Soldiers became a class apart, enrolled for long terms, paid wages, professional in their outlook, and highly trained. They lived in barracks or great forts and were dressed in bright uniforms (like the British "redcoats"), which, since camouflage was unnecessary, they wore even in battle. Weapons were not powerful; infantry was predominant and was armed with the smooth-bore musket to which the bayonet could be attached. In war the troops depended on great supply depots built up beforehand, which were practically immovable with the transportation available, so that armies, at least in central and western Europe, rarely operated more than a few days' march from their bases. Soldiers fought methodically for pay. Generals hesitated to risk their troops, which took years to train and equip and were very expensive. Strategy took the form not of seeking out the enemy's main force to destroy it in battle but of maneuvering for advantages of position, applying a cumulative and subtle pressure somewhat as in a game of chess.

Little national feeling

There was little national feeling, or feeling of any kind. The Prussian army recruited half or more of its enlisted personnel outside Prussia; the British army was largely made up of Hanoverian or other German regiments; even the French army had German units incorporated in it. Deserters from one side were enlisted by the other. War was between governments, or between the oligarchies and aristocracies which governments represented, not between whole peoples. It was fought for power, prestige, or calculated practical interests, not for ideologies, moral principles, world conquest, national survival, or ways of life. Popular nationalism had developed farthest in England, where "Rule Britannia" and "God Save the King," both breathing a low opinion of foreigners, became popular songs during these mid-eighteenth-century wars.

Civilians were little affected, except in India or the American wilderness where European conditions did not prevail. In Europe, a government aspiring to conquer a neighboring province did not wish to ruin or antagonize it beforehand. The fact that the west-European struggle was largely naval kept it well outside civilian experience. Never had war been so harmless, certainly not in the religious wars of earlier times or in the national wars initiated later. This was one reason why governments went to war so lightly. On the other hand governments also withdrew from war much more readily than in later times. Their treasuries might be exhausted, their trained soldiers used up; only practical or rational questions were at stake; there was no war hysteria or pressure of mass opinion; the enemy of today might be the ally of tomorrow. Peace was almost as easy to make as war. Peace treaties were negotiated, not imposed. So the eighteenth century saw a series of wars and treaties and rearrangements of alliances, all arising over much the same issues and with exactly the same powers present at the end as at the beginning.

The War of the Austrian Succession, 1740–1748

The War of the Austrian Succession was started by the king of Prussia. Frederick II, or the "Great," was a young man of 28 when he became king in 1740. His youth had not been happy; he was temperamentally incompat-

Frederick II

ible with his father. His tastes as a prince had run to playing the flute, corresponding with French authors, and writing prose and verse in the French language. His father, the sober, military-minded Frederick William I, thought him frivolous and effeminate and dealt with him so clumsily that at the age of 18 he tried to escape from the kingdom. Caught and brought back, he was forced to witness the execution, by his father's order, of the friend and companion who had shared in his attempted flight. Frederick changed as the years passed from a jaunty youth to an aged cynic, equally undeceived by himself, his friends, or his enemies, and seeing no reason to expect much from human nature. Though his greatest reputation was made as a soldier, he retained his literary interests all his life, became a historian of merit, and is perhaps of all modern monarchs the only one who would have a respectable standing if considered only as a writer. An unabashed freethinker, like many others of his day, he considered all religions ridiculous and laughed at the divine right of kings; but he would have no nonsense about the rights of the house of Brandenburg, and he took a solemn view of the majesty of the state.

Frederick lost no time in showing a boldness which his father would have surely dreaded. He decided to conquer Silesia, and on December 16, 1740, he invaded that province, a region adjoining Prussia, lying in the upper valley of the Oder, and belonging to the kingdom of Bohemia and hence to the Danubian empire of the Habsburgs (see map, p. 208, panel 3). The Pragmatic Sanction, a general agreement signed by the European powers, including Prussia, had stipulated that all domains of the Austrian Habsburgs should be inherited integrally by the new heiress, Maria Theresa. The issue was between law and force. Frederick in attacking Silesia could invoke nothing better than "reason of state," the welfare and expansion of the state of which he was ruler.

The young Frederick II of Prussia, who would later be called Frederick the Great, was more interested in music and literature than in the military and political tasks of a monarch — which he nevertheless pursued boldly after becoming king in 1740. This painting by Antoine Pesne portrays the "Crown Prince" in the year before he inherited the Prussian throne.
(Bettmann/CORBIS)

The Pragmatic Sanction was universally disregarded. All turned against Maria Theresa. Bavaria and Saxony put in claims. Spain, still hoping to revise the Peace of Utrecht, saw another chance to win back former Spanish holdings in Italy. The decisive intervention was that of France. It was the fate of France to be torn between ambitions on the European continent and ambitions on the sea and beyond the seas. Economic and commercial advantage might dictate concentration on the impending struggle with Britain. But the French nobles were less interested than the British aristocrats in commercial considerations. They were influential because they furnished practically all the army officers and diplomats. They saw in Austria the traditional enemy, in Europe the traditional field of valor, and in Belgium, which now belonged to the Austrians, the traditional object for annexation to France. Cardinal Fleury, much against his will and judgment, found himself forced into war against the Habsburgs.

Maria Theresa

Maria Theresa was at this time a young woman of 23. She proved to be one of the most capable rulers ever produced by the house of Habsburg. She bore 16 children, and set a model of conscientious family living at a time of much indifference to such matters among the upper classes. She was as devout and as earnest as Frederick of Prussia was irreligious and seemingly flip. She dominated her husband and her grown sons as she did her kingdoms and her duchies. With a good deal of practical sense, she reconstructed her empire without having any doctrinaire program, and she accomplished more in her methodical way than more brilliant contemporaries with more spectacular projects of reform.

Soon after Frederick invaded Silesia, she gave birth to her first son, the future emperor Joseph II, in March 1741. She was preoccupied at the same time by the political crisis. Her dominions were assailed by half a dozen outside powers and her two kingdoms of Hungary and Bohemia (both of which had accepted the Pragmatic Sanction) were waiting to see which way their advantage lay. She betook herself to Hungary to be crowned with the crown of St. Stephen—and to rally support. She made a carefully arranged and dramatic appearance before the Hungarian political elite, implored them to defend her, and swore to uphold the liberties of the Hungarian nobles and the separate constitution of the kingdom of Hungary. All Europe told how the young queen, by raising aloft the infant Joseph, who was to be heir to the throne, at a session of the Hungarian parliament, had thrown the dour Magyars into paroxysms of chivalrous resolve. The story was not quite true, but it is true that she made an eloquent address to the Magyars and that she took her baby with her and proudly exhibited him. The Hungarian magnates pledged their "blood and life" and delivered 100,000 soldiers.

The war, as it worked out in Europe, was reminiscent of the struggles of the time of Louis XIV, or even of the Thirty Years' War now a century in the past. It was, again, a kind of civil struggle within the Holy Roman Empire, in which a league of German princes banded together against the monarchy of Vienna. This time they included the new kingdom of Prussia. It was, again, a *Parallels with past wars* collision of Bourbons and Habsburgs, in which the French pursued their old policy of maintaining division in Germany by supporting the German princes against the Habsburgs. The basic aim of French policy, according to instructions given by the French foreign office to its ambassador in Vienna in 1725, was to keep the Empire divided, preventing the union of German powers into "one and the same body, which would in fact become formidable to all the other powers of Europe." This time France had Spain on its side. Maria Theresa was supported only by Britain and Holland, which subsidized her financially but had inadequate land forces. The Franco-German-Spanish combination was highly successful. In 1742 Maria Theresa, hard pressed, accepted the proposals of Frederick for a separate peace. She temporarily granted him Silesia, and he temporarily slipped out of the war which he had been the first to enter. The French and Bavarians moved into Bohemia and almost organized a puppet kingdom with the aid of Bohemian nobles. The French obtained the election of their Bavarian satellite as Holy Roman Emperor, Charles VII. In 1745 the French won the battle of Fontenoy in Belgium, the greatest battle of the war; they dominated Belgium, which neither the Dutch nor British were able to defend. In the same year they fomented the Jacobite rebellion in Scotland to weaken or overthrow the British monarch.

But the situation overseas offset the situation in Europe. It was America that tilted the balance. The French fortress of Louisburg on Cape Breton Island was captured by an expedition of New Englanders in conjunction with the British navy. British warships drove French and Spanish shipping from the seas. The French West Indies were blockaded. The French government, in danger of losing the wealth and taxes drawn from the sugar and slave trades, announced its willingness to negotiate.

Peace was made at Aix-la-Chapelle in 1748. It was based on an Anglo-French agreement in which Maria Theresa was obliged to concur. Britain *Peace of Aix-la-Chapelle* and France arranged their differences by a return to the prewar *status quo*. The British returned Louisburg despite the protests of the Americans and relaxed their stranglehold on the Caribbean. The French returned Madras, which they had captured, and gave up their hold on Belgium. The Atlantic powers recognized Frederick's annexation of Silesia and required Maria Theresa to cede some Italian duchies to a Spanish Bourbon. Belgium was returned to Maria Theresa at the insistence of Britain and the Dutch. She and her ministers were very dissatisfied. They would infinitely have preferred to lose Belgium and keep Silesia. They were required, in the interest of a European or even intercontinental balance of power, to give up Silesia and to hold Belgium for the benefit of the Dutch against the French.

MARIA THERESA AND HER FAMILY
by Martin van Meytens (Austrian, 1695–1770)
Maria Theresa had an imposing public image in her dual roles as Queen in the Austrian house of Habsburg and mother in a large household of 16 children. This portrait of the Queen with her husband and many of her children shows her devotion to family life as well as the power she exercised in governing her empire.
(Scala/Art Resource, NY)

The war had been more decisive than the few readjustments of the map seemed to show. It proved the weakness of the French position, straddled as it was between Europe and the overseas world. Maintaining a huge army for use in Europe, the French could not, like Britain, concentrate upon the sea. On the other hand, because they were vulnerable on the sea, they could not hold their gains in Europe or conquer Belgium. The Austrians, though bitter, had reason for satisfaction. The war had been a war to partition the Habsburg empire. The Habsburg empire still stood. Hungary had thrown in its lot with Vienna, a fact of much subsequent importance. Bohemia was won back. In 1745 Maria Theresa got her husband elected Holy Roman Emperor as Francis I, a position for which, as a woman, she could not qualify. But the loss of Silesia was momentous. Silesia was as populous as the Dutch Republic, heavily German, and industrially the most advanced region east of the Elbe. Prussia by acquiring it doubled its population and more than doubled its resources. Prussia with Silesia was unquestionably a great power. Since Austria was still a great power, there were henceforth two great powers in the vague world known as "Germany," a situation which came to be known as the German dualism. But the transfer of Silesia, which doubled the number of Germans ruled by the king of Prussia, made the Habsburg empire less German, more Slavic and Hungarian, more Danubian and international. Silesia was the keystone of Germany. Frederick was determined to hold it; Maria Theresa was determined to win it back. A new war was therefore foreseeable in central Europe. As for Britain and France, the peace of Aix-la-Chapelle was clearly only a truce.

The next years passed in a busy diplomacy, leading to what is known as the "reversal of alliances" and Diplomatic Revolution of 1756. The Austrians set themselves to checking the growth of Prussia. Maria Theresa's foreign minister, Count Kaunitz, perhaps the most artful diplomat of the century, concluded that the rise of Prussia had revolutionized the balance of power. Kaunitz, dramatically reversing traditional policy, proposed an alliance between Austria and France—between the Habsburgs and the Bourbons. He encouraged French aspirations for Belgium in return for French support in the destruction of Prussia. The overtures between Austria and France obliged Britain, Austria's former ally, to reconsider its position in Europe; the British had Hanover to protect and were favorably impressed by the Prussian army. An alliance of Great Britain and Prussia was concluded in January 1756. Meanwhile Kaunitz consummated his alliance with France. One consequence was to marry the future Louis XVI to one of Maria Theresa's daughters, Marie Antoinette, the "Austrian woman" of French Revolutionary fame. The Austrian alliance was never popular in France. Some French thought that the ruin of Prussia would only enhance the Austrian control of Germany and so undo the fundamental "Westphalia system." The French progressive thinkers, known as "philosophes," believed Austria to be priest-ridden and backward and were for ideological reasons admirers of the freethinking Frederick II. Dissatisfaction with its foreign policy was one reason for the growth of internal opposition to the Bourbon government.

The Diplomatic Revolution of 1756

In any case, when the Seven Years' War broke out in 1756, though it was a continuation of the preceding war in that Prussia fought Austria, and Britain fought France, the belligerents had all changed partners. Great Britain and Prussia were now allies, as were, more remarkably, the Bourbons and the Habsburgs. In addition, Austria had concluded a treaty with the Russian empire for the annihilation of Prussia.

The Seven Years' War, 1756–1763: In Europe and America

Although the Seven Years' War began in America, let us turn first to Europe, where the war was another war of "partition." As a league of powers had but recently attempted to partition the empire of Maria Theresa, and a generation before had in fact partitioned the empires of Sweden and Spain, so now Austria, Russia, and France set out to partition the newly created kingdom of Prussia. Their aim was to relegate the Hohenzollerns to the territory of Brandenburg. Even with Silesia, Prussia had less than 6,000,000 people; each of its three principal enemies had 20,000,000 or more. But war was less an affair of peoples

Schönbrunn Palace, near Vienna, was the great palace of the Austrian Habsburgs. It was planned to compete with the vast palace of their French Bourbon rivals, but the plan was never completed because Maria Theresa (1740–1780) thought that the building seen here was adequate for her needs.

(Kunsthistoriches Museum, Vienna)

Frederick's military triumphs

than of states and standing armies, and the Prussian state and Prussian army were the most efficient in Europe. Frederick fought brilliant campaigns, won victories as at Rossbach in 1757, moved rapidly along interior lines, and eluded, surprised, and reattacked the badly coordinated armies opposed to him. He proved himself the great military genius of his day. But genius was scarcely enough. Against three such powers, reinforced by Sweden and the German states, and with no ally except Great Britain (and Hanover) whose aid was almost entirely financial, the kingdom of Prussia by any reasonable estimate had no chance of survival. There were times when Frederick believed all to be lost, yet he went on fighting, and his strength of character in these years of adversity, as much as his ultimate triumph, later made him a hero and symbol for the Germans. His subjects, Junkers and even serfs, advanced in patriotic spirit under pressure. The coalition tended to fall apart. The French lacked enthusiasm; they were fighting Britain, the Austrian alliance was unpopular, and Kaunitz would not plainly promise them Belgium. The Russians found that the more they moved westward the more they alarmed their Austrian allies. Frederick was left to deal only with the implacable Austrians, for whom he was more than a match. By the peace of Hubertusburg in 1763 not only did he lose nothing but he also retained Silesia.

The Masters of the Cloth Guild
by **Rembrandt van Rijn** (Dutch, 1606–1669)
This painting was done on commission for the guild of "clothiers" in Amsterdam; these men are the prosperous leaders of the guild.
(Rijksmuseum, Amsterdam)

Portrait of the Artist with Isabelle Brant
by **Peter Paul Rubens** (Flemish, 1577–1640)
Isabelle Brant married Rubens about the time he painted this dual portrait, which conveys the affection in an early seventeenth-century marriage.
(Bayerische Staatsgemäldesammlungen. Alte Pinakothek, Munich, Kustdia-Archive ARTOTHEK, D-Peissenberg)

The Artist's Studio
by **Jan Vermeer** (Dutch, 1632–1675)
The shadings of light and the textures of cloth are joined with the mysteries of human character in Vermeer's painting of the creative artist and his subject.
(Kunsthistorisches Museum, Vienna)

Old Woman Cooking Eggs
by **Diego Velásquez** (Spanish, 1559–1660)
Velásquez was best known for his portraits of people at the Spanish royal court, but he also portrayed the lives and character of the lower classes—as in this painting of an unknown woman preparing food.
(National Galleries of Scotland)

Self-Portrait
by **Elisabeth Vigée-Lebrun** (French, 1755–1842)
Vigée-Lebrun boldly represented her creative ambitions, looking directly toward the viewer and claiming her place in the mostly male world of eighteenth-century art.
(Scala/Art Resource, NY)

Mrs. Philip Thicknesse
by **Thomas Gainsborough** (English, 1727–1788)
Although eighteenth-century women could not enter politics, their role in the fine
arts became a theme in paintings such as Gainsborough's portrait of the fashionable
Mrs. Thicknesse.
(Cincinnati Art Museum, Bequest of Mary M. Emery)

1-6

A Woman of the Revolution
by **Jacques-Louis David** (French, 1748–1825)
David's portrait of a lower-class French woman in 1795 suggests the determination of the women who joined the revolutionary Parisian crowds and clubs during the French Revolution.
(Giraudon/Art Resource, NY)

The Gleaners
by **Jean-François Millet** (French, 1814–1875)
Most French women still worked in the countryside during the nineteenth century, as Millet
showed in this painting of poor peasants who gleaned the fields for a few stalks of grain.
(Art Resource, NY)

CHRONOLOGY OF NOTABLE EVENTS, 1619–1763

1619	First enslaved Africans arrive in Virginia
1720	The "Mississippi Bubble" in France and "South Sea Bubble" in Britain
1740–1748	War of Austrian Succession in Europe
1740–1780	Queen Maria Theresa rules and expands the Austrian Empire
1740–1786	Frederick II (the Great) rules and expands the kingdom of Prussia
1756–1763	The Seven Years' War; expansion of British power in India and America

For the rest, the Seven Years' War was a phase in the long dispute between France and Great Britain. Its stakes were supremacy in the growing world economy, control of colonies, and command of the sea. The two empires had been left unchanged in 1748 by the peace of Aix-la-Chapelle. Both held possessions in India, in the West Indies, and on the American mainland (see maps, pp. 187, 295). In India both British and French possessed only disconnected commercial establishments on the coast, infinitesimal specks on the giant body of India. Both also traded with China at Canton. Both occupied way stations on the route to Asia—the British in St. Helena and Ascension Island in the south Atlantic, the French in the more valuable islands of Mauritius and Reunion in the Indian Ocean. The French were active also on the coasts of Madagascar. The greatest way station, the Cape of Good Hope, belonged to the Dutch. In the West Indies the British plantations were mainly in Jamaica, Barbados, and some of the Leeward Islands; the French, in Santo Domingo, Guadeloupe, and Martinique. All were supported by the booming slave trade in Africa.

British and French colonial interests

On the American mainland the French had more territory and the British had more people. In the British colonies from Georgia to Nova Scotia lived perhaps two million Europeans, predominantly English but with strong infusions of Scots-Irish, Dutch, Germans, French, and Swedes. Philadelphia, with some 40,000 people, was as large as any city in England except London. The colonies in population bulked about a quarter as large as the mother country. But they were provincial, locally minded, and incapable of concerted action. In 1754 the British government called a congress at Albany in New York, hoping that the colonies would assume some collective responsibility for the coming war. The congress adopted an "Albany plan of union" drawn up by Benjamin Franklin, but the colonial legislatures declined to accept it, through fear of losing their separate identity. The colonials were willing, in a politically immature way, to rely on Britain for military action against France.

The French were still in possession of Louisburg on Cape Breton Island, a stronghold established by Louis XIV, located in the Gulf of St. Lawrence. It was designed for naval domination of the north Atlantic and to control access to the St. Lawrence River, the Great Lakes, and the vast region now called the Middle West. Through all this tract of country the French constantly came and went, but there were sizable French settlements only around New Orleans in the south and Quebec in the north. One source of French strength was that the French were more successful than the British in gaining the support of the Indians. This was probably because the French, being few in numbers, did not threaten to expropriate their lands and also because Catholics at this time were incomparably more active than Protestants in Christian missions among non-European peoples.

Mercantilist regulations

Both empires, French and British, were held together by mercantilist regulations framed mainly in the interest of the home countries. In some ways the British empire was more liberal than the French; it allowed local self-government and permitted immigration from all parts of Europe. In other ways the British system was stricter. British subjects, for example, were required by the Navigation Acts to use British ships and seamen—English, Scottish, or colonial—whereas the French were freer to use the transport services of other nations. British sugar planters had to ship raw sugar to the home country, there to be refined and sold to Europe, whereas French planters were free to refine their sugar in the islands. The mainland British colonials were forbidden to manufacture ironware and numerous other articles for sale; they were expected to buy such objects from England. Since the British sold little to the West Indies, where the slave population had no income with which to buy, the mainland colonies, though less valued as a source of wealth, were a far more important market for British goods. The colonials, though they had prospered under the restrictive system, were beginning to find much of it irksome at the time of the Seven Years' War, and indeed evaded it when they could.

Fighting was endemic even in the years of peace in Europe. Nova Scotia was a trouble spot. French in population, it had been annexed by Britain at the Peace of Utrecht. Its proximity to Louisburg made it a scene of perpetual agitation. The British government in 1755, foreseeing war with France, bodily removed about 7,000 of the mostly French-speaking inhabitants of Acadia, originally a French colony and part of Nova Scotia. Although they were dispersed throughout Britain's North American colonies, some of these displaced people eventually migrated to Louisiana and preserved a distinctive identity in the French Cajun culture that developed there. But the great disputed area was the Alleghenies. British colonials were beginning to feel their way westward through the mountains. French traders, soldiers, and empire builders were moving eastward toward the same mountains from points on the Mississippi and the Great Lakes. In 1749, at the request of Virginia and London capitalists, the British government chartered a land-exploitation company, the Ohio Company, to operate in territory claimed also by the French. The French built a fort at the point where the Ohio River is formed by the junction of two smaller rivers—Fort Duquesne, later called Pittsburgh. A force of colonials and British regular troops, under General Braddock, started through the wilderness to dislodge the French. It was defeated in July 1755, perhaps through its commander's unwillingness to take advice from the colonial officers, one of whom was George Washington.

A year later France and Britain declared war. The British were brilliantly led by William Pitt, subsequently the Earl of Chatham, a man of wide vision and superb confidence. "I know that I can save the country," he said, "and I know that no one else can." He concentrated British effort on the navy and colonies, while subsidizing Frederick of Prussia to fight in Europe, so that England, as he put it, might win an empire on the plains of Germany. Only the enormous financial credit of the British government made such a policy feasible. In 1758 British forces successfully took Fort Duquesne. Louisburg fell again in the same year. Gaining entry to the St. Lawrence, the British moved upstream to Quebec, and in 1759 a force under General Wolfe, stealthily scaling the heights, appeared by surprise on the Plains of Abraham outside the fortress, forcing the garrison to accept a battle, which the British won. With the fall of Quebec no further French resistance was possible on the American mainland. The British also, with superior naval power, occupied Guadeloupe and Martinique in the Caribbean and the French slave stations in Africa.

The Seven Years' War, 1756–1763: In India

Both British and French interests meanwhile profited from disturbed conditions in India. As large as Europe without Russia, India was a congested country of impoverished masses, speaking hundreds of languages and following many religions and subreligions, the two greatest being the Hindu and the Muslim. Waves of invasion through the northwest frontier since the Christian year A.D. 1001 had produced a Muslim empire, whose capital was at Delhi and which for a time held jurisdiction over most of the country. These Muslim emperors were known as Great Moguls. The greatest was Akbar, who ruled from 1556 to 1605, built roads, reformed the taxes, patronized the arts, and attempted to minimize religious differences among his peoples. The Muslim artistic culture flourished for a time after Akbar. One of his successors, Shah Jehan (1628–1658), built the beautiful Taj Mahal near Agra and at Delhi built the delicately carved alabaster palace of the Moguls, in which he placed the Peacock Throne made of solid gold and studded with gems.

But meanwhile there was restlessness among the Hindus. The Sikhs, who had originated in the fifteenth century as a reform movement in Hinduism, went to war with the Mogul emperor in the seventeenth century. They became one of the most ferociously warlike of Indian peoples. Hindu princes in central India meanwhile formed a "Mahratta confederacy" against the Muslim emperor at Delhi. Matters were made worse when Aurungzeb, the last significant Mogul emperor (1658–1707), adopted repressive measures against the Hindus. After Aurungzeb, India fell into political dissolution. Many of the modern princely states originated or became autonomous at this time. Hindu princes rebelled against the Mogul. Muslims, beginning as governors or commanders under the Mogul, set up as rulers in their own right. Thus originated Hyderabad, which included the fabulous diamond mines of Golconda and whose ruler long was called the wealthiest man in the world. Princes and would-be princes fought with each other and with the emperor. New Muslim invaders also poured across the northwest frontier. In 1739 a Persian force occupied Delhi, slaughtered 30,000 people, and departed with the Peacock Throne. Between 1747 and 1761 came a series of forays from Afghanistan, which again resulted in the looting of Delhi and the massacre of thousands.

Religious and political upheaval in India

The situation in India resembled, on a larger and more frightful scale, what had happened in Europe in the Holy Roman Empire, where irreconcilable religious differences (of Catholics and Protestants) had also torn the country asunder, ambitious princes and city-states had won a chaotic independence, and foreign armies appeared repeatedly as invaders. India, like central Europe, suffered chronically from war, intrigue, and rival pretensions to territory; and in India, as in the Holy Roman Empire, outsiders and ambitious insiders benefited together.

The instability and violence in the interior had repercussions on the Indian coasts. Here handfuls of Europeans were established in the coastal cities. By the troubles in the interior the Indian authorities along the coasts were reduced, so to speak, to a size and power with which the Europeans could deal. The Europeans—British and French—were agents of their respective East India companies. The companies built forts, maintained soldiers, coined money, and entered into treaties with surrounding Indian powers, under charter of their home governments and with no one to deny them the exercise of such sovereign rights. Agents of the companies, like Indians themselves, ignored or respected the Mogul emperor as suited their own purpose. They were, at first, only one of the many elements in the flux and reflux of Indian affairs. Their presence in India showed the international reach

The battle of Quebec, depicted here in an English illustration of the British army's surprise approach to the Plains of Abraham, allowed Britain to gain control over most of North America and to increase its power in the expanding, global system of eighteenth-century trade.
(Courtesy of the Director, National Army Museum, London)

of European companies, the worldwide competition between British and French interests, and the growing importance of India in the global economic system.

Intentions of the British and the French

Neither the British nor the French government, during the Seven Years' War, had any intention of territorial conquest in India, their policy in this respect differing radically from policy toward America. Nor were the two trading companies pushing their agents toward imperialistic political interventions. The company directors in London and Paris disapproved of fantastic schemes to intervene in Indian politics, insisted that their agents should attend to business only, and resented every penny and every sou not spent to bring in commercial profit. But it took a year or more to exchange messages between Europe and India, and company representatives in India, caught up in the Indian vortex and overcome by the chance to make personal fortunes or by dreams of empire, acted very much on their own, committing their home offices without compunction. Involvement in Indian affairs was not exactly new. We have seen how "Diamond" Pitt, in 1702, purchased the goodwill of the local ruler of the Carnatic when he threatened by military force to reduce the English traders at Madras to submission.

The first European to exploit the possibilities of the changing situation in mid-eighteenth-century India was the Frenchman Joseph-François Dupleix, who believed that the funds sent out by the company in Paris to finance the Indian trade were insufficient. His idea seems to have been not empire-building but to make the company into a local territorial power in order that, from taxes and other political revenues, it might have more capital for its commercial operations. In any case, during the years of peace in Europe after 1748, Dupleix found himself with about 2,000 French troops in the Carnatic. He lent them out to neighboring local rulers in return for territorial concessions. He also began to drill Indian soldiers by European methods, thereby creating the first regiments of "sepoys"—Indian troops who served in the military forces of the European companies. Following a program of backing claimants to various Indian thrones, he built up a clientele of local rulers under obligation to himself. He was very successful, for a few well-armed European troops or sepoys could overcome much larger, poorly armed Indian forces in pitched battle. But he was recalled to France in 1754, after the company became apprehensive of war with Britain and other trouble; and he died in disgrace.

When war came in 1756, British interests in India were advanced chiefly by Robert Clive. He had come to India many years before as a clerk for the East India Company but had shown military talents and an ability to comprehend Indian politics. He had maneuvered, with little success, against Dupleix in the Carnatic in the 1740s. In 1756, on hearing the news of war in Europe, he shifted his attention to Bengal, hoping to drive the French from their trading stations there. The French were favored in Bengal by the local Muslim ruler, Suraja Dowla, who proceeded to anticipate Clive's arrival by expelling the British from Calcutta. Capturing the city, he shut up 146 Englishmen in a small room without windows (soon known in England as the "Black Hole of Calcutta") and kept them there all night, during which most of them died of suffocation. Clive, soon appearing with a small force of British and sepoys, routed Suraja Dowla at the battle of Plassey in 1757. He put his own puppet on the Bengal throne and extorted huge reparations both for the company and for himself. Returning to England, he was received with mixed feelings; but he was given a new title (Baron Clive of Passy) and appointed the "governor" of Bengal. He strove in India to reduce the almost incredible corruption of company employees there, individuals normal enough but demoralized by irresistible chances for easy riches. Finally he committed suicide in 1774.

Robert Clive

It was British sea power, more fundamentally than Clive's tactics, that assured the triumph of British over French ambitions in the East. The British government still had no intention of conquest in India, but it could not see its East India Company forced out by agents of the French company in collaboration with Indian princes. Naval forces were therefore dispatched to the Indian Ocean, and they not only allowed Clive to shift from Madras to Calcutta at will but also gradually cut off the French posts in India from Europe and from each other. By the end of the war all the French establishments in India, as in Africa and America, were at the mercy of the British. The French overseas lay prostrate, and France itself was again detached from the overseas world on which much of its economy rested. In 1761 France made an alliance with Spain, which was alarmed for the safety of its own American empire after the British victories at Quebec and in the Caribbean. But the British also defeated Spain.

The Peace Settlement of 1763

The British armed forces had been spectacularly successful. Yet the peace treaty, signed at Paris in February 1763, five days before the Austro-Prussian peace of Hubertusburg, was by no means unfavorable to the defeated. The French Duke of Choiseul was a

Britain's imperial role in late eighteenth-century India is represented in this Indian miniature of a British officer's wife surrounded by Indian servants. The social hierarchies within the growing empire appear in this scene of domestic order and wealth, which dates from about 1785.
(Werner Forman Archive/Art Resource, NY)

French concessions

skillful and single-minded negotiator. The British, Pitt having fallen from office in 1761, were represented by a confused group of parliamentary favorites of the new king, George III. France ceded to Britain all French territory on the North American mainland east of the Mississippi. Canada thereby became British, and the colonials of the thirteen colonies were relieved of the French presence beyond the Alleghenies. To Spain, in return for aid in the last days of the war, France ceded all holdings west of the Mississippi and at its mouth. France thereby virtually abandoned the North American continent. But these almost empty regions were of minor commercial importance, and the French, in return for surrendering them, retained many economically more valuable establishments elsewhere. In the West Indies the British planters, and in England the powerful "West India interest," feared competition from the French sugar islands and wanted to exclude them from the protected economic system of

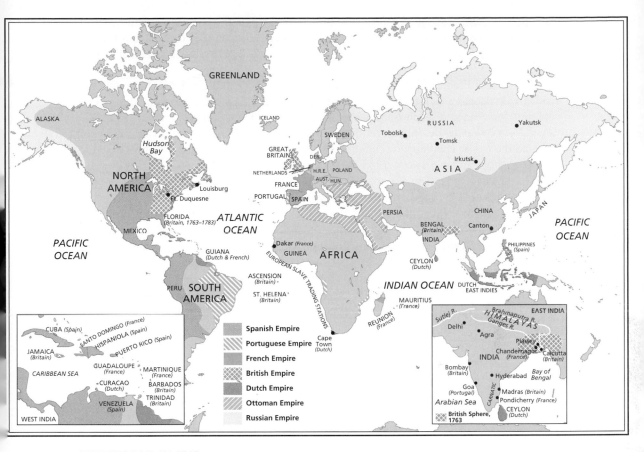

THE WORLD IN 1763

At the Peace of Paris of 1763 the British overseas empire trimphed over the French. The French ceded their holdings on the North American mainland east of the Mississippi to Britain, those west of the Mississippi to Spain. Britain also took Florida from Spain in 1763, but lost it, returning it to Spain in 1783, at the close of the War of American Independence. The French retained their sugar islands in the West Indies and their trading stations in India; they were stopped from empire-building but did not greatly suffer commercially from the Seven Years' War. The British proceeded to build their empire in India.

the British empire. France therefore received back Guadeloupe and Martinique, as well as most of its slave stations in Africa. In India, the French remained in possession of their commercial installations—offices, warehouses, and docks—at Pondicherry and other towns. They were forbidden to erect fortifications or pursue political ambitions among Indian princes—a practice which neither the French nor the British government had hitherto much favored in any case.

The treaties of Paris and Hubertusburg, closing the prolonged war of the mid-century, made the year 1763 a memorable turning point. Prussia was to remain a major power, which meant that the dualism of Germany would continue. Austria and Prussia eyed each other as rivals. Frederick's aggression of 1740 was legalized and even given a new moral status in Prussia by the heroic defense that had proved necessary to retain the plunder.

Frederick himself, from 1763 until his death in 1786, was a man of peace, philosophical and even benign. But the German crucible had boiled, and out of it had come a Prussia even more disposed by its escape from annihilation to glorify its army as the steel framework of its life.

The Anglo-French settlement was far-reaching and rather curious. Although the British won decisive victories everywhere in the global war, it resulted in no commercial calamity for France. French trade with America and the East grew as rapidly after the Seven Years' War as before it, and in 1785 was double what it had been in 1755. For England the war opened up new commercial channels. British trade with America and the East probably tripled between 1755 and 1785. But the outstanding British gains were imperial and strategic. The European balance of power was preserved, the French had been kept out of Belgium, British subjects in North America seemed secure, and Britain had again vindicated its command of the sea. British sea power implied, in turn, that British sea-borne commerce was safe in peace or war, while the seaborne commerce for the French, or of any others, depended ultimately on the political requirements of the British. But the French still had a few cards to play and were to play them in the American and French revolutions.

For America and India the peace of 1763 was decisive in pushing the peoples of these two vast territories toward closer connections with the political and commercial

Repercussions of the settlement

institutions of the British empire. America north of Mexico was to become part of an English-speaking world. In India the British government was drawn increasingly into a policy of territorial occupation; a British "paramount power" eventually emerged in place of the empire of the Moguls. British political rule in India stimulated and protected British business there, until in the greatest days of British prosperity India was one of the main pillars of the British economic system, and the road to India became in a real sense the lifeline of the British empire. But in 1763 this state of affairs was still in the future and was to be reached by many intermediate steps.

   For interactive exercises, glossary, chronologies, and more, go to the *Online Learning Center* at **www.mhhe.com/palmer10.**

Chapter **8**

THE AGE
OF ENLIGHTENMENT

The eighteenth century, or at least the years of that century preceding the French Revolution of 1789, is commonly known in European history as the Age of Enlightenment, and though that name raises some difficulties, still there is no other that describes so many features of the time so well. People strongly felt that theirs was an enlightened age, and it is from their own evaluation of themselves that our term Age of Enlightenment is derived. Everywhere there was a feeling that Europeans had at last emerged from a long twilight. The past was generally regarded as a time of barbarism and darkness. The sense of progress was all but universal among the educated classes. It was the belief both of the forward-looking thinkers and writers known as the philosophes and of the forward-looking monarchs, the "enlightened despots," together with their ministers and officials.

The leading ideas of the Enlightenment—optimistic beliefs in the historical advance of reason, science, education, social reform, tolerance, and enlightened government—have been constant themes in the modern world. The Enlightenment, in short, remains a dynamic tradition in cultural and political life. Intellectual debates since the eighteenth century have almost always returned, explicitly or implicitly, to questions about the validity and legacy of Enlightenment conceptions of truth, knowledge, and progress. The Enlightenment has often been challenged or condemned by influential cultural movements (for example, romanticism, postmodernism, religious revivals) and by modern political ideologies (for example, fascism, ethnic nationalisms). Yet the vehemence of its modern critics confirms the Enlightenment's exceptional, enduring importance in the cultures and politics of modern societies.

Eighteenth-century critiques of existing regimes and cultural traditions drew increasingly on the ideas of the Enlightenment; indeed, such ideas were contributing by

Chapter emblem: Detail from a portrait of Jean-Jacques Rousseau by Allan Ramsay (1713–1784).
(Giraudon/Art Resource, NY)

the end of the century to explosive political revolutions in America and Europe. In later centuries, Enlightenment ideas continued to generate opposition to unpopular governments or dominant cultural ideologies or hierarchical social systems, but the Enlightenment was also condemned in many cultures. For its advocates and critics alike, however, the "Age of Enlightenment" has always represented a decisive historical moment or force in the development of "modernity."

35.   THE PHILOSOPHES—AND OTHERS

The Spirit of Progress and Improvement

The spirit of the eighteenth-century Enlightenment was drawn from the scientific and intellectual revolution of the seventeenth century. The Enlightenment carried over and popularized the ideas of Bacon and Descartes, of Bayle and Spinoza, and, above all, of Locke and Newton. It carried over the philosophy of natural law and of natural right. There had never been an age in which Europeans were so skeptical toward tradition, so confident in the powers of human reason and of science, so firmly convinced of the regularity and harmony of nature, and so deeply imbued with the sense of civilization's advance and progress.

Faith in progress

The idea of progress has often been described as the dominant or characteristic idea of European civilization in the modern era, or since the late seventeenth century. It is a belief, a kind of nonreligious faith, that the conditions of human life become better as time goes on, that in general each generation is better off than its predecessors and will contribute by its labor to an even better life for generations to come, and that in the long run all humankind will share in the same advance. All the elements of this belief had been present by 1700. It was after 1700, however, that the idea of progress became explicit. In the seventeenth century it had shown itself in a more rudimentary way in the sporadic intellectual dispute in England and France known as the quarrel of Ancients and Moderns (which, as noted earlier, also became part of the challenge to official theorists in Louis XIV's academies). The Ancients held that the works of the Greeks and Romans had never been surpassed. The Moderns, pointing to science, art, literature, and invention, declared that their own time was the best, that it was natural for people of their time to do better than the ancients because they came later and built upon their predecessors' achievements. The quarrel was never exactly settled, but a great many people in 1700 were Moderns.

Far-reaching also was the faith of the age in the natural faculties of the human mind. Extreme skepticism, but not a skeptical outlook, was rejected. Nor were the educated, after 1700, likely to be superstitious, terrified by the unknown, or addicted to magic. The witchcraft mania abruptly died. Indeed all sense of the supernatural became dim for many Europeans. "Modern" people not only ceased to fear the devil but also to fear God. They thought of God less as a Father than as a First Cause of the physical universe. There was less sense of a personal God, or of the inscrutable imminence of divine Providence, or of the human need for saving grace. God was less the God of Love than the inconceivably intelligent Being who had made the amazing universe now discovered by human reason. The great symbol of the Christian God was the Cross, on which a divine being had suffered in human form. The symbol which occurred to people of scientific view was the Watchmaker. The intricacies of the physical universe were compared to the intricacies of a watch, and it was argued that just as a watch could not exist without a watchmaker, so the universe as discovered by Newton could not exist without a God who created it and set it moving by its mathematical laws. It was almighty intelligence that was thought divine.

Of course not everyone was primarily moved by such ideas. The first half of the eighteenth century was in fact also a time of continuing religious fervor. Isaac Watts wrote many hymns that are still familiar in English-speaking churches; the great church music of J. S. Bach was composed

Religious fervor and Pietism

mainly in the 1720s; Handel's oratorio, *The Messiah,* was first performed in 1741; and it was at about this time that congregations first sang the *Adeste fideles* ("O Come, All Ye Faithful"), originally Catholic in inspiration but soon adopted by Protestants also. The Lutherans of Germany were stirred by the movement known as Pietism, which stressed the inner spiritual experience of ordinary persons as distinct from the doctrines taught and debated in theological faculties. The quest for an "inner light," or illumination of the soul rather than of the reason, was somewhat contrary to the main thrust of the Age of Enlightenment, and a religious urge for improvement of the individual rather than of social institutions was hardly central to the ideas of the age, but such ideas were by no means merely conservative, for they were in general highly critical of the existing order.

Within the Church of England John Wesley, while a student at Oxford, joined a group of like-minded young men for prayer and meditation. They engaged in good works to relieve the sufferings of prisoners and the poor, to whom they distributed food and clothing, while also teaching them how

John Wesley and Methodism

to read. Going outside the restrictive system of parishes, Wesley and others took to "itinerant" preaching, often to immense crowds in open fields. Wesley is said to have traveled 250,000 miles within Great Britain over a period of 50 years. He and George Whitfield, who shared his views, preached also in the English American colonies, where they helped to arouse the Great Awakening of the 1740s. Such movements had a democratizing effect in stressing individual worth and spiritual consciousness independently of the established religious authorities. Indeed, the spokesmen for older churches dismissed such movements as "enthusiasm," which was then a word of reproach. By the time he died in 1791, Wesley had about half a million followers in what were called Methodist societies. Wesley himself tried to keep them within the Church of England, but separate Methodist churches were already founded in England and the United States.

In a way these expressions of religious feeling reflected differences between the popular and elite cultures that have already been described. While some of the elite joined in the new movements, it was on the whole the least comfortable classes who did so. The official churches, Anglican, Lutheran, Catholic, did not wish to be disturbed by religious revivalism. Bishops were cultivated gentlemen of the age. But the most vehement intellectual leaders pushed all churches aside.

The science and new learning in this "age of reason" did not end the popular interest in magic or mystification. A Swiss pastor, J. C. Lavater, attracted attention with his supposed science of "physiognomy," by which a person's character could be read in the play of the facial features. An Austrian physician, F. A. Mesmer, created a stir in Paris by arranging séances where people were touched by a wand, or sat in tubs, to receive "animal magnetism" in the hope of curing various ills. His "mesmerism" was an early stage in the discovery of hypnosis, but it is significant that a committee of the Royal Academy of Sciences, after investigation, concluded that Mesmer's own theories to explain these strange phenomena were without foundation.

Freemasonry

More in the mainstream was Freemasonry, which took form in England and soon spread to the Continent. The Masons were generally persons who held typical Enlightenment views, well disposed toward reason, progress, toleration, and humane reforms, and respectful toward God as architect of the universe; but they met secretly in lodges, in an atmosphere of mysterious rituals and occult knowledge. People of all walks of life, nobles, clergy, and middle classes, belonged to the lodges (a few also allowed women to join). Freemasonry thus had the effect of bringing persons of different social classes together, somewhat harmlessly for self-improvement and the improvement of others. It aroused suspicion, however, because of its secrecy; and a small deviant offshoot, the Illuminati of south Germany, was considered so dangerous that the Bavarian government suppressed it in 1786. There were later some who insisted that the French Revolution had been caused by a conspiracy of Illuminati, philosophes, and other clandestine plotters, but this idea was never any more than the belief of a few frightened conservative critics. The word *Illuminati* meant "the enlightened ones," but the notion of secrecy was foreign to the Enlightenment, which relied above all else on publicity and the reading public.

The Philosophes

Philosophe is simply French for philosopher, but to be "philosophical" in the eighteenth century meant to approach any subject in a critical and inquiring spirit. The French word is used in English to denote a group of writers who were not philosophers in the sense of treating ultimate questions of knowledge or existence. They were social or literary critics, popularizers, and publicists. Most philosophes were men, but many women also participated in Enlightenment culture. The French writer Emilie du Châtelet, for example, translated Newton and explained the significance of the new theories in her scientific essays. Though often learned, the philosophes wrote to gain attention, and it was through the philosophes that the ideas of the Enlightenment spread. Formerly authors had generally been persons of leisure, or talented protégés of aristocratic or royal patrons, or professors or clerics supported by the income from religious foundations. In the Age of Enlightenment a great many were freelancers, grub-streeters, or journalists. They wrote for "the publick."

The reading public

The reading public had greatly expanded; by the 1780s in France, literacy rates had risen to 47 percent among men and 27 percent among women. The educated middle class, commercial and professional, was much larger than ever before. Women readers formed a growing audience for novels and literary journals, country gentlemen sought new scientific advice on agriculture, and even noblemen wished to keep informed. Newspapers and magazines multiplied, and people who could not read them at home could read them in coffeehouses or in reading rooms organized for that purpose. There was a great demand also for dictionaries, encyclopedias, and surveys of all fields of knowledge. The new readers wanted matters made interesting and clear. They appreciated wit and lightness of touch. From such a public, literature itself greatly benefited.

The style of the eighteenth century became admirably fluent, clear, and exact, neither ponderous on the one hand nor frothy on the other. And from writings of this kind the readers benefited also, from the interior of Europe to the America of Benjamin Franklin. People began to talk of "public opinion" as a kind of critical tribunal that judged the significance of new books and established or destroyed the reputations of ambitious authors. This new public opinion, the French writer Malesherbes explained, was an independent social force "that all powers respect, that appreciates all talents, that pronounces on all people of merit." Critical reviews of literature, art, and music provoked debates in newspapers, journals, and coffeehouses, all of which contributed to an expanding public sphere beyond the personal world of private households and outside the official world of government institutions. The bourgeois middle class was becoming not only educated but also thoughtful and critical. But the movement was not a class movement only.

There was another way in which writings of the day were affected by social conditions. They were all written under censorship. The theory of censorship was to protect people from harmful ideas as they were protected from shoddy merchandise or dishonest weights and measures. In England the censorship was so mild as to have little effect. Other countries, such as Spain, had a powerful censorship. France, the center of the Enlightenment, had both a complicated censorship and a large reading and writing public. The church, the Parlement of Paris, the royal officials, and the printers' guilds all had a hand in the censoring of books. French censorship, however, was loosely administered, and after 1750 writers were little disturbed by it. It cannot be compared to censorship in some countries in the twentieth century. Yet in one way it had an unfavorable effect on French thought and letters. It discouraged writers from openly or explicitly addressing concrete public questions. Legally forbidden to criticize church or state, they threw their criticisms on an abstract level. Barred from attacking matters in particular, they tended to attack matters in general. Or they talked of the customs of the Persians and the Iroquois but not the French. Their works became full of double meanings, sly digs, innuendoes, and jokes by which authors, if questioned, could declare that they did not mean what all the world knew they did mean. As for readers, they developed a taste for forbidden books, which were always easy enough to obtain through illicit channels and foreign booksellers.

Censorship

Paris was the heart of the movement. Here, in the town houses of the well-to-do, literary and social celebrities gathered for literate conversation. It might occasionally happen that a notable philosophe was also wealthy; such was the case of Helvétius, who not only wrote books *On the Mind* and *On Man* but also gave grand entertainments at which such matters were discussed. Mainly, however, this mingling of people and ideas went on in salons conducted by women who became famous as hostesses, or salonnières, and who played a crucial mediating role in what came to be called the "Republic of Letters." Madame de Geoffrin, for example, for a period of 25 years beginning about 1750, organized conversations of artists and writers at dinner, sometimes helped them financially, and introduced them to persons of influence in high society or in government. She welcomed visiting foreigners also, such as Horace Walpole and David Hume from England and young Stanislas Poniatowski before he became king of Poland. Since other women held similar salons, philosophes and other writers had frequent opportunity to meet and exchange ideas.

Paris: the heart of the Enlightenment

Salons became well-organized meeting places at which authors introduced new works to critical readers, salonnières read letters from travelers or distant correspondents, and lively conversation spread the reputations of aspiring philosophes. The leading salonnières gave careful attention to the intellectual themes and social continuities of their salons. Suzanne Necker, whose salon met on Friday afternoons during the 1770s and 1780s, prepared for her weekly conversations by listing in her journal the ideas and books that she wanted to discuss. Julie de Lespinasse provided opportunities for almost constant discussion at her Parisian home, where she received visitors every evening of the week for 12 years. "Her great art," wrote one admirer, "was to show to advantage the minds of others, and she enjoyed doing that more than revealing her own." Salons and salonnières promoted the ideals of a cosmopolitan Republic of Letters in which talent and creativity counted for more than noble lineage; and though women lost much of their cultural influence after the 1780s, some salons of this kind survived the Revolution. In 1795, after the Terror, the widows of two eminent philosophes, Helvétius and Condorcet, opened or reopened their salons in Paris for people of moderate republican or liberal sentiments. Sophie Condorcet became a writer herself and a translator of Adam Smith. Her salon remained a center of liberal opposition during the years of Napoleon. More short-lived was the salon of the even more famous Germaine de Staël, who also wrote widely read books and who, among her many other ideas, deplored the subordination of women that the Revolution had done little to change. In these post-Revolutionary salons much of the French liberalism of the nineteenth century was born.

Diderot's Encyclopédie

In Paris also, in the mid–eighteenth century, the most serious of all philosophe enterprises, the *Encyclopédie,* was published in 17 large volumes and completed over the years 1751 to 1772. Edited by Denis Diderot, it was a great compendium of scientific, technical, and historical knowledge, carrying a strong undertone of criticism of existing society and institutions and epitomizing the skeptical, rational, and scientific spirit of the age. It was not the first encyclopedia, but it was the first to have a distinguished list of contributors or to be conceived as a positive force for social progress. Virtually all the French philosophes contributed—Voltaire, Montesquieu, Rousseau, d'Alembert (who assisted in the editing), Buffon, Turgot, Quesnay, and many others, all sometimes collectively called the Encyclopedists. Although edited in Paris, the *Encyclopédie* became very widely known and read. About 25,000 multivolumed sets were sold before the Revolution, about half of them outside France, since French had become an international language understood by educated persons all over Europe. Within France itself the *Encyclopédie* was read in all parts of the country and in the most influential ranks of society. At Besançon, for example, a city of about 28,000 inhabitants, 137 sets were sold to local residents, of whom 15 were members of the clergy, 53 were of the nobility, and 69 were lawyers, doctors, merchants, government officials, or others of what was called the Third Estate. The privileged groups of whom the Encyclopedists were the most critical, that is, the clergy and the nobility, read it or at least purchased it far out of proportion to their numbers in the population as a whole.

Men and women who considered themselves philosophes, or close to the philosophes in spirit, were found all over Europe. Frederick the Great was an eminent philosophe; not only was he the friend of Voltaire and host to a circle of literary and scientific men at Potsdam, but he also wrote epigrams, satires, dissertations, and histories, as well as works on military science; and he had a gift of wit, a sharp tongue, and a certain impishness toward the traditional and the pompous. Catherine the Great, empress of Russia, was also a philosophe for much the same reason. Maria Theresa, of Austria, was not a philosophe; she was too religious and too little concerned with general ideas. Her son Joseph, on the other hand, as we shall see, proved to be virtually a philosophe enthroned. In England Bishop Warburton was considered by some of his friends as a philosophe; he held that the Church of England of his day, as a social institution, was exactly what pure reason would have invented. The Scottish skeptical philosopher David Hume counted as a philosophe, as did Edward Gibbon, who shocked the pious by his attacks on Christianity in his famous *Decline and Fall of the Roman Empire*. Dr. Samuel Johnson was not a philosophe, though he was best known for a typical eighteenth-century project—the compilation of a new dictionary of the English language. Johnson worried over the supernatural, adhered to the

The salon of Madame de Geoffrin, depicted here by the artist Lemonnier, became one of the best-known meeting places for writers and artists in mid-eighteenth-century Paris. This imagined scene of an author reading from his work was painted early in the following century, but it shows the cultural reputation of famous salons and salonnières.
(Réunion des Musées Nationaux/Art Resource, NY)

established church, deflated pretentious authors, and even declared that Voltaire and Rousseau were evil men who should be sent "to the plantations." There were also Italian and German philosophes, like the Marquis di Beccaria, who sought to humanize the criminal law, or Baron Grimm, who sent a literary newsletter from Paris to his many subscribers.

Montesquieu, Voltaire, and Rousseau

Most famous of all philosophes were the French trio, Montesquieu (1689–1755), Voltaire (1694–1778), and Rousseau (1712–1778). They differed vehemently with each other. All were hailed as literary geniuses in their own day. All turned from pure literature to works of political commentary and social analysis. All thought that the existing state of society could be improved.

Montesquieu, twice a baron, was a landed aristocrat, a seigneur or manorial lord of southern France. He inherited from his uncle a seat in the Parlement of Bordeaux and sat actively in that parlement after the death of Louis XIV. He was part of the noble resurgence that began about 1715 and continued on through the eighteenth century. Although he shared many of the ideas in the stream of aristocratic and antiabsolutist thought, he went beyond a mere self-centered class philosophy. In his great work, *The Spirit of*

This portrait of Voltaire (c. 1736) by Maurice-Quentin de La Tour suggests the playful, ironic style that made his works accessible and popular, even when he was attacking religious persecutions or the suppression of controversial ideas. (Réunion des Musées Nationaux/Art Resource, NY)

Montesquieu's The Spirit of Laws

Laws, published in 1748, he developed two principal ideas. One was that forms of government varied according to climate and circumstances, for example, that despotism was suited only to large empires in hot climates, and that democracy would work only in small city-states. His other great doctrine, aimed against royal absolutism in France (which he called "despotism"), was the separation and balance of powers. In France he believed that power should be divided between the king and a great many "intermediate bodies"—parlements, provincial estates, organized nobility, chartered towns, and even the church. His position as a judge in parlement, a provincial, and a nobleman gave him good reasons to favor the first three, and his work in Bordeaux helped him to recognize the importance of the bourgeoisie in French towns; as for the church, he observed that, while he took no stock in its teachings, he thought it useful as a barrier to undue centralization of government. He greatly admired the English constitution as he understood it, believing that England carried over, more successfully than any other country, the feudal liberties of the early Middle Ages. He thought that in England the necessary separation and balance of powers was obtained by an ingenious mixture of monarchy, aristocracy, and democracy (king, lords, and commons) and by a separation of the functions of the executive, legislature, and judiciary. This doctrine had a wide influence and was well known to the Americans who in 1787 wrote the Constitution of the United States. Montesquieu's own philosophe friends thought him too conservative and even tried to dissuade him from publishing his ideas. He was, indeed, technically a reactionary, favoring a scheme of things that antedated Louis XIV, and he was unusual among contemporaries in his admiration of the "barbarous" Middle Ages.

Voltaire

Voltaire was born in 1694 into a comfortable bourgeois family and christened François-Marie Arouet; "Voltaire," an invented name, is simply the most famous of all pen names. Until he was over 40 he was known only as a clever writer of epigrams, tragedies in verse, and an epic. Thereafter he turned increasingly to philosophical and public questions. His strength throughout lay in the facility of his pen. He is the easiest of all great writers to read. He was always trenchant, logical, and incisive, sometimes scurrilous; mocking and sarcastic when he wished, equally a master of deft irony and of withering ridicule. However serious in his purpose, he achieved it by getting his readers to laugh.

In his youth Voltaire spent 11 months in the Bastille for what was considered to be impertinence to the Regent, who, however, in the next year rewarded him with a pension for one of his dramas. He was again arrested after a fracas with a nobleman, the Chevalier de Rohan. He remained an incorrigible bourgeois, while never deeply objecting to the aristocracy on principle. Through his admirer Mme. de Pompadour (another bourgeois, though the king's favorite) he became a gentleman of the bedchamber and royal historian to Louis XV. These functions he fulfilled *in absentia,* when at all, for Paris and Versailles were too unsafe for him. He was the personal friend of Frederick the Great, in whose household he lived for about two years at Potsdam. The two finally quarreled, for no stage was big enough to hold two such prima donnas for long. Voltaire made a fortune from his writings, pensions, speculations, and practical business sense. In his later years he purchased a manor at Ferney near the Swiss frontier. Here he became, as he said, the "hotel keeper of Europe," receiving the streams of distinguished admirers, favor hunters, and distressed persons who came to seek him out. He died at Paris in 1778, at the age of 84, by far the most famous man of letters in Europe. His collected writings fill over 70 volumes.

Voltaire was mainly interested in the freedom of thought. Like Montesquieu, he was an admirer of England. He spent three years in that country, where, in 1727, he witnessed the state funeral accorded to Sir Isaac Newton and his burial in Westminster Abbey. Voltaire's *Philosophical Letters on the English* (1733) and *Elements of the Philosophy of Newton* (1738) not only brought England increasingly before the consciousness of the rest of Europe but also popularized the new scientific ideas—the inductive philosophy of Bacon, the physics of Newton, and the psychology of Locke, whose doctrine that all true ideas arose from sense experience undercut the authority of religious belief. What Voltaire mainly admired in England was its religious liberty, its tolerance for diverse ideas and scientific inquiry, its relative freedom of the press, and its respect for men of letters like himself. Political liberty concerned him much less than it did Montesquieu. Louis XIV, a villain for Montesquieu and the neoaristocratic school, was a hero for Voltaire, who wrote a laudatory *Age of Louis XIV* (1751) praising the Sun King for the splendor of art and literature in his reign. Voltaire likewise continued to esteem Frederick the Great, though he quarreled with him personally. Frederick was in fact almost his ideal of the enlightened ruler, a man who sponsored the arts and sciences, recognized no religious authority, and granted toleration to all creeds, welcoming Protestants and Catholics on equal terms if only they would be socially useful.

After about 1740 Voltaire became more definitely the crusader, preaching the cause of religious toleration. He fought to clear the memory of Jean Calas, a Protestant put to death on the charge of murdering a son to prevent his conversion to Rome. He wrote also to exonerate a youth named La Barre, who had been executed for defiling a wayside cross. *Écrasez l'infâme!* became the famous Voltairean war cry—"crush the infamous thing!" The *infâme* for him was bigotry, intolerance, and superstition and behind these the power of an organized clergy. He assaulted not only the Catholic church but the whole traditional Christian view of the world as well. He argued for "natural religion" and "natural morality," holding that belief in God and the difference between good and evil arose from reason itself. This doctrine had in fact long been taught by the Catholic church. But Voltaire insisted that no supernatural revelation in addition to reason was desirable or necessary; belief in a special supernatural revelation, he argued, made people intolerant, stupid, and cruel.

Voltaire was also the first to present a purely secular conception of world history. In his *Essai sur les moeurs,* or "Universal History," he began with ancient China and surveyed the great civilizations in turn. Earlier writers of world history had put human events within a Christian framework. Following the Bible, they began with the Creation, proceeded to the Fall, recounted the rise of Israel, and so on. Voltaire put Judeo-Christian history within a much broader world history and placed religious thought in a sociological framework. He represented Christianity and all other organized religions as social phenomena or mere human inventions. Spinoza had said as much; Voltaire spread these ideas through Europe.

Voltaire on politics

In matters of politics and self-government Voltaire was neither a liberal nor a democrat. His opinion of the human race was about as low as his friend Frederick's. If only a government was enlightened, he did not care how powerful it was. By an enlightened government he meant one that fought against sloth and stupidity, kept the clergy in a subordinate place, allowed freedom of thought and religion, and advanced the cause of material and technical progress. He had no developed political theory, but his ideal for large civilized countries approached that of enlightened or rational despotism. Believing that only a few could be enlightened, he thought that these few, a king and his advisers, should have the power to carry out their program against all opposition. To overcome ignorance, credulity, and priestcraft it was necessary for the state to be strong. What Voltaire most desired was liberty for the enlightened, or for people like himself.

Jean-Jacques Rousseau

Jean-Jacques Rousseau was very different. Born in Geneva in 1712, he was a Swiss, a Protestant, and almost of lower-class origin. He never felt at ease in France or in Paris society. Neglected as a child, a runaway at 16, he lived for years by odd jobs, such as copying music, and not until the age of 40 did he have any success as a writer. He was always the little man, the outsider. In addition, his personal relations with women were difficult and unstable; he finally settled down with an uneducated woman named Thérèse Levasseur and with her mother, who kept interfering in his affairs. By Thérèse he had five children, whom he deposited at an orphanage. He had no social status, no money; and no sense of money; and after he became famous he lived largely by the generosity of his friends. He was pathetically and painfully maladjusted. He came to feel that he could trust no one, that those who tried to befriend him were deriding or betraying him behind his back. He condemned the cultural influence of French women, criticizing especially their prominent role in Parisian salons ("they do not know anything, although they judge everything"). He suffered from what would now be termed psychological complexes; possibly he was paranoid. He talked endlessly of his own virtue and innocence and complained bitterly that he was misunderstood.

But unbalanced though he was, he was possibly the most profound writer of the age and was certainly the most permanently influential. Rousseau felt, from his own experience, that in society as it existed a good person could not be happy. He therefore attacked society, declaring that it was artificial and corrupt. He even attacked reason, calling it a false guide when followed alone. He felt doubts on all the progress which gave satisfaction to his contemporaries. In two "discourses," one on the *Arts and Sciences* (1750), the other on the *Origin of Inequality Among Men* (1753), he argued that civilization was the source of much evil and that life in a "state of nature," were it only possible, would be much better. As Voltaire said, when Rousseau sent him a copy of his second discourse (Voltaire who relished civilization in every form), it made him "feel like going on all fours." To Rousseau

Rousseau's "discourses"

the best traits of human character, such as kindness, unselfishness, honesty, and true understanding, were products of nature. Deep below reason, he sensed the presence of feeling. He delighted in the warmth of sympathy, the quick flash of intuition, the clear message of conscience. He was religious by temperament, for though he believed in no church, no clergy, and no revelation, he had a respect for the Bible, a reverent awe toward the cosmos, a love of solitary meditation, and a belief in a God who was not merely a "first cause" but also a God of love and beauty. Rousseau thus made it easier for serious-minded people to slip away from orthodoxy and all forms of churchly discipline. He was feared by the churches as the most dangerous of all "infidels" and was condemned both in Catholic France and at Protestant Geneva.

In general, in most of his books, Rousseau, unlike so many of his contemporaries, gave the impression that impulse is more reliable than considered judgment, spontaneous feeling more to be trusted than critical thought. Mystical insights were for him more truthful than rational or clear ideas. He became the "man of feeling," the "child of nature," the forerunner of the coming age of romanticism, and an important source of all modern emphasis on the nonrational and the subconscious. He thus became an early, influential critic of the Enlightenment, even as he resembled other philosophes in his desire to change the existing social order.

In the *Social Contract* (1762) Rousseau seemed to contradict much of his famous sentiment for nature. In this book he held, somewhat like Hobbes, that the "state of nature" was a brutish condition without law or

The Social Contract

morality. In other works he had held that human evil was due to the evils of society. He now held that good people could be produced only by an improved society. Earlier thinkers, such as John Locke, for example, had thought of the "contract" as an agreement between a ruler and a people. Rousseau thought of it as an agreement among the people themselves. It was a social, not merely a political, contract. Organized civil society, that is, the community, rested upon it. The social contract was an understanding by which all individuals surrendered their natural liberty to each other, fused their individual wills into a combined General Will, and agreed to accept the rulings of this General Will as final. This General Will was the sovereign; and true sovereign power, rightly understood, was "absolute," "sacred," and "inviolable." Government was secondary; kings, officials, or elected representatives were only delegates of a sovereign people. Rousseau devoted many difficult and abstruse pages to explaining how the *real* General Will could be known. It was not necessarily determined by vote of a majority. "What generalizes the will," he said, "is not the number of voices but the common interest that unites them." He said little of the mechanism of government and had no admiration for parliamentary institutions. He was concerned with something deeper. Maladjusted outsider that he was, he craved a commonwealth in which every person could feel that he or she belonged. He wished a state in which all persons had a sense of membership and participation.

By these ideas Rousseau made himself the prophet of both democracy and nationalism. Indeed, in his *Considerations on Poland,* written at the request of Poles who were fighting against the partitions of their nation's territories by foreign powers, Rousseau applied the ideas of the *Social Contract* in more concrete form and became the first systematic theorist of a conscious and calculated nationalism. In writing the *Social Contract* he had in mind a small city-state like his native Geneva. But what he did, in effect, was to generalize and make applicable to large territories the psychology of small city republics—the sense of membership, of community and fellowship, of responsible citizenship and intimate participation in public affairs—in short, of common will. All modern states, democratic or undemocratic, strive to impart this sense of moral solidarity to their peoples. Whereas in democratic states the General Will can in some way be identified with the sovereignty of the people, in dictatorships it becomes possible for individuals (or parties) to arrogate to themselves the right to serve as spokesmen and interpreters of the General Will. Both totalitarians and democrats have regarded Rousseau as one of their prophets.

Rousseau's influence on his contemporaries was spread also by his other writings and especially his novels, *Émile* (1762) and the *Nouvelle Héloïse* (1760). The novels were widely read in all literate classes of society, especially by women, who made a kind of cult of Jean-Jacques. He was a literary master, able to evoke shades of thought and feeling that few writers had touched before, and by his literary writings he spread in the highest circles a new respect for the common person, a love of common things, an impulse of human pity and compassion, a sense of artifice and superficiality in aristocratic life. Women took to nursing their own babies, as Rousseau said they should. Men began describing the delicacy of their sentiments. Tears became the fashion. The queen, Marie Antoinette, built herself a village in the gardens at Versailles, where she pretended to be a simple milkmaid. In all this there was much that was ridiculous or shallow. Yet it was the wellspring of modern humanitarianism, the force leading to a new sense of human equality. Rousseau estranged the French upper classes from their own mode of life. He made many of them lose faith in their own superiority. That was his main direct contribution to the French Revolution.

Political Economists

Physiocrats

In France, somewhat apart from the philosophes, were the Physiocrats, whom their critics called "economists," a word originally thought to be mildly insulting. Many of the Physiocrats, unlike the philosophes, were close to the government as administrators or advisers. Quesnay was physician to Louis XV, Turgot was an experienced official who became minister to Louis XVI, and Dupont de Nemours, an associate of Turgot's, became the founder of the industrial family of the Du Ponts in the United States. Such men concerned themselves with fiscal and tax reform and with measures to increase the national wealth of France. They opposed guild regulations and price controls as impediments to the production and circulation of goods, and so were the first to use the term laissez-faire ("let them do as they see fit") as a principle of economic activity. They favored strong government, however, relying on it to overcome traditional obstacles and to provide inducements for the establishment of new industries.

Economics, or what was long called political economy, arose from these activities of the Physiocrats, from the somewhat similar work of "cameralists" in the German states, and from the collection and analysis of quantitative data, that is, the birth of statistics. Economic thinking flourished especially in Great Britain, and notably in Scotland, where Adam Smith's *Wealth of Nations* appeared in 1776. By 1800 the *Wealth of Nations* had been translated into every west-European language except Portuguese.

Adam Smith

Adam Smith's purpose, like that of the French Physiocrats, was to increase the national wealth by the reduction of barriers that hindered its growth. He undercut the premises of what we have called "the struggle for wealth and empire" in Chapter 7, since he argued that to build up a nation's wealth it was unnecessary to have an empire. He attacked most of the program of mercantilism that had obtained since the sixteenth century, and he expected that Britain's American colonies would soon become independent without loss to British trade. Where others

JEAN-JACQUES ROUSSEAU by Allan Ramsay (Scottish, 1713–1784)

Some hints of the complexities of Rousseau's personality and thought appear in this portrait by a Scottish artist who admired the famous writers of the French Enlightenment.
(Giraudon/Art Resource, NY)

looked to planning by an enlightened government, Adam Smith preferred to limit the functions of government to defense, internal security, and the provision of reasonable laws and fair law courts by which private differences could be adjudicated. For innovation and enterprise he counted more on private persons than on the state. He became the philosopher of the free market, the prophet of free trade. If there was a shortage of a given commodity, its price would rise and so stimulate producers to produce more, while also attracting new persons into that line of production. If there was an excess, if more was produced than purchasers would buy, both capital and labor would withdraw and gradually move into another area where demand was stronger. Demand would increase with lower prices, which depended on lower costs, which in turn depended on the specialization of labor. His most famous example was that of the pin factory of his time, where each of a dozen workers engaged in only one part of the process of manufacture, so that together they produced far more pins than if each worker produced whole pins; the price of pins then fell, and more pins could be used by more people. The same principle held in international trade; some countries or climates could produce an article more cheaply than others, so that if each specialized and then exchanged with the others, all would have more. Each nation could use its comparative advantage in certain spheres of production or trade to compensate for economic weaknesses in other spheres and also to increase its national wealth.

The motivation for all such production and exchange was to be the self-interest of the participants. As he said, we rely for our meat not on the goodwill of the butcher but on his concern for his own income. To those who might object that this was a system of selfishness Adam Smith would reply (being a professor of moral philosophy at the University of

Glasgow) that it was at least realistic, describing how people really behaved, and that it was morally justified since it ultimately produced a maximum both of freedom and of abundance. The mutual interaction of the enlightened self-interest of millions of persons would in the end, as if by an "invisible hand," he said, result in the highest welfare of all. Among problems that Smith minimized, or accepted as lesser evils, were the insecurity of individuals and the dangers of excessive dependence of a whole country on imports of essentials, such as food; and if the visible hand of government continued to regulate the price of bread, it should not be for economic reasons, but to prevent rioting and maintain social peace.

Main Currents of Enlightenment Thought

It is clear that the currents of thought in France and Europe were divergent and inconsistent. There was a general belief in progress, reason, science, and civilization. Rousseau had his doubts and praised the imagined conditions in a precivilized state of nature. Montesquieu thought the church useful but did not believe in religion; Rousseau believed in religion but saw no need for any church. Montesquieu was concerned about practical political liberty; Voltaire would surrender political liberty in return for guarantees of intellectual freedom; Rousseau wanted emancipation from the restraints of society and sought the freedom that consists in merging with nature and with one's fellows. Most philosophes were closest to Voltaire. They favored more tolerance for intellectual differences and more equality in European societies. It was not a very far-reaching equality, but it meant equality of rights for persons of different religions, a reduction of privileges enjoyed by nobles but not by commoners, greater equality of status in law courts and in the payment of taxes, and more opportunity for middle-class persons to rise to positions of social or political importance.

France was the main center of the Enlightenment. French philosophes traveled all over Europe. Frederick II and Catherine II invited French thinkers to their courts. French was the language of the academies of St. Petersburg and Berlin. Frederick wrote his philosophical works in the French language. The upper classes of Europe shared a uniform cosmopolitan culture, and this culture was predominantly French. But Britain was important also. Hitherto somewhat on the fringes of the European consciousness, Britain now moved closer to the center. Montesquieu and Voltaire may be said to have "discovered" Britain for Europe. Through them the ideas of Bacon, Newton, and Locke, and the whole theory of British liberty and parliamentary government became matters for general discussion and comment. We have seen, too, how Adam Smith's *Wealth of Nations* was soon translated into many languages.

The main agency of progress was thought to be the state. Whether in the form of limited monarchy on the British model favored by Montesquieu, or of enlightened despotism preferred by Voltaire, or of the idealized republican commonwealth portrayed by Rousseau, the rightly ordered government was considered the best guarantee of social welfare. Even the political economists needed the state to shake people out of the habits of ages, sweep away a mass of local regulation, preserve law and order and the enforcement of contracts, and so assure the existence of a free market. But if they relied on the state,

Belief in the unity of humankind

they were not nationalists in any later sense of the word. As "universalists," they believed in the unity of humankind under a natural law of right and reason and thus they carried over the classical and Christian outlook in a secular way. They supposed that all peoples would participate eventually in the same progress. No nation was thought to have a peculiar message. French ideas enjoyed a wide currency, but no one thought of them as peculiarly French, arising from a French "national character." It was simply thought that the French at the time were in the vanguard of civilized thinking. Such was the idea of Condorcet, one of the later philosophes, a leading spokesman of the Enlightenment who became an active figure in the French Revolution, and also one of its victims, and who in 1794, while in hiding from the guillotine, wrote the great testament to the Enlightenment, his *Sketch of the Progress of the Human Mind*.

36. ENLIGHTENED DESPOTISM: FRANCE, AUSTRIA, PRUSSIA

The Meaning of Enlightened Despotism

Enlightened despotism is hard to define, because it grew out of earlier forms of absolutism that Louis XIV and Peter the Great had established in France and Russia. Characteristically, the enlightened despots drained marshes, built roads and bridges, codified the laws, repressed provincial autonomy and localism, curtailed the independence of church and nobles, and developed a trained and salaried officialdom. All these things had been done by kings before. Enlightened despots differed from their "unenlightened" predecessors mainly in attitude and tempo. They said little of a divine right to the throne. They might even not emphasize hereditary or dynastic family rights. They justified their authority on grounds of usefulness to society, calling themselves, as Frederick the Great did, the "first servant of the state."

The secular outlook

Enlightened despotism was secular; it claimed no mandate from heaven and recognized no special responsibility to God or church. The typical enlightened despot consequently favored toleration in religion, and this was an important new emphasis after about 1740; but here again there was precedent in the older absolutism, for the rulers of Prussia had been inclined toward toleration before Frederick, and even the French Bourbons had recognized a degree of religious liberty for almost a century following the Edict of Nantes in 1598. The secular outlook of the enlightened governments is again seen in the common front they adopted against the Jesuits. High papalists, affirming the authority of a universal church in Rome and asserting themselves in other ways as the strongest religious order in the Catholic world, the Jesuits were distasteful to the enlightened monarchs. In the 1760s the order was banned in almost all Catholic countries. In 1773 the pope was persuaded to dissolve the Society of Jesus entirely. Governments in France, Austria, Spain, Portugal, and Naples confiscated Jesuit property and took over the Jesuit schools. Not until 1814 was the order reconstituted.

Enlightened despotism was also rational and reformist. The typical monarch set out to reconstruct the state by the use of reason. Sharing the widespread eighteenth-century view of the past as benighted, the new monarchs were impatient of custom and of all that was imbedded in custom or claimed as a heritage from the past, such as systems of customary law and the rights and privileges of church, nobles, towns, guilds, provinces, assemblies of estates, or, in France, the judicial bodies called parlements. The complex of such institutions was disparagingly referred to as "feudalism." Monarchs had long struggled against feudalism in this sense, but in the past they had usually compromised. The enlightened despot was less willing to compromise, and herein lay the difference in tempo. The new monarchs acted abruptly, desiring quicker results.

Enlightened despotism, in short, was an acceleration of the old central-izing institution of monarchy, which now put aside its quasi-sacred mantle and undertook to justify itself in the cold light of reason and secular useful-ness. In theory even the dynastic claim was awkward, for it rested on inher-itance from the past. Under enlightened despotism the idea of the state itself was changing, from the older notion of an estate belonging by a kind of sanctified property right to its ruler, to a newer notion of an abstract and impersonal authority exercised by public offi-cers, of whom the king was simply the highest.

The trend to enlightened despotism after 1740 owed a great deal to writers and philosophes, but it arose also out of a very practical situation, namely, the great war of the mid-eighteenth century. War, in modern history, has usually led to concentration and rationalizing of government power, and the wars of 1740–1748 and 1756–1763 were no exception. Under their impact even governments where the rulers were not considered by philosophes to be enlightened, notably those of Louis XV and Maria Theresa, and even the government of Great Britain, which was certainly not despotic, embarked on programs that all bear features in common. They attempted to augment their revenues, devise new taxes, tax persons or regions hitherto more or less tax-exempt, limit the autonomy of out-lying political bodies, and centralize and renovate their respective political systems. The workings of enlightened despotism might be seen in many states, but the new policies had the most far-reaching influence in the larger Continental countries—France and Austria, Prussia and Russia—and in the rather different, yet not wholly different, course of events in the British empire.

The Failure of Enlightened Despotism in France

It was in France that enlightened despotism had the least success. Louis XV, who had inherited the throne as a child in 1715 and lived until 1774, though by no means stupid, was indifferent to most serious questions, absorbed in the daily rounds at Versailles, disin-clined to make trouble for people with whom he had personal contact, and interested in government only by fits and starts. His reputed remark, *après moi le déluge,* whether or not he really said it, sufficiently characterizes his personal attitude to conditions in France. Yet the French government was not unenlightened, and many capable officials carried on its affairs all through the century. These officials generally knew what the basic trouble was. Most of the practical difficulties of the French monarchy could be traced to its meth-ods of raising revenue. It derived some income from the sale of offices and privileges,

which had the perverse effect of building up vested interests in the existing system. Of actual taxes the most important was the *taille,* a kind of land tax, generally paid only by peasants. Nobles were exempt from it on principle, and officeholders and bourgeois, for one reason or another, were generally

EUROPE, 1740

Boundaries are as of 1740. There were now three Bourbon monarchies (France, Spain, and the Two Sicilies), while the Austrian monarchy possessed most of what is now Belgium, and in Italy the duchy of Milan and grand duchy of Tuscany, where the Medici family had recently died out. Prussia expanded by acquiring Silesia in the war of the 1740s. The first partition of Poland in 1772 enlarged Prussia, Austria, and Russia. France acquired Lorraine in 1766 and Corsica in 1768. Otherwise there were no changes until the Revolutionary-Napoleonic wars of 1792–1814.

Bourbon Dominions

Habsburg Dominions

Boundary of Holy Roman Empire

NORWAY

SWEDEN

KINGDOM OF
DENMARK AND NORWAY

St. Petersburg

Stockholm

SCOTLAND

Edinburgh

*North
Sea*

Riga

LITHUANIA

Minsk

IRELAND

Dublin

GREAT BRITAIN

Liverpool

DENMARK

Copenhagen

Baltic Sea

PRUSSIA

Memel

ENGLAND

London

SCHLESWIG

Hamburg

Danzig

EAST
PRUSSIA

WALES

Amsterdam

UNITED
PROVINCES

Brennen

HANOVER
(Britain)

Elbe R.

Magdeburg

BRANDENBURG

Berlin

Thorn

Warsaw

POLAND

Lublin

Utrecht

AUSTRIAN
NETHERLANDS

Oudenarde

Antwerp

Cologne

MINOR

GERMAN STATES

Leipzig

SAXONY

Dresden

SILESIA

Breslau

Oder R.

Cracow

Lemberg

*ATLANTIC
OCEAN*

*CHANNEL I.
(Britain)*

Cape
de la Hogue

Malplaquet

Ramilles

Rhine R.

Frankfurt

BOHEMIA

Prague

MORAVIA

Vistula R.

PODOLIA

Rouen

Reims

PALATI-
NATE

Munkacz

Quiberon

Paris

Metz

Blenheim

AUSTRIA

Orléans

Seine R.

LORRAINE
(France 1766)

Strasbourg

BAVARIA

Vienna

Pressburg

Budapest

Tours

Besançon

Munich

TYROL

AUSTRIAN MONARCHY

TRANSYLVANIA

FRANCE

Limoges

Geneva

SWITZERLAND

KINGDOM
OF HUNGARY

Santiago

Bordeaux

Lyons

Rhône R.

SAVOY

MILAN

Po R.

VENETIA

Venice

CROATIA

Save R.

BANAT

Belgrade

WALLACHIA

León

Pamplona

Garonne R.

Toulouse

Turin

PARMA

Genoa

Bologna

BOSNIA

SERBIA

Danube R.

Burgos

Avignon

Marseille

TUSCANY

PAPAL
STATES

DALMATIA
(Venice)

Adriatic Sea

MONTENEGRO

OTTOMAN EMPIRE

Sofia

PORTUGAL

SPAIN

Madrid

Ebro R.

Barcelona

KINGDOM OF SARDINIA

Corsica
(Genoa)

Rome

ALBANIA

Salonica

Lisbon

Tagus R.

Toledo

BALEARIC I.

Minorca
(Britain)

Sardinia

Benevento

Bari

IONIAN I.
(Venice)

Athens

Almanza

Majorca
(Spain)

Cagliari

Naples

NAPLES

MOREA

Guadalquivir R.

Seville

Granada

KINGDOM
OF THE TWO SICILIES

Cadiz

Tangier

Gibraltar (Britain)

Mediterranean

Palermo

SICILY

Algiers

MOROCCO
(Independent)

ALGERIA
(Turkish)

Tunis

TUNISIA
(Turkish)

MALTA (Knights of St. John)

Sea

0   200   400 miles

exempt also. In addition, the church, which owned between five and ten percent of the land of the country, insisted that its property was not taxable by the state; it granted to the king a periodic "free gift" which, though sizable, was less than the government might expect from direct taxation. The consequence of the tax exemptions was that, although France itself was wealthy and prosperous, the government was chronically poor, because the social classes which enjoyed most of the wealth and prosperity did not pay taxes corresponding to their incomes.

Louis XIV, under pressure of war, had tried to tax everybody alike by creating new levies—the capitation or poll tax and the *dixième* or tenth, both of which were assessed in proportion to income; but these taxes had been widely evaded. A similar effort was made in 1726, but it too had failed. The propertied classes resisted taxation because they thought it degrading. France had succumbed to the appalling principle that to pay direct taxes was the sure mark of inferior status. Nobles, churchmen, and bourgeois also resisted taxation because they were kept out of policymaking functions of government and so had no sense of political responsibility or control.

In the 1740s, under pressure of heavy war costs, a new tax was introduced, the *vingtième* or twentieth, which imposed a five percent tax on income from all forms of property and was to be paid irrespective of class status, provincial liberties, or previous exemptions of any kind. In practice, the *vingtième* amounted to less than five percent and fell only upon land, but it was paid by nobles and bourgeois alike and lasted until the Revolution. During the Seven Years' War the government tried to increase it, without success. A clamor arose from the Parlement of Paris, the provincial parlements, the estates of Brittany, and the church. All these were now stronger than in the days of Louis XIV, and they could now cite Montesquieu to justify their opposition to the crown. The parlements ruled the tax increase to be incompatible with the laws of France, that is, unconstitutional; and the *pays d'états,* or provinces having assemblies of estates, declared that their historic liberties were being violated. After several years of wrangling, Louis XV decided to push the matter no further.

But after the Seven Years' War, burdened with war debts, the government sought to win effective central control by eliminating the parlements as a political force. In 1768 Louis XV called to the chancellorship a man named Maupeou, who simply abrogated the old parlements and set up new ones in their place. Maupeou had the sympathy of Voltaire and most of the philosophes. In the "Maupeou parlements" the judges had no property rights in their seats but became salaried officials appointed by the crown with assurances of secure tenure; and they were forbidden to reject government edicts or to pass on their constitutionality, being confined to purely judicial functions. Maupeou proposed to make the laws and judicial procedure more uniform throughout the whole country. Meanwhile, with the old parlements out of the way, another attempt was made to tax the privileged and exempted groups.

The "Maupeou parlements"

Louis XVI

But Louis XV died in 1774. His grandson and successor, Louis XVI, though more conscientious than his grandfather and possessed by a genuine desire to govern well, resembled Louis XV in that he lacked sustained will power and could not bear to offend the people who could get to see him personally. In any case he was only 20 in 1774. The kingdom resounded with outcries against Maupeou and his colleagues as minions of despotism and with demands for the immediate restoration of the old Parlement of Paris and the others. Louis XVI, fearful of beginning his reign as a "despot," therefore recalled the old parlements and abolished those of Maupeou. The abortive Maupeou parlements represented the farthest step taken by enlightened despotism in France. It was arbitrary, high-handed, and despotic for Louis XV to destroy the old parlements, but it was certainly "enlightened" in the sense then connoted by the word, for the old parlements were strongholds of aristocracy and privilege and had for decades blocked programs of reform.

Louis XVI, in recalling the old parlements in 1774, began his reign by pacifying the privileged classes. At the same time he appointed a reforming ministry. At its head was Turgot, a philosophe and a Physiocrat and a widely experienced government administrator. Turgot undertook to suppress the guilds and their privileged municipal monopolies in their several trades. He allowed greater freedom to the internal commerce in grain. He planned to abolish the royal *corvée* (a requirement that certain peasants labor on the roads a few days each year), replacing it by a money tax which would fall on all classes. He began to review the whole system of taxation and in religious matters was known even to favor the legal toleration of Protestants. The Parlement of Paris, supported by the Provincial Estates and the church, vociferously opposed him, and in 1776 he resigned. Louis XVI, by recalling the parlements, had made reform impossible. In 1778 France again went to war with Britain. The same cycle was repeated: war costs, debt, deficit, new projects of taxation, resistance from the parlements and other semiautonomous bodies. In the 1780s the clash led to revolution.

Austria: The Reforms of Maria Theresa (1740–1780) and of Joseph II (1780–1790)

For Maria Theresa the European war of the 1740s proved the extraordinary flimsiness of her empire and the Austrian monarchy. Her subjects did not show much inclination to remain united under her rule, even when threatened by invading armies. The empire was only a loose bundle of territories without common purpose or common will. The Pragmatic Sanction devised by Charles VI, it should be recalled, had been meant not only to guarantee the Habsburg inheritance against foreign attack but also to secure the assent of the several parts of the empire to remain united under the Habsburg dynasty.

The war of the 1740s led to internal consolidation. The reign of Maria Theresa set the course of all later development of the Austrian empire and hence of the many peoples who lived within its borders. She was aided by a notable team of ministers, whose origin illustrated the nonnational character of the Habsburg system. Her most trusted adviser in foreign relations, the astute Kaunitz, was a Moravian; her main assistants in domestic affairs were a Silesian and a Bohemian-Czech. They worked smoothly with the German archduchess-queen and with German officials in Vienna. Their aim was to prevent dissolution of the monarchy by enlarging and guaranteeing the flow of taxes and soldiers. This involved breaking the local control of territorial nobles in their diets. Hungary, profoundly separatist, was left alone. But the Bohemian and Austrian provinces were welded together, and a unified state bureaucracy took the place of local self-government. Officials (following the form of mercantilist doctrine called "cameralism" in central Europe) planned to augment the economic strength of the empire by increasing production. They checked the local guild monopolies; suppressed brigandage on the roads; and in 1775 created a tariff union of Bohemia, Moravia, and the Austrian duchies. This region became the largest area of free trade on the European continent, since even France was still divided by internal tariffs. Bohemia, industrially the most advanced part of the empire, benefited substantially; one of its cotton manufacturing plants, at the end of Maria Theresa's reign, employed 4,000 persons.

Internal consolidation of the empire

Le Roy Louis XVI. tenant son Lit de Justice pour la I.ᵉ   Fois au Palais a Paris le 12 de Novembre 1774. pour

The restoration of the traditional parlements at the beginning of the reign of Louis XVI was an important political victory for the privileged classes in French society, whose power had been challenged by the Maupeou ministry in the early 1770s. This illustration of the young king at the first session of the restored Parlement of Paris (he occupies the elevated seat on the upper left side of the assembly) offers an early example of his lifelong tendency to align himself with older elites and to oppose reformers who wanted to reduce the power or privileges of the old nobility. The caption lists the royal officials and dignitaries who accompanied the king at this meeting of the Parlement in November 1774.

(Bibliothèque Nationale de France, Paris)

The great social fact, both in the Habsburg lands and in all eastern Europe, was the serfdom into which the rural masses had progressively fallen during the past 200 years. Serfdom meant that the peasant belonged more to the landlord than to the state. The serf owed labor to the lord, often unspecified in amount or kind. The tendency, so long as the landlords ruled locally through their diets, was for the serf to do six days a week of forced labor on the lord's land. Maria Theresa, from humane motives and also from a desire to control the manpower from which her armies were recruited, launched a systematic attack on the institutions of serfdom, which meant also an attack on the landed aristocracy of the empire. With the diets reduced in power, the protests of the nobles were less effective; still, the whole agricultural labor system of her territories was involved, and Maria Theresa proceeded with caution. Laws were passed against abuse of peasants by lords or their overseers. Other laws regularized the labor obligations, requiring that they be publicly registered and usually limiting them to three days a week. The laws were often evaded. But the peasant was to some extent freed from arbitrary exactions of the lord. Maria Theresa accomplished more to alleviate serfdom than any other ruler of the eighteenth century in eastern Europe, with the single exception of her own son, Joseph II.

Attacks on serfdom

The great archduchess-queen died in 1780, having reigned for 40 years. Her son, who had been co-regent with his mother since 1765, had little patience with her methods. Maria Theresa, though steady enough in aim, had always been content with partial measures. Instead of advertising her purposes by philosophical pronouncements, she disguised or understated them, never carrying matters to the point of arousing an unmanageable reaction or of uniting against her the vested interests that she undermined. She watched and waited. Joseph II was more impatient. Though he thought the French philosophes frivolous, and Frederick of Prussia a mere clever cynic, he was himself a pure representative of the Age of Enlightenment, and it is in his brief reign of 10 years that the character and the limitations of enlightened despotism can best be seen. He was a solemn, earnest, good man, who sensed the misery and hopelessness of the lowest classes. He believed existing conditions to be bad, and he would not regulate or improve them; he would end them. Right and reason, in his mind, lay with the views which he himself adopted; upholders of the old order were self-seeking or mistaken and to yield to them would be to compromise with evil.

Joseph II: the "revolutionary emperor"

"The state," said Joseph, anticipating the later Philosophical Radicals in England, meant "the greatest good for the greatest number." He acted accordingly. His 10 years of rule passed in a quick succession of decrees. Maria Theresa had regulated serfdom. Joseph abolished it. His mother had collected taxes from nobles as well as peasants, though not equally. Joseph decreed absolute equality of taxation. He insisted on equal punishment for equal crimes whatever the class status of the offender; an aristocratic army officer, who had stolen 97,000 gulden, was exhibited in the pillory, and Count Podstacky, a forger, was made to sweep the streets of Vienna chained to common convicts. At the same time many legal punishments were made less physically cruel. Joseph granted complete liberty of the press. He ordered toleration of all religions, except for a few popular sects that he thought too ignorant to allow. He granted equal civil rights to the Jews, and equal duties, making Jews liable, for the first time in Europe, to service in the army. He even created Jewish nobles, an amazing phenomenon to those of aristocratic "blood."

Joseph clashed openly and rudely with the pope. He demanded increased powers in the appointment and supervision of Catholic bishops, and he suppressed a good many monasteries, using their property to finance secular hospitals in Vienna, and thus laying the foundations of Viennese excellence as a medical center. He attempted also to develop the empire economically and built up the port of Trieste, where he even established an East India Company, which soon failed for obvious reasons—neither capital nor naval support being forthcoming from central Europe. His attempts to reach the sea commercially through Belgium, like those of his grandfather at the time of the Ostend Company, were blocked by Dutch and British interests.

To force through his program Joseph had to centralize his state, like earlier rulers, except that he went further. Regional diets and aristocratic self-government fared even worse than under his mother. Where she had always sagaciously let Hungary go its own way, he applied most of his measures to Hungary also—what was right must be right everywhere. His ideal was a perfectly uniform and rational empire, with all irregularities smoothed out as if under a steamroller. He thought it reasonable to have a single language for administration and naturally chose German; this led to a program of Germanizing the Czechs, Poles, Magyars, and others, which in turn aroused their nationalistic resistance. Using the German language, and pushing the emperor's program against regional and class opposition, was a hard-pressed, constantly growing, and increasingly disciplined body of officials. Bureaucracy became recognizably modern, with training courses, promotion schedules, retirement pensions, efficiency reports, and visits by inspectors. The clergy likewise were employed as representatives of the state to explain new laws to their parishioners and teach due respect for the government. To watch over the whole structure Joseph created a secret police, whose agents, soliciting the confidential aid of spies and informers, reported on the performance of government employees or on the ideas and actions of nobles, clergy, or others from whom trouble might be expected. The police state, so infamous to the liberal world, was first systematically built up under Joseph as an instrument of enlightenment and reform.

Joseph II, the "revolutionary emperor," anticipated much that was done in France by the Revolution and under Napoleon. He could not abide "feudalism" or "medieval-

*Limitations of
Joseph's reforms*

ism"; he personally detested the nobility and the church. But few of his reforms proved lasting. He died prematurely in 1790, at the age of 49, disillusioned and broken-hearted. Joseph was a revolutionist without a party. He failed because he could not be everywhere and do everything himself, and because he was opposed by the most powerful social groups in his empire. His reign demonstrated the limitations of a merely despotic enlightenment. It showed that a legally absolute ruler could not really do as he pleased. It suggested that drastic and abrupt reform could perhaps come only with a true revolution, on a wave of public opinion, and under the leadership of persons who shared in a coherent body of ideas.

Joseph was succeeded by his brother Leopold, one of the ablest rulers of the century, who for many years as grand duke of Tuscany had given that country the best government known in Italy for generations. Now, in 1790, Leopold was plagued by outcries from his sister, Marie Antoinette, caught in the toils of a real revolution in France. He refused to interfere in French affairs; in any case, he was busy dealing with the uproar left by Joseph. He abrogated most of Joseph's edicts, but he did not yield entirely. The nobles did not win back full powers in their diets. The peasants were not wholly consigned to the old serfdom; Joseph's efforts to provide them with land and to rid them of forced labor had to be given up, but they remained legally free to migrate, marry, or choose an occupation at will. Leopold died in 1792 and was followed by his son Francis II. Under Francis the aristocratic and clerical reaction gathered strength, terrified by the memory of Joseph II and by the spectacle of revolutionary France, with which Austria went to war soon after Leopold's death.

Prussia under Frederick the Great (1740–1786)

In Prussia, Frederick the Great continued to reign for 23 years after the close of the Seven Years' War in 1763. "Old Fritz," as he was called, spent the time peaceably, writing memoirs and histories, rehabilitating his shattered country, promoting agriculture and industry, replenishing his treasury, drilling his army, and assimilating his huge conquest of Silesia, and, after 1772, the Polish lands which fell to him in the first partition of Poland. Frederick's fame as one of the most eminent of enlightened despots rests, however, not so much on his actual innovations as on his own intellectual gifts, which were considerable, and on the admiring publicity which he received from such literary friends as Voltaire. "My chief occupation," he wrote to Voltaire, "is to fight ignorance and prejudices in this country. . . . I must enlighten my people, cultivate their manners and morals, and make them as happy as human beings can be, or as happy as the means at my disposal permit." He did not conceive that sweeping changes were necessary to happiness in Prussia. The country was docile, for its Lutheran church had long been subordinate to the state, its relatively few burghers were largely dependents of the crown, and the independence of the Junker landlords, as expressed in provincial diets, had been curtailed by Frederick's predecessors. Frederick simplified and codified the many laws of the kingdom and made the law courts cheaper, more expeditious, and more honest. He kept up a wholesome and energetic tone in his civil service. He protected religious freedom, and he decreed, though he did not achieve, a modicum of elementary education for all children of all classes. Prussia under Frederick was attractive enough for some 300,000 immigrants to seek it out.

But society remained stratified in a way hardly known in western Europe. Nobles, peasants, and burghers lived side by side in a kind of segregation. Each group paid different taxes and owed different duties to the state, and no person could buy property of the type owned by one of the other two groups. Property was legally classified, as well as persons; there was little movement from one group to another. These policies served a specific military purpose. They preserved a distinct peasant class from which to draw soldiers and a distinct aristocratic class from which to draw officers. The peasants, except in the western extremities of the kingdom, were serfs holding patches of land on precarious terms with obligations to labor on the estates of the lords. They were likewise considered the lord's "hereditary subjects" and were not free to leave the lord's estate, to marry, or to learn a trade except with his permission. Frederick in his early years considered steps to relieve the burden of serfdom. He did relieve it on his own manors, those belonging to the Prussian crown domain, which comprised a quarter of the area of the kingdom. But he did nothing for serfs belonging to the private landlords or Junkers. No king of Prussia could antagonize the Junker class which commanded the army. On the other hand, even in Prussia, the existence of a monarchical state was of some advantage for the common person; the serf in Prussia was not so badly off as in adjoining areas—Poland, Livonia, Mecklenburg, or Swedish Pomerania—where the will of the landlords was the law of the land, and which therefore have been called Junker republics. In these countries cases came to light in which owners sold their serfs as movable property or gambled or gave them away, breaking up families in the process, as Russian landlords might do with their serfs or American plantation owners with their slaves. Such abuses were unknown in Prussia.

Social stratification in Prussia

Frederick's system was centralized not merely at Potsdam but in his own head. He himself attended to all business and made all important decisions. None of his ministers or generals ever achieved an independent reputation. As he said of his army, "no one reasons, everyone executes"—that is, no one reasoned except the king himself. Or again, as Frederick put it, if Newton had had to consult with Descartes he would never have discovered the law of universal gravitation. To have to take into account other people's ideas, or to entrust responsibilities to people less capable than himself, seemed to Frederick wasteful and anarchic. He died in 1786, after ruling 46 years and having trained no successors. Twenty years later Prussia was all but destroyed by Napoleon. It was not surprising that Napoleon should defeat Prussia, but Europe was amazed, in 1806, to see Prussia collapse totally and abruptly. It was then concluded in Prussia and elsewhere that government by a mastermind working in lofty and isolated superiority did not offer a viable form of state under modern conditions.

37.   ENLIGHTENED DESPOTISM: RUSSIA

The Russian empire has long been out of sight in the preceding pages. There are reasons for its absence, for it played no part in the intellectual revolution of the seventeenth century, and its role in the struggle for wealth and empire, which reached a climax in the Seven Years' War, was somewhat incidental. In the Age of Enlightenment the role of Russia was passive. No Russian thinker was known to western Europe, but western European thinkers were well known in Russia. The French-dominated cosmopolitan culture of the European upper classes spread to the upper classes of Russia. The Russian court and aristocracy took over French as their common conversational language. With French (German was also known, and sometimes English, for the Russian aristocrats were remarkable linguists) all the ideas boiling up in western Europe streamed into Russia. The Enlightenment, if it did not affect Russia profoundly, affected it significantly. It continued the westernization so forcibly pushed forward by Peter and carried further the estrangement of the Russian upper classes from their own people and their own native scene.

Russia absorbs French culture

Russia after Peter the Great

Peter the Great died in 1725. To secure his revolution he had decreed that each tsar should name his successor, but he himself had named none and had put to death his own son Alexis to prevent social reaction. Peter's long reign was therefore followed by a period of political instability. Rival factions at court—a German party and a native Russian party— struggled for control over successive tsars, tsarinas, and short-lived governments until a palace revolution in 1741 brought to the throne Peter the Great's daughter, Elizabeth, who managed to hold power until her death 21 years later. In her reign the military power of Russia expanded, and she entered into European diplomacy and joined in the Seven Years' War against Prussia, fearing that the continued growth of Prussia would endanger the new Russian position on the Baltic. Her nephew, Peter III, was almost immediately dethroned, and probably assassinated, by a group acting in the name of his young wife Catherine. The victorious coterie gave it out that Peter III had been almost a half-wit, who at the age of 24 still played with paper soldiers. Catherine was proclaimed the Empress Catherine II and is called "the Great." She enjoyed a long reign from 1762 to 1796, during which she acquired a somewhat exaggerated reputation as an enlightened despot.

The names of the tsars and tsarinas between Peter I and Catherine II are of slight importance, but their violent and rapid sequence tells a story. With no principle of succession, dynastic or other, the empire fell into a lawless struggle of parties, in which plots against rulers while living alternated with palace revolutions upon their death. In all the confusion an underlying issue was always how the westernizing reform program of Peter would turn out. To most people in western Europe Russia still seemed alien or even barbaric.

Catherine the Great (1762–1796): Domestic Program

Catherine the Great was a German woman of a small princely house of the Holy Roman Empire. She had gone to Russia at the age of 15 to be married. She had immediately cultivated the goodwill of the Russians, learned the language, and embraced the Orthodox church. Early in her married life, disgusted with her husband, she foresaw the chance of becoming empress herself. Like the other prominent woman ruler of this era in Europe, Maria Theresa, she approached political issues with a strong practical sense and great energy (though she did not share Maria Theresa's devotion to family life). Catherine's intellectual powers were as remarkable as her physical vigor; even after becoming empress she often got up at five in the morning, lit her own fire, and turned to her books, making a digest, for example, of Blackstone's *Commentaries on the Laws of England,* published in 1765. She corresponded with Voltaire and invited Diderot, editor of the *Encyclopédie,* to visit her at St. Petersburg, where, she reported, he thumped her so hard on the knee in the energy of his conversation that she had to put a table between them. She bought Diderot's library, allowing him to keep it during his lifetime, and in other ways won renown by her benefactions to the philosophes, whom she regarded as useful press agents for Russia.

When she first came to power, she publicized an intention to introduce certain enlightened reforms. She summoned a great consultative assembly, called a Legislative Commission, which met in the summer of 1767. From its numerous proposals Catherine obtained a good deal of information on *Catherine's reforms* conditions in the country and concluded, from the profuse loyalty exhibited by the deputies, that though a usurper and a foreigner she possessed a strong hold upon Russia. The reforms which she subsequently enacted consisted in a measure of legal codification, restrictions on the use of torture, and a certain support of religious toleration, though she would not allow Old Believers to build their own chapels. Such innovations were enough to raise an admiring chorus from the philosophes, who saw in her, as they saw retrospectively in Peter the Great, the standard-bearer of an enlightened civilization among a backward people.

Whatever ideas Catherine may conceivably have had at first, as a thoughtful and progressive young woman, on the fundamental subject of reforming serfdom in Russia, did not last long after she became empress and dissolved with the great peasant insurrection of 1773, known as Pugachev's rebellion. The condition of the Russian serfs was deteriorating. Serf owners were increasingly selling them apart from the land, breaking up families, using them in mines or manufactures, disciplining and punishing them at will, or exiling them to Siberia. The serf population was restless, worked upon by Old Believers and cherishing distorted popular memories of the mighty hero, Stephen Razin, who a century before had led an uprising against the landlords. Class antagonism, though latent, was profound, nor was it made less when the rough muzhik, in some places, heard the lord and his family talking French so as not to be understood by the servants or saw them wearing European clothes, reading European books, and adopting the manners of a foreign way of life.

In 1773 a Don Cossack, Emelian Pugachev, a former soldier, appeared at the head of an insurrection in the Urals. Following an old Russian custom, he announced himself as the true tsar, Peter III (Catherine's deceased *Pugachev's rebellion* husband), now returned after long travels in Egypt and the Holy Land. He surrounded himself with his own imperial family, courtiers, and even a secretary of state, He issued an imperial manifesto proclaiming the end of serfdom and of taxes and military conscription. Tens of hundreds of thousands, in the Urals and Volga regions, Tartars, Kirghiz, Cossacks, agricultural serfs, servile workers in the Ural mines, fishermen in the rivers and in the Caspian Sea, flocked to Pugachev's banner. The great host surged through eastern Russia, burning and pillaging, killing priests and landlords. The upper classes in Moscow were terrified; 100,000 serfs lived in the city as domestic servants or industrial workers and their

CATHERINE THE GREAT
by Alexander Roslin (Swedish, 1718–1793)

Catherine's forceful character and slightly whimsical smile are represented in this portrait, which was painted shortly after the powerful tsarina suppressed the great peasant rebellion of 1773–1774.

(Giraudon/Art Resource, NY)

sympathies went out to Pugachev and his militant supporters. Armies sent against him were at first unsuccessful. But famine along the Volga in 1774 dispersed the rebels. Pugachev, betrayed by some of his own followers, was brought to Moscow in an iron cage. Catherine forbade the use of torture at his trial, but he was executed by the drawing and quartering of his body, a punishment, it should perhaps be noted, used at the time in western Europe in cases of flagrant treason.

Pugachev's rebellion was the most violent peasant uprising in the history of Russia, and the most formidable mass upheaval in Europe in the century before 1789. Catherine replied to it by repression. She conceded more powers to the landlords. The nobles shook off the last vestiges of the compulsory state service to which Peter had bound them. The peasants were henceforth the only bound or unfree class. As in Prussia, the state came more than ever to rest on an understanding between ruler and gentry, by which the gentry accepted the monarchy, with its laws, officials, army, and foreign policy, and received from it, in return, the assurance of full authority over the rural masses. Government reached down through the aristocracy and the scattered towns, but it stopped short at the manor; there the lord took over and was himself a kind of government in his own person. Under these conditions the number of serfs increased, and the load on each became heavier. Catherine's reign saw the culmination of Russian serfdom, which now ceased to differ in any important respect from the chattel slavery to which blacks were subject in the Americas. One might read in the Moscow *Gazette* such advertisements as the following: "For sale, two plump coachmen; two girls 18 and 15 years, quick at manual work. Two

Emelian Pugachev, leader of the most violent, widespread peasant uprising in Russian history, was held in an iron cage before his trial and execution for treason.

barbers; one, 21, knows how to read and write and play a musical instrument; the other can do ladies' and gentlemen's hair."

Catherine the Great: Foreign Affairs

Territorially Catherine was one of the main builders of modern Russia. When she became tsarina in 1762, the empire reached to the Pacific and into central Asia, and it touched upon the Gulf of Riga and the Gulf of Finland on the Baltic, but westward from Moscow one could go only 200 miles before reaching Poland, and no one standing on Russian soil could see the waters of the Black Sea (see map, pp. 222–223). Russia was separated from central Europe by a wide band of loosely organized domains, extending from the Baltic to the Black Sea and the Mediterranean and nominally belonging to the Polish and Turkish states. Poland was an old enemy, which had once threatened Muscovy, and in both Poland and the Ottoman Empire there were many Greek Orthodox Christians with whom Russians felt an ideological tie. In western Europe the disposal of the whole Polish-Turkish tract, which stretched through Asia Minor, Syria, and Palestine into Egypt, came to be called the Eastern Question. Though the name went out of use after 1900, the question of who would control these lands remained a contentious issue in the modern history of both Europe and the Middle East.

Catherine's supreme plan was to penetrate the entire area, Polish and Turkish alike. In a war with Turkey in 1772 she developed her "Greek project," in which "Greeks," that is, members of the Greek Orthodox Church, would replace Muslims as the dominant element throughout the Middle East. She defeated the Turks in the war, but was herself checked by the diplomatic pressures of the European

Territorial expansion

balance of power. The result was the first partition of Poland—a seizure of land and people in which the monarchs of Prussia, Russia, and Austria began to divide up Polish territory between them. Frederick took Pomerelia, which he renamed West Prussia; Catherine took parts of Byelorussia; Maria Theresa, Galicia. Frederick digested his portion with relish, realizing an old dream of the Brandenburg house; Catherine swallowed hers with some-what less appetite, since she had satisfactorily controlled the whole of Poland before; to Maria Theresa the dish was distasteful, and even shocking, but she could not see her neighbors go ahead without her, and she shared in the feast by suppressing her moral scru-ples. "She wept," said Frederick cynically, "but she kept on taking." Catherine, in 1774, signed a peace treaty with the defeated Turks at Kuchuk Kainarji on the Danube. The sul-tan ceded his rights over the Tartar principalities on the north coast of the Black Sea, where the Russians soon founded the seaport of Odessa.

Catherine had only delayed, not altered, her plans with respect to Turkey. She decided to neutralize the opposition of Austria. She invited Joseph II to visit her in Russia, and the two sovereigns proceeded together on a tour of her newly won Black Sea provinces. Her long-time adviser and lover, Grigory Potemkin, accompanied Catherine on this tour, which included visits to numerous towns and fortresses that Potemkin had established in the Crimea. Although the Russians had actually made significant progress in developing the region, Potemkin's enemies claimed that the new towns were nothing but a facade—thus creating the famous phrase "Potemkin villages" to mean bogus evidence of a nonexistent prosperity. At Kherson Catherine and Joseph II passed through a gate marked "The Road to Byzantium." "What I want is Silesia," said Joseph II, but the tsarina induced him to join in a war of conquest against Turkey.

This war with Turkey was interrupted by the French Revolution. Both governments reduced their commitments in the Balkans to await developments in western Europe. It became Catherine's policy to incite Austria and Prussia into a war with revolutionary France, in the name of monarchy and civilization, in order that she might have a free hand in the Polish-Turkish sphere. Meanwhile she contributed to killing off the nationalist and reforming movement among the Poles. In 1793 she arranged with Prussia for the second partition, and in 1795, with both Prussia and Austria, for the third. She was the only ruler who lived to take part in all three partitions of Poland (which are described later in this chapter).

Catherine's reign evaluated

Her protestations of enlightenment tempt one to an ironic judgment of her career. Her foreign policy was purely expansionist and unscrupulous, and the net effect of her domestic policy, aside from a few reforms of detail, was to favor the half-Europeanized aristocracy and to extend serfdom among the people. In her defense it may be observed that unscrupulous expansion was the accepted practice of the time, and that, domestically, probably no ruler could have corrected the social evils from which Russia suffered. If there was to be a Russian empire, it had to be with the consent of the serf-owning gentry, which was the only politically significant class. As Catherine observed to Diderot on the subject of reforms: "You write only on paper, but I have to write on human skin, which is incomparably more irritable and tick-lish." She had reason to know how easily tsars and tsarinas could be unseated and even murdered and that the danger of overthrow came not from the peasants but from cliques of army officers and landlords.

Yet she remained attuned to the West. She never thought that the peculiar institutions of Russia should become a model for others. She continued to recognize the standards of the Enlightenment. In her later years she gave careful attention to her favorite grandson,

Alexander, closely supervising his education, which she planned on the Western model. She gave him as a tutor the Swiss philosophe La Harpe, who filled his mind with humane and liberal sentiments on the duties of princes. Trained by Catherine as a kind of ideal ruler, Alexander I was destined to cut a wide circle in the affairs of Europe, to help defeat Napoleon Bonaparte, preach peace and freedom, and suffer from the same internal cultural divisions and frustrations by which educated Russians seemed characteristically to be afflicted.

The Limitations of Enlightened Despotism

Enlightened despotism, seen in retrospect, foreshadowed an age of revolution and even signified a preliminary effort to revolutionize society by authoritative action from above. People were told by their own governments that reforms were needed, that many privileges, special liberties, or tax exemptions were bad, that the past was a source of confusion, injustice, or inefficiency in the present. The state rose up as more completely sovereign, whether acting frankly in its own interest or claiming to act in the interest of its people. All old and established rights were brought into question—rights of kingdoms and provinces, orders and classes, legal bodies and corporate groups. Enlightened despotism overrode or exterminated the Society of Jesus, the Parlement of Paris, the autonomy of Bohemia, and the independence of Poland. Customary and common law was pushed aside by authoritative legal codes. Governments, by opposing the special powers of the church and the feudal interests, tended to make all persons into uniform and equal subjects. To this extent enlightened despotism favored equality before the law. But it could go only a certain distance in this direction. The king was after all a hereditary aristocrat himself, and no government can be revolutionary to the point of breaking up its own foundations.

Even before the French Revolution enlightened despotism had run its course. Everywhere the "despots," for reasons of politics if not of principle, had reached a point beyond which they could not go. In France Louis XVI had appeased the privileged classes; in the Austrian empire Joseph's failure to appease them threw them into open revolt; in Prussia and in Russia the brilliant reigns of Frederick and Catherine wound up in an aggravation of landlordism for the mass of the people. Almost everywhere there was an aristocratic and even feudal revival. Religion also was renewing itself in many ways. Many were again saying that kingship was in a sense divine, and a new alliance was forming between "the throne and the altar." The French Revolution, by terrifying the old vested interests, was to accelerate and embitter a reaction which had already begun. Monarchy in Europe, ever since the Middle Ages, had generally been a centralizing but progressive institution that set itself against the feudal and ecclesiastical powers. Enlightened despotism was the culmination of the historic institution of monarchy. After the enlightened despots, and after the French Revolution, monarchy became on the whole nostalgic and backward-looking, supported most ardently by the churches and aristocracies that it had once tried to subdue and least of all by those who felt in themselves the surge of the future.

38.   THE PARTITIONS OF POLAND

The fate of eighteenth-century Poland has been mentioned as a consequence of the growing power of the newer Central European monarchies, but the partitions of Polish territories also illustrate the assumptions and practices of the so-called "enlightened despots." Apart from the still somewhat non-European state of Russia, Poland in the eighteenth century was by far the largest state in Europe. It reached at the beginning of the century from the Baltic almost to the Black Sea and extended eastward for 800 miles across the north-European plain. But it was the classic example, along with the Holy Roman Empire, of an older political structure which failed to develop modern organs of government (see maps, pp. 193, 194). It fell into ever deeper anarchy and confusion. Without army, revenues, or administration and internally divided among parties forever at cross-purposes, the country was a perpetual theater for foreign diplomatic maneuvering and was finally absorbed by its growing neighbors.

The Polish kings were chosen in elections that became an object of regular international interference. A movement for reform therefore began to gather strength after the 1730s, and Polish patriots sought to do away with the *liberum veto* and other elements in the constitution that made government impossible. The reformers were repeatedly frustrated, however, by the influence of Catherine the Great and other foreign rulers who preferred a Poland in which they could intervene at will. Catherine's candidate for the Polish throne, Stanislas Poniatowski, won an election in 1763, thereby giving her new influence over Poland's domestic affairs. She declared herself protector of the Polish liberties. It was to the Russian advantage to maintain the existing state of affairs in Poland rather than to divide the country with neighbors who might exclude Russian influence from their own spheres. The Prussian government, which was eager to join the old duchy of Prussia with its other territories in the east, developed a greater interest in dividing Poland as a means to enhance its own strategic position.

Interference in Polish elections

The opportunity for Prussia presented itself in 1772, when Russia's war with Turkey destabilized the situation in eastern Europe. The Russian victories in this war were so overwhelming that both Austrians and Prussians feared an enduring Russian disruption of the balance of power. The Prussians therefore came forward with a proposal. It was a proposal to prevent an Austro-Russian war and to preserve the balance in Eastern Europe by leaving the Ottoman Empire more or less intact, but to have all three European powers annex territory from Poland instead. The proposition was accepted by all three parties.

Poland was thus sacrificed. By the first partition in 1772, its outer territories were cut away. Russia took an eastern slice around the city of Vitebsk. Austria took a southern slice, the region known as Galicia. Prussia realized its territorial ambitions by taking the Pomerelian borderland in West Prussia and creating a solid Prussian block from the Elbe to the borders of Lithuania (see map, p. 208, panel 4). The partition sobered the Poles, who renewed their efforts at a national revival, hoping to create an effective sovereignty which could secure the country against outsiders. But the Polish movement lacked deep popular strength, for it was confined mainly to nobles, whose conflicts had brought the country to ruin. The mass of the serf population and the numerous Jews did not much care at this time whether they were governed by Poles, Russians, or Germans.

Nevertheless, beginning in 1788, a reform party gathered strength. One of its members was King Stanislas Poniatowski himself, who had begun his reign as a protégé of the Russian empress. The reformers produced a new constitution in 1791. It made the Polish kingship hereditary, thus strengthening the executive government, and it reduced the powers of the great magnates while giving political rights to many burghers in the towns. By this time, however, the governments of eastern Europe were afraid of the French Revolution, which they saw as an outbreak of "Jacobinism." Denouncing the Polish reformers as Jacobins, Catherine the Great said she would "fight Jacobinism and beat it in Poland." In collusion with a few disgruntled Polish noblemen she sent an army into Poland and destroyed the constitution of 1791. In agreement with Prussia she then carried out the Second Partition in 1793. In 1794 Thaddeus Kosciusko led a more revolutionary political movement, which included even a proposed abolition of serfdom. Although it received no aid from the revolutionaries then governing France, it was crushed in the general European counterrevolution when Russian and Prussian armies again invaded Poland, defeated Kosciusko, and in a Third Partition in 1795 divided what remained of the country among themselves and Austria. Poland as a political entity ceased to exist.

Many advanced thinkers of the day praised the partitions of Poland as a triumph of enlightened rulers, putting an end to an old nuisance. The three partitioning powers justified their conduct on various grounds and even took pride in it as an enlightened diplomatic achievement by which war was prevented among them. It was argued also that the partitions of Poland put an end to an old cause of international rivalry and war, replacing anarchy with more stable governments in a large area of eastern Europe. It is a fact that Poland had been scarcely more independent before the partitions than after. It is to be noted also, though nationalist arguments were not used at the time, that on national grounds the Poles themselves had no claim to large parts of the old Poland. The regions taken by Russia were inhabited overwhelmingly by Byelorussians and Ukrainians, among whom the Poles were mainly a landlord class. Russia, even after the third partition, reached only to the true ethnic border of Poland. But later, after the fall of Napoleon, by general international agreement, the Russian sphere was extended deep into the territory inhabited by Poles.

Debate over the partitions

The partitions of Poland, however extenuated, were nevertheless a great shock to the old system of Europe. Edmund Burke, in England, prophetically saw in the first partition the crumbling of the old international order. His diagnosis was a shrewd one. The principle of the balance of power had been historically invoked to preserve the independence of European states and to secure weak or small ones against universal monarchy. It was now used to destroy the independence of a weak but ancient kingdom. Poland was not the first European kingdom to be "partitioned," but it was the first to be partitioned without war and the first to disappear totally. That Poland was partitioned without war, a source of great satisfaction to the partitioning powers, was still a very unsettling fact. It was alarming for a huge state to vanish simply by cold diplomatic calculation. It seemed that no established rights were safe even in peacetime. The partitions of Poland showed that in a world where great powers had arisen in control of a modern state apparatus it was dangerous not to be strong. They suggested that any area failing to develop a sovereign state capable of keeping out foreign infiltration, and so situated as to be within the reach of the great powers of Europe, was unlikely to retain its independence. In this way the history of eighteenth-century Poland anticipated, for example, the partitions of Africa a century later, when Africa too, lacking strong governments, was almost totally divided, without war, among half a dozen states of Europe.

Moreover the partitions of Poland, while maintaining a balance of power in eastern Europe, profoundly changed the balance of Europe as a whole. The disappearance of Poland was a blow to France, which had long used Poland, as it had used Hungary and Turkey, as an outpost of French influence in eastern Europe. The three Eastern powers expanded their territory, while France enjoyed henceforth no permanent growth. Eastern Europe bulked larger than ever before in the affairs of Europe. Prussia, Russia, and the Austrian empire became contiguous. Although they had drawn somewhat differently on western European methods of statecraft and military organization to build their power, they had a common interest and objective in eastern Europe, the repression of Polish resistance to their rule. Polish resistance, dating from before the partitions and continuing thereafter, was the earliest example of modern revolutionary nationalism in Europe.

The independence of Poland, and of other submerged nationalities, later became a popular cause in western Europe, while the three great monarchies of eastern Europe were

POLAND SINCE THE EIGHTEENTH CENTURY

The top panel shows, in simplified form, the ethnic composition of the area included in the Poland of 1772. In addition to languages shown, Yiddish was spoken by the large scattered Jewish population. The line set in 1795 as the western boundary of Russia persists through later changes. It reappears as the eastern border of Napoleon's Grand Duchy and of Congress Poland. After the First World War the victorious Allies contemplated much this same line as Poland's eastern frontier (the dotted line in the fourth panel, known as the Curzon Line); but the Poles in 1920–1921 conquered territory farther east. After the Second World War the Russians pushed the Poles back to the same basic line, but compensated Poland with territory taken from Germany, as far west as the river Oder and its tributary, the Neisse. The position of Warsaw in each panel shows how Poland has been shoved westward.

drawn together in common opposition to national liberation; this fact, plus the fact that the eastern monarchies were primarily landlord states, accentuated the political and social division of Europe in the nineteenth century between a western Europe that inclined to be liberal and an eastern Europe that inclined to be reactionary. The first great assault on the older social order and political system in eighteenth-century Europe, however, came from the "enlightened despots" who destroyed the kingdom of Poland.

39. NEW STIRRINGS: THE BRITISH REFORM MOVEMENT

It was not only by monarchs and their ministers that the older privileged, feudal, and ecclesiastical interests were threatened. Beginning about 1760 they were challenged also in more popular quarters. Growing out of the Enlightenment, and out of the failure of governments to cope with grave social and fiscal problems, a new era of revolutionary disturbance was about to open. It was marked above all by the great French Revolution of 1789, but the American Revolution of 1776 was also of international importance. In Great Britain, too, the long-drawn-out movement for parliamentary reform that began in the 1760s was in effect revolutionary in character, though nonviolent, since it questioned the foundations of traditional English government and society. In addition, in the last third of the eighteenth century, there was revolutionary agitation in Switzerland, Belgium, and Holland, in Ireland, Poland, Hungary, Italy, and in lesser degree elsewhere. After 1800 revolutionary ferment was increasingly evident in Germany, Spain, and Latin America. This general wave of revolution may be said not to have ended until after the revolutions of 1848.

Onset of an Age of "Democratic Revolution"

For the whole period the term "Atlantic Revolution" has sometimes been used, since countries on both sides of the Atlantic were affected. It has been called also an age of "Democratic Revolution," since in all the diversity of these upheavals, from the American Revolution to those of 1848, certain principles of the modern democratic society were in one way or another affirmed. In this view, the particular revolutions, attempted revolutions, or basic reform movements are seen as aspects of one great revolutionary wave by which virtually the whole area of Western civilization was transformed. There is also another view of this revolutionary age, namely, that each country presented a special case, which can be misunderstood if specific national events are described only as part of a vague general international turmoil. Thus the American Revolution, it is argued, was essentially a movement for independence, conservative in its objectives, and entirely different from the French Revolution, in which a thorough renovation of all society and ideas was contemplated; and both were utterly different from what happened in England, where there was no revolution at all. It need only be stressed here, however, that the American revolutionaries, the French Jacobins, the United Irish, the Dutch Patriots, and similar groups, though differing from each other, shared much in common that can only be characterized as revolutionary and as contributing to a revolutionary age.

   It is important to see in what ways the movement that began about 1760 was and was not "democratic." It did not generally demand universal suffrage, though a handful of persons in England did so as early as the 1770s and some of the American states practiced an almost universal male suffrage after 1776, as did the more militant French revolutionaries

"Age of Democratic Revolution"

in 1792. It did not aim at a welfare state, nor question the right of property, though there were signs pointing in these directions in the extreme wing of the French Revolution. It was not especially directed against monarchy as such. The quarrel of the Americans was primarily with the British Parliament, not the king; the French proclaimed a republic by default in 1792, three years after their revolution began; the revolutionary Poles after 1788 tried to strengthen their king's position, not weaken it; and revolutionary groups could come into action where no monarchy existed at all, as in the Dutch provinces before the French Revolution, and the Swiss cantons, the Venetian Republic, or again in Holland, under French influence after 1795. Indeed the first revolutionary outbreak of the period occurred in 1768 at Geneva, a very nonmonarchical small city-republic, ruled by a close-knit circle of hereditary patricians. Royal power, where it existed, became the victim of revolutionaries only where it was used to support various privileged social groups.

Liberty and equality

The revolutionary movement announced itself everywhere as a demand for "liberty and equality." It favored declarations of rights and explicit written constitutions. It proclaimed the sovereignty of the people, or "nation," and it formulated the idea of national citizenship. In this context the "people" were essentially classless; it was a legal term, signifying not government but the community over which public authority was exercised and from which government itself was in principle derived. To say that citizens were equal meant originally that there was no difference between noble and commoner. To say that the people were sovereign meant that neither the king, nor the British Parliament, nor any group of nobles, patricians, regents, or other elite possessed power of government in their own right; that all public officers were removable and exercised a delegated authority within limits defined by the constitution. There must be no "magistrate" above the people, no self-perpetuation or cooptation in office, no rank derived from birth and acknowledged in the law. Social distinctions, as the French said in their Declaration of Rights of 1789, were to be based only "on common utility." Elites of talent or function there might be, but none of birth, privilege, or estate. "Aristocracy" in every form must be shunned. In representative bodies, there could be no special representation for special groups; representatives should be elected by frequent elections, not indeed by universal suffrage, but by a body of voters, however defined, in which each voter should count for one in a system of equal representation. Representation by numbers, with majority rule, replaced the older idea of representation of social classes, privileged towns, or other corporate groups.

In short, everything associated with absolutism, feudalism, or inherited right (except the right of property) was repudiated. Likewise rejected was any connection between religion and citizenship, or civil rights. The Democratic Revolution undermined the special position of the Catholic church in France, the Anglican in England and Ireland, and the Dutch Reformed in the United Provinces. This was also the great period of what has been called Jewish "emancipation," which gave Jews political and social rights that had been denied to them throughout the Middle Ages and early modern era. The whole idea that government, or any human authority, was somehow willed by God and protected by religion faded away. A general liberty of opinion on all subjects was countenanced, in the belief that it was necessary to progress. Here again the secularism of the Enlightenment was carried from science and philosophy into many of the new political and cultural institutions that emerged during this era of revolutionary change.

On the whole, the Democratic Revolution was a middle-class movement, and indeed the term "bourgeois revolution" was later invented to describe it. Many of its leaders in Europe were in fact nobles who were willing to forgo the historic privileges of nobility; and many of its supporters were of the poorer classes, especially in the great French Revolution. But the middle classes were the great beneficiaries, and it was a kind of middle-class or bourgeois society that emerged. Persons of noble ancestry continued to exist after the storm was over, but the world of noble values was gone; and they either took part in various activities on much the same terms as others or retreated into exclusive drawing rooms to enjoy their aristocratic distinctions in private. The main drive of the working classes was still to come.

The English-Speaking Countries: Parliament and Reform

If the American Revolution was the first act of a larger drama, it must be understood also in connection with the broader British world of which the American colonies formed a part. The British Empire in the middle of the century was decentralized and composite. Thirty-one governments were directly subordinate to Westminster, ranging from the separate kingdom of Ireland through all the crown and charter colonies to the various political establishments maintained in the East by the East India Company. The whole empire, with about 15,000,000 people of all colors in 1750, was less populous than France or the Austrian monarchy. The whole tract of the American mainland from Georgia to Nova Scotia compared in the number of its white population with Ireland or Scotland—or with Brittany or Bohemia—a figure of about 2,000,000 being roughly applicable in each case.

Britain had its own way of passing through the Age of Enlightenment. There was general contentment with the arrangements that followed the English Revolution of 1688—it has often been remarked that nothing is so conservative as a successful revolution. British thought generally lacked the asperity of thought on the Continent. The writers who most resembled French philosophes, such as the Scottish philosopher David Hume and the English historian Edward Gibbon, were moderate in their political ideas. The prevailing mood, however, was one of complacency, a self-satisfaction in the glories of the unwritten British constitution by which Englishmen enjoyed liberties unknown on the Continent.

In Britain, Parliament was as supreme as the monarchs in most Continental countries. It had the power, as one facetious journalist put it, to do all things except change a man into a woman. The British Parliament was indeed more sovereign than any European ruler, since less that could be called feudalism remained in England than on the Continent. Nor was there

The monarchy in Great Britain

any "despotism" in England, enlightened or otherwise. The young George III, who inherited the throne in 1760, did feel himself to be a "patriot king." He did wish to heighten the influence of the crown and to overcome the factionalism of parties. But it was through Parliament that he had to work. He had to descend into the political arena himself, buy up or otherwise control votes in the Commons, grant pensions and favors, and make promises and deals with other parliamentary politicians. What he did in effect was to create a new faction, the "king's friends." This faction was in power during the ministry of Lord North from 1770 to 1782. It is worth noting that all factions were factions of Whigs, that the Tory party was practically defunct, that Britain did not yet have a two-party system, and that the word "Tory," as it came to be used by American revolutionaries, was little more than a term of abuse.

While Parliament was supreme, and constitutional questions apparently settled, there were nevertheless numerous undercurrents of discontent. These were expressed, since the press was freer in England than elsewhere, in many books and pamphlets which were read in the American colonies and helped to form the psychology of the American Revolution. There was, for example, a school of Anglo-Irish Protestant writers who argued that since Ireland was in

English discontent

any case a separate kingdom, with its own parliament, it ought to be less dependent on the central government at Westminster. The possibility of a similar separate state remaining within the British Empire, was one of the alternatives considered by Americans before they settled on independence. In England there was the considerable body of Dissenters, or Protestants not accepting the Church of England, who had enjoyed religious toleration since 1689 but continued to labor (until 1828) under various forms of political exclusion. They overlapped with two other amorphous groups, a small number of "commonwealth-men" and a larger and growing number of parliamentary reformers. The commonwealth-men, increasingly eccentric and largely ignored, looked back nostalgically to the Puritan Revolution and the republican era of Oliver Cromwell. They kept alive memories of the Levellers and ideals of equality, well mixed with a pseudo-history of a simple Anglo-Saxon England that had been crushed by the despotism of the Norman Conquest. They had less influence in England than in the American colonies and especially New England, whose origins were closely connected to the Puritan Revolution. The parliamentary reformers were a more diverse and influential group. They were condemned in the eigh-teenth century to repeated frustration; not until the First Reform Bill of 1832 did they begin to accomplish their goals.

Parliamentary politics

The very power of Parliament meant that political leaders had to take strong measures to assure its votes. These measures were generally denounced by their critics as "corruption," on the grounds that Parliament, whether or not truly representative, should at least be free. Control of Parliament, and especially of the House of Commons, was assured by various devices, such as patronage or the giving of government jobs (called "places"), or awarding contracts, or having infrequent general elections (every seven years after 1716); or the fact that in many con-stituencies there were no real elections at all. The distribution of seats in the Commons bore no relation to numbers of inhabitants. A town having the right to send members to Parliament was called a "borough," but no new borough was created after 1688 (or until 1832). Thus localities that had been important in the medieval or Tudor periods were rep-resented, but towns that had grown up recently, such as Manchester and Birmingham, were not. A few boroughs were populous and democratic, but many had few inhabitants or none, so that influential "borough mongers" decided who should represent them in Parliament.

The reform movement

The reform movement began in England before the American Revolu-tion, with which it was closely associated. Since complaints were diverse, it attracted people of different kinds. The first agitation centered about John Wilkes, a journalist and member of Parliament who vehemently attacked the policies of King George III. He was vindicated when the courts pronounced the arrest of his publisher illegal, but the king's supporters expelled him from the House of Com-mons. Wilkes became a political hero, however, and was later reelected three times to the House, which refused to seat him. A whirl of protests, public meetings, and petitions sup-ported him against the exclusionary actions of Parliament. His followers in 1769 founded the Supporters of the Bill of Rights, the first of many societies dedicated to parliamentary reform. His case raised the question of whether the House of Commons should be depen-dent on the electorate and on the propriety of mass agitation "out of doors" on political questions. It was in this connection, also, that debates in Parliament for the first time came to be reported in the London press. Parliament stood on the eve of a long transition, by which it was to be converted from a select body meeting in private to a modern represen-tative institution answerable to the public and its constituents. Wilkes himself finally

THE HON. MRS. GRAHAM
by Thomas Gainsborough (English, 1727–1788)

High social status is very evident in this portrayal of a young English gentlewoman. The wealth of her social class is apparent in the brooch, the plumes, the silks, bows and ruffles, and in the strings of pearls. Her delicate hands and the classical colonnade suggest a life of leisure and cultural importance. This is the way that English aristocrats of the eighteenth century liked to imagine themselves and to be portrayed for posterity.

(National Galleries of Scotland)

regained his parliamentary seat in 1774 and soon introduced the first of many reform bills, none of which passed for over half a century.

Meanwhile, the important Whig leaders, who had previously managed Parliament by manipulating elections in lightly populated boroughs, began to sense "corruption" in such methods after control passed to George III and his "friends." Their most eloquent spokesman was Edmund Burke. Other reformers called for more frequent elections, "annual parliaments," a wider and more equal or even universal male suffrage, with dissolution of some boroughs in which no one was really represented. Burke favored none of these things; in fact he came strenuously to oppose them. A founder of philosophical conservatism, he was yet in his way a reformer. He was more concerned that the House of Commons should be independent and responsible than that it should be mathematically representative. He thought that the landowning interest should govern. But he pleaded for a strong sense of party in opposition to royal encroachments, and he argued that members of Parliament should follow their own best judgment of the country's interests, bound neither by the king on the one hand nor by their own constituents on the other. Like other reformers, he objected to "placemen," or jobholders dependent on their ministerial patrons, and he objected to the use made, for political purposes, of a bewildering array of pensions, sinecures, honorific appointments, and ornamental offices, ranks, and titles. In his Economical Reform of 1782, which curtailed crown patronage, he got many of these abolished.

Edmund Burke

The reform movement, though ineffectual, remained strong. Even William Pitt, as prime minister in the 1780s, gave it his sponsorship. It took on new strength at the time of the French Revolution, spreading then to more popular levels, as members of the skilled artisan class responded to events in France by demanding a more adequate "representation of the people" in England. They then had upper-class support from Charles James Fox and a minority of the Whigs. But conservatism, satisfaction with the British constitution, patriotism engendered by a new round of French wars, and reaction against the French Revolution all raised an impassable barrier. Reform was delayed for another generation.

After the American Revolution, which in a way was a civil struggle within the English-speaking world, the English reformers generally blamed the trouble with America on King George III. This was less than fair, since Parliament on the American question was never dragooned by the king. The most ardent reformers later argued that if Parliament had been truly representative of the British people, the Americans would not have been driven to independence. This seems unlikely. In any case, reformers of various kinds, from Wilkes to Burke, were sympathetic to the complaints of the American colonials after 1763. There was much busy correspondence across the Atlantic. Wilkes was a hero in Boston as well as London. Burke pleaded for conciliation with the colonies in a famous speech of 1775. His very insistence on the powers and dignity of Parliament, however, made it hard for him to find a workable solution; and after the colonies became independent, he showed no interest in the political ideas of the new American states. It was the more radical reformers in England, as in Scotland and Ireland, who most consistently favored the Americans, both before and after independence. They of course had no power. On the American side, for a decade before independence, the increasingly discontented colonials, reading English books and pamphlets and reports of speeches, heard George III denounced for despotism and Parliament accused of incorrigible corruption. All this seemed to confirm what Americans had long been reading anyway in the works of English Dissenters or old commonwealthmen, now on the fringes of English society but sure of a receptive audience in the American colonies. The result was to make Americans suspicious

Edmund Burke's insistence on the political and social value of inherited traditions made him a key figure in the emergence of modern conservatism. Although he favored an independent Parliament in Britain, he wrote a famous critique of the revolution that abolished traditional royal prerogatives in France. He appears here in an engraving from the 1770s, after a painting by Sir Joshua Reynolds.
(Getty Images)

of all actions by the British government, to sense tyranny everywhere, to magnify such things as the Stamp Act into a kind of plot against American liberties.

The real drift in England in the eighteenth century, however, despite the chronic criticism of Parliament, was for Parliament to extend its powers in a general centralization of the empire. The British government faced somewhat the same problems as governments on the Continent. All had to deal with the issues raised by the great war of the mid-century, in its two phases of the Austrian Succession and Seven Years' War. Everywhere the solution adopted by governments was to increase their own central power. We have seen how the French government, in attempting to tap new sources of revenue, tried to encroach on the liberties of Brittany and other provinces and to subordinate the bodies which in France were called parlements. We have likewise seen how the Habsburg government, also in an effort to raise more taxes, repressed local self-government in the empire and consolidated power in a more centralized bureaucracy. The same tendency showed itself in the British system. The Habsburg revocation of a constitutional charter in Bohemia in 1749 had its parallel in the revocation of the charter of Massachusetts in 1774. The disputes of the French king with the estates of Brittany or Languedoc had their parallel in the disputes of the British Parliament with the provincial assemblies of Virginia or New York.

British centralization

Scotland, Ireland, India

The British also faced problems nearer home. Scotland proved a source of weakness in the War of the Austrian Succession. The Lowlanders were loyal enough, but the Highlanders revolted with French assistance in the Jacobite rising of 1745 and by invading England threatened to attack the British government in the rear as it was locked in the struggle with France. The Highlands had never really been under any government, even under the old Scottish monarchy before

British rule in Scotland

CHRONOLOGY OF NOTABLE EVENTS, 1733–1795

1733	Voltaire publishes *Philosophical Letters on the English*
1741	Montesquieu publishes *The Spirit of Laws*
1751–1772	Publication of the *Encyclopedia* in Paris
1753	Jean-Jacques Rousseau publishes *Origin of Inequality Among Men*
1762	Rousseau publishes *The Social Contract* and *Émile*
1762–1796	Tsarina Catherine the Great reigns as "enlightened despot" in Russia
1769	Emergence of Reform Movement in British Parliament
1772	Prussia, Austria, and Russia impose the First Partition of Poland
1773	Emelian Pugachev leads a rebellion of the lower classes in Russia
1774–1792	King Louis XVI reigns in France
1776	Adam Smith publishes *The Wealth of Nations*
1776–1783	Revolutionary War achieves American independence from Britain
1780–1790	Emperor Joseph II introduces "enlightened" reforms in Austria
1784	Britain creates the India Office to manage British interests in India
1787	Written Constitution establishes new government in the United States
1793, 1795	Second and Third Partitions of Poland destroy the Polish state

the union of 1707 with England. Men in the Highlands looked to their chiefs, the heads of the clans, to tell them whom and when to fight. The chiefs had hereditary jurisdiction, often including powers of life and death, over their clans. A few leaders could throw the whole region to the Stuarts or the French. The British government, after 1745, proceeded to make its sovereignty effective in the Highlands. Troops were quartered there for years. Roads were pushed across the moors and through the glens. Law courts enforced the law of the Scottish Lowlands. Revenue officers collected funds for the treasury of Great Britain. The chiefs lost their old quasi-feudal jurisdiction. The old system of land tenure was broken up, and the holding of land from clannish chiefs was ended. Fighting High-landers were incorporated into newly formed Highland regiments of the British army, under the usual discipline imposed by the modern state on its fighting forces. For 30 years the Scots were forbidden to wear the kilt or play the bagpipes.

The British in Ireland

In Ireland the process of centralization worked itself out more slowly. How Ireland was subjected after the battle of the Boyne has already been described. It was a French army that had landed in Ireland, supported James II, and been defeated in 1690. The new English constitutional arrangements, the Hanoverian succession, the Protestant ascendancy, the church and the land settlement in Ireland, together with the prosperity of British commerce, were all secured by the subordination of the smaller island. The native or Catholic Irish remained generally pro-French. The Presbyterian Irish disliked both the French and popery, but they were alienated from England also; many in fact emigrated to America in the generation before the American Revolution. Ireland remained quiet in the mid-century wars. When the trouble began between the

British Parliament and the American colonies, the Presbyterian Irish generally took the American side. They were greatly stirred by the example of American independence. Thousands formed themselves into Volunteer Companies; they wore uniforms, armed, and drilled; they demanded both internal reform of the Irish parliament (which was even less representative than the British) and greater autonomy for the Irish parliament as against the central government at Westminster.

Faced with these demands, and fearing a French invasion of Ireland during the War of American Independence, the British government made concessions. It allowed an increase of power to the Irish parliament at Dublin. But from the English parliament Catholics were still excluded. In the next war between France and Great Britain, which began in 1793, many Irish felt a warm sympathy for the French Revolution. Catholics and Presbyterians, at last combining, formed a network of United Irish societies throughout the whole island. They sought French aid, and the French barely failed to land a sizable army. Even without French military support, the United Irish rose in 1798 to drive out the English and establish an independent republic. The British, suppressing the rebellion, now turned to centralization. The separate kingdom of Ireland, and the Irish parliament, ceased to exist. The Irish were thereafter represented in the imperial Parliament at Westminster. These provisions were incorporated in the Act of Union of 1801, creating the United Kingdom of Great Britain and Ireland, which lasted until 1922.

British establishments in India also felt the hand of Parliament increasingly upon them. At the close of the Seven Years' War the various British posts in and around Bombay, Madras, and Calcutta were unconnected with *Intervention in India*
each other and subordinate only to the board of directors of the East India Company in London. Company employees interfered at will in the wars and politics of the Indian states and enriched themselves by such means as they could, not excluding graft, trickery, intimidation, rapine, and extortion. In 1773 the ministry of Lord North passed a Regulating Act, of which the main purpose was to regulate the British subjects in India, whom no Indian government could control. The company was left with its trading activities, but its political activities were brought under parliamentary supervision. The act gathered all the British establishments under a single governor general, set up a new supreme court with British judges at Calcutta, and required the company to submit its correspondence on political matters for review by the ministers of His Majesty's Government. Warren Hastings became the first British governor general in India. He was so high-handed with some of the Indian princes, and made so many enemies among jealous English residents in Bengal, that he was denounced at home, impeached, and subjected to a trial which dragged on for seven years in the House of Lords. He was finally acquitted. After Clive, whose interventions had rapidly expanded British power there during the 1750s, Hastings was the main author of British supremacy in India. Meanwhile, in 1784 an India office was created in the British ministry at home. The governor general henceforth ruled the growing British sphere in India almost as an absolute monarch but only as the agent of the ministry and Parliament of Great Britain.

Thus the trend in the British world was to centralization. Despite the flutter of royalism under George III, it was to a centralization of all British territories under the authority of Parliament. What was happening in empire affairs, as in domestic politics in England, was a continuing application of the principles of 1689. The parliamentary sovereignty established in 1689 was now, after the middle of the eighteenth century, being applied to regions where it had heretofore had little effect. And it was against the authority of the British Parliament that the Americans primarily rebelled.

✣ 40.   THE AMERICAN REVOLUTION

Background to the Revolution

The behavior of the Americans in the Seven Years' War, as viewed by the British government, left much to be desired. The several colonial legislatures rejected the Albany Plan of Union drafted by Franklin and commended to them by British officials. During the war it was the British regular army and navy, financed by taxes and loans in Great Britain, that drove the French out of America. The war effort of the Anglo-Americans was desultory at best. After the defeat of the French the colonials had still to reckon with the Indians of the interior, who preferred French rule to that of their new British and British-colonial masters. Many tribes joined in an uprising led by Pontiac, a western chief, and they carried their attacks on colonial and British outposts as far eastward as the Pennsylvania and Virginia frontiers. Again, the colonials proved unable to deal with a problem vital to their own future, and peace was brought about by officials and army units taking their orders from Great Britain.

The British government tried to make the colonials pay a larger share toward the expenses of the empire. The colonials had hitherto paid only local taxes. They were liable to customs duties, of which the proceeds went in principle to Great Britain; but these duties were levied to enforce the Acts of Trade and Navigation and to direct the flow of commerce, not to raise revenue; and they were seldom paid, because the Acts of Trade and Navigation were persistently ignored. American merchants, for example, commonly imported sugar from the French West Indies, contrary to law, and even shipped in return the iron wares which it was against the law for Americans to manufacture for export. The colonials in practice paid only such taxes as were approved by their own local legislature for local purposes. The Americans in effect enjoyed a degree of tax exemption within the empire, and it was against this form of provincial privilege that Parliament began to move.

By the Revenue Act of 1764 (the "Sugar" Act), the British ministry, while reducing and liberalizing the customs duties payable in America, entered upon a program of actual and systematic collection. In the following year the ministry attempted to extend to British subjects in America a tax peaceably accepted by those in Great Britain and commonplace in most of Europe. This imposed on all uses of paper, as in newspapers and commercial and legal documents, the payment of a fee that was certified by the affixing of a stamp. The Stamp Act aroused violent and concerted resistance in the colonies, especially among the businessmen, lawyers, and editors who were the most articulate class. It therefore was repealed in 1766. In 1767 Parliament, clumsily casting about to find a tax acceptable to the Americans, hit upon the "Townshend duties," which taxed colonial imports of paper, paint, lead, and tea. Another outcry went up, and the Townshend duties were repealed, except the one on tea, which was kept as a token of the sovereign power of Parliament to tax all persons in the empire.

Colonial resistance to new taxes

The colonials had proved stubborn, the government pliable but lacking in constructive ideas. The Americans argued that Parliament had no authority to tax them because they were not represented in it. The British replied that Parliament represented America as much as it represented Great Britain. If Philadelphia sent no actually elected deputies to the Commons, so this argument ran, neither did Manchester in England. Both places enjoyed a kind of "virtual representation," since members of the Commons did not merely speak for local constituencies but made themselves responsible for imperial interests as a whole. To this

Debate over representation

many Americans retorted that if Manchester was not "really" represented it ought to be, which was of course also the belief of the English reformers. Meanwhile the strictly Anglo-American question subsided after the repeal of the Stamp Act and the Townshend program. There had been no clarification of principle on either side. But in practice the Americans had resisted significant taxation, and Parliament had refrained from making any drastic use of its sovereign power.

The calm was shattered in 1773 by an event which proved, to the more dissatisfied Americans, the disadvantages of belonging to a global economic system in which the main policies were made on the other side of the ocean. The East India Company was in difficulties. It had a great surplus of Chinese tea, and in any case it wanted new commercial privileges in return for the political privileges which it was losing in India by the Regulating Act of 1773. In the past the company had been required to sell its wares at public auction in London; other merchants had handled distribution from that point on. Now, in 1773, Parliament granted the company the exclusive right to sell tea through its own agents in America to American local dealers. Tea was a large item of business in the commercial capitalism of the time. The colonial consumer might pay less for it, but the intermediary American merchant would be shut out. The company's tea was boycotted in all American ports. In Boston, to prevent its forcible landing, a party of disguised men invaded the tea ships and dumped the chests into the harbor. To this act of vandalism the British government replied by measures far out of proportion to the offense. It "closed" the port of Boston, thus threatening the city with economic ruin. It virtually rescinded the charter of Massachusetts, forbidding certain local elections and the holding of town meetings.

The Boston Tea Party

And at the same time, in 1774, apparently by coincidence, Parliament enacted the Quebec Act. The wisest piece of British legislation in these troubled years, the Quebec Act provided a government for the newly conquered Canadian French, granting them security in their French civil law and Catholic religion and laying foundations for the British Empire that was to come. But the act defined the boundaries of Quebec somewhat as the French themselves would have defined them, including in them all territory north of the Ohio River—the present states of Wisconsin, Michigan, Illinois, Indiana, and Ohio. In the view of British legislators these boundaries were perfectly reasonable, since the few Europeans in the area were French, and since, in the age before canals or railways, the obvious means of reaching the whole region was by way of the St. Lawrence valley and the Lakes. But to the Americans the Quebec Act was a pro-French and pro-Catholic outrage, and at a time when the powers of juries and assemblies in the old colonies were threatened, it was disquieting that the Quebec Act made no mention of such representative institutions for the new northern province. It was lumped with the closing of an American port and the destruction of the Massachusetts government as one of the "Intolerable Acts" to be resisted.

The Quebec Act

And indeed the implications of parliamentary sovereignty and centralized planning were now apparent. It was no longer merely an affair of taxation. A government that had to take account of the East India Company, the French Canadians, and the British taxpayers, even if more prudent and enlightened than Lord North's ministry of 1774, could not possibly at the same time have satisfied the Americans of the thirteen seaboard colonies. These Americans, since 1763 no longer afraid of the French empire, were less inclined to forgo their own interests in order to remain under British protection or control. British policies had aroused antagonism in the coastal towns and in the backwoods, among wealthy land speculators and poor squatter frontiersmen, among merchants and the workers who depended on the business of merchants. The freedom of Americans to determine their own

MRS. ISAAC SMITH

by John Singleton Copley (American, then English, 1737–1815)

The wife of a Boston merchant, Mrs. Smith represents the bourgeois family background of many leaders in the American and French revolutions. In general, it was a background of substance, comfort, and hard work. Mrs. Smith's costume and surroundings (though less elegant than those portrayed in the painting of Mrs. Graham on p. 333) suggest her high station in New England society. Copley disliked the rising revolutionary agitation in America and emigrated permanently to England in 1774.

(Yale University Art Gallery, Gift of Maitland Fuller Griggs, B.A. 1869, LHD 1938 (1941.74), (detail)) political life was in question. Yet there were few in 1774, or even later, prepared to face the thought of independence.

The War of American Independence

After the "Intolerable Acts," self-authorized groups met in the several colonies and sent delegates to a "continental congress" in Philadelphia. This body adopted a boycott of British goods, to be enforced on unwilling Americans by local organizers of resistance. Fighting began in the next year, 1775, when the British commander at Boston sent a detachment to seize unauthorized stores of weapons at Concord. On the way, at Lexington, in a brush between soldiers and partisans, or "minute-men," someone fired the "shot heard round the world." The Second Continental Congress, meeting a few weeks later, proceeded to raise an American army, appointed George Washington as the commanding general of its troops, dispatched an expedition to force Quebec into the revolutionary union, and entered into overtures with Bourbon France.

The "shot heard round the world"

The Congress was still reluctant to repudiate the tie with Britain. But passions grew fierce in consequence of the fighting. Radicals convinced moderates that the choice now lay between independence and enslavement. It appeared that the French, naturally uninterested in a reconciliation of British subjects, would give help if the avowed aim of American rebels was to dismember the British Empire. In January 1776 Thomas Paine, in his pamphlet *Common Sense,* made his debut as a kind of international revolutionary; he was to figure in the French Revolution and to work for revolution in England. He had come from England less than two years before, and he detested English society for its injustices. Eloquent and vitriolic, *Common Sense* identified the independence of the American colonies with the cause of liberty for all humankind. It pitted freedom against tyranny in the person of "the royal brute of Great Britain." It was "repugnant to reason," said Paine, "to suppose that this Continent can long remain subject to any external power. . . . There is something absurd in supposing a Continent to be perpetually governed by an island." *Common Sense* was read everywhere in the colonies, and its slashing arguments unquestionably spread a sense of proud isolation from the Old World. Such ideas also gained wide support in the Continental Congress, where Thomas Jefferson and other members of a special committee began drafting a theoretical and historical justification for America's separation from Britain. Like Paine, the authors linked their specific grievances to broad Enlightenment claims for universal human rights, thus giving the widest possible significance to the armed rebellion of some sparsely settled colonies in Britain's far-flung eighteenth-century empire. On July 4, 1776, the Congress adopted the Declaration of Independence, by which the United States assumed its separate and equal station among the powers of the earth.

Role of the European powers

The War of American Independence thereupon turned into another European struggle for empire. For two years more the French government remained ostensibly noninterventionist but meanwhile poured munitions into the colonies through an especially rigged-up commercial concern. Nine-tenths of the arms used by the Americans at the battle of Saratoga came from France. After the American victory in this battle the French government concluded, in 1778, that the insurgents were a good political risk, recognized them, signed an alliance with them, and declared war on Great Britain. Spain soon followed, hoping to drive the British from Gibraltar and deciding that its overseas empire was more threatened by a restoration of British supremacy in North America than by the disturbing example of an independent American republic. The Dutch were drawn into hostilities through their trade with the Americans, which flowed mostly by way of the Dutch West Indies. Other powers—Russia, Sweden, Denmark, Prussia, Portugal, and Turkey—irked at British employment of blockade and sea power in time of war, formed an "Armed Neutrality" to protect their commerce from dictation by the British fleet. The French, in a brief revival of their own sea power, landed an expeditionary force of 6,000 men in Rhode Island. The Americans suffered from the internal differences inseparable from all revolutions and were in any case still unable to govern themselves to any effect, meeting with the old difficulties in raising both troops and money. It was therefore the participation of regiments of the French army, in conjunction with squadrons of the French fleet, that made possible the defeat of the armed forces of the British Empire and so persuaded the British government to recognize the independence of the United States. By the peace treaty of 1783, though the British were still in possession of New York and Savannah and though the governments befriending the Americans would just as soon have confined them east of the mountains, the new republic obtained territory as far west as the Mississippi. Canada remained British. It received an English-speaking population by the settlement of over 60,000 refugee Americans who remained loyal to Great Britain.

Significance of the Revolution

The upheaval in America was a revolution as well as a war of independence. The cry for liberty against Great Britain raised echoes within the colonies themselves. The Declaration of Independence was more than an announcement of secession from the empire; it was a justification of rebellion against established authority. Curiously, although the American quarrel had been with the Parliament, the Declaration arraigned no one but the king. One reason was that the Congress, not recognizing the authority of Parliament, could separate from Great Britain only by a denunciation of the British crown; another reason was that the cry of "tyrant" made a more popular and flaming issue. Boldly voicing the natural right philosophy of the age, the Declaration held as "self-evident"—that is, as evident to all reasonable people—that "all men are created equal, that they are endowed by their Creator with certain unalienable rights, that among these are life, liberty, and the pursuit of happiness." These electrifying words leaped inward into America and outward to the world.

The Declaration of Independence

In the new states democratic equality made many advances. It was subject, however, to a great limitation, in that it long applied only to white males of European origin. It was more than a century before women received the vote. American Indians were relatively few in number, but the black population at the time of the Revolution comprised about a fifth of the whole. Many American whites of the revolutionary generation were indeed troubled by the institution of slavery. It was abolished outright in Massachusetts, and all states north of Maryland took steps toward its gradual extinction. But application of the principles of liberty and equality without regard to race or gender went far beyond the political and cultural assumptions of even the most enlightened white Americans at the time. In the South, all censuses from 1790 to 1850 showed a third of the population to be slaves. In the North, free blacks found that in fact, and often in law, they were debarred from voting, from adequate schooling, and from the widening opportunities in which white Americans saw the essence of their national life and their superiority to Europe.

Equality advances and limitations

Brief, violent clashes in Massachusetts in April 1775 launched the long military struggle of the American Revolution. This picture shows the local militia exchanging fire in the village of Lexington with a detachment of the British army that had been sent from Boston to search for arms that American rebels were collecting in the area.

(Photo from the collection of the Lexington, Massachusetts, Historical Society)

For the white male population the Revolution had a democratizing effect in many ways. Lawyers, landowners, and businessmen who led the movement against England needed the support of numbers and to obtain it were willing to make promises and concessions to the lower classes. Or the popular elements, workmen and mechanics, farmers and frontiersmen, often dissidents in religion, extorted concessions by force or threats. There was a good deal of violence, as in all revolutions; the new states confiscated property from the counterrevolutionaries, called Tories, some of whom were tarred and feathered by infuriated mobs. The dissolution of the old

Democratization

colonial governments threw open all political questions. In some states more men became qualified to vote. In some, governors and senators were now popularly elected, in addition to the lower houses of the legislatures as in colonial times. The principle was adopted, still unknown to the parliamentary bodies of Europe, that each member of a legislative assembly should represent about the same number of citizens. Primogeniture and entail, which landed families aspiring to an aristocratic mode of life sometimes favored, went down before the demands of democrats and small property owners. Tithes were done away with, and the established churches—Anglican in the South, Congregationalist in New England—lost their privileged position in varying degree. But the Revolution was not socially as profound as the revolution soon to come in France, or as the revolution in Russia in 1917. Property changed hands, but the law of property was modified only in detail. There had been no such thing in British America as a native nobleman or even a bishop; clergy and aristocracy had been incomparably less ingrained in American than in European society, and the rebellion against them was less devastating in its effect.

The main importance of the American Revolution remained political and even constitutional in a strict sense. The American leaders were themselves part of the Age of Enlightenment, sharing fully in its humane and secular spirit. But probably the only non-British thinker by whom they were influenced was Montesquieu, and Montesquieu owed his popularity to his philosophizing upon English institutions. The Americans drew heavily on the writings of John Locke, but their cast of mind went back before Locke to the English Puritan movement of the first half of the seventeenth century. Their thought was formed not only by Locke's ideas of human nature and government, but, as already noted, by the dissenting literature and the neorepublican writings that had never quite died out in England. The realities of life for five generations in America had sharpened the old insistence upon personal liberty and equality. When the dispute with Britain came to a head, the Americans found themselves arguing both for the historic and chartered rights of the English and for the timeless and universal rights of man, both of which were held up as barriers against the inroads of parliamentary sovereignty. The Americans came to believe, more than any other people, that government should possess limited powers and operate only within the terms of a fixed and written constitutional document.

Influence of Enlightenment thinkers

All 13 of the new states lost no time in providing themselves with written constitutions (in Connecticut and Rhode Island merely the old charters reaffirmed), all of which enshrined virtually the same principles. All followed the thought stated in the great Declaration, that it was to protect "unalienable" rights that governments were instituted among men and that whenever government became destructive to this end the people had a right to "institute new government" for their safety and happiness. All the constitutions undertook to limit government by a separation of executive, legislative, and judicial powers. Most appended a bill of rights, stating the natural rights of the citizens and the actions which no government might justly take. None of the constitutions were as yet fully democratic; even the most liberal gave some advantage in public affairs to the owners of property.

Constitutionalism and federalism

Federalism, or the allocation of power between central and outlying governments, went along with the idea of written constitutions as a principal offering of the Americans to the world. Like constitutionalism, federalism developed in the atmosphere of protest against a centralized sovereign power. It was a hard idea for Americans to work out, since the new states carried over the old separatism which had so distracted the British. Until 1789 the states remained banded together in the

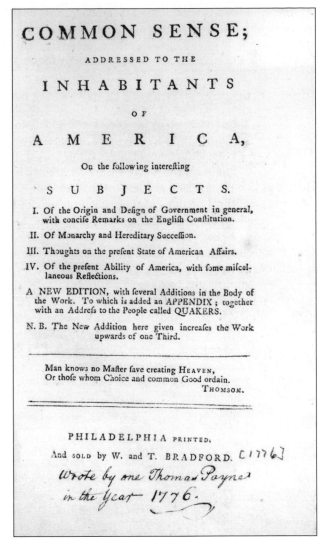

COMMON SENSE;

ADDRESSED TO THE

INHABITANTS

OF

AMERICA,

On the following interesting

SUBJECTS.

I. Of the Origin and Design of Government in general,
with concise Remarks on the English Constitution.

II. Of Monarchy and Hereditary Succession.

III. Thoughts on the present State of American Affairs.

IV. Of the present Ability of America, with some miscellaneous Reflections.

A NEW EDITION, with several Additions in the Body of
the Work. To which is added an APPENDIX ; together
with an Address to the People called QUAKERS.

N. B. The New Addition here given increases the Work
upwards of one Third.

Man knows no Master save creating HEAVEN,
Or those whom Choice and common Good ordain.
THOMSON.

PHILADELPHIA PRINTED,

And SOLD by W. and T. BRADFORD. [1776]

*Wrote by one Thomas Payne
in the year — 1776.*

Thomas Paine (1737–1809) lived in England until he arrived in Philadelphia in 1774. He published his *Common Sense* anonymously two years later, after the armed conflict had begun. Widely read, it helped persuade Americans to fight for complete independence from Britain.
(Library of Congress)

Articles of Confederation. The United States was a union of 13 independent republics. Disadvantages in this scheme becoming apparent, a constitutional convention met at Philadelphia in 1787 and drew up the constitution which is today the world's oldest written instrument of government still in operation. In it the United States was conceived not merely as a league of states but as a union in which individuals were citizens of the United States of America for some purposes and of their particular states for others. Persons, not states, composed the federal republic, and the laws of the United States fell not merely on the states but on the people.

The consequences of the American Revolution can hardly be overstated. By overburdening the French treasury, the American war became a direct cause of the French Revolution. Beyond that, it ushered in the age of predominantly liberal or democratic revolution which lasted through the European revolutions of 1848. The American doctrine, like most thought in the Age of Enlightenment, was expressed in universal terms of "man" and "nature." All peoples regardless of their own history could apply it to themselves, because, as Alexander Hamilton once put it in his youth, "the sacred rights of man are not to be rummaged for among old parchments or musty records. They are written, as with a sunbeam, in the whole volume of human nature, by the hand of Divinity itself, and can never be erased or obscured by mortal power." The Americans, in freeing themselves, had done what all peoples ought to do.

Significance of American Revolution

The revolt in America offered a dramatic judgment on the old colonial system, convincing some, in England and elsewhere, that the empires for which they had long been struggling were hardly worth acquiring, since colonies in time, in the words of Turgot, fell away from the mother country "like ripe fruit." The idea spread, since trade between Britain and America continued to prosper, that one could do business with a country without exerting political influence or control, and this idea became fundamental to the coming movement of economic liberalism and free trade. By coincidence, the book that became the gospel of the free trade movement, Adam Smith's *Wealth of Nations,* was published in England in the year 1776. The American example was pointed to by other peoples wishing to throw off colonial status—first by the Latin Americans, then by the peoples of the older British dominions, and, finally, in the twentieth century, by those of Asia and Africa also. In Europe, the American example encouraged the type of nationalism in which subjugated nations aspire to be free. And at home the Revolution did much to determine the spirit and method by which the new nation spread across the North American continent and the ideas by which the United States, when it became a leading power a century and a half later, would explain and justify its national actions in the modern world.

More immediately, the American example was not lost on the many Europeans who sojourned in the new states during and after the war. Of these the Marquis de Lafayette was the most famous, but there were many others: Thomas Paine, who returned to Europe in 1787; the future French revolutionist Brissot; the future Polish national leader Kosciusko; the future marshals of Napoleon, Jourdan and Berthier; the future reformer of the Prussian army Gneisenau. Contrariwise various Americans went to Europe, notably the aging Benjamin Franklin, who in the 1780s was incredibly lionized in the fashionable and literary world of Paris.

Vindication of Enlightenment ideas

The establishment of the United States was taken in Europe to prove that many ideas of the Enlightenment were practicable. Rationalists declared that here was a people, free of past errors and superstitions, who showed how enlightened beings could plan their affairs. Rousseauists saw in America the very paradise of natural equality, unspoiled innocence, and patriotic virtue. But nothing so much impressed Europeans, and especially the French, as the spectacle of the Americans meeting in solemn conclave to draft their state constitutions. These, along with the Declaration of Independence, were translated and published in 1778 by a French nobleman, the Duke de la Rochefoucauld. They were endlessly and excitedly discussed. Constitutionalism, federalism, and limited government were not new ideas in Europe. They came out of the Middle Ages and were currently set forth in many quarters, for example, in Hungary, the Holy Roman Empire, and the Parlement of Paris. But in their prevailing form, and even in the philosophy of Montesquieu, they were associated with feudalism and aristocracy. The American Revolution made such ideas progressive. The American influence, added to the force of developments in Europe, made the thought of the later Enlightenment more democratic. The United States replaced England as the model country of advanced thinkers. On the Continent there was less passive trust in

DECLARATION OF INDEPENDENCE
by John Trumbull (American, 1756–1843)

Trumbull's painting shows the committee that presented America's Declaration of Independence to the Continental Congress in 1776. Although Franklin and Adams are standing with the committee, Thomas Jefferson is presenting the document. Trumbull met often with Jefferson in Paris when he was at work on this painting in the late 1780s, and the picture conveys a Jeffersonian view of the event it portrays.

(Yale University Art Gallery, Trumbull Collection (1832.3))

the enlightened despotism of the official state. Confidence in self-government was aroused.

The American constitutions seemed a demonstration of the social contract. They offered a picture of men in a "state of nature," having cast off their old government, deliberately sitting down to contrive a new one, weighing and judging each branch of government on its merits, assigning due powers to legislature, executive, and judiciary, declaring that all government was created by the people and in possession of a merely delegated authority, and listing specifically the inalienable human rights—inalienable in that they could not conceivably be taken away, since all persons possessed them even if denied them by force. And these rights were the very same rights that many Europeans wanted secured for themselves—freedom of religion, freedom of press, freedom of assembly, freedom from arbitrary arrest at the discretion of officials. And they were all based on the rigorous principle of equality before the law. The American example crystallized and made tangible the ideas that were strongly blowing in Europe, and the American example was one reason why the French, in 1789, began their revolution with a declaration of human rights and with the drafting of a written constitution.

And more deeply still, America became a kind of mirage or ideal vision for Europe, land of open opportunity and of new beginnings, free from the load of history and of the past, wistfully addressed by Goethe:

> *America, thou hast it better*
> *Than has our Continent, the old one.*

It is evident that this was only part of the picture. The United States, as its later history was to show, bore a heavy load of inherited burdens and unsolved problems, especially slavery and pervasive racial discrimination. But in a general way, until new revolutionary and radical social movements set in a century later, America stood as a kind of utopian opportunity for common people, not only for the millions who emigrated to it but for other millions who stayed at home, who often wished that their own countries might become more like it, and many of whom might even agree with Abraham Lincoln in calling it the last best hope of earth.

For interactive exercises, glossary, chronologies, and more, go to the *Online Learning Center* at **www.mhhe.com/palmer10.**

Chapter 9

THE FRENCH REVOLUTION

In 1789 France fell into revolution, and the world has never since been the same. The French Revolution was by far the most momentous upheaval of the whole revolutionary age. It replaced the "old regime" with "modern society," and at its extreme phase it became very radical, so much so that later revolutionary movements often looked back to it as a predecessor. The ideas of the French Revolution, spreading far beyond France itself, decisively influenced the subsequent development of political parties and ideological conflicts throughout much of Europe and elsewhere; indeed, the Revolution still provokes highly charged debates about the characteristics or consequences of social reform, political radicalism, and revolutionary violence. At the time, in the age of the Democratic or Atlantic Revolution from the 1760s to 1848, the role of France was decisive. Even the Americans, without French military intervention, would hardly have won such a clear settlement from England or been so free to set up the new states and new constitutions that have just been described. And while revolutionary disturbances in Ireland and Poland, or among the Dutch, Italians, and others, were by no means caused by the French example, it was the presence or absence of French aid that usually determined whatever successes they achieved.

The French Revolution, unlike the Russian or Chinese revolutions of the twentieth century, occurred in what was in many ways the most advanced country of the day. France was the center of the intellectual movement of the Enlightenment. French science then led the world. French books were read everywhere, and the newspapers and political journals that became very numerous after 1789 carried a message that hardly needed translation.

Chapter emblem: Detail from *The Tennis Court Oath* by Jacques-Louis David (1748–1825). (Giraudon/Art Resource, NY)

French was a kind of international spoken language in the educated and aristocratic circles of many countries. France was also, potentially before 1789 and actually after 1793, the most powerful country in Europe. It may have been the wealthiest, though not per capita. With a population of 24,000,000 the French were the most numerous of all European peoples under a single government. Even Russia was hardly more populous until after the partitions of Poland. The Germans were divided, the subjects of the Habsburgs were of diverse nationalities, and the English and Scots together numbered only 10,000,000. Paris, though smaller than London, was over twice as large as Vienna or Amsterdam. French exports to Europe were larger than those of Great Britain. It is said that half the goldpieces circulating in Europe were French. Europeans in the eighteenth century were in the habit of taking ideas from France; they were therefore, depending on their social position, the more excited, encouraged, alarmed, or horrified when revolution broke out in that country.

41.   BACKGROUNDS

The Old Regime: The Three Estates

Some remarks have already been made about the Old Regime, as the prerevolutionary society came to be called after it disappeared, and about the failure of enlightened despotism in France to alter it in any fundamental way. The essential fact about the Old Regime was that it was still legally aristocratic and in some ways feudal. Everyone belonged legally to an "estate" or "order" of society. The First Estate was the clergy, the Second Estate was the nobility, and the Third Estate included everyone else—from the wealthiest business and professional classes to the poorest peasantry and city workers. These categories were important in that the individual's legal rights and personal prestige depended on the category to which he or she belonged. Politically, they were obsolescent; not since 1614 had the estates assembled in an Estates General of the whole kingdom, though in some provinces they had continued to meet as provincial bodies. Socially, they were obsolescent also, for the threefold division no longer corresponded to the real distribution of interest, influence, property, or productive activity among the French people.

The church

Conditions in the church and the position of the clergy have in the past been much exaggerated as a cause of the French Revolution. The church in France levied a tithe on all agricultural products, but so did the church in England; the French bishops often played a part in government affairs, but so did bishops in England through the House of Lords. The French bishoprics of 1789 were in reality no wealthier than those of the Church of England were found to be when investigated 40 years later. In actual numbers, in the secular atmosphere of the Age of Enlightenment, the clergy, especially the monastic orders, had greatly declined, so that by 1789 there were probably not more than 100,000 Catholic clergy of all types in the entire population. But if the importance of the clergy has been overemphasized, still it must be said that the church was deeply involved in the prevailing social system. For one thing, church bodies—bishoprics, abbeys, convents, schools, and other religious foundations—owned between 5 and 10 percent of the land of the country, which meant that collectively the church was the greatest of all landowners. Moreover, the income from church properties, like all income, was divided very unequally, and much of it found its way into the hands of the aristocratic occupants of the higher ecclesiastical offices.

This image of French peasants shows how farmers prepared their fields and planted seeds during the 1760s, when the picture was published in a French book. The agrarian system shaped property rights and social hierarchies as well as the supply of food in French cities—all of which created resentments or fears that contributed to the coming of the French Revolution.

(Ann Ronan Picture Library/HIP/ The Image Works)

The noble order, which in 1789 comprised about 400,000 persons, including women and children, had enjoyed a great resurgence since the death of Louis XIV in 1715. Distinguished government service, higher church offices, army, parlements, and most other public and semipublic honors were almost monopolized by the nobility in the time of Louis XVI, who, it will be recalled, had mounted the throne in 1774. Repeatedly, through parlements, Provincial Estates, or the assembly of the clergy dominated by the noble bishops, the aristocracy had blocked royal plans for taxation and shown a desire to control the policies of state. At the same time the bourgeoisie, or upper crust of the Third Estate, had never been so influential. Although the "bourgeoisie" was an amorphous social category (indeed, some historians argue that "bourgeois" refers to a class that never had a real social identity), the number of French merchants, lawyers, and other professional groups clearly grew over the course of the eighteenth century. The fivefold increase of French foreign trade between 1713 and 1789 suggests the growth of the merchant class and of the legal and governmental classes associated with it. As members of the bourgeoisie became stronger, more widely read, and more self-confident, they resented the distinctions enjoyed by the nobles. Some of these were financial: nobles were exempt on principle from the most important direct tax, the taille, whereas bourgeois obtained exemption with more effort; but so many bourgeois enjoyed tax privileges that purely monetary self-interest was not

The nobility

primary in their psychology. The bourgeois resented the nobleman for his superiority and his arrogance. What had formerly been customary respect was now felt as humiliation. And they felt that they were being shut out from office and honors and that the nobles were seeking more power in government as a class. The Revolution thus began in the social and political collision of two moving objects, a rising aristocracy and a rising bourgeoisie.

The Third Estate

The common people, below the commercial and professional families in the Third Estate, were probably as well off as in most countries. But they were not well off compared with the upper classes. Wage earners had by no means shared in the wave of business prosperity. Between the 1730s and the 1780s the prices of consumers' goods rose about 65 percent, whereas wages rose only 22 percent. Persons dependent on wages were therefore badly pinched, but they were less numerous than today, for in the country there were many small farmers and in the towns many small craftsmen who made a living not by wages but by selling the product of their own labor at market prices. Yet in both town and country there was a significant wage-earning population, which was to play a decisive part in the Revolution.

The Agrarian System of the Old Regime

Over four-fifths of the people were rural. The agrarian system had developed so that there was no serfdom in France as it was known in eastern Europe. The peasant owed no labor to the lord—except a few token services in some cases. The peasants worked for themselves, either on their own land or on rented land; or they worked as sharecroppers (*métayers*); or they hired themselves out to the lord or to another peasant.

Survival of feudal privileges

The manor, however, still retained certain surviving features of the feudal age. The noble owner of a manor enjoyed "hunting rights," or the privilege of keeping game preserves and of hunting on his own and the peasants' land. He usually had a monopoly over the village mill, bakeshop, or wine press, for the use of which he collected fees called *banalités*. He possessed certain vestigial powers of jurisdiction in the manorial court and certain local police powers, from which fees and fines were collected. These seigneurial privileges were of course the survivals of a day when the local manor had been a unit of government and the noble had performed the functions of government, an age that had long passed with the development of the centralized modern state.

There was another special feature to the property system of the Old Regime. Every owner of a manor (there were some bourgeois and even wealthy peasants who had purchased manors) possessed what was called a right of "eminent property" with respect to all land located in the manorial village. This meant that lesser landowners within the manor "owned" their land in that they could freely buy, sell, lease, and inherit or bequeath it; but they owed to the owner of the manor, in recognition of his "eminent property" rights, certain rents, payable annually, as well as transfer fees that were payable whenever the land changed owners by sale or death. Subject to these "eminent property" rights, landownership was fairly widespread. Peasants directly owned about two-fifths of the soil of the country; bourgeois, a little under a fifth. The nobility owned perhaps a little over a fifth and the church owned somewhat under a tenth, the remainder being crown lands, wastelands, or commons. Finally, all property rights were subject also to certain "collective" rights by which villagers might cut firewood, run their pigs in the commons, or pasture cattle on land belonging to other owners after the crops were in, which they could easily do because there were usually no fences or enclosures.

All this may seem rather complex, but it is important to realize that property is a changing institution. Even today, in industrialized countries, a high proportion of all property is in land, including natural resources in and below the soil. In the eighteenth century property meant land even more than it does today. The bourgeois class, whose wealth was so largely in ships, merchandise, or commercial paper, also invested heavily in land, and in 1789 they owned almost as much land in France as the nobility and more than the church. The Revolution was to revolutionize the law of property by freeing the private ownership of land from all the indirect encumbrances described—manorial fees, "eminent property" rights, communal village agricultural practices, and church tithes. It also was to abolish other older forms of property, such as property in public office or in masterships in the guilds, which had worked to the advantage mainly of closed and privileged groups. In final effect the Revolution defined and established the institutions of private property in the modern sense and therefore mostly benefited the landowning peasants and the bourgeoisie.

The peasants not only owned two-fifths of the soil but also worked almost all of it on their own initiative and risk. In effect, the land owned by the nobility, the church, the bourgeoisie, and the crown was divided up and leased to peasants in small parcels. France was already a country of small farmers. There was no "big agriculture" as in England, eastern Europe, or the plantations of America. The manorial lord performed no economic function. He lived (there were of course exceptions) not by managing an estate and selling his own crops and cattle but by receiving innumerable dues and fees. During the eighteenth century, in connection with the general aristocratic resurgence, there took place a phenomenon often called the "feudal reaction." Manorial lords, faced with rising living costs and acquiring higher living standards because of the general material progress, collected their dues more

The "feudal reaction"

rigorously or revived old ones that had fallen into disuse. Leases and sharecropping arrangements also became less favorable to the peasants. The farmers, like the wage earners, were under a steadily increasing pressure. At the same time the peasants resented the "feudal dues" more than ever because they regarded themselves as in many cases the real owners of the land and viewed the lord as a gentleman of the neighborhood who for no reason enjoyed a special income and a status different from their own. The trouble was that much of the property system no longer bore any relation to real economic usefulness or activity.

The political unity of France, achieved over the centuries by the monarchy, was likewise a fundamental prerequisite, and even a cause, of the Revolution. Whatever social conditions might have existed, they could give rise to nationwide public opinion, nationwide agitation, nationwide policies, and nationwide legislation only in a country already politically unified as a nation. These conditions were lacking in central Europe. In France a centralized French state existed. Reformers did not have to create it but only capture and remodel it. The French in the eighteenth century already had the sense of membership in a political entity called France. The Revolution saw a tremendous stirring of this sense of membership and of fraternity, turning it into a passion for citizenship, civic rights, voting powers, and the use of the state and its sovereignty for the public advantage. At the very outbreak of the Revolution people saluted each other as *citoyen* or *citoyenne* and shouted *vive la nation!*

Political Culture and Public Opinion after 1770

The social and economic resentments that existed among ambitious people in French cities and among peasants in the French countryside could finally explode in a revolutionary upheaval because eighteenth-century writers had created a culture that

The Revolution and the Enlightenment

encouraged political and social criticism. Educated persons in the Third Estate could draw on Enlightenment conceptions of reason, natural rights, and historical progress to complain about the irrationality of ancient privileges or the injustice of noble prerogatives. Enlightenment thought provided a language in which people could now describe their dissatisfactions with the obstacles that stymied professional or economic ambitions.

It has been argued that the famous works of the French philosophes led directly to the revolutionary events of 1789; it was the "fault" of Voltaire, critics explained; it was the "fault" of Rousseau. Many who supported the Revolution also made such claims for its intellectual origins, so that the history of the French Revolution has always been linked in complex ways with the legacy of the Enlightenment. Yet most historians now argue that the connections between the philosophes and the Revolution were by no means as direct as people once imagined. The philosophes themselves favored enlightened social reforms, but they were not revolutionaries and, except perhaps for Rousseau, they rarely promoted the political rights of the lower classes. Their most important publications, including the famous *Encyclopédie,* often attracted more readers among the nobility than among the middle classes. Political theory was far less popular than novels or social satires; there was an enormous audience for Rousseau's *Nouvelle Héloise,* for example, but few persons read the *Social Contract.* The notion that great Enlightenment writers "caused" the French Revolution is therefore an inadequate explanation for what happened (much as claims that bourgeois economic interests "caused" the Revolution are also inadequate). It is nevertheless true that the Enlightenment contributed widely to new forms of criticism, public debate, and "public opinion," most of which challenged the traditional authority of the French king and nobles.

The last two decades of the Old Regime were filled with intense political controversy as the monarchy sought unsuccessfully to suppress the traditional French parlements, as successive ministries sought to raise new revenues, as French journals reported on the new American state constitutions, and as pamphleteers increasingly attacked the officials and courtiers at Versailles. The critical spirit that had developed in salons, cof-

Critical spirit

feehouses, and literary arguments spread rapidly into a developing public sphere of political debate. The new political pamphlets were scarcely concerned with the subtle nuances of political theory; in fact, many consisted of little more than scandalous rumors of sexual misconduct or financial corruption in the affairs of the royal family and government ministries. Stories of corruption in high places stripped away the once sacred image of the monarchy, the church, and the social hierarchy. At the same time, the reading public developed an interest in scandalous legal cases that pitted members of the aristocracy against aggrieved persons of the Third Estate or that revealed immorality and decadence among ancient noble families. Lawyers could publish their legal briefs without securing the approval of government censors, and, using this freedom, they bolstered their legal arguments with appeals to popular sentiment or natural rights. The injustice of inherited privilege thus became a recurring theme in the scandalous stories of social and personal disputes that French lawyers carried from French courtrooms to the tribunal of "public opinion."

By 1789, in France, educated persons in all social classes were coming to believe what Voltaire had said after the famous Calas Affair in the 1760s: "Opinion governs the world." Campaigns to influence public opinion became a powerful political force in French society during the last decades of the Old Regime, and most such campaigns appealed for public support in the name of reason, rights, or justice. In these ways, the critical thought of Enlightenment culture entered into bitter political conflicts that led finally and unexpectedly to the Revolution.

42. THE REVOLUTION AND THE REORGANIZATION OF FRANCE

The Financial Crisis

The Revolution was precipitated by a financial collapse of the government. What overburdened the government was by no means the costly magnificence of the court of Versailles. Only five percent of public expenditures in 1788 was devoted to the upkeep of the entire royal establishment. What overburdened all governments was war costs, both current upkeep of armies and navies and the burden of public debt, which in all countries was due almost totally to the war costs of the past. In 1788 the French government devoted about a quarter of its annual expenditure to maintenance of the armed forces and about half to the payment of its debts. British expenditures showed almost the same distribution. The French debt stood at almost four billion livres. It had been greatly swollen by the War of American Independence. Yet it was only half as great as the national debt of Great Britain, and less than a fifth as heavy per capita. It was less than the debt of the Dutch Republic. It was apparently no greater than the debt left by Louis XIV three-quarters of a century before. At that time the debt had been lightened by repudiation. No responsible French official in the 1780s even considered repudiation, a sure sign of the progress in the interim of the well-to-do classes, who were the main government creditors.

Yet the debt could not be carried, for the simple reason that revenues fell short of necessary expenditures. This in turn was not due to national poverty but to the tax exemptions and tax evasions of privileged elements and to complications in the fiscal system, or lack of system, by which *Problems of taxation* much of what taxpayers paid never came into the hands of the Treasury. We have already described how the most important tax, the taille, was generally paid only by the peasants—the nobles being exempt by virtue of their class privilege, and office holders and bourgeois obtaining exemption in various ways. The church too insisted that its property was not taxable by the state; and its periodic "free gift" to the king, though substantial, was less than might have been obtained from direct taxation of the church's land. Thus, although the country itself was prosperous, the government treasury was empty. The social classes which enjoyed most of the wealth of the country did not pay taxes corresponding to their income—and, even worse, they resisted taxation as a sign of inferior status.

A long series of responsible persons—Louis XIV himself, John Law, Maupeou, Turgot—had seen the need for taxing the privileged classes. Jacques Necker, a Swiss banker made director of the finances in 1777 by Louis XVI, made moves in the same direction and, like his predecessors, was dismissed. His successor, Calonne, as the crisis mounted, came to even more revolutionary conclusions. In 1786 he produced a program in which enlightened despotism was tempered by a modest resort to representative institutions. He proposed, in place of the taille, a general tax to fall on all landowners without exemption, a lightening of indirect taxes and abolition of internal tariffs to stimulate economic production, and a confiscation of some properties of the church. He also sought to give the propertied elements a greater interest in the government by proposing the establishment of provincial assemblies in which all landowners should be represented without regard to estate or order.

Calonne's program, if carried out, might have solved the fiscal problem and averted the Revolution. But it struck not only at privileges in taxation—noble, provincial, and others—but also at the threefold hierarchic organization of society. Knowing from experience that the Parlement of Paris would never accept it, Calonne in 1787 convened an "assembly of notables," hoping to win its endorsement of his ideas. The notables insisted on concessions in return, for they wished to share in control of the government. A deadlock followed; the king dismissed Calonne and appointed as his successor Loménie de Brienne, the exceedingly worldly-wise archbishop of Toulouse. Brienne tried to push the same program through the Parlement of Paris. The Parlement rejected it, declaring that only the three estates of the realm, assembled in an Estates General, had authority to consent to new taxes. Brienne and Louis XVI at first refused, believing that the Estates General, if convened, would be dominated by the nobility. Like Maupeou and Louis XV, Brienne and Louis XVI tried to break the parlements, replacing them with a modernized judicial system in which the law courts should have no influence over policy. This led to a veritable revolt of the nobles. All the parlements and Provincial Estates resisted; army officers refused to serve; the intendants hesitated to act; and noblemen began to organize political clubs and committees of correspondence. With his government brought to a standstill, and unable to borrow money or collect taxes, Louis XVI on July 5, 1788, promised to call the Estates General for the following May. The various classes were invited to elect representatives and also to draw up lists of their grievances.

Resistance of the nobles

From Estates General to National Assembly

Since no Estates General had met in over a century and a half, the king asked for proposals on how such an assembly should be organized under modern conditions. This led to an outburst of public discussion, which soon expanded far beyond all previous campaigns to influence public opinion. Hundreds of political pamphlets appeared, many of them demanding a change in the old system by which the three estates sat in separate chambers, each chamber voting as a unit. This voting system was widely criticized because it meant, in practice, that the chamber of the Third Estate was always outnumbered. But in September 1788 the Parlement of Paris, restored to its functions, ruled that the Estates General should meet and vote as in 1614, in three separate orders.

The aims of the nobility

The nobility, through the Parlement, thus revealed its aim. It had forced the summoning of the Estates General, and in this way the French nobility initiated the Revolution. The Revolution began as another victory in the aristocratic resurgence against the absolutism of the king. The nobles actually had a liberal program: they demanded constitutional government, guarantees of personal liberty for all, freedom of speech and press, freedom from arbitrary arrest and confinement. Many now were even prepared to give up special privileges in taxation; this might have worked itself out in time. But in return they hoped to become the preponderant political element in the state. It was their idea not merely to have the Estates General meet in 1789 but for France to be henceforth governed through the Estates General, a supreme body in three chambers—one for nobles, one for a clergy in which the higher officers were also nobles, and one for the Third Estate.

This was precisely what the Third Estate wished to avoid. Lawyers, bankers, business owners, government creditors, shopkeepers, artisans, working people, and peasants had no desire to be governed by lords temporal and spiritual. Their hopes of a new era, formed by the philosophy of the Enlightenment, stirred by the revolution in America, rose to the utmost excitement when "good king Louis" called the Estates General. The ruling of the Parlement of Paris in September 1788 came to them as a slap in the face—an unprovoked class insult. The whole Third Estate turned on the nobility with detestation and distrust. The Abbé Sieyès in January 1789 launched his famous pamphlet *What Is the Third Estate?*, declaring that the nobility was a useless caste which could be abolished without loss, that the Third Estate was the one necessary element of society, that it was identical with the nation, and that the nation was absolutely and unqualifiedly sovereign. Through Sieyès the ideas of Rousseau's *Social Contract* entered the thought of the Revolution. At the same time, even before the Estates General actually met, and not from the books of philosophes so much as from actual events and conditions, nobles and commoners viewed each other with fear and suspicion. The Third Estate, which had at first supported the nobles against the "despotism" of the king's ministers, now ascribed to the former the worst possible motives. Bourgeois critics vehemently rejected the political program and ambitions of the nobility. Class antagonism poisoned the Revolution at the outset, made peaceful reform impossible, and threw many bourgeois without delay into a radical and destructive mood.

The Third Estate reacts

The Estates General met as planned in May 1789 at Versailles. The Third Estate, most of whose representatives were lawyers, would not accept the division of the orders into three separate chambers. It insisted that deputies of all three orders should sit as a single house and vote as individuals; this procedure would be of advantage to the Third Estate, since the king had granted it as many deputies as the other two orders combined. For six weeks a deadlock was maintained. On June 13 a few priests, leaving the chamber of the First Estate, came over and sat with the Third. They were greeted with jubilation. On June 17 the Third Estate declared itself the "National Assembly." Louis XVI, under pressure from the nobles, closed the hall in which it met. The members found a neighboring indoor tennis court and there, milling about in a babel of confusion and apprehension, swore and signed the Oath of the Tennis Court on June 20, 1789, affirming that wherever they foregathered the National Assembly was in existence and that they would not disband until they had drafted a constitution. This was a revolutionary step, for it assumed virtually sovereign power for a body that had no legal authority. The king ordered members of the three estates to sit in their separate houses. He now somewhat tardily presented a reforming program of his own, too late to win the confidence of the disaffected and in any case continuing the organization of French society in legal classes. The self-entitled National Assembly refused to back down. The king faltered, failed to enforce his commands promptly, and allowed the Assembly to remain in being. In the following days, at the end of June, he summoned about 18,000 soldiers to Versailles.

What had happened was that the king of France, in the dispute raging between nobles and commoners, chose the nobles. It was traditional in France for the king to oppose feudalism. For centuries the French monarchy had drawn strength from the bourgeoisie. All through the eighteenth century the royal ministers had carried on the struggle against the privileged interests. Only a year before, Louis XVI had been almost at war with his rebellious aristocracy. In 1789 he failed to assert himself. He lost control

OUVERTURE DES ÉTATS GÉNÉRAUX.
(D'après C. Monet.)

Convoked for the first time in 175 years, the Estates General met in a large hall at Versailles in May 1789. This picture shows Louis XVI seated on his throne, with deputies of the clergy seated on his right, those of the nobility on his left, and those of the Third Estate facing him at the other end of the hall.
(Culver Pictures)

over the Estates General, exerted no leadership, offered no program until it was too late, and provided no symbol behind which parties could rally. He failed to make use of the profound loyalty to himself felt by the bourgeoisie and common people, who yearned for nothing so much as a king who would stand up for them, as in days of yore, against an aristocracy of birth and status. He tried instead, at first, to compromise and postpone a crisis; then he found himself in the position of having issued orders which the Third Estate boldly defied; and in this embarrassing predicament he yielded to his wife Marie Antoinette, to his brothers, and to the court nobles with whom he lived and who told him that his dignity and authority were outraged and undermined. At the end of June Louis XVI undoubtedly intended to dissolve the Estates General by military force. But what the Third Estate most feared was not a return to the old theoretically absolute monarchy. It was a future in which the aristocracy should control the government of the country. There was now no going back; the revolt of the Third Estate had allied Louis XVI with the nobles, and the Third Estate now feared the nobles more than ever, believing with good reason that they now had the king in their hands.

Failure of royal leadership

The Lower Classes in Action

The country meanwhile was falling into dissolution. The lower classes, below the bourgeoisie, were out of hand. For them too the convocation of the Estates General had seemed to herald a new era. The grievances of ages, and those which existed equally in other countries than France, rose to the surface. Short-run conditions were bad. The harvest of 1788 had been poor; the price of bread, by July 1789, was higher than at any time since the death of Louis XIV. The year 1789 was also one of depression; the rapid growth of trade since the American war had suddenly halted, so that wages fell and unemployment spread while scarcity drove food prices up. The government, paralyzed at the center, could not take such measures of relief as were customary under the Old Regime. The masses were everywhere restless. Labor trouble broke out; in April a riot of workers devastated a wallpaper factory in Paris. In the rural districts there was much disorder. Peasants declared that they would pay no more manorial dues and were refusing to pay taxes. In the best of times the countryside was troubled by vagrants, beggars, and smugglers who flourished along the many tariff frontiers. Now the business depression reduced the income of honest peasants who engaged in weaving or other domestic industries in their homes; unemployment and indigence spread in the country; people were uprooted; and the result was to raise the number of vagrants to terrifying proportions. It was believed, since nothing was too bad to believe of the aristocrats (though it was not true), that they were secretly recruiting these "brigands" for their own purposes to intimidate the Third Estate. The economic and social crises thus became acutely political.

The towns were afraid of being swamped by beggars and desperadoes. This was true even of Paris, the largest city in Europe except London. The Parisians were also alarmed by the concentration of troops about Versailles. They began to arm in self-defense. All classes of the Third Estate took part. Crowds began to look for weapons in arsenals and public buildings. On July 14 they came to the Bastille, a stronghold built in the Middle Ages to overawe the city, like the Tower of London in England. It was used as a place of detention for persons with enough influence to escape the common jails but was otherwise in normal times considered harmless; in fact there had been talk, some years before, of tearing it down to make room *The storming of the Bastille* for a public park. Now, in the general turbulence, the governor had placed cannon in the embrasures. The crowd requested him to remove his cannon and to furnish them with arms. He refused. Through a series of misunderstandings, reinforced by the vehemence of a few firebrands, the crowd turned into a mob, which assaulted the fortress and which, when helped by a handful of trained soldiers and five artillery pieces, persuaded the governor to surrender. The mob, enraged by the death of 98 of its members, streamed in and murdered six soldiers of the garrison in cold blood. The governor was murdered while under escort to the Town Hall. A few other officials met the same fate. Their heads were cut off, stuck on the ends of pikes, and paraded about the city. While all this happened, the regular army units on the outskirts of Paris did not stir; their reliability was open to question and the authorities were in any case unaccustomed to firing on the people.

The capture of the Bastille, though not so intended, had the effect of saving the Assembly at Versailles. The king, not knowing what to do, accepted the new situation in Paris. He recognized a citizens' committee, which had formed there, as the new municipal government. He sent away the troops that he had summoned and commanded the recalcitrants among nobles and clergy to join in the National Assembly. In Paris and other cities a

THE TENNIS COURT OATH
by Jacques-Louis David (French, 1748–1825)
This famous picture portrays the momentous decision by members of the Third Estate to continue meeting as the National Assembly of France until they had written a new constitution. The deputies swore their oath at an indoor tennis court because the king had closed the hall in which they had been holding their sessions.
(Giraudon/Art Resource, NY)

bourgeois or national guard was established to keep order. The Assembly appointed the Marquis de Lafayette, "the hero of two worlds," to command the guard in Paris. For insignia he combined the colors of the city of Paris, red and blue, with the white of the house of Bourbon. The French tricolor, emblem of the Revolution, thus originated in a fusion of old and new.

The Great Fear of 1789

In the rural districts matters went from bad to worse. Vague insecurity rose to the proportions of panic in the Great Fear of 1789, which spread over the country late in July in the wake of travelers, postal couriers, and others. The cry was relayed from point to point that "the brigands were coming." Peasants, armed to protect their homes and crops and gathered together and working upon each other's feelings, turned their attention to the manor houses, burning them in some cases and in others simply destroying the manorial archives in which fees and dues were recorded. The Great Fear became part of a general agrarian insurrection, in which peasants, far from being motivated by wild alarms, knew perfectly well what they were doing. They intended to destroy the manorial regime by force.

The Initial Reforms of the National Assembly

The Assembly at Versailles could restore order only by meeting the demands of the peasants. To wipe out all manorial payments would deprive the landed aristocracy of much of its income. Many bourgeois also owned manors. There was therefore much perplexity. A small group of deputies prepared a surprise move in the Assembly, choosing an evening session from which many would be absent. Hence came the "night of August 4." A few liberal noblemen, by prearrangement, arose and surrendered their hunting rights, their *banalités,* their rights in manorial courts, and feudal and seigneurial privileges generally. What was left of serfdom and all personal servitude was declared ended. Tithes were abolished. Other deputies repudiated the special privileges of their provinces. All personal tax privileges were given up. On the main matter, the dues arising from "eminent property" in the manors, a compromise was adopted. These dues were all abolished but compensation was to be paid by the peasants to the former owners. The compensation was in most cases never paid. Eventually, in 1793, in the radical phase of the Revolution, the provision for compensation was repealed. In the end French peasant landowners rid themselves of their manorial obligations without cost to themselves. This was in contrast to what later happened in most other countries, where peasants, when liberated from manorial obligations, either lost part of their land or were burdened with installment payments lasting many years.

In a decree summarizing the resolutions of August 4 the Assembly declared flatly that "feudalism is abolished." With legal privilege replaced by legal equality, it proceeded to map the principles of the new order. On August 26, 1789, it issued the Declaration of the Rights of Man and Citizen.

The Declaration of 1789 was meant to affirm the principles of the new state, which were essentially the rule of law, equal individual citizenship, and collective sovereignty of the people. "Men are born and remain," declared Article I, "free and equal in rights." Man's natural rights were held

The Declaration of the Rights of Man and Citizen

to be "liberty, property, security, and resistance to oppression." Freedom of thought and religion was guaranteed; no one might be arrested or punished except by process of law; all persons were declared eligible for any public office for which they met the requirements. Liberty was defined as the freedom to do anything not injurious to others, which in turn was to be determined only by law. Law must fall equally upon all persons. Law was the expression of the general will, to be made by all citizens or their representatives. The only sovereign was the nation itself, and all public officials and armed forces acted only in its name. Taxes might be raised only by common consent, all public servants were accountable for their conduct in office, and the powers of government were to be separated among different branches. Finally, the state might for public purposes, and under law, confiscate the property of private persons, but only with fair compensation. The Declaration, printed in thousands of leaflets, pamphlets, and books, read aloud in public places, or framed and hung on walls, became the catechism of the Revolution in France. When translated into other languages it soon carried the same message to all of Europe. Thomas Paine's book *The Rights of Man,* published in 1791 to defend the French Revolution, gave the phrase a powerful impact in English.

The "rights of man" had become a motto or watchword for potentially revolutionary ideas well before 1789. The thinkers of the Enlightenment had used it, and during the American Revolution even Alexander Hamilton had spoken of "the sacred rights of man" with enthusiasm. "Man" in this sense was meant to apply abstractly, regardless of nationality, race, or sex. In French as in English the word "man" was used to designate all human beings, and the Declaration of 1789 was not intended to refer to males alone. In German,

The capture of the Bastille—the prison-fortress that became a symbol of Old Regime repression—marked the dramatic entry of the Parisian crowd into the rapidly evolving Revolution. Violence in the streets of Paris in July 1789 saved the National Assembly from the king's intention to dissolve it.
(Bibliothèque Nationale de France, Paris)

for example, where a distinction is made between *Mensch* as a human being and *Mann* as an adult male, the "rights of man" was always translated as *Menschenrechte*. Similarly the word "citizen" in its general sense applied to women, as is shown by the frequency of the feminine *citoyenne* during the Revolution, in which a great many women were very active. But when it came to the exercise of specific legal rights the Revolutionaries went no farther than contemporary opinion. Thus they assigned the right to vote and hold office only to men, and in most matters of property, family law, and education it was the boys and men who benefited most. Very few persons at the time argued for legal equality between the sexes.

The Rights of Woman

One of them, however, was Olympe de Gouges, a woman who had gained prominence as a writer for the theater and who in 1791 published *The Rights of Woman*. Following the official Declaration in each of its 17 articles, she applied them to women explicitly in each case, and she asserted also, in addition, the right of women to divorce under certain conditions, to the control of property in marriage, and for equal access with men to higher education and to civilian careers and public employment. Mary Wollstonecraft in England published a similar *Vindication of the Rights of Woman* in 1792. In France some of the secondary figures in the Revolution, and some of the teachers in boys' schools, thought that women should have greater opportunities at least in education. And there were in fact a few reforms that improved the social rights of women. The revolutionary government redefined marriage as a civil contract and legalized divorce in 1792, thereby enabling women to leave abusive or unhappy marriages (until divorce was banned again in 1816). Inheritance laws were also changed in ways that gave women the legal right to equal inheritance of their family's property.

But among the leaders of the Revolution, only Condorcet argued for legal equality of the sexes. Intent on political change, the Revolutionaries thought that politics, government, law, and war were a masculine business, for which only boys and young men needed to be educated or prepared. The Revolution generally reduced or restricted the cultural and political influence that some women had exercised in the elite circles of Old Regime society. The new political order, as most revolutionaries defined it, was to develop through "manly" opposition to the "feminine" corruptions of the Old Regime court and social hierarchies. "Women are disposed . . . to an over-excitation which would be deadly in public affairs," one revolutionary deputy argued in a typical justification for excluding women from government institutions. Such assumptions led to restrictions on the rights of women to petition or gather in political meetings; finally, in 1793, the revolutionary government closed all women's political clubs.

Shortly after adoption of the Declaration of the Rights of Man the Revolutionary leadership fell apart. In September 1789 the Assembly began the actual planning of the new government. Some wanted a strong veto power for the king and a legislative body in two houses, as in England. Others, the "patriots," wanted only a delaying veto for the king and a legislative body of one chamber. Here again, it was suspicion of the aristocracy that proved decisive. The "patriots" were afraid that an upper chamber would bring back the nobility as a collective force, and they were afraid to make the king constitutionally strong by giving him a full veto, because they believed him to be in sympathy with the nobles. He was, at the moment, hesitating to accept both the August 4th decrees and the Declaration of Rights. His brother, the Count of Artois, followed by many aristocrats, had already emigrated to foreign parts and, along with these other émigrés, was preparing to agitate against the Revolution with all the governments of Europe. The patriot party would concede nothing; the more conservative party could gain nothing. The debate was interrupted again, as in July, by insurrection and violence. On October 4, a crowd of market women and revolutionary militants, followed by the revolutionary Paris national guard, took the road from Paris to Versailles. Besieging and invading the château, they obliged Louis XVI to take up his residence in Paris, where he could be watched. The National Assembly also shifted itself to Paris, where it too soon fell under the influence of radical elements in the city. The champions of a one-chamber legislative body and of a suspensive veto for the king won out.

The more conservative revolutionaries, if such they may be called, disillusioned at seeing constitutional questions settled by mobs, began to drop out of the Assembly. Men who on June 20 had bravely sworn the Oath of the Tennis Court now felt that the Revolution was falling into unworthy hands. Some even emigrated, forming a second wave of émigrés that would have nothing to do with the first. The counterrevolution gathered strength.

But those who wanted still to go forward, and they were many, began to organize in clubs. Most important of all was the Society of Friends of the Constitution, called the Jacobin club for short, since it met in an old Jacobin monastery in Paris. The dues were at first so high that only substantial bourgeois belonged; the dues were later lowered but never enough to include persons of the poorest classes, who therefore formed clubs of their own. The most advanced members of the Assembly were Jacobins, who used the club as a caucus in which to discuss their policies and

The Jacobins

lay their plans. They remained a middle-class group even during the later and more radical phase of the Revolution. Madame Rosalie Jullien, for example, who was as dedicated a revolutionary as her husband and son, attended a meeting of the Paris Jacobin club on August 5, 1792. Tell your friends in the provinces, she wrote to her husband, that these Jacobins are "the flower of the Paris bourgeoisie, to judge by the fancy jackets they wear. There were also two or three hundred women present, dressed as if for the theater, who made an impression by their proud attitude and forceful speech."

Constitutional Changes

In the two years from October 1789 to September 1791 the National Assembly (or the Constituent Assembly, as it had come to be called because it was preparing a constitution) continued its work of simultaneously governing the country, devising a written constitution, and destroying in detail the institutions of the Old Regime. The Assembly soon discarded most of the political and legal institutions that had governed French affairs for centuries—the old monarchical ministries, the organization of government bureaus, the taxes, the property in office, the titles of nobility, the parlements, the hundreds of regional systems of law, the internal tariffs, the provinces, and the urban municipalities. Contemporaries, like Edmund Burke, were appalled at the thoroughness with which the French seemed determined to eradicate their national institutions. Why, asked Burke, should the French fanatics cut to pieces the living body of Normandy or Provence? The truth is that the provinces, like everything else, formed part of the whole system of special privilege and unequal rights. All had to disappear if the hope of equal citizenship under national sovereignty was to be attained. In place of the provinces the Constituent Assembly divided France into 83 equal "departments." In place of the old towns, with their quaint old magistrates, it introduced a uniform municipal organization, all towns henceforth having the same form of government, varying only according to size. All local officials, even prosecuting attorneys and tax collectors, were elected locally. Administratively the country was decentralized in reaction against the bureaucracy of the Old Regime. No one outside Paris now really acted for the central government, and local communities enforced the national legislation, or declined to enforce it, as they chose. This proved ruinous when the war came, and although the "departments" created by the Constituent Assembly still exist, it became traditional in France after the Revolution, as it was before, to keep local officials under strong control by ministers in Paris.

Under the constitution that was prepared, sometimes called the Constitution of 1791 because it went into effect at that date, the sovereign power of the nation was to be exercised by a unicameral elected assembly called the Legislative Assembly.

The Constitution of 1791

The king was given only a suspensive veto power by which legislation desired by the Assembly could be postponed. In general, the executive branch, that is, king and ministers, was kept weak, partly in reaction against "ministerial despotism," partly from a well-founded distrust of Louis XVI. In June 1791 Louis attempted to escape from the kingdom, join with émigré noblemen, and seek help from foreign powers. He left behind him a written message in which he explicitly repudiated the Revolution. Arrested at Varennes in eastern France, he was brought back to Paris and forced to accept his status as a constitutional monarch. The hostile attitude of Louis XVI greatly disoriented the Revolution, for it made impossible the creation of a strong executive power and left the country to be ruled by a debating society which under revolutionary conditions contained more than the usual number of hotheads.

Not all this machinery of state was democratic. As noted above, women did not receive the right to vote or hold public office; and in the granting of political rights to men

The three men at an anvil are a noble, a cleric, and a commoner hammering out a new constitution together. At the beginning of the Revolution, most people expected the three estates to fraternize in the redefined French nation.
(Bibliothèque Nationale de France, Paris)

the abstract principles of the great Declaration were seriously modified for practical reasons. Since most people were illiterate, it was thought that they could have no reasonable political views. Since the small man was often a domestic servant or shop assistant, it was assumed that in politics he would merely follow the views of his employer. The Constituent Assembly therefore distinguished in the new constitution between "active" and "passive" citizens. Both had the same civil rights, but only active citizens had the right to vote. These active citizens chose "electors" on the basis of one elector for every hundred active citizens. The electors convened in the chief town of their new "department" and there chose deputies to the national legislature as well as certain local officials. Males over 25 years of age, and wealthy enough to pay a small direct tax, qualified as "active" citizens; well over half the adult male population could so qualify. Of these, men paying a somewhat higher tax qualified as "electors"; even so, almost half the adult males qualified for this role. In practice, what limited the number of available electors was that, to function as such, a man had to have enough education, interest, and leisure to attend an electoral assembly at a distance from home and remain in attendance for several days. In any case, only about 50,000 persons served as electors in 1790–1791 because a proportion of one for every hundred active citizens yielded that figure.

Economic and Cultural Policies

Economic policies favored the middle rather than the lowest classes. The public debt had precipitated the Revolution, but the revolutionary leaders, even the most extreme Jacobins, never disowned the debt of the Old Regime. The reason is that the bourgeois class, on the whole, were the people to whom the money was owed. To secure the debt, and to pay current expenses of government, since tax collections had become very sporadic, the Constituent Assembly as early as November 1789 resorted to a device by no means new in Europe, though never before used on so extensive a scale. It confiscated all the property of the church. Against this property, it issued negotiable instruments

Assignats

called *assignats,* first regarded as bonds and issued only in large denominations, later regarded as currency and issued in small bills. Holders of *assignats* could use them, or any money, to buy parcels of the former church lands. None of the confiscated land was given away; all was in fact sold, since the interest of the government was fiscal rather than social. The peasants, even when they had the money, could not easily buy land because the lands were sold at distant auctions or in large undivided blocks. The peasants were disgruntled, though they did acquire a good deal of the former church lands through middlemen. Peasant landowners were likewise expected, until 1793, to pay compensation for many of their old manorial fees. And the landless peasants were aroused when the government, with its modern ideas, encouraged the dividing up of the village commons and extinction of various collective village rights in the interest of individual private property.

The revolutionary leadership favored free economic individualism. It had had enough, under the Old Regime, of government regulation over the sale or quality of goods and of privileged companies and other economic monopolies. Reforming economic thought at the time in France and in Britain, where Adam Smith had published his epoch-making *Wealth of Nations* in 1776, held that organized special interests were bad for society and that all prices and wages should be determined by free arrangement between the individuals concerned. The more prominent leaders of the French Revolution believed firmly in this freedom from control. The Constituent Assembly thus abolished the guilds, which were mainly monopolistic organizations of small businessmen or master craftsmen, interested in keeping up prices and averse to new machinery or new methods.

There was also in France what we would now call an organized labor movement. Since the masterships in the guilds were practically hereditary (as a form of property and privilege), the journeymen had formed their own associations, or trade unions, called *compagnonnages,* outside the guilds. Many trades were so organized—the carpenters, plasterers, paper workers, hatters, saddlers, cutlers, nail makers, carters, tanners, locksmiths, and glassworkers. Some were organized nationally; some, only locally. All these journeymen's unions had been illegal under the Old Regime, but they had flourished nevertheless. They collected dues and maintained officers. They often dealt collectively with the guild masters or other employers, requiring the payment of a stipulated wage or change of working conditions. Sometimes they even imposed closed shops. Organized strikes were quite common. The labor troubles of 1789 continued on into the Revolution. Business fell off in the atmosphere of disorder. In 1791 there was another wave of strikes. The Assembly, in the Le Chapelier law of that year, renewed the old prohibitions of the *compagnonnages.* The same law restated the abolition of the guilds and forbade the organization of special economic interests of any kind. All trades, it declared, were free for all to enter. All persons, without belonging to any organization, had the right to work at any occupation or business they might choose. All wages were to be settled privately by the worker and his or her employer. This was not at all what the workers, at that time or any other, really wanted. Nevertheless the provisions of the Le Chapelier law remained a part of French law for three-quarters of a century. The embryonic trade unions continued to exist secretly, though with more difficulty than under the hit-and-miss law enforcement of the Old Regime.

Banning labor organizations

Meanwhile, revolutionary activists set about transforming the symbols, rituals, dress, and holidays of Old Regime society. Seeking to break from the hierarchies and privileges of the past, they developed a new political culture that would be symbolized by a new flag,

The revolutionary government used paper money to finance its policies. The notes were called *assignats* because they were assigned to, or secured by, real estate confiscated during the Revolution, mostly from the church. Inflation rose rapidly after 1794, so that even notes with denominations as high as 10,000 livres, as shown in this picture, became worthless. The assignats were therefore abolished, and a new, more stable French currency came into use in 1796. (Bibliothèque Nationale de France, Paris)

new forms of democratic language, new clothing, new festivals, and new public monuments. The art and imagery of the traditional monarchy and church rapidly disappeared from public life. Great festivals of national unity were organized, beginning with the famous "Festival of the Federation," which brought together a vast crowd in Paris to mark the first anniversary of the assault on the Bastille (July 14, 1790), to celebrate the new liberties of the French people and to begin creating rituals for what would eventually become the French national holiday.

A revolutionary political culture

Supporters of the Revolution planted "liberty trees" in towns throughout France, and they began to wear "liberty caps" and tricolor cockades to show their political allegiances. Later revolutionary governments encouraged new artwork in which the nation came to be represented by a female symbol of liberty, Marianne. Statues of Marianne offered alternatives to traditional Catholic icons of the Virgin Mary and gave illiterate persons new visual images by which they could understand that national sovereignty and liberty had replaced the king and church at the symbolic center of French political life. A profusion of revolutionary plays, novels, and songs conveyed the same message. By promoting the new political ideas and symbols in every sphere of daily life, the French Revolution created a new national identity and "nationalized" the French people through the use of cultural rituals that would later become common in other national movements of the modern world.

The Quarrel with the Church

Most fatefully of all, the Constituent Assembly quarreled with the Catholic church. The confiscation of church properties naturally came as a shock to the clergy. The village priests, whose support had made possible the revolt of the Third Estate, now found that the very buildings in which they worshipped with their parishioners on Sunday belonged to the "nation." The loss of income-producing properties undercut the religious orders and ruined the schools, in which thousands of boys had received free education before the Revolution. Yet it was not on the question of material wealth that the church and the Revolution came to blows. Members of the Constituent Assembly took the view of the church that the great monarchies had taken before them. The idea of separation of church and state was far from their minds. They regarded the church as a form of public authority and as such subordinate to the sovereign power. They frankly argued that the poor needed religion if they were to respect the property of the more wealthy. In any case, having deprived the church of its own income, they had to provide for its maintenance. For the schools many generous and democratic projects of state-sponsored education were drawn up, though under the troubled conditions of the time little was accomplished. For the clergy the new program was mapped out in the Civil Constitution of the Clergy of 1790.

The Civil Constitution of the Clergy

This document went far toward setting up a French national church. Under its provisions the parish priests and bishops were elected, the latter by the same 50,000 electors who chose other important officials. Protestants, Jews, and agnostics could legally take part in the elections, purely on the ground of citizenship and property qualifications. Archbishoprics were abolished, and all the borders of existing bishoprics were redrawn. The number of dioceses was reduced from over 130 to 83, so that one would be coterminous with each department. Bishops were allowed merely to notify the pope of their elevation; they were forbidden to acknowledge any papal authority on their assumption of office, and no papal letter or decree was to be published or enforced in France except with government permission. All clergy received salaries from the state; the average income of bishops was somewhat reduced and that of parish clergymen was raised. Sinecures, plural holdings, and other abuses by which the church had supported noble families were done away with. The Constituent Assembly (independently of the Civil Constitution) also prohibited the taking of religious vows and dissolved all monastic houses.

Some of all this was not in principle alarmingly new, since before the Revolution the civil authority of the king had designated the French bishops and passed judgement on the admission of papal documents into France. French bishops, in the old spirit of the "Gallican liberties," were traditionally jealous of papal power in France. Many were now willing to accept something like the Civil Constitution if allowed to produce it on their own authority. The Assembly refused to concede so much jurisdiction to the Gallican church and applied instead to the pope, hoping to force its plans upon the French clergy by invoking the authority of the Vatican. But the Vatican pronounced the Civil Constitution a wanton usurpation of power over the Catholic church. Unfortunately, the pope also went further, condemning the whole Revolution and all its works. The Constituent Assembly retorted by requiring all French clergy to swear an oath of loyalty to the constitution, including the Civil Constitution of the Clergy. Half took the oath and half refused it, the latter half including all but seven of the bishops. One of the seven willing to accept the new arrangements was Talleyrand, soon to be famous as foreign minister of numerous French governments.

There were now two churches in France, one clandestine, the other official, one maintained by voluntary offerings or by funds smuggled in from abroad, the other financed and sponsored by the government. The former, comprising the nonjuring, unsworn, or "refractory" clergy, turned violently counterrevolutionary. To protect themselves from the Revolution they insisted, with an emphasis quite new in France, on the universal religious supremacy of the Roman pontiff. They denounced the "constitutional" clergy as schismatics who spurned the pope and as mere careerists willing to hold jobs on the government's

The revolutionaries created rituals and symbols to celebrate the new nation they were trying to establish. The great festival of the Federation in Paris on July 14, 1790, assembled the king, the National Guard, and a huge crowd in a symbolic expression of the national unity and national liberties that the new political institutions were supposed to protect.
(Giraudon/Art Resource, NY)

terms. The constitutional clergy, those taking the oath and upholding the Civil Constitution, considered themselves to be patriots and defenders of the rights of man; and they insisted that the Gallican church had always enjoyed a degree of liberty from Rome. The Catholic laity were terrified and puzzled. Many were sufficiently attached to the Revolution to prefer the constitutional clergy but to do so meant to defy the pope, and Catholics who persisted in defying the pope were on the whole those least zealous in their religion. The constitutional clergy therefore stood on shaky foundations. Many of their followers, under stress of the times, eventually turned against Christianity itself.

"Constitutional" and "refractory" clergy

Good Catholics tended to favor the "refractory" clergy. The outstanding example was the king himself. He personally used the services of refractory priests, and thus gave a new reason for the revolutionaries to distrust him. Whatever chance there was that Louis XVI might go along with the Revolution was exploded, for he concluded that he could do so only by endangering his immortal soul. Former aristocrats also naturally preferred the refractory clergy. They now put aside the Voltairean levities of the Age of Enlightenment, and the "best people" began to exhibit a new piety in religious matters. The peasants, who found little in the Revolution to interest them after their own insurrection of 1789 and the consequent abolition of the manorial regime, also favored the old-fashioned or refractory clergy. Much the same was true of the urban working-class families, in which both men and women might shout against priests and yet want to be sure that their marriages were valid and their children were properly baptized. The Constituent Assembly, and its successors, could never finally decide what to do. Sometimes they shut their eyes at the intrigues of refractory clergy, in which case the constitutional clergy then became fearful. Sometimes they hunted out and persecuted the refractories; in that case they only stirred up religious fanaticism.

The Civil Constitution of the Clergy has been called the greatest tactical blunder of the Revolution. Certainly its consequences were unfortunate in the extreme, and they spread to much of Europe. In the nineteenth century the church was to be officially antidemocratic and antiliberal; and democrats and liberals in most cases became outspokenly anticlerical. The main beneficiary was the papacy. The French church, which had clung for ages to its Gallican liberties, was thrown by the Revolution into the arms of the pope. Even Napoleon, when he healed the schism a decade later, acknowledged powers in the papacy that had never been acknowledged by the French kings. These were steps in the process, leading through the proclamation of papal infallibility in 1870, by which the affairs of the modern Catholic church became increasingly centralized at the Vatican.

With the proclamation of the constitution in September 1791, the Constituent Assembly disbanded. Before dissolving, it ruled that none of its members might sit in the forthcoming Legislative Assembly. This body was therefore made up of men who still wished to make their mark in the Revolution. The new regime went into effect in October 1791. It was a constitutional monarchy in which a unicameral Legislative Assembly confronted a king unconverted to the new order. Designed as the permanent solution to France's problems, it was to collapse in 10 months, in August 1792, as a result of popular insurrection four months after France became involved in war. A group of Jacobins, known as Girondins, for a time became the left or advanced party of the Revolution and in the Legislative Assembly led France into war.

43.   THE REVOLUTION AND EUROPE: THE WAR AND THE "SECOND" REVOLUTION, 1792

The International Impact of the Revolution

The European governments were long reluctant to become involved with France. They were under considerable pressure. On the one hand, pro-French and pro-revolutionary groups appeared immediately in many quarters. The doctrines of the French Revolution, as of the American, were highly exportable: they took the form of a universal philosophy, proclaiming the rights of man regardless of time or place, race or nation. Moreover, depending on what one was looking for, one might see in the first disturbances in France a revolt of either the nobility, the bourgeoisie, the common people, or the entire nation. In Poland those who were trying to reorganize the country against further partition hailed the French example. The Hungarian landlords pointed to it in their reaction against Joseph II. In England, for a time, those who controlled Parliament complacently believed that the French were attempting to imitate them.

Inspiration of the Revolution

But it was the excluded classes of European society who were most inspired. The hard-pressed Silesian weavers were said to hope that "the French would come." Strikes broke out at Hamburg, and peasants rebelled elsewhere. One English diplomat found that even the Prussian army had "a strong taint of democracy among officers and men." In Belgium, where the privileged elements were already in revolt against the Austrian emperor, a second revolt broke out, inspired by events in France and aimed at the privileged elements. In England the newly developing "radicals," men like Thomas Paine and Dr. Richard Price, who wished a thorough overhauling of Parliament and the established church, entered into correspondence with the Assembly in Paris. Business leaders of importance, including Watt and Boulton, the pioneers of the steam engine, were likewise pro-French since they had no representation in the House of Commons. The Irish too were excited and presently revolted. Everywhere the young were aroused, the young Hegel in Germany or in England the young Wordsworth, who later recalled the sense of a new era that had captivated so many spirits in 1789:

Bliss was it in that dawn to be alive,
But to be young was very heaven!

On the other hand the anti-Revolutionary movement gathered strength. Edmund Burke, frightened by the French proclivities of English radicals, published as early as 1790 his *Reflections on the Revolution in France*. For France, he predicted anarchy and dictatorship. For England, he sternly advised the English to accept a slow adaptation of their own English liberties. For all the world, he denounced a political philosophy that rested on abstract principles of right and wrong, declaring that every people must be shaped by its own national circumstances, national history, and national character. He drew an eloquent reply and a defense of France from Thomas Paine in the *Rights of Man*. Burke soon began to preach the necessity of war, urging a kind of ideological struggle against French barbarism and violence. His *Reflections* was translated and widely read, becoming in the long run an influential work in the emergence of modern conservative thought. In the short run it fell on willing ears. The king of Sweden, Gustavus III, offered to lead a monarchist crusade. In Russia Empress Catherine was appalled; she forbade further translations of her erstwhile friend Voltaire, she called the French "vile riffraff" and "brutish cannibals," and she packed off to Siberia a Russian named Radischev, who in his *Voyage from St. Petersburg to Moscow* pointed out the evils of serfdom. The terrors were heightened by plaintive messages from Louis XVI and Marie Antoinette and by the émigrés who kept bursting out of France, led as early as July 1789 by the king's own brother, the Count of Artois. The émigrés, who at first were nobles, settled in various parts of Europe and began using their international aristocratic connections. They preached a kind of holy war against the evils of revolution. They bemoaned the sad plight of the king, but what they most wanted was to get back their manorial incomes and other rights. Extremists among the émigrés even hinted that Louis XVI himself was a dangerous revolutionary and much preferred his brother, the unyielding Count of Artois.

In short, Europe was soon split by a division that overran all frontiers. The same was true of America also. In the United States the rising party of Jefferson was branded as Jacobin and pro-French, that of Hamilton as aristocratic and pro-British, while in colonial Latin America there was new interest in ideas of independence, and the Venezuelan Miranda became a general in the French army. In all countries of the European world, though least of all in eastern and southern Europe, there were revolutionary or pro-French elements that were feared by their own governments. In all countries, including France, there were implacable enemies of the French Revolution. In all countries were people whose loyalties or sympathies lay abroad. There had been no such situation since the Protestant Reformation, nor was there anything like it again until after the Russian Revolution of the twentieth century.

The Coming of the War, April 1792

Yet the European governments were slow to move. Catherine had no intention of becoming involved in western Europe. She only wished to involve her neighbors. William Pitt, the British prime minister, resisted the war cries of Burke. Pitt had tried and failed to carry a plan for reform of Parliament and was now concentrating on a policy of orderly finance and systematic economy. His domestic program would be ruined by war. He insisted that the internal affairs of France were of no concern to the British government. The key position was occupied by the Habsburg emperor, Leopold II, brother to the French queen.

Leopold at first answered Marie Antoinette's pleas for help by telling her to adjust herself to conditions in France. He resisted the furious demands of the émigrés, whom he understood perfectly, having inherited from Joseph II a fractious aristocracy himself.

Still, the new French government was a disturbing phenomenon. It openly encouraged malcontents all over Europe. It showed a tendency to settle international affairs by unilateral action. For example, it annexed Avignon at the request of local revolutionaries but without the consent of its historic sovereign, the pope. Or again, in Alsace there had been much overlapping jurisdiction between France and Germany ever since the Peace of Westphalia in 1648 (see maps, pp. 142–143, 180, 313). The Constituent Assembly abolished feudalism and manorial dues in Alsace as elsewhere in France. To German princes who had feudal rights in Alsace the Assembly offered compensation, but it did not ask their consent. Moreover, after the arrest of Louis XVI at Varennes, after his attempted flight in June 1791, it became impossible to deny that the French king and queen were prisoners of the revolutionaries.

The Declaration of Pillnitz

In August Leopold met with the king of Prussia at Pillnitz in Saxony. The resulting Declaration of Pillnitz rested on a famous *if:* Leopold would take military steps to restore order in France if all the other powers would join him. Knowing the attitude of Pitt, he believed that this could never materialize. His aim was mainly to rid himself of the French émigrés, but the émigrés perversely received the Declaration with delight. They used it as an open threat to their enemies in France, announcing that they would soon return alongside the forces of civilized Europe to punish the guilty and right the wrongs that had been done to them.

In France the upholders of the Revolution were alarmed. They were ignorant of what Leopold really meant and took the dire menaces of the émigrés at their face value. The Declaration of Pillnitz, far from cowing the French, enraged them against all the crowned heads of Europe. It gave a political advantage to the then dominant faction of Jacobins, known to history as the Girondins. These included the philosophe Condorcet, the humanitarian lawyer Brissot, and the civil servant Roland and his more famous wife, Madame Roland, whose house became a kind of headquarters of the group. They attracted many foreigners also, such as Thomas Paine and the German Anacharsis Cloots, the "representative of the human race." In December 1791 a deputation of English radicals, led by James Watt, son of the inventor of the steam engine, received a wild ovation at the Paris Jacobin club.

France goes to war

The Girondins became the party of international revolution. They declared that the Revolution could never be secure in France until it spread to the world. In their view, once war had come, the peoples of states at war with France would not support their own governments. There was reason for this belief, since revolutionary elements antedating the French Revolution already existed in both the Dutch and the Austrian Netherlands, and to a lesser degree in parts of Switzerland, Poland, and elsewhere. Some Girondins therefore contemplated a war in which French armies should enter neighboring countries, unite with local revolutionaries, overthrow the established governments, and set up a federation of republics. War was also favored by a very different group, led by Lafayette, which wished to curb the Revolution by holding it at the line of constitutional monarchy. This group mistakenly believed that war might restore the much damaged popularity of Louis XVI, unite the country under the new government, and make it possible to put down the continuing Jacobin agitation. As the war spirit boiled up in France, the Emperor Leopold II died. He was succeeded by Francis II, a man much more inclined than Leopold to yield to the clamors of the old aristocracy. Francis resumed negotiations with Prussia. In France all who dreaded a return of the Old Regime listened more readily to the Girondins. Among the Jacobins as a whole, only a few, generally a handful of radical democrats, opposed the war. On April 20, 1792, without serious opposition, the Assembly declared war on "the king of Hungary and Bohemia," that is, the Austrian monarchy.

The "Second" Revolution: August 10, 1792

The war intensified the existing unrest and dissatisfaction of the unpropertied classes. Both peasants and urban workers felt that the Constituent and the Legislative Assembly had served the propertied interests and had done little for them. Peasants were dissatisfied with the inadequate measures taken to facilitate land distribution; workers felt especially the pinch of soaring prices, which by 1792 had greatly risen. Gold had been taken out of the country by the émigrés; paper money, the *assignats,* was almost the sole currency, and the future of the government was so uncertain that it steadily lost value. Peasants concealed their food products rather than sell them for depreciating paper. Actual scarcity combined with the falling value of money to drive up the cost of living. The lowest income groups suffered the most. But dissatisfied though they were, when the war began they were threatened with a return of the émigrés and a vindictive restoration of the Old Regime, which at least for the peasants would be the worst of all possible eventualities. The working classes—peasants, artisans, mechanics, shopkeepers, wage workers—rallied to the Revolution but not to the revolutionary government in power. The Legislative Assembly and the constitutional monarchy lacked the confidence of large elements of the population.

In addition, the war at first went very unfavorably for the French. Prussia joined immediately with Austria, and by the summer of 1792 the two powers were on the point of invading France. They issued a proclamation to the French people, the Brunswick Manifesto of July 25 declaring that if any harm befell the French king and queen the Austro-Prussian forces, upon their arrival in Paris, would exact the most severe retribution from the inhabitants of that city. Such menaces, compounding the military emergency, only played into the hands of the most violent activists. Masses of the French people, roused and guided by bourgeois Jacobin leaders, notably Robespierre, Danton, and the vitriolic journalist Marat, burst out in a passion of patriotic excitement. They turned against the king because he was identified with powers at war with France and also because, in France itself, those who still supported him were using the monarchy as defense against the lower classes. Republicanism in France was partly a rather sudden historical accident, in that France was at war under a king who could not be trusted, and partly a kind of popular lower-class movement, in which, however, many bourgeois revolutionaries shared.

Feeling ran high during the summer of 1792. Recruits streamed into Paris from all quarters on their way to the frontiers. One detachment, from Marseilles, brought with them a new marching song, known ever since as the *Marseillaise,* a fierce call to war upon tyranny. The transient provincials stirred up the agitation in Paris. On August 10, 1792, the working-class quarters of the city rose in revolt, supported by the recruits from Marseilles and elsewhere. They stormed the Tuileries against resistance by the Swiss Guard, many of whom were massacred, and seized and imprisoned the king and the royal family. A revolutionary municipal government, or "Commune," was set up in Paris. Usurping the powers of the Legislative Assembly, it forced the abrogation of the constitution and the election, by universal male suffrage, of a Constitutional Convention that was to govern France and prepare a new and more democratic constitution. The very word Convention was used in

Agitation and violence in Paris

recollection of the American Constitutional Convention in 1787. Meanwhile hysteria, anarchy, and terror reigned in Paris; mobs of insurrectionary volunteers, declaring that they would not fight enemies on the frontiers until they had disposed of enemies in Paris, dragged about 1,100 persons—refractory priests and other counterrevolutionaries—from the prisons of the city and killed them after drumhead trials, in brutal executions known as the "September massacres."

For nearly three years, since October 1789, there had been an abatement of popular violence. Now the coming of the war and the dissatisfaction of the lower classes with the course of events so far had led to new explosions. The insurrection of August 10, 1792, the "second" French Revolution, initiated the most advanced phase of the Revolution.

44. THE EMERGENCY REPUBLIC, 1792–1795: THE TERROR

The National Convention

The National Convention met on September 20, 1792; it was to sit for three years. It immediately proclaimed the Year One of the French Republic. The disorganized French armies, also on September 20, won a great moral victory in the "cannonade of Valmy," a battle that was hardly more than an artillery duel, but which induced the Prussian commander to give up his march on Paris. The French soon occupied Belgium (the Austrian Netherlands), the Savoy region near the Swiss-Italian border (which belonged to the king of Sardinia who had joined with the Austrians), and Mainz and other cities on the German Left Bank of the Rhine. Revolutionary sympathizers in these places appealed for French aid. The National Convention decreed assistance to "all peoples wishing to recover their liberty." It also ordered that French generals, in the occupied areas, should dissolve the old governments; confiscate government and church property; abolish tithes, hunting rights, and seigneurial dues; and set up provisional administrations. Thus revolution spread in the wake of the successful French armies.

Spread of the Revolution

The British and Dutch now prepared to resist. Pitt, still insisting that the French might have any domestic regime that they chose, declared that Great Britain could not tolerate the French occupation of Belgium. The British and Dutch began conversations with Prussia and Austria, and the French declared war on them on February 1, 1793. Within a few weeks the Republic had annexed Savoy and Nice, as well as Belgium, and had much of the German Rhineland under its military government (see map, p. 388). Meanwhile, in eastern Europe, while denouncing the rapacity of the French savages, the rulers of Russia and Prussia, as we have seen, came to an arrangement of their own, each appropriating a portion of Poland in the second partition in January 1793. The Austrians, excluded from the second partition, became anxious about their interests in eastern Europe. The infant French Republic, now at war with all Europe, was saved by the weakness of the Coalition, for Britain and Holland had no land forces of consequence and Prussia and Austria were too jealous of each other, and too preoccupied with Poland, to commit the bulk of their armies against France.

The Jacobins split

In the Convention all the leaders were Jacobins, but the Jacobins were again splitting. The Girondins were no longer the most advanced revolutionary group as they had been in the Legislative Assembly. Beside the Girondins appeared a new group, whose members preferred to sit in the highest seats in the hall, and therefore were dubbed the "Mountain" in the political language of the day. The leading Girondins came from the great provincial cities; the leading Montagnards, though mostly of provincial birth, represented Paris and owed most of their political strength to the radical and popular elements in that city.

These popular revolutionists, outside the Convention, proudly called themselves "sans-culottes," since they wore the workingman's long trousers, not the knee breeches or *culottes* of the middle and upper classes. They were the working class of a preindustrial age, shopkeepers and shop assistants, skilled artisans in various trades, including some who were owners of small manufacturing or handicraft enterprises. For two years their militancy and their activism pressed the Revolution forward. They demanded an equality that should be meaningful for people like themselves, they called for a mighty effort against foreign powers that presumed to intervene in the French Revolution, and they denounced the now deposed king and queen (correctly enough) for collusion with the Austrian enemy. The sans-culottes feared that the Convention might be too moderate. They favored direct democracy in their neighborhood clubs and assemblies, together with a mass rising if necessary against the Convention itself. The Girondins in the Convention began to dismiss these popular militants as anarchists. The group known as the Mountain was more willing to work with them, so long at least as the emergency lasted.

The Convention put Louis XVI on trial for treason in December 1792. On January 15 it unanimously pronounced him guilty, but on the next day, out of 721 deputies present, only 361 voted for immediate execution, a majority of one. Louis XVI died on the guillotine forthwith. The 361 deputies were henceforth branded for life as regicides; never could they *The execution of the king* allow, in safety to themselves, a restoration of the Bourbon monarchy in France. The other 360 deputies were not similarly compromised; their rivals called them Girondins, "moderatists," counterrevolutionaries. All who still wanted more from the Revolution, or who feared that the slightest wavering would bring the Allies and the émigrés into France, now looked to the Mountain wing of the Jacobins.

Background to the Terror

In April 1793 the most prominent French general, Dumouriez, who had won the victories in Belgium five months before, defected to Austria. The Allied armies now drove the French from Belgium and again threatened to invade France. Counterrevolutionaries in France exulted. From the revolutionaries went up the cry, "We are betrayed!" Prices continued to rise, the currency fell, food was harder to obtain, and the working classes were increasingly restless. The sans-culottes demanded price controls, currency controls, rationing, legislation against the hoarding of food, and requisitioning to enforce the circulation of goods. They denounced bourgeois traders as profiteers and exploiters of the people. While the Girondins resisted, the Mountain went along with the sans-culottes, partly from sympathy with their ideas, partly to win mass support for the war, and partly as a maneuver against the Girondins. On May 31, 1793, the Commune of Paris, under pressure from the sans-culottes assembled a host of demonstrators and insurrectionists who invaded the Convention and forced the arrest of the Girondin leaders. Other Girondins fled to the provinces, including Condorcet, who, while in hiding, and before his death, found occasion to write his famous book on the *Progress of the Human Mind*.

The Mountain now ruled in the Convention, but the Convention itself ruled very little. Not only were the foreign armies and the émigrés at the gates bent on destroying the Convention as a band of regicides and social incendiaries, but the authority of the Convention

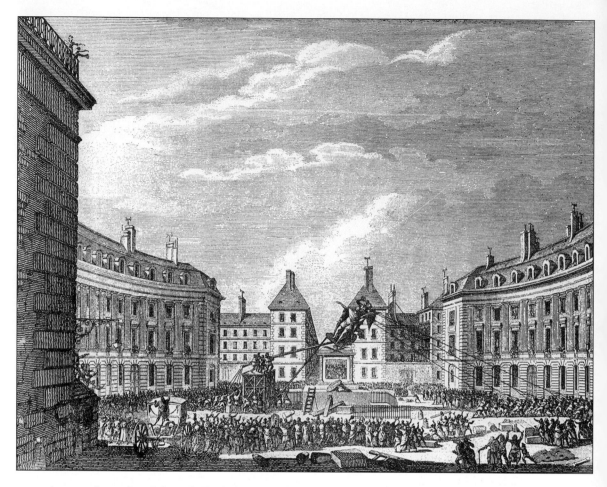

A wave of popular violence in Paris in 1792 led to the fall of the monarchy and the proclamation of a new French republic. Angry crowds pulled down the symbols of the old regime, including this statue of Louis XIV.
(Stock Montage, Inc.)

was also widely repudiated in France itself. In the west, in the Vendée, the peasants had revolted against military conscription; they were worked upon by refractory priests, British agents, and royalist emissaries of the Count of Artois. The great provincial cities, Lyons, Bordeaux, Marseilles, and others, had also rebelled, especially after the fugitive Girondins reached them. These "federalist" rebels demanded a more "federal" or decentralized republic. Like the Vendéans, with whom they had no connection, they objected to the ascendancy of Paris, having been accustomed to more regional independence under the Old Regime. These rebellions became counterrevolutionary, since all sorts of foreigners, royalists, émigrés, and clericals streamed in to assist them.

The Convention under attack

The Convention had to defend itself against extremists of the Left as well. To the genuine mass action of the sans-culottes were now added the voices of even more excited militants called *enragés*. Various organizers, enthusiasts, agitators, and neighborhood politicians declared that parliamentary methods were useless. Generally they were men outside the Convention—and also women, for women were particularly sensitive to the crisis of food shortage and soaring prices, and an organization of Revolutionary Republican Women helped to mobilize the sans-culottes in 1793 (until the suppression of women's political clubs). All such activists worked through units of local government in Paris and elsewhere as well as in thousands of "popular societies" and provincial clubs throughout the whole country. They also formed "revolutionary armies," semimilitary bands that scoured the rural areas for food, searched the barns of peasants, denounced suspects, and preached revolution.

As for the Convention, while it cannot be said ever to have had any commanding leaders, the program it followed for about a year was on the whole that of Maximilien Robespierre, himself a Jacobin but not one to go along forever with popular revolution or anarchy. Robespierre is one of the most argued about *Robespierre* and least understood figures in history. Persons accustomed to stable conditions dismiss him with a shudder as a bloodthirsty fanatic, dictator, and demagogue. Others have considered him an idealist, a visionary, and an ardent patriot whose goals and ideals were at least avowedly democratic. All agree on his personal honesty and integrity and on his revolutionary zeal. He was by origin a lawyer from northern France, educated with the aid of scholarships in Paris. He had been elected in 1789 to sit for the Third Estate in the Estates General, and in the ensuing Constituent Assembly played a minor role, though calling attention to himself by his views against capital punishment and in favor of universal suffrage. During the time of the Legislative Assembly, in 1791–1792, he continued to agitate for democracy and vainly pleaded against the declaration of war. In the Convention, elected in September 1792, he sat for a Paris constituency. He became a prominent member of the Mountain and welcomed the purge of the Girondins. He had always kept free of the bribery and graft in which some others became involved and for this reason was known as the Incorruptible. He was a great believer in the importance of "virtue," a term that the philosophes had used in a specialized way. Both Montesquieu and Rousseau, for example, had held that republics depended upon "virtue," or unselfish public spirit and civic zeal, to which was added, under Rousseauist influence, a somewhat sentimentalized idea of personal uprightness and purity of life. Robespierre was determined, in 1793 and 1794, to bring about a democratic republic made up of good, virtuous, and honest citizens.

The Program of the Convention, 1793–1794: The Terror

The program of the Convention, which Robespierre helped to form, was to repress anarchy, civil strife, and counterrevolution at home and to win the war by a great national mobilization of the country's people and resources. It would prepare a democratic constitution and initiate legislation for the lower classes, but it would not yield to the Paris Commune and other agencies of direct revolutionary action. To conduct the government, the Convention granted wide powers to a Committee of Public Safety, a group of 12 members of the Convention who were reelected every month. Robespierre was an influential member; others were the youthful St. Just, the militant lawyer Couthon, and the army officer Carnot, "organizer of victory."

To repress the "counterrevolution," the Convention and the Committee of Public Safety set up what is popularly known as the "Reign of Terror." Revolutionary courts were instituted as an alternative to the lynch law of *The "Reign of Terror"* the September massacres. A Committee of General Security was created as a kind of supreme political police. Designed to protect the Revolutionary Republic from its internal enemies, the Terror struck at those who were in league against the Republic and at those who were merely suspected of hostile activities. Its victims ranged from Marie Antoinette and other royalists to the former revolutionary colleagues of the Mountain, the Girondin leaders; and before the year 1793–1794 was over, some of the old Jacobins of the Mountain who had helped inaugurate the program also went to the guillotine.

Many thousands of people died in France at the height of the Revolution. Most deaths were in places in open revolt against the Convention, as in the Vendée in western France. Some resulted from acts of private vengeance. But if the Terror is understood to mean the official program of the government, which at one time decreed "terror the order of the day," the number who died in it was not large by the brutal standards of the twentieth century, in which dictatorial governments attempted to wipe out not only their political opponents but whole social classes or ethnic groups. About 40,000 persons perished in the Terror thus defined, and many others were temporarily imprisoned. About 8 percent of the

Victims of the "Terror"

victims of the "official" Terror were nobles, but nobles as a class were not molested unless suspected of political agitation; 14 percent of the victims were classifiable as bourgeois, mainly of the rebellious southern cities; 6 percent were clergy, while no less than 70 percent were of the peasant and laboring classes. A democratic republic, founded on the Declaration of the Rights of Man, was in principle to follow the Terror once the war and the emergency were over, but meanwhile, the Terror was inhuman at best and in some places atrocious, as at Nantes where 2,000 persons were loaded on barges and deliberately drowned. The Terror left long memories in France and created much of the enduring antipathy to the Revolution and to republicanism.

The Committee of Public Safety

To conduct the government in the midst of the war emergency the Committee of Public Safety operated as a joint dictatorship and war cabinet. It prepared and guided legislation through the Convention. It gained control over the "representatives on mission," who were members of the Convention on duty with the armies and in the insurgent areas of France. It established the *Bulletin des loix,* so that all persons might know what laws they were supposed to enforce or to obey. It centralized the administration, converting the swarm of locally elected officials left over from the Constituent Assembly (who were royalists in some places, wild extremists, in others) into centrally appointed "national agents" named by the Committee of Public Safety.

To win the war the Committee proclaimed the *levée en masse,* calling on all able-bodied men to rally to the colors. It recruited scientists to work on armaments and munitions. The most prominent French scientists of the day, including Lagrange and Lamarck, worked for or were protected by the government of the Terror, though one, Lavoisier, "father of modern chemistry," was guillotined in 1794 because he had been involved in tax farming before 1789. For military reasons also the Committee instituted economic controls, which at the same time met the demands of the *enragés* and other working-class spokesmen. The value of the *assignats* ceased to fall during the year of the Terror. Thus the government protected both its own purchasing power and that of the masses. It did so by controlling the export of gold, by confiscating specie and foreign currency from French citizens, to whom it paid assignats in return, and by legislation against hoarding or the withholding of goods from the market. Food and supplies for the armies, and for civilians in the towns, were raised and allocated by a system of requisitions, centralized in a Subsistence Commission under the Committee of Public Safety. A "general maximum" set ceilings for prices and wages. It helped to check inflation during the crisis, but it did not work very well; the Committee believed, in principle, in a free market economy and lacked the technical and administrative machinery to enforce thorough controls. By 1794 it was giving freer rein to private enterprise and to the peasants to encourage production. It tried also to hold down wages and in that respect lost the adherence of many working-class leaders.

In June 1793 the Committee produced, and the Convention adopted, a republican constitution which provided for universal male suffrage. But the new constitution was suspended indefinitely, and the government was declared "revolutionary until the peace," "revolutionary" meaning extraconstitutional or of an emergency character. In other ways the Committee showed intentions of legislating on behalf of the lower economic classes. The price controls and other economic regulations answered the demands of the sans-culottes. The last of the manorial regime was done away with; the peasants were relieved of having to pay compensation for the obligations that had been abolished at the opening of the Revolution. The Committee busied itself also with social services and measures of public improvement. It issued pamphlets to teach farmers to improve their crops, selected promising youths to receive instruction in useful trades, opened a military school for boys of all classes, even the humblest, and certainly intended to introduce universal elementary education.

It was also at this time, in 1794, that the National Convention decreed the abolition of slavery in the French colonies, meaning chiefly Saint-Domingue, the modern Haiti, the richest of all the sugar islands in the Caribbean. Free blacks in the colonies had already received civic rights earlier in the Revolution. The black slaves had in fact already liberated themselves in a massive rebellion in 1791. They had produced a leader in Toussaint L'Ouverture, born a slave, who after the French abolished slavery served as a general in the French army against the Spanish and British who had ambitions in Haiti. Amid the ensuing political and military conflicts Toussaint became France's governor-general in Haiti, but his new government soon broke away from all French control. Under pressure from the slave-owning and commercial interests (and the European demand for sugar) the government of Napoleon in 1802 reestablished slavery in the French colonies, sent troops to reassert French authority in Haiti, captured Toussaint, and took him to France, where he died in prison. Unable in any case to defeat the armed rebellion of the black population, most of the French army sent out in this operation perished of yellow fever. Haitian leaders, in 1804, established an independent Republic of Haiti. An unexpected consequence of the French defeat in Haiti was that Napoleon sold the remaining French possessions on the North American mainland ("Louisiana") to the United States in 1803. Slavery was not effectively abolished in the French colonies until 1848.

Slavery abolished in French colonies

At the climax of the Revolution, in 1793–1794, the Committee of Public Safety was determined to concentrate revolutionary initiative in itself. It had no patience with unauthorized revolutionary violence. With a democratic program of its own, it disapproved of the turbulent democracy of popular clubs and local assemblies. In the fall of 1793, at the time of its prohibition of revolutionary women's organizations, the Committee arrested the leading *enragés*. Extreme revolutionary demands were expressed by Jacques Hébert, a journalist and officer of the Paris Commune. Robespierre called such people "ultra revolutionaries." They were a large and indefinable group and included many members of the Convention. They indiscriminately denounced merchants and bourgeoisie. They were the party of extreme Terror; an Hébertist brought about the drownings at Nantes. Believing all religion to be counterrevolutionary, they launched the movement of Dechristianization and strongly supported the creation of a new republican calendar. The Convention adopted this calendar as part of its campaign to strengthen popular allegiance to the republic and to establish a new national organization of daily life that would replace the Christian cycle of Sundays, saints' days, and holidays such as Christmas and Easter. The new calendar thus counted years from the founding of the French Republic, divided each year into new months of 30 days each, and even abolished the week, which it replaced with the 10-day *décade*.[1]

The Revolution and religion

Dechristianization also contributed to the development of the cult of reason, which sprang up all over France at the end of 1793. In Paris the bishop resigned his office, declaring that he had been deluded; and the Commune put on ceremonies in the cathedral of Notre Dame, in which Reason was impersonated by an actress who was the wife of one of the city officials. But Dechristianization was severely frowned upon by Robespierre. He believed that it would alienate the masses from the Republic and ruin such sympathy as was still felt for the Revolution abroad. The Committee of Public Safety, therefore, ordered the toleration of peaceable Catholics, and in June 1794 Robespierre introduced the cult of the Supreme Being, a deistic natural religion, in which the Republic was declared to recognize the existence of God and the immortality of the soul. Robespierre hoped that both Catholics and agnostic anticlericals could become reconciled on this ground. But Catholics were now beyond reconciliation, and the freethinkers, appealing to the tradition of Voltaire, regarded Robespierre as a reactionary mystery monger and were instrumental in bringing about his fall.

Meanwhile the Committee proceeded relentlessly against the Hébertists, whose main champions it sent to the guillotine in March 1794. The paramilitary "revolutionary armies" were suppressed. The extreme Terrorists were recalled from the provinces. The revolutionary Paris Commune was destroyed. Robespierre filled the municipal offices of Paris with his own appointees. This Robespierrist commune disapproved of strikes and tried to hold down wages, on the plea of military necessity; it failed to win over the ex-Hébertists and working-class leaders, who became disillusioned with the Revolution and dismissed it as a bourgeois movement. Probably to prevent just such a conclusion, and to avoid the appearance of deviation to the Right, Robespierre and the Committee, after liquidating the left-wing Hébertists, also liquidated certain right-wing members of the Mountain who were known as Dantonists. Danton and his followers were accused of financial dishonesty and of dealing with counterrevolutionaries; the charges contained some truth but were not the main reason for the executions.

By the spring of 1794 the French Republic possessed an army of 800,000 men, the largest ever raised up to that time by a European power. It was a national army representing a people in arms, commanded by officers who had been promoted rapidly on grounds of merit and composed of troops who felt themselves to be citizens fighting for their own cause. Its intense political-mindedness made it the more formidable and contrasted strongly with the indifference of the opposing troops, some of whom were in fact serfs and none of whom had any sense of membership in their own political systems. The Allied governments, each pursuing its own ends and still distracted by their ambitions in Poland, where the third partition was impending, could not combine their forces against France. In

Revolutionary military victories

June 1794 the French won the battle of Fleurus in Belgium. The Republican hosts again streamed into the Low Countries; in six months their calvary rode into Amsterdam on the ice. A revolutionary Batavian Republic soon replaced the old Dutch provinces. The opposite occurred at this time

---

[1]Though not adopted until October 1793, the revolutionary calendar dated the Year I of the French Republic from September 22, 1792. The names of the months, in order and corresponding to the seasons of the year, were Vendémiaire, Brumaire, Frimaire (autumn); Nivôse, Pluviôse, Ventôse (winter); Germinal, Floréal, Prairial (spring); Messidor, Thermidor, Fructidor (summer).

The French army won a great victory at the battle of Fleurus in June 1794, thus opening the way for republican troops to enter the Low Countries and easing the external threats that had pushed the Revolution toward internal repression and the Terror. This picture shows how the French used a balloon to observe enemy forces during the battle, but the results must have been disappointing, since balloons were not thereafter used by either side.

(Picture Collection, The New York Public Library, Astor, Lenox and Tilden Foundations)

in eastern Europe, where Russian and Prussian armies stamped out the attempted revolution that Kosciusko led in Poland. All Polish lands and people were finally merged into the east-European empires in 1795.

Military success made the French less willing to put up with the dictatorial rule and economic regimentation of the Terror. Robespierre and the Committee of Public Safety had antagonized all significant parties. The working-class radicals of Paris would no longer support him, and after the death of Danton the National Convention was afraid of its own ruling committee. A group in the Convention obtained the "outlawing" of Robespierre on 9 Thermidor (July 27, 1794); he was guillotined with some of his associates on the following day. Many who turned against Robespierre believed they were pushing the Revolution farther forward, as

Fall of Robespierre

The guillotine was used during the most radical phase of the Revolution to execute persons judged to be enemies of the republic. First adopted as a more humane way of inflicting capital punishment, it became a permanent symbol of revolutionary violence and it claimed victims from every part of the Revolution itself. This picture illustrates the execution of Robespierre and four others who were denounced as conspirators against liberty and sent to the guillotine in July 1794.
(Bettmann/Corbis)

in destroying the Girondins the year before. Others thought, or said, that they were stopping a dictator and a tyrant. All agreed, to absolve themselves, in heaping all blame upon Robespierre. The idea that Robespierre was an ogre originated more with his former colleagues than with conservatives of the time.

The Thermidorian Reaction

The fall of Robespierre stunned the country, but its effects manifested themselves during the following months as the "Thermidorian reaction." The Terror subsided. The Convention reduced the powers of the Committee of Public Safety, and it closed the Jacobin club. Price controls and other regulations were removed. Inflation resumed its course, prices again rose, and the disoriented and leaderless working classes suffered more than ever. Sporadic uprisings broke out, of which the greatest was the insurrection of Prairial in the Year III (May 1795), when a mob all but dispersed the Convention by force. Troops were called to Paris for the first time since 1789. Insurrectionists in the working-class quarters threw up barricades in the streets. The army prevailed without much bloodshed, but the Convention arrested, imprisoned, or deported 10,000 of the insurgents. A few organizers were guillotined. The affair of Prairial gave a foretaste of modern social revolution.

The triumphant element consisted mostly of the bourgeois class which had guided the Revolution since the Constituent Assembly and had not been really unseated even during the Terror. It was not mainly a bourgeoisie of modern capitalists, eager to make a financial profit by developing new factories or machinery. The political victors after Thermidor were "bourgeois" in an older social sense, those who had not been noble or aristocratic before 1789 yet had held a secure position under the Old Regime, many of them lawyers or officeholders and often drawing income from the ownership of land. To them were now added new elements produced by the Revolution itself, parvenus and *nouveaux riches,* who had made money by wartime government contracts or had profited by inflation or by buying up former church lands at bargain prices. Such people, often joined by former aristocrats, and in reaction against Robespierrist virtue, set an extravagant and ostentatious style of living that gave a bad name to the new order. They also unleashed a "white terror" in which many ex-Jacobins were simply murdered.

Politics and society after Thermidor

But the Thermidorians, disreputable though a few of them were, had not lost faith in the Revolution. Democracy they associated with red terror and mob rule, but they still believed in individual legal rights and in a written constitution. Conditions were rather adverse, for the country was still unsettled, and although the Convention made a separate peace with Spain and Prussia, France still remained at war with Great Britain and the Habsburg empire. But the men of the Convention were determined to make another attempt at constitutional government. They set aside the democratic constitution written in 1793 (and never used) and produced the Constitution of the Year III, which went into effect at the end of 1795.

45. THE CONSTITUTIONAL REPUBLIC: THE DIRECTORY, 1795–1799

The Weakness of the Directory

The first formally constituted French Republic, known as the Directory, lasted only four years. Its weakness was that it rested on an extremely narrow social base and that it presupposed certain military conquests. The new constitution applied not only to France but also to Belgium, which was now regarded as incorporated constitutionally into France, though the Habsburgs had not yet ceded these "Austrian Netherlands," nor had the British yielded in their refusal to accept French occupation. The constitution of 1795 thus committed the republic to a program of successful expansion. At the same time it restricted the politically active class. It gave almost all adult males the vote, but they voted only for "electors." Persons chosen as electors were usually men of some means, able to give their time and willing to take part in public life; this in effect meant men of the upper middle class, since the old aristocracy was disaffected. The electors chose all important department officials and also the members of the national Legislative Assembly, which this time was divided

The constitution of 1795

into two chambers. The lower chamber was called the Council of Five Hundred; the upper, composed of 250 members, the Council of Ancients—"ancients" being those over 40. The chambers chose the executive, which was called the Directory (from which the whole regime took its name) and was made up of five Directors.

The government was thus constitutionally in the hands of substantial property owners, rural and urban, but its real base was narrower still. In the reaction after Thermidor many people began to consider restoring the monarchy. The Convention, to protect its own members, had ruled that two-thirds of the men initially elected to the Council of Five Hundred and Council of Ancients must be ex-members of the Convention. This interference with the freedom of the elections provoked serious disturbances in Paris, instigated mainly by royalists. The Convention, having now accustomed itself to using the army, instructed a young general named Bonaparte, who happened to be in Paris, to put down the royalist mob. He did so with a "whiff of grapeshot." The constitutional republic thus made itself dependent on military protection at the outset.

The regime had enemies to both Right and Left. On the Right, undisguised royalists agitated in Paris and even in the two councils; and they were in continuous touch with the late king's brother, the Count of Provence, whom they regarded as Louis XVIII (Louis XVI's son, who died in prison, was counted as Louis XVII). Louis XVIII had installed himself at Verona in Italy, where he headed a propaganda agency financed largely by British money. The worst obstacle to the resurgence of royalism in France was Louis XVIII himself. In 1795, on assuming the title, he had issued a Declaration of Verona, in which he announced his intention to restore the Old Regime and punish all involved in the Revolution back to 1789. It has been said, correctly enough in this connection, that the Bourbons "learned nothing and forgot nothing." Had Louis XVIII offered in 1795 what he offered in 1814, it is quite conceivable that his partisans in France might have brought about his restoration and terminated the war. As it was, the bulk of the French adhered not exactly to the republic as set up in 1795, but more negatively to any system that would shut out the Bourbons and privileged nobility, prevent a reimposition of the manorial system, and secure the new landowners, peasant and bourgeois, in the possession of the church properties which they had purchased.

The Left was made up of persons from various levels of society who still favored the more democratic ideas expressed earlier in the Revolution. Some of them thought that the fall of Robespierre had been a great misfortune. A tiny group of extremists formed the Conspiracy of Equals, organized in 1796 by "Gracchus" Babeuf. His intention was to overthrow the Directory and replace it with a dictatorial government which he called "democratic," in which private property would be abolished and equality would be decreed. For these ideas, and for his activist program, he has been regarded as a political precursor to modern communism. The Directory repressed the Conspiracy of Equals without difficulty and guillotined Babeuf and one other. Meanwhile it did nothing to relieve the distress of the lower classes, who showed little inclination to follow Babeuf even though they suffered from the ravages of scarcity and inflation.

The Political Crisis of 1797

In March 1797 occurred the first really free election ever held in France under republican auspices. The successful candidates were for the most part constitutional monarchists or at least vaguely royalist. A change of the balance within the Five Hundred and the Ancients, in favor of royalism, seemed to be impending. This was precisely what most of the republicans of 1793, including the regicides, could not endure, even though they had to violate the constitution to prevent it. Nor was it endurable, for other reasons, to General Napoleon Bonaparte.

Bonaparte had been born in 1769 into the minor nobility of Corsica, shortly after the annexation of Corsica to France. He had studied in French military schools and been commissioned in the Bourbon army but would never have reached high rank under the conditions of the Old Regime. In 1793 he was a fervent young Jacobin officer, who had been useful in driving the British from Toulon and who was consequently made a brigadier general by the government of the Terror. In 1795, as noted, he rendered service to the Convention by breaking up a demonstration of royalists. In 1796 he received command of an army, with which, in two brilliant campaigns, he crossed the Alps and drove the Austrians from north Italy. Like other generals he soon became independent from the government in Paris, which was financially too harassed to pay his troops or to supply him. He lived by local requisitions in Italy, became self-supporting, and in fact made the civilian government in Paris dependent on him.

Napoleon Bonaparte

He developed a foreign policy of his own. Many Italians had become dissatisfied with their old governments, so that the arrival of the French republican armies threw north Italy into a turmoil. The Venetian cities revolted against Venice, Bologna against the pope, Milan against Austria, and in Piedmont the Savoy monarchy was threatened by uprisings of its own subjects. Combining with some of these revolutionaries, while rejecting others, Bonaparte established a "Cisalpine" Republic in the Po valley, modeled on the French system, with Milan as its capital. Where the Directory, on the whole, had originally meant to return Milan to the Austrians in compensation for Austrian recognition of the French conquest of Belgium, Bonaparte insisted that France hold its position in both Belgium and Italy. He therefore needed expansionist republicans in the government in Paris and was perturbed by the royalist victories in the elections of 1797.

The Austrians negotiated with Bonaparte because they had been beaten by him in battle. The British also, in conferences with the French at Lille, discussed peace in 1796 and 1797. The war had gone badly for England; a party of Whigs led by Charles James Fox had always openly disapproved it, and the pro-French and republican radicals were so active that the government suspended habeas corpus in 1794, and thereafter imprisoned political agitators at its discretion. Crops were bad and bread was scarce and costly. England too suffered from inflation, for Pitt at first financed the war by extensive loans, and a good deal of gold was shipped to the Continent to finance the Allied armies. In February 1797 the Bank of England suspended gold payments to private citizens. Famine threatened, the populace was restless, and there were even mutinies in the fleet. Ireland was in rebellion; the French came close to landing a republican army there, and it could be supposed that the next attempt might be more successful. The Austrians, Britain's only remaining ally, had been routed by Bonaparte, and at the moment the British could subsidize them no further. The British had every reason to make peace.

Prospects for peace

Prospects for peace therefore seemed good in the summer of 1797, but, as always, it would be peace upon certain conditions. It was the royalists in France that were the peace party, since a restored king could easily return the conquests of the republic and would in any case abandon the new republics in Holland and the Po valley. The republicans in the French government could make peace with difficulty, if at all. They were constitutionally bound to retain Belgium. They were losing control of their own generals. Nor could the supreme question be evaded: Was peace dear enough to purchase by a return of the Old Regime, such as Louis XVIII had himself promised?

CHRONOLOGY OF NOTABLE EVENTS, 1789–1804

May 1789	Estates General convenes at Versailles
June 1789	The Third Estate declares itself to be the National Assembly
July 1789	Crowd assaults and captures the Bastille fortress in Paris
August 1789	National Assembly issues "Declaration of the Rights of Man and Citizen" and abolishes "feudal privileges"
September 1791	New French Constitution establishes a constitutional monarchy
April 1791	France declares war on Austria and Prussia
September 1792	New National Convention meets in Paris; France becomes a republic
January 1793	King Louis XVI is executed in Paris
1793–1794	The Radical Revolution and the "Reign of Terror"
July 1794	Robespierre and his Jacobin allies are executed
1795–1799	Republic called "the Directory" governs France and sends armies to spread revolutionary republicanism in Europe
November 1799	Napoleon Bonaparte seizes power in a coup d'état
1799–1804	Napoleon is "First Consul" in French government called the Consulate; laws are codified in Napoleonic Code
1801	Napoleon's Concordat with the Roman Catholic Church
1804	France becomes an empire under Emperor Napoleon I

The coup d'état of Fructidor

The coup d'état of Fructidor (September 4, 1797) resolved all these many issues. It was the turning point of the constitutional republic and was decisive for all Europe. The Directory asked for help from Bonaparte, who sent one of his generals, Augereau, to Paris. While Augereau stood by with a force of soldiers, the councils annulled most of the elections of the preceding spring. On the whole, it was the old republicans of the Convention who secured themselves in power. Their justification was that they were defending the revolution, keeping out Louis XVIII and the Old Regime. But to do so they had violated their own constitution and quashed the first free election ever held in a constitutional French republic. And they had become more than ever dependent on the army.

After the coup d'état the "Fructidorian" government broke off negotiations with England. With Austria it signed the treaty of Campo Formio on October 17, 1797, incorporating Bonaparte's ideas. By the new treaty Austria recognized the French annexation of Belgium (the former Austrian Netherlands), the French right to incorporate the Left Bank of the Rhine, and the French-dominated Cisalpine Republic in Italy. In return, Bonaparte allowed the Austrians to annex Venice and most of mainland Venetia.

Revolutionary republicanism spreads

In the following months, under French auspices, revolutionary republicanism spread rapidly through much of Italy, creating new republics with classical names. The old patrician republic of Genoa turned into a Ligurian Republic on the French model. At Rome the pope was deposed from his temporal power and a Roman Republic was established. In southern Italy a Neapolitan Republic, also called Parthenopean, was set up. In Switzerland at the same time, Swiss reformers cooperated with the French to create a new Helvetic Republic.

The Left Bank of the Rhine, in the atomistic Holy Roman Empire, was occupied by a great many German princes who now had to vacate. The treaty of Campo Formio provided that they be compensated by church territories in Germany east of the Rhine and that France have a hand in the redistribution. The German princes turned greedy eyes on the German bishops and abbots, and the almost 1,000-year-old empire, hardly more than a solemn form since the Peace of Westphalia, sank to the level of a land rush or real estate speculation, while France became involved in the territorial reconstruction of Germany.

The Coup d'État of 1799: Bonaparte

After Fructidor the idea of maintaining the republic as a free or constitutional government was given up. There were more uprisings, more quashed elections, more purgings both to Left and Right. The Directory turned into an ineffective dictatorship. It repudiated most of the assignats and the debt but failed to restore financial confidence or stability. Guerrilla activity flared up again in the Vendée and other parts of western France. The religious schism became more acute; the Directory had to take severe measures toward the refractory clergy.

Meanwhile Bonaparte waited for the situation to ripen. Returning from Italy a conquering hero, he was assigned to command the army in training to invade England. He concluded that invasion was premature and decided to strike indirectly at England, by threatening India in a spectacular invasion of Egypt. In 1798, outwitting the British fleet, he landed a French army at the mouth of the Nile. Egypt was part of the Ottoman Empire, and the French occupation of it alarmed the Russians, who had their own designs on the Middle East. The Austrians objected to the French rearrangement of Germany. A year and a half after the treaty of Campo Formio, Austria, Russia, and Great Britain formed an alliance known as the Second Coalition. The French Republic was again involved in a general war. And the war went unfavorably, for in August 1798 the British fleet had cut off the French army in Egypt by winning the battle of the Nile (or Aboukir), and in 1799 Russian forces, under Marshal Suvorov, were operating as far west as Switzerland and north Italy, where the Cisalpine Republic went down in ruin.

General Bonaparte's opportunity had now come. He left his army in Egypt and, slipping through the British fleet, reappeared unexpectedly in France. He found that certain civilian leaders in the Directory were planning a change. They included Sieyès, of whom little had been heard since he wrote *What Is the Third Estate?* in 1789, but who had sat in the Convention and voted for the death of Louis XVI. Sieyès' formula was now "confidence from below, authority from above"—what he now wanted of the people was acquiescence, and of the government, power to act. This group was looking about for a general, and their choice fell on the sensational young Bonaparte, who was still only 30. Dictatorship by an army officer was repugnant to most republicans of the Five Hundred and the Ancients. Bonaparte, Sieyès, and their followers resorted to force, executing the coup d'état of Brumaire (November 9, 1799), in which armed soldiers drove the legislators from the chambers. They proclaimed a new form of the republic, which Bonaparte entitled the Consulate. It was headed by three consuls, with Bonaparte as the First Consul.

The Directory turns to Bonaparte

THE FRENCH REPUBLIC AND ITS SATELLITES, 1798–1799

By 1799 the French Republic had annexed Belgium (the Austrian Netherlands) and the small German bishoprics and principalities west of the Rhine, and had created, with the aid of native sympathizers, a string of lesser revolutionary republics in the Dutch Netherlands, Switzerland, and most of Italy. With the treaty of Campo Formio between France and Austria in 1797, the Holy Roman Empire began to disintegrate, for the German princes of the Left Bank of the Rhine, who were dispossessed when their territories went to France, began to be compensated with territory of the church-states of the Holy Roman Empire. These developments were carried further by Napoleon (see map, p. 430).

46. THE AUTHORITARIAN REPUBLIC: THE CONSULATE, 1799–1804

The next chapter takes up the affairs of Europe as a whole in the time of Napoleon Bonaparte, the purpose at present being only to tell how he closed, in a way, the Revolution in France.

It happened that the French Republic, in falling into the hands of a general, fell also to a man of such remarkable talents as are often denominated genius. Bonaparte was a short man who would never have looked impressive in civilian clothing. His manners were rather coarse; he lost his temper, cheated at cards, and pinched people by the ear in a kind of formidable play—he was no "gentleman." A child of the Enlightenment and the Revolution, he was entirely emancipated not only from customary ideas but from moral scruples as well. He regarded the world as a flux to be formed by his own mind. He had an exalted belief in his own destinies, which became more mystical and exaggerated as the years went on. He claimed to follow his "star." His ideas of the good and the beautiful were rather blunt, but he was a man of extraordinary intellectual capacity, which impressed all with whom he came in contact. "Never speak unless you know you are the ablest man in the room," he once advised his stepson, on making him viceroy of Italy, a maxim which, if he followed it himself, still allowed him to do most of the talking. His interests ran to solid subjects, history, law, military science, public administration. His mind was tenacious and perfectly orderly; he once declared that it was like a chest of drawers, which he could open or close at will, forgetting any subject when its drawer was closed and finding it ready with all necessary detail when its drawer was opened. He had all the masterful qualities associated with leadership; he could dazzle and captivate those who had any inclination to follow him at all. Some of the most humane men of the day, including Goethe and Beethoven in Germany, and Lazare Carnot among the former revolutionary leaders, at first looked on him with high approval. He inspired confidence by his crisp speech, rapid decisions, and quick grasp of complex problems when they were newly presented to him. He was, or seemed, just what many people in France were looking for after ten years of upheaval.

Napoleon's genius

Under the Consulate France reverted to a form of enlightened despotism, and Bonaparte may be thought of as the last and most eminent of the enlightened despots. Despotic the new regime undoubtedly was from the start. Self-government through elected bodies was ruthlessly pushed aside. Bonaparte delighted in affirming the sovereignty of the people; but to his mind the people were a sovereign, like Voltaire's God, who somehow created the world but never thereafter interfered in it. He clearly saw that a government's authority was greater when it was held to represent the entire nation. In the weeks after Brumaire he assured himself of a popular mandate by devising a written constitution and submitting it to a general referendum or "plebiscite." The voters could take it—or nothing. They took it by a majority officially reported as 3,011,007 to 1,562.

Bonaparte as First Consul

The new constitution set up a make-believe of parliamentary institutions. It provided for universal male suffrage, but the citizens merely chose "notables"; men on the lists of notables were then appointed by the government itself to public position. The notables had no powers of their own. They were merely available for appointment to office. They might sit in a Legislative Body, where they could neither initiate nor discuss legislation but only mutely reject or enact it. There was also a Tribunate which discussed public policies but had no enacting powers. There was a Conservative Senate, which had rights of appointment of notables to office ("patronage" in American terms) and in which numerous storm-tossed regicides found a haven. The main agency in the new government was the Council of State, imitated from the Old Regime; it prepared the significant legislation, often under the presidency of the First Consul himself, who always gave the impression that he understood everything. The First Consul made all the decisions and ran the state. The regime did not openly represent anybody, and that was its strength, for it provoked the less opposition. In any case, the political machinery just described fell rapidly into disuse.

Bonaparte entrenched himself also by promising and obtaining peace. The military problem at the close of 1799 was much simplified by the attitude of the Russians, who in effect withdrew from the war with France. In the Italian theater Bonaparte had to deal only with the Austrians, whom he again defeated, by again crossing the Alps, at the battle of Marengo in June 1800. In February 1801 the Austrians signed the treaty of Lunéville, in which the terms of Campo Formio were confirmed. A year later, in March 1802, peace was made even with Britain.

Peace was made also at home. Bonaparte kept internal order, partly by a secret political police but more especially through a powerful and centralized administrative machine in which a "prefect," under direct orders of the minister of the interior, ruled firmly over each of the regional departments created by the Constituent Assembly. The new government put down the guerrillas in the west. Its laws and taxes were imposed on Brittany and the Vendée. Peasants there were no longer terrorized by marauding partisans. A new peace settled down on the factions left by the Revolution. Bonaparte offered a general amnesty and invited back to France, with a few exceptions, exiles of all stripes, from the first aristocratic émigrés to the refugees and deportees of the republican coups d'état. Requiring only that they work for him and stop quarreling with each other, he picked reasonable men from all camps. His Second Consul was Cambacérès, a regicide of the Terror; his Third Consul was Lebrun, who had been Maupeou's colleague in the days of Louis XV. Fouché emerged as minister of police; he had been an Hébertist and extreme terrorist in 1793 and had done as much as anyone to bring about the fall of Robespierre. Before 1789 he had been an obscure bourgeois professor of physics. Talleyrand appeared as minister of foreign affairs; he had spent the Terror in safe seclusion in the United States, and his principles, if he had any, were those of constitutional monarchy. Before 1789 he had been a bishop, and he descended from an old and famous aristocratic lineage—no one who had not known the Old Regime, he once said, could realize how pleasant it had been. Men of this kind were now willing, for a few years beginning in 1800, to forget the past and work in common toward the future.

Disturbers of the new order the First Consul ruthlessly put down. Indeed, he concocted alarms to make himself more welcome as a pillar of order. On Christmas Eve, 1800, on the way to the opera, he was nearly killed by a bomb, or "infernal machine," as people then called such bombs. It had been set by royalists, but Bonaparte represented it as the work of Jacobin conspiracy, being most afraid at the moment of some of the old republicans; and over 100 former Jacobins were deported. Contrariwise, in 1804, he greatly exaggerated certain royalist plots against him, invaded the independent state of Baden, and there arrested the Duke of Enghien, who was related to the Bourbons. Though he knew Enghien to be innocent, he had him shot. His purpose now was to please the old Jacobins by staining his own hands with Bourbon blood; Fouché and the regicides concluded that they were secure so long as Bonaparte was in power.

After repeatedly winning battles against all the powers of Europe, Napoleon developed even more grandiose ideas of himself and the imperial power of France. This painting was completed in 1806 by Jacques-Louis David, the aging revolutionary whose work had once portrayed the Tennis Court Oath and the faces of common people in Paris. Here he presents an idealized image of Napoleon as a young republican hero who crossed the Alps in 1800 to win the battle of Marengo.

(Giraudon/Art Resource, NY)

The Settlement with the Church; Other Reforms

For all but the most convinced royalists and republicans, reconciliation was made easier by the establishment of peace with the church. Bonaparte himself was a pure eighteenth-century rationalist. He regarded religion as a convenience. He advertised himself as a Muslim in Egypt, as a Catholic in France, and as a freethinker among the professors at the Institute in Paris. But a Catholic revival was in full swing and he saw its importance. The refractory clergy were the spiritual force animating all forms of counter-revolution. "Fifty émigré bishops, paid by England," he once said, "lead the French clergy today. Their influence must be destroyed. For this we need the authority of the pope." Ignoring the horrified outcries of the old Jacobins, in 1801 he signed a concordat with the Vatican.

Concordat with the Vatican

Both parties gained from the settlement. The autonomy of the prerevolutionary Gallican church came to an end. The pope received the right to depose French bishops, since before the schism could be healed both constitutional and refractory bishops had to be obliged to resign. The constitutional or pro-revolutionary clergy came under the discipline of the Holy See. Publicity of Catholic worship, in such forms as processions in the streets, was again allowed. Church seminaries were again permitted. But Bonaparte and the heirs of the Revolution gained even more. The pope, by signing the concordat, virtually recognized the Republic. The Vatican agreed to raise no question over the former tithes and the former church lands. The new owners of former church properties thus obtained clear titles. Nor was there any further question of Avignon, an enclave within France, formerly papal, annexed to France in 1791. Nor were the papal negotiators able to undermine religious toleration; all that Bonaparte would concede was a clause that was purely factual, and hence harmless, stating that Catholicism was the religion of the majority of the French people. The clergy, in compensation for loss of their tithes and property, were assured of receiving salaries from the state. But Bonaparte, to dispel the notion of an established church, put Protestant ministers of all denominations on the state payroll also. He thus checkmated the Vatican on important points. At the same time, simply by signing an agreement with Rome, he disarmed the counterrevolution. It could no longer be said that the Republic was godless. Good relations did not, indeed, last very long, for Bonaparte and the papacy were soon at odds. But the terms of the concordat proved lasting.

With peace and order established, the constructive work of the Consulate turned to the fields of law and administration. The First Consul and his advisers combined what they conceived to be the best of the Revolution and of the Old Regime. The modern state took on clearer form. It was the reverse of everything feudal. All public authority was concentrated in officially employed agents of government, no person was held to be under any legal authority except that of the state, and the authority of government fell on all persons alike. There were no more estates, legal classes, privileges, local liberties, hereditary offices, guilds, or manors. Judges, officials, and army officers received specified salaries. Neither military commissions nor civil offices could be bought and sold. Citizens were to rise in government service according to their abilities rather than their wealth or priveleged birth.

Consulate reforms

"Careers open to talent"

This was the doctrine of "careers open to talent"; it was what the bourgeoisie had wanted before the Revolution, and a few persons of quite humble birth profited also. For sons of the old aristocracy, it meant that pedigree was not enough; they must also show individual capacity to obtain employment. Qualification came to depend increasingly on education, and the secondary and higher schools were reorganized in these years, with a view to preparing young men for government service and the learned professions. Scholarships were provided, but it was mainly the upper middle class that benefited. Education, in fact, in France and in Europe generally, came to be an important determinant of social standing, with one system for those who could spend a dozen or more years at school, and another for those who were to enter the workforce at the age of 12 or 14. Meanwhile, French intellectual life was strictly regulated and censored. When a few professors at the National Institute began to question certain government policies, for example, Bonaparte suppressed both their writings and the section of the Institute in which they worked; and when the liberal critic Germaine de Staël published books that displeased the First Consul, she was sent off to exile in Switzerland. Creative, critical intellectual debate thus became impossible in France during these years, though Bonaparte satisfied many of the popular demands for education and professional advancement.

Another deep demand of the French people, deeper than the demand for the vote, was for more reason, order, and economy in public finance and taxation. The Consulate gave these also. There were no tax exemptions because of birth, status, or special arrangement. Everyone was supposed to pay, so that no disgrace attached to payment, and there was less evasion. In principle these changes had been introduced in 1789; after 1799 they began to work. For the first time in ten years the government really collected the taxes that it levied and so could rationally plan its financial affairs. Order was introduced also into expenditure, and accounting methods were improved. There was no longer a haphazard assortment of different "funds" on which various officials drew independently and confidentially as they needed money, but a concentration of financial management in the treasury and even in a kind of budget. The revolutionary uncertainties over the value of money were also ended. Because the Directory had shouldered the odium of repudiating the paper money and government debt, the Consulate was able to establish a sound currency and public credit. To assist in government financing, one of the banks of the Old Regime was revived and established as the Bank of France.

Like all enlightened despots, Bonaparte codified the laws, and of all law codes since the Romans the Napoleonic codes are the most famous. To the 300 legal systems of the Old Regime and the mass of royal ordinances were now added the thousands of laws enacted but seldom implemented by the revolutionary assemblies. Five codes emerged—the Civil Code (often called simply the Code Napoleon), the codes of civil and of criminal procedure, and the commercial and penal codes. The codes made France legally and judicially uniform. They assured legal equality; all French citizens had the same civil rights. They formulated the new law of property and set forth the law of contracts, debts, leases, stock companies, and similar matters in such a way as to create the legal framework for an economy of private enterprise. They repeated the ban of all previous regimes on organized labor unions and were severe with individual workers, their word not being acceptable in court against that of the employer—a significant departure from equality before the law. The criminal code was somewhat freer in giving the government the means to detect crime than in granting the individual the means of defense against legal charges. As for the family, the codes recognized civil marriage and divorce but left the wife with very restricted powers over property and the father with extensive authority over minor children; the legal system codified a paternalistic view of all family relations. The codes reflected much of French life under the Old Regime. They also set the character of France as it has been ever since, socially bourgeois, legally egalitarian, and administratively bureaucratic.

The Napoleonic Codes

In France, with the Consulate, the Revolution was over. If its highest hopes had not been accomplished, the worst evils of the Old Regime had at least been cured. The beneficiaries of the Revolution felt secure. Even former aristocrats were rallying. The working-class movement, repeatedly frustrated under all the revolutionary regimes, now vanished from the political scene to reappear as socialism 30 years later. What the Third Estate had most wanted in 1789 was now both codified and enforced, with the exception of parliamentary government, which after ten years of turmoil many people were temporarily willing to forgo. Moreover, in 1802, the French Republic was at peace with the papacy, Great Britain, and all Continental powers. It reached to the Rhine and had dependent republics in Holland and Italy. So popular was the First Consul that in 1802, by another plebiscite, he had himself elected consul for life. A new constitution, in 1804, again ratified by plebiscite, declared that "the government of the republic is entrusted to an emperor." The Consulate became the Empire, and Bonaparte emerged as Napoleon I, Emperor of the French.

From Consulate to Empire

But France, no longer revolutionary at home, was revolutionary outside its borders. Napoleon became a terror to the patricians of Europe. They called him the "Jacobin." And the France which he ruled, and used as his arsenal, was an incomparably formidable state. Even before the Revolution it had been the most populous in Europe, perhaps the most wealthy, in the front rank of scientific enterprise and intellectual leadership. Now all the old barriers of privilege, tax exemption, localism, and caste exclusiveness had disappeared. The new France could tap the wealth of its citizens and put able men into positions without inquiring into their origins. Every private, boasted Napoleon, carried a marshal's baton in his knapsack. The French looked with disdain on their caste-ridden adversaries. The principle of civic equality proved not only to have the appeal of justice, but also to be politically useful, and the resources of France were hurled against Europe with a force which for many years nothing could check.

For interactive exercises, glossary, chronologies, and more, go to the *Online Learning Center* at **www.mhhe.com/palmer10.**

Chapter 10

NAPOLEONIC EUROPE

The repercussions of the French Revolution had been felt throughout Europe since the fall of the Bastille, and even more definitely after the outbreak of war in 1792 and the ensuing victories of the republican armies. They became even more evident after the republican General Bonaparte turned into Napoleon I, Emperor of the French, King of Italy, and Protector of the Confederation of the Rhine. Napoleon surpassed all previous European rulers in imposing a broad political unity on the European continent. Although his imperial power collapsed in less than fifteen years, his military campaigns and political ascendancy transformed both international relations in Europe and the internal development of the various European peoples. The French impact on other nations, though based on military success, represented more than mere forcible subjugation. Innovations of a kind made in France by revolution were brought to other countries by administrative decree. There were for several years Germans, Italians, Dutch, and Poles who worked with the French emperor to introduce the changes that he demanded, and which they themselves often desired. In Prussia it was resistance to Napoleon that gave the incentive to internal reorganization and fostered the emergence of a new German nationalism. Whether by collaboration or resistance, Europe was transformed.

It is convenient to think of the fighting from 1792 to 1814 as a "world war," as indeed it was, affecting not only all of Europe but also places as far away as Latin America, where the wars of independence began, or the interior of North America, where the United States purchased Louisiana in 1803 and attempted a conquest of Canada in the War of 1812. But it is important to realize that this world war was actually a series of wars, most of them quite short and distinct. Only Great Britain remained continually at war with France, except for about a year of peace in 1802–1803. Never were the four

Chapter emblem: Detail from a nineteenth-century illustration of Napoleon and Tsar Alexander I meeting on the Niemen River in 1807. (Rare Book Collection, University of North Carolina–Chapel Hill (Hoyt IC-187))

great European powers, Britain, Austria, Russia, and Prussia, simultaneously in the field against France until 1813.

The history of the Napoleonic period would be much simpler if the European governments had fought merely to protect themselves against the aggressive French. Each, however, in its way, was as dynamic and expansive as Napoleon himself. For some generations Great Britain had been building a commercial empire, Russia had been pushing upon Poland and Turkey, and Prussia had been consolidating its territories and striving for leadership in north Germany. Austria was less aggressive, but the Austrians were not without their own dreams of ascendancy in Germany, the Balkans, and the Adriatic. None of these ambitions ceased during the Napoleonic years. Governments, in pursuit of their own aims, were quite as willing to ally with Napoleon as to fight him. Only gradually, and under repeated provocation, did they conclude that their main interest was to dispose of the French emperor entirely.

47. THE FORMATION OF THE FRENCH IMPERIAL SYSTEM

The Dissolution of the First and Second Coalitions, 1792–1802

The conflicting purposes of the powers had been apparent from almost the beginning of the French Revolution. Leopold of Austria, in issuing the Declaration of Pillnitz in 1791, had believed a general European coalition against France to be impossible. When war began in 1792, the Austrians and Prussians kept their main forces in eastern Europe, more afraid of each other and of Russia, in the matter of Poland, than of the French revolutionary republic. Indeed, the main accomplishment of the First Coalition was the partition of Poland and the dissolution of the Polish state.

The First Coalition disintegrates

In 1795 the French broke up the coalition. The British withdrew their army from the Continent. Prussia and Spain each made a separate peace with France. Indeed, Bourbon Spain—acting for reasons of strategic self-interest that ignored all ideology or principle—formed an alliance with the French republic that had guillotined Louis XVI and kept Louis XVIII from his monarchic rights. Spain simply reverted to the eighteenth-century pattern in allying with France because of hostility to Great Britain, whose possession of Gibraltar, naval influence in the Mediterranean, and attitude toward the Spanish empire were disquieting to the Spanish government. When Austria signed the peace of Campo Formio in 1797, the First Coalition was totally dissipated, only British naval forces remaining engaged with the French.

The Second Coalition of 1799 fared no better. After the British fleet defeated the French at the battle of the Nile, cutting off the French army in Egypt, the Russians saw their ambitions in the Mediterranean blocked mainly by the British and withdrew Suvorov's army from western Europe. Austria's acceptance of the peace of Lunéville in 1801 dissolved the Second Coalition, and in 1802 Great Britain signed the peace of Amiens. For the only time between 1792 and 1814 no European power was at war with another.

Peace Interim, 1802–1803

Never had a peace been so advantageous to France as the peace of 1802. But Bonaparte gave it no chance. He used peace as he did war to advance his interests. He dispatched a sizable army to Haiti, ostensibly to suppress Toussaint L'Ouverture and the Haitian military campaign to establish an independent republic. But he also sent this army with the further thought (since Louisiana had been ceded back by Spain to France in 1800) of reviving the French colonial empire in America. He reorganized the Cisalpine Republic into an "Italian" Republic with himself as president. He reorganized the Helvetic Republic, making himself "mediator" of the Confederation of Switzerland. He reorganized Germany; that is to say, he and his agents closely watched the rearrangement of territory which the Germans themselves had been carrying out since 1797.

By the treaty of Campo Formio, it will be recalled, German princes of the Left Bank of the Rhine, expropriated by the annexation of their dominions to the French Republic, were to receive new territories on the Right Bank. The result was a scramble called by patriotic German historians the "shame of the princes." The German rulers, far from opposing Bonaparte or upholding any national interests, competed desperately for the absorption of German territory, each bribing and fawning upon the French (Talleyrand made over 10,000,000 francs in the process) to win French support against other Germans. The Holy Roman Empire was fatally mauled by the Germans themselves. Most of its ecclesiastical principalities and 45 out of its 51 free cities disappeared, annexed by their larger neighbors. The number of states in the Holy Empire was greatly reduced, but Prussia, Bavaria, Württemberg, and Baden consolidated and enlarged themselves. These arrangements were ratified in February 1803 by the diet of the Empire. The enlarged German states now depended on Bonaparte for the maintenance of their new position.

The "shame of the princes"

Formation of the Third Coalition in 1805

Britain and France went to war again in 1803. Bonaparte, his communications with America menaced by the British navy, and his army in Haiti decimated by disease and by the military campaigns of the Haitian independence movement, suspended his ideas for recreating an American empire and sold Louisiana to the United States. Great Britain began to seek allies for a Third Coalition. In May 1804 Napoleon pronounced himself Emperor of the French to ensure the hereditary permanency of his system, though at the time he had no heir. Francis II of Austria, seeing the Holy Roman Empire in ruins, promulgated the Austrian Empire in August 1804. He thus advanced the long process of integrating the Danubian monarchy. In 1805 Austria signed an alliance with Great Britain. The Third Coalition was completed by the accession of the Russian Tsar Alexander I, who, after Napoleon himself, was to become the most considerable figure on the European stage.

Tsar Alexander I

Alexander was the grandson of Catherine the Great, educated by her to be a kind of enlightened despot on the eighteenth-century model. The Swiss tutor of his boyhood, La Harpe, later turned up as a pro-French revolutionary in the Helvetic Republic of 1798. Alexander became tsar in 1801, at the age of 24, through a palace revolution which implicated him in the murder of his father Paul. He still corresponded with La Harpe, and he surrounded himself with a circle of liberal and zealous young men of various nationalities, of whom the most prominent was a Polish youth, Czartoryski. Alexander regarded the still recent partitions of Poland as a crime. He wished to restore the unity of Poland with himself as a constitutional king. In Germany many who had first warmed to the French Revolution, but had been disillusioned, began to hail the new liberal tsar as the protector of Germany and hope of the future. Alexander conceived of himself as a rival to Napoleon in

Toussaint L'Ouverture, pictured here with a sword and documents to symbolize his independence, led the political and military movement that created a new Republic of Haiti. Although Toussaint himself was captured and sent to a prison in France (where he died in 1803), the French defeat in Haiti made Napoleon abandon his plans for an American empire and sell Louisiana to the United States.
(Library of Congress)

guiding the destinies of Europe in an age of change. Moralistic and self-righteous, he puzzled and disturbed the statesmen of Europe, who generally saw, behind his humane and republican utterances, either an enthroned leader of all the "Jacobins" of Europe or the familiar specter of Russian aggrandizement.

Yet Alexander, more than his contemporaries, formed a conception of international collective security and the indivisibility of peace. He was shocked when Napoleon in 1804, in order to seize the duke of Enghien, rudely violated the sovereignty of Baden. He declared that the issue in Europe was clearly between law and force—between an international society in which the rights of each member were secured by international agreement and organization and a society in which all trembled before the rule of cynicism and conquest embodied in the French usurper.

Alexander was therefore ready to enter a Third Coalition with Great Britain. Picturing himself as a future arbiter of central Europe, and with secret designs on the Ottoman Empire and the Mediterranean, he signed a treaty with England in April 1805. The British agreed to pay Russia £1,250,000 for each 100,000 soldiers that the Russians raised.

The Third Coalition, 1805–1807: The Peace of Tilsit

Napoleon meanwhile, since the resumption of hostilities in 1803, had been making preparations to invade England. He concentrated large forces on the Channel coast, together with thousands of boats and barges in which he gave the troops amphibious training in embarkation and debarkation. He reasoned that if his own fleet could divert or cripple the British fleet for a few days he could place enough soldiers on the defenseless island to force its capitulation. The British, sensing mortal danger, lined their coasts with lookouts and signal beacons and set to drilling a home guard. Their main defense was twofold: the Austro-Russian armies and the British fleet under Lord Nelson. The Russian and Austrian armies moved westward in the summer of 1805. In August Napoleon relieved the pressure upon England, shifting seven army corps from the Channel to the upper Danube. On October 15 he surrounded an Austrian force of 50,000 men at Ulm in Bavaria, forcing it to surrender without resistance. On October 21 Lord Nelson, off Cape Trafalgar on the Spanish coast, caught and annihilated the main body of the combined fleets of France and Spain.

The battle of Trafalgar established the supremacy of the British navy for over a century—but only on the proviso that Napoleon be prevented from controlling the bulk of Europe, which would furnish an ample base *British victory at Trafalgar* for eventual construction of a greater navy than the British. And to control Europe was precisely what Napoleon proceeded to do. Moving east from Ulm he came upon the Russian and Austrian armies in Moravia, where on December 2 he won the great victory of Austerlitz. The broken Russian army withdrew into Poland, and Austria made peace. By the treaty of Pressburg Napoleon took Venetia from the Austrians, to whom he had given it in 1797, and annexed it to his kingdom of Italy (the former Cisalpine and Italian Republic), which now included a good deal of Italy north of Rome. Venice and Trieste soon resounded with the hammers of shipwrights rebuilding the Napoleonic fleet. In Germany, early in 1806, the French emperor raised Bavaria and Württemberg to the stature of kingdoms and Baden to a grand duchy. The Holy Roman Empire was finally, formally, and irrevocably dissolved. In its place Napoleon began to gather his German client states into a new kind of Germanic federation, the Confederation of the Rhine, of which he made himself the "protector."

Prussia, at peace with France for ten years, had declined to join the Third Coalition. But as Napoleon's program for controlling Germany became clear after Austerlitz, the war party in Prussia became irresistible, and the Prussian government, outwitted and distraught, went to war with the French unaided and alone. The French smashed the famous Prussian army at the battles of Jena and Auerstädt in October 1806. The French cavalry galloped all over north Germany *The Third Coalition collapses* unopposed. The Prussian king and his government took refuge in the east, at Königsberg, where the tsar and the re-forming Russian army might protect them. But the terrible Corsican pursued the Russians also. Marching through western Poland and into East Prussia, he met the Russian army first at the sanguinary but indecisive battle of Eylau and then defeated it on June 14, 1807, at Friedland. Alexander I was unwilling to retreat into Russia. He was unsure of his own resources; if the country were invaded, there might be a revolt of the nobles or even of the serfs—for people still remembered the great serf rebellion of the 1770s. Alexander feared also merely playing the game of the British. He put aside his war aims of 1804 and signified his willingness to negotiate with Napoleon. The Third Coalition had gone the way of the two before it.

The Emperor of the French and the Autocrat of All the Russias met privately on a raft in the Niemen River, not far from the border between Prussia and Russia, the very easternmost frontier of civilized Europe, as the triumphant Napoleon gleefully imagined it. The hapless Prussian king, Frederick William III, paced nervously on the bank. Bonaparte turned all his charm upon Alexander, denouncing England as the author of all the troubles of Europe and captivating him by flights of Latin imagination, in which he set before Alexander a boundless destiny as Emperor of the East, intimating that Russia's future lay toward Turkey, Persia, Afghanistan, and India. The result of their conversations was the treaty of Tilsit of July 1807, in many ways the high point of Napoleon's success. The French and Russian empires became allies, mainly against Great Britain. Ostensibly this alliance lasted for five years. Alexander accepted Napoleon as a kind of Emperor of the West. As for Prussia, Napoleon continued to occupy Berlin with his troops, and he took away all Prussian territories west of the Elbe, combining them with others taken from Hanover to make a new kingdom of Westphalia, which became part of his Confederation of the Rhine.

The Treaty of Tilsit

The Continental System and the War in Spain

Hardly had the "peace of the continent" been reestablished on the foundation of a Franco-Russian alliance when Napoleon began to have serious trouble. He was bent on subduing the British who, secure on their island, seemed beyond his reach. Since the French naval disaster at Trafalgar, there was no possibility of invading England in the foreseeable future. Napoleon therefore turned to economic warfare. He would fight sea power with land power, using his political control of the Continent to shut out British goods and shipping from all European ports. He would destroy the British trade in exports to Europe, both exports of British products and the profitable British reexport of goods from America and Asia. Thereby, he hoped, he would ruin British commercial firms and cause a violent business depression, marked by overloaded warehouses, unemployment, runs on the banks, a fall of the currency, rising prices, and revolutionary agitation. The British government, which would simultaneously be losing revenues from its customs duties, would thus find itself unable to carry the enormous national debt, or to borrow additional funds from its subjects, or to continue its financial subsidies to the military powers of Europe. At Berlin, in 1806, after the battle of Jena, Napoleon issued the Berlin Decree, forbidding the importation of British goods into any part of Europe allied with or dependent on himself. He in that way formally established the Continental System.

Economic warfare

To make the Continental System effective Napoleon believed that it must extend to all continental Europe without exception. By the treaty of Tilsit, in 1807, he required both Russia and Prussia to adhere to it. They agreed to exclude all British goods; in fact, in the following months Russia, Prussia, and Austria all declared war on Great Britain. Napoleon then ordered two neutral states, Denmark and Portugal, to adhere. Denmark was an important entrepôt for all central Europe, and the British, fearing Danish compliance, dispatched a fleet to Copenhagen, bombarded the city for four days, and took captive the Danish fleet. The outraged Danes allied with Napoleon and joined the Continental System. Portugal, long a satellite of Britain, refused compliance; Napoleon invaded it. To control the whole European coastline from St. Petersburg around to Trieste he now had only to control the ports of Spain. By a series of deceptions he got both the Bourbon Charles IV and his son Ferdinand to abdicate the Spanish throne. He made his brother Joseph king of Spain in 1808 and reinforced him with a large French army.

He thus involved himself in an entanglement from which he never escaped. The Spanish regarded the Napoleonic soldiers as godless villians who desecrated churches. Fierce guerrillas took the field. Cruelties of one side were answered by atrocities of the

This meeting between Napoleon and Russia's Alexander I on the Niemen River produced an alliance and the Continental System. The new system was aimed against the British, but Alexander soon disliked the restrictions on Anglo-Russian commerce. His withdrawal from the Continental System provoked Napoleon's disastrous invasion of Russia in 1812.
(Rare Book Collection, University of North Carolina–Chapel Hill (Hoyt IC-187))

other. The British sent an expeditionary force of their small regular army, eventually under the Duke of Wellington, to sustain the Spanish guerrillas; the resulting Peninsular War dragged on for five years. But from the beginning the affair went badly for Napoleon. In July 1808 a French general, for the first time since the Revolution, surrendered an army corps,

The Peninsular War in Spain

without fighting, by the capitulation at Baylen. In August another French force surrendered to the British army in Portugal. And these events raised hopes in the rest of Europe. An anti-French movement swept over Germany. It was felt strongly in Austria, where the Habsburg government, undaunted by three defeats and hoping to lead a general German national resistance, prepared for a fourth time since 1792 to go to war with France.

The Austrian War of Liberation, 1809

Napoleon summoned a general congress which met at Erfurt in Saxony in September 1808. His main purpose was to talk with his ally of a year, Alexander; but he assembled numerous dependent monarchs as well, by whose presence he hoped to overawe the tsar. He even had Talma, the leading actor of the day, play in the theater of Erfurt before "a parterre of kings." Alexander was unimpressed. He was hurt in a sensitive spot because Napoleon, a few months before, had made moves to re-create a Polish state, setting up what was called the Grand Duchy of Warsaw. He had found Napoleon unwilling, despite the grandiose language of Tilsit, really to support his expansion into the Balkans. In addi-

Talleyrand

tion, Alexander was taken aside by Talleyrand, Napoleon's foreign minister. Talleyrand had concluded that Napoleon was overreaching himself and said so confidentially to the tsar, advising him to wait. Talleyrand thus betrayed the man whom he ostensibly served and prepared a safe place for himself in the event of Napoleon's fall; but he acted also as an aristocrat of the prenationalistic Old Regime, seeing his own country as only one part of the whole of Europe, believing a balance among the several parts to be necessary and holding that peace would be possible only when the exaggerated reach of French power would be reduced. For France and Russia, the two strongest states, to combine against all other states was contrary to all principles of the older diplomacy.

Austria proclaimed a war of liberation in April 1809. Napoleon advanced rapidly along the familiar route to Vienna. The German princes, indebted to the French, declined to join in a general German war against him. Alexander stood watchfully on the sidelines. Napoleon won the battle of Wagram in July. In October Austria made peace. The short war of 1809 was over. The Danubian monarchy, by no means as fragile as it seemed, survived a fourth defeat at the hands of the French without internal revolution or disloyalty to the Habsburg house. From it, in punishment, Napoleon took considerable portions of its territory. Part of Austrian Poland was used to enlarge Napoleon's Grand Duchy of Warsaw, and parts of Dalmatia, Slovenia, and Croatia, on the south, were erected into a new creation which Napoleon called the Illyrian Provinces (see map, p. 407).

Napoleon at His Peak, 1809–1811

Metternich

The next two years saw the Napoleonic empire at its peak. In Austria after the defeat of 1809 the conduct of foreign affairs fell to Clemens von Metternich, who was to remain the Austrian foreign minister for 40 years. He was a German from west of the Rhine, whose ancestral territories had been annexed to the French Republic, but he had entered the Austrian service and even married the granddaughter of Kaunitz, the old model of diplomatic savoir-faire, of which Metternich now became a model himself. Austria had been repeatedly humiliated and even partitioned by Napoleon, most of all in the treaty of 1809. But Metternich was not a man to conduct diplomacy by grudges. Believing that Russia was the really permanent problem for a state situated in the Danube valley, Metternich thought it wise to renew good relations with France. He was quite willing to go along with Napoleon, whom he knew personally, having been Austrian ambassador to Paris before the short war of 1809.

The French emperor, who in 1809 was exactly 40, was increasingly concerned by the fact that he was childless. He had made an empire which he pronounced hereditary. Yet he had no heir. Between him and his wife Josephine whom he had married in youth, and who

THE THIRD OF MAY 1808
by Francisco de Goya (Spanish, 1746–1808)
Facing steadfast resistance to their military occupation of Spain, the French army committed atrocities such as the brutal scene that Goya portrayed in this image of the Peninsular War.
(Erich Lessing/Art Resource, NY)

was six years his senior, there had long since ceased to be affection or even fidelity on either side. He divorced her in 1809, though since she had two children by a first husband she naturally protested that Napoleon's childlessness was not her fault. He intended to marry a younger woman who might bear him offspring. He intended also to make a spectacular marriage, to extort for himself, a self-made Corsican army officer, the highest and most exclusive recognition that aristocratic Europe could bestow. He debated between Habsburgs and Romanovs, between an archduchess and a grand duchess. Tactful inquiries at St. Petersburg concerning the availability of Alexander's sister were tactfully rebuffed; the tsar intimated that his mother would never allow it. The Russian alliance again showed its limitations. Napoleon was thrown into the arms of Metternich—and of Marie Louise, the 18-year-old daughter of the Austrian emperor and niece of another "Austrian woman," Marie Antoinette. They were married in 1810. In a year she bore him a son, whom he entitled the King of Rome.

Napoleon assumed ever more pompous airs of imperial majesty. He was now, by marriage, the nephew of Louis XVI. He showed more consideration to French noblemen of the Old Regime—only they, he said, knew really how to serve. He surrounded himself with a newly made hereditary Napoleonic nobility, hoping that the new families, as time went on, would bind their own fortunes to the house of Bonaparte. The marshals became dukes and princes; Talleyrand became the Prince of Benevento; and the bourgeois Fouché, an Hébertist radical in 1793 and more latterly a police official, was now solemnly addressed as the Duke of Otranto. In foreign affairs also the cycle had been run. With one significant exception, all the powers of the successive coalitions were allied with the French, and the Son of the Revolution now gravely referred to the emperor of Austria as "my father."

48. THE GRAND EMPIRE: SPREAD OF THE REVOLUTION

The Organization of the Napoleonic Empire

The empire at its height

Territorially Napoleon's influence enjoyed its farthest reach in 1810 and 1811, when it included the entire European mainland except the Balkan peninsula. The Napoleonic domain was in two parts. Its core was the French empire; then came thick layers of dependent states, which together with France comprised the Grand Empire. In addition, to the north and east were the "allied states" under their traditional governments—the three great powers, Prussia, Austria, and Russia, and also Denmark and Sweden. The allied states were at war with Great Britain, though not engaged in positive hostilities; their populations were supposed to do without British goods under the Continental System, but otherwise Napoleon had no direct lawful influence upon their internal affairs.

The French empire, as successor to the French Republic, included Belgium and the Left Bank of the Rhine. In addition, by 1810, it had developed two appendages which on a map looked like tentacles outstretched from it (see the map on p. 407). When he proclaimed France an empire and turned its dependent republics into kingdoms, Napoleon had set up his brother Louis as king of Holland; but Louis had shown such a tendency to ingratiate himself with the Dutch, and such a willingness to let Dutch businessmen trade secretly with the British, that Napoleon dethroned him and incorporated Holland into the French empire. In his endless war upon British goods he found it useful to exert more direct control over the ports of Bremen, Hamburg, Lübeck, Genoa, and Leghorn; he therefore annexed directly to the French empire the German coast as far as the western Baltic, and the Italian coast far enough to include Rome, which he desired for its imperial rather that its commercial value. Harking back to traditions as old as Charlemagne, he considered Rome the second city of his empire and entitled his son the "King of Rome." When Pope Pius VII protested, Napoleon took him prisoner and interned him in France. The whole French empire, from Lübeck to Rome, was governed directly by departmental prefects who reported to Paris, and the 83 departments of France, created by the Constituent Assembly, had risen in 1810 to 130.

The dependent states, forming with France the Grand Empire, were of different kinds. The Swiss federation remained republican in form. The Illyrian Provinces, which included Trieste and the Dalmatian coast, were administered in their brief two years almost like departments of France. In Poland, since the Russians objected to a revived kingdom of Poland, Napoleon called his creation the Grand Duchy of Warsaw. Among the most important of the dependent states in the Grand Empire were the German states organized into the

Confederation of the Rhine. Too modestly named, the Confederation included all Germany between what the French annexed on the west and what Prussia and Austria retained on the east. It was a league of all the German princes in this region who were regarded as sovereign and who now numbered only about 20, the most important being the four newly made kings of Saxony, Bavaria, Württemberg, and Westphalia. Westphalia was an entirely new and synthetic state, made up of Hanoverian and Prussian territories and of various small parts of the old Germany. Its king was Napoleon's youngest brother, Jerome.

Napoleon liked to use his family as a means of rule. The Corsican clan became the Bonaparte dynasty. His brother Joseph from 1804 to 1808 functioned as king of Naples and after 1808 as king of Spain. Louis Bonaparte was for six years king of Holland; Jerome was king of Westphalia. Sister Caroline became queen of Naples after brother Joseph's transfer to Spain; for Napoleon, running out of brothers (having quarreled with his remaining brother, Lucien), gave the throne of Naples to his brother-in-law, Joachim Murat, a cavalry officer who was Caroline's husband. In the "Kingdom of Italy," which in 1810 included Lombardy, Venetia, and most of the former papal states, Napoleon himself retained the title of king, but set up his stepson, Eugène Beauharnais (Josephine's son) as viceroy. The mother of the Bonapartes, Letitia, who had brought up all these children under very different circumstances in Corsica, was suitably installed at the imperial court as Madame Mère. According to legend she kept repeating to herself, "If only it lasts!"; she outlived Napoleon by 15 years.

Napoleon and the Spread of the Revolution

In all the states of the Grand Empire the same course of events tended to repeat itself. First came the stage of military conquest and occupation by French troops. Then came the establishment of a native satellite government with the support of local persons who were willing to collaborate with the French and who helped in the drafting of a constitution specifying the powers of the new government and regularizing its relationships with France. In some areas these two stages had been accomplished under the republican governments before Napoleon came to power. In some regions no more than these two stages really occurred, notably in Spain and the Grand Duchy of Warsaw.

Stages of French occupation

The third stage of French influence was one of sweeping internal reform and reorganization, modeled on Bonaparte's program for France and hence derivatively on the French Revolution. Belgium and the German territories west of the Rhine underwent this stage most thoroughly, since they were annexed directly to France for 20 years. Italy and the main bulk of Germany west of Prussia and Austria also experienced the third stage.

Napoleon considered himself a great reformer and man of the Enlightenment. He called his system "liberal," and though the word to him meant almost the reverse of what it meant later to liberals, he was possibly the first to use it in a political sense. He believed also in "constitutions"; not that he favored representative assemblies or limited government, but he wanted government to be rationally "constituted," that is, deliberately mapped out and planned, not merely inherited from the jumble of the past. Man on horseback though he was, he believed firmly in the rule of law. He insisted with the zeal of conviction on transplanting his Civil Code to the dependent states. He assumed that this code was based on the very nature of justice and human relationships, and he believed that it must therefore be applicable to all countries with no more than minor adaptation. The idea that a country's laws must mirror its peculiar

Napoleon as reformer

national character and history was foreign to his mind, for he carried over the rationalist and universalist outlook of the Age of Enlightenment. He thought that people everywhere wanted, and deserved, much the same thing. As he wrote to his brother Jerome, on making him king of Westphalia, "the peoples of Germany, as of France, Italy and Spain, want equality and liberal ideas. For some years now I have been managing the affairs of Europe, and I am convinced that the crowing of the privileged classes was everywhere disliked. Be a constitutional king."

The same plan of reform was initiated, with some variation, in all the dependent states from Spain to Poland and from the mouth of the Elbe to the Straits of Messina. The reforms were directed, in a word, against everything feudal. They established the legal equality of individual persons and gave governments more complete authority over their individual subjects. Legal classes were wiped out, as in France in 1789; the theory of a society made up of "estates of the realm" gave way to the theory of a society made up of legally equal individuals. The nobility lost its privileges in taxation, officeholding, and military command. Careers were "opened to talent."

The manorial system, bulwark of the old aristocracy, was virtually liquidated. Lords lost all legal jurisdiction over their peasants; peasants became subjects of the state, personally free to move, migrate, or marry, and able to bring suit in the courts of law. The manorial fees, along with tithes, were generally abolished, as in France in 1789. In France the peasants escaped from these burdens without having to pay compensation, in part because they had themselves risen in rebellion in 1789 and in part because France passed through a radical popular revolution in 1793. In other parts of the Grand Empire, however, the peasants were committed to payment of indemnities, and the former feudal class continued to receive income from its abolished rights. Only in Belgium and the Rhineland, incorporated into France under the republic, did the manorial regime disappear without compensation as in France, leaving a numerous entrenched class of small landowning farmers. East of the Rhine Napoleon had to compromise with the aristocracy that he assailed. In Poland, the only country in the Grand Empire where a thoroughgoing serfdom had prevailed, the peasants received legal freedom during the French occupation; but the Polish landlords remained economically unharmed, since they owned all the land. Napoleon had to conciliate them, for there was no other effective class in Poland to which he could look for support. In general, outside of France, the assault upon feudal traditions was not socially as revolutionary as it had been in France. The lord was gone, but the landlord remained.

Everywhere in the Grand Empire the church lost its position as a public authority alongside the state. Church courts were abolished or restricted; the Inquisition was outlawed in Spain. Tithes were done away with, church property was confiscated, and monastic orders were dissolved or severely regulated. Toleration became the law; Catholics, Protestants, Jews, and unbelievers received the same civil rights. The state was to be based not on the idea of religious community but on the idea of territorial residence. With the nobility, or on

NAPOLEONIC EUROPE, 1810

Napoleon extended the sphere of French power well beyond the earlier expansion of the French Republic. By 1810 he dominated the whole continent except Portugal and the Balkan peninsula. Russia, Prussia, and Austria had been forced into alliance with him, and he had made his brothers kings of Spain, Holland, and Westphalia; his brother-in-law king of Naples; and his stepson viceroy of Italy. The old Holy Roman Empire disappeared into other states, including Napoleon's Confederation of the Rhine. In Poland, Napoleon undid the partitions of the 1770s by setting up the Grand Duchy of Warsaw.

Napoleon's Russian Campaign
June to December, 1812

RUSSIAN EMPIRE

Baltic Sea

0   100   200 miles

Moscow
Borodino
Riga   Vitebsk
Tilsit   Vilna   Smolensk
Königsberg   Kovno   Borisov
Warsaw   Brest-Litovsk

NORWAY

SWEDEN

FINLAND

St. Petersburg

ESTONIA

LIVONIA

COURLAND

Stockholm

Baltic Sea

SCOTLAND

Edinburgh

KINGDOM OF DENMARK
AND NORWAY

North
Sea

DENMARK   Copenhagen

Memel
Tilsit   Nieman R.   Vilna
Königsberg   Friedland
Danzig   Eylau

RUSSIA

IRELAND

GREAT
BRITAIN

ENGLAND

London

Plymouth

Dover

Amsterdam

HELIGOLAND
(Britain)

Lübeck
Hamburg
Bremen

SWEDISH
POMERANIA

MECKLEN-
BURG

Berlin

PRUSSIA

Posen   Vistula R.

Brest-Litovsk

Warsaw

Elbe R.

KINGDOM OF
HOLLAND

Rhine R.

BERG

K. OF
WESTPHALIA

Auerstaedt

K. OF
SAXONY
Leipzig   Dresden

Oder R.

GRAND DUCHY
OF WARSAW

Breslau

GALICIA

Cracow

Tarnapol

ATLANTIC
OCEAN

CHANNEL I.
(Britain)

Boulogne
Cherbourg

Brussels

Cologne

Antwerp

English Channel

Amiens

Seine R.

Versailles   Paris

Fontainebleau

Nantes   Loire   R.   Orléans

Mainz

Erfurt   Jena

Valmy

Metz

Strasbourg

CONFEDERATION
OF THE
RHINE

BADEN

WÜRTTEMBERG

Prague

BOHEMIA

Austerlitz

Wagram

FRENCH EMPIRE

Rochefort

Bordeaux

Lyons

Basel

Ulm
Munich   Hohenlinden

SWITZERLAND

K. OF BAVARIA

Vienna

AUSTRIA

Budapest

HUNGARY

SAVOY

PIEDMONT

Rhone R.

Garonne R.

Toulouse

Avignon

Marseille

Nice

Toulon

Genoa

Po R.

LOMBARDY
Milan

VENETIA

Trieste

ILLYRIAN

SLOVENIA

Drave R.

Save R.

CROATIA

BOSNIA

Belgrade

SERBIA

WALLACHIA

Danube R.

CAPE
FINISTERRE

La Coruña

Oporto

Burgos

Douro R.

Ebro R.

Almeida   Ciudad Rodrigo

PORTUGAL

Lisbon   Tagus R.

Elvas

Albuera

Seville

Cadiz

TRAFALGAR

Tangier

MOROCCO

Saragossa

SPAIN

Talavera   Madrid

Guadiana R.

Ocaña

Valencia

Baylen

ANDALUSIA

Gibraltar (Britain)

Algiers

ALGERIA
(Turkish)

Barcelona

BALEARIC IS.
(Spain)

IVIZA

MINORCA

MAJORCA

CORSICA

Elba

Rome

KINGDOM OF
SARDINIA

Cagliari

LUCCA
Leghorn

Florence

Naples

Bari

Taranto

KINGDOM OF
NAPLES

Palermo

KINGDOM OF
SICILY

Tunis

TUNISIA
(Turkish)

MALTA
(Britain)

DALMATIA

MONTENEGRO

OTTOMAN EMPIRE

ALBANIA

Salonica

CORFU

IONIAN I.
(Britain)

MOREA

CERIGO

Mediterranean Sea

KINGDOM
OF
ITALY

French Empire

Grand Empire

Allied with Napoleon

0   100   200   300 miles

economic matters, Napoleon would compromise; but he would not compromise with the Catholic clergy on the principle of a secular state. Even in Spain he insisted on these fundamentals of his system, a sure indication that he was not motivated by expediency only, since it was largely his antireligious program that provoked the Spanish populace to rebellion.

Guilds were generally abolished or reduced to empty forms, and the individual's right to work was generally proclaimed. Peasants, gaining legal freedom, might learn and enter any trade they chose. The old town oligarchies and bourgeois patriciates were broken up. Towns and provinces lost their antique liberties and came under general legislation. Internal tariffs were removed, and free trade within state frontiers was encouraged. Some countries shifted to a decimal system of money; and the heterogeneous weights and measures which had originated in the Middle Ages, and of which the Anglo-American bushels, yards, ounces, and pints are living survivals, yielded to the Cartesian regularities of the metric system. Ancient and diverse legal systems gave way to the Napoleonic codes. Law courts were separated from the administration. Hereditary office and the sale of office were done away with. Officials received salaries large enough to shield them from the temptations of corruption. Kings were put on civil lists, with their personal expenses separated from those of the government. Taxes and finances were modernized. The common tax became a land tax, paid by every landowner; and governments knew how much land each owner really possessed, for they developed systematic methods of appraisal and assessment. Tax farming was replaced by direct collection. New methods of accounting and of collecting statistics were introduced.

In general, in all countries of the Grand Empire, some of the main principles of the French Revolution were introduced under Napoleon, with the notable exception that there

Support for Napoleon

was no self-government through elected legislative bodies. In all countries Napoleon found numerous natives willing to support him, mainly among people in the commercial and professional classes, who were generally aware of Enlightenment writers, often anticlerical, desirous of more equality with the nobility, and eager to break down the old localisms that interfered with trade and the exchange of ideas. He found supporters also among many progressive nobles and, in the Confederation of the Rhine, among the German rulers. His program appealed to some people everywhere and in all parts of the Grand Empire was executed mainly by local leaders. Repression went with it, though hardly on the same scale as the repressions of later dictatorships. There were no vast internment camps, and Fouché's police were engaged more in spying and submitting reports than in the brutalizing of the disaffected. The execution of a single Bavarian bookseller, named Palm, became a famous outrage.

In short, there was at first a good deal of pro-Napoleonic feeling in the Grand Empire. The French influence (outside Belgium and the Rhineland) struck deepest in north Italy, where there were no native monarchist traditions and where the old Italian city-states had produced a strong and often anticlerical burgher class. In south Germany also the French influence was profound. The French system had the least appeal in Spain, where Catholic royalist sentiment produced a kind of counterrevolutionary movement of independence. Nor did it appeal to agrarian eastern Europe, the land of lord and serf. Yet even in Prussia, as will be seen, the state was remodeled along French lines. In Russia, during the Tilsit alliance, Alexander gave his backing to a pro-French reforming minister, Speranski. The Napoleonic influence was pervasive because it carried over the older movement of enlightened despotism and seemed to confer the advantages of the French Revolution without the violence and the disorder. Napoleon, it seemed to Goethe, "was the expression of all that was reasonable, legitimate and European in the revolutionary movement."

But the Napoleonic reforms were also weapons of war. All the dependent states were required by Napoleon to supply him with money and soldiers. Germans, Dutch, Belgians,

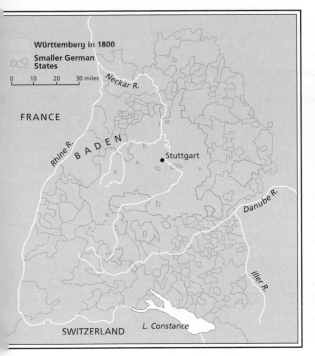

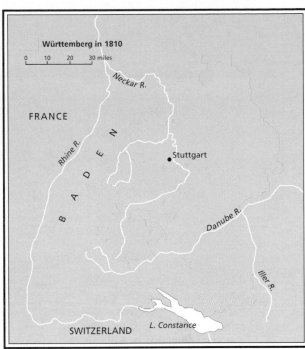

NAPOLEONIC GERMANY

In the panel at the left are shown, by shading, territories of the Duchy of Württemberg in 1800. Note how Württemberg had "islands" of territory unconnected with its main mass, and "holes" or enclaves formed by smaller states enclosed within the mass of Württemberg. Note, too, how Württemberg, itself only 50 miles wide, was surrounded by a mosaic of tiny jurisdictions—free cities, counties, duchies, principalities, abbacies, commanderies, bishoprics, archbishoprics, etc.—all "independent" within the Holy Roman Empire. The right-hand panel shows the Kingdom of Württemberg as consolidated and enlarged in the time of Napoleon. Similar consolidations all over Germany greatly reduced the number of states and added to the efficiency of law and government.

Italians, Poles, and even Spaniards fought in his armies. In addition, the dependent states defrayed much of the cost of the French army, most of which was stationed outside France. This meant that taxes in France could remain low, to the general satisfaction of the propertied interests that had issued from the Revolution.

49. THE CONTINENTAL SYSTEM: BRITAIN AND EUROPE

Beyond the tributary states of the Grand Empire lay the countries nominally independent, joined under Napoleon in the Continental System. Napoleon thought of his allies as at best subordinate partners in a common project. The great project was to crush Great Britain, and it was for this purpose that the Continental System had been established. But the crushing of Britain became in Napoleon's mind a means to a further end, the unification and mastery of all of Europe. This in turn, had he achieved it, would doubtless have merely opened the way to further conquests.

Germaine de Staël was an influential leader of the liberal opposition to Napoleon's repressive cultural policies. She was forced to live in exile in Switzerland, but both her Swiss home and her writings provided crucial support for Napoleon's critics.

(Ken Welsh/Bridgeman Art Library)

Continental unity

At the point where he stood in 1807 or 1810 the unification of continental Europe seemed a not impossible objective. He cast about for an ideology to inspire both his Grand Empire and his allies. He held out the cosmopolitan doctrines of the eighteenth century, spoke endlessly of the enlightenment of the age, and urged all peoples to work with him against the medievalism, ignorance, and obscurantism by which they were surrounded. Although he disliked and even suppressed the creative work of writers such as his vehement critic Germaine de Staël, Napoleon encouraged innovative scientific research and rewarded the scientists who pursued it. He viewed science as the essential, rational foundation of modern knowledge. And while appealing to ideas of modernity or progress he dwelt also on the grandeur of Roman times. The Roman inspiration appeared in the arts of the day and in the architecture that expressed Napoleon's conception of imperial glory. The massive "empire" furniture, the heroic canvases of David, the church of the Madeleine in Paris (resembling a classical temple and converted to a Temple of Glory); and the Arch of Triumph in the same city (begun in 1806) all evoked the atmosphere of far-spreading majesty in which Napoleon would have liked the peoples of Europe to live. In addition, to arouse an all-European feeling, Napoleon worked upon the latent hostility to Great Britain. The British, in winning out in the eighteenth-century struggle for wealth and empire, had made themselves disliked in many quarters. There was the natural jealousy felt toward the successful, and resentment against the high-handedness by which success had been won and maintained. Such feelings were present among almost all Europeans. It was believed that the British were really using their sea power to win a larger permanent share of the world's seaborne commerce for themselves. Nor, in truth, was this belief mistaken.

British Blockade and Napoleon's Continental System

The British, in the Revolutionary and Napoleonic wars, when they declared France and its allies in a state of blockade, did not expect either to starve them or to deprive them of necessary materials of war. Western Europe was still self-sufficient in food, and armaments were to a large extent produced locally from simple materials like iron, copper, and saltpeter. Europe required almost nothing indispensable from overseas. The chief aim of the British blockade was not, therefore, to keep imports out of enemy countries; it was to keep the trade in such imports out of enemy hands. It was to kill off enemy commerce and shipping, in the short run to weaken the war-making powers of the enemy government by undermining its revenues and its navy and in the long run to weaken the enemy's position in the markets of the world. Economic warfare was trade warfare. The British were willing enough to have British goods pass through to the enemy either by smuggling or by the mediation of neutrals.

Anti-British sentiments

As early as 1793 the French republicans had denounced England as the "modern Carthage," a ruthless mercantile and profit-seeking power which aspired to enslave Europe to its financial and commercial system. With the wars, the British in fact obtained a monopoly over the shipment of overseas commodities into Europe. At the same time, being relatively advanced in the new techniques of industrial production, they could produce cotton cloth and certain other articles, by power machinery, more cheaply than other peoples of Europe and so threatened to monopolize the European market for such manufactured goods. There was much feeling in Europe against the modern Carthage, especially among the bourgeois and commercial classes who were in competition with it. The upper classes were perhaps less hostile, not caring where the goods that they consumed had originated, but aristocracies and governments were susceptible to the argument that Britain was a money power, a "nation of shopkeepers" as Napoleon put it, which fought its wars with pounds sterling instead of blood and was always in search of dupes in Europe.

It was on all these feelings that Napoleon played, reiterating time and again that England was the real enemy of all Europe, and that Europe would never be prosperous or independent until relieved of the incubus of British "monopoly." To prevent the flow of goods into Britain was no more the purpose of the Continental System than to prevent the flow of goods into France was the purpose of the British blockade. The purpose of each was to destroy the enemy's commerce, credit, and public revenues by the destruction of its exports—and also to build up markets for oneself.

Trade warfare

To destroy British exports Napoleon prohibited, by the Berlin Decree of 1806, the importation of British goods into the continent of Europe. Counted as British, if of British or British colonial origin, were goods brought to Europe in neutral ships as the property of neutrals. The British, in response, ruled by an "order in council" of November 1807 that neutrals might enter Napoleonic ports only if they first stopped in Great Britain, where the regulations were such as to encourage their loading with British goods. The British thus tried to move their exports into enemy territory through neutral channels, which was precisely what Napoleon intended to prevent. He announced, by the Milan Decree of December 1807, that any neutral vessel that had stopped at a British port, or submitted to search by a British warship at sea, would be confiscated upon its appearance in a Continental harbor.

With all Europe at war, virtually the only major trading neutral nation was the United States, which could now trade with neither England nor Europe except by violating the regulations of one belligerent or the other. It would thus become liable to reprisals, and hence to involvement in war. President Jefferson, to avoid war, attempted a self-imposed policy of commercial isolation which proved so ruinous to American foreign trade that the United States government took steps to renew trade relations with whichever belligerent first removed its controls over neutral commerce. Napoleon offered to do so, on condition that the United States would defend itself against the enforcement of British controls. At the same time an expansionist party among the Americans, ambitious to annex Canada, considered that with the British army engaged in Spain the time was ripe to complete the

The War of 1812

War of Independence by driving Britain from the North American mainland. The result was the Anglo-American War of 1812, which had few results, except to demonstrate the distressing inefficiency of military institutions in the new republic.

But the Continental System was more than a device for destroying the export trade of Great Britain. It was also a scheme for developing the economy of continental Europe, around France as its main center. The Continental System, if successful, would replace the national economies with an integrated economy for the Continent as a whole. It would create the framework for a European civilization. And it would ruin the British sea power and commercial monopoly; for a unified Europe, Napoleon thought, would itself soon take to the sea.

The Failure of the Continental System

But the Continental System failed; it was worse than a failure, for it caused widespread antagonism to the Napoleonic regime. The dream of a united Europe, under French rule, was not sufficiently attractive to inspire the necessary sacrifice—even a sacrifice more of comforts than of necessities. As Napoleon impatiently said, one would suppose that the destinies of Europe turned upon a barrel of sugar. It was true, as he and his propagandists insisted, that Britain monopolized the sale of sugar, tobacco, and other overseas goods, but people preferred to deal clandestinely with the British rather than go without them. The charms of America destroyed the Continental System.

British manufactures were somewhat easier than colonial goods to replace. Raw cotton was brought by land from the Middle East through the Balkans, and the cotton manufacturers of France, Saxony, Switzerland, and north Italy were stimulated by the relief from British competition. There was a great expansion of Danish woolens and German hardware. The cultivation of sugar beets, to replace cane sugar, spread in France, central Europe, Holland, and even Russia. Thus infant industries and investments were built up which, after Napoleon's fall, clamored for tariff protection. In general, the European industrial interests were well disposed toward the Continental System.

Consequences of the Continental System

Yet they could never adequately replace the British in supplying the market. One obstacle was transportation. Much trading between parts of the Continent had always been by sea; this coastal traffic was now blocked by the British. Land routes were increasingly used, even in the faraway Balkans and Illyrian Provinces, through which raw cotton was brought; and improved roads were built through the Simplon and Mont Cenis passes in the Alps. No less than 17,000 wheeled vehicles crossed the Mont Cenis pass in 1810. But land transport, at best, was no substitute for the sea. Without railroads, introduced some 30 years later, a purely Continental modern economy was impossible to maintain.

Construction on the Arch of Triumph began in 1806, but it was not completed until 1836. It became a monument of French nationalism, symbolizing both the Republic and the Empire. The continuous band of bas reliefs above the curve of the arch represented 172 battles since Valmy in 1792.
(Culver Pictures)

Another obstacle was tariffs. The idea of a Continental tariff union was put forward by some of his subordinates, but Napoleon never adopted it. The dependent states remained insistent on their ostensible sovereignty. Each had widened its trading area by demolishing former internal tariffs, but each kept a tariff against the others. The kingdoms of Italy and Naples enjoyed no free trade with each other nor did the German states of the Confederation of the Rhine. France remained protectionist; and when Napoleon annexed Holland and parts of Italy to France, he kept them outside the French customs. At the same time Napoleon forbade the satellite states to raise high tariffs against France. France was his base, and he meant to favor French industry, which was much crippled by its loss of its Middle Eastern and American markets.

Shippers, shipbuilders, and dealers in overseas goods, a powerful element of the older bourgeoisie, were ruined by the Continental System. The French ports were idle and their populations were distressed and disgruntled. The same problems befell all ports of Europe where the blockade was strictly enforced; at Trieste, total annual tonnage fell from 208,000 in 1807 to 60,000 in 1812. Eastern Europe was especially hard hit. In the West there was the stimulus to new manufactures. Eastern Europe, long dependent on western Europe for manufactured goods, could no longer obtain them from England legally, nor from France, Germany, or Bohemia because of the difficulties of land transport and the British control of the Baltic.

Economic stagnation

Napoleon used architecture to show that Paris was the capital of modern Europe and that his empire replicated the imperial grandeur of ancient Rome. He built the multicolumned Madeleine to be a temple of glory, but after his fall from power it became a church. (Bettmann/Corbis)

Nor could the landowners of Prussia, Poland, and Russia market their produce. The aristocracy of eastern Europe, which was the principal spending and importing class, had additional reason to dislike the French and to sympathize with the British.

As a war measure against Britain the Continental System also failed. British trade with Europe was significantly reduced, but the loss was made up elsewhere because of British control of the sea. Exports to Latin America rose from £300,000 in 1805 to £6,300,000 in 1809. Here again the existence of the overseas world frustrated the Continental System. Despite the System, export of British cotton goods, rising on a continuous tide of the rapidly developing Industrial Revolution, more than doubled in four years from 1805 to 1809. And while part of the increase was due to mere inflation and rising prices, it is estimated that the annual income of the British people more than doubled in the Revolutionary and Napoleonic wars, growing from £140,000,000 in 1792 to £335,000,000 in 1814.

50.   THE NATIONAL MOVEMENTS: GERMANY

The Resistance to Napoleon: Nationalism

From the beginning, as far back as 1792, the French met with resistance as well as collaboration in the countries they occupied. There was resentment when the invading armies plundered and laid requisitions upon the occupied countries, which were required to pay tribute in men and money, and whose policies were dictated by French residents or ambassadors. The Continental System was also resented because it was used for the benefit of French manufacturers. Europeans began to feel that Napoleon was employing them merely as tools against England. And in all countries, including France itself, people grew tired of the peace that was no peace, the wars and rumors of war, the conscription and the taxes, the loss of lives and local liberties, the aloof bureaucratic government, and the obviously growing and insatiable appetite of Napoleon for power and self-exaltation. Movements of protest and independence showed themselves even within the Napoleonic structure. We have seen how the dependent states protected themselves by tariffs. Even the emperor's proconsuls tried to root themselves in local opinion, as when Louis Bonaparte, king of Holland, tried to defend Dutch interests against Napoleon's demands, or when Murat, king of Naples, appealed to Italian sentiment to secure his own throne.

Nationalism developed as a movement of resistance against the forcible internationalism of the Napoleonic empire. Since the international system was essentially French, the nationalistic movements were anti-French; and since Napoleon was an autocrat, they were antiautocratic. The nationalism of the period was a mixture of the conservative and the liberal. Some nationalists, predominantly conservative, insisted on the value of their own peculiar institutions, customs, folkways, and historical development, which they feared might be obliterated under the French and Napoleonic system. Others, or indeed the same persons, insisted on more self-determination, more participation in government, more representative institutions, more freedom for the individual against the bureaucratic interference of the state. Both conservatism and liberalism rose up against Napoleon, destroyed him, outlasted him, and shaped the history of the following generations.

Anti-French nationalism

Nationalism was thus very complex and appeared in different countries in different ways. In England the profound solidarity of the country exhibited itself; all classes rallied and stood shoulder to shoulder against "Boney"; and ideas of reforming Parliament or tampering with historic English liberties were resolutely put aside. It is possible that the Napoleonic wars helped England through a very difficult social crisis, for the Industrial Revolution was causing dislocation, misery, unemployment, and even revolutionary agitation among a small minority, all of which were eclipsed by the patriotic need for resistance to Bonaparte. In Spain, nationalism took the form of implacable resistance to the French armies that desolated the land. Some Spanish nationalists were liberal; a bourgeois group at Cádiz, rebelling against the French regime, proclaimed the Spanish constitution of 1812, modeled on the French constitution of 1791. But Spanish nationalism drew its greatest strength from sentiments that were counterrevolutionary, aiming to restore the clergy and the Bourbons. In Italy the Napoleonic regime was better liked and national feeling was less anti-French than in Spain. Bourgeois of the Italian cities generally prized the efficiency and enlightenment of French methods and often shared in the anticlericalism of the French Revolution. The French regime, which lasted in Italy from 1796 to 1814, broke the habit of loyalty to the various duchies, oligarchic republics, papal states, and foreign dynasties by which Italy had long been ruled. Napoleon never unified Italy, but he consolidated it into only three parts, and the French influence brought the notion of a politically united Italy within the bounds of reasonable aspiration. With the Poles, Napoleon positively encouraged national feeling. He repeatedly told them that they might win a restored and united Poland by faithfully fighting in his cause. A few Polish nationalists, like the aging patriot Kosciusko, never trusted Napoleon, and some others, like Czartoryski, looked rather to the Russian tsar for a restoration of the Polish kingdom; but in general the

Poles, for their own national reasons, were exceptionally devoted to the emperor of the French and lamented his passing.

The Movement of Thought in Napoleonic Germany

The national movement in Germany

By far the most momentous new national movement developed in Germany. The Germans rebelled not only against the Napoleonic rule but also against the century-old ascendancy of French civilization. They rebelled not only against the French armies but also against much of the philosophy of the Age of Enlightenment. The years of the French Revolution and Napoleon were for Germany the years of great cultural efflorescence, the years of Beethoven, Goethe, and Schiller, of Herder, Kant, Fichte, Hegel, Schleiermacher, and many others. German ideas fell in with all the ferment of the new cultural movement known as "romanticism," which was everywhere challenging the "dry abstractions" of the Age of Reason and shaping the new themes of literature, music, art, and historical research. Germany became the most "romantic" of all countries, and German influence spread throughout Europe. In the nineteenth century the Germans came to be widely regarded as intellectual leaders, somewhat as the French had been in the century before. And most of the distinctive features of German thought were somehow connected with nationalism in a broad sense.

Formerly, especially in the century following the Peace of Westphalia, the Germans had been the least nationally minded of all the larger European peoples. They prided themselves on their world citizenship or cosmopolitan outlook. Looking out from the tiny states in which they lived, they were conscious of Europe, conscious of other countries, but hardly conscious of Germany. The Holy Roman Empire was neither a forceful political power nor the public embodiment of a well-defined national culture. The German world had no tangible frontiers; the area of German speech simply faded out into Alsace or the Austrian Netherlands, or into Poland, Bohemia, or the upper Balkans. That "Germany" ever did, thought, or hoped anything never crossed the German mind. The upper classes, becoming contemptuous of much that was German, took over French fashions, dress, etiquette, manners, ideas, and language, regarding them as an international norm of civilized living. Frederick the Great hired French tax collectors and wrote his own books in French.

About 1780 signs of a change set in. Even Frederick, in his later years, predicted a golden age of German literature, proudly declaring that Germans could do what other nations had done. In 1784 appeared a book by J. G. Herder called *Ideas on the Philosophy of the History of Mankind*. Herder was an earnest soul, a Protestant pastor and theologian who thought the French somewhat frivolous. He concluded that imitation of foreign ways made people

Herder's cultural nationalism

shallow and artificial. He declared that German ways were indeed different from French but not for that reason the less worthy of respect. All true culture or civilization, he held, must arise from native roots. It must arise also from the life of the common people, the *Volk,* not from the cosmopolitan and artificial life of the upper classes. Each people, he thought, meaning by a people a group sharing the same language, had its own attitudes, spirit, or genius. A sound civilization must express a national character or *Volksgeist*. And the character of each people was special to itself. Herder did not believe the nations to be in conflict; quite the contrary, he simply insisted that they were different. He did not believe German culture to be the best; many other peoples, notably the Slavs, later found his ideas applicable to their own needs. His philosophy of history was very different from that of Voltaire and the philosophes, who had

Nationalism grew rapidly in all the European countries that resisted Napoleon's expansionist military policies. This image of Britannia "blowing up the Corsican Bottle Conjurer" expressed British national pride during this era. The bottle's label says "British spirits, composed of True Liberty, Courage, Loyalty and Religion."
(Rare Book Collection, University of North Carolina–Chapel Hill (Hoyt 11-192))

BRITANNIA
*Blowing up the
Corsican Bottle Conjuror*

expected all people to progress along the same path of reason and enlightenment toward a similar civilization. Herder thought that all peoples should develop their own genius in their own way, each slowly unfolding with the inevitability of plantlike growth, avoiding sudden change or distortion by outside influence, and all ultimately reflecting, in their endless diversity, the infinite richness of humanity and of God.

The idea of the *Volksgeist* was reinforced from other and non-German sources and soon passed to other countries in the general movement of romantic thought. Like much else in romanticism, it emphasized genius or intuition rather than reason. It stressed the differences rather than the similarity of mankind. It broke down that sense of human similarity or universality which had been characteristic of the Age of Enlightenment, and which revealed itself in French and American doctrines of the rights of man, or again in the law codes of Napoleon. In the past it had been usually thought that what was good was good for all peoples. Good poetry was poetry written according to certain classical principles or "rules" of composition, which were the same for all writers from the Greeks on down. Now, according to Herder and to romantics in all countries, good poetry was poetry that expressed an inner genius, either an individual genius or the genius of a people—there were no more rigid, classical "rules." Good and just laws, according to the older philosophy of natural law, somehow corresponded to a standard of justice that was the same for all people. But now, according to Herder and the romantic school of jurisprudence, good laws were those that reflected local conditions or national idiosyncrasies. Here again there were no "rules," except possibly the rule that each nation should follow its own path.

Herder's philosophy set forth a cultural nationalism, without a political message. The Germans had long been a nonpolitical people. In the microscopic states of the Holy Roman Empire they had had no significant political questions to think about; in the more sizable ones they had been excluded from public affairs. The French Revolution made the Germans acutely conscious of the state. It showed what a people could do with a state, once they took it over and used it for their own purposes. For one thing, the French had raised themselves to the dignity of citizenship; they had become free individuals, responsible for themselves, taking part in the affairs of their country. For another, because they had a unified state which included all French people, and one in which a whole nation surged with a new sense of freedom, they were able to rise above all the other nations of Europe. Many in Germany were beginning to feel humiliation at the paternalism of their governments. The futilities of the Holy Roman Empire, which had made Germany for centuries the battlefield of Europe, now filled them with shame and indignation. They saw with disgust how their German princes, forever squabbling with each other for control over German subjects, disgraced themselves before the French to promote their own interests. The national awakening in Germany, which set in strongly after 1800, was therefore directed not only against Napoleon and the French but also against the German rulers and many of the half-Frenchified German upper classes. It was democratic in that it stressed the superior virtue of the common people.

Germans became fascinated by the idea of political and national greatness, precisely because they had neither. A great national German state, expressing the deep moral will and distinctive culture of the German people, seemed to them the solution to all their problems. It would give moral dignity to the individual German, solve the vexatious question of the selfish petty princes, protect the deep German *Volksgeist* from violation, and secure the Germans from subjection to outside powers. The nationalist philosophy remained somewhat vague, because in practice there was little that one could do. "Father" Jahn organized a kind of youth movement, had his young men do calisthenics for the Fatherland and led them on open-air expeditions into the country, where they made fun of aristocrats in French costume. He taught them to be suspicious of foreigners, Jews, and internationalists, and indeed of everything that might corrupt the purity of the German *Volk*. Most Germans thought him too extreme. Others collected wonderful stories of the rich medieval German past. There was an anonymous anti-French work, *Germany in Its Deep Humiliation,* for selling which the publisher Palm was put to death. Others founded the Moral and Scientific Union, generally known as the *Tugendbund* or league of virtue or manliness, whose members, by developing their own moral character, were to contribute to the future of Germany.

Fichte and the German national spirit

The career of J. G. Fichte illustrates the course of German thought in these years. Fichte was a moral and metaphysical philosopher, a professor at the University of Jena. His doctrine that the inner spirit of the individual creates its own moral universe was much admired in many countries. In America, for example, it entered into the transcendental philosophy of Ralph Waldo Emerson. Fichte at first was practically without national feeling. He enthusiastically approved of the French Revolution, as did many other German intellectuals at the time. In 1793, with the Revolution at its height, Fichte published a laudatory tract on the French Republic. He saw it as an emancipation of the human spirit, a step upward in the elevation of human dignity and moral stature. He accepted the idea of the Terror, that of "forcing men to be free," and he shared Rousseau's conception of the state as the embodiment of the sovereign will of a people. He came to see the state as the means of human salvation. In 1800, in his *Closed Commercial State,* he sketched a kind of totalitarian system in which the state planned and operated the whole economy of the country, shutting itself off from the rest of the world in order that, at home, it might freely develop the character of its own citizens. When the French conquered Germany Fichte became intensely and self-consciously German. He took over the idea of the *Volksgeist:* not only did the individual spirit create its own moral universe, but the spirit of a people created a kind of moral universe as well, manifested in its language, history, arts, folkways, customs, institutions, and ideas.

At Berlin, in 1808, Fichte delivered a series of *Addresses to the German Nation,* declaring that there was an ineradicable German spirit, a primordial and immutable national character, more noble than that of other peoples (thus going beyond Herder), to be kept pure at all costs from all outside influence, either international or French. The German spirit, he held, had always been profoundly different from that of France and western Europe; it had never yet really been heard from but would be some day. The French army commander then occupying the city thought the lectures too academic to be worth suppression. They attracted only small audiences; but his published lectures provided an enduring philosophical argument for German nationalism, and many Germans later regarded him as a national hero.

Reforms in Prussia

Politically, the revolt against the French led to major transformations in Prussia and the Prussian state. After the death of Frederick the Great in 1786 Prussia had fallen into a period of satisfied inertia, such as is likely to follow upon rapid growth or spectacular success. Then in 1806, at Jena-Auerstädt, the kingdom collapsed in a single battle. Its western and most of its Polish territories were taken away. It was relegated by Napoleon to its old holdings east of the Elbe River. Even here the French remained in occupation, for Napoleon stationed his Ninth Corps in Berlin. But in the eyes of German nationalists Prussia had a moral advantage. Of all the German states it was the least compromised by collaboration with the French. Toward Prussia, as toward a haven, German patriots therefore made their way. Prussia, east of the Elbe, formerly the least German of German lands, became the center of an all-German movement for national freedom. The years after Jena contributed to the "Prussianizing" of Germany; but it is to be observed that neither Fichte nor Hegel, Gneisenau nor Scharnhorst, Stein nor Hardenberg, all rebuilders of Prussia, was a native Prussian.

The reform movement in Prussia

The main problem for Prussia was military, since Napoleon could be overthrown only by military force. And as always in Prussia, the requirements of the army shaped the form taken by the state. The problem was conceived to be one of morale and personnel. The old Prussia of Frederick, which had fallen ingloriously, had been mechanical, arbitrary, soulless. Its people had lacked the sense of membership in the state, and in the army its soldiers had held no hope of promotion and felt no patriotism or spirit. To produce this spirit was the aim of the army reformers Scharnhorst and Gneisenau. Gneisenau, a Saxon, had served in one of the British "Hessian" regiments in the War of American Independence, during which he had observed the military value of patriotic feeling in the American soldiers. He was a close observer also of the consequences of the French Revolution, which, he said, had "set in action the national energy of the entire French people, putting the different classes on an equal social and fiscal basis." If Prussia was to strengthen itself against France, or indeed to avoid revolution in the long run in Prussia

CHRONOLOGY OF NOTABLE EVENTS, 1799–1815

1799–1801	Second Coalition (Austria, Russia, Britain) wages war with France
1803	Napoleon's army is defeated in Haiti and France sells Louisiana to the United States
1805–1807	Third Coalition (Austria, Russia, Britain) wages war with France
1806	Napoleon defeats Prussian armies and occupies Berlin
1806–1825	Latin American countries pursue successful campaigns for national independence from Spain and Portugal
1807	Treaty of Tilsit creates French-Russian alliance; Napoleon proclaims "Continental System" to exclude trade with Britain
1808–1814	Peninsular War leads to French defeats in Spain
1810	Napoleon marries Marie Louise, daughter of Austrian Emperor
1812	Napoleon's "Grand Army" invades Russia and is destroyed in winter retreat
1813	French army loses decisive battle of Leipzig in Germany
1814	Abdication of Napoleon and restoration of Bourbon Monarchy in France
1814–1815	Congress of Vienna reorganizes the political order in Europe
1815	Napoleon returns to power for "100 Days"; final defeat at the battle of Waterloo

itself, it must find a means to inspire a similar feeling of equal participation in its own people and to allow capable individuals to fill important positions in the army and government without regard to their social status.

The reconstruction of the state, prerequisite to the reconstruction of the army, was initiated by Baron Stein and continued by his successor, Hardenberg. Like Metternich, Stein came from western Germany, and he was long hostile to what he considered a barely civilized Prussia, but he finally turned to the Prussian state as the best hope to lead Germany as a whole into the future. Deeply committed to the philosophy of Kant and Fichte, he dwelt on the concepts of duty, service, moral character, and responsibility. He thought that the common people must be awakened to moral life and raised from a brutalized servility to the level of self-determination and membership in the community. This, he believed, required an equality more of duties than of rights.

Under Stein the old caste structure of Prussia became somewhat less rigid. Property became interchangeable between social classes, and soldiers of all classes could now serve as officers in the army. The burghers, to develop a sense of citizenship and participation in the state, were given extensive freedom of self-government in the cities; the municipal systems of Prussia, and later of Germany, became a model for much of Europe in the following century.

Stein's most famous work was the "abolition of serfdom." It was naturally impossible, since the whole reform program was aimed at strengthening Prussia for a war of liberation against the French, to antagonize the Junkers who commanded the army. Stein's ordinance of 1807 abolished serfdom only in that it abolished the "hereditary subjection" of peasants to their manorial lords. It gave peasants the right to move and migrate, marry, and take up trades without the lord's approval. If, however, they remained on the land, they were still subject to all the old services of forced labor in the fields of the lord. Peasants enjoying small tenures of their own continued to be liable for the old dues and fees. By an edict of 1810, they might convert their tenure into private property, getting rid of the manorial obligations, but only on condition that one-third of the land held should become the private property of the lord. In the following decades many such conversions took place; as a result, the estates of the Junkers grew considerably larger. The reforms in Prussia somewhat reduced the old patriarchal powers of the lords and gave legal status and freedom of movement to the mass of the population, thus laying the foundation for a modern state and modern economy. But the peasants tended to become mere hired agricultural laborers and the position of the Junkers was heightened, not reduced. Prussia avoided the Revolution. Stein himself, because Napoleon feared him, was obliged to go into exile in 1808, but his reforms endured.

51. THE OVERTHROW OF NAPOLEON: THE CONGRESS OF VIENNA

The situation at the close of 1811 may be summarized as follows. Napoleon had the mainland of Europe in his grip. Russia and Turkey were at war on the Danube, but otherwise there was no war except in Spain, where four years of fighting remained inconclusive. The Continental System was working badly. Britain was hurt by it only in that, without it, British exports to Europe would have risen rapidly in these years. Well launched in the economic growth of the Industrial Revolution, Britain was amassing a vast store of national wealth that could be used to assist European governments financially against Napoleon. The peoples of Europe were growing restless, dreaming increasingly of national freedom. In Germany especially, many awaited the opportunity to rise in a war of independence. But Napoleon could be overthrown only by the destruction of his army, over which neither British wealth nor British sea power, nor the European patriots and nationalists, nor the Prussian nor the Austrian armed forces were able to prevail. All eyes turned to Russia. Alexander I had long been dissatisfied with his French alliance. He had obtained from it nothing but the annexation of Finland in 1809. He received no assistance from France in his war with Turkey; he saw Napoleon marry into the Austrian house; he had to tolerate the existence of a French-oriented Poland at his very door. The articulate classes in Russia, namely, the landowners and serf owners, loudly denounced the French alliance and demanded a resumption of open trade relations with England. An international clientele of émigrés and anti-Bonapartists, including Baron Stein, also gradually congregated at St. Petersburg, where they poured into the tsar's ears the welcome message that Europe looked to him for its salvation.

Europe in 1811

The Russian Campaign and the War of Liberation

On December 31, 1810, Russia formally withdrew from the Continental System. Anglo-Russian commercial relations were resumed. Napoleon resolved to crush the tsar. He concentrated the Grand Army in eastern Germany and Poland, a vast force of 700,000 men, the largest ever assembled up to that time for a single military operation. It was an all-European host. Hardly more than a third was French; another third was German, from German regions annexed to France, from the states of the Confederation of the Rhine, and with token forces from Prussia and Austria; and the remaining third was drawn from all other nationalities of the Grand Empire, including 90,000 Poles.

Napoleon at first hoped to meet the Russians in Poland or Prussia. This time, however, they decided to fight on their own ground, and they needed in any case to delay until their forces on the lower Danube could be recalled. In June 1812 Napoleon led the Grand Army into Russia.

He intended a short, sharp war, such as most of his wars had been in the past, and carried with him only three weeks' supplies. But from the beginning everything went wrong. It was Napoleon's principle to force a decisive battle; but the Russian army simply melted away. It was his principle to live on the country, so as to reduce the need for supply trains; but the Russians destroyed as they retreated, and in any case, in Russia, even in the summer, it was hard to find sustenance for so many men and horses. Finally, not far from Moscow, Napoleon was able to join battle with the main Russian force at Borodino. Here again everything miscarried. It was his principle always to outnumber the enemy at the decisive spot, but the Grand Army had left so many detachments along its line of march that at Borodino the Russians outnumbered it. It was Napoleon's principle to concentrate his artillery, but here he scattered it instead. His principle was to throw in his last reserves at the critical moment, but at Borodino, so far from home, he refused the risk of ordering the Old Guard into action. Napoleon won the battle, at a cost of 30,000 men, as against 50,000 lost by the Russians; but the Russian army was able to withdraw in good order.

On September 14, 1812, the French emperor entered Moscow. Almost immediately the city broke into flames. Napoleon found himself camping in a ruin, with troops strewn along a long line all the way back to Poland, and with a hostile army maneuvering near at hand. Baffled, he tried to negotiate with Alexander, who refused all overtures. After five weeks, not knowing what to do and fearful of remaining isolated in Moscow over the winter, Napoleon ordered a retreat. Prevented by the Russians from taking a more southerly route, the Grand Army retired by the same way it had come, but it could no longer live off the land. The cold weather set in early and was unusually severe. For a century after 1812 the retreat from Moscow remained the last word in military horror. Men froze and starved, horses slipped and died, vehicles could not be moved, and equipment was abandoned. Discipline broke down toward the end; the army dissolved into a horde of individual fugitives, speaking a babel of languages, harassed by bands of Russian irregulars, picking their way on foot over ice and snow, most of the time in the dark, for the nights are long in these latitudes in December. Of 611,000 who entered Russia 400,000 died of battle casualties, starvation, and exposure, and 100,000 were taken prisoner. The Grand Army no longer existed.

The retreat from Moscow

Now at last all the anti-Napoleon forces rushed together. The Russians pushed westward into central Europe. The Prussian and Austrian governments, which in 1812 had halfheartedly supplied troops for the invasion of Russia, switched over in 1813 and joined the tsar. Throughout Germany, the patriots, often half-trained boys, marched off in the War of Liberation, though it was the professional armies of the German states that made the difference. Anti-French riots broke out in Italy. In Spain Wellington at last pushed rapidly forward; in June 1813 he crossed the Pyrenees into France. The British government, in three years from 1813 to 1815, poured £32,000,000 as subsidies into Europe, more than half of all the funds granted during the 22 years of the wars. An incongruous alliance of British capitalism and east-European agrarian feudalism, of the British navy and the Russian army, of Spanish clericalism and German nationalism, of divine-right monarchies and newly aroused democrats and liberals, combined at last to bring the Man of Destiny to the ground.

Napoleon, who had left his army in Russia in December 1812 and rushed across Europe to Paris by sleigh and coach in the remarkable time of 13 days, raised a new army in France in the early months of 1813. But it was untrained and unsteady, and he himself had lost some of his genius for command. His new army was smashed in October at the battle of Leipzig, known to the Germans as the Battle of the Nations, the greatest battle in number of men engaged ever fought until the twentieth century. The allies drove Napoleon back upon France. But the closer they came to defeating him the more they began to fear and distrust each other.

The "Battle of the Nations"

The Restoration of the Bourbons

The coalition already showed signs of splitting. Should the allies, together or singly, negotiate with Napoleon? How strong should the France of the future be? What should be its new frontiers? What form of government should it have? There was no agreement on these questions. Alexander wanted to dethrone Napoleon and dictate peace in Paris, in dramatic retribution for the destruction of Moscow. He had a scheme for giving the French throne to Bernadotte, a former French marshal, now crown prince of Sweden, who as king of France would depend on Russian support. Metternich preferred to keep Napoleon or his son as French emperor, after clearing the French out of central Europe; for a Bonaparte dynasty in a reduced France would be dependent on Austria. The Prussian counsels were divided. The British, with an eye to one of their main strategic concerns, declared that the French must get out of Belgium and that Napoleon must go; they held that the French might then choose their own government but believed a restoration of the Bourbons to be the best solution. The three Continental monarchies had no concern for the Bourbons, and both Alexander and Metternich, if they could make France dependent respectively on themselves, were willing to see it remain strong to the extent of including Belgium.

The British foreign minister, Viscount Castlereagh, arrived on the Continent for consultations in January 1814. He held a number of strong cards. For one thing, Napoleon continued to fight, and the allies therefore continued to ask for British financial aid. Castlereagh skillfully used the promise of British subsidies to win acceptance of the British war aims, which included France's expulsion from Belgium. In addition, he found a common ground for agreement with Metternich, both Britain and Austria fearing the domination of Europe by Russia. Castlereagh's first great problem was to hold the alliance together, for without Continental allies the British could not defeat France. He succeeded, on March 9, 1814, in getting Russia, Prussia, Austria, and Great Britain to sign the treaty of Chaumont. Each power bound itself for 20 years to a Quadruple Alliance against France, and each agreed to provide 150,000 soldiers to enforce such peace terms as might be arrived at. For the first time since 1792 a solid coalition of the four great powers now existed against France. Three weeks later the allies entered Paris, and on April 4 Napoleon abdicated at Fontainebleau.

The Quadruple Alliance

He was forced to this step by lack of support in France itself. Twenty years before, in 1793 and 1794, France had fought off the combined powers of Europe—minus Russia. It could not and would not do so in 1814. The country cried for peace. Even the imperial marshals advised the emperor's abdication. But what was to follow him? For over 25 years the French had had one regime after another. Now they were divided. Some wanted a republic; other wished to retain the empire under Napoleon's infant son; still others desired

The French army's retreat from Russia in 1812 shattered Napoleon's image of military invincibility and brought the anti-Napoleonic forces together for a decisive victory in the following year. This French painting portrays the misery that gave the retreat of 1812 its lasting reputation for military horror.
(Alinari/Art Resource, NY)

a constitutional monarchy; and there were even those who longed for the old regime. Talleyrand stepped into the breach. The "legitimate" king, he said, Louis XVIII, was the man who would provoke the least factionalism and opposition. The powers, likewise, had by this time concluded in favor of the Bourbons. A Bourbon king would be peaceable, under no impulse to win back the conquests of the republic and empire. He would also, as the native and rightful king of France, need no foreign support to bolster him, so that the control of France would not arise as an issue to divide the victorious powers.

The Bourbons restored

The Bourbon dynasty was thus restored. Louis XVIII, ignored and disregarded for a whole generation, both by most people in France and by the governments of Europe, returned to the throne of his brother and his fathers. He issued a "constitutional charter," partly at the insistence of the liberal tsar and partly because, having actually learned from his long exile, he sought the support of influential people in France. The charter of 1814 made no concession to the principle of popular or national sovereignty. It was represented as the gracious gift of a theoretically absolute king. But in practice it granted what most of the French wanted. It promised legal equality, eligibility of all to public office without regard to class, and a parliamentary government in two chambers. It recognized the Napoleonic law codes, the Napoleonic settlement with the church, and the redistribution of property effected during the Revolution. It carried over the abolition of all feudal privileges and manorial rights. It confined the vote, to be sure, to a very few large landowners; but for the time being, except for a few irreconcilables, France settled down to enjoy the blessings of a chastened revolution—and peace.

The Settlement before the Vienna Congress

It was with the government of the restored Bourbons that the powers, on May 30, 1814, signed a treaty. This document, the "first" Treaty of Paris, confined France to its boundaries of 1792, those obtaining before the wars. The allied statesmen disregarded cries for vengeance and punishment, imposed no indemnity or reparations, and even allowed the works of art gathered from Europe during the wars to remain in Paris. It was not the desire of the victors to handicap the new French government on which they placed their hopes. Napoleon meanwhile was exiled to the island of Elba on the Italian coast.

To deal with other questions, the powers had agreed, before signing the Alliance of Chaumont, to hold an international congress at Vienna after defeating Napoleon. The recession of the French flood left the future of much of Europe fluid and uncertain. Both Russia and Great Britain, however, before consenting to a general conference, specified certain matters that they would decide for themselves as not susceptible to international consideration. The Russians refused to discuss Turkey and the Balkans; they retained Bessarabia as the prize of their recent war with the Turks. They also kept Finland, as an autonomous constitutional grand duchy, as well as certain conquests in the Caucasus almost unknown to Europe, namely Georgia and Azerbaijan. The British refused any discussion of the freedom of the seas. They also barred all colonial and overseas questions. The British government simply announced which of its colonial and insular conquests it would keep and which it would return. The revolts in Latin America were left to run their course.

In Europe, the British remained in possession of Malta, the Ionian Islands, and Heligoland; in America, they kept St. Lucia, Trinidad, and Tobago in the West Indies. Of former French possessions, the British kept the island of Mauritius in the Indian Ocean. Of former Dutch territories, they kept the Cape of Good Hope and Ceylon, but returned the Netherlands Indies. During the Revolutionary and Napoleonic wars in Europe the British had also made extensive conquests in India, bringing much of the Deccan and the upper Ganges valley under their rule. The British emerged, in 1814, as the controlling power in both India and the Indian Ocean.

British supremacy

Indeed, of all the colonial empires founded by Europeans in the sixteenth and seventeenth centuries, only the British now remained as a growing and dynamic system. The old French, Spanish, and Portuguese empires were reduced to mere scraps of their former selves; the Dutch still held vast establishments in the East Indies, but all the intermediate positions—the Cape, Ceylon, Mauritius, Singapore—were now British. Nor, in 1814, did any people except the British have a significant navy. With Napoleon and the Continental System defeated, with the Industrial Revolution bringing power machinery to the manufacturers of England, with no rival left in the contest for overseas dominion, and with a virtual monopoly of naval power, whose use they studiously kept free from international regulation, the British embarked on their century of world leadership, which may be said to have lasted from 1814 to 1914.

The Congress of Vienna, 1814–1815

The Congress of Vienna assembled in September 1814. Never had such a brilliant gathering been seen. All the states of Europe sent representatives; and many defunct states, such as the formerly sovereign princes and ecclesiastics of the late Holy Roman Empire, sent lobbyists to urge their restoration. But procedure was so arranged that all important matters were decided by the four triumphant Great Powers. Indeed it was at the Congress of Vienna that the terms great and small powers entered clearly into the diplomatic vocabulary. Europe was at peace, a treaty having been signed with the late enemy, but France was represented at the Congress, by none other than Talleyrand, now minister to Louis XVIII. Castlereagh, Metternich, and Alexander spoke for their respective countries; Prussia was represented by Hardenberg. The Prussians hoped, as always, to enlarge the kingdom of Prussia. Alexander was a question mark, but it could be surmised that he wanted Poland, that he favored constitutional governments in Europe, and that he sought some kind of international system of collective security. Castlereagh and Metternich, with support from Talleyrand, were most especially concerned to produce a balance of power on the Continent. Aristocrats of the Old Regime, they applied eighteenth-century diplomatic principles to the existing problem. They by no means desired to restore the territorial boundaries obtaining before the wars. They did desire, as they put it, to restore the "liberties of Europe," meaning the freedom of European states from domination by a single power; and it was hoped that a proper balance of power would also produce a lasting peace.

Containing France

The chief menace to peace, and most likely claimant for the domination of Europe, naturally seemed to be the late troublemaker, France. The Congress of Vienna, without much disagreement, erected a barrier of strong states along the French eastern frontier. The historic Dutch Republic, extinct since 1795, was revived as the kingdom of the Netherlands, with the house of Orange as a hereditary monarchy; to it was added Belgium, the old Austrian Netherlands with which Austria had long been willing to part. It was hoped that the combined Dutch-Belgian kingdom would be strong enough to discourage the perennial French drive into the Low Countries. On the south, the kingdom of Sardinia (or Piedmont) was restored and strengthened by the incorporation of Genoa. Behind the Netherlands and Piedmont, and further to discourage a renewal of French pressure upon Germany and Italy, two great powers were installed. Almost all the German left bank of the Rhine was ceded to Prussia, which was to be, in Castlereagh's words, a kind of "bridge" spanning central Europe, a bulwark against both France in the West and Russia in the East. In Italy, again as a kind of secondary barrier against France, the Austrians were firmly installed. They not only took back Tuscany and the Milanese, which they had held before 1796, but also annexed the extinct republic of Venice. The Austrian empire now included a Lombardo-Venetian kingdom in north Italy, which lasted for almost half a century. In the rest of Italy the Congress recognized the restoration of the pope in the papal states and of former rulers in the smaller duchies; but it did not insist on a restoration of the Bourbons in the kingdom of Naples. There Napoleon's brother-in-law Murat, with support from Metternich, managed for a time to retain his throne. The Bourbon and Braganza rulers restored themselves in Spain and Portugal, respectively, and were recognized by the Congress.

Germany remains divided

As for Germany, the Congress made no attempt to put together again the Humpty Dumpty of the Holy Roman Empire. The French and Napoleonic reorganization of Germany was substantially confirmed, and the kings of Bavaria, Württemberg, and Saxony kept the royal crowns that Napoleon had bestowed on them. The king of England, George III, was now recognized as

The Congress of Vienna combined complex diplomatic negotiations with the cultural elegance of traditional elites. This picture shows the social status of the diplomats who sought to establish peace and order in Europe after 25 years of revolution and warfare.
(akg-images)

king, not "elector," of Hanover. The German states, 39 in number, including Prussia and Austria, were joined in a loose confederation in which the members remained virtually sovereign. The Congress ignored the yearnings of German nationalists for a great unified Fatherland; Metternich especially feared nationalistic agitation; and in any case the nationalists themselves had no practical answer to concrete questions, such as the government and frontiers that a united Germany should have.

The Polish-Saxon Question

The question of Poland, reopened by the fall of Napoleon's Grand Duchy of Warsaw, brought the Congress almost to disaster. Alexander still insisted on undoing the crime of the partitions, which to his mind meant reconstituting the Polish kingdom with himself as constitutional king, in a merely personal union with the Russian empire. To reunite Poland required that Austria and Prussia surrender their respective segments of the old Poland, most of which they had lost to Napoleon. The Prussians were willing, with the proviso, which Alexander supported, that Prussia receive instead the whole of the kingdom of Saxony, which was considered available because the king of Saxony had been the last German ruler to abandon Napoleon. The issue presented itself as the Polish-Saxon question, with

Russia and Prussia standing together to demand all Poland for Russia and all Saxony for Prussia.

Such a prospect horrified Metternich. For Prussia to absorb Saxony would raise Prussia prodigiously in the eyes of all Germans, and it would greatly lengthen the common frontier between Prussia and the Austrian Empire. Furthermore, for Alexander to become king of all Poland, and incidentally the protector of an extended Prussia, would incalculably augment the influence of Russia in the affairs of Europe. Metternich found that

Diplomatic maneuvers

Castlereagh shared these views. To Castlereagh it seemed that the main problem at Vienna was to restrain Russia. The British had not fought the French emperor only to have Europe fall to the Russian tsar. For months the Polish-Saxon question was debated, Metternich and Castlereagh exploring every device of argument to dissuade the Russo-Prussian combination from its expansionist designs.

Finally they accepted the proffered assistance of Talleyrand, who shrewdly used the rift between the victors to bring France back into the diplomatic circle as a power in its own right. On January 3, 1815, Castlereagh, Metternich, and Talleyrand signed a secret treaty, pledging themselves to go to war if necessary against Russia and Prussia. So, in the very midst of the peace conference, war again reared its head.

No sooner had news of the secret treaty leaked out than Alexander offered to compromise. In his complicated nature he was, among other things, a man of peace, and he agreed to content himself with a reduced Polish kingdom. The Congress therefore created a new

"Congress Poland"

Poland (called "Congress Poland," which lasted for 15 years); Alexander became its king, and he gave it a constitution. It comprised much the same area as Napoleon's Grand Duchy, representing in effect a transfer of this region from French to Russian control. It reached 250 miles farther west into Europe than had the Russian segment of the third partition of 1795. Some Poles still remained in Prussia and some remained in the Austrian Empire; Poland was not reunited. With the tsar thus content, Prussia too had to back down. It received about two-fifths of Saxony, the rest remaining to the Saxon king. The addition of both Saxon and Rhineland territories brought the Prussian monarchy into the most advanced parts of Germany. The net effect of the peace settlement, and of the Napoleonic wars, in this connection, was to shift the center of gravity of both Russia and Prussia farther west—Russia almost to the Oder River and Prussia to the borders of France (see maps, pp. 208–209, 222–223).

With the solution of the Polish-Saxon question the main political work of the Congress was completed, and various committees of the Congress set to work to draft the Final Act. But at this point the whole settlement was unexpectedly brought into jeopardy.

The Hundred Days and Their Aftermath

Napoleon escaped from Elba, landed in France on March 1, 1815, and again proclaimed the empire. In the year since the return of the Bourbons discontent had been spreading in France. Louis XVIII proved to be a sensible man, but a swarm of unreasonable and vindictive émigrés had come back with him. Reaction and a "white terror" were raging through the country. Adherents of the Revolution rallied to the emperor on his dramatic reappearance. Napoleon reached Paris, took over the government and army, and headed for Belgium. He would, if he could, disperse the pompous assemblage at Vienna. To the victors of the year before, and to most of Europe, it seemed that the Revolution was again stirring, that the old horror of toppling thrones and recurring warfare might not after all be ended. The opposing forces met in Belgium at Waterloo, where the Duke of Wellington, commanding an allied force, won a great victory. Napoleon again abdicated and was again exiled, this time to distant St. Helena in the south Atlantic. A new peace treaty was made with France, the "second" Treaty of Paris. It was more severe than the first, since the French seemed to have shown themselves incorrigible and unrepentant. The new treaty imposed minor changes of the frontiers, an indemnity of 700,000,000 francs, and an army of occupation.

The effect of the Hundred Days, as the episode following Napoleon's return from Elba is called, was to renew the dread of revolution, war, and aggression. Britain, Russia, Austria, and Prussia, after being almost at war with each other in January, again joined forces to get rid of the apparition from Elba, and in November 1815 they solemnly reconfirmed the Quadruple Alliance of Chaumont, adding a provision that no Bonaparte should ever govern France. They agreed also to hold future congresses to review the political situation and enforce the peace. No change was made in the arrangements agreed to at Vienna, except that Murat, who fought for Napoleon during the Hundred Days, was captured and shot, and an extremely unenlightened Bourbon monarchy was restored in Naples. In addition to the Quadruple Alliance of the Great Powers, bound specifically to enforce or amend the terms of the peace treaty by international action, Alexander devised a vaguer scheme which he called the Holy Alliance. Long attracted to the idea of an international order, *Alliances against Napoleon* appalled by the return of Napoleon, and influenced at the moment by the pious Baroness von Krüdener, the tsar proposed, for all monarchs to sign, a statement by which they promised to uphold Christian principles of charity and peace. All signed except the pope, the sultan of the Ottoman Empire, and the prince regent of Great Britain. The Holy Alliance, probably sincerely meant by Alexander as a condemnation of violence, and at first not taken seriously by the others who signed it and who thought it absurd to mix Christianity with politics, soon came to signify, in the minds of liberals, a kind of unholy alliance of monarchies against liberty and progress.

The Peace of Vienna, including generally the Treaty of Vienna itself, the treaties of Paris, and the British and colonial settlement, was the most *The Peace of Vienna* far-reaching diplomatic agreement between the Peace of Westphalia of 1648 and the Peace of Paris, which closed the First World War in 1919. It had its strong points and its weak ones. It produced a minimum of resentment in France; the late enemy accepted the new arrangements. It ended almost two centuries of European conflicts over the control of colonial territories in Asia and the Americas; for 60 or 70 years no colonial empire seriously challenged the British. Two other causes of friction in the eighteenth century—the control of Poland and the Austro-Prussian dualism in Germany—were smoothed over for 50 years. With past issues the peace of 1815 dealt rather effectively; with future issues, not unnaturally, it was less successful. The Vienna treaty was not illiberal in its day; it was by no means entirely reactionary, for the Congress showed little desire to restore the state of affairs in existence before the wars. The reaction that gathered strength after 1815 was not written into the treaty itself.

But the treaty gave no satisfaction to nationalists and democrats. It was a disappointment even to many liberals, especially in Germany. The transfer of peoples from government to government without consultation of their wishes opened the way under nineteenth-century conditions to a good deal of subsequent trouble. The peacemakers were in fact hostile both to nationalism and to democracy, the potent forces of the coming age; they regarded them, with reason, as leading to revolution and war. The problem to which they addressed themselves was to restore the balance of power, the "liberties of Europe," and to make a lasting peace. In this they were successful. They restored the European state system, a system in which a number of sovereign and independent states existed without

fear of conquest or domination. And the peace they made, though some details broke down in 1830 and others in 1848, on the whole subsisted for half a century; and not for a full century, not until 1914, was there a war in Europe that lasted longer than a few months or in which all the great powers were involved.

The Peace of Vienna thus brought to a close the great political and military upheavals that had spread across Europe in the wake of the French Revolution. Yet even the most conservative diplomats at Vienna recognized that the revolutionary events and legacy would not simply vanish from European culture or history; indeed the Holy Alliance and the vigilance of the conservative European states after 1815 showed how deeply the French Revolution had affected all of Europe and those places outside Europe where revolutionary ideas had become popular and influential. The Latin American struggle for independence from Spain, for example, continued to draw on the new conceptions of national sovereignty and continued to spread across the New World while diplomats in Vienna were working to restore stability and order in Europe.

Legacy of the Revolution

The French Revolution and the Napoleonic empire had demonstrated how a new, more open system of social and professional advancement enabled a nation to exercise power more effectively than any of the traditional, monarchical states. The revolutionary regimes had introduced new methods for mobilizing national economic resources, military forces, and large populations, all of which would reappear in the national mobilizations of other modern states. The Revolution and Napoleon, in short, gave the modern world new models of political organization and authoritarian rule. At the same time, however, the famous revolutionary events also helped to spread new conceptions of human rights, political participation, democratic government, and economic organization that would remain powerful cultural ideals throughout much of the modern world; and the popular ideology of nationalism, which developed among both supporters and opponents of the French Revolution and Napoleon, rapidly became one of the most pervasive political and cultural forces in modern world history.

All of these ideas helped to produce and reshape the characteristic institutions of modern societies. They continued to attract fervent supporters after the Congress of Vienna and after all other attempts to defend or revive the old order. The French Revolution and the Napoleonic wars, for all their turmoil and terrible destructive violence, created a lasting political and cultural legacy that has influenced modern nations almost everywhere, down to our own time.

For interactive exercises, glossary, chronologies, and more, go to the *Online Learning Center* at **www.mhhe.com/palmer10.**

EUROPE, 1815

Boundaries are those set by the Congress of Vienna. France was reduced to the borders it had in 1789. Prussia was firmly installed on both banks of the Rhine, but South Germany remained as reorganized by Napoleon. Poland was again partitioned, with a larger share than in 1795 going to Russia—which also acquired Finland and Bessarabia. The Austrians added Venetia to what they had held before 1796. The union of the Dutch and Belgian Netherlands lasted only until 1831, when the kingdom of Belgium was established. Otherwise, the boundaries of 1815 lasted until the Italian war of 1859, which led to the unification of Italy.

Chapter 11

INDUSTRIES, IDEAS, AND THE STRUGGLE FOR REFORM, 1815–1848

In the period of some 30 years preceding 1815 two "revolutions" had been taking place. One was the upheaval associated with the French Revolution and the Napoleonic empire. Basically, it was mainly political, having to do with the organization of government, public power and authority, public finance, taxation, administration, law, individual rights, and the legal position of social classes. The other "revolution," a revolution in a more metaphorical sense, was primarily economic, having to do with the production of wealth, the techniques of manufacture, the exploitation of natural resources, the development of new technologies, the formation of capital, and the distribution of products to consumers. The political and the economic revolutions in these years went on somewhat independently of each other. Until 1815 the political revolution affected mainly the Continent, while the economic revolution was most active in England. The Continent, while renewing itself politically, remained economically less advanced than England. England, transformed economically, remained conservative in other respects. Hence it has been possible to deal with the political significance of the French Revolution and its Napoleonic sequel without much discussion of the Industrial Revolution, as the economic changes then occurring in England are always called.

It may be (the matter is arguable) that the Industrial Revolution was more important than the French Revolution or any other. In a telescopic view of world history the two biggest changes experienced by the human race in the past 10,000 years may have been the agricultural or Neolithic revolution, which, beginning about 8000 B.C., ushered in the first civilizations, and the Industrial Revolution, which ushered in the modern global civilization of the last two centuries. However that may be, it proves on closer examination that

Chapter emblem: Detail from an engraving, *Young Saint-Simonienne* (1832), by Malreuve. (Bibliothèque Nationale de France, Paris)

433

the economic and the political, the Industrial Revolution (or industrialization) and the other institutions of a society, cannot be kept apart in the historical study of modern times. The Industrial Revolution occurred first in England, becoming evident about 1780, because of certain political characteristics of English society, because earlier commercial and naval successes had expanded England's access to world markets, and because English life offered rewards to the individual for a spirit of risk-taking and innovation. Nor can the effects of political and economic revolution, in England or elsewhere, be kept apart for the years after 1815.

With the defeat of Napoleon and signing of the peace treaty at Vienna in 1815, it seemed that the French Revolution was at last over. European conservatism had triumphed; since it restored European monarchies and frankly opposed the new "French ideas," it can appropriately be called "reaction." But the processes of industrialization, as they accelerated in England and spread to the Continent, worked against the politically conservative settlement. Industrialization greatly enlarged both the business and wage-earning classes, and made it harder for monarchs and landed aristocrats to maintain their control over public power. Industrial development in the nineteenth century was often called "progress," and economic progress proved stronger than political reaction.

Industrial society arose in England, Western Europe, and the United States in the nineteenth century, within the system known as capitalism. In the twentieth century, after the Russian Revolution in 1917, industrial societies were created in which capitalism was vehemently rejected. Industrialism and capitalism are therefore by no means the same. Yet all industrial societies use capital, which is defined as wealth that is not consumed but is used to produce more wealth, or future wealth. An automobile is a consumer's good; the automobile factory is the capital. What distinguishes a capitalist from a noncapitalist society is not the existence of capital but the ways in which the capital is controlled. The distinctions sometimes become blurred. In one form of society the control of capital is through private ownership, or institutions of private property, by which capital is owned by individuals, families, or corporations that are in turn owned by shareholders—in any case not by the state. In such societies, though ownership may be widespread, most capital is controlled by relatively few people, responding to market forces. In the other form of society productive capital in principle belongs to the public and is in effect owned and controlled by the state or its agencies; such societies usually call themselves socialist, because the first socialists rejected the principle of private ownership of the means of production, that is, of capital. In these societies the control of capital, or decisions on saving, investment, and production, are also in the hands of relatively few under some form of central plan.

In Europe the institutions of secure private property had developed gradually since the Middle Ages, and much that happened in the French Revolution was designed to protect property from the demands of the state. Possession of property was held to be the basis of personal independence and political liberty, and the expectation of keeping future profits inspired, in some, a willingness to commit their capital to new and uncertain ventures. It made possible an entrepreneurial spirit. There had been a commercial capitalism in Europe at least since the sixteenth century. Industrialization in Europe was therefore capitalist. Countries outside the West-European orbit, and industrializing later, faced a different problem. A country in which little capital had accumulated from the trade and agriculture of previous generations, and which had few owners of capital or enterprising individuals, could hardly industrialize by European methods. If it lacked the European background, in which various political, social, legal, and organizational features were as important as the economic, it would have to achieve industrialization by a combination of other methods. This usually meant that innovation, planning, decision making, control, and even domination rested largely with the state.

In the short run, within a few years, the Industrial Revolution in Western Europe favored the liberal, modernizing principles and legal rights proclaimed in the French Revolution. In the middle run, or in half a century, it made Europe overwhelmingly more powerful than other parts of the world, leading to a worldwide European ascendancy in the form of imperialism. In the still longer run, by the twentieth century, it provoked a retaliation, in which other countries tried hastily to industrialize in self-protection, or to improve the condition of their peoples, hoping to catch up with Western economies and nation-states while loudly denouncing the West as imperialist and capitalist. Of these newer industrial societies the Soviet Union, until its dissolution in 1991, and the People's Republic of China, from 1949 into the twenty-first century, would be the most prominent.

52.   THE INDUSTRIAL REVOLUTION IN BRITAIN

On the whole, from the beginning of history until about 1800, the work of the world was done with hand tools. Since then it has been increasingly done by machines. Before about 1800 power was supplied by human or animal muscle, reinforced by levers or pulleys, and supplemented by the force of running water or moving air. Since then power has been supplied by the human manipulation of forms of energy found in steam, electricity, the combustion of gases, and most recently within the atom. The process of shifting from hand tools to power machinery is what is meant by the Industrial Revolution. Its beginning cannot be dated exactly. It grew gradually out of the technical practices of earlier times. It is still going on, for in some countries industrialization has barely begun, and even in the most highly developed it is still making advances. But the first country to be profoundly affected by industrialization was Great Britain, where its effects became manifest in the half-century following 1780.

It seems likely, despite the emphasis placed on revolutionary upheavals by historians, that people are habitually quite conservative. Working people do not put off their old way of life, move to strange and overcrowded towns, or enter the deadly rounds of mine and factory except under strong incentive. Well-to-do people, living in comfort on assured incomes, do not readily risk their wealth in new and untried ventures. The shifting to modern machine production requires in any country a certain mobility of people and of wealth. Such mobility may be produced by state pressure, as in the twentieth-century industrialization of the Soviet Union or the People's Republic of China. In eighteenth-century England a high degree of social mobility developed from a long historical process of social change.

The Agricultural Revolution in Britain

The English Revolution of 1688, confirming the ascendancy of Parliament over the king, meant in economic terms the ascendancy of the more well-to-do property-owning classes. Among these the landowners were by far the most important, though they counted the great London merchants among their allies. For a century and a half, from 1688 to 1832, the British government was substantially in the hands of these landowners—the "squirearchy" or "gentlemen of England." The result was a thorough transformation of farming, an Agricultural Revolution without which the Industrial Revolution could not have occurred.

Agricultural experimentation

Many landowners, seeking to increase their money incomes, began experimenting with improved methods of cultivation and stock raising. They made more use of fertilizers such as animal manure; they introduced new implements such as the drill seeder and horse-hoe; they brought in new crops, such as turnips, and a more scientific system of crop rotation; they attempted to breed larger sheep and fatter cattle. An improving landlord, to introduce such changes successfully, needed full control over his land. He saw only a barrier to progress in the old village system of open fields, common lands, and semicollective methods of cultivation. Improvement also required an investment of capital, which was impossible so long as the soil was tilled by numerous poor and custom-bound small farmers.

The old common rights of the villagers were part of the English common law. Only an act of Parliament could modify or extinguish them. It was the great landowners who controlled Parliament, which therefore passed hundreds of "enclosure acts," authorizing the

The enclosure acts

enclosure, by fences, walls, or hedges, of the old common lands and unfenced open fields. Land thus came under a strict regime of private ownership and individual management. At the same time small owners sold out or were excluded in various ways, the more easily since the larger owners had so much local authority as justices of the peace. Ownership of land in England, more than anywhere else in central or western Europe, became concentrated in the hands of a relatively small class of wealthy landlords, who leased it out in large blocks to a relatively small class of substantial farmers. This development, though in progress throughout the eighteenth century, reached its height during the Napoleonic wars.

One result was greatly to raise the productivity of land and of farm labor. Fatter cattle yielded more meat; more assiduous cultivation yielded more cereals. The food supply of England was increased, while a smaller percentage of the population was needed to produce it. Labor was thus released for other pursuits. The greater number of the English country people became wage earners, working for the farmers and landlords, or spinning or weaving in their cottages for merchants in the towns. English working men and women were therefore dependent on daily wages long before the coming of the factory and the machine. Working people became mobile; they would go where the jobs were, or where the wages were slightly higher. They also became available for new kinds of work because fewer of them were needed on the land to produce food. Such conditions hardly obtained except in Great Britain. On the Continent agricultural methods were less productive, and the rural workers were more established on the soil, whether by institutions of serfdom as in eastern Europe or by the possession of property or firm leaseholds as in France.

Industrialism in Britain: Incentives and Inventions

Meanwhile, as the Agricultural Revolution ran its course in the eighteenth century and into the nineteenth, the British had conquered a colonial empire, staked out markets all over the Americas and Europe, built up a huge mercantile marine, and won command of the sea. The British merchant could sell more, if only more could be produced. He had the customers, he had the ships, and moreover he could obtain the capital with which to finance new ideas. The profit motive prompted the search for more rapid methods of production. The old English staple export, woolen cloth, could be marketed indefinitely if only more could be woven. The possibilities in cotton cloth were enormous. The taste of Europeans for cottons had been already formed by imports from Asia. Using hand methods, Europeans could not produce cotton cloth in competition with the East. But the market was

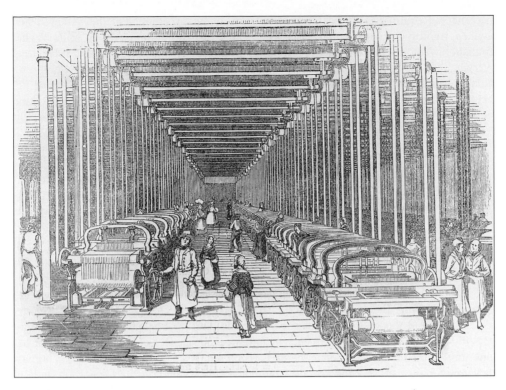

The construction of cotton mills led to a rapid increase in the production of textiles and brought large numbers of workers together in new cities. This illustration of an English cotton mill in the early 1830s shows the technology of industrialization and the women workers who moved from older cottage industries into the new factories.

(Mary Evans Picture Library/The Image Works)

endless if cotton could be spun, woven, and printed with less labor, that is, by machines. Capital was available, mobile, and fluid because of the rise of banking, credit, and stock companies. Funds could be shifted from one enterprise to another. Wealthy landowners and merchants could divert some of their profits to industry. If an invention proved a total loss, as sometimes happened, or if it required years of development before producing any income, the investment could still be afforded. Only a country already wealthy from commerce and agriculture could have been the first to initiate the machine age. England was such a country.

These conditions induced a series of successful inventions in the textile industry. In 1733 a man named John Kay invented the fly shuttle, by which only one person instead of two was needed to weave cloth on a loom. The resulting increase in the output of weaving set up a strong demand for yarn. This was met in the 1760s by the invention of the spinning jenny, a kind of mechanized spinning wheel that enabled workers to increase their production of yarn. The new shuttles and jennies were first operated by hand and used by domestic workers in their homes. But in 1769 Richard Arkwright patented the water frame, a device for the multiple spinning of many threads. At first it was operated by water power, but in the 1780s Arkwright introduced the steam engine to drive his spinning

Inventions in the textile industry

machinery. Requiring a considerable installation of heavy equipment, he gathered his engines, frames, and workers into large and usually dismal buildings, called mills by the English, or factories in subsequent American usage. Mechanical spinning now for a time overwhelmed the hand weavers with yarn. This led to the development of the power loom, which became economically practicable shortly after 1800. Weaving as well as spinning therefore took place increasingly in factories. These improvements in the finishing process put a heavy strain on the production of raw cotton. An ingenious Connecticut inventor, Eli Whitney, while employed as a children's tutor on a Georgia plantation in 1793, produced a cotton gin, which by speeding up the removal of seeds greatly increased the output of cotton. The gin soon spread through the American South, where the almost decaying plantation economy was abruptly revived, becoming an adjunct to the Industrial Revolution in England. British imports of raw cotton multiplied fivefold in the 30 years following 1790. In value of manufactures, cotton cloth rose from ninth to first place among British industries in the same years. By 1820 it made up almost half of all British exports.

The steam engine

The steam engine, applied to the cotton mills in the 1780s, had for a century been going through a development of its own. Scientific and technical experiments with steam pressures had been fairly common in the seventeenth century, but what gave the economic impetus to invention was the gradual dwindling of Europe's primeval stocks of timber. The wood shortage became acute in England about 1700, so that it was more difficult to obtain the charcoal needed in smelting iron, and smelters turned increasingly to coal. Deeper coal shafts could not be sunk until someone devised better methods of pumping out water. About 1702 Thomas Newcomen built the first economically significant steam engine, which was soon widely used to drive pumps in the coal mines. However, it consumed so much fuel in proportion to power delivered that it could generally be used only in the coal fields themselves. In 1763 James Watt, a technician at the University of Glasgow, began to make improvements on Newcomen's engine. He formed a business partnership with Matthew Boulton. Boulton, originally a manufacturer of toys, buttons, and shoe buckles, provided the funds to finance Watt's rather costly experiments, handmade equipment, and slowly germinating ideas. By the 1780s the firm of Boulton and Watt was eminently successful, manufacturing steam engines both for British use and for the export trade.

At first, until further refinements and greater precision could be obtained in the working of iron, the engines were so cumbersome that they could be used as stationary engines only, as in the new spinning mills of Arkwright and others. Soon after 1800 the steam engine was successfully used to propel river boats, notably on the Hudson River in 1807, by Robert Fulton, who employed an imported Boulton and Watt engine. Experiments with steam power for land transportation began at the same time. Just as Newcomen's engine had been put to practical uses in the coal fields of England a century before, so now it was in the coal fields that Watt's engine first became a locomotive. Well before 1800 the mines had taken to using railways, on which wagons with flanged wheels, drawn by horses, carried coal to canals or to the sea. In the 1820s steam engines were successfully placed on moving vehicles. The first fully satisfactory locomotive was George Stephenson's *Rocket,* which in 1829, on the newly built Liverpool and Manchester Railway, not only reached an impressive speed of 16 miles per hour but met more important safety tests as well. By the 1840s the era of railroad construction was under way in both Europe and the United States.

Transportation

The Industrial Revolution in Great Britain in its early phase, down to 1830 or 1840, took place principally in the manufacture of textiles, with accompanying developments in the exploitation of iron and coal. The early factories were principally textile factories, and indeed mainly cotton mills; for cotton was an entirely new industry to Europe and hence easily mechanized, whereas the long established woolen trade, in which both employers and workers hesitated to abandon their customary ways, was mechanized more slowly. The suddenness of the change must not be exaggerated. It is often said that the Industrial Revolution was not a revolution at all. As late as the 1830s only a small fraction of the British working people were employed in factories. But the factory and the factory system were even then regarded as the coming mode of production, destined to grow and expand and symbolize the irresistible march of progress.

Some Social Consequences of Industrialism in Britain

The Britain that emerged fundamentally unscathed and in fact strengthened from the wars with Napoleon was no longer the "merrie England" of days of yore. The island was becoming crowded with people, as was the lesser island of Ireland. The combined population of Great Britain and Ireland tripled in the century from 1750 to 1850, rising from about 10 million in 1750 to about 30 million in 1850. The growth was distributed very unevenly. Formerly, in England, most people had lived in the south. But the coal and iron, and hence the steam power, lay in the Midlands and the north. Here whole new cities rose seemingly out of nowhere. In 1785 it was estimated that in England and Scotland, outside of London, there were only three cities with more than 50,000 people. Seventy years later, the span of one lifetime, there were 31 British cities of this size.

Preeminent among them was Manchester in Lancashire, the first and most famous of the new industrial cities. Manchester, before the coming of the cotton mills, was a rather large market town. Though very ancient, it *Manchester* had not been significant enough to be recognized as a borough for representation in Parliament. Locally it was organized as a manor. Not until 1845 did the inhabitants extinguish the manorial rights, buying them out at that time from the last lord. In population Manchester grew from 25,000 in 1772 to 455,000 in 1851. But until 1835 there was no regular procedure in England for the incorporation of cities. Urban organization was more backward than in Prussia or France. Unless inherited from the Middle Ages, a city had no legal existence. It lacked proper officials and adequate tax-raising and lawmaking powers. It was therefore difficult for Manchester and the other new factory towns to deal with problems of rapid urbanization, such as provision for police protection, water and sewers, or the disposal of garbage.

The new urban agglomerations were drab places, blackened with the heavy soot of the early coal age, settling alike on the mills and the workers' quarters, which were dark at best, for the climate of the Midlands is not sunny. Housing for workers was hastily built, closely packed, and always in short supply, as in all rapidly growing communities. Entire families lived in single rooms, and family life tended to disintegrate. A police officer in Glasgow observed that there were whole blocks of tenements in the city, each swarming with a thousand ragged children who had first names only, usually nicknames—like animals, as he put it.

The distressing feature of the new factories was that for the most part they required unskilled labor only. Skilled workers found themselves degraded in status. Hand weavers and spinners, thrown out of work by the new machines, either languished in a misery that was the deepest of that of any class in the *Unskilled labor* Industrial Revolution or else went off to a factory to find a job. The factories paid good wages by the standards for unskilled labor at the time. But these standards were very low, too low to allow a man to support his wife and children. This had generally

The invention of the steam locomotive and railways contributed decisively to early nineteenth-century industrialization. These primitive trains, about 1840, are running on wooden rails with "guidance wheels" at a strange angle to keep them on the track.
(Time Life Pictures/Getty Images)

been true for unskilled labor, in England and elsewhere, under earlier economic systems also. In the new factories the work was so mechanical that children as young as six years old were often preferred. Women, too, worked for less and were often more adept at handling a bobbin, which brought many women spinners from the older, displaced "cottage industries" into the new industrial working class.

Hours in the factories were long, 14 a day or occasionally more; and though such hours were familiar to persons who had worked on farms, or at domestic industry in rural households, they became more tedious and oppressive in the more regimented conditions that were necessary in the mills. Holidays were few, except for the unwelcome leisure of unemployment, which was a common scourge, because the short-run ups and downs of

Population Density: Persons per Square Mile

250 to 500

Over 500

• Cities over 100,000

ABOUT 1700

IN 1911

BRITAIN BEFORE AND AFTER THE INDUSTRIAL REVOLUTION

In 1700 England, Scotland, and Wales had only one city with a population of more than 100,000. In 1911 they had nearly 30, most of which were located in the industrialized Midlands (the area within the small rectangle).

business were very erratic. A day without work produced nothing to live on, but even where the daily wage was relatively attractive, the worker's real income was chronically insufficient. Workers in the factories, as in the mines, were almost entirely unorganized. They were a mass of recently assembled humanity without traditions or common ties. They bargained individually with their employers who, usually small business people themselves, faced ferocious competition with others. The employers were often in debt for the equipment in their own factories, or they were determined to save money in order to purchase more, and so held their wages bill to the lowest possible figure.

The factory owners, the new "cotton lords," were the first industrial capitalists. They were often self-made men, who owed their position to their own intelligence, persistence, and foresight. They lived in comfort

The cotton lords

without ostentation or luxury, saving from each year's income to build up their factories and their machines. Hard-working themselves, they thought that landed gentlemen were usually idlers and that the poor tended to be lazy. They were usually honest, in a hard and exacting way; they would make money by any means the law allowed, but not beyond it. They were neither brutal nor knowingly hard-hearted. They gave to charitable and philanthropic causes. They believed that they did the poor a favor by furnishing them with work and by seeing to it that they worked diligently and productively. Most of them disapproved of public regulation of their business, though a few, driven by competition to expedients that they did not like, such as the employment of small children, would have accepted some regulation that fell on all competitors equally. It was a cotton magnate, the elder Robert Peel, who in 1802 pushed the first Factory Act through Parliament. This act purported to regulate the conditions in which pauper children were employed in the textile mills, but it was a dead letter from the beginning, since it provided no adequate body of factory inspectors. The English at this time, alone among the leading European peoples, had no class of trained, paid, and professional government administrators; nor did they yet want such a class, preferring self-government and local initiative. To have inspectors for one's affairs smacked of Continental bureaucracy. The fact that the older methods of economic regulation were obsolescent, actually unsuited to the new age, had the effect of discrediting the idea of regulation itself. The new industrialists wanted to be left alone. They considered it unnatural to interfere with business and believed that, if allowed to follow their own judgment, they would assure the future prosperity and progress of the country.

Classical Economics: "Laissez-Faire"

The industrialists were strengthened in these beliefs by the emerging science of political economy. In 1776 Adam Smith published his epochal *Wealth of Nations,* which criticized the older mercantilism, with its regulatory and monopolistic practices, and urged, though with moderation, that certain "natural laws" of production and exchange be allowed to work freely in economic markets. Smith was followed by Thomas R. Malthus, David Ricardo, and the so-called Manchester School. Their doctrine was dubbed (by its opponents) laissez-faire and in its elaborated form is still called classical economics. It held, basically, that there is a world of economic relationships autonomous and separable from government or politics. It is the world of the free market and is regulated within itself by certain "natural laws," such as the law of supply and demand. All persons should follow their own enlightened self-interest; all know their own interests better than anyone else; and the sum total of individual interests will add up to the general welfare and liberty of all. Government should do as little as possible; it should confine itself to preserving security of life and property, providing reasonable laws and reliable courts, thus ensuring the discharge of private contracts, debts, and obligations. Not only business but education, charity, and personal matters generally should be left to private initiative. There should be no tariffs; free trade should reign everywhere, for the economic system is worldwide, unaffected by political barriers or national differences. As for workers, according to classical economists before about 1850, they should not expect to make more than a bare minimum living; an "iron law of wages," they argued, shows that as soon as workers receive more than a subsistence wage they breed more children, who eat up the excess, so that they reduce themselves, and the working class generally, again to a subsistence level. Workers, if discontented, should see the folly of changing the system, for this *is* the system, the natural system—there is no other. Political economy as taught in grim Manchester was not without reason called the "dismal science."

Self-interest and free trade

For working people in England the Industrial Revolution was a hard experience. It should be remembered, however, that neither low wages, nor the 14-hour day, nor the labor of women and children, nor the ravages of unemployment were anything new. All had existed for centuries, in England and western Europe, as agricultural and commercial capitalism replaced the more self-sufficient economies of the Middle Ages. The factory towns were in some ways better places than the rural slums from which many of their people came. Factory routine was psychologically deadening, but the textile mills were not always worse than the domestic

Working people's experiences

sweatshops in which manufacturing processes had previously been carried on. The concentration of working people in city and factory opened the way to improvement in their condition. It made their misery apparent; philanthropic sentiment gradually arose among the more fortunate. Gathered in cities, workers obtained more knowledge of the world. Mingling and talking together, they developed a sense of solidarity, class interest, and common political aims; and in time they became organized, establishing labor unions by which to obtain a larger share of the national income.

Britain after the fall of Napoleon became the workshop of the world. Though factories using steam power sprang up in France, Belgium, New England, and elsewhere, it was really not until after 1870 that Great Britain faced major industrial competition from abroad. The British had a virtual monopoly in textiles and machine tools. The English Midlands and Scottish Lowlands shipped cotton thread and steam engines to all the world. British capital was exported to all countries, there to call new enterprises into being. London became the world's clearinghouse and financial center. Progressive people in other lands looked to Britain as their model, hoping to learn from its advanced industrial methods, and to imitate its parliamentary political system.

53. THE ADVENT OF THE "ISMS"

The combined forces of industrialization and of the French Revolution led after 1815 to a proliferation of new doctrines and movements, most of which contributed to a general European revolution in 1848. As for the 33 years from 1815 to 1848, there is no better way of grasping their long-run meaning than to reflect on the number of enduring "isms" that arose at that time.

So far as is known the word "liberalism" first appeared in the English language in 1819, "radicalism" in 1820, "socialism" in 1832, "conservatism" in 1835. The 1830s first saw "individualism," "constitutionalism," "humanitarianism," "feminism," and "monarchism." "Nationalism" and "communism" date from the 1840s. Not until the 1850s did the English-speaking world use the word "capitalism" (French *capitalisme* is much older); and not until even later had it heard of "Marxism," though the doctrines of Marx grew out of and reflected the troubled times of the 1840s.

The rapid coinage of new "isms" does not in every case mean that the ideas they conveyed were new. Many of them had their origin in the Enlightenment, if not before. People had loved liberty before talking of liberalism and been conservative without defining their ideas as conservatism. The appearance of so many "isms" shows rather that people were making their ideas more systematic. To the "philosophy" of the Enlightenment were now added an intense activism and partisanship generated during the French Revolution. People were obliged to reconsider and analyze society as a whole. The social sciences were taking form. An "ism" (excluding such words as "hypnotism" or "favoritism") may be defined as the conscious espousal of a doctrine in competition with other doctrines. Without the "isms" created in the 30-odd years after the peace of Vienna it is impossible to understand or even talk about the history of the world since that event, so that a brief characterization of some of the most important is in order.

Romanticism

One of the "isms" was not political. It was called "romanticism," a word first used in English in the 1840s to describe a movement then half a century old. Romanticism was primarily a theory of literature and the arts. Its great exponents included William Wordsworth,

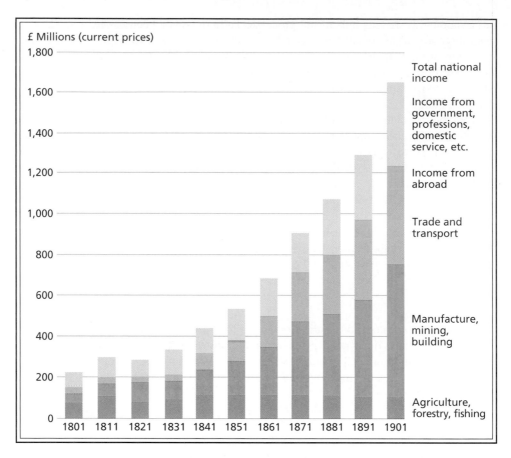

£ Millions (current prices)

THE INDUSTRIAL REVOLUTION IN BRITAIN (AS SHOWN BY SOURCES OF INCOME)

British national income grew about eightfold in the nineteenth century. Income derived from agriculture, forestry, and the like remained about the same, but the income from these activities sank from one-third to one-sixteenth of all income. By 1851 half the national income came from manufacturing, trade, and transportation, and by 1901 three-quarters came from these sources. The category "income from abroad" refers to interest and dividends on loans and investments outside Great Britain, which grew rapidly after the 1850s.

Source: P. Deane and W. A. Cole, *British Economic Growth* (Cambridge, England: Cambridge University Press, 1962), pp. 166–167.

Lord Byron, Percy Bysshe Shelley, and Mary Wollstonecraft Shelley in England; Victor Hugo, René Chateaubriand, and George Sand in France; and Friedrich von Schiller, Friedrich Schlegel, and many others in Germany. As a theory of art it raised basic questions on the nature of significant truth, on the importance of various human faculties, on the relation of thought and feeling, on the meaning of the past and of time itself. Romanticism rejected the emphasis on classical rules and rational order that had shaped aesthetic theory during much of the eighteenth century. Romantics celebrated the idiosyncratic visions of creative individuals rather than the symmetries of classical art and literature. They helped produce the modern image of defiant artistic rebels. Representing a new way of sensing all human experience, romanticism affected much thinking on social and public questions.

Possibly the most fundamental romantic attitude was a love of the unclassifiable—of moods or impressions, scenes or stories, sights or sounds or things concretely experienced, personal idiosyncrasies or peculiar customs which the intellect could never classify, box up, explain away, or reduce to an abstract generalization. The romantics, characteristically, insisted on the value of feeling as well as of reason. They were aware of the importance of the subconscious. They were likely to suspect a perfectly lucid idea as somehow superficial. They loved the mysterious, the unknown, the half-seen figures on the far horizon. Hence romanticism contributed to a new interest in strange and distant societies and in strange and distant historical epochs. Where the philosophes of the Enlightenment had deplored the Middle Ages as a time of intellectual error, the romantic generation looked back upon them with respect and even nostalgia, finding in them a fascination, a colorfulness, or a spiritual depth which they missed in their own time. The "Gothic," which rationalists thought barbarous, had a strong appeal for romantics. A Gothic Revival emerged in the arts, of which one example was the British Parliament buildings, built in the 1830s.

Love of the unclassifiable

In medieval art and institutions, as in the art and institutions of every age and people, the romantics saw the expression of an inner genius. The idea of original or creative genius was in fact another of the most fundamental romantic beliefs. A genius was a dynamic spirit that no rules could hem in, one that no analysis or classification could ever fully explain. Genius, it was thought, made its own rules and laws. The genius might be that of the individual person, such as the artist, writer, or Napoleonic mover of the world. It might be the genius or spirit of an age. Or it might be the genius of a people or nation, the *Volksgeist* of Herder, an inherent national character making each people grow in its own distinctive way, which could be known only by a study of its history; romanticism thus merged in many places with new forms of nationalism. Here again romanticism gave a new impetus to study of the past. Politically, romantics could be found in all camps, conservative, liberal, and radical, but the emphasis on individual creativity led most romantics toward a critical view of rigid social and cultural hierarchies. Romanticism thus added cultural and emotional passions to the more political "isms" that evolved rapidly after 1815.

Creative genius

Classical Liberalism

The first Liberals, calling themselves by that name (though Napoleon used that word for his own system), arose in Spain among opponents of the Napoleonic occupation. The word passed to France, where it denoted opposition to royalism after the restoration of the Bourbons in 1814 and where it gained intellectual influence through the work of liberal writers such as Benjamin Constant. In England, many Whigs became increasingly liberal, as did even a few Tories. Liberal political theorists also had influence in England, most notably in the writings of John Stuart Mill, and a new Liberal Party became an important force in British politics during the 1850s. Nineteenth-century, or "classical," liberalism varied from country to country, but it showed many basic similarities, including an emphasis on the rights and liberties that individuals should possess in every well-ordered, modern society.

Liberals were generally persons of the business and professional classes, together with enterprising landowners wishing to improve their estates. They believed in what was modern, enlightened, efficient, reasonable, and fair. They had confidence in the human capacity for self-government and self-control. They set a high value on parliamentary or representative government,

Liberal beliefs

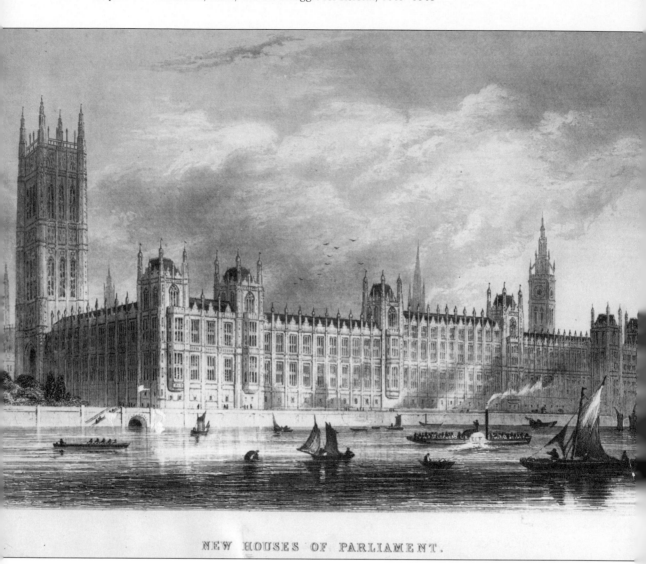

NEW HOUSES OF PARLIAMENT.

The new British Houses of Parliament were built during the 1830s. They became a prominent example of the Gothic revival in architecture and of the early nineteenth-century romantic fascination with the Middle Ages.
(Getty Images)

working through reasonable discussion and legislation, with responsible ministries and an impartial and law-abiding administration. They demanded full publicity for all actions of government, and to ensure such publicity they insisted on freedom of the press and free rights of assembly. All these political advantages they thought most likely to be realized under a good constitutional monarchy. Outside England they favored explicit written constitutions. They were not democrats; they generally opposed giving every man the vote, fearing the excesses of mob rule or of irrational political action. Only as the nineteenth century progressed did liberals gradually and reluctantly come to accept the idea of universal male suffrage. Many continued to oppose female suffrage, though some liberals such as John Stuart Mill argued that women should have the same voting rights as men. Liberals subscribed to the doctrines of the "rights of man" as set forth in the American and French revolutions, but with a clear emphasis on the right of property, and in their economic views they typically followed the British Manchester School or the French economist J. B. Say. They favored laissez-faire, were suspicious of the ability of government to regulate business, wanted to get rid of the guild system where it still existed, and disapproved of attempts on the part of the new industrial laborers to organize unions.

Internationally they advocated freedom of trade, to be accomplished by the lowering or abolition of tariffs, so that all countries might exchange their products easily with each other and with industrial England. In this way, they thought, each country would produce what it was most fitted for, and so best increase its wealth and standards of living. From the growth of wealth, production, invention, and scientific progress they believed that the general progress of humanity would ensue. They generally frowned upon the established churches and landed aristocracies as obstacles to advancement. They believed in the spread of tolerance and education. They were also profoundly civilian in attitude, disliking wars, conquerors, army officers, standing armies, and military expenditures. They wanted orderly change by processes of legislation. They shrank before the idea of revolution. Liberals on the Continent usually admired Great Britain.

Radicalism, Republicanism, Socialism

Radicalism, at least as a word, originated in England, where about 1820 the Philosophical Radicals proudly applied the term to themselves. These Radicals in the 1820s included not only the few working-class leaders who were beginning to emerge but also many of the new industrial capitalists, who were still unrepresented in Parliament. They took up where such English "Jacobins" as Thomas Paine had left off a generation earlier, before the long crisis of the French wars had discredited all radicalism as pro-French; and they wanted to extend many of the liberal arguments for individual rights to much wider segments of the population.

The Philosophical Radicals were a good deal like the rationalist French philosophes before the Revolution. They were followers of an elderly sage, Jeremy Bentham, who in prolific writings from 1776 to 1832 undertook to reform the English criminal and civil law, church, Parliament, and constitution. The English Radicals professed to deduce the right form of institutions from the fundamental traits of human nature and psychology. They impatiently waved aside all arguments based on history, usage, or custom. They went to the roots of things. ("Radical" is from the Latin word for "root.") They wanted a total reconstruction of laws, courts, prisons, poor relief, municipal organization, rotten boroughs, and fox-hunting clergy. Their demand for the reform of *Demands for radical reforms* Parliament was vehement and insistent. They detested the Church of England, the peerage, and the squirearchy. Many radicals would just as soon abolish royalty also; not until the long reign of Queen Victoria (1837–1901) did the British monarchy become undeniably popular in all quarters. Above all, radicalism was democratic; it demanded a vote for every adult Englishman. After the Reform Bill of 1832 the industrial capitalists generally turned into liberals, but the working-class leaders remained radical democrats, as will be seen.

On the Continent radicalism was represented by militant republicanism. The years of the First French Republic, which to liberals and conservatives signified horrors associated with the Reign of Terror, were for the *Republican ideals* republicans years of hope and progress, cut short by forces of reaction. Republicans were a minority even in France; elsewhere, as in Italy and Germany, they were fewer still, though they existed. Mostly the republicans were drawn from intelligentsia such as students and writers, from working-class leaders protesting social injustice, and from elderly veterans, or the descendants of veterans, to whom the Republic of '93, with its wars and its glory, was a living thing. Because of police repression, republicans often joined together in secret societies. They looked with equanimity on the prospect of further revolutionary upheaval, by which they felt that the cause of liberty, equality, and fraternity would be advanced. Strong believers in political equality, they were democrats demanding universal male suffrage. They favored parliamentary government but were much less primarily concerned with its successful operation than were the liberals. Most republicans were bitterly anticlerical. Remembering the internecine struggle between the church and the republic during the French Revolution, and still facing the political influence of the Catholic clergy (for republicanism was most common in Catholic countries), they regarded the Catholic church as the implacable enemy of reason and liberty. Opposed to monarchy of any kind, even to constitutional monarchy, intensely hostile to church and aristocracy, conscious heirs of the great French Revolution, organized in national and international secret societies, not averse to overthrowing existing regimes by force, the more militant republicans were considered by most other people, including the liberals, to be little better than anarchists.

Socialist views

Republicanism shaded off into socialism. Socialists generally shared the political attitudes of republicanism but added other views besides. The early socialists, those before the Revolution of 1848, were of many kinds, but all had certain ideas in common. All of them regarded the existing economic system as aimless, chaotic, and outrageously unjust. All thought it improper for owners of wealth to have so much economic power—to give or deny work to the worker, to set wages and hours in their own interests, to guide all the labors of society in the interests of private profit. All therefore questioned the value of private enterprise, favoring some degree of communal ownership of productive assets—banks, factories, machines, land, and transportation. All disliked competition as a governing economic or social principle and set forth principles of harmony, cooperation or association instead. All flatly and absolutely rejected the laissez-faire of the liberals and the political economists. Where the latter thought mainly of increasing production, without much concern over distribution, the early socialists thought mainly of a fairer or more equal distribution of income among all useful members of society. They believed that beyond the civil and legal equality brought by the French Revolution a further step toward social and economic equality had yet to be taken.

One of the first socialists was also one of the first cotton lords, Robert Owen (1771–1858) of Manchester and the Scottish Lowlands. Appalled at the condition of the mill-hands, he created a kind of model community for his own employees, paying high wages, reducing hours, sternly correcting vice and drunkenness, building schools and housing and company stores for the cheap sale of workers' necessities. From such paternalistic capitalism in his early years he passed on to a long lifetime spent in crusading for social reforms, in which he was somewhat handicapped, not only by the opposition of industrialists, but also by his unpopular radicalism in matters of religion.

Saint-Simonians and Fourier

Most of the early socialists were French, spurred onward by the sense of an uncompleted revolution. One was a nobleman, the Count de Saint-Simon (1760–1825), who had fought in the War of American Independence, accepted the French Revolution, and in his later years wrote many books on social problems. He and his followers, who called themselves not socialists but Saint-Simonians, were among the first clear exponents of a planned society. They advocated the public ownership of industrial equipment and other capital, with control vested in the hands of great captains of industry or social engineers, who should plan vast projects like the digging of a canal at Suez, and in general coordinate the labor and resources of society to productive ends. Of a different type was Charles Fourier (1772–1837), a somewhat doctrinaire thinker who subjected all social institutions to a sweeping condemnation. His positive program took the form of proposing that society be organized in small units which he termed "phalansteries." Each of these he conceived to contain 1,620 persons, each doing the work suited to his or her natural inclination. Among the practical French no phalanstery was ever successfully organized. A number were established in the United States, still the land of Europe's utopian dream; the best known, since it was operated by literary people, was the Brook Farm "movement" in Massachusetts, which ran through a troubled existence of five years from 1842 to 1847. Robert Owen also, in 1825, had founded an experimental colony in America, at New Harmony, Indiana, on the then remote and unspoiled banks of the Wabash; it, too, lasted only about five years. Such schemes, as their critics pointed out, presupposed the withdrawal of select spirits to live by themselves and really had little to say about the problems of society as a whole in an industrial age.

Politically the most significant form of socialism before 1848 was the movement stirring among the working classes of France, a compound of revolutionary republicanism and socialism. The politically minded Paris workers had been republican since 1792. For them the Revolution, in the 1820s, 1830s, 1840s, was not finished but only momentarily interrupted.

The French working classes

Reduced to political impotence, discriminated against in the law courts, obliged to carry identity papers signed by their employers, and goaded by the pressures of industrialization as new factories spread across France, they developed a deep hostility to the owning classes of the bourgeoisie. They found a spokesman in the Paris journalist Louis Blanc, editor of the *Revue de progrès* and author of the *Organization of Work* (1839), one of the most constructive of the early socialist writings. He proposed a system of "social workshops," or state-supported manufacturing centers, in which the workers should labor by and for themselves without the intervention of private capitalists. Of this kind of socialism we shall hear more.

As for "communism," it was at this time an uncertain synonym for socialism. A small group of German revolutionaries, mainly exiles in France, took the name for themselves in the 1840s. They would have been historically forgotten had they not included Karl Marx and Friedrich Engels among their members. Marx and Engels consciously used the word in 1848 to differentiate their variety of socialism from that of such utopians as Saint-Simon, Fourier, and Owen. But the word *communism* went out of general use after 1848, to be revived after the Russian Revolution of 1917, at which time it received a somewhat new meaning.

Feminism

Feminism emerged as a new political and cultural movement in the early nineteenth century, though the term itself did not appear until some women in France began to refer to themselves as "feminists" during the 1830s. There were several strands of feminism, as there were several strands of all significant "isms," but most feminists shared various ideas with liberals, radicals, or socialists. Feminism sought to expand the rights of women in both public and private life. Drawing on the legacy of the French Revolution and its conceptions of human rights, feminists argued that the "rights of man" existed also for women (much as republicans and socialists claimed that such rights must also exist for poor people and workers). Some feminists, extending the arguments of Mary Wollstonecraft's influential book, *A Vindication of the Rights of Women* (1792), worked mainly to secure new voting and civil rights for women. Other feminists, though they might also support the quest for voting rights, worked mainly to reform the laws that regulated family life or to advance the rights of women in education, cultural life, and the economy. Both of these tendencies in early nineteenth-century feminism drew on Enlightenment ideas about human rights, reform, education, and progress, so that feminism resembled republicanism, radicalism, and socialism in its links to eighteenth-century predecessors, including French writers such as Condorcet and Olympe de Gouges.

Egalitarian feminism

The writers and activists who sought new political rights for women tended to be "egalitarian" feminists; that is, they stressed the ways in which women and men shared the use of reason and universal human rights. Despite the obvious connection to themes of the French Revolution, the campaign for women's political rights developed more rapidly in early nineteenth-century England and America. These national differences may have reflected the fact that voting rights generally became more widespread in England and America in the decades before 1848; or the different feminisms may have developed because French republicanism had become hostile to female political activities during the later stages of the French Revolution, and because the Napoleonic Code had given French women a subordinate position in the patriarchical legal system that regulated family relations. In any case, French feminists in the nineteenth century tended to focus on the social, cultural, or legal rights of women rather than on campaigns to win the vote.

English feminists

The first nineteenth-century advocates for women's rights in England were Philosophical Radicals and followers of the socialist leader Robert Owen. The socialists Anne Wheeler and William Thompson, for example, published an important statement of the new feminist themes in their *Appeal on Behalf of Women* (1825), which traced the inferior status of women to flaws in the economic system. Similar arguments appeared also in the writings of Owen himself and in the publications of his feminist friend, the Scottish writer Frances Wright. But the most influential English argument for women's political rights emerged in the works of the liberal writers Harriet Taylor and John Stuart Mill, who worked together as close intellectual partners for more than 20 years (they ultimately married after the death of her husband). Beginning in the 1830s, Taylor and Mill produced important works on the social, legal, and political inequalities that women faced in even the most advanced modern societies. Their collaboration led finally to Mill's famous book, *The Subjection of Women* (1869), in which Mill referred to the decisive influence of Taylor's ideas, though she had died before its publication. Mill built his case for women's political and social rights on the claim that women were inherently equal to men (hence entitled to the same rights) and on the utilitarian argument that society could only benefit from the increased participation of women in public life. Translated into all the major European languages, his book had much subsequent influence on feminist campaigns for the political and legal rights of women in other nations as well as in England. Meanwhile, American women launched their own campaign for voting rights at a convention in Seneca Falls, New York, where leaders such as Elizabeth Cady Stanton declared, in 1848, that women were entitled to vote because they were "created equal" with men.

Feminists also entered public life on the Continent during the 1830s and 1840s, especially in France. Socialists such as Saint-Simon and Fourier gave critical attention to the history of the family, thereby encouraging their followers to develop a social analysis of traditional restrictions on the rights of women. Women activists in the Saint-Simonian groups of the 1830s established journals whose titles asserted new feminist identities: *The Free Woman* and *The New Woman*. A new generation of women writers also began to extend the earlier work of Germaine de Staël, who had argued that "it is useful to society's enlightenment and happiness that women should carefully develop their intelligence and their reason." All feminists advocated better education for young women, reforms in property and divorce laws to enhance women's independence, and the right of women to participate in public debates. Many feminists in France, however, moved away from the egalitarian arguments for women's rights by stressing certain differences between men and women. The special responsibilities of motherhood, for example, gave women a distinctive, essential task in educating the rising generation, but only well-educated, competent women could raise intelligent, well-educated children. Feminists thus strongly supported the creation of new schools for girls and began seeking women's access to higher education (public secondary schools for girls were not established in France until the 1880s).

In addition to the campaigns for education and legal reforms, many feminists became writers in order to describe the social lives of women or to assert their claims for a place in public life. The travel writings of Flora Tristan, for instance, examined the social constraints that women faced in both South America and Europe. Another French writer of Tristan's generation, George Sand, became the most influential literary woman of the 1840s. Her many novels and essays often portrayed independent women, but her own life was almost as famous and controversial as her books. Critics mocked her for wearing male clothing, smoking cigars, and living with men outside marriage; yet Sand also won the admiring support of readers throughout Europe, many of whom saw her as a model for new forms of female cultural and political expression. She therefore became a famous symbol for both supporters and enemies of the new feminism; indeed, the term "George Sandism" was used to condemn women whose behavior seemed radical or unconventional. Such hostility indicates how feminism had become one of the postrevolutionary "isms," though the political campaign for women's voting rights and other legal reforms would not achieve its main objectives until the twentieth century.

French feminism

Nationalism: Western Europe

Nationalism first arose in many places as part of the general reaction against the international Napoleonic system, but it also drew its strength from specific cultural and political traditions in each country. It was the most pervasive and the least crystallized of the new "isms," in part because it usually overlapped with various forms of romanticism, republicanism, or liberalism. In western Europe — Britain, France, or Spain — where national unity already existed, nationalism was not a doctrine for nation-building so much as a set of political and cultural beliefs, easily aroused when national interests were questioned but normally taken for granted. Elsewhere — in Italy, Germany, Poland, the Austrian and Turkish empires — where peoples of the same nationality were politically divided or subject to foreign rule, nationalism was becoming a deliberate and conscious program for political action. It was undoubtedly the example of the West, of Great Britain and France, successful and flourishing because they were unified nations, that stimulated the ambitions of

The Saint-Simonian movement in France produced early feminist publications and also helped to launch a new social analysis of the restrictions on women's rights. This engraving by the artist Malreuve in 1832 suggests the unconventional behavior of the Saint-Simonian feminists; the woman is wearing a dress short for its time and standing beside a document that says simply "Doctrine of St. Simon. The Free Woman?"
(Bibliothèque Nationale de France, Paris)

other peoples to become unified nations too. The period after 1815 was in Germany a time of rising agitation over the national question; in Italy, of the Risorgimento or "resurgence"; in eastern Europe, of the Slavic Revival.

The movement was led by intellectuals, who often found it necessary to instill in their compatriots the very idea of nationality itself. They seized upon Herder's conception of the *Volksgeist*, or national spirit, applying its emphasis on national differences to their own people. Usually they began with a cultural nationalism, holding that each people had a language, history, world view, and culture of its own, which must be preserved and perfected. They then usually passed on to a political nationalism, holding that to preserve this national culture, and to ensure liberty and justice for its individual members, each nation should create for itself a sovereign state. Governing authorities, they held, should be of the same nationality and language as those they governed; and all persons of the same national language should be encompassed within the same state.

Volksgeist

Since such ideas could not be fully realized without the overthrow of every government in Europe east of France, thoroughgoing nationalism was inherently revolutionary.

Outspoken nationalists were therefore persecuted by the authorities, which drove them everywhere into secret nationalist societies. The Carbonari, organized in Italy in the time of Napoleon, was the best known, but there

Secret societies

MIROIR DROLATIQUE.

Si de Georges Sand ce portrait
Laisse l'esprit un peu perplexe,
C'est que le génie est abstrait,
Et comme on sait n'a pas de sexe.

This caricature of George Sand, which appeared in a lithograph by Alcide Lorentz in 1842, mocks the famous author for her apparently "masculine" actions. Dressed in pants, holding a cigarette, and surrounded by her writings and political concerns, Sand is ridiculed in both the image and in a sarcastic caption—which alludes to her claim that genius "has no sex."
(Bibliothèque Nationale de France, Paris)

were many others—like the *Veri Italiani,* the Apophasimenes, and the Sublime and Perfect Masters. In some regions Masonic lodges might serve the same purpose. In many of the societies nationalism was mixed with liberalism, socialism, or revolutionary republicanism in an undifferentiated way. Members were initiated by a complex ritual intended to impress upon them the dire consequences of betraying the society's secrets. They used special grips and passwords and adopted revolutionary names to conceal their identity and baffle the police. They were usually so organized that the ordinary member knew the identity of only a few others, and never of the higher-ups, so that those arrested could reveal nothing important. The societies kept busy, circulating forbidden literature and generally maintaining a revolutionary ferment. Conservatives dreaded them, but they were not really dangerous to any government that enjoyed the support of its people.

Best known of the nationalist philosophers in western Europe was the Italian Joseph Mazzini (1805–1872), who spent most of his adult life in exile in France and England. In his youth he joined the Carbonari, but in 1831 he founded a society of his own, called Young Italy, and he edited and smuggled into Italy copies of a journal of the same name. Young Italy was soon imitated by other

Mazzini

societies of similar aim, such as Young Germany. In 1834 Mazzini tried unsuccessfully to bring about an uprising against the kingdom of Sardinia, which he viewed as a key obstacle to the unification of Italy. Undeterred by the total failure of this plan, he continued to organize, to conspire, and to write. For Mazzini nationality and revolution were a holy cause in which the most generous and humane qualities were to find expression. He was a moral philosopher, as may be judged from the title of his most widely read book, *The Duties of Man,* in which he placed duty to the nation intermediate between duty to family and to God.

To the Germans, divided and frustrated, nationality became almost an obsession. It affected everything from folklore to metaphysics. *Grimm's Fairy Tales*, for example, was first published in 1812. It was the work of the two Grimm brothers, founders of the modern science of comparative linguistics, who traveled about Germany to study the popular dialects and in doing so collected the folktales that for generations had been current among the common people. They hoped in this way to find the ancient, native, indigenous "spirit" of Germany, deep and unspoiled in the bosom of the *Volk*. The same preoccupation with nationhood revealed itself in the philosophy of Hegel (1770–1831), possibly the most extraordinary of all nineteenth-century thinkers.

To Hegel, witnessing the spectacle of the Napoleonic years, it was evident that for a people to enjoy freedom, order, or dignity it must possess a potent and independent state.

Hegel's philosophy

The state, for him, became the institutional embodiment of reason and liberty—the "march of God through the world," as he put it, meaning not an expansion in space through vulgar conquest, but a march through time and through the processes of history. Hegel conceived of reality itself as a process of endless change, a development having an inner logic and necessary sequence of its own. He thus broke with the more static and mechanical philosophy of the eighteenth century, with its fixed categories of unchangeable right and wrong. He became a philosopher of history, in which he saw the unfolding of a "Universal Spirit" or "Idea" across time, and he linked this evolving Spirit in complex ways to reason and freedom. He held that change came about through a historical "dialectic," or irresistible tendency of the Universal Spirit and the human mind to move forward by the creation of opposites. A given state of affairs (the *thesis*) would in this view inevitably produce the conception of an opposite state of affairs (the *antithesis*), which would be followed by a reconciliation and fusion of the two (the *synthesis*). This new synthesis became the starting point for a new "thesis" in the next stage of dialectical change. Thus, for example, the very disunity of Germany, by producing the opposing idea of unity, would ultimately lead toward the creation of a more unified German state.

The Hegelian dialectic was soon to be appropriated by Karl Marx to new uses, but meanwhile Hegel's philosophy, with other currents in Germany, made the study of history more philosophically meaningful than it had ever been before. History, the study of time process, seemed to be the very key with which to unlock the true significance of the world; it could show the unfolding of the Universal Spirit in specific times and places. Historical studies were stimulated, and the German universities became centers of historical learning, attracting scholars from many countries. Most eminent of the German historians was Leopold von Ranke (1795–1886), founder of the "scientific" school of historical writing. Ranke, too, though intellectually scrupulous to the last degree, owed much of his incentive to his national feeling. His first youthful work was a study of the *Latin and Teutonic Peoples;* and one of his main ideas, throughout his long life, was that Europe owed its unique greatness to the coexistence and interplay of several distinct nations, which had always resisted the attempts of any one nation to control the whole. By the latter Ranke really meant France—the France of Louis XIV and Napoleon. The Germans, said Ranke in 1830, had a mission from God to develop a culture and a political system entirely different from those of the French. They were destined to "create the pure German state corresponding to the genius of the nation." Whether Western constitutional, parliamentary, and individualist principles were suited to the national character of Germany seemed to Ranke very doubtful.

List's economics

In economics Friedrich List, in his *National System of Political Economy* (1840), held that political economy as taught in England was suited

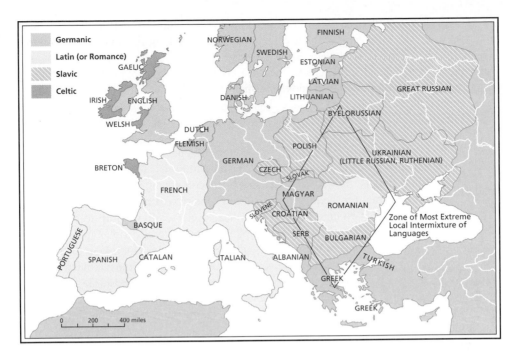

LANGUAGES OF EUROPE

National movements in modern Europe often referred to the distinctive languages of various national groups, but there are only three main European language families: Germanic, Latin, and Slav. The map shows language areas in the early twentieth century. It does not show the overlap of adjoining languages, bilingual areas, or the existence of small language "pockets" such as Turkish in the Balkans, Greek in Asia Minor, Yiddish in Poland, or German in scattered parts of eastern Europe. In the extreme northwest is the "Celtic fringe," to which the Breton, Welsh, and Gaelic languages were pushed back in the early Middle Ages. For the area within the diamond-shaped zone no map on this scale can give a realistic idea of the overlapping languages. During the Second World War and its aftermath, however, many language pockets in eastern Europe were wiped out through exchange, transportation, or destruction of peoples.

only to England. It was not an abstract truth but a body of ideas developed in a certain historical stage in a certain country. List thus became a founder of the historical or institutional school of economics. The doctrine of free trade, he said, was designed to make England the world's industrial center by keeping other countries in the status of suppliers of raw material and food. But any country, he held, if it was to be civilized and develop its own national culture, must have cities, factories, industries, and capital of its own. It must therefore put up high tariffs (at least temporarily, in theory) for protection. List, it should be remarked, had developed his ideas during a sojourn in the United States, where Henry Clay's "American system" was in fact a national system of political economy.

Nationalism: Eastern Europe

In eastern Europe the Poles and the Magyars had long been active political nationalists, the Poles wishing to undo the partitions of Polish territories and reestablish their Polish state, the Magyars insisting on autonomy for their kingdom of Hungary within the Habsburg empire. But for the most part nationalism in eastern Europe long remained more cultural than political. Centuries of development had tended to submerge the Czechs, Slovaks, Ruthenians, Romanians, Serbs, Croats, Slovenes—and even the Poles and Magyars in lesser degree. Their upper classes spoke German or French and looked to Vienna or to Paris for their ideas. The native languages had remained peasant languages, barely known outside the isolated peasant cultures in which they were spoken. It seemed that many of these languages would disappear.

Preservation of historic cultures

But early in the nineteenth century the new national patriots began to demand the preservation of their historic cultures. They collected folktales and ballads; they studied the languages, composing grammars and dictionaries, often for the first time; and they took to writing books in their mother tongues. They urged their own educated classes to give up foreign ways. They wrote histories showing the famous exploits of their several peoples in the Middle Ages. A new nationalism stirred the Magyars; in 1837 a national Hungarian theater was established at Budapest. In what was to become Romania a former Transylvanian peasant youth named George Lazar began as early as 1816 to teach at Bucharest. He lectured in Romanian (to the surprise of the upper classes, who preferred Greek), telling how Romania had a distinguished history back to the Roman emperor Trajan. As for the Greeks, they entertained visions of restoring the medieval Greek empire (known to Westerners as the Byzantine Empire) in which persons of Greek language or Greek Orthodox religion should become the predominant people of the Balkans.

The Slavic Revival

The most far-reaching of the East European movements was the Slavic Revival. The Slavs included the Russians, Poles, Ukrainians, Byelorussians, and Ruthenians; the Czechs and Slovaks; and the South Slavs, consisting of the Slovenes, Croats, Serbs, and Bulgars. All branches of the Slavs began to develop new nationalisms. In 1814 the Serb Vuk Karajich published a grammar of his native tongue and a collection of *Popular Songs and Epics of the Serbs;* he worked out a Serbian alphabet, translated the New Testament, and declared that the dialect spoken in the city of Ragusa (now Dubrovnik) should become the literary language of all South Slavs. In 1836 the Czech historian Francis Palacky published the first volume of his *History of Bohemia,* designed to give the Czechs a new pride in their national past. He first wrote his book in German, the common reading language of educated Czechs. But he soon recast it into Czech, significantly reentitling it a *History of the Czech People.* Among Poles the poet and revolutionary Adam Mickiewicz must be mentioned. Arrested by the Russians in 1823 for membership in a secret society, he was later allowed by the tsarist government to pass into western Europe. From 1840 to 1844 he taught Slavic literature at the Collège de France, using his lecture platform as a rostrum to deliver eloquent pleas for the liberation of all peoples and overthrow of autocracy. He wrote epic poems on Polish historical themes and continued to be active among the revolutionary Polish exiles settled in France.

Russia itself, which Poles and Czechs regarded as backward, was slower to develop a pronounced national sense. Under Tsar Alexander I a Western or European orientation prevailed, but in Alexander's last years and after his death in 1825 the doctrines of Slavophilism began to spread. Russian Slavophilism, or the idea that Russia possessed a way of life of its own, different from and not to be corrupted by that of Europe, became a Russian affirmation of the fundamental idea of the *Volksgeist.* Such views in Russia were at least as old as the opposition to the reforms of Peter the Great. In the nationalistic nineteenth century they crystallized

Russian Slavophilism

more systematically into an "ism," and they tended to merge into Pan-Slavism, which made substantially the same assertions for the Slavic peoples as a whole. But Pan-Slavism, before 1848, was no more than embryonic.

Other "Isms"

Romanticism, liberalism, radical republicanism, socialism, feminism, and nationalism were the political and cultural forces driving many of the new European political and cultural conflicts in the era between 1815 and 1848. Of other "isms" less need be said. Conservatism remained strong. Politically, on the Continent, conservatism upheld the institutions of absolute monarchy, aristocracy, and church and opposed the constitutional and representative government *Conservatism* sought by liberals. As a political philosophy, conservatism built upon the ideas of Edmund Burke, who had held that every people must change its institutions by gradual adaptation and that no people could suddenly realize in the present any freedoms not already well prepared for in the past. This doctrine lacked appeal for those to whom the past had been a series of misfortunes, but it gained support among others who sought to define and defend long-evolving social or political traditions. Conservatism sometimes passed into nationalism, since it stressed the firmness and continuity of national character. But nationalists at this time were more often liberals or republicans. Monarchism was conservative and even reactionary. Gone was the enlightened despotism of the previous century, when kings had boldly irritated their nobles and defied their churches. After the thunders of the French Revolution aristocracy and monarchy huddled together, and their new watchword was to maintain "the throne and the altar."

Deeper than other "isms," a feeling shared in varying ways by people of all parties, was the profound current of humanitarianism. It consisted in a *Humanitarianism* heightened concern about the cruelty inflicted upon others. Here the thought of the Age of Enlightenment suffered no reversal. Torture was gone, and even conservative monarchical governments showed no inclination to restore it. Conditions in prisons, hospitals, insane asylums, and orphanages improved. People became determined to change the miserable social position of pauper children, chimney sweeps, women in the mines, and enslaved people in the Americas. Russian serf owners and American slave owners began to show psychological signs of moral doubt. To degrade human beings, use them as work animals, torture them, confine them unjustly, hold them as hostages for others, tear apart their families, and punish their relatives were increasingly regarded by Europeans as foreign to true civilization. The Christian sense of the inviolability of the human person was now again, in a more secular, mundane way, beginning to relieve the sufferings of humanity.

54. THE DIKE AND THE FLOOD: DOMESTIC

It is now time to look more specifically at the most influential political reactions and reform movements that emerged after the European peace settlement of 1814–1815. The governments that defeated Napoleon wanted to assure themselves above all else that the disturbances of the past 25 years would not be renewed. In France the restored Bourbon king, Louis XVIII, aspired to keep his throne for himself and his successors. In Great Britain the Tory governing class hoped to preserve the old England that they had so valiantly saved from the clutches of Bonaparte. In Germany, Austria, Italy, and central Europe the chief aim of Metternich, who for another 33 years remained the dominant political figure in these regions, was to maintain a system in which the prestige of the Habsburg dynasty should be supreme. The aims of the tsar, Alexander, were less clear. He was feared by representatives of the other powers as a dreamer, a self-chosen world savior, a man who said he wanted to bring Christianity into politics, a crowned Jacobin, and even a liberal. It became one of Metternich's chief hopes to convert Alexander to conservatism.

The arrangements made by the victorious powers were in some ways moderate, at least when the provocations they had undergone in the Napoleonic wars are considered. Partly by the tsar's insistence written constitutions existed after 1814 in France and in Russian or "Congress" Poland. Some of the rulers of south German states allowed a measure of representative government. Even the king of Prussia promised a representative assembly for his kingdom, though the promise was not kept. But it was difficult to maintain any kind of stability. The forces of the political right, the privileged classes (or in France the former privileged classes) denounced all signs of liberalism as dangerous concessions to revolution. Those of the political left—liberals, nationalists, republicans—regarded the newly installed regimes as hopelessly reactionary and inadequate. Statesmen were jittery on the subject of revolution. They therefore met every sign of agitation with attempts at repression, which, though they might drive agitation temporarily underground, really only made it worse by creating additional grievances. A vicious circle was set endlessly revolving.

Reaction after 1815: France, Poland

In France Louis XVIII began his reign in 1814 with an amnesty to the regicides of 1793. But the regicides, like all republicans, found the France of 1814 an uncomfortable place to live in, exposed as they were to the unofficial vengeance of counterrevolutionaries, and in 1815 most of them rallied to Napoleon when he returned from Elba. This exasperated the royalist counterrevolutionaries beyond all measure. A brutal "white terror" broke out. Upper-class youths murdered Bonapartists and republicans; Catholic mobs seized and killed Protestants at Marseilles and Toulouse. The Chamber of Deputies chosen in 1815 (by the tiny electorate of 100,000 well-to-do landowners) proved to be more reactionary and royalist than the king. The king himself could not control the mounting frenzy of reaction, which he was sensible enough to realize would only infuriate the revolutionary element still further, as in fact happened. In 1820 a fanatical workingman assassinated the king's nephew, the Duke de Berry. Those who said that all partisans of the French Revolution were criminal extremists seemed to be justified. The reaction deepened, until in 1824 Louis XVIII died and was succeeded by his brother Charles X. Not only was Charles X the father of the recently murdered Duke de Berry, but for over 30 years he had also been the acknowledged leader of implacable counterrevolution. As the Count of Artois, youngest brother of Louis XVI, he had been among the first to emigrate in 1789. He was the favorite Bourbon among the most obstinate exseigneurs, nobles, and churchmen. Regarding himself as hereditary absolute monarch by the grace of God, he had himself crowned at Reims with all the romantic pomp of ages past, and proceeded to stamp out not only revolutionary republicanism but liberalism and constitutionalism as well.

In Poland, it will be recalled, the Vienna settlement created a constitutional kingdom, with the Russian tsar Alexander as king, joined in merely personal union with the Russian empire. The new machinery did not work very well. The Polish constitution provided for an elected diet, a wide suffrage by the standards of the day, the Napoleonic civil code, freedom of press and religion, and exclusive use of the Polish language. But the Poles discovered that Alexander, though favoring liberty, did not like to have anyone disagree with

The "white terror"

him. They could make little use of their much touted freedom in any actual legislation. The elected diet could not get along with the viceroy, who was a Russian. In Russia the serf-owning aristocracy viewed Alexander's idea of a constitutional kingdom in Poland with a jaundiced eye. They wanted no experimentation with liberty on the very borders of Russia.

The Poles themselves played into the hands of their enemies. For the Poles were nationalist at least as much as they were liberal. They were dissatisfied with the boundaries accorded to Congress Poland, and they dreamed of the vast kingdom that had existed before the First Partition in 1772. At the University of Vilna *Polish ambitions* professors and students began to join secret societies. Some members of these societies were revolutionaries who wanted to drive out Alexander, reunite with Prussian and Austrian Poland, and reconstitute an independent Polish state. It was in the discovery and breaking up of one such society that Adam Mickiewicz was arrested in 1823. Reaction and repression now struck the University of Vilna.

Reaction after 1815: The German States, Britain

In Germany those who had felt national stirrings during the Wars of Liberation were disillusioned by the peace treaty, which maintained the several German principalities about as Napoleon had left them and purposely united them only in a loose federation, or Bund. National ideas were most common in the numerous universities, where students and professors were more susceptible than most people to the doctrines of an eternal *Volksgeist* and a far-flung *Deutschtum*. National ideas tended to glorify the German common people and thus carried with them a kind of democratic opposition to aristocrats, princes, and kings. Students in many of the universities in 1815 formed college clubs, called collectively the *Burschenschaft,* which, as centers of serious political discussion, were to replace the older clubs devoted to drinking and dueling. The *Burschenschaft,* a kind of German youth movement, held a nationwide congress at Wartburg in 1817. Students listened to rousing speeches by patriotic professors, marched about in "Teutonic" costume, and burned a few reactionary books. This undergraduate performance was no immediate threat to any established state, but the nervous governments took alarm. In 1819 a theology student assassinated the German writer Kotzebue, known as an informer in the service of the tsar. The assassin received hundreds of letters of congratulation, and at Nassau the head of the local government barely escaped the same fate at the hands of a pharmacy student.

Metternich now chose to intervene. He had no authority in Germany except in that Austria was a member of the Germanic federation. He *Metternich intervenes* regarded all these manifestations of German national spirit, or of any demand for a more solidly unified Germany, as a threat to the favorable position of the Austrian Empire and to the whole balance of Europe. He called a conference of the principal German states at Carlsbad in Bohemia; the frightened conferees adopted certain resolutions, proposed by Metternich, which were soon enacted by the diet of the Bund. These Carlsbad Decrees (1819) dissolved the *Burschenschaft* and the equally nationalistic gymnastic clubs (some of whose members thereupon joined secret societies). They provided for government officials to be placed in the universities and for censors to control the contents of books and the periodical and newspaper press. The Carlsbad Decrees remained in force for many years, and they imposed an effective check on the growth of liberal and nationalist ideas in Germany.

Nor did Great Britain escape the dreary rounds of agitation and repression. As elsewhere, radicalism produced reaction and vice versa. Britain after *Economic crisis spurs radicalism* Waterloo was a country devoted to its old traditions but also afflicted by the

German students celebrated their conception of German nationhood at a festival in 1817. Gathering near a castle at Wartburg where Martin Luther had once lived, they commemorated the beginning of the Protestant Reformation in 1517 and also burned books that were deemed hostile to German liberty.
(akg-images)

most advanced social problems of a rapidly developing industrial economy. In 1815, at the close of the wars, the landed classes feared an inrush of imported agricultural products and consequent collapse of farm prices and rentals. The landowning gentry who controlled Parliament enacted a new Corn Law, raising the protective tariff to the point where import of grain became impossible unless prices were very high. Landlords and their farmers benefited, but wage earners and industrial workers found the price of breadstuffs soaring out of reach. At the same time there was a postwar depression in industry. Wages fell and many were thrown out of work. These conditions naturally contributed to the spread of political radicalism, which looked first of all to a drastic reform of the House of Commons in order that thereafter a radical program of social and economic legislation might be enacted.

A riot broke out in London in December 1816. In the following February the Prince Regent was attacked in his carriage. The government suspended habeas corpus and employed *agents provocateurs* to obtain evidence against the agitators. Industrialists of Manchester and the new factory towns, determined to force through the reform of parliamentary representation, took the chance offered by the distress of the working classes to organize mass meetings of protest. At Birmingham a crowd elected a mock member of Parliament. At sprawling Manchester 80,000 people staged an enormous demonstration at St. Peter's Fields in 1819; they demanded universal male suffrage, annual election of the House of Commons, and the repeal of the Corn Laws. Although perfectly orderly they were fired upon by soldiers; 11 persons were killed and about 400 were wounded, including 113 women. Radicals called this episode the Peterloo massacre in derisive comparison with the battle of Waterloo.

The Peterloo massacre

The frightened government thanked the soldiers for their brave upholding of the social order. Parliament rushed through the Six Acts (1819), which outlawed "seditious and blasphemous" literature, put a heavy stamp tax on newspapers, authorized the search of private houses for arms, and rigidly restricted the right of public meeting. A group of revolutionaries thereupon plotted to assassinate the whole cabinet at a dinner; they were caught in Cato Street in London in 1820—whence the name "Cato Street Conspiracy." Five of them were hanged. Meanwhile, for publishing the writings of Thomas Paine, Richard Carlisle spent seven years in prison.

"Our example," wrote the Duke of Wellington to a Continental correspondent in 1819, "will be of value in France and Germany, and it is to be hoped that the world will escape from the general revolution with which we all seem to be threatened."

In summary, the various European governments promoted reactionary policies everywhere they could reach in the years following the peace of 1815. The reaction was due only in part to memories of the French Revolution. It was due even more to the living fear of revolution in the present. This fear, though exaggerated, was no mere hallucination. Sensing the rising flood, the established interests desperately built dikes against it in every country. The same is true of international politics at the time.

55.   THE DIKE AND THE FLOOD: INTERNATIONAL

At the Congress of Vienna in 1814–1815 the powers agreed to hold meetings in the future to enforce the treaty and take up new issues as they arose. A number of congresses of the Great Powers resulted, which are of significance as an experimental step toward international regulation of the affairs of Europe. The congresses resembled, in a tentative and partial way, the League of Nations that arose after the First World War of 1914–1918, or the United Nations that followed after the war of 1939–1945. The powers had also, in 1815, in alarm after the return of Napoleon, subscribed to Alexander I's Holy Alliance, which became the popular term for the collaboration of the European states in the congresses. The Holy Alliance, on the face of it a statement of Christian purpose and international concord, gradually became an alliance for the suppression of revolutionary and even liberal activity, following in that respect the trend of the governments which made it up.

The Congress of Aix-la-Chapelle, 1818

The first general postwar assemblage of the powers took place at the congress of Aix-la-Chapelle (or Aachen) in 1818. The principal item on the agenda was to withdraw the allied army of occupation from France. The French argued that Louis XVIII would never be popular in France so long as he was supported by a foreign army. The other powers, since they all desired the French to forget the past and accept the Bourbons, withdrew their military forces without disagreement. They arranged also to have private bankers take over the French reparations debt (the 700 million francs imposed by the second Treaty of Paris); the bankers paid the allied governments, and the French in due time paid the bankers.

Tsar Alexander was still the most advanced internationalist of the day. He suggested at Aix-la-Chapelle a kind of permanent European union and even proposed the maintenance of international military forces to safeguard recognized states against changes by violence. Governments if thus reassured against revolution, he argued, would more willingly grant constitutional and liberal reforms. But the others demurred, especially the British foreign minister Lord Castlereagh. The British declared themselves willing to make international commitments against specified contingencies, such as a revival of aggression on the part of

Alexander's internationalism

The "Peterloo Massacre" of 1819 was condemned in this caricature by the English artist George Cruikshank. A peaceable crowd gathered in St. Peter's Fields, Manchester, to demand political reforms and repeal of the Corn Laws (which placed high tariffs on imported grains), but a militia of part-time soldiers opened fire on the protesters, causing numerous casualties. The British government responded by commending the soldiers and passing new restrictions on public meetings.
(Getty Images)

France. But they would assume no obligations to act upon indefinite and unforeseeable future events. They reserved the right of independent judgment in foreign policy.

Concretely, the congress addressed itself to the problems of the Atlantic slave trade and of the recurring nuisance of the Barbary pirates. It was unanimously agreed that both should be suppressed. To suppress them required naval forces, which only the British possessed in adequate amount, and it meant also that naval captains must be authorized to stop and search vessels at sea. The continental states, always touchy on the subject of British sea power, refused to countenance any such uses of the British fleet. They feared for the freedom of the seas. As for the British, they would not even discuss placing British warships in an international naval pool or putting British squadrons under the authority of an international body. Nothing therefore was done; the slave trade continued, booming illicitly with the endless demand for cotton; and the Barbary pirates were not disposed of until the French occupied and annexed Algeria some years later. The growth of international institutions was blocked by the separate interests of the sovereign states.

Revolution in Southern Europe: The Congress of Troppau, 1820

Scarcely had the Congress of Aix-la-Chapelle disbanded when revolutionary agitation came to a crisis in southern Europe. It was not that revolutionary or liberal sentiment was stronger here than in the north, but rather that the governments in question, those of Spain, Naples, and the Ottoman Empire, were inefficient, flimsy, and corrupt. Many of the revolutionaries were hardly more than middle-class liberals; indeed, the Spaniards, as we have noted, were the first to use the word "liberal" in this modern political sense. Many of them had at first accepted the Napoleonic occupation of Spain as a progressive development but had then turned against it and proclaimed a new constitution in 1812, modeled on the French revolutionary constitution of 1789–1791. After Napoleon's final defeat they attempted to force the restored Bourbon kings of Spain and Naples to adopt this constitution of 1812.

Revolution in Spain and Naples

In 1820 the governments of both Spain and Naples collapsed with remarkable ease before the demonstrations of revolutionaries. The kings of both countries reluctantly took oaths to the Spanish constitution of 1812. But Metternich saw the insurrections as the first symptoms of a revolutionary seizure against which Europe should be quarantined. It was a fact that revolutionary agitation was international, easily leaping across frontiers, because of the operations of secret societies and of political exiles and because in any case the same ideas had been aroused in all countries by the French Revolution. Metternich considered Italy in particular to be within the legitimate sphere of influence of the Austrian Empire. He therefore called a meeting of the Great Powers at Troppau in the Austrian-controlled region in Silesia, hoping to use the authority of an international congress to put down the revolution in Naples. The governments of Great Britain and France, not eager to play Austria's game, sent only observers to the congress. Metternich's main problem was, as usual, Alexander. What would be the attitude of the liberal tsar, the friend and patron of constitutions, toward the idea of a constitutional monarchy in Naples? At an inn in Troppau Metternich and Alexander met alone, and there held a momentous interview over the teacups. Metternich reviewed the horrors of revolutionism, the unwisdom of granting any concessions lest revolutionaries be encouraged. Alexander was already somewhat disillusioned by the ungrateful feelings of the Poles, and the upheaval in Naples posed a new threat to his view of royal authority. He had always believed that constitutions should be granted by legitimate sovereigns, not extorted from them by revolutionaries, as had happened in Naples. He allowed himself to be persuaded by Metternich. He declared that he had always been wrong and that Metternich had always been right; and he announced himself ready to follow Metternich's political judgment.

Thus fortified, Metternich drew up a document, the protocol of Troppau, for consideration and acceptance by the five Great Powers. It held that all recognized European states should be protected by collective international action, in the interests of general peace and stability, from internal changes brought about by force. It was a statement of collective security against revolution. Neither France nor Great Britain accepted it. Castlereagh wrote to Metternich that if Austria felt its interests to be threatened in Naples it should intervene in its own name only. The British Tories did not object to the repression of the Neapolitan revolution, but they rejected the principle of a binding international collaboration.

Metternich could get only Russia and Prussia to endorse his protocol, in addition to Austria. These three, acting as the Congress of Troppau, authorized Metternich to dispatch an Austrian army into Naples. He did so; the Neapolitan revolutionaries were arrested or put to flight; the incompetent and brutal Ferdinand I was restored as "absolute" king; the demon of revolution was seemingly exorcised. But the Congress of Troppau, ostensibly a Europewide international body, had in effect functioned as an antirevolutionary alliance of Austria, Russia, and Prussia. A gap opened between the three Eastern autocracies and the two Western powers—even when the latter consisted of Tories and Bourbons.

A gap opens between East and West

Spain and the Near East: The Congress of Verona, 1822

Thousands of revolutionaries and liberals fled from the terror raging in Italy. Many went to Spain, now dreaded by conservatives as the main seat of revolutionary infection. The Middle East also seemed about to ignite in conflagration. Alexander Ypsilanti, a Greek who had spent his adult life in the military service of Russia, in 1821 led a band of armed followers from Russia into Romania (then still a part of Turkey), hoping that all Greeks and pro-Greeks in the Turkish empire would join him. He expected Russian support, since Russia had long wanted to use Greek Christians in a campaign to weaken the Turkish empire. The possibility of a Turkish empire converted into a "Greek" empire and dependent on Russia was naturally unpleasant to Metternich. To deal with all these matters an international congress met at Verona in 1822.

Alexander, in shifting from liberal to reactionary views, had not changed his belief in the need for concerted international action. Had pure power politics determined his decisions, he would doubtless have favored Ypsilanti's Grecophile revolution. But he stood by the principle of international solidarity against revolutionary violence. He refused to support Ypsilanti, who found less enthusiasm for Greek culture among the Romanians and Balkan peoples than he had expected and was soon defeated by the Turks. As for intervention to repress the uprising in Greece itself, the question did not arise since the Turkish government proved quite able for a time to handle the matter without assistance.

Ypsilanti refused support

The question of the revolution in Spain was settled by foreign intervention. The Bourbon regime in France had no taste for a Spain in which revolutionaries, republicans, political exiles, and members of secret societies might be harbored. The French government proposed to the Congress of Verona that it be authorized to dispatch an army across the Pyrenees. The Congress welcomed the offer, and despite many dire predictions of ruin, arising from memories of Napoleon's disaster, a French army of 200,000 men moved into Spain in 1823. The campaign proved to be a military promenade through a cheering country. Spanish liberals, constitutionalists, or revolutionaries were a helpless minority. The mass of the people saw the invasion as a deliverance from Masons, Carbonari, and heretics and shouted with satisfaction at the restoration of church and king. Ferdinand VII, unscrupulous and narrow-minded, repudiated his constitutional oath and let the most reactionary Spaniards have their way. The revolutionaries were savagely persecuted, exiled, or jailed.

The French invade Spain

Latin American Independence

The Napoleonic wars and later political disturbances in Europe had their repercussions in all parts of America. While Great Britain was engaged against Napoleon, the United States fought its inconclusive War of 1812 against the former mother country, and a few years later, after minor military operations, obtained the cession of Florida from Spain. During these same years, new movements for national independence emerged in Latin America and used the turmoil in Europe as an opportunity to break free from the weakening Portuguese and Spanish empires. The Portuguese royal family, to escape Napoleon, had taken refuge in its Brazilian empire, but when the dynasty was restored at Lisbon, one of its members refused to leave Brazil, which remained as an "empire" independent of Portugal; in 1889 the imperial regime gave way to a new Brazilian republic.

Spanish America reached over the enormous area from San Francisco to Buenos Aires. Here, too, the thought of the Enlightenment, the news of the American and French revolutions, the Napoleonic occupation of Spain, and the restoration in 1814 of the Bourbon Ferdinand VII to the Spanish throne all had their effects. The British had been commercially active in Spanish America for over a century, and during the Napoleonic wars they had increased their exports to it twentyfold. There were thus business interests in Spanish America that resisted *Motives for revolt* any return to the old Spanish imperial system of trade controls. More fundamental was the political and social resentment that Creoles felt for the peninsulars. The Creoles were the white population of Spanish descent born in America, and they found their ambitions blocked by the peninsulars who were sent out from Spain to occupy the highest offices in the empire. In many places most of the people were native Indians or mestizos of mixed Spanish and Indian origin, often living in depressed economic conditions and far from the capital cities. The movement for independence in most of Latin America therefore lacked the more widespread popular character that it had developed in the British colonies that became the United States. It was mainly led by Creoles who were active in municipal governments in the towns. At times, the movement for independence recruited some very conservative elements among large landowners and high churchmen. But the important leaders, such as Simón Bolívar and José de San Martín, were men who had spent years in Europe and preferred the new constitutional principles but were in the end frustrated in their aspirations for their own country. The dissensions that long continued to afflict Spanish America were all present within the independence movement itself.

Because of its vast extent, over 6,000 miles interrupted by mountain barriers, there could be less unity in the liberation of Spanish America than had been possible, however difficult, in the North American rebellion against England. There could be no Continental Congress such as had met in Philadelphia in 1774. Revolts took place separately within the great vice-royalties: New Spain (Mexico), New Granada (Colombia and Venezuela), Peru (including Ecuador and most of Bolivia and Chile), and La Plata (Argentina, with claims over what are now Uruguay and Paraguay).

The first revolts were against Joseph Bonaparte after Napoleon made him king of Spain in 1808. The rebels proclaimed their loyalty to the deposed Ferdinand VII, who, however, when restored in 1814, refused to make any concessions to American demands, so that revolutionary sentiment turned against him also. There followed a series of disconnected struggles between those fighting for independence (with or without much internal change) and combinations of officials, army officers, landowners, and churchmen who remained loyal to the Spanish crown. Bolívar became the liberator of Venezuela and Colombia. San Martín became the liberator of Argentina and Chile, and both combined in the liberation of Peru. In Mexico, by way of exception, there was a true mass rising of Indians and mestizos, which was put down by the middle- and upper-class leaders. This conservative repression of a more popular revolutionary movement led to a long period of turmoil in the newly independent Mexican state, but Mexico was by no means the only postcolonial society that faced such problems. All Spanish America was troubled by disputes over boundaries, regional

Simón Bolívar (1783–1830) was known as "The Liberator" for his leadership of the South American revolutionary movements. He had lived in Europe, where he was strongly influenced by the political ideas of the French Revolution. Although his revolutionary campaigns secured the independence of several new nations, Bolívar's attempts to establish stable, constitutional governments were generally stymied during the 1820s.
(Getty Images)

conflicts and attempted conquests and secessions, so that it was only later in the nineteenth century that the map of South and Central America took form as we know it today.

In addition to these complex conflicts among themselves, the emerging Latin American nations remained vulnerable to the imperial interventions of outside powers. Let us return to the congress of European powers meeting in Verona in 1822. At the very time when a French army suppressed the revolution in Spain, the revolutionaries in Spanish America were declaring their independence. At Verona, Tsar Alexander urged the Congress to mediate between Spain and its colonies. This was a euphemistic way of suggesting

British favor Spanish American independence

military intervention in Spanish America, following the principle of repressing revolutions that had been announced at Troppau. The British objected. Even the Tory government favored revolutions that might break up the Spanish empire into independent states, with which free trade treaties might be negotiated. Without at least benevolent neutrality from the British fleet no armed force could sail to America. The Spanish Americans therefore maintained their independence, thanks in part to the use made by the British of their sea power on this occasion.

The Monroe Doctrine

The new republics also received strong moral support from the United States. In December 1823 President James Monroe, in a message to Congress, announced the "Monroe Doctrine." It stated that attempts by European powers to return parts of America to colonial status would be viewed as an unfriendly act by the United States. The British foreign minister George Canning (who had just succeeded Castlereagh) had at first proposed a joint statement by Great Britain and the United States against the East European powers on the Spanish-American question. President Monroe, at the advice of his secretary of state, John Quincy Adams, decided instead to make a unilateral statement in the form of a message to Congress. They intended to aim their "doctrine" at Great Britain as well as the Continental states, since the British, with their command of the sea, were in fact the only power that could actually threaten the independence of American states at this time. Canning, having no such threats in mind, and concerned more with the Congress of Verona, accepted the line taken by the United States. Indeed, he declared with a flourish that he had "called the New World into existence to redress the balance of the Old." The Monroe Doctrine, at its inception, was a kind of counterblast to the Metternich doctrine of the protocol of Troppau. Where the latter announced the principle of intervention against revolution, the Monroe Doctrine announced that revolutions in America, if they resulted in regimes recognized by the United States, were outside the pale of attention of European powers. In any case, the efficacy of the Monroe Doctrine long depended on the tacit cooperation of the British fleet.

Over 300 years of European colonial empires in America now came to an end, with few exceptions, in the half-century following the United States declaration of independence. One exception was Canada, where membership in the British empire was voluntary, at least for the English-speaking inhabitants, and where both the English and French Canadians resisted threats of annexation by the United States. The other exceptions were in the West Indies, where Haiti was independent; the smaller islands remained British, French, or Dutch; and the large islands of Cuba and Puerto Rico remained Spanish until the Spanish-American War of 1898.

The End of the Congress System

After the Congress of Verona no more such meetings were held. The attempt at a formal international regulation of European affairs was given up. In the broadest retrospect, the congresses failed to make progress toward an international order because, especially after Alexander's conversion to Metternich's conservatism, they came to stand for nothing except preservation of the status quo. They made no attempt at accommodation with the new forces that were shaping Europe. It was not the policy of the congresses to forestall revolution by demanding that governments institute reforms. They simply repressed or punished all revolutionary agitation. They propped up governments that could not stand on their own feet.

In any case the congresses never succeeded in subordinating the separate interests of the Great Powers. Perhaps Alexander's repudiation of Ypsilanti was a sacrifice of Russian advantage to international principle; but when the Austrian government intervened to crush the revolution in Naples, and when the French government crushed the revolution in Spain, though in both cases they acted with an international mandate, each was really promoting what it conceived to be its own interests. The interest of Great Britain was to pull away from the system entirely. As defined by Castlereagh and by Canning after him, it was to stand aloof from permanent international commitments, to preserve a free exercise of sea power and foreign policy, and to take a benevolent view toward revolution in other countries. Since France eventually pulled away also, the Holy Alliance ceased to be even ostensibly a European system and became no more than a counterrevolutionary league of the three East European autocracies. The cause of liberalism in Europe was thus advanced by the collapse of this highly

Liberalism advances

conservative international system. At the same time the collapse of this system opened the way to the uncontrolled nationalism of the sovereign states. "Things are getting back to a wholesome state again," wrote George Canning in 1822. "Every nation for itself and God for us all!"

Russia: The Decembrist Revolt, 1825

Alexander I, "the man who defeated Napoleon," the ruler who had led his armies from Moscow to Paris, who had frightened the diplomats by the Russian shadow that he threw over the Continent, and who yet in his way had been the great pillar of constitutional liberalism and international order, died in 1825. His death was the signal for revolution in Russia. Officers of the Russian army, during the campaigns of 1812–1815 in Europe, had become acquainted with many unsettling ideas. Secret societies were formed even in the Russian officer corps; their members held all sorts of conflicting ideas, some wanting a constitutional tsardom in Russia, some demanding a republic, some even dreaming of an emancipation of the serfs. When Alexander died it was for a time uncertain which of his two brothers, Constantine or Nicholas, should succeed him. The restless coteries in the army preferred Constantine, who was thought to be more favorable to innovations in the state. In December 1825 they proclaimed Constantine at St. Petersburg, having their soldiers shout "Constantine and Constitution!" The soldiers, it is said, thought that Constitution was Constantine's wife.

Constantine and Nicholas

But the fact was that Constantine had already renounced his claims in favor of Nicholas, who was the rightful heir. The uprising, known as the Decembrist revolt, was soon put down. Five of the mutinous officers were hanged; many others were condemned to forced labor or interned in Siberia. The Decembrist revolt was the first manifestation of the modern revolutionary movement in Russia—of a revolutionary movement inspired by an ideological program, as distinguished from the elemental mass upheavals of Pugachev or Stephen Razin in earlier times. But the immediate effect of the Decembrist revolt was to clamp repression upon Russia more firmly. Nicholas I (1825–1855) maintained an unconditional and despotic autocracy.

Ten years after the defeat of Napoleon the new forces issuing from the French Revolution seemed to be routed, and reaction, repression, and political immobility seemed to prevail everywhere in Europe. The dike—a massive dike—seemed to be containing the flood.

56.   THE BREAKTHROUGH OF LIBERALISM IN THE WEST: REVOLUTIONS OF 1830–1832

The reactionary dike broke in 1830, and in western Europe the stream thereafter never stopped. The seepage, indeed, had already begun. By 1825 Spanish America was independent. The British and the French had pulled away from the congress system. The Greek nationalist movement against the Turks had broken out in the early 1820s.

With the defeat of Ypsilanti in 1821 the Greek nationalists turned somewhat away from the idea of a neo-Greek empire and more toward the idea of independence for Greece proper, the islands and peninsulas where Greek was the predominant language. Tsar Nicholas was more willing than Alexander to assist this movement. The governments of Great Britain and France were not inclined to let Russia stand as the only champion of Balkan peoples. Moreover, liberals in the West thought of the embattled Greeks as ancient Athenians fighting the modern oriental despotism of the Turkish empire.

The result was a joint Anglo-French-Russian naval intervention, which destroyed the Turkish fleet at Navarino Bay in 1827. Russia again, as often in the past, sent armies into the Balkans. A Russo-Turkish war and a great Middle Eastern crisis followed, in the course of which the rival powers agreed in 1829 to recognize Greece as an independent kingdom. The Balkan states of Serbia, Wallachia, and Moldavia were also recognized as autonomous principalities within the badly shaken Ottoman Empire (see map p. 649). From the same crisis Egypt emerged as an autonomous region under Mehemet Ali. Egypt in time became a center of Arabic nationalism, which reduced Ottoman power in the south just as Balkan nationalism did in the north.

France, 1824–1830: The July Revolution, 1830

It was in 1830, and first of all in France, that the wall of reaction really collapsed. Charles X became king in 1824. In the next year the legislative chambers voted an indemnity, in the form of perpetual annuities totaling 30 million francs a year, to those who as émigrés thirty-odd years before had had their property confiscated by the revolutionary state. Catholic clergy began to take over classrooms in the schools. A law pronounced the death penalty for sacrilege committed in church buildings. But the France of the restored Bourbons was still a free country, and against these apparent efforts to revive the Old Regime a strong opposition developed in the newspapers and in the chambers. In March 1830 the Chamber of Deputies, in which the bankers Laffitte and Casimier-Périer led the "leftist" opposition, passed a vote of no confidence in the government. The king, as was his legal right, dissolved the Chamber and called for new elections. The elections repudiated the king's policies. He replied on July 26, 1830, with four ordinances issued on his own authority. One dissolved the newly elected Chamber before it had ever met; another imposed censorship on the press; the third so amended the suffrage as to reduce the voting power of bankers, merchants, and industrialists and to concentrate it in the hands of the old-fashioned aristocracy; the fourth called for an election on the new basis.

These July Ordinances produced on the very next day the July Revolution. The upper bourgeois class was of course desperate at being thus brazenly ousted from political life. But it was the republicans—the nucleus of revolutionary workers, students, and intelligentsia in Paris—who actually moved. For three days, from July 27 to 29, barricades were erected in the city, behind which a swarming populace defied the army and the police. Most of the army refused to fire. Charles X, in no mood to be made captive by a revolution like his long-dead brother Louis XVI, precipitately abdicated and headed for England.

Charles X abdicates

Some of the leaders wished to proclaim a democratic republic. Working people hoped for better conditions of employment. The political liberals, supported by bankers, industrialists, various journalists, and intellectuals, had other aims. They had been satisfied in general with the constitutional charter of 1814; it was only to the policies and personnel of the government that they had objected, and they wished now to continue with constitutional monarchy, somewhat liberalized, and with a king whom they could trust. A solution to the deadlock was found by Lafayette, the aging hero of the American and the French revolutions, who became commander of the reorganized National Guard and a popular symbol of national unity. Lafayette produced the Duke of Orleans on the balcony of the Paris Hôtel de Ville, embraced him before a great concourse of people, and offered him as the answer to France's need. The duke was a collateral relative of the Bourbons; he had also, as a young man, served in the republican army of 1792. The militant republicans accepted him, willing to see what would develop; and the Chamber of Deputies on August 7 offered him the throne, on condition that he observe faithfully the constitutional charter of 1814. He reigned, until 1848, under the title of Louis Philippe.

The July Monarchy

The regime of Louis Philippe, called the Orléanist, bourgeois, or July Monarchy, was viewed very differently by different groups in France and in Europe. To the other states of Europe and to the clergy and legitimists within France, it seemed shockingly revolutionary. The new king owed his throne to an insurrection, to a bargain made with republicans, and to promises made to the Chamber of Deputies. He called himself not king of France but king of the French, and he flew the tricolor flag of the Revolution in place of the Bourbon lily. The tricolor produced an effect on the established classes not unlike that of the hammer and sickle after the Russian Revolution. He cultivated a popular manner, wore sober dark clothing (the ancestor of the modern business suit), and carried an umbrella. Though in private he worked stubbornly to maintain his royal position, in public he adhered scrupulously to the constitution.

The constitution remained substantially what it had been in 1814. The main political change was one of tone; there would be no more absolutism, with its notion that constitutional guarantees could be abrogated by a reigning prince. Legally the main change was that the Chamber of Peers ceased to be hereditary, to the chagrin of the old nobility, and that the Chamber of Deputies was to be elected by a somewhat enlarged body of voters. Where before 1830 there had been 100,000 voters, there were now about 200,000. The right to vote was still based on the ownership of a considerable quantity of real estate. About one-thirtieth of the adult male population (the top thirtieth in the possession of real property) now elected the Chamber of Deputies. The beneficiaries of the new system were the upper bourgeoisie—the bankers, merchants, and industrialists. The big property owners constituted the *pays légal*, the "legal country," and to them the July Monarchy was the consummation and stopping place of political progress. To others, and especially to the radical democrats, it proved as the years passed to be a disillusionment and an annoyance.

Revolutions of 1830: Belgium and Poland

The immediate effect of the three-day Paris revolution of 1830 was to set off a series of similar explosions throughout Europe, most notably in Belgium and Poland. These in turn, coming after the collapse of the Bourbons in France, brought the whole peace settlement of 1815 into jeopardy. It will be recalled that the Congress of Vienna had joined Belgium with the Dutch Netherlands to create a strong buffer state against a resurgent France and had also done what it could to prevent direct pressure of Russian power upon central Europe by way of Poland. Both these arrangements were now undone.

The benefits of the Dutch-Belgian union

The Dutch-Belgium union proved economically beneficial, for Belgian industry complemented the commercial and shipping activity of the Dutch, but politically it worked poorly, especially since the Dutch king had absolutist and centralizing ideas. The Belgians, though they had never been independent, had always stood stiffly for their local liberties under former Austrian rulers (and Spanish before them); now they did the same against the Dutch. The Catholic Belgians disliked Dutch Protestantism; those Belgians who spoke French (the Walloons) objected to regulations requiring the use of Dutch. About a month after the July Revolution in Paris disturbances broke out in Brussels. The leaders asked only for local Belgian self-government, but when the king took arms against them, they went on to proclaim independence. A national assembly met and drafted a constitution.

LIBERTY LEADING THE PEOPLE
by Eugène Delacroix (French, 1798–1863)

Delacroix, a founder of the romantic school in nineteenth-century French art, painted this picture soon after the July Revolution in Paris in 1830. It well illustrates the idealistic conception of revolution that prevailed among revolutionaries before 1848. Revolution is shown as a noble and moral act on behalf of the abstract ideals of liberty. The figures express determination and courage but show no sign of hatred or even anger. They are not a class; they are the people, affirming the rights of man. Liberty, holding the tricolor aloft, is a composed and even rational goddess.

(Giraudon/Art Resource, NY)

Nicholas of Russia wished to send troops to stamp out the Belgian uprising. But he could not get his forces safely through Poland. In Poland, too, in 1830, a revolution broke out. The Polish nationalists saw in the fall of the French Bourbons a timely moment for them to strike. They objected also to the appearance of Russian troops bound presumably to suppress freedom in western Europe. One incident led to another, until in January 1831 the Polish diet proclaimed the dethronement of the Polish king (i.e., Nicholas), who thereupon sent in a large army. The Poles, outnumbered and divided among themselves, could put up no successful resistance. They obtained no support from the West. The British government was unsettled by agitation at home. The French government, newly installed under Louis Philippe, had no wish to appear disturbingly revolutionary, and in any case feared the Polish agents who

Revolution in Poland

sought its backing as international firebrands and republicans. The Polish revolution was therefore crushed. Congress Poland disappeared; its constitution was abrogated, and it was merged into the Russian empire. Thousands of Poles settled in western Europe, where they became familiar figures in republican circles. In Poland the engines of repression rolled. The tsar's government exiled some thousands to Siberia, began to Russify the Eastern Border, and closed the universities of Warsaw and Vilna. Since it was too late for the tsar any longer to contemplate intervention in Belgium, it may be said that the sacrifice of the Poles contributed to the success of the West European revolution of 1830, as it had to that of the French Revolution of 1789–1795.

It was true enough, as Nicholas maintained, that an independent Belgium presented great international problems. Belgium for 20 years before 1815 had been part of France. A few Belgians now favored reunion with it, and in France the republican left, which regarded the Vienna treaty as an insult to the French nation, saw an opportunity to win back this first and dearest conquest of the First Republic. In 1831, by a small majority, the Belgian national assembly elected as their king the son of Louis Philippe, who, however, not wishing trouble with the British, forbade his son to accept it. The Belgians thereupon elected Leopold of Saxe-Coburg, a German princeling who had married into the British royal family and became a British subject. He was in fact the uncle of a 12-year-old girl who was to be Queen Victoria. The British negotiated with Talleyrand, sent over by the French government (it was his last public service); and the result was a treaty of 1831 (confirmed in 1839) setting up Belgium as a perpetually neutral state, incapable of forming alliances and guaranteed against invasion by all five of the Great Powers. The aim intended by the Treaty of Vienna, to prevent the annexation of Belgium to France, was thus again realized in a new way. Internally Belgium presently settled down to a stable parliamentary system, somewhat more democratic than the July Monarchy in France but fundamentally offering the same type of bourgeois and liberal rule.

Reform in Great Britain

The three-day Paris revolution of 1830 had direct repercussions across the Channel. The quick results following on working-class insurrection gave radical leaders in England the idea that threats of violence might be useful. On the other hand, the ease and speed with which the French bourgeoisie gained the upper hand reassured the British middle classes, who concluded that they might unsparingly embarrass the government without courting a mass upheaval.

The Tory regime

The Tory regime in England had in fact already begun to loosen up. A group of new Tory leaders came forward in the 1820s, notably George Canning, the foreign minister, and Robert Peel, son of one of the first cotton manufacturers. This group was sensitive to the needs of British business and to the liberal doctrines of free trade. They reduced tariffs and liberalized the old Navigation Acts, permitting British colonies to trade with countries other than Britain. The Liberal Tories also undermined the legal position of the Church of England, forwarding the conception of a secular state, though such was hardly their purpose. They repealed the old laws (which dated from the seventeenth century) forbidding dissenting Protestants to hold public office except through a legal fiction by which they pretended to be Anglicans. They even allowed the Test Act of 1673 to be repealed and Catholic Emancipation to be adopted. Catholics in Great Britain and Ireland received the same rights as others. Capital punishment was abolished for about a hundred offenses. A professional police force was introduced in place of the old-fashioned and ineffectual local constables. (It is after Robert Peel that London policemen came to be called "bobbies.") The new police were expected to handle protest meetings, angry crowds, or occasional riots without having to call for military assistance.

There were two things that the Liberal Tories could not do. They could not question the Corn Laws, and they could not reform the House of Commons. By the Corn Laws, which set the tariff on imported grain, a tariff raised to new heights in 1815, the gentlemen of England protected their rent rolls; and by the existing structure of the House of Commons they governed the country, expecting the working class and the business interests to look to them as natural leaders.

Never in 500 years of its history had the Commons been so unrepresentative. No new borough had been created since the Revolution of 1688. The boroughs, or urban centers having the right to elect members of Parliament, were heavily concentrated in southern England. Although the Industrial Revolution was shifting population noticeably to the north, the new factory towns were not represented in Parliament. In a few boroughs real elections took place, but in some of them it was the town corporation, and in others the owners of certain pieces of real estate, that had the right to name members of Parliament. Each borough was different, carrying over the local liberties of the Middle Ages. Many boroughs were entirely dominated by influential persons called borough-mongers by their critics. As for the rural districts, the "forty-shilling freeholders" chose two members of Parliament for each county, in a convivial assembly much influenced by the gentlefolk. It was estimated about 1820 that fewer than 500 men, most of them members of the House of Lords, really selected a majority of the House of Commons.

Problems of representation

Some two dozen bills to reform the House of Commons had been introduced in the half-century preceding 1830. They had all failed to pass. In 1830, after the Paris revolution, the issue was again raised by the minority party, the Whigs. The Tory prime minister, the Duke of Wellington, the victor of Waterloo and a most extreme conservative, so immoderately defended the existing system that he lost the confidence even of some of his own followers. The existing methods of election in England, he declared, were more perfect than any that human intelligence could contrive at a single stroke. After this outburst a Whig ministry took over the government. It introduced a reform bill. The House of Commons rejected it. The Whig ministry thereupon resigned. The Tories, fearing popular violence, refused to take the responsibility for forming a cabinet. The Whigs resumed office and again introduced their reform bill. This time it passed the Commons but failed in the House of Lords. An angry roar went up over the country. Crowds milled in the London streets, rioters for several days were in control at Bristol, the jail at Derby was sacked, and Nottingham castle was burned. Only the passage of the reform bill, it seemed, could prevent an actual revolution. Using this argument, the Whigs got the king to promise to create enough new peers to change the majority in the House of Lords. The Lords yielded rather than be swamped, and in April 1832 the bill became law.

The Reform Bill of 1832

The Reform Bill of 1832 was a very English measure. It adapted the English or medieval system rather than following the new ideas of the French Revolution. On the Continent, constitutional political systems in countries such as France rested on the idea that each representative should represent roughly the same number of voters and that voters should qualify to vote by a flat uniform qualification, usually the payment of a stated amount of property taxes. The British held to the idea that members of the House of Commons represented boroughs and counties, in general without regard to size of population (with exceptions). In other words, no attempt was made to create equal electoral districts, and the vote was still distributed in the reformed boroughs and counties on the basis of economic status, reliability, and permanence. The total effect on the size of the electorate was to raise the number of voters in the British Isles from about 500,000 to about 813,000. Some persons actually lost their votes, namely, the poorer elements in the handful of old boroughs which had been fairly democratic, like the borough of Westminster in greater London.

The most important change was not the increased size of the electorate but its redistribution by region and by class. The Reform Bill reallocated the seats in the House of Commons. Fifty-six of the smallest older boroughs were abolished, their inhabitants thereafter voting as residents of their counties. Thirty other small boroughs kept the right to send only one burgess to Parliament instead of the historic two. The 143 seats thus made available were given to the new industrial towns, where the middle classes now gained the right to vote—factory owners and businessmen and their principal employees, doctors, lawyers, brokers, merchants, and newspaper people, relatives and connections of the well-to-do.

The ambiguous impact of reform

The Reform Bill of 1832 was more sweeping than the Whigs would have favored except for their fear or revolution. It was more conservative than the democratic radicals would have accepted, except for their belief that the suffrage might be widened in the future. Whether Great Britain in 1830 was in danger of any real revolution can never be known. A distressed mass of workers was led by an irate manufacturing class that was unwilling to tolerate any longer its exclusion from political life, yet neither the workers nor the industrialists turned toward violence and revolution. The reason probably lies first of all in the existence of the historic institution of Parliament, which, erratic though it was before the Reform Bill, provided the means by which social changes could be legally accomplished and continued, in principle, to enjoy universal respect. Conservatives, driven to the wall, would yield; they could allow a revision of the suffrage because they could expect to remain themselves in public life. Radicals, using enough violence to scare the established interest, did not thereafter face a blank wall; they could expect, once the breach was made, to carry some day a further democratization of Parliament and with it their social and economic program by orderly legislation.

Britain after 1832

But the Reform Bill of 1832 was in its way a revolution. The new business interests, created by industrialization, took their place alongside the old aristocracy in the governing elite of the country. The aristocratic Whigs who had carried the Reform Bill gradually merged with formerly radical industrialists and with a few Liberal Tories to form the Liberal party. The main body of the Tories, joined by a few old Whigs and even a few former radicals, gradually turned into the Conservative party. The two parties alternated in power at short intervals from 1832 to the First World War, this being the classic period in Great Britain of the Liberal-Conservative two-party system.

Liberals and Conservatives

In 1833 slavery was abolished in the British Empire. In 1834 a new Poor Law was adopted. In 1835 the Municipal Corporations Act, second only to the Reform Bill in basic importance, modernized the local government of English cities; it broke up the old local oligarchies and brought in uniform electoral and administrative machinery, enabling city dwellers to grapple more effectively with the problems of

CHRONOLOGY OF NOTABLE EVENTS, 1780–1869

1780s	Mechanical spinning of cotton spreads across England
1792	Mary Wollstonecraft publishes *A Vindication of the Rights of Women*
1807	Robert Fulton uses the steam engine to propel river boats
1819	"Peterloo Massacre" suppresses protesting English workers in Manchester
1819	Metternich's "Carlsbad Decrees" suppress the German nationalist movement
1820	Congress of Troppau calls for international action against all revolutions
1823	Monroe Doctrine opposes European intervention in Latin America
1825	Decembrist Revolt of military officers is put down in Russia
1829	Steam locomotive is tested safely in England
1830	July Revolution in France forces abdication of Charles X; Louis-Philippe becomes king
1831	Russia suppresses national movement in Poland
1832	Reform Bill widens British suffrage; alters representation in Parliament
1839	Louis Blanc's *Organization of Work* promotes new socialist ideas
1846	Repeal of Corn Laws marks ascendancy of British industrial interests
1869	John Stuart Mill argues for women's rights in *The Subjection of Women*

urban life. In 1836 the House of Commons allowed the newspapers to report how its members voted—a long step toward publicity of government proceedings was thus taken. Meanwhile an ecclesiastical commission reviewed the affairs of the Church of England; financial and administrative irregularities were corrected, together with the grosser inequalities between the income of upper and lower clergy, all of which had made the church formerly a kind of closed preserve for the landed gentry.

The Tories, thus assaulted in their immemorial strongholds of local government and the established church, carried a counteroffensive into the strongholds of the new liberal manufacturing class, namely, the factories and the mines. Tories became champions of the industrial workers. Landed gentlemen, of whom the most famous was Lord Ashley, later seventh Earl of Shaftesbury, took the lead in publicizing the social evils of a rapid and even ruthless

The Tory counteroffensive

industrialization. They received some support from a few humanitarian industrialists; indeed, the early legislation tended to follow practices already established by the best or strongest business firms. A Factory Act of 1833 forbade the labor of children less than nine years old in the textile mills. It was the first effective piece of legislation on the subject because it provided for paid inspectors and procedures for enforcement. An act of 1842 initiated significant regulation in the coal mines; the employment underground of women and girls, and of boys under ten, was forbidden.

The greatest victory of the working classes came in 1847 with the Ten Hours Act, which limited the labor of women and children in all industrial establishments to ten hours a day. Thereafter men commonly worked only ten hours also, since the work of men, women, and young people was too closely coordinated for the men to work alone. The

Liberal John Bright, Quaker and cotton magnate, called the Ten Hours Act "a delusion practiced on the working classes." To regulate the hours of labor was contrary to the accepted principles of laissez-faire, economic law, the free market, freedom of trade, and individual liberty for employer and worker. Yet the Ten Hours Act stood, and British industry continued to prosper.

The Anti–Corn Law League

Gathering their strength, the Whig-liberal-radical combination established in 1838 an Anti-Corn Law League. Wage earners objected to the Corn Laws because the tariff on grain imports kept up the price of food. Industrial employers objected to them because, in keeping up food prices, they also kept up wages and the cost of industrial production in England, thus working to England's disadvantage in the export trade. Defenders of the Corn Laws argued that protection of agriculture was necessary to maintain the natural landowning aristocracy of the country, but they also sometimes used more widely framed economic arguments, affirming that Britain should preserve an economic balance between industry and farming and avoid becoming too exclusively dependent on imported food. The issue became a straight contest between the industrialists, acting with working-class support, and the aristocratic and predominantly Tory landowning interest. The Anti–Corn Law League, whose headquarters were at Manchester, operated like a modern political party. It had plenty of money, supplied by large donations from manufacturers and small ones from laboring people. It sent lecturers on tour, agitated in the newspapers, and issued a stream of polemical pamphlets and educational books. It held political teas, torchlight processions, and open-air mass meetings. The pressure proved irresistible and received a final impetus from a famine in Ireland. It was a Tory government, headed by Sir Robert Peel, which in 1846 yielded before so vociferous a demand.

The repeal of the Corn Laws in 1846 stands as a symbol of the change that had come over England. It reaffirmed the revolutionary consequences of the Reform Bill of 1832. Industry was now a governing element in the country. Free trade was henceforth the rule. Great Britain, in return for the export of manufacturers, became deliberately dependent on imports for its very life. It was committed henceforth to an international and even worldwide economic system. The first to undergo the Industrial Revolution, possessing mechanical power and methods of mass production, the British could produce yarn and cloth, machine tools and railroad equipment, more efficiently and more cheaply than any other people. In Britain, the early industrial workshop of the world, people would pour increasingly into mine, factory, and city; live by selling manufactures, coal, shipping, and financial services to the other peoples of the earth; and obtain raw cotton, rare ores, meat, cereals, and thousands of lesser but still vital necessities from the rest of the earth in exchange. The welfare of Britain depended on the maintenance of a freely exchanging worldwide economic system and, as always, on the British navy's control of the sea.

57.   TRIUMPH OF THE WEST EUROPEAN BOURGEOISIE

In general, the decades following 1830 may be thought of as a kind of golden age of the West-European bourgeoisie, or what in English would be called the upper middle class. In the older meaning, in French, a *bourgeois* had been someone who was not of the nobility but enjoyed an income from business, a profession, or the ownership of property. After the French Revolution, and even more after 1830, the word took on new meanings, not all of them consistent. Artists, literary people, and old-line aristocrats might disdain the bourgeois as a person of uncultivated tastes, supposedly interested only in making money. From another point of view, shared by social theorists and working-class leaders, the bourgeois was someone who could hire the labor of other people for business enterprises, recreational activities, or household service. In a word, the bourgeois was the employer. In any case, the bourgeoisie and the aristocracy tended to become more alike in the nineteenth century in their daily pursuits and style of life, and to draw income from the possession of income-producing property or capital. The bourgeoisie, formerly identified in contrast to the nobility, was now identified in contrast to the working class, that is, those whose whole income depended on daily labor in shops, offices, farms, or factories.

The reigning liberal doctrine was the "stake in society" theory; those who govern should have something to lose. In the France of the July Monarchy (1830–1848), only about one adult male in 30 had the vote. In the Britain of the first Reform Bill (1832–1867), one man in eight could vote for a member of the House of Commons. In France only the most well-to-do were enfranchised; in Britain, virtually the whole middle class, which, however, long supported members of the aristocracy for the highest public positions. In Britain the continuation of the Tory landed interest in politics somewhat blunted the edge of capitalist and managerial rule, resulting in the passage of significant legislation for the protection of industrial labor. In France the aristocratic landed interest, weaker and less public spirited than in England, lost much of its influence by the Revolution of 1830, and less was done to relieve the condition of labor.

"Stake in society" theory

The bourgeois age left its mark on Europe in many ways. For one thing, western Europe continued to accumulate capital and build up its industrial plant. National income was constantly rising, but a relatively small share went to the laboring class and a relatively large share went to owners of capital. This meant that less was spent on consumers' goods—housing, clothing, food, recreation—and that more was saved and available for reinvestment. New stock companies were constantly formed, and the law of corporations was amended, allowing for the extension of corporate enterprise to new fields. The factory system spread from Britain to the Continent and within Britain from the textile industry to other lines of production. The output of iron, a good index to economic advancement in this phase of industrialism, rose about 300 percent in Great Britain between 1830 and 1848 and about 65 percent in France between 1830 and 1845. (All the German states combined, at the latter date, produced about a tenth as much iron as Great Britain and less than half as much as France.) Railroad building began in earnest after 1840. In 1840 Samuel Cunard put four steamships into regular transatlantic service. Much capital was exported; as early as 1839 an American estimated that Europeans (mainly British) owned $200,000,000 worth of stocks in American companies. Such investments financed the purchase of British and other goods and helped to rivet together a world economic system, in which western Europe and especially England took the lead, with other regions remaining in a somewhat subordinate status.

The Frustration and Challenge of Labor

The bourgeois age had the effect also of estranging the world of labor. The state in Britain and France was as near as it has ever been to what Karl Marx was soon to call it—a committee of the bourgeois class. Already in France people spoke worriedly of the

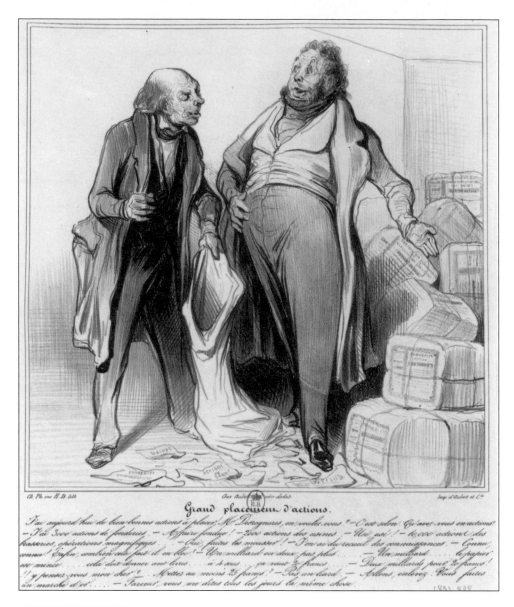

BIG INVESTMENTS

by Honoré Daumier (French, 1808–1879)

The Revolution of 1830, romanticized at first by Delacroix and most European liberals, was in fact followed by a period of moneymaking and business ferment (as well as rapid economic development), made famous by the novels of Balzac and the graphic art of Daumier. This lithograph of 1837 shows a financier with bundles of stock certificates piled beside him, offering to sell shares in factories, foundries, and breweries to a skeptical client. Daumier's satirical images provided vivid, memorable critiques of the corruptions and hypocrisies in nineteenth-century political and economic life.

(Bibliothèque Nationale de France, Paris)

prolétaires, those at the bottom of society, who had nothing to lose. Republicans in France, radical democrats in Britain, felt cheated and imposed upon in the 1830s and 1840s. They had in each country forced through a virtual revolution by their insurrections and demonstrations and then in each country had been left without the vote. Some lost interest in representative institutions. Excluded from government, they were tempted to seek political ends through extragovernmental, which is to say revolutionary or utopian, channels. Social and economic reforms seemed to the average worker far more important, as a final aim, than mere governmental innovations. Workers were told by respected economists that they could not hope to change the system in their own favor. They were tempted, therefore, to destroy the system, to replace it utterly with some new system conceived mainly in the minds of thinkers. They were told by the Manchester School, and by its equivalent in France, that the income of labor was set by ineluctable natural laws, that it was best and indeed necessary for wages to remain low, and that the way to rise in the world was to get out of the laboring class altogether, by becoming the owner of a profitable business and leaving working people about where they were.

The labor market

The reigning doctrine emphasized the conception of a labor market. The worker sold labor; the employer bought it. The price of labor, or wage, was to be agreed upon by the two individual parties. The price would naturally fluctuate according to changes in supply and demand. When a great deal of a certain kind of labor was required, the wage would go up until new persons moved into the market offering more labor of this type, with the result that something like the old wage would again be established. When no labor was needed, none should be hired, and persons who could not sell labor might then subsist for a time by poor relief.

The Poor Law of 1834

The new Poor Law of 1834 was especially repugnant to the British working class. It corrected crying evils of the old poor laws that had left millions of people in habitual poverty but did nothing constructive to relieve productive workers suffering from occasional or cyclical unemployment. The new law followed the stern precepts of the dismal science; its main principle was to safeguard the labor market by making relief more unpleasant than any job. It granted relief only to persons willing to enter a workhouse, or poorhouse; and in these establishments the sexes were segregated and life was in other ways made noticeably less attractive than in the outside world. The workers considered the new law an abomination. They called the workhouses "bastilles." They resented the whole conception of a labor market, in which labor was to be bought and sold (or remain unsold) like any other commodity. The fluctuating, cyclical labor market contributed to the social instability of working-class families and may also have created new tensions between women and men. Court records from early nineteenth-century England suggest that violent family disputes became more common when women earned significant portions of the working family's household income or found work more readily than their unemployed husbands; such situations challenged the traditional relations in English family life, though women almost always received lower wages than men.

In the long run it would be the increase in productivity that would improve the condition of the workers. Meanwhile the friends of the working class offered two means of escape. One was to improve the position of labor in the market. This led to the formation of labor unions for control of the labor supply and collective bargaining with employers. Such unions, illegal in France, were barely legal in Great Britain after 1825, though it was still illegal in both countries to strike. The other means of escape was to repudiate the whole idea of a market economy and of the capitalist system. It was to conceive of a system in which goods were to be produced for use, not for sale; and in which working people should be compensated according to need, not according to the requirements of an employer. This was the basis of most forms of nineteenth-century socialism.

Socialism and Chartism

Socialism spread rapidly among the working classes after 1830. In France it blended with revolutionary republicanism. There was a revival of interest in the great Revolution and the democratic Republic of 1793. Cheap reprints of the writings of Robespierre began to circulate in the working-class quarters of Paris. Robespierre was now seen as a people's hero. The socialist Louis Blanc, for example, who in 1839 published his *Organization of Work* recommending the formation of "social workshops," also wrote a long history of the French Revolution, in which he pointed out the egalitarian ideals that had inspired the National Convention in 1793. In Britain, as befitted the different background of the country, socialistic ideas blended in with the movement for further parliamentary reform. This was advanced by the working-class group known as the Chartists, from the People's Charter which they drafted in 1838.

Chartism was far more of a mass movement than the French socialism of the day. Only a few Chartists were clearly socialists in their own minds. But all were anticapitalistic. All could agree that the first step toward social reform must be to win working-class representation in Parliament. The Charter of 1838 consisted of six points. It demanded (1) the annual election of the House of Commons by (2) universal suffrage for all adult males, through (3) a secret ballot and (4) equal electoral districts; and it called for (5) the abolition of property qualifications for membership in the House of Commons, which perpetuated the old idea that Parliament should be composed of gentlemen of independent income, and urged instead (6) the payment of salaries to the elected members of Parliament, in order that people of small means might serve. A convention composed of delegates sent by labor unions, mass meetings, and radical societies all over the country met in London in 1839. Convention was an ominous word, with French revolutionary and even terrorist overtones; some members of this British convention regarded it as the body really representing the people and favored armed violence and a general strike, while others stood only for moral pressure upon Parliament.

The Charter of 1838

A petition bearing over a million signatures, urging acceptance of the Charter, was submitted to the House of Commons. The violent and revolutionary wing, or "physical force" Chartists, precipitated a wave of riots which were effectively quelled by the authorities. In 1842 the petition was again submitted. This time, according to the best estimate, it was signed by 3,317,702 persons. Since the entire population of Great Britain was about 19 million, it is clear that the Charter, whatever the exact number of signatures, commanded the explicit adherence of half the adult males of the country. The House of Commons nevertheless rejected the petition by 287 votes to 49. It was feared that political democracy would threaten property rights and the whole economic system as they then existed. The Chartist movement gradually died down in the face of firm opposition by the government and the business classes and was weakened by mutual fears and disagreements among its own supporters. It had not been entirely fruitless; for without popular agitation and the publicizing of working-class grievances, the Mines Act of 1842 and the Ten Hours Act of

Petitions and the defeat of the Chartists

The newly organized London police await the arrival of a Chartist procession in the 1840s. The British government introduced a more disciplined police force to avoid incidents such as the Peterloo Massacre and to manage the mass demonstrations of groups such as the Chartists, who campaigned (unsuccessfully) for more democratic electoral laws.
(Getty Images)

1847 might not have been enacted. These measures in turn alleviated the distress of industrial workers and kept alive a degree of confidence in the future of the economic system. Chartism revived briefly in 1848, as will be seen in the next chapter; but in general, in the 1840s, British working people turned from political agitation to the forming and strengthening of labor unions by which they could deal directly with employers without having to appeal to the government. Not until 1867 was the suffrage extended in Great Britain, and it took about 80 years to realize the full program of the Charter of 1838, except for the annual election of Parliament, for which there soon ceased to be any demand.

It is not easy to summarize the history of Europe between 1815 and 1848. Among all the forces set free by the French and Industrial revolutions—liberalism, conservatism, nationalism, republicanism, socialism, feminism, democracy—no stabilization had been achieved. No international system had been created; Europe had instead fallen increasingly into two political camps, which represented both geographical and ideological divisions in nineteenth-century European societies. In general, the political ideas of classical liberalism advanced most rapidly in the nations of western Europe, whereas eastern Europe was mostly dominated by three autocratic monarchies. Western Europe generally adhered more closely to the principles of nationality; governments in central and eastern

Europe still opposed them. The countries of northwestern Europe were growing collectively richer, more industrialized, more liberal, more bourgeois. Middle-class people in Germany, central Europe, and Italy (as well as in Spain and Portugal) did not usually enjoy the dignities and emoluments that they enjoyed in Great Britain or France. But the industrializing societies in northwestern Europe had not solved their social problem; their whole material civilization rested upon a restless and sorely tried working class. Everywhere there was repression, in varying degree, and everywhere apprehension, more in some places than in others; but there was also hope, confidence in the progress of an industrial and scientific society, and faith in the unfinished liberal program of the rights of individuals. The result was the general Revolution of 1848.

 For interactive exercises, glossary, chronologies, and more, go to the *Online Learning Center* at **www.mhhe.com/palmer10.**

Chapter 12

REVOLUTIONS AND THE REIMPOSITION OF ORDER, 1848–1870

Fears haunting the established classes of Europe for 30 years came true in 1848. Governments collapsed all over the Continent. Remembered horrors appeared again, as in a recurring dream, in much the same sequence as after 1789 only at a much faster rate of speed. Revolutionaries milled in the streets, kings fled, republics were declared, and within four years there was another Napoleon. Soon thereafter came a series of short wars.

Never before or since has Europe seen so truly universal an upheaval as in 1848. While the French Revolution of 1789 and the Russian Revolution of 1917 both had immediate international repercussions, in each of these cases a single country took the lead. In 1848 the revolutionary movements broke out spontaneously from Copenhagen to Palermo and from Paris to Budapest. Contemporaries sometimes attributed the universality of the phenomenon to the machinations of secret societies, and it is true that the faint beginnings of an international revolutionary movement existed before 1848; but the fact is that revolutionary plotters had little influence upon what actually happened, and the nearly simultaneous fall of governments is quite understandable from other causes. Many people in Europe sought substantially the same goals—constitutional government, the independence and unification of national groups, an end to serfdom and manorial restraints where they still existed. With some variation, there was a common body of ideas among politically conscious elements of all countries. Some of the powers that the new forces had to combat were themselves international, notably the Catholic church and the far-spreading influence of the Habsburgs, so that resistance to them arose independently in many places. In any case, only the Russian

Chapter emblem: Detail from a nineteenth-century illustration of the crowd marching on the Tuileries in Paris during the Revolution of 1848. (Snark/Art Resource, NY)

empire and Great Britain escaped the European revolutionary contagion of 1848, and the British received a very bad scare.

But the Revolutions of 1848, though they shook the whole Continent, lacked enduring political and social strength. They failed almost as rapidly as they succeeded. Their main consequence, at least in the short run, was to strengthen the more conservative forces that viewed all revolution with alarm. Revolutionary ideals succumbed to military repression. To some extent the governments of the 1850s and 1860s, while hostile to revolution, satisfied some of the aims of 1848, notably in national unification and constitutional government with limited representation, but they did so in a mood of calculated realism that firmly reasserted their own authority. The repressed Revolutions of 1848 left a legacy of class fears and class conflict, in which prophets of a new society also became more realistic, as when Karl Marx, branding earlier forms of socialism as "utopian," offered his own views as hard-headed and "scientific." New "isms" arose in response to the evolving nineteenth-century political and cultural order, but power also remained firmly with the institutions and national ideologies of the various European states and their centralizing governments.

58.   PARIS: THE SPECTER OF SOCIAL REVOLUTION IN THE WEST

The July Monarchy in France was a platform of boards built over a volcano. Under it burned the repressed fires of the republicanism put down in 1830, which since 1830 had become steadily more socialistic.

Politics in the July Monarchy became increasingly separated from the changing social classes in French society. So few interests were represented in the Chamber of Deputies that the most basic social or political issues were seldom debated. Even most of the bourgeois class had no representation. Graft and corruption were more common than they should have been, as economic expansion favored stock swindles and fraud by business promoters and politicians in combination. A strong movement set in to give the vote to more people. Radicals wanted universal male suffrage and a republic, but liberals asked only for a broadening of voting rights within the existing constitutional monarchy. The king, Louis Philippe, and his prime minister, Guizot, instead of allying with the liberals against the radicals, resolutely and obtusely opposed any change whatsoever.

The "February" Revolution in France

Reformers, against the king's expressed wishes, planned a great banquet in Paris for February 22, 1848, to be accompanied by demonstrations in the streets. The government on February 21 forbade all such meetings. That night barricades were built in the working-class quarters. Paving blocks, building stones, or large pieces of furniture were thrown together across the narrow streets and intersections of the old city, constituting a maze within which insurgents prepared to resist the authorities. The government called out the National Guard, which refused to move. The king now promised electoral reform, but republican firebrands took charge of the working-class elements, who demonstrated outside the house of Guizot. Someone shot at the guards placed around the house; the guards replied, killing 20 persons. The republican organizers put some of the corpses on a torch-lit cart and paraded them through the city, which, armed and barricaded, soon began to erupt in an enormous riot. On February 24 Louis Philippe, like Charles X before him, abdicated and made for England. The February Revolution of 1848, like the July Revolution of 1830, had unseated a monarch in three days.

The constitutional reformers hoped to carry on with Louis Philippe's young grandson as king, but the republicans, now aroused and armed, poured into the Chamber of Deputies and forced the proclamation of the Republic. Republican leaders set up a provisional government of 10 men, pending election by all France of a Constituent Assembly that would write the new constitution for the second French Republic. Seven of the 10 were "political" republicans, the most notable being the poet Lamartine. Three were "social" republicans, the most notable being Louis Blanc. A huge crowd of workers appeared before the Hôtel de Ville, or city hall, demanding that France adopt the new socialist emblem—the red flag. They were dissuaded by the eloquence of Lamartine, and the tricolor remained the republican standard.

Proclamation of the Republic

Louis Blanc urged the Provisional Government to push through a bold economic and social program without delay. But since the "social" republicans were in a minority in the Provisional Government (though probably not among Paris republicans generally), Louis Blanc's ideas were very much watered down in the application. He wanted a Ministry of Progress to organize a network of "social workshops," the state-supported and collectivist manufacturing establishments that he had projected in his writings. The new government, however, would only create a more limited Labor Commission and a system of shops significantly entitled "national" rather than "social." The National Workshops, as they are always called in English (though "workshop" suggests something more insignificant than Louis Blanc had in mind), were established as a political concession to the "social" republicans, but no significant work was ever assigned them for fear of competition with private enterprise and dislocation of the economic system. Indeed, the man placed in charge of them admitted that his purpose was to prove the fallacies of socialism. Meanwhile the Labor Commission was unable to win public acceptance for the ten-hour day, which the British Parliament had enacted the year before. One action of the Provisional Government, however, had permanent effect: the final abolition of slavery in the French colonies.

Louis Blanc

The National Workshops became in practice only an extensive project in unemployment relief. Women were excluded from the workshops, but men of all trades, skilled and unskilled, were set to work digging on the roads and fortifications outside Paris. They were paid two francs a day. The number of legitimate unemployed increased rapidly, for 1847 had been a year of depression and the revolution prevented the return of business confidence. Other needy persons also presented themselves for remuneration, and soon there were too many men for the amount of work made available. From 25,000 enrolled in the workshops by the middle of March, the number climbed to 120,000 by mid-June, by which time there were also in Paris another 50,000 whom the bulging workshops could no longer accommodate. In June there were probably almost 200,000 essentially idle but able-bodied men in a city of about a million people.

The National Workshops

The Constituent Assembly, elected in April by universal male suffrage throughout France, met on May 4. It immediately replaced the Provisional Government with a temporary executive board of its own. The main body of France, a land of provincial bourgeois and peasant landowners, was not socialist in the least. The temporary executive board,

There was in Paris a well-established tradition of revolutionary agitation, so that a conflict between political activists and the police in February 1848 could lead quickly toward the well-known patterns of radical political upheaval: crowds and barricades in the streets, publications calling for revolutionary change, and emotional responses to popular national symbols such as the tricolor flag. This nineteenth-century illustration depicts part of the Parisian crowd that marched on the Tuileries, forcing King Louis-Philippe to abdicate power and leave the country.

(Snark/Art Resource, NY)

chosen by the Constituent Assembly in May, included no "social" republicans. All five of its members were known as outspoken enemies of Louis Blanc; the socialists could no longer expect even the grudging concessions that they had earlier obtained.

The battle lines were now drawn after only three months of revolution, somewhat as they had been drawn in 1792 after three years. Paris again stood for revolutionary actions in which the rest of the country was not prepared to share. Revolutionary leaders in Paris, in 1848 as in 1792, were unwilling to accept the processes of majority rule or slow parliamentary deliberation. But the crisis in 1848 was more acute than in 1792. A larger proportion of the population were wage earners. Under a system of predominantly merchant capitalism, in which machine industry and factory concentration were only just emerging, the workers were tormented by the same evils as the more industrialized working classes of England. Hours were if anything longer, and pay was less, in France than in Great Britain; insecurity and unemployment were at least as great; and the belief that a capitalist economy held no future for the laborer was the same. In addition, where the English worker shrank from an actual assault on Parliament, the French worker saw nothing very sacrilegious in the violation of elected assemblies. Too many regimes in France since 1789, including those preferred by the comfortable classes, had been based on insurrectionary violence for the French workers to feel much compunction over using it for their own ends.

The "June Days" of 1848

On the one hand stood the nationally elected Constituent Assembly. On the other, the National Workshops had mobilized in Paris the most distressed elements of the working class. Tens of thousands had been brought together where they could talk, read journals, listen to speeches, and concert common action. Agitators and organizers naturally made use of the opportunity thus presented to them. Men in the workshops began to feel desperate, to sense that the social republic was slipping from them perhaps forever. On May 15 they attacked the Constituent Assembly, drove its members out of the hall, declared it dissolved, and set up a new provisional government of their own. They announced that a social revolution must follow the purely political revolution of February. But the National Guard, a kind of civilian militia, turned against the insurgents and restored the Constituent Assembly. The Assembly, to root out socialism, now prepared to get rid of the National Workshops. It offered those enrolled in them the alternatives of enlistment in the army, transfer to provincial workshops, or expulsion from Paris by force. The whole laboring class in the city began to resist. The government proclaimed martial law, the civilian executive board resigned, and all power was given to General Cavaignac and the regular army.

Paris on the verge of revolution

There followed the "Bloody June Days"—June 24 to 26, 1848—three days during which a terrifying class war raged in Paris. Over 20,000 men from the workshops took to arms, and they were joined by thousands of men and women from the working-class districts of the city. Half or more of Paris became a labyrinth of barricades defended by determined men and equally resolute women. Military methods of the time made it possible for civilians to shoot it out openly with soldiers in the narrow streets; small arms were the main weapons, and armies still lacked the military advantage of armored vehicles. The soldiers found it a difficult operation, but after three days the outcome was in doubt no longer. Ten thousand persons had been killed or wounded. Eleven thousand insurgents were taken prisoner. The Assembly, refusing all clemency, decreed their immediate deportation to the colonies.

Class war

The June Days sent a shudder throughout France and Europe. Whether the battle in Paris had been a true class struggle, how large a portion of the laboring class had really participated (it was large in any case), how much they had fought for permanent objectives, and how much over the temporary issue of the workshops—all these were secondary questions. It was widely understood that a class war had in fact broken out. Militant workers were confirmed in a hatred of the bourgeois class and in a belief that capitalism ultimately survived by shooting working-class men and women in the streets. People above the laboring class were thrown into a panic. They were sure that they had narrowly escaped a ghastly upheaval. The very ground of civilized living seemed to have quaked. After June 1848, wrote a Frenchwoman of the time, society was "a prey to a feeling of terror incomparable to anything since the invasion of Rome by the barbarians."

The revival of Chartist agitation

Nor were the signs in England much more reassuring. There the Chartist agitation for electoral reforms was revived by the February Revolution in Paris. "France is a Republic!" cried the Chartist Ernest Jones; the Chartist petition was again circulated and was soon said to have six million signatures. Another Chartist convention met, considered by its leaders to be the forerunner of a Constituent Assembly as in France. The violent minority was the most active; it began to gather arms and to drill. The old Duke of Wellington swore in 70,000 special constables to uphold the social order. Clashes occurred at Liverpool and elsewhere; in London the revolutionary committee laid plans for systematic arson and organized men to break up the pavements for barricades. Meanwhile the petition, weighing 584 pounds, was carried in three cabs to the House of Commons, which estimated that it contained "only" two million signatures and again summarily rejected it. The revolutionary menace passed. One of the secret organizers in London proved to be a government spy; he revealed the whole plan at the critical moment, and the revolutionary committee was arrested on the day set for insurrection. Most Chartists had in any case refused to support the militants, but the truculent minority of radical workers and journalists had a deeper sense of envenomed class consciousness. The word "proletarian" was imported from France. "Every proletarian," wrote the Chartist editor of *Red Revolution,* "who does not see and feel that he belongs to an enslaved and degraded class is a *fool.*"

The specter of social revolution thus hung over western Europe in the summer of 1848, though in all probability there could have been no successful socialist revolution at the time. But the specter was there, and it spread a sinking fear among all who had something to lose. This fear shaped the whole subsequent course of the Second Republic in France and of the revolutionary movements that had by this time begun in other countries as well.

The Emergence of Louis Napoleon Bonaparte

In France, after the June Days, the Constituent Assembly (with General Cavaignac as a virtual dictator) set about drafting a republican constitution. It was decided, in view of the disturbances just passed, to create a strong executive power in the hands of a president to be elected by universal male suffrage. It was decided also to have this president elected immediately, even before the rest of the constitution was finished. Four candidates presented themselves: Lamartine, Cavaignac, Ledru-Rollin—and Louis Napoleon Bonaparte. The poet Lamartine stood for a somewhat vaguely moral and idealistic republic; Cavaignac, for a republic of disciplined order; Ledru-Rollin, for somewhat chastened social ideas. What Bonaparte stood for was not so clear. He was, however, elected by an avalanche of votes in December 1848, receiving over 5,400,000, compared to only 1,500,000 for Cavaignac, 370,000 for Ledru-Rollin, and a mere 18,000 for Lamartine.

Bonaparte's background

Thus entered upon the European stage the second Napoleon. Born in 1808, Louis Napoleon Bonaparte was the nephew of the great Napoleon. His father, Louis Bonaparte, was at the time of his birth the king of Holland. When Napoleon's own son died in 1832, Louis Napoleon assumed the headship of the Bonaparte family. He resolved to restore the glories of the empire. With a handful of followers he tried to seize power at Strasbourg in 1836 and at Boulogne in 1840, leading what the following century would know as *Putsches.* Both failed ridiculously. Sentenced to life imprisonment in the fortress of Ham, he had escaped from it as recently as 1846 by simply walking off the grounds dressed as a stonemason. He professed advanced social and political ideas, and he wrote two books. *Napoleonic Ideas* claimed that his famous uncle had been misunderstood and checkmated by reactionary forces; his other book, *Extinction of Poverty,* was a somewhat anticapitalist tract like so many others of its time. But he was no friend of "anarchists," and in the spring of 1848, while still a refugee in England, he enrolled as one of Wellington's special constables to oppose the Chartist agitation. He soon returned to France. Compromised neither by the June Days nor by their repression, he was supposed to be a friend of the common people and at the same time a believer in order; and his name was Napoleon Bonaparte.

For 20 years a groundswell had been stirring the popular mind. It is known as the Napoleonic Legend. Peasants put up pictures of the emperor in their cottages, fondly imagining that it had been Napoleon who gave them the free ownership of their land. The completion of the Arch of Triumph in 1836 drove home the memory of imperial glories, and in 1840 the remains of the emperor were brought from St. Helena and majestically interred at the Invalides on the banks of the Seine. All this happened in a country where, with government in the hands of a few, most people had little political experience or political sense except what they had gained in revolution. When millions were suddenly, for the first time in their lives, asked to vote for a president in 1848, the name of Bonaparte was the only one they had ever heard of. "How should I not vote for this gentleman," said an old peasant, "I whose nose was frozen at Moscow?"

So Prince Louis Napoleon became president of the Second Republic, by an overwhelming popular mandate, in which an army officer was his only even faintly successful rival. He soon saw the way the wind was blowing. The Constituent Assembly dissolved itself in May 1849 and was replaced by the Legislative Assembly. Although this new legislative body was established under the provisions of the new republican constitution and was elected by universal male suffrage, it was a strange assembly for a republic. Five hundred of the Second Republic's newly elected deputies, or two-thirds, were really monarchists, but they were divided into irreconcilable factions—the Legitimists, who favored the line of Charles X, and the Orléanists, who favored that of Louis Philippe. One-third of the deputies called themselves republicans. Of these, in turn, about 180 were socialists of one kind of another; and only about 70 were political or old-fashioned republicans to whom the main issue was the form of government rather than the form of society itself.

President by popular mandate

The president and the Assembly at first combined to conjure away the specter of socialism with which republicanism itself was now clearly associated. An abortive insurrection of June 1849 provided the chance. The Assembly, backed by the president, ousted 33 socialist deputies, suppressed public meetings, and imposed controls on the press. In 1850 it went so far as to rescind universal male suffrage, taking the vote away from about a third of the electorate—naturally the poorest and hence most socialistic third. The Falloux Law of 1850 put the schools at all levels of the education system under supervision of the Catholic clergy; for, as M. Falloux said in the Assembly, "lay teachers have made the principles of social revolution popular in the most distant villages," and it was necessary "to rally around religion to strengthen the foundations of society against those who want to divide up property." The French Republic, now actually an antirepublican government, likewise intervened forcefully against the revolutionary republic that Mazzini had established in the city of Rome. French military forces were sent to Rome to protect the pope; they remained there 20 years.

Antirepublican government

To the conservatives Bonaparte knew that he was virtually indispensable. They were so sharply divided between two sets of monarchists—Legitimist and Orléanist—that each would accept any antisocialist regime rather than yield to the other. Bonaparte's problem was to win over the radicals. He did so by urging in 1851 the restoration of universal suffrage, which he had himself helped repeal in 1850. He now posed as the people's friend, the one man in public life who trusted the common man. He let it be thought that greedy plutocrats controlled the Assembly and hoodwinked France. He put his lieutenants in as ministers of war and of the interior, thus controlling the army, the bureaucracy, and the police. On December 2, 1851, the anniversary of his uncle's famous victory at the battle of Austerlitz, he sprang his coup d'état. Placards appeared all over Paris. They declared the Assembly dissolved and the vote for every adult Frenchman reinstated. When members of the Assembly tried to meet, they were attacked, dispersed, or arrested by the soldiers. The country did not submit without fighting. One hundred and fifty persons were killed in Paris, and throughout France probably 100,000 were put under arrest. But on December 20 the voters elected Louis Napoleon president for a term of 10 years, by a vote officially stated as 7,439,216 to 646,737. A year later the new Bonaparte proclaimed the empire, with himself as Emperor of the French. Remembering Napoleon's son, who had died, he called himself Napoleon III.

How the empire functioned will be seen below. Not only was the Second Republic dead. The republic as republicans understood it, an egalitarian, anticlerical regime with socialist or at least antibourgeois tendencies, had been dead since June 1848. Feeble anyway, it was killed by its reputation for radicalism. Liberalism and constitutionalism were dead also, at least in the political institutions by which the new Napoleon now governed France. Republicans and monarchists were all pushed aside, and for the first time since 1815 France ceased to have any significant parliamentary life.

The demise of parliamentary government

∽ℒ 59.   VIENNA: THE NATIONALIST REVOLUTIONS IN CENTRAL EUROPE AND ITALY

The Austrian Empire in 1848

The Austrian Empire of the Habsburgs, with its capital at Vienna, was in 1848 the most populous European state except Russia. Its peoples, living principally in the three major geographical divisions of the empire (Austria, Bohemia, and Hungary) were of about a dozen recognizably different nationalities or language groups—Germans, Czechs, Magyars, Poles, Ruthenians, Slovaks, Serbs, Croats, Slovenes, Dalmatians, Romanians, and Italians (see map, p. 455). In some parts of the empire the nationalities lived in solid blocks, but in many regions two or more were interlaced together, the language changing from village to village, or even from house to house, in a way quite unknown in western Europe.

Germans were the most numerous national group. They occupied all of Austria proper and considerable parts of Bohemia and were scattered also in small pockets throughout Hungary. The Czechs occupied Bohemia and the adjoining Moravia. The Magyars were the dominant group in the historic kingdom of Hungary, which contained a mixture of nationalities with a considerable number of Slavic peoples. Two of the most advanced parts of Italy

The diversity of the empire

also belonged to the empire—Venetia, with its capital at Venice, and Lombardy, whose chief city was Milan.

The Czechs, Poles, Ruthenians, Slovaks, Serbs, Croats, Slovenes, and Dalmatians in the empire were all Slavs; that is, their languages were all related to one another and to the several forms of Russian. Neither the Magyars nor the Romanians were Slavs. The Magyars, as national sentiment grew, prided themselves on the uniqueness of their language in Europe, and the Romanians prided themselves on their linguistic affiliations with the Latin peoples of the West. Romanians, Magyars, and Germans formed a thick belt separating the South Slavs from those of the north. The peoples of the empire represented every cultural level known to Europe. Vienna, where the Waltz King Johann Strauss was reigning, recognized no peer except Paris itself. Milan was a great center of trade. Bohemia had long had an important textile industry, which was beginning to be mechanized in the 1840s; but 200 miles to the south a Croatian intellectual remarked, about the same time, that the first steam engine he ever saw was in a picture printed on a cotton handkerchief imported from Manchester.

Thus the empire ruled from Vienna included, according to political frontiers established 70 years later, in 1918, all of Austria, Hungary, and Czechoslovakia, with adjoining portions of Poland, Romania, Yugoslavia, and Italy. But the political authority of Vienna reached far beyond the borders of the empire. Austria since 1815 had been the most influential member of the German confederation, for Prussia in these years was content to look with deference upon the Habsburgs. The influence of Vienna was felt throughout Germany in many *Vienna's authority and leadership* ways, as in the enactment and enforcement of Metternich's repressive Carlsbad Decrees described in the last chapter. It reached also through the length of Italy. Lombardy and Venetia were part of the Austrian Empire. Tuscany, ostensibly independent, was governed by a Habsburg grand duke. The kingdom of Naples or the Two Sicilies, comprising all Italy south of Rome, was virtually a protectorate of Vienna. The papal states looked politically to Vienna for leadership, at least until 1846, when the College of Cardinals elected a liberal-minded pope, Pius IX—the one contingency upon which Metternich confessed he had failed to reckon. In all Italy there was only one state ruled by a native Italian dynasty and attempting any consistent independence of policy—the kingdom of Sardinia (called also Savoy or Piedmont) tucked away in the northwest corner around Turin. Italy, said Metternich blandly, was only a "geographical expression," a mere regional name. He might have said the same of Poland, or even of Germany, though Germany was tenuously joined in the Bund, or loose confederation, of 1815.

These peoples since the turn of the century had all felt the flutters of the *Volksgeist*, persistent stirrings of a cultural nationalism; and among Germans, Italians, Poles, and Hungarians a good deal of political agitation and liberal reformism had been at work. Metternich, in Vienna, had discouraged such manifestations for over 30 years, ominously predicting that if allowed to break out they would produce the *bellum omnium contra omnes*—"the war of all against all." As a prophet he was not wholly mistaken, but if it is the business of statesmanship not merely to prophesy events but to control them, it cannot be said that the regime of Metternich was very successful. The whole nationalities question was evaded. The fundamental problem of the century, the bringing of peoples into some kind of mutual relationship with their governments—the problem of which nationalism, liberalism, constitutionalism, and democracy were diverse aspects—remained unconsidered by the responsible authorities of central Europe. Metternich believed that a reigning house, with an official bureaucracy, should rule benevolently over peoples with whom it need have no connection and who need have no connection with each other. Such ideas could be found everywhere among the governing elites in eighteenth-century Europe. They dated from before the French Revolution, and they were best suited to the agricultural, locally oriented societies that by 1848 were giving way to cities, cultural nationalisms, and new commercial institutions.

The March Days

In March 1848 most of the political institutions in central Europe collapsed with incredible swiftness. At that time the diet of Hungary had been sitting for some months, considering constitutional reforms and, as usual, debating further means of keeping German influence out of Hungary. Then came news of the February Revolution in Paris. The radical party in the Hungarian diet was aroused. Its leader, Louis Kossuth, on March 3 made an impassioned speech on the virtues of liberty. This speech was immediately printed in German and read in Vienna, where restlessness was also heightened by the news from Paris. On March 13 workers and students rose in insurrection in Vienna, erected barricades, fought off soldiers, and invaded the imperial palace. So flabbergasted and terrified was the government that Metternich, to the amazement of Europe, resigned and fled in disguise to England.

Metternich's fall

The fall of Metternich proved that the Vienna government was completely disoriented. Revolution swept through the empire and through all Italy and Germany. On March 15 rioting began in Berlin; the king of Prussia promised a constitution. The lesser German governments collapsed in sequence. On the last day of March a pre-Parliament met to arrange the calling of an all-German national assembly. In Hungary, aroused by Kossuth's national party, the diet on March 15 enacted the March Laws, by which Hungary sought complete constitutional separatism within the empire, while still recognizing the Habsburg house. The harassed Emperor Ferdinand a few days later granted substantially the same status to Bohemia. At Milan between March 18 and 22 the populace drove out the Austrian garrison. Venice proclaimed itself an independent republic. Tuscany drove out its grand duke and also established a republic. Charles Albert was king of Sardinia, a kingdom also called Piedmont because its capital Turin and much of its territory apart from the island of Sardinia lay in northwest Italy at the foot of the Alps. Stimulated by events in Paris, Charles Albert had granted a constitution to his small country. He now declared war on Austria on March 23 and invaded Lombardy-Venetia, hoping to bring that area under his house of Savoy. Italian troops streamed up from Tuscany, from Naples (where revolution had broken out as early as January), and even from the papal states (the new pope being in some sympathy with national and liberal aims) to join in an all-Italian war against the seemingly helpless Austrian government.

Thus in the brief span of these phenomenal March Days in 1848 the whole political structure based on Vienna went to pieces. The Austrian Empire had fallen into its main components, Prussia had yielded to revolutionaries, all Germany was preparing to unify itself, and war raged in Italy. Everywhere constitutions had been widely promised by stupefied governments, constitutional assemblies were meeting, and independent or autonomous nations struggled into existence. Patriots everywhere demanded liberal government and national freedom—written constitutions, representative assemblies, responsible ministries, a more or less extended suffrage, restrictions upon police action, jury trial, civil liberty, freedom of press and assembly. And where it still existed—in Prussia, Gali-

The Revolution of 1848 spread rapidly across the European continent, provoking an uprising in Vienna by mid-March. Workers, students, and even soldiers joined together to erect barricades and resist the king's loyal troops. This nineteenth-century image of the Viennese crowd, however, suggests the tensions within a movement that rallied behind a banner for "King, Freedom, and Fatherland."
(Snark/Art Resource, NY)

cia, Bohemia, Hungary—serfdom was declared abolished and the peasant masses became legally free from control by their local lords.

The Turning of the Tide after June

The revolution, as in France, surged forward until the month of June and then began to ebb. For its steady reflux there are many reasons. The old governments had been stunned in the March Days, but not really broken. They merely awaited the opportunity to take back promises extorted by force. The pressure originally imposed by the revolutionaries could not be sustained. The revolutionary leaders lacked a strong social base. Middle-class, bourgeois, property-owning, and commercial interests were nowhere nearly as highly developed as in western Europe. The revolutionary leaders were to a large extent writers, editors, professors, and students—intellectuals rather than the representatives of powerful social and economic interests. In Vienna, Milan, and a few other cities the working class was numerous and socialist ideas were fairly common, but the workers were not as literate, organized, or politically conscious as in Paris or Great Britain. They were strong enough, however, to disquiet the middle classes; and especially after the specter of social revolution rose over western Europe, the middle-class and lower-class revolutionaries began to be afraid of each other. The liberated nationalities also began to disagree. The peasants, once emancipated, had no further interest in revolution. Nor were the peasants at this time conscious of nationality; nationalism was primarily a doctrine of the educated

EUROPEAN REVOLUTIONS, 1848

The map shows cities in which notable revolutionary upheavals occurred during 1848. Although opponents of the revolutionary agitation suspected an international conspiracy, the revolutions erupted more or less spontaneously as urban populations took to the streets with demands for constitutional government, national independence, or new civil rights. It should be noted that the revolutions of 1848 took place mainly in central and eastern Europe—a pattern that suggests the spreading influence of ideas that had appeared earlier in the American and French revolutions. But the failure of these revolutions led to a resurgence of conservatism and delayed or prevented the development of liberal, constitutional governments in most of central and eastern Europe.

middle classes or of the aristocratic landowning classes in Poland and Hungary. Since the old internationally minded aristocracy furnished the bulk of officers in the armies, and the peasants the bulk of the soldiers, the armies remained almost immune to nationalist aspirations. This attitude of the armies was decisive.

The tide first turned in Prague. The all-German national assembly met at Frankfurt in May. Representatives from Bohemia had been invited to come to Frankfurt, since many Germans had always lived in Bohemia and since Bohemia formed part of the confederation of 1815 as it had of the Holy Roman Empire before it. Many of the Germans in Bohemia, the Sudeten Germans, were attracted to the Frankfurt Assembly, but the idea of belonging to a national German state, a Germany based on the principle that the inhabitants embodied a German nationality, did not appeal to the Czechs in Bohemia. They refused to go to the all-German congress at Frankfurt. Instead, they called an all-Slav

The first Pan-Slav assembly

congress of their own. At Prague, in June 1848, this first Pan-Slav assembly met. Most of the delegates were from Slav communities within the Austrian Empire, but a few came from the Balkans and non-Austrian Poland.

The spirit of the Prague congress was that of the Slavic Revival described in the last chapter; the Czech historian Palacky was in fact one of its most active figures. The congress was profoundly anti-German, since the essence of the Slavic Revival was resistance to Germanization. But it was not profoundly anti-Austrian or anti-Habsburg. A few extremists, indeed, maintained that Slavdom should be the basis of political regeneration, and that the world therefore had no place for an Austrian Empire. But the great majority at the Prague congress were Austroslavs who held that the many Slavic peoples, pressed on two sides by the Russians and Germans, needed the Austrian Empire as a political frame within which to develop their own national life. It demanded that the Slavic peoples be admitted as equals with the other nationalities in the Austrian Empire, enjoying local autonomy and constitutional guarantees.

Victories of the Counterrevolution, June–December, 1848

But the Emperor Ferdinand, and the advisers on whom he chose to rely, would have nothing to do with the liberal national movements or with the restrictions they wanted to impose upon the powers of the state. All therefore were to be resisted. The first victory of the old government came at Prague. In that city a Czech insurrection broke out on June 12, at the time when the Slav congress was sitting, and the conflict was made worse by local animosities between Czechs and Germans. Windischgrätz, the local army commander, bombarded and subdued the city, thereby reasserting Habsburg military control. The Slav congress dispersed.

The next victory of the counterrevolution came in north Italy in the following month. Only Lombardy-Venetia, of all parts of the empire, had declared independence from the Habsburgs during the upheavals of March. The diminutive kingdom of Sardinia had lent support and had declared war on Austria. Italians from all over the peninsula had flocked in to fight; and until after the June Days in Paris it even seemed possible that republican France might intervene to befriend fellow revolutionaries as in 1796. But in France no radical or expansionist revolution succeeded. The Italians were left to themselves. Radetsky, the Austrian commander in Italy, overwhelmingly defeated the king of Sardinia at Custozza on July 25. The Sardinian king, Charles Albert, retreated into his own country. Lombardy and Venetia were restored with savage vengeance to the Austrian Empire.

The Italians defeated

The third victory of the counterrevolution came in September and October. The Hungarian radical party of Louis Kossuth was liberal and even democratic in many of its principles, but it was a Magyar nationalist party above all else. Triumphant in the March Days, it completely shook off the German connection. It moved the capital from Pressburg near the Austrian border to Budapest in the center of Hungary. It changed the official language of Hungary from Latin to Magyar. Less than half the people of Hungary were Magyars, and Magyar is a difficult language, quite alien to the Indo-European tongues of Europe. It soon became clear that one must be a Magyar to benefit from the new liberal constitution and that the Magyars intended to repress the national ambitions of all others with whom they shared the country. Slovaks, Romanians, Germans, Serbs, and Croats violently resisted, each group determined to keep its national identity unimpaired. The Croats, who had enjoyed certain liberties before the Magyar revolution, took the lead under Count Jellachich, the "ban," or provincial governor, of Croatia. In September Jellachich raised a civil war in Hungary, leading a force of Serbo-Croatians, supported by the whole non-Magyar half of the population. Half of Hungary, alarmed by Magyar nationalism, now

Magyar nationalism

looked to the Habsburgs and the empire to protect them. Emperor Ferdinand made Jellachich his military commander against the Magyars. Hungary dissolved into the war of all against all.

At Vienna the more clear-sighted revolutionaries, who had led the March rising, now saw that Jellachich's army, if successful against the Magyars, would soon be turned against them. They therefore rose in a second mass insurrection in October 1848. The emperor fled; never had the Viennese revolution gone so far. But it was already too late. The Austrian military leader Windischgrätz brought his intact forces down from Bohemia. He besieged Vienna for five days and forced its surrender on October 31.

Vienna recaptured

With the recapture of Vienna the upholders of the old order took heart. Counterrevolutionary leaders—large estate holders, Catholic clergy, high-ranking army men—decided to clear the way by getting rid of the Emperor Ferdinand, considering that promises made in March by Ferdinand might be more easily repudiated by his successor. Ferdinand abdicated and on December 2, 1848, was succeeded by Francis Joseph, a boy of 18, destined to live until 1916 and to end his reign in a crisis even more shattering than that in which he began it.

Final Outburst and Repression, 1849

For a time in the first part of 1849 the revolution in many places seemed to blaze more fiercely than ever. Republican riots broke out in parts of Germany. In Rome someone assassinated the reforming minister of Pius IX. The pope fled from the city, and a radical Roman Republic was proclaimed under three Triumvirs, one of whom was Mazzini, who hastened from England to take part in the republican upheaval. In north Italy Charles Albert of Sardinia again invaded Lombardy. In Hungary, after the revived Habsburg authorities repudiated the new Magyar constitution, the Magyars, led by the inflamed Kossuth, went on to declare absolute independence. But all these manifestations proved short-lived. German republicanism flickered out. A French army drove Mazzini and his republican allies from Rome, thereby restoring Pope Pius IX to his traditional powers. The Sardinian king was again defeated by an Austrian army, but in Hungary the Magyars put up a terrific resistance, which Austria's imperial army and the anti-Magyar native irregulars could not overcome. The Habsburg authorities now renewed the procedures of the Holy Alliance. The new Emperor Francis Joseph invited the Tsar Nicholas to intervene. In August 1849 over 100,000 Russian troops poured over the mountains into Hungary, defeated the Magyars, and laid the prostrate country at the feet of the court of Vienna.

The nationalist upheaval of 1848 in central Europe and Italy was now over. The Habsburgs had reasserted their imperial authority over Czech nationalists in Prague, Magyars in Hungary, Italian patriots in north Italy, and liberal revolutionists in Vienna itself. Reaction, or antirevolutionism, became the order of the day. Pius IX, the "liberal pope" of 1846, returned to the papal throne and rejected all of his earlier liberal ideas. The breach between liberalism and Roman Catholicism, which had opened wide in the first French Revolution, was made a yawning chasm by the revolutionary violence of Mazzini's Roman Republic and by the measures taken to repress it. Pius IX now reiterated the anathemas of his predecessors. He codified them in 1864 in the *Syllabus of Errors,* which warned all Catholics, on the authority of the Vatican, against everything that went under the names of liberalism, progress, and modern civilization. As for the nationalists in Italy, many were disillu-

Antirevolutionism

Joseph Mazzini (1805–1872) led the short-lived Republic in Rome during the Italian upheavals of 1849, but his new regime was soon suppressed by foreign powers and he retreated to the life of an exile in England. Although Mazzini's Romantic nationalism lost favor in Italy after about 1850, his writings and political activities gave him a prominent place in the intellectual life of London, where this photograph was taken in the early 1860s.
(The Granger Collection, New York)

sioned with the firecracker methods of romantic republicans and were inclined to conclude that Italy would be liberated from Austrian influence only by an old-fashioned war between established powers.

In the Austrian Empire, under Prince Schwarzenberg, the emperor's chief minister, the main policy was now to oppose all forms of popular self-expression with a more candid reliance on military force. Constitutionalism was to be rooted out, as well as all forms of nationalism—Slavism, Magyarism, Italianism, and also Germanism, which would draw the Austrian Germans away from the Habsburg empire to the great kindred body of the German people. The regime came to be called the Bach system, after Alexander Bach, the minister of the interior. Under it, the government was rigidly centralized. Hungary lost the separate rights it had held before 1848. *The Bach system* The ideal was to create a perfectly solid and unitary political system. Bach insisted on maintaining the emancipation of the peasants, which had converted the mass of the people from subjects of their landlords into subjects of the state. He drove through a reform of the legal system and law courts, created a free trading area of the whole empire with only a common external tariff, and subsidized and encouraged the building of highways and railroads. The aim, as in France at the same time under Louis Napoleon, was to make people forget liberty in an overwhelming demonstration of administrative efficiency and material progress. But some, at that time, would not forget. A liberal said of the Bach system that it consisted of "a standing army of soldiers, a sitting army of officials, a kneeling army of priests, and a creeping army of informers."

60.   FRANKFURT AND BERLIN: THE QUESTION OF A LIBERAL GERMANY

The German States

Meanwhile, from May 1848 to May 1849, the Frankfurt Assembly was sitting at the historic city on the Main. It was attempting to bring a unified German state into being, one which should also be liberal and constitutional, assuring civil rights to its citizens and possessing a government responsive to popular will as manifested in free elections and open parliamentary debate. The mid-nineteenth-century failure to produce a democratic Germany became one of the overshadowing facts of modern times.

The convocation of the Frankfurt Assembly was made possible by the collapse of the existing German governments in the March Days of 1848. These governments, the 39 states recognized after the Congress of Vienna, enjoyed their political independence and formed the main obstacles in the way of unification. The German states resisted the surrender of sovereignty to a united Germany just as national states in later eras were to resist the surrender of sovereignty to a United Nations. In another way the German world was a miniature of the wider political world. It consisted of both great and small powers. Its great powers were Prussia and Austria. Austria was the miscellaneous empire described earlier. Prussia after 1815 included the Rhineland, the central regions around Berlin, West Prussia and Posen (acquired in the partitions of Poland), and historic East Prussia. The former Polish areas were inhabited by a mixture of Germans and Poles. Neither of these great powers could submit to the other or allow the other to dominate its lesser German neighbors.

Obstacles to unification

This German "dualism," or polarity between Berlin and Vienna, had become somewhat less intense under the common menace of the Napoleonic empire. The whole German question had lain dormant so far as the governments were concerned, nor did it agitate the old aristocracies. In Prussia the Junkers, the owners of great landed estates east of the Elbe, were singularly indifferent to the all-German dream. Their political feeling was not German but Prussian. They were satisfied with their dominant position in Prussia and could expect only to lose by absorption into Germany as a whole, for in Germany west of the Elbe the small peasant holding was the basis of society, and there was no landowning element corresponding to the Junkers. The rest of Germany looked upon Prussia as somewhat uncouth and eastern; but this feeling, too, had diminished in the time of Napoleon, when patriots from all over Germany enlisted in the Prussian service.

German dualism

Berlin: Failure of the Revolution in Prussia

Prussia was illiberal but not backward. Frederick William III repeatedly evaded his promise to grant a modern constitution. His successor, Frederick William IV, who inherited the throne in 1840 and from whom much was at first expected by liberals, was equally determined not to share his authority with his subjects. At the same time the government, administratively speaking, was efficient, progressive, and fair. The universities and elementary school system surpassed those of western Europe. Literacy was higher than in England or France. The government followed in mercantilist traditions of evoking, planning, and supporting economic life. In 1818 it initiated a tariff union, at first with tiny states (or enclaves) wholly enclosed within Prussia. This tariff union, or *Zollverein,* was extended in the following decades to include almost all Germany.

On March 15, 1848, the rioting and street fighting that we have noted broke out in Berlin. For a time it seemed as if the army would master the situation. But the erratically conscientious king, Frederick William IV, called off the soldiers and allowed his subjects to elect the first all-Prussian legislative assembly. Thus though the army remained intact, and its Junker officers remained unconvinced, revolution proceeded superficially on its way. The new Prussian Assembly proved surprisingly radical, since it was dominated by anti-Junker lower-class extremists from East Prussia. These men were supporting Polish revolutionaries and exiles who sought the restoration of Polish freedom. Their main belief was that the fortress of reaction was tsarist Russia—that the whole structure of Junkerdom, landlordism, serf-owning, and repression of national freedom depended ultimately on the armed might of the tsarist empire. (The subsequent intervention of Russia in Hungary indicated the truth of their diagnosis.) Prussian radicals, like many elsewhere, hoped to smash the old Holy Alliance by raising an all-German or even European revolutionary war against Russia, to precipitate which they supported the claims of the Poles.

Radical assemblies

Meanwhile the radical-dominated Berlin Assembly granted local self-government to the Poles of West Prussia and Posen. But in those areas Germans and Slavs had long lived side by side. The Germans in Posen now refused to respect the authority of Polish officials. Prussian army units stationed in Posen supported the German element. As early as April 1848, a month after the "revolution," the army crushed the new pro-Polish institutions set up in Posen by the Berlin Assembly. It was clear where the only real power lay. By the end of 1848, in Prussia as in Austria, the revolution was over. The king again changed his mind; and the old authorities, acting through the army, were again in control.

The Frankfurt Assembly

Meanwhile a similar story was enacted on the larger stage of Germany as a whole. The disabling of the old governments left a power vacuum. A self-appointed committee convoked a preliminary parliament, which in turn arranged for the election of an all-German assembly. Bypassing the existing sovereignties, voters throughout Germany sent delegates to Frankfurt to create a federated superstate. The strength and weakness of the resulting Frankfurt Assembly originated in the manner in which it was elected. The Assembly represented the moral sentiment of people at large, the liberal and national aspirations of many Germans. It stood for an idea. Politically it represented nothing. The delegates had no power to issue orders or expect compliance. Superficially resembling the National Assembly which met in France in 1789, the German National Assembly at Frankfurt was really in a very different position. There was no preexisting national structure for it to work with. There was no all-German army or civil service for the Assembly to take over. The Frankfurt Assembly, having no power of its own, became dependent on the power of the very sovereign states that it was attempting to supersede.

The Assembly met in May 1848. Its members with a handful of exceptions were not at all revolutionary. They were overwhelmingly professional people—professors, judges, lawyers, government administrators, clergy both Protestant and Catholic, and prominent businessmen. They wanted a liberal, self-governing, federally unified, and "democratic" though not egalitarian Germany. Their outlook was earnest, peaceable, and legalistic; they hoped to succeed by persuasion. Violence was abhorrent to them. The example of the June Days in Paris, and the Chartist agitation in Great Britain, coinciding with the early weeks of the Frankfurt Assembly, increased the dread of that body for radicalism and republicanism in Germany. The fate of Germany (and hence of Europe) lay in the fact that this German revolution came at a time when social revolutionaries had already begun to declare war on the bourgeoisie and the bourgeoisie was already afraid of the lower classes. It was the worker or artisan, not the professor or respectable merchant, who in unsettled times had actually seized firearms and shouted revolutionary utterances in the streets. Without lower-class insurrection not even middle-class revolutions have been successful.

An untimely revolution

The combination effected in France between 1789 and 1794, an unwilling and divergent combination of bourgeois and lower-class revolutionaries, could not be effected in Germany in 1848. One form of revolutionary power—controlled popular turbulence—the Germans of the Frankfurt Assembly would not or could not use. Quite the contrary: when radical riots broke out in Frankfurt itself in September 1848, the Assembly undertook to repress them. Having no force of its own, it appealed to the Prussian army. The Prussian army put down the riots, and thereafter the Assembly met under its protection.

Questions of territory

But the most troublesome question facing the Frankfurt Assembly was not social but national. What, after all, was this "Germany" which so far existed only in the mind? The assembly at Frankfurt, eager to create a real Germany, naturally could not propose a German state that would be smaller than the shadow Germany that they so much deplored. Most members of the Assembly were therefore Great Germans; they thought that the Germany for which they were writing a constitution should include the Austrian lands, except Hungary. This would mean that the federal crown must be offered to the Habsburgs. Others, at first a minority, were Little Germans; they thought that Austria should be excluded and that the new Germany should comprise the smaller states and the entire kingdom of Prussia. In that case the king of Prussia would become the federal emperor.

Dependence on Austrian and Prussian armies

The desire of the Frankfurt Assembly to retain non-German peoples in the new Germany, at a time when these peoples also were feeling national ambitions, was another reason for its fatal dependency upon the Austrian and Prussian armies. The Frankfurt Assembly applauded when Windischgrätz broke the Czech revolution and when Prussian forces put down the Poles in Posen. On this matter the National Assembly at Frankfurt and the Prussian Assembly at Berlin did not agree. The men of Frankfurt, thinking the Prussian revolutionary assembly was too radical and pro-Polish, in effect supported the Prussian army and the Junkers against the Berlin revolution, without which the Frankfurt Assembly itself could never have existed. The Assembly, in short, turned against the revolutionary movement in Berlin and lost its earlier base of popular support. When radical riots later broke out against the Junkers, the tsar, and the Frankfurt Assembly itself, the Assembly acknowledged its weak and vulnerable position by calling in Prussian forces for its own protection.

The Failure of the Frankfurt Assembly

By the end of 1848 the debacle was approaching. The nationalists had checkmated each other. Everywhere in central Europe, from Denmark to Naples and from the Rhineland to Romania, the awakening nationalities had failed to respect each other's aspirations, had delighted in each other's defeats, and by quarreling with each other had hastened the return of the old absolutist and nonnational order. At Berlin and at Vienna the counterrevolution, backed by the army, was in the saddle. At this very time, in December, the Frankfurt Assembly at last issued a Declaration of the Rights of the German People. It was a humane and high-minded document, announcing numerous individual rights, civil liber-

The Frankfurt Assembly that convened in May 1848 (as depicted in this nineteenth-century illustration) consisted mostly of professional people who feared the working classes almost as much as or more than they feared the political powers of kings and Prussian aristocrats. The members of the Assembly wrote a constitution and sought to create a constitutional monarchy for all Germany outside Austria. But the Prussian king would not accept this kind of constitutional appointment to royal power and the Frankfurt Assembly's national, democratic aspirations were destroyed when the Assembly was dissolved in 1849.

(akg-images)

ties, and constitutional guarantees, much along the line of the French and American declarations of the eighteenth century, but with one significant difference—the French and Americans spoke of the rights of man, while even the liberal Germans spoke of the rights of Germans. In April 1849 the Frankfurt Assembly completed its constitution. It was now clear that Austria must be excluded, for the simple reason that the restored Habsburg government refused to come in. The Little Germans in the Assembly therefore had their way. The hereditary headship of a new German empire, a constitutional and federal union of German states minus Austria, was now offered to Frederick William IV, the king of Prussia.

Frederick William was tempted. The Prussian army officers and East Elbian landlords were not. They had no wish to lose Prussia in Germany. The king himself had his scruples.

Frederick William tempted

If he took the proffered crown, he would still have to impose himself by force on the lesser states, which the Frankfurt Assembly did not represent and could not bind and which were in fact still the actual powers in the country. He could also expect trouble with Austria. He did not want war.

Nor was it proper for an heir to the Hohenzollerns to accept a throne circumscribed with constitutional limitations and representing the revolutionary conception of the sovereignty of the people. Declaring that he could not "pick up a crown from the gutter," he turned it down. It would have to be offered freely by his equals, the sovereign princes of Germany.

The failure of liberal nationalism

Thus all the work of the Frankfurt Assembly went for nothing. Most members of the Assembly, having never dreamed of using violence in the first place, concluded that they were beaten and went home. A handful of extremists remained at Frankfurt, promulgated the constitution on their own authority, urged revolutionary outbreaks, and called for elections. Riots broke out in various places. The Prussian army put them down—in Saxony, in Bavaria, in Baden. The same army drove the rump Assembly out of Frankfurt, and that was the end of it.

In summary, liberal nationalism failed to produce a unified constitutional German state in 1848, and a less liberal kind of nationalism soon replaced it. The weakness and failures of German liberalism in 1848–1849 in the long run contributed to a complex estrangement between Germany and western Europe. The failed revolutions of 1848 also pushed thousands of disappointed German liberals and revolutionaries toward the United States, where the stream of liberal immigrants came to be known as the "forty-eighters."

In Prussia itself the ingenious monarch undertook to placate everybody by issuing a constitution of his own, one that should be peculiarly Prussian. It remained in effect from 1850 to 1918. The Constitution established a single parliament for all the miscellaneous regions of Prussia and divided the parliament into two chambers. The lower chamber was elected by universal male suffrage, but the system of elections in effect divided the population into three estates—the wealthy, the less wealthy, and the general run of the people. Those few big taxpayers who together contributed a third of the tax returns chose a third of the members of district electoral colleges, which in turn chose deputies to the Prussian lower house. In this way one large property owner had as much voting power as hundreds of working people. Large property in Prussia in 1850 still meant mainly the landed estates of the East Elbian Junkers, but as time went on, it came to include industrial property in the Rhineland also. The Junkers likewise were not harmed by the final liquidation of serfdom. They increased the acreage of their holdings, and the former servile agricultural workers turned into free wage earners economically dependent on the great landowners.

The Prussian Constitution of 1850

For 1850 the Prussian constitution was fairly progressive. If the mass of the people could elect very few deputies under the indirect system described, the mass of the British people, until 1867 or even 1884, could elect no deputies to Parliament at all. But the Prussian constitution remained in force until 1918. By the close of the nineteenth century, with democratic advances making their appearance elsewhere, the electoral system in Prussia came to be reactionary and illiberal, giving the great landowners and industrialists an unusual position of special privilege within the state.

CHRONOLOGY OF NOTABLE EVENTS, 1848–1857

January 1848	Marx and Engels publish the *Communist Manifesto*
February 1848	Revolution in Paris; proclamation of the Second French Republic
March 1848	Revolutions in Vienna, Berlin, Bohemia, and Hungary; Metternich flees from Vienna to England
March 1848	Italians rise against Austrian rule in northern Italy
March–April 1848	Prussian Legislative Assembly meets in Berlin
May 1848	All-German Frankfurt Assembly convenes to draft constitution for a unified German state
June 1848	Thousands die in worker-army clashes in Paris
June–December 1848	Counterrevolutionary forces regain control of Austrian empire: Bohemia, northern Italy, Hungary, Vienna
December 1848	Louis Napoleon Bonaparte is elected president of French Republic; Francis Joseph becomes emperor of Austrian empire
April 1849	King Frederick William IV of Prussia rejects Frankfurt Assembly's constitution and offer of hereditary rule in a federal German state; Frankfurt Assembly is dissolved
1852	Louis Napoleon Bonaparte becomes "Emperor Napoleon III" and establishes Second French Empire
1853–1870	Baron Haussmann supervises the modern rebuilding of Paris
1857	Gustave Flaubert publishes *Madame Bovary*

61. THE NEW EUROPEAN "ISMS": REALISM, POSITIVISM, MARXISM

The revolutions of 1848 failed not only in Germany but also in Hungary, Italy, and France. The "springtime of peoples," as it was called, was followed by chilling blasts of winter. The dreams of half a century, visions of a humane nationalism, aspirations for liberalism without violence, ideals of a peaceful and democratic republican commonwealth, were all exploded. Everywhere the cry had been for constitutional government, but only in a few small states—Denmark, Holland, Belgium, Switzerland, Piedmont—was constitutional liberty more firmly secured by the revolutions of 1848. Everywhere the cry had been for the freedom of nations, to unify national groups or rid them of foreign rule; but nowhere was national liberty more advanced in 1850 than it had been two years before. France obtained universal male suffrage in 1848 and kept it permanently thereafter (except for a brief reversion to a restricted suffrage in 1850–1851), but it did not obtain democracy; it obtained a kind of popular dictatorship under Louis Napoleon Bonaparte. One accomplishment, however, was real enough. The peasantry was emancipated in the German states and the Austrian Empire. Serfdom and manorial restraints were abolished, nor were they reimposed after the failure of the revolutions. This was the most fundamental accomplishment of the whole movement. The peasant masses of central Europe were thereafter free to move about, find new jobs, enter a labor market, take part in a money economy, receive and spend

New freedoms for peasants

wages, migrate to growing cities—or even go to the United States. But the peasants, once freed, showed little concern for constitutional or bourgeois ideas. Peasant emancipation, in fact, strengthened the forces of political counterrevolution.

The most immediate and far-reaching consequence of the 1848 revolutions, or of their failure, was a new kind of intellectual and political realism. Idealism and romanticism were discredited in European culture and politics. Revolutionaries became less optimistic; conservatives, more willing to exercise repression. It was now a point of pride to be realistic, emancipated from illusions, willing to face facts as they were. The future, it was thought, would be determined by present realities rather than by imaginings of what ought to be. Industrialization went forward, with England still far in the lead, but now spreading across the Continent and initiating the momentous transformation of Germany. The 1850s were a period of rising prices and wages, thanks in part to the gold rush in California. There was more prosperity than in the 1840s; the propertied classes felt secure, and spokesmen for labor turned from theories of society to the organizing of viable unions, especially in the skilled trades.

Materialism, Realism, Positivism

In basic philosophy the new intellectual themes appeared as materialism, holding that everything mental, spiritual, or ideal was an outgrowth of physical or physiological forces. In literature and the arts it was called realism. Writers and painters broke away from romanticism, which they said colored things out of all relation to the real facts. They attempted to describe and reproduce life as they found it, without intimation of a better or nobler world. The French writer Gustave Flaubert, for example, wrote meticulous descriptions of a provincial woman's tedious, unhappy marriage in his famous novel *Madame Bovary* (1857), a book that both mocked the illusions of romantic literature and showed the new artistic desire for a precise, unsentimental literary language. More people came to trust science, not merely for an understanding of nature but for insights into the true meaning of human life and social relations. In religion the movement was toward skepticism, renewing skeptical trends of the eighteenth century, which had been somewhat interrupted during the intervening period of romanticism. It was variously held, not by all but by many, that religion was unscientific and hence not to be taken seriously; or that it was a mere historical growth among peoples in certain stages of development and hence irrelevant to modern civilization; or that one ought to go to church and lead a decent life, without taking the priest or clergyman too seriously, because religion was necessary to preserve the social order against radicalism and anarchy. To this idea the radical counterpart was of course that religion was a bourgeois invention to delude the people.

Auguste Comte

"Positivism" was another term used to describe the new attitude. It originated with the French philosopher Auguste Comte, who had begun to publish his numerous volumes on *Positive Philosophy* as long ago as 1830 and was still writing in the 1850s. He saw human history as a series of three stages, the theological, the metaphysical, and the scientific. The French revolutions of 1789 and 1848 suffered, in his view, from an excess of metaphysical abstractions, empty words, and unverifiable high-flying principles. Those who worked for the improvement of society must adopt a strictly scientific outlook, and Comte produced an elaborate classification of the sciences, of which the highest would be the science of society, for which he coined the word "sociology." This new science would build upon observation of actual "positive" facts to develop broad scientific laws of social progress. Comte himself, and his closest disciples, envisaged a final scientific Religion of Humanity, which, stripped of archaic theological and metaphysical concerns, would serve as the basis for a better world of the future. More generally, however, positivism came to mean an insistence on verifiable facts, an avoidance of wishful thinking, a questioning of all assumptions, and a dislike of unprovable generalizations. Positivism in a broad sense, both in its demand for observation of facts and testing of ideas, and in its aspiration to be humanly useful, contributed to the growth of the social sciences as a branch of learning.

In politics the new emphasis on realism came to be known by the German term *Realpolitik*. This simply meant a "politics of reality." In domestic affairs it meant that people should give up utopian dreams, such as had caused the debacle of 1848, and content themselves with the blessings of an orderly, honest, hard-working government. For radicals it meant that people should stop imagining that the new society would result from goodness or the love of justice and that social reformers must resort to the methods of politics—power and calculation. In international affairs *Realpolitik* meant that governments should not be guided by ideology, or by any system of "natural" enemies or "natural" allies, or by any desire to defend or promote any particular view of the world; but that they should follow their own practical or strategic interests, meet facts and situations as they arose, make any alliances that seemed useful, disregard ethical theories and scruples, and use any practical means to achieve their ends. The same persons who before 1848 had been not ashamed to express pacifist and cosmopolitan hopes now dismissed such ideas as a little softheaded. War, which governments since the overthrow of Napoleon had successfully tried to prevent, was accepted in the 1850s as a strategic option that was sometimes needed to achieve a political purpose. It was not especially glorious; it was not an end in itself; it was simply one of the tools of realistic statesmanship. *Realpolitik* was by no means confined to Germany, despite its German name and despite the fact that the famous German chancellor Bismarck became its most famous practitioner. Two other tough-minded thinkers, each in his own way, were Karl Marx and Louis Napoleon Bonaparte.

| Realpolitik |

Early Marxism

Karl Marx and Friedrich Engels were among the disappointed revolutionaries of 1848. Marx (1818–1883) was the son of a lawyer in the Prussian Rhineland. He studied law and philosophy at several German universities and received a doctoral degree in 1841. Unable to find an academic job, Marx associated with radical German intellectuals, began writing for left-wing journals, and soon moved to Paris with other Germans who wanted to produce philosophical publications in the historic birthplace of modern revolutions. Engels (1820–1893), the son of a well-to-do German textile manufacturer, was sent as a young man to Manchester in England where his father owned a factory, to learn the business and then manage it. Marx and Engels met in Paris in 1844. There they began a collaboration in thinking and writing that lasted for 40 years.

In 1847 they joined the Communist League, a tiny secret group of revolutionaries, mainly Germans in exile in the more liberal cities of Western Europe. The word "communist" then had only a vague and uncertain meaning, and the League, as Engels later recalled, was at first "not actually much more than the German branch of the French secret societies." It agitated like other societies during the revolutions of 1848 and issued a set of "Demands of the Communist Party in Germany," which urged a unified indivisible German republic; democratic suffrage;

| The Communist League |

A BURIAL AT ORNANS
by Gustave Courbet (French, 1819–1877)
A new "realism" emerged in many spheres of European culture after the failure of the revolutions in 1848. The artist Courbet in fact began to use the term "realism" in this period to describe his work, which frequently depicted ordinary people and peasants on monumental canvasses. Paintings such as this portrayal of a funeral in the French countryside disturbed many nineteenth-century critics because Courbet painted images of the lower classes and also because he refused to romanticize his subjects or to portray common people in sentimental poses.
(Giraudon/Art Resource, NY)

universal free education; arming of the people; a progressive income tax; limitations upon inheritance; state ownership of banks, railroads, canals, mines, and the like; and a degree of large-scale, scientific, collectivized agriculture. It was such obscurely voiced radicalism that alarmed the Frankfurt Assembly. With the triumph of counterrevolution in Germany the Communist League was crushed.

It was for this League that Marx and Engels wrote their *Communist Manifesto,* which was published in January 1848. But there was as yet no Marxism, and Marxism played no role in the revolutions of 1848. As a historical force Marxism set in during the 1870s. Meanwhile, with the failure of the revolutions, Engels returned to his factory at Manchester. Marx also settled in England, spending the rest of his life in London, where, after long labors in the library of the British Museum, he finally produced his huge work called *Capital,* of which the first volume was published in German in 1867. The final two volumes were edited by Engels and published after Marx's death.

Sources and Content of Marxism

Marxism may be said to have had three sources or to have merged three national streams of early nineteenth-century European history: German philosophy, French revolutionism, and the British Industrial Revolution. As a student in Germany, and for a while thereafter, Marx mingled with a group known as Young Hegelians, who were actually critics of Hegel in that they expected the

The Young Hegelians

Workers in Manchester came to be known as some of the most impoverished in the new industrial age, partly because writers such as Friedrich Engels focused on the city in their critiques of the capitalist economy. This image of a demoralized worker was published in Elizabeth Gaskell's novel *Mary Barton* (1848), a popular work that portrayed the miseries of the heroine's unhappy working-class father in Manchester.
(Lebrecht/The Image Works)

course of history to lead to a free and democratic society, instead of to the existing Prussian state as Hegel had maintained. They joined with liberals in resisting the repressive measures that prevailed in Germany after the defeat of Napoleon. Like democrats and republicans, they believed that the promise of the French Revolution had not yet been fulfilled, since social and economic equality should follow the civil and legal equality already won. In keeping with the general movement of romanticism, they hoped for a more personal emancipation from the trammels of society, government, and religion.

In the mid 1840s, elaborating on Hegel, Marx developed the idea of the alienation of labor, a social experience and state of mind produced when human beings in the historic process of mechanization become estranged from the objects on which they work. This alienation, as Marx described it, was a distinctive feature of modern capitalist societies. The economic system of wage labor and private ownership of the means of production kept workers from identifying with or benefiting from the products of their labor. In fact, Marx argued, the wealth (or capital) that workers produced was regularly used against them in the social and political institutions of capitalist societies. It followed that true freedom would become possible only when private property in capital goods was abolished. Some of the early writings in which these ideas were worked out in the 1840s were not published until a century later. They then led to a reconsideration of Marxism, in which the early Marx was seen more as a social analyst and critical historian than as a revolutionary.

Engels and British industrialism

But they had little impact on the growth of Marxism as a program for revolutionary socialism in the nineteenth century.

Engels, engaged in the Manchester cotton industry, possessed a personal knowledge of the new industrial and factory system in England. He was in touch with some of the most radical Chartists, though he had no confidence in Chartism as a constructive movement. In 1844 he published a revealing book, *The Condition of the Working Classes in England*. He drew from his observations much the same conclusions that Marx drew from philosophical analysis and historical study. The depressed condition of labor was an actual fact. It was a fact that labor received a relatively small portion of the national income and that much of the product of society was being reinvested in capital goods, which belonged as private property to private persons. Government and parliamentary institutions, also as a matter of fact, were in the hands of the well-to-do in both Great Britain and France. Religion was commonly viewed as necessary for keeping the lower classes in order, but such views did not encourage the kinds of reform movements that religious groups had often led in other centuries and in other cultures. The churches at the time actually took little interest in problems of the workers. The family, as an institution, was indeed disintegrating among laboring people in the cities, through exploitation of women and children and the overcrowding in inadequate and unsanitary living quarters.

Much of this was seized upon and dramatized in the *Communist Manifesto* as a summons to revolution. The outbreak of revolution in France in February, and its rapid spread to other countries, naturally confirmed Marx and Engels in their beliefs. They interpreted the actual class war that shook Paris in the June Days as a manifestation of a universal class struggle, in which the workers or proletariat would rise against the owners of capital, the bourgeoisie.

The Communist Manifesto

As a call to action, the *Communist Manifesto* was meant to be inflammatory. It went beyond facts to denunciation and exhortation. It said that workers were deprived of the wealth they had themselves created. It called the state a committee of the bourgeoisie for the exploitation of the people. Religion was a drug to keep the worker quietly dreaming upon imaginary heavenly rewards. The women and children in working-class families had been brutalized by the bourgeoisie, and many women were forced into prostitution. It seemed to Marx and Engels that uprooted workers should be loyal to nothing—except their own class. Even country had become meaningless. The proletarian had no country. Workers everywhere had the same problems and faced everywhere the same enemy. Therefore "let the ruling classes tremble at a communist revolution. The proletarians have nothing to lose but their chains. They have a world to win. Workingmen of all countries, unite!" So closed the *Manifesto*.

But Marx was no mere revolutionary schemer like the "revolution-makers," as he later scornfully called them. His mature thought was a system for producing revolution, but it showed how revolution would necessarily come by operation of vast historical forces.

British political economy

It was from English sources that Marx developed much of his economic theory, as expounded at length in *Capital*. From British political economy he adopted the subsistence theory of wages, or Iron Law (which orthodox economists presently abandoned since wages did in fact begin to rise). It held that the average worker could never obtain more than a minimum living standard—of which the corollary, for those who wished to draw it, was that the existing economic system held out no better future for the laboring class as a class. Marx likewise took over from orthodox economists the labor theory of value, holding that the value of any human-made object depended ultimately on the amount of labor put into it—capital being regarded as the stored up labor of former times. Orthodox economists, it must be said, soon discarded the theory that economic value is produced by the input of labor alone. Marx, from the labor theory, developed his doctrine of surplus value, which, to simplify, meant in effect that workers were being robbed. They received in wages only a fraction of the value of the products which their labor produced. The difference was expropriated by the bourgeois capitalists—the private owners of the factories and the machines. And because workers never received in wages the equivalent of what they produced, capitalism was constantly menaced by overproduction, the accumulation of goods that people could not afford to buy. Hence it ran repeatedly into crises and depressions and was obliged also to be constantly expanding in search of new markets. It was the depression of 1847, according to Marx, that had precipitated the revolutions of 1848; and with every such depression during the rest of his lifetime Marx hoped that the day of the great social revolution was drawing nearer.

What brought all these observations together in a unified and compelling doctrine was the philosophy of dialectical materialism. By dialectic, Marx meant what the German philosopher Hegel had meant, that all things are in movement and in evolution and that all change comes through the clash of antagonistic elements. The word itself, coming from the Greek, meant originally a way of arriving at a higher conclusion through a series of propositions, as in a logical argument. The implications of the dialectic, for both Hegel and Marx, were that all history, and indeed all reality, is a process of development through time, a single and meaningful unfolding of events in a clear historical direction; that every event happens for good and sufficient reasons; and that history—though not exactly predetermined—is always shaped by impersonal forces and deep structural changes rather than by individuals or chance events.

Dialectical materialism

Marx differed from Hegel in one vital respect. Whereas Hegel emphasized the primacy of ideas in social change, Marx gave emphasis to the primacy of material conditions, or the relations of production, which included technology, inventions, natural resources, and property systems. These material realities create the social world in which people live. It is the relations of production that determine what kind of religions, philosophies, governments, laws, and moral values are accepted. To believe that ideas precede and generate actualities was, according to Marx, the error of Hegel. Hegel had thought, for example, that the mind conceives the idea of freedom, which it then realizes in the Greek city-state, in Christianity, in the French Revolution, and in the kingdom of Prussia. Not at all, according to Marx: the idea of freedom, or any other idea, is generated by the actual economic and social conditions. Conditions are the roots; ideas, the trees. Hegel had held the ideas to be the roots and the resulting actual conditions to be the trees. Or as Marx and Engels said, they found Hegel standing on his head and set him on his feet again.

Historical development

In the picture of historical development offered by Marx material conditions, or the relations of production, give rise to economic classes. Agrarian conditions produce a landholding or feudal class, but with changes in trade routes, money, and productive techniques a new commercial or bourgeois class arises. Each class, feudal and bourgeois, develops an ideology suited to its needs. Prevailing religions, governments, laws, and morals reflect the outlook of these classes. The two classes inevitably clash. Bourgeois revolutions against feudal interests break out—in England in 1642, in France in 1789, in Germany in 1848, though the bourgeois revolution in Germany proved abortive.

Karl Marx as he appeared near the end of his life. By the time he sat for this photograph in the early 1880s, he had been living in London for about 30 years, but he had developed many of his social and historical theories while living on the European continent in the political, economic, and revolutionary context of the 1840s.
(Getty Images)

Meanwhile, as the bourgeois class develops, it inevitably calls another class into being, its dialectical antithesis, the proletariat. The bourgeois is defined as the private owner of capital, the proletarian as the wage worker who possesses nothing but his or her own hands. The more a country becomes bourgeois, the more it becomes proletarian. The more production is concentrated in factories, the more the revolutionary laboring class is built up. Under competitive conditions the bourgeois tend to devour and absorb each other; ownership of the factories, mines, machines, and railroads (capital) becomes concentrated into very few hands. Others sink into the proletariat. In the end the proletarianized mass simply takes over from the remaining bourgeois. It "expropriates the expropriators," and abolishes private property in the means of production.

The social revolution is thus accomplished. Marx assumed that this revolution would create a classless society, because class arises from economic differences which will disappear. The state and religion, being outgrowths of bourgeois interests, also disappear. For a time, until all vestiges of bourgeois interests have been rooted out, or until the danger of counterrevolution against socialism has been overcome, there will be a "dictatorship of the proletariat." After that the state will "wither away," since there is no longer an exploiting class to require it.

Class war between bourgeois and proletariat

Meanwhile the call is to war. Bourgeois and proletarian are locked in a universal struggle, which means that workers and labor unions must be kept in a belligerent and revolutionary mood. They must never forget that the employer is their class enemy and that government, law, morality, and religion are merely so much artillery directed against them. Morals are "bourgeois morals," law is "bourgeois law," government is an instrument of class power, and religion is a form of psychological warfare, a means of providing "opium" for the masses. Workers must not let themselves be fooled; they must learn how to detect the class interest underlying the most exalted institutions and beliefs. In this form of military intelligence, ferreting out the ways of the enemy, they will be helped by intellectuals especially trained in explaining it to them.

Like all fighting forces, the workers need a disciplined solidarity. Individuals must lose themselves in the whole—in their class. It is a betrayal of their class for workers to rise above the proletariat, to "improve themselves," as the bourgeois says. It is dangerous for labor unions merely to obtain better wages or hours by negotiation with employers, for by such little gains the war itself may be forgotten. It is likewise dangerous, and even treasonous, for workers to put faith in democratic machinery or "social legislation," for the state, an engine of repression, can never be made into an instrument of welfare. Law simply expresses the will of the stronger class; "right" and "justice" are thin emanations of class interest. We must hold, wrote Marx in 1875, to "the realistic outlook which has cost so much effort to instill into the party, but which has now taken root in it"; and we must not let this outlook be perverted "by means of ideological nonsense about 'right' and other trash common among the democrats and French Socialists."

Worker solidarity

The Appeal of Marxism: Its Strength and Weaknesses

The original Marxism was a hard doctrine, with both advantages and handicaps in the winning of adherents. One of its advantages was its claim to be scientific. Marx classified earlier and rival forms of socialism as utopian: they rested on moral indignation, and their formula for reforming society was for human beings to become more just, or for the upper classes to be converted to sympathy for the lower. His own doctrine, Marx insisted, had nothing to do with ethical ideas; it was purely scientific, resting upon the study of actual facts and real processes, and it showed that socialism would be not a miraculous reversal but a historical continuation of what was already taking place. He also considered it utopian and unscientific to describe the future socialist society in any detail. It would be classless, with neither bourgeois nor proletarian; but to lay any specific plans would be idle dreaming. Let the revolution come, and socialism would take care of itself.

Marxism was a strong compound of the scientific, the historical, the metaphysical, and the apocalyptic. But some elements of Marxism stood in the way of its natural propagation. The working people of Europe were not really in the frame of mind of an army in battle. They hesitated to subordinate all else to the distant prospect of a class revolution. They were not exclusively class-people, nor did they behave as such. They still held to religious beliefs or to a political faith in natural rights that could not portray morality as simply a class weapon or right and justice as "trash." Increasingly, they had national loyalties to country. Only with great difficulty could they associate themselves emotionally with a world proletariat in an unrelenting struggle against their own neighbors.

Conflicting working-class values

The cure for the revolutionism of 1848 proved in time to be the admission of the laboring classes to a fuller membership in society. Wages generally rose after 1850, labor unions were organized, and by 1870 in the principal European countries the workingman very generally had gained the right to vote. Through their unions, workers were often able to get better wages and working conditions by direct pressure upon employers. Having the vote, they gradually formed working-class parties, and as they proceeded to act through the state, they had less inclination to destroy it. Marx's dismissive term for these maneuvers was "opportunism," but such political campaigns gained increasing support among

Opportunism

workers, most of whom wanted to better themselves by dealing with employers and by obtaining social reforms through existing government institutions rather than by waging class war. From Marxism the working class absorbed much, including a watchful hostility to employers and a sense of working-class solidarity; but on the whole, as Marxism spread at the close of the nineteenth century, it ceased to be really revolutionary. Had the old Europe not gone to pieces in the twentieth-century wars, and had Marxism not been revived by Lenin and transplanted to Russia, it is probable that Marx's ideas would have been domesticated into the general body of European thought and that much less would have been said about them in later years in Europe or elsewhere.

62.   BONAPARTISM: THE SECOND FRENCH EMPIRE, 1852–1870

The new "realism" in European culture after 1848 extended also to the exercise of post-revolutionary political power. We have seen how Louis Napoleon Bonaparte, elected president of the French republic in 1848, soon made himself Emperor of the French with the title of Napoleon III. Those willing to fight for the parliamentary and liberal institutions which he crushed were silenced. He became chief of state and then Emperor (in 1852) on a wave of popular acclaim.

Political Institutions of the Second Empire

Napoleon III, like Napoleon I, came to power because of the fear of radicalism in a discredited republic. Otherwise he bore little resemblance to his famous uncle. He was not a professional soldier or a great organizer. When he became president of the republic at the age of 40 he had been an adventurer and a conspirator, but he undoubtedly felt more concern than Napoleon I for the plight of the working classes. Where Napoleon I had been disdainful of public opinion, his nephew recognized it as an opportunity, not a nuisance. Though journalists and intellectuals generally distrusted him, he drew some of them to his side; he tried to placate the Catholic interests; and he appealed to the masses by giving them the vote (however useless), by promises of prosperity, and by pageantry. He understood perfectly that a single leader exerts more magnetism than an elected assembly. And he knew that a Europe still shuddering over the June Days was hoping desperately for order in France.

Modern progress

He gloried in modern progress. Toward the changes coming over Europe the monarchs of the old school usually showed an attitude of timidity and doubt if not positive opposition. Napoleon III boldly offered himself as the strong leader in a brave new world. Like his uncle, he announced that he embodied the sovereignty of the people. He said that he had found a solution to the problem of mass democracy. In all the other great Continental states and in Great Britain, in 1852, universal suffrage was thought to be incompatible with intelligent government and economic prosperity. Napoleon III claimed to put them together. Like Marx and other "realists" after 1848 he held that elected parliamentary bodies, far from representing an abstract "people," only accentuated class divisions within a country. He declared that the regime of the restored Bourbons and the July Monarchy had been dominated by special interests; that the Republic of 1848 had first been violent and anarchic and then had fallen into the hands of a distrustful assembly that robbed the laboring man of his vote; and that France would find in the empire the permanent, popular, and modern system for which it had been vainly searching since 1789. He affirmed that he stood above classes and would govern equally in the interests of all. In any case, like many other political leaders after 1848, he held that forms of government were less important than economic and social realities.

The political institutions of the Second Empire were therefore authoritarian, modeled on those of the Consulate of the first Bonaparte. There was a Council of State, composed of experts who drafted legislation and advised on technical matters. There was also an appointive Senate and a Legislative Body, which was elected by universal male suffrage in carefully managed elections. But the Legislative Body had no real power to make laws, set the budget, or control the army. Parliamentary life was reduced almost to absolute zero.

Authoritarian political institutions

To captivate public attention and glorify the Napoleonic name the new emperor set up a sumptuous court at the Tuileries. Balked in the ambition to marry into one of the great dynasties, Napoleon III chose as his empress a young Spanish noblewoman, Eugénie, who was destined to outlive the empire by 50 years, dying in 1920. It was said to be a love match—a sure sign of popularized royalty. The court life of the empire was brilliant and showy beyond anything known at the time in St. Petersburg or Vienna. The note of pageantry was further struck in the embellishment of the city of Paris. Baron Haussmann, one of the most creative of city planners, gave Paris much of the appearance that it has today. He built roomy railway stations with broad approaches, and he constructed a system of boulevards and public squares offering long vistas ending in fine buildings or monuments, as at the Place de l'Opéra. He also modernized the sewers and the water supply. The building program, like the expensive court, had the additional advantage of stimulating business and employment. And the cutting of wide avenues through the crooked streets and congested old houses would permit easier military operations against insurrectionists entrenched behind barricades, should the events of 1848 ever be repeated.

Economic Developments under the Empire

It was as a great social engineer that Napoleon III preferred to be known. In his youth he had tried to read the riddle of modern industrialism, and now, as emperor, he found some of his main backers in former Saint-Simonians, who called him their "socialist emperor." Saint-Simon, it may be recalled, had been among the first to conceive of a centrally planned industrial system. But the Saint-Simonians of the 1850s shared in the new sense of being realistic, and their most signal triumph was the invention of investment banking, by which they hoped to guide economic growth through the concentration of financial resources. They founded a novel kind of banking institution, the *Crédit Mobilier,* which raised funds by selling its shares to the public, and with the funds thus obtained bought stock in such new industrial enterprises as it wished to develop. France entered a new phase of rapid economic development—a distinctive French version of the Industrial Revolution.

The times were exceedingly favorable for expansion, for the discovery of gold in California in 1849, and in Australia soon afterward, together with the newly organized credit facilities, brought a substantial increase in the European money supply, which had a mildly inflationary effect. The steady rise of prices and all money values encouraged company promotion and investment of capital. Railway mileage, increasing everywhere in the Western world, increased in France from 3,000 to 16,000 kilometers in the 1850s. The demand for rolling stock, iron rails,

Expansion

auxiliary equipment, and building materials for stations and freight houses kept the mines and factories busy. The railway network was rationalized, 55 small lines in France being merged into six big regional trunks. Iron steamboats replaced wooden sailing ships. Between 1859 and 1869 a French company built the Suez Canal, which it continued to own for almost a century, though the British government after 1875 was the principal stockholder.

Large corporations made their appearance, in railroads and banking first of all. In 1863 the law granted the right of "limited liability," by which a stockholder could not lose more than the par value of the stock, however insolvent or debt-burdened the corporation might become. This encouraged investment by persons of small means, and by capitalists large and small in enterprises of which they knew very little; thus the wealth and savings of the country were more effectively mobilized and put to work. Stocks and shares became more numerous and diversified. The Stock Exchange boomed. Financiers—those whose business was to handle money, credit, and securities—assumed a new eminence in the capitalistic world. A good many people became very rich, richer perhaps than anyone had ever been in France before.

The emperor aspired also to do something for the working class, within the limits of the existing system. Jobs were plentiful and wages were good, by the ideas of the day, at least until the temporary depression of 1857. The emperor had a plan, as did some of the Saint-Simonians, for organizing forces of workers in military fashion and setting them to clear and develop uncultivated land. Not much was done in this direction. More was accomplished in the humanitarian relief of suffering. Hospitals and asylums were established, and free medicines were distributed. The outlines of a social-welfare state began somewhat vaguely to appear. Meanwhile the workers were building up unions. All combinations of workers had been prohibited during the French Revolution, a prohibition that was deemed to be still in force until the ambiguous legal position of labor unions began to change. In 1864 it even became legal for organized workers to go on strike. Large labor units, or unions, and large business units, or corporations, were thus legalized at the same time. Napoleon III hardly did enough for labor to rank as a working-class hero, but he did enough to be suspected as "socialistic" by many middle-class people of the day.

Napoleon's "socialistic" initiatives

Later authoritarian regimes, bent like the Second Empire on a program of economic development, were usually highly protectionist, unwilling to face open competition with the rest of the world. Napoleon III believed in freedom of international trade. He had a project for a tariff union with Belgium, which some Belgians also supported. Belgium was already well industrialized, and a Franco-Belgium union, especially since Belgium had the coal that France lacked, would have formed a trading area of very great strength. But the plan was blocked by private interests in both countries and strongly opposed by both Great Britain and the German *Zollverein*. The emperor then turned to an all-around reduction of import duties. Since the repeal of the Corn Laws in 1846 the free traders were in power in England. They were eager to abolish trade barriers between Britain and France. Napoleon III, overriding unusual opposition in his Legislative Body, concluded a free trade treaty with Great Britain in 1860. He set aside 40 million francs of government funds to assist French manufacturers in making adjustments to British competition; but this sum was never spent in full, which suggests that French industry was generally able to compete successfully with the more intensively mechanized industry of Britain. The Anglo-French treaty was accompanied by lesser trade agreements with other countries.

Free trade treaty with Britain

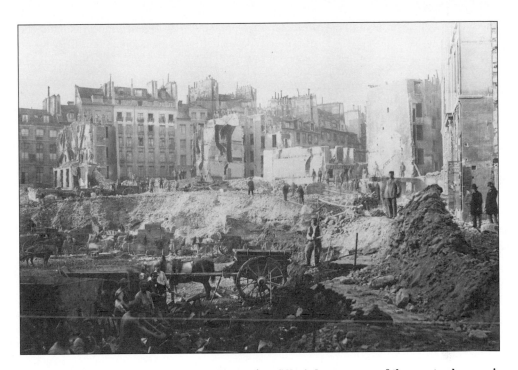

Napoleon III's ambitious plan to rebuild the city of Paris became one of the great urban projects of modern times. Organized by the strong-willed Baron Haussmann, the systematic, controversial reconstruction of Parisian streets, parks, buildings, sewers, and monuments transformed the city and produced an aesthetic grandeur that has drawn visitors ever since. This photograph shows some of the construction workers and the tools they used to build the new streets.
(Giraudon/Art Resource, New York)

It looked, in the 1860s, as if Europe might actually be about to enter the promised land of freedom of trade.

Internal Difficulties and War

But by 1860 the empire was running into trouble. It took a few years to overcome the depression of 1857. By his free trade policy the emperor made enemies among certain industrialists. The Catholics objected to his intervention in Italy, where he briefly joined an anti-Austrian military campaign in 1859. After 1860 opposition mounted. The emperor granted more leeway to the Legislative Body. The 1860s are called the decade of the Liberal Empire—all such terms being relative. How the empire would have fared had purely internal causes been left free scope we shall never know. Louis Napoleon actually ruined himself by war. His empire evaporated on the battlefield in 1870. But he was at war long before that.

"The empire means peace," he had assured his audiences in 1852: *l'Empire, c'est la paix*. But war is after all a supreme form of pageantry (or was then); France was the strongest country in Europe, and the emperor's name was Napoleon. Less than a year and a half after the proclamation of the empire France was at war with a European state for the first time since Waterloo. The enemy was

"The Empire means peace"

Russia, and the war was the Crimean War. Napoleon III did not alone instigate the Crimean War. Many forces in Europe after 1848 made for war; but Napoleon III was one of these forces. In 1859 the new Napoleon was fighting in Italy, from 1862 to 1867 in Mexico, and in 1870 in France itself, in a war with Prussia which he could easily have avoided. These wars form part of the story of the following chapter.

It is enough to say here that in 1870 the Second Empire went the way of the First, into the limbo of governments tried and discarded by the French. It had lasted 18 years, exactly as long as the July Monarchy, and longer than any other regime known in France, up to that time, since the fall of the Bastille. Not until the twentieth century, when dictators sprouted all over Europe, did people begin to recognize that Louis Napoleon had been an omen of the future rather than a bizarre reincarnation of the past.

For interactive exercises, glossary, chronologies, and more, go to the *Online Learning Center* at **www.mhhe.com/palmer10.**

Chapter **13**

THE GLOBAL CONSOLIDATION OF LARGE NATION-STATES, 1859–1871

The rise of nineteenth-century nationalism and the quest for unified national governments led to a remarkable consolidation of nation-states during the 12 years after 1859. Notable political unifications and reforms in this period included the formation of a new German empire, a unified kingdom of Italy, the Dual Monarchy of Austria-Hungary, and the introduction of drastic internal changes in tsarist Russia; the triumph of central authority after a civil war in the United States; the creation of an independent, united Dominion of Canada; and the emergence of a modernizing government and economy in the empire of Japan. All these disparate events reflected profound changes brought by the railroad, steamship, and telegraph. The communication of ideas, exchange of goods, and movement of people over wide areas became more frequent and easier than ever before. New technologies and the rapid development of new industries strengthened the political power of nation-states, which gained increasing influence in the evolving social and economic life of all modern societies.

63. BACKGROUNDS: THE IDEA OF THE NATION-STATE

Before 1860 there were two prominent nation-states in Europe—Great Britain and France. Spain, united on the map, was internally so miscellaneous as to belong to a different category. Portugal, Switzerland, the Netherlands, and the Scandinavian countries

Chapter emblem: Detail from a photograph of Giuseppe Garibaldi, a leader of the Italian movement for national unification in the early 1860s. (Getty Images)

were nation-states, but small and peripheral. The characteristic political organizations were small states comprising fragments of a nation, such as were strewn across the middle of Europe—Hanover, Baden, Sardinia, Tuscany, or the Two Sicilies—and large sprawling empires made up of all sorts of peoples, distantly ruled from above by dynasties and bureaucracies, such as the Romanov, Habsburg, and Ottoman domains. Except for recent developments in the Americas the same mixture of small nonnational states and of large nonnational empires was to be found in most of the rest of the world.

Since 1860 or 1870 a nation-state system has prevailed. The consolidation of large nations became a model for other peoples large and small. In time, in the following century, other large groups of people undertook to establish nation-states in India, Pakistan, Indonesia, Iran, and Nigeria. Small and middle-sized populations increasingly thought of themselves as nations, entitled to their own sovereignty and independence. Some of these sovereignties that emerged after 1945 comprise fewer people than a small modern city.

Unity and disunity

The idea of the nation-state has served both to bring people together into larger units and to break them apart into smaller ones. In the nineteenth century, outside the disintegrating Ottoman Empire, from which Greece, Serbia, Bulgaria, and Romania became independent, and in which an Arab national movement also began to stir, the national idea served mainly to create larger units in place of small ones. The map of Europe from 1871 to 1918 was the simplest it has ever been before or since (see map, pp. 538–539).

This book has already had much to say about the idea of the nation-state and the movement of nationalism. Earlier chapters have described the ferment of national ideas and movements stirred up by the French Revolution and by the Napoleonic domination of Europe, the nationalist agitation and repression of the years after 1815, and the frustration and failure of patriotic aspirations in Germany, Italy, and central Europe in the Revolution of 1848. For many in the nineteenth century, nationalism, the winning of national unity and independence and the creation of the nation-state, became a kind of secular faith. For most devout nationalists, the nation represented higher truths as well as collective and personal aspirations for a better future life.

Characteristics of nation-states

A nation-state may be thought of as one in which supreme political authority somehow rests upon and represents the will and feeling of its inhabitants. There must be a people, not merely a swarm of human beings. The people must basically will and feel something in common. They must sense that they belong—that they are members of a community, participating somehow in a common social and cultural life, that the government is their government, and that outsiders are "foreign." The outsiders or foreigners are usually (though not always) those who speak a different language. The nation is usually (though not always) composed of persons sharing the same speech. A nation may also possess a belief in common descent or racial origin (however mistaken), or a sense of a common history (sometimes imagined), a common future, a common religion, a common geographical home, or a common external menace. Nations take form in many ways. But all are alike in feeling or imagining themselves to be communities, permanent communities in which individual persons, together with their children and their children's children, are committed to a collective destiny on earth.

Consolidation and constitutionalism

In the nineteenth century governments found that they could not effectively rule or develop the full powers of state except by enlisting this sense of membership and support among their subjects. The consolidation of large nation-states had two distinguishable phases. Territorially, it meant the union of preexisting smaller states. Morally and psychologically it meant the creation of new ties between government and governed, the admission of new segments of the population to political life, through the creation or extension of liberal and representative institutions. This process of national integration and institution-building was repeated in widely disparate cultures, including Japan, tsarist Russia, and the frontier societies of North America. Although there was considerable variation in the real power of the new political institutions and in the extent of self-government actually realized, parliaments were set up for the new Italy, the new Germany, the new Japan, the new Canada; and the movement in Russia was in the same direction. In Europe, some of the aims which the revolutionists of 1848 had failed to achieve were now brought about by the established authorities.

They were brought about, however, only through a series of wars. To create an all-German or an all-Italian state, as the revolutions of 1848 had already shown, it was necessary to break the power of Austria, render Russia at least temporarily ineffective, and overthrow or intimidate those German and Italian governments which refused to surrender their sovereignty. In the United States, to maintain national unity as understood by President Lincoln, it was necessary to repress the movement for Southern independence by force of arms. For almost 40 years after 1815 there had been no war between established powers of Europe. Then in 1854 came the Crimean War; in 1859, the Italian War; in 1864, the Danish War; in 1866, the Austro-Prussian War; and in 1870, the Franco-Prussian War. Concurrently the Civil War raged in the United States. After 1871, for 43 years there was again no war between the major European powers.

The Crimean War, 1854–1856

Before moving on to the first of the national consolidation movements, the Italian, we must examine the Crimean War which, though seemingly remote and unconnected, helped to make possible the success of the European national movements. Its chief significance for Europe is that it seriously weakened both Austria and Russia, the two powers most bent on preserving the peace settlement of 1815 and on preventing national changes. It was also the first war covered by newspaper correspondents, and the first in which women, led by Florence Nightingale, established their position as army nurses.

The pressure of Russia upon Turkey was an old story. Every generation saw its Russo-Turkish war. In the last Russo-Turkish war, to go back no further, that of 1828–1829, Tsar Nicholas I protected the independence *Russian pressure* newly won by Greece and annexed the left bank of the mouth of the Danube. Now, in 1853, Nicholas again made demands upon the still large but decaying Ottoman Empire, moving in on the two Danubian principalities, Wallachia and Moldavia (later to be known as Romania), with military forces (see map, p. 649). The dispute this time ostensibly involved the protection of Christians in the Ottoman Empire, including the foreign Christians at Jerusalem and in Palestine. Over these Christians the French also claimed a certain protective jurisdiction. The French had for centuries been the principal Western people in the Middle East. They had often furnished money and advisers to the sultan, they carried on a huge volume of trade, they staffed and financed Christian missions, and they were continually talking of building a Suez canal. Napoleon III thus had his own aspirations in the eastern Mediterranean, and he encouraged the Turkish government to resist Russian claims to protect Christians within Turkey. War between Russia and Turkey broke out late in 1853. In 1854 France joined the side of the Turks, as did Great Britain, whose settled policy was to uphold Turkey and the Middle East against penetration by Russia. The two

Western powers were soon joined by a small ally, the kingdom of Sardinia, better known because of its Italian mainland territory and seat of government as Piedmont. Sardinia had no visible interest in the issues in the Middle East, but it entered the war as a means to influence the Italian question.

The British fleet successfully blockaded Russia in both its Baltic and Black Sea outlets. French and British armies invaded Russia itself, landing in the Crimean peninsula, to which all the important fighting was confined. The Austrian Empire had its own reasons not to want Russia to conquer the Balkans and Constantinople, or to see Britain and France master the situation alone; Austria therefore, though not yet recovered from the upheaval of 1848–1849, mobilized its armed forces at a great effort to itself and occupied Wallachia and Moldavia, which the Russians evacuated under this threat of attack by a new enemy. Tsar Nicholas died in 1855, and his successor, Alexander II, sued for peace.

Peace in 1856

A congress of all the great powers made peace at Paris in 1856. By the treaty the powers pledged themselves jointly to maintain the "integrity of the Ottoman Empire." The Russian tide ebbed a little. Russia ceded the left bank of the mouth of the Danube to Moldavia and gave up its claim to the special protection of Christians in the

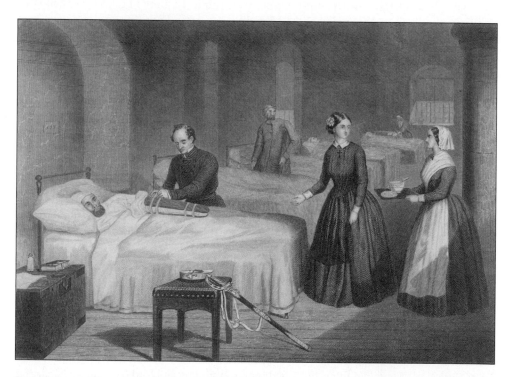

The Crimean War weakened the international position of Austria and Russia, but its most enduring effect on nations such as Britain may have come in the ways that wars were described in the popular press and in the new role of women nurses. Florence Nightingale arrived in the Crimea with 36 nurses and was at first opposed by army doctors. She is pictured here in one of the hospitals where she began to create the new military and social identity of the female nurse.

(Getty Images)

Turkish empire. Moldavia and Wallachia (united as Romania in 1858), together with Serbia, were recognized as self-governing principalities under protection of the European powers. At the Congress of Paris European diplomacy seemed to be achieving a more harmonious international system.

But trouble was in the making. Napoleon III needed glory. The Italians wanted some kind of unified Italy. The Prussians, who had done nothing in the Crimean War and were only tardily invited to the Congress of Paris, feared that their status as a great power might be slipping away. Napoleon III, the Italian nationalists, and the Prussians all stood to gain by change. Change in central Europe and Italy meant a tearing up of the Treaty of Vienna of 1815, long guarded by Metternich and unsuccessfully challenged by the revolutionaries of 1848. Now, after the Crimean War, the forces opposing change were very weak. It was the Russian and Austrian empires that had stood firmly for the status quo. But these two powers, which had most seriously attempted to uphold the Vienna settlement, could do so no longer. The first proof came in Italy.

64. CAVOUR AND THE ITALIAN WAR OF 1859: THE UNIFICATION OF ITALY

Italian Nationalism: The Program of Cavour

In Italy there had long been about a dozen sizable states, together with a few very small ones. Several of them had dissolved in the Italian movements that accompanied the wars of the French Revolution. All had been reorganized, first by Napoleon and then by the Congress of Vienna. The governments of these states were generally content with their separate independence. But the governments were remote from their peoples.

There was a widespread disgust in Italy with the existing authorities, and a growing desire for a liberal national state in which all Italy might be embodied and which might resurrect the Italian grandeur of ancient times and of the Renaissance. This sentiment, the dream of an Italian Risorgimento, or resurgence, had become very heated at the time of the French Revolution and Napoleon, and had then been transformed by the writings of Mazzini into an intensely moral campaign for Italian national unity. Mazzini had seen his hopes for a unified republican Italy elevated for a brief moment and then blasted in the general debacle of 1848. In the stormy events of 1848 the papacy vehemently rejected the radical romantic republicanism of Mazzini, Garibaldi, and other firebrands; and the pope could no longer be expected to support the cause of Italian nationalism. The same events had shown that Austria could not be ousted from the Italian peninsula without the aid of an outside power.

Italian Risorgimento

These lessons were not lost on the prime minister of Piedmont, which was ruled since 1848 as a constitutional monarchy and was now under King Victor Emmanuel. This prime minister after 1852 was Camillo di Cavour, one of the shrewdest political tacticians of that or any age. Cavour was a liberal of Western type. He tried to make the state a model of progress, efficiency, and fair government that other Italians would admire. He worked hard to plant constitutional and parliamentary practices. He favored the building of railroads and docks, the improvement of agriculture, and emancipation of trade. He followed a strongly anticlerical policy, cutting down the number of religious holidays, limiting the right of church bodies to own real estate, abolishing the church courts—all without negotiation with the Holy See. A liberal and constitutional monarchist, a wealthy landowner in

Cavour's "politics of
reality"
his own right, he had no sympathy for the revolutionary, romantic, and
republican nationalism of Mazzini.

Cavour shared in that new realism described in the last chapter. He did
not approve of romantic republicans but was willing to work with them surreptitiously. He did not idealize war but was willing to make war to unify Italy under the
house of Savoy. With unruffled calculation he took Piedmont into the Crimean War, sending troops to Russia in the hope of winning a place at the peace table and raising the Italian
question at the Congress of Paris. It was evident to him that against one great power one
must pit another and that the only way to get Austria out of Italy was to use the French
army. He therefore developed a master plan to provoke war with Austria, after having
assured himself of French military support.

It was not difficult to persuade Napoleon III to collaborate. The Bonapartes looked
upon Italy as their ancestral country, and Napoleon III, in his adventurous youth, had
traveled in conspiratorial Italian circles and even participated in an Italian insurrection
in 1831. Now, as emperor, in his role of apostle of modernity, he entertained a "doctrine
of nationalities" which held the consolidation of nations to be a forward step at the existing stage of history. To fight reactionary Austria for the freedom of Italy would also mollify liberal opinion in France, which in other ways Napoleon was engaged in
suppressing. The last note in persuasion was furnished by an Italian republican named
Orsini, who in 1858, finding the French emperor too slow to make up his mind,
attempted to assassinate him with a bomb. Napoleon III reached a secret agreement with
Cavour. In April 1859, Cavour tricked Austria into a declaration of war. The French
army poured over the Alps.

There were two battles, Magenta and Solferino, both won by the French and Piedmontese. But Napoleon III was now in a quandary. In Italy, with the defeat of the Austrians, revolutionary agitation broke out all over the peninsula, as it had a decade
before—and the French emperor was no patron of popular revolution. The revolutionaries
overthrew or denounced the existing governments and clamored for annexation to Piedmont. In France, as elsewhere, the Catholics, fearful that the pope's temporal power would
be lost, upbraided the emperor for his godless and unnecessary war. The French position
was indeed odd, for while the bulk of the French army fought Austria in the north, a
detachment of it was still stationed in Rome, sent there in 1849 to protect the pope against
Italian republicanism. Napoleon III, in July 1859, at the height of his victories, stupefied
Cavour. He made a separate peace with the Austrians.

Franco-Austrian
agreement
The Franco-Austrian agreement gave Lombardy to Piedmont but left
Venetia within the Austrian Empire. It offered a compromise solution to the
Italian question, in the form of a federal union of the existing Italian governments, to be presided over by the pope. This was not what Cavour or the
Piedmontese or the more fiery Italian patriots wanted. Revolution continued to spread across the northern Italian states. Tuscany, Modena, Parma, and Romagna
drove out their old rulers. They were annexed to Piedmont, after plebiscites or general
elections in these regions had shown an overwhelming popular favor for this step. Since
Romagna belonged to the papal states, the pope excommunicated the organizers of the
new Italy. Undeterred, representatives of all north Italy except Venetia met at the Piedmontese capital of Turin in 1860 in the first parliament of the enlarged kingdom. The British
government hailed these events with enthusiasm, and Napoleon III also recognized the
expanded Piedmontese state, in return for the transfer to France of Nice and Savoy, where
plebiscites disclosed enormous majorities for annexation to France.

The Completion of Italian Unity

There were now, in 1860, a north Italian kingdom, the papal states in the middle, and the kingdom of the Two Sicilies, ruled by a Bourbon king in Naples and still standing in the south. The latter was being undermined by revolutionary agitation, as often in the past. A Piedmontese republican, Giuseppe Garibaldi, brought matters to a head. Somewhat like Lafayette, Garibaldi was a "hero of two worlds," who had fought for the independence of Uruguay, lived in the United States, and been one of the Triumvirs in the short-lived Roman Republic of 1849. He now organized a group of about 1,150 personal followers—Garibaldi's Thousand, or the Red Shirts—for an armed expedition to the south. Cavour, unable openly to favor such action against a neighboring state, connived at Garibaldi's preparations and departure. Garibaldi landed in Sicily and soon crossed to the mainland. Revolutionists hastened to join him, and the government of the Two Sicilies, backward and corrupt, commanding little loyalty from its population, collapsed before this picturesque intrusion.

Garibaldi now prepared to push from Naples up to Rome. Here, of course, he would meet not only the pope but also the French army, and the international scandal would reverberate throughout the globe. Cavour decided that so extreme a step must be averted, but that Garibaldi's successes must at the same time be used. Garibaldi, though not all his followers, was now ready to accept a monarchy as the best solution to the problem of Italian unification. The chief of the Red Shirts, the one-time foe of kings, consented to ride in an open carriage with Victor Emmanuel through the streets of Naples amid cheering thousands. Plebiscites held in the Two Sicilies showed an almost unanimous willingness to join with Piedmont. In the remainder of the papal states, except for Rome and its environs, plebiscites were held also, with the same result. A parliament representing all Italy except Rome and Venetia met in 1861, and the Kingdom of Italy was formally proclaimed, with Victor Emmanuel II as king "by grace of God and the will of the nation." Venetia was added in 1866, as a reward for Italian aid to Prussia in a war against Austria. Rome was annexed in 1870 after the withdrawal of French troops in the Franco-Prussian War of 1870.

Garibaldi's compromise

So Italy was "made," as the phrase of the time expressed it. It had been made by the high-minded cultural nationalism of Mazzini, the audacity of Garibaldi, and the cold policy of Cavour. In the end, however, the Italians also achieved national unification through insurrections, armed violence, and the endorsement of popular votes.

Persistent Problems after Unification

Very little was settled or ended by unification. Even territorially, the more pronounced nationalists refused to believe that Italian unity was completed. They looked beyond to regions of mixed population where Italians were numerous or preponderant—to the Trentino, to Trieste, to certain Dalmatian islands, or to Nice and Savoy. They saw in these regions an *Italia irredenta*, "an unredeemed Italy," awaiting in its turn the day of incorporation. Irredentism even passed into the English language as a word signifying a vociferous demand, on nationalist grounds, for annexation of regions beyond one's own frontiers.

The occupation of Rome in 1870 by the Italian government opened the rift between church and state still wider. The pope, deprived of territories the papacy had held for a thousand years, renewed his condemnations and chose to remain in lifelong seclusion in the Vatican. His successors followed the same policy until 1929. Hence good Italian patriots were bound to be anticlerical, and good Catholics were bound to look upon the Italian state with unfriendly eyes.

Occupation of Rome

UNIFICATION OF ITALY, 1859–1870

PIEDMONT
LOMBARDY
VENETIA
Turin
Milan
Venice
PARMA
MODENA
Florence
TUSCANY
PAPAL
STATES
KINGDOM OF SARDINIA
ROME
SARDINIA
NAPLES
SICILY

FORMATION OF DUAL MONARCHY OF AUSTRIA-HUNGARY, 1867

A U S T R I A
Vienna
Budapest
H U N G A R Y

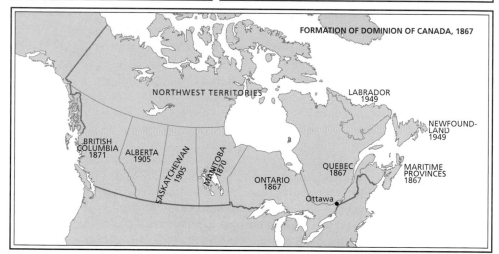

FORMATION OF DOMINION OF CANADA, 1867

NORTHWEST TERRITORIES

LABRADOR
1949

NEWFOUND-
LAND
1949

BRITISH
COLUMBIA
1871

ALBERTA
1905

SASKATCHEWAN
1905

MANITOBA
1870

ONTARIO
1867

QUEBEC
1867

MARITIME
PROVINCES
1867

Ottawa

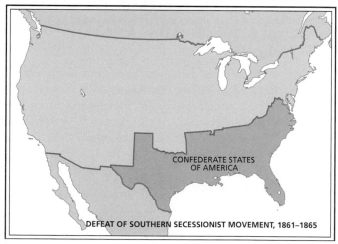

CONFEDERATE STATES
OF AMERICA

DEFEAT OF SOUTHERN SECESSIONIST MOVEMENT, 1861–1865

This photograph of Giuseppe Garibaldi suggests the confident, charismatic personal style that enabled him to lead a spirited group of Italian nationalists or "Red Shirts" into southern Italy, to form an alliance with King Victor Emmanuel of Piedmont, and to help establish a unified Italian nation-state.
(Getty Images)

The regional differences between northern and southern Italy did not disappear with unification. The north looked upon the agrarian south—the land of priest, landlord, and impoverished peasant—as disgracefully backward.

The new Italy was parliamentary but not democratic. At first the vote was only given to some 600,000 persons out of more than 20 million. Not until 1913 was the suffrage significantly broadened. Meanwhile parliamentary life, confined to a few, was somewhat isolated from the mass of the population and frequently corrupt. But the dream of ages was realized. Italy was one. The period that seemed so shameful to patriots, the long centuries that had elapsed since the Renaissance, were now terminated in the glories of a successful Risorgimento.

65. THE FOUNDING OF A GERMAN EMPIRE AND THE DUAL MONARCHY OF AUSTRIA-HUNGARY

To play upon the divisions among the Germans, keeping them in rivalry with each other and dependent upon outside powers, had been the policy of France ever since the Reformation and of Russia since it began to take part in the affairs of Europe. To keep the Germanic world divided was in fact a kind of negative prerequisite to the development of modern history as we know it, for without it the economic and cultural leadership of Europe would hardly have become concentrated along the Atlantic seaboard; nor would a great military empire have arisen in Russia and spread along the Baltic and into Poland.

Gradually, as we have seen, the Germans became dissatisfied with their position. They became nationalistic during and after the Napoleonic wars. Many German thinkers held

NATION BUILDING, 1859–1867

In the eight years after 1859 Italy was unified (except for the city of Rome, annexed in 1870), the Habsburg government tried to solve its nationalities problem by creating the Dual Monarchy of Austria-Hungary, the United States affirmed its unity by defeating a Southern secessionist movement, and the Dominion of Canada was formed to include all of British North America (dates show the accession of provinces) except Newfoundland and Labrador, which were added in 1949.

that Germany was different from the West, destined someday to work out a peculiarly German way of life and political system of its own. To the Slavs the Germans felt immeasurably superior. German philosophy, as shown most clearly in Hegel, took on a certain characteristic tone. It tended to criticize modern individualism and to skip lightly over liberal conceptions of individual liberty; it also tended to glorify group loyalties, the nation, and the state. It emphasized the progressive evolution of history, which in the thought of Hegel, and after him Marx, became a vast impersonal force almost independent of human beings. History was said to ordain, require, condemn, justify, or excuse. What one did not like could be dismissed as a mere historical phase, opening into a quite different and more attractive future. What one wanted, in the present or future, could be described as historically necessary and bound to come.

The German States after 1848

In 1848 a series of revolutions had unseated the several governments of Germany. At the Frankfurt Assembly a group composed essentially of private citizens tried to organize a united Germany by constitutional methods. They failed because they had no power. Hence after 1848 the Germans began to think in terms of power, developing a somewhat excessive admiration for *die Macht*. The men of Frankfurt failed also, perhaps, because they were insufficiently revolutionary. The Germans were still attached emotionally to their several states. What happened in Italy, a revolutionary destruction of all the old governments except that of Piedmont, could not readily happen in Germany.

After the failure of the 1848 revolution German nationalists and liberals were confused. By 1850 the old states were restored—Austria and Prussia, the kingdoms of Hanover, Saxony, Bavaria, and Württemberg, together with about 30 other states ranging in size down to the free cities of Hamburg and Frankfurt. The loose confederation of 1815, linking all these states together, was restored also (see map, p. 530). But within this framework great economic and social changes were occurring. Between 1850 and 1870 the output of both coal and iron in Germany multiplied sixfold. In 1850 Germany produced less iron than France; in 1870, more. Germany was rapidly gaining economic unity and overcoming the economic and social lag which had separated Germans from the fast-developing industrial and global commerce in northwestern Europe. The German cities were growing, bound together by railroad and telegraph, requiring larger supporting areas on which to live. Industrial capitalists and industrial workers were becoming more numerous. With the advantages of unity more obvious than ever, with the ideals of 1848 badly compromised, with a strong philosophical respect for the state and for power, and with a habit of accepting the successful event as the "judgment of history," the Germans were ripe for what happened. They did not unify themselves by their own exertions. They fell into the arms of Prussia.

Advantages of unity

Prussia in the 1860s: Bismarck

Prussia had always been the smallest and most precarious of the great powers. Ruined by Napoleon, it had risen again. It owed its international influence and internal character to its army. Actually it had fought rather fewer wars than other great powers, but its army enabled Prussia to expand by conquest or diplomacy. The taking of Silesia in 1740 by force, the acquisition of parts of Poland in the partitions of the 1770s and 1790s, and the addition of the Rhineland in 1815 by diplomatic or international agreement were the highlights of Prussian growth. After 1850 those who controlled the destinies of Prussia were apprehensive. Their state had been shaken by revolution. In the Crimean War and at the

Congress of Paris they were hardly more than spectators. It seemed as if the hard-won and still relatively recent position of Prussia might be waning.

Since 1815 the population of Prussia had grown from 11 to 18 million, but the size of the army had not changed. Merely to enforce existing principles of conscription would therefore almost double the army. But this would require increased financial appropriations. After 1850 Prussia had a parliament. It was a parliament, to be sure, dominated by men of wealth; but some of the wealthy Prussians, notably the industrialists of the Rhineland, were liberals who wished the parliament to have control over government policies. These men did not like professional armies and considered the Prussian Junkers, from whom the officer corps was recruited, as their main rivals in the state. The parliament refused the necessary appropriations. The king at this juncture, in 1862, appointed a new chief minister, Otto von Bismarck.

Parliamentary politics

Bismarck was a Junker from old Brandenburg east of the Elbe. He cultivated the gruff manner of an honest country squire, though he was in fact an accomplished man of the world. Intellectually he was far superior to the rather unsophisticated landlord class from which he sprang and for which he often felt an impatient contempt. He shared in many Junker ideas. He advocated, and even felt, a kind of stout Protestant piety. Although he cared for the world's opinion, it never deterred him in his actions; criticism and denunciation left him untouched. He was in fact obstinate. He was not a nationalist. He did not look upon all Germany as his Fatherland. He was a Prussian. His social affinities, as with the Junkers generally, lay to the East with corresponding landowning elements of the Baltic provinces and Russia. Western Europe, including the bulk of Germany, he neither understood nor trusted; it seemed to him revolutionary, freethinking, and materialistic. Parliamentary bodies he considered ignorant and irresponsible as organs of government. Individual liberty seemed to him disorderly selfishness. Liberalism, democracy, socialism were repugnant to him. He preferred to stress duty, service, order, and the fear of God. The idea of forming a new German union developed only gradually in his mind and then as an adjunct to the strengthening of Prussia.

Bismarck

Bismarck thus had his predilections and even his principles. But no principle bound him; no ideology seemed to him an end in itself. He became the classic practitioner of *Realpolitik*. First he made wars; then he insisted upon peace. Enmities and alliances were to him only matters of passing convenience. The enemy of today might be the friend of tomorrow. Far from planning out a long train of events, then following it step by step to a grand consummation, he seems to have been practical and opportunistic, taking advantage of situations as they emerged and prepared to act in any one of several directions as events might suggest.

In 1862, as minister president, it was his job, or duty, to thwart the liberals in the Prussian parliament. For four years, from 1862 to 1866, Bismarck waged this constitutional struggle. The parliament refused to vote the proposed taxes. The government collected them anyway. The taxpayers paid them without protest—it was the orderly thing to do, and the collectors represented public authority. The limitations of Prussian liberalism, the docility of the population, the respect for officialdom, the belief that the king and his ministers were wiser than the elected deputies—all clearly revealed themselves in this triumph of military policy over the theory of government by consent. The army was enlarged, reorganized, retrained, and reequipped. Bismarck fended off the showers of abuse from the liberal majority in the chamber. The liberals declared that the government's policy was flagrantly unconstitutional. The constitution, said Bismarck, could not have been meant to

Constitutional struggle

Otto von Bismarck's pragmatic use of power and his successful campaign to create a unified German nation-state made him the most successful practitioner of *Realpolitik* in late nineteenth-century Europe. This photograph suggests the talent for well-focused observation that enabled Bismarck to see clearly what was at stake in the many political and diplomatic conflicts of his generation.
(Getty Images)

undermine the state. The government, said the liberals, was itself undermining Prussia, for the rest of Germany hoped to find in Prussia, as Italy had found in Piedmont, a model of political freedom. What the Germans admired in Prussia, replied Bismarck coldly, was not its liberalism but its power. He declared that the Prussian boundaries as set in 1815 were unsound, that Prussia must be prepared to seize favorable opportunities for further growth. And he added one of his most memorable utterances: "Not by speeches and majority votes are the great questions of the day decided—that was the great error of 1848 and 1849—but by blood and iron."

Bismarck's Wars: The Creation of the North German Confederation, 1867

A favorable opportunity was not long in presenting itself. The Danes, engaged in a process of national consolidation of their own, wished to make the duchy of Schleswig an integral part of Denmark. The population of Schleswig was part Dane and part German. The diet of the German confederation, unwilling to see Germans thus annexed outright to Denmark, called for an all-German war upon the Danes. Bismarck had no desire to support or strengthen the existing German confederation. He wanted not an all-German war but a Prussian war. To disguise his aims he acted jointly with Austria, a fellow member of the German confederation. In 1864 Prussia and Austria together went to war with Denmark, which they soon defeated. It was Bismarck's intention to annex both Schleswig and the duchy of Holstein to Prussia, gaining whatever other advantages might present themselves from future trouble with Austria. He arranged a provisional occupation of Schleswig by Prussia and of Holstein by Austria. Disputes soon arose over rights of passage, the keeping of internal order, and other problems with which occupying forces are commonly afflicted. While pretending to try to regulate these disputes he allowed them to ripen.

He now proceeded to discredit and isolate Austria. The British government was at the time following a policy of nonintervention in the affairs of the Continent. The Russian empire was in no position for action; it was divided internally by a reform program then at its height; it was in a mood of hostility to Austria, because of events of the Crimean War, and well disposed toward Prussia and Bismarck, because Bismarck in 1863 took care to support it against an uprising of the Poles. To win over the new kingdom of Italy Bismarck held out the lure of Venetia. As for France, Napoleon III was embarrassed by domestic discontents and his army was committed to adventures in Mexico. In addition, Bismarck charmed him at a confidential interview at Biarritz, where vague oral intimations of French expansion were exchanged, and the two men seemed to agree to a needed modernization of the map of Europe. To weaken Austria within Germany, Bismarck presented himself as a democrat. He proposed a reform of the German confederation, recommending that it have a popular chamber elected by universal male suffrage. He calculated that the mass of the German people were wedded neither to the well-to-do capitalistic liberals, nor to the existing government structures of the German states, nor to the house of Habsburg. He would use "democracy" to undermine all established interests that stood in his way.

Bismarck as democrat

Meanwhile the occupying powers continued to quarrel over Schleswig-Holstein. Austria finally raised the matter formally in the German federal diet, one of whose functions was to prevent war between its members. Bismarck declared that the diet had no authority, accused the Austrians of aggression, and ordered the Prussian army to enter Holstein. The Austrians called for federal sanctions in the form of an all-German force to be sent against Prussia. The result was that Prussia, in 1866, was at war not only with Austria but also with most of the other German states. The Prussian army soon proved its superiority. Trained to an unprecedented precision, equipped with the new needle-gun, by which the infantryman could deliver five rounds a minute, brought into the zone of combat by an imaginative strategy that made use of the new railroads, and skillfully commanded, the Prussian army overwhelmed the Austrians and defeated the other German states soon thereafter. The Austro-Prussian, or Seven Weeks' War, was amazing in its brevity. Bismarck hastened to make peace before the other European powers could realize what had happened.

Seven Weeks' War

Prussia annexed outright, together with Schleswig-Holstein, the whole kingdom of Hanover, the duchies of Nassau and Hesse-Cassel, and the free city of Frankfurt. Here the old governments simply disappeared before the axe of the "red reactionary." The German federal union disappeared likewise. In its place, in 1867, Bismarck organized a North German Confederation, in which the newly enlarged Prussia joined with 21 other states, all of which combined it greatly outweighed. The German states south of the river Main—Austria, Bavaria, Baden, Württemberg, and Hesse-Darmstadt—remained outside the new organization, with no kind of union among themselves. Meanwhile the kingdom of Italy annexed Venetia.

For the North German Confederation Bismarck produced a constitution. The new structure, though a federal one, was much stronger than the now defunct Confederation of 1815. The king of Prussia became its hereditary head. Ministers were responsible to him. There was a parliament with two chambers. The upper chamber, as in the United States, represented the

A new constitution

states as such, though not equally. The lower chamber, or Reichstag, was deemed to represent the people and was elected by universal male suffrage. Such flirting with democracy seemed madness to both conservative Junker and liberal bourgeois. It was indeed a bold step, for only France at the time exemplified universal suffrage in Europe on a large scale, and in the France of Napoleon III neither old-fashioned conservatives nor genuine liberals could take much satisfaction. As for Great Britain, where voting rights were extended in this same year, 1867, they were still given to fewer than half the adult male population. Bismarck sensed in the "masses" an ally of strong government against private interests. He negotiated even with the socialists, who had arisen with the industrialization of the past decade, and who, in Germany at this time, were mainly followers of Ferdinand Lassalle. The Lassallean socialists, unlike the Marxian, believed it possible to improve working-class conditions through the action of existing governments. To the great annoyance of Marx, then in England (his *Capital* first appeared in 1867), the bulk

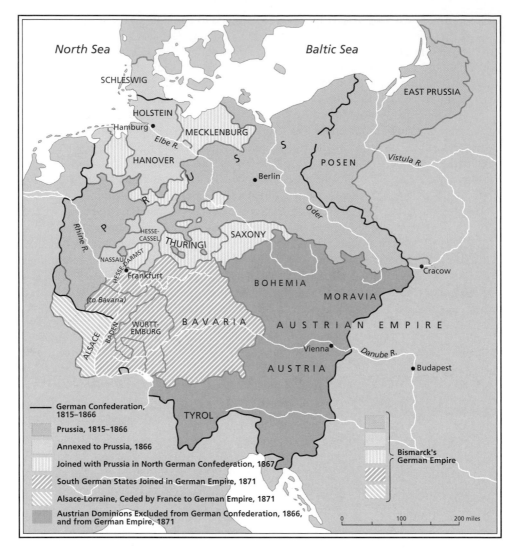

THE GERMAN QUESTION, 1815–1871

From 1815 to 1866 there were 39 German states joined in the German Confederation (the largest states are shown here). The movement to create a unified Germany gave rise in this era to opposing nationalist groups: the Great Germans, who favored an all-German union that would include Austria; and the Little Germans, who were willing to exclude Austria and its empire from a new German nation-state. Bismarck was a Little German but a Great Prussian. He (1) enlarged Prussia by conquest in 1866; (2) joined Mecklenburg, Saxony, and other regions with Prussia in the North German Confederation of 1867; and (3) combined this Confederation with Bavaria, Württemberg, and other southern states to form the German Empire in 1871. He also (4) conquered Alsace-Lorraine from France and (5) excluded Austria from the new German empire. These boundaries remained unchanged until 1918.

of the German socialists reached an understanding with Bismarck. In return for a democratic suffrage they agreed to accept the North German Confederation. Bismarck, for his part, by making use of democratic and socialist sentiment, won popular approval for his emerging empire.

The Franco-Prussian War

It was clear that the situation was not yet stable. The small south German states were left floating in empty space; they would sooner or later have to gravitate into some orbit or other, whether Austrian, Prussian, or French. In France there were angry criticisms of Napoleon III's foreign policy. French intervention in Mexico had proved a fiasco. A united Italy had been allowed to rise on France's borders. And now, contrary to all principles of French national interest observed by French governments for hundreds of years, a strong and independent power was being allowed to spread over virtually the whole of Germany. Everywhere people began to feel that war was inevitable between France and Prussia. Bismarck played on the fears of France felt in the south German states. South Germany, though in former times often a willing satellite of France, was now sufficiently nationalistic to consider such subservience to a foreign people disgraceful. To Bismarck it seemed that a war between Prussia and France would frighten the small south German states into a union with Prussia, leaving only Austria outside— which was what he wanted. To Napoleon III, or at least to some of his advisers, it seemed that such a war, if successful, would restore public approval of the Bonapartist empire. In this inflammable situation the responsible persons of neither country worked for peace.

Meanwhile, in a totally unexpected chain of events, a revolution in Spain had driven the reigning queen into exile, and a Spanish provisional government invited Prince Leopold of Hohenzollern, the king of Prussia's cousin, to be constitutional king of Spain. To entrench the Prussian royal house in Spain would naturally be distasteful to France. Three times the Hohenzollern family refused the Spanish offer. Bismarck, who could not control such family decisions but who foresaw the possibility of a usable incident, deviously persuaded the Spanish to issue the invitation still a fourth time. On July 2, 1870, Paris heard that Prince Leopold had accepted. The French ambassador to Prussia, Benedetti, at the direction of his government, met the king of Prussia at the bathing resort of Ems, where he formally demanded that Prince Leopold's acceptance be withdrawn. It was withdrawn on July 12. The French seemed to have their way. Bismarck was disappointed.

France thwarts new Spanish king

The French government went still further. It instructed Benedetti to approach the king again at Ems and demand that at no time in the future would any Hohenzollern ever become a candidate for the Spanish throne. The king politely declined any such commitment and telegraphed a full report of the conversation to Bismarck at Berlin. Bismarck, receiving the telegram, which became famous as the "Ems dispatch," saw a new opportunity, as he put it, to wave a red flag before the Gallic bull. He condensed the Ems telegram for publication, so reducing and abridging it that it seemed to newspaper readers as if a curt exchange had occurred at Ems, in which the Prussians believed that their king had been insulted and the French believed that their ambassador had been snubbed. In both countries the war party demanded satisfaction. On July 19, 1870, on these trivial grounds, and with the ostensible issue of the Spanish throne already settled, the irresponsible and decaying government of Napoleon III declared war on Prussia.

The French suffered a crushing defeat at Sedan in northeastern France during the brief Franco-Prussian War in 1870. Napoleon III was captured along with much of his army. French civilians fled from both the battle and advancing Prussian troops, as can be seen in this German engraving of terrified people crossing a dangerous, crowded bridge.

(The Art Archive/Musée Carnavalet Paris/Dagli Orti)

A short war

Again the war was short. Again Bismarck had taken care to isolate his enemy in advance. The British generally felt France to be in the wrong. They had been alarmed by French operations in Mexico, which suggested an ambition to re-create a French American empire. The Italians had long been awaiting the chance to seize Rome; they did so in 1870, when the French withdrew their troops from Rome for use against Prussia. The Russians had been awaiting the chance to upset a clause of the Peace of 1856 that forbade them to keep naval vessels in the Black Sea. They did so in 1870.

The War of 1870, like the others of the time, failed to become a general European struggle. Prussia was supported by the south German states. France had no allies. The French army proved to be technically backward compared with the Prussian. War began on July 19; on September 2, after the battle of Sedan, the principal French army surrendered to the Germans. Napoleon III was himself taken prisoner. On September 4 an insurrection in Paris proclaimed the Third Republic. The Prussian and German forces moved into France and laid siege to the capital. Though the French armies dissolved, Paris refused to capitulate. For four months it was surrounded and besieged.

The German Empire, 1871

With their guns encircling Paris, the German rulers or their representatives assembled at Versailles. The château and gardens of Versailles, since Louis XVI's unceremonious departure in October 1789, had been little more than a vacant monument to a society long since dead. Here, in the most sumptuous room of the palace, the resplendent Hall of Mirrors, where the Sun King had once received the deferential approaches of German princes, Bismarck on January 18, 1871, arranged for the German Empire to be proclaimed. The king of Prussia received the hereditary title of German emperor. The other German rulers (excepting, to be sure, the ruler of Austria, and those whom Bismarck had himself dethroned) accepted his imperial authority. Ten days later the people of Paris, shivering, hungry, and helpless, opened their gates to the enemy. France had no government with which Bismarck could make peace. It was not at all clear what kind of government the country wanted.

Bismarck insisted on the election of a Constituent Assembly by universal suffrage. He demanded that France pay the German Empire a war indemnity of five billion gold francs (then an enormous and unprecedented sum) and cede to it the border region of Alsace and most of Lorraine. *Bismarck's demands* Though the Alsatians spoke German, most of them felt themselves to be French, having shared in the general history of France since the seventeenth century. There was strong local protest at the transfer to Germany, and the French never reconciled themselves to this cold-blooded amputation of their frontier. The peace dictated by Bismarck was embodied in the treaty of Frankfurt of May 10, 1871. Thereafter, as will be seen, the French Constituent Assembly gradually proceeded to construct the Third Republic.

The consolidation of Germany transformed the face of Europe. It reversed the dictum not only of the Peace of Vienna but even of the Peace of Westphalia. The German Empire, no sooner born, was the strongest state on the continent of Europe. Rapidly industrialized after 1870, it became more potent still. Bismarck had astutely exploited the conflicting ambitions of other European states and used three *The strength of the German state* short wars to bring about a German unification that most European governments had long sought at all costs to prevent. He outwitted everybody in turn, including the Germans. The united all-German state that issued from the nationalist movement was a Germany conquered by Prussia. Within the new empire Prussia directly controlled about two-thirds of the whole imperial territory. Before such unanswerable success the Prussian liberals capitulated, and the Prussian parliament passed an indemnity act; the gist of it was that Bismarck admitted to a certain high-handedness during the constitutional struggle but that the parliament legalized the disputed tax collections *ex post facto,* agreeing to forgive and forget, in view of the victory over Austria and its consequences. Thus liberalism withered away before nationalism.

The German Empire received substantially the constitution of the North German Confederation. It was a federation of monarchies, each based in theory on divine or hereditary right. At the same time, in the Reichstag elected by universal male suffrage, the empire rested on a kind of mass appeal and was in a sense democratic. Yet the country's ministers were responsible to the emperor and not to the elected chamber. Moreover, it was the rulers who joined the empire, not the peoples. There were no popular plebiscites as in Italy. Each state kept its own laws, government, and constitution. The people of Prussia, for example, remained for Prussian affairs under the rather illiberal constitution of 1850 with its three-class system of voting; in affairs of the Reich, or empire, however, they enjoyed an equal vote by universal suffrage. The emperor, who was also the king of Prussia, had

The new German Empire was officially proclaimed in January 1871 at the historic French palace in Versailles. King Wilhelm of Prussia became the German Emperor. This picture shows how Bismarck assembled his military officers and representatives from all of the constituent German states in the famous "Hall of Mirrors"—a symbolic site of past French grandeur that made the German celebration all the more humiliating for the French.
(Bismarck Museum/Bildarchiv Preussicher Kulturbesitz/Art Resource, NY)

legal control over the foreign and military policy of the empire. The German Empire in effect served as a mechanism to magnify the role of Prussia, the Prussian army, and the East Elbian Prussian aristocracy in world affairs.

The Habsburg Empire after 1848

Bismarck united Germany, but he also divided it, for he left about a sixth of the Germans outside his German Empire. These Germans of Austria and Bohemia had now to work out a common future with the dozen other nationalities in the Danubian domain. The clumsiness of the old Habsburg multinational empire is clear enough, but more impressive is its astonishing capacity to live and to survive. Having survived repeated attempts to dismember it during the eighteenth century,

Habsburg resilience

the Napoleonic wars, and the revolutions of 1848, the empire held together until the cataclysm of the First World War. But the events of the 1850s and 1860s greatly altered its character.

The essential question, in a nationalist age, was how the Habsburg government would react to the problems raised by national self-expression. By Habsburg, in this period, one means primarily Francis Joseph, who as emperor from 1848 to 1916 reigned even longer than his famous contemporary, Queen Victoria. Francis Joseph, like many others, could never shake off his own tradition. His thoughts turned on his house and on its rights. Buffeted unmercifully by the waves of change and by central European nationalisms, he cordially disliked everything liberal, progressive, or modern. Personally, Francis Joseph was incapable of enlarged views, ambitious projects, bold decisions, or persevering action. And he lived in a pompous dream world, surrounded in the imperial court by great noblemen, high churchmen, and bespangled personages of the army.

Yet the government was not idle; it was, if anything, too fertile in devising new deals and new dispensations. Various expedients were tried after 1849, but none was tried long enough to see if it would work. For several years the ruling idea was centralization—to govern the empire through the German language and with German efficiency, maintaining the abolition of serfdom as accomplished in 1848 (and which required a strong official control over the landlords if it was to work in practice) and favoring the building of railroads and other

Germanic centralization

forms of material progress. This Germanic and bureaucratic centralization was distasteful to the non-German nationalities, and especially to the Magyars. It is important to say Magyars, not Hungarians, because the Magyars composed less than half of the very mixed population within the then existing borders of Hungary. Nevertheless the Magyars, as the strongest of the non-German groups, and hence the most able to maintain a political system of their own, felt the Germanic influence as most oppressive.

The Compromise of 1867

In 1867 a compromise was worked out between the Germans of Austria-Bohemia and the Magyars of Hungary. It worked to the common disadvantage of the Slavs, who were viewed as a backward, less civilized people by both the Germans and the Magyars. The compromise created a Dual Monarchy, of a kind unparalleled in Europe. West of the river Leith was the Empire of Austria; east of it was the Kingdom of Hungary. The two were now judged exactly equal. Each

A dual monarchy

had its own constitution and its own parliament, to which in each country the governing ministry was henceforth to be responsible. The administrative language of Austria would be German; of Hungary, Magyar. Neither state might intervene in the other's affairs. The two were joined by the fact that the same Habsburg ruler should always be emperor in Austria and king in Hungary. Yet the union was not personal only; for, though there was no common parliament, delegates of the two parliaments were to meet together alternately in Vienna and Budapest, and there was to be a common ministry for finance, foreign affairs, and war. To this common ministry of Austria-Hungary both Austrians and Hungarians were to be appointed.

Both Austria and Hungary under the Dual Monarchy were in form constitutional parliamentary states, although the principle of ministerial responsibility was not consistently honored. Neither was democratic. In Austria, after much juggling with voting

**Hungary and Austria formed a political union under a Dual Monarchy and common govern-
ment ministries after 1867, but most of the population continued to live a traditional agrarian
life. This painting by the Hungarian artist Miklos Barabas,** *The Arrival of the Bride* **(1856),
portrays one of the enduring rituals of rural societies, which were often romanticized in
nineteenth-century nationalism.**
(Magyar Nemzeti Galeria, Budapest, Hungary/Bridgeman Art Library (*The Arrival of the Bride,* 1856 by Miklos
Barabas, 1810–98))

systems, a true universal male suffrage was instituted in 1907. In Hungary, when the
First World War came in 1914, still only a quarter of the adult male population had the
vote. Socially, the great reform of 1848, the abolition of serfdom, was not allowed to
lead on to upsetting conclusions. The owners of great landed estates, especially in Hungary (but also in parts of the Austrian Empire) remained the unquestionably dominant class. They were surrounded by landless peasants, an
agrarian proletariat, composed partly of lower classes of their own
nationality and partly of entire peasant peoples, like the Slovaks and
Serbs, who had no educated or wealthy class of their own. National and
social questions therefore came together. For some nationalities, especially the Magyars, not only a national but also a social and economic ascendancy was at stake. Landlordism became the basic social issue. A landowning class, educated and civilized,
faced a depressed peasant mass that was generally left out of the advancing civilization
of the day.

*National and social
questions*

ᕗ 66.   LIBERALIZATION IN TSARIST RUSSIA: ALEXANDER II

Tsarist Russia after 1856

For Russia also the Crimean War set off a series of changes. The ungainly empire, an "enormous village" as it has been called, stretching from Poland to the Pacific, had proved unable to repel a localized attack by France and Great Britain, into which neither of the Western powers had put anything like its full resources. Alexander II (1855–1881), who became tsar during the war, was no liberal by nature or conviction. But he saw that something drastic must be done. The prestige of western Europe was at its height. There the most successful and even enviable nations were to be found. The reforms in Russia therefore followed, at some distance, the European model.

Imperial Russia was a political organization very difficult to describe. Its own subjects did not know what to make of it. Some, called Westernizers in the mid–nineteenth century, believed Russia destined to become more like Europe. Others, the Slavophiles, believed Russia to be entrusted with a special destiny of its own, which imitation of Europe would only weaken or pervert.

That Russia differed from Europe at least in degree was doubted by nobody. The leading institution was the autocracy of the tsar. This was not exactly the absolutism known in the West. In Russia certain very old European conceptions were missing, such as the idea that spiritual authority is independent of even the mightiest prince or the old feudal idea of reciprocal duties between king and subject. The notion that people have certain rights or claims for justice at the hands of power, which no one in Europe had ever expressly repudiated, was in Russia a somewhat doctrinaire importation from the West. The tsardom did not rule by law; it ran the country by ukase, police action, and the army. The tsars, since Peter and before, had built up their state very largely by importing European technical methods and technical experts, often against strong objection by native Russians of all classes, upon whom the new methods were, when necessary, simply forced. More than any state in Europe, the Russian empire was a machine superimposed upon its people without organic connection—bureaucracy pure and simple. But as the contacts with Europe were joined, many Russians acquired European ideas in which the autocracy was not interested—ideas of liberty and fraternity, of a just and classless society, of individual personality enriched by humane culture and moral freedom. Many people with such sentiments found themselves chronically critical of the government and of Russia itself. The government, massive though it seemed, was afraid of such people. Any idea arising outside official circles seemed pernicious, and the press and the universities were as a rule severely censored.

Autocracy of the tsar

A second fundamental institution, which had grown up with the tsardom, was legalized bondage or serfdom. The bulk of the population were serfs dependent upon masters. Russian serfdom was more onerous than the serfdom that existed in east-central Europe until 1848. It resembled the slavery of the Americas in that serfs were "owned"; they could be bought and sold and used in occupations other than agriculture. Some serfs worked the soil, rendering unpaid labor service to the gentry. Others could be used by their owners in factories or mines or rented out for such purposes. Others were more independent, working as artisans or mechanics, and even traveling about or residing in the cities, but from their earnings they had to remit certain fees to the lord or return home when he called them. The owners had a certain paternalistic responsibility for their serfs, and in the villages the gentry constituted a kind of personal local government. The law, as in the American South, did little or nothing to interfere

The severity of Russian serfdom

EUROPE, 1871

This map shows the existence of the newly unified German Empire and a unified Kingdom of Italy. The German domain was enlarged by the incorporation of Schleswig (in the neck of the Danish peninsula) and the annexation from France of Alsace and parts of Lorraine (the regions around Strassburg and Metz on the map). From 1871 to 1914, Europe had fewer separate states than at any other time in its history. There were no further changes in national borders during this period except for the voluntary separation of Norway and Sweden in 1905 and various realignments in southeastern Europe as the Ottoman Empire withdrew from the Balkans.

between gentry and servile mass, so that the serfs' day-to-day fortunes depended on the personality or economic circumstances of their owners.

By the mid–nineteenth century most Russians agreed that serfdom must some day end. Serfdom was in any case ceasing to be profitable; some two-thirds of all the privately owned serfs (that is, those not belonging to the tsar or state) were mortgaged as security for loans at the time of Alexander II's accession. Increasingly serfdom was recognized as a bad system of labor relations, making the muzhiks into illiterate and stolid drudges, without incentive, initiative, self-respect, or pride of workmanship, and also very poor soldiers for the army.

Educated Russians, full of Western ideas, were estranged from the government, from the Orthodox church, which was an arm of the tsar, and from the common people of their own country. They felt ill at ease in a nation of uneducated peasants and a pang of guilt at the virtual slavery on which their own position rested. Hence arose another distinctive feature of nineteenth-century Russian life, the intelligentsia. In Russia it was thought so exciting to be educated, to have ideas, to subscribe to magazines, or engage in critical conversation that the intelligentsia sensed themselves as a class apart. They were made up of students, university graduates, and persons who had a good deal of leisure to read. Such people, while not very free to think, were more free to think than to do almost anything else. The Russian intelligentsia tended to sweeping and all-embracing philosophies. They believed that intellectuals should play a large role in society. They formed an exaggerated idea of how thinkers could direct the course of historical change. Their characteristic attitude was one of opposition. Some, overwhelmed by the mammoth immobility of the tsardom and of serfdom, turned to revolutionary and even terroristic philosophies. This only made the bureaucrats more anxious and fearful, and the government more fitfully repressive.

Western ideas and education

The Emancipation Act of 1861 and Other Reforms

Alexander II, on becoming tsar in 1855, attempted to enlist the support of the liberals among the intelligentsia by implementing a whole series of significant reforms. He gave permission to travel outside Russia, eased the controls on the universities, and allowed the censorship to go relatively unenforced. Newspapers and journals were founded, and those written by Russian revolutionaries abroad, like the *Polar Star* of Alexander Herzen in London, penetrated more freely into the country. The result was a great outburst of public opinion, which was agreed at least on one point, the necessity of emancipating the peasants. This was in principle hardly a party question. Alexander's father, Nicholas I, had been a noted reactionary, who abhorred Western liberalism and organized a system of secret political police until then unparalleled in Europe for its arbitrary and inquisitorial methods. Yet Nicholas I had taken serious measures to alleviate serfdom. Alexander II, basically conservative on Russian affairs, proceeded to set up a special branch of the government to study the question. The government did not wish to throw the whole labor system and economy of the country into chaos, nor to ruin the gentry class without which it could not govern at all. After many discussions, proposals, and memoranda, an imperial ukase of 1861 declared serfdom abolished and the peasants free.

By this great decree the peasants became legally free in the Western sense. They were henceforth subjects of the government, not subjects of their owners. It was hoped that they would be stirred by a new sense of human dignity. As one enthusiastic official put it shortly after emancipation: "The people are erect and transformed; the look, the walk, the speech, everything is changed." The gentry lost their old quasi-manorial jurisdiction over the villages. They could no longer exact forced and unpaid labor or receive fees arising from servitude.

It is important to realize what the Act of Emancipation did and did not do. Roughly (with great differences from region to region) it allocated about half the cultivated land to the gentry and half to the former serfs. The latter had to pay redemption money for the land they received and for the fees which the gentry lost. The Russian aristocracy was far from weakened; in place of a kind of human property largely mortgaged anyway, they now had clear possession of some half the land, they received the redemption money, and they were rid of obligations to the peasants.

Land allocation

The peasants, on the other hand, now owned some half the arable land in their own right—a considerable amount by the standards of almost any European country. They did not, however, possess it according to the principles of private property or independent farming that had become prevalent in Europe. The peasant land, when redeemed, became the collective property of the ancient peasant village assembly, or *mir.* The village, as a unit, was responsible to the government for payment of the redemption and for collection of the necessary sums from its individual members. The village assembly, in default of collection, might require forced labor from the defaulter or a member of his family; and it could prevent peasants from moving away from the village, lest those remaining bear the whole burden of payment. It could (as in the past) assign and reassign certain lands to its members for tillage and otherwise supervise cultivation as a joint concern. To keep the village community intact, the government presently forbade the selling or mortgaging of land to persons outside the village. This tended to preserve the peasant society but also to discourage the investment of outside capital, with which equipment might be purchased, and so to retard agricultural improvement and the growth of wealth.

Not all peasants within the village unit were equal. As in France before the Revolution, some had the right to work more land than others. Some were only day laborers. Others had rights of inheritance in the soil (for not all land was subject to reassignment by the commune) or rented additional parcels of land belonging to the gentry. These lands they worked by hiring other peasants for wages. None of the Russian peasants, however, after the emancipation, possessed full individual freedom of action. In their movements and obligations, as in their thoughts, they were restricted by their villages as they had once been restricted by their lords.

Inequality among peasants

Alexander II proceeded to overhaul and westernize the legal system of the country. With the disappearance of the lord's jurisdiction over his peasants a new system of local courts was needed in any case, but the opportunity was taken to reform the courts from bottom to top. The arbitrariness of authority and defenselessness of the subject were the inveterate evils. They were greatly mitigated by the edict of 1864. Trials were made public, and private persons received the right to be represented in court by lawyers of their own choosing. All class distinctions in judicial matters were abolished, although in practice peasants continued to be subject to harsh disadvantages. A clear sequence of lower and higher courts was established. Requirements were laid down for the professional training of judges, who henceforth received stated salaries and were protected from administrative pressure. A system of juries on the English model was introduced.

While thus attempting to establish a rule of law, the tsar also moved in the direction of allowing self-government. He hoped to win over the liberals and to shoulder the upper and middle classes with some degree of public responsibility. He created, again by an edict of 1864, a system of provincial

A system of self-government

The emancipation of the peasants in Russia transformed the legal status of the former serfs and opened opportunities for the development of more prosperous peasant communities. There was still much poverty in the Russian countryside after 1861, but the people who are drinking and playing music outside this rural Russian house seem to be part of the prospering post-emancipation peasant class.

(Library of Congress)

and district councils called zemstvos. Elected by various elements, including the peasants, the zemstvos gradually went into operation and took up matters of education, medical relief, public welfare, food supply, and road maintenance in their localities. Their great value was in developing civic sentiment among those who took part in them. Many liberals urged a representative body for all Russia, a Zemsky Sobor or Duma, which, however, Alexander II refused to concede. After 1864 his policy became more cautious. A rebellion in Poland in 1863 inclined him to take advice from those who favored repression. He began to mollify the vested interests that had been disgruntled by the reforms and to whittle down some of the concessions already granted. But the essence of the reforms remained unaffected.

Revolutionism in Russia

The autocrat who thus undertook to liberalize Russia barely escaped assassination in 1866, had five shots fired at him in 1873, missed death by half an hour in 1880 when his imperial dining room was dynamited, and in 1881 was to be killed by a bomb. The revolutionaries were not pleased with the reforms, which if successful would merely strengthen the existing order. Dissatisfied intelligentsia in the 1860s began to call themselves "nihilists": they believed in "nothing"—except science—and took a cynical view of the reforming tsar and his zemstvos. The peasants, saddled with heavy redemption payments, remained basically unsatisfied, and intellectuals toured the villages fanning this discontent. Revolutionaries developed a mystic conception of the revolutionary role of the Russian masses. Socialists, after the failure of socialism in Europe in the Revolution of 1848, came in many cases to believe, as Alexander Herzen wrote, that the true future of socialism lay in Russia, because of the very weakness of capitalism in Russia and the existence of a kind of collectivism already established in the village assemblies or communes.

More radical than Herzen were the anarchist Bakunin and his disciple Nechaiev. In their *People's Justice* these two called for terrorism not only against tsarist officials but against liberals also. As they wrote in the *Catechism of a Revolutionist,* the true revolutionary "is devoured by one purpose, one thought, one passion—the revolution. . . . He has severed every link with the social order and with the entire civilized world. . . . Everything which promotes the success of the revolution is moral, everything which hinders it is immoral." Terrorism (which in that time generally meant assassination) was rejected by many of the revolutionaries, especially by those who in the 1870s took up the scientific socialism of Karl Marx. To Marx it did not seem that frantic violence would advance an inevitable social process. But other groups, recognizing the inspiration of men like Bakunin and Nechaiev, organized secret terrorist societies. One of these, the People's Will, determined to assassinate the tsar. In an autocratic state, they held, there was no other road to justice and freedom.

Bakunin and anarchism

Alexander II, alarmed by this underground menace, which of course did not escape the attention of the police, again turned for support to the liberals. The liberals, who were themselves threatened by the revolutionaries, had become estranged from the government by its failure to follow through with the reforms of the early 1860s. Now, in 1880, to rally support, the tsar again relaxed the autocratic system. He abolished the dreaded secret police set up by his father, allowed the press to discuss most political subjects freely, and encouraged the zemstvos to do the same. Further to associate representatives of the public with the government, he proposed, not exactly a parliament, but two nationally elected commissions to sit with the council of state. He signed the edict to this effect on March 13, 1881, and on the same day was assassinated, not by a demented individual acting wildly and alone, but by the joint efforts of the highly trained members of the terrorist society, the People's Will.

Alexander III, upon his father's death, abandoned the project for elected commissions and during his whole reign, from 1881 to 1894, reverted to a program of brutal resistance to liberals and revolutionaries alike. The new regime established by peasant emancipation, judicial reform, and the zemstvos was nevertheless allowed to continue. How Russia finally received a parliament in 1905 is explained below in the chapter on the Russian Revolution. At present it is enough to have seen how even tsarist Russia, under Alexander II, shared in a liberal movement that was then at its height. The abolition of serfdom, putting both aristo-

Between autocracy and revolutionism

crat and peasant more fully into a money economy, opened the way for capitalistic development within the empire. And between the two confining walls of autocracy and revolutionism—equally hard and unyielding—European ideas of law, liberty, and humanity began to spread in a tentative way.

67.   THE UNITED STATES: THE AMERICAN CIVIL WAR

The history of Europe, long interconnected with that of the rest of the world, by the early twentieth century became merged with it entirely. Similarly the development of non-European regions, long a collection of separate stories, was to fuse into a single worldwide theme, to which later chapters of this book are largely devoted. It is no great leap at this point to pass to a treatment of areas outside Europe, some of which underwent in the 1860s the same process of national consolidation, or attempted consolidation, already traced in Italy and Germany, Austria, Hungary, and the Russian empire. In particular, foundations were laid for two new powerful nation-states like those of Europe—the United States of America and the Empire of Japan. The huge Dominion of Canada was also established.

Growth of the United States

As in the time of the American Revolution and Napoleon, the history of the United States in the nineteenth century resembled the evolving history of the European world, to which it was closely connected. The most basic fact, besides territorial expansion, was rapid growth. This was so obvious as to lead a French observer in the 1830s, Alexis de Tocqueville, to make a famous prediction: that within a century the United States would have 100 million people and would, along with Russia, be one of the two leading powers of the world. By 1860, with 31 million, the United States was almost as populous as France and more so than Great Britain.

Immigration

The growth in numbers was due to a prolific birth rate, but also to the arrival of immigrants, who became prolific in their turn. The immigrants in this era—except for an uncounted, because illegal, importation of slaves—came almost entirely from Europe, and before 1860 almost entirely from Great Britain, Ireland, and Germany. The immigrants did not desire to surrender their native ways. Some brought skills that the new country greatly needed, but immigration also presented a true social problem, obliging peoples to live together without common traditions. On the whole, it appears that most older Americans accepted the immigrants and the reshaping of their country rather calmly, with antiforeign movements occasionally surfacing but then quickly subsiding. Few concessions were made to the immigrant populations. English was the language of the public schools, the police, law courts, local government, and public notices and announcements. Usually the immigrant had to know some

English to hold a job. On the other hand no one was exactly forced to become "Americanized"—the new arrivals were free to maintain churches, newspapers, and social gatherings in their own tongues. The fact that the English, Scots, and Irish already spoke English, and that the Germans readily learned it, alleviated the language issue. The immigrants did not constitute minorities in the European sense. They were more than willing to embrace American national attitudes as formed in the eighteenth century—the national traditions of republicanism and self-government, of individual liberty, free enterprise, and unbounded opportunity for self-improvement. They also accepted the optimistic American creed—which preached that the future would be better than either the present or the past. The old America impressed itself on the new, being somewhat impressed itself in the process. In this sense a new nationality was steadily consolidated.

The Estrangement of North and South

But at the same time the nation was falling to pieces. North and South became completely estranged. The Industrial Revolution had contrary effects on the two regions. It turned the South into an economic associate of Great Britain. The South became the world's chief producer of raw cotton for the Lancashire mills. The Southerners, living by the export of a cash crop and producing virtually no manufactures, wished to purchase manufactured goods as cheaply as possible. Hence they favored free trade, especially with Great Britain. In the North, the Industrial Revolution led to the building of factories. Northern factory owners, usually backed by their workers, demanded protection from the inflow of British goods, with which no other country at the time could easily compete. The North therefore favored a high tariff, which the South declared to be ruinous.

More fundamental was the difference in the status of labor. As the demand for raw cotton reached unprecedented magnitudes the South fell more deeply under the great hereditary social problem of the Americas—the slave and plantation system. In the nineteenth century slavery increasingly revolted the moral conscience of thoughtful people on both sides of the Atlantic. It was abolished in the British colonies in 1833, in the French colonies in 1848, and in the Spanish American republics at different dates in the first half of the century.

Slave labor and the plantation system

Similarly, serfdom was abolished in the Habsburg possessions in 1848 and in Russia in 1861. The American South could not, and after about 1830 no longer even wished to, free itself of the system. The South was the Cotton Kingdom whose "peculiar institution" controlled the unfree labor of blacks. Whites were hurt by the system as well as blacks. Few free workers could prosper alongside a mass of subservient and virtually uncompensated labor. The incoming Europeans settled overwhelmingly in the North, the South remaining more purely "Anglo-Saxon"—except that in its most densely peopled areas some half of the people were of African descent.

In the movement westward, common in North and South, the pressure in the South came mainly from planters wishing to establish new plantations and in the North from persons hoping to set up small farms and from businessmen bent on founding new towns, building railroads, and creating markets. As once France and Great Britain had fought for control beyond the Alleghenies, so now North and South fought for control beyond the Mississippi. In 1846 the United States made war upon Mexico by methods that anticipated the aggressive tactics that Bismarck would soon use to expand the territories of Prussia. The North widely denounced the war as an act of Southern aggression but was willing enough to take the ensuing territorial conquests, which comprised the region from Texas to the Pacific.

The first new state created in this region, California, prohibited slavery. Since 1820 the United States had held together precariously by the Missouri Compromise, under which new states, as set up in the West, were admitted to the Union in pairs, one slave and one free, so that a rough equality was maintained in the Senate and in the presidential electoral vote.

The compromise of 1850

With the creation of California this balance of power was upset in favor of the North, so that in return, by the "compromise of 1850," the North agreed to enforce the laws on runaway slaves to the satisfaction of the South. But the new strictness toward fugitive slaves ran against mounting anti-slavery sentiment in the North. Attempts to arrest blacks in free states and return them to slavery aroused abolitionist anger to a higher pitch. The abolitionists, a branch of the humanitarian movement then sweeping the European world, and somewhat resembling the radical democrats who came forward in Europe in 1848, demanded the immediate and total elimination of slavery, without concession, compromise, or compensation for the property interests of the slave owners. Abolitionists denounced the Union itself as the unholy accomplice in a social abomination.

By 1860 a sense of sectionalism had developed in the South not different in principle from the nationalism felt by many peoples in Europe. In their proud insistence on states' rights and constitutional liberties, their aristocratic and warlike codes of ethics, their demand for independence from outside influence and for freedom in ruling their own subject people, the Southern white elites can be compared to the Magyars of the Austrian Empire. They now wondered whether their way of life could be safely maintained within the Union which they had helped to create. They viewed Northerners as outsiders, unsympathetic, foreign, hostile, and the South as potentially an independent and distinct nation. They were aware that within the Union they were increasingly a minority; for where in 1790 North and South had been approximately equal, by 1860 the North had outrun the South in population, mainly because of the stream of migration from Europe. The incipient nationalism of the South resembled the nationalist sentiments of a small nation struggling against a great empire. In the North, nationalism favored maintaining the whole existing territory of the United States. Northerners by 1860, with a few exceptions, refused to admit that any state of the Union could withdraw, or secede, for any reason.

In 1860 the new Republican party elected Abraham Lincoln president. It advanced a program of free Western lands for small farmers, a higher tariff, transcontinental railroad building, and economic and capitalistic development on a national scale. The new party's radical wing, to which Lincoln himself did not belong, was vehemently abolitionist and anti-Southern in sentiment. Southern leaders, after the election of Lincoln, brought about the formal withdrawal of their states from the United States of America and the creation of

Lincoln and the secession of the South

the Confederate States of America reaching from Virginia to Texas. Lincoln ordered the armed forces to defend the territory of the United States, and the resulting Civil War, or war of Southern independence, lasting four years and involving battles as great as those of Napoleon, was the most harrowing struggle of the nineteenth century with the exception of the Tai-ping rebellion in China, which lasted from 1853 to 1864.

European governments, while never recognizing the Confederacy, were partial to the South. The United States stood for principles still considered revolutionary in Europe, so that while the European working classes generally favored the North, the upper classes were willing enough to see the North American republic end in collapse and failure. In addition, Great Britain and France saw in the breakup of the United States the same advantages that they had formerly seen in the breakup of the Spanish empire. In the Confederate States the British, and the French to a lesser degree, expected to find another free trade country, supplying western Europe with raw materials and buying its manufactures; in short, they saw not a competitor like the North, but a complementary partner to the industry of the Old World. It was likewise during the American Civil War that a French army sent by Napoleon III invaded Mexico to create a puppet empire under an Austrian archduke. Thus the only serious attempt to ignore the Monroe Doctrine, violate the independence of Latin America, and revive European colonialism in the Americas occurred at the time when the United States was in dissolution.

But the North won the war and the Union was upheld. The power and influence of the United States continued to grow, and people in the Americas reaffirmed their independence from the Old World. The Mexicans rid themselves of their unwanted European emperor. Tsar Alexander II sold Alaska to the United States. The war ended the idea of the Union as a confederation of member states from which members might withdraw at will. In its place triumphed the idea that the United States was a national state, composed not of member states but of a unitary people irrevocably bound together. This doctrine was written explicitly into the Fourteenth Amendment to the Constitution, which pronounced all Americans to be citizens not only of their several states but of the United States and forbade any state to "deprive any person of life, liberty or property without due process of law"—"due process" to be determined by authority of the national government. The new force of central authority was felt first of all in the South. President Lincoln, using his war powers, issued the Emancipation Proclamation in 1863, abolishing slavery in areas engaged in hostilities against the United States. The Thirteenth Amendment in 1865 abolished slavery everywhere in the country. No compensation was paid to the slave owners, who were therefore financially ruined. The abolitionist campaign for the human rights of black Americans prevailed over the historic American deference to the rights of property.

The Union upheld

After the Civil War: Reconstruction, Industrial Growth

The assassination of Lincoln in 1865 by a fanatical Southern patriot strengthened those radical Republicans who said that the South must be drastically reformed. With the old Southern upper class completely ruined, Northerners of many types poured into the defeated country. Some came to represent the federal government, some to dabble in local politics, some to make money, and a great many out of democratic and humanitarian impulses to teach the distressed ex-slaves the elements of reading and writing or of useful trades. Blacks in the South voted, sat in legislatures, and occupied public office. This period, called Reconstruction, may be compared to the most advanced phase of the French Revolution in that "radical republicans" undertook to press liberty and equality upon a recalcitrant country, under conditions of emergency rule and under the auspices of a highly centralized national government with a mobilized army. The Southern whites strenuously objected. Some of the Northern radicals discredited themselves and most gradually lost their zeal. Reconstruction was abandoned in the 1870s, and, by what Europeans would call a counterrevolution, the Southern whites and even members of the old planter class gradually regained control.

The Northern business interests—financiers, bankers, company promoters, railway builders, manufacturers—expanded greatly with the wartime demand for munitions and military provisioning. They received protection by the Morrill tariff of 1861. In the next year, partly as a war measure, the Union Pacific Railroad was incorporated, and in 1869, at a remote spot in Utah, the last spike was driven in the first railroad to span the American continent. The

The dominance of business and finance

Les nègres affranchis colportant le décret d'affranchissement du président Lincoln.

The victories of Union armies during the American Civil War preserved the unity of the United States and also gave the national government the power to abolish slavery. This illustration from a French journal in 1863 provides a European image of newly freed people celebrating President Lincoln's Emancipation Proclamation and leaving the places where they had been enslaved. Lincoln's proclamation is posted on the side of the coach.

Homestead Act, providing farms to settlers on easy conditions, and the granting of public lands to certain colleges (ever since called land-grant colleges), largely for the promotion of agricultural sciences, encouraged the push of the eastern population into the West. Vast tracts of land were given by the government to subsidize railway building. With the destruction of the Southern slaveholders, who before the war had counterbalanced the rising industrialists, it was now industry and finance that dominated national politics in the increasingly centralized United States. The Fourteenth Amendment, for many years, was mainly interpreted not to protect the civil rights of individual persons but the property rights of business corporations against restrictive legislation by the states. The shift of political power from the states to the federal government accompanied and protected the shift of economic enterprise from local businesses to far-flung and continent-embracing corporations. As in France under Napoleon III, there was a good deal of corruption, fraud, speculation, and dishonestly or rapaciously acquired wealth; but industry boomed, the cities grew, and the American mass market was created. On Fifth Avenue in New York, and in other Northern cities, rose the pretentious and gaudy mansions of the excessively rich.

In short, the American Civil War, which might have reduced English-speaking America to a scramble of jealously competing minor republics, resulted instead in the economic and political consolidation of a large nation-state, liberal and democratic in its political principles, and committed enthusiastically to private enterprise in its economic system.

68.   THE DOMINION OF CANADA, 1867

North of the United States, at the time of the Civil War, lay a number of British provinces unconnected with one another and each in varying degree dependent on Great Britain. The European population in this vast territory had originated in three great streams. One part was French, settled in the St. Lawrence valley since the seventeenth century. A second part was made up of descendants of United Empire Loyalists, old seaboard colonists who, remaining faithful to Britain, had fled from the United States during the American Revolution. They were numerous in the Maritime Provinces and in Upper Canada, as Ontario was then called (see map, p. 524). A third part consisted of recent immigrants from Great Britain, men and women of the working classes who had left the home country to improve their lives in America.

The French firmly resisted assimilation to the English-speaking world around them. Their statute of freedom was the Quebec Act of 1774, which had been denounced as "intolerable" by the aroused inhabitants of the thirteen colonies, but which put the French civil law, French language, and French Catholic church under the protection of the British Crown. The *French resistance to assimilation*
French looked with apprehension upon the stream of immigrants, English-speaking and Protestant, which began to flow into Canada about 1780 and thereafter never stopped. There was constant irritation between the two nationalities.

The British government tried various expedients. In 1791 it created two provinces in the St. Lawrence and Great Lakes region—a Lower Canada to remain French, and an Upper Canada to be English. They received the same form of government as that enjoyed by the thirteen colonies before their break from the empire. *Upper and Lower Canada*
Each colony, that is, had a locally elected assembly with certain powers of taxation and lawmaking, subject to veto by the British authorities, as represented either by the governor or by the London government itself. For many years there was no objection to these arrangements. The War of 1812, in which the United States embarked on the conquest of Canada, aroused a national sentiment among both French and English in that country, together with a willingness to depend politically upon Great Britain for military security. But the internal political differences continued. In Lower Canada the French feared the English-speaking minority. In Upper Canada the old aristocracy of United Empire Loyalists, who had carved the province from the wilderness, hesitated to share control with the new immigrants from Great Britain. Between the provinces there were grievances also, since Lower Canada stood in the way of Upper Canada's outlet to the sea. In 1837 a superficial rebellion broke out in both provinces. It was put down virtually without bloodshed.

Lord Durham's Report

In Great Britain at this time the reforming Whigs were busily renovating many ancient English institutions. Some of them had definite views on the administration of colonies. In general, they held that it was not necessary to control a region politically to trade with it. This was an aspect of the free trade doctrine, separating economics from politics, business from power. The Whig reformers were rather indifferent to empire, unconcerned with military, naval, or strategic considerations. A few even thought it natural for colonies, when mature, to drop away entirely from the mother country. Whigs, liberals, and radicals all wished to economize on military expenditure, to relieve British taxpayers by cutting down British garrisons overseas.

After the Canadian insurrection of 1837 the Whig government sent out the Earl of Durham as governor. Durham, one of the framers of the parliamentary Reform Bill of 1832, published his views on Canadian affairs in 1839. Durham's Report was long regarded as one of the classic documents in the rise of the British Commonwealth of Nations. He held that in the long run French separatist feeling in Canada should disappear and all Canadians should be brought to feel a common citizenship and national character.

He therefore called for the reuniting of the two Canadas into one province. To consolidate this province he proposed an intensive development of railways and canals. In political matters he urged the granting of virtual self-government for Canada and the introduction of the British system of "responsible government," in which the prime minister and cabinet should be responsible to and under the control of the elected assembly in the province, the governor becoming a kind of legal and ceremonial figure like the sovereign in Great Britain.

Call for reuniting the provinces

Most of Durham's Report was accepted immediately. Upper and Lower Canada were combined into one province, with the machinery of self-government, in 1840. The British army was withdrawn. The Canadians undertook to maintain their own military establishment, still regarded as necessary, since the era of the famous undefended frontier between Canada and the United States had not yet dawned. The principle of responsible government was established in the late 1840s, the governors of Canada allowing the elected assembly to adopt policies and appoint or remove ministers as it chose. Responsible government, still confined to internal matters, worked satisfactorily from the beginning. But one feature of the new plan, the union of the two Canadas, began to produce friction as the English-speaking immigration continued. The French were afraid of being outnumbered in their own country. Many Canadians therefore turned to the idea of a federation, in which the French and English areas might each conduct their own local affairs, while remaining joined for larger purposes in a central government.

The appeal of a federation

Founding of the Dominion of Canada

Federalism in Canada was thus partly a decentralizing idea, aimed at satisfying the French element by returning to a division into two provinces, and in part a plan for a new centralization or unification, because it contemplated bringing all the provinces of British North America into union with the St. Lawrence and Great Lakes region, to which alone the term Canada had hitherto been applied. While the people of British North America discussed federation, the Civil War was tearing apart the United States. In the face of this example, the Canadians formed a strong union in which all powers were to rest in the central government except those specifically assigned to the provinces. The federal constitution, drafted in

The Dominion of Canada united English and French provinces under a federal constitution. The French-Canadian Prime Minister Wilfred Laurier, pictured here toward the end of his long political career in the early twentieth century, helped extend the union of the English and French populations from a constitutional document into the daily affairs of a modern national government.
(Getty Images)

Canada by Canadians, was passed by the British Parliament in 1867 as the British North America Act, which constitutionally established the Dominion of Canada. The eastern maritime provinces (Nova Scotia, New Brunswick, and Prince Edward Island) joined Quebec and Ontario in the Dominion, and the new political arrangements facilitated Canada's rapid westward expansion to the Pacific coast. In 1982 the British North America Act was replaced by a new agreement, which explicitly recognized the sovereign independence of Canada and its power to frame a constitution for itself. By the 1980s, however, the French speakers of Quebec had become more determined to defend the autonomy of their own province and culture, so it was again necessary to recognize a special status for Quebec. The western provinces had also grown and become more protective of their interests. The relationship between the central and provincial governments, along with bilingualism, or the equal recognition of the French and English languages, has never been completely resolved.

By the legislation of 1867 the new dominion received a common federal parliament, in which a ministry responsible to the majority in parliament governed according to British principles of "responsible," or cabinet, government. The new Canadian government was generally controlled by the Conservative Party, but the Liberal Party eventually came to a long term of power (1896–1911) under the leadership of an energetic French Canadian named Wilfred Laurier, whose political prominence showed the increasing collaboration between the French and English populations. The Dominion of Canada, though at first not large in population, possessed from the beginning a significance beyond the mere number of its people. It was the first example of successful devolution, or granting of political liberty, within one of the European colonial empires. It embodied principles which Edmund Burke and Benjamin Franklin had vainly recommended a century before to keep the thirteen colonies loyal to Great Britain. The dominion after 1867 moved forward from independence in internal matters to independence in such external affairs as tariffs, diplomacy, and the decisions of war and peace. It thus pioneered in the development of "dominion status," working out precedents later applied in Australia (1901), New Zealand (1907), the

Pioneering dominion status
Union of South Africa (1910), and in the 1920s, temporarily, in Ireland. By the middle of the twentieth century the same idea, or what may be called the Canadian idea, was also applied to the worldwide process of decolonization as it affected non-European peoples, notably in India, Pakistan, Sri Lanka, and the former British colonies in Africa, until all these peoples chose to become republics, though still loosely and voluntarily joined together and to Great Britain in a Commonwealth of Nations.

More immediately, in America, the founding of the dominion, a solid band of self-governing territory stretching from ocean to ocean, stabilized the relations between British North America and the United States. The United States regarded its northern borders as final. The withdrawal of British control from Canadian affairs also furthered the long-developing conception of an American continent entirely free from European political influence.

69.   JAPAN AND THE WEST

The Japanese, when they allowed the Westerners to discover them, were a highly civilized people living in a complex society. They had many large cities, they enjoyed the contemplation of natural scenery, they went to the theater, and they read novels. With their stylized manners, their fans and their wooden temples, their lacquer work and their painting on screens, their tiny rice fields and their curious and ineffectual firearms, they seemed to Europeans to be the very acme of everything quaint. This European view of traditional Japan is immortalized in *The Mikado* of Gilbert and Sullivan, first performed in 1885. Not long thereafter the idea of Japanese quaintness, like the idea of the Germans as an impractical people given mainly to music and metaphysics, had to be revised. The Europeans, in "opening" Japan, opened up more than they knew.

In 1853, the American Commodore Perry forced his way with a fleet of naval vessels into Yedo Bay, insisted upon landing, and demanded of the Japanese government that it engage in commercial relations with the United States and other Western powers. In the next year the Japanese began to comply, and in 1867 an internal revolution took place, of which the most conspicuous consequence was a rapid modernizing of Japanese life and institutions. But if it looked as if the country had been "opened" by Westerners, actually Japan had exploded from within.

Background: Two Centuries of Isolation, 1640–1854

For over two centuries Japan had followed a program of self-imposed isolation. No Japanese was allowed to leave the islands or even to build a ship large enough to navigate the high seas. No foreigner, except for handfuls of Dutch and Chinese, was allowed to enter. Japan remained a sealed book to the West. The contrary is not quite so true, for the Japanese knew rather more about Europe than Europeans did about Japan. The Japanese policy of systematic exclusions was not merely based upon ignorance. Initially, at least, it was based on experience.

The first Europeans—three Portuguese in a Chinese junk—are thought to have arrived in Japan in 1542. For about a century thereafter there was considerable coming and going.

Early contact with Europeans
The Japanese showed a strong desire to trade with the foreigners, from whom they obtained clocks and maps, learned about printing and ship-building, and took over the use of tobacco and potatoes. Thousands also adopted the Christian religion as preached to them by Spanish and Por-

CHRONOLOGY OF NOTABLE EVENTS, 1853–1871

1853	American Commodore Perry arrives in Yedo (Tokyo) Bay, "opening" Japan to foreign commercial exchanges
1854–1856	France and Britain join with Turkey to defeat Russia in the Crimean War
1861	Italians establish the unified Kingdom of Italy
1861	Tsar Alexander II abolishes serfdom in Russia
1861–1865	Civil War in the United States; federal union is upheld and slavery is abolished
1867	Austria and Hungary join together in "Dual Monarchy" under the Habsburg ruler Francis Joseph
1867	Creation of the independent Dominion of Canada
1868	New Japanese emperor Mutsuhito begins the Meiji era; Japan enters process of rapid economic and political change
1870	Prussia defeats France in brief war; Napoleon III abdicates and Parisians proclaim a Third French Republic
1871	King Wilhelm of Prussia becomes emperor in newly established German Empire

tuguese Jesuits. Japanese traveled to the Dutch Indies and even to Europe. The Japanese in fact proved more receptive to European ideas than other Asian peoples. But shortly after 1600 the government began to drive Christianity underground; in 1624 it expelled the Spaniards, in 1639 it expelled the Portuguese, and in 1640 it expelled all Europeans except for a few Dutch merchants who were allowed to remain at Nagasaki under strict control. From 1640 to 1854 these few Dutch at Nagasaki were the only channel of communication with the West.

The reasons for self-seclusion, as for its abandonment later, arose from the course of political events in Japan. The history of Japan showed some similarities to that of Europe. In Japan, as in Europe, a period of feudal warfare was followed by a period of government absolutism, during which civil peace was kept by a bureaucracy, an obsolescent warrior class was maintained as a privileged element in society, and a commercial class of native merchants grew wealthier, stronger, and more insistent upon its position.

When the first Europeans arrived, the islands were still torn by the wars and rivalries of the numerous clans into which the Japanese were organized. Gradually one clan, the Tokugawa, gained control, taking over the office of "shogun." The shogun was a kind of military head who governed in the name of the emperor, and the hereditary Tokugawa shogunate, founded in 1603, lasted until 1867. The early Tokugawa shoguns concluded from a good deal of evidence that the Europeans in Japan, both merchants and missionaries, were engaging in feudal or interclan politics and even aspiring to dominate Japan by helping Christian or pro-European Japanese to get into power. The first three Tokugawa shoguns, to establish their own dynasty, to pacify and stabilize the country, and to keep Japan free from European penetration, undertook to eliminate Christianity and adopted the rigid policy of nonintercourse with the rest of the world.

The Tokugawa shoguns

Under the Tokugawa Japan enjoyed peace, a long peace, for the first time in centuries. The Tokugawa shoguns completed the detachment of the emperor from politics, building him up as a divine and legendary being, too august and too remote for the hurly-burly of the world. The emperor remained shut in at Kyoto on a modest allowance furnished by the shoguns. The shoguns established their own court and government at Yedo (later called Tokyo); and as Louis XIV brought nobles to Versailles, or Peter the Great forced his uncouth lords to build town houses in St. Petersburg, so the shoguns required the great feudal chieftains and their men-at-arms to reside at least part of the year in Yedo.

Military dictatorship

The shoguns administered the country through a kind of military bureaucracy or dictatorship. This formidable instrument of state watched over the great lords (called daimyo), who, however, retained a good deal of feudal authority over their subjects in the regions most distant from Yedo. The great lords and their armed retainers (the samurai), having no further fighting to occupy them, turned into a landed aristocracy which spent a good deal of its time in Yedo and other cities. As a leisure class, they developed new tastes and standards of living and hence needed more income, which they obtained by squeezing the peasants, and which they spent by buying from the merchants.

The merchant class greatly expanded by catering to the government and the gentry. Japan in the seventeenth century developed a money economy. Many lords fell seriously into debt to the merchants. Many samurai, like lesser nobles in France, Spain, or Poland at the time, were almost ridiculously impoverished, hard-pressed to keep up appearances, with nothing except social status to distinguish them from commoners. The law, as in Europe under the Old Regime, drew a sharp line between classes. Nobles, merchants, and peasants were subject to different taxes and were differently punished for different offenses. What was a crime for a commoner would be excusable for a samurai; or what in a samurai would be a punishable breach of honor would be accepted in a commoner. The samurai had the right to carry two swords as a mark of class and could in theory cut down an impudent commoner without arousing further inquiry. In practice the shoguns repressed violence of this kind, but there was much less development of law and justice than in the European monarchies of the Old Regime. Economically the merchants and artisans prospered. By 1723 Yedo was a city with 500,000 people; by 1800 with over 1,000,000, it was larger than London or Paris, and 20 times as large as the largest city in the United States. After 1800 some merchants were able to purchase the rank of samurai for money. The old class lines were beginning to blur.

Class divisions

Though deliberately secluded, the economic and social life of Japan was thus by no means static. The same is true of its intellectual life. Buddhism, the historic religion, lost its hold on many people during the Tokugawa period, so that Japan in its way underwent, like the West, a secularization of ideas. As a code of personal conduct there was a new emphasis on Bushido, the "way of the warrior," a kind of nonreligious moral teaching which exalted the samurai virtues of honor and loyalty. With the decline of Buddhism went

Secularization and Shinto

also a revival of the cult of Shinto, the "way of the gods," the ancient indigenous religion of Japan, which held, among much else, that the emperor was veritably the Son of Heaven. There was much activity in the study and writing of history, arousing, as in Europe, an acute interest in the national past. History, like Shinto, led to a feeling that shoguns were usurpers and that the emperor, obscurely relegated to Kyoto, was the true representative of everything highest and most lasting in the life of Japan.

Meanwhile, through the crack left open at Nagasaki, Western ideas trickled in. The shogun Yoshimune in the mid–eighteenth century permitted the importation of Occidental books, except those relating to Christianity. A few Japanese learned Dutch and began to decipher Dutch books on anatomy, surgery, astronomy, and other subjects. In 1745 a

Dutch-Japanese dictionary was completed. For European manufactures also—watches, glassware, velvets, woolens, telescopes, barometers—there came to be an eager demand, satisfied as much as possible by the methodical Dutch. Nor were the Japanese wholly uninformed about politics in the West. While the most assiduous Westerner could learn nothing of the internal affairs of Japan, an educated Japanese could, if he wished, arrive at some idea of the French Revolution, or know who was president of the United States.

The Opening of Japan

When Perry sailed into Yedo Bay in 1853, he therefore had many potential allies within Japan. There were nobles, heavily in debt, unable to draw more income from agriculture, willing to embark upon foreign trade and to exploit their property by introducing new enterprises. There were penurious samurai, with no future in the old system, ready and willing to enter upon new careers as army officers or civil officials. There were merchants hoping to add to their business by dealing in Western goods. There were scholars eager to learn more of Western science and medicine. There were patriots fearful that Japan was becoming defenseless against Western guns. Spiritually the country was already adrift from its moorings, already set toward a course of national self-assertion, restlessly susceptible to hazily understood new ideas. Under such pressures, and from downright fear of a bombardment of Yedo by the Americans, which if it would not subdue Japan would at least ruin the declining prestige of the shogunate, the shogun Iesada in 1854 signed a commercial treaty with the United States. Similar treaties were soon signed with the Europeans.

In the following years were sown the seeds of much later misunderstanding between Japan and the West. The Europeans and Americans tended to be trigger-happy in the discharge of naval ordnance against less well-armed peoples. The Japanese, a proud and elaborately civilized nation, *The seeds of conflict* soon found that Western people considered them backward. They quickly found, for example, as soon as they learned more of the West by reading and travel, that the treaties they signed in the 1850s were not treaties between equals as understood in the West. These first treaties provided that Japan should maintain a low tariff on imports and not change it except with the consent of the foreign powers. To give outsiders a voice in determining tariff policy was not the custom among sovereign states of the West. The early treaties also provided for extraterritoriality. This meant that Europeans and Americans residing in Japan were not subject to Japanese law but remained under the jurisdiction of their respective homelands as represented by consular officials. Such extraterritorial provisions had long been established in Turkey and were currently taking root in China. Europeans insisted upon them in countries where European principles of property, debt, or security of life and person did not prevail. At the same time, of course, no European state ever permitted a foreign power to exercise jurisdiction within its borders. Extraterritoriality was a mark of inferiority, as the Japanese soon discovered.

A strong antiforeign reaction developed after 1854. It was at first led *Antiforeign reaction* by certain nobles of the western islands, the lords of Choshu and Satsuma, who had never been fully subordinated to the shogun at Yedo, and who now dreamed of overturning the Tokugawa shogunate and leading a national revival with the emperor as its rallying point. Their first idea was to check Western penetration (as two and a half centuries before) by driving the Westerners out. But in 1862 some Englishmen unintentionally violated a small point of Japanese etiquette. One of them was killed. The

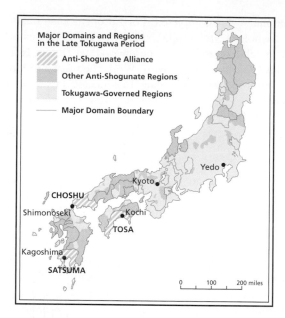

JAPAN IN THE LATE TOKUGAWA PERIOD

The Tokugawa regime lasted from 1603 to 1867. The map shows the divisions and power rivalries within Japan around the time that Western nations began to enter the region in the mid–nineteenth century. The Tokugawa shogunate controlled the territory around Yedo (later called Tokyo), but independent nobles in Choshu, Satsuma, and other parts of the country controlled large areas that the shogun at Yedo could not bring under his authority. As the Western powers entered Japan after 1854, a strong demand for reforms emerged in Choshu and Satsuma, leading to the overthrow of the Tokugawa shogun in 1867, the establishment of a new national ("Meiji") government, and the rapid development of a new industrial economy.

British government demanded punishment for the offending Japanese, who were followers of the lord of Satsuma. The shogun proved unable to arrange this, and the British navy thereupon bombarded the capital of Satsuma. In the same year the lord of Choshu, who commanded the straits of Shimonoseki with some ancient artillery, ordered it to fire on passing vessels. The British, French, Dutch, and United States governments immediately protested, and, when the embarrassed shogun proved unable to discipline Choshu, they dispatched an allied naval force to Shimonoseki. The forts and shipping of Choshu were destroyed, and an indemnity of $3,000,000 was imposed. These incidents were remembered in Japan long after they were forgotten in Europe and the United States. It was likewise remembered that the Western powers, discovering that the shogun was not the supreme ruler of the country, sent a naval expedition to Kyoto itself and required the emperor to confirm the treaties signed by the shogun and to reduce import duties, under threat of naval bombardment.

The Meiji Era (1868–1912): The Modernization of Japan

The lords of Choshu and Satsuma now concluded that the only way to deal with the West was to adopt the military and technical equipment of the West itself. They would save Japan for the Japanese by learning the secrets of modern Western power. First they forced the resignation of the shogun, whose prestige had long been undermined anyway and who had now discredited himself first by signing undesirable treaties with the West and then failing to protect the country from outrage. The last shogun abdicated in 1867. The reformers declared the emperor restored to his full authority. It was their intention to use the imperial throne to consolidate and fortify Japan for its new position in the world. In 1868 a new emperor inherited the throne; his name was Mutsuhito; according to Japanese custom a name was given to his reign also, which was called Meiji ("enlightened peace"). The Meiji era (1868–1912) was the first great era of modernization in Japan.

Japan turned into a modern nation-state. Feudalism was abolished, most of the great lords voluntarily surrendering into the emperor's hands their control over samurai and common people. "We abolish the clans and convert them into prefectures," declared one imperial decree. The legal system was reorganized and equality before the law was introduced, in the sense that all persons became subject to the same rules regardless of class. In part with the hope of getting rid of extraterritoriality, the reformers recast the criminal law along Western lines, deleting the bizarre and cruel punishments which Europeans considered barbaric. A new army was established, modeled mainly on the Prussian. The samurai in 1871 lost his historic right to carry two swords; he now served as an army officer, not as the retainer of a clannish chief. A navy, modeled on the British, followed somewhat later. Control of money and currency passed to the central government, and a national currency with decimal units was adopted. A national postal service began to function, and above all the government developed a national school system, which soon brought a high rate of literacy to Japan. Buddhism was discouraged, and the property of Buddhist monasteries was confiscated. Shinto was the cult favored by the government. Shinto gave a religious tincture to national sentiment and led to a renewed veneration of the imperial family.

A modern nation-state

In 1889 a constitution was promulgated. It confirmed the civil liberties then common in the West and provided for a parliament in two chambers, but it stressed also the supreme and eternal authority of the emperor, to whom the ministers were legally responsible. In practice, in the new Japan, the emperor never actively governed. He remained aloof, as in the past; and political leaders, never fully responsible to the parliament, tended to govern freely in what they conceived to be the interests of the state.

Industrial and financial modernization went along with and even preceded the political revolution. In 1858 the first steamship was purchased from the Dutch. In 1859 Japan placed its first foreign loan, borrowing five million yen by a bond issue floated in England. In 1869 the first telegraph connected Yokohama and Tokyo. The first railroad, between the same two cities, was completed in 1872. In 1870 appeared the first spinning machinery. Foreign trade, almost literally zero in 1854, was valued at $200 million a year by the end of the century. The population rose from 33 million in 1872 to 46 million in 1902. The island empire, like Great Britain, became dependent on exports and imports to sustain its dense population at the level of living to which it aspired.

Industrial and financial modernization

The modernization of Japanese society still stands as the most remarkable transformation ever undergone by any people in so short a time. It recalls the "westernizing" of Russia under Peter over a century before, though conducted somewhat less brutally, more rapidly, and with a wider consent among the population. For Japan, as formerly for Russia, the motive was in large measure defense against Western penetration, together with an admiration for Western statecraft and an ambition to become an international power. The new government institutions helped to produce a more unified nation-state of the type then

Distinctive characteristics of Japan's new industrial economy appear in this illustration of a silk reeling factory by the artist Ichiyosai. Working in a Western-style brick building under the supervision of factory foremen, women produce silk within the structures of a modern industrial system, but they continue to wear Japanese clothing (in contrast to the visitors in the left foreground), thereby expressing the cultural mixtures of an older society and a new economic order.

(Laurie Platt Winfrey, Inc.)

developing throughout Europe and the Americas. What the Japanese wanted from the West was primarily science, technology, and organization. They were content enough with the innermost substance of their culture, their moral ideas, their family life, their arts and amusements, their religious conceptions, though even in these they showed an uncommon adaptability. Essentially it was to protect their internal substance, their Japanese culture, that they took over the external apparatus of modern Western civilization. This apparatus—science, technology, machinery, arms, political and legal organization—was the part of Western civilization for which other peoples generally felt a need, which they hoped to adopt without losing their own cultural and spiritual independence, and which therefore, though sometimes rather scornfully dismissed as materialistic, became the common ground for the interdependent worldwide civilization that emerged at the close of the nineteenth century.

In brief, the world between 1850 and 1870, revolutionized economically by the rail-road and steamship, was revolutionized politically by the formation and expansion of large, consolidated nation-states. These states at the time all embodied certain liberal and constitutional principles, or at least the machinery of parliamentary and representative government. But the whole earth had also become an arena in which certain nations or powers sought to promote their economic and political interests. The Great Powers in 1871 were Great Britain, Germany, France, Austria-Hungary, and Russia. Britain had produced a daughter nation in Canada. Whether Italy was to be called a Great Power was not yet clear. No one knew what Japan would do. All agreed that the United States would one day play a large role in international affairs, but the time was not yet.

For interactive exercises, glossary, chronologies, and more, go to the *Online Learning Center* at **www.mhhe.com/palmer10.**

Chapter 14

EUROPEAN CIVILIZATION, 1871–1914: ECONOMY AND POLITICS

Half a century elapsed between the period of national consolidation described in the last chapter and the outbreak of the First World War in 1914. In this half-century European civilization achieved its greatest power in global politics, developed its leading role in the global economy, and also exerted its maximum influence upon peoples outside Europe.

For Europe and the European world the years 1871 to 1914 were marked by hitherto unparalleled material and industrial growth; international peace; domestic stability; the advance of constitutional, representative, and democratic government; and continued faith in science, reason, and progress. But in these very years, in politics, economics, philosophy, and the arts, there were also new trends operating to undermine the liberal premises and tenets of this European civilization. Meanwhile, a new wave of European imperialism spread across Africa and Asia, creating new colonial empires, new global economic connections, and new international and cultural conflicts. All of these developments contributed to and reflected the European ascendancy before 1914, and all produced a legacy that has decisively influenced the modern world down to our own time.

For purposes of historical analysis, we must separate this complex era into different thematic strands. This chapter therefore examines economic and political trends in Europe after 1871, the next describes European social and cultural movements in this era, and the following one discusses the worldwide impact of European imperialism. By 1914, the institutions and ideas of modern European civilization were spreading across most of the world, but these same institutions and ideas were also facing new critical challenges from within Europe and from people on other continents who resented the European domination of their economies, governments, and cultures.

Chapter emblem: Detail from a photograph of Italian immigrants arriving in New York about 1900. (Snark/Art Resource, NY)

✑ 70.   THE MODERN "CIVILIZED WORLD"

Materialistic and Nonmaterialistic Ideals

With the extension of the nation-state system Europe was politically more divided than ever. Its unity lay in the sharing by almost all Europeans of a similar way of life and outlook, which existed also in such "European" countries as the United States, Canada, Australia, and New Zealand. Europe and its offshoots constituted what Europeans and North Americans called the "civilized world" or the "West." Other regions—mostly in Asia, Africa, and Latin America—were described by Europeans as "backward." Europeans and other Westerners were extremely conscious and inordinately proud of their civilization in the half-century before 1914. They believed it to be the well-deserved outcome of centuries of progress. Believing themselves to be the most advanced branch of mankind in the most important areas of human endeavor, they assumed that all peoples should respect the same social ideals—that so far as they were unwilling or unable to adopt them, they were "backward," and that so far as they did adopt them, they became "civilized" in their turn.

Such ideas shaped the ideology and practice of imperialism, which entered a dynamic new phase in the late nineteenth century.

The ideal of civilization

The ideals of European or "Western" civilization were in part materialistic. If Europeans and Westerners considered their civilization to be better in 1900 than in 1800, or better than the ways of non-Western peoples at the same time, it was because they generally had a higher standard of living, ate and dressed more adequately, slept in softer beds, and had more satisfactory sanitary facilities. It was because they possessed ocean liners, railroads, and streetcars and after about 1880, telephones and electric lights. But the ideal of civilization was by no means exclusively materialistic. Knowledge as such, correct or truthful knowledge, was held to be a civilized attainment—scientific knowledge of nature, in place of superstition or demonology; geographical knowledge, by which civilized people were aware of the earth as a whole with its general contours and diverse inhabitants. The ideal was also profoundly moral, derived from Christianity, but now secularized and detached from religion. An Englishman, Isaac Taylor, in his *Ultimate Civilization,* published in 1860, defined this moral ideal by listing the contrasting "relics of barbarism" which he thought were due to disappear—"Polygamy, Infanticide, Legalized Prostitution, Capricious Divorce, Sanguinary and Immoral Games, Infliction of Torture, Caste and Slavery." Several of these had been unknown to the approved customs of Europe at least since the coming of Christianity (though prostitution was more or less tolerated in almost all European societies). Torture went out of use about 1800, even in the illiberal European states; and legalized caste and slavery were gradually abolished by Western countries in the course of the nineteenth century. But there were few non-Western peoples, in 1860, among whom two or three of Taylor's "relics" could not be found.

Indices of advancement

There are certain other indices, more purely quantitative, worked out by sociologists to show the level of advancement of a given society. One of these is the death rate, or number of persons per thousand of population who die each year. In England, France, and Sweden the "true" death rate (or death rate regardless of the proportion of infants and old people, who are most susceptible to death) is known to have fallen from about 25 (per 1,000 per year) before 1850, to 19 in 1914 and 18 in the 1930s. Indeed, before the Second World War, it stood seemingly stabilized at about 18 in all countries of northwestern Europe, the United States, and the British dominions.

Death rates in countries not "modern" usually run over 40 even in favorable times. A closely related index is infant mortality, which fell rapidly after 1870 in all countries affected by medical science. Thus a woman under more modern conditions had to go through pregnancy and childbirth less often to produce the same number of surviving children. Another index is life expectancy, or the age that a person has an even chance of attaining. In England life expectancy at birth rose from 40 years in the 1840s to 59 in 1933 and to 78 at the beginning of the twenty-first century. In India in 1931 it was less than 27 years. It had risen to about 62 in 2001. Still another index is the literacy rate, or proportion of persons above a certain age (such as ten) able to read and write. In northwestern Europe by 1900 the literacy rate approached 100, whereas in some countries of the world it had still not risen very far above zero. A further basic index is the productivity of labor, or amount produced by one worker in a given expenditure of time. This is difficult to compute, especially for earlier periods for which statistical data are lacking. In the 1930s, however, the productivity of a farmer in Denmark was over ten times that of a farmer in Albania. All northwestern Europe was above the European average in this respect with the exception of Ireland, whereas Ireland, Spain, Portugal, Italy and all eastern Europe were below it.

The essence of civilized living doubtless is in the intangibles, in the way in which people use their minds and in the attitudes they form toward others or toward the conditions and planning of their own lives. The intangibles, however, are not always agreed upon by persons of different cultures or ideologies. On the quantitative criteria there is less disagreement; all, with few exceptions, wish to lower the death rate, raise the literacy rate, and increase the productivity of human exertion. Whatever we might say about the intangible qualities of a civilized society, if we apply quantitative or sociological indices alone, we can say that for about four decades after 1870 Europe was in fact (and not merely in the opinion of Europeans) the center of a modern civilization that was expanding rapidly around the world.

The "Zones" of Civilization

Or rather, a certain region of Europe was the center. For there were really two Europes, an inner zone and an outer. A Frenchman writing in the 1920s describing the two Europes that had risen since 1870, called the inner zone the "Europe of steam," and bounded it by an imaginary line joining Glasgow, Stockholm, Danzig, Trieste, Florence, and Barcelona. It included not only Great Britain but Belgium, Germany, France, northern Italy, and the western portions of the Austrian Empire. Virtually all heavy European industry was located in this zone. Here the railway network was thickest. Here the wealth of Europe was concentrated, in the form both of a high living standard and of accumulations of capital. Here likewise were almost all the laboratories and scientific activity of Europe. Here, in the same zone, lay the strength of constitutional and parliamentary government and of liberal, humanitarian, socialist, and reformist movements of many kinds. In this zone the death rate was low, life expectancy was high, conditions of health and sanitation were at their best, literacy was almost universal, productivity of labor was impressive. To the same zone, for practical purposes, belonged certain regions of European settlement overseas, especially the post-Civil War United States.

The outer zone

The outer zone included most of Ireland, most of the Iberian and Italian peninsulas, and all Europe east of what was then Germany, Bohemia, and Austria proper. The outer zone was agricultural, though the productivity of agriculture, per farm worker or per acre, was far less than in the inner zone. The people were poorer, more illiterate, and more likely to die young. The wealthy were landlords, often absentees.

TRAIN IN THE SNOW
by Claude Monet (French, 1840–1926)

Trains became one of the new symbols of modernity during the nineteenth century, but few artists saw them as appropriate subjects for paintings. Monet and other Impressionists, however, wanted to apply their artistic techniques to the familiar objects of everyday life, including the iron shapes of a passing locomotive. In this typical Impressionist rendering of modern technology, the solid mass of the train melts into the play of light and the indeterminate grays of a dull winter day.
(Giraudon/Art Resource, NY)

The outer zone lived increasingly after 1870 by selling grain, livestock, wool, or lumber to the more industrialized inner zone but was too poor to purchase many manufactured products in return. To obtain capital it borrowed in London or Paris. Its social and political philosophies were characteristically imported from Germany and the West. It borrowed engineers and technicians from the first zone to build its bridges and install its telegraph systems and sent its youth to universities in the first zone to study medicine or other professions. Many areas of European settlement overseas, for example in Latin America and the agrarian parts of the United States, may also be thought of at that time as belonging to this outer zone.

Beyond the European world lay a third zone, the immense reaches of Asia and Africa, all viewed as "backward" by the standards or cultural assumptions of Europe, with the exception of modernizing Japan, and destined for the most part to become heavily dependent upon or colonized by Europe in the half-century after 1870. Much of the world's history since 1870 could be written as the story of relations among these three zones; but it is necessary in all human matters to guard against formulas that are too simple. And there are always changes as well as continuities in the histories of all human societies.

71. BASIC DEMOGRAPHY: THE INCREASE OF THE EUROPEANS

European and World Population Growth since 1650

All continents except Africa gained enormously in population in the three centuries following 1650, but it was Europe that grew the most. There is little doubt that the proportion of Europeans in the world's total, including those of European origin in other continents, reached its maximum for all time between 1850 and the Second World War. Estimates are given in the table on page 566, beginning with 1650.

Causes of demographic growth

The causes of the rise in population after 1650 cannot be positively known. Some of them obviously operated in Asia as well as Europe. In Europe the organized sovereign states, as established in the seventeenth century, put an end to a long period of civil wars, stopping the chronic violence and marauding, with the accompanying insecurity of agriculture and family life, which were more deadly than wars fought between governments. Similarly, the Tokugawa kept peace in Japan, and the Manchu or Qing dynasty (1644–1912) brought a long period of order in China. The British rule in India and the Dutch in Java, by curbing famine and violence, allowed populations to grow very rapidly. All such factors, which allowed more people to remain alive longer, also favored the stability of families and the birth and raising of children. Death rates could fall and birth rates could rise from similar causes. The great exception to the swelling rise of population was Africa, where the slave trade removed over 10 million people (and what would have been an even larger number of their descendants) in three or four centuries, and where slave raiding led to the disruption of African cultures. In the Americas the native Indians were devastated by diseases brought from Europe to which at first they had no immunity.

Improved living conditions

In Europe, sooner than elsewhere, other causes of growth were at work beyond the maintenance of civil peace. They included liberation from certain endemic afflictions, beginning with the subsiding of bubonic plague in the seventeenth century and the use of vaccination against smallpox in the eighteenth. Agricultural improvement produced more food, notably in England about 1750. The improvement of transportation by road, canal, and railroad made localized famine a thing of the past, since food could be moved into areas of temporary shortage. With the Industrial Revolution larger populations could subsist in Europe by importing food from overseas. In the cities of Europe and North America, by 1900, the supply of pure drinking water and facilities for the disposal of garbage and sewage were better than in the past.

Hence population grew for several generations more substantially in Europe and its offshoots than elsewhere. Approximate percentages are given in the table. Asia, by these estimates, increased less than threefold between 1650 and 1900, but Europe increased fourfold, and the total number of Europeans, including the descendants of those who

ESTIMATED POPULATION OF THE WORLD BY CONTINENTAL AREAS

	Millions					
	1650	**1750**	**1850**	**1900**	**1950**	**2000**
Europe	100	150	263	396	532	729
United States and Canada	1	2	26	82	166	304
Australasia-Oceania	2	2	2	6	13	53
Predominantly "European"	103	154	291	484	711	1086
Latin America	12	16	38	74	162	519
Africa	100	106	111	133	217	785
Asia	330	515	822	959	1396	3683
Predominantly "Non-European"	442	637	971	1166	1775	4987
World Total	545	791	1262	1650	2486	6073
	Percentages					
Europe	18.3%	19.1%	20.8%	24.0%	21.5%	12.0%
United States and Canada	.2	.2	2.1	5.0	6.7	5.0
Australasia-Oceania	.4	.2	.2	.3	.5	1.0
Predominantly "European"	18.9	19.5	23.1	29.3	28.7	18.0
Latin America	2.2	2.0	3.0	4.5	6.5	8.5
Africa	18.3	13.0	8.8	8.1	8.7	12.9
Asia	60.6	65.0	65.1	58.1	56.1	60.6
Predominantly "Non-European"	81.1	80.0	76.9	70.7	71.3	82.0
World Total	100.0	100.0	100.0	100.0	100.0	100.0

*This table is designed to show only the numbers and proportion of people living in predominantly "European" cultures (that is, descended from societies with European languages and traditions) and "non-European" cultures over the modern period. It reveals the rapid increase in the proportion of "Europeans" in this sense from 1750 to 1900, and a steady decline in the "European" proportion during the twentieth century. The table is subject to serious reservations. The population of the former Soviet Union is divided between Europe and Asia, but millions of Russian "Europeans" have long lived in the Asian parts of the former U.S.S.R. It must also be remembered that the population of the United States consists of Africans and Asians as well as Europeans, that the people in Latin American countries now generally speak a European language and differ widely in their racial composition, and that there are well over four million persons of European origin in southern Africa. In short, the table has nothing to do with race, for there are many whites who do not live in "European" cultural zones and many "nonwhite" people in the Americas and elsewhere (including Europe) who participate fully in institutions and languages derived from Europe.

Source: For 1650 to 1900, A. N. Carr-Sanders, *World Population* (Oxford: Oxford University Press, 1936); for 1750, 1850, and 1900, John D. Durand, "The Modern Expansion of World Population," in *Proceedings of the American Philosophical Society,* vol. 111 (1967); and for 1950 and 2000, *United Nations Demographic Yearbook and World Population Prospects* (United Nations: New York, 1989) and *The New York Times 2001 Almanac* (New York, 2000).

migrated to other continents, multiplied fivefold. The ascendancy of European civilization in the two and a half centuries after 1650 was due in some measure to demographic growth. But while in 1900 the proportion of "Europeans" in all continents was approaching a third of the human race, after 1900 this proportion began to fall. By the beginning of the twenty-first century it could be projected that "Europeans" would constitute only a tenth of the human beings on the planet in the year 2100.

Stabilization of European Population

The stabilization and relative decline of the European population followed from a fall in the birth rate. As early as 1830 the birth rate began noticeably to drop in France, with the result that France, long the most populous European state, was surpassed in population by Germany about 1870, by the British Isles about 1895, and by Italy about 1930. France, once thought to be decadent for this reason, was in fact only the leading country in a population cycle through which the European countries seemed to pass. The birth rate, which had fallen below 30 per hundred in France in the 1830s, fell to that level in Sweden in the 1880s; in England in the 1890s; and in Germany and the Netherlands between 1900 and 1910. After the Second World War there was a temporary rise, but by 2000 the birth rate was less than 15 per 1,000 in Europe and North America, hardly sufficient to maintain existing population levels. In much of the rest of the world it was still well over 25 or even 30.

The reduced birth rate is not a mere dry statistical item, nor does it affect populations merely in the mass. It is one of the indices of modern civilization, first appearing in that inner European zone in which the other indices were also highest, and thence spreading outward in a kind of wave. Concretely, a low birth rate in the nineteenth century meant that families averaged from two to four children, where in former times, families might consist of ten children or even more. The low birth rate reflects the small family system, and few institutions were more fundamental to modern life. The principal means used to hold down the birth rate, or to limit the family, is the practice of contraception. But the true causes or reasons why parents wish to limit their families were deeply embedded in the codes of modernizing societies.

Historical demographers have detected a "European family pattern" as far back as the seventeenth century. It was a pattern in which, in comparison to other societies, Europeans married later, and a larger number never married at all. Late marriage shortened the number of years during which a woman bore children and enabled young people to acquire skills or accumulate savings (as in tools and household goods) before setting up new families. The effect was less-explosive population growth, and less-extreme poverty, than in other parts of the world. Evidence indicating the use of various forms of contraception can be found in the eighteenth century among the upper classes, by study of the number and spacing of their children. The practice seems to have spread to other social classes during the French Revolution. The Code Napoleon that followed required that inheritances be divided among all sons and daughters. The French peasants, many of them owners of land, began to limit themselves to two or three children in order that all children (by inheritance, marriage, and dowries) might remain in as high an economic and social position as their parents. It was thus the quest for economic security and higher living standards that led to the reduced birth rate in France and subsequently in other parts of Europe.

A European family pattern

In the great cities of the nineteenth century, in which standards of life for the working classes often collapsed, the effect might at first be a proliferation of offspring. But life in the city, under crowded conditions of housing, also set a premium on the small family. There were many activities in the city that people with many children could only with difficulty enjoy. After about 1880 child labor became much less frequent among the working classes. When children ceased to earn part of the family income, parents tended to have fewer of them. About the same time governments in the advanced countries began to require universal compulsory schooling. The number of years spent in education, and hence in economic dependency

Life in the city

upon parents, grew longer and longer until it became common even for young adults to be still engaged in study. Each child represented many years of expense for its parents. The ever rising idea of what it was necessary to do for one's children and the desire of parents to give them every possible advantage in a competitive world were probably the most basic causes of voluntary limitation of the family. Hardly less basic was the desire to lighten the burdens upon mothers. The small family system, together with the decline of infant mortality, since they combined to free women from the interminable bearing and tending of infants, probably did more than anything else to improve the position of women in modern societies. Freed at least in part from the traditional cycles of pregnancy and child care, middle-class women were eventually able to pursue advanced education, new professions, and new kinds of social or political activities. The use of contraception also spread widely among the working class during the early twentieth century; demographic research in England, for example, suggests that almost 70 percent of working-class couples were using contraception by the 1930s (compared to fewer than 20 percent in 1900).

The effects of the small family system upon total population became manifest only slowly. More people lived on into the middle and older age groups, and the fall of the birth rate was gradual, so that in all the leading countries total numbers continued to rise, except in France, which hardly grew between 1900 and 1945. The persistent note was one of superabundant increase. In five generations, between 1800 and 1950, some 200 million "Europeans" grew into 700 million "Europeans" around the globe. Since productivity increased even more rapidly, the standard of living for most of these "Europeans" rose in spite of the increase of numbers, and there was no general problem of overpopulation.

Growth of Cities and Urban Life

Where did so many people go? Some stayed in the rural areas where most people had always lived. Rural populations in the inner zone became more dense, turning to the more intensive agriculture of truck gardening or dairy farming, leaving products like wool and cereal grains to be raised elsewhere and then imported. But it is estimated that of every seven persons added to the western European population only one stayed on the land. Of the other six, one left Europe altogether and five went to the growing cities.

The nineteenth-century city was mostly the child of the railroad, for with the railroads it became possible for the first time to concentrate manufacturing in large towns, to which bulky goods such as foods and fuel could now be moved in great volume. The growth of cities between 1850 and 1914 was phenomenal. In England two-thirds of the people lived in places of 20,000 or less in 1830; in 1914 two-thirds lived in places of 20,000 or more. Germany, the historic land of archaic towns carried over from the Middle Ages, rivaled England after 1870 in modern industrial urbanization. Whereas in 1840 only London and Paris had a million people, the same could be said by 1914 of Berlin, Vienna, St. Petersburg, and Moscow; and outside Europe, of cities such as New York, Chicago, Philadelphia, Rio de Janeiro, Buenos Aires, Calcutta, Tokyo, and Osaka. Some places, like the English Midlands and the Ruhr valley in Germany, became a mass of contiguous smaller cities, vast urban agglomerations divided only by municipal lines.

Impact of urban life

The great city set the tone of modern society. City life was impersonal and anonymous; people were uprooted, less tied to home or church than in the country. They lacked the country person's feeling of deference for aristocratic families. They lacked the sense of self-help characteristic of older rural communities. It was in the city that the daily newspaper press, which spread rapidly in the wake of

The evolving demographic pattern in nineteenth-century European bourgeois families may be seen in this portrait of a Victorian-era English family sitting in their garden. The declining number of children eventually gave women more time and freedom for diverse activities because they were less tied to long cycles of pregnancies and childrearing.
(Getty Images)

the telegraph after 1850, found its most habitual readers. The so-called yellow or sensational press appeared about 1900. Articulate public opinion was formed in the cities, and city people were on the whole disrespectful of tradition, receptive to new ideas, having in many cases deliberately altered their own lives by moving from the country or from smaller towns. It is hardly surprising that the new conditions of urban life fostered the spread of socialism among the industrial masses in European cities. Some of the more blatant nationalism that arose after 1870 was also stimulated by city life, for people felt increasingly detached from all institutions except the state. At the same time city life, by its greater facilities for schooling, reading, and discussion, made for a more alert and informed public opinion of an enlightened kind.

Migration from Europe, 1850–1940

During the same period in which cities were growing, almost 60 million people left Europe altogether, of whom possibly a fifth sooner or later returned. The Atlantic Migration—aptly so called, because all crossed the ocean except those who moved from European to Asian Russia—towers above all others in magnitude, and possibly also in significance, for it was by this means that earlier colonial offshoots of Europe were transformed into new societies that carried the very strong influence of European political, social, religious, and cultural traditions. All parts of Europe contributed to the migration, as shown in the table below, which comprises the years from 1850 to 1940. Before 1850 the mass movement had scarcely begun, though by that time over a million immigrants had entered the United States since the close of the Napoleonic wars. After 1940 the character of intercontinental migration was greatly transformed. In recent decades, since the Second World War, there have been large migrations into Europe from Africa, the Middle East, and Asia, and into the Americas from places outside Europe. But in the century before 1940 the migration of European peoples was a key force in the dissemination of European institutions and cultures.

It is hard to give satisfactory figures for emigration from Europe. In the statistical sources the English, Scots, Welsh, and Irish are mixed, and until the First World War, that is until 1914, the Poles, Czechs, other Slavic peoples, Hungarians, East European Jews, and others were not counted as such but were included among emigrants from the Russian, Austro-Hungarian, and German empires. Millions of Jews, Irish, Poles, and many thousands of others are therefore invisible in the figures, which also include several million Russians who moved from European to Asian parts of Russia. It must be remembered also that some intercontinental migration did not involve Europeans. For a

<table>
<tr><td colspan="3">EMIGRATION FROM EUROPE, 1850–1940</td></tr>
<tr><td>From:</td><td>British Isles</td><td>18,300,000</td></tr>
<tr><td></td><td>Italy</td><td>10,200,000</td></tr>
<tr><td></td><td>Russia</td><td>9,000,000</td></tr>
<tr><td></td><td>Germany</td><td>5,000,000</td></tr>
<tr><td></td><td>Spain</td><td>4,500,000</td></tr>
<tr><td></td><td>Austria-Hungary</td><td>4,200,000</td></tr>
<tr><td></td><td>Portugal</td><td>2,500,000</td></tr>
<tr><td></td><td>Sweden</td><td>1,200,000</td></tr>
<tr><td></td><td>Norway</td><td>750,000</td></tr>
<tr><td></td><td>Denmark</td><td>470,000</td></tr>
<tr><td></td><td>Finland</td><td>390,000</td></tr>
<tr><td></td><td>France</td><td>390,000</td></tr>
<tr><td></td><td>Switzerland</td><td>340,000</td></tr>
<tr><td></td><td>Netherlands</td><td>210,000</td></tr>
<tr><td></td><td>Belgium</td><td>150,000</td></tr>
<tr><td></td><td></td><td>57,600,000</td></tr>
</table>

Source: William Woodruff, *The Impact of Western Man* (New York: St. Martin's Press, 1966), p. 106.

few years after 1850 black slaves were still brought illegally to the United States and Brazil. Workers went from India to the West Indies and South Africa, and many Chinese settled in the United States and southeast Asia. With these reservations, the table on this page shows the pattern of European emigration in the 90 years preceding the Second World War.

The British and Irish went to the British dominions and the United States. The Italians divided between the United States and Latin America. Spaniards settled overwhelmingly in the Spanish American republics, and the Portuguese settled in Brazil. The Germans moved overwhelmingly to the United States, though some went to Argentina and Brazil. The extraordinary preponderance of the United States is apparent. At the same time, it should be noted that almost half of the European migration went to other countries around the world. The new countries received the following influxes of people:

IMMIGRATION INTO VARIOUS COUNTRIES, 1850–1940

To:	United States	32,300,000
	Asian Russia	7,000,000
	Argentina	6,600,000
	Brazil	4,700,000
	Canada	4,300,000
	Australia	2,900,000
	New Zealand	650,000
	Uruguay	600,000
	Cuba	600,000
	South Africa	250,000
	Mexico	250,000

Source: Woodruff, *Impact of Western Man,* p. 108.

The exodus from Europe was due to a remarkable and temporary juxtaposition of causes. One fundamental cause, or precondition, was that before 1914 the new countries welcomed immigration. Hands were wanted to farm the land, build houses, dig in the mines. This was least true of Australia and New Zealand, which preferred to limit themselves to English-speaking settlers and which also pioneered as social democracies, becoming models even before 1900 of legislation to protect the working classes. One result was that no inrush of outsiders to compete for jobs at low wages was desired. A similar combination of national preferences and labor protectionism led to laws restricting immigration in the United States in 1921 and 1924. Thereafter immigrants could enter only under quotas, and the quotas were lowest for eastern and southern Europe, the areas from which most emigration had been coming.

Causes of the exodus

In Europe there were many conditions propelling emigrants outward. Physically, the steamship made it easier and cheaper to cross the sea, and the railroad helped people to get to the ports as well as to distribute themselves after landing in the new countries. Economically, people in the mass could for the first time afford a long journey. People migrated to improve their material circumstances; but some high points in the wave of emigration coincided with high points in the business cycle in Europe, when jobs in Europe were

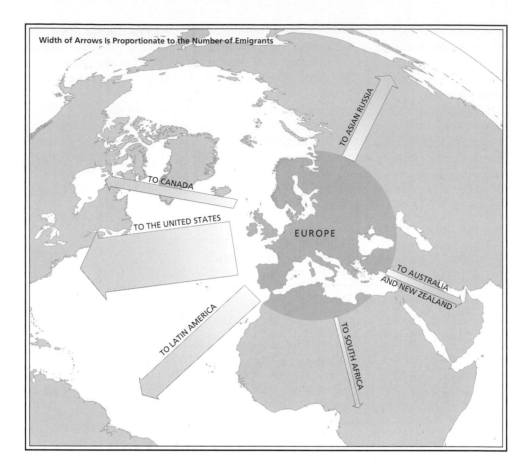

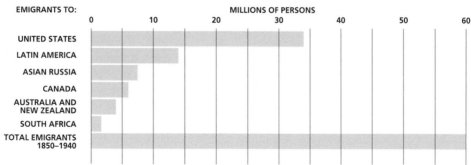

MIGRATION FROM EUROPE, 1850–1940

About 60 million people left Europe in the century preceding the Second World War, distributing themselves as shown in the diagram above. (See figures on p. 571.) About half went to the United States, but the migration of European peoples also built up "European" societies in other regions of the world. These overseas "European" societies produced food and raw materials for Europe and borrowed capital or bought manufactured goods from Europe, thus helping to support European economic development and to expand the modern worldwide economic system.

The mass migration of people is one of the distinctive social patterns of the modern world. This Italian woman and her children, who arrived in New York about 1900, were part of a vast emigration out of Europe that affected societies and economies on every continent.
(Snark/Art Resource, NY)

plentiful and wages were at their highest. Of the opposite case, of actual flight from economic ruin or starvation, the emigration from Ireland after 1846 is the best example. In the "great potato famine" of 1845–1849 nearly 1 million Irish died of starvation and disease, and more than 1.5 million emigrated to the United States in the next few years. After the revolutions of 1848 a certain number of Europeans left Europe for political reasons, and, later on, to avoid compulsory military service. The best example of flight from segregation and discrimination, and from direct persecution in government-encouraged pogroms, is that of the Jews of Russia and Russian Poland, of whom a million and a half moved to the United States in the 15 years preceding the First World War.

But perhaps most basic in the whole European exodus was the underlying liberalism of the age. Never before (nor since) had people been legally so free to move. Old laws requiring skilled workmen to stay in their own countries were repealed, as in England in 1824. The old semicommunal agricultural villages, with collective rights and obligations, holding individuals to their

Freedom of movement

native groups, fell into disuse except in Russia. The disappearance of serfdom allowed the peasants of eastern Europe to change residences without obtaining a lord's permission. Governments permitted their subjects to emigrate, to take with them their savings of shillings, marks, kronen, or lire, and to change nationality by becoming naturalized in their new homes. The rise of liberty in Europe, as well as the hope of enjoying it in America, made possible the great emigration. For so huge a mass movement the most remarkable fact is that it took place by private initiative and at private expense. Individuals, families, and small local groups (to borrow the metaphor of one authority) detached themselves atom by atom from the mass of Europe, crossed the seas on their own, and reattached themselves atom by atom to the accumulating mass of the New World. The mass migrations of the late nineteenth century thus launched a worldwide movement of people that continues to the present day, grows in importance, and remains one of the most characteristic social patterns of the modern world.

72.   THE WORLD ECONOMY
OF THE NINETEENTH CENTURY

How did the swelling population of Europeans manage to feed itself? How, in fact, did it not merely feed itself but enjoy an incomparably higher standard of living in 1900 than in 1800? By science, industry, transportation, communications, and the expansion of global trading systems. And by organization—in business, finance, and labor.

The "New Industrial Revolution"

The Industrial Revolution and the global economy entered upon a new phase. The use of steam power, the growth of the textile and metallurgical industries, and the advent of the railroad had characterized the early part of the century. Now, after 1870, new sources of power were tapped, the already mechanized industries expanded, new industries appeared, and industry spread geographically.

The steam engine itself was refined and improved. By 1914 it still predominated over other power machinery, but electricity with its incomparable advantages came into use. The invention of the internal combustion (or gasoline) engine and the diesel engine gave the world automobiles, airplanes, and submarines in the two decades before 1914; the advent of the automotive and aviation industries made oil one of the most coveted of natural resources. In the new chemical industries industrial research laboratories were replacing the individual inventor. Chemists discovered new fertilizers and from coal tar alone produced a bewildering array of new products ranging from artificial food flavors to high explosives. With explosives the first great tunnels were built, the Mount Cenis in 1873, the Simplon in 1906—both in the Alps; and great new canals, the Suez in 1869, the Kiel in 1895, the Panama in 1914. Chemistry made possible the production of synthetic fabrics like rayon, which revolutionized the textile industry. Electricity transformed all indoor and outdoor lighting. There was a communications revolution too. The telephone appeared in the 1870s. Marconi brought the continents closer together, successfully transmitting wireless signals across the Atlantic in 1901. The moving picture and the radio modestly presented themselves before 1914. Medicine ran the alphabetical gamut from anesthetics to X-rays; yellow fever was overcome. Vastly improved processes for refining iron ore made possible a great expansion in the production of steel, the key product of the new industrial age; aluminum and other metal alloys were also produced through new industrial processes. Railroad mileage multiplied; the European network, including the Russian, increased from 140,000 miles in 1890 to 213,000 in 1914.

Industrial advances

In the new phase of the Industrial Revolution machine industry spread geographically from Britain and Belgium, the only truly industrial countries in 1870, to France, Italy, Russia, Japan, and, most markedly, to Germany and the United States. In Europe industrial production was concentrated in the "inner zone." Three powers alone—Britain, Germany, and France—accounted in 1914 for more than seven-tenths of all European manufactures and produced over four-fifths of all European coal, steel, and machinery. Of the major European powers Germany was now forging ahead. To use steel alone as a criterion, in 1871 Germany was producing

The industrial powers

annually three-fifths as much steel as Britain; by 1900 it was producing more, and by 1914 it was producing twice as much as Britain — but only half as much as the new industrial giant, the United States. By 1914 American steel output was greater than that of Germany, Britain, and France combined. Britain, the pioneer in mechanization, was being outstripped in both the Old World and the New. The three European powers increased their industrial production by about 50 percent in the two decades before 1914, but the United States had a far higher annual growth rate from 1870 to 1913, 4.3 percent as compared to the next leading powers, Germany with 2.9 percent, Britain with 2.2 percent, and France with 1.6 percent. By 1914 the United States had moved ahead of Europe in the mechanization of agriculture, in manufactures, and in coal and steel production, in which it was producing over two-fifths of the world's output. The Americans were pioneering also in assembly-line, conveyor-belt techniques for the mass production of automobiles and all kinds of consumer goods.

Free Trade and the European "Balance of Payments"

It was Britain in the mid-nineteenth century, then the workshop of the world, that had inaugurated the movement toward free trade. It will be recalled that in 1846, by the repeal of the Corn Laws, the British embarked upon a systematic free trade policy, deliberately choosing to become dependent upon overseas imports for their food. France adopted free trade in 1860. Other countries soon followed. It is true that by 1880 there was a movement back to protective tariffs except in Britain, Holland, and Belgium. But the tariffs were impediments rather than barriers, and until 1914 the characteristic of the economic system was the extreme mobility of goods across political frontiers. Politically, Europe was more than ever nationalistic; but economic activity, under generally liberal conditions in which business was supposed to be free from the political state, remained predominantly international and globe-encircling.

Broadly speaking, the great economic accomplishment of Europe before 1914 was to create a system by which the huge imports used by industrial Europe could be acquired and paid for. All European countries except Russia, Austria-Hungary, and the Balkan states imported more than they exported. It was the British again who led in this direction. Britain had been a predominantly importing country since the close of the eighteenth century. Despite the expanding export of cotton manufactures and other products of the Industrial Revolution, Britain consumed more goods from abroad than it sent out. Industrialization and urbanization in the nineteenth century confirmed the same situation. Between 1800 and 1900 the value of British exports multiplied eightfold, but the value of imports into Great Britain multiplied tenfold, and in the decade before 1914 the British had an import surplus of about three-quarters of a billion dollars a year. Great Britain and the industrial countries of Europe together (roughly Europe's "inner zone"), at the beginning of the twentieth century, were drawing in an import surplus, measured in dollars, of almost $2 billion every year (the dollar then representing far more goods than it came to represent later). The imports into Europe's inner zone consisted of raw materials for its industries and of food and amenities for its people.

Imports versus exports

How were the imports paid for? How did Europe enjoy a favorable "balance of payments" despite an unfavorable balance of trade in commodities? Export of European manufactures paid for most imports, but not all. It was the so-called invisible exports that made up the difference, that is, shipping and insurance services rendered to foreigners, and interest on money lent out or invested,

Invisible exports

The Bessemer steel-making process enhanced the production of steel and rapidly became an important component of industrial expansion during the later decades of the nineteenth century. Its importance for Britain is suggested by this illustration of the future King Edward VII and his wife, who are observing the new methods of steel production from box seats at a factory in Sheffield in 1875.
(Getty Images)

all bringing in foreign exchange. Shipping and insurance were important. An Argentine merchant in Buenos Aires, to ship hides to Germany, might employ a British vessel; he would pay the freight charges in Argentine pesos, which might be credited to the account of the British shipowner in an Argentine bank; the British shipowner would sell the pesos to someone, in England or elsewhere in Europe, who needed them to buy Argentine meat. The far-flung British merchant marine thus earned a considerable amount of the food and raw materials needed by Britain. To insure themselves against risks of every conceivable kind people all over the world turned to Lloyds of London. With the profits drawn from selling insurance the British could buy what they wished. Governments or business enterprises borrowed money in Europe, mainly in England; the interest payments, putting foreign currencies into European and British hands, constituted another invisible export by which large quantities of imports could be financed. But the lending of money to foreigners is only part of a larger phenomenon, the export of capital.

The Export of European Capital

The migration of millions of Europeans had the effect of creating new societies, basically European in character, which both purchased manufactures from Europe and produced the food, wool, cotton, and minerals that Europe needed. It could not have had this effect if

CLASSIC LANDSCAPE
by Charles Sheeler (American, 1883–1965)

This landscape depicts an American plant of the Ford Motor Company in 1931, but it also symbolizes what has been called the Second Industrial Revolution. In this phase of industrialization, electricity, the internal combustion engine, and the automobile were especially important, and industry spread far beyond its early centers in Britain and western Europe. The picture is "classic" in its clear delineation, its array of familiar mathematical forms, and the universality of its message. The plant seems rational and precise, but there are no human beings. It is as if the machine had a life of its own and could do without human hands.

(Collection of Mr. and Mrs. Barney A. Ebsworth, Photograph © 2000 Board of Trustees, National Gallery of Art, Washington, 1931 (2000.39.2))

Europe had exported people only, especially people of such small means as most emigrants were. Europe also exported the capital that enabled the new settlers to develop productive economies.

The export of capital meant that an older and wealthier country, instead of using its whole annual income to raise its own standard of living, or to add to its own capital by expanding or improving its houses, factories, machinery, mines, and transportation, diverted some of its income to expanding or improving the houses, factories, machinery, mines, and transportation of foreign countries. It meant that British, French, Dutch, Belgian, Swiss, and eventually German investors bought the stocks of foreign business enterprises and the bonds of foreign businesses and governments; or they organized companies of their own to operate in foreign countries; or their banks granted loans to banks in New York or Tokyo, which then lent the funds to local users.

Capital arose in Europe to some extent from the savings of quite small people, especially in France, where peasants and modest bourgeois families were notably thrifty. But most capital accumulated from savings by the well-to-do. The owners of a business concern, for example, instead of spending the concern's income by paying higher wages, took a portion of it in profits or dividends, and instead of spending all this on their own living, reinvested part of it in domestic or foreign enterprises. The gap between rich and poor was thus one cause of the rapid accumulation of capital, though the accumulation of capital, in the nineteenth century, produced in turn a steady rise of living standards for the working classes. In a sense, however, the common people of western Europe, by forgoing the better housing, diet, education, or pleasures that a more democratic or consumer-oriented society might have planned for them, made possible the export of capital and hence the financing and building up of other regions of the world.

Capital accumulation

The British were the chief exporters of capital, followed at some distance by the French, and at the close of the century by the Germans. As early as the 1840s half the annual increase of wealth in Great Britain was going into foreign investments. By 1914 the British had $20 billion in foreign investments, the French had about $8.7 billion, and the Germans had about $6 billion. A quarter of all the wealth owned by the inhabitants of Great Britain consisted in 1914 of holdings outside the country. Almost a sixth of the French national wealth lay in investments outside France. All three countries had given hostages to fortune, and fortune proved unkind, for in the First World War the British lost about a quarter of their foreign investments, the French lost about a third, and the Germans lost all.

These huge sums, pouring out from Europe's inner zone for a century before 1914, at first went mainly to finance the Americas and the less affluent regions of Europe. European capital was also invested in Asia and Africa, especially after the rapid expansion of Europe's colonial empires in the 1890s. No country except Great Britain completely built its railways with its own resources. In the United States the railway system was built very largely with capital obtained from England. In central and eastern Europe British companies often constructed the first railways, then sold out to native operating companies or to governments which subsequently ran them. In the Argentine Republic the British not merely financed and built the railways, but long continued to operate and own them. In addition, up to 1914 the British sold about 75 million tons of coal a year to South America to keep the railways going, not to mention items for replacement and upkeep of equipment. Docks, warehouses, mines, plantations, processing and manufacturing establishments all over the world were similarly built up with capital drawn from Europe. European capital also helped emigrants in the new countries to develop public services and institutions that required major financial investments. In the United States, for example, state and local governments very commonly sold their bonds in Europe to build roads, pave streets, or construct school systems for the westward-moving population. A few of these American bonds proved a partial or total loss to European investors. On the whole, by 1914, the United States had paid back a good deal of its indebtedness. Even so, in 1914, Americans

The recipients of European capital

still owed about $4 billion to Europeans—a sum three times as large as the national debt of the United States at the time.

An International Money System: The Gold Standard

The international economy rested upon an international money system, based in turn upon the almost universal acceptance of the gold standard. England had adopted the gold standard in 1821, when the pound sterling was legally defined as the equivalent of 113 grains of fine gold. Western Europe and the United States adopted an exclusively gold standard in the 1870s. A person holding any "civilized" money—pounds, francs, dollars, marks, and the like—could turn it into gold at will, and a person holding gold could turn it into any money. The currencies were like so many different languages all expressing the same thing. All had substantially the same value, and until 1914 the exchange rates between currencies remained highly stable. It was assumed that no modern industrial country's currency ever "fell"; such things might happen in Turkey or China, or in the French Revolution, but not in the world of modern progress and civilized affairs.

Currency exchange

The important currencies were all freely exchangeable. A French merchant selling silks to a German, and hence receiving German marks, could turn the marks into francs, pounds sterling, or dollars. That is, he was not obliged to buy from Germany or spend his money in Germany but could use the proceeds of his German sale to buy French, British, or American goods or services as he chose. Trade was multilateral. A country needing imports from another country, such as American cotton, did not have to sell to that country to obtain them; it could sell its own goods anywhere and then import according to its needs.

Effects of the gold standard

It was the acceptance of the gold standard, and the fact that all important countries possessed a sufficient share of gold to support their currencies, that made possible so fluid an interchange. At the same time the gold standard had less wholesome effects. It was hard on countries that lacked gold. And it produced a gradual fall of prices, especially between 1870 and 1900, because (until the gold discoveries in South Africa, Australia, and Alaska in the 1890s) the world's production of gold lagged behind the expanding production of industrial and agricultural goods. Persistently declining prices were a hardship to those who habitually worked with borrowed money—many farmers, many businessmen, and debtor nations as a whole. A famous speech of William Jennings Bryan in the United States in 1896, declaring that mankind should not be crucified "upon this cross of gold," expressed a common, worldwide anger about a financial system that worked against the interests of indebted persons and indebted nations. But falling prices were an advantage to the wage-earning class, which generally improved its position in these years, and also to the wealthy, the owners and lenders of capital, the bankers and financiers, who so long as prices were falling were repaid in money of more value than that which they had lent.

London at the center

The center of the global economic and financial system was London. The London banks prospered in consequence of the defeat of Napoleon, the older financial centers in Amsterdam having been ruined in the Revolutionary and Napoleonic wars. It may be recalled also that the victors in 1815 imposed upon France an indemnity of 700 million francs, which in 1818 was taken over by a syndicate of private bankers; the London banks played a leading part in this affair and so developed their connections with many government treasuries. In the Crimean War of 1854–1856, with England at war with Russia, the London banks floated loans for the Russian government—so independent were business and politics at the time. The early adoption of the gold standard in England meant that many people, British and foreign, kept their funds in the form of sterling on deposit in London, where quantities of available capital therefore accumulated. London became the apex of a financial pyramid which had the world for its base. It was the main center for the exchange of currencies, the clearing-house of the world's debts, the depository from which all the world borrowed, the banker's bank, as well as the world's shipping center and the headquarters of many international corporations.

A World Market: Unity, Competition—and Insecurity

Never had the earth been so unified economically, with each region playing specific roles in a global specialization. Western Europe, and in 1870 mainly Great Britain, was the world's industrial workshop. Other parts of the earth supplied its many needs. An English economist marveled in 1866 that Britain now had its granaries in Chicago and Odessa, its forests in Canada and the Baltic, its sheep farms in Australia, and its gold and silver mines in California and Peru, while drinking tea brought from China and coffee from East Indian plantations. The same could have been said of most of Europe's inner zone by the time of the First World War.

A true global market

A true global market had been created. Goods, services, commodities, money, capital, people moved back and forth almost without regard to national boundaries. Articles were bought and sold at uniform world prices. Dealers in wheat, for example, followed prices in Minneapolis, Liverpool, Buenos Aires, and Danzig as reported by telegraph and cable from day to day. They bought where it was cheapest, and sold where it was dearest. In this way the world's wheat supply was distributed roughly according to need or ability to pay. The worker of Milan, if the Italian crop was poor and prices were high, was fed from another source. On the other hand, the Italian wheat grower would in this case feel the pinch of world competition. The world market, while it organized the world into a unified economic system, at the same time brought distant regions into competition for the first time. The producers of goods and commodities—whether entrepreneur, factory employee, farmer, or coffee planter—had no secure outlet for their products, as had generally been true in the past. They were in competition not only with persons across the street or down the road but also with other producers throughout the world. It was this worldwide system of production and consumption that established the modern economic foundation for what is now called "globalization."

The creation of an integrated world market, the financing and building up of countries outside of Europe, and the consequent feeding and support of Europe's increasing population were the great triumphs of the nineteenth-century system of unregulated capitalism. The system was intricate, with thousands and even millions of individuals and business firms supplying each other's wants without central planning. But it was extremely precarious, and the position of most people in this network of global economic exchanges was exceedingly vulnerable. Region competed against region and person against person. A fall of grain prices in the American Middle West, besides ruining a few speculators, might oblige German or Argentine wheat growers to sell at a price at which they could not live. Factory owners might be driven out of business if competitors successfully undersold them or if a new commodity made their own product obsolete. The workers, hired only when needed by an employer, faced unemployment when business slackened or when jobs disappeared because of labor-saving inventions.

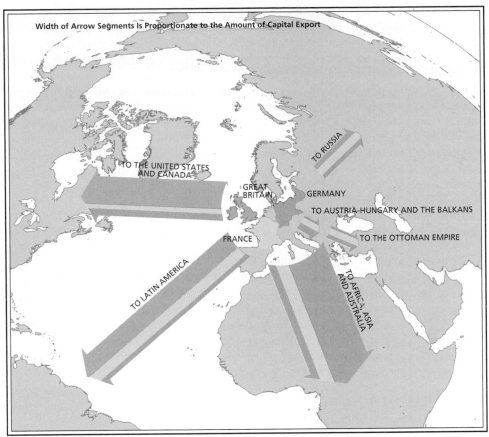

Width of Arrow Segments Is Proportionate to the Amount of Capital Export

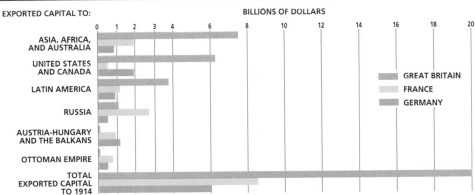

EXPORT OF EUROPEAN CAPITAL TO 1914

In 1914 the British, French, and Germans held upwards of $30 billion in foreign and colonial loans and investments, distributed as shown on the map. Dutch investments, especially in the West Indies, together with Swiss, Belgian, and Scandinavian holdings, would add several billion dollars more. Proceeds from such investments helped Europeans to pay for the excess of their imports over exports. British capital predominated in the overseas world, while the less-developed regions of eastern Europe and the Middle East were financed mainly from Germany and France. Much of the investment shown here was lost or expended in the First World War.

Cycles of boom and depression

The system went through cycles of boom and depression, the most notable example of the latter being the "long depression" that set in about 1873 and lasted to about 1893. The new global economy depended on expansion and on credit; but sometimes people could not pay their debts, so that credit collapsed; and sometimes expansion failed to keep pace with expectations, and anticipated profits proved to be losses. To combat the essential insecurity of private capitalism, all manner of devices were resorted to. Against competition from other countries governments established protective tariffs; business enterprises entered into acquisitions and mergers, sometimes approaching monopolies. For the working classes governments adopted social insurance measures as protection against accidents, illness, and unemployment. Labor meanwhile turned increasingly to its own trade unions and socialist parties. All this signalized the gradual decline in the years after 1880 of nineteenth-century unregulated, laissez-faire capitalism.

Changes in Organization: Big Business

A great change came over capitalism itself about 1880 or 1890. Formerly characterized by a large number of small units, small businesses run by individuals, partnerships, or small companies, it was increasingly characterized by large and impersonal corporations. The

The "limited liability" corporation

attractions of the "limited liability" corporation as a form of business organization and as a means of encouraging investment arose from laws enacted by most countries in the nineteenth century that limited the individual investor's personal loss in the event of a bankruptcy to the amount of his or her shares of stock in the enterprise. The corporation, in its modern form appearing first with the railroads, became the usual form of organization for industry and commerce. As machinery grew more complicated, only a large pool of capital could finance it. And as corporations grew in size and number, relying on the sale of stock and the issue of bonds, the influence of banking and financial circles was enhanced. Financiers, using not so much their own money as the savings of others, had a new power to create or to destroy, to stimulate, discourage, or combine corporate enterprises in various industries. Industrial capitalism brought finance capitalism with it.

Corporate organization made it possible to concentrate diverse economic processes under unified management. In retail commerce, large department stores appeared after about 1870 in the United States and France, selling all kinds of goods that were formerly sold only in small shops and establishing a fixed price for each piece of merchandise. In industry, steel offers a good example. Steel became in any case a big business when heavy blast furnaces were introduced. It was not safe for the steel business, or for the blast furnaces, to rely for iron and coal on independent producers. The steel works therefore began to operate mines of their own or to buy out or otherwise reduce coal and iron mines to subsidiary status. Some, to assure their markets, began to produce not merely steel but steel

Vertical integration

manufactures as well—steel ships, railway equipment, naval and military ordnance. Thus entire processes from mining to finished product became concentrated in a "vertical" integration.

"Horizontal" integration meant that concerns at the same level combined with each other to reduce competition and to protect themselves against fluctuations in prices and markets. Some fixed prices, some agreed to restrict production, and some divided up markets among themselves. They were called trusts in the United States; cartels, in Europe. They were common in the steel industry and in many other new industries at the close of the century, such as chemicals, aluminum, and oil. It was in the United

The new world market strongly encouraged the development of export industries and commodity production in agrarian societies that mainly produced food in earlier times. During the decades before 1914, the colonized areas of Asia, Africa, and the Americas rapidly increased their production of commodities such as tea, coffee, sugar, and cocoa, most of which flowed into the more industrialized, capitalist economies of Europe and North America. These workers in India collected tea for export and thus participated, though with low wages, in a global trading system that transformed agriculture and daily life in almost every part of the world. (The Art Archive)

"Captains" of industry, "titans" of finance

States that such big business developed furthest, headed by "captains" of industry and "titans" of finance. Andrew Carnegie, by origin a poor Scottish immigrant boy, produced more steel than all England; in 1901 he sold out to an even more colossal organization, the United States Steel Corporation, formed by the financier J. P. Morgan. It was in the United States, too, that concern over monopoly and the power of big business in general was felt most strongly; antitrust legislation, beginning with the Sherman Act of 1890, was enacted but never with any substantial effect.

Many of the new combinations were beneficial in making the ups and downs of business less erratic, and so providing more stable prices and more continuous and secure employment. Generally they reduced the costs of production; but whether the savings went into higher profits, higher wages, or lower prices depended on numerous factors. Some trusts were greedier than others or were confronted with only weakly organized or unorganized labor. In any case, for good or ill, decisions rested with management and finance. A new kind of private power had arisen, which its critics like to call "feudal." Since no economic system had ever been so centralized up to that time, never in fact had so few people exercised so much economic power over so many. The middle class, with the rise of great corporations, came typically to consist of salaried employees; the salaried person might spend a lifetime with the same company, and feel toward it, in its disputes with labor or government, a loyalty not unlike that of a lord's retainer in feudal times. The laboring class was less amenable; labor attempted to organize unions capable of dealing with increasingly gigantic employers. It also after about 1880 played an increasingly decisive role in the politics of all advanced nations.

73.   THE ADVANCE OF DEMOCRACY: THIRD FRENCH REPUBLIC, UNITED KINGDOM, GERMAN EMPIRE

In the years from 1815 to 1870 European political life had been marked by liberal agitation for constitutional government, representative assemblies, responsible ministries, and guarantees of individual liberties. In the years from 1871 to 1914 the most notable political development was the democratic extension of the vote to working class men—the adoption of universal male suffrage, which in turn meant for the first time the creation of mass political parties and the need for political leaders to appeal to a wide electorate. Although there was growing agitation for voting rights for women in the decades before 1914, that reform would not be achieved until after the First World War. The extension of male suffrage and democratization often took place in a continuing monarchical and aristocratic framework, but almost everywhere in Europe by 1914 some machinery of democratic self-government was being introduced. In addition, to counter the growing strength of socialism after 1871, and for humanitarian reasons, governments were also assuming responsibility for the social and economic problems arising from industrialism. The welfare state in its modern form was taking shape.

France: The Establishment of the Third Republic

In France the democratic republic was not easily established, and its troubled early years left deep cleavages within the country. It will be recalled that in September 1870, when the empire of Napoleon III revealed its helplessness in the Franco-Prussian War,

The Bon Marché department store in Paris became a well-known example of the new, large stores that began to displace smaller shops and independent merchants. The new era is evident in this late nineteenth-century illustration of the store's vast expanse, proliferation of merchandise, and affluent shoppers. Department stores provided a safe meeting place for women as well as lower prices for the many new products of the industrial era.

(Picture Collection, The New York Public Library, Astor, Lenox and Tilden Foundations) insurrectionaries in Paris, as in 1792 and 1848, again proclaimed the Republic. A provisional government of national defense sought desperately to continue the war, but the cause was hopeless. By January 1871, a bitter siege of Paris came to an end and an armistice was signed. Bismarck, insisting that only a properly constituted government could make peace, permitted the election, by universal male suffrage, of a National Assembly which was to consider his peace terms and draft a constitution for the new French state. When the elections were held in February, it was found, as in 1848 (and, indeed, 1797), that republicanism was so distrusted by the French people as a whole, and most especially in the provinces and rural areas, that a free election brought monarchist elements into power. Republicanism was still thought to be violent—bellicose in its foreign policy, turbulent in its political workings, unfriendly to the church, and socialistic or at least egalitarian in its views of property and private wealth. The new Assembly contained only about 200 republicans out of more than 600 deputies.

But the Paris republicans, who had defended France when Napoleon III failed to do so, who for four months had been besieged, starved, and frozen by the Germans, and who still refused to make peace on the harsh terms imposed by Bismarck and about to be accepted by the Assembly, refused to recognize the latter's authority. A civil war broke out between the National Assembly, now sitting at Versailles, and the city of Paris, where a revolutionary municipal council or "Commune" was set up. Paris, so lately attacked by German soldiers, was now attacked by French.

The Paris Commune

The Paris Commune, which lasted from March to May 1871, seemed to be another explosion of social revolution. Actually, it was in essence a revival of the Jacobinism of 1793. It was fiercely patriotic and republican; anti-German; opposed to wealthy bourgeois, aristocrats, and clergy; in favor of government controls of prices, wages, and working conditions, but still not socialist in any sweeping or systematic way. Among its leaders, however, there were a few of the new international revolutionary socialists who saw in a Jacobin or democratic republic a step toward their new order. Marx in England, and others elsewhere, hopefully read into the Commune the impending doom of the bourgeoisie. This was precisely what more conservative elements feared. To many of the French middle and peasant class, and to people like them all over Europe, it seemed that the Communards were wild and savage destroyers of nineteenth-century civilization. The fighting in Paris was atrocious beyond anything known in any preceding French revolution. The Communards, in final desperation, burned a number of public buildings and put to death the archbishop of Paris, whom they held as a hostage. The armed forces of the National Assembly, when finally triumphant, were determined to root out the inveterate revolutionism of Paris. Some 330,000 persons were denounced, 38,000 were arrested, 20,000 were put to death, and 7,500 were deported to New Caledonia. The Third Republic was born in an atmosphere of class hate and social terror.

The form of government for the new regime still had to be established. The monarchist majority in the Assembly was itself evenly divided between those who favored a restoration of the Bourbon family and those who favored the Orléanist. The monarchists thus checkmated each other and, in effect, opened the way toward a new French republic. Meanwhile, after extended discussion of various constitutional projects, the Assembly adopted in 1875 not a constitution, but certain constitutive laws. By a margin of one vote, a resolution indirectly amounting to the establishment of a republic was passed. The new laws provided for a president, a parliament in two chambers, and a council of ministers, or cabinet, headed by a premier. The two legislative bodies were to emerge from different electoral processes: the Senate was to be elected by a complicated and indirect system of election, the Chamber of Deputies, by universal, direct, male suffrage.

Within two years, in 1877, the role of the president, the ministers, and the parliament was further clarified as a result of an unsuccessful attempt by an early president, Marshal MacMahon, to dismiss a premier of whom he did not approve but who had the backing of the Chamber. MacMahon proceeded to dissolve the Chamber and to hold new elections, but the example of Napoleon III's transformation of the Second Republic into an authoritarian regime was still fresh. The elections vindicated the principle of parliamentary primacy and of the responsibility of the premier and his cabinet to the legislature, a responsibility which meant generally but not exclusively to the lower house. The true executive in republican France for a long time was not the president, who became a ceremonial figure, but the premier and the cabinet, themselves held strictly to account by a majority of the legislature. Unfortunately, that majority, in a parliament where a dozen or so parties were represented, was always difficult to form and could be created only by unstable, temporary, shifting party alliances, coalitions, or blocs. No president, and indeed no premier, could henceforth dissolve the Chamber in order to hold new elections and consult the country as could be done in Britain. Actually, under the Third Republic the substantial machinery of state — ministries, prefectures, law courts, police, army, bureaucracy, all under highly centralized control — was carried over virtually untouched as in all upheavals since the time of Napoleon I. France in the nineteenth century, although volatile in appearance, in effect underwent less extensive governmental reorganization than any other leading country in Europe.

Parliamentary primacy

Troubles of the Third French Republic

Yet the Third Republic was precarious. The government had changed so often since 1789 that all forms of government seemed to be transitory. Questions that in other countries were questions about specific government policies or party programs became in France fundamental questions of "regime" — monarchy versus republic. Many people, especially those influenced by the upper classes, the Catholic clergy, and the professional army officers, continued to harbor a positive aversion to the republic. On the other hand, the unmerciful and vindictive repression of the Commune made many middle-class people sympathetic to the republicans. Many turned republican simply because no other form of government established itself or because it was the form of government that divided the country the least. As republicanism took in wider elements of society, it became less revolutionary and less fearsome. In 1879, for the first time, republicans won control of both houses of the government. In the 1880s their radicalism hardly went further than the founding of a democratic and compulsory school system at government expense and the passage of anticlerical legislation intended to curb church influence in education.

For over a quarter of a century, however, republican energies had to be expended in defense of republican institutions in order to ensure the survival of the regime. An initial crisis arose in 1886–1889, when General Boulanger gathered around him an incongruous following that included not only Bonapartists, monarchists, and aristocrats but also extreme radical republicans who wished a war of revenge against Germany and workers disgruntled over their unhappy lot. Boulanger became a popular figure and seemed for a moment about to seize power. But the menace collapsed in a comical failure as the general lost heart at the crucial hour and fled into exile. Meanwhile, in the 1880s and 1890s scandals and revelations of corruption in high republican circles provided ammunition for the antirepublicans. Moreover, the hope that unsympathetic French Catholics would "rally" to the republic, as urged by French prelates and by Pope Leo XIII in 1892, was shattered by

This barricade and its defenders suggest the revolutionary fervor of the Paris Commune, which controlled the French capital in the spring of 1871. The Commune was in many respects a revival of revolutionary Jacobinism rather than a precursor of social revolution, but it provoked intense fear and brutal repression from more conservative forces in French society. Revolutionary images of Parisian radicals in the streets—as seen in this photograph—made the Paris Commune a symbol of political idealism and martyrdom for many socialists and a symbol of dreadful social dangers for the middle and upper classes.
(akg-images)

The Dreyfus Affair   the Dreyfus Affair, which in the late 1890s rocked the country and attracted wide attention outside France as well.

In 1894 a French military court found Captain Alfred Dreyfus, a Jewish army officer, guilty of treason for leaking secret military documents to the German embassy in Paris. Dreyfus was deported to life imprisonment at Devil's Island, but evidence accumulated to show his innocence and to indicate the guilt of another officer, Major Esterhazy, an adventurer known to be riddled with gambling debts. But the army refused to reopen the case, unwilling to admit it had erred; a staff officer, Major Henry, even forged documents to confirm Dreyfus's guilt. Meanwhile anti-Semites, royalists, traditionalists, militarists, and most of the "best" people fought the reopening of the case, deeming it unpatriotic to shake the nation's confidence in the army and wishing also to disgrace the republican regime. The partisans of Dreyfus stubbornly upheld him, both because they believed in justice and because they wished to discredit their antirepublican

This photograph of Alfred Dreyfus shows the French army captain after he was found guilty of treason in 1894. Stripped of his army rank and deported to prison on an island near French Guiana, his unjust conviction sparked bitter debates in France, a surge of anti-Semitism, and protracted legal campaigns that ultimately led to his complete exoneration and return to the French army.
(Getty Images)

adversaries. The country was deeply split into political and cultural factions that defended or attacked republicanism with arguments that repeated the bitter ideological conflicts of every French revolution since 1789. Finally, following a passionate pro-Dreyfus campaign by writers such as Emile Zola, Dreyfus was pardoned by the French president in 1899 and granted complete legal exoneration in 1906. In the aftermath of the affair, leftist republicans and socialists held power in the Chamber of Deputies and revenged themselves by blocking the promotions of antirepublican officers and by anticlerical legislation. In 1905, in a series of laic laws, they "separated" church and state, unilaterally ending the close relationship established under Napoleon's concordat a century earlier. All ties between church and state were severed, priests and bishops were no longer to be paid by the state, church property was taken over ("even the chandeliers") by the government, and Catholic laymen were to administer each parish. The Pope retaliated by excommunicating all deputies who had voted for these measures. Gradually compromises were worked out; some provisions were made less stringent, and tensions, if they did not disappear, at least eased.

The Strength and Weakness of the Republic

The Third Republic, when the First World War came in 1914, had lasted over twice as long as any French regime since 1789. Born unwanted and accidentally, though it still had opponents, it now commanded the loyalty of the overwhelming mass of the French people. What it had done, since 1871, was to domesticate democratic republicanism in Europe. Republicanism, one of the most

Domesticating republicanism

militant of revolutionary movements down to 1870, had been shown in France to be compatible with order, law, parliamentary government, economic prosperity, and a mutual tolerance between classes, to the extent at least that they no longer butchered each other in the streets. Industrial workers were in many ways less well off than in England or Germany, but there were fewer of them; and for most people France in these years was a pleasant country, where painters, writers, scholars, and scientists flourished, where bankers, bourgeois and well-established farmers could freely pursue their economic interests, a country living comfortably and unhurriedly on the savings of generations, and one in which, in close-knit family groups, average men and women could plan securely for their own and their children's future.

But the comforts and values of bourgeois France were not those that would equip it for leadership in the modern age of technology and industrial power. Though substantial economic progress was made, the country lagged behind Germany in industrial development; the French entrepreneur showed little inclination to take the business risks needed for industrial growth. Politically, the fragmentation of political parties, itself a democratic reflection of a divided public opinion, and the distrust for historic reasons of a strong executive power led to the rise and fall of numerous short-lived ministries—no fewer than 50 in the years between 1871 and 1914. Ministerial instability was to be a chronic problem of the Third Republic both before and after 1914; continuity of government policy was, however, generally maintained because of stability in certain key ministries and because of the permanent civil service.

French labor remained a steady source of discontent. Although French workers benefited from some labor legislation in the two decades after 1890, they continued to feel frustrated at the failure to establish a "social republic." Socialist representation in the Chamber grew, strengthening the antiroyalist factions in the French government. However, the most important single party of the republic, the Radicals, or Radical Socialists, were in actuality radical republicans—patriotic, anticlerical spokesmen for the small shopkeepers and the lesser propertied interests; they drew the line at the advanced social legislation that labor expected from them, and on occasion their leaders even took positive steps to prevent unionization and to suppress strikes. Since some of these Radicals had started out as socialists, the distrust of French workers for all politicians and even for political processes was intensified. But the difficulties of the republic went deeper. The political energies of the republican statesmen had gone into liquidating the past, into curbing the political strength of the monarchists, the church, and the army; by the turn of the century, even before these older issues were fully resolved, the republic was compelled to meet the challenge of labor and to face other domestic and international pressures that were to try it sorely. The Third Republic was to weather the crisis of the First World War but not that of the Second.

The Radical
Socialists

The British Constitutional Monarchy

The British constitutional monarchy in the half-century before 1914 was the great exemplar of reasonable, orderly, and peaceable self-government through parliamentary methods. For over 60 years, spanning two-thirds of the nineteenth century, Victoria reigned (1837–1901) and gave her name to a distinguished era of material progress, literary accomplishment, and political stability. The two great parties, Liberal and Conservative, the heirs roughly of the Whigs and Tories, took form in the 1850s, the former producing its great leader in William E. Gladstone; the latter, a series of leaders of whom the most colorful was Benjamin Disraeli.

The advance toward an egalitarian political democracy in Britain was more cautious and slower than in France. The Reform Bill of 1832 had granted the vote to about an eighth of the adult male population. The democratic Chartist agitation of the 1830s and 1840s attracted wide popular support but failed to produce further reforms in the electoral system. In 1867, however, in response to continued demand for a wider suffrage, the Second Reform Bill was passed, Conservatives as well as Liberals outdoing one another in an effort to satisfy the country and to win new political strength for their own party. The bill, adopted under Disraeli's Conservative ministry, extended the suffrage from about 1 million eligible voters to about 2 million, or over a third of the adult males in the United Kingdom, reaching down far enough to include most workers in the cities. Disraeli's colleague Lord Derby called it a "leap in the dark." In 1884, under Liberal auspices, the suffrage was again broadened, this time in the rural areas, adding some 2 million additional voters and enfranchising over three-fourths of all adult males in the country. Not until 1918 did Great Britain adopt universal male suffrage, as generally understood; and at that time the long campaign for women's political rights gained at least a partial victory when women over the age of 30 received the right to vote.

The extension of suffrage

The leadership of the country at the turn of the century was still in the hands of men of the upper and wealthier classes. Until 1911 the government paid no salaries to members of the House of Commons, who therefore, in both great parties, were usually gentlemen with private incomes, possessing the same family background and education. An attitude of sportsmanship and good feeling was characteristic of British politics. The two parties alternated in power at regular intervals, each indulgent toward the other, carrying over and developing rather than reversing the policies of its predecessor in office. Both parties sought support where they could find it, the Liberals leaning somewhat more on the industrial and commercial interests; the Conservatives on the landed aristocracy; both sought and succeeded in winning their share of the new working-class vote.

The Liberals were usually the more willing to pioneer, the first of the four ministries of Gladstone being especially notable in this respect. Gladstone in this first ministry (1868–1874) developed the principle of state-supported public education under the Forster Education Act of 1870, introduced the secret ballot, formally legalized labor unions, promoted competitive examinations for civil service posts, reorganized the upper judiciary, eliminated the purchase and sale of commissions in the army (a form of property in office), and by abolishing religious tests enabled persons who were not members of the Church of England to graduate from Oxford and Cambridge. The Conservative party, less sensitive to pressure from business interests for a laissez-faire policy in economic matters, and continuing the tradition of early Tory reformers, took the initiative in further labor legislation. Under Disraeli's second ministry (1874–1880), the existing acts regulating public sanitation and conditions in mines and factories were extended and codified, safety measures were enacted to protect sailors, and the first attempt to regulate housing conditions for the poorer classes was initiated. But the Liberals, it must be added, sought to protect the workers' interests too. In Gladstone's second ministry (1880–1885), for example, workers were assured of compensation for injuries not of their own responsibility, and Gladstone later campaigned to reduce labor hours and to extend employers' liability in accidents.

Liberals and Conservatives

British Political Changes after 1900

Rise of British labor

At the turn of the century important changes were discernible on the British political scene. Labor emerged as an independent political force, the Labour party itself being organized shortly after 1900. The rise of labor had a deep impact upon the Liberal party and indeed upon liberalism itself. With many persons insisting that protective measures be taken to counteract the poor health, low income, and economic insecurity of British workers, the Liberals abandoned their traditional position of laissez-faire and sponsored a policy of government intervention and social legislation in behalf of working people. The Liberals, though they acted in part for humanitarian reasons, were aware that with the emergence of the Labour party workers who customarily had voted for them might readily transfer their allegiance.

The Liberals, in control of the government from 1906 to 1916, with Herbert Asquith as prime minister and David Lloyd George as chancellor of the exchequer during most of this time, put through a spectacular program of social welfare. Sickness, accident, and old-age insurance, and a degree of unemployment insurance were adopted, and a moderate minimum wage law was enacted. Labor exchanges, or employment bureaus, were established throughout the country. Restrictions on strikes and other trade union activities were removed. To meet the costs of the new program as well as of other government expenditures, Lloyd George's budget of 1909 called for progressive income and inheritance taxes: wealthier taxpayers would be taxed at progressively higher rates. He was in effect advancing the then novel idea of using taxation to modify the social extremes of wealth and poverty. It was a "war budget," he said, intended "to wage war against poverty." Its fiscal measures were directed primarily at the landed aristocracy, and it aroused great opposition, especially in the House of Lords, where the contest over the budget led to a further constitutional curtailment of the power of the upper house. The Parliament Act of 1911 deprived the Lords of all veto power in money matters and of all but a two-year delaying veto on action of the Commons on other legislation. At this time, too, the government voted to pay salaries to members of the House of Commons, making it possible for workers and others without independent incomes to take seats in Parliament.

A war against poverty

State intervention

The Liberal party was embracing a program of positive state intervention in social and economic matters that the older liberalism, nurtured on the doctrines of laissez-faire and the Manchester School, would not have accepted. With the Liberals actively seeking the support of labor and altering much in their traditional program, the Conservatives in the twentieth century tended to become the party of industry as well as of landed wealth and to replace the Liberals as the champions of economic liberalism and laissez-faire. In the next generation, after the First World War, the Conservatives were to remain one of the two major parties of the country; the Liberals were to be far outstripped by the Labour party.

Meanwhile, despite its gains, labor was not pacified. Real wages showed a tendency to fall after 1900, and great coal and railway strikes broke out in 1911 and 1912. The British capacity to survive crises without violence, while still conspicuous, was being strained. An even more serious threat came from Ireland.

The Irish Question

Britain suffered from one of the most bitter minorities conflicts in Europe—what the British called the Irish question. After 1801 Britain was known as the United Kingdom of

SUNDAY AFTERNOON ON THE ISLAND OF LA GRANDE JATTE
by Georges Seurat (French, 1859–1891)

This picture of sunny calm, painted in 1886, conveys the well-being that many Europeans enjoyed in the late nineteenth century. The people portrayed here seem to live in a peaceable world that is far removed from a later age of speed and mechanical amusements. Technically, this is one of the most remarkable pictures ever painted. The artist created it without the use of lines by filling the canvas with thousands of minute dots of the primary colors, which blur and mix in the eye to produce the forms, hues, light, and shadows of nature.

(George Seurat, French, 1859–1891, *A Sunday on La Grande Jatte—1884*, 1884–1886, oil on canvas, 207.6 × 308 cm., photograph © 2001, The Art Institute of Chicago, 1926.224 (E28490))

Great Britain and Ireland, Ireland having been incorporated into the United Kingdom as a defensive measure against pro-French sympathies in Ireland during the wars of the French Revolution. The Irish representatives who sat in Parliament were generally obstructionist in their tactics. The Irish had many substantial grievances, among which two were conspicuous. The Irish peasants were defenseless against their landlords, far more so, for example, than the French peasants before 1789; and the Irish people, though predominantly Catholic, were obliged to pay tithes to the established Church of Ireland

Real wages for British workers tended to fall in first decade of the twentieth century, causing hardships for people such as these coal miners in Wales. Miners joined in strikes throughout Britain after 1910, contributing to economic and political crises that altered the older doctrines and policies of laissez-faire liberalism.

(Getty Images)

(an Anglican sister church to the Church of England), which also owned a good deal of the land.

Gladstone, in his first ministry, disestablished the Church of Ireland. He also initiated measures to protect the Irish farm tenant. By 1900, under Conservative auspices, Irish tenants were being assisted by the British government to buy out their landlords—

Home rule

often English or Anglicized and absentee Irish landowners. The Irish also wanted home rule, or a parliament of their own. Gladstone, in trying to give it to them in 1886, split his Liberal party, part of which went along with the Conservatives in opposing a political division of the British Isles. Home rule was finally granted to Ireland in 1914. But the Ulstermen, Protestants of northern Ireland, objected vehemently to inclusion in an autonomous Ireland, in which they would be outnumbered by the Catholics of the south. The latter, however, insisted with equal vehemence on the inclusion of Ulster, not wishing to see a political division of Ireland.

The Ulstermen, backed by British Conservatives, started arming and drilling to resist the act of Parliament that authorized home rule. Great Britain, in 1914, was about to see a civil war on its own doorstep. It suffered from something like the insoluble nationalist disputes that afflicted Austria-Hungary. During the First World War home rule was suspended. After considerable violence on both sides Catholic Ireland (which for a time called itself Eire) received dominion status in 1922, but eventually dissolved all ties with Britain and became the Republic of Ireland. Northern Ireland remained in the United Kingdom and was dominated by Protestants, so that its Catholic minority continued to be an alienated, discontented population within the British state. The "Irish question" remained an unresolved issue, generating bitter resentments and violent conflicts during all of the twentieth century and beyond.

Bismarck and the German Empire, 1871–1890

The German Empire, as put together by Bismarck in 1871 with William I, king of Prussia, as Kaiser, was a federation of monarchies, a union of 25 German states, in which the weight of monarchical Prussia, the Prussian army, and the Prussian landed aristocracy was preponderant. It developed neither the strong constitutionalism of England nor the democratic equality that was characteristic of France. To win popular support for his projects, Bismarck exploited existing democratic and socialist sentiment and provided that members of the Reichstag, the lower chamber, be elected by universal male suffrage. Remaining chancellor of the united empire for some 20 years, from 1871 to 1890, he usually tried to have a majority in the Reichstag on his side, but he recognized no dependence on a majority in principle, holding to the doctrine that it was the emperor and his chancellor who were to govern the country. Moreover, in practice, the legislative powers of the lower house were severely restricted, and the upper chamber, representing the princes and not the people, and favored by the government, tended to be more important. Despite the nature of the empire, the Prussian conservatives, the East Elbian Junker landlords, were at first by no means enthusiastic over Bismarck's unified Germany. They opposed his democratic concessions and were left horrified when in 1872 he undertook to abolish what was left of their manorial jurisdiction over their peasants.

Bismarck in the 1870s therefore leaned not on the Conservatives but on the National Liberals. With their aid he put through a number of economic and legal measures designed to consolidate the unity of the new empire. Bismarck's first serious conflict developed with the Catholic church. At the very time that he was bent on subordinating all groups within the state to the sovereign power of the new empire, the church had spoken out. In 1864 in the *Syllabus of Errors,* it denounced the encroachment of all governments on educational and

The Catholic church

church affairs; in 1870 the new dogma of papal infallibility made it incumbent on Catholics to accept unreservedly the pope's pronouncements in matters of faith and morals. To many, the implication was that the new empire could not count on the undivided loyalty of its Catholic citizens. To defend Catholic interests and those of the south German states where Catholicism predominated, Catholic elements had organized the strong Center party, which now upheld the church pronouncements. In 1871 Bismarck launched the *Kulturkampf,* or "battle for modern civilization." The Liberals joined in eagerly. Like nineteenth-century liberals elsewhere (Gladstone's campaign against Anglican privilege and the French laic laws have just been mentioned), they were strongly anticlerical and disapproved of the influence of organized churches in public and private life. Laws were put through imposing restrictions upon Catholic worship and education, the Jesuits were expelled, and many Catholic bishops throughout Germany were arrested or went into exile. But Bismarck gradually concluded that the anti-Catholic legislation was fruitless, that he had overestimated the danger to the state of

CHRONOLOGY OF NOTABLE EVENTS, 1850–1914

1850–1940	About 60 million people migrate from Europe
1869	Opening of Suez Canal in Egypt facilitates global trade
1870s	Western Europe and United States adopt the "gold standard" for global currency exchanges
1871	The revolutionary Paris Commune is violently suppressed in France
1890	Kaiser William II dismisses Bismarck and begins to shape policies of the German Empire
1894–1899	Dreyfus Affair bitterly divides republican and antirepublican factions in France
c. 1900	European population reaches its highest percentage of world population
1906–1916	Liberal government in Britain introduces broad program of social welfare
1914	Opening of Panama Canal facilitates global trade in the Americas

organized Catholicism, and that he needed the support of the Center party for other parts of his program. Meanwhile, the country's rapid and spectacular industrial expansion had stimulated the growth of the German working class, and to Bismarck's alarm, socialism was spreading.

The German Social Democratic party had been founded in 1875 by a fusion of Marxian socialists and the reformist followers of Ferdinand Lassalle on an essentially moderate program which Marx had denounced. But even a moderate socialism was mistrusted by Bismarck. He shared in the European horror at the recent Paris Commune, he feared socialism as anarchy, and he knew that socialism was in any case republican, which made it a potentially revolutionary movement in an empire of monarchies. Two radical attempts on the emperor's life (in neither case by Social Democrats) provided him with all the excuse he needed. In 1878, having already made peace with the Catholics, he set out to eradicate socialism. Antisocialist laws from 1878 to 1890 prohibited socialist meetings and socialist newspapers. For 12 years socialism was driven underground. But repression was not his only weapon; he turned also to another tactic. Bismarck sought to persuade the workers to place their faith in him and the German Empire rather than in Marx and the prophets of socialism. To that end, in the 1880s, he initiated an extensive program of social legislation. Workers were insured by the state against sickness, accident, and incapacity in old age. "Our democratic friends," said Bismarck, "will pipe in vain when the people see princes concerned with their well-being." In social insurance imperial Germany was, from whatever motives, years ahead of more democratic England, France, and the United States.

Repression of socialism

Bismarck failed to kill socialism. The number of socialists elected to the Reichstag was greater in 1890 than in 1878. It seems, however, that Bismarck by the later 1880s was more apprehensive than ever of social revolution that would destroy his empire and contemplated some kind of coup d'état in which the Reichstag would be throttled. He never reached this point because in 1890, at the age of 75, he was obliged by the new emperor, William II, to retire.

The German Empire after 1890: William II

William I died in 1888 and was succeeded by his son Frederick III, who had been married for many years to Victoria, the eldest daughter of England's Queen Victoria. Incurably ill of cancer, he died some three months after his accession. Frederick's son, William II, the last king of Prussia and the last German Kaiser, began his reign (1888–1918) as a young man of 29, full of startling ideas about his personal power and privileges, somewhat in contrast to his father. He was also uncomfortable in the presence of an elder statesman who had made the German Empire, who had been his grandfather's aide and adviser, and whom he regarded partly with veneration and partly as an old fogy. William soon quarreled with Bismarck over continuation of the antisocialist laws and over matters of foreign affairs. When Bismarck forbade his ministers to meet with the emperor on policy matters unless he was present, William resolved that he, and not Bismarck, would rule the empire, and in 1890 he ordered Bismarck to resign, "dropping the pilot," in the celebrated phrase. Under the four chancellors who succeeded Bismarck, it was William who dominated policy.

William II

After 1890 Germany embarked upon what was termed a "new course." In foreign affairs this meant a more aggressive and ambitious colonial, naval, and diplomatic policy. In domestic affairs it meant a more concilia- tory attitude toward the laboring class. The antisocialist laws were dropped, and the system of social security legislation was enlarged and codified. But no expansion of parliamentary democracy seemed possible. William II believed in the divinely ordained prerogatives of the house of Hohenzollern, and the empire still rested on the power of the federated princes, the Junkers, the army, and the new industrial magnates. But the Social Democrats, the Progressive party, and other democratic forces were growing in strength. They demanded, for Prussia, a reform of the illiberal constitution of 1850, and for the Reich, real control over the federal chancellor by the majority party in the Reichstag. In the election of 1912 the Social Democrats reached a new high by polling four and a quar- ter million votes, about one-third of the total, and by electing 110 members to the Reich- stag, in which they now formed the largest single party; yet they were excluded from the highest posts of government. Even had war not come in 1914, it is clear that the imperial Germany created by Bismarck, and now ruled by William II, was moving toward a consti- tutional crisis in which political democracy would be the issue.

A "new course"

Developments Elsewhere; General Observations

Of political developments in other European states before 1914, something has already been said in the preceding chapter. Italy had become a constitutional monarchy in the 1860s and completed its unification by the forceful seizure of Rome in 1870. Despite parliamentary reforms, Italian political life in substance was characterized by unstable majorities and by opportunistic maneuvering and manipulation by moderate liberal political leaders who maintained them- selves in office for long periods of time by shuffling and reshuffling politi- cal coalitions. The liberal leaders were anticlerical, and the quarrel with the papacy over the seizure of the papal territories remained unsettled. The popes refused to recognize the Italian kingdom and forbade Catholics to participate in its affairs or even to vote in elec- tions. Catholics voted nonetheless and in 1907 bishops in each diocese were permitted to relax the ban, as they increasingly did.

Political scene in Italy

Kaiser William II's decision to remove Bismarck from his powerful position in Germany's government was widely described as "dropping the pilot" of the German Empire. This theme was conveyed by the British cartoonist John Tenniel, who portrayed William expelling Bismarck from the ship of state in this famous illustration for the British magazine *Punch*.
(Getty Images)

Industry had begun to make an appearance in the northern cities like Milan. More as a matter of expediency than out of any democratic impulse, the government moved to extend the franchise to the working classes. The narrow suffrage of 1861 was broadened, first in 1882, and then in 1912, when the new reform increased the number of eligible voters from 3 to 8 million, or virtually universal male suffrage. Because of illiteracy and political inertia not all of the newly enfranchised hastened to exercise their voting privilege. The social problem remained serious, too, despite some modest labor legislation. Poverty and illiteracy, especially in the agrarian south, were widespread, and radical unrest appeared in the industrial cities. The first manifestations of an antiparliamentary ideology, chauvinistic nationalism, and explosive irrationalism appeared in the writings and political activism of literary men such as Gabriele d'Annunzio and Filippo Marinetti, the latter publishing in 1909 the manifesto of a violently nihilistic movement he called "futurism." The machinery of political democracy was established in Italy, but there could be no assurance about the evolution of a stable Italian parliamentary democracy.

Austria-Hungary

In the Dual Monarchy of Austria-Hungary, created by the political compromise of 1867, Austria and Hungary were each in form constitutional parliamentary states. In theory, the Emperor-King Francis Joseph ruled through ministries responsible to the legislature in each state. However, in the important sphere of matters affecting the empire as a whole, such as foreign affairs and military questions, there was little parliamentary restraint on the emperor. Here he had virtually final authority; moreover, in all matters he still had broad powers to govern by decree, which he exercised. As in Germany, the tide of socialism was held back both by repressive laws and by social insurance and benevolent legislation. The most serious problem in the empire remained not socialism but agitation by the various subject nationalities, the Czechs and other Slavic peoples. Political democracy took a different course in Austria than in Hungary. In the former, partly as an effort to placate nationalist sentiment, universal male suffrage was introduced in 1907. In the latter it was bitterly and successfully resisted by the Magyars, who saw in it a weapon that could be employed by the Slavs to contest and destroy the Magyar preponderance. Austria itself, despite the democratic suffrage, was ruled very much like the German Empire, with the legislature able to debate and criticize but not control policy.

Of other countries it can be said that the political forms of democracy showed signs of advancing everywhere. Universal male suffrage was adopted in Switzerland in 1874, in Belgium in 1893, in the Netherlands in 1896, and in the next few years in Norway and Sweden (Norway was *Democratic advances* peacefully separated in 1905 from Sweden). In southern Europe, besides Italy, universal male suffrage was introduced in Spain, Greece, Bulgaria, Serbia, and, after the revolt of 1908, in Turkey. Even tsarist Russia, after the Revolution of 1905, received a Duma, or national parliament, elected on a wide franchise but on an indirect and undemocratic class basis and with narrow powers. Among states west of the Russian empire, only Hungary and Romania had a highly restricted suffrage on the eve of the First World War. The vote for women progressed more slowly. Women voted before 1914 only in certain western states of the United States, in Australia, New Zealand, Finland, and Norway. Not until after the First World War did female suffrage begin to make significant advances, and women did not gain the right to vote in France and Italy until after the Second World War.

The progress of representative and democratic institutions did not mean an end to the rule of monarchs, landed aristocrats, and other minority interests. For one thing, with the exception of France and Switzerland, Europe remained monarchical. Second, despite the growing importance of parliaments, parliamentary control over political life was far from guaranteed; emperors and kings still ruled through their chancellors and prime ministers. Of the major world powers it was mainly in the United States (at least for white males), Britain, and France that democratic and popular control was something of a reality. But the extension of the suffrage, by the *Expansion of the* relaxation of property qualifications, had a dynamic of its own and was *suffrage* altering the framework of politics everywhere; mass political parties, including socialist parties and confessional, or religious-oriented, parties were replacing the older narrow oligarchic political organizations, and support now had to be sought on a wider electoral basis. In almost all Europe, and in many of the outlying areas peopled by European descendants, democracy was advancing, even within the older framework. By 1871, most European nations, with the notable exception of Russia, had already won written constitutions, guarantees of personal freedom, parliamentary and representative institutions, and limitations on absolutism; in the years between 1871 and 1914 the most significant new political factor was the advance of male suffrage.

The growing populations and economies of European nations thus created a social stability in which political institutions gradually became more democratic and more responsive to public opinion. Wealth and resources flowed into Europe from all parts of the world, so that the middle classes and even workers had more comforts and material goods than ever before—and more opportunities to participate in the political institutions of their various nations. Europe's dominant role in the global economy, the massive migration of European people, and the military power of European nation-states gave European civilization its extraordinary world influence in the decades after 1871.

During these same years, however, the growing power of industrial corporations and capitalist financial institutions as well as the traditional power of older European social hierarchies and cultural attitudes also provoked opposition, which appeared in popular political movements, as in socialism, and in criticisms of imperialism. The critics eventually influenced many people outside Europe, gaining a following wherever European economic and cultural institutions had appeared. European criticisms of Western capitalism, traditions, and ideas became another aspect of Europe's global influence at the end of the nineteenth century.

For interactive exercises, glossary, chronologies, and more, go to the *Online Learning Center* at **www.mhhe.com/palmer10.**

Chapter 15

EUROPEAN CIVILIZATION, 1871–1914:

SOCIETY AND CULTURE

The belief in progress has been at the center of modern thought since the Scientific Revolution of the seventeenth century. Although some romantic poets, conservatives, and socialists questioned the consequences of modern technologies and industry, most people in the nineteenth century assumed that progress was both inevitable and beneficial. Liberals were especially optimistic about progressive developments in all the main spheres of modern life: scientific knowledge, technological inventions, economic expansion, constitutional government, and protection for fundamental human rights. But the liberals were by no means alone in seeing the late nineteenth-century European ascendancy as the historical confirmation of human progress.

There were also many Europeans, however, who believed that whole groups of human beings were denied the benefits of modern civilization, that workers were not receiving their rightful share of modern wealth, or that women were not entering their rightful place in modern political life. The popular new political movements in these decades were therefore convinced that they were on the side of progress, and in fact they were often able to gain new rights or benefits for the groups they represented.

Meanwhile, science itself continued to produce advances in both the theoretical understanding of nature and the technological inventions that were transforming modern societies. Yet it was also at this time that various thinkers began to question the certitudes of scientific knowledge and to stress the limits of human reason, thus challenging many of the cultural assumptions that sustained the popular belief in human progress. These new trends in European intellectual life before 1914 began to erode some of the confidence in the progressive evolution of human history (at least among certain philosophers or artists) and to undermine the optimism of classical liberalism. The idea of progress remained a powerful theme in all modern cultures, but by the early twentieth century the limits and

Chapter emblem: Albert Einstein as he appeared after he had published scientific papers on the theory of relativity in 1905 and 1916. (Getty Images)

consequences of progress were also becoming subjects for historical reflection, artistic representation, and cultural debate.

✑ 74. THE ADVANCE OF DEMOCRACY: SOCIALISM, LABOR UNIONS, AND FEMINISM

The artisan and laboring classes had always been suspicious of "bourgeois" liberalism's optimistic view of free competition, unrestrained private enterprise, the Manchester School, laissez-faire, the laws of supply and demand, the free market for goods and labor,

Opponents of liberalism

and the idea of an economy independent of states and governments. These were the ideas of middle-class liberals, not of radical democrats. Popular leaders had opposed them in the French Revolution in 1793. The English Chartists had been outspokenly anticapitalistic, and on the Continent the ideas of socialism had been spreading. In 1848 there was a strong movement among the working classes for a "social" republic, and, though the social revolution failed in 1848, the force of it was enough to terrify the possessing classes and shape the philosophy of Karl Marx. With the advent of the ballot, workers pressed for social legislation and used their political power to gain a greater measure of social democracy.

But in addition, before and after obtaining the ballot, working people resorted to other devices for the improvement of their position. Against the owners of capital, who controlled the giving of jobs, there were two principal lines of action. One was to abolish the capitalists; the other, to bargain with them. The former led to radical forms of socialism; the latter, to the formation of labor unions. Socialism, in logic, meant the extinction of the private employer as such, or at least to the dissolution of the larger capitalist corporations. Trade unionism, in logic, meant that the workers had every reason to keep their employers prospering in business in order that bargaining with them might produce better economic results. The working-class movement thus contained an internal contradiction which was never completely resolved.

Workers and intellectuals

Middle-class and educated people who took up the workers' cause, the "intellectuals" of the movement—Karl Marx, Friedrich Engels, Louis Blanc, Ferdinand Lassalle, and thousands of less famous names—tended more to socialism than to unionism. They thought of society as a whole, they saw the economy as a complex social system, they thought of the future in long-run terms, and their time scale allowed generously for whole historical epochs to come and go. The actual workers, put to work at an early age, barely educated if at all, with the waking hours of their adult lives spent on manual jobs, were inclined to keep their attention more on unionism than on socialism. To earn a shilling more every week beginning next week, to be spared the nervous strain and physical danger of constant exposure to unprotected machinery, to have 15 minutes more every day for lunch, were likely to seem more tangible and important than far-reaching but distant plans for a reconstructed society. The worker looked on the intellectual as an outsider, however welcome; the intellectual looked on the worker as shortsighted and timid, however much in need of help.

After the failures of 1848 the socialist and trade union movements diverged for a generation. The 1850s, compared with the hungry '40s, were a time of full employment, rising wages, and increasing prosperity for all classes. Workers set to organizing unions, socialist thinkers to perfecting their doctrines.

The Trade Union Movement and Rise of British Labor

Organizations of wage workers, or labor unions in the modern sense (as distinguished from medieval craft guilds), had long maintained a shadowy and sporadic existence. But they had always been extralegal, frowned upon or actually prohibited by governments. French revolutionaries in the Le Chapelier Act of 1791 and British Tories in the Combination Act of 1799 had been as one in forbidding workers to unite. It was the rise of "bourgeois" liberalism, so insensitive to the worker in most ways, that first gave legal freedom to labor unions. The British unions received a tacit recognition from the Liberal Tories in 1825 and explicit recognition from Gladstone's Liberal ministry in 1871. French unions were recognized by Napoleon III in 1864, then restrained in the reaction caused by the Commune, then fully legalized in 1884. In Germany Bismarck negotiated with labor leaders to find support against the vested interests that stood in his way.

The prosperity of the 1850s favored the formation of unions, for workers can always organize most easily when employers are most in need of their services. The craft union — or union of skilled workers in the same trade, such as carpenters — was at first the typical organization. It was most fully developed in England, where a "new model" unionism was introduced by the Amalgamated Society of Engineers (i.e., machinists) in 1851. It was the policy of the "new model" union officials to take the unions out of politics, to forget the semisocialism of the Chartists, to abandon Robert Owen's grandiose idea of "one big union" for all workers, and to concentrate on advancing the interests of each separate trade. The new leaders proposed to be reasonable with employers, avoid strikes, accumulate union funds, and build up their membership. In this they were successful; the unions took root; and the two governing parties in England, reassured by the unexpected moderation of working-class representatives, combined to give the town worker the vote in 1867.

"New model" unionism

In the 1880s, and especially with the great London dock strike of 1889, which closed the port of London for the first time since the French Revolution, unions of unskilled workers began to form. Industrial unionism, or the joining in one union of all workers in one industry, such as coal or transportation, regardless of the skill or job of the individual worker, began to take shape at the same time. In some cases the older skilled unionists joined with unskilled laborers who worked beside them. By 1900 there were about 2,000,000 union members in Great Britain, compared with only 850,000 in Germany and 250,000 in France.

It was largely because British workers were so far advanced in trade unionism, and so successful in forcing collective bargaining upon their employers, that they were much slower than their Continental counterparts in forming a workers' political party. By the 1880s, when avowed socialists were already sitting in French, Belgian, and German parliaments, the only corresponding persons in Britain were a half-dozen "Lib-Labs," as they were called, laboring men elected on the Liberal ticket. The British Labour party was formed at the turn of the century by the joint efforts of trade union officials and middle-class intellectuals. Where on the Continent the labor unions were often led, and even brought into being, by the socialist political parties, in Britain it was the labor unions that brought into being, and subsequently led, the Labour party. The influence of British labor unions made the Labour party less socialistic than working-class parties on the Continent. Its origin and rapid growth were due in large measure to a desire to defend the unions as established and respectable institutions.

The British Labour party

A steady rise in the membership of labor unions transformed political life in all industrialized societies. This illustration of British miners voting to strike was published in an Italian newspaper, but it depicts the kind of worker activism that became common in most European nations and in other parts of the modern world by the early twentieth century.

(The Art Archive/Domenica del Corriere/Dagli Orti(A))

The Taff Vale decision

The unions were threatened in their very existence by a ruling of the British courts in 1901, the Taff Vale decision, which held a union financially responsible for business losses incurred by an employer during a strike. The shortest and most orderly strike, by exhausting a union's funds, might ruin the union. Opposition to the Taff Vale decision unified the unions and all other existing labor and socialist organizations and precipitated the formation of the modern Labour party. In the election of 1906 the new Labour party sent 29 members to Parliament, which thereupon overruled the Taff Vale decision by new legislation. The social legislation put through Parliament by the Liberal party government in the next few years, in good part under pressure from labor, has been described in the last chapter.

European Socialism after 1850

As for socialism, which had so frightened the middle and upper classes in 1848, it seemed in the 1850s to go into abeyance. Karl Marx, after issuing the *Communist Manifesto* with Engels in 1848, and agitating as a journalist in the German revolution of that year, withdrew to the secure haven offered by England, where, after years of painstaking research, he published the first volume of his *Capital* in 1867. This work, of which the succeeding two volumes were published after his death, gave body, substance, and argument to the principles announced earlier in the *Communist Manifesto*. Marx, during more than 30 years in London, scarcely mixed with the labor leaders then building up the English unions. Hardly known to the English, he associated mainly with political exiles and temporary visitors of numerous nationalities. The first volume of *Capital* was not even published in English until 1886.

In 1864 there took place in London the first meeting of the International Working Men's Association, commonly known as the First International. It was sponsored by a heterogeneous group, including the secretary of the British carpenters' union, Robert Applegarth; the aging Italian revolutionary, Mazzini; and Karl Marx. With the union officials absorbed in union business, leadership in the Association gradually passed to Marx, who used it as a means of publicizing the ideas about to appear in his *Capital*. At subsequent annual congresses, at Geneva, Lausanne, Brussels, and Basel, Marx built up his position. He made the Mazzinians unwelcome, and he denounced the German Lassalleans for their willingness to cooperate with Bismarck, arguing that it was not the business of socialists to cooperate with the state but to seize it. His sharpest struggle was with the Russian Bakunin. Drawing on his experience in tsarist Russia, Bakunin viewed the state as the cause of the worker's afflictions; he was hence an "anarchist," holding that the state should be attacked and abolished. To Marx anarchism was abhorrent; the correct doctrine was that the state—tsarist or bourgeois—was a product of economic conditions and a weapon of the propertied interests, so that the true target for revolutionary action must be not the state but the capitalist economic system. Marx drove Bakunin from the International in 1872.

The First International

Meanwhile members of the First International watched with great excitement the Paris Commune of 1871, which they hoped might be the opening act of a European working-class upheaval. Members of the International infiltrated the Commune, and the connection between the two, though rather incidental, was one reason why the French Provisional Government repressed the Commune with such terrified ferocity. But the Commune actually destroyed the First International. The Commune had been bloody and violent, an armed rebellion against the democratically elected National Assembly of France. Marx praised it as a stage in the international class war. He even saw in it a foretaste of what he was coming to call the "dictatorship of the proletariat." He thus frightened away many possible followers. Certainly British trade unionists, sober and steady individuals, could have nothing to do with such doings or such doctrines. The First International faded out of existence after 1872.

The Paris Commune

But in 1875, at the Gotha conference, Marxian and Lassallean socialists united to found the German Social Democratic party, whose remarkable growth thereafter, against Bismarck's attempts to stop it, has already been noted. About 1880 socialist parties sprouted in many countries. In Belgium, highly industrialized, a Belgian Socialist party appeared in 1879. In the industrial regions of France some workers were attracted to Jules Guesde, a self-taught worker, former Communard, and now a rigid Marxist, who held it impossible to emancipate the working class by compromise of any sort; others followed Paul Brousse, who thought it possible for workers to arrive at socialism through parliamentary methods; still others supported Jean Jaurès, who eloquently linked social reform to the French revolutionary tradition and the defense of republican institutions. Not until 1905 did the socialist groups in France form a unified Socialist party. In England, in 1881, H. M. Hyndman founded a Social Democratic Federation on the German model and with a Marxist program; it never had more than a handful of members. In 1883 two Russian exiles in Switzerland, Plekhanov and Axelrod, recent converts to Marxism, founded the Russian Social Democratic party, from which the communism of the following century was eventually to be derived. The socialist parties all came together to establish an international league in 1889, known as the Second International, which thereafter met every three years and lasted until 1914.

Revisionist and Revolutionary Socialism, 1880–1914

The new socialist parties of the 1880s were all Marxist in inspiration. Marx died in 1883. Marxism or "scientific socialism," by the force of its social analysis, the mass of Marx's writings over 40 years, and an attitude of unyielding hostility to competing socialist doctrines, had become the only widely current form of systematic socialism. Strongest in Germany and France, Marxism was relatively unsuccessful in Italy and Spain, where the working class, less industrialized anyway, more illiterate, unable to place its hopes in the ballot, and habituated to insurrectionism in the manner of Garibaldi, turned more frequently to the anarchism preached by Bakunin.

Nor was Marxism at all successful in England; workers stood by their trade unions, and middle-class critics of capitalism followed the Fabian Society, established in 1883. The Fabians (so called from the ancient Roman general Fabius Cunctator, the "delayer," or strategist of gradual methods) were very English and very un-Marxist. George Bernard

Shaw, H. G. Wells, and Sidney and Beatrice Webb were among early members of the Society. For them socialism was the social and economic counterpart to political democracy, as well as its inevitable outcome. They held that no class conflict was necessary or even existed, that gradual and reasonable and conciliatory measures would in due time bring about a socialist state, and that improvement of local government, or municipal ownership of such things as waterworks and electric lighting, were steps toward this consummation. The Fabians, like the trade union officials, were content with small and immediate satisfactions. They joined with the unions to form the Labour party. At the same time, by patient and detailed research into economic realities, they provided a mass of practical information on which a legislative program could be based.

The Marxist or Social Democratic parties on the Continent grew rapidly. Marxism turned into a less revolutionary "parliamentary socialism"— except indeed for the Russian Social Democratic party, since Russia had no parliamentary government. The growth of socialist parties meant that true workers, and not merely intellectuals, were voting for socialist candidates for the Reichstag, Chamber of Deputies, or whatever the lower house of parliament might be called; and this in turn meant that the moderating influence of labor unions within the parties was increased. The workers and their union officials might in theory consider themselves locked in an enormous struggle with capital; but in practice their aim was to gain more for themselves out of their employers' business. They might believe in the internationalism of the workers' interests; but in practice, acting through the parliaments of national states, they would work for orderly legislation benefiting the workers of their own country only—social insurance, factory regulation, minimum wages, or maximum hours.

By the close of the nineteenth century it was becoming apparent that Marx's prediction of growing worker impoverishment (based initially on conditions of the 1840s) had not come true, at least not yet; the bourgeois was getting richer, but the proletarian was not getting poorer. Real wages—or what the wage earner's income would actually buy, even allowing for the losses due to unemployment—are estimated to have risen about 50 percent in the industrialized countries between 1870 and 1900. The increase was due to the greater productivity of labor through mechanization, the growth of the world economy, the accumulation of capital wealth, and the gradual fall in prices of food and other items that the workers had to buy.

Marxism began in the 1890s to undergo a movement of revisionism, led in France by Jean Jaurès, Socialist leader in the Chamber of Deputies, and in Germany by Eduard Bernstein, Social Democratic member of the Reichstag and author in 1898 of *Evolutionary Socialism,* an important tract setting forth the new views. The revisionists held that the class conflict might not be absolutely inevitable, that capitalism might be gradually transformed in the workers' interest, and that now that the workers had not only the vote but also a political party of their own, they could obtain their ends through democratic channels, without revolution and without any dictatorship of the proletariat. Most socialists or social democrats followed the revisionists. Repeatedly, but in vain, the Second International had to warn its component socialist parties against collaboration with the bourgeoisie.

The revisionists

This tendency to "opportunism" among Marxists drove the really revolutionary spirits into new directions. Thus there arose revolutionary syndicalism, of which the main intellectual exponent was a Frenchman, Georges Sorel. "Syndicalism" is simply the French word for trade unionism (*syndicat,* a union), and the idea was that the workers' unions might themselves become the supreme authoritative institutions in society, replacing not only property and the market economy, but also government itself. The means to this end was to be a stupendous general strike, in which all workers in all industries would simultaneously stop work, thus paralyzing society and forcing acceptance of their will. Syndicalism made most headway where the unions were weakest, as in Italy, Spain, and France, since here the unions had the least to lose and were most in need of sensational doctrines to attract members. Its strongest base was in the French General Confederation of Labor, founded in 1895.

Syndicalism

Among orthodox Marxists there was also a revival of Marxist fundamentals in protest against revisionism. In Germany Karl Kautsky arraigned the revisionists as compromisers who betrayed Marxism for pettybourgeois ends. In 1904 he and other rigorists prevailed upon the Second International to condemn the political behavior of the French socialist Alexandre Millerand, who in 1899 had accepted a ministerial post in a French cabinet. Socialists might use parliaments as a forum, the International ruled, but socialists who entered the government itself were unpardonably identifying themselves with the enemy bourgeois state. Not until the First World War did socialists henceforth join the cabinet of any European country. In the Russian Social Democratic party the issue of revisionism came to a head in 1903 at a party congress held in London—for the most prominent Russian Marxists were mainly exiles. Here a group led by the committed revolutionist V. I. Lenin demanded that revisionism be stamped out. Lenin won a majority, at the moment at least, and hence the uncompromising Marxists were called Bolsheviks (from the Russian word for majority), while the revisionist Russian Marxists, those willing to work with bourgeois liberals and democrats, were subsequently known as Mensheviks or the "minority" group. But in 1903 the Russian Marxists were considered unimportant.

Orthodoxy vs. Revisionism

In general, in Europe's inner zone, by the turn of the century, most people who called themselves Marxists were no longer actively revolutionary. As revolutionary republicanism had quieted down in the Third French Republic, so revolutionary Marxism seemed to have quieted down into the milder doctrines of social democracy. What would have happened except for the coming of war in

Marxism transformed

1914 cannot be known; possibly social revolutionism would have revived, since real wages no longer generally rose between 1900 and 1914, and considerable restlessness developed in labor circles, punctuated by great strikes. But in 1914 the working class as a whole was in no revolutionary mood. Workers still sought a greater measure of social justice, but the social agitation so feared or hoped for in 1848 had subsided. There seem to have been three principal reasons. Capitalism had worked well enough to raise the workers' living standard above what they could remember of their parents' or grandparents'; workers had gained the right to vote, so they expected to benefit from new public policies rather than from the overthrow of their governments; and they had created political parties and increasingly powerful labor unions, all of which protected their interests and helped them acquire a larger share of the national income.

Feminism, 1880–1914

The campaign for women's rights also became more international and better organized during the same decades that the new workers' parties were spreading across Europe. Women received less pay than men for the work they performed in the new industrial economy, and in most places they still faced numerous restrictions on their rights to own property, participate in political meetings, vote in elections, and attend universities. The movement for women's rights therefore continued to promote the kind of reforms that feminists had been advocating since the early nineteenth century, including more access to education and the right to vote. Women's groups on the Continent tended to emphasize legal and social reforms rather than voting rights, whereas British and American feminists gave more attention to the campaign for women's suffrage. But activists in all industrialized societies were increasingly drawn to national and international organizations, in part because such groups created useful networks for spreading information and political ideas. American women such as Susan B. Anthony and Elizabeth Cady Stanton joined with European feminists to establish an International Council of Women in 1888, and the growing demand for women's rights crossed the borders of all modern nations.

Although some feminists worked to make birth control available to more women or to improve the conditions of women workers, the quest for voting rights attracted the most public attention, especially in the United States and Britain. New organizations such as the National American Woman Suffrage Association and, in Britain, the Women's Social and Political Union sponsored petitions, mass meetings, and protests that demanded equal voting rights in both local and national elections. The suffrage movement in Britain became especially militant after the British Parliament rejected every legislative proposal to grant women the vote—a pattern of official opposition that had become a recurring theme in British politics since the 1860s. Frustrated by the stubborn resistance of male politicians, the energetic leader of the Women's Social and Political Union, Emmeline Pankhurst, led a radical wing of the suffrage movement in a campaign of violent protests in the years before 1914. Pankhurst's supporters and allies disrupted sessions of Parliament, broke store windows, destroyed mailboxes, and damaged government buildings to protest the exclusion of women from British elections and political institutions. When arrested, the "suffragettes" went on hunger strikes, to which the police responded by painful forcible feedings.

Pankhurst and other suffragettes were widely ridiculed in the British press and Parliament, but their campaign attracted growing support during the First World War (when the

Suffragettes seek the vote

The British campaign for women's voting rights often mobilized women for marches in the streets, public demonstrations, and confrontations with government officials. The protestors at this march in 1913 were following a woman who had been arrested at an early suffragist demonstration, and the presence of the police is an example of the close government surveillance that was part of every such event.

(Getty Images)

militant protests were suspended), and, as noted earlier, British women over the age of 30 finally received the right to vote in 1918. Women also gained the right to vote in Germany, the United States, and other Western nations in the early years of this postwar era. The campaign for voting rights was only one component of modern feminism, however; and the movement to enhance women's rights in the economy, legal system, family, and education would develop new themes and new political strategies throughout the twentieth century.

75. SCIENCE, PHILOSOPHY, THE ARTS, AND RELIGION

Faith in the powers of natural science has been characteristic of modern society for over three centuries, but never was there a time when this faith spread to so many people or was held so firmly and with so few mental reservations as in the half-century preceding the First World War. Science lay at the bottom of the whole movement of industrialization; and if science gained wide popularity after about 1870, in that persons ignorant of science came to look upon it as an oracle of wisdom, it was because it manifested itself to everybody in the new wonders of daily life. Hardly had the world's more industrialized regions digested the railroad, the steamship, and the telegraph when a whole series of new inventions began to appear. In the 30 years following 1875 the number of patents tripled in the United States, quadrupled in Germany, and multiplied in all modern countries. The scientific and technical advance was as completely international (though confined mainly to the "inner zone") as any movement the world has ever seen. Never had the rush of scientific invention been so fundamentally useful, so helpful to the constructive labors and serious problems of mankind.

Changing conceptions in science

In more basic scientific thinking important changes set in about 1860 or 1870. Up to that time, generally speaking, the underlying ideas had been those set forth by Isaac Newton almost two centuries before. The law of universal gravitation reigned unquestioned, and with it, hardly less so, the geometry of Euclid and a physics that was basically mechanics. The ultimate nature of the universe was thought to be regular, orderly, predictable, and harmonious; it was also timeless, in that the passage of ages brought no change or development. By the end of the epoch considered here, that is, by 1914, the old conceptions had begun to yield on every side.

The Impact of Evolution

Charles Darwin

In impact upon general thinking the greatest change came in the new emphasis upon biology and the life sciences. Here the great symbolic date is the publication by Charles Darwin of the *Origin of Species* in 1859. Evolution, after Darwin, became the most influential intellectual theme of the era. Evolutionary philosophies, holding that the way to understand anything was to understand its development, were not new in 1859. Hegel had introduced the evolutionary conception into metaphysics; and he and Marx, into historical theories of human society. The idea of progress, taken over from the Age of Enlightenment, was a kind of evolutionary philosophy; and the great activity in historical studies, under romantic and nationalist auspices, had made people think of human affairs in terms of a time process. In the world of nature, the rise of geology after 1800 had opened the way to evolutionary ideas, and venturesome biologists had allowed themselves to speculate on an evolutionary development of living forms. What Darwin did was to stamp evolution with the seal of science, marshaling the evidence for it and offering an explanation of how it worked. In 1871, in *The Descent of Man,* he applied the same hypotheses to human beings.

By evolution, Darwin meant that species are mutable; that no species is created to remain unchanged once and for all; and that all species of living organisms, plant and animal, microscopic or elephantine in dimensions, living or extinct, have developed by successive small changes from other species that went before them. An important corollary was that all life was interrelated and subject to the same laws. Another corollary was that the whole history of living things on earth, generally held by scientists in Darwin's time to be many millions of years, was a unified history unfolding continuously in a single complex process of evolution.

Darwin thought that species changed, not by any intelligent or purposeful activity in the organism, but essentially by a kind of chance. Individual organisms, through the play of heredity, inherited slightly different characteristics, some more useful than others in food getting, fighting, or mating; and the organisms that had the most useful characteristics tended to survive, so that their characteristics were passed on to offspring, until the whole

Charles Darwin's *Origin of Species* (1859) set forth scientific arguments for the biological evolution of living organisms and provoked cultural debates far beyond the academic sphere of natural scientists. Darwin is portrayed here as an ageing, somewhat detached scientific expert whose grandfatherly appearance scarcely suggests the intellectual revolution that he launched through his research and writings.
(Library of Congress)

species gradually changed. Certain phrases, not all of them invented by Darwin, summed up the theory. There was a "struggle for existence" resulting in the "survival of the fittest" through "natural selection" of the "most favored races"—races meaning not human races but the strains within a species. The struggle for existence referred to the fact that in nature more *"Survival of the fittest"*

individuals were born in each species than could live out a normal life span; the "fittest" were those individual specimens of a species having the most useful characteristics, such as fleetness in deer or ferocity in tigers; "natural" selection meant that the fittest survived without purpose in themselves or in a Creator; the "favored races" were the strains within a species having good survival powers.

Darwin's ideas precipitated a great outcry. Scientists rushed to defend and churchmen to attack him. The biologist T. H. Huxley became the chief spokesman for Darwin—"Darwin's bulldog." He debated with, among others, the bishop of Oxford. Darwin was denounced, with less than fairness, for saying that human beings came from monkeys. It was feared that all grounds of human dignity, morality, and religion would collapse. Darwin himself remained complacent on this score. Under civilized conditions, he said, the social and cooperative virtues were useful characteristics assisting in survival, so that "we may expect that virtuous habits will grow stronger, becoming perhaps fixed by inheritance." Much of the outburst against Darwin was somewhat trivial, nor were those who attacked him generally noted for spiritual insight; yet they were not mistaken in sensing a profound danger.

That Darwinism said nothing of God, Providence, creative (or intelligent) design, or salvation was not surprising; no science ever did. That evolution did not square with the first chapter of Genesis was disturbing but not fatal; much of the Old Testament was already regarded as symbolic, at least outside fundamentalist circles. Even the idea that humans and animals were of one piece was not ruinous; the animal side of human nature had not escaped the notice of theologians. The novel and upsetting effect of evolutionary biology was to change the conception of nature. Nature was no longer a harmony; it was a scene of struggle, "nature red in tooth and claw." Elimination of the weak was natural, and it might even be considered good insofar as it contributed to evolutionary development. Such conceptions of what was good or beneficial for evolutionary progress profoundly challenged traditional religious ideas about morality and virtue. There were no fixed species or perfected forms, but only an unending flux. Change was everlasting; and everything seemed relative to time, place, and environment. There were no norms of good and bad; a good organism was one that survived where others perished; adaptation replaced virtue; outside it there was nothing "right." The test was, in short, success; the "fit" were the successful; and here Darwinism merged with the new realism, or *Realpolitik,* and other social doctrines which were appearing in Europe at the same time from other causes.

Changing views of nature

Such at least were the implications if one generalized from science, carrying over scientific findings into human affairs, and the prestige of science was so great that this is precisely what many people wished to do. With the popularization of biological evolution, a school known as Social Darwinists actively applied the ideas of the struggle for existence and survival of the fittest to human society. Social Darwinists were found all over Europe and the United States. Their doctrines were put to various political and cultural uses, to show that some peoples were naturally superior to others, such as whites to blacks, or Nordics to Latins, or Germans to Slavs (or vice versa), or non-Jews to Jews; or that the upper and middle classes, comfortable and contented, deserved these blessings because they had proved themselves "fitter" than the shiftless poor; or that big business in the nature of things had to take over smaller concerns; or that some states, such as the British or German Empires, were bound to rise, or that war was morally a fine thing, proving the virility and survival value of those who fought.

Social Darwinism

Genetics, Anthropology, and Psychology

Meanwhile Gregor Mendel (1822–1884), an Austrian monk patiently experimenting with the cross-pollination of garden peas in his Augustinian monastery, arrived at an explanation of how heredity operates and how hybridization can take place. Unlike Darwin, his findings, published in 1866, were ignored until 1900, when they were rediscovered and became the basis for the new science of genetics. Mendel's ideas foreshadowed the amazing breakthroughs in the scientific study of heredity and control over genetic materials in the second half of the twentieth century and in our own day.

Gregor Mendel

Anthropologists began to study the physical and cultural characteristics of all branches of humankind. Physical anthropologists became interested in the several human "races," some of which they considered might be "favored" in the Darwinian sense, that is, superior in inheritance and survival value. Some European scientists and intellectuals in this era argued that the whites were the most competent race, and among the whites the Nordics, or Germans and Anglo-Saxons. The public became more race conscious than Europeans had ever been before. On the other hand the cultural anthropologists, surveying all manner of primitive or complex societies with scientific disinterest, seemed sometimes to teach a more deflating doctrine. Scientifically, it seemed, no culture or society was "better" than any other, all being adaptations to an environment, or merely a matter of custom—of the *mores*, as people said in careful distinction from "morals." The effect was again a kind of relativism or skepticism—a negation of values, a belief that right and wrong were matters of social convention, psychological conditioning, mere opinion, or point of view. We are describing, let it be emphasized, not the history of science itself but the effects of science upon European civilization at the time.

The impact of anthropology was felt keenly in religion too. Sir James Frazer (1854–1941) in his multivolumed *The Golden Bough* could demonstrate that some of the most sacred practices, rites, and ideas of Christianity were not unique but could be found among numerous premodern societies and that, moreover, only the thinnest of lines divided magic from religion. Anthropology, like Darwinian evolution, undermined traditional religious beliefs.

Anthropology and religion

Psychology, as a science of human behavior, led to thoroughly upsetting implications about the very nature of human freedom and rationality. It was launched in the 1870s as a natural science by the German physiologist Wilhelm Wundt (1832–1920), who developed various new experimental techniques. The Russian Ivan Pavlov (1849–1936) conducted a famous series of experiments in which he "conditioned" dogs to salivate automatically at the ringing of a bell once they had become accustomed over a period of time to associate the sound with the serving of their food. Pavlov's observations were important. They implied that a great part of animal behavior, and presumably human behavior, could be explained on the basis of conditioned responses. In the case of human beings these are responses which humans make automatically by virtue of their earlier environment and training and not through choice or conscious reasoning.

Most significant of all the developments in the study of human behavior was the work of Sigmund Freud (1856–1939) and those influenced by him. Freud, a Viennese physician, founded psychoanalysis at the turn of the century. He came to believe that certain forms of emotional disturbance like hysteria were traceable to earlier forgotten episodes of patients' lives. After first trying various techniques such as hypnosis, which he soon abandoned, he employed free association, or free recall. If patients could be helped to bring these suppressed experiences into conscious recall, the symptoms of illness would often disappear.

Sigmund Freud

From these beginnings Freud and his followers explored the role that the unconscious played in all human behavior, he himself stressing the sexual drive. In one of his most famous books, *The Interpretation of Dreams* (1900), he stressed dreams as a key to understanding the unconscious; elsewhere he related his findings to religion, war, education, art, and literature. Freud and Freudian ideas had great influence on the social and behavioral sciences, and a good deal of the Freudian vocabulary later entered into everyday modern language and popular culture. In its deepest significance psychoanalysis, by revealing the wide areas of human behavior outside conscious control, suggested that human beings were not essentially rational creatures at all. Although Freud identified with the scientific traditions of the Enlightenment, his theory of the unconscious called into question the classical liberal and Enlightenment assumptions about how reasonable, free persons developed, explained, and acted upon their individual interests or beliefs.

The New Physics

The revolution in biology of the nineteenth century, together with the developments in psychology and anthropology, were soon to be matched and surpassed by the revolution in physics. In the late 1890s physics was on the threshold of a revolutionary transformation.

Sigmund Freud's description of the unconscious mind reshaped modern conceptions of human psychology and influenced the arts, literature, and social theories as well as the medical treatment of mental illnesses. As this photograph suggests, however, the "revolutionary" Dr. Freud was also a typical member of his own cultural milieu—the professional class in early twentieth-century Vienna.
(Culver Pictures, Inc.)

Like Newtonian mechanics in the seventeenth century and Darwinian evolution in the nineteenth, the new physics represented one of the great scientific revolutions of all time. There was no single work comparable to Newton's *Principia* or Darwin's *Origin of Species* unless Albert Einstein's theory of relativity, propounded in a series of scientific papers in 1905 and 1916, might be considered as such. Instead there were a series of discoveries and findings, partly mathematical and then increasingly empirical, that threw new light on the nature of matter and energy. In Newtonian physics the atom, the basic unit of all matter, which the Greeks had hypothesized in ancient times, was like a hard, solid, unstructured billiard ball, permanent and unchanging; and matter and energy were separate and distinct.

Einstein's theory of relativity

But a series of discoveries from 1896 on profoundly altered this view. In 1896 the French scientist Antoine Henri Becquerel discovered radioactivity, observing that uranium emitted particles or rays of energy. In the years immediately following, from the observations and discoveries of the French scientists Pierre and Marie Curie and the Englishmen J. J. Thomson and Lord Rutherford, there emerged the notion that atoms were not simple but complex and, moreover, that various radioactive atoms were by nature unstable, releasing energy as they disintegrated. The German physicist Max Planck demonstrated in 1900 that energy was emitted or absorbed in specific and discrete units or bundles, each called a quantum; moreover, energy was not emitted smoothly and continuously as previously thought, nor was it as distinguishable from matter as once supposed. In 1913, the Danish physicist Niels Bohr postulated an atom consisting of a nucleus of protons surrounded by electrically charged units, called electrons, rotating around the nucleus, each in its orbit, like a minuscule solar system.

With radioactivity scientists were returning to an idea long rejected, the favored view of the alchemists, that matter was transmutable; in a way undreamed of even by the alchemists, it was convertible into energy. This the German-born Jewish scientific genius Albert Einstein (1879–1955) expressed in a famous formula $e = mc^2$. From his theory of relativity emerged also the profoundly

$e = mc^2$

The new theories that emerged in physics after 1900 transformed earlier Newtonian science and gave the young Albert Einstein an international reputation. This picture shows Einstein standing next to his personal books and papers in the 1920s, several years before he moved to the United States to escape the intolerance and repression in Nazi Germany.
(Getty Images)

revolutionary notion that time, space, and motion were not absolute in character but were relative to the observer and the observer's own movement in space. In later years, in 1929 and in 1954, Einstein brought together into one common set of laws, as Newton formerly had done, a unified field theory, an explanation of gravitation, electromagnetism, and subatomic behavior. Difficult as it was for even the serious-minded to grasp, and a great deal was still the subject of scientific controversy, it modified much that had been taken for granted since Newton. The Newtonian world was being replaced by a four-dimensional world, a kind of space-time continuum; and in mathematics, non-Euclidian geometries were being developed.

It turned out, too, that neither cause and effect nor time and space nor Newton's law of universal gravitation meant very much in the subatomic world nor indeed in the cosmos when objects moved with the speed of light. It was impossible, as the German scientist Werner Heisenberg demonstrated a little later, in 1927, by his principle of uncertainty, or indeterminacy, to ascertain simultaneously both the position and the velocity of the individual electron. On these foundations established before the First World War there developed the new science of nuclear physics and the tapping of the atom's energy. The atom and its world of subatomic particles were discovered to be even more complex than conceived of before 1914.

Trends in Philosophy and the Arts

Although some writers and artists resembled earlier Romantic thinkers in criticizing Enlightenment ideas or modern science, most European intellectuals in this period viewed science as the model for all forms of knowledge. They were drawn to positivism or to the belief that scientific methods provided the only "positive" knowledge of the world. Anything unknowable to science must therefore remain unknowable forever— a doctrine called agnosticism, or the acknowledgment of ignorance. Herbert Spencer (1820–1903) in England and Ernst Haeckel (1834–1919) in Germany were widely read popularizers of agnosticism; both also pictured a universe governed by Darwinian evolution. For Spencer especially, all philosophy could be unified, organized, and coordinated through the doctrine of evolution; this

Agnosticism

doctrine he applied not only to all living things but also to sociology, government, and economics as well. The evolution of society, he felt, was toward the increasing freedom of the individual, the role of governments being merely to maintain freedom and justice; they were not to interfere with natural social and economic processes, nor to coddle the weak and unfit. Yet, like Darwin himself, Spencer believed that altruism, charity, and goodwill as individual ethical virtues were themselves useful and laudable products of evolutionary development.

These latter views were not shared by another of the serious writers of the age, also much influenced by evolutionary ideas, the German philosopher Friedrich Nietzsche (1844–1900). Drawing upon many intellectual currents of the century, Nietzsche was an unsystematic, radical thinker to whom it is easy to do less than justice. It is evident, however, that he held a low opinion of modern, democratic societies. From a background of evolutionary thinking he developed the concept of a Superman, a new kind of noble being who would create new ethical values and philosophical truths that would enable him to dominate and dazzle the multitude. Qualities of humility, patience, helpfulness, hope, and love, in short the specifically Christian virtues, Nietzsche described as a slave morality concocted by the weak to disarm the strong. Qualities of courage, love of danger, intellectual excellence, and beauty of character he prized more highly. Indeed he argued that all humans, even philosophers, were driven more by their instincts and a "will to power" than by reason or rational thought. His critique of religion revived and revised some forms of classical paganism. Nietzsche was neither much read nor much respected by his contemporaries, many of whom considered him unbalanced or even insane; but he nevertheless expressed with unshrinking frankness many implications of the new evolutionary ideas. And his critique of reason and rationality had wide influence among anti-Enlightenment thinkers both before and after the First World War.

Friedrich Nietzsche

As in the sciences and philosophy, so in works of creative imagination—literature, drama and the fine arts—the changes at the dawn of the twentieth century ushered in the contemporary age. Some writers, like Emile Zola in France or Henrik Ibsen in Scandinavia, turned to the portrayal of social problems, producing a realistic literature that dealt with industrial strife, strikes, prostitution, divorce, or insanity. New psychological theories appeared in fictional portraits of troubled characters and irrational human behavior. The new novels and plays were indeed often truer to life than the older forms of European literature. But some literary movements—for example, the symbolist poets in France—were experimenting with language in works that moved modern writing far away from the literal representation of social realities. In a sense the arts followed the intellectual developments of the age, reflecting, as they do today, diverse attitudes of relativism, irrationalism, social determinism, linguistic ambiguity, and interest in the operations of the unconscious mind. On the other hand, never had artist and society been so far apart. The painter Paul Gaugin, an extreme case, fled to the South Seas, abandoned his family and modern European life, and reveled in the stark violence of tropical colors (see Gaugin's painting *Ia Orana Maria* in the color insert following p. 792). Others became absorbed in technicalities or mere capricious self-expression. Art at its extreme fringe became almost incomprehensible and the average person seemed deprived of a visual means (as old as the cave paintings of the Stone Age) of perceiving and enjoying the world.

The artistic movement known as Impressionism did not sever all links between painting and the external world, however, and the Impressionists became perhaps the most influential artists in late nineteenth-century Europe. Rising to prominence in the 1870s and 1880s, painters such as Claude Monet, Pierre-Auguste Renoir, Camille Pissaro, Berthe

A distinctive fascination with light can be seen in most Impressionist works, as in Claude Monet's paintings of the cathedral at Rouen. This view of the cathedral in the evening light was one of a series that Monet painted in the 1890s, when he portrayed the different appearances and colors of objects in various shades of light over the course of a single day.
(The Art Archive/Musée d'Orsay Paris/Dagli Orti (*Rouen Cathedral, brown harmony, effect of evening,* 1894 by Claude Monet (1840–1926))

Morisot, and Mary Cassatt rejected traditional styles of academic painting in France and turned instead to the representation of everyday life and the colorful play of light in the natural world. In contrast to earlier painters who had worked in studios and depicted scenes from mythology, classical history, or exotic cultures, the Impressionists preferred to paint outdoors and to portray the streets or buildings of modern France, the daily activities of ordinary people, or the pleasures of a modern café. Monet was especially adept at representing the same object in various shades of light (see, for example, the *Rouen Cathedral* at the top of this page, but all Impressionists used light and color rather than classical lines or themes to convey their "impressions" of the modern world. Most Impressionist painters were French and most were men, though women such as Morisot and the American-born Cassatt also produced innovative works, often portraying women in the different phases of their lives (see Morisot's *Little Girl Reading* on p. 618 and Cassatt's *The Boating Party* in the color insert following p. 792; another famous Impressionist painting, Renoir's *Le Moulin de La Galette* is also in this color insert).

Impressionism gradually gained international influence and became the aesthetic starting point for other artists, usually called Post-Impressionists, who portrayed people and objects in novel and increasingly abstract forms and surprising colors. The works of

The French painter Berthe Morisot was one of the first women to adopt the methods and perspectives of Impressionist art. This painting, *Little Girl Reading* (1888), exemplifies the movement's characteristic concern with light and color, but the portrait of a young girl was typical of Morisot's particular interest in representing the experiences and memories of women.
(Museum of Fine Arts, St. Petersburg, FL. Museum purchase in memory of Margaret Acheson Stuart 1981.2 (*La Lecture (Reading)*, 1888 By Berthe Morisot (French, 1841–1895)))

Paul Cézanne are influential examples of the "post-impressionist" art that pushed steadily beyond Impressionism in a continuing attempt to represent the artist's distinctive personal vision of human experience (see Cézanne's *Self-Portrait with Beret* in the color insert following p. 792). By the early twentieth century, artists such as Pablo Picasso, Georges Braque, and Vasily Kandinsky were painting "Cubist" or "Abstract Expressionist" works that represented natural objects and the human body in highly abstract forms and splashes of color, most of which bore little or no resemblance to what scientists might have called objective reality (see Picasso's *Les Demoiselles d'Avignon* on p. 619; Braque's *Composition with the Ace of Clubs* and Kandinsky's *Panel for Edwin R. Campbell No. 1, 1914* are both in the color insert following p. 792).

After the First World War, and on into the present, the same trends of subjectivism in the arts attracted a wider, less-skeptical audience. People read books without punctuation (or with peculiar punctuation); listened to music called atonal, composed for effects of discord and dissonance; and studied intently abstract or "nonobjective" paintings and sculpture to which the artists themselves often refused to give titles. Increasingly remote from modern industrial society, artists and their art exemplified the specialization of the modern

Pablo Picasso's representations of the human body in paintings such as this disorienting collective portrait, *Les Demoiselles d'Avignon* (1907), became the best-known works of early "Cubism." The Cubist painters portrayed objects from multiple perspectives and used abstract shapes or unexpected colors to convey the subjective visions of the artist rather than a realistic image of the external world.

(Digital Image © The Museum of Modern Art/Licensed by SCALA/Art Resource, NY. © 2007 The Estate of Pablo Picasso/Artists Rights Society (ARS), New York (*Les Demoiselles d'Avignon*, 1907 by Pablo Picasso (1881–1973)))

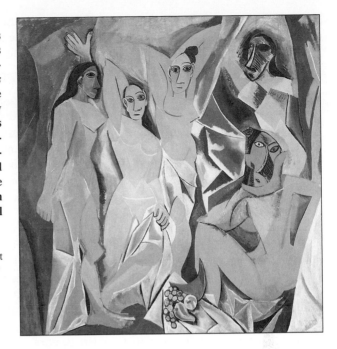

world. Artists were no longer speaking for society or creating art for common use or enjoyment but were specialists plying their trade and pursuing their own concerns—like other specialists whose work was often incomprehensible to outsiders.

The Churches and the Modern Age

Religion, too, was displaced. It was now a long time since almost everyone had looked to religion for guidance. But religion was more threatened after 1860 or 1870 than ever in the past, because never before had science, or philosophies drawing upon science, addressed themselves so directly to the nature of life and of human existence. Never before had so many of the fundamental premises of traditional religion been questioned or denied. Darwinian evolution challenged the value of Christian ethics as well as the traditional picture of Creation, and anthropologists questioned the uniqueness of the most sacred Christian tenets. There developed also the "higher" criticism of the Bible, an effort to apply to the Scriptures the techniques of scholarship long applied to secular documents, to incorporate archeological discoveries, and to reconstruct a naturalistic, historical account of ancient religious times. This form of critical, textual analysis, going back at least to the seventeenth century, now took on significant proportions and was applied both to the Old Testament and the New. In the case of the Old Testament the patient scrutiny of style and language cast doubt on the validity of certain prophecies; and in the New the inconsistencies of the several Gospel sources were demonstrated by a new generation of scholars and critics. The German theologian David Friedrich Strauss (1808–1874), one such critical scholar, was the author of a widely discussed *Life of Jesus*, in which many miraculous and supernatural episodes were reverently but firmly explained away as myth. The sensitive French historian and man of letters Ernest Renan (1823–1892) in a somewhat similar vein wrote on Jesus and the origins of

Threats to religion

Christianity and on the life of ancient Israel, giving secular explanations for the oldest religious stories and beliefs. Moreover, the whole tenor of the time, its absorption in material progress, kept people away from church; and the wholesale uprooting, the movement from country to city, often broke religious ties.

Challenges to Protestantism

The Protestant churches were less successful than the Catholic in protecting their membership from the disintegrating effects of the age. Church attendance among Protestants became increasingly casual, and the doctrines set forth in sermons seemed increasingly remote. Protestants traditionally trusted their own private judgment and regarded their clergy as their own agents, not as authoritative teachers placed above them. Protestants also had always set special emphasis on the Bible as the source of religious belief; and as doubts accumulated on the literal truth of Biblical narratives there seemed no other authoritative source on which to rely.

Protestants tended to divide between modernists and fundamentalists. The fundamentalists, as they were called in the United States, in an effort to defend the literal word of Scripture, were often obliged to deny the most indubitable findings of science. The modernists were willing enough to accept science and to interpret much of the Bible as allegory, but only with difficulty could they recapture a strong sense of spirituality or urgent feeling of Christian truth. Most Protestant churches were slow to face the social problems and wholesale injustices produced by the economic system, though a group of "Christian socialists" had emerged by the early twentieth century in some Protestant denominations. Because both education and the care for orphans, sick, and mentally disturbed persons generally passed to the state, Protestant groups had less to do in the relief of suffering and the upbringing of the young. Protestantism, to the regret of many Protestants, became increasingly a customary observance by people whose minds were elsewhere. Not until after the First World War could a strong Protestant revival be discerned, with a reaffirmation of basic doctrines by theologians such as Karl Barth, and an ecumenical movement on the part of divergent Protestant churches to combine.

Catholicism resists

The Roman Catholic church proved more resistant to the trends of the age. We have seen how Pope Pius IX (1846–1878), after being driven from Rome by republicans in 1848, gave up his inclinations to liberalism. In 1864, in the *Syllabus of Errors,* he denounced as erroneous a long list of widely current ideas, including the faith in rationalism and science, and he vigorously denied that the head of the church "should reconcile and align himself with progress, liberalism, and modern civilization." The *Syllabus* was a warning to Catholics, not a matter of dogma incumbent upon them to believe. In dogma, the Immaculate Conception of the Virgin Mary was announced as dogmatic truth in 1854; a century later, in 1950, the bodily assumption of Mary into heaven was proclaimed. Thus the Catholic church reaffirmed in a skeptical age, and against Christian modernists, its faith in the supernatural and miraculous.

Pius IX also convened a general church council, which met at the Vatican in 1870. It was the first such council since the Council of Trent some 300 years before. The Vatican Council proclaimed the dogma of papal infallibility, which holds that the pope, when speaking *ex cathedra* on matters of faith and morals, speaks with a final and supernatural authority that no Catholic may question or reject. The Vatican Council, and the acceptance of papal infallibility by Catholics, was the climax of centuries of development within the church. In brief, as the world grew more national, Catholicism became more international. As state sovereignty and secularism grew, Catholic clergy looked increasingly to the spiritual powers of Rome for protection against alien forces. Much in the past 300 years had

made Catholics distrustful of their own governments or of non-Catholics in their midst—
the Protestantism and the state churches of the sixteenth century, the Jansenist movement
of the seventeenth, the anticlericalism of enlightened despotism in the eighteenth, the hostility to the church shown by the French Revolution, and by liberalism, republicanism, and
socialism in the nineteenth century. By 1870 the net effect was to throw Catholics into the
arms of the Holy See. Ultramontanism, the unconditional acceptance of papal jurisdiction,
prevailed over the old Gallican and other national tendencies that had long existed within
the Catholic church.

In 1870, while the 600 prelates of the Vatican Council were sitting, the new Italian
state unceremoniously entered and annexed the city of Rome. The pope's temporal power
thus disappeared. It is now widely agreed that with the loss of local temporal interests the
spiritual hold of the papacy on Catholics throughout the world was ultimately enhanced.
The popes long refused, however, to recognize the loss of Rome; and each pope in turn,
from 1870 to 1929, adopted a policy of self-imprisonment in the Vatican
grounds. By the Lateran treaty of 1929 the papacy finally recognized the   *Vatican City*
Italian state, and Italy conceded the existence of a Vatican City about a
square mile in area, as an independent state not legally within Italy at all.
The papacy thus gained the independence from national or secular authority deemed necessary by Catholics to the performance of its role.

Pius IX's successor, Leo XIII (1878–1903), carried on the counteroffensive against
irreligion and instituted a revival of medieval philosophy as represented by Thomas
Aquinas. But Leo XIII is chiefly remembered for formulating Catholic
social doctrine, especially in the encyclical *Rerum Novarum* ("of modern   Rerum Novarum
things") of 1891, to which subsequent pontiffs have adhered, and from
which various movements of Catholic socialism are derived. *Rerum
Novarum* upheld private property as a natural right, within the limits of justice; but it found
fault with capitalism for the poverty, insecurity, and even degradation in which many of
the laboring classes were left. It declared that much in socialism was Christian in principle;
but it criticized socialism insofar as (like Marxism) it was materialistic and antireligious.
The pope therefore recommended that Catholics, if they wished, form socialist parties of
their own and that Catholic workers form labor unions under Catholic auspices.

As for Judaism, the Jews were a small minority, but their condition had always been a
kind of barometer reflecting changes in the atmosphere of tolerance as a
whole. In the nineteenth century the basic trend was toward emancipation
and assimilation. Science and secularism had the same dissolving effect   *Jewish emancipation*
upon Orthodox Judaism as upon traditional Christianity. Reform Judaism
grew up as the Jewish counterpart to modernism in other faiths. Secular Jews moved away
from worship altogether. In society at large, the prevalence of liberalism allowed them to
act as citizens and to enter business or the professions like everybody else, freed from old
legal discriminations that had been imposed on them for centuries.

Toward the end of the century two important new tendencies began to challenge or
counter earlier trends that were leading to the assimilation of Jewish communities and
individuals. One, a cultural and political nationalism, originated with Jews themselves,
some of whom feared an assimilation that would lead to a loss of Jewish identity and
perhaps even the disappearance of Judaism itself. The other counter-
tendency, or barrier to assimilation, was the rise of a virulent new anti-   *The rise of anti-*
Semitism, noticeable in many quarters by 1900. Racist theories, dislike   *Semitism*
for Jewish competitors in business and the professions, socialist scorn for

This is a photograph of the Jewish journalist Theodor Herzl (1860–1904), who responded to anti-Semitic ideologies in central Europe and the anti-Semitism of the Dreyfus Affair in France by launching a new Zionist movement in late nineteenth-century Europe. Herzl organized the first international Zionist congress and called for the creation of a new Jewish state in Palestine, which was at this time part of the Ottoman Empire and occupied by a predominantly Arab population.

(Zionist Archives and Library)

Jewish capitalists like the Rothschilds, upper-class fears of Jewish revolutionists and Marxists, together with a growth of ethnic nationalism, which held that France should be purely French and Latin, Germany purely German and Nordic, or Russia purely Russian and Slav, all combined to raise an anti-Semitic hue and cry. In Russia there were fierce pogroms, or massacres of Jews. In France the Dreyfus case, which dragged on from 1894 to 1906, revealed unsuspected depths of anti-Semitic fury. Many Jews were forced by such hostility into a new sense of Jewish identity. The Hungarian-born Jewish journalist Theodor Herzl was one. Appalled by the turbulence of the Dreyfus affair in civilized France, which he observed firsthand as a reporter for a Vienna newspaper, he founded modern, or political, Zionism when he organized the first international Zionist congress at Basel in 1897. Zionists hoped to establish a Jewish state in Palestine, in which Jews from all the world might find refuge, although there had been no independent Jewish state there since ancient times.

Many Jews, wishing civic assimilation yet despairing of obtaining it, began to sympathize with the Jewish nationalist movement, looking to Zionism and a Jewish renascence as a way to maintain their own dignity. Others insisted that Judaism was a religious faith, not a nationality by itself; that Jews and non-Jews within the same country shared in exactly the same nationality, citizenship, and political or social outlook. On the integration of Jews into the larger community the traditions of the Enlightenment, the American and French revolutions, the empire of Napoleon I, and the liberalism of the nineteenth century all agreed.

76. THE WANING OF CLASSICAL LIBERALISM

The net effect of the political, economic, and intellectual trends described above was twofold. There was a continued advance of much that was basic to classical liberalism and at the same time a weakening of the grounds on which liberalism had firmly rested ever since the seventeenth and eighteenth centuries. A third effect might be noted too. Even where the essentials of liberalism persisted, in program and doctrine it underwent impor-

The English political writer John Stuart Mill, who appears here in a photograph from the early 1850s, was one of the most influential advocates of classical liberalism. By the last years of his career, however, he had also become a prominent supporter of political rights for women and of social reforms that broke with some of the individualism in classical liberal theory.
(Getty Images)

tant changes; liberalism persisted but the classical type of liberalism was in eclipse.

Liberalism changed

    Classical liberalism, the liberalism in its heyday in the nineteenth century, went back at least as far as John Locke in the seventeenth century and the philosophes of the eighteenth. It found its highest nineteenth-century expression in political philosophers such as John Stuart Mill and in the outlook of political leaders such as William Gladstone. Classical liberalism had as its deepest principle the liberty of the individual. Man, or each specimen of humankind according to liberals, was or could become a freestanding being. "Man" meant for them any member of the human race, *homo sapiens,* though in practice, except for a few like Mill, they were usually thinking of adult males. The very principle of liberalism, however, with its stress on the autonomy of the individual, also contributed to the growing movement for women's rights.

    The individual, in this view, was not simply formed by race, class, church, nation, or state but was ultimately independent of all such collective identities. Individuals did not hold their ideas because they belonged to particular ethnic or social groups. They were viewed as autonomous persons who were capable of the free use of reason or of thinking matters out independently, apart from their own interests, prejudices, or unconscious drives. And, since this was the nature of rational human behavior, people of different interests could reasonably and profitably discuss their differences, make compromises, and reach solutions by peaceable agreement. It was because they thought all persons potentially reasonable that liberals favored education. They opposed all imposition of force upon the individual, from physical torture to mental indoctrination.

The rational individual

    In religion, liberals thought each individual should adopt any faith or no faith as he or she chose and that churches and clergy should play little or no part in public affairs. In politics, they thought that governments should be constitutional and limited in power, with individuals governing themselves through their chosen representatives, with issues discussed and decided by the use of intelligence, both by the voters in election campaigns and by elected deputies in parliamentary debate. The will of a majority, or larger number of individuals, was taken as decisive, with the understanding that the minority might become a majority in its turn as individuals changed opinions. At first distrustful of democracy, fearing the excesses of popular rule, and eager to limit political power and the suffrage to the propertied classes, in the course of the nineteenth century liberals had accepted the democratic principle of universal male suffrage, if not yet the vote for women. In economics, liberals thought of the whole world as peopled by individuals doing business with one another—buying and selling, borrowing and lending, hiring and firing—without interference from governments and without regard to religion or politics, both of which were thought to impose superficial differences upon the underlying uniformity of mankind. The practical consequences of liberalism were toleration, constitutionalism, laissez-faire, free trade, and an international economic system. It was thought that all peoples would progress to these same ends, though the era's pervasive racism and the attitudes of imperialism blocked the actual application of liberal principles to the non-European peoples who lived under European rule in old and new colonial empires.

There never was a time, even in one country, when all liberal ideas were simultaneously triumphant. Pure liberalism, like most other cultural and political ideologies, has never existed except as a doctrine. Advancing in one way, liberalism would be blocked or reversed in another. On the whole, Europe before 1914 was predominantly liberal. But signs of the wane of liberalism set in clearly about 1880; some, like the changing conceptions of human behavior and the new interest in the irrational, have already been mentioned.

The Decline of Nineteenth-Century Liberalism: Economic Trends

The free economy produced many hardships. Workers tossed by the ups and downs of a labor market and producers caught in the uncertainties of a world commodity market clamored for protection against exposure. A severe depression in 1873 sent prices and wages into collapse, and the economy did not fully recover until 1893. European farmers, both small French farm owners and big Junker landlords of East Germany, demanded tariff protection; they could not compete with the American Middle West or the steppes of South Russia, both of which after 1870 poured their cereals at low prices into Europe. The revival of tariffs and decline of free trade, very marked in Europe about 1880, thus began with the protection of agricultural interests. Industry soon demanded the same favors. In Germany the Junkers and the rising Rhineland industrialists joined forces in 1879 to extort a tariff from Bismarck. The French in 1892 adopted a high tariff to shelter both manufacturing and agricultural interests. The United States, rapidly industrializing, also adopted protective tariffs beginning in the 1860s, the earliest of all.

The Industrial Revolution was now definitely at work in countries other than Great Britain. There was an increasing resistance to buying manufactures from England, selling only raw materials and foodstuffs in return. Everywhere there was a revival of the arguments of the German economist Friedrich List, who a half-century before,

A revival of List

in his *National System of Political Economy* (1840), had branded free trade as a system mainly advantageous to the British and declared that no country could become strong, independent, or even fully civilized if it remained an agrarian supplier of unfinished goods. With Germany, the United States, and Japan manufacturing for export, a nationalist competition for world markets set in, contributing also to

CHRONOLOGY OF NOTABLE EVENTS, 1859–1920

1859	Charles Darwin publishes *Origin of Species;* "evolution" becomes a key theme in modern intellectual life
1880s–1890s	Claude Monet portrays the nuances of light and color in Impressionist paintings such as *Rouen Cathedral*
1889	European socialist parties establish the Second International
1897	Theodor Herzl organizes the first international Zionist congress
1900	Sigmund Freud develops his theory of the unconscious mind in *The Interpretation of Dreams*
1905	Albert Einstein introduces the theory of relativity in physics
1907	Pablo Picasso advances his new Cubist style of painting in works such as *Les Demoiselles d'Avignon*
1918–1920	Women gain the right to vote in Britain, Germany, and the United States

the drive for colonies and the new imperialism described in the next chapter. The new imperialism itself was another sign of the waning of liberalism, which had been largely indifferent to colonies.

In all these respects the division between politics and economics, postulated by liberals, began to fade. A kind of neomercantilism arose, recalling the attempts of governments in the seventeenth and eighteenth centuries to subordinate economic activity to political ends. A better term is economic nationalism, which became noticeable by 1900. Nations struggled to strengthen themselves by tariffs, by trade competition and by internal regulation, without regard to the effect upon other nations. Workers and business entrepreneurs were now very much affected in purely economic matters by the nation to which they belonged and by the government or laws under which they lived.

Economic nationalism

It was of course to protect themselves against insecurity and abuse as individuals that workers formed labor unions. It was likewise to protect themselves against the uncertainties of uncontrolled markets that business interests began to merge; to concentrate in large corporations; or to form monopolies, trusts, or cartels. The rise of big business and organized labor undermined the theory and practice of individual competition to which classical liberalism had been attached. Organized labor, socialist parties, universal male suffrage, and a sensitivity to social distress all obliged political leaders to intervene increasingly in economic matters. Factory codes became more detailed and better enforced. Social insurance, initiated by Bismarck, spread to other countries. Governments regulated the purity of foods and drugs. The social service state developed, a state assuming responsibility for the social and economic welfare of the mass of its own subjects. The "new" liberalism, that of the Liberals in England of the David Lloyd George era, of the Republican President Theodore Roosevelt and the Democratic President Woodrow Wilson in the United States, accepted the enlarged role of the government in social and economic matters. Both Roosevelt and Wilson, and others, sought also to reestablish economic competition by government action against monopolies and trusts. The new liberals were generally

The "new" liberalism and the welfare state

more favorably disposed toward workers and the disadvantaged classes than toward business; the improvement of the workers' lot would vindicate the old humanitarian concern of liberalism with the dignity and worth of the individual person. The welfare state with an enlarged role for government, remote as it was from classical liberalism, was the direction taken by the new liberals. Advocates of the older or classical liberalism, however, often opposed the growing power of governments and centralized authority and were apprehensive for individual liberties.

Intellectual and Other Currents

Liberalism, both old and new, was undermined also by many developments in the field of thought described earlier in this chapter—Darwinian evolution, the new psychology, trends in philosophy and the arts. Paradoxically, this great age of science found that the human being was not a rational animal. Darwinian theory implied that the human species was merely a highly evolved organism whose faculties were merely adaptations to an environment. Psychology seemed to teach that what was called reason was often only rationalization, or a finding of alleged "reasons" to justify material wants or emotional and unconscious needs, and that conscious reflection dominated only a narrow part of human behavior. Ideas themselves were said to be the products of cultural conditioning or of social power. There were English ideas or Anglo-Saxon ideas, or bourgeois or progressive or reactionary ideas. In politics, some believed that parties or nations with conflicting interests could never reasonably agree on a program common to both, since neither could ever get beyond the limitations of its own outlook. It became common to dismiss the arguments of an adversary without further thought and without any expectation that thought could overcome difficulties. This insidious "anti-intellectualism" was destructive to liberal principles. If, because of prior conditioning, it was impossible to change one's mind, then there was no hope of settling matters by persuasion.

From the view that the human being was not essentially a rational creature, which in itself was only a scientific attempt at a better understanding of human behavior, it was but a short step deliberately to reject reason and to emphasize and cultivate the irrational; to stress the will, intuition, impulse, and emotion; and to place a new value on violence and conflict. A philosophy of "realism," a kind of unreasoning faith in the constructive value of struggle and a tough-minded rejection of ideas and ideals, spread. It was not new. Marxism, since the 1840s, had taught that class war, latent or open, was the motivating force of history. Now Nietzsche rejected the ordinary ethical virtues in favor of personal courage and daring; and the Social Darwinists glorified the successful and the dominant in all phases of human activity as the most "fit" in a perpetual struggle for existence. Other thinkers embraced a frank irrationalism. Georges Sorel, the philosopher of syndicalism, in his *Reflections on Violence* in 1908, declared that violence was good irrespective of the end accomplished and that workers should believe in the "myth" of a future general strike, with its attendant debacle of bourgeois civilization, even though it was known to be only a "myth." The function of thought, in this philosophy of the social myth, was to keep people agitated and excited and ready for action, not to achieve any correspondence with rational or objective truth. Such ideas passed into the fascism and other activist movements of the twentieth century.

Thus, the end of the nineteenth century, the greatest age of peace in Europe's history, abounded in philosophies glorifying struggle. People who had never heard a shot fired in anger solemnly announced that world history moved forward by violence and antagonism. They said not merely that struggle existed (which would have been a purely factual state-

These miners, who were on strike at a coal mine in northern France in 1906, represent the militancy of the early twentieth-century European labor movement. Demanding better wages, better working conditions, and a greater role in public life, labor became an important force in the political cultures of all major European states during this era.
(Roger-Viollet)

ment) but that struggle was a positive good through which progress was to be accomplished. The popularity of struggle was due not only to the intellectuals but also in part to actual historical events. People remembered that before 1871 certain weighty questions had been settled by force, that the movements of social revolution in 1848 and in the Paris Commune of 1871 had been put down by the military, and that the unity of Italy and Germany, as well as of the United States, had been confirmed by war. In addition, after 1871, all continental European states maintained large standing armies, the largest ever maintained until then in time of peace.

The popularity of struggle

In economic and political matters, even in England, the homeland of classical liberalism, there were numerous signs between 1900 and 1914 that the older liberalism was on the wane. Joseph Chamberlain led a movement to return to tariff protection (to repeal, so to speak, the repeal of the Corn Laws); it failed at the time, but was strong enough to disorient the Conservative party in 1906. The Liberal party abandoned its traditional laissez-faire policy in sponsoring the labor legislation of the years following 1906. The new Labour party required its members in Parliament to vote as directed by the party, thus initiating a system of party solidarity, eventually copied by others, that hardened the lines of opposition, denied that individuals should freely change sides, and hence reduced the practical significance of parliamentary discussion. The Irish nationalists had long used unparliamentary methods; in 1914, when Parliament at last enacted Irish home rule, the anti-Irish and conservative interests prepared to resist parliamentary action by force. The English suffragettes, despairing of ever getting the men to listen to reason, resorted to the amazingly "un-English," violent political actions noted earlier. And in 1911 and 1912 great railway and coal strikes disclosed the sheer power of organized labor.

The persistence of liberalism

Still, it is the persistence of liberalism rather than its wane that should be emphasized at the close of two chapters on European history in the half-century before 1914. Tariffs existed, but goods still circulated freely in world trade. Nationalism was heightened, but there was nothing like totalitarianism. Racist ideas were in the air, but they still had little political importance within Europe itself. Anti-Semitism was sometimes vocal; but all governments except the Russian protected the rights of Jews, and the years from 1848 to 1914 were in fact the great period of Jewish integration into general society. The laissez-faire state was disappearing, but social legislation continued the humanitarian strain that had always been an essential part of liberalism. A few advanced revolutionaries preached social catastrophism, but social democrats and working people were overwhelmingly revisionist, loyal to parliamentary procedures and to their existing states. Doctrinaires exalted the grim beauty of war, but all governments down to 1914 tried to prevent war among the great powers. And despite the skepticism of some radical philosophers, artists, and intellectuals, there was still a supreme popular faith in progress.

For interactive exercises, glossary, chronologies, and more, go to the *Online Learning Center* at **www.mhhe.com/palmer10.**

Chapter 16

EUROPE'S WORLD SUPREMACY, 1871–1914

The economic, political, and cultural institutions and ideas of modern European civilization, as described in the last two chapters, spread steadily across most of the world after about 1870. The large European nation-states, which were now equipped with the overwhelming new powers of science and industry, gained empires for themselves throughout the globe. The history of Europe—as of Asia, Africa, and the Americas—became more closely involved than ever before in the history of the world.

For a while the most active of the imperialist nation-states were located in Europe, and the 40 years preceding the First World War were the years of Europe's world supremacy. With the rise of the United States the term "Western" came into use, signifying European in an expanded sense. The modernization of Japan made the term "Western" inappropriate in some ways, as did other later developments. By the mid–twentieth century it was customary to speak of "developed" parts of the world, in comparison with which others were seen as "less developed" or "developing." There even came to be a "Third World," with no specific geographic identity of its own, but which came to mean the developing countries in the later decades of the twentieth century. These terms represented efforts to deal with the same basic reality, namely, a bifurcation between modern and traditional societies, rich countries and poor ones, or between the powerful and the weak.

The Third World

For the first time in human history, by 1900, it was possible to speak of a world civilization. Although retaining important differences in languages, culture, and social practices, all countries were drawn into a world economy and a world market. The attributes of political and economic modernity were much the same everywhere—modern science,

Chapter emblem: Detail from a Chinese illustration of an attack on Europeans during China's anticolonial "Boxer Uprising" in 1899. (© Trustees of the British Museum)

629

modern weapons of warfare, machine industry, fast communications, industrial organization, efficient taxation and law enforcement, and modern public health, sanitation, and medicine.

But not all peoples participated in this global evolution on equal terms. It was the Europeans, or "Westerners," who reaped the greatest rewards. Elsewhere, tribal societies and massive old civilizations alike began to come apart, reacting to the pressures of modern economic and social changes. Scientific ideas changed ways of thinking everywhere, as they had in Europe. In India, China, or Africa local industries often suffered, and many people found it harder than ever to subsist even at a low level. The building of railways in China, for example, threw boatmen, carters, and innkeepers out of work. In India, the hand spinners and weavers of cotton could not compete in their own villages with the machine-made products of Lancashire. In parts of Africa, tribal groups that had lived by owning herds of cattle, moving from place to place to obtain grazing lands, found white farmers or plantation or mine owners occupying their country and were often forced by the white man's law to give up their migratory habits. Peoples of all races began to produce for export—rubber, raw cotton, jute, petroleum, tin, gold—and hence were exposed to the rise and fall of world prices. A depression tended to become a world depression, dragging all down alike.

Imperialism

Imperialism, or the colonialism of the late nineteenth century, may be briefly defined as the government of one people by another. As a specific form of political control, European imperialism proved to be transitory, weakening and disappearing in this form after the Second World War. But the economic and cultural aspects of the colonial systems continued to influence "post-colonial" societies after they regained their political independence. Imperialism and empire-building were a phase in the worldwide spread of the industrial and scientific civilization which had originated in Europe's "inner zone." That it was not the last phase became clear as the twentieth century unfolded. The subordinated peoples, forcibly introduced to the West by imperialism, came to sense a need for modernizing and industrializing their own countries and for the aid of Western science, technology, and capital; but they wished to get rid of imperialists, govern themselves, and control the conditions under which modernization and borrowing should take place. In opposition to European empires, subject peoples began to assert ideas learned from Europe—ideas of liberty and democracy, and of an anticapitalism that passed easily into socialism. Many such ideas were derived from the French and American revolutions, or from Marxism, or from the whole modern history of Europe itself; but these ideas were transformed or challenged as they entered into the political and cultural traditions of other civilizations.

The present chapter deals only with the imperialist phase of this global transformation. By one of the ironies of history, the imperialist rivalries of the European powers, while representing Europe's world supremacy, also contributed to the disaster of the First World War, and so to the collapse of such supremacy as Europe had enjoyed.

77.   IMPERIALISM: ITS NATURE AND CAUSES

European civilization had always shown a tendency to expand. In the Middle Ages Latin Christendom spread by conquest and conversion to include the whole area from Spain to Finland. Then came the age of overseas discoveries and the founding of colonial empires, whose struggles filled the seventeenth and eighteenth centuries and whose most far-reaching consequence was the gradual "Europeanization" of the Americas. At the same time European culture spread among the upper classes of Russia. The defeat of Napoleon left only one of the old colonial empires standing in any strength, namely, the British. For 60 years after 1815 there were no significant colonial rivalries. In many circles there was an indifference to overseas empire. Under principles of free trade, it was thought unnecessary to exercise political influence in areas in which one did business. During these years, however, the French took control of Algeria, the British strengthened their Indian empire, the Dutch developed Java and the neighboring islands more intensively, and the Western powers "opened" Japan and began to penetrate China. But these developments did not lead to overt imperial conflicts among Europeans, and there was no systematic imperial program, doctrine, or "ism."

Rather suddenly, about 1870 or 1880, colonial questions came again to the fore. In the short space of two decades, by 1900, the advanced industrial countries partitioned most of the earth among themselves. A world map by 1900 showed their possessions in some nine or ten colors.

The New Imperialism

The new imperialism differed both economically and politically from the colonialism of earlier times. The older empires had been maritime and mercantile. European traders in India, Java, or Canton had simply purchased the wares brought to them by local merchants as produced by local methods. They operated on a kind of cash-and-carry basis. European governments had had no territorial ambitions beyond the protection of way stations and trading centers. To these generalizations America, the Philippines, and Australia had been exceptions. They had neither native states which Europeans respected, nor native industries in which Europeans were interested. Europeans therefore developed territorial claims and invested capital and brought in their own methods of production and management, especially in the then booming sugar islands of the West Indies.

New imperialism versus old colonialism

Under the new imperialism Europeans were by no means content simply to purchase what local merchants provided. They wanted goods of a kind or in a quantity that preindustrial handicraft methods could not supply. They moved into the so-called "backward" countries more thoroughly. They invested capital in them, setting up mines, plantations, docks, warehouses, factories, refineries, railroads, river steamships, and banks. They built offices, homes, hotels, clubs, and cool mountain resorts for European officials and visitors. Taking over the productive life of the country, they transformed large elements of the local population into the wage employees of foreign owners and so introduced the class problems of industrial Europe in a form accentuated by racial differences. Or they lent money to non-European rulers—the khedive of Egypt, the shah of Persia, the emperor of China— to enable them to hold up their tottering thrones or simply to live with more pleasure and magnificence than they could from their usual revenues. Europeans thus developed a huge financial stake in governments and economic enterprises outside the West.

To secure these investments, and for other reasons, in contrast to what had happened under the older colonialism, the Europeans now aspired to political and territorial domination. Some areas became outright colonies, directly governed by European states and their appointed government officials. Others became protectorates: here the native chief, sultan, bey, rajah, or prince was maintained and guaranteed against internal upheaval or external conquest. A European "resident" or "commissioner" usually told him what to do. In other regions, as in China or Persia, where no single European state could make good its claims against the

Political and territorial domination

European access to colonial territories in the period of the "new imperialism" often depended on the construction of new railroads, which carried both people and goods into and out of the interior districts of the European colonies. This picture portrays the arrival of a locomotive that a team of elephants pulled into central India when a new railroad track was built in the region of Indore.
(Picture Collection, The New York Public Library, Astor, Lenox and Tilden Foundations)

others, they arranged to divide the country into "spheres of influence," each European power having advisory privileges and investment and trade opportunities within its own sphere. The sphere of influence was the vaguest of all forms of imperial control; supposedly, it left the country independent.

An enormous differential opened up, about 1875, between the power of European and non-European states. Queen Elizabeth had dealt with the Great Mogul of the Indian subcontinent with genuine respect, at least in part because his revenues in the early seventeenth century were some 20 times greater than those of the English monarchy. Even Napoleon had pretended to regard the shah of Persia as an equal. Then came the Industrial Revolution in Europe, iron and steel ships, heavier naval guns, and more accurate rifles. Democratic and nationalist movements produced large and unified European peoples, united in the service and financial support of their governments. Seemingly endless wealth, with modern administration, allowed European governments to tax, borrow, and spend without apparent limit. The modern nation-states loomed as enormous power complexes without precedent in the world's history. At the same time it so happened that all the principal non-European empires were in decay. They were receiving a minimum of support from their own subjects. As in the eighteenth century when the disintegration of the Mogul empire had enabled the British to take over India, so in the nineteenth century the political weakness and vulnerabilities of the sultan of Turkey, the sultan of Zanzibar, the shah of Persia, the emperor of China, and the shogun of Japan made European intervention remarkably easy. Only the Japanese were able to revolutionize their government in time to ward off imperialist penetration. Even the Japanese, however, were restricted by early treaties that controlled their tariff policies until after 1900.

So great was the difference in the sheer mechanics of power that usually a mere show of force allowed the Europeans to impose their will. A garrison of only 75,000 troops long held India for the British. Numerous sporadic little wars were constantly fought—Afghan wars, Burmese wars, Zulu wars—which passed unnoticed by Europeans in the home country and were no more like a true national war or national military mobilization than the operations of the United States army against the Indians of the western plains. The Spanish-American War of 1898 and the Boer War of 1899 were also wars of colonial type, fought between entirely unequal parties. Often a show of naval strength was enough. It was the classic age of the punitive bombardment. We have seen how the American Commodore Perry threatened to bombard Tokyo in 1854. In 1856 the British consul at Canton, to punish acts of violence against Europeans, called upon the local British admiral to bombard that Chinese city. In 1863 the British bombarded Satsuma, and in 1864 an allied force including Americans bombarded Choshu—precipitating revolution in Japan. Similarly, Alexandria was bombarded in 1882 and Zanzibar in 1896. The usual consequence was that the local ruler signed a treaty, reorganized the government, or accepted a European (usually British) adviser.

Europeans impose their will

Incentives and Motives

Behind the aggressiveness lay many pressures. The Europeans could not maintain for themselves the style of life to which they had become accustomed except by bringing the rest of the world within their orbit. But many other needs felt in Europe drove people into distant, unknown places. Catholic and Protestant groups sent growing numbers of missionaries to remote regions, where they sometimes got into trouble with the local people and where some missionaries were even killed. Public opinion in the home countries, soon learning of such events by ocean cable, might clamor for political action to suppress such outbreaks of anti-Christian violence. Similarly, scientists required geographical expeditions for their observations and discoveries. Wealthy persons traveled more, now that travel was so easy; they hunted tigers or elephants, or simply went to see the sights. It seemed only reasonable at the close of the nineteenth century that all Europeans wherever they might choose to go should enjoy the personal security and the orderly legal procedures that European governments sought to provide for the Western people who visited or lived in their overseas empires.

Economically, European life required material goods, many of which only tropical regions could supply. Even the working classes now drank tea or coffee every day. After the American Civil War Europe relied for its cotton increasingly on Africa and the East. Rubber and petroleum became staple needs. The lowly jute, which grew only in India, was used to make burlap, twine, carpets, and the millions of jute bags employed in commerce. The lordly coconut tree had innumerable common uses, which led to its intensive cultivation in the Dutch Indies. Various parts of it could be eaten, or manufactured into bags, brushes, cables, rope, sails, or doormats or converted into coconut oil, which in turn went into the making of candles, soap, margarine, and many other products.

Raw materials

Europe's overseas colonies gave European travelers new places to visit and new forms of "exotic" adventure that developed within the social and legal hierarchies of imperial political systems. The Englishwomen depicted here are going into an Asian forest for a picnic, accompanied by servants who carry their food and handle their horses and by escorts whose pith helmets symbolize the heyday of the British Empire.
(Getty Images)

Industrial countries also attempted to sell their own products, and one of the reasons given by imperialists, in support of imperialism, was the urgent necessity of finding new markets. The industrialization of Germany, the United States, Japan, and other countries, after about 1870, meant that they competed with each other and with Great Britain for foreign trade. The slowly declining price level after 1873 meant that a business firm had to sell more goods to turn over the same amount of money. Competition was more intense. The advanced industrial countries, as we have seen, raised tariffs to keep out each other's products. It was therefore argued that each industrialized nation must develop a colonial empire, an area of "sheltered markets," as the phrase went in England, in which the home country would supply manufactured goods in return for raw materials. The idea was to create a large self-sufficient trading unit, embracing various climates and types of resources, protected if necessary from outside competition by tariffs, guaranteeing a market for all its members and wealth and prosperity for the home country. This phase of imperialism is often called neomercantilism, since it revived in substance the mercantilism, or national economic systems, of the sixteenth to the eighteenth centuries.

Neomercantilism

Purely financial considerations also characterized the new imperialism. Money invested in the so-called "backward" countries by the close of the nineteenth century brought a higher rate of return than if invested in the more industrialized ones. For this there were many reasons, including the cheap labor of non-European regions, the heavy and unsatisfied demand for non-European products, and the greater risk of losses in half-unknown areas where European ideas of law and order did not prevail. By 1900 western Europe and the northeastern United States were equipped with their basic industrial apparatus. Their railway networks and first factories were built. Opportunities for investment in these countries became stabilized. At the same time, these countries themselves accumulated capital seeking an outlet. In the mid-century most exported capital was British-owned. By the close of the century more French, German, American, Dutch, Belgian, and Swiss investors were investing or lending outside their own borders. In 1850, most exported capital went to build up Europe, the United States, Canada, Australia, or Argentina. By 1900 more of it was going to undeveloped regions in other parts of the world. This capital was the property of individual small savers or of large banking combinations. Investors preferred "civilized" political control over the parts of Asia, Africa, or Latin America in which their railroads, mines, plantations, government loans, or other investments were situated. Hence the profit motive, or desire to invest "surplus" capital, promoted imperialism.

The profit motive

This analysis was put forward by critics like the English socialist J. A. Hobson, who wrote an influential book on imperialism in 1903, and later by Lenin, in his *Imperialism, the Highest Stage of World Capitalism,* written in 1916. They ascribed imperialism primarily to the accumulation of surplus capital and condemned it on socialist grounds. Hobson argued that a change in the domestic economy would remove the main motive for imperialism: if more of the national income went to workers as wages, and less of it to capitalists as interest and dividends, or if wealthy people were more heavily taxed and the money used for social welfare, there would be no surplus of capital and no real imperialism. Since the working class, if this were done, would also have more purchasing power, it would be less necessary to look endlessly for new markets outside the country. But the surplus capital explanation of imperialism was not entirely convincing. That investors and exporters were instrumental in the rise of imperialism was of course very true. That imperialism arose essentially from the capitalists' pressure to invest abroad was more doubtful. Perhaps even more basic was Europe's need for imports—only by enormous imports could Europe sustain its dense population, complex industry, and high standard of living. It was the demand for such imports—cotton, cocoa, coffee, copper, and the like drawn from the colonies—that made investment in the colonies financially profitable. Moreover, non-Europeans themselves often asked for the capital, glad though the European lenders were to lend it at high rates. In 1890 this might mean merely that a shah or sultan wanted to build himself a new palace, but the need of non-Europeans for Western capital was basic, nor was it to decline in later times. Lastly, the imperialism of some countries, notably Russia and Italy, which had little capital and few modern-type capitalists of their own, could not reasonably be attributed to pressure for lucrative foreign investments.

Socialist critics

For the British, however, the capitalistic incentive was of great importance. We have seen how the British, in 1914, had $20 billion invested outside Great Britain, a quarter of all their wealth. About half, or $10 billion, was invested in the British Empire. Only a tenth of French foreign investments was in French colonies. French investment in the colonial world in general, however, including Egypt, Suez, South Africa, and Asia in addition to the

French colonies, amounted to about a fifth of all French foreign investments. Only an infinitesimal fraction of German foreign investment in 1914 was in German colonies, which were of slight value. A fifth of German foreign investments, however, was placed in Africa, Asia, and the Ottoman Empire. These sums are enough to suggest the pressures upon the European governments to assert political influence in Africa, Turkey, or China.

Foreign economic interests in Russia

In addition, French investors (including small bourgeois and even affluent peasants) had in 1914 a huge stake in the Russian empire. Russia, an imperial power with respect to adjoining countries in the Balkans and Asia, occupied an almost semicolonial status with respect to western Europe. The tsardom until its demise in 1917, not unlike the Ottoman sultanate or the Qing dynasty in China, was kept going by foreign loans, predominantly French. The French in 1914 had lent over $2 billion to Russia, more than to all colonial regions combined. For these huge outlays the motivation was at least as much political as economic. The French government urged French banks to buy Russian bonds. The aim was not merely to make a profit for bankers and small investors but to build up and hold together a military ally against Germany.

Joseph Chamberlain

Politics went along with economics in the whole process of imperialist expansion. National security, both political and economic, was as important an aim as the accumulation of private wealth. So, too, was the growing concern in many quarters over the economic security and welfare of the working classes. The ideas of the British statesman Joseph Chamberlain (1836–1914) illustrated how these motives entered into imperialist thinking.

Chamberlain, father of Neville Chamberlain, who was to be prime minister of Britain in the years just prior to the Second World War, began as a Birmingham manufacturer, the type of man who a generation before would have been a staunch free trader and upholder of laissez-faire. Discarding the old individualism, he came to believe that the community should and could take better care of its members and that the British community (or empire) could advance the welfare of Britons. As mayor of Birmingham he introduced a kind of municipal socialism, including public ownership of utilities. As colonial secretary from 1895 to 1903, he preached Britain's need for "a great self-sustaining and self-protecting empire" in an age of rising international competition—a worldwide British trading area, developed by British capital, which would give a secure source of raw materials and food, markets for exports, and a steady level of profits, wages, and employment.

Chamberlain saw with misgivings the tendencies toward independence in Canada, New Zealand, and the Australian Commonwealth. For these dominions he favored complete self-government, but he hoped that, once assured of virtual independence, they would reknit their ties with each other and with Great Britain. Britain and its dominions, in Chamberlain's view, should pool their resources not only for military defense but also for economic well-being. The dominions had already levied tariffs against British manufacturers in order to build up their own. Chamberlain urged the dominions to charge a lower duty on British wares than on the same wares coming from foreign countries. In return, he even proposed that Great Britain adopt a protective tariff, so that it might then favor Canadian or Australian goods by offering them a lower rate. His plan was to bind the empire together by economic bonds, making it a kind of tariff union, or system of "imperial preference." Since Britain imported mainly meat and cereals from the dominions, Chamberlain was obliged to recommend a tariff even upon these products—to "tax the people's food," repudiating the very ark of the covenant of Free Trade upon which the British economy had rested for half a century. The proposal was rejected. Chamberlain died in 1914, his goal unaccomplished. But after the First World War the British Empire, or Commonwealth of Nations, followed closely the proposals he had mapped out.

Whether the economic welfare and security of the European working classes was advanced by imperialism is still debated. It is probable that the worker in western Europe did gain economic benefits from imperialism. Socially conservative imperialists were joined in this belief by thinkers of the extreme Left. Marx himself, followed by Lenin, thought that the European worker obtained higher real wages through the inflow of low-priced colonial goods. To Marxists this was unfortunate, for it gave European workers a vested interest in imperialism, made the European proletariat "opportunistic" (i.e., unrevolutionary), and blocked the formation of a true international world proletariat of all races.

Working classes and imperialism

Another imperialist argument much heard at the time held that European countries must acquire colonies to which surplus population could migrate without altogether abandoning the native land. It seemed unfortunate, for example, that so many Germans or Italians emigrating to the United States should be lost to the fatherland. This argument was purely specious. No European country after 1870 acquired any colony to which European families in any numbers wished to move. The millions who were still leaving Europe persisted in heading for the Americas, where in the circumstances no European colony could be founded.

The competitive nature of the European state system introduced other almost exclusively political features. The European states had to guard their security against each other. They had to keep some kind of balance among themselves, in the overseas world as in Europe. Hence, as in the scramble for Africa, one government often hurriedly annexed territory simply for fear that another might do so first. Or again, colonies came to have an intangible but momentous value in symbolism and prestige. To have colonies was a normal criterion of greatness. It was the sign of having arrived as a Great Power. Britain and France had had colonies for centuries. Therefore the new powers formed in the 1860s—Germany, Italy, Japan, and in a sense the United States—came to believe they had to have colonies also.

Diplomacy and imperialism

Imperialism as Crusade

Imperialism arose from the commercial, industrial, financial, scientific, political, journalistic, intellectual, religious, and humanitarian impulses of Europe compounded together. It was an outthrust of modern Western civilization, and its advocates claimed that it would bring civilization and enlightenment to those who still sat in darkness. Faith in "modern civilization" had become a kind of substitute religion. Imperialism was its crusade.

So the British spoke of the White Man's Burden; the French, of their *mission civilisatrice;* the Germans, of diffusing *Kultur;* the Americans, of the "blessings of Anglo-Saxon protection." Social Darwinism and popular anthropology taught the racist doctrine that the white races were "fitter" or more gifted than the peoples of other races. Some imperialists argued, more reasonably, that the "backwardness" of non-European societies was due to historic, and hence temporary, causes but that for a long period into the future the civilized whites must keep a guardianship over their darker protégés. The psychology of imperialism contained strands of idealism and humanitarianism as well as greed, and numerous Europeans went to the colonies to build schools or hospitals rather than railroads or mines. Young people of good family left the pleasant lands of Devonshire or Poitou to spend long and lonely years in hot, isolated places, sustained by the thought that they were advancing the work of humanity. It

Trade missions

A belief in the cultural or religious mission of European civilization led to the establishment of European schools, churches, and hospitals in much of Africa and Asia. The Englishwoman in this photograph, Elizabeth Mort, was a Protestant deaconess at a Christian mission in Fukien, China; the man standing behind her suggests the important presence of local workers and assistants in all overseas European institutions.
(Church Mission Society Archives, London)

was a good thing to put down slave raiding, torture, and famine; to combat degrading superstitions; to fight the diseases of neglect and filth; and to promote the ideas and institutions of legal justice (even though colonial legal systems did not treat the colonizers and native people in the same way). But these accomplishments, however real, went along all too obviously with European self-interest and were expressed with unbearable complacency and gross condescension to the larger part of the human race. As Rudyard Kipling wrote in 1899 (in his exhortation to Americans after their taking over of the Philippines):

> *Take up the White Man's burden—*
> *Send out the best ye breed—*
> *Go bind your sons to exile,*
> *To serve your captives' need;*
> *To wait in heavy harness,*
> *On fluttered folk and wild—*
> *Your new-caught sullen peoples,*
> *Half devil and half child.*

78. THE AMERICAS

After the general considerations above, let us examine each of the earth's great regions in turn, and first the Americas, where we must begin our discussion earlier in the century, before the age of the "new imperialism."

In America the breakup of the Spanish and Portuguese empires in the first quarter of the nineteenth century, during and after the Napoleonic wars, left the vast tract from Colorado to Cape Horn very unsettled. Most of the people were Indian or a mixture of Indian and white *(mestizo)*, with clusters here and there of pure European stock, which the nineteenth-century immigration was greatly to increase. In the former Spanish empire, except in inaccessible spots, the Spanish culture and language predominated. In Brazil, in the former Portuguese empire, the culture was Portuguese, and the country, though independent after 1822, remained a monarchy (or "empire") until 1889, when it became a republic. In the former Spanish domains the disappearance of royal control left a large number of weak and unstable republics, chronically engaged in border disputes with one another. Fortunately for these republics, at the time of independence in the 1820s, European imperialism was at a low ebb. We have seen how the Congress of Verona considered ways of returning them to Spain but was opposed by Great Britain and how the United States, in 1823, supplemented the British action by announcing the Monroe Doctrine. But the first external military threat to one of the new republics actually came from the United States.

The United States and Mexico

Mexico, on becoming independent of Spain, reached almost to the Mississippi and the Rocky Mountains. Hardly was it independent when land seekers from the United States swarmed over its northeastern borders. They brought with them their slaves, to grow the cotton so voraciously demanded in industrial England. The Mexican Republic did not allow slavery. The newcomers proclaimed their own republic, which they called Texas. Agitation developed for annexation to the United States. Mexico objected, but in 1845 the United States annexed Texas. A war followed, in which Mexico lost to the United States not only Texas but the whole region from Texas to the California coast. As is usual in such affairs, the loser preserved a longer memory than the winner. It soon seemed only natural in the United States to possess these regions; in Mexico many decades had to pass before the wound was healed. Mexico had lost half its territory to an aggressive neighbor within the first generation of its independence. Meanwhile, though some Americans condemned the war, most people in the United States justified this vast annexation of Mexican territory by arguing that their nation was far better prepared than Mexico to develop a modern economy and government in the region.

The Mexican-American War

The next threat to Mexico came from Europe. Mexico, at a time of internal disorders, had contracted large loans on exorbitant terms. When the liberal president Benito Juárez (a pure-blooded Indian and thus at least racially "non-European") repudiated the loans, the European bondholders demanded satisfaction from their governments. The United States was paralyzed by the Civil War. Great Britain, France, and Spain, which had never recognized the Monroe Doctrine, in 1861 sent combined military forces to Veracruz. The British proposed seizure of the customs houses in Mexican ports and appropriation of the custom revenues to pay off the debt (an expedient introduced in China three years before); but the French had more ambitious designs. Unknown both to the British, who wanted only to collect debts, and to the Spanish, who dreamed of setting up a new Bourbon monarchy in Mexico, the Emperor Napoleon III had a secret project for establishing a French satellite state in Mexico, which French capital and exports might subsequently develop. He planned to create a Mexican empire with the Austrian archduke Maximilian as its figurehead emperor. The

European intervention in Mexico

Benito Juárez was born into a Zapotec Indian family in the Mexican city of Oaxaca. His picture conveys the determination of a liberal reformer who opposed the traditional power of the Catholic Church, led the national resistance to a French-backed regime that Napoleon III imposed on Mexico, and became president of the Mexican republic after that regime was overthrown in 1867.
(Getty Images)

British and Spanish disapprovingly withdrew their forces. The French army proceeded into the interior and installed Maximilian on a very shaky imperial throne. Maximilian reigned for some years, but Napoleon III gradually concluded that conquest of Mexico was impossible or too expensive. It further appeared, by 1865, that the United States was not going to collapse after all, as expected and even hoped for by the European governing classes. The United States protested strongly to the French government. The French withdrew, Maximilian was captured and shot, and Juárez and the Mexican liberals came back to power.

The United States before 1870 had thus in turn both despoiled and protected the adjoining part of Latin America. This ambivalent situation became characteristic of the New World. As the United States became a great power, the Monroe Doctrine became an effective barrier to European territorial ambitions. Latin America never became subject to imperialism as completely as did Asia and Africa. On the other hand, the United States became the imperialist power feared above all others south of the border. It was the *Yanqui* menace, the Colossus of the North.

The Monroe Doctrine

In the 1870s in the course of its turbulent politics, both citizens of Mexico and foreign residents were obliged to pay forced loans to rival leaders. The State Department in Washington demanded that American citizens be reimbursed by the Mexican government. The double standard characteristic of imperialism—one standard for "civilized" and one for "uncivilized" states—became clear in the exchange of notes. The Mexican government under Porfirio Díaz attempted to lay down the principle that "foreigners locating in a country accepted the mode of life of the people . . . and participated not only in the benefits of such residence but also in the adversities. Foreigners should enjoy the same guarantees and the same legal protection as natives, but no more." The Mexicans observed that the United States had never recognized the claims of foreigners for losses sustained in its Civil War. The United

Imperialism's double standard

States, under President Hayes, held on the other hand that citizens of advanced states, operating in more primitive regions, should continue to enjoy the security of property characteristic of their home countries. When on another occasion the United States sent troops to the border, and the Mexicans objected, the secretary of state remarked on "the volatile and childish character of these people and their incapacity to treat a general question with calmness and without prejudice." Mexico retorted that the United States had "disregarded all the rules of international law and practice of civilized nations and treated the Mexicans as savages, as Kaffirs of Africa."

It was, in fact, a principle of international law in the nineteenth century that "civilized" states might not intervene in each other's affairs but had the right of intervention in so-called "backward" countries. In the dispute of 1877 the United States classified Mexico as backward and as "volatile and childish." The Mexicans objected to being treated like "savages and Kaffirs," and not like a civilized nation. The leaders of both nations thus agreed that there were different legal standards for "civilized" and "uncivilized" nations, but they strongly disagreed on which of the two standards should apply in Mexico.

United States Imperialism in the 1890s

The 1890s saw a crescendo of imperialism both in Europe and in the United States. In 1895, in a resounding restatement of the Monroe Doctrine, President Cleveland forbade the British to deal directly with Venezuela in a boundary dispute affecting British Guiana. The British were obliged to accept international arbitration. When, however, adjacent Colombia faced a revolution in the Isthmus of Panama, the United States supported the revolutionaries and, consulting nobody, recognized Panama as an independent republic. Here the United States leased and fortified a Canal Zone, over which it long kept control, and proceeded to build the Panama Canal. Panama became in effect a protectorate of the United States.

The Panama Canal

Meanwhile what was left of the old Spanish American empire, confined to Cuba and Puerto Rico, was agitated by revolutionary movements that were fighting for national independence. Sympathies in the United States lay with the revolutionaries, but every sign of the new imperialism showed itself unmistakably in the American response to these conflicts. Americans had $50 million invested in Cuba. They bought the bonds issued by Cuban revolutionaries in New York. Cuban sugar, whose production was disrupted by political troubles, was necessary to the famed American standard of living. An orderly and amenable Cuba was vital to American strategic interests in the Caribbean, in the soon-to-be-built canal and in the Pacific. The barbarity of the Spanish authorities was deplored as an outrage to modern civilization. The newspapers, especially the new "yellow" press, roused the American public to a fury of moral indignation and imperial self-assertion. The climax came when an American warship, the *Maine*, sank under mysterious circumstances in Havana harbor. (Most historians now believe the ship exploded because of a mechanical flaw.)

The Spanish-American War

The United States easily won the ensuing war with Spain in 1898. Puerto Rico was annexed outright, as were the Philippine Islands on the other side of the world. Filipino nationalists fought against the American annexation in a bloody six-year insurgency that took the lives of more than 4,000 Americans, 20,000 Filipino insurgents, and some 200,000 civilians; but the United States eventually managed to turn the Philippines into a new East Asian colony. Meanwhile, Cuba was set up as an independent republic, subject to the Platt Amendment, a series of provisions by which the United States obtained the right to oversee Cuba's relations with foreign powers and to intervene in Cuba on matters pertaining to "life, property, individual liberty," and "Cuban independence." Thus the United States obtained another protectorate in the Caribbean. The American government proceeded to intervene directly in Cuba on several occasions during the following two decades—interventions that were remembered much longer in Cuba than in the United States. The growth of Cuban nationalism and the subsiding of American imperialism led to repeal of the Platt Amendment in 1934 and recognition of Cuban independence. The United States retained only the right to a permanent lease on a naval base in Guantanamo Bay. Later, after the Second World War, the Philippines formally received independence in 1946 and Puerto Rico became a self-governing commonwealth in 1952.

It was under President Theodore Roosevelt, the peppery "hero of San Juan hill," that the imperial power of the United States was most emphatically trumpeted. He announced in 1904 that weakness or misbehavior "which results in a general loosening of the ties of civilized society may . . . require intervention by some civilized nation," and that the Monroe Doctrine might force the United States "to the exercise of an international police power." In the following year Santo Domingo fell into such financial disorder that European creditors were alarmed. To forestall any pretext for European intervention, the United States sent a financial administrator to Santo Domingo, reformed the economy of the country, and impounded half the customs receipts to pay its debts. Roosevelt declared—in what came to be known as the "Roosevelt Corollary" to the Monroe Doctrine—that, because the United States would not permit European states to intervene in America to collect debts, it must itself assume the duty of intervention to safeguard the investments of the

The Roosevelt corollary

civilized world. The Monroe Doctrine, initially a negative warning to Europe, now stood with the new corollary as a positive notice of supervision of all the Americas by the United States. A quarter of a century of "dollar diplomacy" followed, in which the United States repeatedly intervened, by military or other means, in the Caribbean and Mexico. But the Roosevelt Corollary, like the Platt Amendment, created so much anger and hostility in Latin America that the Washington government finally repudiated it.

The Hawaiian Islands

The story of American intervention in the Hawaiian Islands was as typical of the new imperialism as any episode in the history of European empires. Known originally to outsiders as the Sandwich Islands, these spots of land long enjoyed isolation in the vastness of the mid-Pacific. The growth of global navigation in the nineteenth century, however, brought a new population of sailors, whalers, missionaries, and vendors of rum and cloth to the islands by 1840. The native ruler, lacking the power to control this new situation, almost accepted a British protectorate in 1843 and in 1875 did accept a virtual protectorate by the United States, which guaranteed Hawaiian independence against any third party, obtained trading privileges, and acquired Pearl Harbor as a naval base. American capital and management entered the island. They created huge sugar and pineapple industries, entirely dependent on export to, and investment by, the United States. In 1891, when Queen Liliuokalani came to the throne, she tried to check westernization and Americanization. The American interests, endangered by her nativist policies, overthrew the queen and set up an independent republic, which soon sought annexation to the United States. It was the story of Texas reenacted. For several years the issue hung in the balance because of lingering disapproval in the United States for such strong-arm methods. But after reconsidering the global situation at a time when Japan was revealing its imperial aspirations in Asia, the

These American soldiers in a trench near Manila were part of the armed force that drove Spain out of the Philippines, repressed the Filipino independence movement, and transformed the Philippine islands into a colony of the United States. The annexation of the Philippines and Hawaii in the 1890s made the United States an influential imperial power in the Pacific and East Asia.

(Getty Images)

European powers were moving into China, the Philippines were becoming an American colony, and the Panama Canal was being planned to facilitate access to the Pacific Ocean, the United States "accepted its destiny" in the Pacific, and annexed the Hawaiian Republic by joint resolution of Congress in 1898. Hawaii became a state in the American union in 1959.

79. THE DISSOLUTION OF THE OTTOMAN EMPIRE

The Ottoman Empire in the 1850s

Of all parts of the non-European world, the Ottoman, or Turkish, Empire was the nearest to Europe. The major European states had a long history of relations with the Ottoman Empire because of its geographical proximity and also because of its strategic dominance in the eastern Mediterranean. The empire still extended in the nineteenth century from Hungary and the Balkan peninsula to the south Russian steppes and from Algeria to the Persian Gulf. The empire was not at all like a European state. Immense in extent, it was a complex social and political system within which people belonged to diverse and often overlapping religious communities. Most of its people were Muslim, including both orthodox Muslims and such reform sects as Druses and Wahabis; some were Jews who had always lived in the Middle East; many were Christian, principally Greek Orthodox and Armenian, who had also always lived there. The Turks were the ruling class and Islam was the dominant religion. Only Muslims, for example, could serve in the army; non-Muslims were known as *raya,* the "flock" or "herd"—they paid the taxes. Persons of different religion lived side by side, each under the laws, courts, and customs of his or her own religious group. Religious officials—patriarchs, bishops, rabbis, imams, ulemas—were responsible to the Turkish government for their own people, over whom therefore they had a great deal of authority.

Western Europeans had their own special rights. Roman Catholic clergy, living mainly in Palestine, looked to the pope in religion and to France for a mundane protector.

The capitulations

Western merchants enjoyed the regime of the "capitulations," or special rights granted by the Ottoman government in numerous treaties going back to the sixteenth century. By the capitulations Turkey could not levy a tariff of more than 8 percent on imported goods. Europeans were exempt from most taxes. Cases involving two Europeans, civil or criminal, could be settled only in a court held by a European consul under European law. Disputes between a European and an Ottoman subject were settled in Turkish courts, but in the presence of a European observer.

The Ottoman Empire, in short, lacked the European idea of nationalism or national unity. European ideas of sovereignty and a uniform law for all its peoples were also absent, as was the idea of the secular state, or of law and citizenship separated from religion. More generally, the empire had fallen behind modern industrial nations in its scientific, mechanical, material, humanitarian, and administrative achievements.

The "sick man of Europe"

Turkey was called the "sick man of Europe," and its long decline constituted the Eastern Question. Since the loss of Hungary in 1699 the Ottoman Empire had entered on a long process of territorial disintegration (see map, p. 649). That the empire lasted another two centuries was due to the European balance of power. But by the 1850s the empire was falling away at the edges. Russia had advanced in the Crimea and the Caucasus. Serbia was autonomous, Greece was independent, and Romania was recognized as a self-governing principality. The French occupied Algeria. A native Arab dynasty, the Sauds, of the Wahabi reform sect, ruled over much of Arabia. A former Turkish governor of Egypt, Mehemet Ali, had established his family as hereditary rulers or "khedives" in the Nile valley. Notwithstanding these changes, the Ottoman Empire in the 1850s was still huge. It encompassed not only the Turkish or Anatolian peninsula (including Armenia and territory south of the Caucasus) but also the central portion of the Balkan peninsula from Constantinople to the Adriatic where many Christians of Slavic nationality lived, Tripoli (as Libya was then called) in North Africa, and the islands of Crete and Cyprus. Egypt and Arabia, though autonomous, were still under the nominal suzerainty of the sultan.

The Crimean War of 1854–1856 opened a new phase in Ottoman history as in that of Europe. We have seen how this war was followed by the consolidation of great nation-states in Europe and how the United States, Canada, and Japan consolidated or modernized themselves at the same time. The Turks tried to do the same between 1856 and 1876.

The Crimean War

In the Crimean War the Turks were on the winning side, but the war affected them as it affected Russia, the loser. Exposing their military and political weakness, it pointed up the need of better organization. The outcome of the war was taken to prove the superiority of the political systems of England and France. It was therefore on Western lines that Turkish reformers wished to remodel. It was not merely that they wished to defend themselves against another of the periodic wars with Russia. They wished also to avoid being periodically saved from Russia by the West, a process which if continued could lead only to French or British control of Turkey.

Attempts at Reform and Revival, 1856–1876

In 1856 the Ottoman government issued the Hatt-i Humayun, the most far-reaching Turkish reform edict of the century. Its purpose was to create an Ottoman national citizenship for all persons in the empire. It abolished the civil authority of religious hierarchs. Equality before the law was guaranteed, as was eligibility to public office without regard to religion. The army was opened to Christians and Muslims alike, and steps were even taken to include both in nonsegregated military units. The edict announced a reform of taxes, security of property for all, abolition of torture, and reform of prisons. It promised to combat the chronic evils of graft, bribery, and extortion by public officials.

For 20 years there were serious efforts to make the reform decree of 1856 a reality. Western and liberal ideas circulated freely. Newspapers were founded. Writers called for a national Turkish revival, threw off the old Persian style in literature, composed histories of the Ottomans, and translated Montesquieu and Rousseau. Foreign loans entered the country. Railroads joined the Black Sea and the Danube. Abdul Aziz (1861–1876), the first sultan to travel to Europe, visited Vienna, London, and the great Paris world's fair of 1867. But powerful resistance developed against such radical changes. Also, the best efforts of the Turkish reformers miscarried. There were too few Turks with skill or experience in the work required, and there was too much dependence on borrowed money. In 1874 the Ottoman government, having recklessly overborrowed, repudiated half its debt.

A new and more determined reforming minister, Midhat Pasha, goaded by opposition and desperate at the weight of inertia, deposed Abdul Aziz in 1876, deposed the latter's nephew three months later, and set up Abdul Hamid II as sultan. The new sultan at first briskly went along with the reform movement, proclaiming a new constitution in 1876. It declared the Ottoman Empire to be indivisible, and promised personal liberty, freedom of conscience, freedom of education and the press, and parliamentary government. The first Turkish parliament met in 1877. Its members earnestly addressed themselves to reform. But they reckoned without Abdul Hamid, who in 1877 revealed his true intentions. The sultan got rid of Midhat, packed off the parliament, and threw away the constitution.

Abdul Hamid II

Repression after 1876

Abdul Hamid reigned for 33 years, from 1876 to 1909. For all this time he lived in fear and isolation, fighting ferociously against forces that he could not understand. Once when a consignment of dynamos reached the Turkish customs, it was held up by fearful officials, because the contents were declared to make several hundred revolutions per minute. Again, chemistry books for use in the new American college were pronounced seditious, because their chemical symbols might be a secret cipher. The sultan sensed that tempering with the old Ottoman way would lead to ruin. He dreaded any moves to check his own whim or power. He was thrown into a panic by Turkish reformers and westernizers, who became increasingly driven to terrorist acts in the face of his opposition. Driven away by Abdul Hamid, some tens of thousands of Young Turks, the activists of the reform era before 1876, or their

Abdul Hamid's fears

The Ottoman Sultan Abdul Hamid II came to power in alliance with a movement for constitutional reform, but he soon became an autocratic ruler who violently suppressed his political opponents, massacred ethnic minorities, and resisted all the currents of modern social and cultural life. He is pictured here in his royal attire, sitting alone in the isolated style that characterized his long reign.
(Bettmann/Corbis)

children and successors, lived in exile in Paris, London, or Geneva, plotting their return to Turkey and vengeance upon Abdul the Damned. The sultan was frightened also by agitation among his non-Turkish subjects. Nationalist Armenians, Bulgars, Macedonians, and Cretans defied and taunted the Ottoman authorities, which responded with the Bulgarian massacres of 1876 and the Armenian massacres of 1894. These horrible butcheries of thousands of peasants by Ottoman troops came as a shock to Europeans, who were no longer accustomed to such violence within their own nation-states. Last, and with good reason, Abdul Hamid lived in a creeping fear of the designs of the imperialist European powers upon his dissolving empire.

A thoroughly reformed, consolidated, and modernized Ottoman Empire was far from what the European governments desired. They might wish for humanitarian reforms in Turkey, for more efficiency and honesty in Turkish government and finance, and even for a Turkish parliamentary system. Such demands were eloquently expressed by liberals like Gladstone in England. But no one in Europe wanted what Turkish reformers wanted, a reinvigorated Ottoman Empire that could deal with Europe politically as an equal.

The Russo-Turkish War of 1877–1878: The Congress of Berlin

In Russia, since the time of Catherine II in the eighteenth century, many had dreamed of installing Russian power on the shores of the Bosporus. Constantinople they called Tsarigrad, the Imperial City, which Orthodoxy was to liberate from the infidel. Crusading

Pan-Slavism

motives, in a nationalist and imperialist age, reappeared anew in the form of Pan-Slavism. This was now a doctrine preached by leading Russians, including the novelist Dostoevski and the publicist Danilevsky.

Danilevsky's *Russia and Europe,* published in 1871, predicted that Russia would enter into a long war with Europe, which would then be followed by the creation of a grand federation of the East. The new eastern federation would include Slavs, Greeks, Hungarians, and parts of Asian Turkey under Russian control. This type of Pan-Slavism was patronized by the Russian government because it diverted attention from internal and revolutionary troubles. As for the Slav peoples of the Ottoman Empire, they were willing to use Russian Pan-Slavism as a means of combating their Turkish rulers. Insurrection against the Turks broke out in the Balkans during the mid-1870s. In 1877 Russia declared war on Turkey. Russia was on the move against the Ottoman Empire for the sixth time in a hundred years.

The British, who had fought Russia over Turkey in 1854, were prepared to do so again. A number of recent developments added to their apprehension. The Suez Canal was completed in 1869, and the Canal's location within the Ottoman Empire restored the Middle East to its ancient position as a crossroads of world trade. In 1874 Benjamin Disraeli, a Conservative and an imperialist, became prime minister of Great Britain. By a sudden coup in the following year he was able to buy up, from the almost bankrupt ruling khedive of Egypt, 44 percent of the shares of the Suez Canal Company. In 1876, in a dramatic affirmation of imperial splendor, he had Queen Victoria take the title of empress of India. British commercial and financial interests in India and the Far East were growing, and the Suez Canal, of which the British government was now the principal stockholder, was becoming the lifeline of the empire. But the Ottoman state, and hence the whole Middle East, was now collapsing before the Russians, whose armies advanced rapidly through the Balkans, reached Constantinople, and forced the Turks to sign a treaty in 1878, the treaty of San Stefano. By this treaty Turkey ceded to Russia strategic territory on the south side of the Caucasus Mountains, gave full independence to Serbia and Romania, promised reforms in Bosnia, and granted autonomy to a new Bulgarian state, whose boundaries were to be very generously drawn and which was expected to fall under Russian domination. England seethed with a popular clamor for war against Russia. The outcry gave the word "jingoism" to the language:

The treaty of San Stefano

> We don't want to fight, but by jingo, if we do,
> We've got the men, we've got the ships, we've
>   got the money too.

It now appeared that Turkey's inability to fend off foreigners from its borders would precipitate at least an Anglo-Russian and possibly a general European war. But war was averted by diplomacy. Bismarck assembled a congress of all the European great powers at Berlin in 1878. Once again Europe attempted to assert itself as a unity, to restore life to the much-battered Concert of Europe by dealing collectively with the common problem presented by the Eastern Question. The congress in effect initiated a partition of the Ottoman domain, thereby keeping peace in Europe at the expense of Turkey. The European balance now both protected and dismembered Turkey at the same time.

Weakness of Turkey

The Russians were persuaded at Berlin to give up the treaty of San Stefano that they had imposed on the Turks, but they held on to the territory they had gained below the Caucasus Mountains and won independence for the Serbs and Romanians. Montenegro, too, was recognized as an independent state. Bulgaria was divided into three zones with varying degrees of autonomy, all still nominally within the Ottoman Empire. Austria-Hungary was authorized by the congress to "occupy and administer" Bosnia (but not annex it) in

The Suez Canal, which was completed in 1869, quickly became Britain's all-important lifeline to its Asian empire and a busy crossing point for the expanding global economy. This picture shows the ship of Edward, Prince of Wales, entering the canal in 1875, when the prince was en route to India.
(Getty Images)

compensation for the spread of Russian influence in the Balkans. To the British the Turks ceded Cyprus, a large island not far from the Suez Canal. The French were told that they might expand from Algeria into Tunisia. To the Italians (who counted least) it was more vaguely hinted that they might later be allowed to expand across the Adriatic into Albania. As Bismarck put it, "the Italians have such a large appetite and such poor teeth." Germany took nothing. Bismarck said he was the "honest broker" with no interest except in European peace.

The continuing Turkish problem

The treaty of Berlin in 1878 dispelled the immediate threat of war. But it left many continuing problems which would contribute to the causes of the First World War 36 years later. Neither the Balkan nationalists nor the Russian Pan-Slavs were satisfied. The Turks, both reactionaries like Abdul Hamid and the revolutionary Young Turks in exile, were indignant that peace had been made by further dismemberment of their territory. The demonstrated weakness of Turkey was a constant temptation to all concerned. In the years before 1914 German influence grew. Germans and German capital entered Turkey, projecting, and partially completing, a great Berlin to Bagdad railway to be accompanied by the exploitation of Middle Eastern resources. The railroad was all but completed before 1914 despite the protests and representations of the Russians, the French, and particularly the British, who saw in it a direct threat to their empire in India.

Egypt and North Africa

For Egypt, technically autonomous within the Ottoman Empire, the 1850s and 1860s were a time of reform and economic development. The Egyptian government modernized its administration, court system, and property law, cooperated with the French in building the Suez Canal, encouraged shipping on the Red Sea, and let British and French interests construct railroads. Between 1861 and 1865, while the American South was unable to export raw cotton, the annual export of Egyptian cotton rose from 60 million to 250 million pounds. Egypt more than Turkey was drawn into the world market, and the khedive of Egypt became a Westernized ruler. The khedive Ismail built himself a fine new opera

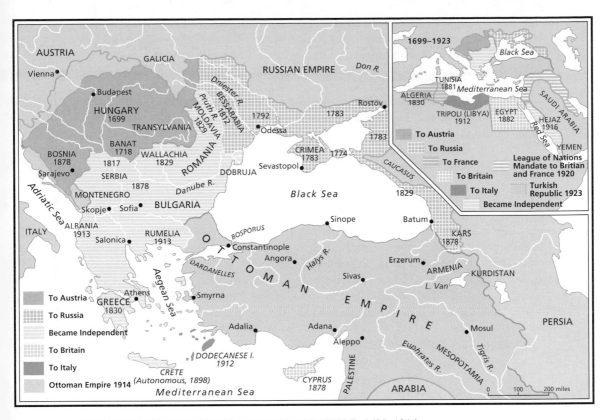

THE DISSOLUTION OF THE OTTOMAN EMPIRE, 1699–1914

Beginning in 1699, with the loss of Hungary to the Austrian Habsburgs, the Ottoman Empire entered upon a long process of territorial disintegration. Dates shown are those at which territories dropped away. In general, regions lost before 1815 were annexed directly by Austria and Russia. European territories lost in the nineteenth century emerged as independent states, owing to the rise of nationalism and rivalries among the great European powers. In the Arab world, reaching from Algeria to the Persian Gulf, regions lost before the First World War were absorbed into European colonial empires; those lost at the end of the First World War were mostly assigned to France and Britain as mandates, but after the Second World War these regions became independent Arab states and the Republic of Israel. A Turkish nationalist movement blocked European attempts to partition Turkey after the First World War, and in 1923 the Turks established the Turkish Republic.

house in Cairo, where, in 1871, two years after the opening of the Suez Canal, Verdi's *Aïda,* written at the khedive's request, was resoundingly performed for the first time.

Such improvements cost a good deal of money, borrowed in England and France. The Egyptian government was soon in financial straits, only temporarily relieved by the sale of canal shares to Disraeli. By 1879 matters reached the point where Western banking interests forced the abdication of Ismail and his replacement by Tewfik, who soon let himself become thoroughly enmeshed by his creditors. This led to nationalistic protests within Egypt, headed by Colonel Arabi. In a pattern repeated in many parts of the colonial world, the nationalists opposed both the foreigners and their own government, charging it with being a mere front for

British intervention

foreign interests. Arabi's movement, an early expression of Arab nationalism, led to riots in Alexandria, where Europeans had to flee aboard British and French shipping in the harbor. A British squadron then unceremoniously bombarded Alexandria. British troops (the French, though invited to take part, refused) disembarked in 1882 at Suez and Alexandria, defeated Arabi, and took Tewfik under their protection. The military intervention of 1882 was said by the British to be temporary, but British troops remained there for a long time,

Egypt as protectorate

through two world wars and well into the twentieth century, not leaving until 1956. Egypt thus became a British protectorate. The British protected the khedive from discontent within his own country, from the claims of the Ottoman court, and from the rival attentions of other European powers.

The French strenuously objected when the British stayed on so long in Egypt. It had long been the French who had the greatest investments in the Middle East, and persons in that region who were at all westernized—Egyptians, Syrians, Turks—overwhelmingly preferred French language and culture to English. The French, harboring deep suspicion of British designs in Egypt, compensated themselves by building a North African empire farther west. They developed Algeria, assumed a protectorate over Tunisia, and began to penetrate Morocco. Upon these French advances the British, and soon the Germans, looked with unmitigated disfavor. Rivalry for the spoils of the Ottoman Empire thus created enmity among the Great Powers and constituted a fertile source of the war scares, fears, and diplomatic maneuvers that preceded the First World War.

The dissolution of the Ottoman Empire became indistinguishable from the whole chronic international crisis before 1914. It is enough to say here, to keep the fate of the

Young Turks

Ottoman Empire in focus, that Abdul Hamid's frantic defensive policies came to nothing and that the Young Turks won control of the Ottoman government in 1908. They forced the restoration of the constitution of 1876 and introduced many reforms. Finally, when all Europe became involved in war in 1914, Russia again declared war on Turkey, and the Turks came into the war on the side of Germany, whose political and economic influence in the empire had been steadily growing. During the war, with British aid, the Arabs detached themselves from the empire, becoming eventually independent Arab states. Egypt, too, ended all connections with the empire. In 1923 a Turkish republic was proclaimed. It was confined to Constantinople and the Anatolian peninsula, where the bulk of the Turkish people lived. The new republic proceeded to undergo a thorough nationalist and secular revolution.

80.   THE PARTITION OF AFRICA

South of Mediterranean Africa lay the Sahara desert, and south of that lay sub-Saharan Africa, of which Europeans knew so little that they called it the Dark Conti-

The "Dark Continent"

nent. Africa is so gigantic that even the part south of the Sahara is almost as large as the whole continent of North America. For centuries Europeans knew only its coasts—the Gold Coast, Ivory Coast, Slave Coast—to which from an inexhaustible interior had come shackled processions of captive slaves, as well as the swelling waters of enormous rivers, like the Nile, Niger, and Congo, whose sources in the dim hinterland were a subject of romantic speculation. The people were black, but diverse both in physique and in culture, and speaking almost a thousand languages. They had been working with iron for more than 2,000 years, and they were adept in many arts, such as bronze sculpture, gold artifacts, weaving, basketry, and the making of ceremonial masks with strikingly symbolic or abstract patterns. Along the northern fringe some had converted to Islam, but mostly they adhered to their traditional religions.

They lived mainly in villages in tribal communities, engaged in agriculture or moving herds of cattle from place to place. But great cities or agglomerations had also arisen, from Timbuktu in the north with its old caravan trade across the Sahara, to the vast complex of buildings at Zimbabwe in the south, which was already in ruins when the Europeans first saw it. There had also been extensive kingdoms whose memory was preserved, in the absence of writing, by specially trained narrators from one generation to the next. But these kingdoms had disappeared or declined. They had been weakened by intertribal wars, by the slave trade which set Africans against one another to satisfy the demand of outsiders, or by demographic causes that are now hard to trace. Hence Africa, somewhat like the Ottoman Empire and China, met the assault of the Europeans at a time when its powers of resistance were reduced. Before the mid–nineteenth century there were no permanently resident whites south of the Sahara except for a few Arabs who had been on the east coast since the seventh century and the Europeans who had been at the Cape of Good Hope since 1652. In the Union of South Africa, when it was established in 1910, some 1.1 million whites lived along with about 5 million blacks.

The Opening of Africa

Missionaries, explorers, and individual adventurers first opened this world to Europe. The historic pair, Livingstone and Stanley, well illustrate the drift of Europe. Before the imperialist age, in 1841, the Scot David Livingstone arrived in southeast Africa as a medical missionary. He gave himself to humanitarian and religious work, with some occasional trading and

Livingstone and Stanley

much travel and exploration, but without political or economic aims. Exploring the Zambesi River, he was the first white man to look upon the Victoria Falls. Fully at home in inner Africa, safe and on friendly terms with its native people, he was quite content to be let alone. But the hectic forces of modern civilization sought him out. Word spread in Europe and America that Dr. Livingstone was lost. The New York *Herald,* to manufacture news, sent the roving journalist H. M. Stanley to find him, which he did in 1871. Livingstone soon died, deeply honored by the Africans among whom he worked. Stanley was a man of the new era. Seeing vast economic possibilities in Africa, he went to Europe to solicit backers. In 1878 he found someone with the same ideas, who happened to be a king, Leopold II, king of the Belgians.

Leopold, for all his royalty, was at heart a commercial promoter. China, Formosa, the Philippines, and Morocco had in turn attracted his fancy, but it was the central African basin of the Congo that he decided to develop. Stanley was exactly the man he was looking for, and the two founded at Brussels, with a few financiers, an International Congo Association in 1878. It was a purely private enterprise; the Belgian government and people had nothing to do with it. Europeans considered all Africa inland from the coasts to be, like America in the time of Columbus, a *terra nullius,* without government and claimed by nobody, wide open to the first Western persons who might arrive. Stanley, returning to the Congo in 1882, in a year or two concluded treaties with over 500 chiefs, who in return for a few trinkets or a few yards of cloth put their marks on his mysterious European papers and accepted the blue-and-gold flag of the Association.

Since the Dark Continent was still innocent of internal frontiers, no one could tell how much territory the Association might soon cover by these methods. The German explorer Karl Peters, working inland from Zanzibar, was signing treaties with the chiefs of East Africa. The Frenchman Brazza, departing from the west coast and distributing the tricolor in every village, was claiming on the Congo River itself a territory larger than France. The

Portuguese aspired to join their ancient colonies of Angola and Mozambique into a trans-African empire, for which they required a generous portion of the interior. Britain supported Portugal. In every case the home governments in Europe were still hesitant over involvement in an Africa of which they knew little. But they were pushed on by small organized minorities of colonizing enthusiasts, and they faced the probability that if they missed the moment it would be too late.

Bismarck, who personally thought African colonies an absurdity but was sensitive to the new pressures, called another conference at Berlin in 1885, this time to submit the African question to international regulation. Most European states, as well as the United

The Berlin conference of 1885

States, attended. The Berlin conference had two goals: to set up the territories of the Congo Association as an international state, under international auspices and restrictions; and to draft a code governing the way in which European powers wishing to acquire African territory should proceed.

The Congo Free State, which in 1885 took the place of the International Congo Association, was not only an international creation but also embodied in some ways what became known in the next century as international mandates or international trusteeships for non-European peoples. The Berlin conference specified that the new state should not be the colony of any power, including Belgium, but delegated its administration to Leopold. It drew the boundaries, making the Congo Free State almost as large as the United States east of the Mississippi, and it added certain specific provisions: the Congo River was internationalized, persons of all nationalities should be free to do business in the Congo state, there should be no tariff levied on imports, and the slave trade should be suppressed. Leopold in 1889 reassembled the signatory powers in a second conference, held at Brussels. The Brussels conference took further steps to root out the slave trade, which remained a stubborn though declining evil, because the Muslim world was several generations behind the Christian in abolishing slavery. The Brussels conference also undertook to protect the rights of the local people, correct certain glaring abuses, and reduce the traffic in liquor and firearms.

But all this effort at internationalism failed because Europe had no international machinery by which the hard daily work of enforcing general agreements could be carried

The Belgian Congo

out. Although slavery was banned, Leopold went his own way in the Congo. His determination to make it commercially profitable for his own benefit led him to unconscionable abuses. Europe and America demanded rubber and the rubber trees of the Congo were at the time one of the world's few sources of supply. The Congo people, already afflicted by the diseases and weakening effects of a lowland equatorial climate, could be made to fulfill assigned quotas of rubber sap only by inhumanly severe coercion. Leopold and his agents, some of whom were African, and the managers of the concessions he leased out extorted forced labor from the native population, compelling them to meet impossible quotas under brutal conditions, with the resulting deaths of thousands. The rubber trees meanwhile were destroyed without any plans for replacement.

Leopold, by ravaging its resources and virtually enslaving its people, was able to draw from the Congo a handsome income and to amass a personal fortune. He nevertheless could not make the entire enterprise profitable and needed investment capital for further development. He therefore borrowed from his own government in 1889 and 1895 in return for giving the government the right to annex the Congo in 1901. The Belgian parliament turned down the opportunity that year, but beginning in 1904 public outrage mounted after European press revelations of the scandalous atrocities in the Congo. A concerted campaign compelled the Belgian government in 1908 to take the Congo over from Leopold,

BEATING RUBBER AND BEATING TIME—TO THE TUNE OF AN OLD LOVE-SONG.

DRAWN BY NORMAN H. HARDY.

Workers in the Congo were forced to remove particles of wood and fiber from the rubber that was harvested for export to Europe and America. This picture of workers, which was published in 1909, shows both the tedious physical labor in the rubber industry and a common Western image of Africans in the era of European colonialism.

(Mary Evans Picture Library/ The Image Works)

THE RUBBER INDUSTRY IN THE BELGIAN CONGO: THUMPING RUBBER TO REMOVE PARTICLES OF WOOD AND FIBRE.

who died the following year. The Congo Free State became the Belgian Congo, a Belgian colony. Under the government's administration the worst excesses of forced labor and other abuses were ended, even though the Congo remained a continuing enticement for enrichment and investment for Europeans and other outsiders.

The Berlin conference of 1885 had also laid down certain rules for imperial claims of African territories—a European power with holdings on the coast had prior rights in the hinterland; occupation must not be on paper only through drawing lines on a map, but must consist in real occupation by administrators or troops; and each power must give proper notice to the others as to what territories it considered its own. A wild scramble for "real occupation" quickly followed. In 15 years the entire continent was parceled out. The sole exceptions were Ethiopia, and, technically, Liberia, founded in 1822 as a colony for emancipated American slaves and virtually a protectorate of the United States.

Everywhere a variant of the same process was repeated. First would appear a handful of white men, bringing their inevitable treaties—sometimes printed forms. To get what they wanted, the Europeans commonly had to ascribe powers to the chief that by the customs of the tribe he did not possess—powers to convey sovereignty, sell land, or grant mining concessions. Thus the Africans were baffled at the outset by foreign legal conceptions. Then the Europeans would build up the position of the chief, since they themselves had no influence over the people. This led to the widespread system of

"Indirect rule"

"indirect rule," by which colonial authorities acted through the existing chiefs and tribal forms. There were many things that only the chief could arrange, such as security for isolated Europeans, porter services, or gangs of workmen to build roads or railroads.

The labor problem

Labor was the overwhelming problem. For pure slavery Europeans now had an abhorrence, and they abolished it wherever they could. But the Africans, so long as they lived in their traditional way, did not react like the free wage earner postulated in European business and economics. They had little expectation of individual gain and almost no use for money. They thus seemed to work only sporadically by European standards, disdaining the continuous and tedious labor that Europeans wanted them to perform. The result was that Europeans all over Africa resorted to forced labor. For road building, systems like the French *corvée* before the Revolution reappeared. Or the chief would be required to supply a quota of able-bodied men for a certain length of time, and frequently he did so gladly to raise his own importance in the eyes of the Europeans. More indirect methods were also used. The colonial government might levy a hut tax or a poll tax, payable only in money, to obtain which the African would have to seek a job. Or the new government, once installed, might allocate so much land to Europeans as private property (another foreign conception) that the local tribe could no longer subsist on the lands that remained to it. Or the whole tribe might be moved to a reservation, like Indians in the United States. In any case, while the women tilled the fields or tended the stock at home, the men would move off to take jobs under the whites for infinitesimal pay. The men then lived in compounds, away from family and tribal kindred; they became demoralized; and the labor they gave, untrained and unwilling, would scarcely have been tolerated in more industrialized societies. In these circumstances everything was done to uproot the Africans, and little was done to benefit them or to protect the social systems in which they had lived before the Europeans arrived.

Conditions improved with the twentieth century as traditions of more enlightened colonial administration were gradually built up. Some colonial officials even came to serve as buffers or protectors of the local peoples against the intruding white man's economic interests. Throughout, it was part of the ethos of imperialism to put down slavery, tribal warfare, superstition, disease, and illiteracy. Slowly a westernized class of Africans grew—chiefs and the sons of chiefs, Catholic priests and Protestant ministers, warehouse clerks and government employees. Young men from Nigeria or Uganda appeared as students at Oxford, the University of Paris, or universities in the United States. Westernized Africans usually resented both exploitation and paternalism. They showed signs of turning nationalistic, like their counterparts in the Ottoman Empire and Asia. If they wanted westernization, it was at a pace and for a purpose of their own, and with methods that recognized the value of their own cultural traditions. As the twentieth century progressed, nationalism in Africa grew more vocal, more intense, and more forceful in challenging the European powers.

Friction and Rivalry between the Powers

Meanwhile, in the 15 years from 1885 to 1900, the Europeans in Africa came dangerously near to open blows. The Portuguese annexed huge domains in Angola and Mozambique. The Italians took over two barren tracts, Italian Somaliland and Eritrea on the Red Sea. They then moved inland, in quest of more imposing possessions, to conquer Ethiopia and the headwaters of the Nile. Some 80,000 Ethiopians, however, defeated and routed 20,000 Ital-

The colonial race in Africa

PRECOLONIAL AFRICA: SITES AND PEOPLES

This map shows Africa before colonization by the Europeans in the nineteenth century. It does not refer to a particular date or to particular kingdoms that the Europeans displaced. Names in burgundy designate important ancient or medieval centers, such as the Ghana and Mali empires, which no longer existed in modern times. Even the most extensive African kingdoms had indefinite and shifting boundaries, which cannot be readily indicated on a map. "Bantu," as used in the phrase "Bantu peoples," refers to a large group of languages spoken from north of the Congo River to the southern African coast. Concentrations of other language groups and peoples are also shown.

ians in pitched battle at Adowa in 1896. It was the first time that Africans successfully defended themselves against the forces of a European imperialist nation, and it discouraged invasion of Ethiopia by the Italians (or other Europeans) for 40 years. Italy and Portugal, like the Congo Free State and Spain (which retained a few vestiges of former days), were able to enjoy sizable holdings in Africa because of mutual fears among the principal contenders. The principal contenders were Great Britain, France, and

African workers built the new European-owned mines that began sending valuable minerals around the world. The laborers in this picture are digging a new gold mine in southern Africa in the late 1880s.
(Getty Images)

Germany. Each preferred to have territory held by a minor power rather than by one of its significant rivals.

The Germans were latecomers in the colonial race, which Bismarck entered with reluctance. By the 1880s all the usual imperialist arguments were heard in Germany, though most of them, such as the need for new markets, for emigration to overseas territories, or for the investment of capital, had little or no application in tropical Africa. The Germans established colonies in German East Africa and in the Cameroons and Togo on the west coast, along with a desert area that came to be called German Southwest Africa (where they ruthlessly suppressed the rebellious Herero people). It did not escape the notice of German imperial planners that someday the Congo and the Portuguese colonies might be joined with their colonies in a solid German belt across the African heartland. The French controlled most of West Africa, from Algeria across the Sahara and the Sudan to various points on the Guinea coast. They also occupied Obok on the Red Sea, and after the Italian defeat in 1896 their influence in Ethiopia grew. French planners therefore dreamed of a solid French belt across Africa from Dakar to the Gulf of Aden. The French government in 1898 dispatched Captain J. B. Marchand with a small party eastward from Lake Chad to hoist the tricolor far away on the upper Nile, in the southern part of the Sudan, which no European power as yet "effectively" occupied.

The two presumptive east-and-west belts, German and French, were cut (presumptively) by a north-and-south belt, projected in the British imperial imagination as an "Africa British from the Cape to Cairo." From the Cape of Good Hope Cecil Rhodes pushed northward into what was later called Rhodesia (now Zimbabwe). Kenya and Uganda in the mid-continent were already under British control. In Egypt, a British protectorate since 1882, the British began to support old Egyptian claims to the upper Nile. The first venture proved a disaster when in 1885 a British general popularly known as "Chinese Gordon" for previous military successes in China, leading an Egyptian force, was killed by Muslim troops at Khartoum. In the following decade British opinion turned imperialist in earnest. Another British officer, General Kitchener (with a young man named Winston Churchill under his command), again started southward up the Nile and defeated the local Muslims in 1898 at Omdurman. He then pushed on further upstream. At Fashoda he met Marchand.

The ensuing Fashoda crisis brought Britain and France to the verge of war. Already at odds over Egypt and Morocco, the two governments used the encounter at Fashoda to force a showdown. It was a test of strength, not only for their respective plans for all Africa but also for their relative position in all imperialist and international issues. Both at first refused to yield. The British virtually threatened to fight. The French, fearful of their insecurity against Germany in Europe, at last decided not to take the risk. They backed down and recalled Marchand from Fashoda. A wave of hatred for the British swept over France.

The Fashoda crisis

The British no sooner won this Pyrrhic victory than they became involved in a major conflict at the other end of the African continent. In 1890 Cecil Rhodes had become prime minister of the Cape Colony. He was a principal sponsor of the Cape-to-Cairo dream. Two small independent neighboring republics, the Transvaal and the Orange Free State, stood in his way. Their people were Afrikaners—descendants of the Dutch who had originally settled the Cape in the seventeenth century and, after 1815, when England annexed the Cape of Good Hope, had made the "great trek" to escape from British rule. The Boers, as the English called them (from the Dutch word for farmer), were simple, obstinate, and old-fashioned. They thought slavery not ungodly and disliked fortune hunters, footloose adventurers, mining-camp people, and other outsiders.

The discovery of diamonds and gold in the Transvaal brought the issue of outsiders to a head. British capital and British people poured in. The Transvaal refused to pass legislation needed by the mining corporations and their employees. In 1895 Rhodes, attempting to precipitate revolution in the Transvaal, sent a party of armed irregulars, under Dr. Jameson, a physician-turned-colonial administrator, over its borders. This Jameson Raid was a failure, but in Europe a great cry went up against British bullying of a small inoffensive republic. The German emperor, William II, dispatched a famous telegram to Paul Kruger, president of the Transvaal, congratulating him on his driving off the invaders "without having to call for the support of friendly powers," that is, Germany. Three years later, in 1899, the British Empire went to war with the two small republics. The South African (or Boer) War lasted until 1902; the British sent in 300,000 troops, and to combat an elusive and irregular adversary they felt obliged to ravage the country and intern about 120,000 women and children in concentration camps, where about 20,000 died. But once subdued and brought within the British system the two republics were left with their self-governing institutions. In 1910 the Transvaal and the Orange Free State were combined with Cape Colony and Natal to form the Union of South Africa, which received semi-independent status along the lines of the Dominion of Canada.

The South African War

The Fashoda crisis and the Boer War, coming in rapid succession, revealed to the British the bottomless depths of their unpopularity in Europe. All European governments and peoples were pro-Boer; only the United States, involved at the time in a similar military conquest of the Philippines, showed any sympathy for the British. The British, after the Boer War, began to rethink their international position, as will soon be seen.

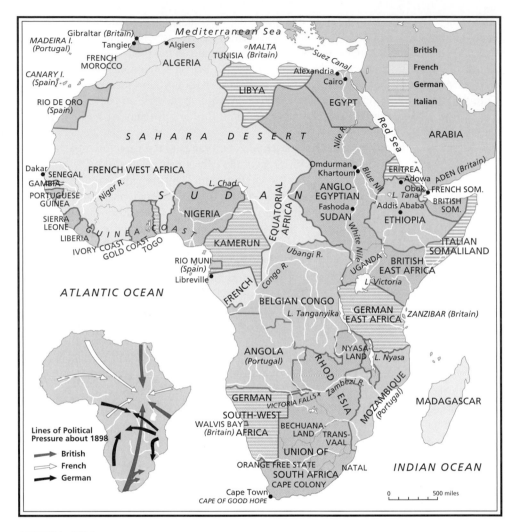

AFRICA, 1914

The map shows the recognized colonial holdings of European nations in 1914. The insert suggests the general directions of European expansion about 1898. These expansionary pressures led to the Fashoda crisis in 1898 and the Boer War in 1899. In 1898 the British and German governments held secret discussions on the possible partitioning of the Portuguese colonies, but no such partitioning took place because the British greatly preferred to have the Portuguese colonies remain in the hands of Portugal.

*Embittered
international relations*

As in the case of the Ottoman Empire, rivalry between the Great Powers over the spoils of Africa embittered international relations and helped prepare the way for the First World War. In Africa as a whole, there was little territorial change after the Boer War, although in 1911 Italy took Libya from the Turks. In 1914 the Germans were excluded from their short-lived empire. Had the Germans won the First World War, the map of Africa would probably have been greatly revised, but since they lost it, the only change was to assign the German colonies, under international mandate, to the French, British, and Belgians. With this

The British military campaign against the Transvaal and the Orange Free State between 1899 and 1902 was widely condemned, in part because it was waged against descendants of seventeenth-century Dutch settlers (the Afrikaners or Boers) in South Africa. This picture of British soldiers crossing a river suggests the scale and costs of the Boer War, which became especially notorious when the British interned Afrikaner women and children in concentration camps, where thousands perished.

(Getty Images)

change, and except for Italy's ephemeral conquest of Ethiopia in 1935, the political map of Africa remained what the brief years of partition had made it until the spectacular end of the European empires after the Second World War.

81.   IMPERIALISM IN ASIA: THE DUTCH, THE BRITISH, AND THE RUSSIANS

The Dutch East Indies and British India

British India and the Dutch East Indies, in the half-century before the First World War, were the Europeans' ideal colonies. They illustrated the kind of empire that all imperialists would have wished to have, and a glance at them suggests the goal toward which imperialism was moving and the system that it was trying to create.

Whereas all countries of western Europe showed a surplus of imports, receiving more goods from the rest of the world than they sent out, India and Indonesia invariably, year after year and decade after decade, showed a surplus of exports, sending out far more goods than they took in. This export surplus was the hallmark of the profitable colonial area, geared closely into the world market, with low purchasing power for the native population and kept going by foreign investment and management. Both regions, in addition, were so large as to have a good deal of internal business—commerce, insurance, banking, transportation—which never appeared in the statistics for world trade, but which, being dominated by Europeans,

Export surplus

added immeasurably to their profits. Both had rich and varied natural resources, tropical in character, so that they never competed with the products of Europe—though India even before 1914 showed tendencies to industrialization. In both regions the people were adept and quick to learn. But they were divided by religion and language, so that, once conquered, they were relatively easy for Europeans to govern.

Neither region before the First World War had any self-government at the highest levels. Both were ruled by a civil service, honest and high-minded by its own lights, in which

European colonial rule

the most influential and best-paying positions were reserved for Europeans. Hence upper-class families in England and the Netherlands valued their empires as fields of opportunity for their sons—somewhat as they had formerly valued an established church. In both India and Indonesia the governments were more or less benevolent despotisms, which, by curbing warfare, plague, and famine, at least allowed the population to grow in numbers. Java, with 5 million people in 1815, had 48 million in 1942. India's population in the same years grew from less than 200 million to almost 400 million. Finally, as the last virtue of a perfect colony, no foreign power directly challenged the British in India or the Dutch in their islands.

The Dutch in 1815 occupied little more than the island of Java itself. In the following decades the British moved into Singapore, the Malay peninsula, and north Borneo, and made claims to Sumatra. The French in the 1860s appeared in Indochina. The Germans in the 1880s annexed eastern New Guinea and the Marshall and Solomon islands. Ultimately it was the mutual jealousy of these three that preserved the Dutch position.

The Dutch took the initiative themselves. To forestall occupation by other Europeans, and to put down native pirates and find raw materials that the world demanded, the Dutch spread their rule over the whole 3,000-mile extent of the archipelago. They created an empire in place of the old chain of coastal trading posts and suppressed internal revolts in 1830, 1849, and 1888; not till the twentieth century was northern Sumatra or the interior of

The "culture system"

Celebes brought under control. For some decades the Dutch exploited their huge empire by a kind of forced labor, the "culture system," in which the authorities required farmers to deliver, as a kind of tax, stated amounts of stated crops, such as sugar or coffee. After 1870 a freer system was introduced. The Dutch also, as an important matter of policy, favored instruction in the Malay and Javanese languages, not in Dutch. This preserved the native cultures from westernizing disintegration but at the same time meant that Western ideas of nationalism and democracy entered more slowly.

In India in 1857, the British faced a dangerous rebellion, commonly called the Indian Mutiny, as if it had been a revolt of undisciplined soldiers

The Indian Mutiny

only. The British army in India, with its "sepoys" (native Indian troops), was the only organization through which Indians could exert any collective pressure. The proportion of sepoys in the army was high in 1857 (about five-sixths) because British units had been withdrawn for the Crimean War and for action in China. Many Indians outside the army had been unhappy with British policies for decades. Rulers had been conquered and dethroned. Landowners had lost their property and been replaced by new ones more friendly to the British. Religious sentiments were inflamed. The British too obviously regarded Indian beliefs as repulsive; they had outlawed suttee, or widow burning, the ancient Hindu practice of a widow burning herself to death on the funeral pyre of her deceased husband; suppressed the Thugs, a small sect of holy assassins; and one British officer even declared that in ten years the government would abolish caste. Many Hindus therefore saw the British as dangerous opponents of their ancient religious traditions. Meanwhile, the Muslims were mobilized by Wahabi fundamentalism, a popular reform movement that sought to purify and defend the religious practices of Islam. Mysterious propaganda circulated over India. It infiltrated the sepoys, announcing to Muslim soldiers that certain newly issued cartridges were greased with the fat of a pig and to Hindus that the same cartridges were greased with the fat of a cow. Since for Hindus the cow was sacred, and for Muslims to touch pork was profane, much agitation was produced. The sepoys mutinied in the Ganges valley; and with them the other injured interests, including the fading Great Mogul and his court, rose against the British.

The British put down the rebellion with much brutality, aided by the fact that western and southern India took no part in it. But the uprising persuaded the British to a radically new course of policy, pursued basically until the end of the Indian empire almost a century later. The British East India Company and the Mogul empire were both finally and forever done away with. British authorities ruled directly, but the British concluded that they must rule India with and through the Indians themselves, not against them. This in practice meant a collaboration between the imperial power and the Indian upper classes. The British began to shelter Indian vested interests. They supported the Indian landlords and became more indulgent toward Indian "superstition." Where before 1857, when they conquered an Indian state, they had simply abolished it and incorporated its territories, after the Mutiny they kept the remaining Indian states as protectorates. States existing in 1857, such as Hyderabad and Kashmir and over 200 others, with their galaxy of rajahs and maharajahs, carried on to the end of British rule in 1947. It was largely to provide a fitting summit for this mountain of Indian royalty that Queen Victoria was proclaimed empress of India in 1877.

British rule in India

India had been a considerable manufacturing country by preindustrial standards, Indian merchants had once been important throughout the Indian Ocean, and before 1800 Indian exports to Europe had included many textiles and other finished goods. The native crafts collapsed before modern industrialism reinforced by political power. "India," observed a British expert in 1837, "can never again be a great manufacturing country, but by cultivating her connection with England she may be one of the greatest agricultural countries in the world." Free trade (made possible by military superiority, usually overlooked by the economists) turned Britain into the world's workshop and India into a supplier of raw materials. Indian exports in the latter part of the nineteenth century consisted increasingly of raw cotton, tea, jute, oilseeds, indigo, and wheat. The British shipped their manufactures in return. Business in India boomed; India came to have the densest railway network outside of Europe and North America. It is important to note, however, as a commentary on European trade with poor countries that Britain in 1914 did far more trading with the 6 million people of Australia and New Zealand than with the 315 million impoverished people of India.

The British, in contrast to the Dutch, decided in 1835 to favor instruction in English, not in the native languages. The historian T. B. Macaulay, one of the commission to make this recommendation, branded the Indian languages as vehicles of barbarous and unenlightened ideas—a bar to progress. The British also, after the Mutiny, admitted Indians to the civil service and to governors' councils—sparingly indeed, but more than the Dutch in Indonesia. There were also many Indian businessmen. A class of westernized Indians grew up speaking perfect English and often were educated in England. They demanded more of a role in the affairs of their country. In 1885 the predominantly Hindu Indian National Congress was organized; in 1906, the All-India Muslim League. Muslim

The great Sepoy Rebellion in 1857 among local troops in India shook the British Empire more profoundly than any other event of the nineteenth century. Although the Indian Mutiny (as the British called it) was eventually suppressed, this illustration suggests why the violence and brutality left bitter memories on all sides and why the British soon restructured the whole system by which they governed Indian society.
(Getty Images)

Indian nationalism

separatism, while favored by the British and sometimes even blamed upon them, was natural to India and exploited by some Indian leaders. Nationalism spread. It became increasingly anti-British; and radical nationalism turned also against the Indian princes, capitalists, and businessmen, as accomplices in imperialism, and so took on the color of socialism. In the period of the First World War, under nationalist pressure, the British granted more representation to Indians, especially in provincial affairs. But the movement toward self-rule was never fast enough to overcome the basic anti-British feeling of the Indian peoples, and Indian nationalism grew rapidly after the First World War.

Conflict of Russian and British Interests

While no outsider yet threatened the British in India, British statecraft discerned in the northern sky a large cloud which was clearly approaching. The Russian empire had occu-

This photograph of the future Indian national leader Jawaharlal Nehru indicates the kind of British education that many young Indians received during the imperial era. Nehru studied at Harrow School (where this picture was taken about 1905) and at Cambridge University before joining Gandhi in the independence movement during the 1920s. He later served as the first prime minister of independent India from 1947 until his death in 1964.
(Getty Images)

pied northern Asia since the seventeenth century. About 1850 Russian pressure on inner Asia resumed. It was a type of imperialism in which neither the demand for markets nor for raw materials, nor for the investment of capital, counted for much. In these matters Russia was itself semicolonial with respect to the West. The Russians had, like the Westerners, a sense of spreading their type of civilization; but Russian expansion was distinctively political in that most of the initiative came from the government. Russia was an icebound empire, craving warm-water ports. It was a landlocked empire, so that whichever way it turned it moved toward one ocean or another. The ocean was the domain of the Westerners, and in particular the British.

In the large picture, Russia pushed by land against the Ottoman Empire, Persia, India, and China, all of which the British (and others) reached by sea. In 1860, on the shores of the Sea of Japan, the Russians founded Vladivostok, the farthest-flung of all Slavic cities, whose name meant Lord of the East. But their advance in the mid-century was mainly in the arid and thinly settled regions of western Asia. The British had already fought two Afghan wars to keep Afghanistan as a no-man's land between Russia and India. Contemporaries called the rivalry between Britain and Russia in Central Asia "the great game." In 1864 the Russians took Tashkent in Turkestan. A decade later they touched India itself but were kept away by an Anglo-Russian agreement, which allotted a long tongue of land to Afghanistan and so separated British India and the Russian empire by 20 miles.

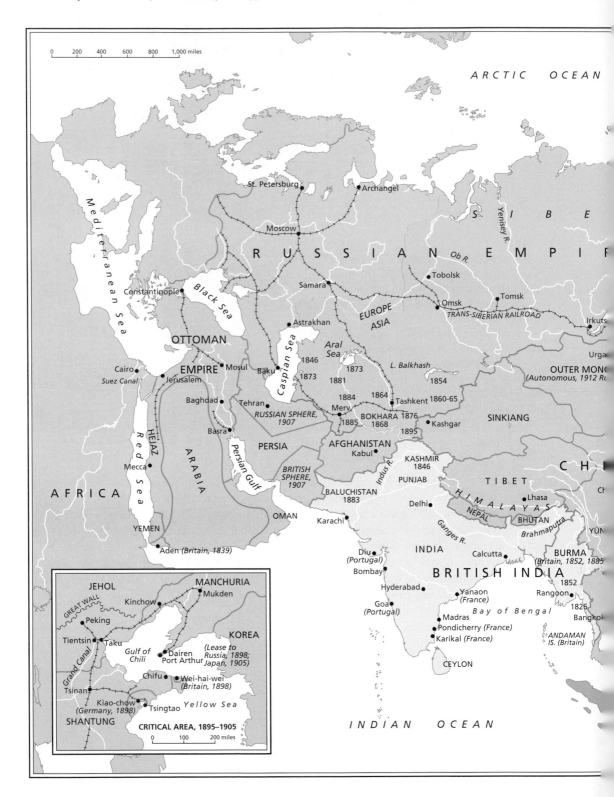

0   200   400   600   800   1,000 miles

ARCTIC   OCEAN

St. Petersburg   •Archangel

Moscow

RUSSIAN   EMPIRE

Ob R.

Tobolsk

Samara   Omsk   Tomsk

EUROPE   TRANS-SIBERIAN RAILROAD   Irkuts

ASIA

Astrakhan

Mediterranean Sea

Black Sea

Constantinople

OTTOMAN   Caspian Sea   Aral Sea

1846   1873   L. Balkhash   Urga

EMPIRE   Mosul   Baku   1873   OUTER MONG

Cairo   1881   1854   (Autonomous, 1912 Ru

Suez Canal   Jerusalem   1884   1864

Baghdad   Tehran   1885   Tashkent 1860-65   SINKIANG

RUSSIAN SPHERE,   Merv

1907   BOKHARA 1876   Kashgar

Basra   1885   1868   CHI

HEJAZ   PERSIA   1895

AFGHANISTAN

BRITISH   Kabul   KASHMIR   TIBET

Red Sea   SPHERE,   Indus R.   1846   Lhasa

1907   PUNJAB   HIMALAYAS

ARABIA   BALUCHISTAN   Delhi   NEPAL   BHUTAN   YÜN

Mecca   Persian Gulf   1883   Brahmaputra

AFRICA   OMAN   Karachi   Ganges R.

YEMEN   INDIA   Calcutta   BURMA

Aden (Britain, 1839)   Diu   (Britain, 1852, 1885

(Portugal)   BRITISH INDIA

Bombay   1852

Hyderabad   Yanaon   Rangoon

(France)   1826

Goa   Bay of Bengal   Bangkol

(Portugal)   Madras

Pondicherry (France)   ANDAMAN

Karikal (France)   IS. (Britain)

CEYLON

INDIAN   OCEAN

JEHOL   MANCHURIA

Mukden

GREAT WALL   Kinchow

Peking

Tientsin   Taku   KOREA

Gulf of   Dairen   (Lease to

Chili   Port Arthur   Russia, 1898;

Chifu   Japan, 1905)

Tsinan   •Wei-hai-wei

Grand Canal   (Britain, 1898)

Kiao-chow   Yellow Sea

(Germany, 1898) Tsingtao

SHANTUNG   CRITICAL AREA, 1895–1905

0   100   200 miles

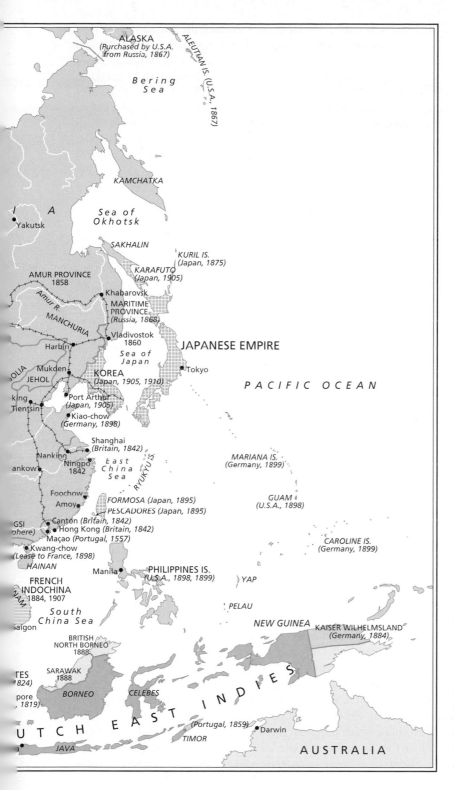

ALASKA
*(Purchased by U.S.A.
from Russia, 1867)*

*Bering
Sea*

ALEUTIAN IS. (U.S.A., 1867)

KAMCHATKA

I   A

•Yakutsk

*Sea of
Okhotsk*

SAKHALIN

KURIL IS.
(Japan, 1875)

*KARAFUTO
(Japan, 1905)*

AMUR PROVINCE
1858

Amur R

Khabarovsk

MARITIME
PROVINCE
(Russia, 1868)

MANCHURIA

Vladivostok
1860

•Harbin

*Sea of
Japan*

JAPANESE EMPIRE

OLIA

•Mukden

KOREA
(Japan, 1905, 1910)

•Tokyo

JEHOL

king•

Port Arthur
(Japan, 1905)

PACIFIC OCEAN

Tientsin•

•Kiao-chow
(Germany, 1898)

Shanghai
(Britain, 1842)

MARIANA IS.
(Germany, 1899)

Nanking•

*East
China
Sea*

•Ningpo
1842

RYUKYU IS.

ankow•

Foochow•

FORMOSA *(Japan, 1895)*

GUAM
(U.S.A., 1898)

Amoy•

PESCADORES *(Japan, 1895)*

GSI
phere)

•Canton *(Britain, 1842)*
•Hong Kong *(Britain, 1842)*
•Maçao *(Portugal, 1557)*

CAROLINE IS.
(Germany, 1899)

•Kwang-chow
(Lease to France, 1898)

HAINAN

Manila•

PHILIPPINES IS.
(U.S.A., 1898, 1899)

) YAP

FRENCH
INDOCHINA
1884, 1907

*South
China Sea*

) PELAU

NEW GUINEA

KAISER WILHELMSLAND
(Germany, 1884)

Saigon

BRITISH
NORTH BORNEO
1888

TES
824)

SARAWAK
1888

BORNEO

CELEBES

E A S T   I N D I E S

pore
1819)

U T C H

(Portugal, 1859) •Darwin

JAVA

TIMOR

AUSTRALIA

IMPERIALISM
IN ASIA, 1840–1914

The map shows boundaries and possessions as they appeared in 1914. During these years the British and Dutch filled out their holdings in India and the East Indies. The Russians pressed southward from Siberia into Central Asia, founded Vladivostok in 1860, and entered Manchuria at the close of the century. The French built their empire in Indochina and the United States took control of the Philippines. The Germans, as latecomers, were confined to miscellaneous parts of the western Pacific. The Japanese won control of Korea and the island of Formosa (now Taiwan). Meanwhile all of the imperial powers obtained special rights and concessions in China.

Russian advances in Turkestan, east of the Caspian, increased the pressure on Persia, which had long felt the same pressure west of the Caspian, where cities like Tiflis and Baku, now Russian, had once been Persian. If Tiflis and Turkestan could fall to the Russian empire, there was no reason why Persia should not do so next—except that Persia had a seacoast and so might also be available for occupancy by the British. In 1864 a British company completed the first Persian telegraph as part of the line from Europe to India. Other British investments and interests followed. Oil became important about 1900. In 1890, to bolster the Persian government against Russia, the British granted it a loan—taking the customs in Persian Gulf ports as collateral. In 1900 the Russian government granted the same favor, making its own loan to Persia, and appropriating as security all Persian customs except those of the Gulf. Clearly Persia was losing control of its own affairs, falling into zones, turning ripe for partition. A Persian nationalist revolution, directed against all foreigners and against the subservient government of the shah, broke out in 1905 and led to the assembly of the first parliament but hardly settled the question of Persian independence. In 1907 the British recognized a Russian "sphere of influence" in northern Persia; the Russians, a British sphere in the south (see map, pp. 664–665).

Foreign interests in Persia

Spheres of influence

Imperial ambitions had deepened the hostility between Great Britain and Russia, with disputes over Persia and the Indian borderlands adding fuel to the quarrel they had long waged over the Ottoman Empire. We have seen how the struggle for Africa had at the same time estranged Britain from France and indeed from all Europe.

82.   IMPERIALISM IN ASIA: CHINA AND THE WEST

China before Western Penetration

In this era of new imperial rivalries, the biggest bone of imperialist contention was China. On this bone every Great Power without exception tried to bite. The Manchu, or Qing (formerly transliterated, and still pronounced, as Ch'ing), dynasty (1644–1912) held a suzerainty over the whole area affected by Chinese civilization, from the mouth of the Amur River (as far north as Labrador) to Burma and Indochina (as far south as Panama), and from the ocean westward into Mongolia and Tibet. In the old Chinese view China was the Middle Kingdom, the civilized center of the world surrounded by less enlightened peoples. The Europeans were outlandish barbarians. A few had trickled through to China since the European Middle Ages. But the Chinese people persistently wanted nothing to do with them.

China was moving into an upheaval of its own even before Western influence became of any importance. For about 4,000 years the country had seen dynasties come and go in cycles. The Qing dynasty in the nineteenth century was clearly nearing its end. It was failing to preserve order or to curb extortion. About 1800 a White Lotus Society revolted and was suppressed. In 1813 a Heavenly Reason Society attempted to seize Peking (now Beijing). In the 1850s a Muslim rebellion set up a temporary independent state in the southwest. Greatest of all the upheavals was the Taiping Rebellion, which lasted for more than a decade (1850–1864) and in which as many as 20 million people are thought to have perished. Except that some fragmentary Christian ideas obtained from missionaries were expressed by some of the Taipings (and its leader claimed to be the younger brother of Jesus), the rebellion was due entirely to Chinese causes. The rebels attacked the Manchus, who had come from

The Taiping Rebellion

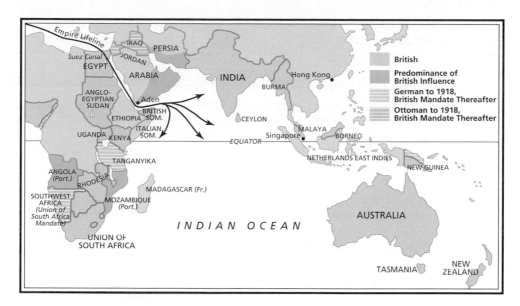

"THE BRITISH LAKE," 1918

This map shows the most important parts of the British Empire except for Canada, the Caribbean islands, and the United Kingdom itself. All shores of the Indian Ocean are shown to be British, except for French Madagascar; the politically weak Portuguese, Italian, and Dutch colonies; and the Arabian and Persian coasts, in which British influence was strong. It is easy to see why the Mediterranean and Suez Canal, leading from Europe into the Indian Ocean, were called the lifeline of the British Empire.

Manchuria two centuries before, as corrupt foreigners ruling over China. Their grievances were poverty, extortion, exorbitant rents, and absentee landlords, and their goal was to establish a new dynasty.

The Taipings set up a state in south China and their armies were at first disciplined, but the fighting lasted so long that both the Taiping leaders and the Manchu commanders sent against them got out of control, and much of the country sank into chronic banditry and disorder. It was in this period that China's war lords, men controlling armed forces but obeying no government, appeared. The Manchus managed to put down organized Taiping resistance after 14 years, with some European assistance, led by the British General Gordon, the "Chinese Gordon" who later died at Khartoum. But it is clear that Chinese social conflict, agrarianism, and nationalism (the latter at first only anti-Manchu) antedated the impact of European imperialism.

Into this distracted China the Europeans began to penetrate about 1840. It became their policy to extort concessions from the Manchu empire but at the same time to defend the Qing dynasty against internal opposition, as was shown in the European response to the Taiping Rebellion. This was because they needed some kind of government in China with which they could make treaties, legalizing their claims and binding upon the whole country.

The Opening of China to the West

The modern phase of Chinese relations with the West was inauspiciously opened by the Opium War of 1839–1841. We have already observed how, though Europeans wanted Chinese products, the Chinese had no interest in buying European products in return. Trade therefore was difficult, and the British East India Company had for decades solved the problem of getting Chinese tea for Europe by shipping Indian-grown opium in return, since opium was one available commodity for which Chinese demand existed. When the Chinese government attempted to control the inflow of opium, the British government went to war. Fifteen years later, in 1857, Britain and France combined in a second war upon China to force the Chinese to receive their diplomats and deal with their traders. The Chinese continued to resist, whereupon 17,000 French and British soldiers entered Beijing and deliberately burned the emperor's very extensive Summer Palace, an appalling act of vandalism from which soldiers brought back enough stolen cultural objects—vases, tapestries, porcelain, enamels, jades, wood carvings—to set a fashion in Europe and America for Chinese art.

From the first of these wars arose the treaty of Nanking (1842); from the second, the treaties of Tientsin (1857), whose terms were soon duplicated in still other treaties signed by China with other European powers and with the United States. The resulting complex of interlocking agreements imposed restrictions on China or conferred rights upon foreigners and came to be known as the "treaty system." To the British in 1842 the Chinese ceded the island of Hong Kong outright and somewhat later granted adjoining territories on a long lease. They opened over a dozen cities, including Shanghai and Canton (now called Guangzhou), to Europeans as "treaty ports." In these cities Europeans were allowed to make settlements of their own, immune to all Chinese law. Europeans traveling in the Chinese empire remained subject only to their own governments, and European and American gunboats began to police the Yangtse River. The Chinese likewise paid large war indemnities, though it was they themselves who suffered most of the damages. They agreed to levy no import duty over 5 percent and so became a free trade market for European products. To administer and collect the customs a staff of European experts was introduced. Money from the customs, collected with a new efficiency on a swelling volume of imports, went in part to the British and French in payment of the indemnities, but part remained with the Qing government, which, as noted, the Europeans had no desire to overthrow.

The treaty system

Annexations and Concessions

While China was thus permeated at the center by the extraterritorial and other insidious privileges for Europeans, whole blocks of its territory were cut away at the outer rim. The Russians moved down the Amur River, established their Maritime Province, and founded Vladivostok in 1860. The Japanese, now sufficiently westernized to behave like Europeans in such matters, in 1876 recognized the independence of Korea. The British annexed Burma in 1886. The French in 1883 assumed a protectorate over Annam despite Chinese protests; they soon combined five areas—Annam, Cochin China, Tonkin, Laos, and Cambodia—into French Indochina. (The first three were known also as Vietnam, a word not familiar in the West until after the Second World War.) These outlying territories had never, it is true, been integral parts of China proper; but it was with China that they had had their most important political and cultural relations and to the Chinese emperor that they had paid tribute.

Japanese imperialism

Japan, whose modernization has been described, lost little time in developing an imperialistic urge. An expansionist party already looked to the Chinese mainland and to the south. Japanese imperialism first revealed itself to the rest of the world in 1894, when Japan went to war with China over disputes in Korea. The Japanese soon won, equipped as they were with modern weapons, training, and organiza-

CHRONOLOGY OF NOTABLE EVENTS, 1850–1906

1850–1864	Taiping Rebellion in China is suppressed by Qing Dynasty; up to 20 million die
1856	Ottoman Empire launches reforms to modernize the legal and military system
1857	"Indian Mutiny" threatens British control of India and leads to reforms in the imperial administration
1864	Napoleon III of France installs Austrian Archduke Maximilian as Emperor of Mexico
1867	Maximilian is overthrown; Benito Juárez returns as Mexican President
1876	Abdul Hamid takes power as sultan in Ottoman Empire; repressive regime lasts for 33 years
1877–1878	Russo-Turkish War leads to Russian gains in the Balkans
1885	Berlin Conference sets European terms for imperial control of Africa
1885	Hindu Indian National Congress is organized to challenge British power in India
1894–1895	Japan goes to war with China and takes Formosa (later called Taiwan)
1898	United States declares war on Spain and takes control of Cuba, Puerto Rico, and the Philippines
1898	French and English forces come to brink of imperial conflict at Fashoda in Sudan—the "Fashoda Crisis"
1899	Chinese revolt against European powers, the "Boxer Uprising," is suppressed by European forces
1899–1902	The Boer War enables Britain to consolidate power in South Africa
1904–1905	Japan defeats Russia in Russo-Japanese War and expands into Manchuria
1906	All-India Muslim League is organized to promote Indian nationalism and Muslim rights

tion. They obliged the Chinese to sign the treaty of Shimonoseki in 1895, by which China ceded Formosa and the Liaotung peninsula to Japan and recognized Korea as an independent state. The Liaotung was a tongue of land reaching down from Manchuria to the sea; at its tip was Port Arthur. Manchuria was the northeastern part of China itself. This sudden Japanese triumph precipitated a crisis in east Asia. No one had realized how strong Japan had become. Europeans were astounded that a people who were not "European" in their culture or race should show such aptitude for modern war and diplomacy. It was to be supposed that Japan had designs on Manchuria.

It so happened that Russia, not long before, in 1891, had begun to build the Trans-Siberian Railway, whose eastern terminus was to be Vladivostok, the "Lord of the East." Manchuria extended northward between central Siberia and Vladivostok. The Russians, whether or not they ever dominated

"Lord of the East"

Manchuria themselves, could not allow its domination by another Great Power. It happened also that Germany was at this time looking for a chance to enter the Far Eastern arena, and that France had formed an alliance with Russia, whose good will it was eager to retain. Russia, Germany, and France joined together in demanding that Japan give up the

Liaotung peninsula. The Japanese hesitated; they were indignant, but they yielded. The Liaotung peninsula went back to China.

In China many alert people were humiliated at the defeat by the Japanese whom they had despised. The Chinese government, at last facing the inevitable, began madly to plan for a program of modernization and reform. Huge loans were obtained from Europe—the customs being pawned as security, following the pattern well established in Turkey, Persia, and Santo Domingo. But the European powers did not wish China to become consolidated too soon. Nor had they forgotten the sudden apparition of Japan. The result was a frantic scramble for further concessions in 1898.

It seemed in 1898 as if the Chinese empire in its turn would be partitioned. The Germans extorted a 99-year lease on Kiaochow Bay, plus exclusive rights in the Shantung peninsula. The Russians took a lease on the Liaotung peninsula from which they had just excluded Japan; they thus obtained Port Arthur and rights to build railroads in Manchuria to interlock with their Trans-Siberian system. The French took Kwangchow and the British Wei-hai-wei, in addition to confirming their sphere of influence in the Yangtse valley. The

The Open Door

Italians demanded a share but were refused. The United States, fearing that all China might soon be parceled out into exclusive spheres, announced its policy of the Open Door. The idea of the Open Door was that China should remain territorially intact and independent and that powers having special concessions or spheres of influence should maintain the five percent Chinese tariff and allow businessmen of all nations to trade without discrimination. The British supported the Open Door as a means of discouraging actual annexations by Japan or Russia, which as the only Great Powers adjacent to China were the only ones that could dispatch real armies into its territory. The Open Door was a program not so much of leaving China to the Chinese as of assuring that all outsiders should find it literally "open."

If readers will imagine what the United States would be like if foreign warships patrolled the Mississippi as far as St. Louis; if foreigners came and went throughout the country without being under its laws; if New York, New Orleans, and other cities contained foreign settlements outside its jurisdiction but in which all banking and management were concentrated; if foreigners determined the tariff policy, collected the proceeds, and remitted much of the money to their own governments; if the western part of the city of Washington had been burned (the Summer Palace), Long Island and California had been annexed to distant empires (Hong Kong and Indochina), and all New England was coveted by two immediate neighbors (Manchuria); if the national authorities were half in collusion with these foreigners and half victimized by them; and if large areas of the country were prey to bandits, guerrillas, and revolutionary secret societies conspiring against the helpless government and occasionally murdering some of the foreigners—then they can understand how observant Chinese felt at the end of the nineteenth century, and why the term "imperialism" came to be held by so many of the world's peoples in abomination.

The Boxer Uprising

One Chinese secret society, its name somewhat literally translated as the Order of Literary Patriotic Harmonious Fists, dubbed the Boxers by hostile Westerners, broke out in insurrection in 1899. The Boxers pulled up railway tracks, fell upon Chinese Christians, besieged the foreign legations, and killed about 300 foreigners. The European powers, joined by Japan and the United States, sent a combined international force against the insurgents, who were put down. The victors imposed still more severe controls on the Chinese government and inflicted an indemnity of $330 million. Of this the United States received $24 million, of which, in 1924, it canceled the balance that was still due. On the other hand, as a

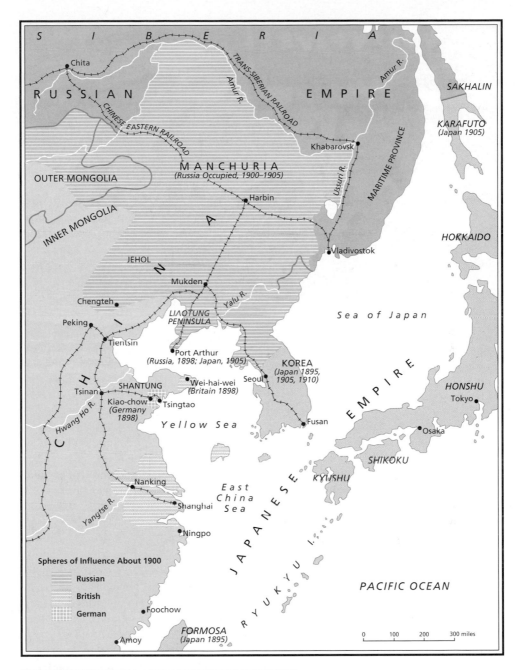

NORTHEAST CHINA AND ADJOINING REGIONS

Manchuria became an object of dispute among China, to which it belonged historically, Russia, and Japan. It was dominated by the Russians from 1898 to 1905, by the Japanese from 1905 to 1945, and again by the Russians from 1945 to 1950, when they transferred it to the People's Republic of China. Korea was dominated by Japan from about 1895 (and formally annexed by Japan in 1910) until the end of the Second World War. It was then divided into Russian and American occupation zones. After the Korean War (1950–1953) it remained divided into two independent states, North Korea under a Communist regime and a Western-supported South Korea.

Chinese resentments against their government's concessions to Western imperialist powers erupted in the violence of the so-called Boxer Uprising in 1899. This Chinese illustration of an attack on a group of Europeans conveys the anger that fueled the movement and the new national identity that was spreading across China.
(© Trustees of the British Museum)

consequence of the Boxer Uprising, the Qing officials strove desperately to strengthen themselves by modernizing the country. Meanwhile, as we shall see in a later chapter, a new revolutionary movement, aiming at expulsion of Manchus and foreigners alike, spread rapidly throughout China, especially in the south, under the leadership of Sun Yat-sen.

83. THE RUSSO-JAPANESE WAR AND ITS CONSEQUENCES

Russia and Japan increasingly opposed each other's intrigues in Manchuria and Korea. The Japanese felt a need for supplying their new factories with raw materials and markets on the Asian mainland, for employment for their modern army and navy and for recognized status as a Great Power in the Western sense. The Russian government needed an atmosphere of crisis and expansion to stifle criticism of tsarism at home; it could not abide the presence of a strong power directly on its East Asian frontier; it could use Manchuria and Korea to strengthen the exposed outpost of Vladivostok, which was somewhat squeezed against the sea and landlocked by Japanese waters. The Russians had obtained a concession from China to build the Chinese Eastern Railway to Vladivostok across the heart of Manchuria. A railway, in Manchuria, implied special zones, railway guards, mining and timber rights, and other auxiliary activities. The Japanese saw the fruits of their successful war of 1895 against China greedily enjoyed by their rival. In 1902 Japan signed a military alliance with Great Britain. We have seen how the British were alarmed by their diplomatic isolation after Fashoda and the Boer War and how for many years they had been expecting to have trouble with Russia. The Anglo-Japanese military alliance lasted 20 years.

Russo-Japanese rivalry

War broke out in 1904, undeclared, by Japanese naval attack on Russian installations at Port Arthur. Both sides sent large armies into Manchuria. The decisive battle of Mukden (which was fought for control of the important Manchurian city now called Shenyang) engaged more troops than any previous battle in human history—624,000 men. Military observers were present from all the major powers, anxiously trying to learn what the next war in Europe would be like. The Russians sent their Baltic fleet around three continents to the Far East, but to the world's amazement the Russian fleet was met and destroyed at Tsushima Strait by the new and untested navy of Japan. Russian communications by sea were thereby broken, and since the Trans-Siberian Railway was unfinished and since the Japanese also won the battle of Mukden, Russia was beaten.

At this point the president of the United States, Theodore Roosevelt, stepped upon the scene. With an outpost in the Philippines and a growing interest in China, it was to the American advantage to have neither side win too overwhelming a victory in the Far East. The most imperially minded of all American presidents offered his mediation, and plenipotentiaries of the two powers met at Portsmouth, New Hampshire. By the treaty of Portsmouth in 1905, Japan recovered from Russia what it had won and lost in 1895, namely Port Arthur and the Liaotung peninsula; a preferred position in Manchuria, which remained nominally Chinese; and a protectorate in Korea, which remained nominally independent until it was

The treaty of Portsmouth

annexed by Japan in 1910. Japan also received from Russia the southern half of the island of Sakhalin. Much of what Russia lost to Japan in 1905 was regained 40 years later at the end of the Second World War.

The Russo-Japanese War was the first war between Great Powers since 1870. It was the first war fought under conditions of developed industrialism. It was the first actual war between modern, westernized powers to be caused by competition in the exploitation of undeveloped countries. Most significant of all (except for the Ethiopian rout of the Italians in 1896), it was the first time that a nation of nonwhite people had defeated a nation of white people in modern times. Asians had shown that they could learn and play, in less than half a century, the geopolitical game of the Europeans.

The Japanese victory set off long chains of repercussions in at least three different directions. First, the Russian government, frustrated in its foreign policy in East Asia, shifted its attention back to Europe, where it resumed an active role in the affairs of the Balkans. This contributed to a

Consequences of Japanese victory

series of international crises in Europe that led to the First World War. Second, the tsarist government was so weakened by the war, both in prestige and in actual military strength, and opinion in Russia was so disgusted at the clumsiness and incompetency with which the war had been handled, that the various underground movements were able to come to the surface, producing the Revolution of 1905. This in turn was a prelude to the great Russian Revolution of 1917, of which Soviet communism was the outcome. Third, news of Japan's victory over Russia electrified those who heard of it throughout the non-European world. The fact that Japan was itself an imperialist power was overlooked in the excited realization that the Japanese were not a European power. Only half a century ago the Japanese, too, had been "backward"—defenseless, bombarded, and bulldozed by the Europeans.

The Japanese victory over the Russians in the battle of Mukden showed the world that Japan had become a major military and industrial power in east Asia. This lithograph from 1905, "Fighting in the Snow," portrays a decisive attack in the battle and illustrates how the Russo-Japanese War quickly gained symbolic significance in the rise of twentieth-century Japanese nationalism.

(The Art Archive/Hibiya Public Library Tokyo/Laurie Platt Winfrey)

The moral was clear. Everywhere leaders of subjugated peoples concluded, from the Japanese precedent, that they must bring Western science and industry to their own countries, but that they must do it, as the Japanese had done, by ending control by the Europeans, supervising the process of modernization themselves, and preserving their own native national character. New "hybrid elites" in colonized societies combined their growing knowledge of Western culture with a growing pride in their own cultures and traditions, thereby creating the new nationalisms that would become a major, worldwide legacy of modern European imperialism. Nationalist revolutions began in Persia in 1905; in Turkey in 1908; in China in 1911. In India and Indonesia many were stirred by the Japanese achievement. In the face of rising agitation, the British admitted an Indian to the

Viceroy's Council in 1909, and in 1916 the Dutch created a People's Council, to include Indonesian members, in the Dutch East Indies. The self-assertion of Asians was to grow in intensity after the First World War.

The Japanese victory and Russian defeat can therefore be seen as steps in three mighty developments: the First World War, the Russian Revolution, and the Revolt of Asia. These three together put an end to Europe's world supremacy and to confident ideas about the inevitable progress and expansion of European civilization; or at least they so transmuted them as to make the world of the twentieth century far different from that of the nineteenth.

Asian self-assertion and nationalism

 For interactive exercises, glossary, chronologies, and more, go to the *Online Learning Center* at **www.mhhe.com/palmer10.**

Chapter 17

THE FIRST WORLD WAR

Somewhere before 1914 Europe went off its course. At the beginning of the twentieth century, most Europeans believed they were heading for a kind of high plateau, full of a benign progress and more abundant civilization, in which the benefits of modern science and invention would be more widely diffused and even competitive struggle would work out somehow for the best. Instead, Europe stumbled in 1914 into disaster. It is not easy to see exactly where Europe went astray, at what point, that is, the First World War became inevitable, or (since the human mind does not know what is truly inevitable) so overwhelmingly probable that only the most Olympian statesmanship could have avoided it. But no such statesmanship appeared, and Europe fell into a deadly, grinding war that consumed much of its wealth, killed millions of its young men, and ultimately weakened or even destroyed much of its power and influence around the world.

84. THE INTERNATIONAL ANARCHY

The great political questions in mid-nineteenth century Europe had been settled by force. The German Empire was the strongest and most obvious of the new structures which armed power had reared, but all European states had concluded that large military forces were essential for their national existence. Never had the European states maintained such huge armies in peacetime as at the beginning of the twentieth century. One, two, or even three years of compulsory military service for all young men became the rule. In 1914 each of the Continental Great Powers had not only a huge standing army but millions of trained reserves among the civilian population. Few people wanted war; all but a few sensational writers preferred peace in Europe, but many took it for granted that war would

Chapter emblem: Soldier in the trenches near Passchendaele, Belgium, in 1917. (Imperial War Museum, London)

come someday. The idea that war was bound to break out sooner or later probably made some statesmen in some countries more willing to unleash it. In any case, the popular expectation of future wars as well as the large standing armies helped to produce the Great War that exploded across Europe in 1914; but the war also came from other causes, including the interlocking system of international alliances, Germany's desire for a greater role in world affairs (which challenged Britain's earlier ascendancy and raised nationalist anxieties in France), and the ongoing conflicts in the Balkans.

Rival Alliances: Triple Alliance versus Triple Entente

Political diagnosticians, from Richelieu to Metternich, had long thought that an effective union of Germany would revolutionize the relationships of Europe's peoples. After 1870 their anticipations were more than confirmed. Once united (or almost united), the Germans entered upon their industrial revolution. Manufacturing, finance, shipping, and population grew phenomenally. By 1900, for example, Germany produced more steel than France and Britain combined, though in 1865 the French alone had produced more than the Germans.

People in Germany felt that they needed and deserved a "place in the sun," by which they vaguely meant some kind of acknowledged supremacy like that of the British. Neither the British nor the French, the leaders of modern Europe since the seventeenth century, could share in such German aspirations. The French nursed the chronic grievance of Alsace and Lorraine, annexed to Germany in 1871. The British as the years passed saw German salesmen appear in their foreign markets, selling goods often at lower prices and using what they viewed as ungentlemanly methods; they saw Germans turn up as colonial rivals in Africa, the Middle East, and the Far East; and they watched other European states gravitate into the Berlin orbit, looking to the mighty German Empire as a friend to advance their interests.

Bismarck after 1871 feared that in another European war his new German Empire might be torn to pieces. He therefore followed, until his retirement in 1890, a policy of diplomacy and peace. We have seen him as the "honest broker" at the Berlin Congress of 1878, helping to adjudicate the Eastern Question, and again offering the facilities of Berlin in 1885 to bring some international order to African affairs. To isolate France, divert it from Europe, and keep it embroiled with Britain, he looked with satisfaction on French colonial expansion. He took no chances, however; in 1879 he formed a military alliance with Austria-Hungary, to which Italy was added in 1882. Thus was formed

the Triple Alliance, which lasted until the First World War. Its terms were, briefly, that if any member became involved in war with two or more powers, its allies should come to its aid by force of arms. To be on the safe side, Bismarck signed a "reinsurance" treaty with Russia also. Since Russia and Austria were enemies (because of the Balkans), Germany needed considerable diplomatic finesse to stay allied to both at the same time. After Bismarck's retirement his system proved too intricate, or too lacking in candor, for his successors to manage. The Russo-German agreement lapsed. The French, faced by the Triple Alliance, soon seized the opportunity to form their own alliance with Russia, the Franco-Russian Alliance signed in 1894. In its time this was regarded as politically almost impossible. The French Republic stood for everything radical; the Russian empire, for everything reactionary and autocratic. But ideology was thrown to the winds, French capital poured into Russia, and the tsar bared his head to the *Marseillaise*.

The Continent was thus divided by 1894 into two opposed camps, the German-Austrian-Italian against the Franco-Russian. For a time it seemed that this rigid division might soften. Germany, France, and Russia cooperated in the Far Eastern crisis of 1895 to stem the expanding power of Japan. All were anti-British at the time of Fashoda and the Boer War. The Kaiser, William II, outlined tempting pictures of a Continental league against the global hegemony of England and its empire.

Much depended on what the British would do. They had long prided themselves on a "splendid isolation," going their own way, disdaining the kind of dependency that alliance with others always brings. European hostility toward Britain during the Fashoda crisis and the Boer War came as a shock. British relations with France and Russia were going badly. Some in England, including Joseph Chamberlain, therefore thought that a better understanding with Germany was to be sought. Arguments of race, in this race-conscious age, made the English and Germans feel akin. But politically it was hard to cooperate. The Kaiser's Kruger Telegram of 1896, expressing support for the South African Boers in their conflict with Britain, was a studied insult. Then in 1898 the Germans decided to build a navy.

"Splendid isolation"

A new kind of race now entered the picture, the naval competition between Germany and Great Britain. British sea power for two centuries had been all too successful. The American Admiral Mahan, teaching at the Naval War College and taking his examples largely from British history, argued that sea power had always been the foundation of Britain's greatness and that in the long run sea power must always choke off and ruin a power operating on land. Nowhere were Mahan's books read with more interest than in Germany. The German naval program, mounting rapidly after 1898, in a few years became a source of concern to the British, and by 1912 was felt as a positive menace. The Germans insisted that they must have a navy to protect their colonies, secure their foreign trade, and "for the general purposes of their greatness." The British held with equal resolution that England, as a densely populated industrial island, dependent even for food upon imports, must at all costs control the sea in both peace and war. They adhered stubbornly to their traditional policy of maintaining a navy as large as the next two combined. The naval race led both sides to enormous and increasing expenditures. In the British it produced a sense of profound insecurity, driving them as the years passed ever more inescapably into the arms of Russia and France.

Naval race

Slowly and cautiously the British emerged from their diplomatic isolation. In 1902 they formed a military alliance with Japan against their common enemy, Russia. The decisive break came in 1904, from which may be dated the immediate series of crises issuing ten years later in the First World War.

In 1904 the British and French governments agreed to forget their conflict at Fashoda and the accumulated bad feeling of the preceding 25 years. The French recognized the British occupation of Egypt, and the British recognized the French penetration of Morocco. They also agreed to support each other against protests by third parties. There was no specific alliance; neither side said what it would do in the event of war; it was only a close understanding, an *entente cordiale*. The French immediately tried to reconcile their new friend to their ally, Russia. After defeat by Japan the Russians proved amenable. The British, increasingly uncertain of German aims, proved likewise willing. In 1907 Britain and Russia, the inveterate adversaries, settled their differences in an Anglo-Russian Convention. In Persia, the British recognized a Russian sphere of influence in the north, while the Russians recognized a British sphere in the south and east. By 1907 England, France,

Triple Entente

and Russia were acting together. The older Triple Alliance faced a newer Triple Entente, the latter somewhat the looser, since the British refused to make any formal military commitments.

The Crises in Morocco and the Balkans

The Germans, who already felt encircled by the alliance of France and Russia, watched with concern the drift of England into the Franco-Russian camp. The entente cordiale was barely concluded when the German government decided to test it by seeing how far the British would go in support of France. The French, now enjoying British backing, were taking over more police powers, concessions, and loans in Morocco. In March 1905 Kaiser William II disembarked from a German warship at Tangier, where he made a startling speech in favor of Moroccan independence. To diplomats everywhere this carefully staged performance was a signal: Germany was attempting to break up the new understanding between France and England. The Germans demanded and obtained an international conference at Algeciras, but the conference, which met in 1906, supported the French claims in Morocco, only Austria voting with Germany.

Testing the Entente

The German government had thus created an incident and been rebuffed. The British, disturbed by German diplomatic tactics, stood by the French all the more firmly. French and British army and naval officers now began to discuss common plans. Distrust of Germany also inclined the British to bury the hatchet with Russia in the next year. The German attempt to break the Entente simply made it more solid. In 1911 came a second Morocco crisis. A German gunboat, the *Panther,* arrived at Agadir "to protect German interests." It soon developed that the move was a holdup; the Germans offered to make no further trouble in Morocco if they could have the French Congo. This crisis also passed, the Germans obtaining some small accessions in Africa, but it increased British hostility to Germany.

Crises in the Balkans

Meanwhile a series of crises rocked the Balkans. The Ottoman Empire, now in an advanced state of dissolution, still held a band of territory from Constantinople westward to the Adriatic (see map, p. 686), which included Bulgarians, Serbs, Albanians, and Macedonians. In the center and west of the peninsula, north of the Turkish belt, was the small, landlocked, independent kingdom of Serbia, adjoined by Bosnia-Herzegovina, which belonged legally to Turkey but had been "occupied and administered" by Austria since 1878. Within the Austro-Hungarian Empire, adjoining Bosnia on the north and west, lay Croatia and Slovenia.

Serbs, Bosnians, Croats, and Slovenes all spoke basically the same language, Serbo-Croatian, the main difference being that Serbs and Bosnians wrote with the eastern or

ANGLO-GERMAN INDUSTRIAL COMPETITION, 1898 AND 1913

This diagram shows the huge increase in world trade in the years before the First World War and also the fact that German exports grew in these years more rapidly than British exports. The exports of both countries together multiplied no less than threefold in these 15 years. The increase reflected a small rise in prices, but it was mainly due to a real increase in volume of business. In 1913, total German exports about equaled the British, but German exports to the United States and Russia greatly exceeded the British. Note how the Germans even gained exports in British India, where the liberalism of British trade policy freely admitted competitive goods. In merchant marine, though the Germans doubled their tonnage, the British continued to enjoy an overwhelming lead.

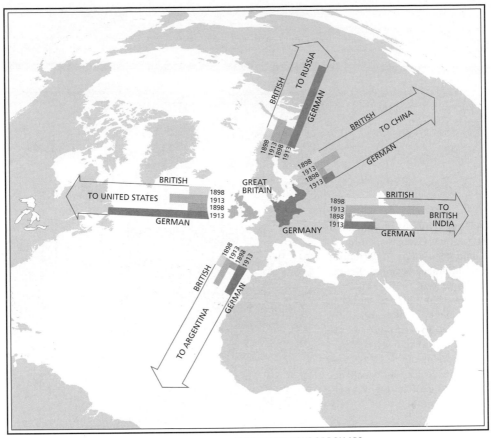

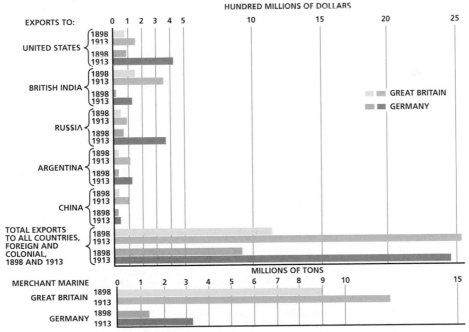

Kaiser William II sought to strengthen Germany's international position by undermining the alliance between France and Britain. His visit to Morocco in 1905, as shown in this image of his arrival at Tangiers, exemplified the Kaiser's assertive style of personal diplomacy, but his call for Moroccan independence failed to weaken the French-British entente.
(Getty Images)

Cyrillic alphabet while the Croats and Slovenes wrote with the western or Roman alphabet. The difference reflected deep differences in religion. The Slovenes and Croats had

Ethnic and religious divisions

long been Roman Catholic, and hence affiliated with Western Europe; the Serbs and many Bosnians were Eastern Orthodox and so closer to Russia; and there were also, especially in Bosnia, large numbers of Slavs who were Muslims, converted during the Ottoman domination. With the Slavic Revival, which emphasized language, many of these peoples came to feel that they were really one people, for which they took the name South Slavs, or Yugoslavs. After the Dual Monarchy was formed in 1867, as we have seen, the Slavs of the Habsburg empire were kept subordinate to the German Austrians and the Hungarian Magyars. By 1900 radical Slav nationalists within the empire had concluded that the Dual Monarchy would never grant them equal status and that all South Slavs should form an independent state of their own. Concretely, this meant that an element of the Austro-Hungarian population, namely, the Croatian and Slovenian nationalists, wished to get out of the empire and join with Serbia across the border. Serbia became the center of South Slav agitation.

This brew was brought to a boil in 1908 by two events. First, the Young Turks, whose long agitation against Abdul Hamid has been noted, managed in that year to carry through a revolution. They obliged the sultan to restore the liberal parliamentary constitution of 1876. They showed, too, that they meant to stop the dissolution of the Ottoman Empire by taking steps to have delegates from Bulgaria and Bosnia sit in the new Ottoman parliament. Second, Russia, its foreign policy in the Far East ruined by the Japanese war, turned actively to the Balkan and Turkish scene. Russia, as always, wanted control at Constantinople. Austria wanted full annexation of Bosnia, the better to discourage pan-Yugoslav ideas.

The Russian and Austrian foreign ministers, Alexander Isvolsky and Alois von Aehrenthal, came to a secret agreement in 1908. They would call an international conference, at which Russia would favor Austrian annexation of Bosnia and Austria would support the opening of the Straits to Russian warships. Austria, without waiting for a conference, proclaimed the annexation of Bosnia without more ado. This infuriated the Serbs, who had marked Bosnia for their own. Meanwhile, that same year, the Bulgarians and the Cretans broke finally with the Ottoman Empire, Bulgaria becoming fully independent, Crete uniting with Greece. Isvolsky was never able to realize the Russian plans for Constantinople. His partners in the Triple Entente, Britain and France, refused to back him, and the projected international conference was never called. In Russia itself public opinion knew nothing of Isvolsky's secret deal. The known fact in Russia was that the Serbs, the little Slav brothers of Russia, had had their toes rudely stepped on by the Austrians by the annexation of Bosnia.

The first Balkan crisis

This "first Balkan crisis" presently passed. The Russians, weakened by the Japanese war and by the domestic revolutionary turmoil of 1905, accepted the Austrian *fait accompli*. Austrian influence in the Balkans seemed to be growing. And South Slav nationalism was frustrated and inflamed.

In 1911 Italy declared war on Turkey, from which it soon conquered Tripoli and the Dodecanese Islands. With the Ottomans thus embarrassed, Bulgaria, Serbia, and Greece joined forces in their own war against Turkey, hoping to annex certain Balkan territories to which they believed they had a right. Turkey was soon defeated, but the Bulgarians claimed more of Macedonia than the Serbs would yield. The first Balkan war of 1912 was followed in 1913 by a second, in which Albania, a mountainous, mainly Muslim region on the Adriatic, was the subject of angry discord. The Serbs occupied part of it in the two Balkan wars, but Greeks also claimed a part, and it had also on several occasions been vaguely promised to Italy. Russia supported the Serbian claim. Austria was determined to shut off the Serbs from access to the sea, which they would obtain by annexation of Albanian territory. An agreement of the great powers conjured up an independent kingdom in Albania. This confirmed the Austrian policy, kept Serbia from the sea, and aroused vehement outcries in both Serbia and Russia. But Russia again backed down. Serbian expansionism was again frustrated and inflamed.

Two Balkan wars

The third Balkan crisis proved to be the fatal one. It was fatal because two others had gone before it, leaving feelings of exasperation in Austria, desperation in Serbia, and humiliation in Russia.

The Sarajevo Crisis and the Outbreak of War

On June 28, 1914, a young Bosnian revolutionary, a member of the Serbian secret society called "Union or Death" and commonly known as the Black Hand, acting with the knowledge of certain Serbian officials, assassinated the heir to the Habsburg empire, the Archduke Francis Ferdinand, in the streets of Sarajevo, the Bosnian capital, in the Austrian Empire. The world was shocked at

The assassination at Sarajevo

this terrorist outrage and at first sympathized with the protests of the Austrian government. Francis Ferdinand, who would soon have become emperor, was known to favor some kind of transformation of Austria-Hungary, in which a more equal place might be given to the Slavs; but the reformer who makes a system work is the most dangerous of all enemies to the implacable revolutionary, and it is perhaps for this reason that the archduke was killed by the Black Hand.

The Austrian government was determined to end the South Slav separatism that was gnawing its empire to pieces. It decided to crush the independence of Serbia, the nucleus of South Slav agitation, though not to annex it, since most Austrians thought too many Slavs were living within the empire already. The Austrian government consulted the German to see how far it might go with the support of its ally. The Germans, issuing their famous "blank check," encouraged the Austrians to be firm. The Austrians,

The German "blank check"

thus reassured of strong German support, dispatched a drastic ultimatum to Serbia, demanding among other things that Austrian officials be permitted to collaborate in investigating and punishing the perpetrators of the assassination. The Serbs counted on Russian support, judging that Russia could not yield in a Balkan crisis, for the third time in six years, without losing its influence in the Balkans altogether. The Russians in turn counted on France; and France, terrified at the possibility of being some day caught alone in a war with Germany and determined to keep Russia as an ally at any cost, in effect gave a blank check to Russia.

The Serbs rejected the critical item in the Austrian ultimatum as an infringement on Serbian sovereignty, and Austria thereupon declared war upon Serbia. Russia prepared to defend Serbia and hence to fight Austria. Expecting that Austria would be joined by Germany, Russia rashly mobilized its army on the German as well as the Austrian frontier. Since the power which first mobilized had all the advantages of a rapid offensive, the German government demanded an end to the Russian mobilization on its border and, receiving no answer, declared war on Russia on August 1, 1914. Convinced that France would in any case enter the war on the side of Russia, Germany also declared war on France on August 3. These German declarations of war would become the basis for later charges that Germany bore complete responsibility, or guilt, for the huge human and financial costs that all European nations would pay over the next four years.

The German decisions were posited on a reckless hope that Great Britain might not enter the war at all. England was bound by no formal military alliance. Even the French did not know for certain, as late as August 3, whether the British would join them in war.

English isolation

The British clung to scraps of their old proud isolation; they hesitated to make a final choice of sides; and as the foreign secretary Sir Edward Grey repeatedly explained, in England only parliament could declare war, so the foreign office could make no binding promise of war in advance. It has often been said that had the German government known as a positive fact that England would fight, the war might not have come. Hence the evasiveness of British policy is made a contributing cause of the war. In reality, the probability that England would fight was so great that to underestimate it, as the Germans did, was an act of supreme folly. The British government was deeply committed to France, especially through naval agreements, but what swept the British public toward the French was the German invasion of Belgium. The German plan to crush France quickly was such that it could succeed only by crossing Belgium. When the Belgians protested, the Germans invaded anyway, violating the treaty of 1839 which had guaranteed Belgian neutrality. England declared war on Germany on August 4.

Archduke Francis Ferdinand of Austria meets here with leaders of the Catholic church during his visit to Sarajevo on June 28, 1914. Shortly after this meeting, the Archduke (the tall man with a moustache) and his wife were assassinated by a Bosnian nationalist. The ensuing diplomatic crisis mobilized all of the nations in the European alliance system and led to the First World War of 1914–1918.
(Getty Images)

The mere narration of successive crises does not explain why the chief nations of Europe within a few days became locked in combat over the murder of an imperial personage. Among more obvious general causes, the alliance system and nationalist ideologies should be emphasized. Europe was divided into two armed camps. Every incident tended to become a test of strength between the two. A specific national incident, such as German intervention in Morocco, or the assassination of Francis Ferdinand, could not be settled on its own merits, merely by the parties concerned. However it was dealt with, one of the two camps was deemed to have lost or gained and hence to have lost or gained influence in other incidents, of perhaps greater importance, that would arise in the future. Each nation felt that it must stand by its allies whatever the specific issue. This was because all lived in the fear of war, of some nameless future war in which allies would be necessary.

Causes of the First World War

The Germans complained of being "encircled" by France and Russia. They dreaded the day when they might have to face a war on two fronts. Willing to accept even a Europeanwide war to break their threatened "encirclement" by the Entente powers, they were obliged to hold to their one ally, Austria-Hungary, which was in turn able to sell its support at its own price. The French dreaded a coming conflict with Germany, which in 40

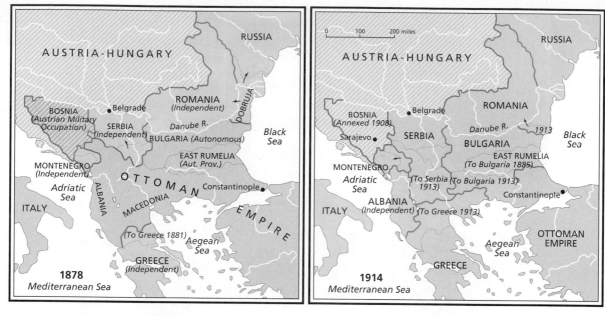

THE BALKANS, 1878 AND 1914

Austria and Russia had gradually pushed the Ottoman Empire out of Europe since 1699. The Congress of Berlin in 1878 attempted to stabilize the situation by recognizing Romania, Serbia, and Montenegro as independent monarchies, and northern Bulgaria as an autonomous principality within the Ottoman Empire. The ambitions and discontents of these new states, of Greece, and of non-Turkish people remaining within the Ottoman Empire culminated in the Balkan Wars of 1912–1913. Albania then became independent, and Serbia, Bulgaria, and Greece became contiguous. Austrian and Russian pressures meanwhile continued; in 1908 Austria annexed Bosnia, where the South Slav population, like the Serbs, was hostile to the Austrian annexation.

years had far surpassed France in population and industrial strength; they were obliged to cling to their ally Russia, which therefore could oblige the French to yield to Russian wishes. As for Russia and Austria, they were both tottering empires. Especially after 1900, the tsarist regime suffered from endemic revolutionism and the Habsburg empire from chronic nationalistic agitation. Authorities in both empires became desperate. Like the Serbs, they had little to lose and were therefore reckless. It was Russia that drew France and hence England into war in 1914, and Austria that drew Germany. Seen in this light, the tragedy of 1914 is that the instability and nationalist conflicts in the politically bankrupt parts of Europe, through the alliance system, dragged the more advanced parts automatically into ruin.

The German Empire, too, faced an internal crisis. The Social Democrats became the largest party in the Reichstag in 1912. Their sentiments for the most part were antimilitarist and antiwar. But the German imperial government recognized no responsibility to a majority in the chamber. Policy was determined by men of the old unreconstructed upper class, in which army and navy interests, now reinforced by new business interests, were strong; and even moderates and liberals shared in the ambition to make Germany a world power, the equal of any. The perplexities the ruling groups faced at home, the feeling that their position was being undermined by the Social Democrats, may have made them more willing to view war as a way out. And while it is not true that Germany alone started the war, as its enemies in 1914 popularly believed, it must be granted that its policies had for some years been peremptory, arrogant, devious, and obstinate. In a broad sense, the emergence of a consolidated industrial Germany after 1870, making its bid for world-power status relatively late, was a distant and basic cause of war.

The alliance system was only a symptom of deeper trouble. In a word, the world had an international economy but an anarchic system of competing, sovereign national states. Economically, each European people now required habitual contact with the world as a whole. Each people was to that extent dependent and insecure. Industrial countries were especially vulnerable, relying as they did on import of raw materials and food and on export of goods, services, or capital in return. There was, however, no world state to police the worldwide system, assuring participation in the world economy to all nations under all conditions. Each nation had to take care of itself. Hence came much of the popular support for nationalist political ideologies and much of the drive for imperialism, in which each Great Power tried to stake out part of the world system for itself. And hence also came the quest for allies and for binding alliances. The alliances, in a world that was in the strict sense anarchic (and seemed likely to remain so), were a means by which each nation attempted to bolster its security; to assure that it would not be cut off, conquered, or subjected to another's will; and to obtain some hope of economic success in the competitive struggle for use of the world's goods.

85.   THE ARMED STALEMATE

The First World War lasted over four years, from 1914 to the end of 1918, the United States entering with effective result in the last year. Germany and its allies were called the Central Powers, while the Entente governments were termed the Allies. The war was appalling in its human costs; on the western front, more men were used and killed in the First World War than in the Second.

At first a short war, as in 1870, was universally expected. The German General Staff had its plans ready for a two-front struggle against France and Russia. The disadvantage of fighting on two fronts was offset by the possession of good rail lines, which allowed the rapid shuttling of troops from one front to the other. The German war plan, known as the Schlieffen Plan, rested upon this fact. The idea was first to defeat France by the rapid wheeling motion of a tremendous army through Belgium and then to turn at more leisure against Russia, whose great size and less-developed railways would make its deployment much slower.

The Schlieffen Plan

The War on Land, 1914–1916

On August 3, 1914, the Germans launched 78 infantry divisions in the West. They were opposed by 72 French divisions, 5 British, and 6 Belgian. The Germans swept irresistibly forward. The Schlieffen Plan seemed to be moving like clockwork. Germany's civilian authorities made plans for the conquest and annexation of large parts of Europe. Then a hitch occurred: the Russians were fulfilling the terms of their alliance; the 10 billion francs invested by the French in Russia now paid their most significant dividend. The Russians pushed two armies into Germany, penetrating into East Prussia. Moltke

THE FIRST WORLD WAR

Land fighting in the First World War was mainly confined to the areas shown by the darker horizontal shading. The huge battles on the western front, which produced more casualties than all of the battles in the West during the Second World War, swayed back and forth over an area less than 100 miles wide.

Almost everyone in 1914 expected a short war and a quick resolution of the international crisis. These German soldiers at the Berlin railway station were preparing to board trains that would take them to the front. Accompanied by their wives or girlfriends and carrying flowers, they departed Berlin amid the optimistic fanfare that spread across all Europe in the early days of the war.

(akg-images)

withdrew forces from the German right wing in France, on August 26, for service in the East. The Germans moved on, but their striking arm was weakened and their lines of communication were already overextended. Joffre, the French commander, regrouping his forces, with strong support from the relatively small British contingent and at exactly the right moment, ordered a counterattack.

The battle of the Marne

The ensuing battle of the Marne, fought from September 5 to 12, changed the whole character of the war. The Germans were obliged to retreat. The hope of felling France at a single blow was ended. Each side now tried to outflank and destroy the other until the battle lines extended to the sea. The Germans failed to win control of the Channel ports; French and British communications remained uninterrupted. For these reverses the great victories meanwhile won by the Germans on the eastern front, though of gigantic proportions (the battles of Tannenberg and the Masurian Lakes, at which 225,000 Russians were captured), were in the long run small consolation.

In the West the war of movement now settled into a war of position. The armies on the western front became almost immobile. The units of horse cavalry—the uhlans, hussars, and lancers that had pranced off to war in high spirits—disappeared from the field. Since aviation was barely beginning, and motor transport was still new (the armies had trucks, but no self-propelled guns, and no tanks until very late in the war), the basic soldier more than ever was the man on foot. The most deadly new weapon was the machine gun, which made it impossible for foot soldiers to advance across open fields without overwhelming artillery preparation. The result was a long military stalemate in which the indispensable infantry sought protection in a vast network of trenches.

War in the trenches

In 1915 the Germans and Austro-Hungarians put their main effort into an attempt to knock out Russia. They pressed far into the tsarist empire. The Russian losses were enormous—two million killed, wounded, or captured in 1915 alone. But at the end of the year the Russian army was still fighting. Meanwhile the British and French, hoping to open up communications with Russia, launched a naval attack on Turkey, aiming at Constantinople by way of the Dardanelles. They poured 450,000 men into the narrow peninsula of Gallipoli, of whom 145,000 were killed or wounded. After almost a year the enterprise was given up as a failure.

In 1916 both sides turned again to northern France in an attempt to break the deadlock. The Allies planned a great offensive along the river Somme, while the Germans prepared one in the neighborhood of Verdun. The Germans attacked Verdun in February. The French commander Joffre put in General Pétain to defend it but resisted committing his main reserves, holding them for the coming offensive on the Somme. Pétain and his troops, held to minimum numbers, thus had to take the full weight of the German army. The battle of Verdun lasted almost ten months, engaged about two million soldiers, and became a legend of determined French resistance ("they shall not pass"). The Germans finally abandoned the attack because they sustained almost as many casualties as the French— 330,000 to 350,000.

The battle of Verdun

The battle of the Somme

While the inferno still raged at Verdun, the Allies opened their offensive on the Somme in July. They brought up unheard of amounts of artillery, and the newly raised British army was present in force. The idea was to break through the German line simply by stupendous pressure. On both sides, Allied and German, the art of generalship had sunk to an all-time low. Despite a weeklong artillery bombardment the British lost 60,000 men on the first day of the attack. In a week they had advanced only one mile along a six-mile front. In a month they had advanced less than three miles. The battle of the Somme, lasting from July to October, cost the Germans about 500,000 men, the British 400,000, and the French 200,000. Nothing of any value had been gained. It was, indeed, at the Somme that the British first used the tank, an armored vehicle with caterpillar tracks that could crash through barbed wire, lunge over trenches, and smash into machine gun nests; but the tanks were introduced in

The miseries and dangers of the muddy trenches on the western front are conveyed in this photograph of soldiers in the battle of Passchendaele in 1917. Human life in such conditions became a raw struggle for survival; most soldiers reported that the grinding, daily experience on a battlefield seemed far removed from the nationalism or political concerns of civilians and government leaders.
(Imperial War Museum, London)

such small numbers, and with such skepticism on the part of many commanders, that they had no effect on the battle.

The War at Sea

With land armies thus helpless, both sides looked to the sea. The long preponderance of British sea power, and the more recent Anglo-German naval race, would now be tested. The British, with French aid, imposed a strict naval blockade. International law at the time placed goods headed for a country at war into two classes. One class was called contraband; it included munitions and certain specified raw materials which might be used in the manufacture of military equipment. The other class, including foodstuffs and raw cotton, was defined as noncontraband. A country was supposed, by international law, to be able to import noncontraband goods even in wartime. These terms of wartime law had been set forth as recently as 1909 at an international conference held in London. The purpose was to make it impossible for a sea power (that is, the British) to starve out an enemy in wartime or even to interfere with normal civilian production. The jealousy of Continental Europe for British sea power was an old story.

Naval blockade

Such law, if observed, would make the blockade of Germany entirely ineffective, and the Allies did not observe it. To starve out the enemy and ruin his economy was precisely their purpose. Economic warfare took its place alongside armed attack as a military weapon, as in the days of Napoleon. The Allies announced a new international law. The distinction between contraband and noncontraband was gradually abolished. The British navy (aided by the French) proceeded to stop all goods of whatever character destined for Germany or its allies. Neutrals, among whom the Americans, Dutch, and Scandinavians were the ones mainly affected, were not allowed to make for German ports at all.

The United States protested vehemently against these regulations and defended the rights of neutrals. It reasserted the distinction between contraband and noncontraband, claimed the right to trade with other neutrals, and upheld the "freedom of the seas." These claims led to mutual bad feelings between the American and British governments in 1915 and 1916. But when the United States entered the war, it adopted the Allied position, and its navy joined in enforcing exactly the same regulations. International law was in fact changed. In the Second World War the very words "contraband" and "freedom of the seas" were never heard.

The Germans countered with an attempt to blockade England. A few isolated German cruisers were able for some time to destroy British shipping in the several oceans of the

Submarine warfare

world. But the Germans relied mainly on the submarine, against which the British naval power at first seemed helpless. The submarine was an unrefined weapon; a submarine commander could not always tell what kind of ship he was attacking, nor could he remove passengers, confiscate cargo, escort the vessel, or indeed do much except sink it. Citing British abuses of international law in justification, the German government in February 1915 declared the waters surrounding the British Isles to be a war zone, in which Allied vessels would be torpedoed and neutral vessels would be in grave danger.

The Lusitania

Three months later the liner *Lusitania* was torpedoed off the Irish coast. About 1,200 persons were drowned, including about 120 American citizens. The *Lusitania* was a British ship; it carried munitions of war manufactured in the United States for Allied use; and the Germans had published ominous warnings in the New York papers that Americans should not take passage on it. Americans then believed that they should be able to sail safely, on peaceable errands, on the ship of a belligerent power in wartime. The loss of life shocked the country. President Wilson informed the Germans that another such act would be considered "deliberately unfriendly." The Germans, to avoid trouble, refrained for two years from making full use of their submarines. For two years the Allied use of the sea was only partly impeded.

Allied access to the sea was confirmed by the one great naval engagement of the war, the battle of Jutland. The German admirals became restless at seeing their newly built navy skulking behind minefields on the German shores, yet they could not presume to challenge the superior British Grand Fleet, posted watchfully at Scapa Flow. They hoped, however, to decoy smaller formations of British ships, destroy them one by one, and perhaps eventually obtain enough of a naval balance in the North Sea to loosen the British blockade by which Germany was slowly being strangled. They were themselves, however, trapped into a major engagement in which the British Grand Fleet of 151 ships took them by surprise in the spring of 1916. After a few hours of furious combat the Germans were able to withdraw into mined waters. They had lost less tonnage and fewer men than the British. They had proved themselves to be dangerously proficient in naval combat. But they had failed to undermine the British preponderance at sea.

Diplomatic Maneuvers and Secret Agreements

With no military solution in sight, both sides looked about for new allies. The Ottoman Empire, fearing Russia, had joined Germany and Austria-Hungary as early as October 1914. The leading new prospect was Italy, which, though formally a member of the Triple Alliance, had long ago drifted away from it. Both sides solicited the Italian government, which bargained imperturbably with both. The Italian public was divided, but extreme nationalists saw a chance to obtain their *irredenta,* the border regions in which Italians lived outside the national territory that had been incorporated at the time of national unification. The Italian government cast its lot with the Allies in the secret treaty of London of 1915. It was agreed that if the Allies won the war, Italy would receive (from Austria) the Trentino, the south Tyrol, Istria and the city of Trieste, and some of the Dalmatian Islands. If Britain and France took over Germany's African colonies, Italy should receive additional territory in Libya and Somaliland. The treaty of London, in short, continued the most brazen prewar practices of territorial expansionism, but the Allies were desperate for additional military support. Italy, thus bought, and probably against the will of most Italians, opened up a front against Austria-Hungary in May 1915.

Italy joins the Allies

The Allies likewise made plans for a final partition of the Ottoman Empire, which still reached from Constantinople through the Middle East into Arabia and into Mesopotamia (modern Iraq). By a secret treaty they agreed that, upon an Allied victory, Mesopotamia was to go to Britain, Syria and southeastern Asia Minor to France, small portions to Italy, and Kurdistan and Armenia to Russia.

Each side tampered with minorities and discontented groups living within the domains of the other. The Germans promised an independent Poland to embarrass Russia. They stirred up local nationalism in the Ukraine. They raised up a pro-German Flemish movement in Belgium. They persuaded the Ottoman sultan, as caliph, to proclaim a holy war in North Africa, hoping that irate Muslims would drive the British from Egypt and the French from Algeria. This had no success. German agents worked in Ireland and one Irish nationalist, Sir Roger Casement, landed in Ireland from a German submarine, precipitating the Easter Rebellion of 1916, which was suppressed by the British.

To Americans the most amazing of similar activities was the Zimmermann telegram. In 1916 an American military force had crossed the Mexican border in pursuit of bandits, against protests by the Mexican government. Relations between the United States and Germany were also deteriorating. In January 1917 the German state secretary for foreign affairs, Arthur Zimmermann, dispatched a telegram to the German minister at Mexico City, telling him what to say to the Mexican president. He was to say that if the United States went to war with Germany, the Germans would form an alliance with Mexico and if possible Japan, enabling Mexico to get back its "lost territories." These latter referred to the region conquered by the United States from Mexico in the 1840s—Texas, New Mexico, and Arizona (California was not mentioned). Zimmermann's telegram was intercepted and decoded by the British, who sent it to Washington. Printed in the newspapers, it shocked public opinion in the United States.

The Zimmermann telegram

The Allies were more successful in appealing to nationalist discontent, for the obvious reason that the most active national minorities were within the lands of their enemies. They were able to promise restoration of Alsace-Lorraine to France without difficulty. They promised independence to the Poles, though anticipating some difficulty as long as

Colonel T. E. Lawrence emerged as the key British liaison to Arab forces fighting for independence from the Ottoman Empire during the First World War. He appears in this photograph at Versailles (wearing a British army uniform and Arab headdress) behind the left shoulder of Prince Faisal, who became the British-appointed King of Iraq in 1921.
(Corbis)

the Russian monarchy stood. It was easier for them to favor national independence for Czechs, Slovaks, and South Slavs, since an Allied victory would dissolve the Austro-Hungarian empire.

But the Allied use of nationalist ambitions also extended from Europe into the Ottoman Empire and beyond. Within the Ottoman Empire the British aroused Arab hopes for independence. The British Colonel T. E. Lawrence led an insurrection against the Turks in the northwestern Arabian peninsula—a region called the Hejaz that includes the Muslim holy city of Mecca. Encouraged by Lawrence and the British to pursue aspirations for an independent Arab state, the emir Hussein of Hejaz in 1916 took the title of King of

Disruption in the Ottoman Empire

the Arabs and established a kingdom that reached from the Red Sea to the Persian Gulf. Meanwhile, Zionists saw in the impending Ottoman collapse the opportunity to realize their dream for a Jewish state in Palestine. Since Palestine was peopled by Arabs (and had been for over 1,000 years) the Zionist program collided with British plans to sponsor Arab nationalism.

Nevertheless, the British Foreign Secretary, Arthur Balfour, issued the famous Balfour Declaration in 1917, promising the British government's support for the idea of a "Jewish homeland" in Palestine (though with protection for the rights of non-Jewish peoples) and also setting the foundations for a clash between Jewish and Arab nationalism, which has afflicted the Middle East down to the present.

For the Armenians these years were especially disastrous. They were a Christian people living in the eastern part of the Anatolian peninsula where it abuts on Russia, and like other peoples in the Ottoman Empire, including the Turks themselves, they had developed aspirations for a national state of their own, which conflicted with the plans of Turkish reformers to Turkify the empire. It was only 20 years since such clashes had produced the horrifying Armenian massacres of 1894. Now in 1915 the Turkish government, as the Russian army threatened its eastern frontier, ordered the deportation of Armenians from the war zone as potential sympathizers with Russia and the Western Allies. Supposedly they were to be resettled in Syria and Palestine. In fact, in the atmosphere of military crisis, political hatred, bureaucratic contempt, and wartime scarcities hundreds of thousands of Armenians perished in what many later defined as a genocidal massacre. Virtually no Armenians remained within what became the Turkish republic a few years later. The surviving Armenians became another of the world's scattered peoples with no state of their own except for a small Armenian republic, briefly independent after 1918, then part of the Soviet Union for 70 years, and finally independent again after 1991.

At the same time that they were seeking to disrupt and dismember the Ottoman Empire, the British and French were using the war as an opportunity to take control of the German colonies in Africa. The British foreign secretary, Sir Edward Grey, revealed to Colonel House, President Wilson's personal emissary, that the Allies did not intend that Germany should ever get its colonies back, though it also became clear that they did not intend to grant true independence to the people who lived there.

In China, too, the third important area of imperialist competition, the war accelerated the tendencies of preceding years. The Japanese saw their own opportunity in the self-slaughter of the Europeans. Japan had been allied to Britain since 1902, and in August 1914 the Japanese declared war on Germany. They soon overran the German concessions in China and the German islands in the Pacific, the Marshalls and Carolines. In January 1915 Japan presented its Twenty-One Demands on China, a secret ultimatum for further concessions, most of which the Chinese were obliged to accept. Japan thereby proceeded to turn Manchuria and north China into an exclusive protectorate.

Japan in China

As for the Germans, their war aims were even more expansionist and more menacing to existing boundaries in Europe itself. Early in September 1914, when a quick victory seemed within their grasp, Bethmann-Hollweg, who remained chancellor until the summer of 1917, drew up a list of German war aims which stayed unaltered until the end of hostilities. The plans called for an enlarged German Empire dominating all central Europe and annexations or satellites in both western and eastern Europe. In the east, Lithuania and other parts of the Baltic coast were to become German dependencies, large sections of Poland were to be directly annexed, and the remainder was to be joined with Austrian Galicia to form a German-dominated Polish state. In the west, Belgium was to become a German dependency to provide more direct access to the Atlantic, and French Lorraine with its rich iron ore was to be added to the already German parts of Alsace-Lorraine. Colonial adjustments, including the acquisition of most of central Africa from coast to coast, were also projected. The political map of Europe and of colonial Africa would thus be transformed in Germany's favor.

German expansionism

All these developments, especially the Allied negotiations, whether accomplished facts or secret agreements, affecting Europe, the Middle East, Asia, or Africa, became very troublesome later at the peace conference. They continued some of the most unsettling tendencies of European politics before the war. It does not appear that the Allies, until driven by Woodrow Wilson, gave any thought to means of controlling nationalism and what could be called international anarchy. As president of the United States, Wilson for a long time could see little to choose between the warring alliances, though his personal sympathies were with England and France. In 1916 he attempted to mediate, entering into confidential discussions with both sides; but both still hoped to win on their own terms, so negotiation was fruitless. Wilson judged that most Americans wished to remain uninvolved, and in November 1916 he was reelected to a second term, on the popular cry "he kept us out of war." Wilson urged a true neutrality of thought and feeling, or a settlement, as he said, that should be a "peace without victory."

A "peace without victory"

As of the end of 1916, it is hard to see how the First World War would have turned out had not two new sets of forces altered the stalemate.

86.   THE COLLAPSE OF RUSSIA
AND THE INTERVENTION OF THE UNITED STATES

The Withdrawal of Russia: Revolution and the Treaty of Brest-Litovsk

The first victim of the First World War, among governments, was the Russian empire. As the Russo Japanese War had led to the Revolution of 1905 in Russia, so the more ruinous conflict in Europe led to the far greater Revolution of 1917. The story of the Russian Revolution is told in the following chapter. It is enough to say here that war offered a test that the tsarist government could not meet. Bungling, dishonest, and secretive, incapable of supplying the materiel required for modern fighting, driving hordes of peasants into battle in some cases even without rifles, losing men by the millions yet offering no goal to inspire sacrifice, the tsarist regime lost the loyalty of all elements of its people.

In March 1917 the troops in St. Petersburg mutinied, while strikes and riots desolated the city. The Duma, or Russian parliament, used the occasion to press its demands for reform. On March 15 Nicholas II abdicated. A Provisional Government took over, made up of liberal noblemen and middle-class leaders, generally democrats and constitutionalists, with at first only one socialist. The Provisional Government held power from March to November 1917.

The Provisional Government

Its members, who shared in the liberalism of western Europe, believed that a liberal and parliamentary regime could not succeed in Russia unless the German Empire were defeated. They took steps, therefore, to prosecute the war with a new vigor. In July 1917 a new offensive was opened, but the demoralized Russian armies again collapsed.

The mass of the Russian people were wearied of a war in which they were asked to suffer so much for so little. Nor did Russian peasants or workers feel any enthusiasm for the westernized intellectuals and professional men who headed the Provisional Government. Ordinary Russians, so far as they had any politics, were drawn to one or another of numerous forms of socialism, Marxist and non-Marxist. The Russian Marxist party, the Social Democrats, was divided between Menshevik and Bolshevik factions, the latter being more radical. The Bolshevik leaders had for some time lived as exiles in western

Europe. Their principal spokesman, V. I. Lenin, with a few others, had spent the war years in Switzerland. In April 1917 the German government offered safe passage to Lenin through Germany to Russia. A railway car full of Bolsheviks, carefully "sealed" to prevent infection of Germany, was thus hauled by a German train to the frontier, whence it passed on to St. Petersburg, or Petrograd, as the city was renamed during the war. The aim of the Germans in this affair, as in the sending of Roger Casement to Ireland in a submarine, was of course to use a kind of psychological warfare against the enemy's home front. It was to promote rebellion against the Provisional Government and thus at last to eliminate Russia.

The Bolsheviks return from exile

The position of the Provisional Government became rapidly more untenable until by November 1917 the situation was so confused that Lenin and the Bolsheviks were able to seize power. The Bolsheviks stood for peace with Germany, partly to win popular favor in Russia and partly because they regarded the war as a struggle among capitalist, imperialist powers which should be left to exhaust and destroy each other for the benefit of socialism. On December 3, 1917, a peace conference opened between the Bolsheviks and the Germans at Brest-Litovsk. Meanwhile the peoples within the western border of the old Russia—Poles, Ukrainians, Bessarabians, Estonians, Latvians, Finns—with German backing, proclaimed their national independence. The Bolsheviks, since they would not or could not fight, were obliged to sign with Germany a treaty to which they vehemently objected, the treaty of Brest-Litovsk of March 3, 1918. By this treaty they acknowledged the "independence," or at least the loss to Russia, of Poland, the Ukraine, Finland, and the Baltic provinces.

The treaty of Brest-Litovsk

For the Germans the treaty of Brest-Litovsk represented their maximum success during the First World War; it accomplished some of the war aims formulated at the beginning of hostilities. Not only had they neutralized Russia, they also now dominated eastern Europe through puppets placed at the head of the new independent states. A certain number of German troops remained in the East to preserve the new arrangements. But it was no longer a two-front war. Masses of the German army were shifted from east to west. The High Command, under Hindenburg and Ludendorff since August 1916, prepared to concentrate for a last blow in France to end the war in 1918.

The year 1918 was essentially a race to see whether American aid could reach Europe soon enough, in sufficient amount, to offset the added strength which Germany drew from the collapse of Russia. In March of that year the Germans, beginning with gas attacks and a bombardment by 6,000 artillery pieces, opened a formidable offensive before which the French and British both recoiled. On May 30, 1918, the Germans again stood at the Marne, 37 miles from Paris. At this time there were only two American divisions in action, though the United States had been at war for over a year. At this point in the story there are therefore two open questions: how the United States entered the war and the length of time required for the buildup of its forces overseas.

American intervention

The United States and the War

We have seen how President Wilson clung persistently to neutrality. The American people were divided. Many had been born in Europe or were the children of immigrants. Those of Irish origin were anti-British; those of German origin were often sympathetic to Germany. On the other hand, since the time of the

America divided

Spanish-American and Boer wars, a noticeable current of friendliness to the English had been running stronger than ever before in American history. The sale of war materiel to the Allies and the purchase of the bonds of Allied governments had given certain limited though influential circles a material interest in an Allied victory. American idealism was on the side of England and France, so far as it was not isolationist. An Allied victory would clearly advance the cause of democracy, freedom, and progress far more than a victory of the German Empire. On the other hand, England and France were suspected of somewhat impure motives, and they were allied with the Russian autocracy, the reactionary and brutal tsardom.

The fall of tsarism made a great impression. Democrats and progressives now came forward even in Russia. No one had ever heard of Lenin or foresaw the Bolshevik Revolution. It seemed in the spring of 1917 that Russia was struggling along the path that England, France, and America had already taken. An ideological barrier had dropped away, and the demand for American intervention to safeguard democracy became more insistent.

The Germans gave up the attempt to keep the United States out. Constricted ever more tightly by the blockade, and failing to get a decision on land, the German government and High Command listened more readily to the submarine experts, who declared that if given a free hand they could force British surrender in six months. It was the chief example in the First World War of the claim that one branch of the service could win the war alone. Civilian and diplomatic members of the government objected, fearing the consequences of war with the United States. They were overruled; it was a good example of

*Unrestricted
submarine warfare*

the way in which, in Germany, the army and navy had taken the highest policy into their hands. Unrestricted submarine warfare was to be resumed on February 1, 1917. It was foreseen that the United States would declare war, but the German High Command believed that this would make no immediate difference. They estimated in 1917 (correctly) that between the time when the United States entered a European war and the time when it could take part with its own army about a year must intervene. Meanwhile, the planners said, in six months they could force Britain to accept defeat.

On January 31, 1917, the Germans notified Wilson of the resumption of unrestricted submarine attacks. They announced that they would sink on sight all merchant vessels found in a zone around the British Isles or in the Mediterranean. Wilson broke off diplomatic relations and ordered the arming of American freighters. Meanwhile, the publication of the Zimmermann telegram convinced many Americans of German aggressiveness. German secret agents also had been at work in America, fomenting strikes and causing explosions in factories engaged in the manufacture of munitions for the Allies. In February and March several American ships were sunk. Americans regarded all these activities as an

*"To make the world
safe for democracy"*

interference with their rights as neutrals. Wilson at last concluded that Germany was a menace. Having made his decision, Wilson saw a clear-cut issue between right and wrong, and he obtained a rousing declaration of war from Congress, on April 6, 1917. The United States went to war "to make the world safe for democracy."

At first the German campaign realized and even exceeded the predictions of its sponsors. In February 1917 the Germans sank 540,000 tons of shipping; in March, 578,000 tons; in April, as the days grew longer, 874,000 tons. Something akin to terror seized the government in London. Britain was reduced to a six-week reserve of food. Gradually countermeasures were developed—mine barges, hydrophones, depth charges, airplane reconnaissance, and most of all the convoy. It was found that a hundred or more freighters

together, though all had to steam at the pace of the slowest, could be protected by a sufficient concentration of warships to keep submarines away. The United States navy, which,
unlike the army, was of considerable size and ready for combat, supplied enough additional force to the Allies to make convoying and other antisubmarine measures highly
effective. By the end of 1917 the submarine was no more than a nuisance. For the Germans the great plan produced the anticipated penalty without the reward—its net result
was only to add America to their enemies.

On the western front in 1917, while the Americans desperately got
themselves ready for the war they had entered, the French and British continued to hold the line. The French, finding in General Nivelle a commander who still believed in the breakthrough, launched an offensive so

*The French and
British hold the line*

unsuccessful and so bloody that mutiny spread through the French army. Pétain replaced
Nivelle and restored discipline to the exhausted and disillusioned soldiers, but he had no
thought of further attack. "I am waiting for the Americans and the tanks," he said. The
British then assumed the main burden. For three months late in 1917 they fought the dismal battle of Passchendaele. They advanced five miles, near Ypres, at a cost of 400,000
men. At the very end of 1917 the British surprised the Germans with a raid by 380 tanks,
which penetrated deep into the German lines, but were obliged to withdraw, since no
reserve of fresh infantry was at hand to exploit their success.

Meanwhile the Austro-Hungarians, strongly reinforced by German troops, overwhelmed the Italians at the disastrous battle of Caporetto. The Central Powers streamed
into northern Italy, but the Italians, with British and French reinforcements, were able to
hold the line. The net effect of the campaigns of 1917 and of the repulse of the submarine
at the same time was to reemphasize the stalemate in Europe, incline the weary Allies to
await the Americans, and give the Americans what they most needed—time.

The Americans made good use of the time given them. Conscription, which was democratically called selective service, was adopted immediately after the declaration of war.
The United States army, whose professionals in 1916 numbered only
130,000, performed the mammoth feat of turning over 3.5 million civilians
into soldiers. With the navy, the United States came to have over 4 million
in its armed services (which may be compared with over 12 million in the

*America mobilizes for
war*

Second World War). Aid flowed to the Allies. To the loans already made
through private bankers were added some $10 billion lent by the American government
itself. The Allies used the money mainly to buy food and munitions in the United States.
American farms and factories, which had already prospered by selling to the Allies during
the period of neutrality, now broke all records for production. Civilian industry was converted to war uses; radiator factories turned out guns, and piano factories manufactured
airplane wings. Every possible means was employed to build up ocean shipping, without
which neither American supplies nor American armies could reach the theater of war.
Available shipping was increased from one million to ten million tons.

Civilian consumption was drastically reduced. Eight thousand tons of steel were
saved in the manufacture of women's corsets and 75,000 tons of tin were spared in the
making of children's toy wagons. Every week people observed meatless Tuesday, and
sugar was rationed. Daylight-saving time, invented in Europe during the war, was introduced to save coal. By such means the United States made enormous stocks available for
its Allies as well as itself, though for some items, notably airplanes and artillery ammunition, the American armies, when they reached France, drew heavily on British and French
manufactures.

The Final Phase of the War

The Germans, as we have seen, victorious in the east, opened a great final offensive in the west in the spring of 1918, hoping to force a decision before American participation turned the balance forever. To oppose it, a unity of command was achieved for the first time when a French general, Ferdinand Foch, was made commander in chief of all Allied forces in France, with the national commanders subordinate to him, including Pershing for the Americans. In June the Germans first made contact with American troops in significant force, meeting the Second Division at Château-Thierry. The German position was so favorable that civilians in the German government thought it opportune to make a last effort at a compromise peace. The military, headed by Hindenburg and Ludendorff, successfully blocked any such attempts; they preferred one final gamble. The German armies reached their farthest advance on July 15 along the Marne.

There were now nine American divisions in the Allied line. Foch used them to spearhead his counterattack on July 18. The badly overstrained Germans began to falter. Over 250,000 American troops were now landing in France every month. The final Allied offensive which opened in September, with American troops in the Argonne occupying an eastern sector, proved more than the Germans could withstand. The German High Command notified its government that it could not win the war. The German foreign office made peace overtures to President Wilson. An armistice was arranged, and on November 11, 1918, firing ceased on the western front.

The armistice

Since Germany's allies had surrendered during the preceding weeks, the deadly, grinding battles were finally over, but the war continued to affect almost every aspect of European politics and society. The horror it brought to individual lives cannot be told by statistics, which dryly report that almost 10 million men had been killed and 20 million had been wounded. Each of the European Great Powers (except Italy) lost from one million to two million in killed alone. The United States, with some 330,000 casualties of all types (of whom 115,000 died) lost in the entire war fewer men than the main combatants had lost in such a single battle as Verdun or Passchendaele. American assistance was decisive in the defeat of Germany. It came late in the war, when the others had been struggling for almost four years, so that the mere beginnings of American military action were enough to turn the scale. On the date of the armistice there were two million American soldiers in France, and another million were on the way. But the American army had really been in combat only four months. During the whole year 1918, out of every hundred artillery shells that were fired by the three Allied armies, the French fired 51, the British fired 43, and the Americans fired only 6.

The war was thus less costly for the United States than for any of the other major military powers. About 50,000 Americans were killed in battle. Most other deaths were caused by disease, including the deadly influenza epidemic of 1918—which killed as many as 43,000 U.S. soldiers over several months. The horrible toll of military deaths in all countries during the World War was actually far surpassed in 1918–1919 by the worldwide influenza pandemic that caused at least 50 million deaths across the globe. A virulent new strain of virus (called the Spanish flu) was the source of the disease, and some historians now believe that perhaps up to 100 million persons died as it moved through much of Africa, Latin America, and Asia as well as Europe and North America. This rapidly spreading pandemic became one of the most deadly events in all of world history, and it added to the profound sense of loss that affected people everywhere after the Great War.

These American soldiers were part of the divisions that began to arrive in France during 1917, but the American military presence did not become significant until the following year. The steady arrival of fresh troops from the United States enabled the Allied commanders to launch a decisive final offensive and forced the German high command to recognize that Germany could not win the war.

(Getty Images)

87. THE COLLAPSE OF THE AUSTRIAN AND GERMAN EMPIRES

The war proved as fatal to the German and Austro-Hungarian empires as to the Russian. The subject nationalities in the Austro-Hungarian Empire, or the "national councils" representing them in the Western capitals, obtained recognition from the Allies, and in October 1918 declared their independence. The last Habsburg emperor, Charles I, abdicated on November 12, and on the next day Austria was proclaimed a republic, as was Hungary in the following week. Before any peace conference could convene, the new states of Czechoslovakia, Yugoslavia, an enlarged Romania, a republican Hungary, and a miniature republican Austria were in existence by their own action.

Nationalities gain independence

The German Empire stood solid until the closing weeks. Liberals, democrats, and socialists had lately begun to press for peace and democratization. Yet it was the High

Command itself that precipitated the debacle. In the last years of the war dictatorial powers had become concentrated in the hands of General Ludendorff, and in September 1918 only he and his closest military associates realized that the German cause was hopeless. On September 29, at supreme headquarters at Spa in Belgium, Ludendorff informed the Kaiser that Germany must ask for peace. He urged that a new government be formed in Berlin reflecting the majority in the Reichstag, on democratic, parliamentary principles.

In calling for immediate peace negotiations, he seems to have had two ideas in mind. First, he might win time to regroup his armies and prepare a new offensive. Or if collapse became unavoidable, then the civilian or democratic elements in Germany would be the ones to sue for peace.

The liberal Prince Max of Baden was found to head a cabinet in which even socialists were included. In October various reforms were enacted, the Bismarckian system was ended, and Germany became a liberal constitutional monarchy. These changes served the purpose of Ludendorff and other generals because the German military caste, at the moment of Germany's crisis, was more eager to save the army than to save the empire. The army must never admit surrender; that was an affair for small men in business suits. Emperor, High Command, officers, and aristocrats were unloading frantically upon civilians.

President Wilson unwittingly played into their hands. Speaking now as the chief of the Allied coalition, the one to whom peace overtures were first made, he insisted that the German government must become more democratic. It may be recalled how Bismarck, after defeating France in 1871, demanded a general election in France before making peace. Wilson, unlike Bismarck, really believed in democracy; but in a practical way his position was the same. He wanted to be sure that he was dealing with the German people rather than with a discredited elite. He wanted it to be the real Germany that applied for and accepted the Allied terms. In Germany, as realization of the military disaster spread, many people began to regard the Kaiser as an obstacle to peace. Or they felt that Germany would obtain better terms if it appeared before the Allies as a republic. Even the officer corps, to halt the fighting before the army disintegrated, began to talk of abdication. Sailors mutinied at Kiel on November 3, and councils of workers and soldiers were formed in various cities. The socialists threatened to withdraw from the newly formed cabinet (that is, go into opposition and end the representative nature of the new government) unless William II abdicated. A general strike, led by minority socialists and syndicalists, began on November 9. "Abdication," Prince Max told the emperor, "is a dreadful thing, but a government without the socialists would be a worse danger for the country." William II abdicated on November 9, and slipped across the frontier into Holland, where despite cries to try him as a "war criminal" he lived quietly until his death in 1941. Germany was proclaimed a republic on the day he abdicated. Two days later the war stopped.

Democracy in Germany

The fall of the empire in Germany, with the consequent adoption of the republic, did not arise from deep revolutionary action or change of basic sentiment in the German people. It was an episode of the war. The republic (soon called the Weimar Republic) arose because the victorious enemy demanded it, because the German people craved peace, because they wished to avoid forcible revolution, and because the old German military class, to save its face and its future strength, wished at least temporarily to be excused. When the war ended, the German army was still in France, its discipline and organization still apparently unimpaired. No hostile shot had been fired on German soil. It was said later, by some, that the army had not been defeated, that it had been "stabbed in the back" by a dissolving civilian home front. This was untrue; it was the panic-stricken Ludendorff who first cried

The Weimar Republic

for "democracy." But the circumstances in which the German republic originated made its later history, and hence all later history, very troubled.

✒ 88.   THE ECONOMIC, SOCIAL, AND CULTURAL IMPACT OF THE WAR

Effects on Capitalism: Government-Regulated Economies

European society was forced by the First World War into many basic changes that were to prove more lasting than the war itself. First of all, the war profoundly affected capitalism as previously known. Essential to the older capitalism (or economic liberalism, or free private enterprise) had been the idea that government should leave business alone, or at the most regulate certain general conditions under which businesses went about their affairs. Before 1914 governments had increasingly entered the economic field. They had put up tariffs, protected national industries, searched for markets or raw materials by imperialist expansion, or passed protective social legislation to benefit the wage-earning classes. During the war all belligerent governments controlled the economic system far more minutely. Indeed, the idea of the "planned economy" was first applied in the First World War as the warring states attempted to direct all the wealth, resources, and moral purpose of their societies to a single end.

The "planned economy"

Since no one had expected a long war, no one had made any plans for industrial mobilization. Everything had to be improvised. By 1916 each government had set up a system of boards, bureaus, councils, and commissions to coordinate its war effort. The aim was to see that all labor was effectively utilized and that all natural resources within the country, and all that could possibly be imported, were employed where they would do the most good. In the stress of war free competition was found to be wasteful; undirected private enterprise was found to be too uncertain and too slow. The profit motive came into disrepute. Those who exploited shortages to make big profits were stigmatized as profiteers. Production for civilian use, or for mere luxury purposes, was cut to a minimum. Businesses were not allowed to set up or close down factories as they chose. It was impossible to start a new business without government approval, because the flotation of stocks and bonds was controlled and raw materials were made available only as the government permitted. It was equally impossible to shut down a business engaged in war production. If a factory was inefficient or unprofitable, the government kept it going anyway, making up the losses, so that in some cases management came to expect government support. Here too the tests of competition and profitability were abandoned.

The "rationalization" of production

The new goal was coordination or "rationalization" of production in the interests of the country as a whole. Labor was discouraged from protesting against hours or wage scales, and the big unions generally agreed to refrain from strikes. For the upper and middle classes it became embarrassing to show their comforts too openly. It was patriotic to eat meagerly and to wear old clothes. War gave a new impetus even to the idea of economic equality, if only to enlist rich and poor alike in a common cause.

Military conscription was the first step in the allocation of manpower. Draft boards told some men to report to the army, granting exemptions to others to work safely in war industries. Given the casualty rates at the front, state determination over individual life could hardly go farther. With the insatiable need

The allocation of manpower

for troops, drawing in men originally exempted or at first rejected as physically inadequate, great numbers of women poured into factories and offices, and in Britain even into
newly organized women's branches of the armed forces. Women took over many jobs
which it had been thought only men could do. Women did not remain in the labor force
after the war in such large numbers, most making way for the returning veterans; but the
wartime experience in this and the Second World War was part of the social transition by
which the labor force in all countries was enlarged, women's place in modern society was
revolutionized, and the lives and outlook of millions of individual women were turned
more actively toward participation in national economies. The First World War thus contributed to the redefinition or reorganization of women's work — a social process that had
begun in the early Industrial Revolution and that would be intensified during the Second
World War and in the years that followed.

During the war governments did not directly force men or women to drop one job
and take another. There was no systematic labor conscription except in Germany. But by
influencing wage scales, granting draft exemptions, forcing some industries to expand
and others to contract or stand still, and propagandizing the idea that work in an arms
factory was patriotic, the state shifted vast numbers of workers to war production.
Impressed or "slave" labor was not used in the First World War, nor were prisoners of
war obliged to give labor service, though there were some abuses of these rules of international law by the Germans, who were possibly the least scrupulous and certainly the
most hard-pressed.

Export controls

Governments controlled all foreign trade. It was intolerable to let private citizens ship off the country's resources at their own whim. It was
equally intolerable to let them use up foreign exchange by importing
unneeded goods or to drive up prices of necessities by competing with one another. Foreign trade became a state monopoly, in which private firms operated under strict licenses
and quotas. The greatest of the exporting countries was the United States, whose annual
exports rose from $2 billion to $6 billion between 1914 and 1918. The endless demand for
American farm and factory products naturally drove up prices, which, however, were fixed
by law in 1917, for the most important items.

As for the European Allies, which even before the war had exported less than they
imported and were now exporting as little as possible, they could make purchases in the
United States only by enormous loans from the American government. British and
French citizens, under pressure from their own governments, sold off their American
stocks and bonds, which were bought up by Americans. The former owners received
pounds sterling or francs from their own governments, which in return took and spent the
dollars paid by the new American owners. In this way the United States ceased to be a
debtor country (it had owed some $4 billion to Europeans in 1914), and became the
world's leading creditor country. By 1919 Europeans were in debt to the United States by
about $10 billion.

Shipping and imports

The Allies controlled the sea, but they never had enough shipping to meet rising
demands, especially with German submarines taking a steady though fluctuating toll. Each government set up a shipping board to expand shipbuilding at any cost and to assign available shipping space to whatever
purposes — troop movements, rubber imports, foodstuffs — the government
considered most urgent in view of overall plans. Control and allocation eventually became
international under the Interallied Shipping Council, of which the United States was a
member after entering the war. In England and France, where all manufactures depended

The need for workers during the First World War opened opportunities for women in jobs that were traditionally open only to men. These German women, who were working in an armaments factory in 1917, exemplified this trend in the workforce and also the general mobilization of an entire population to serve the demands of modern warfare.
(akg-images)

on imports, government control of shipping and hence of imports was itself enough to give control over the whole economy.

Germany, denied access to the sea and also to Russia and western Europe, was obliged to adopt unprecedented measures of self-sufficiency. The Germans went with less food than other belligerents. Their government controls became more thorough and more efficient, producing what they called "war socialism." In Walter Rathenau they found a man with the necessary ideas. He was a Jewish industrialist, son of the head of the German electrical trust. One of the first to foresee a long war, he launched a program for the mobilization of raw materials. Early in the war it seemed that Germany might be soon defeated by lack of nitrogen, necessary to make explosives. Rathenau sweepingly requisitioned every conceivable natural source, including the very manure from the farmers' barnyards, until German chemists succeeded in extracting nitrogen from the air. The German chemical industry developed many other substitute products, such as synthetic rubber. German production was organized into war companies, one for each line of industry, with private business firms working under close government supervision.

German "war socialism"

The other belligerent governments also replaced competition between individual firms and factories with coordination. Consortiums of industrialists in France allocated raw materials and government orders within each industry. The War Industries Board did the same in the United States. In Britain, similar methods became so efficient that by 1918, for example, the country produced every two weeks as many shells as in the whole first year of the war and turned out 70 times as much heavy artillery.

Inflation, Industrial Changes, Control of Ideas

No government, even by heavy taxes, could raise all the funds it needed except by printing paper money, selling huge bond issues, or obliging banks to grant it credit. The result, given heavy demand and acute shortages, was rapid inflation of prices. Prices and wages were regulated but were never again so low as before 1914. The hardest hit by this development were those whose money income could not easily be augmented—people living on supposedly safe investments, those drawing annual salaries, professional people, government employees. These classes had been one of the most stabilizing influences in Europe before the war. Everywhere the war threatened their status, prestige, and standard of living. The huge national debts meant higher taxes for years to come. The debt was most

Mortgaging the future

serious when it was owed to a foreign country. During the war the Continental Allies borrowed from Britain, and they and the British both borrowed from the United States. They thereby mortgaged their future. To pay the debt, they were bound for years to export more than they imported—or, roughly, to produce more than they consumed. It may be recalled that in 1914 every advanced European country habitually imported more than it exported. That fact, basic to the European standard of life, was now threatened with reversal.

Industry spreads

Moreover, with Europe torn by war for four years, the rest of the world accelerated its own industrialization. The productive capacity of the United States increased immensely. The Japanese began to sell in China, in India, and in South America the cotton textiles and other civilian goods which these countries for the time being could not obtain from Europe. Argentina and Brazil, unable to get locomotive parts or mining machinery from England, created their own industries to manufacture such items for themselves. In India the Tata family, controlling $250 million of native Indian capital, developed numerous manufacturing enterprises, one of which became the largest iron and steel works in the British Empire. With Germany entirely out of the world market, with Britain and France producing desperately for their armies, and with the world's shipping commandeered for war uses, the position of western Europe as the world's workshop was undermined. After the war Europe had new competitors. The economic foundations of the nineteenth century had slipped away. The age of European supremacy was in its twilight.

All the belligerent governments during the war attempted to control ideas as they did economic production. Freedom of thought, respected everywhere in Europe for half a century, was discarded. Propaganda and censorship became more effective than any government, however despotic, had ever been able to devise. No one was allowed to sow doubt by raising any basic questions.

It must be remembered that the facts of the prewar crises, as related above, were then largely unknown. People were trapped in a nightmare whose causes they could not comprehend. Each side wildly charged the other with having started the war from

Propaganda and public opinion

pure malevolence. The long attrition, the fruitless fighting, the unchanging battle lines, and the appalling casualties were a severe ordeal to morale. Civilians, deprived of their usual liberties, working harder, eating dull food, seeing no victory, had to be kept emotionally at a high pitch. Placards, posters, diplomatic white papers, schoolbooks, public lectures, solemn editorials, and slanted news reports conveyed the message. The new mass press and the new motion pictures proved to be ideal media for the direction of popular thinking. Intellectuals and professors advanced complicated reasons, usually historical, for loathing and crushing the enemy. In

Every nation in the First World War used propaganda posters to rally public support, recruit soldiers, and show the evil actions of the enemy. The picture on the left is an Austrian postcard with the typical image of a soldier defending the "Fatherland, Family, and Future." The child represents the nation's future. The poster on the right portrays the female symbol of the French Republic, Marianne, who is calling on the French to buy war bonds "for the flag and for victory." This money will support the soldiers who stand behind Marianne and defend the French nation.

(Left: akg-images; right: Corbis)

Allied countries the Kaiser was portrayed as a demon, with glaring eyes and abnormally bristling mustaches, bent on the mad project of conquest of the world. In Germany people were taught to dread the day when Cossacks and Senegalese should rape German women and to hate England as the inveterate enemy which inhumanly starved little children with its blockade. Each side convinced itself that all right was on its side and all wrong, wickedness, and barbarity were on the other. An inflamed opinion helped to sustain men and women in such a fearsome struggle. But when it came time to make peace the rooted convictions, fixed ideas, profound aversions, hates, and fears became an obstacle to political judgment.

Cultural Pessimism

We have seen how many European intellectuals in the decades before 1914 began to question the theories of classical liberalism and to celebrate the social value of human struggle

Wilfred Owen, pictured here in his army uniform, was one of the English war poets who described the horrors of the First World War. He was killed in France, one week before the armistice in November 1918.
(Imperial War Museum, London (Q79045))

and violence. Such ideas, widely disseminated by popular writers and intellectuals, contributed to the public enthusiasm that accompanied each nation's entry into the Great War. Indeed, some of the best-known younger writers, including Charles Péguy in France and Rupert Brooke in England, went off to die in the early battles, leaving literary testaments about the spiritual nobility of sacrifices for the nation. But as the war dragged on through more than four murderous years, much of the early literary patriotism turned into cynicism, pessimism, and despair. By 1918, famous war poets such as Siegfried Sassoon and Wilfred Owen were condemning the horrors of a senseless war and mocking the propaganda that flowed from every national government. Irony and bitterness became pervasive themes in the creative works of post–World War I European culture.

War poets

The war's most widespread cultural consequence thus emerged in new forms of cultural pessimism. The psychological studies of Sigmund Freud, for example, increasingly emphasized the raw power of human aggression—what Freud began to call the death instinct—which could never be completely tamed in even the most advanced modern societies. His famous postwar book, *Civilization and its Discontents,* offered pessimistic descriptions of the endless struggle between humanity's deep irrational drives and civilized moral standards, a struggle in which the unconscious instincts of both individuals and social groups seemed constantly to overwhelm the precarious defenses of civilization. A different kind of pessimism appeared in the influential work of Oswald Spengler, the German philosopher-historian whose book *The Decline of the West* (1918) became a best-selling account of how Western civilization had fallen into crisis and decay. Drawing on cyclical theories of life and

Freud and Spengler

death, Spengler traced the history of the West from its energetic youth (the Renaissance) to a creative middle passage (the eighteenth century) to a declining old age (the twentieth century). Spengler's historical theories, so alien to the nineteenth-century liberal confidence in Western progress and expansion, attracted attention far beyond Germany because they offered explanations for events that seemed otherwise to be simply chaotic and absurd.

This sense of a crisis in Western culture spread also through new literary and artistic movements, most notably perhaps, in the nonsensical productions of Dadaism. The Dada movement, developing in Switzerland after 1915 and promoted by the poet Tristan Tzara, rejected the structures of traditional literature and generated nihilistic criticisms of Western rationality, aesthetic ideals, and social conventions. After a brief moment of postwar popularity in Paris, Dadaism vanished from the scene, but its fascination with irrational impulses, "spontaneous" writing, and strange dreams passed into the more enduring ideas of Surrealism. Meanwhile, even the most sober-minded European authors believed that the war had exposed a sickness in the heart of European civilization. The great German writer Thomas Mann, for example, set his postwar novel *The Magic Mountain* within a Swiss sanatorium, where everyone is ill and where tubercular characters from all parts of Europe debate the flawed traditions of Western civilization. And the Irish poet W. B. Yeats, also seeing that something in Europe had gone terribly wrong, summarized the anxiety of a whole generation in his famous poem "The Second Coming" (1919):

Tzara, Mann, Yeats

> *Mere anarchy is loosed upon the World,*
> *The blood-dimmed tide is loosed, and everywhere*
> *The ceremony of innocence is drowned;*
> *The best lack all conviction, while the worst*
> *Are full of passionate intensity.*

89. THE PEACE OF PARIS, 1919

The late ally, Russia, was in the hands of the Bolsheviks by 1919, ostracized like a leper colony, and taking no part in international relations. The late German and Austro-Hungarian empires were already defunct, and more or less revolutionary regimes struggled to replace them. New republics already existed along the Baltic coast, in Poland, and in the Danube basin but without effective governments or acknowledged frontiers. Europe east of France and Italy was in a state approaching chaos, with revolution on the Russian style threatening. Western Europe was wrenched out of all resemblance to its former self. The Allied blockade of Germany continued. In these circumstances the victors assembled in Paris, in the bleak winter of 1919, to reconstruct the world. During 1919 they signed five treaties, all named after Paris suburbs—St.-Germain with Austria, Trianon with Hungary, Neuilly with Bulgaria, Sèvres with Turkey (1920), and most especially, with Germany the Treaty of Versailles.

The world looked with awe and expectation to one man—the president of the United States. Woodrow Wilson occupied a lone eminence and enjoyed a universal prestige. Victors, vanquished, and neutrals admitted that American intervention had decided the conflict. Everywhere people who had been long tried, confused, bereaved, were stirred by Wilson's thrilling language in favor of a higher cause, of a great concert of right in which peace would be forever

Woodrow Wilson

secure and the world itself would be at last free. Wilson reached Europe in January 1919, visiting several Allied capitals. He was wildly acclaimed, and almost mobbed, greeted as the man who would lead civilization out of its wasteland.

The Fourteen Points and the Treaty of Versailles

Wilson's views were well known. He had stated them in January 1918 in his Fourteen Points—principles upon which, after victory, peace was to be established. The Fourteen Points demanded an end to secret treaties and secret diplomacy (or in Wilsonian language, "open covenants openly arrived at"); freedom of the seas "alike in peace and in war"; removal of barriers and inequalities in international trade; reduction of armaments by all powers; colonial readjustments; evacuation of occupied territory; self-determination of nationalities and a redrawing of European boundaries along national lines; and, last but not least, an international political organization to prevent war. On the whole, Wilson stood for the fruition of the democratic, liberal, progressive, and nationalistic movements of the century past, for the ideals of the Enlightenment, the French Revolution, and the revolutions of 1848. As Wilson saw it, and as many believed, the World War should end in a new type of treaty. There was thought to be something sinister about peace conferences of the past, for example, the Congress of Vienna of 1815. The old diplomacy was blamed for leading to war. Lenin in his own way and for his own purposes was saying this in Russia too. It was felt that treaties had too long been wrongly based on a politics of power or on unprincipled deals and bargains made without regard to the people concerned. Democracy having defeated the Central Powers, people hoped that a new settlement, made in a democratic age, might be reached by general agreement in an atmosphere of mutual confidence. There was a real sense that a new political era was dawning.

A new era

Wilson had had some difficulty, however, in persuading the Allied governments to accept his Fourteen Points. The French demanded a guarantee of German payment for war damages. The British vetoed the freedom of the seas "in peace and war"; it was naval rivalry that had estranged them from Germany, and they had fought the war to preserve British command of the sea. But with these two reservations the Allies expressed their willingness to follow Wilson's lead. The Germans who asked for the armistice believed that peace would be made along the lines of the Fourteen Points with only the two modifications described. In addition, the socialists and democrats now trying to rule Germany thought that having overthrown the Kaiser and the war lords, they would be treated by the victors with moderation and that a new democratic Germany would reemerge to take its rightful place in the world.

Twenty-seven nations assembled at Paris in January 1919, but the full or plenary sessions were unimportant. Matters were decided by conferences among the Big Four—Wilson himself, Lloyd George for England, Clemenceau for France, Orlando for Italy. The conjunction of personalities was not a happy one. Wilson was stern and stubbornly righteous; Lloyd George, a fiery and unpredictable Welshman; Clemenceau, an aged patriot, the "tiger of France," who had been politically active since the Franco-Prussian War of 1870; Orlando, a passing phenomenon of Italian politics. None of them was especially equipped for the task in hand. Clemenceau was a pronounced nationalist, Lloyd George had always been concerned with domestic reforms, Orlando was by training a professor like Wilson, and Wilson, a former college president, imbued with a sense of mission, lacked concrete knowledge of peoples other than his own. However, they democratically represented the governments and peoples of their respective countries, and thus spoke with an authority denied to professional diplomats of the old school.

CHRONOLOGY OF NOTABLE EVENTS, 1879–1920

1879	Germany signs military alliance with Austria-Hungary
1894	France and Russia create the Franco-Russian alliance
1904	France and Britain establish close relations in the *entente cordiale*
1905	Germany challenges French-English relations by calling for Moroccan independence from France
1912–1913	Two Balkan wars contribute to Serbian and Russian hostility toward Austria
June 1914	Austrian Archduke Francis Ferdinand is assassinated by Bosnian terrorist in Sarajevo
August 1914	Germany declares war on Russia and France; England declares war on Germany
September 1914	Battle of the Marne stops German advance in France and leads to trench warfare on the Western front
1916	Battles of Verdun and the Somme confirm military stalemate in France
March 1917	Revolution in Russia overthrows Tsar Nicholas II; provisional government takes power and continues the war
April 1917	United States declares war on Germany
November 1917	Britain issues "Balfour Declaration," promising support for a Jewish homeland in Palestine
March 1918	Treaty of Brest-Litovsk ends war between Russia and Germany
November 1918	Collapse of German and Austrian Empires
November 1918	Armistice ends the fighting on the Western Front
March 1919	Western Allies complete the Versailles Treaty, creating new nations in eastern Europe; Germany is charged with "war guilt" and reparations
1920	Treaty of Sèvres breaks up the Ottoman Empire and leads to French and British "mandates" in Middle East

Wilson first fought a hard battle for a League of Nations, a permanent international body in which all nations, without sacrificing their sovereignty, should meet together to discuss and settle disputes, each promising
A League of Nations
not to resort to war. Few European statesmen had any confidence in such a League. But they yielded to Wilson, and the covenant of the League of Nations was written into the treaty with Germany. In return, Wilson had to make concessions to Lloyd George, Clemenceau, Orlando, and the Japanese. He was thus obliged to compromise the idealism of the Fourteen Points. Probably compromise and bargaining would have been necessary anyway, for such general principles as national self-determination and colonial readjustment invariably led to differences of opinion in concrete cases. Wilson allowed himself to believe that if a League of Nations were established and operating, faults in the treaty could later be corrected at leisure by international discussion.

A special kind of disagreement arose over the covenant of the League. Wilson wished to include a clause endorsing religious freedom. The Japanese insisted that it be broadened to condemn racial discrimination as well. The Americans and British were opposed to the latter for fear that an international authority might interfere with their immigration practices. In the end both proposals were abandoned.

The great demand of the French at the peace conference was for security against Germany. On this subject the French were almost rabid. The war in the West had been fought almost entirely on their soil. To trim Germany down more nearly to French size, they proposed that the part of Germany west of the Rhine be set up as an independent state under Allied auspices. Wilson and Lloyd George objected, sagely observing that the resulting German resentment would only lead to another war. The French yielded, but only on condition that they obtain their security in another way, namely, by a promise from both Britain and the United States to join them immediately if they were again attacked by the Germans. An Anglo-French-American guarantee treaty, with these provisions, was in fact

Alsace and Lorraine

signed at Paris. France obtained control over the Saar coal mines for 15 years; during that time, a League commission would administer the Saar territory and in 1935 a plebiscite would be held. Lorraine and Alsace were returned to France. German fortifications and troops were banned from a wide belt in the Rhineland. Allied troops would occupy the Rhineland for 15 years to ensure German compliance with the treaty.

In eastern Europe the Allies wished to set up strong buffer states against Bolshevism in Russia. Sympathies with Poland ran high. Those parts of the former German Empire that were inhabited by Poles, or by mixed populations of Poles and Germans—Posen and West Prussia—were assigned to the new Polish state. This gave Poland a corridor to the sea, but at the same time cut off the bulk of Germany from East Prussia. Danzig, an old German town, became a free city, belonging to no country. Upper Silesia, a rich mining country, went to Poland after a disputed plebiscite. In Austria and among the Sudeten Germans of Bohemia, now that there was no longer a Habsburg empire (whose existence had blocked an all-German union in 1848 and also a few years later in the time of Bismarck), a feeling developed for annexation to the new German republic. But the feeling was unorganized, and in any case the Allies naturally refused to make Germany bigger than it had been in 1914. Austria remained a dwarf republic; and Vienna, a former imperial capital cut off from its empire—a head severed from its body and scarcely more capable of sustaining life. The Sudeten Germans became disgruntled citizens of the new state of Czechoslovakia.

Germany loses its colonies

Germany lost all its colonies. Wilson and the South African General Smuts, to preserve the principle of internationalism against any imputation of raw conquest, saw to it that the colonies were actually awarded to the League of Nations. The League, under "mandates," then assigned them to various powers for administration. In this way France and Great Britain divided the best of the African colonies; the Belgian Congo was slightly enlarged; and the Union of South Africa took over German Southwest Africa. In the colonial world, Italy got nothing. Japan received the mandate for the German Pacific islands north of the equator; Australia, for German New Guinea and the Solomon Islands; New Zealand, for German Samoa. The Japanese claimed rights over the German concessions in China. The Chinese at the Paris conference tried to get all special concessions and extraterritorial rights in China abolished. No one listened to such proposals. By a compromise, Japan received about half the former German rights. The Japanese were dissatisfied, and the Chinese walked out of the conference. Meanwhile, the young Vietnamese nationalist Ho Chi Minh, who was then living in Paris, wanted Wilson to recognize that France was violating the principles of national self-determination in Indochina, but such criticisms of European colonialism were ignored at Versailles.

The Allies took over the German fleet, but the German crews, rather than surrender it, solemnly scuttled it at Scapa Flow. The German army was limited to 100,000. Since the Allies forbade conscription, or the annual training of successive groups of young civilians, the army became exclusively professional, the officer class retained political influence in it, and the means used by the Allies to demilitarize Germany served if anything the contrary purpose. The treaty forbade Germany to have any heavy artillery, aviation, or submarines. Wilson saw his plan for universal disarmament applied to Germany alone.

The French, even before the armistice, had stipulated that Germany must pay for war damages. The other Allies made the same demand. Wilson, at the conference, was stupefied at the size of the bills presented. The Belgians suggested, for their own share, a sum larger than the entire wealth of all Belgium according to officially published Belgian statistics. The French and British proposed to *War damages* charge Germany with the entire expenses, including war pensions, incurred by them during the war. Wilson observed that "total" reparation, while not strictly unjust, was absolutely impossible, and even Clemenceau noted that "to ask for over a trillion francs would lead to nothing practical." The insistence on enormous reparations was in fact largely emotional. No one knew or considered how Germany would pay, though all dimly realized that such sums could only be made up by German exports, which would then compete with the Allies' own economic interests. The Germans, to avoid worse, even offered to repair physical damages in Belgium and France, but were brusquely refused on the ground that the Belgians and French would thereby lose jobs and business. No monetary total was set for reparations in the treaty; it was made clear that the sum would be very large, but it was left for a future commission to determine. The Allies, maddened by the war and themselves loaded with fantastic debts to the United States, had no desire to listen to economic reason and regarded the reparations as simply another means of righting a wrong and of putting off the dangers of a German revival. As a first payment on the reparations account the treaty required Germany to surrender most of its merchant marine, make coal deliveries, and give up all property owned by German private citizens abroad. This last proviso ended Germany's prewar career as an exporter of capital.

It was with the specific purpose of justifying the reparations that the famous "war guilt" clause was written into the treaty. By this clause Germany explicitly "accepted the responsibility" for all loss and damage resulting from the war *The "war guilt"* "imposed upon them (the Allies) by the aggression of Germany and her *clause* allies." The Germans themselves felt no such responsibility as they were now obliged formally to accept. They considered their honor as a people to be impugned. The war guilt clause gave a ready opening to agitators in Germany and made even moderate Germans regard the treaty as something to be escaped from as a matter of self-respect.

The Treaty of Versailles was completed in three months. The absence of the Russians, the decision not to give the Germans a hearing, and the *The Treaty of* willingness of Wilson to make concessions in return for obtaining the *Versailles* League of Nations, made it possible to dispose of intricate matters with considerable facility. The Germans, when presented with the completed document in May 1919, refused to sign. The Allies threatened a renewal of hostilities. A government crisis ensued in Berlin. No German wished to damn himself, his party, or his principles, in German eyes, by putting his name to a document which all Germans regarded as outrageous. A combination drawn from the Social Democratic and Catholic parties finally consented to shoulder the hateful burden. Two abashed and virtually

These four men represented the leading Allied powers at the Versailles peace conference in 1918: (from left to right) Vittorio Emanuele Orlando of Italy, David Lloyd George of Great Britain, Georges Clemenceau of France, and Woodrow Wilson of the United States. Neither the Germans nor the Russians were represented at Versailles. The decisions of the peace conference, including a "war guilt" clause that blamed Germany for the recent war, produced deep resentments among the excluded peoples.
(Corbis)

unknown representatives appeared at the Hall of Mirrors at Versailles and signed the treaty for Germany in the presence of a large concourse of Allied dignitaries.

The other treaties drafted by the Paris conference, in conjunction with the Versailles treaty, laid out a new map for eastern Europe and registered the recession of the Russian, Austrian, and Turkish empires. Seven new independent states now existed: Finland, Estonia, Latvia, Lithuania, Poland, Czechoslovakia, and Yugoslavia. Romania was enlarged by adding areas formerly Hungarian and Russian; Greece was enlarged at the expense of Turkey. Austria and Hungary were now small states, and there was no connection between them. The belt of states from Finland to Romania was regarded as a *cordon sanitaire,* a quarantine zone, to prevent the infection of Europe by communism. The creation of Yugoslavia (or the Kingdom of the Serbs, Croats, and Slovenes, as it was called until 1929), although dominated by the Serbs and under the Serbian monarchy, seemed to fulfill the aims of the South Slav movement which had set off the fatal crisis of 1914. The fact, however, that Italy received Trieste and some of the Dalmatian Islands (in keeping with the secret treaty of 1915) left the more ambitious South Slavs discontented.

The treaty of Sèvres transformed the political order in the Middle East. The Ottoman Empire completely disappeared. Turkey emerged as a republic confined to Asia Minor and the area around Constantinople, but most other people in the former Empire fell under the control of France or Britain. Syria and Lebanon went to France as mandates of the League of Nations. Palestine and Iraq went to Great Britain on the same basis, though the British had to suppress strong nationalist resistance in Iraq before they could establish a cooperative government under the ruler they had chosen, King Faisal. The Kingdom of Hejaz in Arabia was recognized as an independent state; by 1924, however, it fell under the control of what was to become the kingdom of Saudi Arabia. In general, the breakup of the Ottoman Empire left a vast area of the Middle East unsettled. Indeed, the complex legacy of the Ottoman Empire as well as the British and French mandates continued to shape the internal conflicts and wars in this region down through the early years of the twenty-first century.

Significance of the Paris Peace Settlement

The most general principle of the Paris settlement was to recognize the right of national self-determination, at least in Europe. Each European people or nation, as defined by language, was in principle set up with its own *National self-determination* sovereign and independent national state. Czechoslovakia, a special case, had two national components, as its originally hyphenated name Czecho-Slovakia made clear. Nationalism triumphed in the belief that it went along naturally with liberalism and democracy. It must be added that the peacemakers at Paris had little choice in this matter, for the new states had already declared their independence. Since in eastern Europe the nationalities were in many places intermixed, and since the peacemakers did not contemplate the actual movement and exchange of populations to sort them out, each new state found alien minorities living within its borders or could claim that people of its own kind still lived in neighboring states under foreign rule. Hence minority problems and irredentism troubled eastern Europe, as they had before 1914. Eventually it was the complaint of Germans in the Sudetenland of Czechoslovakia that they were an oppressed minority, together with the irredentist demand of Germany to join these outlying Germans to the fatherland, that produced the Munich crisis preceding the Second World War.

The Treaty of Versailles was designed to put an end to the German menace. It was not a successful treaty. The wisdom of the treaty has been debated without end, but a few comments may safely be made. For practical purposes, with respect to Germany, the treaty was either too severe or too lenient. It was too severe to conciliate and not severe enough to destroy. *The failure of Versailles* Possibly the victors should have dealt more moderately with the new German republic, which professed their own ideals, as the monarchical victors over Napoleon, in 1814, had dealt moderately with the France of the restored Bourbons, regarding it as a regime akin to their own. As it was, the Allies imposed upon the German Republic about the same terms that they might have imposed upon the German Empire. They innocently played the game of Ludendorff and the German reactionaries; it was the Social Democrats and liberals who bore the "shame" of Versailles. The Germans from the beginning showed no real intention to live up to the treaty. On the other hand, the treaty was not sufficiently disabling to destroy Germany's economic and political strength. Even the degree of severity that it incorporated soon proved to be more than the Allies were willing to enforce.

The treaty makers at Paris in 1919, working hastily and still in the heat of war, under pressure from press and propaganda in their own countries, drafted a set of terms which

Areas Lost by Germany
Areas Lost by Russia
Areas Lost by Ottoman Empire
Austria and Hungary plus Areas Lost by Austro-Hungarian Empire

EUROPE, 1923

The map shows European boundaries between the two World Wars after the Peace of Versailles and certain other agreements. Germany returned Alsace-Lorraine to France and lost the region around Danzig (the "Polish corridor") to Poland. In place of the Austro-Hungarian empire we find the "succession states"—Austria, Hungary, Czechoslovakia, Yugoslavia, and Romania. Poland regained its independence, and Finland and the three Baltic states—Estonia, Latvia, and Lithuania—emerged from the tsarist empire. Most of Ireland became a "free state" in the British Commonwealth of Nations, only Ulster remaining in the United Kingdom. These boundaries lasted until 1938, when Germany annexed Austria and the Sudeten part of Czechoslovakia.

the test of time showed that they themselves did not in the long run wish to impose. As the years passed, many people in Allied countries declared various provisions of the Versailles treaty to be unfair or unworkable. The loss of faith by the Allies in their own treaty only made easier the task of those German agitators who demanded its repudiation. The door was opened for Adolf Hitler.

Victors' uneasiness

Even at the beginning the Allies showed doubts. Lloyd George, in the last weeks before the signing, tardily called for certain amendments, though in vain; for in 1919 British opinion shifted somewhat from fear of Germany to the fear of Bolshevism, and already the idea of using Germany as a bulwark against communism was expressed. The Italians disliked the whole settlement from the beginning; they observed that the spoils of Africa and the Middle East went only to France and Great Britain. The Chinese were also deeply dissatisfied. The Russians, when they reentered the international arena some years later, found a situation that they did not like and had had no part in making. They objected to being faced with a *cordon sanitaire* from Finland to Romania and soon remembered that most of this territory had once belonged to the Russian empire.

The United States never ratified the Treaty of Versailles at all. A wave of isolationism and disgust with Europe spread over the country; and this feeling, together with some rational criticism of the terms and a good deal of party politics, caused the Senate to repudiate Wilson's work. The Senate likewise refused to make any advance promises of military intervention in a future war between Germany and France and hence also declined to ratify the Anglo-French-American guarantee treaty on which Wilson had persuaded Clemenceau to rely. The French considered themselves duped, deprived both of the Rhineland and of the Anglo-American guarantee. They raised more anguished cries over their insecurity. This led them to try to hold Germany down while it was still weak, in turn raising many further complications.

The League of Nations

The League of Nations was established at Geneva. Its mere existence marked a great step beyond the international anarchy before 1914. Wilson's vision did not die. But the United States never joined; Germany was not admitted until 1926, nor was Russia until 1934. The League could handle and dispatch only such business as the Great Powers were willing to allow. It was associated with a West European ascendancy that no longer corresponded to the facts of the world situation. Its covenant was part of the Versailles treaty, and many people in many countries, on both sides in the late war, saw in it not so much a system for international adjudication as a means for maintaining a new status quo in favor of Britain and France.

The First World War dealt a last blow to the ancient institutions of monarchy and aristocratic feudalism. Thrones toppled in Turkey, in Russia, in Austria-Hungary, in the German Empire and the individual German states; and with the kings went the courtly retainers and all the social preeminence and special advantage of the old landed aristocracies. The war was indeed a victory for democracy, though a bitter one. It carried further a process as old as the French and American revolutions. But for the basic problems of modern civilization, industrialism and nationalism, economic security and international stability, it gave no answer. And it left the major European nations much weaker than before to face the rising economic power of the United States, the revolutionary government of the Soviet Union, and the emerging anticolonial movements of Africa and Asia.

For interactive exercises, glossary, chronologies, and more, go to the *Online Learning Center* at **www.mhhe.com/palmer10.**

Chapter 18

THE RUSSIAN
REVOLUTION AND
THE SOVIET UNION

The Russian Revolution became almost as important as the First World War in its influence on later twentieth-century events and global conflicts. Although the war of 1914–1918 was one of the decisive, short-term causes of the revolution, the far-reaching upheaval came also from numerous other social and political problems in Russian society—and the revolutionary ideas of the Bolshevik party attracted followers far beyond Russia itself. The Russian Revolution of 1917 can thus be compared in its historical magnitude with the French Revolution of 1789. Both originated in deep-lying and distant causes, and both made their repercussions felt in many countries for many years. The present chapter will examine the revolutionary process in Russia over half a century. We begin with the old regime before 1900, pass through the two revolutions of 1905 and 1917, and survey the Union of Soviet Socialist Republics down to 1939, at which time a new order had been consolidated under Joseph Stalin, a form of "planned economy" had been realized, and the last of the original revolutionaries, or Old Bolsheviks, either had been silenced or put to death.

The comparison of the Russian Revolution to the French is enlightening in many ways. Both claimed to be movements of liberation—the one against "feudalism" and "despotism"; the other against "capitalism" and "imperialism." Neither was a strictly national movement dealing with merely domestic troubles; both addressed their message to all the world.

French and Russian revolutions

Both attracted followers in all countries. Both aroused a strong reaction on the part of those whose view of life was endangered. And both showed the same pattern of revolutionary politics: a relative unity of opinion so long as the problem was to overthrow the old regime, followed by disunity and conflict over the founding of the new, so that one set

Chapter emblem: Families of soldiers marching in St. Petersburg in 1917 to demand more rations for Russian troops. (SOVFOTO)

of revolutionaries eliminated others, until a small, organized, and determined minority (Jacobin democrats in 1793; Bolshevik communists in 1918) suppressed all opposition in order to defend or advance the revolutionary cause; and in short order (within a matter of months in France; years in Russia), many of the most intensely revolutionary leaders were themselves suppressed or liquidated.

The differences are equally deserving of notice. Relatively speaking, or compared by many criteria with other European countries. Russia in 1900 was in the rear, and France in 1780 in many ways was in the lead. The main strength of the French Revolution lay in the middle classes, who soon managed to prevail over more extreme pressures. In the Russian Revolution middle-class people were also active, especially at first, but they proved unable to cope with mass discontents and succumbed to a more radical party which appealed to workers and peasants. In France the Revolution just "happened," so to speak, in that ordinary people from many walks of life unexpectedly found themselves in a revolutionary situation, and even the Jacobin dictatorship was improvised by individuals who had spent their lives thinking of other things. In Russia professional revolutionaries worked for the revolution long in advance, and the dictatorship of the Bolsheviks realized the plans and preparations of 20 years.

In France the revolution was followed by a reaction in which émigrés returned, dispossessed classes reappeared in politics, and even the Bourbons were restored. The French Revolution was followed by a century of uneasy compromise. The Russian Revolution effectively wiped out its opposition; few émigrés returned; no Romanovs regained their throne. The Russian Revolution was in this sense more immediately successful. But in the long run the differences reemerged. By the 1990s the ideas proclaimed in Russia in 1917 were in ruins, while those proclaimed in France in 1789 were widely accepted—representative constitutional government, equal civil rights under national sovereignty, and legal safeguards for persons and property.

Repercussions of the revolution in Russia

The repercussions of the Russian Revolution were felt widely around the world because of Russia's special position in global politics and economic affairs. Since the days of Peter the Great and before, it had always faced toward both Europe and Asia. It was European, yet it was also outside Europe and even opposed to it. If about 1900 it was the least developed of the major European countries, it was at the same time one of the most developed, industrialized, or modernized parts of the non-European world. Its revolution could win sympathy on the left in Europe because it reinforced the old European socialist objections to capitalism. It aroused the interests of peoples in other continents because it also denounced economic imperialism and the possession of colonies by Europeans, affirming that imperialism was merely the "highest stage" of capitalism and that both must be overthrown together. The Soviet Union, once established, came to occupy an intermediate position between the West and the colonial world (or what later came to be called the Third World). In the West it would long be feared or admired as the last word in social revolution. In the colonial, or formerly colonial, world it suggested new beginnings, a new way to become modern without being capitalistic or Western, a step in a worldwide rebellion against Western supremacy. The Russian Revolution thus not only produced communism and hence fascism in Europe but also added strength to the emerging anticolonial movements in Asia and elsewhere.

Although professional revolutionaries worked for revolution in Russia, they did not "cause" it. Lenin and the Bolsheviks did not bring about the Russian Revolution. They captured it after it had begun. They boarded the ship in midstream. The Russian Revolution, like all great revolutions, originated in a totality of previous history, in diverse local causes, and in the prolonged dissatisfaction of many kinds of people.

∞ 90. BACKGROUNDS

Russia after 1881: Reaction and Progress

We have seen in earlier chapters how the tsarist autocracy arose, how it ruled as a machine superimposed upon its subjects, how the upper class became westernized while the masses sank further into serfdom, and how an intelligentsia developed, divorced both from the work of government and the activities of the people. It has been explained in Chapter 13 how Alexander II freed the serfs in 1861 and created provincial and district councils or zemstvos, elected mainly by landowners, which attended to such matters as roads, schools, and hospitals.

In 1881 Alexander II was assassinated by members of the revolutionary group called the People's Will. His son, Alexander III (1881–1894), tried to stamp out revolutionism and to silence even peaceable criticism of the government. Revolutionaries and terrorists were driven into exile. The People's Will as an organized group became extinct. Jews were subjected to pogroms, by far the worst of any (until then) in modern times. For the first time the empire adopted a program of systematic Russification. Poles, Ukrainians, Lithuanians, the peoples of the Caucasus, the scattered German communities, the Muslim groups in central Asia—all faced the prospect of forcible assimilation to Russian culture. The philosopher and chief official of this movement was Pobiedonostsev, procurator of the Holy Synod, or layman head, under the tsar, of the Russian Orthodox church. Pobiedonostsev saw in the West something alien and doomed; and he dreamed of turning Holy Russia into a kind of churchly community, in which a disciplined clergy should protect the faithful from the insidious influence of the West.

Russification in the old regime

This is not, however, what happened. In the closing decades of the nineteenth century Russia became more than ever before a part of European civilization. Almost overnight it presented Europe with great works of literature and music that Europeans could appreciate. The nineteenth-century Russian novel became known throughout the Western world. All could read the novels of Tolstoy (1828–1910) without a feeling of strangeness; and if characters in the novels of Turgenev (1818–1883) and of Dostoevski (1821–1881) behaved more strangely, the authors themselves were obviously within the great European cultural family. The melodies of Tchaikovsky (1840–1893) and of Rimsky-Korsakov (1844–1908) became familiar throughout Europe and America; if they sometimes seemed hauntingly wild, distant, or sad, they still betrayed no more than the usual amount of national idiosyncrasy. Russians also contributed to the sciences, notably chemistry. They were known to be especially talented in the more abstruse intellectual exercises, such as higher mathematics, physics, or chess.

Russia also, from the 1880s, began to pass through the Industrial Revolution and take its place as an integral part of the world economic system. European capital entered the country, financing railways, mines, and factories (as well as government and the army) until by 1914 Europeans had about the same amount invested in Russia as in the United States, some $4 billion in each case. In 1897, under the reforming ministry of Count Witte, Russia adopted the gold standard, making its currency readily convertible with all others. In

Industrialization before 1914

the quarter-century between 1888 and 1913 the Russian railway mileage more than doubled, the miles of telegraph wires multiplied fivefold, the number of post offices trebled, and the number of letters carried by the mails multiplied seven times.

Although still industrially undeveloped by Western standards, Russia was industrializing rapidly. Exports rose in value from 400 million rubles in 1880 to 1.6 billion in 1913. Imports, though smaller, grew more rapidly, quintupling in the same period. They consisted of such items as tea and coffee and of the machines and industrial goods made in western Europe.

Industrialization, in Russia as in all countries, brought an increase both of the business and of the wage-earning classes, or, in socialist terminology, of the bourgeoisie and of the proletariat. Though growing, they were still not numerous by standards of the West. Factory workers, laboring for 11 or more hours a day for low wages under hard conditions, were in somewhat the same position as in England or France before 1850. Unions were illegal and strikes were prohibited. Nevertheless, great strikes in the 1890s called attention to the misery of the new industrial workers. There was one distinctive feature to the Russian proletariat. Russian industry was heavily concentrated; half of Russia's industrial workers were employed in factories employing over 500 persons. It was easier for workers under such circumstances to be organized economically and at the proper time to be mobilized politically. As for the Russian business and capitalist class, it was relatively the weaker because of several features in the situation. Ownership of much of Russia's new industrial plant was in foreign hands. Much was owned by the tsarist government itself; Russia already had the largest state-operated economic system in the world. Moreover, in Russia (unlike the United States at the time) the government itself was a heavy borrower from Europe; hence it was less dependent financially on its own people and more able to maintain an absolutist regime.

Nevertheless, the rising business and professional classes, reinforced by enterprising landowners, were strong enough to form a liberal segment of public opinion, which emerged in 1905 as the Constitutional Democratic party (or "Cadets").

The "Cadets"

Many of those who were active in the provincial zemstvos also became Constitutional Democrats. They were liberals, progressives, or constitutionalists in the Western sense, thinking less about the troubles of factory workers and peasants than about the need for a nationally elected parliament to control the policies of state.

Russia remained predominantly agricultural. Its huge exports were mainly farm and forest products. The peasants formed four-fifths of the population. Free from their former lords since 1861, they lived in village communes called *mirs*. In most communes much of the land was divided and redivided among peasant households by agreement of the village community, nor could anyone leave without communal permission. The peasants still carried a considerable burden. Until 1906 they paid redemption money arising from the Emancipation of 1861, and even after that, other forms of onerous payments. They also paid high taxes, for the government defrayed the interest on its foreign loans from taxes raised at home. The constantly rising export of cereals (also used to pay off debts contracted by Russia in the West) tended to keep food from the farmer's table; many peasants raised the best wheat for sale and ate black bread themselves. The farm population, in short (as in other countries in similar stages of their development), bore a considerable share of the costs of industrialization.

Peasant demands

Under such pressures, and because of their crude methods of cultivation, the peasants were forever demanding more land. "Land hunger" was felt both by individual families and by the *mirs*. The Emancipation had turned over roughly half the land to peasant ownership, individual and collective; and in the following half-century the peasants added to their share by buying from nonpeasant owners. The *mirs* were by no means obsolescent. They were in fact flourishing; they acquired far more land by purchase than did individual buyers, and perhaps half or more of the peasants valued communal security above the uncertain pleasures of private property. The exceptions were the minority of more enterprising and wealthier peasants, later called the kulaks. These "big farmers" stood out conspicuously from the impoverished mass of peasants, by whom they were often disliked.

The Emergence of Revolutionary Parties

The peasants were the ancient source of revolutionary disturbance in Russia. After the Emancipation in 1861 they continued to believe that they had some kind of rights in *all* the land of former estates on which they had formerly been serfs—not merely in the portion that had been allotted to peasant possession. They demanded (and obtained) credit from the government to buy from the big landowners or former masters. Their land hunger could not be appeased. They remained jealous of the landed aristocrat's very existence. In Russia, as elsewhere in Europe, and unlike the United States, the rural population was divided into two sharply distinct classes—on the one hand, the peasants of all types who worked the soil, and on the other, the gentry who resided upon it. The two never intermarried. They differed not merely economically but in speech, dress, and manners, and even in the looks of their faces and hands. But in the last three decades of the nineteenth century the Russian peasants were notably quiet. Insurrectionism seemingly subsided.

The other traditional source of revolutionary disturbance lay among the intelligentsia. Revolutionary intelligentsia (as distinguished from those who were simply liberal or progressive) held a violent contempt for the Russian empire and yearned for a catastrophic overthrow of the tsardom. Since the days of the Decembrists in 1825 they had formed secret organizations, comprising a few hundred or thousands of members, engaged in outwitting the tsarist police, by whom they were bafflingly interpenetrated. At a Bolshevik party congress held in 1913, out of 22 delegates present, no fewer than five, unknown to the others, were government spies.

The intelligentsia

The revolutionary intelligentsia, since there was normally little that they could do, spent their time in vehement discussion and interminable refinement of doctrine. By 1890 the terrorism and nihilism of the 1870s were somewhat passé. The great question was where these willing officers of a revolutionary movement could find an army. Disputation turned upon such topics as whether the peasants or the new factory workers were the true revolutionary class, whether the peasants were potentially proletarian or incurably petty bourgeois, whether Russia was bound to experience the same historical process as the West, or whether it was different; and, specifically, whether Russia had to go through capitalism or might simply skip the capitalist stage in reaching the socialist society.

Most of the revolutionary intelligentsia were "populists." Some had once belonged to the now broken People's Will. Some continued to approve of terrorism and assassination as morally necessary in an autocratic country. They generally had a mystical faith in the vast inchoate might of the Russian people, and since most Russians were peasants, the populists were interested in peasant problems and peasant welfare. They believed that a great native revolutionary tradition existed in Russia, of which the peasant rebellion of Pugachev, in 1773, was the chief example. The populists admired the *mir,* in which they saw the European

Populism

Although new industries began to develop in Russia during the early twentieth century, most people continued to live and work in the countryside. This picture of peasants harvesting hay before the First World War shows that women performed much of the labor and that modern machinery had not yet reached Russian farms.
(Library of Congress)

socialist idea of a "commune" represented. They read and respected Marx and Engels (indeed, a populist first translated the *Communist Manifesto* into Russian); but they did not believe that an urban proletariat was the only true revolutionary class or that socialism had to evolve historically out of capitalism. They said that in Russia the horrors of capitalism could be skipped. They addressed themselves to the plight of the farmer and the evils of landlordism, favored strengthening the *mir* and equalizing the shares of all peasants in it; and, since they did not believe that socialism would have to emerge from the prior triumph of capitalism in Russia, they thought that revolution might come quite soon. This populist sentiment crystallized in the founding in 1901 of the Social Revolutionary party.

Two populists, Plekhanov and Axelrod, fleeing to Switzerland in the 1870s, founded in exile the organization from which the Russian Social Democratic or Marxist party was to grow. A few Marxists began to declare themselves (though not publicly) in Russia itself. When the youthful Lenin met his future wife N. K. Krupskaya in 1894, she already belonged to a circle of argumentative Marxists. The fact that the peasants in the 1890s were disappointingly quiescent while machine industry, factor labor, and strikes were developing rapidly turned many of the revolutionary intelligentsia, though only a minority, from populism to Marxism. To Plekhanov and Axelrod were added, as young leaders, Vladimir Ilyich Lenin (1870–1924), Leon Trotsky (1879–1940), Joseph V. Stalin (1879–1953), and others.

Marxism

Of these it was Lenin who, after Marx, was to be claimed by communism as a father. Lenin was a short almost rotund man, with a bounding quickness and intense, penetrating gaze. High cheekbones and somewhat slanting eyes showed an Asian strain on the paternal side. His hair receded in early youth, leaving a massive forehead, behind which a restless mind was inexhaustibly at work. Even in his 20s he was called the Old One. He was of upper-middle-class origin, son of an inspector of schools who rose in the civilian bureaucracy to a rank equivalent to major general. His boyhood was comfortable and even happy, until the age of 17, when his elder brother, a student at St. Petersburg, became somewhat incidentally involved in a plot to assassinate Alexander III, for which he was put to death by order of the tsar himself. Because of the blot on the family record it became impossible for Lenin to continue with his law studies. He soon joined the ranks of professional revolutionaries, having no other occupation and living precariously from the party funds, which came mainly from the donations of well-to-do sympathizers.

Lenin

Arrested as a revolutionary, he spent three years of exile in Siberia. Here the tsarist government treated educated political prisoners with an indulgence not later shown by the Soviet regime. Lenin and most of the others lived in cottages of their own or boarded with local residents. No labor was required of them. They borrowed books from Europe; met and visited with one another; debated, played chess, went hunting, and wrote. They chafed, however, at being cut off from the mainstream of Russian political life back home. Lenin, his term over, proceeded in 1900 to western Europe, where except for short secret trips to Russia he remained until 1917. His intellectual vigor, irresistible drive, and shrewdness as a tactician soon made him a force in the party. Genius has been called the faculty for everlasting concentration upon one thing. Lenin, said his one-time close associate Axelrod, "for twenty-four hours of the day is taken up with the revolution, has no thoughts but thoughts of revolution, and even in his sleep dreams of nothing but revolution."

In 1898 the Marxists in Russia, spurred on by émigrés, founded the Social Democratic Labor party. They were not more revolutionary than the larger group of Social Revolutionaries. They simply had a different conception of the revolution. First of all, as good Marxists, they were more inclined to see the revolution as an international movement, part of the dialectical process of world history in which all countries were involved. Russia for them was no different from other countries except that is was less advanced. They expected the world revolution to break out first in the industrial societies of western Europe. They particularly admired the German Social Democratic party, the largest and most flourishing of all the parties that acknowledged the fatherhood of Marx.

The Social Democrats

If the Social Democrats were more oriented to Europe than the Social Revolutionaries, it was because so many of their spokesmen lived there in exile. They tended to think that Russia must develop capitalism, an industrialist proletariat, and the modern form of class struggle before there could be any revolution. Seeing in the urban proletariat the true revolutionary class, they looked upon the peasantry with suspicion, ridiculed the *mir,* and abhorred the Social Revolutionaries. Like Marx himself, the Russian Marxists disapproved of sporadic terrorism and assassination. For this reason, and because their doctrine seemed somewhat academic and their revolution seemed rather conditional and far in the future, the Marxists were for a time actually favored by the tsarist police, who regarded them as less dangerous than the Social Revolutionaries.

Split in the Social Democrats: Bolsheviks and Mensheviks

The Russian Marxists held a second party congress in Brussels and London in 1903, attended by émigrés like Lenin and delegates from the underground in Russia, and by Social Democrats and members of lesser organizations. The purpose of the congress was to unify all Russian Marxism, but in fact it split it forever. The two resulting factions called themselves Bolshevik, or majority, and Menshevik, or minority. Lenin was the main author of the split and hence the founder of Bolshevism. Although after 1903 it was usually the Mensheviks who had the majority, Lenin clung proudly and stubbornly to the term Bolshevism, with its favorable connotation of a majority in his support. For a number of years after 1903 the Social Democrats remained at least formally a single Marxist party, but they were now irreconcilably divided into two wings. In 1912 the Bolshevik wing organized itself as a separate party.

Leninism

Bolshevism, or Leninism, originally differed from Menshevism mainly on matters of organization and tactics. Lenin believed that the party should be a small revolutionary elite, a hard core of reliable and zealous workers. Those who favored a larger and more open party, with membership for mere sympathizers, became Mensheviks. Lenin insisted upon a strongly centralized party, without autonomy for national or other component groups. He demanded strong authority at the top, by which the central committee would determine the doctrine (or party line) and control personnel at all levels of the organization. The Mensheviks favored a greater degree of influence by the membership as a whole. Lenin thought that the party would strengthen itself by purges, expelling all who developed deviations of opinion. The Mensheviks favored covering up or bridging over all but the most fundamental disagreements. The Mensheviks came to recommend cooperation with liberals, progressives, and bourgeois democrats. Lenin regarded such cooperation as purely tactical and temporary, never concealing that in the end the Bolsheviks must impose their views through a dictatorship of the proletariat. The Mensheviks, in short, came to resemble the Marxists of western Europe, so far as that was possible under Russian conditions. Lenin stood for the rigid reaffirmation of Marxian fundamentals—dialectical materialism and irreconcilable class struggle.

Lenin accepted and added little to Marx's governing ideas: that capitalism exploited the workers; that history was shaped by economic forces and was moving toward socialism; that class struggle was the law of society; and that existing forms of religion, government, philosophy, and morals were weapons of the ruling class. He did, however, develop and transform certain theories of imperialism and of the "uneven development of capitalism" that had been propounded in only general terms by Marx and Engels.

Imperialism and development

According to this Leninist elaboration of earlier Marxist theory, "imperialism" was exclusively a product of monopoly capitalism, that is, capitalism in its "highest" and "final" stage, which develops differently and at different times in each country. Monopoly capitalism was bent on exporting surplus capital and investing it in underdeveloped areas for greater profits. The unceasing drive for colonies and markets in a world already almost completely partitioned leads inevitably to international imperialist wars for the redistribution of colonies, as well as to

Lenin built the Russian Bolshevik party into a disciplined revolutionary movement by insisting that a small, centralized elite should make all of the party's key strategic decisions. When the opportunity for revolutionary action finally arrived during the First World War, the Bolsheviks had an effective, centralized political organization, a well-defined Marxist conception of class conflict, and the strong-willed leadership of Lenin—who is shown here addressing a crowd in the spring of 1920.
(SOVFOTO)

intensified national colonial struggles for independence; both provide new revolutionary opportunities for the proletariat.

In other respects, Lenin roundly denounced all who attempted to "add" anything to the fundamental principles of Marx. Nothing infuriated him so much as revisionist efforts to tone down the class struggle or hints that Marxism might in the last analysis perhaps find room for some kind of religion. As he wrote in 1908: "From the philosophy of Marxism, cast of one piece of steel, it is impossible to expunge a single basic premise, a single essential part, without deviating from objective truth, without falling into the arms of bourgeois-reactionary falsehood." Lenin was a convert. He discovered Marxism; he did not invent it. He found in it a theory of revolution which he accepted without reservation as scientific and on which he was more outspokenly dogmatic even than Marx himself. His powers of mind, which were great, were spent in demonstrating how the unfolding events of the twentieth century confirmed the analysis of the master.

It was by his powers of will that Lenin was most distinguished, and if Leninism contributed little to Marxism as a theory, it contributed a great deal to it as a movement. Lenin was an activist. He was the supreme agitator, a field commander in the class war who could dash off a polemical pamphlet, dominate a party congress, or address throngs of workers with equal ease.

Lenin as activist

Beside him, Marx and Engels seem almost to be mere recluses or sociologists. Marx and Engels had preferred to believe that the dictatorship of the proletariat, when it came, would represent the wishes of the great majority in a society in which most people had become proletarians. Lenin more frankly foresaw the possibility that the proletarian dictatorship might represent the conscious wishes of a small vanguard and might have to impose itself on great masses by an unshrinking use of force.

The party

Above all, Lenin developed Marx's idea of the role of the party. He drew on the rich experience of pre-Marxist revolutionaries in Russia—the mysterious use of false names, invisible ink, secret ciphers, forged passports, and hidden meeting places—the whole conspiratorial wonderland which, when it existed to a lesser degree in the West before 1848, drew Marx's scorn and laughter. Lenin's conception of the party was basically Marx's, reinforced by his own experience as a Russian. The party was an organization in which intellectuals provided leadership and understanding for workers, who could not see so clearly for themselves. For trade unionism, concerned only with the day-to-day demands of workers, Lenin had even less patience than Marx. "The unconscious growth of the labor movement," he wrote, "takes the form of trade unionism, and trade unionism signifies the mental enslavement of the workers to the bourgeoisie." The task of intellectuals in the party was to make the trade unions and the workers class-conscious and hence revolutionary. Armed with "objective" knowledge, known to be correct, the party leadership naturally could not listen to the subjective opinions of others—the passing ideas of laborers, peasants, mistaken party subordinates, or other parties pretending to know more than Marx himself. The idea that intellectuals supply the brains and workers the brawn, that an elite leads while the toilers meekly follow, is understandable enough in view of the Russian background, which had created on the one hand a highly self-conscious intelligentsia and on the other a repressed working class and peasantry deprived of all opportunity for political experience of their own. The insistence on a leading and powerful role for the party elite became one of the most distinctive traits of Leninism and one of the most foreign to the democratic movements of the West.

Leninism accomplished the marriage of Russian revolutionary traditions with the Western doctrine of Marxism. It was an improbable marriage, whose momentous offspring was to be communism. But at the time, when Bolshevism first appeared in 1903, it had little or no effect. When revolution first broke out in Russia in 1905, it took the revolutionary émigrés almost entirely by surprise.

91.   THE REVOLUTION OF 1905

Background and Revolutionary Events

The almost simultaneous founding at the turn of the century of the Constitutional Democratic, Social Revolutionary, and Social Democratic parties was clearly a sign of mounting discontent. None of these was as yet a party that tried to get candidates elected to office, for there were no elections in Russia above the provincial zemstvo level. All three parties were propaganda agencies, made up of leaders without followers, intellectuals who followed various lines of thought. All, even those who became Constitutional Democrats,

Growing discontent

were watched by the police and obliged to do most of their work underground. At the same time, after 1900, there were signs of growing popular unrest. Peasants were trespassing on lands of the gentry and even rising in local insurrections against landlords and tax collectors. Factory workers sporadically refused to work. But with these popular movements none of the new parties had formed any solid links.

The government refused to make concessions of any kind. The tsar, Nicholas II, who had mounted the throne in 1894, was a man of narrow outlook. Tutored in his youth by Pobiedonostsev, the lay leader of the Russian Orthodox church, he regarded all ideas questioning autocracy, Orthodoxy, and Great Russian nationalism as un-Russian. That persons in the government should be controlled by interests outside the government—the mildest liberalism or most orderly democracy—seemed to the tsar, the tsarina, and the leading officials to be a monstrous aberration. Autocracy, for them, was the best and only, as it was the God-given, form of government for Russia.

The chief minister, Plehve, and the circles at court hoped that a short successful war with Japan would create more attachment to the government. The war went so badly that its effect was the reverse. Critics of the regime (except for the handful of the most internationalist Marxists) were sufficiently patriotic to be ashamed at the ease with which Russia was defeated by an upstart, Asian power. As after the Crimean War, there was a general feeling that the government had exposed its incompetence to all the world. Liberals believed that its secret methods, its immunity to criticism or control, had made it sluggish, obstinate, and inefficient, unable either to win a war or to lead the economic modernization that was taking place in Russia. But there was little that the liberals could do.

Response to military defeat

The police had recently allowed a priest, Father Gapon, to try to organize the St. Petersburg factory workers, hoping thus to counter the propaganda of revolutionaries. Father Gapon took up their grievances in all seriousness. They believed, as uneducated peasants only recently transplanted to the city, that if only they could reach the ear of the tsar, whom they called the Little Father, he would hear their complaints with shocked surprise and rectify the evils that afflicted Russia. They drew up a petition, asking for an eight-hour day, a minimum daily wage of one ruble (50 cents), a repudiation of bungling bureaucrats, and a democratically elected Constituent Assembly to introduce representative government into the empire. Unarmed, peaceable, respectful, singing "God save the Tsar," a crowd of 200,000—men, women, and children—gathered before the tsar's Winter Palace one Sunday in January 1905. But the tsar was not in the city, and his officials were fearful. Troops marched up and shot down the demonstrators in cold blood, killing several hundred.

"Bloody Sunday" in St. Petersburg snapped the moral bond upon which all stable government rests. The horrified workers saw that the tsar was not their friend. The autocracy stood revealed as the force behind the hated officials, the tax collectors, the landlords, and the owners of the industrial plants. A wave of political strikes broke out. Social Democrats (more Mensheviks than Bolsheviks) appeared from the underground or from exile to give revolutionary direction to these movements. Councils or "soviets" of workers were formed in Moscow and St. Petersburg. The peasants, too, in many parts of the country spontaneously began to erupt, overrunning the lands of the gentry, burning manor houses and doing violence to their owners. Social Revolutionaries naturally tried to take over this movement. The liberal Constitutional Democrats—professors, engineers, business people, lawyers, and leaders in the provincial zemstvos founded 40 years before—tried also to seize leadership or at least use the crisis to force the government's hand. All agreed on one demand: that there should be more democratic representation in the government.

Reactions to "Bloody Sunday"

The tsar yielded grudgingly and as little as possible. In March 1905 he promised to call to office men "enjoying the confidence of the nation." In August (after the ruinous defeat in the naval battle of Tsushima) he agreed to call a kind of Estates General, for which peasants, landowners, and city people should vote as separate classes. Still the revolution raged unchecked. The St. Petersburg Soviet, or workers' council, led mainly by Mensheviks (Lenin had not yet reached Russia), declared a great general strike in October.

The angry response to "Bloody Sunday" in early 1905 erupted in a wave of strikes, demands for political reform, and militant demonstrations, including this protest march in St. Petersburg. Most of the protestors in this photograph were students, and they were marching behind red flags that had become a modern symbol for revolutionary political movements. (SOVFOTO)

Railroads stopped, banks closed, newspapers ceased to appear, and even lawyers refused to go to their offices. The strike spread to other cities and to the peasants. With the government paralyzed, the tsar issued his October Manifesto. It promised a constitution, civil liberties, and a Duma to be elected by all classes alike, with powers to enact laws and control the administration.

The October Manifesto

The tsar and his advisers intended to divide the opposition by releasing the October Manifesto, and in this they succeeded. The Constitutional Democrats, with a Duma promised, allowed themselves to hope that social problems could henceforth be dealt with by parliamentary methods. Liberals were now afraid of revolutionaries, industrialists feared the strength shown by labor in the general strike, and landowners demanded a restoration of order among the peasants. Aroused peasants and workers were not yet satisfied: the former still wanted more land and less taxation; the latter, a shorter working day and a living wage. The several branches of revolutionary intellectuals worked upon the continuing popular agitation, hoping to carry matters forward until the tsarist monarchy was abolished and a socialist republic was established with themselves at its head. They believed also (and correctly) that the October Manifesto was in any case a deception, which the tsar would refuse to adhere to as soon as revolutionary pressure was removed. The soviets continued to seethe, local strikes went on, and there were mutinies among soldiers at Kronstadt and sailors in the Black Sea fleet.

But the government was able to maintain itself. With the middle-class liberals now inactive or demanding order, the authorities arrested the members of the St. Petersburg Soviet. Peace was hastily made with Japan, and reliable troops were recalled from the Far East. The revolutionary leaders fled back to Europe, or again went underground, or were caught and sent to prison or to Siberia; executions were carried out in the countryside. The Revolution of 1905 would prove to be only a dress rehearsal for the revolution to come in 1917.

The Results of 1905: The Duma

The chief apparent result of the Revolution of 1905 was to make Russia, at least ostensibly, into a parliamentary type of state like the rest of Europe. The promised Duma was convoked. For ten years, from 1906 to 1916, Russia had at least the superficial attributes of a semiconstitutional monarchy.

But Nicholas II soon showed that he did not intend to yield much. He drew the teeth of the new Duma before the assembly could even be born, by announcing in advance, in 1906, that it would have no power over foreign policy, the budget, or government personnel. His attitude toward constitutional monarchy continued until 1917 to be entirely negative; the one concession that tsarism would not allow was any real participation in government by the public. Within this "public" the two extreme fringes were equally impervious to liberal constitutionalism. On the Right, stubborn upholders of pure autocracy and the Orthodox church organized the Black Hundreds, terrorizing the peasantry and urging them to boycott the Duma. On the Left, in 1906, the Social Revolutionaries and both the Bolshevik and Menshevik wings of the Social Democrats likewise refused to recognize the Duma, urged workers to boycott it, and refused to put up any candidates for election.

The short-lived first Duma was elected in 1906 by a system of indirect and unequal voting, in which peasants and workers voted as separate classes, and with proportionately far less representation than was granted to the landlords. In the absence of socialist candidates, workers and peasants voted for all sorts of people, including the liberal Constitutional Democrats (the Cadets), who obtained a sweeping majority. The Cadets, when the Duma met, found themselves still fighting for the bare principle of constitutional government. They demanded true universal male suffrage and the responsibility of ministers to a parliamentary majority. The tsar's response was to dismiss the Duma after two months.

The first Duma

A second Duma was elected in 1907, with the government trying to control the elections through suppression of party meetings and newspapers, but since Social Revolutionaries and Mensheviks now consented to take part, some 83 socialists were elected. The Cadets, becoming fearful of the revolutionary Left, concluded that constitutional progress must be gradual and showed a willingness to cooperate with the government. But the Duma came to an abrupt end when the government denounced and arrested some 50 socialists as revolutionaries bent only on destruction. A third Duma, elected after an electoral change that gave increased representation to the landed propertied class and guaranteed a conservative majority, managed to hold several sessions between 1907 and 1912, as did a fourth Duma from 1912 to 1916. The deputies, by following the lead of the government, by addressing themselves only to concrete issues, by losing themselves in committee work, and by avoiding the basic question of where supreme power lay, kept precariously alive a modicum of parliamentary institutions in the tsarist empire.

The second Duma

The Stolypin Reforms

Some officials believed that the way to checkmate the revolutionaries and strengthen the hold of the monarchy was for the government, while keeping all controls in its own hands, to attract the support of reasonable and moderate people by a program of reforms. One of these reformers was Peter Stolypin, whom the tsar retained as his principal minister from 1906 to 1911. It was Stolypin who dissolved the first two Dumas. But it was not his policy merely to stand still. His aim was to build up the propertied classes as friends of the state. He believed, perhaps rightly, that a state actively supported by widespread private property had little to fear from doctrinaire intellectuals, conspirators, and émigrés. He therefore favored and broadened the powers of the provincial zemstvos, in which the larger landowners took part in administering local affairs. For the peasantry he put through legislation more sweeping than any since the Emancipation, allowing peasants to sell their shares in the communal land of the *mirs* and leave their villages. Peasants also gained the right to acquire private control over land and to buy property from the communes or the gentry.

Success of the Stolypin program

The Stolypin policy was successful. Between 1907 and 1916, 6.2 million families out of 16 million who were eligible applied for legal separation from the *mir*. There was no mistaking the trend toward individual property and independent farming. But the results of the Stolypin program must not be exaggerated. The *mir* was far from broken. A vast majority of peasants were still involved in the old system of common rights and communal restrictions. The land shortage was still acute in the agricultural areas where yields were highest. Land hunger and poverty continued in the countryside. There were the new big farmers—the *kulaks*—to be resented and envied, but the largest landed proprietors were still the gentry. About 30,000 landlords owned nearly 200 million acres of land, and another 200 million acres made up other large landed estates.

Stolypin was not left long to carry on his program. The tsar gave him only an unwilling support. Reactionary circles disliked his tampering ways and his Western orientation. Social Revolutionaries naturally cried out against dissolution of the communes. Even Marxists, who should in theory have applauded the advance of capitalism in Russia, feared that Stolypin's reforms might do away with agrarian discontent. "I do not expect to live to see the revolution," said Lenin in these years. Stolypin was shot dead while attending the theater in Kiev, in the presence of the tsar and tsarina, in 1911. The assassin, a member of the terrorist wing of the Social Revolutionaries, is thought also to have been a secret agent of the reactionary tsarist police. It may be added that Stolypin's predecessor, Plehve, and about a dozen other high officials within the past few years had similarly died at the hands of assassins.

Westernization

But all in all, despite its violence and repression, the Russian empire on the eve of the First World War was moving in a Western direction. Its industries were growing, its railways were expanding, and its exports were almost half as great in value as those of the United States. It had a parliament, if not a parliamentary government. Private property and individualist capitalism were spreading to new layers of the people. There was a guarded freedom of the press, illustrated, for example, by the legal and open establishment of the Bolshevik party paper, *Pravda* (or *Truth*), in St. Petersburg in 1912. It is not possible to say how far this development might have gone, for it was menaced on both the Right and the Left by obstinate reactionaries upholding the absolute tsardom and by revolutionaries whom nothing but the end of tsardom and wholesale transformation of society could appease. But both extremes were discouraged. The desperation of extreme reactionaries in the government, the feeling that they might in any case soon lose their position, perhaps made them the more willing to precipitate a European war by armed support of Serbian nationalists. As for the revolutionary parties, and especially the Bolsheviks, they were losing in membership on the eve of the war; their leaders lived year after year in exile, dreaming of the great days of 1905 which stubbornly failed to repeat themselves and sometimes pessimistically admitting, as Lenin did, that there might be no revolution in their time.

ℰ︎ 92.   THE REVOLUTION OF 1917

End of the Tsardom: The Revolution of March 1917

War again put the tsarist regime to a test that it could not meet. In this war, more total than any had ever been, willing cooperation between government and people was indispensable to success. This essential prerequisite the tsarist empire did not have. National minorities—Poles, Ukrainians, the peoples of the Caucasus, Jews, and others—were disaffected. As for the socialists, who in every other European parliament voted for funds to finance the war, the dozen otherwise disunited socialists in the Duma refused to do so and were promptly jailed. The ordinary worker and peasant marched off with the army, but without the sense of personal conviction felt by common people in Germany and the West. More decisive was the attitude of the middle class. Because they patriotically wished Russia to win, the glaring mismanagement of the government was the more intolerable to them. The Russian disasters at the battles of Tannenberg and the Masurian Lakes, with which the war opened in 1914, were followed by the advance of the Central Powers into Russia in 1915, at the cost of 2 million Russian soldiers killed, wounded, or captured.

At the war's outbreak middle-class people, as in all countries, offered their assistance to the government. The provincial zemstvos formed a union of all zemstvos in the empire to facilitate the mobilization of agriculture and industry. Business groups at Petrograd (as St. Petersburg was renamed during the war) formed a commercial and industrial committee to get the factories into maximum production. The government distrusted these signs of public activity arising outside official circles. On the other hand, organized in this way, middle-class people became conscious of their own strength and more critical of the bureaucracy. Rumors spread that some officials in the war ministry itself were pro-German, reactionaries who feared the liberalism of England and France with which Russia was allied. *Middle-class support*

Life at court was bizarre even for Russia. The tsarina Alexandra, German by origin, looked upon all Russians outside her own circle with contempt, incited her husband to play the proud and pitiless autocrat, and took advice from a self-appointed holy man, the mysterious Rasputin. She was convinced that Rasputin possessed supernatural and prophetic powers, because he had apparently cured her young son of hemophilia. Rasputin, by his influence over her, had a voice in appointments to high office. All who wished an audience with the imperial pair had to go through him. Patriotic and enlightened persons of all classes vainly protested. In these circumstances, and given the military defeats, the union of zemstvos and other such wartime bodies complained not merely of faults of administration but of fundamental conditions in the state. The government responded by holding them at arm's length. The tsarist regime, caught in a total war, was afraid of the help offered by its own people.

During the war, in September 1915, the Duma was suspended. The war thus revived all the basic political issues that had been latent since the Revolution of 1905. The union of zemstvos demanded restoration of the Duma, which reassembled in November 1916 and expressed loud indignation at the way affairs were conducted. Among all elements of the population, *Deepening of political divisions*

Tsar Nicholas II, the last of the Romanov rulers in Russia, sought to wage war against Germany without mobilizing the popular support of the Russian people. This photograph shows the tsar with his wife and children during the first year of the war. Nicholas abdicated the throne in March 1917, and the Bolsheviks put the entire family to death in the following year. (TASS/SOVFOTO)

The mystical monk Rasputin gained a much-resented influence over tsarina Alexandra and the affairs of the Russian government because he seemed to cure the illness of the royal family's young son. Rasputin's mysterious personality is evoked in this picture, which was taken shortly before his enemies at court murdered him in 1916.
(The Art Archive/Musée des 2 Guerres Mondiales Paris/Dagli Orti)

dissatisfaction with the course of the war and with the government's ineptitude mounted. In December Rasputin was assassinated by nobles at the court. The tsar began to consider repression and again adjourned the Duma. Machine guns were issued to the police. Members of the Duma and of the new extragovernmental bodies concluded that the situation could be saved only by force. It is when moderate persons, normally concerned with their own business, come to such conclusions that revolution becomes a political possibility. The shift of moderates and liberals, their need of a coup d'état to save themselves from reactionaries, likewise raised the long-awaited prospects of the minority of professional revolutionaries.

Again it was the workers of Petrograd who precipitated the crisis. Food had become scarce, as in all the belligerent countries. But the tsarist administration was too clumsy and too demoralized by graft to institute the controls that had become usual elsewhere, such as maximum prices and ration cards. It was the poorest who felt the food shortage most keenly. On March 8, 1917, food riots broke out, which soon developed, doubtless with the help of revolutionary intellectuals, into political insurrection. Crowds shouted, "Down with the tsar!" Troops within the city refused to fire on the insurgents; mutiny and insubordination spread from unit to unit. Within a few days a Soviet of Workers' and Soldiers' Deputies, on the model of 1905, had been organized in Petrograd.

Middle-class leaders, with the government now helpless, demanded dismissal of the ministry and formation of a new one commanding the confidence of a majority of the Duma. The tsar retaliated by disbanding the Duma. The Duma set up an executive committee to take charge until the situation clarified. There were now two new authorities in the city: one, the Duma committee, essentially moderate, constitutionalist, and relatively legal; the other, the Petrograd Soviet, representing revolutionary forces arising by spontaneous upsurge from below. The Petrograd Soviet (or workers' "council") was to play in 1917 a role like that of the Paris Commune of 1792, constantly pushing the supposedly higher and more nationwide authority to the left. The Soviet became the public auditorium and administrative center of the working-class upheaval. Since it was generally socialist in its outlook, all the factions of doctrinaire socialists—Social Revolutionaries, Mensheviks, Bolsheviks—tried to win it over and utilize it for their own ends.

The Petrograd Soviet

The Duma committee, under pressure from the Petrograd Soviet, on March 14 set up a Provisional Government under Prince Lvov. The Duma liberals, as a concession to the Soviet, admitted one socialist to the new government, Alexander Kerensky, a moderate, legal-minded Social Revolutionary; and they furthermore consented to demand the abdication of Nicholas II. The tsar was then at the front. He tried to return to his palace near Petrograd, but the imperial train was stopped and turned back by troops. The army, fatefully, was taking the side of the revolution. The very generals in the field, unable to vouch for the loyalty of their men, advised abdication. Nicholas yielded; his brother, the grand duke, declined to succeed him; and on March 17, 1917, Russia became a republic.

The Bolshevik Revolution: November 1917

The Provisional Government, following the best precedents of European revolutions, called for elections by universal male suffrage to a Constituent Assembly, which was to meet late in the year and prepare a constitution for the new regime. It tried also to continue the war against Germany. In July an offensive was mounted, but the demoralized Russian armies were quickly routed. Pending final decision by the Constituent Assembly, the Provisional Government promised wholesale redistribution of land to the peasants but took no action. Meanwhile, the peasants, driven by the old land hunger, were already overrunning the rural districts, burning and looting. At the front the armies melted away; many high officers refused to serve the republic, and masses of peasant soldiers simply turned their backs and went home, unwilling to be absent while land was being handed out. The Petrograd Soviet, opposing the Provisional Government, called for speedy termination of the war. Fearing reactionary officers, it issued on March 14 its Order No. 1, entrusting command within the army to committees elected by both officers and soldiers. Discipline collapsed.

Russia's costly military defeats and the food shortages that developed because of the long war contributed decisively to the revolutionary uprising that overthrew Tsar Nicholas II. Similar discontents soon undermined popular support for the Provisional Government, which tried to continue the war. These women in Petrograd were demanding increased food rations for Russian soldiers, but their demonstration in 1917 is an example of the wider political mobilization that swept across Russia during that revolutionary year.
(SOVFOTO)

Revolution advancing

The revolution was thus already well advanced when Lenin and the other Bolsheviks arrived in Petrograd in the middle of April. They immediately took sides with the Petrograd Soviet against the Provisional Government, and with similar soviets that had sprung up in other parts of the country. In July an armed uprising of soldiers and sailors, which the Bolshevik central committee disapproved of as premature, was put down. The Bolsheviks were blamed, and Lenin had to flee to Finland. But as a bid for popular support the Provisional Government named the socialist Alexander Kerensky as its head in place of Prince Lvov in an uneasy coalition of moderate socialists and liberals. Kerensky's middle position was next threatened from the Right. The newly appointed military commander, General Kornilov, dispatched a force of cavalry to restore order. Not only conservatives but liberals wished him success in the hope that he would suppress the soviets. Kornilov's movement was defeated, but with the aid of the Bolsheviks, who rallied with other socialists, and of revolutionary-minded soldiers in the city who offered armed resistance. Radicals denounced liberals as accomplices in Kornilov's attempt at counterrevolution, and both camps blamed Kerensky for having allowed the plot to be hatched under his government. Both liberals and moderate socialists abandoned Kerensky, and he had to form a government of uncertain political support. Meanwhile the food shortage worsened with transport disarranged and the farm population in turmoil, so that workers in the city listened more willingly to the most extreme speakers.

The Bolsheviks adapted their program to what the most aroused elements in a revolutionary people seemed to want. Lenin concentrated on four points: first, immediate peace with the Central Powers; second, redistribution of land to the peasants; third, transfer of factories, mines, and other industrial plants from the capitalists to committees of workers in each plant; and, fourth, recognition of the soviets as the supreme power instead of the Provisional Government. Lenin, though a rigid dogmatist on abstract questions, was a flexible and bold tactician, and his program in 1917 was dictated more by the immediate situation in Russia than by considerations of theoretical Marxism. What was needed was to win over soldiers, peasants, and workers by promising them "peace, land, and bread." With this program, and by infiltration and parliamentary stratagems, as well as by their accuracy as political prophets—predicting the Kornilov counterrevolution and "unmasking" the trend of middle-way liberals to support it—the Bolsheviks won a majority in the Petrograd Soviet and in soviets all over the country.

Lenin thereupon raised the cry, "All power to the Soviets!" to crush Kerensky and forestall the coming Constituent Assembly. Kerensky, to broaden the base on which he stood, and unable to wait for the Constituent Assembly, convoked a kind of pre-parliament representing all parties, labor unions, and zemstvos. Lenin and the Bolsheviks boycotted his pre-parliament. Instead they called an all-Russian Congress of Soviets.

"All power to the Soviets!"

Lenin now judged that the hour had come for the seizure of power. The Bolsheviks themselves were divided, but Lenin was backed by Trotsky, Stalin, and a majority of the party Central Committee. Troops garrisoned in Petrograd voted to support the soviets, which the Bolsheviks now controlled. On the night of November 6–7, 1917, the Bolsheviks took over telephone exchanges, railway stations, and electric power plants in the city. A warship turned its guns on the Winter Palace, where Kerensky's government sat. The latter could find almost no one to defend it. The hastily assembled Congress of Soviets pronounced the Provisional Government defunct and named in its place a Council of People's Commissars, of which Lenin became the head. Trotsky was named commissar for foreign affairs; Stalin, commissar for nationalities. Kerensky fled, eventually arriving in the United States, where he died in 1970.

At the Congress of Soviets Lenin introduced two resolutions. One called upon the belligerent governments to negotiate a "just democratic peace," without annexations and without indemnities; the second "abolished all landlord property" immediately and without compensation. Although determined to establish a proletarian dictatorship, the Bolsheviks knew the importance of the Russian peasants. The millions of acres belonging to the large estates that were now expropriated provided a base of support for the new regime without which it could hardly have survived.

Resolutions on peace and property

Thus was accomplished the Bolshevik or November Revolution.[1] But the long awaited Constituent Assembly remained to be dealt with. It met in January 1918. Thirty-six million persons had voted for it. Of these, 9 million had voted for Bolshevik deputies,

---

[1] Also known as the October Revolution, since according to the Julian calendar used in Russia until 1918, the events described took place in October.

showing that the Bolshevik program, launched less than a year before by a small band of émigrés, had a widespread mass appeal. But almost 21 million had voted for Kerensky's party, the agrarian, populist, peasant-oriented Social Revolutionaries. However, said Lenin, "to hand over power to the Constituent Assembly would again be compromising with the malignant bourgeoisie." The Assembly was broken up on the second day of its sessions; armed sailors dispatched by the people's commissars simply surrounded it. The dissolution of the Constituent Assembly was a frank repudiation of majority rule in favor of "class rule"—to be exercised for the proletariat by the Bolsheviks. The dictatorship of the proletariat was now established. Two months later, in March 1918, the Bolsheviks renamed themselves the Communist party.

The New Regime: The Civil War, 1918–1922

In these same months, the Communists, or Bolsheviks, signed the peace of Brest-Litovsk with Germany, surrendering to Germany control over the Baltic provinces, Poland, and the Ukraine. The Russian conquests of two centuries were thus abandoned, but to Lenin it made no difference. He was convinced that the events that he had just mastered in Russia were the prelude to a general upheaval; that the war, still raging in the West, would bring all Europe to the inevitable proletarian or Marxist revolution; that Imperial Germany was therefore doomed; and that Poles, Ukrainians, and others would soon emerge, like the Germans themselves, as free socialist peoples. In any case, it was largely by promising peace that Lenin had won enough backing to overthrow Kerensky, who on this deep popular demand had delayed too long, waiting for England and France to release Russia from its treaty obligations as an ally. But real peace did not come, for the country sank immediately into civil war.

Not only old tsarist reactionaries, and not only liberals, bourgeois, zemstvo members, and Constitutional Democrats, but all types of anti-Leninist socialists as well, Mensheviks and Social Revolutionaries, scattered in all directions to organize resistance against the regime of soviets and people's commissars; and they obtained aid from the Western Allies. Both sides competed for the support of the peasants.

As for the new regime, the oldest of its institutions was the party, founded as a wing of the Social Democrats in 1903; the next oldest were the soviets, dating from 1905 and 1917; and then came the Council of People's Commissars set up on the day of the coup d'état. The first institution founded under the new order was a political police, an Extraordinary All-Russian Commission of Struggle Against Counterrevolution, Speculation, and Sabotage, commonly known from its Russian initials as the Cheka and in later years, without basic change of methods or purpose, under such successive names as the OGPU, the NKVD, the MVD, and the KGB. It was established on December 7, 1917. In January 1918 the Red Army was founded, with Leon Trotsky as war commissar and virtually its creator. In July a constitution was promulgated.

In social policy the Bolsheviks at first adopted no long-range plans, contenting themselves with a mixture of principle and expediency known as "war communism." They nationalized some of the largest industrial enterprises but left the bulk under the control of workers' committees. The pressing problem was to find food, which had ceased to move through any normal channels.

"War communism"

The peasants, very much as in the French Revolution under similar conditions—worthless money, insecure property titles, unruly hired hands, armed marauding, and a doubtful future—were producing less food than usual, consuming it themselves, or hoarding it on their own farms. The response of the government and city workers was also much as in

1793. The new government levied requisitions, required the peasants to make stated "deliveries," and invited labor unions to send armed detachments into the country to procure food by force. Since it was naturally the big farmers who had the surplus, they came into disrepute as starvers of the people. Class war broke out, rabid, ferocious, and elemental, between farmers who feared that their very subsistence as well as their property would be taken away and city people, often supported by hungry agricultural laborers, who were driven to desperation by famine. Many peasants, especially the larger farmers, therefore rallied to anti-Bolshevik political leaders.

Centers of resistance developed on every side. In the Don valley a small force assembled under Generals Kornilov and Denikin, with many army officers, gentry landowners, and expropriated business people taking part in it. The Social Revolutionaries gathered followers on the middle Volga. Their most significant military support came from a force of some 45,000 Czechs, who had deserted or been captured from the Austro-Hungarian armies and had then been organized as a Czech Legion to fight on the side of Russia and the Allies. After the November Revolution and the peace of Brest-Litovsk, these Czechs decided to leave Russia by way of the Trans-Siberian Railroad, return to Europe by sea, and resume fighting on the western front. When Bolshevik officials undertook to disarm them, they allied with the Social Revolutionaries on the Volga.

The Allied governments believed that Bolshevism was a temporary madness that with little effort could be stopped. They wished above all to bring Russia back into the war against Germany, an objective they sought to achieve by launching a military intervention in East Asia, through Vladivostok. The Japanese, who had declined military aid to their allies in any other theater, viewed this action favorably, seeing in the ruin of the Russian empire a rare opportunity to develop their sphere of influence in East Asia. It was agreed that an interallied military force should land at Vladivostok, cross Siberia, join with the Czechs, break up Bolshevism, and fall upon the Germans in eastern Europe. For this ambitious scheme Britain and France could supply no soldiers, engaged as they were on the western front. The force turned out to be American and Japanese, but predominantly Japanese; Japan contributed 72,000 men and the United States only 8,000. They landed at Vladivostok in August 1918.

Allied responses

The civil war lasted until 1920, or even later in some places. It became a confused melee in which the Bolsheviks struggled against Russian opponents, independence-minded nationalities, and foreign intervention. The Red Army fought in Ukraine first against the Germans and then against the French, who occupied Odessa as soon as the war ended in Europe. It reconquered Ukraine, Armenia, Georgia, and Azerbaijan, all of which had declared their independence in 1918; put to flight a hundred thousand "Whites," as the counterrevolutionaries were called, in the south; and fought off Admiral Kolchak, who in Siberia proclaimed himself ruler of all Russia. In 1920, the Bolsheviks carried on a war with the new republic of Poland, which was scarcely organized when it set out to recover the huge Ukrainian and Byelorussian territories that had been Polish before 1772. A small force of British, French, and American troops occupied the northern Russian city of Archangel until the end of 1919, and the Japanese remained at Vladivostok until the end of 1922.

But the anti-Bolshevik forces could never unite. The anti-Communist Russians represented every hue of the political spectrum from unregenerate tsarists to left-wing Social Revolutionaries. Many of the rightist anti-Bolsheviks openly antagonized the peasants by proceeding to restore expropriated landed estates in areas they occupied; many engaged in vindictive reprisals in a kind of "white terror." Leon Trotsky, on the other hand, shaped in the

Disunity among anti-Bolshevik forces

Leon Trotsky commanded the Red Army that defeated the Bolsheviks' many enemies in the Civil War of 1918–1922. He is seen here in the early years of the revolution, when he emerged as a key political and military leader of the Bolshevik party and an influential theorist of international communism.
(Getty Images)

civil wars a disciplined, effective Red Army, recruiting it, organizing it, unifying it, and equipping it as best he could, assigning political commissars to watch it, and assuring that trustworthy officers occupied its high command. The Bolsheviks could denounce the foreign intervention and appeal to national patriotism, and they could win peasant support by the distribution of land.

By 1922 the Bolsheviks, or Communists, had established themselves up to the frontiers of the former tsarist empire in every direction except on the European side. There the band of Baltic states—Finland, Estonia, Latvia, and Lithuania—remained independent; Romania had acquired Bessarabia, the new Romanian frontier reaching now almost to Odessa. Poland, as a result of the war of 1920, retained a frontier farther east than the Allies themselves had intended. Russia thus lost thousands of square miles of territory and buffer areas acquired over the centuries by the tsars. They remained lost until the Second World War. But peace was won and the regime stood.

The Red Terror

It was during these civil wars that the Red Terror broke out in Russia. Like the famous Terror in France in 1793, it was in part a response to civil and foreign war. Before the Bolshevik Terror, however, the old Jacobin Terror paled. Thousands were shot in Russia merely as hostages (a practice unknown to Europe for some time); and other thousands were killed without even the summary formalities of revolutionary tribunals. The Cheka was the most formidable political police that had yet appeared. The Bolshevik Terror was aimed at the physical extermination of all who opposed the new regime. A bourgeois class background would go far to confirm the guilt of the person charged with conspiring against the Soviet state. As a chief of the Cheka said: "The first questions you should put to the accused person

The Bolsheviks' consolidation of power depended on the carefully controlled Red Army. This is a Red Army artillery battalion that was engaged in the suppression of the Kronstadt sailors' uprising in 1921.
(ITAR-TASS/SOVFOTO)

are, To what class does he belong, what is his origin, what was his education, and what is his profession? These should determine the fate of the accused. This is the essence of the Red Terror."

But a working-class background for a man or a woman made little difference. In 1918 a young woman named Fanny Kaplan shot at Lenin and wounded him. She deposed that she had favored the Constituent Assembly, that her parents had emigrated to America in 1911, that she had six working-class brothers and sisters; and she admitted that she had intended to kill Lenin. She was of course executed, as were others in Petrograd. When the sailors at Kronstadt, who were among the first adherents of the Bolsheviks, rose in 1921, objecting to domination of the soviets by the party (threatening a kind of leftist renewal of the revolution, like the Hébertists who had opposed Robespierre), they were branded as petty bourgeois and shot down by the thousands. The Terror struck at the revolutionists themselves quite as much as it did the bourgeoisie; it was to continue to do so long after the revolution was secure.

The Terror succeeded in its purpose. Together with the victories of the Red Army, it established the new regime. Those "bourgeois" who survived took on the protective coloration of "toilers." No bourgeois as such presumed to take part in the politics of Russia. Mensheviks and other socialists fleeing to

A new regime

Europe told appalling stories of the human toll taken by Lenin. Horrified European socialists repudiated communism as an atrocious, Russian perversion of Marxism. But, at whatever cost, Lenin and his followers were now able to start building the socialist society as they understood it.

93.   THE UNION OF SOVIET SOCIALIST REPUBLICS

Government: The Nationalities and Federalism

With the end of the civil wars and foreign intervention, and with the termination of the war with Poland, it became possible in 1922 to establish the Union of Soviet Socialist Republics. There were at first four such republics in the Union, but political reorganization and the occupation of new territories at the beginning of the Second World War increased the number to 15 (see map, pp. 746–747). Although many of these new republics were established in central Asia, most of the Soviet Union's population lived in three large Slavic regions: the Russian Soviet Federated Socialist Republic, the Ukrainian Soviet Socialist Republic, and the Byelorussian Soviet Socialist Republic. In the new Union, which geographically replaced the old Russian empire, the name Russia was not officially used. The guiding conception was a blend of the national and the international: to recognize nationality by granting autonomy to national groups, while holding these groups together in a higher union and allowing new groups to enter regardless of historic frontiers. In 1922 the expectation of world revolution was still alive. The constitution, formally adopted in 1924, pronounced the founding of the U.S.S.R. to be "a decisive step by way of uniting the workers of all countries into one World Soviet Socialist Republic." It made the Union, in principle, fluid and expansible, declared that any member republic might secede and that newly formed soviet socialist republics might join (none ever did voluntarily). When the U.S.S.R. occupied contiguous territories (once part of the tsarist empire) after the outbreak of the Second World War, these territories were also transformed into Soviet Socialist republics—the three independent Baltic states, Estonia, Latvia, and Lithuania; Bessarabia, detached from Romania; and Karelia, taken from Finland after the Russo-Finnish War. Bessarabia became the Moldavian S.S.R., and Karelia temporarily, from 1940 to 1956, had the status of a Karelo-Finnish S.S.R., a 16th Soviet Socialist republic.

An answer to the problem of nationalism

The federal principle in the U.S.S.R. was designed to resolve the problem of nationalism. The tsardom, in its last decades, had tried to deal with this problem by systematic Russification. The nationalities had resisted, and nationalist discontent had been one of the forces fatally weakening the empire. Nationalism, the demand that national groups should have their own political sovereignty, had not only broken up the Austro-Hungarian empire but "Balkanized" central and eastern Europe. This might have happened after 1917 in Russia except for the fact that the Red Army during the civil wars occupied large parts of the tsarist empire which had broken away and declared their independence. As it turned out, by 1922 the U.S.S.R. occupied a sixth of the world's land area.

A hundred languages were spoken in the Soviet Union, and 50 distinct nationalities were recognized within its borders. Many of these were small splinter groups or isolated communities left by the ebb and flow of humanity in inner Asia over thousands of years. All recognized nationalities received a cultural autonomy, or the right to use their own language, have their own schools, wear their own dress, and follow their own folkways with-

A good example of early "socialist realism" in Soviet art, this Soviet political poster from 1918 celebrates "One Year of Proletarian Dictatorship," and portrays the early achievements of the revolution. A worker and a peasant stand on the symbols and chains of the old regime. The happy people in the background are celebrating their triumph and moving confidently toward a prosperous, industrialized future. (SOVFOTO)

out interference. Indeed, the Soviet authorities favored the growth of cultural nationalism, and some 50 local languages were put into written form for the first time.

Administratively the nationalities were put on various levels, with varying degrees of separate identity according to their size and importance. The most important were the soviet republics themselves, but in practice *The Soviet republics* the Russian S.F.S.R., with over half the population and three-fourths of the territory of the Union, predominated over all the others. When to the Russian were added the Ukrainian and the Byelorussian republics, the overwhelmingly Russian and Slavic character of the Union was marked. Moreover all political and economic rights were severely limited by the concentration of authority in the hands of the central government. There was little substance in the formal claim that each constituent republic was sovereign and had the right to conduct its own foreign affairs. During the Second World War there was evidence that separatism had not wholly died down, remaining especially alive in Ukraine, and several autonomous areas were officially dissolved for separatist activities or even for collusion with the German invaders. By the late 1980s it became increasingly apparent that the Soviets could not prevent the disintegration of the multinational empire that they had inherited from the tsars.

Government: State and Party

Government in the Union, and in each component republic, followed a pattern worked out during the revolution and written into the constitutions of 1924 and 1936. In theory, a principle of parallelism was adopted. On the one hand was the state: on the other, paralleling the state but technically not part of it, was the party. But the close interlocking relationship between the two made the parallelism virtually meaningless because the party actually controlled all of the state institutions.

Elections

The distinctive state institution was the council or soviet. Here elections took place, and authority proceeded from the bottom upward to the top through an ascending hierarchy of local, provincial, and national soviets. Under the constitution of 1924 only "toilers" had the right to vote. In the later constitution of 1936 a more direct democratic procedure was introduced. Voters henceforth directly elected members of the higher soviets, a secret ballot was adopted, no class was any longer denied the vote, and a bicameral parliament was created. On the state side, as set forth in the constitution of 1936, the government embodied many seemingly democratic features.

The Central Committee of the party

Yet alongside the state, at all levels and in all localities, was the party. Only one party was allowed, the Communist, though nonparty members might be elected to the soviets or to other official positions. In the party, authority began at the top and proceeded downward. At its apex stood the Central Committee, whose membership varied from about 70 in the 1930s to more than double that in later years. Within the Central Committee a powerful Politburo, or political bureau, of about a dozen members dominated discussions of policy and personnel. An even more powerful general secretary, the office that Stalin virtually fashioned, dominated the entire structure and apparatus with authority over appointments, assignments, and decisions at all levels. Thus power and authority in the Communist Party flowed downward and outward, as in an army, or as in a highly centralized government agency or large private corporation in the West, except that the party was not subject to any outside control. Discipline was likewise enforced in ways not used in liberal countries, the fearsome machinery of the secret police being available for use against party members as well as those outside.

Growth and nature of the party

The number of party members, men and women, which could not have been more than 70,000 at the time of the revolution, rose to about 2 million by 1930, 3 million by 1940, and to 19 million in the late 1980s. The Leninist ideal of a highly disciplined party, made up of faithful and zealous workers who willingly carried out orders, the ideal on which the Bolsheviks had separated from the Mensheviks in 1903, continued to characterize the Communist party in the Soviet Union. A party of 2 million members, though small in contrast to the population of the U.S.S.R., still represented an enormous growth for the party itself; for each old member who had joined before 1917 there were thousands of new ones. To preserve party unity under the new conditions strict uniformity was enforced. Members intensively studied the principles of Marxism-Leninism, embraced dialectical materialism as a philosophy and even as a kind of religion, learned to take orders without question or compunction and to give authoritative leadership to the mass of nonparty members among whom they worked. The base of the party structure consisted of small nuclei or cells. In each factory, in each mine, in each office, in each class at the universities and technical schools, in each labor union, in each at least of the larger villages, a few people belonged to the party and imparted party views and party momentum to the whole.

The function of the party, in Marxist terms, was to carry out the dictatorship of the proletariat. It was to lead the people as a whole to the realization of socialism and, in day-to-day affairs, to coordinate the ponderous mechanism of government and make it work. Party members were present at all levels of the government. Throughout the whole structure, the party decided what the state should do.

The party in the U.S.S.R. by the 1930s functioned as a tightly knit, highly disciplined leadership group. Those who joined it were willing to work hard, devote themselves to party matters day and night, absorb and communicate the party policy (or "party line"), go where they were sent, attend meetings, speak up, perceive and explain the significance of passing events for the Soviet Union or the world revolution, and master intricate technical details of farming, manufacturing, or the care of machinery. The party was a specially trained elite whose members were in constant touch with each other. It was the thin stream of lifeblood which, by circulating through all the diverse tissues of the U.S.S.R., kept the whole complex body unified, functioning, and alive.

The party's leadership role

If the party was a leadership group, the corollary was that more than 95 out of 100 persons were condemned to be followers, and while it is perhaps true (as apologists for the system maintained) that under any system true leadership is exercised by a tiny fraction of people, the difference between Communist and non-Communist in the U.S.S.R. became a clear matter of social status. As the years passed, many Communists in the U.S.S.R. were less the revolutionary firebrand type than the successful and efficient man or woman in any social system. They represented the satisfied, not the dissatisfied. They enjoyed extensive material privileges, not only for themselves but also for their children. They became a new vested interest. Within the party, members had to be not so much leaders as followers. A homogeneous and monolithic organization had to present a solid front to the far more numerous outsiders. From time to time a good deal of difference of opinion and open discussion was tolerated (since there was only one party all political questions were intraparty disputes), but in the end the entire membership had to conform. The party favored a certain fertility of mind in looking for ways to get tasks accomplished, but it did not favor, and in fact repressed, originality, boldness, risk taking, or freedom of thought or action. The dangers of stagnation in such a system became apparent within the Soviet Union itself in later times.

The New Economic Policy, 1921–1927

By 1920 "war communism" had hopelessly antagonized the peasants, who were cultivating less than two-thirds as much land as in 1914. This fact, together with a severe drought and the breakdown of transportation, produced a great famine. Millions of people died. The ravages of eight years—of the First World War, the revolution, the civil wars, the Terror, the famine—had left the country in ruins, its productive facilities thrown back by decades as compared with 1914. The mutiny of the Kronstadt sailors in 1921 revealed profound disillusionment in the revolutionary ranks themselves. Lenin concluded that socialization had advanced too fast. He openly advocated a compromise with capitalism, a strategic retreat. The New Economic Policy, or NEP, adopted in 1921, lasted until 1927. Most of the decade of the 1920s saw a relaxation of tempo (and of terror) for most people in the U.S.S.R.

Under the NEP, while the state controlled the "commanding heights" of the economy, maintaining state ownership of the basic productive industries, it allowed a great deal of private trading for private profit. The basic problem was to restore trade between town and country. The peasants would produce only for their own subsistence unless they could exchange a surplus for

Private enterprise under the NEP

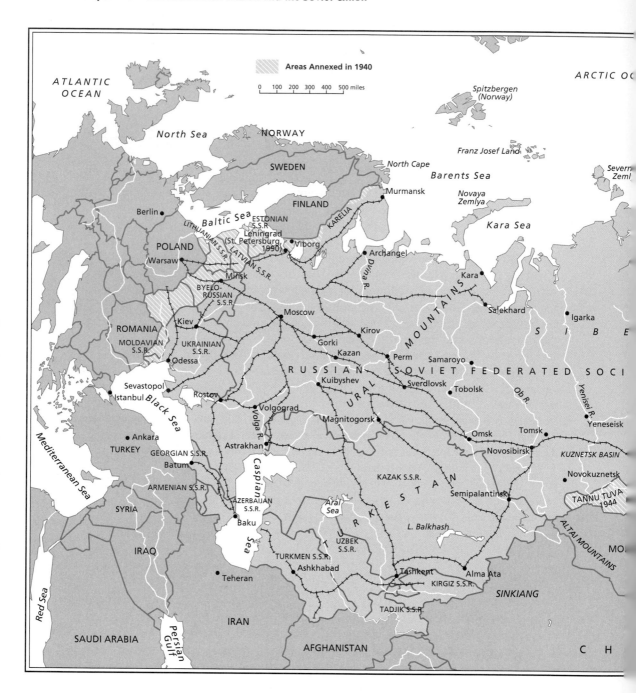

city-made wares such as clothing or tools. The city people had to be fed from the country if they were to turn out factory products or even continue to live in the city. Under the NEP, peasants were allowed to sell their farm products freely. Middlemen were allowed to buy and sell farm products and manufactured articles at will, selling to whom they pleased at market prices and at a profit to themselves. The NEP thus fostered a new commercial class in the cities and favored the big individualist farmer or kulak in the countryside. Indeed, rural

The U.S.S.R. was over 5,000 miles long and covered one-sixth of the land area of the globe. It was the only state that immediately adjoined so many important political areas—Europe in the west, the Middle East in the south, China along a long frontier, Japan across a narrow sea, and the United States on the coast near Alaska. The Union had 15 member republics (for a short time 16), of which the Russian was by far the largest. Most of it lay farther north than the Great Lakes of North America, but around Tashkent, in the latitude of New York and Chicago, cotton and citrus fruits were grown by irrigation. The diversion of rivers for this purpose led to environmental disasters such as the spread of deserts and the gradual drying up of the Aral Sea.

changes initiated before 1914 were still at work; peasant families consolidated millions of acres as private property in 1922, 1923, and 1924. Correspondingly, other peasants became "proletarians," wage-earning hired hands. Under the NEP the worst damages of war and revolution were repaired. But there was no real progress, for in 1928 Russia was producing only about as much grain, raw cotton, cattle, coal, and oil as in 1913, and far less than it presumably would have produced (given the rate of growth before 1913) had there been no revolution.

Social and Cultural Changes after the Revolution

Most Bolsheviks wanted their revolution to accomplish much more than the reconstruction of the state and economy; they wanted to revolutionize the daily lives of the workers, peasants, and "toilers," whom they now expected to construct a new classless society. The new Soviet society was supposed to destroy traditional gender hierarchies as well as the hierarchies of class and wealth. Under the legal reforms of the revolutionary regime, women received equal voting rights, the right to divorce, and access to birth control and abortion—which was legalized in 1920. The new theoretical rights, however, did not have much immediate effect on the social or economic lives of most women in the Soviet Union. Some of the new rights soon lost significance (for example, the right to vote) or disappeared (for example, abortion became illegal again in the 1930s and 1940s), and traditional social relations among the rural masses could not simply be transformed by revolutionary decrees. But it is also true that many girls and young women, like the boys and young men from the working classes, began to receive more education, especially after the turmoil of the Civil War subsided in the early 1920s.

Women's rights

The campaign to improve prerevolutionary literacy rates was only one example of the early Bolshevik aspirations for radical cultural changes. Writers and artists rallied to the revolutionary cause, seeing the social upheaval as part of a wider rejection of traditional ideas and artistic forms. The creative film director, Sergei Eisenstein, joined with avant-garde theatrical groups to create imaginative new techniques for editing films, portraying dramatic action, and representing political themes. Using his new techniques, Eisenstein produced a famous film about the Russian Revolution of 1905, *Potemkin* (1925), which was commissioned by the Soviet government and which is still regarded by many critics as one of the most innovative films in the history of cinema. Meanwhile, some radical artists sought to combine "futurist" art with the socialist revolution, and the young Russian poet Vladimir Mayakovsky moved on from a famous "Ode to Revolution" to innovative experiments with a new poetic language. In the end, though, Mayakovsky fell into despair and committed suicide as Soviet society entered the Stalinist era of rigid social control. By the late 1920s the period of experimental art was over, and the new cultural orthodoxy of "socialist realism" was celebrating the beauty of large factories and tractors rather than the abstract mysteries of the artistic avant-garde. Like all other spheres of Soviet life, art fell under the strict control of the Communist party and government institutions.

Art, literature, and film

Stalin and Trotsky

Lenin died in 1924 prematurely at the age of 54 after a series of paralyzing strokes that left him incapacitated in the last two years of his life. His embalmed remains were put permanently on view in the Kremlin; Petrograd was renamed Leningrad; a leader cult was built up around his name and image. The party presented him as a deified equal of Marx himself, and it became necessary for all schools of communist thought to claim unflinching fidelity to the Leninist tradition. Actually, in his own lifetime, the Old Bolsheviks had never regarded Lenin as infallible. They had often differed with him and with each other. As he lay dying, and after his death, his old companions and contemporaries, carrying on the feuding habits of the émigré days, fought with each other for control of the party in Lenin's name. They disputed over Lenin's intentions, but behind the scenes, the general secretary of the party, Joseph Stalin, whom Lenin had warned against, was drawing all the strings of party control into his own hands. More openly and vociferously, Leon Trotsky, who as war commissar in the critical years had been only less conspicuous than Lenin himself, raised the basic issues of the whole nature and future of the movement.

Trotsky, in 1925 and 1926, inveighed against the lassitude that had descended upon socialism.[2] The NEP with its tolerance of bourgeois and kulaks excited his contempt. He developed his doctrine of "permanent revolution," an incessant drive for proletarian objectives on all fronts in all parts of the world. He championed world revolution, which many in the party were beginning to discard in favor of first building socialism in one country. He denounced the tendency to bureaucratic ossification in the party and urged a new movement of the masses to give it life. He called for more forceful development of industry and for the collectivization of agriculture, which had figured in Communist manifestos ever since 1848. Above all, he demanded immediate adoption of an overall plan, a central control and operation of the whole economic life of the country.

Permanent revolution

Trotsky failed to carry the party with him. He was charged with leftist deviationism, machinations against the Central Committee, and inciting public discussion of controversial issues outside the party. Stalin wove his web. At a party congress in1927, 95 percent of the delegates dutifully voted for Stalin and the Central Committee and fewer than 5 percent voted for Trotsky. Trotsky was first exiled to Siberia, then banished from the U.S.S.R.; he lived in Europe and then in Mexico, writing and propagandizing for the "permanent revolution," stigmatizing developments in the U.S.S.R. as a monstrous betrayal of Marxism-Leninism, and organizing an underground against Stalin as he had done in former days against the tsar. He was murdered in Mexico in 1940 under mysterious circumstances, presumably by a Soviet agent. Not until the late 1980s was anyone in the U.S.S.R. permitted to talk or write about him and his contributions to the revolution.

94.   STALIN: THE FIVE-YEAR PLANS AND THE PURGES

Economic Planning

Hardly had Trotsky been expelled when Stalin and the party appropriated certain fragments of his program. In 1928 the party launched the First Five-Year Plan, aimed at rapid industrialization and the collectivization of agriculture. "Planning," or the central planning of a country's whole economic life by government officials, was to become the distinctive feature of Soviet economics and the one that for a time was to have the greatest influence on other parts of the world.

In retrospect, it seems strange that the Communists waited ten years before adopting a plan. The truth seems to be that the Bolsheviks had only vague ideas of what to do after their seizure of power. Marxism for the most part gave only general descriptions of a future classless society, which offered no specific guidance for the operation of a modern industrial system. The main constructive idea had been mapped out, most clearly by Engels. *Within* each private enterprise, Engels had observed, harmony and order reigned; it was only *between* private enterprises that capitalism was chaotic. In the individual factory, he noted, the various departments did not compete with each other; the output of all

[2]For communists, though not for socialists, the terms "communism" and "socialism" were almost interchangeable, since Russian Communists regarded their own system as true socialism and all other socialism as opportunistic, reactionary, or false. Communism was also defined, in the U.S.S.R., as a future state of society toward which socialism, that is, Soviet socialism, was the intermediate stage.

departments was planned and coordinated by management. In an approximate way, the great capitalist mergers and trusts, controlling many factories, prevented competition between them, assigned specific quotas to each, anticipated, coordinated, and stabilized the work of each plant and each person by an overall policy. With the growth of large corporate enterprise, observed Engels, the area of economic life under free competition was

Engels' centralized economy

constantly reduced, and the area brought under rational planning was constantly enlarged. The obvious next step, according to Engels and other socialists, was to treat *all* the economic life of a country as a single factory with many departments, a single enormous monopoly with many members under one unified, far-seeing management.

During the First World War the governments of belligerent countries had in fact adopted such centralized controls, not because they were socialist but because in time of war people were willing to subordinate their usual liberties to a single undisputed social purpose — victory. The "planned society" therefore made its first actual

Wartime conditions and economic planning

(though incomplete) appearance in the First World War. It was partly from socialist doctrine as exemplified by Engels, partly from experience of the war, and in even larger measure from the pressure to meet the continuing chronic problems of the country by raising its productive level that Stalin and the party in Russia developed the idea of an economic plan.

The U.S.S.R. decided to plan for five years into the future, beginning with the First Five-Year Plan in 1928. The aim of the plan was to strengthen and enrich the country, make it militarily and industrially self-sufficient, lay the groundwork for a true workers' society, and overcome the Russian reputation for backwardness. As Stalin said in a speech in 1929: "We are becoming a country of metal, a country of automobiles, a country of tractors. And when we have put the U.S.S.R. in a motor car and the *muzhik* in a tractor. . . . we shall see which countries may then be 'classified' as backward and which as advanced." The Plan was declared fulfilled in 1932, and a Second Five-Year Plan was launched, lasting until 1937. The Third, inaugurated in 1938, was interrupted by the war with Germany in 1941. New plans were introduced after 1945.

The First Five-Year Plan

The First Five-Year Plan (like its successors) listed the economic goals to be achieved. It was administered by an agency called the Gosplan. Within the frame of general policy set by the party, the Gosplan determined how much of every article the country should produce, what wages all classes of workers should receive, and at what prices all goods should be exchanged. Because all decisions were made at the top, it was as much a command economy as a planned economy. At the bottom level, in the individual factory, the local management drew up its requirements, or estimates of what it would need, in raw material, machinery, trained workers, plant facilities, and fuel, if it was to deliver the planned quantity of its product at a stated date. Thousands of estimates were passed up the planning ladder until they reached the Gosplan, which, balancing them against each other and against other needs as seen at the top, determined what should be produced and in what qualities and grades; how many workers should be trained in technical schools and in what particular skills; how many machines should be manufactured and how many spare parts; and how, where, when, and to whom the workers and manufactured goods should be made available. The plan, in short, undertook to control, by conscious management, the flow of resources and workforce which was regulated in capitalist economies by shifts in demand and supply and through changes in prices, wage levels, profits, and interest rates.

The system was exceedingly intricate. It was not easy to have the right number of ball bearings, for example, arrive at the right place at the right time, in exact correspondence to the amounts of other materials or to the number of workers waiting to use them. Sometimes there was overproduction; sometimes, underproduction. Countless reports, check-ups, and exchanges of information were necessary. A huge class of bureaucrats came into existence to handle the paperwork. The plan achieved some of its goals, exceeded a few, and failed in some. The criteria for fulfillment were almost always quantitative, often to the complete neglect of quality control.

The primary objective of the First Five-Year Plan was to build up the heavy industry, or capital wealth, of the U.S.S.R. The aim was to industrialize without the use of foreign loans.[3] Russia in 1928 was still chiefly an agricultural country. The world offered hardly any case of a country shifting from agriculture to industry without borrowing capital from abroad. Britain, the original home of the Industrial Revolution, was the best example, although even there in the eighteenth century a great deal of capital invested in England was owned by the Dutch. An agricultural country could industrialize from its own resources only by drawing upon agriculture itself. An agricultural revolution had been prerequisite to an industrial revolution in England. By enclosure of land, the squeezing out of small independent farmers, the introduction of scientific cultivation, and under the auspices of a growing class of wealthy landowners, England had both increased its production of food and released many of the rural population to find employment in industry. The First Five-Year Plan called for a similar agricultural revolution in Russia, without benefit to landlords and under the auspices of the state, but no one forsaw its consequences.

Building capital wealth

The Collectivization of Agriculture

The agricultural plan of 1929 set up collective farms, averaging a few thousand acres apiece, which were considered to be the property not of the state but of the peasants collectively who resided on them. (A few state-operated collective farms were also established, as models for the others.) Individual peasants were to pool their privately owned fields and livestock in these collectives. When those peasants who possessed fields or stock in considerable amount—the prosperous peasants or kulaks—resisted surrendering them to the new collectives, they were ruthlessly liquidated as a class. Zealous detachments of Communists from the cities used violence; poor peasants turned upon rich ones; hundreds of thousands of kulaks and their families were killed and many more were transported to labor camps in remote parts of the Soviet Union. The trend that had gone on since the nineteenth-century Emancipation, building up a class of property-owning, labor-hiring, and "bourgeois" peasants, was now abruptly reversed. Collectivization was intended to convert the peasantry into a class more nearly resembling the proletariat of Marxian doctrine, a class of people who as individuals owned no capital and employed no labor, and so would better fit into a proletarian, socialist state. The year 1929, not 1917, was the memorable revolutionary year for most people in Russia.

Collectivization was accomplished at the cost of village class war in which many of the most capable farmers perished and at the cost also of a wholesale destruction of livestock. The big farmers slaughtered their horses, cattle, pigs, and poultry rather than give them up. Even middling and small farmers did the same, caring nothing about animals that were no longer their

The human costs of collectivization

---

[3]The Bolsheviks had repudiated the entire debt of the tsarist empire. Their credit in capitalist countries was therefore not good, so that, in addition to fearing dependence upon foreign lenders, they were in any case for a long time unable to borrow large sums.

The creation of collective farms during Stalin's First Five-Year Plan was one of the most radical and most resented economic actions of the new Communist regime. Millions of farm animals were destroyed by angry peasants and millions of people died in the subsequent period of repression and famine. But the creation of large-scale agriculture and tractor stations gradually made it possible for farmers to use new machinery in Russian fields. These farmers were heading for work on new tractors in the early 1930s.
(SOVFOTO)

own. The ruinous loss of animals was the worst unforeseen calamity of the First Five-Year Plan. The agricultural disorders led to a deadly famine in southeast Russia and the Ukraine in 1932 that cost millions of lives. Despite the famine Stalin refused to cut back on cereal and other food exports because they were needed to pay for industrial imports under the Five-Year Plan.

By introducing thousand-acre units in place of small ones, collectivization made it possible to apply capital to the soil. Formerly the average peasant had been far too poor to buy a tractor and his fields had been too tiny and dispersed for him to use one; only a few kulaks had employed any such machinery. In the course of the First Five-Year Plan hundreds of Machine Tractor Stations were organized throughout the country. In its region each maintained a force of tractors, harvesting combines, and expert agronomists, which could be dispatched from one collective farm to another by local arrangement. The new collectivized system made it easier

Mechanization of agriculture

for higher authorities to control the agricultural surplus (products not consumed by the village itself). Each collective was assigned a quota. Members of the collective could sell in a free market any products they raised beyond this quota. Meanwhile the government knew the quantity of agricultural produce it could count on, either to feed the cities and other regions that did not produce their own food or for export in the world market to pay for imports of machinery from the West. By 1939 all but a negligible fraction of the peasantry was collectivized, but collectivization failed to increase agricultural output. The new collectives denied peasants the freedom to make their own economic decisions, destroyed their incentive to improve the land they worked, and prevented them from passing land on to their heirs. Agriculture therefore remained a troubled sector of the economy. Collectivization made possible, however, the success of industrialization by augmenting the supply of industrial workers. Since the villages needed less labor, 20 million people moved from country to city between the years 1926 and 1939 and were available for jobs in the new industries.

The Growth of Industry

While the agricultural base was being revolutionized, industrialization went rapidly forward. At first there was considerable dependence on the capitalist countries. Engineers and other technicians from western Europe and the United States went to work in the Soviet Union. Much machinery was imported. But the worldwide depression that set in about 1931, bringing a catastrophic fall of agricultural prices, made foreign-made machines more costly in terms of the cereals that were the chief Soviet export. The international situation also deteriorated. While the U.S.S.R. always considered the whole outside world hostile to it, both Japan and Germany in the 1930s showed overt hostility and posed a new military threat. The Second Five-Year Plan, launched in 1933, though in some ways less ambitious than the first, showed an even greater determination to cut down imports and achieve national self-sufficiency, especially in the heavy industry basic to war production.

No ten years in the history of any Western country ever showed such a rate of industrial growth as the decade of the first two plans in the Soviet Union. In Great Britain industrialization had been gradual; in Germany and the United States it had been more rapid, and in each country there had been decades in which output of coal or iron doubled; but in the U.S.S.R., *Rates of industrial growth* from 1928 to 1938, production of iron and steel expanded four times and that of coal expanded three and a half times. In 1938 the U.S.S.R. was the world's largest producer of farm tractors and railway locomotives. Four-fifths of all its industrial output came from plants built in the preceding ten years. In 1939 the U.S.S.R., as measured by purely quantitative standards, was surpassed in gross industrial output only by the United States and Germany.

The plans called for a marked development of industry east of the Urals and brought a modernization of life for the first time to inner Asia. New industrial cities rose in the old Turkestan (divided into the five Central Asian Soviet socialist republics) and in Siberia. The opening of all these new areas demanded a revolution in transportation, and by 1938 the railroads were carrying five times as much freight as in 1913.

These astounding developments were enough to change the relative economic strength of the world's peoples with respect to one another. It *Changes brought by modernization* was significant that inner Asia was for the first time turning industrial. In part because of these developments in Asia, the Russia that went to war with Germany in 1941 proved to be a different antagonist from the Russia of 1914.

CHRONOLOGY OF NOTABLE EVENTS, 1894–1937

1894	Creation of Russian Marxist organization, the Social Democratic Party
1903	Social Democrats split into two factions, Bolsheviks and Mensheviks; Lenin leads Bolsheviks
January 1905	Economic hardship, "Bloody Sunday," and Russo-Japanese War spark Revolution of 1905 in St. Petersburg
October 1905	Tsar's "October Manifesto" establishes new parliamentary body, the Duma
1906–1911	Stolypin's reforms promote growth of prosperous farmers (*kulaks*)
1914	Russia enters war with Germany and suffers crushing military defeats
March 1917	Tsar Nicholas II abdicates; Russia becomes a republic under provisional government and continues war with Germany
April 1917	Germany provides safe passage for Bolshevik leaders to enter Russia
November 1917	The Bolshevik Revolution: Lenin and followers overthrow the provisional government in Petrograd
January 1918	Bolsheviks dissolve Constituent Assembly and establish the Red Army
1918–1922	Bolsheviks consolidate power and suppress all opponents in Civil War and "Red Terror"
1919–1920	Creation of Third, or Communist, International (the Comintern)
1921–1927	New Economic Policy allows more independent commercial activity
1922	Establishment of the Union of Soviet Socialist Republics (USSR)
1925–1927	Stalin prevails over Trotsky to take control of the Bolshevik Central Committee
1928	Stalin launches the first Five-Year Plan for economic development
1929	Soviet regime begins the collectivization of agriculture; resistance from *kulaks* and others leads to widespread repression and famine
1936–1937	Public "purge trials" remove Old Bolsheviks from Communist party; many are executed or imprisoned

Industrialization in the Urals and in Asia enabled the U.S.S.R. (with Allied assistance) to survive the German occupation and destruction of the older industrial areas in the Don valley. The new "socialist fatherland" proved able to absorb terrible losses and strike back. A great deal of the increased industrial output had gone to equip and modernize the Red Army.

At the same time, the degree of industrialization of the U.S.S.R. can easily be exaggerated. It was phenomenal because it started from so little. Qualitatively, by Western criteria, standards of production were low. Many of the hastily constructed new plants were shoddy and suffered from rapid depreciation. In efficiency, as shown by output per worker employed, the U.S.S.R. continued to lag behind the West. In intensity of modernization, as shown by output of certain items in proportion to the whole population, it also lagged. Per capita comparisons with other industrial nations, in 1937, show that the U.S.S.R. produced less coal, electricity, cottons, woolens, leather shoes, or soap than did the United States, Britain, Germany, France, or Japan, and less iron and steel than any of them except Japan. Production of paper is revealing because paper is used in so many different aspects of modern education, economic activity, communications, government affairs, and household life. Where the United States about 1937 produced 103 pounds of paper per person, Germany and Great Britain each produced 92, France produced 51, and Japan produced 17, the U.S.S.R. produced only 11.

Social Costs and Social Effects of the Plans

Industrialization in Russia demanded huge and continuing sacrifices on the part of the people. It was not merely that kulaks lost their lives, or that millions of others, whose exact numbers have never been known, were found to be enemies of the system and sent off to correctional labor camps. All were required to accept a program of austerity and self-denial, going without the better food, housing, and other consumer goods that might have been produced, in order that the capital wealth and heavy industry of the country might be built up. The plan required hard work and low wages. Better housing, better food, better clothing, and more leisure would follow once the basic industries had been built. Morale was sustained by propaganda. One of the chief functions of party members was to explain why sacrifices were necessary. In the late 1930s life began to ease; food rationing was abolished in 1935, and a few more products of light industry, such as dishes and fountain pens, began to appear in Soviet retail stores. Living standards were at least up to those of 1927 with prospects brighter for raising them. But the need for war preparations, as the world again approached chaos, again drove back the vision of the Promised Land.

Sacrifices and rewards

Socialism, as realized in the plans, did away with some of the evils of unrestrained free enterprise. There was no acknowledged unemployment. There was no cycle of boom and depression. There was less misuse of women and children than in the early days of industrialism in the West. There was a minimum below which no one was supposed to fall. On the other hand, there was no economic equality. Marxism, indeed, had never seen complete equality of income as a principal objective. While there were no very rich people, as in the West (where the income of the very rich often came from inherited property), the differences in income were nevertheless great. High government officials, managers, engineers, and favored artists and intellectuals received the highest rewards. People with large incomes could build precarious little fortunes for themselves and their children. They could not, however, under socialism, own any industrial capital, that is, buy shares of stock or other equities. There was, of course, no stock exchange.

Competition of a special kind developed. In 1935 a miner named Stakhanov greatly increased his daily output of coal by devising improvements in his methods of work. He also greatly increased his wages, since Soviet workers were paid at piece rates. His example proved contagious; workers all over the country began to break records of all kinds. The government publicized their achievements, called them Stakhanovites and "labor heroes," and pronounced the movement to be "a new and higher stage of socialist competition." In labor circles in the United States such straining to increase output was called a speed-up, and piecework wages had long been anathema to the organized labor of all countries. Nor was management free from competitive pressure. A factory manager who failed to show the net income (or "profit") upon

Competition

The rapid industrialization of the Soviet Union emphasized heavy machinery rather than consumer goods, but the Soviets also began to produce their own cars. This automobile factory in the city of Gorky (a city renamed by the Soviets for the Russian writer) represented the new industrial economy and also expressed the requisite political loyalty to Stalin. (SOVFOTO)

which the plan counted, or who failed to meet his quota of output, might lose not only his job but also his social status—or even his life.

The price of solidarity

Solidarity was purchased at the price of totalitarianism. The government supervised everything. There was no room for skepticism, independence of thought, or any criticism that weakened the will to achieve. As in tsarist times, no one could leave the country without special permission, which was given far more rarely than before 1914. There was, of course, only one political party. There were no free labor unions, no free press, no freedom of association, and at best only an irritable tolerance for religion. Soviet Jews who adapted to the system found themselves in a more favorable position than ever before; some even attained positions of high importance. Many still faced lingering suspicion and distrust, however, and in religious matters they met harassment. Art, literature, and even science became vehicles of political propaganda; creative, experimental works— and the people who promoted them—disappeared from Soviet cultural life. Conformity was the ideal, and the very passion for solidarity made for fear and suspicion of all who might go astray. As for the number of people sacrificed to Stalin's brutal Juggernaut— liquidated bourgeois, liquidated peasants, purged party members, disaffected persons sentenced to long terms in labor camps—a precise figure is difficult to arrive at, but it certainly reached many millions over the years in which the various Soviet plans were implemented.

The Purge Trials of the 1930s

In 1936 socialism was judged to have proved so successful that a new constitution for the U.S.S.R. was proclaimed. It enumerated, as rights of Soviet citizens, not merely the usual civil liberties of Western democracy but the rights to steady employment, rest, leisure, economic security, and a comfortable old age. All forms of racism were condemned. It reorganized the Soviet republics and granted equal and direct universal suffrage. The constitution of 1936 received favorable comment in the West, where it was hoped that the Russian Revolution, like former revolutions, had at last turned into more peaceable and quiet channels. It was nonetheless apparent that the Communist party remained the sole governing group in the country, that Stalin was tightening his dictatorship, and that the party was racked by internal troubles.

It was natural that the rapid changes of the 1930s should provide divergences of opinion among the party leaders, but Stalin acted preemptorily to suppress all dissent. As early as 1933, the party underwent a drastic purge, *Diverging opinions* in which a third of its members were expelled. Even the faithful were appalled at Stalin's growing ruthlessness. Serge Kirov, an old friend and revolutionary companion of Stalin since 1909, head of the Leningrad party apparatus, and member of the Politburo since 1930, showed signs of leading the disaffected. In 1934 he was assassinated in his office, it is now thought by a police agent of Stalin's. Stalin used the assassination as an excuse to strike out at his opponents, imagined or real, by a revival of terror, immediately executing over a hundred persons and launching the extraordinary purges of the next four years.

A series of sensational trials took place. In 1936 sixteen Old Bolsheviks were brought to trial. Some, like Zinoviev and Kamenev, had been expelled from the party in 1927 for supporting Trotsky and subsequently, *Trials of the Old* *Bolsheviks* after the proper recantations, had been readmitted. Now they were charged with the murder of Kirov, with plotting the murder of Stalin, and with having organized in 1932 under Trotsky's inspiration a secret group to disrupt and terrorize the Central Committee. To the amazement of the world, all the accused made full confession to the charges in open court. All blamed themselves as unworthy and erring reprobates. All were put to death. In 1937, after similar trials, 17 other Old Bolsheviks met the same fate or received long prison sentences; and in 1938 a group of "rightists" were executed after they were charged with wanting to restore bourgeois capitalism. The same confessions and self-accusations followed in almost every case, with no other verifiable evidence adduced. How these confessions were obtained in open court from hardened revolutionaries apparently in full possession of their faculties and bearing no sign of physical harm mystified the outside world. Only later did it become clear that psychological torture had broken the will of those accused and that threats against their families (or promises to spare them) had played the major part.

In addition to these public trials there were other arrests, private inquisitions, and executions. In 1937, in a secret court martial, Marshal Tukhachevski and seven other top generals were accused of Trotskyism and of conspiring with the Germans and Japanese and were summarily shot. The purges embraced the highest levels of the party, government, military, intellectual, and scientific circles and reached down to the lesser echelons as well. In later years the KGB itself disclosed that in the years 1930–1953 (the year of Stalin's

Soviet propaganda depicted Stalin as the benevolent national leader and as the worthy successor to Lenin. This typical poster shows a thoughtful, visionary Stalin with a new hydroelectric plant in the background. The artist, Konstantin Ivanov, quoted Lenin on the poster and gave this work a straightforward political title: "To communism—along the path laid by Lenin."
(SOVFOTO)

death) 3,778,334 persons had been tried and sentenced for "counterrevolutionary" activity and crimes against the state, most of them in the Great Terror of 1934–1938, and that 786,098 were executed; unknown others died in prison camps, later to be known as the Gulag. In later years, the innocence of many of Stalin's victims was officially confirmed and their reputations posthumously restored.

Reinforcing the dictatorship

By these purges Stalin rid himself of all possible rivals for his own position. He disposed of the embarrassment of having colleagues about him who could remember the old days, who could quote Lenin as a former friend, or belittle the reality of 1937 by recalling the dreams of 1917. After 1938 there were virtually no Old Bolsheviks left. The aging but still explosive professional revolutionaries were now dead. A younger group, products of the new order, practical, constructive, impatient of "agitators," and acquiescing in Stalin's dictatorship, were operating what was now an established system.

✑ 95.   THE INTERNATIONAL IMPACT OF COMMUNISM, 1919–1939

The Background: Socialism and the First World War

Marxism had always been international in its outlook. To Marx and the early Marxists existing states (like other institutions) owed their character to the class struggle. They were no more than committees of the bourgeoisie to govern the proletariat, destined to be dismantled and pass away in the course of inevitable historic processes. After Marx's death, as Marxist parties grew in numbers, and as states of western Europe became more democratic, most people who called themselves Marxists accepted the national state, seeing in it a means by which the workers' lot could be gradually improved. This view was part of the movement of revisionism, or what more rigorous Marxists called "opportunism." In the First World War national loyalty proved its strength. The socialist parties in the Reichstag, the French Chamber, and other parliamentary bodies voted for war credits without hesitation. Socialist workers reported for mobilization like everyone else.

Small minorities of socialists in every country, however, refused to accept the war. Marxian socialism had long taught that workers of all nations were bound by the supreme loyalty of class, that their real enemies were the capitalists of their own countries, that international wars were capitalist and imperialist quarrels, and that class struggle was the only kind of warfare that the proletarian should accept. These socialists denounced the action of the socialist majorities as a sellout to capitalism and imperialism. They met in international conferences with each other and with socialists from the neutral countries. Active among them had been Lenin and other Russian Social Democrats then in Switzerland. "The only task for socialists," wrote Lenin in 1914, "is to convert the war of peoples into a civil war." The minority or antiwar socialists met at the small Swiss town of Zimmerwald in 1915, where they drew up a "Zimmerwald program," calling for immediate peace without annexations or indemnities. This had no effect on most socialists in the belligerent countries. The Zimmerwald group itself soon began to split. Most Zimmerwalders regarded peace, or the repudiation of the war, as their aim. But a "Zimmerwald Left" began to develop, inspired mainly by Lenin and the Russian émigrés. This faction made its aim not peace but revolution. It hoped that the war would go on until it caused social revolution in the belligerent countries.

Class solidarity versus nationalism

Then in April 1917, as we have seen, with the German imperial government arranging their trip, Lenin and the other Bolsheviks went back to Russia and accomplished the November Revolution. Lenin, until his death in 1924, believed that the Russian Revolution was only a local phase of a world revolution—of *the* revolution of strict Marxian doctrine. Russia, for him, was the theater of currently most active operations in the international class war. Because he expected proletarian upheaval to follow soon in Germany, Poland, the Danube valley, and the Baltic regions, he accepted the treaty of Brest-Litovsk. He took no pride in Russia; he was no patriot or "social-chauvinist," to use his own term. In the founding of the U.S.S.R. in 1922 he saw a nucleus around which other and greater soviet republics of any nationality might coalesce.

The First World War was in fact followed by attempted revolutions in Germany and eastern Europe. With the German and Austro-Hungarian empires wrecked, socialists and liberals of all descriptions strove to establish new regimes. Among socialists the old differences persisted, between those favoring gradual, nonviolent, and parliamentary methods and a more extreme group

Attempted revolutions in Europe

who saw in postwar disintegration a chance to realize the international proletarian revolution. The first group looked upon the Bolshevik Revolution with horror; the second looked upon it with admiration. The first group included not only trade union officials and practical socialist politicians but also such prewar giants of Marxian exegesis as Karl Kautsky and Eduard Bernstein. Even Kautsky, who had upheld pure Marxism against the revisionism of Bernstein, could not stomach the methods of Lenin. The mass of European socialists, with their fiercest leaders removed, were to remain characterized by relative moderation. Marxist in principle, they were in fact more than ever wedded to gradual, peaceable, and parliamentary methods. The second group, radical Leninists, continued to agitate for the forcible overthrow of European capitalism and European political institutions; and they began to join together in the Bolsheviks' new organization for promoting world revolution, the Third, or Communist, International, which was created in March 1919.

The Founding of the Third International

The Second International, which since its foundation in 1889 had met every two or three years until 1914, held its first postwar meeting at Berne in 1919. It represented socialist parties and labor organizations of all countries. The Berne meeting was stormy, for a small minority vehemently demanded "revolution as in Russia, socialization of property as in Russia, application of Marxism as in Russia." Overruled at Berne, they repaired to Moscow and there founded a new International in conjunction with the Russian Communist party, and with Lenin and the Russians dominating it completely. It was Lenin's hope, by founding a new International of his own, to discredit moderate socialism and to claim for the Communists the true line of succession from the First International of Karl Marx.

The Third International

The first congress of the Third International in 1919 was somewhat haphazard, but at the second, in 1920, the extreme left parties of 37 countries were represented. The Russian party was supposedly only one component. Actually, it supplied most of the personnel and most of the funds; the Bolshevik Zinoviev was its first president, remaining in this office until his disgrace as a Trotskyist in 1927. The Third, or Communist, International—the Comintern—was in part a spontaneous rallying of Marxists from all countries who accepted the Bolshevik Revolution as the true fruition of Marxism and were willing to follow the Russian lead; but, even more, it was the creation and weapon of the Bolsheviks themselves, by which they wished to discredit and isolate the moderate socialists and bring about world revolution. Of all enemies the Communists hated the socialists most, reserving for them even stronger epithets than they bestowed upon capitalists and imperialists, because Communists and socialists were competing for the same objective, the leadership of the world's working class.

Lenin's Twenty-One Points

The second congress of the International, in 1920, endorsed a program of Twenty-One Points, written by Lenin. These included the requirements that each national party must call itself Communist, repudiate "reformist" socialism, propagandize labor unions and get Communists into the important union offices, infiltrate the army, impose an iron discipline upon members, require submission to the orders of the international Executive, use both legal channels and secret underground methods, and expel promptly any member not hewing to the party line. Making no pretense of respect for parliamentary democracy, the second congress ruled that "the only question can be that of utilizing bourgeois state institutions

The Russian Revolution brought about a split between socialists who favored parliamentary politics and those who supported the revolutionary methods of the Bolsheviks. The latter group met in Russia to form the Third, or Communist, International. It adhered to the views of Lenin, who is speaking here to a meeting of the Third International in 1920.
(Hulton-Deutsch Collection/Corbis)

for their own destruction." The Comintern was not an assemblage of humanitarians engaged in welfare work; it was a weapon for revolution, organized by revolutionaries who knew what revolution was. In most countries, as in France, there were many socialists who could not accept the Twenty-One Points. Once unified socialist parties therefore broke up. Communists and socialists went their separate ways.

For several years the U.S.S.R., using the Comintern or more conventional diplomatic channels, promoted world revolution as best it could. Communists from many countries went to Russia for indoctrination. Native-born or Russian agents proceeded to the Dutch Indies, China, Europe, and America. Until 1927 the Chinese revolutionists welcomed

Promoting world revolution

assistance from Moscow; the Russian Borodin became an adviser in their affairs. In 1924, in England, publication of the "Zinoviev letter," in which the Comintern allegedly urged British workers to provoke revolution, led to a great electoral victory for the Conservative party. The Bolshevik menace, real and imagined, produced everywhere a strong reaction. It was basic to the rise of fascism described in the chapters to follow.

In 1927, with the suppression of Trotskyism and world revolutionism in Russia, and with the concentration under Stalin on a program of building socialism in one country, the Comintern moderated its activities. In 1935, as fascist dictators became noisily bellicose and threatened the Soviet Union, the U.S.S.R. through the Comintern instructed all Communist parties to enter into coalitions with socialists and activist liberals in what were called "popular fronts" to combat fascism and reaction and support the national defense of their own countries. During the Second World War (in 1943), as a gesture of goodwill to Great Britain and the United States, the U.S.S.R. abolished the Comintern entirely. It reappeared for a few years from 1947 to 1956 under a new name, the Communist Information Bureau or Cominform, and was then disbanded.

The U.S.S.R.'s impact

It was not through the Comintern that the U.S.S.R. exerted its greatest influence on the world in the years after 1917. It exerted its influence by the massive fact of its very existence. By 1939 it was clear that a new type of economic system had emerged. Before 1917 no one in Europe or Asia had thought that anything was to be learned from Russia. Twenty years later even critics of the U.S.S.R. feared that it might represent the wave of the future. Its sheer power was soon demonstrated in the Second World War. Marxism was no longer merely a theory; there was an actual society, embracing a sixth of the globe, which called itself Marxist.

In every country those who were most critical of capitalist institutions compared them unfavorably to those of the Soviet Union. Some believed that something like Soviet results might be obtained without the use of Soviet methods, which were dismissed as typically Russian, a deplorable heritage from the tsars. With the appearance of Communism and Communist parties, socialism and socialist ideas seemed in contrast to be middling and respectable. Everywhere in the 1930s the idea of planning began to find favor. Workers obtained more security against the fluctuations of capitalism. Colonial and formerly colonial peoples, especially in Asia, were particularly impressed by the achievement of the U.S.S.R., which had shown how a traditional society could modernize without falling under the influence of foreign capital or foreign guidance.

For a long time the Communist party in the Soviet Union presented itself as the leader of world revolution and tried to exert control over Communist parties in all other countries. This became increasingly difficult. Over the years the U.S.S.R. pursued diplomatic

Waning Soviet influence in later years

and military policies and engaged in acts of aggression and territorial expansion, such as the tsarist state might have done. By the late 1980s the U.S.S.R. was no longer an innovative, or some would say, a viable society. Its economic system was in a shambles; the component republics demanded autonomy or independence. The revelation from within the Soviet Union itself of the persecution and deaths of tens of millions of innocent victims, along with the restiveness of its own nationalities, undermined its role as leader of oppressed peoples elsewhere. European Communist parties proclaimed their independence from Moscow. Meanwhile a new form of dynamic communism emerged in 1949 in the People's Republic of China. Yet all Communist parties, including the Chinese, are derived from Marxism and from the Russian Revolution of 1917, once hailed as the first great victory over capitalism and imperialism. It was thus a revolution that profoundly influenced fervent supporters and passionate opponents throughout the twentieth century. But the repressive political system, stifling cultural policies, and economic failures of the Soviet state also produced a widespread hostility to Communism, even among many of its former advocates and supporters.

For interactive exercises, glossary, chronologies, and more, go to the *Online Learning Center* at **www.mhhe.com/palmer10.**

Chapter 19

DEMOCRACY, ANTI-IMPERIALISM, AND THE ECONOMIC CRISIS AFTER THE FIRST WORLD WAR

We have followed events in the Soviet Union in detail to about the year 1939 but have left the story of Europe and the rest of the world at the signing of the peace treaties of 1919. We turn now to the wider history of political and economic change during the period of just 20 years that elapsed between the formal close of the First World War in 1919 and the outbreak of the Second World War in 1939. In these 20 years the world made a dizzy passage from confidence to disillusionment and from hope to fear. It went through a few years of superficial prosperity, abruptly followed by unparalleled economic disaster. For a time, in the 1920s, democracy and democratic reforms seemed to be advancing; then, in the difficult economic conditions of the 1930s, dictatorship began to spread in countries that had earlier tried to move toward greater democracy. Let us first examine the apparent triumphs of democracy and the growing opposition to European imperialism in the 1920s, turn next to the devastating worldwide effects of the Great Depression that began in 1929, and then, in the following chapter, trace the new conflicts and rising dangers of the 1930s.

96. THE ADVANCE OF DEMOCRACY AFTER 1919

The first years following the war were troubled. The victors and losers alike faced serious difficulties in reconversion from war to peace. Veterans demobilized from the huge armies found themselves unemployed and psychologically restless. Farms and factories geared to maximum production during the war faced a sudden disappearance of markets. They produced more than could now be sold, so that the war was followed by a sharp postwar depression, which, however, had run its course by 1922. Basically, the economic position even of the victors was seriously damaged, for the war had disjointed the world of 1914, in

Chapter emblem: Mahatma Gandhi leading a group of nonviolent protestors in 1930 during the political campaign for India's national independence. (Bettmann/Corbis)

which industrial western Europe had lived by exchange with eastern Europe and with overseas countries.

Gains of Democracy and Social Democracy

The war, President Wilson had said, was fought to make the world safe for democracy. Political democracy, to be sure, now made numerous advances. The new states that emerged from the war all adopted liberal democratic principles such as written constitutions and universal suffrage. Democracy made advances even in countries that had long been in large measure democratic. Great Britain, for example, dropped the last barriers to universal male suffrage in 1918. The most conspicuous innovation in many countries was the growing enfranchisement of women. We have seen how the women's suffrage movement in Great Britain achieved an important breakthrough in 1918, when women received a somewhat restricted right to vote; in 1928 the restrictions were dropped and the vote was granted on an equal basis with men. In 1920, through an amendment to the constitution, female suffrage became general in the United States. Women voted also in Germany and in most of the new states of Europe. In the Soviet Union women received the vote on an equal basis with men after the revolution in 1917.

In most European countries the successors of the old prewar socialists gained in strength. With the left wings of the old socialists generally seceding, calling themselves Communists, and affiliated with each other and with Moscow in the Communist International, the European socialists or social democrats were preponderantly parties of peaceable or revisionist Marxism, entirely willing to pursue their political and social goals by parliamentary and legislative methods. Labor unions, with new self-confidence gained from the role they had played in the war, grew in membership, prestige, and importance.

Social legislation enacted

Social legislation that before the war would have seemed radical was now enacted in many places. An eight-hour legal working day became common; and government-sponsored insurance programs against sickness, accident, and old age were either adopted or extended; an act of 1930, in France, insured almost 10 million workers. An air of progressive democracy pervaded Europe and the European world. The social service, or welfare, state, already under way in the late nineteenth century, was becoming more firmly established.

Only in Italy in the early postwar years, of the states that might have been expected to continue their prewar democratic gains, did democracy receive a sharp setback. Italy had been a parliamentary state since 1861 and had introduced a democratic male suffrage in the elections of 1913. In 1919 the Italians held their second such elections. But Italian

Mussolini

democracy soon abruptly ended. In 1922 an agitator named Benito Mussolini, leading a movement which he called Fascism (thereby adding a new word to the world's political vocabulary), ended Italian parliamentary government and founded his Fascist regime. Lenin in his way had already created the first single-party state; Mussolini became the first of the dictators of postwar Europe outside the Soviet Union. Fascist Italy in the 1920s was the chief exception in what seemed to be a rising tide of democracy.

The New States of Central and East-Central Europe

In central and east-central Europe—in Germany, in the territory of the former Austro-Hungarian empire, and in the western fringe of former tsarist Russia—new states and new governments struggled to establish themselves. The new postwar states included, besides

The 19th amendment to the Constitution gave American women the right to vote in all elections. This poster, which was published by the League of Women Voters shortly after the amendment was approved in 1920, urged women to use their new voting rights by going to the polls.
(Getty Images)

republican Germany, the four successor states to the Habsburg empire—Austria, Hungary, Czechoslovakia, and Yugoslavia; and the five states that had broken away from the Russian empire—Poland, Finland, Estonia, Latvia, and Lithuania (see map, pp. 716–717). The other small states in eastern Europe, Romania, Bulgaria, Greece, and Albania, had already been independent before 1914; their boundaries underwent some modification and their governments underwent considerable reorganization after the war. Turkey, the successor to the Ottoman Empire, was also a new republic.

Allthough many people in all countries had developed nationalist identities and aspirations, the new states in Europe were to a large extent accidents of the war. Nowhere, except possibly in Poland, did they represent a deeply felt, long-maturing, or widespread revolutionary sentiment. *Accidents of war* Only an infinitesimal number of Germans in 1914 would have voted for a republic. Even among the nationalities of Austria-Hungary in 1914 few persons would have chosen the complete breakup of the Habsburg empire. The republicans, moderate socialists, agrarians, or nationalists who now found themselves in power had to improvise governments for which there had been little preparation. They had to contend with reactionaries, monarchists, and members of the old aristocracy. They had also to deal with the real revolutionaries, who, inspired by Lenin's success, hoped to bring about a dictatorship of the proletariat. A Communist revolt broke out in Germany in 1919 but was quickly suppressed; Soviet regimes that were actually set up were soon crushed in Hungary and in the German state of Bavaria; and as late as 1923 there was a Communist uprising in the German state of Saxony.

Self-determination

The new states all embodied the principle of national self-determination, which held that each nationality should enjoy political sovereignty—one nation, one government. But people in this region were and always had been locally intermixed. Each of the new states therefore included minority nationalities; with the exception of an exchange of populations between Greece and Turkey arranged in 1923, there was no thought of the actual physical removal of "alien" groups. Poland, Czechoslovakia, and Yugoslavia were the most composite of the new states. Poland and Czechoslovakia each had many disaffected Germans. In Czechoslovakia the Slovaks resented Czech domination and in Yugoslavia, where the Serbs were in control, Croatian and other separatist movements actively opposed the Serb domination.

Nevertheless, despite economic and nationalist troubles, the new states and governments attempted at the outset to make themselves democratic. All the newly created states were republics except Yugoslavia, where the monarchy was under the older Serbian dynasty. Hungary started out in 1918 as a republic, but the attempt of the Communist leader Béla Kun to found a Hungarian Soviet Republic in 1919 brought back the counter-revolutionaries who restored the Habsburg monarchy in principle, though they were prevented by foreign pressure from restoring the king in person. Hungary emerged in 1920 as a monarchy with a perennially vacant throne, under an authoritarian regency exercised by Admiral Horthy. All smaller states of Europe, including Hungary, possessed at least the machinery of democracy until the 1930s; that is, they had constitutions, parliaments, elections, and a diversity of political parties. If civil liberty was sometimes violated, the right to civil liberty was not denied; and if elections were sometimes rigged, they were at least in principle supposed to be free.

Economic Problems of Eastern Europe; Land Reform

Eastern Europe for centuries had been an agrarian region of large landed estates, which supported on the one hand a wealthy landowning aristocracy of almost feudal outlook, and on the other an impoverished mass of agricultural workers with little or no property of their own. The landed aristocracy had been the chief support of the Austro-Hungarian empire and an important pillar of the old order in the tsarist empire and in eastern Prussia. The mass of the rural population through all this region had been free from serfdom only since the middle of the preceding century. The middle class of business and professional people was small except in Austria and Bohemia, the western portion of Czechoslovakia. In general, the whole region was conscious of lagging behind western Europe, not only in industry, factories, railroads, and great cities, but also in literacy, schooling, reading habits, health, death rates, length of life, and material standard of living.

Obstacles to modernization

The new states set out to modernize themselves, generally on the model of the West. In addition to introducing democratic and constitutional ideas, they put up protective tariffs, behind which they tried to develop factories and industries of their own. But the new national boundaries created difficulties. Where Europe had 6,000 miles of frontiers in 1913, it had almost 10,000 after the war, and all the increase was in eastern Europe. Goods circulated much less easily. Protected industries in the old agricultural regions produced inefficiently and at high cost. Old and established industries in Austria, Czechoslovakia, and western Poland, cut off by the new frontiers and new tariffs from their former markets, fell upon hard times. The working class of Vienna lived in misery. Vienna, a city of 2 million persons, formerly the capital of an empire of 50 million, was now the capital of a republic of 6 million. In Czechoslovakia the German minority living in the Sudetenland complained that in hard times the German businesspeople and workers, because of government policies, always suffered more than their Czech counterparts. Economically, the carving up of eastern Europe into a dozen independent states was self-defeating.

The greatest of reforms undertaken by the new east-European states was the reform of landownership. Although it far from solved basic economic problems in the area, it did have substantial effect on the pattern of land distribution. The whole traditional agrarian base of society was overturned. The work of the revolutions of 1848, which, in the Habsburg lands, had liberated the peasants but left them landless, was now carried a step further. The example of the Russian Revolution provided a powerful stimulus, for in Russia in 1917 peasants had driven off landlords, and Communists won a hearing among discontented and property-less peasants from Finland to the Balkans. Not until 1929, it should be recalled, did the Soviet Union embark on the collectivization of agriculture; until then, communism appeared to favor the small individual farmer. But it may be said with equal truth that the model for agrarian reform lay in the West, especially in France, the historic land of the small peasant proprietor.

Land reform

Land reform worked out differently in different countries, but large estates were generally broken into smaller farms throughout the Baltic states and in much of Czechoslovakia. This transformation reflected nationalist sentiment as well as a new social policy because most of the large landowners in all of these places were German. In Romania and Yugoslavia the breakup of large estates, though considerable, was less thorough. In Finland, Bulgaria, and Greece the issue hardly arose, since small landownership was already common. Land reform had least success in Poland and Hungary, where the landed magnates were exceptionally strong and well-rooted.

After the land reforms, political parties of small landholders became the chief democratic force within the various states on the western border of Russia. Often they inclined to socialism, especially since capitalism was associated in their minds with foreign investors and outsiders. On the other hand, the great landowners, the former aristocrats of the prewar empires, whether already expropriated or merely threatened with expropriation, were confirmed in a reactionary outlook. The land reforms did not solve basic economic problems. The new small farms were small, frequently no more than ten acres. The peasant owners lacked capital, agricultural skill, and knowledge of the market. Farm productivity did not rise. In place of old differences between landlord and tenant there developed new differences between the more comfortable peasants and the proletarian hired hands. The continuance of relative poverty, the obstinacy of reactionary upper classes, the new economic tensions among the peasants themselves, the economic distortions produced by numerous tariff walls, and the lack of any sustained tradition of self-government all helped to frustrate the democratic experiments launched in the 1920s.

Peasant and smallholder parties

97.   THE GERMAN REPUBLIC
AND THE SPIRIT OF LOCARNO

The keystone of Europe was Germany, which also had its revolution in 1918. But it was a revolution without revolutionaries, a negative revolution caused more by the disappearance of the old than by any decisive arrival of the new. The emperor and the High Command of the army, in the last weeks of the war, had bowed out of the picture, leaving it to others to face defeat and humiliation. For a time after November 1918, the political leaders in charge of affairs were mainly Social Democrats. The Social Democrats were Marxists, but their Marxism was the tamed, toned down, and revisionist Marxism that had prevailed for 20 years before the advent of Lenin. They were trade union officials and party managers. They could look back, in 1918, on decades spent in developing labor organizations and building up the Social Democratic party, which in 1912 had become the largest single party in the Reichstag. Now, in 1918, they were a cautious and prudent group, essentially conservative, more anxious to preserve what they had already achieved than to launch audacious new social experiments. Before 1917 the Social Democrats considered themselves well to the Left. But the Bolshevik Revolution in Russia and the emergence of a pro-Bolshevik or Communist element in Germany put the Social Democrats in the middle. The middle is an awkward spot, especially in disturbed times; the Communists regarded the Social Democrats as reactionaries, despicable traitors to the working-class movement, whereas the true reactionaries, recruited from old monarchists, army officers, Junker landowners, and big business groups, saw in social democracy, or professed to see in it, a dangerous flirtation with Bolshevism.

The middle group in Germany, the Social Democrats reinforced by the Catholic Center party and others, was more afraid of the Left than of the Right. They were appalled in 1918 and 1919 by the stories brought out of Russia, not merely by fugitive bourgeois or tsarist aristocrats but by refugee Social Democrats, Mensheviks, and anti-Leninist Bolsheviks, many of whom the socialists had long known and trusted in the Second International.

The Spartacists

In January 1919 the Spartacists,[1] led by Karl Liebknecht and Rosa Luxemburg, attempted to bring about a German proletarian revolution, like that in Russia. Lenin and the Russian Bolsheviks aided them. For a time, there seemed to be a possibility that the Spartacists might succeed in imposing a communist dictatorship of the proletariat in Germany. But the Social Democratic Provisional Government crushed the Spartacist uprising, turning for that purpose to demobilized army officers and volunteer vigilantes recruited from the disbanding army. The Spartacist leaders Liebknecht and Luxemburg were arrested and shot while in police custody. The events of "Spartacus Week" widened the chasm between Social Democrats and Communists.

Shortly after, elections were held for a National Constituent Assembly. No single party received a majority, but the Social Democrats were the leading party. A coalition of Social Democrats, Center party, and liberal democrats dominated the Assembly. After several months of deliberations at the city of Weimar, in July 1919, a constitution was adopted establishing a democratic republic. The Weimar Republic (as the regime in Germany from 1919 to the advent of Hitler in 1933 is called) was soon threatened ominously from the Right. In 1920 a group of disaffected army officers staged a *Putsch,* or armed revolt, put the republican government to flight, and attempted to place a puppet of their own, one Dr.

---

[1]So named from Spartacus, a Roman slave who led a slave revolt in south Italy in 72 B.C.

The Spartacists in Germany tried to provoke a Soviet-style, Communist revolution in early 1919, but their uprising was suppressed by the Social Democratic Provisional Government. These people are burning political pamphlets that they had seized from Spartacist newspaper offices.
(Getty Images)

Kapp, at the head of the state. The Berlin workers, by turning off public utilities, stopped the Kapp *Putsch* and saved the republic. But the Weimar government never took sufficiently firm measures to put down private armed bands led by reactionary or outspokenly antidemocratic agitators. One of these was soon to be Adolf Hitler, who as early as 1923 staged an abortive revolt in Munich. Being democratic and liberal, the Weimar government would not deny the rights of free speech or of election to the Reichstag to even the most radical antidemocratic groups on the Left or the Right.

The Weimar Republic was in principle highly democratic. The constitution embodied all the devices then favored by the most advanced democrats, not only universal suffrage, including the vote for women, but also proportional representation and the initiative, referendum, and recall. But

The Weimar Republic

except for the legal eight-hour day and a few other such safeguards to the workers' welfare (and traditional demands of organized labor) the republic of which the Social Democrats were the main architects in its formative years was remote from anything socialist. No industries were nationalized. No property changed hands. No land laws or agrarian reforms were undertaken, as in the new states of eastern Europe; the East Elbian Junkers remained untouched in their landed estates. The very statues of emperors, kings, princes, and grand dukes were left standing in the streets and squares. Officials, civil servants, police agents, professors, and schoolteachers of old imperial Germany remained at their respective duties. The army, though limited by the Versailles treaty to 100,000 men, remained the old army in miniature, with all its essential organs intact, and lacking only in numbers. In the officer corps the old professional and aristocratic influences remained strong.

Never had there been a revolution so mild, so reasonable, so tolerant. There was no terror, no fanaticism, no stirring faith, no expropriation, and no émigré migration. There had in truth been no revolution at all in the sense in which England, France, the United States, Russia, and other countries either recently or in the more distant past had experienced revolutions.

The German Democracy and Versailles

The supreme question for Europe and the world was how Germany would adjust to the postwar conditions. How would the Germans accept the new internal regime of democracy? How would they accept the new German frontiers and other provisions of the Treaty of Versailles? The two questions were unfortunately interconnected. The Weimar Republic and the Treaty of Versailles were both products of the defeat of Germany in the war. There were many in Germany who favored democracy, notably the numerous Social Democrats, and many more possibly could have been won over to it, given time and favorable conditions. But no one, not even the Social Democrats, accepted the Treaty of Versailles or the new German frontiers as either just or final. If democracy in Germany meant the perpetual acceptance of the treaty without amendment, or if it meant economic distress or hardship which could either reasonably or unreasonably be explained as consequences of the treaty, then democracy would lose such appeal as it had for the Germans.

The German republicans, we have seen, protested against the Versailles treaty before signing, and signed only under pressure. The Allies continued the wartime naval blockade after the armistice; this confirmed, in German eyes, the argument that the Treaty of Versailles was a *Diktat,* a vengeful, dictated peace. The "war guilt" clause, while it perhaps on the one hand satisfied a peculiar Anglo-American sense of morality, on the other hand offended a peculiar German sense of honor. Neither the reparations demanded of them nor the new frontiers were accepted by the Germans as settled. Reparations they regarded as a perpetual mortgage on their future. They generally expected some day to revise their eastern frontier, recover at least the Polish corridor, and merge with German-speaking Austria.

The Versailles treaty as "Diktat"

The French lived in fear of the day when Germany would recover. Their plans for their own security and for the collective security of Europe against a German revival had been disappointed. They had been unable to detach the Rhineland from Germany. The United States Senate had refused to ratify the treaty signed at Paris by Wilson, by which the United States was to guarantee France against German invasion in the future. Both Britain and the United States showed a tendency to isolation, to pull away from the Continent, to get back to "normalcy," to work mainly for a restored trade in which a strong Germany would be a large customer. The League of Nations, of which the United States was not a member and in which every member nation had a veto, offered little assurance of safety to the French. The French began to form alliances against a potentially resurgent Germany with Poland, Czechoslovakia, and other East European states. They insisted also on German payment of reparations. The amount of reparations, left unstated in the treaty, was fixed by a Reparations Commission in 1921 at 132 billion gold marks (the equivalent of $35 billion), a sum that even non-German economists said was more than Germany could possibly pay.

French fear

The Weimar government in these circumstances looked to the Soviet Union, which had been no party to the Versailles treaty and claimed no reparations. The Soviet government meanwhile, concluding from the failure of proletarian revolution in Germany and Hungary that the time was not ripe for the sovietizing of Europe, prepared to enter into normal diplomatic relations with established governments. Germany and the Soviet Union, despite ideological repugnance, thus signed the treaty of Rapallo in 1922. In the following years the Soviet Union obtained needed manufactures from Germany, and German factories and workers were kept busy by orders from the Soviets. The German army dispatched officers and technicians to give instruction to the Red Army. Obliged by the Treaty of Versailles to restrict its activities, the German army was in fact able, through its work in Russia and through a number of subterfuges at home, to maintain a high standard of training and technical knowledge of new weapons and equipment.

Soviet-German relations

Reparations, the German Inflation of 1923, Recovery

The French, blocked in the attempt to collect reparations and assisted by the Belgians, in 1923 sent units of the French army to occupy the industrial sites of the Ruhr valley. The Germans responded by general strikes and passive resistance. To sustain the workers the Weimar government paid them benefits, grinding paper money off the printing presses for this purpose. Germany, like other belligerent countries, had suffered from inflation during and after the war; neither the imperial nor the Weimar government had been willing to impose heavier taxes to offset it. But what now swept Germany was different from ordinary inflation. It was of catastrophic and utterly ruinous proportions. Paper money became literally worthless. By the end of 1923 it took over 4 trillion paper marks to equal a dollar.

A social revolution

This inflation brought far more of a social revolution than the fall of the Hohenzollern empire had ever done. Debtors paid off debts in worthless money. Creditors received baskets full of meaningless paper. Salaries even when raised lagged behind the soaring cost of living. Annuities, pensions, proceeds of insurance policies, savings accounts in the banks, income from bonds and mortgages—every form of revenue which had been arranged for at some time in the past, and which often represented the economy, foresight, and personal planning of many years—now turned to nothing. The middle class was pauperized and demoralized. Middle-class people were now materially in much the position of workers and proletarians. Their whole view of life, however, made it impossible for them to identify themselves with the laboring class or to accept its Marxist or socialist ideologies. They had lost faith in society itself, in the future, in the old burgher codes of self-reliance and rational planning of their own lives in an understandable world. A kind of moral void was created, with nothing for them to believe in, hope for, or respect.

The inflation, however, by wiping out all outstanding indebtedness within the country, made it possible, once the losses were written off and accepted, to start up economic production afresh. The United States was persuaded to play a reluctant role, in part because it was demanding the payment of huge war debts by the Allies. The Allies—Britain, France, Belgium—insisted that they could not pay these debts to the United States unless they collected reparations from Germany. In 1924 the Dawes Plan, named for the American Charles G. Dawes, was instituted in Germany to assure the flow of reparations. By the Dawes Plan the French evacuated the

The Dawes Plan

Ruhr, the reparations payments were cut down, and arrangements were made for the German republic to borrow abroad. A good deal of American private capital was invested in Germany in the following years, both in German government bonds and in German industrial enterprises. Gradually, so at least it seemed, Germany was put on its feet. For four or five years the Weimar Republic even enjoyed a bustling prosperity, and there was a good deal of new construction in roads, housing, factories, and ocean liners. But the prosperity rested in good measure on foreign loans, and the Great Depression that began in 1929 reopened all the old questions.

The Spirit of Locarno

These years of economic prosperity were years also of relative international calm. Yet none of the fundamental international issues were addressed or resolved. The universal German hatred for the Treaty of Versailles elicited no concessions from the Allies.

The catastrophic German inflation of 1923 destroyed the value of wages, savings, and investments. Consumers paid for goods with baskets of paper money, forcing merchants such as this baker and his employees to calculate their daily sales with trillions of almost worthless German marks.
(akg-images)

Conceivably, had the Allies been willing at this time to amend the treaty by international agreement, they might have taken the wind from the sails of nationalistic rabble-rousers in Germany and so spared themselves much later grief. It may be, however, that no possible concession would have sufficed. The great problem was to prevent a German overthrow of the treaty structure by violence, especially in eastern Europe where the Germans regarded the new frontiers as very much subject to reconsideration. After the Ruhr incident in 1923 and adoption of the Dawes Plan in 1924, a group of moderate and peaceloving men shaped the foreign policy of the principal countries—Gustav Stresemann in Germany, Édouard Herriot and Aristide Briand in France, and Ramsay MacDonald in England.

The charter of the League of Nations provided for international sanctions against potential aggressors. Like the system of congresses after the Peace of Vienna, the League was designed to assure compliance with the peace treaties or at the very least their modification without resort to force. No one expected the League, by any authority of its own, to prevent war between Great Powers; but the League achieved various minor pacifications in the 1920s, and in any case its headquarters at Geneva offered a convenient meeting place in which statesmen could talk.

As a further assurance against war, in 1925, the European powers signed a number of treaties at Locarno, Switzerland. These marked the highest point in international goodwill reached between the two World Wars. Germany signed a treaty with France and Belgium guaranteeing their respective frontiers unconditionally. It signed arbitration treaties with Poland and Czechoslovakia— not guaranteeing these frontiers as they stood but undertaking to attempt changes in them only by international discussion, agreement, or arbitration. France signed treaties with Poland and Czechoslovakia promising military aid if they were attacked by Germany. France thus fortified its policy of balancing German power in the East by its own diplomatic alliances and by supporting the Little Entente, as the alliance of Czechoslovakia, Yugoslavia, and Romania was called. Great Britain "guaranteed"—that is, promised military aid in the event of violation—the frontiers of Belgium and France against Germany. It did not give an equivalent guarantee with respect to Czechoslovakia or Poland. The British policy was based on the view that their security would be threatened by German expansion westward, but not by German expansion to the east. It was on the borders of Czechoslovakia and Poland, 14 years later, that the Second World War began. Had Britain gone along with France in 1925 in guaranteeing these two countries, then abided by the guarantee, the Second World War might possibly have been prevented. On the other hand, no war ever depends on any single decision; it is the accumulation of many decisions that matters.

The Locarno treaties

In 1925 people talked with relief of the "spirit of Locarno." In 1928 international harmony was again strengthened when the French foreign minister Briand and the United States Secretary of State Frank B. Kellogg arranged for the Pact of Paris. Ultimately signed by 65 nations, it condemned recourse to war for the solution of international controversies (though it provided no measures of enforcement).

In the mid-1920s the outlook was therefore full of hope. At Locarno, Germany had of its own volition accepted its borders both east and west, to the extent of abjuring violence and unilateral action even in the east. In 1926 Germany joined the League of Nations. Germany appeared to be a going concern as a democratic republic. Democracy seemed to work, as well as could be expected, in most of the new states of eastern Europe, and Communist Russia itself had halted its postwar revolutionary offensive. The world was again prosperous, or seemed to be. World production was at or above the prewar level. World trade, by 1929, measured in hard money— gold—had almost doubled since 1913. The war and the postwar troubles were remembered as a nightmare from which Europe had finally escaped. It seemed that, after all, the world had been made safe for democracy.

A hopeful outlook

But complacency was shattered by the great world depression, by the growth of a malignant nationalism in Germany, due in part to the depression, and by the assertion of a new militancy in Japan, which also was not unrelated to the depression. But let us turn first to the postwar years in Asia, where new nationalisms and political movements confronted Europe's colonial empires and challenged its once-dominant position in the global economy.

98. ANTI-IMPERIALIST MOVEMENTS IN ASIA

Resentments in Asia

The peoples of Asia had never been satisfied with the position in which they found themselves after the great European expansion of the nineteenth century. Increasingly they condemned everything associated with "imperialism." In this respect there was little difference between countries actually governed by Europeans as parts of European empires in the nineteenth century, such as British India, the Netherlands Indies, French Indochina (or the American Philippines), and countries that remained nominally independent under their own government, such as China, Persia, and the Ottoman Empire. In the former, as new national movements began to develop, there was objection to the monopoly of Europeans in the important offices of government. In the latter, there was objection to the special rights and privileges enjoyed by Europeans, the widespread impounding of customs revenues to pay foreign debts, the special privileges for foreigners in Turkey, the extraterritorial rights in China, and the spheres of influence in Persia which divided the country between British and Russians.

Imperialism in Asia

By imperialism, in either case, aroused Asians meant a system whereby the affairs of their own country were conducted, its resources exploited, and its people employed for the benefit of foreigners, Europeans, or white people. They meant the system of absentee capitalism, by which the plantations, docks, or factories on which they themselves labored, were the property of owners thousands of miles away whose main interest was a regular flow of profits. They meant the constant threat that an alien civilization would disintegrate and eat away their own ancient cultures. They meant the burden of having to speak a European language or the disagreeable prospect of having to fight in wars originated by Europeans. And they meant the airs of superiority assumed by whites, the race consciousness exhibited by all Westerners, though perhaps most of all by the British and Americans, the color line that was everywhere drawn, the attitudes varying between contempt and condescension, the relation of native "boy" and European "sahib." Imperialism to them signified the gentlemen's clubs in Calcutta to which no Indian was ever admitted, the hotels in Shanghai from which Chinese were carefully kept out, or the park benches in various cities on which no "native" could ever sit. In deeper psychology, as well as in economics and politics, the revolt of self-conscious Asians was a rebellion against an imperial system that reduced them to social inferiority and humiliation in their own societies.

The revolt against the West was generally ambivalent or two-sided. It was a revolt against Western supremacy; but at the same time, in most cases those who revolted meant to learn from and imitate the West in order that, by taking over Western science, industry, organization, and other sources of Western power, they might preserve their own identity and achieve political and economic equality with the Western nation-states. Anti-imperialist movements and intellectuals thus borrowed from Western culture even as they vehemently rejected Western ideologies that assumed the superiority of European institutions or races.

The crisis in Asia had broken out with the Russo-Japanese War, when an Asian people in 1905 defeated a great European power for the first time. In 1906 revolution began in Persia, leading to the assembly of the first *majlis,* or parliament. In 1908 the Young Turks staged a successful revolution in Constantinople and summoned a parliamentary assembly to represent all regions then in the Ottoman Empire. In 1911 the revolutionists in China, led by Sun Yat-sen, overthrew the Manchu (or Qing) dynasty and proclaimed the Chinese Republic. In each case the rebels charged their old monarchs—shah, sultan, emperor— with subservience to Western imperialists. In each case they summoned national assemblies on the prevailing democratic model of Europe, and they proposed to revive, modernize, and westernize their countries to the degree necessary to avoid domination by the West.

Anti-imperialist revolts

First World War and Russian Revolution

In the First World War almost all the Asian peoples were somehow involved. The Ottoman Empire, allied with Germany, immediately repudiated all the capitulations, or special legal rights of Europeans. In Persia, where Russian and British intervention in 1907 had blocked the developing movement for constitutional reform, there was a concerted attempt to maintain Persian neutrality in the war and to get rid of the foreign spheres of influence that Russia and Britain had imposed through agreements between themselves. Persian territory became a battleground of British, Russian, and Turkish forces; and a large number of Persians died from wartime violence, disruption, and disease. China, which joined the Allies, attempted at the peace conference to have the extraterritorial rights in China abolished. We have seen how this request of the Chinese Republic was refused, and how the Allies instead transferred many of the prewar German concessions to the Japanese. The dependent regions of Asia, the Dutch, French, and British possessions, were stimulated economically by the war. The Netherlands Indies, though remaining neutral, increased its output of foodstuffs, oil, and raw materials. India developed its steel industry and textile manufactures and contributed over a million soldiers, combat and service troops, to the British cause. All the dependent regions were stirred by Woodrow Wilson's call to make the world safe for democracy.

The home governments made concessions. They were naturally afraid to go too far; they insisted that their subject peoples were not yet capable of self-government. Huge investments were at stake, and the whole world economy depended on the continuing flow of raw materials from tropical and subtropical countries. But they did compromise. In 1916 the Dutch created a legislative assembly to advise the governor general of the Indies; half its members were Indonesians. In 1917 the British agreed to a measure of self-government in India; an Indian legislative assembly was set up with 140 members, of whom 100 were elected, and in the provinces of British India the number of elected representatives and of local Indian officials was increased. The French in 1922 provided for a somewhat similar assembly in Indochina. Thus all three colonial powers at about the same time began to experiment with consultative bodies whose membership was partly elective and partly appointive, partly non-European and partly European. The United States introduced an elected assembly in the Philippine Islands in 1916.

Home government concessions

The Russian Revolution added a new stimulus to unrest in Asia. The Bolsheviks denounced not only capitalism but also imperialism. In Marxist-Leninist ideology imperialism was an aspect of capitalism, which Lenin had called the "highest" or "final" phase of capitalist societies. Colonial peoples also tended to identify the two, not so much for Marxist reasons as because modern capitalism was a foreign or "imperialist" phenomenon in colonial countries, where the ownership and the management of large enterprises were foreign. Nationalism in Asia, the movement for independence or for more equality with the West, thus easily shaded off into socialism and the denunciation of capitalist exploitation. The Bolsheviks were quick to see the advantages for themselves in this situation. As it became clear that the world revolution, as expected by Lenin, would not soon come to pass in Europe, the Russian Communists turned to Asia as the theater in which world capitalism might be attacked by a great flanking movement. In September 1920 a "congress of oppressed Eastern peoples" assembled at Baku, on the coast of the Caspian Sea. Zinoviev, head of the Communist International, called for war upon "the wild beasts of British capitalism." In the following years a few future radical leaders from Asian countries sojourned

Bolshevik anti-imperialism

in Moscow. Meanwhile, Communists dispatched from Moscow stirred up the discontents which existed, quite without Russian instigation, all over Asia.

The postwar situation in Asia was thus extremely fluid. People who were not Communists hailed communism as a liberating force. Anti-Westerners declared that their countries must westernize, at least in certain aspects of science, technology, and social organization. Nationalism overshadowed all other "isms." In the Indian National Congress rich Indian capitalists worked together with socialist leaders in relative harmony so long as the common enemy was the British.

The Turkish and Persian Revolutions

The most immediately successful of the revolutionary movements took place in Turkey. The Young Turks at first, in 1908, had meant to prevent the further dissolution of the Ottoman Empire. This proved to be impossible. In the Balkan wars of 1912–1913 the Ottoman power was almost totally excluded from the Balkan peninsula. In the First World War, in which the Turks were on the losing side, the Arabs with a great deal of British assistance broke away. After the war, in 1921, the Greeks invaded the Anatolian peninsula. They dreamed of a greater Greece embracing both sides of the Aegean. Europeans still regarded Turkey as the sick man of Europe, the Ottoman state as doomed to extinction, and the Turkish people as barbarous and incompetent. The Allies had agreed in 1915 to partition Turkey; and after the war the Western powers favored the Greek invasion. Italian and French forces occupied parts of Anatolia; and Italians, French, and British undertook to take Constantinople from Turkish rule, though its disposition remained uncertain. In these circumstances a powerful army officer named Mustapha Kemal rallied Turkish national resistance. Within two years, and with aid from the Soviet Union, the Turks drove out the Greeks and the Western Allies. They affirmed their hold on the Anatolian peninsula, and on both shores of the Straits, including Constantinople, which in 1930 was renamed Istanbul.

The Turkish Republic

The Nationalists, under the energetic drive of Mustapha Kemal, now put through a sweeping revolution. They abolished the sultanate and the caliphate, since the sultan had compromised himself with foreigners and was also, as caliph or commander of the faithful, a religious leader for all Islam and hence a conservative link with the past. The Turkish Republic was promulgated in 1923.

Whereas the Ottoman Empire had been a composite organization made up of diverse religious communities, among which the Muslims were the ruling group, the Turkish Republic was conceived as a national state in which the "people," that is, the Turkish people, were sovereign. Universal suffrage was introduced, along with a parliament, a ministry, and a president with strong powers. Non-Turks in Asia Minor now became "foreign" in a way they had not been before. We have seen that the Armenians were deported and massacred during the First World War. The other large non-Turkish and Christian people were the Greeks. After the war about 1.4 million Greeks either fled or were officially transported from Asia Minor to Greece and in exchange some 400,000 Turks residing in northern Greece were transported to Turkey. The exchange of populations caused great hardship, it uprooted most of the Greek population that had lived in Asia Minor since antiquity, and it overwhelmed the impoverished Greek kingdom by obliging it suddenly to absorb a mass of destitute refugees, who were a quarter as numerous as the population of Greece itself. But it enabled the Turkish Republic to acquire a relatively homogeneous population (except for a Kurdish minority in eastern Turkey), and it ended minority disputes between Greece and Turkey until new problems arose after the Second World War.

For the first time in any Muslim country the spheres of government and religion were sharply distinguished. The Turkish Republic affirmed the total separation of church and state. It declared religion to be a private belief, and it tolerated all religions. Government was reorganized on secular and nonreligious principles stemming from the French Revolution. The law of the Qur'an was thrust aside. The new law was modeled on the Swiss Code, the most recently codified European legislation, itself derived from the Code Napoleon.

Separation of church and state

Mustapha Kemal urged women to put aside the veil, to come out of the harem, to vote, and to occupy public office. He made polygamy a crime. Men he required by law to discard the fez. He fought against the fez as Peter the Great had fought against the beard, and for the same reason, seeing in it the symbol of backward habits. The hat, "headgear of civilization," correspondingly became the symbol of progress. The people shifted to Western dress. The Western alphabet became mandatory; literate Turks had to learn to read again, and illiteracy was reduced. The Western calendar and the metric system were adopted. Turks were required to assume hereditary family surnames, like Westerners; Kemal himself took the name Atatürk, or Great Turk. The capital was moved from Istanbul to Ankara. The republic put up a high tariff. In 1933 it adopted a five-year plan for economic development. The Turks, having shaken off foreign influence, were determined not to become again dependent on Western capital or capitalism. The five-year plan provided for mines, railroads, and factories, mainly under government ownership. At the same time, while willing to accept Russian aid against the Western powers, the republic had no patience with communism, which it suppressed. The Turks wanted a modern Turkey—by and for the Turks.

Persia experienced a different kind of political revolution, but there were comparable attempts to reduce the influence of foreign powers. When the British tried to establish a postwar colonial protectorate there in 1919, they were stymied by strong national resistance. Meanwhile, the new Soviet regime withdrew from Persia and renounced all claims of the previous Russian government. In 1921 an army officer named Reza Khan overthrew the older ruling Qajar dynasty and in 1925 became shah (with British and Soviet support). Henceforth known as Reza Shah Pahlavi, he established a repressive regime that sought to modernize the country and to break away from various agreements with the British government. Earlier concessions, capitulations, and spheres of influence were abolished, and Reza Shah renegotiated the British oil contracts. There were also efforts to assert greater control over foreign corporations and to collect more taxes, though revenues still fell below what the shah hoped to extract. Beginning in 1935, the government affirmed its national identity by changing the country's official international name to Iran, which had for some time been used within the nation itself.

New regime in Persia

The National Movement in India: Gandhi and Nehru

India at the close of the First World War was on the verge of revolution against British rule. Discontented Indians looked for leadership to Mohandas K. Gandhi, the Mahatma, or Holy One, who in the following decades, though hardly typical of modern Asia, attained a worldwide eminence as the champion of subjected peoples. Gandhi had been educated in England in the 1890s and had practiced law in South Africa, where he became aware of

The president of the new Turkish Republic, Mustapha Kemal Atatürk, sought to reduce the influence of Islam. In this photograph from about 1925, he shows his support for Westernizing policies by wearing European-style clothes and by dancing at his daughter's wedding.
(Getty Images)

racial discrimination as a worldwide problem. In India, after 1919, he led a movement for self-government and economic and spiritual independence from Great Britain. He also sought greater tolerance within India itself, both between Hindus and Muslims, and between upper-caste Hindus and the depressed outcastes and untouchables. The weapons he favored were those of nonviolence, passive resistance, civil disobedience, and the boycott. He took to self-imposed fasts and hunger strikes to cope with his British jailers and later with the Indians themselves.

Gandhi and his most loyal followers, as the troubles mounted, refused to be elected to or take part in the partially representative institutions that the British had cautiously introduced. They also undermined the British economic position in India by refusing to buy or use goods imported from England. The latter touched the British in a sensitive spot. Before the World War half of all exports of British cotton cloth went to India, but by 1932 this proportion had fallen to a quarter. Gandhi turned against all industrialism, even the mechanized industry that was growing up in India itself. He put aside Western costume, took to using a spinning wheel and living on goat's milk, urged Indian peasants to revive their old handicrafts, and appeared on solemn occasions clad in no more than a homespun loincloth. By the high level of his principles Gandhi made himself an inspiration to many groups that differed on more mundane matters. Even in the West he was regarded as one of the great spiritual leaders of all time.

Gandhi's campaign

India was very much divided within, and the British maintained that because of these divisions the ending of British rule would precipitate anarchy. There were Hindus and Muslims, between whom clashes and terrorist outrages were chronic. (Gandhi was himself assassinated in 1948 by an anti-Muslim Hindu fanatic.) There were the hundreds of minor potentates

Divisions in society and politics

of the native states. There were Indian capitalists and wealthy industrialists, like the Tata family, and growing masses of proletarians produced by Indian industrialization. There were the higher castes and the outcastes, and there were hundreds of millions of peasants living in rural poverty. In politics, there were those who demanded full independence, boycotted the British, and spent years in jail, as did Gandhi and his more practical-minded but devoted follower Jawaharlal Nehru; and there were the moderates who believed that they might best advance the welfare of India by accepting government office, cooperating with the British, and working for dominion status within the British Empire. Marxism exerted a strong appeal, not indeed on the spiritual and pacific Gandhi, but on Nehru and even many of the less radical leaders. In the 1920s the Soviet Union stood in their eyes for the overthrow of imperialism; in the 1930s it pointed the way toward economic development by its adoption of five-year plans. For a people wishing to move from poverty to industrial strength and higher living standards without loss of time, and without dependence on foreign capital and capitalism, the Soviet Union with its economic planning seemed to offer a more appropriate model and more practical lessons than the rich democracies of the West, with their centuries of gradual progress behind them.

The 20 years between world wars were years of repeated disturbance, rioting and repression, sporadic violence despite the exhortations of Gandhi, conferences and round tables, reforms and promises of reform, with a shift in the 1930s toward more participation of Indians in the affairs of the Indian empire. Independence was not won until after the Second World War; with it took place a partition of the Indian subcontinent into two new nations, a predominantly Hindu India and a predominantly Muslim Pakistan.

Continuing struggle for independence

In the Netherlands Indies, where the nationalist movement was less developed, the interwar years were quieter than in India. A serious rebellion, in which communists took part, broke out in 1922 but was suppressed by the Dutch. The peoples of the Indonesian archipelago were almost as diverse as those of India. Only the Dutch empire had brought them politically together. Opposition to the Dutch gave them a common program. In 1937 the legislative council petitioned for dominion status. But not until after the Second World War and the failure of a military effort to repress the nationalists did the Dutch, in 1949, concede independence.

The Chinese Revolution: The Three People's Principles

The Chinese Revolution had opened in 1911 with the overthrow of the Manchu (Qing) dynasty, which itself had belatedly begun to introduce modernizing reforms. The Chinese Republic was proclaimed, but the first immediate result was the establishment in Peking (now Beijing) of a military dictatorship exercised by General Yüan Shih-kai, who had been a close adviser to the Manchus and who, until his death in 1916, never ceased to cast covetous eyes on the now empty imperial throne itself. In the south the veteran revolutionary Dr. Sun Yat-sen reorganized the Guomindang (National People's, or Nationalist party), successor to the prerevolutionary network of underground societies of which he had been the chief architect.[2] Sun,

Sun Yat-sen and the Nationalists

---

[2]The Pinyin system, adopted in 1979 by The People's Republic of China, is now widely used for the transliteration of Chinese into languages like English that use the Latin alphabet, replacing the older Wade-Giles spelling. Kuomintang is now rendered as Guomindang, Mao Tse-tung as Mao Zedong, Peking as Beijing, Nanking as Nanjing, Chou En-lai as Zhou Enlai, Teng Hsiao-p'ing as Deng Xiaoping, and so on. For a few names like Sun Yat-sen or Chiang Kai-shek the original spellings are often retained.

The nonviolent principles of Mohandas Gandhi profoundly shaped the Indian movement for national independence after the First World War. He is shown here in typically simple clothing as he led his followers on a "walk to the sea" to collect salt as part of a boycott of British goods and to promote his nonviolent campaign for Indian national independence.
(Corbis)

elected the first president of the republic by a revolutionary provisional assembly, resigned within a few months in favor of General Yüan, who he mistakenly believed would unite the country under a parliamentary regime. Subsequently, in the confusion that followed the struggle for power in Peking after Yüan's death in 1916, Sun was proclaimed president of a rival government in the south at Canton (now Guangzhou), which exercised a nominal power over the southern provinces. Not until 1928 could any government have any basis for claiming actual rule over China—and even then, there were important exceptions. For most of these years the country was virtually in the hands of contending war lords, each of whom pocketed the customary taxes in his own locality, maintained his own army, and recognized no superior authority.

It was Sun Yat-sen who best expressed the ideas of this phase of the Chinese Revolution. Born in 1867 and educated under American influence in the Hawaiian Islands, he had received a medical degree at Hong Kong, had traveled and lived around the world, studied Western ideas, lectured to Chinese audiences in America, collected money for his conspiracies against the Manchus, and had returned from Europe to take part in the revolution. Shortly before his death in 1925 Sun gathered the lectures which he had been expounding for years into a book, *The Three People's Principles*. The book sheds much light on the revolt of China and of all Asia against the supremacy of the West.

The three people's principles, according to Sun Yat-sen, were democracy, nationalism, and livelihood. Livelihood meant social welfare and economic reform—a more equitable distribution of wealth and land, a gradual end to poverty and unjust economic exploitation. By nationalism Dr. Sun meant that the Chinese who had always lived mainly in the clan and family had now to learn the importance of the nation and the state. They were in *Democracy, nationalism, livelihood* fact a great nation, he taught, the world's most cultured, and had once prevailed from the mouth of the Amur to the East Indies. But they had never been cohesive. The Chinese had been "a sheet of loose sand"; they must now "break down individual liberty and become pressed together into an unyielding body like the firm rock which is formed by the addition of cement to sand."

By democracy Sun Yat-sen meant the sovereignty of the people. Like Rousseau, he gave little attention to voting, elections, or parliamentary processes. He believed that while the people were sovereign, the able should govern. Adhering in this respect to traditional Confucian teachings, he believed that government should be conducted by experts, a principle he criticized the West for neglecting. Dr. Sun felt a warm sympathy for Lenin. Yet he was by no means a doctrinaire Marxist. Marxism he thought inapplicable to China, arguing that the Chinese must take Marxism as they took all other Western ideas, avoiding slavish imitation, using, adapting, amending, or rejecting as they saw fit. China had no native capitalism in any Marxist or Western sense. The "capitalists" in China, he said, were owners of land, especially in cities such as Shanghai, where the coming of Westerners had raised land values to dizzy heights. Hence if China could get rid of imperialism it would take a long step toward getting rid of capitalism also; it could begin to equalize landowning and confiscate unearned rents. Since China, he observed, had no true capitalists, the state itself must undertake capitalist and industrial development. This would require loans of foreign capital and the services of foreign managers and technicians, adding another reason why the Chinese state, to maintain control, must be strong.

With Sun Yat-sen, in short, democracy easily shaded off into a theory of benevolent and constructive dictatorship. Marxism, communism, socialism, "livelihood," the planned society, welfare economics, and antiforeign and anti-imperialist sentiment were all mixed together—in some ways as many of the ideas of the Chinese Communists would later be.

The first aim of Sun Yat-sen and of the revolutionists in China was to shake off the "treaty system" that had bound China to outside interests since 1842. In this respect the Paris peace conference had been disappointing; the Chinese not only failed to obtain the abolition of Western privileges and extraterritorial rights but also could not win back the former German concessions that the Japanese had taken over during the war. Widespread student and worker demonstrations directed against the Western powers took place at the time of the Paris peace conference on May 4, 1919. The May Fourth movement heightened antiforeign consciousness.

Antiforeign sentiments

As the Western powers proved obdurate, Sun and the Guomindang turned to Russia. They declared the Russian and Chinese revolutions to be two aspects of the same worldwide movement of liberation. The Chinese Communist party, organized in 1921, became allied with the Guomindang in 1923. The latter accepted Russian Communist advisers, notably the veteran revolutionist Borodin, whom Sun Yat-sen had known years before in the United States. The Soviet Union, following its strategy of outflanking world capitalism by penetrating Asia, sent military equipment, army instructors, and party organizers into China. It also surrendered the Russian concessions and extraterritorial rights acquired in China by the tsars. The Chinese policy of friendliness to Russia began to produce the hoped-for effects; the British, to draw China from Russia, gave up a few of their lesser concessions at Hankow and other cities.

Alliances with Russia

China: Nationalists and Communists

The Guomindang, its armies reorganized and strengthened, displayed a fresh vitality and after 1924 launched a military and political offensive. The new offensive was planned by the ever-active Russian advisers, supported by the Chinese Communists, and headed by Chiang Kai-shek, who succeeded to the leadership of the Nationalist party upon Sun's death in 1925. Chiang's main objectives were to compel the independent war lords and the regime still holding office in Beijing to accept the authority of a single Nationalist government. By the end of 1928 Chiang's armies had swept northward, occupied Beijing, and transferred the seat of government to Nanjing. Chiang now exercised at least nominal control over most of China, although effective control was still limited by the recalcitrance of many provincial war lords. The outside powers, acknowledging the accomplishments of the Guomindang, extended diplomatic recognition to the Nanjing government and conceded its right to organize and run the country's tariff and customs affairs. They also partially surrendered their extraterritorial privileges and pledged to abolish them completely in the near future.

In 1927, while a measure of national unity was being forged in the country, an open break occurred between the Guomindang and its left wing. In the course of the northern military campaign, and particularly in the seizure of Nanjing, popular disturbance and excesses, including the killing of a number of foreigners, had taken place, allegedly fomented by the Communists. These radical disturbances frightened and alienated the wealthier and more conservative element in the Guomindang and jeopardized Chiang's chief source of financial assistance for his government and army. Chiang himself had never apparently considered the alliance with either the Communists or the Russians as anything more than one of convenience. He now took decisive action, purging Communists and Russian advisers from the party, and executing many people who were affiliated with left-wing groups. Borodin and others fled to Moscow, and a Communist-led uprising in Guangzhou was forcefully suppressed. A number of armed Communist groups fled to the safety of the mountain

Communists purged from the Guomindang

regions in the south and joined other guerrilla contingents. In that way the Chinese Red Army was formed; among its leaders was Mao Zedong, a former librarian, teacher, newspaper editor, and union organizer, who had been one of the founding members of the party.

Chiang, with the renewed financial and moral support of the Guomindang bankers, resumed the northern offensive. But the original revolutionary impulse of the Guomindang was now dissipated. Made up of men who feared social upheaval and who often regarded their own maintenance in power as their chief goal, it exercised a kind of one-party dictatorship over most of China under Chiang's leadership. Chiang himself recognized mounting popular dissatisfaction with the reluctance or inability of the party to initiate reforms, but he was busy consolidating the regime and after 1931 he had to contend with Japanese aggression. During these years he developed a deadly hatred for Communists and those who agitated for revolutionary reform.

The Communists, operating in southeast China, fed on popular discontent and drew support from the peasantry by a systematic policy of expropriation and distribution of large landed estates as well as by intensive propaganda. They succeeded in fighting off Chiang's armies and even in winning over part of his troops. Organizing a network of local soviets, in 1931 they proclaimed a Chinese Soviet Republic in the southeast. When the Nationalist armies succeeded in dislodging them, the Communists, under Mao's leadership, undertook in 1934–1935 an amazing 6,000-mile march over near-insuperable terrain to north-central Yenan, where they were closer to Soviet supply lines. About 90,000 began the Long March, of which only half survived. They entrenched themselves again, fought off the Nationalist armies, and built up a popular following among the rural masses. With the Japanese invasion of north China under way, they abandoned their revolutionary offensive and pressed Chiang to end the civil war and to create a united front against the Japanese aggressor. Chiang reluctantly consented. By 1937 an alliance was formed between the Nationalists and the Communists, and the Chinese Red Army was placed under Nationalist control; a united China would face the Japanese. But the uneasy alliance was not to last even until the defeat of Japan in the Second World War. Guomindang and Communists would soon engage in a deadly struggle for power.

A united front against Japan

Japan: Militarism and Aggression

The Nationalist movement in China caused apprehension in Japan, whose rise as a modern power has already been traced. The Japanese, at least since the Sino-Japanese War of 1895, had looked upon the political weakness and disorder in China as a field for expansion of their own interests, in this scarcely differing from Europeans except that they were closer to the scene. During the First World War they had presented their Twenty-One Demands on China, had taken over the German concessions in Shantung, and had sent troops into eastern Siberia. During the war the industrialization of Japan proceeded rapidly; Japan captured new markets while the Europeans were locked in struggle; and after the war the Japanese remained one of the chief suppliers of textiles for Asia. The Japanese could produce at lower prices than the Europeans, prices at which the penniless masses of Asia were more able to buy. They themselves sustained their standard of living by importing raw materials and selling manufactures. But the Chinese Nationalists hoped to erect a protective tariff; it was for this reason, among others, that they denounced the treaty system, which for almost a century had bound China to international free trade. The Chinese, like the Turks, hoped to industrialize and develop their own country behind a high tariff wall, which would shut out Japanese manufactures as well as others.

Mao Zedong and Zhou Enlai led nearly 100,000 Communists on the famous "Long March" from southeast China to the northwest province of Yenan in 1934–1935. They were escaping the armies of the Nationalist Guomindang and seeking to establish new bases near the Soviet Union. This picture shows Mao and Zhou as they appeared at the time of the march, which crossed almost 6,000 miles of remote terrain and became a legendary event in the history of the Chinese Communist party.
(Getty Images)

During the 1920s the civilian, liberal, Western-oriented element in Japan remained in control of the government. In 1925 universal male suffrage was adopted. Europeans and Americans generally viewed the Japanese with sympathetic approval, as the most progressive of all non-Europeans, the one Asian people who had ably learned to play its part in the advancing worldwide civilization. But there was another facet to Japan. The constitution of 1889 and the parliamentary system were a façade that concealed the true nature of Japanese political power. Only in Japan of all modern countries did a constitutional law prescribe that the war and navy ministers must be active generals or admirals. The diet itself functioned under sharply restricted powers. Ministers governed in the name of the supreme and sacred authority of the emperor, to whom they were alone responsible. Economically, the government's sponsorship of industrial growth had resulted in a tremendous concentration of economic power in the hands of four family trusts known collectively as the Zaibatsu. The business interests and the civilian political leaders all looked to an expanding empire and growing markets. The most restless group in Japan drew its strength from the nationalist revival which, even before the "opening" of Japan in 1854, had cultivated Shinto, emperor worship, and the way of the warrior as a new and modern way of life. This group was recruited in large part from the old clansmen and samurai, whom the "abolition of feudalism" had uprooted from their accustomed ways and who in many cases found no outlet for their energies in the new regime. Many of these men now served as officers in the army. Often they regarded the West as decadent. They dreamed of the day when Japan would dominate all East Asia.

Nationalist revival

About 1927 this group began to hold ministries in the Japanese government and to turn Japanese policy into increasingly aggressive and militaristic attitudes toward China. In 1931 Japanese army units in southern Manchuria (where the Japanese had been stationed since defeat of the Russians in 1905), alleging the murder of a Japanese officer at Mukden, seized Chinese arsenals and spread northward over Manchuria. In 1932, charging the Chinese with economic warfare against Japan (Chinese boycotts were in fact damaging the Japanese export trade), the Japanese landed 70,000 troops at Shanghai. They soon withdrew, preferring to concentrate at this stage on the occupation of northern China. They declared Manchuria to be an independent state under an emperor they selected (they chose the last Chinese emperor, the "boy-emperor" Pu Yi, who had been deposed in 1911) and renamed the state Manchukuo.

To protest the Japanese invasion of Manchuria the Chinese appealed to the League of Nations. The League sent a commission of inquiry, which found Japan at fault for disturbing the peace. Japan defiantly withdrew from the League. The small powers in the League called for military sanctions, but the Great Powers, knowing that they would bear the burden of military intervention against Japan, and in any case inclined to see no threat to their own immediate security, refused to take any stronger measures. The Japanese remained in occupation of Manchuria and northeast China. With the Japanese conquest of Manchuria one tributary of the coming military torrent had begun to flow. But the world at this time was also stunned by economic depression. Each government was preoccupied with its own internal social problems.

The invasion of Manchuria

𝒪ℓ 99.   THE GREAT DEPRESSION: COLLAPSE OF THE WORLD ECONOMY

The capitalist economic system was a delicate and interlocking mechanism in which any disturbance was rapidly transmitted with accelerating impact through all the parts. For many basic commodities prices were determined by the free play of supply and demand in a worldwide market. There was much regional division of labor; large areas lived by producing a few specialized articles for sale to the world as a whole. A great deal of production, both local and international, especially in the 1920s, was financed by credit, that is, by promises of repayment in the future. The system rested upon mutual confidence in the processes of mutual exchange—on the belief of lenders, creditors, and investors that they would get their money back and on the belief of borrowers that they could pay their debts. This vast interlocking system also depended on the ability of farms and factories to market their products at prices high enough to bring a net return, so that farmers and factory people might purchase the output of other factories and farms—all this round and round in countless circles of mutual interdependence and throughout the world as a whole.

The Prosperity of the 1920s and Its Weaknesses

The five years after 1924 were a period of prosperity in that there was a good deal of international trade, building, and development of new industries. The automobile, for example, still an oddity in 1914, became an article of mass production after the war. Its widespread use increased the demand for oil, steel, rubber, and electrical equipment, caused the building of tens of thousands of miles of roads, and created whole new occupations for truck-drivers, garage mechanics, and filling-station attendants. Similarly the new mass popularity of radios and movies had repercussions in all directions. The economic expansion was most phenomenal in the United States, but almost all countries enjoyed it in

CHRONOLOGY OF NOTABLE EVENTS, 1911–1935

1911	Revolution in China ends the Qing (Manchu) Dynasty
January 1919	Spartacist attempt at proletarian revolution is suppressed in Berlin
July 1919	Weimar Republic is established in Germany
1919	Gandhi launches campaign in India for independence from Britain
1922	Germany and the Soviet Union agree to diplomatic relations in Treaty of Rapollo
1923	French occupation of the Ruhr Valley and ruinous German inflation
1923	Turkish Republic is established under the leadership of Kemal Atatürk, who launches modernizing reforms
1925	Treaties at Locarno recognize the postwar European national borders
1925	Reza Khan becomes shah of Iran and seeks to curb British and other foreign concessions
1925	Death of Sun Yat-sen is followed by conflicts between Nationalists and Communists in China
October 1929	Stock market crash in New York leads to the Great Depression
1931–1932	Japanese forces expand control of Manchuria
1932	Governments respond to economic crisis with national protectionism
1932–1939	Writers respond to social crisis with new "social realism"
1934–1935	Chinese communists make the 6,000-mile Long March

greater or lesser degree. "Prosperity" became a magical term, and some thought that it would last indefinitely, that the secret of human plenty and of progress had been found, and that science and invention were at last realizing the hopes of ages.

But there were weaknesses in this prosperity, various imperfections in this or that gear or valve of the mechanism, flaws which, under stress, were to bring the whole intricate structure to a halt. The expansion was largely financed by credit, or borrowing. Laboring people received less than a proportionate share; wages lagged behind profits and dividends; mass purchasing power, even when inflated by installment buying (another form of credit), was inadequate to pay for the vast output that it was technically possible to produce. And throughout the world the whole decade of the 1920s was a time of chronic agricultural depression, so that farmers could neither pay their debts nor purchase manufactures to the degree required for the smooth functioning of the system.

A prosperity financed by credit

Military operations in the First World War had reduced wheat fields under cultivation in Europe by a fifth. The world price of wheat went up, and farmers in the United States, Canada, and elsewhere increased their acreage. Often, to acquire land at high prices, they assumed mortgages which in later years they were unable to repay. After the war Europe restored its wheat production, and eastern Europe reentered the world market. Agriculture everywhere was increasingly mechanized, and farmers rapidly increased their output of wheat by using a tractor-drawn harvester-thresher combine. At the same

Worldwide agricultural depression

Movie companies used their distinctive, popular form of modern entertainment to develop one of the prosperous, expansive industries of the 1920s. The cinema attracted large audiences in all modern cities, including this festive crowd that gathered at a New York theater in 1926 for the premiere of *Don Juan*—starring the famous actor John Barrymore.
(The Art Archive/National Archives, Washington, D.C.)

time dry farming opened up new land, and science increased the yield per acre. The result of all these agricultural developments was a superabundant output of wheat. But the demand for wheat was what economists call "inelastic." By and large, within the area of the Western world, people already ate as much bread as they wanted and would buy no more; and the undernourished masses of Asia, who in pure theory could have consumed the excess, could not pay even low costs of production or transportation. The world price of wheat fell incredibly. In 1930 a bushel of wheat, in terms of gold, sold for the lowest price in 400 years.

Wheat growers in all continents were faced with ruin. Growers of many other crops faced the same dismal prospect. Cotton and corn, coffee and cocoa all collapsed. Brazilian and African planters were caught by overproduction and falling prices. In Java, where the acreage in sugar had been extended and the unit yield from the sugar cane had also multiplied ten times under scientific cultivation over the past century, prices bottomed out of the world market. There were indeed other and more profitable forms of agricultural production—for example, in oranges and eggs, of which world consumption was steadily growing. But the coffee planter could not shift to eggs, nor the Iowa farmer to oranges. Not to mention the requirements of climate, the ordinary farmer or peasant lacked the capital, the special knowledge, or the access to refrigerated transportation that these newer branches of agriculture demanded. For the one thing that the average farmer or peasant knew how to do—grow wheat and other cereals—the new wonderful world of science and machinery had little place.

The acute phase of the Great Depression, which began in 1929, was made worse by this chronic background of agricultural distress, since there was no reserve of purchasing power on the farms. The farmer's plight became even worse when city people, struck by depression in industry, cut down their expenditures for food. Agricultural depression, rather than industrial depression, was at the root of widespread troubles in the inter-war years throughout eastern Europe and the colonial world.

The Crash of 1929 and the Spread of Economic Crisis

The depression, in the strict sense, began as a stock market and financial crisis. Prices of stocks had been pushed upward by years of continuing expansion and high dividends. At the beginning of 1929 prices on the European stock exchanges began to weaken. But the real crisis, or turning point, came with the crash on the New York Stock Exchange in October 1929. Here values had been driven to fantastic heights by excessive speculation. Not only professional speculators, but quite ordinary people bought stock with borrowed funds. Often trading on "margin," they "owned" five or ten times as much stock as the amount of their own money put into it; the rest they borrowed from brokers, and the brokers borrowed from banks, the purchased stock in each case serving as collateral. With money so easy to obtain, people pushed up American stock prices by bidding against each other and enjoyed huge fortunes on paper; but if prices fell, even a little, the hapless owners would be obliged to sell their stock to pay off the money they had borrowed. Hence the weakening of values on the New York Stock Exchange set off uncontrollable tidal waves of selling, which drove stock prices down irresistibly and disastrously. In a month stock values dropped by 40 percent, and in three years, from 1929 to 1932, the average value of 50 industrial stocks traded on the New York Stock Exchange dropped from 252 to 61. In these same three years 5,000 American banks closed their doors.

Crisis reaches the rest of the world

The crisis passed from finance to industry and from the United States to the rest of the world. The export of American capital came to an end. Americans not only ceased to invest in Europe but sold the foreign securities that they had. This pulled the foundations from under the postwar revival of Germany and hence indirectly of much of Europe. Americans, their incomes falling, ceased to buy foreign goods; people everywhere saw their American markets slip away, and prices tumbled. In 1931 the failure of a leading Vienna bank, the *Creditanstalt,* sent a wave of shivers, bankruptcies, and business calamities over Europe. Everywhere business firms and private people could not collect what was owed them or even draw on money that they thought they had in the bank. They could not buy, and so the factories could not sell. Factories slowed down or closed entirely. Between 1929 and 1932, the latter year representing the depth of the depression, world production is estimated to have declined by 38 percent, and the world's international trade fell by two-thirds. In the United States national income fell from $85 billion to $37 billion.

Unemployment

Unemployment, a chronic disease ever since the war, assumed the proportion of a plague. In 1932 there were 30 million unemployed persons reported in the world; and this figure did not include the further millions who could find work only for a few hours in the week, or the masses in Asia or Africa for whom no statistics were to be had. The worker's wages were gone, the farmer's income touched bottom; and the decline of mass purchasing power forced more idleness of machinery and more unemployment. People in the prime of life spent years out of work. Young people could not find jobs or establish themselves in an occupation. Skills and talents of older people grew rusty. Millions were reduced to living and supporting their families on the pittances of charity, doles, or relief. Great modern cities saw an outburst of sidewalk art, in which jobless able-bodied men drew pictures on the pavement with colored chalk, in the hope of attracting a few sixpence or dimes. People were crushed in spirit by a feeling of uselessness; months and years of fruitless job hunting left them demoralized, bored, embittered, and resentful. Never had there been such waste, not merely of machinery which now stood idle but also of the trained and disciplined labor force on which all modern societies were built. And people chronically out of work turned to new and disturbing political ideas.

Political and Economic Reactions to the Crisis

Optimists at the time, of whom President Herbert Hoover in the United States was one, declared that this depression, though a severe one, was basically only another periodic low point in the business cycle, or alternation of expansion and contraction, which had ebbed and flowed in the Western world for over a century. Prosperity, they blithely said, was "just around the corner." Others came to believe that the crisis represented the breakdown of the whole system of capitalism and free private enterprise. These people in many cases looked for signs of the future in the planned economy then being introduced in the U.S.S.R. There was some truth in both views. After 1932, in part for purely cyclical reasons—because the depression cut down indebtedness and reduced the costs of doing business—it again became possible to produce and sell. World steel production, for example, which had stood at 121 million tons in 1929, and then collapsed to 50 million in 1932, by 1936 again reached 122 million. To a considerable degree, to be sure, revival was due to rearmament. On the other hand, the Great Depression did put an end to some aspects of the older free–market economic system. Even if such a stricken economy had internal powers of full recuperation, people would not stand for such terrifying insecurity in their personal lives. The horrors of mass unemployment were long remembered.

All governments took new steps to provide work and incomes for their people. All in one way or another strove to free themselves from dependency on the uncertainties of the world market. The interlocking world economy collapsed both from the depression itself and from the measures adopted to cure it. One of the most marked economic consequences of the depression was a strong movement toward economic nationalism— toward greater self-sufficiency within the sphere which each government could hope to control.

Economic nationalism

The internationalism of money, the gold standard, and the free convertibility of currencies were gradually abandoned. Countries specializing in agricultural exports were among the first to be pinched. Agricultural prices were so low that even a large quantity of exports failed to produce enough foreign currency to pay for needed imports; hence the exporting country's currency fell in value. The currencies of Argentina, Uruguay, Chile, Australia, and New Zealand all depreciated in 1929 and 1930. Then came the turn of the industrial countries. England, also, as the depression went on, could not sell enough exports to pay for imports. It had to pay for imports in part by sending gold out of the country; thus the gold reserve supporting the pound sterling declined, and people who

This picture by the American photographer Dorthea Lange conveys some of the personal dimensions of the social and economic crisis of the 1930s. An idle, unemployed man stands outside a vacant store on an empty street in San Francisco. The photograph suggests the sense of failure and social disorientation that spread across much of the industrialized world during the decade of the Great Depression.

had pounds sterling began to convert their pounds into dollars or other currencies for which they thought the gold basis was more secure. This was known, in the poetic language of economics, as the "flight from the pound." In 1931 Great Britain went off the gold standard, which is to say that it devalued the pound. But after Britain devalued, some 20 odd other countries, to protect their own exports and their own industries, did the same. Hence somewhat the same relative position reappeared. Even the United States, which possessed most of the world's gold supply, renounced the gold standard and devalued the dollar in 1934. The purpose was mainly to help American farmers; with dollars cheaper in terms of foreign currencies, foreigners could afford to buy more American agricultural products. But it became harder for foreigners to sell to the United States.

Hence the depression, adding its effects to those of the World War and postwar inflation, led to chaos in the international monetary exchanges. Governments manipulated their currencies to uphold their sagging exports. Or they imposed exchange controls, which required that foreigners from whom their own people purchased, and to whom they gave their own currency, should use this currency to buy from them in return. Trade, which had been multilateral, became increasingly bilateral. Where Brazilian importers of steel, for example, had formerly bought steel wherever they wished at the prices or quality they preferred, they now had to obtain steel, often regardless of price or precise quality, from a country to which Brazil had sold enough of its own products to make payment possible. Sometimes, notably in the relations between Germany and East European countries in the 1930s, bilateralism degenerated into actual barter. The Germans would exchange a certain number of cameras with Yugoslavia in return for a certain number of pigs. In such cases the very conception of a market disappeared.

International monetary exchanges in chaos

Currency control was one means of keeping one's own factories from idleness by holding or capturing export markets in time of depression. Another way of keeping one's own factories going was to shut out competitive imports by the old device of protective tariffs. The United States enacted the unprecedentedly high Hawley-Smoot tariff in 1930, which soon contributed to the further decline of international trade. Other countries, equally or more distressed, now could sell less to America and hence buy fewer American goods. Other countries likewise raised their own tariffs in the desperate hope of reserving national markets for their own people. Even Great Britain, citadel of free trade in the nineteenth century, turned to protectionism. It also revived and adopted Joseph Chamberlain's old idea of an imperial tariff union. In 1932, by the Ottawa agreements, Britain and the British dominions adopted a policy of lower tariffs against one another and higher tariffs against the rest of the world.

Even tariffs were not always enough for economic nationalists. Quotas or quantitative restrictions were adopted in many nations. By this system a government said in effect not merely that goods brought into the country must pay a high tariff duty but that above a certain amount no goods could be brought in at all. Increasingly both importers and exporters worked under government licenses, in order that a country's entire foreign trade could be centrally planned and managed.

Quotas

Thus the world economy disintegrated into fiercely competing national economic systems. In the oceanic wreckage of the Great Depression, each state tried to create an island of economic security for its own people. Some efforts were made to break down the rising barriers. An International Monetary and Economic Conference, meeting in London in 1933, attempted to open the clogged channels of world trade; it ended in failure, as did attempts to stabilize the exchange rates of various currencies. Soon thereafter, the wartime Allies defaulted on their postwar debt payments to the United States. Legislation in Congress then denied them the right to float bonds or obtain new loans in the American securities market. American actions thus reinforced economic nationalism. The era that had opened with Woodrow Wilson's dream of international economic cooperation was ending with an unprecedented intensification of economic rivalry and national self-centeredness; it was only one of the promises of the postwar world to be blasted by the Great Depression.

Cultural Reactions to the Crisis

The effects of the economic crisis spread to the cultural and intellectual life of the 1930s. Responding to the despair and social dislocation of the masses of unemployed, artists and

AUTOUR D'ELLE

by Marc Chagall (Russian, then French, 1887–1984)

Although this painting clearly does not represent the social realism that emerged in the 1930s, it exemplifies the diversity of twentieth-century art. It was painted by Chagall in 1945 in memory of his wife. At the center is the Russian city of Smolensk, where they had been married 30 years before. The surrounding faces and figures are individually quite distinct, but they float disconnectedly like the vivid images in a dream. Past and present, memory and perception, fantastic and real objects flow together in a free play of the unconscious mind. These qualities characterized surrealism, of which the younger Chagall had been a forerunner.

(Scala/Art Resource, NY/© 2007 Artists Rights Society (ARS), New York/ADAGP, Paris)

Le Moulin de La Galette
by **Pierre-Auguste Renoir** (French, 1841–1919)
Renoir helped create the impressionist style of painting, which used contrasting colors to convey subtle variations of sunlight and shadows. This painting of dancers and friends at a popular Parisian dancehall is an example of the impressionists' interest in the everyday life and leisure of late nineteenth-century French society.

(Scala/Art Resource, NY)

Ia Orana Maria
by **Paul Gauguin** (French, 1848–1903)
Gauguin moved to Tahiti in the early 1890s, searching for non-European alternatives
to the culture and art he had known in France. His use of color and his portrayal
of Tahitians influenced avant-garde European artists, but Gauguin also continued to
draw on (classical) Western artistic themes. The title of this painting means "Hail
Mary," an allusion to the Biblical Annunciation in which the angel Gabriel told the
Virgin Mary that she would give birth to a child.
(The Metropolitan Museum of Art, Bequest of Sam A. Lewisohn, 1951 (51.112.2) Photograph ©1983 The
Metropolitan Museum of Art)

The Boating Party, 1893
by **Mary Cassatt** (American, then in France, 1844–1926)
Cassatt developed her most distinctive works under the influence of both Impressionism and the traditions of Japanese art. She painted many pictures of mothers with their children, including this colorful and slightly mysterious image of a man rowing two people across a European lake.
([The Boating Party, 1893, Mary Cassatt.*]* Chester Dale Collection, Photograph © 2001 Board of Trustees, National Gallery of Art, Washington [1963.10.94])

Self-Portrait with Beret, 1898-1899
by **Paul Cézanne** (French, 1839–1906)
Cézanne went beyond early Impressionist art to develop a new emphasis on the shapes or
contours of natural objects, buildings, and people. He also applied his innovative techniques
to portraits of himself, striving to depict his identity as a painter through both the style and the
content of such works.

(Charles H. Bayley Picture and Painting Fund and partial Gift of Elizabeth Paine Metcalf, 1972. Courtesy, Museum of
Fine Arts, Boston [1972.950]. Reproduced with permission. ©2001 Museum of Fine Arts Boston. All Rights Reserved.)

Panel for Edwin R. Campbell No. 1, 1914
by **Vasily Kandinsky** (Russian, then in Germany and France, 1866–1944)
Kandinsky was one of the first artists to paint purely abstract works. This painting, which Kandinsky completed in 1914, conveys an early twentieth-century artistic desire to use shapes and colors without reference to physical objects. Modernist artists wanted their colors to represent a personal vision rather than objective, external realities.

(Vasily Kandinsky, *Panel for Edwin R. Campbell No. 1.* 1914. Oil on canvas, 64 x 31 1/2" [162.5 x 80 cm]. The Museum of Modern Art, New York. Mrs. Simon Guggenheim Fund. Photograph ©2001 The Museum of Modern Art, New York/©2001 Artists Rights Society [ARS], New York/ADAGP, Paris)

Composition With The Ace of Clubs
by **Georges Braque** (French, 1883–1963)
This painting is an example of the Cubist movement in the early twentieth century. Braque
and the Cubists broke up the visual world into lines and planes, stressing almost mathematical
patterns and multiple perspectives rather than the bursts of color or pure abstractions that
appeared in other works of modern art.

(Giraudon/Art Resource, NY/© 2001 Artists Rights Society [ARS], New York/ADAGP, Paris)

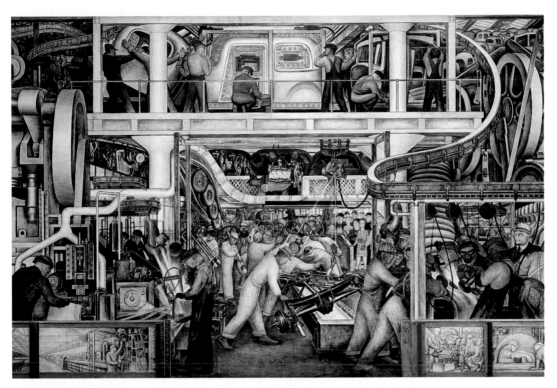

The Assembly Line

by **Diego Rivera** (Mexican, 1886–1957)

Twentieth-century artists have often depicted modern social realities as well as personal visions or abstract uses of color. This detail from a mural, Detroit Industry, that Diego Rivera painted in Detroit during the 1930s emphasizes stark social divisions between the workers on an automobile assembly line and the visitors who are watching them work.

The Survivor
by **George Grosz** (German, then American, 1893–1959)
Grosz was a refugee from Nazi Germany. This picture, which he painted in 1945, vividly
portrays the horrors of modern warfare, the brutal collapse of civilization, and the terrified
emotions of an isolated, filthy survivor. Note the symbolism of a broken swastika in the
arrangement of the man's body and the debris.

(AKG London/© Estate of George Grosz/Licensed by VAGA, New York, NY) writers turned to describing painful social realities and committed themselves to political activity.

All this was in contrast to the 1920s. The postwar decade had been a period of great achievement in what is generally called "modernist" art and literature. Painters projected disjointed dreamlike scenes evoking their personal memories or disorienting personal experiences and writers emphasized their own personal vision and the innermost lives of the characters whom they depicted. These writers were responsible for remarkable explorations of memory, time, and the internal workings of the human mind. The Irish writer James Joyce published his famous novel *Ulysses* portraying the life and thoughts of its leading character during a single day in Dublin, contributing with it to a new literary fascination with interior monologues and "stream of consciousness" writing, which was soon followed by the dramas of the American playwright Eugene O'Neill. The French novelist Marcel Proust developed lengthy descriptions of personal and emotional experiences in his multivolume *Remembrance of Things Past,* and the English writer Virginia Woolf examined the complex passage of time through the characters she created in novels such as *To the Lighthouse*. A generation of American writers, including Gertrude Stein and Ernest Hemingway, had even settled in Paris after the First World War to pursue experimental forms of literature and art. The political and social world by no means disappeared from "modernist" literature, but these writers were more concerned with exploring the inner complexities of human psychology.

Modernism

Now, under the harsh economic conditions of the 1930s, it became common to reject the literary exploration of psychological anxieties as inadequate or even as self-indulgent. A new kind of "realist" literature and a literature of political engagement won support from intellectuals in all industrial societies, especially among those who believed that the Great Depression had grown out of fundamental flaws and injustices in the capitalist economy. Some writers, like the French novelist André Gide, as well as some poets, artists, and film-makers, temporarily embraced communism and praised the social experiments of the Soviet Union. Others simply decided that they should set aside the arcane language of the literary avant-garde and write about the social suffering of the day. A new genre of proletarian literature came into being. Many who had settled in Paris returned to the United States in the early 1930s. As the American critic Malcolm Cowley noted in his *Exile's Return,* the new social problems called for new kinds of writing. Where *Ulysses* was a classic modernist work of the 1920s, John Steinbeck's *The Grapes of Wrath* may be seen as a classic "social novel" of the 1930s. Steinbeck wrote about the social miseries of America's impoverished, displaced farmers rather than the personal memories of an alienated intellectual. His themes and those elaborated by others exemplified the cultural anxiety that spread across the world in the wake of the unprecedented economic crisis. Meanwhile, the anxiety that fostered a new literary and artistic "realism" also contributed in very different ways to the rise of an angry political extremism, which, as we shall see, was now attracting new support in Europe, the United States, and other parts of the world.

Realism

For interactive exercises, glossary, chronologies, and more, go to the *Online Learning Center* at **www.mhhe.com/palmer10.**

Chapter *C h a p t e r* **20**

DEMOCRACY
AND DICTATORSHIP
IN THE 1930S

In the 1920s, people in a general way believed that despite the horrors of the World War the twentieth century was realizing the material and political goals summed up in the idea of progress. In the 1930s, they began to fear that "progress" was a phantom, to speak the word self-consciously with mental quotation marks, and to be content if only they could prevent a relapse into positive barbarism and a new world war.

The Great Depression ushered in the nightmare of the 1930s. Everywhere the demand was for security. Each nation tried to live, so far as possible, within itself. Each regulated, controlled, guided, planned, and tried to rescue its own economic system, attempting to be as little influenced as possible by the unpredictable behavior of other countries. Within each country the same search for security encouraged the advancement of the welfare state and social democracy.

Where democratic institutions were strong and resilient, governments took steps to protect individuals against the ravages of unemployment and destitution and to help guard against future catastrophes. On the other hand, where democratic governments were not well established or taken for granted, which was the case in many countries after the First World War, dictatorship spread alarmingly in the 1930s with the coming of the depression. Democracy was said to be suited only to wealthy or prosperous countries. Unemployed people generally cared far more for economic help or for promises of economic help than for any theory of how persons wielding public power should be selected. The cry was for a leader, someone who would act, make decisions, get results, inspire confidence, and restore national pride. The Great Depression opened the way for unscrupulous and ambitious political adventurers, for dictators like Adolf Hitler in Germany, whose solution to all political and international problems, it turned out, was war.

Chapter emblem: Benito Mussolini addressing a Fascist meeting in Italy in 1932. (Getty Images)

❧ 100.   THE UNITED STATES:
DEPRESSION AND NEW DEAL

Profound changes took place in the United States, where the stock market crash of 1929 had precipitated the great economic collapse. In 1932 national income had dropped to less than half of what it had been in 1929; 12 million to 14 million were unemployed. The Republican President Herbert Hoover, elected in 1928 at the floodtide of prosperity, was identified in the public mind with the hard times. Hoover viewed with disfavor any large-scale government intervention, convinced that the business cycle that had brought the depression would in turn bring prosperity and that once business confidence was restored, recovery would begin. His administration did act, proposing for the world economy a one-year suspension of payments on all intergovernmental debts and at home giving financial assistance to banks and railroads, expanding credit facilities, and helping to save the mortgages of some farmers and small home owners.

But Hoover would go no further; he opposed immediate direct federal relief to the jobless; veterans seeking payment of their wartime bonuses to tide them over the bad times were forcibly ejected from Washington; unemployment, business failures, and farm foreclosures continued. In the election of 1932 the millions of unemployed workers, disheartened urban lower middle classes, and distressed farmers swept the Republican administration from office and elected the first Democratic president since Woodrow Wilson. The new president was Franklin Delano Roosevelt. The combination of recovery, relief, and reform legislation that he introduced is known as the New Deal.

FDR's recovery, relief, and reform legislation

The new president embarked rapidly on a program of improvisation and experimentation, but with such dispatch and vigor as to generate at once an electric enthusiasm. Within a short time an impressive array of legislation was put through Congress. The modest program of assistance to farmers, small home owners, and industry initiated under the Hoover administration was expanded so widely that it was no longer recognizable.

The government provided financial assistance for the relief of the unemployed and sponsored a broad public works program to absorb the jobless, first by loans to the states for the construction of housing, roads, bridges, and schools; later by a direct federal works program. To meet the financial crisis, the banks were temporarily closed and then reopened under stricter supervision. The dollar was taken off the gold standard and devalued, principally to help the farmers compete in foreign markets. In agriculture, the government offered subsidies to farmers who agreed to curtail farm production, even to the point of subsidizing the destruction of crops and livestock, so that ruinous surpluses which had been one cause of the agricultural distress might be eliminated. It was a paradox, to be sure, for the government to reduce acreage and destroy farm products while city populations were in want. But the administration sought to confront the deep-seated agricultural crisis that antedated the depression as well as to cope with the immediate situation. Subsequently, farmers received subsidies mostly for devoting part of their land to soil-conserving crops. A Civilian Conservation Corps promoted conservation and reforestation and helped relieve unemployment by giving jobs to almost 3 million young people. For industry a National Recovery Administration (the NRA) encouraged business firms to set up voluntary "codes of fair competition," which helped to regulate prices and production.

All these measures were designed to set the ailing capitalist system on its feet again by creating purchasing power and stimulating industrial activity. The major innovation was government spending, or "deficit financing." Although never following any consistent economic philosophy, the New Deal policies indirectly reflected the theories of the British economist John Maynard Keynes. In his earlier writings and in his most famous book *The General Theory of Employment, Interest, and Money* published in 1936, he argued that if private investment funds were idle, government funds must be employed to encourage economic activity and to increase purchasing power until such time as private funds flowed again. In order to get money into circulation and to "prime the pump" of industrial production, the New Deal government undertook a huge borrowing and spending program. Unorthodox as deficit financing was, it seemed to many at the time (and to many since) the only direct and rapid method of preventing economic collapse in a capitalist system. In all these recovery and reform activities the federal government assumed a role that it had hitherto played only in wartime. New government agencies proliferated, the federal payroll grew, and the government debt more than doubled between 1932 and 1940.

Keynes's "deficit financing"

From the beginning some longer-range reform measures were adopted in addition to the recovery measures. To prevent overspeculation and the recurrence of a stock market crash such as that of 1929, a Securities and Exchange Commission was created to regulate the issuance of stock and to supervise the operations of the stock exchange. Bank deposits were guaranteed by federal insurance so that depositors would not lose their lifetime savings. A Tennessee Valley Authority served as a pilot program in flood control, regional economic development, and cheap public power production, bringing electricity to farms and rural households.

After 1935 the focus shifted to regulation and reform. Sound economic recovery had not been achieved; there were still at least 5 million persons who could not find jobs in private industry. Business leaders who at first had been responsive to the government's new role in the economy now resisted the government's regulation of finance and industry. The Supreme Court declared the NRA and other New Deal measures unconstitutional.

Resistance to regulation and reform

The major New Deal reforms after 1935 were designed to improve the condition of labor and to cope with various kinds of economic insecurity. A broad national Social Security Act in 1935 provided for unemployment, old-age, and disability insurance. Here the United States was a latecomer. Germany, Britain, and other European countries had already enacted such legislation before the First World War. A Fair Labor Standards Act established 40 hours as a maximum normal workweek and set a minimum hourly wage; child labor was ended. A third measure, the National Labor Relations (or Wagner) Act, virtually transformed the American industrial scene. The act guaranteed the right of workers to set up and bargain through unions of their choice, outlawed company unions, and prohibited employers from interfering with union organizing or discriminating against union members. Under its aegis the older American Federation of Labor (AFL) was revitalized and a new vigorous Congress of Industrial Organizations (CIO) came into being, which now organized workers on an industrywide basis and reached down to unskilled workers in such industries as automobile, steel, textile, maritime, and rubber. Millions never before organized became part of powerful labor unions with expanding treasuries. Total union membership rose from about 4 million in 1929 to 9 million by 1940. Militant and conscious of its new strength but hardly touched by revolutionary ideology, American labor chose not to create a third party but to operate within the traditional two-party system, generally supporting Roosevelt's Democratic party.

Labor and unions

The economic crisis of the 1930s and changes in the laws governing labor relations contributed to the rapid growth and new militancy of labor unions in the United States. This picture of an automobile factory in Flint, Michigan, in the late 1930s shows workers engaged in a sit-down strike. Such strikes became one of the strategies that workers used to express their grievances about wages, working conditions, or restrictions on the organizing of labor unions.
(Library of Congress)

Slow and partial recovery

Government spending and renewed confidence in the soundness of the country's institutions created a slow and partial recovery. By 1939 national income had risen to double what it had been at the depth of the depression but still short of June 1929. Resistance from the business community itself may have played a part in the failure to achieve full recovery. The rising public debt, antibusiness pronouncements by the government, heavier corporate and income taxes, and the concessions to labor undoubtedly frightened off business investments and led to what was called a "sit-down strike" of capital. Some claimed that wage rates had risen too sharply, adding to production costs and therefore discouraging business expansion. The New Deal did much to help economic recovery, but it did not end the depression. Complete recovery, the elimination of unemployment, and the full use (and expansion) of the nation's productive capacity had to wait upon the huge war expenditures to come. By 1938 or so the New Deal was virtually over; the administration turned its attention from domestic reform to the gathering storm in Europe and the Far East.

The changes were substantial under what some called the "Roosevelt Revolution." Enlarging the role of the federal government as no previous administration had done, the New Deal helped transform the noninterventionist state into a social service or welfare state. The government imposed controls on business, increased labor's power and influence and its share of the national income, and introduced a broad social security system. It established the responsibility of public authority for the social and economic welfare of the people. When the Republican party later returned to power, it opposed in principle the further growth of the welfare state and the expanding role of the federal government, but it retained many of the New Deal reforms, a tacit admission that the New Deal had not intended to destroy capitalism but to preserve and revive it.

The New Deal, however, engendered violent feelings, which lingered on. Roosevelt, himself of patrician and well-to-do background, denounced the "economic royalists"; in turn he was called a "traitor to his class." When the Supreme Court declared some New Deal measures unconstitutional, he made plans to reorganize (or "pack") the Court, which aroused more political hostility. Despite vociferous opposition, in the election of 1936 Roosevelt won all but two states, and he was subsequently reelected in 1940 and 1944 (during the war, to be sure), for unprecedented third and fourth terms. A constitutional amendment in 1951 limited presidents to two terms.

Reelection of Roosevelt

Roosevelt's opponents, at the time and later, argued that the New Deal had created an enormous regulatory bureaucracy, which was expensive, cumbersome, and a threat to the freedom and self-reliance of the citizenry. Others contended that despite its unorthodox financial policies, enlargement of the executive power, and expansion of the bureaucracy, it represented a bold and humanitarian way of meeting the economic crisis, and that it also preserved and reaffirmed American faith in its democratic system at a time when democracy was succumbing or was threatened elsewhere.

101. TRIALS AND ADJUSTMENTS OF DEMOCRACY IN BRITAIN AND FRANCE

British Politics: The 1920s and the Depression

Britain, like the United States, even in the troubles of the depression, remained firmly attached to representative institutions and democratic principles. The Great Depression aggravated and intensified Britain's older economic difficulties. More dependent on overseas markets than any other people, the British until 1914 had managed to hold their lead, exporting industrial products and investment capital, selling insurance and other services, and importing foodstuffs. But in the years before 1914 the British were increasingly losing markets because of the emergence of other economically aggressive industrial nations, the growth of tariff barriers, the development of indigenous textile and other industries in India and elsewhere in the East, the competition of new textile products with British cottons and woolens, and the substitution of new sources of fuel for British coal. The losses were accelerated by the economic disruption of the First World War, the disappearance of many overseas investments, and the postwar disorganization and impoverishment of markets. The widespread rise in tariffs after the war and the customs barriers in the new small states of Europe also hurt British exports. After 1918 Britain lived in a world no longer

The British coal miners' strike in 1926 generated a massive "general strike" by sympathetic workers throughout Britain. These striking engineers marched across London to show their solidarity with the miners, but the government soon responded to this broad-based labor action with legislation that made all such sympathy strikes illegal.
(Getty Images)

dependent on, or eager for, its manufactures. Britain's very historical primacy as the pioneer industrial country was also a handicap. Both labor and management had become adjusted to older conditions, and the more recently industrialized countries had newer techniques and machinery.

The net result of all this was that in the interwar years, even in times of relative prosperity for the rest of the world, Britain was in depression and suffered severely from unemployment. The unemployment insurance adopted in 1911 was called heavily into play. By 1921 over 2 million unemployed were receiving benefit payments, contemptuously called the "dole" by those who disliked it. Unemployment insurance, an expanded old-age pension system, medical aid, government-subsidized housing, and other social welfare measures helped to relieve economic distress and to prevent any drastic decline in the living standards of British workers. The welfare state was well established in Britain before the Labour party took office after the Second World War.

Unemployment insurance

The labor unions made a strenuous effort to retain wage gains and other concessions won in wartime. Industry, hard-pressed itself, resisted. This situation reached a climax in 1926 in the coal-mining industry, which was in a particularly bad plight; government subsidies had not helped and even conservative investigators had recommended some form of amalgamation and public management. A strike by the coal miners led to a "general strike" supported by the other British unions; about half of the 6 million organized workers in Britain left their jobs as a token of sympathy and solidarity. But the government declared a state of emergency and made use of army and navy personnel and middle-class volunteers to take over essential services. The strike ended in failure, and even in a setback for the trade unions. They were put under stricter control by the Trades Disputes Act of 1927, which declared all general or sympathy strikes illegal and even forbade the unions from raising money for political purposes.

After the election of 1922, the Labour party displaced the Liberal party as the second of the two great parties of the country and faced the Conservatives as the official opposition. The Labour party, which had been no more *The Labour party* than a loose federation of trade union and socialist organizations before the war, tightened its organizational structure, promoted labor legislation, and, bridging the gap between the trade unionists and the socialists, committed itself to a program of socialism. But it was a program of gradualist, democratic socialism operating through customary British parliamentary procedures and hence able to gain the goodwill of large sections of the middle classes.

Twice, in 1924 and in 1929, Labour governed the country with Ramsay MacDonald as prime minister, in each case as a coalition government. In 1924 Labour demonstrated its moderation. It did no more than extend unemployment relief and inaugurate housing and public works projects; indeed it acted firmly in the face of strikes that broke out. But it aroused opposition when it gave diplomatic recognition to the Soviet Union and pledged a loan to the Soviets for the purchase of British goods. Meanwhile newspapers published the so-called Red (or Zinoviev) letter purporting to be secret instructions from the head of the Communist International for British Labour groups to prepare for a Communist uprising in Britain. The document's authenticity has never been established, but the Conservatives successfully exploited it and won the election of 1924.

In the election of May 1929, however, Labour's representation almost doubled, and the Conservative representation dropped proportionately. MacDonald again became prime minister. The Wall Street crash and the worldwide depression came while the Labour party government was in office. The effects of the depression were quickly felt. Unemployment, which had hovered about the 1 million mark in 1929, soon approached the 3 million figure. The government expended large sums to supplement the unemployment insurance payments, and the public debt began to grow. Alarmed by the mounting deficit, MacDonald made plans to introduce a severe retrenchment policy, even to the extent of reducing the "dole" payments. The Labour party was outraged; some of the Labour ministers in his cabinet refused to support him. He was read out of the party, along with those ministers who had gone along with him. *The formation of the* MacDonald thereupon formed an all-party coalition cabinet known as the *National government* National government, which in an election of 1931 won an overwhelming victory, but it was the Conservative members of the coalition who took a majority of the seats in Parliament.

The National government coped with the depression chiefly along retrenchment lines, under Ramsay MacDonald from 1931 to 1935, Stanley Baldwin to 1937, and Neville Chamberlain after 1937. In addition to retrenchment and budget balancing, the government encouraged industry to reorganize and rationalize production by providing low-interest loans. Mainly, the government concentrated on economic nationalist measures rather than on fundamental changes in the capitalist economic system. As in the United States, despite some recovery from the depths of the depression, none of the steps taken brought full recovery or full employment. Unemployment persisted until military conscription and an expanded armament program absorbed the jobless.

Britain and the Commonwealth: Imperial Relations

To the older British Empire—India, the crown colonies, protectorates, and spheres of influence—the postwar settlement added a number of League of Nations mandates. British rule in its various forms extended to almost 500 million people, a fourth of the earth's population and land surface. It was principally in Palestine, Egypt, India, and Ireland that the British faced complex imperial problems after the First World War. In Palestine, where Britain exercised a League of Nations mandate following the breakup of the Ottoman Empire, a bitter conflict developed as Jewish emigrants moved into the territory after 1919 (at which time there had been a relatively small population of about 570,000 Muslims, 75,000 Christians, and 60,000 Jews). The emigration increased rapidly during the 1930s, when Jews were escaping from Nazism and the rising anti-Semitism in Europe. Arabs and Jews began to struggle with each other and with Britain for control of lands that both groups claimed on the basis of long ancestries and ancient religions, inflamed now by modern nationalisms. In Egypt in 1922, Britain, although retaining the right to station some troops there, formally ended the protectorate it had established 40 years earlier; but many questions, especially the status of the Sudan, remained unresolved. In India the agitation for national independence, as we have seen, grew more intense. In all of these areas, from the Middle East to South Asia, nothing resembling a solution was arrived at until after the Second World War. In Ireland the independence movement managed to establish a separate republic.

The Irish question   The Irish question had disoriented English politics for 40 years. Home rule, authorized by Parliament in 1914, had been deferred for the duration of the war. During the hostilities the Irish nationalists even accepted German support and rose in rebellion against the British in 1916. The rebellion was suppressed, but after the war the Irish nationalists, led by the Sinn Fein party, fought a small but savage war of independence against the British. In 1922 the British finally recognized the Irish Free State, granting it dominion status within the British Commonwealth. But the Protestants in Ulster, the northern counties of Ireland where Presbyterians of Scottish origin had lived for three centuries and where they comprised a majority of the population, insisted on remaining outside the new state. Despite the vehement dissatisfaction of Irish nationalists, Ulster continued to be part of what was now called the United Kingdom of Great Britain and Northern Ireland. In 1937 the Irish Free State affirmed its full sovereignty and took the name Eire. In 1949 it broke all ties with the British Commonwealth and renamed itself the Republic of Ireland. The Irish question, however, remained unsettled throughout the rest of the century and beyond because the Irish agitated for the annexation of Ulster. The conflict pitted Irish moderates against Irish extremists, the latter perpetrating assassinations, bombings, and other disturbances to further their cause of uniting all Ireland with the Irish Republic. The Protestants in Ulster meanwhile remained obdurate about retaining their own religious and cultural identity and maintaining their political affiliation with Britain.

The dominions   As for the dominions, the political status of these areas of European settlement overseas was now more clearly defined than ever before. The dominions—Canada, Australia, New Zealand, and the Union of South Africa—had long pursued their own independent policies, even levying tariffs against British goods. They had all joined loyally with Great Britain in the First World War, but all were stirred by a nationalism of their own and desired their independence to be regularized and promulgated to the world. An imperial conference in 1926 defined "dominion status," which was then corroborated by the Statute of Westminster of 1931. The dominions became legally equal with each other and with Great Britain. No act passed by the British Parliament would apply to a dominion except by the dominion's own consent. Despite independent policies in economic matters and even in foreign affairs, the bonds between the dominions and Britain remained firm; the support of the dominions in the Second World War was to be vital in Britain's survival. In the postwar world, with decolonization, the Commonwealth became a larger, more heterogeneous, and even more flexible institution.

France: The 1920s and the Coming of the Depression

When the depression came to France, right-wing agitation of fascist type made more headway than in Britain or the United States. Earlier, in the 1920s, France was preoccupied with recovery from the physical destruction of the war, the instability of public finances, and the fear of a resurgent Germany. Immediately after 1919, and for most of the 1920s, the government was run by coalitions of parties of the conservative Right, that is, parties supported by business and financial interests, well disposed toward the army and church, and determined to maintain stability in domestic affairs. For a brief time, from 1924 to 1926, the Radical Socialists were in control; this party of the moderate left, whose leader was Edouard Herriot, served as spokesman for the lower classes, small business, and farmers; it advocated progressive social legislation but only so long as increased taxes were not necessary. Despite its name, a carryover from an earlier era, it was firmly committed to private enterprise and private property (and was often described as "neither radical nor socialist"); it was staunch in its defense of individual liberties and fervently anticlerical; sometimes, it seemed, its anticlericalism was a substitute for any more positive program.

Although the Radical Socialists cooperated in parliamentary elections with the Socialists, the other major party of the Left, the two parties differed too profoundly on economic policies to preserve stable coalitions. In the 1920s the Socialists were still recovering from the secession of the more orthodox Marxists who had formed a French Communist party. Both Left and Right in France shaded off into antidemocratic groups that were hostile to the parliamentary republic. These included the Communists on the Left, who sat in Parliament and took part in elections; and on the extreme Right, royalists of the *Action Française* and other antirepublican organizations, which operated principally outside the Chamber as militant and noisy pressure groups.

Hostility to the republic

The outstanding figure of the moderate conservative right was Raymond Poincaré, who sent troops into the Ruhr in 1923 when the Germans failed to pay reparations, and who also "saved" the franc. The reparations question was extremely important for French finances. The country had undertaken a large-scale reconstruction program to repair the wartime devastation of northern and eastern France and had counted upon the defeated enemy to pay. When German reparations were not paid as anticipated, the public debt mounted, a balanced budget became impossible, and the franc declined precipitously. The huge war expenditures, heavy loss of foreign investments, notably in Russia, and an outmoded taxation program which invited widespread evasion added to French difficulties. After 1926, when the financial crisis reached a climax, a "national union" ministry under Poincaré inaugurated new taxes, tightened tax collection, cut down drastically on government expenditures to balance the budget, and eventually stabilized the franc—at about one-fifth its prewar value. The internal debt was thus in effect largely repudiated, to the despair of many bondholders, but the threat of a runaway inflation like that of the Weimar Republic was avoided. From

Poincaré's measures

Britain repeatedly used its armed forces to suppress the movement for Irish independence during and after the First World War. The British army thus operated in Ireland's cities as a kind of special police force. These troops were holding back the crowd in a Dublin street while other soldiers conducted a raid on Irish nationalists in 1921.
(Getty Images)

1926 to 1929 the country prospered. New factories, replacing those destroyed in the war, were modern and up to date. The index of industrial production rose; tourists flocked in. As in many other countries, however, workers did not share proportionately in the prosperity of the 1920s, and labor unions still had little influence on the French government's social policies.

The Great Depression came later to France and was less severe than in the United States or Germany. Trade declined. Unemployment increased; in 1935, close to 1 million workers were unemployed, and half of those employed worked part-time. Industrial production, which in 1930 was 40 percent above the prewar level, sank by 1932 to 1913 figures. The government displayed its older pattern of unstable, short-lived ministries; in 1933 five ministries rapidly succeeded one another (there were some 40 in the 20 interwar years). The depression cabinets followed a policy of retrenchment and economy, clung to the gold standard, and faced the threat of an aggressive new government in Germany, where Adolf Hitler had become chancellor in 1933.

Depression Ferment and the Popular Front

In the uneasy years of the depression, the latent right-wing hostility to the republic came to the surface. Fascist-type "leagues" appeared in open imitation of Italian and German fascist organizations, many obtaining funds from wealthy industrialists; the older *Action Française* and right-wing veterans' associations like Colonel de le Rocque's *Croix de Feu* continued to be active. The same elements that had been antirepublican, antidemocratic, or monarchist since the French Revolution, and which in the nineteenth century had rallied behind Boulanger and denounced Dreyfus, now grew more strident in their attacks on the parliamentary republic.

In 1934 it seemed for a moment that the opportunity awaited by the antirepublican elements had come. A political and financial scandal shook the country. A financial manipulator and adventurer with important political connections, Serge Alexandre Stavisky, induced the municipal authorities at Bayonne to launch a flotation of worthless bonds. Faced with exposure, he fled and apparently committed suicide; the sensationalist press and right-wing political agitators encouraged the rumor that Stavisky had been shot by the police to prevent the implication of high-ranking politicians. A clamor went up accusing the government of involvement in the financial scandal. Where elsewhere such an affair would have called only for turning the incumbents out of office, in France it supplied ammunition for those who demanded the end of the republic itself, which they now equated with corruption and venality.

Scandals

The agitation reached a climax in the riots of February 1934. A crowd of angry antirepublican activists and other right-wing extremists assembled in Paris at the Place de la Concorde, where they threatened the nearby Chamber of Deputies and battled violently with the police; several were killed and hundreds were injured. French liberals and democrats, organized labor, and socialists were outraged by the threat to the republic from violent agitators who resembled the fascist groups that had seized power elsewhere in Europe. The Communists, hostile to the fascist groups, were unfriendly to the government too, but soon, guided by the Comintern, they sensed the danger to the Soviet Union in the event of a French fascist triumph and joined with the antifascists. As elsewhere, in the 1930s the Communists emerged from their sectarian revolutionary isolation, adopted patriotic programs, and widened their prestige, influence, and appeal. An impressive labor-sponsored general strike was held a week after the riots. Shortly thereafter, Radical Socialists, Socialists, and Communists drew together in a political coalition that came to be known as the Popular Front, of the kind that was being organized, or advocated, in many countries in the 1930s. It campaigned on a pledge to defend the republic against fascism, to take measures against the depression, and to introduce labor reforms. In the spring of 1936 it won a decisive victory at the polls. The French Socialists for the first time in their history became the leading party in the Chamber; their chief, Léon Blum, long a spokesman for democratic and reformist

The emergence of the French Socialists

The French Popular Front brought the leftist, antifascist political parties together in a governing coalition that held power for about a year in 1936–1937. Despite its brevity, the Popular Front government introduced numerous reforms that became permanent features of French social and economic life. This photograph shows Premier Léon Blum addressing supporters of the Popular Front on Bastille Day in 1936.
(akg-images)

socialism, became premier of a coalition cabinet of Socialists and Radical Socialists; the Communists, who had increased their representation in the Chamber from 10 to 72 seats, did not join the cabinet but pledged their support.

The Popular Front and After

Blum's Popular Front ministry, although it lasted little more than a year, put through a program of far-reaching legislation. In part, this was due to the Popular Front election program, in part to unforeseen events, for the tremendous enthusiasm generated by the victory led to a spontaneous nationwide wave of "sit-down strikes," in which the striking workers refused to leave their factories or shops until Blum pledged a number of immediate reforms.

Parliament in short order passed laws providing for a 40-hour week, vacations with pay, and a collective bargaining law. As in the case of the Wagner Act in the United States, the encouragement given to collective bargaining led to the nationwide signing of collective contracts for the first time in the country's history and to enormous growth in trade union membership, from about 1 million to 5 million in a year's time. Other legislation was important too. Steps were taken to nationalize the armaments and aviation industry; the fascist armed leagues were, at least in theory, dissolved; the Bank of France was reorganized and placed under government control to break the power of the nation's close-knit economic elite, the so-called "two hundred families." Machinery was established for the arbitration of labor disputes. Aid was given to farmers through price fixing and government purchases of wheat. As in the United States all these measures aimed at both recovery and reform; Blum spoke openly of his program as a "French New Deal." But French conservatives, and the quasi-fascists to their Right, cried revolution; they uttered dark predictions that a French Lenin would follow Blum. They did not conceal their sullen resentment at what had come to pass: the fate of Catholic France in the hands of a leftist, a Socialist, and a Jew. Even salvation by a warrior from outside the country, one who had demonstrated his anti-Bolshevism, would be preferable. They envied the protection given to established interests by Mussolini, and there were those who, it was said, even muttered "better Hitler than Léon Blum."

Overdue measures for reform and recovery

The Popular Front reforms, long overdue though they were, came to France at a time when the sands were rapidly running out. While France had a 40-hour week, German arms plants were operating at full capacity. In the shadow of Nazi remilitarization a rearmament program had to be undertaken at the very same time as reform; even moderates argued that the country could not afford both. Opposition from many quarters hindered success. French employers balked at cooperating in the new labor reforms and tried to pass on rising production costs to the consumer. Labor was disgruntled at the price rises that canceled out its wage gains. Both employers and labor applied the 40-hour week in such a manner that plants were shut down for two days a week instead of operating in shifts, as the law had made possible. Nothing could check the flight of gold from the country. Industrial production hardly rose; even in 1938, when it had shown substantial recovery in other countries, it was only 5 percent higher in France than at the depth of the depression.

In July 1936 the Spanish Civil War had broken out. The Communists attacked the Blum government for refusing aid to the hard-pressed Spanish Popular Front government, which was fighting fascist forces across the Pyrenees; Blum, following the lead of Britain and fearful also of involving a divided France, resisted. In 1937, after a year in office, the Blum government was overthrown by the Senate, which refused to grant it emergency financial powers. The Popular Front coalition rapidly disintegrated. By mid-1938 the Radical Socialists had abandoned their allies on the Left and under Edouard Daladier formed a conservative ministry, whose attention was increasingly occupied by the international crisis. Little remained of the Popular Front, or indeed of the strength of labor, which declined rapidly and exhausted itself further by an unsuccessful general strike in 1938 in protest against nullification of the 40-hour week. Although the conservative government did not overturn all of the recent social reforms, French workers found that 1936 had gone the way of other "great years" in French history; the comfortable classes had been thrown into panic by the social turmoil; internal division and class hatreds had grown sharper. Yet the French democracy, the Third Republic itself, had been successfully preserved and its domestic enemies repulsed, at least for a time.

The overthrow of Blum's government

Western Europe and the Depression

Britain and France, and indeed all western Europe, Europe's inner zone, never fully recovered from the Great Depression before the Second World War. When economic expansion resumed after the war, the interwar years seemed like a deep trough in Europe's economic history. Western Europe barely maintained its old industrial equipment in the depression and was unable to utilize even its existing machinery to capacity. Moreover, as the events of 1929 had clearly shown, Europe's economic dependence on the United States was pronounced, and the U.S.S.R. was becoming an industrial giant. The economic destiny of Europeans in the 1930s was very much in doubt.

There were other signs of decline. The birth rate in western Europe in the 1930s fell to its lowest recorded levels as people postponed marriage or limited the size of their families because of economic and psychological stresses. Birth rates did not run significantly higher than death rates; the population was stagnating and growing older. There was a scarcity of middle-age men because of the casualties of the First World War. Politically neither British nor French democratic political leaders were able to cope with the economic dilemmas of the depression era. Nor could the

Other signs of decline

Socialists, who found little practical guidance in the ideas of Marxian economics or class struggle, but failed to renew or reinvigorate their own doctrines in any significant way.

102.   ITALIAN FASCISM

Though they shade into each other imperceptibly, it is possible to distinguish dictatorship from totalitarianism. Dictatorship, an old phenomenon in history, has commonly been regarded as a mere expedient, designed for emergencies and believed to be temporary; at most, it is a theory of government to justify the authoritarian exercise of state power. Totalitarianism, as it arose after the First World War, was not merely a theory of government but a theory of life and of human nature. It claimed to be no expedient but a permanent form of society and civilization, and so far as it appealed to emergency for justification, it regarded life itself as an everlasting emergency. This new kind of totalitarianism, when it emerged in Western Europe, came from the political Right and carried significant theoretical differences from Russian Communism—which it vehemently rejected and yet in its repressive methods, its cult of the leader, and its one-party rule it often resembled. The first of the new right-wing totalitarian movements to seize power in Europe appeared somewhat unexpectedly in Italy in the form of fascism.

Mussolini and the Fascist Seizure of Power

The belief widely held in the 1920s that democracy was generally advancing was not deeply disturbed by the failure of Russia or Turkey or China to develop effective parliaments or liberal institutions. These were regarded as "backward" countries, in the throes of revolution; someday, when conditions quieted down, it could be supposed, they would move forward to democracy as known in the West. Italy thus became a jarring exception to the apparent victory of democracy in western societies because the Italians had always been an integral part of Europe and European history. Although Italy had accepted parliamentary liberalism and other democratic institutions since 1861, Benito Mussolini seized control of the Italian government in 1921 and proclaimed the new ruling ideology and political system of *Fascismo*.

The birth of Fascismo

Mussolini, born in 1883, the son of a blacksmith, was a fiery and pugnacious character, who before the war had followed the career of professional revolutionary, left-wing socialist, and radical journalist. He had read and digested Marxist writings but also works such as Sorel's *Reflections on Violence* and the writings of Nietzsche. During the war he turned intensely nationalist, clamored for Italian intervention on the side of the Allies, and demanded the conquest from Austria of *Italia irredenta,* the "unredeemed" Italian lands to the north and across the Adriatic. In the war he served as a corporal. In March 1919 he organized, mainly from demobilized and restless ex-soldiers, his first fighting band, or *fascio di combattimento. Fascio* meant a bunch or bundle, as of sticks; it called to mind the Latin *fasces,* or bundle of rods, carried by the lictors in ancient Rome as a symbol of state power—for Mussolini loved to conjure up ancient glories.

In 1919 Italian glories were dim. Italy had entered the war on the side of the Allies quite frankly for territorial and colonial spoils; the secret treaty of London in 1915 had promised the Italians certain Austrian lands and a share in German and Turkish possessions. During the war Italian arms did not especially shine; Italian troops were routed at Caporetto in 1917. Yet Italy lost over 600,000 lives in the war, and the Italian delegates came to the peace conference confident that their sacrifices would be recognized and their territorial aspirations would be satisfied. They were rapidly disappointed. Wilson refused to honor the provisions of the London secret treaty and other demands of the Italians. Britain and France displayed no eagerness to side with Italy. The Italians received some of the Austrian territories promised to them, but to their resentment they were given no part of the former German or Turkish possessions as mandates.

After the war Italy, like other countries, suffered from the burden of wartime debt and from acute postwar depression and unemployment. Social unrest spread. In the countryside land seizures took place, not in any significant proportions but enough to spread concern among landowners; tenant farmers refused to pay rents; peasants burned crops and destroyed livestock. In the cities great strikes broke out in heavy industry and in transportation. Some of the strikes turned into sit-down strikes, the workers refusing to leave the plants; demands were raised even for worker control of the factories. Moderate socialist and labor leaders disavowed all such extremism, but left-wing socialists who, as elsewhere, had turned Communist and joined the Third International, fanned the existing discontents. Meanwhile, armed bands of young men, most prominent of whom were the Blackshirts or Fascists, brawled with Communists and ordinary workers in the streets. By the late summer of 1920 the strikes and the agrarian unrest had subsided, although violence in the streets persisted.

Social unrest

During the months of turmoil the government refrained from any bold action, and the already low respect for Italy's parliamentary system sank even lower. In 1919 the first postwar election gave impressive victories to the Socialists and a new Catholic Popular party (the latter were also called Christian Socialists). In 1921, in the wake of the postwar disturbances, new elections were held. Despite concerns about the recent social turmoil, liberals and democrats, moderate socialists, and the Catholic Popular Party were all returned in large numbers. Mussolini's Fascist movement won only 35 of the 500-odd seats. This less than impressive showing was the best the Fascists ever achieved in a free election, but the Fascist ranks were nonetheless swelling outside the regular channels of electoral politics—in the backwash, as it were, of the postwar unrest.

Mussolini and the Fascists at first went along with the radical tide; they did not disapprove the factory seizures; they inveighed against plutocracy and war profiteers and called for a high levy on capital and profits. But Mussolini, never one to sacrifice opportunity for principles or doctrine, soon came forward with his Fascists as the upholders of national law and order, and hence property; he now pledged battle "against the forces dissolving victory and nation." Although the social agitation subsided, burning itself out on its own, and there had never been any real threat of a Soviet-style revolution, the propertied classes had gone through a great fright; they found comfort in the Fascist movement and were willing to lend it financial support. Patriots and nationalists of all classes rallied to it, as well as the lower middle class, which was pinched by economic inflation and, as elsewhere, was unable to find protection or solace in labor unions or socialist movements. The blackshirted upholders of national order proceeded methodically to administer beatings (and doses of castor oil) to Communists and alleged Communists, to Socialists and Christian Socialists, and to ordinary persons who did not support them; nor did they refrain from arson and murder. Vigilante fascist squadrons, the *squadristi,* broke up strikes, demolished labor union headquarters, and drove from office duly elected Socialist and Communist mayors and town officials. Mussolini nevertheless reinforced his claim as paladin of law,

Mussolini: upholding order and property

Fascist groups joined a "March on Rome" that sought to displace Italy's liberal-democratic government in October 1922. Mussolini joined the March as the Blackshirts entered the capital, and he is seen here (in civilian clothes) leading his fascist followers through the city — shortly before he became prime minister in a new coalition ministry.
(akg-images)

authority, and order by declaring his loyalty to king and church; a few years earlier he had been a rabid republican and anticlerical.

The "March on Rome"

In October 1922 the "March on Rome" took place. The Blackshirts mobilized for a threatened coup and began to converge from various directions on the capital; Mussolini remained at a safe distance in Milan. The liberal-democratic coalition cabinet had viewed the events of the past two years with disapproval but at the same time saw with satisfaction that the Blackshirts were serving a useful national purpose by suppressing troublemakers on the Left. Now they made belated but ineffectual gestures to save the situation by an effort to have martial law declared, but the king refused to approve. The cabinet resigned and Mussolini was named premier. It was all quite legal, or almost so. Indeed Italy was still in form a constitutional and parliamentary monarchy. Mussolini headed only a coalition ministry and received from parliament no more than a year's grant of full emergency powers to restore order and introduce reforms.

But soon it was clear in whose hands power rested. Before the expiration of his emergency powers Mussolini forced through parliament a law providing that any party securing the largest number of votes in an election should automatically receive two-thirds of the seats in the legislature. The two-thirds law was not even necessary. In the 1924 elections, although seven opposition slates appeared, the Fascists, aided by control of the electoral machinery and the use of *squadristi,* received well over three-fifths of the total vote.

Benito Mussolini liked to portray his Fascist regime in Italy as a restoration of the power and grandeur of ancient Rome. Speaking here at a Fascist rally in 1932 and surrounded by uniformed followers as well as symbols of the Roman Empire, Mussolini struck a characteristic stance to convey a public image of decisive, powerful leadership in the authoritarian Italian state.
(Getty Images)

After the elections of 1924 the highly respected Socialist deputy Matteotti publicly exposed hundreds of cases of armed Fascist violence, fraud, and chicanery. He was murdered by Fascists. There was widespread indignation in the country, and the press clamored for Mussolini's resignation. The left and centrist parties, in an act that proved to be a serious miscalculation, seceded in protest from the Chamber, wanting to have nothing to do with such a government. Mussolini, not directly involved in the assassination, expressed a willingness to punish the perpetrators but eventually took full responsibility and moved to consolidate his dictatorship. Within a few years he reduced the Italian parliament to a nonentity, placed the press under censorship, abolished the labor unions, deprived labor of the right to strike, and abolished all political parties except the Fascist party.

Matteotti's murder

The Fascist State

Fascism in the 1920s was an innovation which the rest of the world was slow to understand. In his more flamboyant moments Mussolini strutted, stuck out his jaw, and glared ferociously; he jumped through flaming hoops to show his virility and had his chief subordinates do likewise; to the outside world this seemed an odd way of demonstrating fitness for public office. He denounced democracy as historically outmoded and declared that it accentuated class struggle, split people into countless minority parties, and led to selfishness, futility, evasion, and empty talk. In place of democracy he preached the need of vigorous action under a strong leader; he himself took the title of Leader, or *Duce*. He denounced liberalism, free trade, laissez-faire, and capitalism, along with Marxism, materialism, socialism, and class consciousness, which he said were the evil offspring of liberal ideas and capitalist economies. In their place he preached national solidarity and state management of economic affairs under the same Leader's farseeing and audacious vision. And in fact Mussolini seemed to bring a limited kind of new efficiency to Italian society; as the saying went, he made the trains run on time.

The corporative state

Mussolini introduced, at least in theory, the syndical, or corporative state, which had been discussed in both left- and right-wing circles for many years. Left-wing syndicalism, especially before the First World War, looked to revolutionary labor unions to expropriate the owners of industry and then to assume the direction of political and economic life. A more conservative syndicalism had been endorsed and encouraged by the Catholic church, with which Mussolini made his peace when he signed with the papacy the Lateran accord in 1929 recognizing the independence and sovereignty of Vatican City. The more conservative type of syndicalism looked nostalgically toward a revival of the medieval guilds, or "corporations," in which master and journeymen, employer and employees, had labored side by side in a supposedly golden age of social peace.

The Fascist corporative system really resembled neither of the older syndicalist theories because in practice the hand of the state was writ large, something that neither of the older corporative doctrines had anticipated. The system went through a number of complicated stages, but as it finally emerged in the 1930s, it provided for the division of all economic life into 22 major areas, for each of which a "corporation" was established. In each corporation representatives of Fascist-organized labor groups, employers, and the government determined working conditions, wages, prices, and industrial policies; and in a national council these representatives were supposed jointly to devise plans for Italy's economic self-sufficiency. In each case the role of government was decisive and the whole structure was under the jurisdiction of a minister of corporations. As a final step, these corporative economic chambers were integrated into the government proper so that in 1938 the old Chamber of Deputies was superseded by a Chamber of Fasces and Corporations representing the corporations and the Fascist party, all of its members selected by the government and not subject to popular ratification. The upper house, the Senate, continued to exist in its older form.

None of this was democratic, but this was an improvement over democracy, the Fascists asserted. A legislature in an advanced economic society, they said, should represent not political parties and geographical constituencies but economic occupations. Organization along such lines would do away with the anarchy and class conflict engendered by free capitalism, which only sap the strength of the national state. In the end real authority rested with the government—the head of the government, the *Duce,* who settled most matters by decree. In point of fact, social unrest and class conflict were "ended," not by the corporative system as such, but by the prohibition of strikes and lockouts and the abolition of independent labor unions. The corporative system represented the most extreme form of

State control of economic life

state control over economic life within a framework of private enterprise and a capitalist economy, that is, one in which ownership continued to rest in private hands. It was the Fascist answer to Western-style democracy and to Soviet proletarian dictatorship. Fascism, said Mussolini, is the "dictatorship of the state over many classes cooperating."

When the depression struck, none of Italy's economic controls availed very much. Mussolini was eager to lay upon the world depression the blame for Italy's continuing economic ills. He turned to a vigorous program of public works and to increasing economic self-sufficiency. A "battle of wheat" was launched to increase food production; progress was made in reclaiming swamp areas in central Italy and in developing hydroelectric power as a substitute for the coal that Italy lacked. Throughout the Fascist era no fundamental reform changed the status of the farmers and peasants. The existing structure of society, which in Italy meant social extremes of wealth and poverty, remained unaltered. Fascism provided neither the economic security nor the material well-being for which it had demanded the sacrifice of individual freedom and democracy. It undeniably, however, substituted a widespread psychological exhilaration, a feeling that Italy was undergoing a heroic national revival; and after 1935 to support that feeling Mussolini turned increasingly to military and imperialist adventures.

Fascism came to be regarded in other countries as a possible alternative to democratic or parliamentary government, as an actual corrective to troubles whose reality no one could deny. All Communists hated it, and so did all Socialists, labor leaders, moderate leftists, idealistic liberals, and many traditional conservatives. Wealthier or established people, because of fear of Bolshevism, made more allowances in its favor. In East European countries, often highly nationalistic, or influenced by disgruntled landowners, or simply unused to settling questions by majority vote, fascism made a considerable appeal. In the Latin countries, in Spain, Portugal, and France, Mussolini's corporative state found champions and admirers. Sometimes, in Europe and elsewhere intellectuals spun sophisticated theories about the new order of discipline and authority, forgetting how Mussolini himself with unusual candor had written, "Fascism was not the nursling of a doctrine worked out beforehand with detailed elaboration; it was born of the need for action."

The appeal of fascism

103. TOTALITARIANISM: GERMANY'S THIRD REICH

The Rise of Adolf Hitler

It was in Germany that Mussolini found his aptest pupil. Born in Austria in 1889, Adolf Hitler did little before the war. He was not an intellectual, like the prewar leftist journalist Mussolini. He was never a socialist, but he fell into a restless and racist type of radicalism. Son of an Austrian customs official, he lost his father at 14 and his mother a few years later. He dropped out of high school at 16 and at 19 came to the great metropolis of Vienna as an art student but was never accepted into the academy to which he sought admission. When the small inheritance left by his parents ran out and a government grant for orphan students ended, he drifted into various menial jobs, occasionally selling a few of his postcard and poster paintings but mainly eking out a marginal existence with hardly any friends, money, or livelihood.

The young Hitler did not like what he saw in Vienna: neither the trappings of the Habsburg court, nor the nobility of eastern Europe who rode by in their carriages, nor the mixed nationalities of the Danubian empire, nor the Vienna worker's attachment to international Marxism, nor above all the Jews, who thanks to a century of liberal influences had become assimilated into the German culture and now occupied many distinguished positions in business, law, medicine, and journalism in the city. He became exceedingly race conscious and racist, not unlike others in many countries at the time. The youthful Hitler took a special satisfaction in thinking of himself as a pure German of the good old German stock. He became violently

Hitler's dislikes

The small Nazi party gained enough followers by 1923 for Adolf Hitler to believe that a popular revolt or *Putsch* might cause the collapse of Germany's Weimar Republic. Hitler appears here (holding a hat) with his supporters at the time of the "beer hall *Putsch*" in Munich, an almost farcical event for which he was sentenced to a brief term in prison. (Getty Images)

anti-Semitic, and he also disliked aristocracy, capitalism, socialism, cosmopolitanism, internationalism, and "hybridization."

His aversion to Austria led him in 1913 to move to Munich, capital of the South German state of Bavaria. Once again he drifted without livelihood except by occasionally selling a few of his watercolors. When the war broke out, he volunteered for the German army. He served as a dispatch runner to the front line, and at one point was the victim of a gas attack that temporarily blinded him and injured his vocal cords. Although he rose in rank only to the rough equivalent of corporal, he received important military decorations. For Hitler, as for Mussolini and others, the war was a thrilling, noble, and liberating experience. The average individual in modern society led a pretty dull existence. Peace, for many, was a drab routine from which war was an exciting emancipation. Human atoms, floating in an impersonal and unfriendly world, they were stirred by the nationalism which the war aroused into a sense of belonging to, believing in, and fighting for something greater than themselves, but which was yet their own. When peace returned, they felt a letdown.

When the war ended, Hitler remained for a time on active duty and was transferred to Munich. Bavaria in 1919 was a principal focus of the Communist expansion in central Europe; a Bavarian Soviet Republic even existed for about three weeks until crushed by the federal government in Berlin. The Communist threat made Bavaria a busy center for anticommunist, antisocialist, antirepublican, and antidemocratic agitation of all kinds, and the seat of a disgruntled illiberalism. It swarmed with secret societies and paramilitary organizations led by discontented army officers or others who fitted with difficulty into the new Weimar democracy. Hitler, working with the army's political instruction program, which had been created to combat socialist and democratic propaganda among the demobilized veterans and workers, joined at the army's behest a tiny party called the German Workers' party and soon became its leader. Early in 1920 he proclaimed its 25-point program, the party now calling itself the National Socialist German Workers' party. Thus were born the Nazis, so called from the German way of pronouncing the first two syllables of "National." Now demobilized, Hitler was fully launched on a career of radical politics.

Nazi origins

We have earlier noted the beginnings of the Weimar Republic and the burdens it was compelled to bear from the start—the Versailles peace, reparations, the catastrophic inflation of 1923. Something has been said also of the failure of the republicans to inaugurate the kind of deeper social changes that might have democratized the political and social structure of German society and thereby strengthened republican forces. For five years after the war, violence remained sporadic in Germany. Communist agitation continued; but more dangerous, because they attracted more sympathy among the Germans, were the maneuvers of monarchist and antirepublican organizations, which maintained armed bands and staged uprisings like the unsuccessful Kapp *Putsch* of 1920. One such private "army" was the Brownshirts or Storm Troopers maintained by the Nazis. Such bands even resorted to assassination. Thus Walter Rathenau was murdered in 1922; he had organized German production during the war, and in 1922 he was foreign minister, but he had democratic and internationalist inclinations—and was a Jew. Another victim was Matthias Erzberger, a leading moderate politician of the Catholic Center party—he had helped "betray" the army by signing the armistice.

In 1923, when reparations payments were not forthcoming, the French army occupied the Ruhr. A clamor of national indignation swept over Germany. Hitler and the National Socialists, who since 1919 had obtained a considerable following, denounced the Weimar government for shameful submission to the French. They judged the moment opportune for seizing power; and at the end of 1923, in imitation of Mussolini's march on Rome the year before, the Brownshirts staged the "beer hall *Putsch*" in Munich. Hitler jumped on the platform, fired a revolver at the ceiling, and shouted that the "national revolution has broken out." But the police suppressed the disturbance, and Hitler was sentenced to five years in prison. He was released in less than a year; the Weimar democracy dealt mildly with its enemies.

The "beer hall Putsch"

In prison Hitler wrote his book, *Mein Kampf (My Struggle),* a turbid stream of personal recollection, racism, nationalism, collectivism, theories of history, Jew–baiting, and political comment. *Mein Kampf* sold widely. The book and the publicity that had accompanied the five-week trial converted Hitler into a political figure of national prominence. The former soldier was not alone in his ideas; no less a person than General Ludendorff, who had distinguished himself in the war, and after the war became one of the most grotesquely unbalanced of the old officer class, gave his warm support to Hitler and even took part in the beer hall *Putsch*.

Mein Kampf

Beginning in 1924, with the French out of the Ruhr, reparations adjusted, a new and stable currency adopted, and loans from foreign countries, mainly the United States, Germany began to enjoy an amazing economic revival. National Socialism lost its appeal; the party lost members, Hitler was regarded as a charlatan, and his followers as a lunatic fringe. All seemed quiet. Then came the Great Depression in 1929. Adolf Hitler, who might have faded out of history, was transformed by the circumstances attending the depression in Germany into a figure of Napoleonic proportions.

No country suffered more than Germany from the worldwide economic collapse. Foreign loans abruptly ceased. Factories ground to a halt. There were 6 million unemployed. The middle class had not really recovered from the great inflation of 1923; struck again, after so brief a respite, they lost all faith in the economic system and in its future. The Communist vote steadily mounted; large numbers of the middling masses, who saw in communism their own death warrant, looked about desperately for someone to save them from Bolshevism. The depression also stirred up the universal German loathing for the Treaty of Versailles. Many Germans explained the ruin of Germany by the postwar treatment it had received from the Allies—the constriction of its frontiers; the loss of its colonies, markets, shipping, and

The crisis confronting Germany

foreign investments; the colossal demand for reparations; the occupation of the Ruhr; the inflation; and much else.

Any people in such a trap would have been bewildered and resentful. But many Germans responded to their crisis with ideas and actions that may have reflected or grown out of Germany's political experience and position in Europe over the previous three or four centuries. Democracy—the agreement to obtain and accept majority verdicts, to discuss and compromise, to adjust conflicting interests without wholly satisfying or wholly crushing either side—was hard enough to maintain in any country in a crisis. In Germany democracy was itself an innovation, which had yet to prove its value, which could easily be called un-German, an artificial and imported doctrine, a foreign system foisted upon Germany by the victors in the late war.

Hitler's propaganda

Hitler inflamed all such feelings by his propaganda. He denounced the Treaty of Versailles as a national humiliation. He denounced the Weimar democracy for producing class struggle, division, weakness, and wordy futility. He called for "true" democracy in a vast and vital stirring of the people, or *Volk,* behind a Leader who was a man of action. He declared that Germans, pure Germans, must rely only on themselves. He inveighed against Marxists, Bolsheviks, communists, and socialists, throwing them all together in a deliberate beclouding of the issues; but he claimed to favor the right kind of socialism for the little man, that is, the doctrine of the National Socialist German Workers' party. He ranted against unearned incomes, war profits, the power of the great trusts and chain stores, land speculators, interest slavery, and unfair taxes. Above all, he denounced the Jews, who, like individuals in other social and religious groups, could be found in all political camps. They now came under attack from anti-Semitic extremists on all sides of the political spectrum. To the Left, Jewish capitalists were anathema. To the Right, Jewish revolutionaries were a horror. In anti-Semitism Hitler found a lowest common denominator upon which to appeal to all parties and classes. At the same time the Jews were a small minority (only 600,000 in all Germany), so that in an age of mass politics it was safe enough to attack them.

In the election of 1930 the Nazis won 107 seats in the Reichstag; in 1928 they had won only 12; their popular vote went up from 800,000 to 6.5 million. The Communist representation rose from 54 to 77. By July 1932 the Nazis more than doubled their popular vote, won 230 seats, and were now by far the largest single party though because of the multiplicity of parties they fell well short of a majority. In another election, in November 1932, the Nazis, though still well out in front, showed some loss of strength, losing 2 million votes, and dropping to 196 seats. The Communist vote had risen progressively to a peak of 100 in November 1932.

After the relative setback of November 1932 Hitler feared that his movement was passing. But certain conservative, nationalist, and antirepublican elements—old aristocrats, Junker landowners, army officers, Rhineland steel magnates, and other industrialists—had conceived the idea that Hitler could be useful to them. From such sources, which supported other reactionary causes as well, came a portion of Nazi funds. This influential group, mainly from the small Nationalist party, was confident that it would be able to control Hitler and hence control the wave of national and mass discontent that he was leading.

After Bruening's resignation in June 1932, Franz von Papen headed a Nationalist cabinet with the backing of the influential army leader General Kurt von Schleicher. In

Hitler named chancellor

December 1932 Schleicher forced Papen's downfall and succeeded him. When he too was compelled to resign a month later, both men, intriguing separately and against each other, prevailed upon President Hindenburg to name Hitler chancellor of a coalition cabinet. On January 30, 1933, by entirely legal means, Adolf Hitler became chancellor of the German Republic; other positions in the new cabinet were filled by the Nationalists, with whom the Nazis were to share power.

But to share power was not the Nazis' aim. Hitler called for another election. A week before election day in March the Reichstag building caught fire. The Nazis, without any real evidence, blamed it on the Communists. They frightened the population with a Red scare, suspended freedom of speech and press, and set loose the Brownshirts to bully the voters. Even so, in the election, the Nazis won only 44 percent of the vote; with their Nationalist allies, they had 52 percent. Hitler, trumpeting a national emergency, was voted dictatorial powers by a pliant Reichstag from which the Communist deputies by now had been excluded. The Nazi revolution began.

The Nazi State

Hitler called his new order the Third Reich. He declared that following the First Reich, or Holy Roman Empire, and the Second Reich, the empire founded by Bismarck that had ended with the war in 1918, the Third Reich would carry on the process of true German history, of which, he said, it was the organic outgrowth and natural culmination. The Third Reich, he prophesied, would last a thousand years.

Like Mussolini, Hitler took the title of Leader, or, in German, the *Führer*. He claimed to represent the absolute sovereignty of the German people. Jews were considered un-German. Democracy, parliamentarianism, and liberalism were condemned and together with communism were labeled as "Jewish." Concentration camps were set up for opponents of the regime. The new "racial science" classified Jews as non-Aryans and included as Jewish anyone who had one Jewish grandparent. Almost at once Jews were driven from public office, the civil service, teaching, and other professions. The Nuremberg laws of 1935 deprived Jews of all citizenship rights and forbade inter-marriage or even sexual relations between Jews and non-Jews. On November 9, 1938, *Kristallnacht,* the "night of broken glass," the anti-Semitism of Nazi Germany turned to fierce violence. When a 17-year-old Polish-Jewish student, distraught by the mistreatment of his parents, shot and killed a German diplomatic official in the German Embassy in Paris, Nazi storm troopers in a savage orgy of vandalism, looting, and incendiarism smashed Jewish shops, businesses, and synagogues in German cities; beat up thousands of Jews; and rounded up 30,000 to be sent to concentration camps. Party and government leaders moved in to control the storm troopers and to use anti-Semitism for their own purposes. The government levied a one billion-mark fine on the Jewish community for provoking the assault and collected the insurance payments for the shattered glass and other property damage. Jews who in the wake of these events belatedly tried to flee the country discovered that neither they nor their families could readily find places of refuge; the doors in Europe and the United States were for the most part closed to them. The events of 1938 in Germany still resembled an older-style pogrom, but they also expressed a radical new racism and foreshadowed the state-organized systematic destruction, in the Holocaust, of six million European Jews and of others in the grisly death camps.

Anti-Semitism

The new totalitarian order was thought of as absolutely solid, and monolithic, like one huge single slab of rock in which no particle had any separate structure. Germany ceased to be federal; all the old states such as Prussia and Bavaria were abolished. All political parties except the National Socialists were destroyed. The Nazi party was itself violently purged on the night of June 30, 1934, when many of the old Brownshirt leaders, those who

The Nazi-orchestrated attack on Jewish shops and businesses in November 1938 carried the official anti-Semitism of the Nazi state to a new level of violence in German cities. The shattered windows and signs at this Jewish store in Berlin convey the meaning of *Kristallnacht*—the night of broken glass.

(akg-images)

represented the more social revolutionary wing of the movement, were accused of plotting against Hitler and were summarily shot. A secret political police, the Gestapo *(Geheime Staatspolizei)* and a system of permanent concentration camps in which thousands were detained without trial or sentence suppressed all persons who were deemed to be "un-German" and all ideas at variance with the Leader's.

Law itself was defined as the will of the German people operating in the interests of the Nazi state (and with the Nazi regime as the sole interpreter of the German "will"). Churches, both Protestant and Catholic, continued to function but were "coordinated" with

"Coordinating" German society

the new regime; their clergy were forbidden to criticize its activities, international religious ties were discouraged, and efforts were made to keep children out of religious schools. The government encouraged anti-Christian pagan movements and worship of the old Teutonic gods, but nothing was sponsored so much as worship of Nazism and its *Führer.* A Nazi Youth Movement and schools and universities indoctrinated the rising generation in the new concepts. The total, all-encompassing repression thwarted the efforts of a few dedicated Germans to develop a broad resistance movement.

Labor unions also were "coordinated"; they were replaced by a National Labor Front. Strikes were forbidden. Under the "leadership principle" employers were set up as small-scale *Führers* in their factories and industries and given extensive control, subject to close government supervision. On the positive side, an extensive public works program was launched, reforestation and swamp drainage projects were organized, housing and super-highways were built. A vast rearmament program absorbed the unemployed and within a short time unemployment disappeared. Even under Nazi statistics labor's share in the national income was reduced, but workers had jobs; and an organization called Strength Through Joy attended to the needs of people with small incomes, providing entertainment, vacations, and travel for many who could never otherwise afford them.

The government assumed increasing controls over industry, while leaving ownership in private hands. In 1936 it adopted a Four-Year Plan of economic development. All countries after the Great Depression tended to economic nationalism, but Nazi Germany set up the goal of autarky and self-sufficiency—absolute independence from foreign trade. German chemists developed artificial rubber, plastics, synthetic textiles, and many other substitute products to enable the country to do without raw materials imported from overseas.

Economic autarky and self-sufficiency

For Europe as a whole one of the basic economic problems, especially after the World War, was that while the Continent was economically a unit dependent on exchange between diverse regions, politically it was cut to pieces by tariff restrictions, currency differences, and hothouse industries artificially nurtured by nationalist ambition. The Nazis claimed to have a solution for this problem in a network of bilateral trade agreements assuring all neighboring peoples an outlet for their products. But it was a solution in which Germans were to be the most industrial and most advanced, the most powerful and wealthiest. Other Europeans were to be relegated to permanently inferior status. What could not be accomplished under trade agreements and economic penetration could be accomplished by conquest and war. Within a few years after 1933, although the regime had its share of bureaucratic confusion and personal rivalries, the Nazi revolution had turned Germany into a huge disciplined war machine, its internal foes liquidated or silenced, its mesmerized masses roaring their approval in giant demonstrations, ready to follow the Führer in storming new Valkyrian heights. "Today Germany," went an ominous phrase; "tomorrow the whole world."

Totalitarianism: Some Origins and Consequences

Totalitarianism was a many-sided thing. It had appeared first with the Bolshevik Revolution, for in the denial of individual liberty the Communist regime did not differ from the most extreme right-wing totalitarianism as manifested in Germany. Although Mussolini was the first to use the term "totalitarian," and advance it explicitly as an ideology, the Fascist regime that he established lacked the all-embracing control over people's lives to merit that term in its full political meaning. The Catholic Church came to terms with the regime, anti-Semitism did not appear until much later, the upper legislative house or Senate continued to function, and the king retained many of his prerogatives. As to the differences between Soviet totalitarianism and Naziism, they were important, at least in principle. Theoretically, the proletarian dictatorship was temporary; it did not at first glorify the individual Leader; and it was not nationalistic, for it rested on a principle of worldwide class struggle in all nations alike. It adopted a democratic-sounding constitution and paid at least lip service to individual rights. Its constitution officially condemned racism, and it did not deliberately and consciously cultivate an ethics of war and violence. But as time passed, Soviet totalitarianism or Communism became harder to distinguish from totalitarian regimes like Naziism. The Soviet dictatorship and one-party state seemed permanent; the hollowness of the constitution and the guarantee of individual rights became more apparent; a cult developed around the person of Stalin; the emphasis became more nationalistic, falling less on the workers of the world and more on the glories of the Soviet motherland; and it sent untold numbers to perish in the harsh labor camps of the Gulag.

The evolution of totalitarianism

Totalitarianism, as distinct from mere dictatorship, though it appeared rather suddenly after the First World War, was no historic freak. It was an outgrowth of a good deal of development in the past. The state was an institution that had continuously acquired new powers ever since the Middle Ages. The First World War continued and advanced the process. The twentieth-century totalitarian state, mammoth and monolithic, claiming absolute dominion over every department of life, carried this old development of state sovereignty to a new extreme. For centuries, for example, the state had clashed with the church. The twentieth-century dictators did the same. In addition, however, they were in most cases not merely anticlerical but explicitly anti-Christian, offering, or imposing, a "total" philosophy of life.

Reliance on historic nationalism

This new philosophy drew heavily upon historic nationalism, which it distorted and exaggerated. It rejected classical liberalism, which stressed the autonomy of rational individuals, and promoted instead an organic theory of society. It held that society was a kind of living organism within which the individual person was but a single cell. Individuals, in this theory, had no independent existence; they received life itself and all their ideas from the society, people, nation, or culture into which they were born and by which they were nurtured. In Marxism, the absolute subordination of individuals to their class came to much the same thing. Individuals were a microscopic cell, meaningless outside the social body. It made little sense, given such theories, to speak of the individual's "reason" or "freedom," to allow individuals to have their own opinions or to count up individual opinions to obtain a merely numerical majority. Valid ideas were those of the group as a whole, of the people or nation (or, in Marxism, the class) as a solid block. Even science was a product of specific societies; there was a "Nazi science" which was bound to differ in its conclusions from democratic bourgeois, Western, or "Jewish" science; and for the Soviets there was a Soviet science, consistent with dialectical materialism and better equipped to see the truth than the decadent bourgeois, capitalistic, or "fascist" science of the non-Soviet world. All art, too—music, painting, poetry, fiction, architecture, sculpture—was good art insofar as it expressed the society or nationality in which it appeared.

The avowed philosophy of totalitarian regimes was subjective. Whether an idea was held to be true depended on whose idea it was. Ideas of truth or beauty or right were not supposed to correspond to any outer or objective reality; they had only to correspond to the inner nature, interests, or point of view of the people, nation, society, or class that entertained such ideas. The older Enlightenment concepts of reason, natural law, natural right, and the ultimate alikeness of all mankind, or of a common path of all mankind in one course of progress, disappeared.

The totalitarian regimes did not simply declare, as a dry finding of social science, that peoples' ideas were shaped by environment. They set about actively shaping ideas through the constant use of propaganda and by establishing propaganda offices as a principal branch of government. Propaganda was hardly new, but in the past, and still in the democratic countries, it had been a piecemeal affair, urging the public to accept this or that political

CHRONOLOGY OF NOTABLE EVENTS, 1922–1938

1922	Britain recognizes the Irish Free State with dominion status; first step toward full sovereignty as Republic of Ireland
October 1922	Mussolini takes power in Italy after the Fascist "March on Rome"
1923	Nazis fail to mobilize political support during an attempted *Putsch* in Munich
1924	First Labour government is elected in Britain under Ramsey MacDonald
January 1933	Hitler comes to power in Germany; Nazis soon take control of all state institutions and suppress opposition
March 1933	Franklin D. Roosevelt introduces the "New Deal" in America to mitigate economic effects of the Great Depression
1934	Right-wing and fascist groups in France challenge the Third Republic with riots during the Stavisky Affair
1935	Nazis adopt Nuremberg laws against Jews
1936	Left-wing "Popular Front" comes to power in France under Léon Blum and enacts notable social reforms
1938	The Nazi regime encourages violent attacks on Jews and Jewish property during *Kristallnacht*—the night of "broken glass"

party, or rally to this or that campaign. Now, like all else, it became "total." Propaganda was monopolized by the state, and it demanded faith in a whole *Propaganda* view of life and in every detail of this coordinated whole. Formerly the control of books and newspapers had been mainly negative; under Napoleon or Metternich, for example, censors had forbidden statements on particular subjects, events, or persons. Now, in totalitarian countries, control of the press became frighteningly positive. The government manufactured thought. It manipulated opinion. It rewrote history. Writers were required to adopt whole ideologies; books, newspapers, magazines, and the radio diffused an endless and overwhelming cloud of words. Loudspeakers blared in the streets; gigantic blown-up photographs of the Leader looked down in public places. The propaganda experts were sometimes fanatics, but often they were cynics like Dr. Joseph Goebbels in Germany, too intelligent to be duped by the rubbish with which they duped their country.

The very idea of empirical truth evaporated. No norm of human utterance remained except political expediency—the wishes and self-interest of those in power. No one could learn anything except what the government wanted people to know. No one could escape the omnipresent official doctrine, the insidious penetration of the very recesses of the mind by ideas planted by outsiders for their own purposes. People came to accept and even to believe the most extravagant statements when they were endlessly repeated, year after year. Barred from all independent sources of information, having no means by which any official allegation could be tested, the peoples of totalitarian countries became increasingly, in fact and not merely in sociological theory, incapable of the use of reason.

Racism, more characteristic of Nazi Germany than of totalitarianism in general, was a further exaggeration, or degradation, of older ideas of *Racism* nationalism and national solidarity. It defined the nation in a tribal sense, as a biological entity, a group of persons possessing the same physical ancestry and the same or similar physical characteristics. Anti-Semitism was the most venomous form of racism

The Nazis promoted racist definitions of German nationhood and created racial propaganda to show the "ideal" German family. This image of the "new people" was produced for a 1938 calendar that conveyed the Nazis' biological view of gender identities as well as the regime's racial portrait of the German nation.
(akg-images)

in Europe. While a latent hostility to Jews had always been present in the Christian world, modern anti-Semitism had little to do with Christianity. It arose in part from the fact that in the nineteenth century with the removal of religious barriers, the Jews entered into general society and many achieved positions of prominence, especially in Germany, so that from the point of view of any resentful individual they could be represented as dangerous competitors in business or the professions. But most of all, anti-Semitism was inflamed by propagandists who wished people to feel their supposed racial purity more keenly or to forget the deeper problems of society, including poverty, class divisions, and economic inequities.

Totalitarianism "resolves" class conflict

Totalitarianism was an escape from the realities of class conflict. It was a way of pretending that differences between rich and poor were of minor importance. Typically, a totalitarian regime came into power by stirring up class fears, then remained in power, and represented itself as indispensable by declaring that it had settled the class problem. Thus Mussolini, Hitler, and certain lesser dictators before seizing office pointed alarmingly to the dark menace of Bolshevism, and once in power, declared that all classes stood shoulder to shoulder in slablike solidarity behind the Leader.

Nor were events in Russia (or in China after the Second World War) altogether different. The Bolsheviks in 1917, armed with the ideas of Marx, aroused the workers against

The Nazi regime used public spectacles to send a message of irresistible national power to both the German people and foreign observers. The annual Nazi rallies at Nuremberg became the most carefully organized expressions of allegiance to the Third Reich and the Nazi ideology. The salute to Hitler, as shown in this photograph of the Führer leading his officers between rows of soldiers at Nuremberg in 1938, was a typical example of the fervent loyalty and emotion that such events were designed to evoke. (Bettmann/Corbis)

capitalists, landlords, the middle classes, and rich peasants; once in power and after extensive liquidations, they declared that the classless society had arrived, that no true social classes any longer existed, and that all citizens stood solidly behind a regime from which, they said, all good citizens benefited equally. Only the democracies admitted that they suffered from internal class problems, from maldistribution of wealth, or from social distinctions between favored and unfavored groups in society.

The dictatorships blamed their troubles on forces outside the country. They accused dissatisfied persons of conspiring with foreigners or refugees—with being the tools of Trotskyism, imperialism, or international Jewry. Or they talked of the struggle (as Mussolini did) between rich nations and poor nations, the "have" and the "have not" countries, and thus transformed the problem of poverty into an international struggle. In the distinction between "have" and "have not" countries there was, of course, more than a grain of truth; in more old-fashioned language some countries (such as the European democracies, as well as the United States and the British dominions of the 1930s) had progressed farther than others in their economic productivity and accumulation of wealth. It is probable that any propaganda is more effective if partly true. But when the totalitarians blamed their troubles on other countries and transformed the conflict between "have" and "have not" into a struggle between nations, they gave the signal that war might be a solution for social ills.

Violence, the acceptance and even glorification of violence, was indeed the characteristic most clearly distinguishing the totalitarian from the democratic systems. We have seen how a cult of violence, or belief that struggle was beneficial, had arisen before the First World War. The war itself habituated people to violence and direct action. Lenin and his followers showed how a small group could seize the helm of state under revolutionary or chaotic conditions. Mussolini in 1922 taught the same lesson, with further refinements; for the Italy in which

The glorification of violence

he seized power was not at war, and it was merely the threat or possibility of revolution, not revolution itself, that provided him with his opportunity. In the 1920s, for the first time since the seventeenth century, some of the most civilized parts of Europe, in time of peace, saw private armies marching about the country, bands of uniformed and organized ruffians, Blackshirts or Brownshirts, who manhandled, abused, and even killed law-abiding citizens with impunity. Nor would anyone in the 1920s have believed that by the 1930s Europe would see the reintroduction of torture.

The very ethics of totalitarianism was violent and neopagan. It borrowed from and distorted Nietzsche and other prewar theoreticians, who, safe and civilized, had declared that people should live dangerously, avoid the flabby weakness of too much thought, and throw themselves with red-blooded vigor into a life of action. The new regimes all instituted youth movements. They appealed to a kind of juvenile idealism in which young people believed that by joining some kind of squad, donning some kind of uniform, and getting into the fresh air they contributed to a great moral resurgence of their country. Young men were taught to value their bodies but not their minds, to be tough and hard, and to regard mass gymnastics as patriotic demonstrations. Young women were taught to breed large families without complaint, to be content in the kitchen, and to look with awe upon their virile mates.

The body cult flourished while the mind decayed. Especially in National Socialism the ideal was to turn the German people into a race of splendid blond Nordics. Contrariwise, euthanasia was adopted for the chronically ill and the insane and was proposed for the aged. Nazi ideologists produced pseudoscientific racist theories to explain and justify their actions. Later, in the Second World War, when the Nazis overran eastern Europe, they committed Jews and others to gas chambers, destroying over six million human beings by the most scientific methods. Human beings were viewed as animals; one bred the kind one wanted and killed the kind one did not.

The Spread of Dictatorship

The trend toward dictatorship, if not necessarily of the totalitarian variety, spread in Europe in the 1930s. By 1938 only 10 out of 27 European countries remained democratic, in the sense that different political parties honestly competed for office and that citizens within generous limits thought and acted as they pleased. They were Great Britain and France; Holland, Belgium, and Switzerland; Czechoslovakia and Finland; and the three Scandinavian countries Denmark, Norway, and Sweden.

The promise of the early 1920s that constitutional and democratic government would flourish was thwarted. The weakness or absence of a parliamentary or democratic tradition, low education and literacy standards, the hostility of reactionary elements, the fear of Bolshevism, and the dissatisfaction of existing national minorities, all coupled with the economic strains resulting from the Great Depression, contributed to the collapse of representative institutions. Apart from the avowedly totalitarian or fascist regimes of Germany and Italy, the new dictatorships and authoritarian systems generally rested on a combination of personal and military power, but several reflected or absorbed some of the ideological features of a generic fascism. In Portugal, Salazar inaugurated a clerical-corporative dictatorship in 1932 that lasted for over four decades. In Austria, Dollfuss fused various right-wing political and military elements into a clerical-fascist "Christian" dictatorship which violently suppressed the Socialists and sought in vain to counter the

The collapse of democratic governments

German threat. In Spain General Franco established a right-wing authoritarian government after a bloody civil war (described in the next chapter). In many respects the dictatorships of Latin America under their caudillos and military juntas resembled the European military dictatorships; and similar repressive one-party regimes have reappeared in other parts of the world down to the present.

The authoritarian regimes were alike in repressing individual liberties, banning opposition parties, and abolishing or nullifying parliamentary institutions. Many borrowed features of fascism, establishing a corporative state, outlawing independent labor organizations, and forbidding strikes; many, like Hungary, Romania, and Poland, enacted anti-Semitic legislation. None of the right-wing regimes went so far as Hitler's Third Reich in the total coordination of all political, economic, intellectual, and biological activities in a revolutionary mass-based dictatorship.

The acceptance and glorification of violence, it has been noted, was the feature most clearly distinguishing the totalitarian from the democratic systems. War in the Nazi and Fascist ethics was a noble thing, and the love of peace a sign of decadence. The Soviet regime by its own theory regarded war with non-Soviet powers as inevitable some day, but did not preach it as a positive moral good. The exaltation of war and struggle, the need for maintaining national solidarity, and the habit of blaming foreign countries for social troubles helped to make violence seem like a normal and appropriate means for strengthening the nation. These general ideological themes were intensified by the considerable armaments programs on which the dictatorships embarked and by the personal ambition and egotistical mania of individual dictators. All of this made the decade of the 1930s a time not only of domestic reaction but of recurrent international crises that led finally, in 1939, to a second and even greater world war.

 For interactive exercises, glossary, chronologies, and more, go to the *Online Learning Center* at **www.mhhe.com/palmer10.**

Chapter $\quad$ 21

THE SECOND
WORLD WAR

Peace in the abstract, the peace that is the mere absence of war, does not exist in international relations. Peace is never found apart from certain conditions; it means peaceable acceptance of given conditions, or peaceable and orderly transformation of conditions by negotiation and agreement. The conditions in the 1930s were basically those laid down by the Paris peace conference of 1919—the states recognized, the frontiers drawn, the terms agreed to, at the close of the First World War. In the 1930s neither Germany, Italy, Japan, nor the U.S.S.R. was content with these conditions; they were "revisionist" or dissatisfied powers; and the first three were willing to undertake war itself to make a change. Great Britain, France, and the United States were satisfied powers, expecting no benefit from change in the conditions; but on the other hand they had lost faith in the conditions and were unwilling to risk war for the sake of upholding them. They had written a treaty in 1919 which a dozen years later they were unwilling to enforce. They stood idly by, as long as they could, while the dissatisfied powers tore to pieces the states recognized, the frontiers drawn, and the terms agreed to at the Peace of Paris. From the Japanese invasion of Manchuria in 1931 to the outbreak of European war in 1939, force was used by those who wished to upset international order, but never by those who wished to maintain it. A new world war was therefore launched by nations that had never accepted the outcome of the last one.

The war that raged across the world from 1939 to 1945 was the most destructive conflict in human history. It was also the most widely dispersed global war that has ever been fought. The Second World War affected nations on every continent; caused the deaths of almost 60 million people (at least two-thirds of whom were civilians); produced vast physical damage in cities, factories, and countrysides; generated new forms of genocidal mass murder as well as new military weapons of mass destruction; and contributed decisively to the new global influence of two superpower nations—the United States and the Soviet Union.

Chapter emblem: German troops entering a destroyed Polish village in September 1939. (akg-images)

Historians often disagree about the social or political consequences of warfare, but the Second World War was unquestionably one of the definitive, shaping events in modern world history. Both the haunting memories and complex legacy of the Second World War still influence modern cultures and people everywhere in the twenty-first century.

104.   THE WEAKNESS OF THE DEMOCRACIES: AGAIN TO WAR

The Pacifism and Disunity of the West

While dictators stormed in the 1930s, the Western democracies were swayed by a profound pacifism, which may be defined as an insistence on peace regardless of consequences. Many people, especially in England and the United States, came to believe that the First World War had been a mistake, that little or nothing had been gained by it, that they had been deluded by wartime propaganda, and that wars were really started by armaments manufacturers. They believed also that Germany had not really caused the war of 1914, that the Treaty of Versailles was too hard on the Germans, that democracy was after all not suited to all nations, that it took two to make a quarrel, and that there need be no war if one side refused to be provoked—a whole system of pacific and tolerant ideas in which there was perhaps both truth and misunderstanding.

The pacifism of the West

The pacifism of the West had other roots, most evident in France. About 1.4 million Frenchmen had died in the First World War; half of all French males between the ages of 20 and 32 in 1914 had been killed. To the French it was inconceivable that such a human disaster should be repeated. French strategy was therefore defensive and sparing of manpower. If war came, the French expected to fight it mainly in the elaborate fortifications, called the Maginot Line, which they built on their eastern frontier facing Germany, from the Swiss to the Belgian border; to its north the Ardennes forest was to be a barrier to any invader. During the depression France was torn by internal class conflict and by fascist and quasi-fascist agitation. Many French on the Right, historically unsympathetic to the republic and seeing, or claiming to see, in such movements as the Popular Front the threat of social revolution, did not conceal their admiration for Mussolini or even for Hitler. Abandoning their traditional role as ardent nationalists, they would do nothing to oppose the dictators. On the other hand, many on the Left looked with sympathy upon the Soviet Union. France was ideologically too divided in the 1930s to possess any firm foreign policy, and all elements took false comfort from the supposed impregnability of the carefully constructed Maginot Line.

A similar situation, in lesser degree, prevailed in Great Britain and the United States. The loss and bloodshed of the First World War were remembered with both mourning and anger. It was well known that another world war would be even more horrible; there was an unspeakable dread of the bombing of cities. Typical of the time was a resolution adopted by students at Oxford in 1933 that they would never take up arms for their country under any conditions; peace movements appeared among American college students too. The pull between Left and Right was felt in England and America. In the 1930s, when any international action seemed to favor either the U.S.S.R. on the one hand, or Hitler and Mussolini on the other, it was hard to establish any foreign policy on a firm basis of national unity. In Britain some members of the upper classes were overtly sympathetic to the fascist dictators or saw in them a bulwark against communism. The government itself tried to be noncommittal; it believed that some means of satisfying or appeasing the more legitimate demands of the dictators might be found. Neville Chamberlain, prime minister after 1937, became the principal architect of the appeasement policy.

The United States government, despite President Roosevelt's repeated denunciation of the aggressors, followed in practice a policy of rigid isolation. Neutrality legislation, enacted by a strong isolationist bloc in Congress in the years 1935 to 1937, forbade loans, export of munitions, and use of American shipping facilities to any belligerent once the president had recognized a state of war in a given area. Many believed that the United States had been drawn into the First World War by such economic involvement. From this American neutrality legislation the aggressors of the 1930s derived great benefit, but not the victims of aggression.

As for the rulers of the U.S.S.R., they were revisionist and dissatisfied in that they did not accept the new frontiers of eastern Europe nor the territorial losses incurred by Russia in the First World War. They resented the *cordon sanitaire* created in 1919 against the spread of Bolshevism, the ring of small states on their borders from Finland to Romania, which were almost without exception vehemently anti-Soviet. They had no fondness for the international status quo, nor had they abandoned their long-range revolutionary objectives. But, as Communists and as Russians, they were obsessed by fear of attack and invasion. Their Marxist doctrine taught the inherent hostility of the entire capitalist world; the intervention of the Western Allies in the revolution and civil wars confirmed their Marxist theory. Resentful and suspicious of the outside world, in the 1930s the men in the Kremlin were alarmed primarily by Germany. Hitler, in *Mein Kampf* and elsewhere, had declared that he meant to obliterate Bolshevism and subordinate large stretches of eastern Europe to Germany.

Russian resentment

The Soviets became interested in collective security, in international action against aggression. In 1934 they joined the League of Nations. They instructed Communist parties to work with socialists and liberals in popular fronts. They offered assistance in checking fascist aggressors, signing mutual assistance pacts with France and Czechoslovakia in 1935. But many people fled from the Soviet embrace with a shudder. They distrusted Soviet motives, or they were convinced that the purges and trials of the 1930s had left the Soviets weak and undependable as allies, or they felt that the fascist dictators might be diverted eastward against the Soviets and so spare the Western democracies. Here again, though the Soviet Union was ostensibly willing, no effective coalition against aggression could be formed.

The March of Nazi and Fascist Aggression

Adolf Hitler perceived these weaknesses with uncanny genius. Determined to wreck the whole treaty system, which most Germans, to be sure, found humiliating, he employed tactics of gradual encroachment that played on the hopes and fears of the democratic peoples. He inspired in them alternating tremors of apprehension and sighs of relief. He would rage and rant, arouse the fear of war, take just a little, declare that it was all he wanted, let the former Allies naïvely hope that he was now satisfied and that peace was secure, then rage again, take a little more, and proceed through the same cycle.

Each year he precipitated some kind of emergency, and each time the French and British saw no alternative except to let him have his way. In 1933, soon after seizing power, he took Germany out of the League and out of the Disarmament Conference then taking place. He successfully wooed Poland, long France's ally, and in 1934 the two countries signed a nonaggression

Hitler's triumphs

Hitler lived in Vienna as an unknown artist before the First World War, but he returned as the all-powerful German *Führer* after the union of Austria and Germany in March 1938. Proceeding through Vienna in this triumphant motorcade, he was hailed by Austrian Nazis and others who celebrated the long-anticipated *Anschluss* on the city's streets.
(akg-images)

treaty. That same year the Nazis of Austria attempted a *Putsch,* assassinated the Austrian chancellor, Dollfuss, and demanded the union of Austria with Germany. The Western powers did nothing. It was Mussolini who acted. Not desiring to see Germany installed at the Brenner Pass, he mobilized large Italian forces on the frontier, discouraged Hitler from intervening openly in Austria, and so preserved the independence of Austria for four more years. In January 1935 a plebiscite was conducted in the Saar by the League of Nations as stipulated under the Versailles treaty. Amidst intense Nazi agitation, the Saar voted for reunion with the Reich. Two months later, in March 1935, Hitler dramatically repudiated those clauses in the Versailles treaty intended to keep Germany disarmed; he now openly built up the German armed forces. France, England, and Italy protested such arbitrary and one-sided denunciation of an international treaty but did nothing about it. Indeed, Great Britain entered into a naval agreement with Germany, to the consternation of the French.

On March 7, 1936, using as his justification the new Franco-Soviet pact, Hitler repudiated the Locarno agreements (which had confirmed post–World War I national borders) and reoccupied the Rhineland; that is, he sent German troops into the German territory west of the Rhine, which by the Treaty of Versailles was supposed to be a demilitarized zone. The French government considered possible military action to force the German army to leave the Rhineland; and at this time Hitler might have been checked, for German military strength was still weak and the German army was prepared to withdraw, or at least consult, at signs of resistance. But the French government was divided and unwilling to act without Britain; and the British would not risk war to keep German troops from occupying

German soil. The next year, 1937, was a quiet one, but Nazi agitation flared up in Danzig, which the Treaty of Versailles had set up as a free city. In March 1938 German forces moved into Austria, and the union of Austria and Germany, the *Anschluss,* was at last consummated. In September 1938 came the turn of Czechoslovakia and the Munich crisis. To understand it we must first pick up other threads in the story.

Mussolini, too, had his ambitions and required sensational foreign triumphs to magnetize the Italian people. Since 1919 the Italians had been dissatisfied with the peace arrangements. They had received nothing of the former Turkish territories and German colonies that had been liberally parceled out as mandates to Great Britain, France, Belgium, Japan, South Africa, Australia, and New Zealand. They had never forgotten the humiliating defeat of Italian forces by Ethiopia at Adowa in 1896, which had blocked Italy's imperial ambitions in northeast Africa. Ethiopia remained the only part of black Africa (with the exception of Liberia) that was still independent.

Mussolini's ambitions

In 1935 Italy invaded Ethiopia. The League of Nations, of which Ethiopia was a member, pronounced the Italian action an unwarranted aggression and imposed sanctions on Italy, by which members of the League were to refrain from selling Italy either arms or raw materials—oil was excepted. The British even gathered large naval forces in the Mediterranean in a show of strength. In France, however, there was considerable sympathy for Mussolini in important quarters, and in England there was the fear that if sanctions became too effective, by refusal of oil or by closure of the Suez Canal, Italy might be provoked into a general war. Mussolini was thus able to defeat Ethiopia in 1936 and to combine it with Italian Somaliland and Eritrea in an Italian East African empire. Haile Selassie, the Ethiopian emperor, made futile pleas for further action at Geneva. The League of Nations again failed, as in the earlier occupation of Manchuria by Japan, to provide machinery for disciplinary action against a wayward Great Power.

The Spanish Civil War, 1936–1939

Hardly had the Ethiopian crisis been disposed of, to the entire satisfaction of the aggressor, when another serious crisis broke out in Spain. In 1931, after a decade of political disturbance, a rather mild revolution had driven out Alfonso XIII, of the Bourbon family, and brought about the establishment of a democratic Spanish Republic. Old hostilities within the country came to a head. The new republican government undertook a program of social and economic reform. To combat the old entrenched power of the church, anticlerical legislation was enacted: church and state were separated, the Jesuit order was dissolved and its property confiscated, and the schools were removed from clerical control. An old movement for Catalan independence was somewhat mollified by the grant of considerable local autonomy. To placate the peasantry the government began to break up some of the larger landed estates and to redistribute the land. The government's program was never pushed vigorously enough to satisfy extremist elements, who manifested their dissatisfaction in strikes and uprisings, particularly in industrial Barcelona, the Catalan capital, and the mining areas of the Asturias, but it was radical enough to antagonize the great property owners and the church. After 1933 the government fell into the hands of rightist and conservative parties, who ruled through ineffective and unpopular ministries. An insurrection of the miners in the Asturias was put down with much brutality. Agitation for Catalan independence was repressed.

In February 1936 new elections were held. All groups of the Left—republicans, socialists, syndicalists, anarchists, communists—joined in a Popular Front against

Right-wing forces launched a military insurrection against Spain's Republican government in July 1936. In the civil war that followed, Germany and Italy sent aid to General Francisco Franco, but anti-fascist groups mobilized everywhere to fight for the Republic. This anti-fascist rally in Spain was one of the many meetings that supported the Republic and the armed forces that were ultimately unable to restore it.
(David Seymour/Magnum Photos)

monarchists, clericals, army officers, other adherents of the old regime, and Falangists, or Spanish fascists. The Left won a victory at the polls, and pressed forward with a reform program. In July 1936, a group of military men led an insurrection against the Republican government; General Francisco Franco emerged as leader. The parties of the Left united in resistance and the whole country fell into civil war. It was the most devastating war in all Spanish history; over 600,000 human beings lost their lives, and it was accompanied by extreme cruelties on both sides. For nearly three years the republican or loyalist forces held their own before finally succumbing to the insurgents led by Franco, who in March 1939 established an authoritarian, fascist-type rule over the exhausted country.

Francisco Franco

Spain provided a rehearsal for the greater struggle soon to come. The republican government could legitimately have looked forward to the purchase of arms abroad to suppress the rebellion, but Britain and France were resolved not to let the war expand into a general conflict. Although pro-republican groups and individuals in Europe and the United States wanted to send military assistance to the antifascist forces, the British and French governments forbade the shipment of all war materials to Spain; even the French Popular Front government put obstacles in the way of aid to the hard-pressed Spanish Popular Front. The United States extended its neutrality legislation to cover civil wars and placed an embargo on the export of arms to Spain. At British and French instigation 27 nations, including all the major European powers, agreed not to intervene or take sides. But the nonintervention policy proved a fiasco. Germany, Italy, and the Soviet Union intervened anyway. The former two supported Franco and denounced the republicans as the tools of Bolshevism, while the U.S.S.R. supported the republic, reinforced the growing strength of the Spanish Communists, and stigmatized the rebels under Franco as the agents of international fascism. Germans, Italians, and Russians sent military equipment to Spain, testing their tanks and planes in battle. The fascist bombings of Guernica, Madrid, and Barcelona horrified the democratic world. The Germans and Italians sent troops (the Italians over 50,000); the Soviets if only for geographical reasons did not send troops but sent technicians and political advisers. Thousands of volunteers of leftist or liberal sympathy from the United States and Europe went to Spain to serve with the republican forces. Spain became the battlefield of contending ideologies. The Spanish Civil War split the world into fascist and antifascist camps.

Spain splits the world

As in the case of Ethiopia, the war in Spain helped bring Germany and Italy together. Mussolini had at first, like others, feared the revival of a militant Germany. He had outfaced Hitler when the latter threatened to absorb Austria in 1934. The Ethiopian war, Italian ambitions in Africa, and a clamorous Italian demand for ascendancy in the Mediterranean, the *mare nostrum* of the ancient Romans, estranged Italy from France and Britain. In 1936, soon after the outbreak of the Spanish Civil War, Mussolini and Hitler came to an understanding, which they called the Rome-Berlin Axis—the diplomatic axis around which they hoped the world might turn. That year Japan signed with Germany an Anti-Comintern Pact, soon ratified by Italy too; ostensibly an agreement to oppose communism, it was actually the foundation for a diplomatic alliance. Each, thus furnished with allies, was able to push its demands with more success. In 1938 Mussolini accepted what he had denied to Hitler in 1934—the German absorption of Austria.

Meanwhile, in 1937, Japan, using as a pretext the firing upon Japanese troops at the Marco Polo Bridge near Beijing, launched a brutal full scale invasion of eastern China and within a short time controlled most of the country. The Japanese occupation of Nanjing in 1937, then the Chinese capital, was accompanied by such violence and atrocities on the part of the Japanese military that it came to be known and long remembered as the "rape of Nanjing." In a terrible prelude to the impending world war, Japanese troops murdered some 250,000 people, raped thousands of Chinese women, and burned huge piles of corpses in the streets. (Government officials in Japan later denied that the Nanjing atrocities took place on the scale that eyewitnesses had reported, which partly explains why the memory of such crimes would become an enduring, contentious issue in Chinese-Japanese relations.)

The "rape of Nanjing"

The Chinese lost their main coastal cities, but they continued to fight from the hinterland. The League of Nations again ineffectually condemned Japan. The United States refrained from applying its neutrality legislation since no war was officially declared. This made possible the extension of loans to China, the victim of aggression, but also made possible the purchase by the Japanese of vitally needed scrap iron, steel, oil, and machinery from American industry. The Japanese were left free to pursue their expansionist ambitions in Asia, in part because the Western nations were distracted and divided by the mounting tensions in Europe.

GUERNICA
by Pablo Picasso (Spanish, 1881–1973)
Picasso painted this famous picture shortly after the fascist bombing of the Spanish city of Guernica in 1937. Although it expressed Picasso's response to a specific event in the Spanish Civil War, its disjointed images of the death, suffering, and destruction in modern warfare quickly gave this work a haunting, universal meaning.
(Art Resource, NY/© 2007 The Estate of Pablo Picasso/Artists Rights Society (ARS), New York)

The Munich Crisis: Climax of Appeasement

Czechs divided

By annexing Austria in March 1938 Hitler added about 6 million Germans to the Reich. Another 3 million Germans lived in Czechoslovakia (see maps, pp. 455, 716–717). All those who were adults in 1938 had been born under the Habsburg empire. They had never, since 1918, been content with their new position as a minority in a Slavic state and had long complained about various forms of subtle discrimination. There were Polish, Ruthenian, and Hungarian minorities also, and since even the Slovaks had a strong sense of separate identity, there was in actuality no preponderant national majority of any kind. The fact that Czechoslovakia had one of the most enlightened minorities policies in Europe, enjoyed the highest living standard east of Germany, and was the only country in central Europe in 1938 that was still democratic only demonstrated the difficulty of maintaining a multinational state even under the most favorable of conditions.

Czechoslovakia was strategically the keystone of Europe. It had a firm alliance with France, by which the French pledged to defend it against German attack, and an alliance with the Soviet Union, which, however, was contingent on the functioning of the French alliance. With Romania and Yugoslavia it formed the Little Entente, upon which France relied to maintain the existing boundaries in that part of Europe. It had a well-trained army, important munitions industries, and strong fortifications against Germany, which, however, were located in precisely the Sudeten border area where the population was almost all German. When Hitler annexed Austria—since Vienna is further east than Prague—he enclosed Czechoslovakia in a vise. From the German point of view it could now be said

Japan's military occupation of Nanjing in 1937 was so violent that it came to be called the "rape of Nanjing." This picture of Japanese soldiers using Chinese prisoners for bayonet drills shows some of the atrocities that were committed during the occupation.
(Bettmann/Corbis)

that western Czechoslovakia, which was almost a third German anyway, formed a bulge protruding into the German Reich.

The Sudeten Germans of Czechoslovakia, whether Nazis or not, fell under the influence of agitators whose aim was less to relieve their grievances than to promote National Socialism. Hitler fomented their demands for union with Germany. In May 1938 rumors of an imminent German invasion caused the Czechs to mobilize; Russia, France, and England issued warnings to Germany. Hitler gave assurances but was nevertheless determined to smash the Czechs in the autumn. France and England were appalled by their narrow escape from war. The nervous French acquiesced in the leadership of Britain, which in the following months strove to avoid any firm stand that might precipitate war. The Czechs, under pressure from Britain and France, accepted British mediation on the Sudeten issue and in the summer of 1938 offered wide concessions to the Sudeten Germans amounting to regional autonomy, but this was not enough to satisfy Hitler, who loudly proclaimed that the plight of the Germans in Czechoslovakia was intolerable and must be corrected. The Soviets urged a firm stand, but the Western powers had little confidence in Soviet military strength and, given the Soviet geographical situation, their ability to render assistance to Czechoslovakia. Moreover, they feared that firmness might mean war. They could not be sure whether Hitler was bluffing. He might, if opposed, back down; but it seemed equally likely, or indeed more so, that he was entirely willing to fight.

As the crisis grew in September 1938, the British prime minister, Neville Chamberlain, who had never flown in his life before, flew to Germany twice to sound out Hitler on his terms. The second time Hitler raised his demands so that even the British and French could not accept them. Mobilization began; war seemed imminent. Suddenly, in the midst of the unbearable tension, Hitler invited Chamberlain and Edouard Daladier, the French premier, to a four-power conference at Munich, to be attended by his ally, Mussolini. The Soviet Union and Czechoslovakia itself were excluded. At Munich Chamberlain and Daladier accepted Hitler's terms and then put enormous pressure on the Czech government to yield—to sign its own death warrant. France, urged on by England in an appeasement course that it was only too willing to follow, repudiated its treaty obligation to protect Czechoslovakia, ignored the Soviets who reaffirmed their willingness to aid the Czechs if the French acted, and abandoned its whole system of a Little Entente in the East. The

Appeasement: the
Munich agreement

Munich agreement permitted Germany to annex the adjoining fringe of Bohemia in which the majority of the people were Germans. This fringe contained the mountainous approaches and the fortifications, so that its loss left Czechoslovakia militarily defenseless. After promises to guarantee the integrity of what remained of Czechoslovakia, the conference disbanded. Chamberlain and Daladier were welcomed home with cheers. Chamberlain reported that he had brought "peace in our time." Again the democracies sighed with relief, hoped that Hitler had made his last demand, and told themselves that, with wise concessions, there need be no war.

Western democratic
weakness

The Munich crisis, with its death sentence to Czechoslovakia, revealed the helpless weakness into which the Western democracies had fallen by 1938. It may be that there was in fact little that the French and British could do at Munich to save Czechoslovakia. Their countries lagged behind Germany in military preparedness. They had little confidence in and were suspicious of the Soviets; and they were impressed by the might of the German army and air force. Bolder leaders than Daladier and Chamberlain, knowing the state of their own armed forces, would have declined to risk a quarrel. They desperately wanted peace and would buy it at a high price, not daring to believe that they were dealing with a blackmailer whose price would always be raised.

They suffered, too, from another moral uncertainty. By the very principle of national self-determination, accepted by the victors after the First World War, Germany could argue that it had a right to all that it had hitherto demanded. Hitler, in sending German troops into the German Rhineland, annexing Austria, stirring up Danzig, and incorporating the Bohemian Germans, had only asserted the right of the German people to have a sovereign German state. Moreover, if Hitler could be diverted eastward, enmeshed in a war with Russia, then communism and fascism might destroy each other—so one might hope. Possibly it was one of Hitler's motives, in the Munich crisis, to isolate Russia from the West and the West from Russia. If so, he succeeded well enough.

End of Appeasement

The final disillusionment came in March 1939. Hitler marched into Bohemia-Moravia, the really Czech part of Czechoslovakia, which he transformed into a German protectorate. Exploiting Slovak nationalism, he declared Slovakia "independent." Czechoslovakia, merely trimmed down at Munich, now disappeared from the map. Having promised to take only a bite, Hitler swallowed the whole. He then seized Memel from Lithuania and raised demands for Danzig and the Polish Corridor. A horrible realization now spread in France and Britain. It was clear that Hitler's most solemn guarantees were worthless, that his designs were not limited to Germans, but reached out to all eastern Europe and beyond, that he was essentially insatiable, that he could not be appeased. In April 1939 his partner in aggression, Mussolini, took over Albania.

The Western powers belatedly began to make preparations for a military stand. Britain, changing its East European policy at the eleventh hour, gave a guarantee to Poland and followed that with guarantees to Romania and Greece. That spring and summer the British tried to form an anti-German alliance with the U.S.S.R. But Poland and the Baltic states were unwilling to allow Soviet armies within their borders, even for the purpose of defending themselves against the Germans. The Anglo-French negotiators refused to put pressure on them. Since the Poles, in 1920, had conquered more territory than the Allies had meant them to have, pushing their eastern border well into Byelorussia, almost to Minsk, the Anglo-French scruples seemed to the Soviets unnecessarily delicate. They did not wish the Germans to launch an attack on them from a point as far east as Minsk. They may have thought also that what the French and British really wanted was for the Soviet Union to take the brunt of the Nazi attack. They considered it an affront that the British sent lesser officials as negotiators to Moscow when the prime minister himself had three times flown personally to deal with Hitler.

The climax came when the Soviets, having quietly undertaken negotiations earlier that spring, on August 23, 1939, openly signed a treaty of nonaggression and friendship with Nazi Germany. In a provision kept secret at the time, it was agreed that in any future territorial rearrangement the Soviet Union and Germany would divide Poland between them, that the Soviet Union would enjoy a preponderant influence in the Baltic states and have its claim to Bessarabia, lost to Romania in 1918, recognized. In return the Soviets pledged to stay out of any war between Germany and Poland or between Germany and the Western democracies.

The Nazi-Soviet Pact

The Nazi-Soviet Pact stupefied the world. Communism and Nazism, supposed to be ideological opposites, had come together. A generation more versed in ideology than in power politics was dumbfounded. The pact was recognized as the signal for war; all last-minute negotiations failed. The Germans invaded Poland on September 1. On September 3 Great Britain and France declared war on Germany. The second European war in a generation, soon to be the Second World War, began.

105. THE YEARS OF AXIS TRIUMPH

Nazi Europe, 1939–1940: Poland and the Fall of France

The Second World War opened with an assault on Poland. German forces totaling over 1 million men, spearheaded by armored divisions and supported by the massed air power of the *Luftwaffe*, rapidly overran western Poland and subdued the ill-equipped Polish armies. The outcome of the campaign, a spectacular example of *Blitzkrieg*, or lightning warfare, was clear within the first few days; organized resistance ended within a month. The Germans set about to integrate their Polish conquest into the Reich.

German Blitzkrieg

Simultaneously, the Soviet Union, acting under the secret clauses of the Nazi-Soviet Pact, moved into the eastern half of Poland two weeks after the German invasion; the territory occupied was roughly equivalent to that lost to Poland in 1920. The Soviets proceeded also to establish fortified bases in the Baltic states—Estonia, Latvia, and Lithuania. Finland resisted Soviet demands. It refused to cede border territories sought by the Russians or to yield military rights within their country. The Soviets insisted; Leningrad, the second major city of the U.S.S.R., lay only 20 miles from the Finnish frontier. When negotiations foundered, the Soviets attacked in November 1939. Finnish resistance was valiant and at first effective, but the small country was no match for the U.S.S.R. Western democratic sympathies were with the Finns; the British and French sent equipment and supplies and planned an expeditionary force. The Soviet Union was expelled from the League of Nations for the act of aggression—the only power ever to be expelled. By March 1940 the

The German army launched the brutal violence of the Second World War with its motorized assault on Poland. The new term *Blitzkrieg* was used to describe this kind of rapid military advance, which is represented here by the arrival of German troops in a bombed-out Polish village. Closely supported by air power and moving quickly on motorcycles, trucks, and armored vehicles, the Germans showed how the new tactics of offensive warfare could overwhelm the defensive strategies that had stopped advancing armies in the First World War.

(akg-images)

fighting was over. Finland had to yield somewhat more territory to the U.S.S.R. than originally demanded but retained its independence.

Meanwhile all was deceptively quiet in the West. The pattern of 1914, when the Germans reached the Marne in the first month of hostilities, failed to repeat itself. The French remained behind their Maginot Line; the British had few troops; the Germans did not stir from behind their Siegfried Line, or West Wall, in the Rhineland. Hardly any air action took place. It was called the "phony war." The Western democracies rejected Hitler's peace overtures after the conquest of Poland but clung to their peacetime outlook. The hope still lingered that somehow a real clash might even yet be averted. During this same strange winter, a cold and bitter one, the Germans put their forces through special training, whose purpose became apparent in the spring.

The "phony war"

On April 9, 1940, the Germans suddenly attacked and overran Norway, ostensibly because the British were laying mines in Norwegian waters in an endeavor to cut off German sources of Swedish iron ore. Denmark, too, was overrun, and an Allied expeditionary force with inadequate air strength had to withdraw. Then on May 10, the Germans delivered their main blow, striking at the Netherlands, Belgium, Luxembourg, and France itself. Nothing could stand against the German armored divisions and dive bombers. The Nazi use of massed tanks, though already demonstrated in Poland, took the French and British by surprise. Strategically, the Allies expected the main advance to be in central Belgium, as in 1914, and indeed as in the original German plan, which had been altered only a few months earlier. Hence the French and British sent into Belgium the best-equipped troops they had.

But the Germans delivered their main armored thrust, seven divisions, through Luxembourg and the Ardennes forest, long considered by the French General Staff impassable to tanks. In France, skirting the northwestern end of the Maginot Line, which had never been extended to the sea, the German armored divisions crossed the Meuse, drove deep into northern France against confused and ineffective resistance and, racing westward toward the Channel ports, cut off the Allied armies in Belgium. The Dutch, fearful of further air attack on their crowded cities, capitulated. The Belgian king sued for an armistice, and a large part of the French armies surrendered. The British fell back upon Dunkirk and could hope only to salvage their broken forces before the trap closed completely. Fortunately Hitler had halted the advance of his overextended armored divisions. In the week ending June 4 an epic evacuation of over 330,000 British and French troops was successfully executed from the beaches of Dunkirk, under air cover, with the help of all kinds of British vessels, manned in part by civilian volunteers, even though the precious equipment of the shattered army was almost totally abandoned.

In June the mechanized German forces drove relentlessly southward. Despite attempts at fragmented resistance by French forces (about 100,000 French soldiers died in the Battle of France), Paris itself was occupied on June 13, and Verdun was occupied two days later; by June 22 France sued for peace and an armistice was signed. Hitler danced with glee.

France, obsessed by a defensive military psychology at the outset of the war, its armies unprepared for mechanized warfare, its government divided, its people split into hostile and suspicious factions, had fallen into the hands of an openly defeatist group of leaders. The fall of France left the world aghast. Everyone knew that France was no longer its former self, but it had still been considered a Great Power, and its collapse in one month seemed inconceivable. Some French, fleeing to England, established a Free French movement under General Charles de Gaulle; others formed a resistance movement in France. The British made the bitter decision to destroy a part of the French fleet anchored in the Algerian harbor of Oran to prevent its falling into enemy hands.

Fall of France

France itself under the terms of the armistice was occupied in its northern two-thirds by the Germans. The Third Republic, its capital now at Vichy in the unoccupied southern third, was transformed by vote of a confused and stunned parliament into an authoritarian regime headed by the 84-year-old Marshal Pétain and the cynical and unscrupulous Pierre Laval. The republic was dead; the very slogan "Liberty, Equality, Fraternity" was banned from official use. French fascist groups, long frustrated in their campaigns to destabilize or destroy the Third Republic, now saw their opportunity to undermine republican traditions in French politics and society. Pétain, Laval, and others, claiming that they were acting to shield France from further suffering, proceeded to collaborate with the Nazis and to integrate Vichy France into the "new order" in Europe (see map, p. 847). The Vichy government cooperated in sending hundreds of thousands of French workers as slave laborers to Germany and even took the initiative in identifying and deporting thousands of French Jews to what were eventually Nazi death camps. The French people themselves had hard choices to make. Some chose to cooperate with the collaborators and the victorious Germans; others chose in a variety of ways to resist, some even joining the underground Resistance; most went about their daily lives waiting out the trying times until the fortunes of war might change. Not for many years after the war did the French admit responsibility as a nation for the misdeeds of the Vichy era.

Vichy France

Mussolini attacked France in June 1940, as soon as it was clear that Hitler had defeated it. Shortly thereafter, he invaded Greece and moved against the British in Africa. The *Duce* tied his own destinies, for good or ill, to those of the *Führer*. Since the Germans were emphatically the senior partner in this combination, since they were on good terms with Franco in Spain, and since the U.S.S.R. was benevolently neutral, they now dominated the European continent.

History seemed to repeat itself, in the distant and unreal way in which it ever repeats. The Germans controlled almost exactly the same geographical area that Napoleon had controlled in the early nineteenth century. Organizing a new "continental system," they made plans to govern, exploit, and coordinate the resources, industry, and labor of Europe. Not having planned for a long war, and only belatedly mobilizing their resources for a sustained military effort, they intensified the exploitation of their conquered subjects. They impressed millions, prisoners of war or civilians, as slave labor, to work under close control in the German war industries. They garrisoned Europe with

their soldiers, creating what they called *Festung Europa,* the Fortress of Europe. In every country they found sympathizers, collaborators, or "quislings"—the prototype was Vidkun Quisling, who had organized a Norwegian Fascist party in 1933 and was Norwegian premier from 1942 to 1945. When Hitler later was at war with the Soviet Union, some Europeans joined Hitler in the crusade against Bolshevism; 500,000 non-Germans fought in the divisions of the Waffen SS.

Festung Europa

The Battle of Britain and American Aid

In 1940, as in 1807, only Great Britain remained at war with the conqueror of Europe. After Dunkirk the British awaited the worst, momentarily expecting invasion. Winston Churchill, who replaced Chamberlain as prime minister in May 1940 during the military debacle, rose to the summit of leadership in adversity. To Parliament and the British people he promised nothing but "blood, toil, tears, and sweat." He pledged implacable war against "a monstrous tyranny, never surpassed in the dark, lamentable catalogue of human crime." To the American democracy across the Atlantic he appealed, "Give us the tools, and we will finish the job." The United States began to respond.

Since 1939, and even before, the American government had been anything but neutral. Opinion was excitedly divided. One group, called isolationist, opposed involvement in the European war, believing that Europe was hopeless, or that the United States could not save it, or that the Germans would win anyway before America could act, or that Hitler, even if victorious in Europe, constituted no danger to the United States. Another group, the interventionists, urged immediate aid to the Allies, believing that Hitler was a menace, that fascism must be destroyed, or that the Nazis, if they subjugated all Europe, would soon tamper with the Latin American republics. President Roosevelt was an interventionist, convinced that American security and vital interests were endangered; he tried to unite national opinion by declaring that the United States might openly assist the Allies without itself fighting, by using "measures short of war."

American "neutrality"

The neutrality legislation of the mid-1930s was amended in November 1939, when the ban on the sale of arms was repealed. Roosevelt described Britain as "the spearhead of resistance to world conquest"; the United States was to be "the great arsenal of democracy." Both were fighting for a world, he said, in which the Four Freedoms were to be secure—freedom of speech,

"The great arsenal of democracy"

The rapid, complete military collapse of France in 1940 stunned the French people and indeed the entire world. Parisians faced this humiliating sight of German troops marching through the great symbol of French nationalism, the Arc de Triomphe, as they began to cope with an oppressive German military occupation that would last more than four years.
(Bettmann/Corbis)

freedom of worship, freedom from want, and freedom from fear. In June 1940, immediately after Dunkirk, the United States sent a small initial shipment of arms to Britain. A few months later the United States gave the British 50 overage destroyers in return for the right to maintain American bases in Newfoundland, the Bermudas, and the British Caribbean islands. In 1941 it adopted Lend-Lease, a policy of providing arms, raw materials, and food to powers at war with the Axis. At the same time, in 1940 and 1941, the United States introduced conscription, built up its army and air force, and projected a two-ocean navy. To protect its shipping it secured bases in Greenland and Iceland and convoyed Allied shipping as far as Iceland.

After the fall of France, the Germans stood poised for an invasion of Britain. But they had not calculated on such rapid and easy successes in Europe, they had no immediately practical plan for an invasion, and they needed to win control of the air before a sea invasion could take place. Moreover, there was always the hope, in Hitler's mind at least, that the British might sue for peace, or even become an ally of Germany. The air assault on Britain began that summer and reached its climax in the autumn of 1940. Never until then had any bombing been so severe. But the Germans were unable to win control over the air in the battle of Britain. Gradually the British Royal Air Force fought off the bombers with more success; new radar devices helped detect the approach of enemy planes. Although Coventry was wiped out, the life and industry of other cities badly disrupted, and thousands of people killed, 20,000 in London alone, still the productive activity of the country carried on. Nor, contrary to the predictions of air power theorists, did the bombings break the morale of the civilian population.

Air war over Britain

In the winter of 1940–1941 the Germans began to shift their weight to the east. Hitler set aside the planned invasion of Britain, for which he seems never to have had much enthusiasm anyway. He had already decided, like Napoleon before him, that before committing his resources to an invasion of England he must dispose of the U.S.S.R., a project much closer to his ideology and his illusions.

The Nazi Invasion of Russia: The Russian Front, 1941–1942

The Nazi-Soviet Pact of 1939, which had precipitated the war, like the alliance between Napoleon and Alexander I, was never a warm or harmonious understanding. Both parties probably entered it mainly to gain time. The Soviets gained space as well, pushing their borders westward. Stalin, incredibly, seems to have convinced himself that he could remain uninvolved in the war going on. But he and the Nazis soon began to dispute over eastern Europe. The Soviets, with the Nazis preoccupied by the war, hoped to win complete control over the Baltic and to gain influence in the Balkans as well. They had already occupied eastern Poland and the three Baltic states and won territory from Finland. In June 1940, to the chagrin of the Germans, they aggressively sovietized and converted the three Baltic states into member republics of the U.S.S.R. The old German landowning class, the famous "Baltic barons," who had lived there for centuries, were uprooted. At the same time, the Soviets seized from Romania the Bessarabian province that they had lost in the First World War and incorporated it too as a Soviet republic. The Russians were expanding toward the Balkans, an area of historic Russian interest, and seemed bent on winning control over eastern Europe.

Hitler takes the Balkans

This the Germans viewed with dismay. They wished to reserve eastern Europe for themselves as a counterpart to industrial Germany. Hitler moved to bring the Balkans under German control. By early 1941 he blackmailed or, by territorial concessions, cajoled Romania, Bulgaria, and Hungary into joining the Axis; they became Axis lesser partners and were occupied by German troops; Yugoslavia also was occupied despite resistance by the army and population. Greece, too, was subjugated, the Germans coming to the rescue of Mussolini's hard-pressed troops. Hitler thus barred Soviet expansion in the Balkans and made the Balkan states part of the Nazi new order. The Balkan campaigns delayed his plans, but now, to crush the Soviets and to gain the wheat harvests of the Ukraine and the oil wells of the Caucasus, the core of the Eurasian "heartland," Hitler struck, and on June 22, 1941, invaded the U.S.S.R. Stalin, refusing to heed several warnings he had received, was caught completely by surprise, and momentarily seemed incapable of mounting any kind of defense.

The German army threw 3 million men into Russia along a vast 2,000-mile front. The Russians gave way. One swift moving battle melted into another. By the autumn of 1941 the Germans had overrun Byelorussia and most of the Ukraine, where the brutal military occupation led immediately to Nazi mass murders of Jews, Bolshevik government officials, and other civilians. In the north, Leningrad was in a state of siege; in the south, the Germans had entered the Crimean peninsula and were besieging Sebastopol. And toward the center of the vast front, the Germans stood, exhausted, but apparently victorious, within 25 miles of Moscow. But the overconfident German forces had not calculated on the stubbornness of Soviet resistance once Stalin recovered from his initial shock, replaced some of his military commanders, and rallied the country to the defense of the Russian motherland. Nor were the Germans prepared to fight in an early and extraordinarily bitter Russian winter, which suddenly descended upon them. A counteroffensive, launched by the Red Army that winter, saved Moscow.

The Nazi invasion of Russia

Hitler, disgusted and impatient with his subordinates, took over direct command of military operations; he shifted the main attack to the south and began a great offensive in the summer of 1942 directed toward the oil fields of the Caucasus. Sebastopol soon fell; the siege of Stalingrad began. After the failure to take Moscow, Hitler, aware now that the war would not be brief, took steps to mobilize the German economy on a fuller wartime basis. Germany had been ready for war in 1939 as no other major power had been, but lacked preparation in depth for a protracted conflict. In the early months of 1942 Hitler found in Albert Speer an organizing genius who, despite all kinds of obstacles from party leaders and government functionaries, coordinated labor and resources in the next two years and tripled armaments production.

1942, the Year of Allied Dismay: Russia, North Africa, the Pacific

A year after the invasion of the Soviet Union, in the summer of 1942, the German line reached from beleaguered Leningrad in the north, past the western outskirts of Moscow, past Stalingrad on the Volga southward to the Caucasus Mountains; the Germans were within a hundred miles of the Caspian Sea. But the Russians had traded space for time. Though the industrial Don basin and the food-producing Ukraine were overrun, and the deliveries of Caucasus oil rendered hazardous and uncertain, the Russians continued to fight. Industries were shifted to the new Ural and Siberian cities; and neither the Soviet economy nor the Soviet government was yet struck in a vital spot. A "scorched earth" policy, in which the retreating Russians destroyed crops and livestock, and guerrilla units wrecked industrial and transportation facilities, guaranteed that Russian resources would not fall into the hands of the advancing conqueror.

Simultaneously, late in 1942 the Axis also moved forward in North Africa. Here the desert campaigns started in September 1940 with an Italian eastward offensive from Libya, which succeeded in crossing over into Egypt. The stakes were high—control over Suez and the Mediterranean. At the height of the battle of Britain, Churchill made the decision to send troops and supplies,

The desert campaigns

The German army's advance across the Soviet Union opened the way for murder squads to execute large civilian populations whom the Nazis deemed to be "inferior" people. These grieving Russians searched for dead family members after the Nazis had moved through their city in early 1942.
(SOVFOTO/EASTFOTO)

much needed at home, to North Africa. A British counteroffensive against vastly superior numbers swept the Italians out of Egypt and by early 1941 the British moved deep into Libya. Shortly thereafter the British overran Ethiopia and ended Mussolini's short-lived East African empire. But in North Africa fortunes were fickle. A German elite force, the Afrika Korps under General Rommel, in the spring of 1941 attacked in Libya and drove the British back to the Egyptian frontier. A few months later, once more on the offensive, the British advanced into Libya. Again fortunes shifted. By mid-1942 Rommel had repulsed the British and penetrated Egypt. The British took up a stand at El Alamein, 70 miles from Alexandria, their backs to the Suez Canal. Here they held the Germans.

But it seemed in 1942 that the Axis armies, breaking through the Soviet Caucasus and across the isthmus of Suez in North Africa, might enclose the whole Mediterranean and Middle East in a gigantic vise, and even, moving farther east, make contact with their allies the Japanese, who were at this time penetrating into the Indian Ocean. For the Pacific situation in the latter half of 1941 had also exploded. It was Japan that finally drew the United States into war.

The Japanese, in 1941, had conducted a war against China for ten years. With the war raging in Europe, Japanese expansionists saw a propitious moment to assert themselves throughout east Asia. In 1940 they cemented their alliance with Germany and Italy in a new three-power pact; the following year they concluded a neutrality treaty with the Soviet Union. From the Vichy French the Japa-

Japan and the Pacific

nese obtained a number of military bases and other concessions in Indochina. The United States belatedly placed an embargo on the export of such materials as scrap iron and steel to Japan. Hesitating to precipitate any all-out drive of the Japanese toward the Dutch East Indies and elsewhere, the United States still sought some definition of Japanese ambitions in southeast Asia. The new Japanese prime minister, General Hideki Tojo, a staunch champion of the Axis, publicly proclaimed that the influence of Britain and the United States was to be totally eliminated from Asia, but he agreed to send representatives to Washington for negotiations.

At the very time that the Japanese representatives in Washington were carrying on conversations with the Americans, on December 7, 1941, without warning, the Japanese launched a heavy air raid on the American naval base at Pearl Harbor in Hawaii and began to invade the Philippines. Simultaneously, they launched attacks on Guam, Midway, Hong Kong, and Malaya. The Americans were caught off guard at Pearl Harbor; close to 2,500 were killed, the fleet was crippled, and the temporary disablement of the American naval forces allowed the Japanese to roam at will in the western Pacific. The United States and Great Britain declared war on Japan on December 8. Three days later Germany and Italy declared war on the United States, as did the Axis puppet states; the war had become a global struggle.

Pearl Harbor

The Japanese, working overland through Malaya, two months later captured Singapore, a British naval base long famous for its supposed impregnability, the veritable Gibraltar of the East. In 1942 the Japanese conquered the Philippines, Malaya, and the Netherlands Indies. They invaded New Guinea and threatened Australia; they moved into the Aleutians. They streamed into the Indian Ocean, occupied Burma, and seemed about to invade India. Everywhere they found ready collaborators among enemies of European imperialism. They held up the idea of a Greater East Asia Co-Prosperity Sphere under Japanese leadership, in which the one clear element (apart from the dominance of Japan) was that the Europeans should be ejected.

Meanwhile, as noted, the Germans stood at the Caucasus and almost at the Nile. And in the Atlantic, German submarines were sinking Allied ships at a disastrous rate. The Mediterranean was unusable. For the Soviet-Western alliance, 1942 was the year of dismay. Despite Allied naval and air victories in the Pacific, the late summer and autumn of 1942 was the worst period of the war. Few realized, wrote the United States Chief of Staff General George C. Marshall some years later, how "close to complete domination of the world" were Germany and Japan and "how thin the thread of Allied survival had been stretched." That Germany and Japan had no plans to concert their strategy and operations was no small factor in the eventual Allied victory.

The year of dismay

106.   THE WESTERN-SOVIET VICTORY

Plans and Preparations, 1942–1943

By January 1942 twenty-six nations, including the three Great Powers—Britain, the United States, and the U.S.S.R.—and representing every continent, were aligned against the Axis, a combination to which President Roosevelt gave the name the United Nations. Each pledged to use all its resources to defeat the Axis and never to make a separate peace. The Grand Alliance against the Axis aggressors, which could not be created in the 1930s, had at last been consummated.

The two Atlantic democracies, the United States and Great Britain, pooled their resources under a Combined Chiefs of Staff. Never had any two sovereign states formed so close a coalition. In contrast with the First World War an overall strategy was in effect from an early date. It was decided that Germany was the main enemy, against which it was necessary to concentrate first. For the time being the Pacific war was relegated to the background. Australia became the chief base for operations against the Japanese. The American navy and air force soon brought Japanese southward expansion to a halt and frustrated Japanese efforts to cut off supply lines to Australia; naval and air victories were won in the spring of 1942 in the battle of the Coral Sea and at Midway, the only relief to the overall gloom of that period. In the summer American forces landed at Guadalcanal in the Solomon Islands. A long ordeal of "island hopping" began.

A unified strategy

In Europe the first point of concentration was an air bombardment of Germany. But meanwhile Stalin called for a true "second front," an immediate invasion by Allied ground forces that would relieve the pressure of the German divisions that were devastating the Soviet Union. Suspicious of the West as ever, the Soviet government regarded the failure to establish a second front as new evidence of anti-Soviet feeling. But neither the United States nor Britain, in 1942, was ready to undertake land action by a direct assault on *Festung Europa*. Although in the Second World War, as in the First, more than two years elapsed between the outbreak of war in Europe and the intervention of the United States; and although in the second war American military preparations began much sooner, the United States in 1942 was still involved in the cumbersome processes of mobilization, converting industry to the production of war materials for itself and its Allies, imposing controls on its economy to prevent a runaway inflation, and giving military training to its profoundly civilian-minded people, of whom over 12 million men and women eventually served in the armed forces—over three times as many as in the First World War.

War preparations

The American home front was transformed like the societies of other warring nations into a war economy. The government carefully rationed the sale of food and essential materials such as oil and rubber, sold millions of "war bonds," distributed thousands of war posters to sustain civilian morale, collected countless tons of scrap metal, and worked closely with the nation's industrial companies to produce vast quantities of ships, warplanes, tanks, and every kind of military armament and equipment. Persons of all racial and ethnic groups found new jobs in the expanding industrial workforce. The total mobilization, however, led also to new forms of racial exclusion. Black Americans remained segregated in the armed forces. More than 100,000 Japanese-Americans on the west coast were forcibly evacuated to internment camps, where they remained until the end of the war. The national mobilization also affected the social and economic positions of women. Large numbers of women, as in Britain, and more so than in the First World War, took wartime jobs in defense and other industries. In contrast, almost to the end, Nazi ideology placed obstacles in the way of utilizing women in German factories.

The home front

During the first year after the United States entered the war, German submarines controlled enough of the Atlantic shipping lanes to threaten the transport of American troops and war supplies. In effect, the risk of Atlantic crossings blockaded much of the American army in the United States. The American and British navies, however, gradually won the battle of the Atlantic; the submarine menace was reduced to tolerable proportions by the first part of 1943. The Americans and British decided to begin the assault upon Germany,

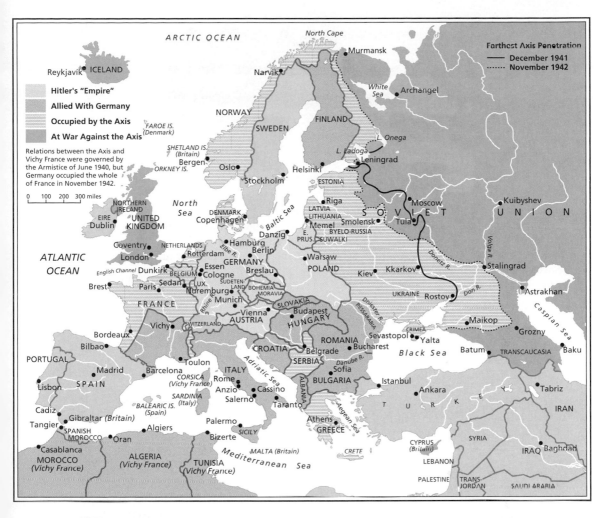

EUROPE 1942

The map shows Europe at the height of Axis military success during the Second World War. Austria, the Sudetenland, Bohemia-Moravia, Poland, and Alsace-Lorraine were all joined to Hitler's Reich. The Atlantic coast from southern France to northern Norway was under German military occupation, as was much of Russia. Southern Europe from Vichy France to Romania was also occupied or allied with Germany.

from Great Britain as a base, with a massive and prolonged air bombardment. Because precision bombardment of factories and other military targets proved difficult either by day or by night, the air assaults became area bombings; German cities were bombed mercilessly and civilians were the largest casualties. In Hamburg in 1943 fires raged on and destroyed most of the city after several days of incessant bombing. Since not everything could be shipped across the Atlantic at the same time, and since the United States and Britain were engaged in war with Japan as well, land invasion had to be deferred until 1944. The embattled Russians questioned whether the Western Allies ever meant to face the German army at all.

The destruction of cities and loss of life on the eastern front during the Second World War went far beyond the destruction and losses in all other theaters of the war. This photograph of Stalingrad at the time of the huge, extended battle for that city suggests the incredible desolation and losses that resulted from the fighting and the vast movement of armies across the Soviet Union and all of eastern Europe.
(akg-images)

The Turning of the Tide, 1942–1943: Stalingrad, North Africa, Sicily

Meanwhile, at the end of 1942 the tide had begun to turn. In November an Anglo-American force under the command of General Dwight D. Eisenhower gained control of the French-held territories in Algeria and Morocco after an amphibious operation of unprecedented proportions. In the competition that developed in the succeeding months for leadership of the French liberation committee, newly established in Algiers, General de Gaulle, though virtually ignored by President Roosevelt, pushed aside all rivals and moved forward with plans for France's revival.

After the North African landings, the Germans took over control of unoccupied France as well; they were frustrated, however, in the effort to seize the remainder of the French fleet when French crews scuttled their ships at Toulon. In North Africa the Allied forces fought their way eastward into Tunisia. Meanwhile British forces under General

Africa cleared of Axis forces

Montgomery, having held the Germans at El Alamein in June 1942, had already launched their third (and final) counteroffensive in October; they now pushed the Germans westward from Egypt until a large German force was crushed between the two Allied armies in Tunisia. By May 1943 Africa was cleared of Axis forces. Mussolini's dream of an African empire had been thwarted; the Mediterranean was open; the threat to Egypt and the Suez Canal ended.

At the same time it became clear, in the winter of 1942–1943, that the Germans had suffered a catastrophic reversal in the Soviet Union in the titanic battle of

Stalingrad

Stalingrad. In August 1942 massive German forces, an army of well over a quarter million, began an all-out assault on Stalingrad, the vital key to all transport on the lower Volga River; by September they had penetrated the city itself. Stalin ordered his namesake city held at all costs; Russian soldiery and the civilian population mounted a desperate defense. Hitler, still gambling on one big victory, was as obstinate in ordering the city taken. After weeks of fighting, the Germans occupied most of the city when suddenly a great Red Army counterattack, led by General Zhukov, trapped the German army and took a terrible toll; fewer than 100,000 were left to surrender in February 1943. The Soviets followed up their victory with a new counteroffensive, a great westward drive that regained for them what they had initially lost in the first year of the war. After Stalingrad, despite some setbacks, the Soviet Union was on the offensive for the remainder of the war. Stalingrad (or Volgograd as it was later renamed) became a turning point not only in the history of the war but in the history of central and eastern Europe as well.

American equipment meanwhile arrived in the Soviet Union in prodigious quantities. The terms of Lend-Lease were liberally extended to the Soviets; a stream of American vehicles, clothing, food, and supplies of all kinds made its way laboriously to the U.S.S.R. through the Arctic Ocean and through the Persian Gulf. Machinery and equipment were sent for the Soviet arms plants, which were themselves vastly increasing their output. Anglo-American bombing meanwhile was cutting into German airplane production at home. The Allied contribution to the Soviet war effort was indispensable, but Russian human losses were tremendous. Between 20 and 25 million people in the Soviet Union died from war-related causes. More than two-thirds of these casualties were civilians; many had been killed early in the war by Nazi murder squads whose assignment was to eliminate all so-called "undesirable" persons from territories occupied by the German army. But the number of battle deaths alone went far beyond Allied losses in other military theaters of the war. The Soviet Union lost more men in the battle of Stalingrad, for example, than the United States lost in combat during the entire war in all theaters combined.

New hope for the Allies

With contemporary American successes against Japanese forces in the Solomon Islands at the end of 1942 and the slow throttling of German submarines in the Atlantic, the beginning of the year 1943 brought new hope for the Allies in all quarters. In a spectacular campaign in July–August 1943, the British, Canadians, and Americans conquered the island of Sicily. Mussolini fell from power, and the 21-year-old Fascist regime came to an end. Mussolini set up an "Italian Social Republic" in the north, but it was no more than a German puppet government. Some months later, in April 1945, the Duce, as he attempted to flee the country, was seized and shot by anti-Fascist Italians. When the new Italian government under Marshal Badoglio, in August 1943, tried to make peace, the German army occupied Italy. The Allies, having crossed to the Italian mainland from Sicily, attacked from the south. In October the Badoglio government declared war on Germany, and Italy was recognized by the Allies as a "cobelligerent." But the Germans stubbornly blocked the advance of the Allies to Rome despite new Allied landings and beachheads. The Italian campaign turned into a long and disheartening stalemate because the Western Allies, concentrating troops in Britain for the approaching cross-Channel invasion, could never spare enough for the Italian front.

The Allied Offensive in Europe, 1944–1945

Festung Europa, especially along its western approaches, the coasts of Holland, Belgium, and France, bristled with every kind of fortification that German scientific and military ingenuity could devise. A seaborne attack upon these coasts clearly differed from the earlier amphibious attacks on Algeria, Sicily, or the Pacific islands in that the defender in Europe, in the very part of Europe where the road and railway network was thickest, could immediately rush overwhelming reserves to the spot attacked—except insofar as feinting tactics kept him uncertain, air power destroyed his transport, or the Russians held the bulk of his forces in the East. Precise and elaborate plans had been worked out. Ten thousand

THE SECOND WORLD WAR

These two maps show the global character of the war and the central position of the United States with respect to the European and Pacific theaters. The numbered legends summarize the successive stages of the war in both the Eastern and Western hemispheres. In 1942, with the Germans reaching as far east as Egypt and Stalingrad and the Japanese as far west as Burma, the great danger to the Soviet-Western alliance was that these two might join forces, dominate southern Asia, control the oil resources of the Persian Gulf, and stop the flow of Western supplies to the Soviet Union from this direction. The almost simultaneous Soviet-Western successes, late in 1942, at Stalingrad and El Alamein, and in the invasion of Morocco-Algeria and of Guadalcanal, proved to be the turning point of the war. In 1943 the German submarine campaign in the Atlantic was defeated, so that American troops and supplies could

move more freely to Europe. **The invasion of Normandy in June 1944, with continuing Russian pressure from the east, brought about the German surrender in May 1945. Meanwhile, in the Pacific, American occupation of the islands and reoccupation of the Philippines prepared the way for the surrender of Japan, which followed the dropping of two atomic bombs in August 1945.**

aircraft were to provide aerial protection, scores of warships were to bombard the coast, 4,000 ships were to carry the invading troops and their supplies across the Channel, and artificial harbors were to be created where none existed.

The invasion of western Europe began before dawn on June 6, 1944. The spot selected was the coast of Normandy directly across the Channel from England; false intelligence reports, planted by the Allies, led the Germans to expect the main thrust, when it occurred, to be at Calais. An

The invasion of Europe

unparalleled combination of forces—British, Canadian, and American, land, sea, and air, backed up by huge accumulations of supplies and troops assembled in Great Britain, and the whole under the unified command of General Eisenhower—assaulted the French coast, established a beachhead, and maintained a front. The Allies poured in their strength, over 130,000 men the first day, 1 million within a month. After heavy fighting around the town of Saint-Lô in early July, the Germans were thrown back more easily than had been expected. By August Paris was liberated, by September the Allies crossed the frontier of Germany itself. In France, Italy, and Belgium the Resistance movements, which had grown up in secret during the years of German occupation, came into the open and drove out Germans and pro-German collaborators. In Germany itself no widespread or deeply rooted Resistance movement ever developed, but a small group of Germans, military and civilian, formed an underground. On July 20, 1944, after the failure of earlier efforts, it attempted to assassinate Hitler by exploding a bomb at his military headquarters in East Prussia; Hitler was only injured and took a fearsome revenge on the conspirators.

In August, in another amphibious operation, the Allies landed on the French Mediterranean coast and swept up from southern France to join the Allied forces advancing against stiffening resistance. At one point, momentarily, the Allied offensive suffered a serious reversal. A sudden German drive under Hitler's direct personal orders in December 1944 was launched against thinly held American lines on the Belgian sector in the Ardennes, created a "bulge" in the advancing armies, and caused heavy losses and confusion. But the Allies rallied, and Hitler used up his armored reserves in the effort. Neither the Ardennes counteroffensive nor the new destructive weapons rained on Britain, jet-propelled flying bombs and rockets, opening up the missile age, availed the Germans. All this time the Americans and British kept up their massive air bombardments, destroying many of Germany's industrial cities and killing over 50,000 civilians in the fire-bombing of Dresden in February 1945. On the ground they pushed on and smashed through the heavily fortified Siegfried Line. The last natural obstacle, the Rhine, was crossed when in March 1945 American forces by a stroke of luck discovered an undestroyed bridge at Remagen; they poured troops over it and established a bridgehead—the first troops to cross the Rhine in combat since the armies of Napoleon. The main crossing, under the British, subsequently took place farther to the north. Soon the Allies were accepting wholesale surrenders in the Ruhr valley.

Meanwhile in 1944 the Russian armies swept the Germans from the Ukraine, Byelorussia, the Baltic states, and eastern Poland. By August they reached the suburbs of Warsaw. The Polish underground rose against the Germans, but the Soviets, determined that Poland not be liberated by non-Communist Polish leadership, refused to permit aid to the rising, and it was crushed, with a heavy loss of Polish lives. Earlier, in 1943, the mass graves of thousands of Polish prisoners of war, mainly officers, had been found by the Germans in the Katyn Forest. Despite continuing Soviet denials at the time, documents in the Russian archives later revealed that they had been shot by the Red Army on Stalin's orders in 1940, after the Soviet Union had joined with Germany in partitioning Poland. The Russians, their lines now overextended, and checked for several months by German strength in Poland, pushed southward into Romania and Bulgaria; both countries changed sides and declared war against Germany. Early in 1945 the Soviets, reopening their offensive, forced their way into East Prussia and Silesia and by February reached the Oder River, 40 miles from Berlin, where Zhukov paused to regroup his forces. In March and April Russian forces occupied Budapest and Vienna.

The eastern front

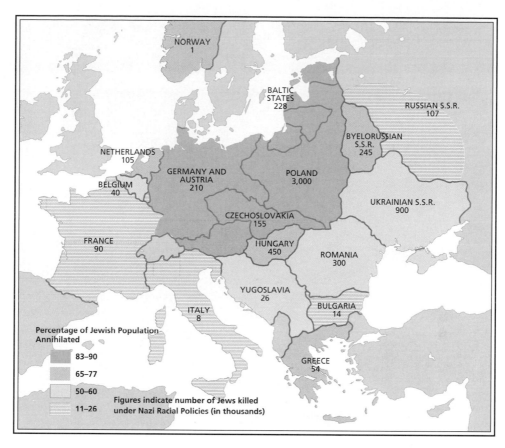

NORWAY
1

BALTIC
STATES
228

RUSSIAN S.S.R.
107

BYELORUSSIAN
S.S.R.
245

NETHERLANDS
105

GERMANY AND
AUSTRIA
210

POLAND
3,000

BELGIUM
40

UKRAINIAN S.S.R.
900

CZECHOSLOVAKIA
155

FRANCE
90

HUNGARY
450

ROMANIA
300

YUGOSLAVIA
26

BULGARIA
14

ITALY
8

Percentage of Jewish Population
Annihilated

83–90

65–77

50–60

11–26   Figures indicate number of Jews killed
         under Nazi Racial Policies (in thousands)

GREECE
54

THE HOLOCAUST

This map shows the loss of life that resulted from what the Nazis called their "Final Solution"—that is, their systematic program of destroying the Jews and Judaism. Before the Second World War most European Jews lived in Poland and the adjoining parts of the Soviet Union. The Germans occupied all of these areas during the war, and most deaths occurred in these territories. The map shows both the number killed in each country and the percentage of its Jewish population that were victims of this deliberate genocide. The numbers add up to about 6 million men, women, and children, or an estimated two-thirds of the Jewish population of Europe as a whole. Although word of this annihilation policy reached the outside world through the Vatican and other sources, the Allied leaders at first disbelieved the reports, and then, giving priority to their military objectives, did nothing to stop the systematic slaughter.

The final drive on Germany began. Hitler moved troops from the collapsing western front to reinforce German positions on the Oder and to protect his capital. In April the Americans reached the Elbe, about 60 miles from Berlin, with hardly any obstacles before them; but here they halted, by decision of General Eisenhower. The Americans, whose supply lines were already overextended, wanted a clear line of demarcation from the Russians; they also believed it necessary to divert forces southward against a possible German last stand in the Alps. But mainly the decision was made as a gesture of goodwill toward the Russians, who were to

The final drive on Germany

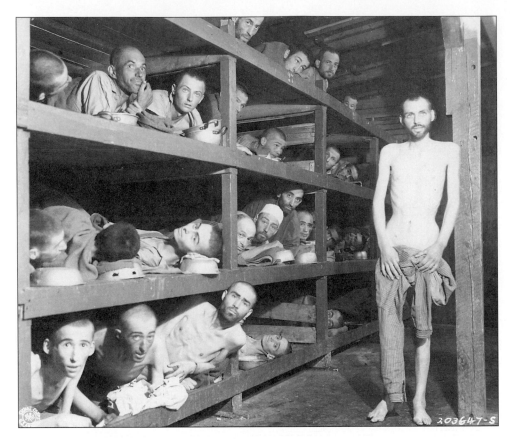

Allied troops found horrifying evidence of mass murder as they entered death camps and concentration camps that the Nazis had constructed throughout Germany and central Europe. These emaciated survivors were liberated from the camp at Buchenwald, where they had been forced to work as slave laborers and where more than 40,000 people had died. This group includes Elie Wiesel (seventh from left in second level, near the vertical beam), who would later write searing descriptions of the camps and of the Holocaust.
(The Art Archive/National Archives, Washington, D.C.)

be permitted to take Berlin as compensation for their heavy sacrifices in the common cause, and to preserve the Western-Soviet coalition until final victory. Similarly, the American troops that moved southward were held back from taking Prague, and the Soviets were permitted to take the Czech capital too. At the end of the war the Soviets were therefore in control of all the major capitals of central and eastern Europe—a military situation that would carry major political consequences.

The Western Allies and the Soviets offered no terms to Hitler nor to any Germans. They demanded unconditional surrender, and the Germans fought on in the very streets of Berlin. On the last day of April Hitler perished by his own hand in the ruins of his capital after denouncing some of his closest party subordinates as traitors. Admiral Doenitz, designated by Hitler as his successor, went through the formalities of surrender on May 8, 1945. Since fighting had already ceased on the Italian front a few days earlier, the war in Europe was over.

The Holocaust

Meanwhile a generation reared to mistrust the fabricated atrocity tales of the First World War painfully and belatedly became aware of the real German horrors of the Second—hostages rounded up and shot in reprisal for resistance; whole villages like Lidice in Czechoslovakia or Oradour-sur-Glane in France razed to the ground and their inhabitants slain or deported; concentration camps like Dachau and Buchenwald, where the prisoners were given minimal rations and worked to death, and where Allied troops found only pitifully emaciated survivors; above all, the mass death camps with gas chambers and crematory ovens at Auschwitz (where at its peak 12,000 victims a day were gassed to death), Treblinka, Belzéc, Sobibor, and others, where peoples whom the Nazis deemed "inferior" could be systematically liquidated.

In the areas of Nazi domination in eastern Europe, the Nazis first used special firing squads and mobile gas units to kill "undesirables," but Hitler's murderous ambitions could not be achieved through such temporary or improvised methods of killing in the countryside. As the war went on, the more unstructured forms of mass murder were replaced by a systematically organized, European-wide system for gathering people at "collection" centers and transporting millions of men, women, and children in railroad cattle cars to the mass death camps where some were worked to death and others were put to death at once. By far the largest proportion killed were some 6 million Jews, but millions of other Poles, Russians, other Slavic peoples, Gypsies, and others were slain as well—either in the death camps or in various killing fields throughout Europe.

Many of the plans for systematic annihilation of the Jews, which would come to be known and remembered after the war as the Holocaust, were decided upon at a high-level Nazi meeting at Wannsee in January 1942. In the genocidal view of Nazi planners such as Heinrich Himmler, these policies would provide the wartime "Final Solution" to the so-called "Jewish problem" that Hitler had agitated with maniacal racist fury for so many years. Genocide, the planned, systematic effort to destroy a whole people, was the greatest of the Nazi sins against humanity. Although there have been mass murders in many other places and eras of human history, the genocidal attack on European Jews had a uniquely modern scale and scientific organization, which explains in part why it has produced such painful memories and questions for later generations. How could such murderous events occur in the heart of modern European civilization? The fact that the Holocaust was carried out by ordinary people and bureaucrats raises pointed questions about individual and collective responsibilities for deadly government policies, about the danger of misused, modern technologies, and about the destructive consequences of racist ideologies.

The "final solution"

Survivors have described extraordinary acts of courage and human will among the prisoners in Nazi death camps, but the Holocaust has become the modern world's most terrifying example and memory of systematic murder and human brutality. And although it was easy enough to blame the Holocaust on Hitler and the other rabid leaders of the Nazi regime, the most haunting aspect of these massive crimes may have come from the unquestioning participation of so many anonymous followers. One of the few survivors from the camp at Auschwitz, the Italian Jewish writer Primo Levi, summarized the problem that reappears constantly in later historical, ethical, and political reflections on the Holocaust and suggests why this event remains so memorable in modern world history. "We must remember," Levi wrote, "that these faithful followers, among them the diligent executors of inhuman orders, were not born torturers, were not (with a few exceptions) monsters: they were ordinary men. Monsters exist, but they are too few in number to be truly dangerous. More dangerous are the common men, the functionaries ready to believe and to act without asking questions."

The Last Phase of the War in the Pacific: 1944—1945

In the Pacific, American operations against Japan had dragged on for three years, hampered by the strategic decision to concentrate against Germany first. Slowly, from points in the Solomon Islands, the easternmost fringe of the Indonesian archipelago, American forces, at first small, worked their way in a northwesterly direction toward faraway Japan. They had to fight in turn for Guadalcanal, for New Guinea, for the reconquest of the Philippines, all against stubborn entrenched Japanese resistance and at heavy cost. They had to fight for the Japanese islands in the mid-Pacific taken by Japan from the Germans after the First World War and converted into powerful naval bases — the Gilbert Islands, the Marshalls, the Carolines, the Marianas. In October 1944 the American navy won a decisive victory over the Japanese in the battle of Leyte Gulf. In March 1945 they fought with heavy casualties to take the eight-square-mile strategic island of Iwo Jima. Finally, in a protracted and bloody battle lasting over 2½ months, in the spring of 1945 they won the island of Okinawa, only 300 miles from Japan itself. Okinawa was captured just as the Germans collapsed in Europe. From the new Allied bases that had been won, from Saipan in the Marianas, from Iwo Jima, from Okinawa, and from aircraft carriers at sea, a crushing air offensive was launched against Japan, shattering Japanese industry, destroying the remnants of the Japanese navy, and compelling the Japanese government to give serious thought to suing for peace. The Allied leaders refused to believe that Japanese defenses were ready to crumble or that the Japanese were ready to negotiate. The American army prepared to shift combat troops from the European theater to Asia. The stage was being set for a full-scale invasion of Japan itself.

The atomic bomb

Then, on August 6, 1945, an American aircraft dropped an atomic bomb — built in the United States in utmost secrecy by European refugee and American scientists — on the city of Hiroshima, with a population of 200,000 people. The city was destroyed in this single explosion, and about 100,000 lives were lost; thousands of others were injured or suffered the long-term effects of radiation. Two days later, the Soviet Union, which had pledged to enter the conflict in the East within three months after the surrender of Germany, declared war on Japan and invaded Manchuria. On August 9 a second American atomic bomb struck Nagasaki and killed approximately 60,000 more. The atomic bombs and the Soviet declaration of war drove the Japanese to make peace at once. On September 2, 1945, the formal surrender was signed. The emperor was permitted to remain as head of state, but Japan was placed under a United States army of occupation.

Meanwhile, the atomic bomb, like the death camps of the Holocaust, soon became another haunting memory and symbol of the new forms of violence and mass destruction that a staggeringly costly global war had bequeathed to humanity. It was probably true, as American leaders insisted at the time and in retrospect, that the atomic bomb was the least costly way (in terms of American lives) for the United States to bring the war in Japan to a rapid, victorious conclusion; but it is also true that the introduction of this hugely destructive weapon created an unprecedented new threat to human survival and an endless danger that has loomed over the modern world ever since.

The human consequences of Nazi brutalities appear in this picture of a Nazi concentration camp near the German city of Ohrdruf in early May 1945. American soldiers were making their way through the camp, where the Nazis had subjected Poles, Czechs, German Jews, and German political prisoners to forced labor and then shot or flogged to death the internees who could no longer work.

(Bettmann/Corbis)

The atomic bomb that was dropped on Hiroshima was the most destructive weapon in the long history of warfare. This photograph shows a view of the city after the single American bomb had reduced the buildings to rubble and killed 100,000 people. The bomb helped to end the Second World War in Japan, but it also created a new and enduring atomic threat to the future of human civilization.
(Associated Press, U.S. SIGNAL CORPS)

The Second World War of the twentieth century was over, the greatest conflict in human history. The same cold impersonal statistics that had recorded 10 million killed in the First World War reported 15 million military deaths and (unlike the First World War) more than twice as many civilian fatalities. Soviet military deaths were estimated at over 6 million, German at 3.5 million, Chinese at 2.2 million, Japanese at 1.3 million, Polish at 700,000. British and Commonwealth losses were over 400,000, American about 300,000, French about 200,000. Over 25 million suffered battle wounds. The military death figures would have been higher except that one of every two of those wounded was saved by new sulfa and penicillin drugs and blood plasma transfusions. None of these statistics could be more than approximate; and no one could estimate the complete toll of human lives lost from Allied and Axis bombings, Nazi mass slayings of Jews in the Holocaust and of other

CHRONOLOGY OF NOTABLE EVENTS, 1935–1945

1935	Mussolini launches an Italian invasion and conquest of Ethiopia
March 1936	German troops enter Rhineland; France and Britain do not intervene
July 1936	Fascist groups under General Franco in Spain rise against the Spanish Republic; Franco takes power after three-year Civil War
March 1938	Hitler annexes Austria to Nazi Germany
September 1938	French and British leaders meet with Hitler in Munich and accept German takeover of Sudetenland in Czechoslovakia
August 1939	Nazi-Soviet Nonaggression Pact includes plan for division of Poland
September 1939	Nazi invasion of Poland begins the Second World War
May–June 1940	Nazis conquer the Netherlands, Belgium, and France
July 1940	French collaborators set up a pro-fascist regime in Vichy
September 1940	German air attacks on Britain are repelled in Battle of Britain
June 1941	Germany launches massive invasion of the Soviet Union
December 1941	Japanese attack on U.S. Pacific fleet at Pearl Harbor brings the United States into war with Japan and then Germany
January 1942	Nazi leaders launch plans to build death camps for genocidal killing of European Jews and others
February 1943	Soviet forces defeat the Germans in decisive battle at Stalingrad
June 1944	Allied Armies open a "western front" in France after D-Day landings at Normandy
February 1945	Churchill, Roosevelt, and Stalin agree on postwar arrangements at meeting in Yalta
May 1945	Germany surrenders after Hitler commits suicide in Berlin
September 1945	Japan surrenders after the United States drops two atomic bombs and the Soviet Union declares war on Japan

people in all the German-occupied nations, Nazi and Soviet deportation policies, and postwar famines and epidemics. Some estimates place the total at 60 million men, women, and children, but at such figures the human mind retreats and human sensitivities are dulled.

107.   THE FOUNDATIONS OF THE PEACE

Whereas the First World War had been concluded by a peace conference a few months after the close of hostilities, the Second World War ended in no such clear-cut settlement. Nothing like the Treaty of Versailles of 1919 followed the defeat of Germany in 1945. The peace terms emerged episodically, at first during a series of conferences among the Allied nations during the war, and then in a series of de facto arrangements in the years after 1945.

The foundations of a peaceable postwar world were being laid, it was thought, at a number of meetings where the strategy of the war itself was being planned. As early as August 1941, before the United States had entered the war, Roosevelt and Churchill met at sea off the coast of Newfoundland and drew up the Atlantic Charter. Later, there were meetings in 1943 at Casablanca, at Cairo, and at Teheran (which was close enough to the Soviet Union for Stalin to participate); and in the final phase of the war, in February 1945, at Yalta (a Crimean resort city in the Soviet Union), and in July 1945 at Potsdam in the environs of shattered Berlin.

The Atlantic Charter, issued jointly by Roosevelt and Churchill at their first meeting, resembled in spirit the Fourteen Points of Woodrow Wilson. It pledged that sovereign rights and self-government would be restored to all who had been forcibly deprived of them, that all nations would have equal access to world trade and world resources, that all peoples would work together to achieve improved living standards and economic security. The postwar peace, it promised, would assure people of all lands freedom from fear and want and end force and aggression in international affairs. Here, and in the Four Freedoms enunciated by President Roosevelt, the ideological basis of the peace was proclaimed. At the 1943 conferences, and through other consultations, the Allies endeavored to concert their military plans. At Casablanca in January 1943, they resolved to accept nothing less than the "unconditional surrender" of the Axis powers. This vague formula, adopted somewhat cavalierly at American initiative, and without much thought to possible political implications, was intended mainly to prevent a recurrence of anything like the ambiguity surrounding the armistice of 1918, when nationalist Germans complained that Germany had not been defeated on the battlefield but had been "stabbed in the back" by a dissolving home front.

"Unconditional surrender"

At Teheran in December 1943, Roosevelt and Churchill met with Stalin for the first of two wartime meetings. They discussed the postwar occupation and demilitarization of Germany, laid plans for a postwar international organization, and debated strategy for winning the war. Throughout the war Roosevelt, unwilling to disturb the unity of the Western-Soviet coalition in the global struggle in which America was engaged, followed a policy of postponing controversial territorial and political decisions until victory was assured. Churchill was more apprehensive. Steeped in traditional balance-of-power politics, he sensed that without prior diplomatic bargaining and political arrangements, the victory over the Nazis would leave Russia dominant over central and eastern Europe. At Teheran he proposed operations in the Mediterranean and an invasion through the Balkans, both for political reasons and out of concern for the casualties that a cross-Channel invasion would involve. But Roosevelt persuaded him otherwise. It was agreed that a landing in France would take place in the spring of 1944; thus the major second front that Stalin had been promised would finally be opened. Stalin pledged that he would launch a simultaneous offensive on the eastern front.

The strategy that would win the war in the next 18 months was decided upon at Teheran, but that strategy, without prior political agreements, all but guaranteed the Soviet domination of eastern Europe. Later, in October 1944, as the Russian armies advanced westward, Churchill visited Stalin and sketched out a demarcation of spheres of influence for the Western powers and the Soviets in the Balkan states (a Soviet preponderance in Romania and Bulgaria, a Western preponderance in Greece, and an even division of influence in Hungary and Yugoslavia). Soviet control over the Baltic states had virtually been conceded by the British earlier. Roosevelt, however, would not agree to any such arrangement, which he considered old-fashioned and a dangerous revival of the worst features of pre-1914 diplomacy.

The two conferences that arrived at the most important political decisions were the meetings at Yalta and at Potsdam in 1945. The Yalta meeting in February 1945 took place when the Allies were close to final victory— closer, events disclosed, than anyone at the time realized. The three Allied statesmen met at the old tsarist Crimean summer resort on the Black Sea, toasted their common triumphs, and, as at Teheran, took the measure of each other. Roosevelt thought of himself as a mediator between Churchill and Stalin where European issues were involved. He took pains to avoid giving Stalin the impression that he and Churchill were in any sense united against him; in point of fact, Roosevelt was suspicious of Churchill's devotion to empire and colonial ties, which he considered anachronistic for the postwar world. Despite differences, the Big Three reached agreements, at least formally, on Poland and eastern Europe, the future of Germany, the war in Asia, and the projected postwar international organization—the United Nations.

The agreements at Yalta

The discussion of Poland and eastern Europe raised the most serious difficulties. Stalin's armies, having driven the Nazi forces to within 40 miles of Berlin, were in control of Poland and of almost all eastern and central Europe. The Russians remembered these areas as anti-Soviet, and Poland particularly as the perpetrator of aggression against Soviet territory in 1920. Stalin had already taken steps to establish a "friendly" government in Poland, that is, a government subservient to the Soviets. Neither Roosevelt nor Churchill had fought the war against the Nazis to leave the Soviet Union the undisputed master of central and eastern Europe and in a position to impose a totalitarian political system on all this vast area. At Yalta, Roosevelt and Churchill extracted from Stalin a number of promises for the areas he controlled. In accordance with the Atlantic Charter, the liberated states were to be permitted provisional governments "broadly representative of all democratic elements in the population," that is, not consisting merely, as in the case of the provisional government of Poland already established, of authorities subservient to the Soviets. They pressed Stalin to pledge also the "earliest possible establishment through free elections of governments responsive to the will of the people." The pledge was a verbal concession that cost the Soviet leader little; he rejected the suggestion of international supervision over the elections. The Declaration on Liberated Europe, promising sovereign rights of democratic self-determination, provided a false sense of agreement; there were to be no free elections in Soviet-controlled eastern Europe.

Poland and eastern Europe

A number of territorial changes were also accepted, pending final settlement at a postwar peace conference. The Russian-Polish boundary would be set roughly at the so-called Curzon line, the Polish frontier contemplated by the Allies in 1919 before the Poles conquered territory to their east. The Poles would be compensated, in the north and west, at the expense of Germany (see map, p. 893). On this and on other matters relating to Germany there was a large area of accord; the three were united in their hatred of German Nazism and militarism. Germany was to be disarmed and divided into four occupation zones under the administration of the Big Three powers and France—the latter at the insistence of Churchill. There was vague talk, at Yalta and earlier, of dismembering Germany, of undoing the work of Bismarck; but the difficulties of such an undertaking were understood and the proposal was eventually discarded. The Americans and British rejected as excessive the Soviet proposals for reparations, a sum of $20 billion to be paid in kind, half to the Soviets. It was agreed, however, that reparations would go to those countries that

The final meeting of Roosevelt, Churchill, and Stalin took place in the Crimean resort city of Yalta in February 1945. Roosevelt's position here between the other two leaders suggests his mediating position at the conference. The agreements reached at Yalta shaped the postwar organization of eastern Europe, laid the foundation for the United Nations, and eventually brought the Soviet Union into the war against Japan, but some critics in the West later complained that the Yalta accords made too many concessions to Stalin and opened the way for Soviet expansion into central Europe.

had borne the main burdens of the war and suffered the heaviest losses. The Soviet Union was to receive half of whatever total sum was set.

To the satisfaction of everyone, the participants agreed on plans for a postwar international organization, to be called the United Nations. Roosevelt believed it essential to win the Soviets over to the idea of an international organization. He was convinced that the Great Powers, cooperating within the framework of the United Nations and acting as international police, could preserve the future peace and security of the world. No less than Stalin or Churchill, he emphasized the importance of the Great Powers in the new organization, although he accepted a dignified role for the smaller nations as well. All agreed that each of the Great Powers, the permanent members of the new organization's Security Council, would have a veto power on important decisions. The Soviets pressed for 16 votes in the General Assembly of the new organization, arguing that their constitution gave sovereign rights to each of their then 16 constituent republics and also that the British dominions would each have a seat. In the interests of harmony, at Churchill's behest, they were given three.

The United Nations

Critical agreements were reached on East Asia. Here political and military decisions were inextricably linked. The Soviets had remained neutral in the Pacific war despite their historic interests in that part of Asia. Given the magnitude of the Soviet war effort on the European front, no one had pressed them to enter the Pacific war earlier. It was agreed to wait at least until the Germans were on the verge of defeat. At Yalta, Stalin agreed to enter the war against Japan, but Soviet "public opinion," he averred, would demand compensation. The U.S.S.R. would enter the war against Japan "two to three months" after Germany had surrendered. In return, the Soviets would receive territories and rights that tsarist Russia had lost to Japan 40 years before in the Russo-Japanese war of 1904–1905 (see map, p. 671), with the addition of the Kurile Islands, which had never been Russian before.

Roosevelt made controversial concessions at Yalta because he believed he needed Soviet support in the last phase of the war against Japan and because he wished to preserve the Western-Soviet coalition until final victory was guaranteed. He believed also that wartime cooperation would produce postwar harmony. Churchill, less sanguine about the future and about "diplomacy by friendship," would have preferred a franker definition of spheres of influence. Such ideas were ruled out as the thinking of a bygone era. Yet the spirit of the Atlantic Charter, so closely identified with the American president, the pledge of sovereign self-determination for all peoples, was already being contravened.

At Potsdam, in July 1945, after the German collapse, the Big Three met again. A new American president, Harry S Truman, represented the United States; President Roosevelt had died in April, on the eve of final victory. Churchill, in the midst of the conference, was replaced by a new British prime minister, Clement Attlee, after the Labour party's victory at the polls. Stalin still represented the Soviet Union. By now, disagreements between the Western Allies and the Soviets had deepened, not only over Soviet control in Poland, eastern Europe, and the Balkans, but over German reparations and other matters. Yet the Western leaders were still prepared to make concessions in the hope of establishing harmonious relations. Agreements were announced on the postwar treatment of Germany—on German disarmament, demilitarization, "denazification," and the punishment of war criminals. Each power could take reparations in kind from its occupation zone and the Russians would get substantial additional deliveries from the Western zones so that the original $10 billion Soviet demand was virtually met.

The Potsdam Conference

Pending the final peace treaty, German territory east of the Oder-Neisse rivers was committed to Polish administration. The details of this decision had earlier been postponed; the Polish-German boundary was now set at the western Neisse, even further west than originally envisaged. Poland thus extended its territorial boundaries about a hundred miles westward as compensation for Russian westward expansion at Polish expense. German East Prussia was divided between the Soviet Union in the north and Poland in the south. Königsberg, founded by the Teutonic Knights and for centuries the coronation city of Prussian kings, became the Russian city of Kaliningrad. The ancient German cities of Stettin and Breslau became the Polish cities of Szczecin and Wrocław. Danzig became Gdansk. The de facto administration of these areas hardened into permanent rule. The transfer of the German population in these eastern areas was supposed to be effected in an orderly and humane fashion, but millions of Germans were driven from their homes or fled within a few months. For them (and for the Sudeten Germans who were expelled from Czechoslovakia) it was the final consummation of the war that Hitler had unleashed.

Germany divided

The Potsdam participants agreed that peace treaties would be signed as soon as possible with the former German satellite states; the task of preparing them was entrusted to a council of foreign ministers representing the United States, Britain, France, the Soviet Union, and China. In the months that followed, the widening chasm between the Soviets and the West manifested itself in stormy meetings in London, Paris, and New York, as well as in a peace conference held in Paris in 1946, at which were represented the 21 states that had contributed substantial military forces to the defeat of the Axis powers. In February 1947 treaties were signed with Italy, Romania, Hungary, Bulgaria, and Finland, all of which paid reparations and agreed to certain territorial adjustments. In 1951 a peace treaty was signed with Japan, but not by the Soviets, who signed their own treaty in 1956. The years went by, but no final treaty was signed with Germany, which for many years to come remained divided into western and eastern zones. The wartime Western-Soviet coalition had fallen apart, shattering the dreams and aspirations for a lasting peace of those who had fought the Second World War to a triumph over one kind of aggression and totalitarianism, and who now found themselves confronted with a new age of crisis.

For interactive exercises, glossary, chronologies, and more, go to the *Online Learning Center* at **www.mhhe.com/palmer10.**

Chapter 22

THE COLD WAR AND RECONSTRUCTION AFTER THE SECOND WORLD WAR

Every age has its share of social conflicts, economic problems, political upheavals, wars, and cultural changes, but the first half of the twentieth century must surely be ranked as one of the most deadly and disorienting periods that people have ever known. During these decades, over the course of a single lifetime, the world passed through the Great War of 1914–1918, a global influenza pandemic (which killed at least 50 million people), the collapse of longstanding dynasties in Europe and the Middle East, the Russian Revolution, a worldwide economic depression, the rise of aggressive fascist and Nazi dictatorships, the Second World War (stretching from Europe and North Africa to all of east and southeast Asia), the Holocaust in Nazi-occupied Europe, the first use of atomic bombs, the rise of Communist China, and the breakup of the Ottoman and European empires into new nations in the eastern Mediterranean and South Asia.

These events brought massive disruptions to individual lives, caused more millions of deaths than can ever be accurately counted, and produced far-reaching changes in global political and economic systems—including the rapid, international ascendancy of the United States and a steady decline in Europe's previous control over people or economies in much of the non-European world. In short, the upheavals of the early twentieth century profoundly transformed the course of modern world history. Yet people everywhere, like their ancestors after earlier upheavals, moved on from these cataclysms to rebuild their lives, their societies, their political institutions, and their economic activities. History did not end, of course, and the age-old resilience of human beings and their cultures appeared again in the decades that followed the Second World War.

Chapter emblem: Hungarian protestors burning a picture of Joseph Stalin in 1956. (Hulton-Deutsch Collection/Corbis)

The end of that titanic war marks a transition for historians as well as for the people who lived through it, because the decades after 1945 or 1950 are the beginning of what historians usually call "contemporary history." Although the postwar era is increasingly distant from our own time, the historical consequences of many events and changes since the Second World War are still evolving and are still part of our contemporary world. Contemporary history arouses strong feelings, leads to many of the world's current conflicts, and directly shapes the experiences and attitudes of most people who are now alive. For historians, the complexities of contemporary history can pose even more challenges than those of earlier eras, because many sources are still unavailable, or because present-day conflicts distort historical perspectives, or because the lasting influence of recent events cannot yet be known. These distinctive, open-ended aspects of contemporary history will begin to emerge in this chapter and those that follow as we examine the unsettled events and trends of the contemporary world, which continues to evolve more rapidly and in more ways than any historical narrative can describe with the long-range perspectives of historical analysis.

108.   THE COLD WAR: THE OPENING DECADE, 1945–1955

Certain issues that had confronted humankind for over a century became even more complex and more urgent in the second half of the twentieth century. Three can be singled out: science, the organization of industrial society, and national sovereignty.

The atomic bomb

The atomic bomb dramatized the new problem of science. The world shuddered at the instantaneous destruction of Hiroshima. The postwar contest to produce more sophisticated nuclear weapons spurred the realization that a third world war would be unthinkable. Human beings now possessed the means to annihilate not only civilization but even human existence on the planet, a thought especially shocking to a world that set one of its highest values on scientific progress.

Science, and its partner, invention, had for a long time transformed both industry and war. It had conquered many of the dreaded plagues and diseases of the world. Everyone had long known that science could be applied either constructively or destructively. It was the magnitude of the new destructive possibilities that now made thoughtful people worry. Scientists themselves, after the first atomic explosion, affirmed the need for a moral regeneration. They insisted that science was neutral, free from blame for the horrors of Hiroshima and Nagasaki, that the trouble lay not with science but with the uses to which scientific knowledge was put.

Organizing industrial society

The problem of organizing industrial society was also unresolved after 1945. There were in theory two opposite social poles. At one, best represented by the Union of Soviet Socialist Republics (until its demise in 1991), all capital was owned by the state and supplied to managers and workers as needed, and all production and interchange were planned in advance by public authorities. In the Soviet form of socialism (as well as in the People's Republic of China after 1949), which the outside world called communism because it had come about through revolution and been maintained through dictatorship, the government's role was all-encompassing. At the other pole, best exemplified by the United States, economic exchange took place through the mechanism of the market, and capital was owned by private persons who chose the channels of investment and determined the availability of jobs. Neither the socialist nor the capitalist system was pure in practice, and even in capitalist countries mixed economies became the rule, with varying degrees of government intervention. The chief drawback in the Soviet system was the lack of political and economic freedom and its stifling of individual initiative; in the American system, its periodic economic crises and its threats to the economic security of individual workers. In the years after the Second World War, Americans expended a good deal more effort trying to correct the lack of economic security than the Soviets did to correct the lack of freedom.

Another postwar question hinged on the unity of the modern world. It was indisputably one world in the sense that there existed a close-knit, interdependent economy, that political events and environmental changes affected the whole globe, and that world cultures and religions interacted as never before. But it was far from homogeneous. All admired the steam turbine and stood in awe of nuclear fission, but beyond the material level schemes of values diverged. No people wished to be subordinated to another, or to an international body, or to lose its way of life in a uniform global civilization.

After the Second World War, as after the First, an international organization was set up to prevent war in the future. A conference of all anti-Axis powers, held at San Francisco in 1945, founded the United Nations (UN) and drew up its charter. The new organization was designed to maintain international peace and security and to encourage cooperative solutions to international problems. Although it was widely acknowledged that peace would depend primarily on the Great Powers, all states, regardless of size, would be represented. Two agencies were central. The General Assembly was a deliberative body in which all member states, however small, had an equal vote. The Security Council, whose primary responsibility was to preserve peace, consisted of the five Great Powers, who were to be permanent members, and ten rotating members chosen for two-year terms. Apart from the two superpowers, the United States and the U.S.S.R., it was not easy to define the Great Powers in 1945, but the permanent seats were assigned to the United States, the Soviet Union, Great Britain, France, and China.[1]

The United Nations

Each permanent member had a veto power. Thus the Security Council could act on important matters only if the Great Powers were unanimous. Although widely criticized, the veto was accepted as necessary. In major crises the agreement of the Great Powers would be needed to maintain world peace. The U.S.S.R. demanded the veto most frankly, but the United States would not have joined without this safeguard. In the following years, however, even small countries refused to abide by judgments of the United Nations. No nation, large or small, was yet willing to forgo its independence or subordinate itself to an international body with the authority to put down violence, but there was much hope, and even confidence, that the authority and prestige of the UN would grow with time.

The United Nations had 51 original members. To symbolize the strong American commitment (and the contrast with America's earlier refusal to join the League of Nations), its headquarters was located in New York. The charter provided for the admission of new members, including the former Axis countries and their satellites, and also wartime neutrals, so that it could be truly international. From 1947 to 1955 a few additional states were

---

[1]Nationalist China (the Republic of China, or Taiwan) occupied the seat until 1971, when the People's Republic of China (Communist China) replaced it. By the early twenty-first century there were growing demands to expand the number of permanent seats on the Security Council by adding other large nations from Asia, Africa, and Latin America.

The United Nations was established to resolve international conflicts and to foster peaceful exchanges between nations, but it also adopted a Declaration of Universal Human Rights. This picture of an early UN meeting shows a representative of the Philippines, Pedro Lopez, calling for the establishment and protection of a free press in all nations of the world.
(Hulton-Deutsch Collection/Corbis)

Membership expands

admitted; in 1955, 16 more; and in the next several decades, after decolonization and other changes, the organization expanded so that by 2005 it counted over 190 members. In 1948, in good part because of the persuasive powers of the American delegate Eleanor Roosevelt, it adopted a sweeping Declaration of Universal Rights, but left unanswered the means of implementing it.

The United Nations and its Security Council failed to fulfill the role projected for it in the early postwar era because of the tensions between the American-led Western powers and the Soviets. Although the UN remained one of the few arenas where the Americans and Soviets could meet and debate, it was powerless to prevent the two superpowers from drifting further and further apart. On the other hand it helped from the beginning to mediate regional disputes and to play a role in peacekeeping missions. With the later expansion of the UN to include the nations of the Third World—a term devised to describe the developing countries, mostly former colonial countries, not directly aligned with either the Western or Soviet camp—the General Assembly became a forum for debate in which the developing nations, critical of the wealthier West, vehemently voiced their social and economic grievances.

The Cold War: Origins and Nature

The Second World War left only the United States and the Soviet Union still standing in any strength. The United States emerged physically unscathed from the war, its economy stronger than ever before. Although it demobilized much of its wartime military force, it alone possessed the atomic bomb. The Soviet Union had been devastated by the war, in which over 20 million of its population had perished, but it was still a formidable military power, with 4 million soldiers under arms and in control of populations and territories in central and eastern Europe well beyond its pre-1939 boundaries. It became common to speak of the two countries as superpowers—continental land giants, possessing enormous resources, overshadowing all other states, including the long-dominant nations of western Europe.

In the kind of two-superpower system that emerged after the Second World War, each power can readily identify its only dangerous enemy. A diplomatic equilibrium is more difficult to sustain in such situations because each views the other power's every action as possible aggression or provocation; and each, ignorant of the other's strength, exaggerates the power and danger of its enemy. After 1945 the United States and the U.S.S.R. fell into this unhappy relationship. It was compounded by a deep-seated ideological tension between capitalist democracy and Marxist-Leninist communism that dated back to the Bolshevik Revolution of 1917. The widening diplomatic, geopolitical, and ideological clash of interests came to be known as the Cold War, so called because the antagonisms and rivalries, intense though they were, always fell short of open or direct military hostilities between the two powers.

The Cold War

It was not possible for anyone to know what Stalin, who dictated all decisions, or his lieutenants in the Kremlin, really believed or intended at the end of the Second World War. Probably they considered a clash between the U.S.S.R. and the Western capitalist powers as inevitable at some point in the future. Probably they were disturbed by the ambitious goals of American capitalism, which sought markets in eastern Europe and elsewhere, and by the American monopoly of the atomic bomb. They themselves undoubtedly saw an opportunity to consolidate their hold over territories gained during the war (or regained, since the new Soviet state had lost control of some of these territories at the end of the First World War), and to create an outer buffer zone for Soviet national security. Undoubtedly they also saw in the aftermath of the Second World War, as of the First, an opportunity to promote the international Communist cause.

Whether the Soviets were acting to protect their national security, fulfill old Russian territorial ambitions antedating communism, or promote communism on a world scale, President Truman and his advisers and a great majority of the American people became convinced that the Soviets were bent on consolidating their grip on central and eastern Europe and then embarking on a worldwide Communist offensive. The American government therefore developed a global strategy of "containment," by which the United States and its allies would seek to "contain" this new Soviet offensive. Although the American government would take direct military steps mainly in reaction to Soviet expansion or threats of expansion, many people in the United States came to ascribe almost all of the complex social and political unrest on the globe to initiatives launched by the Kremlin.

Containment

In Europe, at the close of hostilities, Soviet armies occupied eastern Europe and Germany as far west as the Elbe River. American, British, and French armies held the remainder of Germany, most of Austria, and all of Italy. During the war, the armed forces liberating an area exercised political authority. In that way, the sweep of the Red Army gave the Soviets political control over much of central and eastern Europe; 100 million people passed under Soviet domination. On the other hand, the United States excluded the Soviets from any active role in its occupation of Italy (and, in Asia, of Japan). For the

The Allied military victory over Nazi Germany was followed by new distrust and conflict in Europe. The Soviet Union took control over Communist satellite states, creating what Winston Churchill called an "iron curtain" against free institutions and ideas. This picture shows Churchill giving a famous speech in March 1946 in Fulton, Missouri, where he first described the new iron curtain that had descended across Eastern Europe.

(Associated Press, AP)

Soviet Union, occupation meant full control over a nation's political, economic, and social institutions and the right to shape the occupied country in its own image. The Western powers, on the other hand, had hoped for pluralist and democratic societies, which would have been open to Western trade and influence. During the war the Americans and British had conceded Soviet predominance in eastern Europe, which the Soviets had liberated from the Nazis, but they soon resented the transformation of Poland and other East European countries into Soviet-dominated Communist states.

For Stalin, however, this kind of transformation was the only way to guarantee "friendly regimes" on his borders. Beginning as early as the Potsdam conference in July 1945, Truman denounced the Soviets for violating their pledge of free elections for the East European states and for failing to cooperate in the joint occupation of Germany. American diplomats began to believe that Soviet control over eastern Europe was similar to the Nazi and Fascist aggression of the 1930s, to which Truman himself frequently compared it. Stalin may have been acting more as a Russian nationalist bent on protecting Russian national security than as a champion of worldwide Communist revolution, but his stubbornness and paranoia about capitalist encirclement, and his lack of concern for world public opinion, made it difficult for the West to deal with him in the Cold War or to distinguish between legitimate Soviet security needs and an expansionist, Communist missionary zeal.

Concerns about Soviet expansion

A series of Soviet actions fed the belief that Stalin's ambitions transcended eastern Europe. In Asia, as pledged at Yalta, the Soviets had declared war on Japan in August 1945 and moved into Manchuria, where they were well positioned to help the Chinese Communists. In Korea, once the Japanese were defeated, the Soviets by agreement occupied the northern part of the country but also took steps to consolidate their occupation zone into a Communist government. Iran was another trouble spot. The Americans, British, and Russians had jointly occupied Iran during the war to forestall a Nazi takeover, but the Soviets refused to evacuate their troops at the stipulated time and pressed for oil concessions (such as the British and Americans already enjoyed).

The Soviets also sought a trusteeship over the former Italian colonies in North Africa, within easy reach of the Suez Canal; and they massed troops on the Turkish border, pressing for joint control over the Black Sea straits and for naval access to the Mediterranean through the Dardanelles—an old tsarist goal. The British, acting again in their earlier role as the "Western" guardians of the Mediterranean and Middle East, bolstered the Turkish defenses despite their own financial weakness. In Greece, in a civil war which raged from 1946 to 1949, Communist guerrillas battled the British-supported royalist, or nationalist, army. Stalin, perhaps recognizing his wartime agreement with Churchill that Greece would remain in the Western sphere of influence, lent little aid to the Communists, but Tito's new Communist regime in Yugoslavia helped the Communist guerrillas. The Communist pressures on Turkey, Greece, and Iran aroused British and American concerns about Soviet strategic designs on the eastern Mediterranean and on the oil reserves of the Middle East.

One casualty of the postwar tension was a plan for international super-vision of nuclear weapons. The United States knew that it was only a mat-ter of time before the Soviets (and other nations) could build the atomic bomb, since the scientific basis for it was known. At the moment the British alone shared the secret. The United States proposed in 1946 that atomic energy be con-trolled by an international authority and that its use be limited to peaceful purposes. Such an international body would have the right to send inspectors into any country to check violations and enforce sanctions that would not be subject to veto in the Security Council. The Soviets objected and would not give up their veto. The idea of foreigners freely exam-ining their society was repugnant to them. They questioned the good faith of the United States, which would not destroy its atomic bombs or halt further testing and production until the proposed international authority was established (many Americans also opposed international controls on their own nuclear arms). The British, in turn, fearful of an Amer-ican relapse into isolationism, undertook to become a nuclear power on their own. The plan for international control foundered on mutual suspicion and mistrust. The Soviets proceeded with their own atomic research (and efficient espionage), which yielded results even sooner than expected. In 1949 the Soviets successfully tested an atomic bomb, and the nuclear arms race, universally dreaded, now began.

Mutual mistrust

The political conflicts had meanwhile deepened in 1946 and 1947. The American pol-icy of containment, as formulated by the State Department, postulated that the Russians would expand wherever a power vacuum existed. Advocates for the strategy of containment argued that the West should show both patience and firmness, and in time Soviet society itself might change. In the meantime, however, the West needed to maintain its military strength and use economic and other counterpressures to resist the Soviets. Containment, the cornerstone of American policy, came to be interpreted in more rigorously military terms than some of its early proponents had intended. Meanwhile Churchill, even before the Soviets had fully completed the transformation of eastern Europe into Communist satellites, made an eloquent speech in March 1946 in which he described the "iron curtain" that had descended between eastern and western Europe—"from Stettin in the Baltic to Trieste in the Adriatic." That spring the United States turned down a pending Soviet request for a recon-struction loan, Congress having decided that Lend-Lease should end with the war, and also cut off reparations deliveries to the Soviets from the American occupation zone of Germany.

In 1947 financially strained Great Britain, forced to cut back on its commitments in the Mediterranean, informed Washington that it could no longer aid the anti-Communist forces in Greece or support Turkey in its resistance to Soviet pressures. The United States quickly moved to fill the vacuum. Truman not only agreed to provide the necessary assis-tance in the Mediterranean but at the same time also formulated in March 1947 a broad national policy to contain communism everywhere—"to assist free peoples who are resist-ing attempted subjugation by armed minorities or by outside pressures." The Truman Doctrine committed the United States to unprecedented involvement in global military and economic affairs. The Marshall Plan, designed to hasten European economic recovery and hence check Commu-nist expansion, was also announced in the spring of 1947.

The Truman Doctrine

The American national security state began to take shape. A National Security Coun-cil was created to advise the president on security matters, and a Central Intelligence Agency (CIA) was created to coordinate the gathering of intelligence. The CIA soon received authorization to conduct covert operations as well. The authority of the executive branch to conduct foreign policy grew. In 1948 the United States adopted its first peace-time military draft.

The Soviets in their turn denounced the American capitalist and imperialist "warmon-gers." With the United States arming Greece and Turkey; American air bases established in the Middle East; American armed forces in occupation of Japan, Okinawa, and South Korea; and the Americans possessing the atomic bomb, the Soviets felt threatened and encircled. Soviet suspicions mounted after 1947, but they also drew on memories that went back to Western intervention in the Russian Revolution and civil war in 1917–1920, the Soviets' exclusion from the Munich Pact, and the delay in opening up a second front in the Second World War as well as the cessation of Lend-Lease at the end of the war and the rejection of a requested post-war loan.

Soviet suspicions

In 1947 the Soviets decided they needed to reassert closer control over all Communist parties in every part of the world. They therefore reestablished in new form the old Com-munist International, or Comintern, which had been abandoned in 1943 as a gesture of wartime cooperation and goodwill, renaming it the Communist Information Bureau, or Cominform. The Soviets also replaced coalition governments in central and eastern Europe, in which the Communists had formerly shared power, with regimes dominated by Communist parties. In Czechoslovakia, for example, where President Benes's democratic coalition had been viewed as a possible bridge between East and West, the Czech Commu-nist party, faced with defeat in a forthcoming election, seized power in February 1948. By this time, the postwar Soviet-American suspicions and conflicts had created a mutual per-ception of permanent dangers, which each side sought to counter by its own assertive political or military actions. The increasingly bitter Cold War therefore spread into the local disputes and political confrontations that were constantly developing in Europe, Asia, and elsewhere around the globe.

Germany: The Berlin Blockade and the Airlift of 1948–1949

The key to the rebuilding of Europe, and the most critical area of Soviet-Western con-tention, was Germany, divided by Allied agreement into four zones and occupied by the United States, the Soviet Union, Britain, and France. The Allies had agreed to joint Allied policies for a defeated Germany, even though each of the four powers was to occupy its separate zone. Berlin also was divided into four separate Allied sectors, with joint admin-istration for the city as a whole. All had agreed that Germany should pay reparations, both in capital equipment and current production, mainly to the Soviet Union, which had suf-fered most from German military destruction, and that limits should be placed on German productive capacity.

The Soviet closure of the railways and roads into Berlin provoked one of the most dramatic events of the early Cold War: the Berlin Airlift. For almost a year (1948–1949) the Americans and their Western allies flew supplies into the isolated city on military aircraft such as the plane in this picture. Images of the airlift became part of the evolving Cold War struggle for international public opinion and an enduring symbol of the links between West Berlin and the Western Allies.
(Hulton-Deutsch Collection/Corbis)

At the war's end the Americans, supported by the British, quickly came to favor the economic reconstruction of Germany to accelerate European recovery and to reduce European dependence on American financial aid. The Ruhr, in the western zone, was still Europe's industrial heartland. The Soviets, on the other hand, were determined to use German resources to repair the devastation in their own country. They removed large amounts of food and stripped entire plants of machinery in their zone. The Western Allies refused to

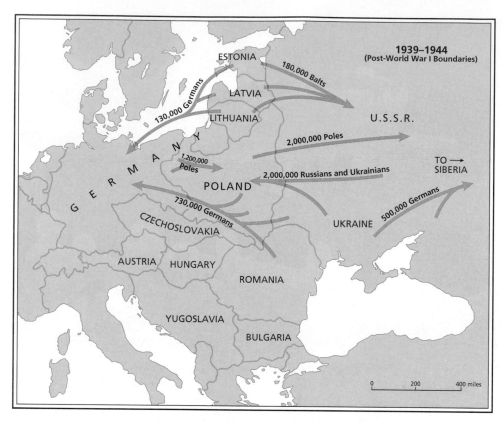

DEPORTATION AND RESETTLEMENT, 1939–1950

The age-old distribution of nationalities in central and eastern Europe was radically transformed between 1939 and 1950. About 6 million Jews died in the Holocaust, with over 300,000 survivors emigrating to Israel by 1950, and millions of Germans, Poles, and others were forcibly uprooted.

Left panel: **The first stage began with the Nazi–Soviet Pact of 1939, after which the Germans occupied western Poland, while the Russians annexed eastern Poland and the three Baltic republics. Western Poland received Poles expelled from Germany, while in eastern Poland about 2 million Poles were deported to Siberia, being replaced by about the same number of Russians and Ukranians. Many Estonians, Latvians, and Lithuanians were moved to other parts of the Soviet Union. Thousands of Germans were "returned" to Germany from the Baltic republics and from places such as Romania, where they had long formed German enclaves. The "Volga Germans," Tatars, and others in south Russia were sent to Siberia.**

permit the dismantling of factories in their zones and insisted that the Soviets take their share of current production only from their own zone. By May 1946 joint administration of Germany had all but broken down. Early in 1947 the United States and Britain united their two zones; the French, overcoming their initial reluctance to see a revived Germany, soon merged their zone as well. The Western powers encouraged the reconstruction of governments in the individual German states and the convening of a constituent assembly to set up a federal republic. The Soviets, in their zone, took steps to establish a Communist-dominated government. Two Germanys were emerging.

Two Germanys emerge

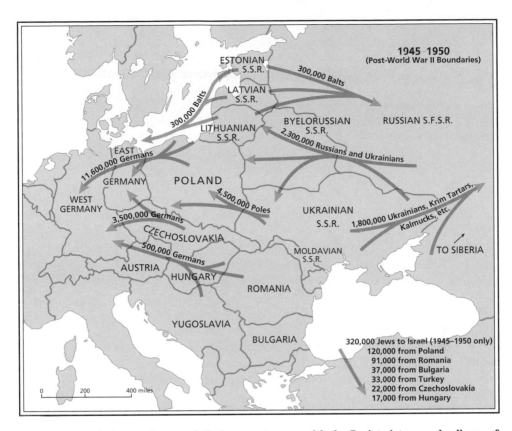

1945 1950
(Post-World War II Boundaries)

Right panel: **A second stage of displacements came with the Soviet victory and collapse of Hitler's Reich. The German–Polish frontier was now moved westward to the Oder River. Millions of Germans from east of the Oder, along with other millions from the Sudeten regions of Czechoslovakia, from Hungary, and from Romania, were thrown back into what remained of Germany, most fleeing to the Western zone. Poles streamed into what had been Germany east of the Oder; others came into Poland from Ukraine. Russians moved into what had been eastern Poland and the Baltic states. Ukranians and various non-Russian minorities were sent to Siberia. Some Balts escaped to the West; others were redistributed to various places in the Soviet Union.**

Amid all of these movements of people, the most conspicuous, long-term changes, in addition to the virtual disappearance of East European Jews, were the expulsion of the Germans from Eastern Europe and a westward movement of Poles and Russians.

(Westermanns Atlas zur Weltgeschichte)

In June 1948 the Western powers, recognizing the need for drastic currency reform to cope with inflation and encourage West German economic revival, suddenly revoked the old worthless currency and at a 1-to-10 ratio issued a new German mark, the Deutsche mark. The Soviets, who had not been consulted, objected to this violation of the wartime agreement to treat Germany as a single economic unit. In retaliation they blockaded all road and rail access to Berlin, which lay 100 miles deep within the Soviet zone. The blockade was a sharp challenge and test of will. If the West abandoned Berlin, it could lose authority in all Europe and open the way for Soviet westward expansion, and perhaps expansion

Berlin blockade and airlift

elsewhere. Knowing that they could not resort to military measures against the much stronger Soviet ground forces, the Allies responded with a massive airlift. For close to a year, American and Western aircraft flew in thousands of tons of food and other supplies to the occupation forces and to the 3 million inhabitants of West Berlin. The Soviets harassed the planes but avoided direct confrontation and, finally, in May 1949 lifted the blockade.

Each side now proceeded with the formation of a German government. The Federal Republic of Germany, its capital in the small Rhineland city of Bonn, came into existence in September 1949; the German Democratic Republic, its capital in the eastern sector of Berlin, one month later. There were now two Germanys, and the division of Europe had hardened along a rigid new political boundary.

The Atlantic Alliance

In 1948 Britain, France, Belgium, the Netherlands, and Luxembourg formed a West European Union for collective self-defense, but it had only limited military resources. In 1949 the United States took the lead in creating a larger military alliance and collective security system. The United States, Canada, and ten European nations met in Washington and agreed to military arrangements for the joint defense of western Europe. The Atlantic Pact was a military alliance of unlimited duration and broad scope: "an armed attack against one or more" was to be considered "an attack against all." The United States formally committed itself to the security of western Europe and agreed to supply funds and equipment for European rearmament. It was the first such military alliance of its kind in American history.

NATO

The North Atlantic Treaty Organization (NATO) emerged with a network of military arrangements and a chain of command headed by General Eisenhower. Because West Germany remained the most vulnerable target for Soviet expansion, large numbers of American troops (eventually over 300,000) were stationed there as the nucleus of the NATO armed forces. But with overwhelming Soviet superiority in ground forces, the NATO defense strategy was based primarily on American air power rather than on ground troops alone. The treaty solemnly affirmed American determination not to abandon the Continent. In later years the West Europeans became restive with American leadership, or, alternatively, feared an American decoupling from Europe, but NATO remained western Europe's shield against Soviet aggression. The Truman Doctrine, the Marshall Plan, and the North Atlantic Treaty Organization were the three prongs of the American and Western response to a potential Soviet challenge.

Meanwhile the West European countries, with the aid of the Marshall Plan, were making an impressive economic recovery and cooperating with each other (the Marshall Plan is discussed in the next section of this chapter). The Soviets could not be expected to view with equanimity the revival and growing unity of western Europe. American financial and military assistance, NATO, the containment policy, all defensive in Western eyes, and indeed provoked by Soviet expansionism, were hostile acts from the Soviet perspective. The Soviet Union drew its six satellite or client states, variously styled people's republics or people's democracies, closer to it. It formalized economic ties by creating in 1949 a Council for Mutual Economic Aid and a few years later coordinated the existing network of military alliances in the Warsaw Pact of 1955. The Soviets added to their military and air power and continued their nuclear research.

By 1949 Stalin's postwar expansion seemed contained and Truman could claim success for his policies. The Soviets had dropped their demands on Turkey and departed from Iran. Insurrectionary strikes launched by Communist parties in western Europe had failed, as did a Communist bid for power in Italy in the elections of 1948, in which the Vatican and the United States strongly supported the anti-Communist camp. Marshal Tito in 1948 successfully defied the Cominform, and Yugoslavia went its separate Communist way. In Greece the American- and British-backed Greek royalists triumphed in 1949 against the Communist guerrillas. The Soviet blockade of Berlin had failed to drive the West from the city.

The rivalry over Europe thus led to a stalemate by about 1950. The Soviet threat to western Europe diminished. The continent remained divided into a western and eastern Europe, Germany into two Germanys, *Stalemate in Europe* Berlin into West and East Berlin. After the failure of the Soviet blockade of Berlin, there was no such overt conflict in Europe. Despite renewed threats to Berlin, each side recognized the strength and security concerns of the other. But any thoughts that the world might settle into peace, no matter how uneasy, were shattered in June 1950. The Western-Soviet struggle shifted to Asia.

The Revival of Japan

In Asia events and new conflicts also developed rapidly in the early postwar years. The Chinese Communists triumphed over the Nationalists and Mao Zedong proclaimed the People's Republic of China in 1949. In Japan the United States used its military occupation from 1945 to 1952 to foster parliamentary institutions and revive the Japanese economy.

Rejecting Soviet demands for a share in the occupation of Japan, the *The occupation of* United States, with British and French approval, lodged full authority in *Japan* General Douglas MacArthur as supreme commander of the occupation forces. Responding in part to the new Cold War tensions, the American occupation encouraged economic revival and political reconstruction, not vindictiveness; and the Japanese, stunned by their disastrous defeat, were willing to cooperate. In the interests of stability the emperor received special status and was shielded from trial or even criticism. A new constitution in 1946 ended divine-right rule, transferred sovereignty from the emperor to the people, established machinery for parliamentary government, gave women the vote, and encouraged local self-government. The constitution "forever" renounced war and the threat or use of force as a means of settling international disputes; the small Japanese armed forces were to be restricted to defensive purposes. Although trials of Japanese war criminals were held, there were no extensive purges. The Japanese paid reparations to Asian nations that had been the victims of Japanese conquest but did not even years later fully acknowledge the brutality that had accompanied these conquests.

Efforts at social and economic reform under the occupation were less sweeping than originally planned. The large family holdings in heavy industry and banking were dissolved, but within a short time new forms of economic concentration replaced them. Labor unions were reinstituted but their powers were curtailed. When the occupation inaugurated a program of land redistribution, with a limit on large landholdings, small farmers lacked the means to purchase the land offered them. Although a moderate Socialist party emerged and militant activists in later years frequently demonstrated their discontent, political control remained in the hands of conservatives drawn from the upper social classes. By the end of the occupation the Liberal Democratic party (a conservative party) dominated the government and long continued to do so.

Economic recovery

The conservative-led political consensus emphasized a strong commitment to economic recovery and growth. Like western Europe, Japan, too, recovered rapidly. In 1945 it had been prostrate, a fourth of its housing destroyed, agricultural and industrial output reduced to half its prewar level, its shipping and financial reserves gone. Under the occupation, and with American help, the economy revived and expanded; by 1954 its gross national product reached prewar levels. Labor self-discipline and social patterns of deference and loyalty kept industrial unrest to a minimum. Close cooperation between government and business encouraged savings, investment, research, and economic growth. The very need to rebuild and renovate the economy from the bottom up proved an advantage.

Beginning in the early 1950s the economy grew at an amazing rate of nearly 10 percent each year; manufacturing output, at 14 percent. Despite the repatriation of millions of Japanese from Manchuria, Korea, and other parts of Asia and the addition of large numbers of rural workers to the labor force, Japan still had a labor shortage. The response was an intense level of automation. Japan became a pioneer in advanced high technology, and technological innovations sustained its economic growth. Japanese consumer products soon entered the world economy, creating a flow of exports that came to rival those of the Americans and the Europeans. Because a large military establishment was forbidden, expenditures that might have gone into the military, as in the past, were now plowed into industrial investments. By the 1950s Japan was once again a major economic power, a bastion of social stability, and a major new element in the global economy. For the Soviets the revival of Japan under American auspices, which they saw as a counterweight to Soviet influence and as a bulwark against revolution in Asia, loomed as still another threat.

Containment in Asia: The Korean War

The Western Allies and the Soviet Union had agreed during the Second World War that Korea, once an object of imperialist rivalry between Japan and tsarist Russia, but under Japanese rule since 1910, would become free and independent after Japan's defeat. In 1945 the United States, for reasons of military expediency, proposed that Soviet troops temporarily occupy the northern part of the country down to the 38th parallel; United States troops would temporarily occupy the southern half. But postwar negotiations for a unified Korea foundered. The U.S.S.R. established a satellite government in its occupation zone under the Communist leader Kim Il Sung and built up North Korean military strength. The United States developed its own client state in the south and lent economic and military assistance. In 1947 a UN commission sought to sponsor nationwide elections, but the Soviet Union would not permit supervision of elections in the north. The elections in the south in May 1948 resulted in the presidency of Syngman Rhee, who, despite superficial forms of democracy, governed autocratically. Anticommunism in Korea and elsewhere did not necessarily equate with democracy. After the elections the United States withdrew its occupation forces but continued to provide military and economic support. The Soviet Union also removed its occupation forces but left behind a well-trained and well-equipped North Korean army. Despite the original intention, two Koreas had come into existence.

By 1950 the situation in East Asia, as we have seen, had altered dra- *East Asia in 1950*
matically. Japan had revived. The United States through its postwar occupation had helped to create a stable Japan, friendly to the West and with a
prospering economy. In addition, the Chinese Communists, with only limited and grudging Soviet support, had triumphed over the Nationalists in a long civil war and in 1949 had
proclaimed the Chinese People's Republic. Although relations between the Chinese Communists and the Soviets were neither warm nor cordial, the two countries shared similar
concerns about the revival of Japan and the growth of American influence in East Asia.
They therefore drew together in a mutual defense pact in February 1950, and the U.S.S.R.
campaigned to have the People's Republic of China replace Nationalist China in the
United Nations. When this campaign failed, the Soviets in protest boycotted the Security
Council meetings.

Although border skirmishes between North and South Korea had been frequent, the
sudden, full-scale North Korean invasion of the south in June 1950 came as a surprise. In
the West it was seen as an open act of military aggression, the first such clear-cut military
aggression of the Cold War. Because of the boldness of their initiative and their superior
forces, the North Koreans expected a quick victory. They gambled that the United States
would not intervene and that the outside world would lodge no more than a moral protest,
thus allowing the Communists to gain control of the entire Korean peninsula.

The precise inspiration for the invasion remains somewhat unclear. North Korea, concerned over the south's avowed ambition to unite the country on pro-Western terms, seems
to have taken the initiative on its own. It is known, however, that Stalin was aware of the
North Korean intentions and even allowed the Soviet military to help plan aspects of the
invasion, counting on a quick victory and a limited international response. Yet the timing
of the invasion seems to have surprised the Soviets who, as noted, were boycotting the
Security Council, unable to exercise their veto when the Council condemned the invasion
and authorized military countermeasures. The Chinese, recovering from their civil war,
barely established in power, and still facing a challenge from the Nationalists in Taiwan,
seemed unlikely to have initiated it. In any case, even if the attack caught their Communist
allies somewhat off guard, the sweeping initial successes of the North Koreans offered the
Soviets and the Chinese an opportunity to check the growing American influence in Japan
and East Asia. The Soviets quietly furnished military aid to North Korea and denounced
the United States for intervening in Asian affairs—on the very doorsteps of the U.S.S.R.
and the People's Republic of China.

For the American government, and for most Americans, it was difficult to believe
that the attack had not been secretly engineered in Moscow or that the North Koreans
were capable of independent action. The Americans assumed that the Soviets, probing in
Asia for weak spots as they had elsewhere, had found one and now must be halted.
Korea, like Berlin, became another test of American and Western will.
Truman, already concerned about the "loss of China" (the formula used at *A test of will*
the time by his political critics for the Chinese Communist victory in
1949), saw the North Korean invasion as a test of the "free world's commitment to liberty." The attack challenged the entire system of collective security and
containment built to stem the tide of Soviet communism. The Soviets, he said, had
passed "beyond the use of subversion" to "armed invasion and war." Without asking for
an American declaration of war because it was deemed to be a "police action," Truman,
in conformity with the Security Council resolution, ordered American combat troops to
Korea and called for air strikes above the 38th parallel. General MacArthur, the wartime

The Korean War was a key test for President Harry Truman's policy of containing communism, yet, like all modern wars, it disrupted the lives of millions of civilians, including those who knew little about the larger political issues at stake. This Korean girl and her baby brother were photographed near an American tank in the summer of 1951, but their expressions convey some of the timeless, local struggle to survive amid the violent international conflicts of governments and global powers.
(Time Life Pictures/Getty Images)

hero of the Pacific who had successfully presided over the occupation of Japan, was named commander of the UN multinational forces, of which the Americans made up the major part.

In the early fighting in the summer of 1950 the American-led United Nations forces were driven south to the very water's edge, where they faced expulsion from the peninsula. But in September MacArthur made a remarkable amphibious landing on the western side of the peninsula, drove the North Koreans back above the 38th parallel, and then rapidly moved north toward the Yalu River, the boundary between Korea and the People's Republic of China. Mao, incensed at the arrival of a multinational army on the Chinese border, took action to assert China's international importance. In late October, a large Chinese "voluntary" army suddenly appeared and within two weeks drove the advancing UN armies back below the 38th parallel. It was an entirely new war, to which China was now committed. The European allies, at first gratified by the American show of determination, grew worried that the war could escalate into a global, possibly nuclear, conflict.

Meanwhile the battle lines seesawed. MacArthur forced the Chinese and North Korean troops to retreat, again crossed the 38th parallel, and demanded unconditional surrender. He proposed to blockade the Chinese coast, bomb Chinese cities, encourage the Chinese Nationalists to attack the Chinese mainland, and even seal off Korea from China by a field of radioactive waste. Truman recognized, however, that MacArthur's threats could lead to full-scale war with China, to Soviet intervention, and to a wider war in which the United States would lack the full support of its European allies. When the general publicly flouted the president's authority, Truman replaced him with another commander and sought to negotiate a truce.

Cease-fire and armistice

In July 1951 a cease-fire agreement brought large-scale fighting to a halt, but armistice negotiations dragged on, deadlocked over the repatriation of North Korean prisoners who did not wish to return home. In July 1953 under General Eisenhower's presidency an armistice was signed, the line of partition drawn roughly where the fighting had begun three years earlier, at the 38th parallel, with provision for a demilitarized buffer zone. The partition hardened into another long-term division. North Korea became a rigid Communist dictatorship, and increasingly so under Kim Il Jong, son of the founder of the North Korean state. South Korea, unable to achieve political democracy under Syngman Rhee or for a long time under his successors, nonetheless developed a dynamic capitalist economy, far outstripping North Korea in economic strength. At the beginning of the next century, many decades later, over 40,000 American troops remained stationed in South Korea and the increasingly isolated North Korean regime was trying to build a small arsenal of nuclear weapons; but negotiations were beginning to reduce some of the tensions between the two Koreas.

The Korean War was costly for all sides. The United States, which furnished half the ground troops and almost all the naval and air power for the 15-nation UN force, suffered over 54,000 deaths in the undeclared war, close to half as many as in the First World War; the American wounded were estimated at over 100,000. But the South Koreans suffered over 1 million casualties in dead, wounded, and missing; and the North Koreans and the Chinese each lost about equal numbers. In all some 3 to 4 million lives may have been lost in a war that the Soviets had fought by proxy.

Results of the Korean War

The war also affected the global economy. The United States alone spent over $15 billion, but the U.S. economy could not by itself supply all of America's military needs. The war therefore stimulated the economic growth of western Europe and Japan, and it also quickened the pressures for German rearmament. In American eyes, such costs were justified because a flagrant act of aggression had been checked, and the global containment strategy had achieved success in Asia. Most people in western Europe, even those who were concerned about MacArthur's recklessness, also found reassurance in the firm American response to a communist military invasion.

As seen in the Communist world, however, and indeed in many of the nonaligned countries in Asia such as India or Indonesia, the Korean War had prevented the United States, the great capitalist power, from reasserting Western imperialist supremacy in the East. In its efforts to create regional security pacts in Asia, the United States found little enthusiasm among the larger non-Communist Asian powers who disliked communism but also distrusted the West. Although the United States had been the least involved of all the Great Powers in nineteenth-century territorial imperialism in Asia, its new leadership of the Western world made it a symbol of Western oppression, buttressed by the suspicion that its free-world rhetoric only masked a drive to create world markets for American capitalism—an image assiduously cultivated by the Soviets and by the Chinese Communists.

On the other hand, its success in checking the North Korean act of aggression by force of arms reinforced the American belief that military strength and decisiveness could check Communist expansion anywhere in the world; containment would be global. The Korean War inaugurated an era of deep American involvement in Asia and served as prelude to an even longer and more costly conflict, the war in Vietnam in the following decade.

American involvement in Asia

The Korean War also had its political repercussions in Europe. Despite continuing misgivings in France and in other parts of Europe over a revival of German military strength, the Americans pressed for West German rearmament. When a French proposal for a European Defense Community (with a "European army," in which the Germans were to serve as "European soldiers") failed to pass the French legislature in 1954, West Germany was authorized to create an army of its own under the overall command of

NATO. Concern over a resurgent German militarism was receding. The West German constitution guaranteed civilian control over the military, and a strong antimilitarist movement had emerged in the country itself. In 1955 the Federal Republic of Germany became a full member of NATO.

Meanwhile, the Korean War hastened a formal peace treaty with Japan. In the peace treaty signed in 1951 in San Francisco by 50 nations, but without Soviet participation, no general reparations were exacted, but individual countries were to work out their own reparations agreements. In a separate security pact the United States retained military rights in Japan and occupied nearby islands, where, under agreement, the United States would remain as long as necessary for peace and security. A year later the American occupation of Japan formally ended. The Soviets made no move to return the Kurile Islands, which they had occupied at the end of the Second World War. The United States meanwhile signed security pacts with Australia, New Zealand, and the Philippines, reinforcing its global commitments.

Peace with Japan

The decades that followed the troubled international relations of the early Cold War brought new confrontations and crises—over Berlin, Cuba, Vietnam, the Middle East, and Africa, to name only the most important—and above all, a mounting nuclear arms race between the two superpowers and the stockpiling of the most formidable weaponry ever assembled. The nuclear arms race moved on to an even more deadly level of competition in late 1952, when the United States successfully tested its first thermonuclear or hydrogen bomb, hundreds of times more powerful than the atomic bomb used at Hiroshima. The Soviets at almost the same time, in 1953, also developed a hydrogen bomb. Both sides developed strategic delivery systems as well, thereby ensuring that neither side could gain a decisive military advantage in the evolving Cold War. But before continuing with the Cold War, we must examine in this and the following chapter many other developments of these years—the remarkable economic recovery and political reconstruction of western Europe, the reshaping of the global economy, the world of the Communist countries, and the emergence of new nations from the old Western colonial empires.

109.   WESTERN EUROPE: ECONOMIC RECONSTRUCTION

The Second World War had left Europe in a worse state of disorder than the First. It had ruined one of the world's chief industrial areas and brought its economic system to collapse. Even when the worst local devastation was repaired, suffering and distress persisted. Europe could no longer pay for the imports that it needed. During the war the West Europeans, and especially the British, had used up their overseas investments and lost a good share of the shipping services they had once provided. Overseas countries had built up their own industries and needed those of Europe less, and the United States had taken over markets once in European hands.

At the same time, western Europe was not to be written off. Its population exceeded that of either of the superpowers. Even in ruins, it still possessed one of the world's leading industrial plants and the skills needed to rehabilitate and run it. The Europeans did not wish to be rescued by either of the superpowers. Most rejected communism as a modern form of enslavement. Yet they feared excessive dependence on the United States. Memories of the stock-market crash of 1929, the economic collapse of Europe after the withdrawal of American capital, and the Great Depression bred skepticism about American capitalism.

The Marshall Plan and European Recovery

For the non-Communist world, the single most important economic reality in the early postwar years was the productivity of the American economic system. The American economy had expanded enormously during the war. At the war's end the United States accounted for two-thirds of the world's industrial production and held two-thirds of the world's gold. Its gross national product was two and a half times higher than in 1939; its exports were three times greater. Despite predictions about postwar economic collapse, its economy grew at unprecedented rates in the 1950s and 1960s.

U.S. economic strength

When Lend-Lease ended after the war, the United States sent billions of dollars worth of goods to western Europe to relieve distress and made loans to individual states, especially to Britain. But the Europeans themselves quickly set about to rebuild their economies. Within two years, by 1947, the economies of western Europe were approaching prewar levels of production. American aid was still desperately needed, however, to continue the purchase of food, fuel, raw materials, and industrial parts essential to full recovery. By the spring of 1947 that recovery appeared at risk. The poorest harvest in a century was feared. With Cold War tensions mounting, Communist parties in France and Italy moved away from earlier cooperation in postwar reconstruction and launched a wave of strikes. Even if the Soviet Union was not actively promoting revolution in western Europe, understanding perhaps that the West would not tolerate overt revolution there, the Americans were concerned about European stability. Between the two superpowers the Soviets had more to gain by chaos in western Europe and the United States had more to gain by its rebuilding.

American economic aid so far had been improvised and piecemeal. In June 1947 Secretary of State George C. Marshall used the occasion of his Harvard commencement address to invite the Europeans to cooperate in drawing up blueprints for a broad program of reconstruction, for which the United States would provide the financial support. The plan, as formulated, was "directed not against country or doctrine, but against hunger, poverty, desperation, and chaos." To reinforce its nonpolitical character, the United States extended the invitation to all European governments, including the Soviet Union and the East European states. The Soviet Union rejected the proposal and forbade the participation of its East European satellites, denouncing the plan as "a new venture in American imperialism."

The Marshall Plan

The West European countries responded eagerly. Under the Marshall Plan, or European Recovery Program, as enacted by Congress, American aid was coordinated with each country's needs and with joint European priorities to maximize the benefits. The Office for European Economic Cooperation (OEEC) in Paris, with which the Americans worked closely, identified projects, coordinated the planning, and allocated the funds.

The results of the Marshall Plan exceeded the boldest anticipations of its American sponsors. The West Europeans utilized their technical and managerial skills to improve transportation facilities, modernize their infrastructure, and expand their productive capacity. They reduced trade barriers among themselves and facilitated trade by setting up a payments union. Hard currency, now available for imports, reduced the financial pressures on West

Results of the Marshall Plan

European governments and the need for further austerity. The Marshall Plan accelerated the recovery already under way, smoothed the recovery process, and encouraged the economic cooperation of the European countries with each other.

While the United States thus used its economic resources to help revive its competitors, the Marshall Plan also served American interests by restoring a world market, of which the United States would be a principal beneficiary. By creating markets for American exports, it helped fuel the postwar economic boom in the United States. The Americans satisfied their humanitarian impulse, served their economic needs, and reduced the drift of Europeans into the Communist camp. At the same time the Marshall Plan sharpened the division between the Soviet bloc and the West.

Economic Growth in Western Europe

For West Germany the currency reform of 1948, Marshall Plan aid, and the economic opportunities opened up by the Korean War ignited a stunning economic revival and expansion, the *Wirtschaftswunder,* or "economic miracle." By 1950 the Federal Republic of Germany was exceeding prewar Germany's production levels, and by 1958 it was the leading industrial country of western Europe. France, Italy, and other West European countries experienced an "economic miracle" also. For two and a half decades, from 1948 to 1974 (when a global recession set in), the western European economies grew at unprecedented and uninterrupted rates of growth. The West Europeans basked in prosperity and rising living standards. Europeans would later speak of the "silver '50s" and the "golden '60s"; the French would speak also of the "30 glorious years." Although Britain's economy, burdened by older industries and the loss of overseas markets, lagged behind the growth in other countries, it too grew faster than at any time in the interwar years.

The silver '50s and golden '60s

The prosperity of western Europe derived from a competitive, capitalist, free-market and private-enterprise economy, but it was accompanied almost everywhere by varying degrees of extensive economic planning, systematic government intervention, and a network of social services to help cope with the instability of competitive capitalism and the business cycle. No one anywhere wished to repeat the hard times and suffering of the Great Depression. Keynes's theories, first formulated in the 1930s but without many adherents at that time, took hold in the postwar era and dominated government policy in the 1950s and 1960s even when conservative governments were in control. Governments kept their economies under close surveillance and used their fiscal and monetary powers to promote investment, production, and employment and to control inflation. They took "countercyclical" measures; that is, at signs of decline in the business cycle they increased government spending. Full employment was accepted as a goal. Improved statistical techniques and economic forecasting, although far from precision instruments, made economic planning and "fine-tuning" feasible. Such planning, however, took the form of guidance and direction, not coercion, and differed markedly from the rigid, detailed, and doctrinaire centralized planning of the Soviet Union and Soviet bloc.

Economic planning and government intervention

In Britain, France, and Italy (less so in West Germany, which had lived through state control under the Nazis), the postwar governments also nationalized a number of the key sectors of the economy to bring them under government control. But even in these mixed economies, the private capitalist sector represented the major share of economic activity. In all western Europe economic growth became virtually an obsession as both governments and people came to expect growth rates far exceeding those of the past.

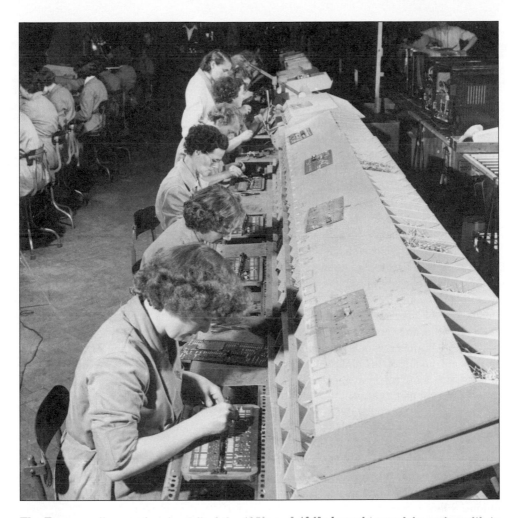

The European "economic miracle" of the 1950s and 1960s brought new jobs and wealth to workers throughout Europe. This picture of British workers in 1957 shows women assembling circuit panels for television sets, one of the important new consumer products in post–World War II economies and social life.

(Getty Images)

When the sustained economic growth led to a labor shortage, West Germany and other countries invited foreign workers to join their labor force. Turks, Greeks, Yugoslavs, Spaniards, Portuguese, and Italians (mostly from southern Italy) were invited in as "guest workers." Four and a half million workers arrived in the Federal Republic of Germany alone, over half of them Turks, who did not return home but often formed large unassimilated enclaves. After the postwar collapse of the European colonial empires, immigrants from the former European colonies in Asia, Africa, and the Caribbean also arrived in western Europe in large numbers. Beginning in the 1950s, a steady stream of immigrants flowed into Britain from India, Pakistan, the West Indies, and Africa. France drew large numbers from its former North African colonies, especially Algeria. The Netherlands became home for many Indonesians.

A steady stream of immigrants

Later political refugees also arrived in Europe from Vietnam and other parts of Asia. The new Europeans were often of different cultures, religion, racial composition, or skin color. Mosques became a common sight in European cities. The influx of guest workers and immigrants by the millions later created new social conflicts and resentments, especially in less affluent times. The growing presence of large immigrant communities led to new social friction, often overtly racial, testing the flexibility and tolerance of a European society that was becoming increasingly multiethnic and multicultural.

A postwar baby boom and an influx of at least 13 million immigrants and refugees increased the population of western Europe by 25 percent between 1945 and 1970. But by the 1960s the birth rate of the West Europeans began to level off and western Europe's population began to show signs of long-term decline.

Growth of the welfare state

In these same postwar years the welfare state grew, going well beyond its pre-1914 origins or its expansion in the interwar years. The postwar governments gave a high priority to social objectives, to what the French Resistance charter had called "a more just social order": the right to a suitable job, government compensation in the event of unemployment or disability, social security in old age, free or subsidized health care, and the redistribution of wealth and income through progressive taxation. The protection of the welfare state was intended to be universal, not confined, as in earlier times, to the poor and disadvantaged. Its social objectives could be achieved in the 1950s and 1960s because of a salutary interplay of government, management, and labor, which all shared in the consensus about investment and growth. Only later, from the late 1970s on, did the argument gather strength that all these entitlements had become excessive and an impediment to economic growth and competitiveness.

⌘ 110.   WESTERN EUROPE: POLITICAL RECONSTRUCTION

Western Europe also confronted overwhelming challenges of political reconstruction at the end of the war. Britain was economically exhausted and in the process of liquidating its empire. France, recovering from the collapse of 1940, the occupation, and the wartime Vichy regime, became engaged in costly colonial wars in Indochina and Algeria. Italy had to renew its political life after two decades of fascism. Germany, after the Nazi defeat, was divided and under military occupation. Nevertheless political reconstruction went forward. Britain resumed its role as the world's oldest parliamentary democracy; France and Italy adopted new constitutions; out of the western zone of occupied Germany the Federal Republic of Germany emerged in 1949.

The smaller states of western Europe also resumed their parliamentary democracies. Only Spain and Portugal remained under prewar dictatorships until those regimes also came to an end in the mid 1970s. The right to participate in political life continued to expand throughout western Europe. Women finally received the vote in France and Italy as the war drew to a close and in Switzerland in 1971. And in another suffrage reform that went almost unnoticed, the legal voting age in most countries was quietly reduced to 18 in the 1970s.

The spirit of reform

The earliest postwar elections showed the political strength of a new desire for social reforms. Wartime Resistance movements had called for a federal union of Europe to prevent future wars and had emphasized the need for economic and social rights as well as political freedom. Postwar governments were therefore asked to provide protection against the insecurities of old age, disability, ill health, and unemployment. Such ideals shaped the political debates and social reforms in the first years after 1945, but politics soon reverted to older patterns of bargain and compromise.

The welfare state idea persisted, as did the impulse for an integrated Europe, but politics became more pragmatic and less ideological. Socialists, following the Scandinavian model, became Social Democratic reformists, accepting capitalism but insisting that they could manage capitalist economies more effectively than liberals, centrists, or conservatives. In France and Italy the presence of large Communist parties, with strong attachments to the Soviet Union in the early postwar years, complicated matters. In the Federal Republic of Germany, Italy, and France, the Christian Democrats, drawing inspiration from Roman Catholic religious and ethical precepts, played a key role in shaping and governing the new regimes. They accepted the welfare state but backed away from the egalitarianism of the socialists and, over time, increasingly came to represent conservative and business interests.

Great Britain: Labour and Conservative

In Great Britain, the first parliamentary elections in ten years, in July 1945, unseated Winston Churchill and the Conservative-led wartime coalition and voted in a Labour government. For the first time in its history Labour had a majority of its own. Governing from 1945 to 1951, with Clement Attlee as prime minister, it set Britain on a new course of parliamentary socialism and the modern welfare state.

On the premise that the country's basic industries could not be left to the unplanned anarchy of capitalism and unregulated competition, the Labour government nationalized the Bank of England, the coal mines, electricity and gas, iron and steel, and other parts of the economy. Because four-fifths of industry remained in private hands, it was a mixed economy that emerged. At the *Labour government* same time Labour greatly expanded and revamped the social insurance program inherited from the Liberal reforms of 1906–1914. During the war, in 1942, the British economist William Henry Beveridge had prepared a government report that proposed to guarantee "full employment in a free society" and social security for all "from the cradle to the grave." Drawing on the Beveridge Report, Labour now extended insurance coverage for unemployment, old age, and other contingencies; inaugurated a comprehensive national health service; and increased income and inheritance taxes.

In the elections of 1951 Labour lost its majority in Parliament. The Conservatives returned to office and governed for the next 13 years under a succession of prime ministers. After 1964 the two parties alternated in office. The shifting electoral fortunes stemmed from disagreement within the country over the welfare state, dissatisfaction with the performance of the economy, and frustration at Britain's diminished global status.

During their years in office, the Conservatives restored some nationalized industries to private control but did little else to dismantle the welfare state. Both parties recognized, however, that the social reforms of the welfare state could be absorbed only if the economy prospered. But there were nagging economic problems. The liquidation of investments to pay for the Second World War, the loss of export markets, and a decline in income from shipping and other services adversely affected Britain's balance of payments and undermined the pound. With American financial aid, an intensified export drive, an austerity program that reduced imports, and a curtailment of military and imperial commitments, the economy improved and the country began to experience a modest

A modest prosperity

prosperity. But the British failed at the time to rebuild their obsolescent capital equipment and infrastructure as effectively as their West European neighbors across the Channel.

Such problems impeded the growth of Britain's economy and made British workers vulnerable to competition from more efficient foreign industries. When inflation set in during the late 1960s and intensified in the 1970s, the trade unions demanded wage increases to match rising prices. Strikes and prolonged work stoppages troubled the economy and divided British society. Until the late 1970s, when a new era opened, the question was whether Labour or the Conservatives could better manage British decline, not how they could overcome it.

Troubles in Northern Ireland

Meanwhile troubles in Northern Ireland persisted. After the partition in 1922, as noted earlier, the six predominately Protestant counties of Northern Ireland, had remained part of the United Kingdom. The Catholic minority, about one-third of the population, protested militantly that they were victims of political and economic discrimination and pressed for annexation to the Republic of Ireland. Open violence broke out in 1969, inflamed by the Irish Republican Army on the one hand and Protestant extremists on the other. In the sectarian violence that followed, over 3,000 persons lost their lives.

The French Republic: Fourth and Fifth

After the liberation of France, General Charles de Gaulle, the very incarnation of the Resistance, became provisional president and elections were held for a Constituent Assembly. Because no one wanted to reestablish the discredited Third Republic, the French undertook the process of creating a new republican government. The parties of the Right were discredited by their role in the Vichy regime, but the Left emerged from the war with new strength and prestige. The Communists, the Socialists, and the Popular Republican Movement (*Mouvement Républicain Populaire,* or MRP), a Catholic progressive party akin to Christian Democrats elsewhere on the Continent, formed the provisional government. The Left pressed for a systematic purge of collaborators, despite the difficul-

Purging collaborators

ties in determining levels of guilt. The purge had begun as soon as the army reached French soil, taking the form of angry drumhead trials and executions. Gradually, the process was brought under more orderly judicial procedures. Even so, the trials of Marshal Pétain and Pierre Laval were impassioned showpieces. The debate over collaboration and trials of collaborators continued to divide the country in later decades, in part because some of the most egregious acts of violence against the French Jews and others had originated with the French Vichy government and not the Nazi occupiers.

The Fourth Republic's machinery of government differed in only a few details from the Third. Once again the presidency was only ceremonial and the premier and cabinet were responsible to an all-powerful National Assembly. De Gaulle made no secret of his dislike for the new constitution, the return of party rivalries, and the dominant role of the legislature, all of which interfered with his vision of a strong France ready to resume a leadership role in world affairs. He resigned in protest in December 1946. The Communists, Socialists, and MRP continued their tripartite coalition under Socialist leadership until the Communists, in the heightened tensions of the Cold War, fomented a series of strikes and were expelled from the cabinet in May 1947.

Parliamentary division and ministerial instability grew more acute. Periodically de Gaulle returned to the political scene, heading a movement called the "Rally of the French People," which he described as "above parties." Except for the brief reform ministry of Pierre Mendès-France in 1954–1955, governmental ineffectiveness in the midst of domestic and foreign crises filled the public with cynicism and hostility.

"Rally of the French People"

Yet despite its record of political instability—25 cabinets from 1946 to 1958—the Fourth Republic enacted significant legislation. The provisional government had nationalized several key industries, and as in Britain a mixed economy gradually emerged. The existing social security legislation was expanded. An economic plan, drawn up by Jean Monnet, a farsighted economist and public official who later played a large role in the creation of the European Economic Community, enlarged and modernized the country's economic base and paved the way for industrial expansion. A flexible form of economic planning, inspired by Monnet, in which government, management, and labor played mutually reinforcing roles, became an accepted part of French economic life. By 1952 production levels were 1½ times those of 1938, and industrial output was growing at an annual rate of over 5 percent. From 1946 to 1966 production tripled. (In the half-century from 1889 to 1940, it had no more than doubled.) The country also displayed a demographic vitality, at least for a time, that confounded pessimists who had long worried about France's low birth rate.

What finally brought down the Fourth Republic was the strain of trying to preserve the old French colonial empire. France alone, of all the major powers, was almost continuously at war for close to 15 years, fighting colonial wars. It could almost envy the lot of Germany, Italy, and Japan who lost the Second World War but emerged from their defeats with no restless colonies to subdue. The new French constitution of 1946 gave the colonies representation in Paris but such reforms did not satisfy nationalists pressing for independence. From 1946 to 1954 the French forces unsuccessfully fought against independence movements in Indochina until they finally had to withdraw. Then, within a matter of months, the Arab movement for independence in Algeria rose up in another anticolonial war, which further drained France's material resources, political morale, and national confidence. The European settlers in Algeria and army leaders adamantly opposed French withdrawal and staged an insurrectionary coup in Algiers in May 1958. When civil war threatened, the country turned to the one man it believed could save the situation—Charles de Gaulle, then living quietly in self-imposed retirement. The army leaders, the settlers in Algeria, and the parties of the Right were convinced, given de Gaulle's solicitude for the army and French national pride, that he would maintain French control of Algeria. De Gaulle accepted the summons. In June 1958 the National Assembly invested him as premier, giving him emergency powers for six months, including the authority to prepare a new constitution.

Colonial wars

The Fifth French Republic thus emerged from the crisis in Algeria and from the political program of Charles de Gaulle. In the autumn of 1958 the new constitution was overwhelmingly accepted in a popular referendum, and de Gaulle was shortly thereafter elected president. The presidency, as de Gaulle had long urged, became the fulcrum of power. The president was the final authority in foreign affairs and national defense. The president named the prime minister (as the premier was now called) and had the right to dissolve the National Assembly, call for new elections, submit important questions to popular referendums, and assume emergency powers, all of which de Gaulle did during his years in office. Political instability disappeared; in the first 11 years of the Fifth Republic there were only three cabinets.

France under De Gaulle

DeGaulle settled the Algerian crisis in his own way. Sensitive to the revolution sweeping the colonial world, he came to recognize that France must accept a policy of independence for Algeria, which the country approved in a referendum in July 1962. Even earlier he granted independence to all of the French colonies in sub-Saharan Africa. With peace, governmental stability, and economic prosperity, the French reconciled themselves to the loss of empire and looked for new ways to play a leading role on the world scene under de Gaulle. France became the world's fifth industrial power in the 1960s, behind only the United States, the U.S.S.R., West Germany, and Japan. In 1960 France became the fourth nation, along with the United States, the U.S.S.R., and Britain, to develop a nuclear bomb. De Gaulle even created an independent nuclear strike force, but France also became western Europe's largest producer of nuclear energy for peacetime energy needs.

After the settlement of the Algerian crisis, de Gaulle built a kind of plebiscitary democracy by direct appeals to the electorate. Although civil liberties were preserved and free elections were maintained, the old democratic ferment disappeared. Skilled technicians ran the affairs of state, and de Gaulle, an uncrowned republican monarch, presided as arbiter over the nation's destinies.

May 1968

The nation grew restless. There was increasing skepticism about de Gaulle's technocratic system of government and his extravagant posturing in world affairs. Suddenly, in May 1968, grievances in the overcrowded universities sparked a revolt that led to demonstrations by hundreds of thousands of students and then brought 10 million workers out on strike, paralyzing the economy and threatening the regime itself. De Gaulle survived the revolt but only after assuring himself of army support. Stressing the threat of communism and domestic chaos, he won an overwhelming majority for his party in new elections. Although there was wide support for institutional reforms in French society, the country as a whole rejected the outburst of radical political agitation, which was similar to revolts of students and young people all over the globe in 1968. Educational reforms and other changes were introduced, but the strikes and social disruptions of 1968 hurt the French economy. In 1969 de Gaulle chose to turn a referendum on various constitutional and regional reforms into a vote of confidence in himself. When his proposed reforms lost by a small margin, he resigned and retired to his country estate, where he died a year later, an august, heroic, austere, and always controversial figure whose exploits in war and peace assured him a lasting place in France's history.

The Federal Republic of Germany

The Nuremberg Trials

To communicate to the German people and to the entire world the enormity of the Nazi crimes, the four wartime Allies had convened an international trial in 1945–1946 at Nuremberg. Hitler, Himmler, and Goebbels were already dead, but 22 other Nazi leaders and the major Nazi organizations were indicted for crimes against peace, that is, plotting and waging a war of aggression; war crimes, which were defined as violations of the accepted laws and conventions of warfare; and crimes against humanity, that is, acts of mass murder and genocide. The evidence of evil deeds, massive and incontrovertible, was set down for posterity in many volumes of recorded testimony. Despite the high moral purpose of the

Demonstrations and strikes swept across France in May 1968, evoking memories of nineteenth-century revolutionary battles in the barricaded streets of Paris, but President de Gaulle was more successful than earlier French kings in quelling crowds and protests. As this photograph suggests, however, clashes between the police and student demonstrators produced strong reactions among all groups in French society during the weeks before de Gaulle and his followers consolidated their power by winning new national elections.
(Sipa Press)

trials and an honest effort to establish fair judicial procedures for the accused, some critics questioned their appropriateness, especially the decision to try the leaders of a defeated sovereign nation for planning and waging war and to indict an agency like the General Staff. Some also questioned the propriety of having the Soviet Union sit in judgment of the Nazis. These critics argued that the Soviets were themselves guilty of crimes because they had contributed to the outbreak of the war, shared in the partition of Poland, and incorporated the Baltic states into the Soviet Union. Others dismissed the trials as victors' justice. Yet the Nuremberg trials served in a singular way to reinforce international standards of civilized behavior. The court condemned 12 of the defendants to execution. Seven received prison terms of varying length, including life sentences; three were acquitted.

The four occupation authorities also carried out a "denazification" program, which produced mixed results. Because so many professional Germans had been members of Nazi organizations, it became difficult to exclude them from public life if the normal processes of government were to resume. Some individuals guilty of the more heinous Nazi crimes fled the country and

Denazification

were still being apprehended and tried many decades after the war's end by the Germans themselves or in French or Israeli courts. But the people who survived the Nazi camps and the families of Nazi victims only began to receive some financial restitution at the end of the twentieth century.

Divided Germany (and Berlin) became a central arena of the Cold War. The German Democratic Republic became one of the most loyal client states of the Soviet Union. The Federal Republic of Germany became a prosperous parliamentary democracy, a full partner of the West. It faced up to and made efforts to atone for the horrors of the Nazi regime.

The West German government encouraged private industry and a capitalist, competitive economy; but it also shaped overall economic policies and provided broad social services, so that West Germany emerged with what became known as a "social market economy." The guaranteed benefits came to exceed those of other major industrial Western countries. The Federal Republic also pioneered in bringing labor and capital together. The labor unions accepted a role as social partners in the expanding economy, moderating wage demands to avoid inflation. A "codetermination" law gave workers seats on the boards of directors of larger firms.

A "social market economy"

After independent state governments had been set up in each state (or *Land*) in West Germany with the encouragement of the occupying powers, a constitutional convention representing the ten German states met in 1948–1949 in Bonn. The convention produced a Basic Law (or *Grundgesetz*) and officially established the Federal Republic of Germany. The Basic Law, by design not called a constitution, was to be temporary, valid only until at some future date the two parts of Germany could be reunited. An extensive bill of rights was one of its most prominent features. Power was decentralized under a federal system.

The founders deliberately set out to avoid the weaknesses of the Weimar Republic. The president, elected indirectly and not by popular vote, was a ceremonial figure with limited political power; a president of stature could, however, as the years revealed, exercise substantial moral authority. The head of government, or real executive, was the chancellor, responsible, along with the cabinet, to the majority in the popularly elected lower house, the *Bundestag*. To avoid instability, a chancellor could be overthrown only when a new majority was ready with an immediate replacement. Proportional representation guaranteed that each party would be apportioned seats equivalent to its share of the popular vote, but to prevent splinter parties and political fragmentation, a party received seats in the legislature only if it won at least five percent of the national vote. The Christian Democratic Union and the Social Democrats emerged as the two chief parties and shared between them a large proportion of the popular vote.

The power of the chancellor

The Christian Democratic Union governed uninterruptedly for 20 years, from 1949 to 1969. In reaction to the Nazi barbarism, it sought to infuse politics with a moral idealism and ethical purpose. Not a confessional party, it appealed to Protestants and Catholics alike, who were almost equally represented in West Germany, and it received strong support from the business community and large segments of the middle classes. The dominating figure in the party and government in the early years was the Christian Democratic leader, Konrad Adenauer, who had begun his career in the pre-1914 imperial era. A patriarchal, strong-willed personality, his ambition was to regain for Germany a position of dignity and international respect. He became chancellor in 1949 at the age of 73 (with only a slim majority)

Christian Democrats and Konrad Adenauer

GERMANY AND ITS BORDERS, 1919–1990

Upper panel: the boundaries established after the Treaty of Versailles. Note the Free City of Danzig and the Polish Corridor. *Middle panel:* Germany's borders at the height of the Second World War in 1942. The Reich proper had then annexed (1) Luxembourg, (2) Alsace and Lorraine from France, (3) Carniola from Yugoslavia, (4) Austria, (5) the Sudeten regions and a Bohemian–Moravian protectorate from Czechoslovakia, (6) the Free City of Danzig, and (7) Poland. *Lower panel:* Germany after Hitler's defeat. East Prussia was divided between Poland and the U.S.S.R., and Poland reached westward almost to Berlin. A Communist East Germany (the German Democratic Republic) and a democratic West Germany (the Federal Republic of Germany) grew out of the zones occupied respectively by the Soviets and the West. After the fall of the Communist regime in East Germany, Germany was reunited in 1990.

and governed for 14 years. Opponents criticized *der Alte* ("the old man") for creating a "chancellor's democracy"; but he provided the resolute leadership, stability, and continuity that made possible the remarkable economic expansion of the 1950s and the regaining of full West German sovereignty.

Adenauer successfully integrated the Federal Republic of Germany into the emerging political, economic, and military structures of western Europe, strengthening ties with France, cooperating in the movement for European economic integration, and winning the

The new spirit of international cooperation in postwar Europe was expressed in the collaboration of French President Charles de Gaulle and German Chancellor Konrad Adenauer (standing next to de Gaulle here and waving to a crowd). The two leaders met often to create a partnership that became the foundation for a new Europe. After fighting three major wars in the heart of Europe over a period of 75 years, Germany and France established a peaceful alliance that brought stability to the continent and eliminated the traditional problem of warfare between two former enemies. (Dalmas/Sipa Press)

support and confidence of the United States and the other Western powers. Indeed, within a decade after the disastrous military defeat that had left a shattered and occupied country, West Germany was a major economic power, a coveted ally of the West and an equal member of the North Atlantic Treaty Organization. The major opposition party, the Social Democrats, heirs to the Social Democratic party founded in the 1870s, criticized Adenauer for his overly close identification with the United States and for ignoring the issue of national reunification. But the Social Democrats abandoned their Marxist ideology at a party congress in 1959 and broadened their appeal to the middle classes and younger voters.

Willy Brandt's "grand coalition"

In 1965 the Social Democrats, who had softened their neutralist stand in foreign affairs, joined the Christian Democrats and the Free Democrats (a small liberal centrist party) in a "grand coalition." Willy Brandt, the former Social Democratic mayor of West Berlin, became foreign minister and launched his "Eastern policy," or *Ostpolitik,* a policy that encouraged building bridges to the Soviet Union and eastern Europe, including East Germany. In 1969, with the support of the Free Democrats, he became chancellor of a new coalition that ended the 20-year tenure of the Christian Democrats. Brandt negotiated treaties with the Soviet Union and Poland in 1971, formally accepting the German eastern frontier at the Oder and West Neisse River line. His government officially recognized the German Democratic Republic and promoted close economic ties with it and other countries of eastern Europe. When a spy scandal in his own entourage cut short his chancellorship in 1974, his Social Democratic colleague Helmut Schmidt took over and continued his policies. Not until 1982 would the Christian Democrats return to office with Helmut Kohl as chancellor. Meanwhile, in the early 1980s, reunification with East Germany still seemed unlikely, only a remote possibility.

The Italian Republic

During the struggle to oust the German armies from the Italian peninsula after the fall of Mussolini in 1943, the Italian political parties, repressed for over two decades under Fascism, sprang to life. All supported the provisional governments in postwar reconstruction and committed themselves to democratic renewal. In 1946 the country voted by a narrow margin to abolish the Savoy monarchy, never distinguished, and now tarnished by its cooperation with the Fascist regime. A constitution for the new Italian Republic established a ceremonial presidency, cabinet government, and legislative supremacy. Proportional representation guaranteed equitable representation for all political parties, large and small.

The Christian Democrats quickly became the dominant party. It appealed to all classes and sectors of Italian society, successfully blending support for democratic political principles, a moderately regulated free-enterprise economy, and the labor tenets of social Catholicism. Although the party remained independent of the Roman Catholic church, it remained close to the hierarchy. In Alcide De Gasperi, who had survived the Fascist years as a librarian in the Vatican, it found an effective leader. For seven formative years from 1946 to 1953 he presided over a series of coalition governments, which made possible postwar economic reconstruction and expansion. In the Cold War he kept Italy firmly in the Western camp. As in France, the Communist party's role in the resistance to Fascism helped to establish its position as a leading party in postwar politics. Communists at first held seats in the cabinet and cooperated in economic reconstruction, but when they fomented politically inspired strikes in 1947, De Gasperi dismissed them from his ministry. In 1948, in the early years of the Cold War, the United States intervened openly for the first time in its history to influence a European election, throwing its weight behind the Christian Democrats to thwart the Communists. The Christian Democrats for the first and only time won an absolute majority in the legislature. The Communists, despite their continuing parliamentary strength and support by a third to a fourth of the electorate, remained excluded from the cabinet.

> Alcide De Gasperi's Christian Democrats

After De Gasperi's disappearance from the political scene in 1953, the Christian Democrats governed under a succession of short-lived coalition cabinets formed with small centrist parties. Over the years the Christian Democrats became faction-ridden and less interested in reform than in patronage. Abandoning their initial idealism, they catered to propertied and narrow interests, and many in the party profited from business connections. In the early 1960s the Socialists became part of the governing coalition, but this "opening to the Left" did not alter political rigidities, and the country grew impatient with the uninterrupted tenure of the Christian Democrats.

The Communists gained further strength in the 1960s. They weakened their ties with Moscow, renounced tenets of Marxist-Leninist orthodoxy such as the dictatorship of the proletariat, and tempered their assault on religion. Architects, with the French party, of what came to be known as "Eurocommunism," they declared that each nation, without deferring to Moscow, must find its own way to a new society through parliamentary democracy and national consensus. The strongest Communist party in the Western world, the Italian party counted 1.8 million members at its peak in the mid-1970s and won the support of 35 percent of the electorate. Communist mayors and municipal councils governed in many major cities, including Rome. But the Christian Democrats continued to reject the Communist bid for seats in the national government.

> Eurocommunism

A prosperous
economy
The unstable political scene did not interfere with unprecedented economic growth and prosperity. The industrial triangle of Genoa, Milan, and Turin in northern Italy provided the nucleus for recovery and expansion. A prosperous economy emerged. By 1949 industrial production reached 1939 levels, and by the early 1950s Italy's rate of industrial growth rivaled that of West Germany and France. Italy was transformed from the primarily agricultural country it had been before the Second World War into one of the world's leading industrial nations. An economic revolution had dramatically elevated living standards for most Italians. Only the underdeveloped south remained a troubled economic region, even in times of advancing prosperity. In general, however, Italy joined the other nations of Western Europe in a remarkably rapid political and economic recovery from the catastrophic events of the Second World War.

111.   RESHAPING THE GLOBAL ECONOMY

Even before the close of hostilities the United States, with British support, developed a bold initiative to reshape the postwar world economy. Determined to avoid the economic nationalism, trade restrictions, and currency instability of the interwar years, the planners sought to restore the free flow of trade and the stable currencies of the pre-1914 era. In 1944 the United States convened an international conference of 44 nations at Bretton Woods, New Hampshire. The participants pledged to reduce trade barriers and work for stable currencies in the postwar world.

An effort to establish a formal world trade organization to oversee international commerce foundered, but an alternative strategy proved successful. The United States had earlier negotiated bilateral trade agreements with a number of countries to reduce tariffs on a reciprocal basis, with each agreement carrying a "most-favored nation" clause whereby concessions to one country were extended to all. These piecemeal arrangements led in 1948 to a broader arrangement, the General Agreement on Tariffs and Trade (GATT), embodying the same negotiating principle. Subscribed to initially by 23 nations, GATT became the foundation of postwar global commerce.

GATT

The General Agreement laid down rules to prevent discrimination in international trade, set up procedures for handling complaints, and provided a framework for continuing negotiation through lengthy bargaining sessions, or "rounds," designed to lower tariffs and remove nontariff barriers. By the 1990s over 100 countries were participating. GATT was only a partial substitute for a formal international trade organization, but it contributed to the vast expansion of world trade beginning in the 1950s. Not until 1997 was a formal World Trade Organization (WTO) established, with enlarged powers to mediate agreements and settle trade disputes. The WTO in its turn faced new problems and recurring controversies as it tried to resolve the conflicting claims of different nations in the global economy.

The "world economy" in the early postwar years meant the world's non-Communist or free-market economies. The strategic centers were North America and western Europe, with the addition of Japan, which doubled its share of world trade between 1951 and 1960. Integrated into the world economy were Latin America, Asia, the Middle East, Australasia, and Africa, so that it was truly an economy of global dimensions. The Soviet Union played no part in any of the postwar trade negotiations and restricted its commerce principally to its East European bloc of satellites. In

Global participation

Japan's dynamic new influence in the postwar global economy grew out of the nation's willingness and ability to develop technological innovations in the 1950s and 1960s. This superexpress train, which went into service between Tokyo and Osaka in 1964 and is shown here passing Mount Fuji, became one of the well-known symbols of modern Japanese society. Reaching speeds of over 150 miles per hour, these trains set a standard for the later development of other very high-speed trains in Europe.
(George Gester/Photo Researchers)

the late 1960s the Soviets and the East European countries opened up trade and economic relations with the West, but not until the late 1980s did they seek integration into the global economy.

Currency Stability: Toward the "Gold-Dollar" Standard

If the first objective of the wartime Bretton Woods conference was to liberalize trade, the second was to stabilize the world's currencies. The chaos of the interwar years when nation after nation abandoned the gold standard and competed in currency devaluations to gain trade advantages haunted everyone. The Bretton Woods conference sought to restore the equivalent of the pre-1914 gold standard, which had provided for fixed exchange rates and the convertibility of all currencies into gold or into the equivalent at the time, British pounds sterling.

Currency stabilization

Currency stabilization, however, turned out to be more difficult than anticipated. The stable conversion of different currencies into gold or dollars at fixed exchange rates did not become possible until the end of 1958. For about a dozen years, until 1971, each major currency had a par value in gold and in dollars. For that same short time the American dollar, like the British pound before 1914, was accepted as the equivalent of gold itself. But the postwar economic scene changed rapidly; the era of the "gold-dollar standard" proved short-lived, and a system of "floating currencies" and fluctuating exchange rates took its place.

The IMF and the World Bank

Meanwhile two important agencies established after the war helped in international financial settlements. The International Monetary Fund (IMF) provided loans to governments to manage temporary balance of payments difficulties and to help reduce the need for currency devaluations. The International Bank for Reconstruction and Development (or World Bank) made long-term loans to the governments of poorer countries for economic development. Both agencies played a larger role in later years than in the immediate postwar era, and both became controversial when critics complained that their policies did not really benefit the world's poorer nations or people. Both were located in Washington, their major funding provided by the United States. The economic center of gravity for the West, like the political and the military, lay after 1945 on the American side of the Atlantic.

European Integration: From the Common Market to the European Community

As western Europe expanded economically, it also drew closer together in a more integrated economic system. There had been numerous proposals in the interwar years for a European federation. The war, the wartime Resistance movements, the Marshall Plan, European cooperative recovery efforts, and the threat from the Soviet Union in the Cold War all reinforced the idea that western Europe's future lay in unity. A number of European leaders pressed for the creation of a "United States of Europe." In 1949 delegates representing the parliaments of ten countries met in Strasbourg to establish a Council of Europe with the hope that it might become a legislative body for a federated Europe. Although the Council of Europe grew in membership over the years and continued to support the idea of federation, it never became an important political force. It confined itself to humanitarian, cultural, and social issues. In 1958 it set up a European Court of Human Rights to protect the rights of individuals in its member nations against arbitrary government actions. It banned corporal punishment in the schools and outlawed the death penalty for convicted criminals.

Expansion and unity

European integration itself took a different path, beginning in the economic area. In 1948 Belgium, the Netherlands, and Luxembourg created a customs union, called Benelux, which provided the benefits of a sizable free trade area for the three small countries. At the same time the visionary but pragmatic French administrator Jean Monnet, who had helped reorganize the postwar French economy, recognized that the first steps toward greater European unity had to develop along modest economic lines and begin with specific objectives.

In 1952, under a plan designed by Monnet, six West European countries—France, the Federal Republic of Germany, Italy, and the three Benelux nations—placed their coal and steel industries under a form of supranational authority. They established the European Coal and Steel Community, its headquarters in Luxembourg. The six nations not only agreed to eliminate import duties and quotas on coal and steel but also placed production under a common High Authority with decision-making powers. A council of ministers represented the six governments, but the High Authority carried out major administrative functions.

The European Coal and Steel Community

Monnet was the first president of the European Coal and Steel Community, which paved the way for economic integration that would extend far beyond a single sector of the West European economy. In a momentous second step, the same six nations on March 25, 1957, signed the Treaty of Rome, creating a large free-trade area or customs union, the European Economic Community, or Common Market, its headquarters in Brussels, with the goal of moving toward full economic and even political integration. The six nations pledged to eliminate tariff barriers, develop a common tariff with respect to the outside world, harmonize social and economic policies, and work toward the free movement of capital and labor. Under a separate treaty the member countries also agreed to coordinate their nonmilitary atomic research and technology in a European Atomic Community.

The Common Market

The six-nation Common Market, encompassing 175 million people in 1958, quickly became one of the thriving economic aggregates of the expanding world economy. By 1968, even earlier than anticipated, the last internal tariff was dropped and trade among the six nations grew at a rate double that of trade with outside countries. Its influence spread to the former European colonies, with which it worked out preferential trade arrangements. Through the Common Market, western Europe set about to recapture a key role in the new configuration of global affairs, which had been dominated since 1945 by the two superpowers. The Common Market also helped further absorb a revived democratic West Germany into western Europe and to nurture reconciliation between France and Germany, ending the internecine rivalries that had devastated the European continent in the first half of the twentieth century.

In 1967 the three "Communities" consolidated themselves into what was now designated the European Community. Their high commissions became the European Commission and their assemblies became the European Parliament, meeting in Strasbourg. The members of the European Parliament took seats by party affiliation and not by nation. In 1979, for the first time, they were not chosen by their respective governments but were elected by a Europeanwide electorate. The Parliament enjoyed only limited legislative authority, but it supervised the budget and the European Commission and kept alive the idea of unity. Final decision making still rested with the council of ministers representing each of the member nations, whose decisions on important matters had to be unanimous.

The European Community

Great Britain initially refrained from joining the Common Market. Its economic ties to the Commonwealth, its dependence on low-priced food imports, and its unwillingness to accept any supranational authority kept both Labour and Conservative governments from joining. But Britain's economy continued to lag behind the economic growth of the major West European nations, prompting the British government eventually to seek Common Market membership in 1963. Britain's request was vetoed by President de Gaulle, however, because he regarded Britain and its admittedly "special relationship" with the

United States as a threat to French leadership on the Continent. Not until after de Gaulle retired from the political scene in 1969 did Britain gain admission.

Advance toward political unity

If the years 1958–1968 showed remarkable gains in economic integration, the advance toward political unity was slower. Although de Gaulle understood the contribution of the Common Market to the prosperity of western Europe and envisioned a strong western Europe as a counterpoise to the two "hegemonic superpowers," he opposed political or supranational authority for the Community. Europe had to be a Europe of sovereign states, a *Europe des patries*. The more dedicated Europeanists were disappointed. Yet the supranational economic and political machinery of the Community, the day-to-day cooperation of the European civil servants or bureaucrats (inevitably called "Eurocrats") in Brussels and Strasbourg, and the close consultation on common interests were favorable signs for unity, even apart from the military and defense ties that brought the western Europeans together in NATO. French-German friendship, cemented by de Gaulle and Adenauer and reinforced by their successors, remained the linchpin of cooperation within the Community.

The Europeans showed no haste to surrender their national sovereignty and independence, but the European Community created a strong sense of common destiny, a shared faith in democratic institutions and market economies and a concern for human rights and social needs. It not only contributed immeasurably to the economic and political strength of western Europe but also helped restore it to a larger role in world affairs; and by the beginning of the twenty-first century the European Community was projecting its own transnational military force.

West European competition

Western Europe accounted in the 1960s for one-fourth of all imports and one-fifth of all exports in the world economy; for a time its exports equaled those of the United States and Japan combined. One-third of the largest multinational corporations, that is, corporations which set up subsidiaries outside their own country for manufacturing or sales, were European. London, Frankfurt, and Paris were again important financial centers. In 1971 West European steel production surpassed that of the United States. European (and Japanese) automobiles cut sharply into American domestic and foreign markets. Self-sufficient in food, western Europe became the world's largest exporter of dairy products. The Federal Republic of Germany, in the 1960s, enjoyed a gross national product exceeded only by the economies of the United States and the U.S.S.R., even though it had only one-fourth the population of each; it accounted for one-third of the Common Market's gross national product. Western Europe and Japan were whittling away at the American economic lead in production and trade and bringing to a close the era of the dollar's supremacy.

End of the Gold-Dollar Standard, 1971

Trade imbalances

The new trading patterns created monetary problems. Because America's exports no longer exceeded its imports, American trade shifted to an unfavorable balance of payments. The United States spent more abroad than it earned abroad. The postwar dollar shortage in other countries gave way to a "dollar glut." Western Europe accumulated large dollar reserves (or "Eurodollars"), some $50 billion by 1971; oil-rich Arab states held "petrodollars." The number of dollars held abroad exceeded American gold reserves.

The shift in the American economic position undermined confidence in a dollar which many now viewed as overvalued. De Gaulle, resentful of American political and economic

The global economy of the 1970s and the "floating" of national currencies gave an ever-growing importance to the world's leading stock exchanges and financial markets. Governments in all parts of the world found their money, debts, and economic stability significantly affected by the speculations or judgments of influential investors and financial traders. This picture of the New York Stock Exchange in 1979 suggests the scale of the modern financial systems and the bustling activity of a typical trading day.
(Bettmann/Corbis)

power, demanded an end to the gold-dollar standard and a return to gold itself. In 1965 France redeemed hundreds of millions of its dollar holdings for gold. Other central banks in Europe and Japan did not follow suit, but private investors speculated against the dollar. American gold and foreign currency reserves dropped precipitously.

In 1971 President Nixon unilaterally suspended gold convertibility and thus devalued the dollar, with a second devaluation in 1973. The global monetary system projected at Bretton Woods ended. Despite many proposals, there was no formal reform. Instead, on a day-to-day basis and with considerable success, the world's major currencies were allowed to "float," that is, to fluctuate daily

Floating currencies

against each other and against the dollar in world markets. Gold itself fluctuated freely and official gold prices were abolished. Although the American dollar remained the world's principal reserve currency, the West German mark and the Japanese yen took their place beside the dollar as key currencies.

The breakdown of the postwar monetary arrangements did not seriously affect the world economy. Currencies did not collapse because they were no longer exchangeable for gold. For currency stability the world learned to rely mainly on international consultation and rapid exchange of information, but governments found their currencies and economic policies vulnerable to a global financial system that crossed all national boundaries.

⚘ 112.   THE COMMUNIST WORLD: THE U.S.S.R. AND EASTERN EUROPE

Stalinism in the Postwar Years

In March 1953 Russia's twentieth-century Peter the Great died. Like his eighteenth-century tsarist predecessor, Stalin had a massive impact during his close to 30 years in power. He was responsible for industrialization in the 1930s, the rallying of the country in the Great Patriotic War, the expansion of the nation's borders, the consolidation of Communist regimes in eastern Europe, and the emergence of the Soviet Union as a nuclear power. But the human costs of the Stalinist transformation of the country were staggering. Millions had fallen victim in the 1930s to his forced collectivization of the countryside and the ensuing famine, and additional millions had died as a result of his purges. Western and Soviet scholars alike have estimated the total figure of Stalin's victims at least as high as 20 million, quite apart from the millions of lives lost in the Second World War. Because the civil war and war communism earlier under Lenin had also taken millions of lives, the Communist regime from its emergence in 1917 to its demise in 1991 must be counted among the costliest experiments in social engineering in all history.

Stalinist terror

The Stalinist terror had continued during the war. Entire ethnic groups like the Crimean Tatars and the Volga Germans, suspected of collaboration with the Nazis, were forcibly moved east to Siberia. Mass deportations took place from Estonia, Latvia, and Lithuania, the three Baltic republics that had been formally annexed in 1940. At the war's end, returning Soviet soldiers who had been prisoners of war and civilian deportees forced to work for the Nazis in Europe were sent off to labor camps because their exposure to the West made them suspect. The unbridled authority of the secret political police (the NKVD, later the KGB) continued to increase, and the network of forced labor camps grew in size. Ideological restrictions tightened. Stalin's personal suspicions, growing sharper with the passage of the years, filled even his closest associates with dismay. In later years, in a freer atmosphere, the country debated whether Stalin's dictatorship represented a logical outgrowth of the Bolshevik Revolution itself and of many of Lenin's policies or was his own personal distortion.

Controls over intellectual life in the postwar years took on a vehemently nationalistic and xenophobic tone; deviations from Stalin's "line" in economics, music, genetics, history, and linguistics were forbidden. An officially inspired anti-Semitism, thinly disguised as anti-Zionism, accused Jewish intellectuals of being "rootless cosmopolitans." The political police meanwhile fabricated conspiracies to justify the terror. In the fictitious "doctors' plot," officially announced in early 1953, a score of Jewish doctors were arrested for plotting to poison Stalin and other Kremlin leaders; one month after Stalin died, his successors withdrew the charges and freed the imprisoned physicians.

Khrushchev: The Abortive Effort at Reform

After Stalin's death the party leaders resolved to exercise collective control, determined that no single leader should again dominate party and government. In the struggle for power, however, authority gradually shifted to Nikita S. Khrushchev. Outwardly jovial and ebullient, Khrushchev was a tough and hardened party stalwart who had enforced Stalin's purges in Ukraine and had long been a member of the Central Committee and Politburo, but he was shrewd enough to recognize the need for change.

In part to win allies against those in the party who were opposed to change, Khrushchev encouraged a greater measure of cultural and intellectual freedom—a "thaw." He put restraints on the still formidable powers of the political police. He surprised many with an attack on Stalin's record. In a speech to the twentieth party congress in 1956, he officially revealed or corroborated the "crimes of the Stalin era," making partial but nonetheless startling disclosures of the Stalinist terror. Stalin had been personally responsible for the purges and executions of the 1930s, and millions of victims had been innocent of the charges against them; his most intimate colleagues had lived in fear for their lives. Khrushchev also revealed Stalin's initial loss of nerve and ineptitude at the time of the German invasion in June 1941.

Khrushchev's "thaw"

Although Khrushchev criticized Stalin, the thaw in Soviet society was never systematic or thorough. In 1958 Boris Pasternak was forbidden to accept the Nobel Prize in literature because his novel, *Dr. Zhivago,* by stressing individual freedom, implicitly condemned the oppressiveness of Soviet society. But in 1962 Alexander Solzhenitsyn was permitted to publish his *One Day in the Life of Ivan Denisovich,* a depiction of human suffering in the world of the forced labor camps. Khrushchev continued the de-Stalinization campaign. Cities named in Stalin's honor were renamed: Stalingrad, the most famous, became Volgograd. Stalin's body was removed from the mausoleum on Red Square, where it had lain next to Lenin's, and buried outside the Kremlin Wall.

For the economy Khrushchev pressed decentralization, attempting to loosen tight central economic controls by creating regional economic councils and offering factory managers greater autonomy and incentives for efficiency and profitability. Meanwhile the country successfully tested the hydrogen bomb; launched its first space satellite, Sputnik, in 1958; and built its first intercontinental ballistic missiles. The Soviet economy was second only to that of the United States in gross national product. Within a decade, Khrushchev boasted in the early 1960s, the Soviet economy would surpass the American. The stress on heavy industry and on military expenditures meant, of course, continuing privation for the ordinary citizen, and the emphasis on quantity to the neglect of quality concealed deep flaws in the system as a whole.

Decentralization

Khrushchev's most ambitious effort lay in agriculture, the weakest sector of the economy ever since Stalin's forced collectivization. He sought to bring under cultivation the "virgin lands" of Soviet Central Asia, in Kazakhstan and elsewhere, but crop failures thwarted the experiment. His reforms did little to alter the bureaucratized system of collective and state farms inherited from Stalin or inspire the collective farmers to increase their

The Cold War did not end after the death of Joseph Stalin, but the new Soviet leader Nikita Khrushchev spoke of "peaceful coexistence" with Western nations and traveled to the United States. Wearing his Soviet medals, Khrushchev appears in a congenial mood during a White House meeting in 1959 with the American President Dwight Eisenhower and Vice President Richard Nixon.
(RIA-Novosti/SOVFOTO)

output. For the party itself he unsuccessfully sought fixed terms of office for important party posts. Few of his reforms were acceptable to the government and party bureaucrats, the *apparatchiki,* who saw their privileged positions threatened and who mustered opposition to his "hare-brained" schemes.

Khrushchev pursued a truculent foreign policy. Proclaiming that war was not inevitable with the United States and other capitalist countries, he spoke of "peaceful coexistence," and relations for a time improved. But in 1960 he scuttled a summit meeting with Allied leaders and in 1962 overreached himself in the confrontation with the United States during the Cuban missile crisis (to be described in a subsequent chapter). He also clashed openly with Communist China. His boastfulness and recklessness, his retreat in Cuba, the failure of his agricultural and other economic policies, and his attempt to reform the party itself led to his downfall. In 1964 the party leadership ousted him from office. He lived quietly in Moscow until his death in 1971. In the post-Stalin era, a reformer did not necessarily have to fear for his life, but there were clear limits to the reforms the party and bureaucracy would tolerate. Leonid I. Brezhnev, who had helped engineer Khrushchev's downfall, soon emerged as the new Soviet leader.

Khrushchev's fall

Eastern Europe: The Decades of Dictatorship

Although nothing like the Russian Revolution of 1917 erupted in Europe after the Second World War, communism made dramatic advances in central and eastern Europe through the Red Army's military presence and the support given to local Communist leaders. Eleven European states and 100 million Europeans fell under Communist-style governments. The areas considered in 1919 by the Allied peacemakers to be a protective buffer against Bolshevism were now under Communist domination.

The three Baltic states, Estonia, Latvia, and Lithuania, came under Soviet control under the terms of the Nazi-Soviet pact, and in 1940 they were incorporated into the U.S.S.R. as Soviet socialist republics. Later, in the sweep of military operations during the last months of the war, Poland, Hungary, Romania, Bulgaria, and Czechoslovakia fell into the orbit of Soviet influence. East Germany, initially part of the joint Allied occupation of Germany, was shaped into a sixth Soviet satellite as the German Democratic Republic. Yugoslavia and Albania, liberated by their own partisan leaders rather than by the Red Army, were governed by Communist regimes but with looser ties to the Soviet Union and soon broke with the Soviets. Despite its defeat in the Soviet-Finnish War in 1940, Finland escaped Communist domination. Accepting its wartime territorial losses, it maintained its independence by a cautious neutrality in foreign policy and a discreetly correct relationship with the Soviets. Austria, after a decade of joint occupation by the four Allied powers, gained independence as a neutral state in 1955.

Soviet satellites

Consolidation of Communist Control

The Soviets consolidated control in eastern Europe in stages. Soviet military occupation made it possible for local Communist leaders, many returning from exile in Moscow, to dominate Left coalition governments. In the early coalition governments everywhere, the Communists shared power but held the key ministries of interior, propaganda, and justice, and controlled the police, the army, and the courts. Individuals alleged to have been "fascist" or to have collaborated with the Nazis were barred from public life and from voting; the loose definition of "fascist" and "reactionary" barred many who were only anti-Communist. In the first elections, in Poland and elsewhere, purges and disfranchisement made a mockery of Stalin's pledge at Yalta to hold "free and unfettered elections" in eastern Europe. Protests by the United States and Great Britain only hardened the Soviet position.

The new regimes confiscated and redistributed large estates and put uncultivated land to use, so that 3 million peasant families acquired about 6 million acres of land; the agrarian reforms were the final blow to the landed aristocracy that had once ruled in eastern Europe. They also nationalized the economy. As they struggled with postwar reconstruction, the new regimes had lent a sympathetic ear to the American invitation in 1947 to accept Marshall Plan aid. But Stalin was not disposed to permit the East European countries to drift into the Western economic orbit. After the summer of 1947, wherever non-Communists were still strong, the Communists ousted their political rivals and banned or reduced to impotence all other political parties. In Czechoslovakia the coalition government lasted longer than elsewhere but fell victim to a Communist coup in February 1948.

Agrarian reform and nationalization

With the Communists in control, the leaders of the opposition political parties were forced into flight, imprisoned, or in other ways silenced. The new regimes, notably in

CHRONOLOGY OF NOTABLE EVENTS, 1945–1967

1945	The United Nations is established at a conference in San Francisco
1947	Secretary of State George C. Marshall announces U.S. plan to aid the rebuilding of Europe
1948–1949	American airlift of supplies sustains West Berlin during Soviet blockade
1949	The Soviet Union successfully tests an atomic bomb
1949	United States and Western Europe create NATO
1949	Mao Zedong and the Communist party proclaim the People's Republic of China
1950–1953	Korean War demonstrates new American policy to "contain" communism
1953	Death of Stalin opens new era in Soviet and East European history
1956	Unsuccessful revolts against Soviet control in Poland and Hungary
1957	Six West–European nations establish a new Common Market for trade
1957	Mao launches "Great Leap Forward" in China; leads to deadly famine
1958	France establishes the Fifth Republic with Charles de Gaulle as president
1962	French war in Algeria ends with recognition of Algerian independence
1966–1967	The "Cultural Revolution" creates disruptions throughout China

Poland and Hungary, clashed also with the Roman Catholic church; high-ranking prelates were brought to public trial and imprisoned, and church property was confiscated. The Communist leaders themselves soon became Stalin's victims. From 1949 to 1953, reflecting the repression in the Soviet Union in Stalin's last years, purges, arrests, trials, confessions, and executions occurred in the highest ranks of each party. Leaders were accused of nationalist deviations and of conspiring with Tito, the independent-minded Communist leader of Yugoslavia.

Collectivization

The new "people's democracies" took steps to collectivize agriculture. In Bulgaria, the most docile of the satellites, over half the arable land was collectivized; but in Hungary, only about a third. In Poland, where resistance was strongest, collectivization was halted after a short time. Agriculture in the people's republics, as in the Soviet Union, remained the weakest part of the economy. Peasants diligently cultivated their individual plots of land but worked reluctantly on the large collectives. All of the East European societies also entered a new phase of industrialization. But the emphasis on heavy industry to the neglect of consumer goods and pressures to complement the economy of the Soviet Union severely limited the improvement of East European living standards.

Economic and political cooperation

The Soviets formalized their economic relationship with Eastern Europe through the Council for Mutual Economic Assistance, but the Council (established in 1949) never worked as cooperation among equals. The Soviets provided low-cost raw materials and oil and provided a large market for East European goods, regardless of their quality, but much of the economic cooperation principally benefited the Soviet Union. Militarily, the Warsaw Pact, signed in 1955, brought the six East European countries together into a mutual defense alliance, and Soviet troops remained stationed in eastern Europe in large numbers.

Yugoslavia, freed from the Nazis largely by its own partisan armies, made a remarkable show of resistance to the Soviets. The Yugoslav Communist leader, Marshal Tito, kept a tight grip on the multinational state but loosened centralized controls over the economy and abandoned collectivization of agriculture. He pursued an independent foreign policy, openly defied Moscow, and took his stand with the neutralist nonaligned nations of Asia and Africa. The first major Communist figure to declare his independence from Moscow, Tito established a model of national autonomy for other Communist leaders and parties to follow.

Ferment and Repression in East Germany, Poland, and Hungary, 1953–1956

The changes in the Soviet Union after Stalin's death directly affected the Soviet satellites. The East Europeans chafed at collectivization, forced industrialization, austere living standards, subservience to the Soviets, and harsh rule by Stalinist-type leaders who remained in power for years after Stalin disappeared. An initial outburst, riots in East Berlin in June 1953, was quickly suppressed. New ferment rose to the surface, however, after Khrushchev denounced the brutal character of the Stalin dictatorship and, in an attempt to win back Yugoslavia, made the official concession that "different roads to socialism" were possible. This concession and his de-Stalinization speech in 1956 opened a Pandora's box; undermining Stalin's infallibility undermined Soviet infallibility as well.

In 1956 open revolt broke out in Poland and Hungary, led by the East European Communist party leaders themselves. In Poland, where national sentiment and church attachments ran deep, pressures for internal freedom and for independence from Moscow led to riots and demonstrations. The Communist leader Wladyslaw Gomulka relaxed political and economic controls, halted collectivization, improved relations with the church, and took steps to loosen the bonds to Moscow. The country welcomed an alternative to direct Soviet control. Khrushchev threatened military action but backed down. For a few years, Gomulka curbed police terror and created a freer atmosphere, but the reform era was short-lived, and Gomulka's regime controlled Poland with growing repression throughout the 1960s.

Revolt in Poland and Hungary

In Hungary, in 1956, events took a tragic turn. When news of Gomulka's success in Poland reached Budapest, demonstrations broke out; young rioters even toppled a statue of Stalin. The reform-minded Communist leader Imre Nagy, who had earlier been driven from the premiership, returned to power. His reform program and release of political prisoners ignited pressures not only for democratization and parliamentary government but also for the severance of ties to Moscow. Alarmed, the Soviets forced the party leadership to remove Nagy from power and to replace him with the more subservient János Kádár, who accepted Soviet intervention. Khrushchev dispatched troops, tanks, and artillery to suppress the "counterrevolution" and forcefully reestablished Communist rule. Severe reprisals followed. Nagy himself was imprisoned, then tried and hanged, and his body was thrown into a mass grave. In the wake of the repression, 200,000 Hungarians fled into exile, mainly to the United States, a larger number than at any time since the crushing of the European revolutions of 1848–1849. The Soviet tanks in Budapest weakened any remaining illusions about the liberalism of Stalin's successors, provoked international condemnation, and drove many Communists in western Europe and elsewhere to renounce their affiliations with Communist parties.

The demand for reforms spread rapidly in Hungary during the fall of 1956. Emboldened by changes in Communist Poland and by the policies of Hungarian reformer Imre Nagy, the people of Budapest protested the repressive policies of the Soviet Union, destroyed statues of Communist leaders, and (like the group in this picture) defiantly burned portraits of Joseph Stalin. The Soviets soon intervened with decisive military force. Nagy was executed, and the new Soviet-supported Hungarian regime crushed all forms of anti-Communist dissent.
(Hulton-Deutsch Collection/Corbis)

113.   THE COMMUNIST WORLD: MAO ZEDONG AND THE PEOPLE'S REPUBLIC OF CHINA

The Civil War

The proclamation on October 1, 1949, of the People's Republic of China by Mao Zedong and the Chinese Communist party was among the most momentous of events shaping the world after 1945.

The long civil war between the Guomindang, or Nationalists, and the Communists had been fought intermittently across much of China since 1927. In 1937 Nationalists and Communists entered into an uneasy alliance to fight the Japanese. Mao agreed to place the People's Liberation Army under the command of Chiang Kai-shek and the Nationalists, but Mao actually waged a separate guerrilla war against the Japanese from the northern bases he controlled and over which he imposed his own Communist regime, winning peasant support through land reforms. The Nationalists, cut off by the Japanese from the urban centers of eastern China, suffered from chaotic economic conditions and severe inflation and became increasingly corrupt, authoritarian, and repressive.

Nationalists and Communists

The victory over Japan in 1945 set the stage for renewed civil war. Nationalist troops, with American aid, returned to eastern China. The Communists, moving out from their guerrilla bases, poured into the northern provinces and made contact with the Russians in Manchuria. When Mao refused to surrender the northern provinces, disband his army, and accept Nationalist political control, the civil war resumed. An American-sponsored truce temporarily halted hostilities, but when the U.S.S.R. withdrew from Manchuria in the spring of 1946 (after removing Manchurian industrial assets as reparations), Nationalists and Communists clashed over control of Manchuria.

In the fighting from 1946 to 1949, the Nationalists, despite substantial American support, lost ground steadily. By the autumn of 1949 the Communists had routed the demoralized Guomindang armies. Chiang withdrew his shattered forces to the island of Taiwan, where he established a small but soon prospering Republic of China. The mainland regime never gave up its claim to Taiwan, and the fate of Taiwan remained a contentious international issue for later generations. In 1971 Taiwan had to surrender to the People's Republic of China the Chinese seat in the United Nations, which also carried with it permanent membership on the Security Council.

Taiwan

Mao: The New Regime

From 1949 until his death in 1976, Chairman Mao, as uncontested head of the party, molded the destinies of China. Much more is known about him now than at the time. He had earlier imposed his iron rule on the party and on the populations under his control. He had ruthlessly eliminated all party rivals in periodic purges during the long struggle with the Guomindang. Having finally gained power over all of China, he was determined to bring about the total transformation of the agrarian and undeveloped Chinese society, which had been the victim of foreign intervention and invasion for well over a century. Mao wanted to create a new proud China in which the social order of domineering landlords and oppressed peasants would be reversed, the country would be industrialized and modernized, and China would be internationally respected. In many ways he personified the Chinese resentment of Western imperialism, which had humiliated China and all but carved the country to pieces in the nineteenth century. He was resolved to set China on the path to modernity, no matter what the cost.

Mao Zedong

In 1949, for the first time since the revolution of 1911, and indeed for generations before that, a unified central government controlled China, able to direct and mobilize the most populous nation in the world. Even before the Communist triumph Chairman Mao, despite his modest title, already saw himself as something of a successor to the ancient Chinese emperors. He would link Marx's world view, which since 1920 he had adopted as the instrument for Chinese liberation, to the 4,000-year-old imperial tradition of an all-powerful emperor ruling together with mandarin scholar-officials. The traditional emperor was to rule with the mandate of Heaven in accordance with Confucian moral precepts, as interpreted by his learned officials. They were obligated to criticize the emperor, but if they went too far they could meet a grim end—in ancient times buried alive. The new regime inherited also an ancient tradition of Chinese preeminence in the East Asian world. With traditional ways of life disrupted by decades of revolution, civil struggle, and the war against Japan, Mao's communism in some ways provided a modern surrogate for the older Confucian values.

The Soviet example
Mao leaned heavily on Soviet experience. The Communist party controlled and policed each level of government and manipulated all organs of information and political indoctrination. The party also added "thought control" and "rectification" labor camps, and it inaugurated a reign of terror. In the first six months of 1950, by Mao's own estimate, some 700,000 "local bullies and evil gentry" labeled "counterrevolutionaries" lost their lives. In the next two years, from 1950 to 1952, a campaign directed against the "landlords" as a class sent some half million more men, women, and children to death or to repressive labor camps. The purges then took a different turn. In 1956, in what seemed to be a burst of enthusiasm for greater diversity and toleration in the country, Mao proclaimed: "Let a hundred flowers bloom, let a hundred schools of thought contend." But as soon as critics were encouraged to come forward, he quickly instituted a new period of repression, an "antirightist" campaign that dispatched more than a half million "rightists," and "class enemies" to prisons or forced labor camps, many never to return.

Mao relentlessly mobilized the nation to rebuild the war-devastated economy and then to transform the country into an industrial power. Eliminating the old land regime in the countryside, the party established agricultural cooperatives as a prelude to collectivization. The country's first Five-Year Plan, launched in 1953 with Soviet economic and technical assistance during an initial period of friendly relations, concentrated on heavy industry, with significant results even if all targets were not reached. In agriculture the same floods and droughts that had troubled China for centuries refused to obey government decrees.

The Great Leap Forward
Impatient with what he considered the slow progress of social change, Mao in 1957 launched the "Great Leap Forward," designed to transform the country's industry and agriculture more rapidly. The program adopted by the Communist party proclaimed that China would "catch up with Britain" in a few years' time. The cooperatives in the countryside were amalgamated into larger "people's communes." Tightly organized in military fashion as production brigades, they were responsible for mechanizing production on the farms and developing local rural industry. Communal kitchens, nurseries, and schools left women freer to work on an equal basis in the fields and factories. Borrowing from some of the discredited Soviet experiments of Stalin, the government ordered farmers to abandon their traditional farming and to plant grain and rice everywhere, whether in suitable soil or not, and to crossbreed crops. Farmers were also encouraged to set up metallurgical furnaces in their backyards and learn to make steel.

The Great Leap Forward turned into disaster. Despite the image Mao had cultivated as the champion of the peasantry, he miscalculated on its ability to resist change. The persistent opposition of the peasants, severe crop failures, and the more bizarre experiments brought a disastrous famine. Up to 30 million died of hunger in what may have been the most disastrous agricultural experiment of all time. The outside world at the time knew little of what was going on. Visitors to China were shielded from the disaster, which later scholars called "Mao's secret famine." Eventually moderates within the party curbed Mao's excessive zeal. Although the land remained collectivized, the party suspended the more rigid aspects of the communal experiment. Farmers were even permitted to sell or barter a portion of their crops.

Industrial gains
But the industrial sector made progress. In the years before the Communist regime, annual steel production had never reached 1 million tons; by 1960 it exceeded 18 million. China's industrial output in 1960 ranked among the top ten powers in the world, and its factories had created a base for further expansion. The

The Cultural Revolution in China was led by millions of young "Red Guards" who—with the encouragement of Mao Zedong—sought to rekindle the revolutionary fervor of the Communist revolution and to disrupt or overthrow the bureaucratic order in Chinese society. These young people in Shanghai demonstrated their militant support for Chairman Mao during a typical Red Guard rally at the height of the Cultural Revolution in early 1967.
(Bettmann/Corbis)

government also marshaled the country's scientific and technological talents for the new technological age. It successfully tested an atomic bomb in 1964 and a hydrogen bomb in 1967, and it orbited space satellites in the 1970s.

The regime transformed modern Chinese life in many ways. Road, rail, and air transport physically unified the country. Public sanitation and public health received a high national priority. Labor gangs systematically drained and filled snail-infested canals, curbing the spread of diseases like schistosomiasis. Progress was made in overcoming illiteracy. The government reformed and simplified the written Chinese language and moved toward a single spoken tongue. It also adopted a new transliteration system for spelling Chinese names and words in the Latin alphabet. Women, encouraged to reject traditional Confucian virtues of obedience and deference, received legal equality with men and could count on new opportunities, even if few entered the higher ranks of political power. Old abuses such as child marriage and concubinage were outlawed; foot-binding had been eliminated earlier in the century. More profoundly than the Russian, the Chinese Revolution refashioned the habits and ethos of a gigantic population, reaching remote villages and hamlets untouched for centuries. Within a generation an agrarian, semifeudal country was developing into a modern industrial society. Mao's transformation was succeeding—at tremendous cost, to be sure.

The Cultural Revolution
Suddenly, beginning in 1966, Mao disrupted the country by unleashing the Cultural Revolution. Fearful that the revolution would not survive him and that its purity was endangered, he called for a purge of the highest ranks of government and party and for the removal of those who had succumbed to bureaucratic routine or lacked the zeal to push on with the social revolution. For his cause he mobilized millions of teenage students and other young people as Red Guards, or armed shock troops. Converging on Beijing and other cities, they denounced bourgeois ways, attacked Western imperialist culture, and brutally harassed and humiliated government and party officials as well as cultural and educational leaders. The worst effects of the Cultural Revolution fell on intellectuals. Men and women of all backgrounds were arrested, marched through the streets in dunce caps, beaten, and maimed.

Because Mao proclaimed the virtues of the land, white-collar workers, teachers, students, and party officials were forcibly sent off to the countryside to labor in the fields and experience rural life. The economy and the entire educational system broke down. When fanatical mobs threatened to tear the country apart, army leaders finally intervened and received Mao's authorization to restore order. By the time the worst disturbances were over in 1969, hundreds of thousands of lives had been lost. Three million persons had been sent to labor camps or to work in the fields. Thousands of high-ranking officials in the government and party, including two-thirds of the party's central committee, had been purged. The impact of the Cultural Revolution lingered on in an authoritarian pall that settled over the country. Mao himself retreated after 1971 into a kind of self-indulgent isolation in Beijing.

The pragmatic and moderate Zhou Enlai, who had little influence in restraining Mao's more radical experiments, faithfully served him for many years as premier and foreign minister. Had he outlived Mao, he might well have been his successor, but Zhou Enlai died in early 1976. Later that same year, Mao died. The Great Helmsman was widely mourned as the towering father of the revolution for over half a century and as one of the giant figures in the history of China. He had forged a revolutionary party and a revolutionary army; fought the Japanese; defeated the Nationalists; and presided over a revolution that had unified, revitalized, and modernized the country. His theoretical teachings on the struggle against imperialism and on the vanguard role of the peasantry, and his practical successes in guerrilla warfare, influenced revolutionaries all over the world. His most famous precept, that "political power grows out of the barrel of a gun," reinforced revolutionary zeal everywhere. His homilies, published in a little red book called *The Living Thoughts of Chairman Mao,* were widely quoted and assiduously studied. Mao's revolution had brought self-respect and self-confidence, industrialization, technological progress, unity, and pride to the country.

The Great Helmsman

But his radical experiments and the uncontrolled violence he had repeatedly unleashed also did irreparable harm. His experiments in social engineering in some ways outdid Stalin's and must also be counted among the most costly in all history. By any criteria he ranks among the most brutal of dictators. His successors a few years later tempered their praise for Mao, still lauding his monumental achievements as a revolutionary leader but criticizing him for his "grave blunders."

Foreign Affairs

The emergence of China as a second major Communist power undermined the ideological leadership of the Soviet Union. Stalin, playing his own game, had not always wholeheartedly supported the Chinese Communists in their civil war with the Guomindang. But once the Communist regime was established, the U.S.S.R. surrendered to it the concessions acquired in Manchuria under the Yalta agreement. In the 1950s the Chinese received military aid, capital loans, and technical assistance from the Soviets. The Korean War, in which Chinese troops fought the Americans as alien intruders who threatened their very borders, for a time drew them closer to the Soviet Union. Western leaders became even more firmly convinced that a monolithic world Communist movement existed. The Chinese Communists resented American support for the regime in Taiwan and the American effort over two decades to bar the People's Republic of China from the United Nations.

Although professing peace, the People's Republic pursued an aggressive foreign policy. In 1950, pressing old Chinese claims of suzerainty over Tibet and in the guise of liberating the country from clerical, that is, Buddhist, despotism, China occupied Tibet and forcibly maintained its rule there over the years. Monasteries were closed; the Dalai Lama, the *An aggressive foreign policy* country's ruler, was forced into exile; and large numbers of Chinese arrived as settlers. Unresolved tensions continued to affect the people of Tibet and the Tibetan borders. In 1962 China clashed with India in border disputes along India's northeastern frontier, although India from the beginning had been one of the staunchest defenders of the Chinese Revolution.

In the 1960s relations with the Soviet Union became strained. The two states hurled polemics at each other in their rivalry for ideological leadership and for control of the lands of inner Asia into which Russia had expanded in the age of the tsars. Mao, undaunted by nuclear arms, accused Khrushchev of pusillanimous behavior in the Cuban missile crisis of 1962. In 1972 the two countries clashed over border territory that divided Manchuria and Russia's maritime provinces, and they continued to confront one another with large armies in other areas. Although both countries supported North Vietnam in the Vietnam War, China after the war opposed the Soviet-backed intervention by Vietnam in Cambodia. Not until the 1980s was there a rapprochement and the promise of troop reductions along the Chinese-Soviet borders.

With time, relations with the United States improved. In 1971, when the United States withdrew its objections, the People's Republic of China replaced Taiwan in the United Nations. The following year Mao welcomed President Nixon on a dramatic visit to China. Diplomatic channels opened and relations were normalized. *Mao meets Nixon* The United States conceded that one day Taiwan would be reunited with the mainland, with its different social and economic system respected, but let it be known that it firmly opposed any forcible annexation.

The Chinese People's Republic had emerged as one of the great potential centers of global power. And in 1976 it was about to embark on an impressive new era of more peaceful modernization under Mao's successors.

Meanwhile, the history of Mao's "anti-imperialist" Chinese revolution had attracted wide interest in many parts of the postwar colonial world, to which we now turn. Most of this far-flung colonial world entered a new stage of nationalist agitation after the Second World War; and the new nations that emerged from this agitation in Asia, Africa, and the Middle East soon entered also into both the global conflicts of the Cold War and the fast-flowing global currents of the turbulent world economy.

For interactive exercises, glossary, chronologies, and more, go to the *Online Learning Center* at **www.mhhe.com/palmer10.**

Chapter 23

POSTCOLONIAL NATIONS IN ASIA AND LATIN AMERICA

❧ *Of all the political changes* in the history of the modern world, affecting hundreds of millions of people, nothing was more revolutionary, more dramatic, or perhaps more unexpected than the end of the European overseas colonial empires in the decades after the Second World War. In 1945 the British, the French, the Dutch, the Belgians, and the Portuguese still governed large parts of the world's population, but within 30 years each of these colonial empires disappeared. Europe's world supremacy came to an end.

The Second World War reinforced nationalist agitation for independence and freedom. It was difficult to wage war in the name of self-determination and democracy, often with the colonial countries as allies, without encouraging the idea of freedom among subject peoples. The Japanese conquests in Asia had also undermined the image of European invincibility. After the war the Europeans, economically exhausted, learned that they could rule only at prohibitive military cost and in embarrassing contradiction to their professed ideals of self-government.

Contradictions of empire

In some instances the colonial powers, bowing to agitation for independence, liquidated their colonial holdings without armed struggle, as in the British withdrawal from the Indian subcontinent in 1947. Elsewhere the European powers withdrew only after protracted bloody wars, as in the case of the Dutch in Indonesia, the French in Indochina and Algeria, and the Portuguese in Angola and Mozambique. The United States also played a part in the transformation. It gave independence to the Philippines, granted Puerto Rico commonwealth status, took in Alaska and Hawaii as equal members of the federal union, and surrendered its privileges in the Panama Canal. The last prominent vestiges of the European empires in Asia ended when Britain surrendered Hong Kong to China in 1997 and Portugal transferred Macao to China in 1999. The second half of the twentieth century witnessed the largest liberation of colonial peoples and transfer of power in all history.

Chapter emblem: Farmers harvesting barley in Ecuador in the 1990s. (Pablo Corral V/Corbis)

The end of the colonial empires and the emergence of over 100 new nations must count among the most far-reaching consequences of the two World Wars, and especially of the Second. But many of the new nations were nations only in a limited sense. They were now sovereign territorial entities, with definite boundaries, internationally recognized, with seats in the United Nations; but many of them lacked the internal coherence and shared experience of nations in the older sense of the word. Nor did nationhood for the most part carry with it democracy, civil rights, or the rule of law, nor alleviate deep-seated social and economic problems—even in Latin America (where most nations had already gained political independence in the nineteenth century).

The imperialist colonial experience left these regions of the world underdeveloped economically. In an uneven exchange they had depended on the industrial nations for capital, technology, and manufactures, while they in turn furnished the industrial countries with raw materials, foodstuffs, minerals, oil, and other primary commodities. With assistance from the industrially developed world, they now undertook modernization programs—against many obstacles and with mixed results. The winning of political independence in Asia and Africa, the mixed record of democratic self-government after independence, the effort to share in the earth's advanced technology and financial riches, and the struggle to reconcile older cultural values with modernization all contributed to the saga of what came to be called the "developing world" in the years after 1945. The emergence of postcolonial nations was affected everywhere by the rapid growth of national populations; the legacy of colonial and regional wars; the struggle to develop modern, competitive economies; and the international conflicts of the Cold War. All of these postcolonial issues continued to affect Latin America as well as the newly independent nations in Asia, Africa, and the Middle East, so that the nations of Latin America were usually included within that broadly defined list of peoples who constituted the "developing world."

The so-called developing nations were also described in the Cold War era as the "Third World," which became a widely used term to distinguish the less economically advanced regions or societies from the two "industrial" worlds: the American-led bloc of capitalist nations and the Soviet-led Communist bloc. In addition to this economic meaning, however, the term "Third World" frequently carried the political connotation of nonalignment in the Cold War. Many of the formerly colonized countries sought to remain uncommitted to either the American-led or Soviet-led alliances as they struggled to establish their own independent states and national cultures. Although this specific political meaning disappeared after the collapse of Soviet communism in 1991, the term "Third World" (in its economic sense) has persisted and may survive as a synonym for the poorer nations in the contemporary global economy.

The present chapter examines the history of the new Asian nations during their first half-century of modern independence and also discusses the post-1945 political and economic changes in Latin America. The Cold War rivalries of this era often affected the course of local political or economic conflicts on both of these continents. The following chapter looks at the history of postcolonial transformations in Africa and the Middle East (where the Cold War also had important consequences) and then returns to the broad problem of economic development that has affected postcolonial and impoverished nations in all parts of the world. The nations that emerged from the various colonial empires differed widely in their struggles for independence, in their later political systems, and in their cultural traditions, but they often faced similar postcolonial economic and political challenges as they sought to establish stable, modern nation-states.

114. THE EMERGENCE OF INDEPENDENT NATIONS IN SOUTH ASIA

The End of British Rule

The end in 1947 of British rule in India, the largest and most populous of all colonial areas ruled by Europeans, was epoch-making. Unfortunately, it fueled an explosion of ethnic and religious conflicts on the Indian subcontinent. The Indian National Congress, founded in 1885, had developed strength in the interwar years under the leadership of Gandhi and Nehru. The Congress party leaders demanded independence but also wished to avoid social revolution in the complex multiethnic country. Along with the British-trained Indian civil service, they considered themselves well prepared to govern an independent state. But the Muslim League, founded in 1906, claimed to speak, under Muhammad Ali Jinnah's leadership, for millions of Muslims unwilling to live in an India dominated by the Hindus and the Congress party. The Muslims insisted on their own national state, rooted in Islam. The Congress leaders, in contrast, pressed for a unified, secular India, with religion separated from politics and with freedom of worship for all religions.

During the Second World War India supported the British, but at the same time the Congress party and the Muslim League stepped up a "quit India" campaign. To retain Indian support for the war effort and to counter Japanese anti-Western propaganda, the British pledged independence. At the war's end, the British under Labour party leadership were poised to honor their pledge, but the Congress party and the Muslim League continued to have irreconcilable differences as plans were developed for an independent Indian state. To end the impasse the British decided on partition. In 1947 Britain granted independence to two nations: to India, predominantly *Partition of India* Hindu, with a population of 350 million at the time, which became the Republic of India; and to Pakistan, mainly Muslim, with a population of 75 million, which became the Islamic Republic of Pakistan. Large Muslim populations were concentrated in two widely separated regions of Britain's former Indian empire, and Pakistan was established as a state with two disconnected parts, West and East Pakistan, separated by a thousand miles of Indian territory. About 60 million Muslims were also left in India, which helped keep India the multireligious secular state that Gandhi and Nehru desired. Ceylon (later renamed Sri Lanka) and Burma (later called Myanmar) in South Asia also received independence from Britain at this time.

The partition, overly hasty and ill-conceived, led immediately to violence and a vast social upheaval. Independence in August 1947 brought with it terrible communal riots between the Hindu and Muslim communities costing at least a million lives in a matter of weeks; some 17 million Hindus and Muslims were caught up in mass expulsions and turbulent migrations. In the worst of the tragedies, in the northern province of Punjab, Hindu and Sikh religious zealots ambushed and slaughtered trainloads of Muslim refugees fleeing west to Pakistan, and Muslim fanatics did the same to Hindus and Sikhs migrating east to India. Gandhi, while praying for civil peace, was himself assassinated in 1948 by a Hindu extremist protesting his program for religious toleration. Only after the uglier features of the communal warfare subsided could the tasks of governing begin.

With his Congress party dominant, Nehru governed India as prime minister from 1947 until his death in 1964, setting the country on the path of British-style parliamentary democracy and even a kind of Fabian socialism. With no effective opposition, Nehru's program was more paternalistic than democratic. The masses looked to him to resolve the country's enormous problems of poverty; rapidly growing population; and ethnic, religious, and linguistic diversity. In addition to Hindi and English, 16 other languages received official recognition. In economic matters Nehru, a moderate socialist, understood the need for private capitalist enterprise but believed that economic planning, government controls, and the nationalization of key industries were also necessary. Under his leadership a modern industrial India with a mixed economy began to take shape and in many ways grew impressively in the years that followed.

Nehru's paternalism

Meanwhile, India and Pakistan fell into a recurring pattern of conflict, centered in part on the former princely state of Kashmir (officially, Jammu and Kashmir) in the Himalayas. Although three-fourths of the population were Muslim, the Hindu maharajah after procrastinating opted to take Kashmir into India. Open fighting over the issue of Kashmir broke out between India and Pakistan in 1948, and tense relations and intermittent conflicts have continued ever since. War again broke out over Kashmir in 1965–1966, ending in an uneasy truce. In 1971 India went to war with Pakistan, but this time to support Bangladesh in its bloody war of secession from Pakistan.

In international affairs Nehru's defense of neutralism and nonalignment in the Cold War, which he forcefully articulated at a milestone conference of emergent Asian and African nations in 1955 in Bandung, Indonesia, struck a responsive chord in many parts of the Third World. Although firmly committed to democracy, Nehru retained a deep antagonism toward Western imperialism and capitalism, which reinforced his neutralism in the Cold War. As to China, although Nehru championed the right of the People's Republic of China to pursue its own path of social development, he condemned the Chinese occupation of Tibet and, as we have seen, actual hostilities broke out over border disputes between India and China in 1962.

Neutralism and nonalignment

Nehru's Successors

When Nehru's immediate successor died in office in 1966, the Congress party leaders chose Nehru's daughter Indira Gandhi to be prime minister. Gandhi was her name through marriage, not through any kinship to the famous founder of Indian nationalism. She turned out to be a strong-willed political leader in her own right, but subordinated some of her father's more idealistic principles to political opportunism. More than Nehru, she looked for support from the masses, who idolized her for her carefully publicized pledges to abolish poverty. To win continuing support at the polls she made deals with Hindu nationalists, Muslims, and Sikhs. Corruption, already common, became even more fully entrenched.

Indira Gandhi

In 1975 Gandhi, fearing losses in a coming election, proclaimed emergency rule, suspended constitutional government, and had hundreds of opponents arrested. This violation of basic democratic principles aroused strong opposition, and after close to two years an outraged parliament drove her from office. But Gandhi retained enough political support to return as prime minister in 1980 and to govern subsequently by constitutional means. Confronting a Sikh secessionist movement in the Punjab, she misguidedly sent army troops to

The British partition of its South Asian colonial empire into mostly Muslim Pakistan and preponderantly Hindu India led to chaotic mass migrations and expulsions as people fled across the new borders in all directions. These trains in Amritsar, India, were swamped with Indian refugees who were trying to move to other Indian cities after fleeing from West Pakistan in October 1947.

(Bettmann/Corbis)

invade their sacred Golden Temple at Amritsar. A few years later, in 1984, she was assassinated by Sikh soldiers of her own personal security guard.

The Congress party turned to her older son, Rajiv Gandhi, who had earlier shown little interest in politics. Governing not very effectively over the next five years, from 1984 to 1989, he seemed at times out of touch with the country's pressing social problems. By now the long-entrenched Congress party was in decline, and in 1989 it lost its parliamentary majority.

The very concept of a tolerant secular India came under siege. A strong Hindu revivalist movement grew in strength during the 1990s, preaching "Hindu values" and pledging to restore India to a Hindu "golden age" antedating the Muslim conquests and British colonial rule. A right-wing political party, the Indian People's party (the Bharatiya Janata, or BJP), used the movement for its own political ends, and through it Hindu

By the early twenty-first century, India had become a leading country in the development of computer software and other technological research. Although much of India's population remained impoverished, skilled workers at facilities such as this computer training center were increasingly prosperous participants in the contemporary global economy.
(Associated Press, AP)

Hindu revivalism

revivalism entered the mainstream of Indian politics. The consequences were hostility, suspicion, and outright violence directed against the country's now 120 million Muslims.

Successfully exploiting widespread dissatisfaction with the Congress party, the BJP continued to increase its strength. Nonetheless, when Rajiv Gandhi was assassinated at a campaign rally in 1991, a sympathetic backlash helped the Congress party to win the new elections.

For the next five years, from 1991 to 1996, the Congress party again held office, but the Nehru-Gandhi dynasty had come to an end. The veteran reform-minded party leader

Congress party reforms

V. Narasimha Rao took steps to reform the party, reduce bureaucracy, and curb widespread corruption. Rao also relaxed the economic controls that had become obstacles to economic growth in a country that was now a major economic power, restoring several nationalized industries to private ownership. He encouraged foreign investment and reduced or eliminated excessive protectionist barriers. In the 1990s India began to emerge as a global leader in the development of new computer technologies, and the Indian economy became steadily more integrated into the worldwide system of transnational commerce.

While the economic results were impressive, the political scene grew more troubled. In December 1992 Hindu extremists clashed with Muslims over religious sites sacred to Islam, and riots erupted in major cities. The Congress Party, which was weakened by internal divisions and new corruption scandals, lost popular support and suffered a crushing electoral defeat in 1996. A series of unstable coalition governments followed until the Hindu revivalist party, the BJP, finally achieved a clear majority in 1999. The leader of the BJP, Atal Bhari Vajpayee, became Prime Minister and sought to enhance India's global standing as both an economic and military power.

Fears of a radical nationalist domestic program gradually dissipated, however, and Vajpayee did not promote the more extreme agenda of activists in the BJP. Meanwhile, the Congress Party reorganized itself for parliamentary elections in 2004 and (somewhat surprisingly) was able to return to power. The new government had to cope with the catastrophic effects of a major tsunami in 2004, which killed thousands of people along the Indian coastline, and it faced the perennial issue of relations with Pakistan—which were slowly improving by 2005, even along the contested borders of Kashmir and even as both nations continued to develop nuclear weapons.

Although Nehru had worked for a non-nuclear India, his successors took a different path. In May 1974, after refusing to sign nonproliferation or comprehensive test ban treaties, India tested an underground nuclear device and became the world's sixth nuclear nation. Two decades later, in 1998, Pakistan demonstrated its nuclear prowess by test detonating a nuclear bomb. India responded with nuclear tests of its own. Armed conflict between India and Pakistan thus took on the dimensions of a global danger, and the older dispute over Kashmir attracted worldwide attention in the early twenty-first century. Despite the welcome progress in Indian-Pakistani relations after 2004, South Asia remained one of the world's threatening trouble spots and a site of continuing religious and nationalist clashes.

Nuclear concerns

Fifty Years of Independence

In 1997 India celebrated 50 years of independence. After over a half-century India remained a land of many contradictions. It could boast of a large, well-educated, ambitious middle class benefiting from an increasingly modern economy. Although the traditional caste system was officially illegal, its effects persisted in many places, and particularly outside the larger cities. But many born into the lower castes had moved into the mainstream of the business and professional world. In 1997 India elected its first president born an "untouchable," President V. R. Narayan.

Through medical advances, better nutrition, and a decline in infant mortality, death rates had declined and population almost tripled in the first 50 years, reaching more than 1 billion by the early twenty-first century. But economic growth and rising consumer standards for some classes hardly affected village India—where most of the population still lived. Poverty, illiteracy, disease, and malnutrition remained widespread. Over half the country was illiterate; for women and girls the number was higher and they labored under additional disadvantages as well. Over 200 million people were without safe drinking water and 650 million were without basic sanitation. Population growth continued to threaten economic advances. A sporadic but ineffective family planning program was still widely resisted. Although poverty had declined in the past 50 years, over 40 percent of the population remained impoverished by internationally accepted standards. The cities were

A land of contradictions

congested and slum-ridden, swollen by millions who had left the villages to find jobs. India, despite its economic and technological advances, remained a Third World country, divided into social groups with very different levels of education, wealth, and access to the products of the global economy.

The status of women

Much remained to be done to improve the status of women. Old forms of discrimination persisted, accompanied at times by outright violence in matters of dowries, divorce, and inheritance, and in the plight of widows who were thrown on the mercy of their husbands' families for survival. The highly visible presence of women in high political ranks in India and elsewhere in South Asia belied their lower status in general. In India, as in Pakistan, Burma, Indonesia, Bangladesh, Sri Lanka, the Philippines, and elsewhere, women became presidents, prime ministers, or opposition leaders; but they almost always came to office as daughters or widows in leading political families similar to the Nehru-Gandhi "dynasty."

The Congress party, in power for most of the years since independence, had undoubtedly provided the stability needed for survival of the diverse country as a united nation. Parliamentary democracy, the rule of law, a free press, and an effective judiciary prevailed; and by the end of the twentieth century over 600 million people were exercising their right to vote (on ballots still marked by party symbols because of the widespread illiteracy). Yet

The invisible majority

bribery, venality, and corruption continued to affect all levels of government, and the country's "invisible majority"—its needy millions—remained neglected. Nehru's appeal at the time of independence for India's "tryst with destiny" had to be postponed. And the enduring problem of ethnic and religious tensions, which continued to disrupt Indian society in the early twenty-first century, often threatened to undermine India's democracy and destroy the multireligious tolerance that India's founders had originally envisaged.

The Islamic Republic of Pakistan

Pakistan's independence leader, Muhammad Ali Jinnah, a British-educated lawyer, was by no means an Islamic extremist and might have made a significant difference in the country's history, but he died shortly after independence, and his successor was assassinated. Despite the machinery of parliamentary democracy, the Islamic Republic of Pakistan soon succumbed to military rule and over the years oscillated between periods of military rule, restoration of constitutional government, which generally meant civilian misrule, and the return of military dictatorship. By the end of the century military dictators had run the country for half of its years of independence. It remained predominantly agricultural, and was still one of Asia's poorest and least developed nations.

Bengali secession and war

The awkward postcolonial arrangement for uniting the widely separated Muslim populations of South Asia in a single nation collapsed in violence. In East Pakistan, which had been carved out of the old Indian state of Bengal during the hasty partition in 1947, most of the population lived in congested, impoverished conditions that fueled political and social resentments against the West Pakistani leaders who dominated the government of Pakistan. These resentments exploded into a war of secession in 1971, when East Pakistan proclaimed its independence as the new state of Bangladesh (or "Bengali nation"). The Pakistani government vehemently opposed the secession movement and dispatched a large army to suppress the rebellion; hundreds of thousands were killed in a brutal and unequal civil war. At that point, however, India massively intervened with military force and compelled the

THE INDIAN SUBCONTINENT, 2000

The map shows nations that emerged from the dissolution of the British Empire in South Asia. East Pakistan was part of Pakistan until its war of secession in 1971 led to the establishment of an independent Bangladesh; Pakistan and Bangladesh are predominantly Muslim. India is predominantly Hindu, but large Muslim and Sikh minorities live there. The political ascendancy of a Hindu nationalist party in the 1990s altered India's pluralistic political culture and also changed the names of cities that have long been known as Bombay, Calcutta, and Madras (Mumbai, Kolkata, and Chennai). Political movements have changed other colonial-era names in the region, including the name of the country now called Myanmar, which was known as Burma throughout the era of British control and early independence. The island once called Ceylon is now Sri Lanka. The dispute between India and Pakistan over the status of Jammu and Kashmir has remained unresolved. Conflicts in this disputed territory, intensified by the development of nuclear weapons in India and Pakistan, as well as continuing internal conflicts in Sri Lanka and Myanmar, made South Asia one of the world's politically volatile regions at the beginning of the twenty-first century.

recognition of independence. Bangladesh became one of the world's most populous, predominantly Muslim nations (the population would grow to about 145 million by 2005), but its high population density contributed to persistent economic problems. It remained one of the world's poorest nations, suffering from floods, drought, and famine as well as recurring cycles of political violence and military coups.

Civilian rule was restored in Pakistan for a short time after the war over Bangladesh, but in 1977 the now familiar Pakistani political pattern continued. The military took power and executed President Ali Bhutto. Even when civilian rule was restored, the army kept a watchful eye on the political scene. In 1988 Benazir Bhutto, the Western-educated daughter of the former president, returned from exile and in new elections became the first woman prime minister of a major Islamic nation. Promising liberalization and reform, she

The steady increase of the population in India—more than 1 billion people at the beginning of the twenty-first century—continued to affect the status of women and the economic conditions of the nation's impoverished classes. Seeking to reduce the rate of population growth, the Indian government has promoted a campaign for family planning. This large sign in New Delhi portrays a woman, but its question seems to be directed at men and women alike: Do you want joy and comfort with two children, or destitution with four?
(François Lochon/Liaison Agency)

provoked opposition from militant Muslim groups and members of the military, who used evidence of corruption to discredit her leadership and eventually force her from office. Meanwhile the Islamic religious movements grew larger and more militant, bolstered by Muslim refugees and guerrilla fighters fleeing Afghanistan after the Soviet Union invaded that country in 1979. Muslim extremism continued to grow, and by the early 1990s the government ruled that Islamic law should take precedence over the constitution.

When the Soviet Union invaded Afghanistan in 1979, Pakistan was caught up in the contest between the superpowers in the Cold War. The United States used Pakistan as a conduit for arms being shipped to the Muslim guerrillas fighting the Soviets, and over 2 million Afghan refugees fled to Pakistan—where they remained until the Soviet army withdrew from Afghanistan in 1989 (and where many returned during later conflicts in the 1990s). The rise of a radical Islamic Afghan regime, the Taliban, contributed to the further development of militant Islamic movements within Pakistan; and the Pakistani government became one of the only governments in the world to establish relations with the Taliban regime.

In 1997 Benazir Bhutto's successor and chief opponent so thoroughly undermined the authority of parliament, the judiciary, and the provincial legislatures that the country was in political disarray and in financial straits. Relations with India, as we have seen, deteriorated. The military suffered a humiliating defeat when it crossed the border into Indian territory in Kashmir in 1999.

Political disarray and financial straits

Later that year, as economic matters worsened and renewed political instability threatened, the army leader General Musharraf staged a military coup. The new government included a number of civilian leaders and promised future elections. The coup was not unpopular because the Pakistani people were desperate for change, but the nation's political record of military rule aroused skepticism about the return to civilian government, let alone to parliamentary democracy.

Musharraf's military regime faced widespread popular opposition after 2001, when Pakistan entered a new era of cooperation with the United States. Following the terrorist attack on the United States by Islamic extremists in September 2001, Musharraf supported the American military campaign that overthrew the Taliban regime which had sheltered the Al Qaeda terrorist organizers of the attacks against America. Although his cooperation with the United States gave Musharraf a prominent new role in international affairs and new sources of foreign support, he faced continuing criticism from Islamic militants, some of whom tried twice to assassinate him. Other Pakistanis resented his unconstitutional hold on the presidency without new elections. The radicals were also unhappy with his efforts to improve relations with India.

The gradual improvement in relations between India and Pakistan offered some promise for a more stable political future in South Asia. At the same time, however, the uncertain future of Pakistan's military government, the presence of foreign Islamic radicals within Pakistani society, the development of nuclear weapons, and the continuing militancy of both Islamic and Hindu radicals all pointed to the danger and likelihood of more upheavals or religious conflicts in South Asia. And the lingering violence in Afghanistan after the overthrow of the Taliban regime gave Pakistan a pivotal (though unpredictable) role in the global political and military strategies of the United States.

115. THE EMERGENCE OF INDEPENDENT NATIONS IN SOUTHEAST ASIA

The Union of Burma (Myanmar)

Burma, India's neighbor to the east, embarked on a unique path of isolation and repression after it gained independence in 1948. Britain had annexed the country to its Indian empire in 1885; and gradually, over the next half century, the British built a railway network, developed the country's mining and forest resources, and encouraged rice cultivation. Burma became for a time the world's largest exporter of rice. In the interwar years the British encouraged limited self-government but also imprisoned nationalist leaders like Aung San who pressed for immediate independence. After the Japanese invasion of Burma in the Second World War the nationalist leaders took up arms against the Japanese but also took advantage of the Japanese conquest to advance Burma's independence from Britain.

Burmese independence

After the war the British recognized Burma's independence, but Aung San, who was to become prime minister, was assassinated and his associate, U Nu, a devout Buddhist and somewhat doctrinaire socialist, became the first prime minister. To the new leaders of the nation anti-imperialism meant anticapitalism and the new government was determined to socialize the country rapidly. With little money, however, it was difficult to import machinery and to train workers; "the Burmese path to socialism," as it was styled, became impossible. In addition to economic chaos, Burma faced armed rebellion from insurgent separatist minorities, many of them reinforced after 1949 by the new Communist regime in China. Ethnic minorities made up about one-third

Aung San Suu Kyi emerged as the charismatic, determined leader and symbol of the democratic movement in Myanmar. She is pictured here in 1989 at the kind of political meeting that led Myanmar's repressive military regime to place her under prolonged house arrest and the Nobel committee to grant her the honor of a Nobel peace prize.
(Time Life Pictures/Getty Images)

of the country's population. Many of these minorities were incensed by Nu's plan to make Buddhism the official state religion.

Despite the official political framework of a multiparty parliamentary democracy, the military exercised a parallel power with the civilian authorities. As the ethnic insurgencies became more threatening in 1962, the army head General Ne Win staged a military takeover. He would retain power for the next 26 years in a one-party state still dedicated to pursuing the "Burmese path to socialism," but in effect a military regime.

Isolation and repression

As economic difficulties and ethnic turbulence steadily worsened, the country retreated into deeper isolation. By the early 1970s insurgent groups controlled one-third of the country. Popular discontent mounted and in the 1980s a new opposition party emerged, the National League for Democracy, headed by Aung San Suu Kyi, the daughter of the country's martyred founder. Educated in India, she also spent some 20 years at Oxford where she pursued graduate studies and married an Oxford don. An immensely popular and charismatic figure, she incorporated in her person the nonviolence of traditional Buddhism with Western democratic values. When in 1988 the military dictator resigned, she addressed large crowds of supporters and proclaimed that Burma's "second struggle for independence" was under way. But in the end a repressive military junta took power and placed her under house arrest. During this same period, in 1989, the military government emphasized its break from the country's previous colonial and national history by changing the nation's name to Myanmar.

Confronted with continuing massive demonstrations, the military agreed to open elections in 1990, the first in 30 years. But when the democratic opposition won 90 percent of the popular vote and over four-fifths of the parliamentary seats, the stunned military declared the elections null and void and took reprisals against the party leaders. Aung San Suu Kyi remained under strict surveillance, her movements and visitors severely restricted. But she became an international symbol of democratic aspirations; in 1991 she received the Nobel Peace Prize. Meanwhile military repression thwarted the popular desire for democratic self-government and civilian rule, and the leaders of the democracy movement remained virtually imprisoned throughout much of the 1990s and into the first decade of the new century. Although international human rights groups protested the regime's repressive policies and helped some refugees escape the country, the military maintained tight control over all aspects of political and public life in Myanmar. The movement for democratic reforms, represented by the determined leadership of Aung San Suu Kyi, was still unable to achieve its political goals almost 60 years after the nation had gained its independence from Britain.

Malaysia

In the Malayan peninsula British plans for independence after the Second World War were delayed because of tensions between the country's Muslim Malay majority and its sizable Chinese and Indian minorities. These large minority populations had lived in Malaysia since the nineteenth century when the British had imported workers from China and India to work in the tin and rubber mines. The Chinese had come to play a dominant role in the economy. At the same time a militant Communist movement had emerged, and the British for several years fought a Communist insurgency. In 1957, with the rebellion mostly subdued, Britain granted independence. Five years later Malaya joined with Singapore and other former British dependencies to create the Federation of Malaysia.

Singapore withdrew in 1965 to become a small island-nation with a flourishing modern economy and high living standards but governed by a semi-authoritarian, paternalistic regime under Lee Kuan Yew. Singapore thus resembled other East Asian countries such as Taiwan and South Korea in making rapid economic advances without establishing full-fledged democracies. There was no absolute repression, but no genuine democracy either. Under more or less authoritarian regimes, the ruler or ruling group brought all political parties under the umbrella of "national unity" and discouraged militant opposition or open dissent. Not until late in the twentieth century did democracy make headway in Taiwan and South Korea. Political life in Singapore also began to evolve, though Lee Kuan Yew remained a guiding force in government affairs and his son became prime minister in 2004.

Ethnic conflicts had flared up in Malaysia in 1969, and riots led to the suppression of parliamentary rule for about two years. After that difficult period, although the Malay political dominance remained clear, multiethnic coalitions gradually helped to ease tensions. Already prospering because of tin, oil, rubber, and lumber resources, Malaysia in the 1980s developed new high-technology industries, and its economy became one of the fastest growing in Asia, attracting foreign investment as well. The long-serving Prime Minister, Mahathir bin Mohamad, promoted an ambitious economic program that included large-scale construction projects. *Economic growth* Malaysia had climbed out of its previous "Third World" economic status by the late 1990s, but a series of financial and currency crises weakened the nation's financial position at the end of the century. Radical Islamic groups became active among the nation's large Muslim population, and the economic problems led to the expulsion of numerous foreign workers. But Malaysia remained one of the most prosperous and stable Asian nations to emerge from the twentieth-century British empire.

The British thus surrendered all but small outposts of their vast empire within a decade or so after the end of the Second World War. However, most of the former British

Malaysia's growing role in the global economy is reflected in the soaring, contemporary office buildings of the capital city, Kuala Lumpur. The Petronas Towers, which rise to a height of almost 1,500 feet and loom over the other offices in this picture, were the tallest buildings in the world at the beginning of the twenty-first century.

(© John Dakers; Eye Ubiquitous/Corbis)

colonies in Asia (as well as in Africa, the Caribbean, and the Pacific) agreed to retain a voluntary association with Britain and each other in a new Commonwealth of Nations. Both Malaysia and Singapore, for example, became members of this Commonwealth, which grew into an association of over 50 independent nations. The Commonwealth did not force its members to act in concert on international issues, but it helped to promote useful interchange between the diverse peoples who had once lived within Britain's far-flung empire.

Indonesia

Another great empire in Southeast Asia, the Dutch East Indies, also came to an end. Agitation for independence, as in India, went back to pre-1914 days, but the Indonesian Nationalist party, founded in 1927, and a growing Communist party had met with little success in the interwar years. The Japanese, as elsewhere in Asia, exploited anti-Western sentiment during the Second World War and found Indonesian nationalist leaders to use as collaborators in their military occupation. At the same time a broad resistance movement emerged in which the Communists played a major part. Once the Japanese were ousted at the war's end in August 1945, before the Dutch could return, the Indonesian Nationalist leader Sukarno (Indonesians often use only their family name in public life) proclaimed the country's independence. For four years the Dutch stubbornly fought the nationalist movement, but they finally ceded independence in 1949.

A large, multiethnic country

By the early twenty-first century Indonesia's population exceeded 240 million, making it the fourth most populous country in the world. An archipelago situated along the equator with thousands of islands strung together over 3,000 miles, it is rich in oil, natural gas, timber, and other resources. A modified form of Malay is the official language, but the people of Indonesia speak over 300 languages and dialects. With some 88 percent of the population Muslim, it has the largest Islamic population in the world. The first and

Indonesian President Sukarno became a leader of the world's new and developing nations during the era of decolonization. He is shown here in 1955, addressing the international meeting at Bandung, where representatives of nonaligned nations affirmed their independence, pledged to remain neutral in the Cold War, and condemned the legacies of Western imperialism.
(Time Life Pictures/Getty Images)

continuing task was to establish and maintain a sense of national identity in so large and multiethnic a country.

Sukarno began with a parliamentary constitutional program and a democratic ideology derived from the struggle against the Dutch, but the democratic phase did not last. In 1959 he dissolved the Constituent Assembly and governed in the following years under a populist dictatorship that he called "guided democracy"; before long he insisted upon being elected "president for life," and he sought to play a prominent, independent role in Cold War diplomacy.

Sukarno's "guided democracy"

Sukarno became one of the chief spokesmen for the developing nations of Asia and Africa. He hosted the meeting in Bandung in 1955 at which leaders of 29 of the new nations celebrated their new sovereignty, condemned Western imperialist and capitalist exploitation, and pledged neutralism and nonalignment in the Cold War. Sukarno cultivated friendship with the Soviet Union and Communist China and loosened economic ties with the West. Meanwhile the Indonesian Communist party, backed by the People's Republic of China, had quietly grown into the third largest Communist party in the world with some 2 million members.

For a time Sukarno managed to work with and control the large Communist party, but in 1965 leftist army officers attempted a coup. A relatively unknown army leader, General Suharto, quickly moved to suppress what was alleged to be a Communist rebellion, but he also ousted Sukarno. What ensued, as the army stood by, was the dreadful slaughter by Islamic militants of hundreds of thousands of Communists and leftists in a bloodbath that ranks among the larger atrocities of the twentieth century. A half million Communists and leftist suspects were murdered, 2 million were arrested and thousands were imprisoned. The violence also took a racial turn when many ethnic Chinese fell victim. The repression destroyed the Indonesian Communist party.

Suharto's war on the Communists

Over the next 32 years General Suharto retained power, running his island empire from the capital in Jakarta under a system of controlled elections in which he was dutifully reelected president every five years. He was supported within the country and abroad by those who claimed that his authoritarian methods were needed to maintain Indonesian unity and to prevent the resurgence of Communism or the spread of Islamic extremism. The military presence, which had loomed in Indonesian politics ever since independence, became pervasive. A single governing party ruled with uncontested power.

Suharto's anti-Communist credentials brought him Western support in the Cold War and attracted foreign investment to the country. He presided over an impressive economy, which showed annual growth rates that became another of the success stories of the developing world. The economy expanded sixfold over 30 years, and Indonesia ranked as one of the ten strongest emerging markets of the world. New construction changed the face of the nation, especially of the capital. A few in Indonesia became very rich; the middle classes grew in number and comfort; and there was a general decline in poverty throughout the country.

An impressive economy

At the same time a culture of corruption grew. Suharto, his family, his political entourage, and an inner circle of bankers, business leaders, and technocrats enriched themselves to the growing resentment of people outside the ruling elite. Suharto aroused opposition in other ways. In 1975, when Portugal withdrew from East Timor, an enclave it had long ruled adjacent to Indonesian territory, Suharto moved aggressively to annex it. The population of almost 1 million, many of whom were Christian, wanted independence and resisted the brutal annexation. Close to 100,000 lives were lost in a violent, systematic repression that provoked worldwide denunciation of Suharto. Indonesia continued to suppress the movement for East Timor's independence until the end of the twentieth century, when the United Nations sent peacekeeping troops and safeguarded a political process that finally established the independent nation of East Timor in 2002.

Spread of corruption

Much of Indonesia's economic success depended on foreign loans, and its foreign debt mounted, but the overexpansion of credit threatened the country's financial stability. In the latter half of 1997 a financial panic swept Indonesia (and other parts of southeast Asia as well). In 1997–1998 the currency lost four-fifths of its value and the poverty rate tripled.

The economic crisis brought about Suharto's downfall. When he insisted on reelection for a seventh term as president and the servile parliament permitted it, riots and demonstrations broke out. Suharto was forced to relinquish power in May 1998, naming as his successor his vice president and protege H. J. Habibie. The country was in economic chaos but also in political ferment. The press was freed, political parties reemerged, new elections were organized, and a new president, Abdurrahman Wahid, took office in 1999. As a concession to the opposition, Megawati Sukarnoputri, the daughter of the country's independence leader and first president (Sukarno), became vice president. Two years later she succeeded Wahid when the legislature removed him from office. President Megawati brought new stability to the Indonesian government and the economy began to revive. Extremist Islamic groups sometimes resorted to terrorism, however, and there were repeated military clashes with rebels who were seeking autonomy or independence for the provinces of Aceh and Papua. Following a pattern that appeared in many parts of the world, the advocates of religious or regional identities challenged the economic and political policies of a government that was seeking to integrate the nation into global economic and political institutions.

Suharto ousted

Steps toward democracy

Mounting political unrest led in 2004 to the election of the first directly elected Indonesian president—a political innovation that exemplified the continuing development of Indonesian democracy. But the new government faced ongoing economic and domestic political challenges as well as the aftereffects of the catastrophic tsunami that struck southeast Asia in December 2004. Indonesia was a rapidly growing and evolving large nation of pivotal importance in Asian affairs and in the global resurgence of Muslim religious identities.

The Independence Movement in Indochina

The French colonial empire also fell apart, not, however, without a long struggle. The first of France's postwar colonial wars, as noted in the previous chapter, was fought over Indochina. When France offered autonomy to the states of Indochina at the end of the Second World War within a French federation, Cambodia and Laos accepted; but Vietnam (as Cochin-China, Tonkin, and Annam jointly came to be called) demanded full independence. Open warfare broke out in 1946, and French armies and Communist-led Vietnamese forces fought each other for over seven years.

The Communist leader Ho Chi Minh, who headed the independence movement in Vietnam, had spent many earlier years in London, in Paris (where he had first called for the "self-determination" of Indochina during the Versailles peace conference and witnessed the founding of the French Communist party in 1920), and in Moscow. He returned to Vietnam in 1941, organized a Vietnamese independence movement (the Viet Minh), and mobilized guerrilla armies to fight the Japanese. At the war's end he proclaimed Vietnam's independence. The French tried to reassert control by using an ineffectual former emperor of Annam as a puppet. When negotiations failed, Ho turned his armies against the French. Because the Communists led the independence movement, the French could claim that they were fighting to stem the tide of world communism, not to preserve nineteenth-century colonial privileges. Yet communism here, as often in Asia, was linked to nationalism, anticolonialism, anti-Westernism, and genuine popular discontent.

Communism and imperialism

Under President Eisenhower the United States, anticolonial but ready to champion anti-Communist causes in the Cold War, aided the French financially but refrained from open military intervention. The war drained French morale and resources. In the spring of 1954 at the very time that an international conference was meeting in Geneva to arrange a settlement in Indochina, the French army after a long, costly siege suffered a severe defeat at the battle of Dien Bien Phu. The conference, with French acquiescence, recognized the independence of Vietnam, as well as of Cambodia and Laos. The colonial empire in French Indochina came to an end.

Vietnam was provisionally partitioned at the 17th parallel into a northern and southern sector until elections could be held for the entire country, but the elections never took place. Neither Ho nor the Western-backed regime in the south was satisfied with the settlement of 1954, and a civil war of increasing intensity soon began. The United States, as we shall see, became deeply involved in the war by the early 1960s, seeing the struggle in Vietnam as part of the global Communist challenge that had to be contained. The Vietnam War became one of the most protracted conflicts of the entire Cold War era, and we shall return to this war when we examine the broader context of American-Soviet confrontations after 1960 in Chapter 25. Meanwhile, by the mid-1950s, France's entire colonial empire in Indochina had given way to new national states.

The Americans and the Philippines

The Americans, too, shared in the liquidation of colonial empires in Asia. In the Philippines a strong independence movement had emerged in the late nineteenth century

Opponents of Ferdinand Marcos rallied in 1986 to Corazón Aquino when she challenged the Filipino president in a contested election after almost two decades of authoritarian rule. Aquino appears here among enthusiastic supporters on the eve of her electoral victory, which Marcos tried to overturn until a popular uprising forced him to flee the Philippines. (AFP/Getty Images)

directed against the decaying Spanish empire. Revolution under the leadership of Emilio Aguinaldo was well under way when the Spanish-American War broke out in 1898. With American encouragement Aguinaldo joined the war against Spain and unilaterally declared independence, promulgating the first democratic and republican constitution in Asia. But Filipino nationalists were stymied when Spain transferred the islands to the United States at the end of the war. Aguinaldo and his followers rebelled and took up arms against the United States. The suppression of the Filipino independence movement over the next three years cost the United States more money and more lives than the war against Spain itself.

Independence remained a pressing issue both in the islands and in the United States, which after semimilitary rule in the 1920s proposed a transition to self-rule and eventual independence. An act of Congress in 1934 granted self-governing commonwealth status with a pledge of full independence in the near future. Delayed by the Second World War, independence was finally granted in July 1946.

Transition to independence

In the early years of independence a succession of governments did little to help the impoverished peasants or even maintain political order. Communist-led guerrilla movements pressing for land redistribution added to instability. President Ferdinand E. Marcos, who was elected in 1965, declared martial law in 1972 and ruled the nation as an authoritarian dictator until the 1980s. The Americans

Marcos as president

cooperated with the Marcos regime because of its staunch anticommunism, but poverty and government corruption steadily increased while Marcos and his family grew wealthy and spent money extravagantly.

After the assassination in 1983 of the popular opposition leader Benigno Aquino upon his return to the islands from exile, his widow Corazón Aquino spearheaded the opposition and contested Marcos in presidential elections that finally took place in 1986. When Marcos, despite clear evidence of fraud, attempted to declare himself the winner, the country turned decisively against him, and his support eroded even in the United States. The ensuing popular upheaval forced him into exile.

President Aquino faced continuing pressures from Right and Left, but restored democratic elections and civil rights. She also slowly inaugurated land and other reforms, setting an example for those who followed her. In the early 1990s the Filipino legislature opposed the renewal of leases for America's military bases, and the United States agreed to withdraw. Another chapter of Western imperialism came to an end. Later governments struggled to develop the Filipino economy, to suppress Muslim secessionist groups in the southern islands, and to overcome persistent charges of corruption and electoral fraud. The Supreme Court forced a later president from office in 2001 because of a corruption scandal; and his successor, Gloria Macapagal-Arroyo, would also arouse widespread suspicion of fraudulent electoral practices. Filipino political life remained unsettled as successive governments lost the confidence of the nation's political elites as well as of the general population.

American withdrawal

The transition from colonialism to postcolonial political and social systems posed complex historical challenges throughout South Asia and Southeast Asia, even after more than a half-century of constant political and economic change. People in all Asian societies had welcomed national independence and celebrated the demise of the Western empires, but the struggles for independence gave way everywhere to new struggles for political stability, democratic institutions, economic development, and national unity. The complex domestic evolution of every newly independent nation-state was further complicated by the international conflicts of the Cold War and by the global pressures of a world economy that often affected the postcolonial nations even more profoundly after they had gained their political freedom from the European imperial systems. More generally, the transition to independence stimulated ongoing debates about cultural, religious, and national identities that were still creating new political movements and conflicts within every postcolonial Asian society in the early twenty-first century.

116.   CHANGING LATIN AMERICA

Unlike the new nations that emerged after the Second World War in Asia, most of the Latin American nations had been independent for well over a century by 1945. Yet the legacy of colonialism had left the region, like other parts of the Third World, with unbalanced economic development, heavily dependent on the outside world, and burdened with unresolved political, social, and economic problems.

A region of over 7 million square miles stretching from the Rio Grande to the southern tip of Argentina and Chile, Latin America includes Mexico, Central America, South America, and the islands of the Caribbean. It is mainly Spanish in language and culture, but Portuguese is the language of Brazil, the continent's largest and most populous country. English and French are spoken

Latin America

CHRONOLOGY OF NOTABLE EVENTS, 1946–2000

1946	The United States grants independence to the Philippines
1947	Britain ends its imperial rule in South Asia, partitioning the region into the two new nations of India and Pakistan
1949	Indonesia wins independence from the Netherlands
1954	France withdraws from Indochina; two governments emerge in North and South Vietnam
1955	Leaders of 29 "new nations" meet in Bandung, Indonesia, and affirm "nonalignment" in the Cold War
1959–1961	Fidel Castro establishes Communist government in Cuba
1965	General Suharto overthrows Sukarno; begins 32-year rule in Indonesia
1970–1973	Leftist government in Chile; overthrown by coup and Pinochet dictatorship
1971	India helps Bangladesh gain independence from Pakistan
1974	India develops nuclear weapons
1976–1983	Dictatorship in Argentina represses leftist opposition
1979	Soviet Union invades Afghanistan and begins war with Muslim guerillas
1989	Soviets withdraw from Afghanistan; radical Muslim (Taliban) government follows
1989	Military rulers in Burma repress dissent; nation is renamed Myanmar
1994	Mexican-U.S.-Canadian Free Trade Agreement (NAFTA) goes into effect
1996–1999	Rising power of Indian People's Party (BJP) fosters Hindu-based nationalism in India
1998	Pakistan detonates a nuclear bomb
1998	General Suharto is ousted from power in Indonesia
1998	Hugo Chávez becomes president of leftist government in Venezuela
2000	Vincente Fox is elected president of Mexico; ends 71 years of rule by Institutional Revolutionary Party (PRI)

in some islands of the Caribbean, and a variant of French is spoken in Haiti. The many indigenous Indian languages and dialects, though still widely used in many rural areas, are generally submerged in the majority cultures; but the indigenous peoples have also reasserted or defended their cultural identities in many parts of Latin America during recent decades.

It is a region of great racial diversity and mixture. Argentina, because of the flood of immigration in the nineteenth century, is overwhelmingly European in composition, but in Bolivia over half the population is of indigenous Indian origin. In Brazil, the population consists of whites of European background, indigenous Indians, blacks, and mainly an amalgam of mixed peoples. Because of the once flourishing slave trade and slavery, half the Brazilian population is wholly or in part of West African ancestry. Almost everywhere, however, European whites and mestizos (that is, people of mixed European and Indian ancestry) tend to dominate their societies. With high growth rates, the population of Latin

America more than tripled after 1945, increasing from 160 million in 1950 to over 500 million by the end of the century. The two largest cities in Latin America, Mexico City and São Paulo, Brazil, were among the ten most populous urban agglomerations in the world at the beginning of the twenty-first century.

The Colonial Experience and the Wars for Independence

The three centuries of colonial rule after the Spanish *conquista* left an ineradicable mark. Wherever the Spanish had found large Indian populations, as in Mexico and in the area then known as Peru, they had incorporated them into their colonial system and imposed upon them the hierarchical social structure of the home country. To encourage settlement the crown had granted (or "entrusted") large estates to Spanish nobles sent out from Spain to the New World.

Spanish colonialism

The arrival of the Europeans had led in many places to demographic disaster. In the first generation the new diseases brought by the Europeans decimated the indigenous Indian populations. To work on the sugar plantations in the lowland areas in South America and throughout the Caribbean, the Europeans imported black slave laborers from Africa, eventually in the millions. Slavery was nominally abolished in most areas by the 1850s (although in Brazil not until 1888), but more or less disguised forms of servitude, like peonage, persisted. Indians and blacks remained at the bottom economic rung of a social system that was dominated by the American-born descendants of European settlers and immigrants—the Creoles.

A long-enduring pattern of economic exchange developed during the colonial period. Mineral wealth and other commodities flowed from the colonies to the mother country, and Spain in turn provided the needed finished goods or arranged for their shipment from other European countries. Although Spain did not develop a strong commercial class either at home or in the colonies, ranching and mining became large-scale colonial operations, and a variety of commercial enterprises sprang up.

The colonial economy

As the years passed, the American-born Creole elite grew wealthy and chafed at European control. They found an opportunity to break away when Napoleon occupied Spain and Portugal and displaced the two royal houses, but the Creole leaders were also frightened by the popular violence of the French Revolution. They intended to control their struggle for independence and protect their privileged social positions and landed wealth. From 1808 to 1826 they fought and won a series of bitterly contested wars for independence; in Brazil members of the Portuguese royal family led the country peacefully into independence. The wars for independence scarcely improved the status of the lower classes who fought the battles, or prepared the way for a more fluid society. Independence, in effect, mainly allowed local elites to wield political power commensurate with their wealth. From the wars for independence and from the subsequent conflicts among the new republics there emerged in Latin America a large military establishment, a powerful military class, and a succession of caudillos, or dictators, emerging from the military.

Latin American independence

The withdrawal of the Spanish and Portuguese transformed Latin America's political elites, but the older patterns of economic exchange and dependency did not disappear. There was, however, a change in the network of trade partners because the British, as pioneers in the Industrial Revolution, were now able to move widely into Latin American markets. Because the Creole landowners wanted low-priced manufactured imports, British-manufactured goods met with little resistance or competition. British capital also financed the infrastructure, the docks, the

Dependency

roads, and eventually the railroads to support the expanding trade. Economic penetration by Britain (and soon by the United States) represented a new form of colonialism, or neo-colonialism, an economic domination that did not require the acquisition of territory. In the late nineteenth century European and American investments and a flood of European immigration further tied Latin America to the outside world.

The Colossus to the North

Independence left the region politically fragmented and unstable, and many of the new republics became mired in civil and national wars. European political control might have been reimposed except for the American Monroe Doctrine, which (with British support) strongly opposed Continental interference with the independence of the new states. Later in the century the United States also made clear that in cases of civil disorder anywhere in the hemisphere it would not permit the Europeans to intervene to restore stability, protect investments, or collect debts, as was their custom in the era of expansive European imperialism. In what came to be known as the corollary to the Monroe Doctrine, President Theodore Roosevelt announced in 1904 that the United States alone would assume the responsibility of intervention for such purposes.

The Monroe Doctrine

Over the next quarter of a century the United States followed a policy of active armed intervention, or "dollar diplomacy," mainly in Central America and the Caribbean until gradually modifying its more overt interventionism in the mid-1930s.

In the opening years of the twentieth century the United States began to rival the British as the dominant trading partner of Latin America, exporting its manufactures and purchasing many of the region's primary agricultural and mineral products. After the First World War it gradually displaced Britain as the leading source of loans and capital investment. Although centers of manufacturing emerged, Latin America remained industrially underdeveloped, in part because of its dependency on the industrial world and in part because its impoverished masses provided a weak consumer base for industrial expansion. Meanwhile prices of the region's agricultural and mining products became increasingly hostage to the world's markets.

Economic Growth and Its Problems

Latin America suffered heavily when commodity prices plummeted in the dismal years of the Great Depression of the 1930s and foreign investment also dried up. The economic crisis encouraged the Latin Americans to look to their own resources and to attempt to industrialize, as Brazil did under the populist dictator Getulio Vargas in the years 1930 to 1945. When during the Second World War the region was cut off from traditional foreign sources of consumer goods, industrialization received additional stimulus.

After 1945 the economic structure of the entire region began to undergo significant transformation. It benefited from the increased demand for its raw materials and agricultural products and from an influx of foreign investment. The Alliance for Progress, sponsored by the United States in the early 1960s under President Kennedy, signaled a new North American commitment to the economic development of the region, even though Latin Americans repeatedly complained of being slighted in favor of other parts of the developing world. In the three decades from 1945 to 1975, Latin American economies grew steadily at impressive rates; steel production multiplied 20 times and electrical energy, metals, and machinery multiplied 10 times.

Alliance for Progress

Mexico, Argentina, Brazil, and Chile, despite many internal problems, could justifiably be classified among the newly industrialized countries of the world. Latin Americans manufactured industrial products in larger volume than ever before and no longer relied heavily on foreign imports for their industrial needs. The presence of American and European multinational corporations further stimulated economic progress. Much of this new industrialization, however, developed within a network of protective tariffs, subsidies, and state-controlled enterprises. Moreover, the region had only begun to utilize advanced technology, and low mass-purchasing power continued to impede growth. Economic expansion mostly benefited the social elites, increasing the gap between rich and poor.

To support economic development the major Latin American governments borrowed heavily in the 1970s from Western (mainly American) banks and international lending agencies, thereby becoming the most heavily indebted nations in the world; for many countries foreign debt nearly quadrupled. By the 1980s the failure to meet debt payments posed a serious financial threat to international creditors, and foreign banks and lending agencies took steps to ease interest payments. The austerity measures imposed by the lending agencies, however, threatened to reduce already depressed living standards. Even in better times many of the Latin American governments assigned a low priority to funding for schools, hospitals, roads, and public health facilities. Large military establishments and bureaucracies also consumed scarce resources. Driven by development ambitions and burdened by other expenditures, many governments simply printed paper money, debasing the currency and promoting extraordinary price rises. In the 1980s several countries suffered "quadruple-digit" annual inflation rates of over 1,000 percent.

Debt and inflation

The social difficulties of these unstable economies were compounded when agricultural commodity prices collapsed in the hyperinflation of the 1980s. Economic growth in Latin America slowed to below one percent, or even at times turned negative. As in other developing areas, the 1980s were in many ways a "lost decade." In 1989 production per capita was lower than in 1980. But growth gradually resumed as many of the Latin American countries abandoned state controls, encouraged freer market economies, introduced sounder public finances, and brought inflation under control. With renewed confidence in the region's economic prospects, foreign bankers and investors once again provided capital for Latin American companies and governments.

A lost decade

Despite economic advances, population growth rates remained a source of concern. As elsewhere in all of the developing world, death rates declined dramatically in the later decades of the twentieth century, and population growth surged. In Latin America it was even more difficult to cope with rising growth rates because of the Catholic church's prohibition of artificial birth control, although such prohibition was often circumvented or ignored by the upper and middle classes. Growing in many years at three percent annually, the population tripled between 1950 and the 1990s, and the increase all but canceled economic and social gains for the masses of people. On the positive side, population began to stabilize in the more industrialized Latin American countries.

Population growth

Over the years landless rural workers fled the impoverished countryside in all parts of Latin America, settling in the slums of the congested and polluted cities. A privileged upper-class minority kept many of its financial assets safely abroad but monopolized land and wealth at home. The per capita income in all Latin American nations still lagged well

Most Latin American nations became steadily more industrialized during the decades after 1945. The workers in this picture are assembling cars at a Volkswagen factory in São Paulo, Brazil. Such factories exemplify the growing role of Latin American cities in the global economy and also the transnational operations of the contemporary world's large industrial corporations.

(Camera Tres/Black Star)

below the incomes of the wealthiest industrialized societies. By the early twenty-first century, the more prosperous countries such as Brazil, Mexico, and Chile had per capita incomes at about one-third the per capita income of nations such as Germany, Japan, France, or the United States. Although the economic elites in Latin America had become wealthy participants in the global economy, countries such as Haiti and Honduras ranked among the very poorest nations in the world. Bolivia, whose mineral wealth had once enriched the Incas and the Spanish, had the lowest per capita income of all the South American republics. Beginning in the 1960s, many priests and nuns responded to the economic inequities in Latin America on their own by preaching "liberation theology," or "the church of the poor." Despite opposition from the Vatican, they threw themselves into efforts to improve the lot of the impoverished. Other reformers showed renewed interest in the economic problems and cultural traditions of the indigenous peoples.

End of Yankee Imperialism?

Did the second half of the twentieth century change relationships with the economic colossus to the north? In its "good neighbor" policy in the 1930s the United States appeared to adopt an important step toward surrendering its interventionist prerogatives. Military interventions before 1933 in Mexico, Nicaragua, Panama, Cuba, the Dominican Republic, and Haiti formed a

American interventions

historical pattern that aroused resentment throughout Latin America. But American marines and troops continued to land in Latin America even after 1945, especially in Central America and the Caribbean, in such countries as Guatemala in 1954, the Dominican Republic in 1965–1966, Grenada in 1983, and Panama in 1989. At times the interventions were tied to American Cold War policies of "containment," which were designed to oppose communism everywhere in the world.

As a goodwill gesture after the Second World War, the United States promoted the establishment in 1948 of the Organization of American States (or OAS). In the OAS 35 nations of the Western Hemisphere, including the United States and Canada, joined together to provide a mechanism for settling disputes among the republics. The OAS provided a more dignified alternative to traditional North American interventionism. Another step signaling a new era was the agreement by the United States in 1977 to hand over the Panama Canal to Panama, which took place in 1999.

Among the signs of change in the Western Hemisphere was a growing sense of economic interdependence. The United States needed a stable and prospering Latin America for its own economy. In 1994, at American initiative, the United States, Canada, and Mexico subscribed to the North American Free Trade Agreement, which over a period of time would eliminate all trade barriers among the three countries, and later be extended to other countries as well. Meanwhile large numbers of immigrants from Mexico, the Caribbean, and other parts of Latin America streamed northward, changing the ethnic composition of the United States itself and expanding the connections among peoples in this region of the world.

Growing sense of interdependence

The Political Systems and Conflicts in Latin American Societies

Politically, the Latin American record for much of the twentieth century was mostly a history of insecure constitutional regimes and repressive military dictatorships, civil wars and social revolutions, ethnic tensions and labor unrest, coups and countercoups, and agitation against foreign, notably American, interests. There were also episodes of broad-based populist dictatorships with wide mass support, as in Brazil under Vargas, mentioned earlier, and in Argentina under Juan Perón from 1946 to 1955 (with *peronismo* exerting a continuing influence in later years). Disheartening cycles of reform and repression recurred. Central America reflected even greater volatility. Instability from the 1950s to the 1980s was intensified by American anti-Communist commitments in the Cold War and by American support for rightist elements in Central America, particularly in Nicaragua and El Salvador.

Cycles of reform and repression

When leftist regimes were overthrown in Latin America in those years, frequently with unofficial United States help, as in Guatemala in 1954, Brazil in 1964, Chile and Uruguay in 1973, Argentina in 1976, and El Salvador in 1980, harsh repression often followed. Political opponents simply "disappeared"—they were imprisoned, tortured, and often executed, as the later record showed. Two of the most extreme examples occurred in Argentina and Chile. Argentina's "Dirty War" against leftists claimed over 30,000 lives between 1976 and 1983. Even under democratic regimes in later years those responsible long went unpunished, although the misdeeds were openly acknowledged. A second striking example of military repression occurred in Chile, where a Left coalition elected in 1970 and committed to land reform as well as the nationalization of American-owned copper mines, was toppled three years later by a military coup with the involvement of the United States. The country's democratically elected leftist president, Salvador Allende,

The Cuban Revolution became a notable event in the Cold War after Fidel Castro's new government broke decisively with the United States, initiated radical social changes, and established a repressive, one-party Communist regime. Castro is shown here addressing a crowd during his revolutionary "March to Havana" in January 1959—before he had declared himself a Communist and forged close ties with the Soviet Union.
(© Bettmann/CORBIS)

and thousands of his supporters lost their lives, and brutal repression followed under a military regime headed for many years by General Augusto Pinochet. The Pinochet era, unlike many dictatorships, left a substantial record of economic growth but also produced bitter memories and a divided country. Arrested in later years while living abroad, Pinochet narrowly escaped trial on human rights charges in Europe but still faced trial in Chile.

The most sweeping attempt at social revolution in Latin America in the second half of the twentieth century occurred in Cuba. In 1933 Cuba had fallen under the heavy-handed

Cuba and Castro

repressive dictatorship of Fulgencio Batista. In 1959 Fidel Castro and a small band of leftist guerrillas returning from exile (among them Castro's chief lieutenant Ernesto Che Guevara) succeeded in overthrowing the Batista dictatorship. Castro pledged to institute land reform and end economic dependence on the United States. When his government confiscated American corporate investments and landholdings, the United States retaliated with a trade embargo. Castro, not initially a Moscow-oriented Communist, moved into the Soviet orbit, and tensions over Cuba in 1962 in the context of the Cold War, as we shall see in Chapter 25, brought the United States and the Soviet Union to the brink of nuclear war.

Cuba became the only professedly Marxist state in the Western Hemisphere. Castro championed anti-imperialism worldwide, aided leftist movements in Bolivia and in Central America, and sent troops across the Atlantic to support anticolonial guerrilla armies in Africa. At home he created an advanced network of social services, promoted public health and literacy, and improved life for the rural masses; but economic failures and totalitarian coercion overshadowed these achievements. He became increasingly dependent on the Soviet bloc for economic aid, receiving favorable terms for the export of sugar and the import of oil. Castro ruled as a dictator. Political opponents fled into exile or were imprisoned. His militarized regime and global adventurism cost him support among the reform-minded in Latin America and elsewhere. When Soviet communism collapsed in 1989–1991, Castro lost the economic subsidies on which he depended and became a somewhat isolated figure in international affairs. Yet *fidelismo* had once been regarded as a threat to the United States and as an opening wedge to communism in the Western Hemisphere. Castro himself continued to govern Cuba in the early twenty-first century, leading a regime that remained in power almost 50 years after the revolution that swept the country in 1959.

Mexico and Brazil at the Beginning of the Twenty-First Century

The political implications of Latin America's long postcolonial struggle for economic development could be seen in the region's most populous nations, Mexico and Brazil. In Mexico, a large proportion of its more than 100 million people lived at subsistence levels at the beginning of the twenty-first century and, as in most of Latin America, wealth remained highly concentrated in the upper echelons of society. Yet Mexico had passed through numerous episodes of social revolution beginning in 1910, during which the power of the church and the military was curbed and land redistribution programs were introduced.

The dominant Mexican political organization, the Institutional Revolutionary Party (PRI), heir to the Revolution of 1910, had long been revolutionary in name only. Opposition parties existed, but the PRI and a small business elite protected their own privileges and interests. The government promoted modernization but slighted social needs; nepotism and corruption flourished. As elsewhere, the human cost of social neglect was malnutrition, disease, infant mortality, limited schooling, illiteracy, and lower life expectancy for all but the social elite. The armed revolt in 1994 of an Indian-led peasant movement in the poor southern state of Chiapas dramatized the broad social and economic problems of Mexico's poorest people. The PRI had retained the allegiance of the poor through subsidies and handouts, but its notorious corruption and its tight grip on power through years of controlled elections had left most Mexicans distrustful of all politicians. Despite industrialization and steadily expanding international trade, the economic gulf between rich and poor, and between north and south, increased in Mexico during the 1990s.

In the presidential election of 2000 the PRI candidate was defeated for the first time by a centrist business leader, Vincente Fox, whose victory brought the more conservative National Action Party to power and ended the 71-year era of PRI control. President Fox promised major economic and political reforms, but he faced strong opposition in the Mexican Congress and was unable to enact most of the changes he wanted to introduce. The Free Trade agreement with the United States (NAFTA), which went into effect in 1994, did not significantly enhance the economic conditions for most poor Mexicans, many of whom sought work by migrating into the United States. Economic problems continued to affect Mexican politics and contributed to the popularity of left-leaning political leaders such as the mayor of Mexico City, who rallied the opposition in a political movement that gained wide support from the nation's lower classes.

Populist opposition to the traditional economic-political elites also emerged in Brazil, where a former leader of the Metalworkers' Union, Lula da Silva, was elected president in 2002. Lula (as he was called) entered office after the first successful transfer of power between elected presidents in Brazil since the early 1960s, raising popular expectations for both the democratic political system and the economic conditions of Brazil's poorest people. The new government's policies were less radical than many had expected, however, and Lula's popular support declined as he struggled to solve the problems of unemployment and to deal with corruption scandals among his own political allies. Brazil's economy nevertheless showed a steady rate of growth, giving this largest of all South American nations an increasingly prominent role in the international economic system. A healthy Brazilian economy and political system had become essential for the stability and development of the whole continent.

The Advance of Latin American Democracy

A diverse region

In the early years of the twenty-first century, Latin America continued to be a diverse region economically and politically. Many Latin American countries were moving toward more stable constitutional government, trying to soften ideological conflict and working to loosen rigid state controls over their economies. Inflation, heavy debt, currency crises, and population growth, however, still made it difficult to meet the fundamental social needs of the region's impoverished lower classes.

The constitutional democracies often remained fragile. In the 1990s military insurrections broke out in Argentina, Ecuador, and Venezuela; and the civilian president of Peru trampled on the constitution before he eventually was forced from office. In Colombia large-scale drug trafficking disrupted orderly government, and a left-wing guerrilla insurgency generated recurring cycles of political violence. In Central America the military often sought to gain or hold on to political power, claiming to protect public order against the dangers of mounting crime or the unrest of impoverished social groups. Poverty and deep-seated social inequities remained legacies of the region's history.

Democracy emergent and receding

Democracy thus continued to emerge and recede and to develop unevenly throughout Latin America. In 1960 virtually every nation in South America had an elected civilian leader, yet by 1976 all but a few countries in Central and South America had fallen under the control of military or rightist dictatorships. In the 1980s and into the 1990s, however, the trend shifted to democracy. For most of the 1990s no elected civilian president was overthrown by the military, but electorates were often frustrated and angered by the ineptitude and corruption of democratic political parties unable to cope effectively with social and economic issues.

Venezuela became an especially significant case of political discontent. Since 1958 it had been a leader in civilian democratic rule and orderly government. Two major parties shared patronage and political spoils for over 40 years, but, despite the country's oil wealth, did little to relieve poverty and inequality. The election of Hugo Chávez in 1998 as president caused alarm in both of the traditional political parties. Chávez, a former colonel and paratrooper who in 1992 had led a bloody but unsuccessful military coup, won a landslide electoral victory, called for a "peaceful social revolution," convened an assembly to write a new constitution, and after 18 months, in the summer of 2000, won reelection. Chávez soon thereafter gained authority from the National Assembly to enact legislation by decree. In the following years, he took new control of Venezuela's state oil company, withstood a prolonged strike in the oil industry, and managed to prevail in a referendum that would have removed him from office. Critics complained bitterly that Chávez had revived the worst practices of past Latin American demagogues and repressive regimes, but he retained significant support among the lower classes, became an ardent supporter of Cuba's Castro, and rallied nationalist sentiment by warning against the dangers of American intervention in Venezuelan politics. As a symbolic identification of his link to the

Despite the growing economic connections between all Latin American nations and the modern, international trading system, many people on the continent continue to live and work in long-established, agricultural communities. Like generations before them, these people were harvesting barley in rural Ecuador during the late 1990s, but their economic lives were also linked to a global economy that profoundly affected the price of their crops as well as the value of their wages.

(© Pablo Corral V/Corbis)

nation's revolutionary past and its nineteenth-century liberator, Simón Bolivar, he officially renamed the country the Bolivarian Republic of Venezuela.

The political practices of earlier eras in Latin American history were therefore still appearing in some places during the first decade of the twenty-first century. By the early years of the new century, however, most of Latin America had followed the lead of other industrial countries in moving toward privatization, free trade, open markets, and globalization. Despite periodic setbacks, democracy was growing to be the prevalent pattern of government. But integration into the global economy had not yet brought prosperity or a more balanced distribution of wealth for the vast majority of Latin Americans. The region was also subject to severe financial crises, including the destabilization of national currencies in countries such as Mexico in 1994 and Brazil in 1998.

A mixed record

A new cluster of leftist governments emerged in the early twenty-first century—Hugo Chavez in Venezuela; Lula da Silva in Brazil; Evo Morales in Bolivia; the first indigenous Indian president ever to be elected to that position in Latin America; and Michelle

Bachelet in Chile, the first woman to be elected president of a major country on the continent, and a Socialist. They and older leftist movements still made their presence felt, and a rising generation of young activists strongly criticized the global free market economy (and the United States as its leading champion) for benefiting only the wealthier nations and neglecting the needs of the impoverished.

Many of the economic and political challenges that confronted the postcolonial nations of Asia after 1945 could therefore be found also in most of Latin America: a legacy of unequal economic exchange with the more industrialized countries, for example, and enduring political conflicts that carried forward an earlier history of political violence from both the left and right wings of the continent's various national and regional cultures. It was nevertheless clear by the early twenty-first century that the nations of Latin America, like the nations of modern Asia, Africa, and the Middle East, had all moved irrevocably into the global economy and the mainstream of contemporary international affairs.

For interactive exercises, glossary, chronologies, and more, go to the *Online Learning Center* at **www.mhhe.com/palmer10.**

Chapter 24

EMPIRES INTO NATIONS: AFRICA AND THE MIDDLE EAST AFTER THE SECOND WORLD WAR

The demise of European empires led to the establishment of new nations throughout Africa and the Middle East after 1945, but this momentous and widely celebrated transition also generated numerous new trouble zones during the Cold War and new regional, ethnic, or religious conflicts that persisted after Soviet-American rivalries faded in the late 1980s. Given their geographical proximity to Europe, the vast lands and diverse populations of Africa and the Middle East had long been affected by waves of European expansion—from the medieval crusades to the imperial competition of powerful nineteenth-century nation-states and the League of Nations' post-1919 distribution of territorial "mandates" to Britain and France. By the mid-twentieth century, however, nationalist movements had emerged everywhere (as in Asia) to oppose such outside intervention. Facing this opposition and weakened by two world wars, Europeans gradually lost the political will and the resources to maintain imperial rule in their African colonies and in the Middle Eastern mandates that they had controlled after the breakup of the Ottoman Empire at the end of the First World War.

Although the French resisted the nationalist upsurge in Algeria, the British suppressed anticolonial militants in Kenya, and the Portuguese fought to keep their colonies in Angola and Mozambique, the new wave of independence movements would ultimately manage to free every African country from European control. The emergence of new nations was nevertheless complicated by the fact that they generally encompassed diverse ethnic and linguistic groups whom the colonial powers had brought together within the artificial boundaries of a single political territory. This legacy of colonial administration often led to ethnic conflicts that destabilized African political systems or produced authoritarian governments.

Meanwhile, the Arab countries of North Africa and the Middle East entered into a prolonged conflict with the new Jewish state of Israel, which was established in 1948 after the British withdrew from the mandate they had exercised over Palestine. The creation of

Chapter emblem: Nelson Mandela taking the oath of office as he became president of South Africa in 1994. (Associated Press, AP)

Israel represented the triumphant fulfillment of a Zionist movement that had grown steadily since the late nineteenth century and gained new support after the devastating Nazi Holocaust, but it also brought about the displacement of a large Palestinian Arab population, a series of regional wars, the resurgence of an Islamic and Arabic religious fervor, and an intractable international issue that would involve the major world powers. The recurring conflicts in Africa and the Middle East also became entangled in the Cold War and in the global competition for key natural resources such as oil and minerals, so that the economic and political stability of the wider global system was much affected by the turmoil in these regions of the world.

We take up the postcolonial history of Africa and the Middle East in the first sections of this chapter and then conclude the chapter with the more general problems of Third World economic development previously encountered in the modern histories of Asia and Latin America. Contemporary analysis of the global economy often focuses on commodity production, labor costs, currency exchanges or the distribution of goods and services; but the modern history of Africa and the Middle East shows that economic history cannot be easily separated from the powerful currents of religion, nationalism, and ethnicity that swirl constantly around the global trade of oil, agricultural products, money, and advanced technologies.

117.   THE AFRICAN REVOLUTION

Africa is a large continent, considerably larger than North and Central America combined. With an estimated population of 220 million in 1950 and almost 900 million in 2000, it has had one of the fastest-growing populations in the world, although the ravages of AIDS have taken a serious toll since the 1980s. A distinction may be made

North and sub-Saharan Africa

between North Africa and sub-Saharan Africa. North Africa, stretching from Mauritania and Morocco to Egypt, mostly Muslim and Arab, belongs as much to the Mediterranean world (and even more to the Islamic Middle East) in ethnic composition, culture, geography, and history. In sub-Saharan Africa, to the south, below the Sahara Desert, lives a population of over 600 million people, where Islam, Christianity, and traditional African animist faiths are found and where the population is predominantly black. An ethnographic and linguistic map of Africa would reveal hundreds of different ethnic groups and some 800 African languages, of which about 50 are spoken by a half million people or more. A large number of Africans since the colonial era also speak English or French, and there are also numerous descendants of European and South Asian settlers and immigrants, most notably in South Africa.

In 1945 the map of Africa was scarcely different from what it had been in 1914. All of Africa was European-governed with the exceptions of Egypt, Liberia, and Ethiopia (the latter had regained its independence from Italy during the Second World

Independence movements

War). By the early 1960s, however, there were 35 independent states, and most of Africa was either independent or close to achieving independence. By the early twenty-first century there were 53 independent African states, making up more than a fourth of the membership of the United Nations. Of the 53 states, all but five were in sub-Saharan Africa.

The new states differed from older nations in many ways. Africa's territorial boundaries, as we have seen, were drawn hastily during the era of European imperial expansion in the late nineteenth century, and the new states often contained highly diverse ethnic and linguistic groups. These groups usually lacked the "national" affinities that are associated with the concept of a "nation-state," while ethnically related peoples were frequently distributed over two or more countries. When independence brought the African states the full panoply of national sovereignty, the people in these states had a less unified national heritage than those in most older nations of Europe and Asia, and the new African governments faced the daunting challenge of welding their disparate ethnic groups into nationhood. The age of imperialism had left the African states economically underdeveloped, dependent on world markets, and with little experience in self-governing institutions; the very rapidity of the transition to independence added to their difficulties. Ethnic or civil wars and regional conflicts marked much of Africa's first half-century of independence. The following survey of important developments in postcolonial Africa can only sketch the broad outlines of African history in these years.

French North Africa

During the Second World War the Allied leaders had made various commitments to self-determination. With Italy defeated (and Ethiopia liberated), the wartime Allies in 1951 granted independence also to the former Italian colony of Libya, and the British took steps to end what was left of their privileged position in Egypt. These events galvanized French North Africa, where Arab nationalist leaders, often French-educated, had pressed for independence since the 1920s. In Morocco, Tunisia, and Algeria—the Maghreb, as these Arab states of northwest Africa are called—the nationalists mounted a vigorous campaign. Morocco and Tunisia were not outright colonies but French protectorates under their traditional rulers, the Moroccan sultan and the Tunisian bey. The French in 1956 granted independence to both countries. The Moroccan sultan became king as a constitutional monarch, but as the years went by, the monarchy increasingly enlarged its powers. Tunisia became a republic and was governed for its first 30 years by Habib Bourguiba, who introduced many democratic reforms (including rights of divorce for women) but insisted on being named president for life. In both countries modernization and pressures for liberalization continued long after independence, often against counterpressures from Muslim traditionalists.

Algeria's story was very different. In the early nineteenth century the French entered Algeria, part of the decaying Ottoman Empire, and after several brutal military campaigns it became a fully controlled French colony by mid-century. Later in the century French and other Europeans settled there in substantial numbers, creating large immigrant communities that came to dominate the political and economic life of the country and its Arab population. The French meanwhile provided a few limited measures for Algerian self-rule and representation along with a promise that further concessions could be made when the country became fully assimilated to French and European ways. Some additional political concessions were granted in the interwar years, but after 1945 Algerian nationalists pressed for full independence. Although Algeria was represented in the French legislature in Paris, the suffrage in Algeria was heavily weighted in favor of the European settlers to the distinct disadvantage of the Arab majority. Of the 9 million or so inhabitants, about 1 million were Europeans. The *colons,* or European settlers, mostly French, like the family of the French writer Albert Camus, had lived there for generations. Because the Europeans controlled the economy and owned most of the land and industry, they feared for their political and economic privileges if Algeria were cut loose from France and governed by an Arab Muslim majority smarting from years of unequal treatment. The

French colons in Algeria

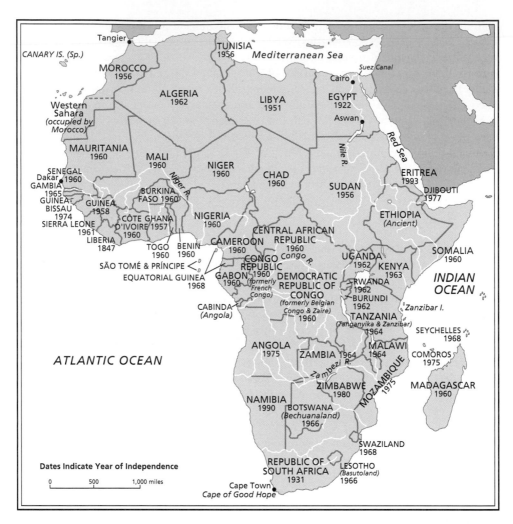

CONTEMPORARY AFRICA

This map shows the emergence of independent African states and may be compared with earlier maps for precolonial Africa (p. 655) and for Africa in 1914 at the height of European imperialism (p. 658). The first of the new sub-Saharan states was Ghana, which gained independence from Britain in 1957 and took its name from a medieval African kingdom that had been located further north. The more recently established states include Zimbabwe (1980) and Namibia (1990) in southern Africa and Eritrea (1993) in northeastern Africa. By the end of the twentieth century all of the European colonial empires had disappeared and the white-controlled apartheid regime in South Africa had given way to a nonracial, democratic political system.

French military suppressed initial postwar uprisings, but the nationalist movement grew, and in the autumn of 1954 the National Liberation Front (FLN) launched a fierce guerrilla war against the French.

The French-Algerian war lasted 7½ years, involving at its peak 500,000 French troops and provoking sharp political divisions within France itself. The Algerian armed forces received aid and support from Egypt and other Arab states. Torture and cruelty became common on both sides. In the spring of 1958, during a French cabinet crisis in which the Europeans in Algeria feared that a negotiated settlement might be arranged, an insurrection by army leaders and diehard settlers in Algiers brought political changes in Paris and General Charles de Gaulle's return to power. To the dismay of the army leaders, however, de Gaulle unexpectedly arranged a cease-fire and soon spoke of autonomy and self-determination for the Algerians. In 1962, in a referendum, he won the backing of the French electorate for full independence. Army leaders thereupon rebelled, and some of his closest former associates helped form a secret army of terrorists who bombed and killed, and even attempted his assassination. Nevertheless, de Gaulle pressed on with negotiations for Algerian independence, and in 1962 French rule ended. The long and brutal war had cost the lives of 10,000 French and 100,000 Algerian combatants as well as many thousands of Algerian civilians.

The French-Algerian War

After independence there was a mass exodus of Europeans from Algeria, but most of the French and Algerians were grateful that de Gaulle had ended the ordeal. The French accepted the loss of Algeria and of other parts of their large African empire, and with a prospering economy in the 1960s turned their attention to other matters. Although staunchly anti-Western, the Algerians accepted French technical assistance for the development of Algeria's extensive oil and natural gas resources.

The FLN retained power and governed the country under a military-dominated one-party regime for the next 30 years. The party became increasingly corrupt, and it mismanaged the cumbersome state-owned planned economy, which survived only through the country's oil and gas revenues. In the 1980s about three-fourths of all young Algerians were without jobs and many were homeless as well. An additional 2 million Algerians migrated in search of jobs, mainly to France, where they were not always warmly welcomed. In 1988 general frustration in Algeria with the political and economic situation exploded into urban riots.

The FLN

In its effort to cement ties with other Arab states, the Algerian military leaders had allowed Islamic fundamentalists to teach and to grow in political influence. Among the parties that emerged was an extremist Islamic Salvation Front. It organized itself into a mass political movement, offered itself as a substitute for the FLN and won broad support. It vehemently opposed the Western-style secularization that had emancipated women from Islamic rules in dress and other matters and pressed for the reimposition of fundamentalist rules of dress and comportment. In late 1991 the Islamic party overwhelmingly won the first multiparty parliamentary elections ever held in the country, but the army leaders peremptorily canceled the election results and declared the Islamic party illegal.

Islamic fundamentalism

After 1992 the social and political life of Algeria entered a violent phase. The armed movement of the Islamic extremists unleashed a reign of terror, attacking whole villages and settlements. Moderate Islamic leaders were helpless. The military responded with brutal terror of its own, and well over 100,000 people died in the insurgent attacks or in the repression that followed. The violence eventually declined after the Islamic radicals

The Algerian war for independence from France was one of the most bitter, protracted struggles for decolonization, in part because a large French population had lived in Algeria for several generations. France had about 500,000 soldiers in Algeria, including these troops in the city of Oran, but the French army could not defeat the Algerian National Liberation Front or regain control of the Algerian countryside. Algeria became an independent nation in 1962.
(Getty Images)

declared a cease-fire and after the government, in 2000, proclaimed a broad amnesty for the rebels. But the large underclass still faced pressing economic problems, and ethnic tensions also strained relations between the nation's Arab and indigenous minority Berber population, which was Muslim but not Arab. Algeria was thus affected by the assertion of local ethnic identities as well as the powerful force of Islamic political movements, and it was still struggling to sustain a stable, democratic state almost a half century after the end of its long war for independence from France.

End of British Rule in West Africa

In North Africa nationalist agitation for independence, already under way in the interwar years, might have been expected, but south of the Sahara the movement for liberation was never as far advanced. Here black African populations still lived in colonial empires that Europeans had carved out either in the colonial age that opened in the fifteenth century or in the "scramble for Africa" in the brief decade and a half of European imperialist competition after 1885.

Ghana was the first African nation to gain independence from Great Britain during the 1950s. The president of the new nation, Kwame Nkrumah, appears in this picture, waving to supporters at a national celebration in 1957. Nkrumah led the struggle for independence and became a key figure in the Pan-African movement, but his autocratic methods of governing and his extravagances provoked a military coup that ousted him from power in 1966.
(Bettmann/Corbis)

Yet independence movements, barely in existence before 1945, soon announced their presence. The British first resisted the mounting nationalist pressures, imprisoning or exiling nationalist leaders, but then, recognizing the strength of the liberation movements and the pressures of their own postwar economic problems, they decided in the 1950s to change their imperial policies. Britain thereafter moved quickly to grant autonomy to its colonies, which soon became dominions and then independent republics.

From colonies to independent republics

For many years the postcolonial republics were mostly ruled by authoritarian governments more interested in sustaining their own power than in developing democratic societies. Although there was a trend toward democratization across parts of the continent in the 1990s, serious economic challenges persisted almost everywhere. African economies remained underindustrialized and therefore highly dependent on international development assistance and on the fluctuating price of commodities in the global economy.

The Gold Coast (soon renamed Ghana) was the first British colony to win independence, and its subsequent history showed the kind of postcolonial economic and political patterns that would reappear in many former African colonies. The British initially resisted a militant civil disobedience movement led by the nationalist leader Kwame Nkrumah and even imprisoned him. But in 1951 they freed Nkrumah and conceded self-government.

Nkrumah's party overwhelmingly won the elections that followed, and he became prime minister. In 1957 the colony won full independence with dominion status, and in 1960 Nkrumah transformed it into a republic with himself as president. With

Nkrumah's Ghana

independence, the country shed the name of Gold Coast, which was too closely identified with the centuries of imperialist exploitation and the slave trade. It called itself Ghana, recalling an African kingdom somewhat to the north which had flourished from the sixth to the eleventh centuries. Nkrumah quickly gathered extensive power into his own hands, banned opposition parties, governed autocratically, and declared himself president for life. The early postcolonial history of Ghana thus showed a pattern that would recur in Africa (and in Asia): charismatic nationalist leaders who led the struggles for independence repeatedly turned into personal dictators once independence was won, and the party of the independence movement often became the basis for one-party governments.

Nkrumah adopted an anti-Western stance, championed a nonalignment policy in the Cold War, and sought a leading role in a pan-African movement, hosting in 1958 the first All-African People's Congress in Ghana's capital, Accra. He cultivated close ties with the Soviet Union and the People's Republic of China. He introduced, and his successors continued, a program of "African socialism," placing the economy under rigorous state control. In these new forms of socialism in Asia, Africa, and the Middle East, the state ran the economy, the ruling elite accumulated power and wealth, and there was little of the egalitarianism promised by traditional socialist doctrines and theories. The Ghanaian economy was generally prosperous when the nation gained its independence, largely because Ghana was the world's largest producer of cocoa and the source of a tenth of the world's gold. But the economy declined in the 1960s, in part because of ill-conceived development projects, and Ghana became heavily dependent on foreign loans.

Power of the military

Fed up with Nkrumah's arbitrary rule, unbridled extravagances, and cult of personality, military leaders ousted him in 1966. There then followed a series of military coups with only brief sporadic efforts to return to constitutional and civilian rule. Finally, in 1979 a junior air force officer, Flight Lieutenant Jerry John Rawlings, seized control. He introduced a program of self-sufficiency and austerity and curbed a number of state controls of the economy. With financial assistance from the World Bank and market reforms the economy in the late 1980s began to show significant growth. By the early 1990s Rawlings was offering the promise of a more liberal political regime, including free, multiparty elections. At the opening of the new century, after two decades in power, Rawlings voluntarily surrendered the presidency in accordance with the terms of a constitution that had been introduced in the early 1990s. His elected successor, John Agyekum Kufuor, was returned to office in democratic elections at the end of 2004, providing new evidence that Ghana was continuing to move toward a more stable and open political system. Every phase of Ghana's postindependence history—especially the gradual evolution from authoritarian rule toward more democratic government in the early twenty-first century—resembled general trends that could be seen in much of postcolonial Africa; the democratization in Ghana became part of a wider African movement for political reform.

Nigeria

Nigeria, the largest British-governed colonial territory in Africa, has remained the most populous country in postcolonial Africa, with a population of over 125 million by the early twenty-first century, and with 250 ethnic groups. The four largest, the Hausa and Fulani in the north and the Yoruba and Ibo in the south, all of which had had distinctive important cultures, trading economies, and city-state organizations in precolonial times, comprise two-thirds of the population. Britain had established its hold over the country through conquests and treaties in the mid–nineteenth century, but it had governed "indirectly" through local traditional rulers, excluding Nigerians from any significant role in self-government at higher levels.

Western-educated Nigerians, who had pressed for political representation in the 1920s, stepped up pressure after the Second World War. In 1960 Britain granted Nigeria independence and in 1963 it became a republic, with the respected nationalist leader Nnandi Azikewe as its first president. To cope with the country's ethnic diversity, the constitution established three large geographical regions and 21 federal states. With a constitution, democratic machinery, a federal structure, political parties, and guarantees of civil rights the Nigerian republic held the promise of serving as a democratic model for the rest of the continent.

The promise of democracy

Unfortunately, regional and ethnic tensions, civil war, and a succession of military coups thwarted that promise. Only six years after independence a brutal civil war broke out. Because the northern region had come to dominate the government, the educated and economically advanced Ibos in the south, mostly Christian, saw themselves as excluded from an appropriate national role. In 1966 Ibo army officers staged a coup, but a Hausa-led military takeover almost immediately followed and became the signal for a widespread slaughter of Ibos. Large numbers of Ibos fled to the east, where in 1967 they proclaimed an independent state of Biafra. A terrible civil war and blockade lasted 2½ years, from 1967 to 1970, and resulted in close to a million deaths from the blockade and starvation. The Ibo secession collapsed. After the war the federal government followed a policy of reconciliation, reintegrated the Ibos into national life, and sought, with some success, to overcome other regional and ethnic differences as well.

But more coups and assassinations took place and the military remained in control. In 1979 General Olusegnu Abusanjo after three years of military rule restored civilian government, but in 1985 a new coup returned the military to power. Although they promised to restore free elections, they did not do so until eight years later.

Coups and assassinations

For a time, in the early 1970s, Nigeria enjoyed a booming economy, based on its large oil resources, which made it the world's sixth largest oil producer. Lagos, the Nigerian capital at the time, quadrupled in size. But the oil wealth failed to stimulate broader economic development and corruption was endemic. Severe drought and a growing population forced dependence on food imports, which led to inflation and debt.

The 1990s brought important political changes. When the military eventually permitted presidential elections in 1993, the popular opposition leader Moshood Abiola clearly won, but the ruling general nullified the results and imprisoned Abiola. His death in prison five years later, allegedly of a heart attack, sparked nationwide protests that eventually brought a restoration of civilian government. In the 1999 elections the voters turned to General Obesanjo, who 20 years earlier had been the first Nigerian military ruler to give up power voluntarily to a civilian regime, and Obesanjo was reelected to the presidency in 2003.

Shift to a civilian regime

Nigeria's early promise of parliamentary democracy, repeatedly frustrated over the past four decades, was showing clear signs of renewal. The widespread

Nigeria has become one of the world's most important producers and exporters of crude oil since the 1970s. This oil derrick in the delta of the Niger River is part of the booming petroleum industry, which accounts for much of Nigeria's income from international trade but also makes the economy vulnerable to rapid, global fluctuations in the price of oil.
(Liaison Agency)

problems of government corruption and poverty persisted, however, and even the steady rise in global oil prices brought little direct economic benefit to most of Nigeria's growing population. The country also suffered from renewed ethnic tensions and from a cycle of violence between Muslims and Christians, which caused numerous deaths in northern Nigeria. Despite such internal problems, the nation's oil production and sheer size gave it a major role in African affairs, which included the dispatch of Nigerian soldiers to serve as peacekeepers in various regional conflicts.

End of British Rule in East Africa: Kenya, Tanzania, Uganda

In East Africa, especially in Kenya, the independence movements after 1945 encountered obstacles, but the struggles to establish new nations moved through the usual political stages to achieve sovereign statehood. European settlers, who had arrived early in the century in considerable numbers, dominated economic and political life. They had dispossessed the Kikiyu and Maasai peoples to create large coffee and tea plantations on the most desirable land. Many Indians had also arrived from South Asia as merchants and traders. Africans, restricted to working as subsistence small farmers, agricultural laborers, and unskilled workers in the cities, resented their second-class economic and social status.

In the 1920s young nationalist leaders, many of whom, like Jomo Kenyatta, had studied abroad, agitated for land reform and African representation in government. After the Second World War a movement for independence led by Kenyatta and his party gathered momentum. When the European settlers stubbornly resisted pressures for independence, the militants responded with violence and acts of terrorism. The settlers retaliated, and as the violence mounted, the British declared a state of emergency and imprisoned or removed from the troubled area many of the nationalist leaders. Eventually, however, the British faced up to the inevitable. They ended the state of emergency, released Kenyatta, and in 1963 granted Kenya independence. Over 55,000 Europeans left the country.

Kenyatta and Kenyan independence

Kenya became a republic in 1964 with Kenyatta as its first president. Until his death 14 years later he completely dominated political life, following the all-too-familiar pattern of the independence leader's turning dictator after independence. Like other new African leaders he championed pan-Africanism and neutralism in the Cold War.

When he died in office in 1978, Daniel arap Moi, who had been his vice president, governed under the same kind of authoritarian one-party regime, rejecting pressures for liberalization. The economy deteriorated and unemployment ran high, but international lending agencies refused to provide aid until reforms were undertaken. Democratic elections were finally instituted in the 1990s, and Moi left office in 2002; but the transfer of power to the opposition leader did not end the country's political unrest. New disputes arose over proposed revisions in the constitution, and there were persistent charges of widespread corruption. Other issues in Kenyan political life, including controversial questions of land ownership and long-term leases, were still influenced by the legacy of British colonialism, so that postcolonial transitions were still affecting Kenya in the early twenty-first century.

Tanzania

The other main East African states, Tanzania and Uganda, also passed through a series of domestic political changes after gaining independence in the early 1960s. Tanzania was established after a revolutionary movement merged the former British-controlled territories of Tanganyika and Zanzibar in 1964. Its political life was dominated by the nationalist leader Julius Nyerere, who did not allow opposition parties or free elections during the 25 years in which he held office. Nyerere therefore stymied the development of democratic political life, but he introduced a number of useful reforms.

By promoting literacy and establishing Swahili along with English as the official language of public life, he helped unite the country's ethnic and linguistic groups. His economic policies were less successful and the country remained impoverished. Also a champion of "African socialism," he nationalized much of the economy, including agriculture. In the Cold War he drew close to the Soviet Union and to China, and for a time Tanzania served as a principal bridgehead for Chinese Communist influence on the African continent. Under Nyerere's successors, the government denationalized many state industries, sought to end overly rigid economic controls, and restored collective farms to family cultivation. In 1995 it held its first multiparty elections, which brought to power another long-serving president—Benjamin William Mkapa. The country's economic problems were soon aggravated by a flood of hundreds of thousands of refugees from civil wars in neighboring states and by the deadly AIDS epidemic, but Mkapa was able to maintain a stable government and to win reelection in 2002.

Uganda

Uganda, which Winston Churchill once described as the "pearl of Africa" because of its natural beauty, won independence in 1962. It, too, encompassed many ethnic groups, who had been brought together in a British protectorate during the 1890s. Uganda was the scene of much missionary activity. Both Protestantism and Roman Catholicism made many converts so that the population became two-thirds Christian. While some permanent European settlers established large plantations, the African farmers cultivated small plots of cotton, tea, and coffee. South Asians arrived to play a leading role as merchants. In 1921 Britain established a legislative council, but the first African members were admitted only in 1945, and not until several years later did they receive a substantial number of seats. Pressure for independence continued.

With independence near, political parties emerged, ethnic rivalries sharpened, and the traditional, central kingdom of Buganda demanded a separate state. Political organizations that were resentful and suspicious of Bugandan intentions coalesced into the leading party, and Milton Obote, its leader, became prime minister. In 1963 a constitution transformed Uganda into a republic. As a compromise, the king of Buganda, the *kabaka,* was elected ceremonial president. But in 1966 Obote, bent on centralizing authority, forced the kabaka to flee the country. Obote promptly concentrated more and more power into his own hands, and over the next five years alienated many in the country. In 1971 a flamboyant, ruthless soldier, Idi Amin, rose from the ranks to become commanding general, seized power, and for eight years brutalized the country, shocking Africa and the world with executions, massacres, and torture. As many as 300,000 Ugandans may have lost their lives; entire ethnic groups were singled out for destruction. A once prosperous agricultural economy with thriving coffee, tea, and cotton exports lay in ruins. Professionals and intellectuals fled. In 1972 he expelled some 60,000 Asians, mostly Indians, who had been a strong presence in the country's commerce and industry. In 1976 he declared himself president for life. At last, in 1979, after he had invaded northern Tanzania over disputed border territory and devastated the area, a Tanzanian army, accompanied by Ugandan exiles, moved into Uganda and overthrew the dictator.

Idi Amin's reign of terror

Obote, the former president, returning with the Tanzanian army, regained power and crushed all opposition forces. Additional tens of thousands lost their lives or fled to neighboring states. Eventually a guerrilla army under Yoweri Museveni, which had fought a guerrilla war against Idi Amin, now helped to overthrow Obote. Museveni took power in 1986 and began to restore a measure of constitutional government. He also took the first steps to rehabilitate the devastated country. Economic production in Uganda in 1989 was one-fifth what it had been at the time of independence; but a measure of political stability, international financial assistance, and foreign investment made economic growth once again possible. The political atmosphere became freer. The government pioneered in aggressive steps to check the spread of the AIDS epidemic that was ravaging the country.

In the early twenty-first century Uganda still faced guerrilla warfare in the countryside led by a fanatical, self-styled Christian religious leader, whose military tactics included the mass abduction of young children who were then used as slave labor or armed as soldiers. Museveni also became involved in the complicated and shifting warfare in Congo. Violence thus remained a problem in Uganda, and the country had not yet established an open, democratic political culture. Museveni disappointed many of his democratic supporters when he took steps in disregard of the constitution to renew his presidency. But Uganda had moved beyond the brutal excesses and ethnic repressions of the 1960s and 1970s.

Southern Africa

In southern Africa the British peacefully transferred power in the early 1960s to black majority governments in Zambia (formerly Northern Rhodesia), Malawi, and Botswana. But elsewhere in this part of the African continent a white colonial minority held out against yielding or even sharing power.

In Southern Rhodesia (now Zimbabwe) the British government in London tried to negotiate political rights for the black majority before granting independence, but the small white community resisted, and in 1965 it unilaterally proclaimed independence from Britain. After 15 years of escalating guerrilla warfare and international political and economic pressure, the white leaders yielded. In 1980 Southern Rhodesia became Zimbabwe, with a black majority government. Within a few years the independence leader Robert Mugabe, combining the posts of president and prime minister, created a one-party state, which he continued to govern for more than twenty-five years. Frustrated by the country's continuing economic difficulties, he allowed and even encouraged armed Africans to seize land that had long been in the hands of white fellow Zimbabweans; violence erupted in many parts of the country, creating alarming episodes of unrest and lawlessness, but opposition political groups were unable to influence government policies or to compete for parliamentary seats in free and fair elections. President Mugabe clung to power in the first decade of the new century — though he was an increasingly isolated "strongman" who had lost the support of both the international community and many of his compatriots who had once supported his leadership of the struggle for national independence.

Zimbabwe

The Union of South Africa

In the extreme south of the continent, in the Union of South Africa, a special drama unfolded. In the late 1980s in a population of just over 40 million, about 6 million whites lived uneasily with 30 million blacks, 3 million people of mixed background (denominated "coloureds"), and 1 million Asians; both of the latter groups were classified as nonwhites. The whites, though a minority, were far more numerous than elsewhere in Africa south of the Sahara and had lived there for a long time. They were numerous enough to constitute a social and cultural outpost of European civilization and to develop an expanding, prosperous economy, but they were greatly outnumbered, and many feared losing their dominant status. About half the whites, the Afrikaners, were mainly descendants of Dutch Calvinist immigrants from as far back as the founding of Cape Town in 1652; the other half represented immigration from Great Britain since the 1820s. The two halves did not easily mix. The Afrikaners, during their long isolation from Europe, developed a new language of their own, Afrikaans, derived from Dutch; and they retained unpleasant memories of British expansion, especially of the Boer war in the late nineteenth century.

In 1948 the Afrikaner-controlled Nationalist party came to power for the first time, campaigning for racial separation and the preservation of a white-dominated society. It legislated a sweeping policy of *apartheid* (the Afrikaans word for separation or segregation). The new laws excluded blacks from political life and imposed blatant forms of racial discrimination in housing, transportation, land ownership, and employment. Between 1950 and 1980 well over 1 million nonwhites in the cities were forced to leave white areas of residence and to relocate. Permits to blacks for urban jobs were granted only as industry required workers. Under a program of "separate development," the government also established four of a projected ten autonomous homelands *(bantustans)* for various black ethnic groups, but they met with little favor or outside acceptance. The land was poor and movement from the "homelands" to the rest of the country was strictly regulated. The practices of apartheid and the racist laws enforcing it were internationally condemned. Finding itself

Apartheid and separate development

increasingly isolated from the rest of the world, the South African government in 1961 broke all official ties with Britain and the Commonwealth and proclaimed itself the Republic of South Africa.

Opponents, black and white, of the restrictive laws encountered police brutality, torture, preventive detention, and prison sentences. Nelson Mandela, the black leader of the African National Congress, was sentenced to life imprisonment. Despite the prolonged detention of Mandela and other leaders, the African National Congress waged a determined campaign for racial equality which included demonstrations, strikes, and armed struggle. The regime attempted to suppress the black movement with military force, and there were tragic clashes at Sharpeville in 1960 and at Soweto in 1976, among others, costing the lives of hundreds of black protesters. By the 1970s increasing numbers of whites were protesting apartheid, and the United Nations had imposed sanctions. The United States, which had gone through its own much needed civil rights movement in the 1960s, joined in the economic sanctions and encouraged business corporations to withdraw or withhold investments.

The international political and economic pressures began to have an impact on the regime. A more enlightened wing of the Nationalist party attempted to moderate the apartheid laws, but initial reforms aroused opposition from Afrikaner diehards. In 1989 President F. W. de Klerk, anxious to defuse the explosive situation and sensitive to international opinion as well as the threatened deterioration of the economy, accelerated the reform program. In 1990 the government freed Nelson Mandela, who had become an

Countdown to democracy

internationally acclaimed hero and martyr after his more than 27 years in prison. In 1991 the government repealed all of the apartheid laws, ending over a half-century of enforced legal segregation. A year later the white electorate voted overwhelmingly in a referendum to end white minority rule. In Mandela's words, the "countdown to democracy" had begun.

In 1994 the first democratic nonracial elections, in which 22 million voters participated, brought Mandela and the African National Congress to power with provisions for a multiparty government of national unity during the period of transition. In 1996 the country adopted a constitution with the broadest bill of rights to be found anywhere in the world. It not only guaranteed political freedoms, but it also proclaimed social and economic entitlement to adequate food, housing, education, and health care. Meanwhile a Truth and Reconciliation Commission held hearings that disclosed the former government's full panoply of cruel abuses and acts of violence. In what many considered a model worthy of imitation in other post-autocratic regimes, amnesty was guaranteed to all who came forward with confessions of wrongdoing.

Freedom and challenges

After its long travail, and with enormous challenges, South Africa at last had the opportunity to create a nonracial democratic political system. The government in its first five years brought electricity and clean water to millions. During the country's second post-apartheid elections, in 1999, the African National Congress party came under heavy criticism for not accomplishing more but again won a sweeping victory and Thabo Mbeki replaced Nelson Mandela, who was voluntarily retiring, as the country's president. Mbeki, who was elected to a second term in 2004, sought to improve economic conditions for the country's black majority; but he lacked Mandela's skills, and he also stubbornly refused to recognize the true dimensions and causes of the AIDS epidemic. South Africa still faced poverty, unemployment, and a high crime rate, all heightened by the continuing spread of AIDS. Land ownership remained predominantly in white hands; 85 percent of the population was

Black protestors often clashed with the police during the long era of official racial segregation under South Africa's apartheid laws. This picture shows one such clash in 1976 in Soweto, where numerous demonstrations were violently repressed and several hundred people were ultimately killed.
(Hulton-Deutsch Collection/Corbis)

black, but they owned only about 20 percent of the land. The standard of living for white South Africans, it was estimated, ranked 24th in the world; that of black South Africans, 126th. But the battle for the most elementary political and social freedoms had been won.

The political transformation in South Africa affected the whole region because the white-dominated earlier regime had intervened to oppose black-led independence movements in other African countries. At the same time it had refused to surrender its international trusteeship over what had once been German Southwest Africa. The black leadership there, with the support of the United Nations, sought independence as the new state of Namibia, but it required a long guerrilla war before Namibia's independence was officially recognized in 1990.

The French Sub-Saharan Empire

The French, largely as a consequence of the bloody war in Algeria, dissolved the remainder of their vast colonial empire in sub-Saharan Africa peacefully. After the Second World War they had hoped that a French-educated and assimilated African elite would maintain ties to France in a loosely organized French Union. They gave the African colonies representation in the French National Assembly and promised self-governing institutions, but

The long campaign for equal civil and political rights in South Africa led finally to democratic, nonracial elections in 1994. The nation's first black president, Nelson Mandela, had emerged from more than 27 years in prison as an internationally known symbol of the struggle for human rights. He is shown here taking the oath of office to lead the first government freely elected by a vote of all South Africans.
(Associated Press, AP)

control remained centralized in Paris, and by the mid-1950s the African colonies, inspired by nationalist movements elsewhere, pressed for independence. De Gaulle recognized the inexorable pressure for independence and offered the sub-Saharan colonies their freedom of choice. By 1960 all 15 colonies had chosen independence.

French aid and cooperation

Many, however, retained close ties with France for economic aid and cultural cooperation. France remained a strong presence among the African francophone nations (and indeed the strongest presence of all the Western countries on the African continent), training the armies of the new states, lending financial assistance, and taking a leading role in economic development.[1] On numerous occasions after 1960 the French intervened in Africa with military force. In 1979, for example, they helped overthrow a brutal dictator who had seized power

---

[1]The francophone, or French-speaking, sub-Saharan African states emerging from the French colonial empire in 1960 were Benin (until 1975 called Dahomey), Cameroon, Central African Republic, Chad, Republic of Congo (Brazzaville), Gabon, Guinea, Ivory Coast, Madagascar (or Malagasy Republic), Mali, Mauritania, Niger, Senegal, Togo, and Burkina Faso (until 1984 called Upper Volta). Comoros became independent in 1975; Djibouti, in 1977. Morocco, Algeria, and Tunisia, in North Africa, are also part of francophone Africa as former French protectorates. The former Belgian colonial territories must also be included: the Democratic Republic of Congo (once the Belgian Congo, and from 1971 to 1997 called Zaire), and Burundi and Rwanda (once Belgian trusteeships).

in the Central African Republic in 1966 and for 13 years ruled as head of a self-proclaimed Central African Empire. In Chad, they intervened when rebels in the north backed by Libya threatened to overthrow the government; and in 2004 they intervened in the Côte d'Ivoire (Ivory Coast), where French peacekeepers were killed during a civil war that unexpectedly erupted in that hitherto peaceful country.

France thus continued to see itself as a key international power in African affairs. The French organized the African Financial Community, helped stabilize African currencies, and became the largest donor of aid to the continent. While some African leaders criticized such actions as neocolonialism, others viewed the French presence more as a partnership than an intrusion. As elsewhere in Africa, the promise of democratic government in the former French colonies turned for the most part into civilian or military dictatorships, even if the degree of repression varied. Here too the independence party often became the sole legally recognized political party. Presidents concentrated power in their own hands, often holding office for 20 years or more.

The Belgian Congo: From Mobutu's Zaire to the Democratic Republic of Congo

The Belgian Congo was a byword for European imperialist exploitation and cruelty in the late nineteenth century. The most abusive features were remedied before 1914, but political control remained concentrated in Brussels and little was done to prepare the large colony (it was 80 times the size of Belgium) for self-government. Agitation for independence intensified when the neighboring French Congo, its capital at Brazzaville, won independence in 1960 and became the Republic of Congo.

Faced with pressure for independence, the Belgian government, which had first proposed a transition period of 30 years, decided against gradualism and in 1960 announced its withdrawal in six months' time. Chaos followed. The two key nationalist leaders, one of them the leftist leader Patrice Lumumba, were at odds with one another. Ethnic and regional antagonisms ran deep, and no one was prepared to carry out governmental responsibilities. The army mutinied, and the soldiers turned against their European officers. Meanwhile the copper-producing province of Shaba (then called Katanga) attempted to secede. Belgian paratroopers hastily flew back, and a United Nations international military force was sent to restore order. When Lumumba was assassinated in 1961 (with evidence of American connivance), the troubled situation became even more volatile because of a threatened Soviet-Western confrontation. The Soviets charged the Europeans and their American supporters with deliberately creating the chaos so that the Europeans might return.

Cold War entanglement

The Shaba secession was halted, but the government with Belgian and American support continued to battle leftist rebels. Eventually, in 1965, Colonel Joseph Désiré Mobutu established a dictatorship that would last for the next 32 years. He at once nationalized the large mining enterprises and other parts of the economy. To symbolize the new era, all geographical and personal names were Africanized. He himself took the name Mobutu Sese Seko. The country became Zaire, as did the famous river. The capital city of Leopoldville and the second largest city, Stanleyville, both carrying names reminiscent of European imperialism, became Kinshasa and Kisangani; Lake Albert became Lake Mobutu.

Mobutu and Zaire

Zaire, the third largest country in size in Africa (second only to Sudan and Algeria), its cities widely separated and with poor, overgrown roads, had vast copper, diamond, cobalt, and other mineral resources; but its potential riches remained undeveloped and

Mobutu's extravagances over the years drove the country to the brink of economic ruin. By his last years it had fallen heavily into debt, was dependent on imported food, and had become increasingly corrupt. The United States, to prevent the expansion of Communist influence, continued its financial assistance and used the country as a base for operations against neighboring countries like Angola, where leftist regimes were fighting to establish themselves.

When in 1987 Mobutu could no longer count on American support, he met his mounting domestic opposition by agreeing to multiparty elections, but he ignored the results and continued his dictatorial rule over the next several years. Meanwhile guerrilla forces, the principal one led by Laurent Kabila, with support from Zaire's neighbors, Rwanda and Uganda, gathered strength and in 1996 swept through the country in a seven-month campaign, meeting little resistance. Kabila's forces gained control of the capital in 1997 and forced Mobutu to flee. Zaire officially became the Democratic Republic of Congo. One of the most repressive, corrupt, and ruthless dictatorships of postcolonial Africa came to an ignominious end and Mobutu died in exile a few months later.

Democratic Republic of Congo

But the country's troubles were not over. Satisfaction over Mobutu's downfall faded when Kabila, assuming a dictatorial role himself, banned all political parties except his own, arrested rival opposition leaders, and refused to permit a UN-sponsored human rights investigation into the repressive actions of his army. Because he relied on troops from neighboring countries and made no effort to build a national army, many in the country came to view him as a puppet of neighboring states who were eager to pillage Congo's vast resources. Because Kabila's weak hold on power disturbed his former allies, Rwanda and Uganda opened a military campaign to overthrow him and soon controlled half the country. By 2000 five separate nations had armed forces warring in Congo, supporting or opposing Kabila, and Rwanda and Uganda were fighting each other. The following year Kabila was assassinated, and a hasty effort was made to provide stability by swearing in his son as his successor. Foreign troops gradually withdrew from the country, but a civil war continued until UN peacekeepers and a tenuous truce agreement brought an end to most of the violence in 2003. President Joseph Kabila remained in office, but elections were postponed and the Democratic Republic of Congo was still far from achieving democratization or peace in the first decade of the new century—as in so many of the other African states that had emerged from European empires during the 1960s.

Burundi and Rwanda

Belgium, which had governed colonial Congo directly, had also administered under a League mandate and a UN trusteeship two small territories that had been part of German East Africa before 1914. In 1962 they became the independent states of Burundi and Rwanda. Both were predominantly Christian, divided between Roman Catholics and Anglicans. Although the two states went their separate ways, there were many parallels. Long-standing tensions between the dominant Tutsi minority and a resentful Hutu majority, partly a legacy of colonial policies, had led to power struggles and internecine warfare over the years but nothing comparable to the tragic events that took place in the mid-1990s.

The Hutu and the Tutsi

The Hutu, a Bantu people, the original settlers, were agricultural farmers. The Tutsi (or Watusi) arrived, possibly from Ethiopia, in the late fifteenth century. A tall warrior people who were cattle herders, they came to dominate the more numerous Hutu who worked the land for them in a kind of semifeudal relation. The German and later the Belgian colonial administrators favored the Tutsi, treating them as an elite group and enlisting their assistance in governing. After the Second World War, however, a new generation of Belgian administrators shifted to the view of redressing the balance in favor of the Hutu majority. When independence came, the Tutsi were still in control of the army and government, but the Hutu saw an opportunity to avenge themselves for the years of subjugation.

In Burundi a series of conflicts between the Tutsi-controlled government and Hutu rebels led to ethnic violence that killed thousands of people, Tutsi and Hutu alike, in the 1970s and early 1980s. Tutsi military regimes succeeded one another. In 1987 one such regime pledged itself to work for ethnic reconciliation and in 1993 allowed presidential elections. A Hutu, the first ever, was elected president. His efforts to form a stable, ethnically balanced government proved difficult. In Rwanda, meanwhile, similar efforts at reconciliation had led to the election of a Hutu president who proceeded to show good faith by appointing Tutsi ministers to the cabinet. In April 1994 an unexpected catastrophe occurred. A plane carrying the Hutu presidents of Burundi and Rwanda returning from a conference was shot down under mysterious circumstances, killing both presidents.

In Rwanda the event set off a wild outburst of revenge by Hutu extremists, who broadcast radio calls for a wholesale massacre of Tutsi. In a few weeks' time over a half million Tutsi were killed, along with Hutu moderates who refused to go along. The killings were accompanied by all kinds *Outburst of revenge*
of atrocities. Men, women, and children seeking refuge in churches were tracked down and slain, at times with the complicity of Hutu Roman Catholic and Anglican clergy. The international community, meanwhile, stood aside while the massacres went on unchecked. The worst carnage ended when Tutsi armed exiles, many of whom had been living in Uganda, swept back into the country, subdued the Hutu extremists, and reestablished a government pledged to work out some form of reconciliation.

But armed Hutu extremists in considerable numbers had fled to the eastern borderlands of neighboring Congo, and Rwanda became enmeshed in Congo's civil war, which soon turned into a regional multinational war. *Regional warfare*
All these events posed problems for the international community. It could not intervene in all cases of civil war to prevent human rights atrocities, but there was wide agreement that some middle ground had to be found between international intervention and the almost complete failure to act during the racist brutality and wholesale slaughter in Rwanda in 1994 that could justifiably be called genocide. Meanwhile, the Rwandan political situation began to stabilize. The Tutsi leader Paul Kagame was elected president in 2003, and in 2005 the largest group of Hutu rebels (many of whom were still in the Democratic Republic of the Congo) decided to end its armed campaign against the government. But the mass murder of the mid-1990s remained a haunting memory for the whole world as well as an impediment to full reconciliation within Rwanda itself.

End of the Portuguese Colonial Empire

Of all the colonial powers Portugal, itself under authoritarian dictatorship until 1974, clung longest to its colonies, symbols of grandeur from the days of Vasco da Gama's explorations and the early age of European expansion. To retain Angola, on the southwestern African coast, and Mozambique, on the southeastern, both of which at one time had been flourishing centers of the slave trade and had been under Portuguese rule for over 400 years, the Portuguese dictatorship stubbornly suppressed anticolonial revolts which broke out in 1961. It was in the course of the fighting that disaffected officers and

The violence of rampaging Hutu extremists in Rwanda sent a flood of refugees into the neighboring countries of central Africa in 1994. Hundreds of thousands of people in Tutsi communities were massacred, along with many thousands of Hutu moderates. Both Tutsi and Hutu families fled from the atrocities and joined other refugees in places such as this makeshift "camp" in the Congolese city of Goma. The people in this group were mostly Hutus, but the violence and displacement tragically affected everyone in Rwanda.
(Mark Peters/Sipa Press)

soldiers in the army, radicalized by the prolonged colonial war, turned against the Portuguese regime and overthrew it in 1974. The following year Portugal granted independence to Angola, Mozambique, and its smaller African colonies. Hundreds of thousands of Portuguese fled.

Angola

In Angola independence touched off a struggle for power by competing groups in which outside powers intervened—the Soviet Union and Cuba on the one side; the United States and South Africa, still under its apartheid regime, on the other. The Soviet bloc provided weapons and advisers to a Marxist faction, and the Cuban dictator Fidel Castro, who projected himself as a Marxist-Leninist defender of oppressed colonial peoples everywhere, dispatched 50,000 troops. Although the leftist group won out, proclaiming a "people's republic" in 1976, anti-Communist rebel groups with the support of the United States and South Africa continued the struggle. The war dragged on and cost hundreds of thousands of lives. Not until the early 1990s did the outside powers withdraw, the arduous task of economic reconstruction begin, and UN-supervised elections take place, but violence continued until antigovernment rebels finally agreed to a cease-fire after the death of a key rebel leader in 2002.

Mozambique

Mozambique, also a "people's republic," became engaged for the next 16 years in similar fighting with a militant rightist insurgency. The continuing wars and natural disasters such as drought and famine cost the small country over half a million lives and created 1½ million refugees. Both Angola and Mozambique gradually abandoned Marxism, loosened economic controls, and turned to the West for desperately needed economic assistance; and both countries were still struggling to recover from their internal wars, even in the first decade of the twenty-first century.

Ethiopia, Eritrea, Somalia, and Sudan

The postcolonial campaign to establish stable governments evolved fitfully over many years in northeastern Africa, where Ethiopia, Eritrea and Somalia had all formed part of Italy's short-lived East African empire. Italian armies, which had occupied Ethiopia after Mussolini invaded the country in 1936, were routed in the early years of the Second World War. Haile Selasse returned as emperor, but he was deposed by a military coup in 1974, whereupon Ethiopia became a client state of the Soviet Union in the Cold War conflicts of the era. The pro-Soviet regime was unable to defeat an Eritrean secessionist movement, however, and by 1993 a new Ethiopian government agreed to recognize the independent state of Eritrea on its northeastern border. Conflicts nevertheless continued to break out along this border in the 1990s, and both countries struggled with droughts, the movement of refugees, and recurring threats to peace and democratic political processes in the next century.

Somalia

Political instability and internal violence also troubled the post-independence history of neighboring Somalia, which had been partly under Italian control before 1914 and eventually under a UN trusteeship before becoming an independent state in 1960. Somalian governments later sent troops into Ethiopia during the period of the Soviet-Ethiopian alliance (seeking control of an area where many Somalians lived), but this intervention failed. Somalia was subsequently disrupted by ongoing rivalries among competing "war lords," who resisted both a strong centralized government and the creation of democratic institutions. Although Somalia would come to be viewed as a dangerous transit point for radical Islamic militants and other anti-Western groups, neither American troops nor UN peacekeeping forces were able to establish political order during their intervention in the 1990s; and regional war lords would continue to dominate Somalia in the first decade of the new century. The American setback in Somalia for a time reinforced American reluctance to intervene in troubled areas elsewhere, including Rwanda.

Sudan

The largest country in Africa, Sudan, entered its own era of internal violence as it gained independence from joint English-Egyptian rule in the late 1950s. The black population in southern Sudan, who were mainly Christian or followers of traditional animist faiths, rose in rebellion against the Arab government in the north, which sought to impose Islamic law on the entire country. Religious and ethnic violence dominated Sudanese life throughout much of the later twentieth century, as people in southern or western Sudan resisted the Islamic regime and as militia groups allied with the central government waged campaigns of violence, rape, and land appropriation. Although rebel groups in southern Sudan finally signed a peace accord with the government in early 2005, the situation was destabilized when the principal southern leader was killed in an accident. Meanwhile, the non-Arab, black peoples in the western Sudanese territory of Darfur came under widespread attacks from Arab militias, whose murderous destruction of whole villages (with the apparent sanction of the Sudanese government) was widely condemned by the international community in 2004–2005.

The recurring wars, government repression, famine, and drought thus kept most of the population of Ethiopia, Eritrea, Somalia, and Sudan in a vulnerable, impoverished condition. The turmoil also displaced a steady stream of refugees and precluded the kind of sustained economic development that was needed to support more stable political institutions.

The African Revolution

The preceding summary of postcolonial African history has stressed political and social conflicts that developed in the former European colonies, but it would be wrong to assume that the African Revolution was only a story of violence and disappointments. Independence provided a deep source of self-esteem. The word *uhuru,* freedom, rang through the continent in the heady days of decolonization. Léopold Senghor, the poet-president of the

Uhuru and négritude

formerly French colony of Senegal, gave voice to the idea of *négritude,* a powerful far-reaching black self-consciousness and pride in ancient cultural roots. This new pride spread far beyond the African continent itself, striking a responsive chord in North and South Americans of African descent whose ancestors had been brought in chains from lands that were now modern sovereign states. Black Africa exulted when the Nigerian playwright, poet, and novelist Wole Soyinka, who blended Yoruba and Western traditions in his writings, received the Nobel Prize for literature in 1986. Meanwhile Chinua Achebe's novel about Nigeria during the early years of European colonialism, *Things Fall Apart* (1959), entered the canon of world literature.

A new era

The African revolution ended Western colonialism and ushered in a new era of independence and national sovereignty, but it did not automatically bring democratic government, civil and human rights, the resolution of ethnic and regional antagonisms (some of which were the residue of Europe's colonial policies and arbitrary boundary divisions), or a meaningful improvement in the quality of human lives. In the countryside ethnic loyalties often transcended national loyalties. Natural disasters, drought and floods, eroding soil, and diseases added to the continent's tribulations, which derived also from the fact that African agriculture and other economic activities remained hostage to world price fluctuations.

The social and economic situation was often grim. At the end of the twentieth century close to one-half of sub-Saharan Africa's population of 600 million survived on less than $1 a day. The continent's debt burdens amounted collectively to $200 billion. Many of the world's older infectious diseases such as malaria and many childhood diseases were still prevalent. The death toll from AIDS and the rate of infection from the HIV virus was devastating. Of the 36 million people in the world living with HIV, the virus that causes AIDS, over two-thirds were in sub-Saharan Africa. Some 15 million Africans had already died from it, and 11 million had been left orphans. Scientists and others agreed that AIDS could well be the most serious infectious disease in recorded human history. For Africa it was described as the worst social disaster since the slave trade. A broad-based campaign to control the pandemic thus gained international support at the beginning of the twenty-first century—in part because of the widespread human suffering and in part because the hard-won gains in development, economic growth, and quality of life were in danger of reversal.

Constitutional governments fall

The new states began independence with constitutions, elected parliaments, independent judiciaries, and formal guarantees of civil liberties. But under the pressure of ethnic conflict, economic burdens, and political instability, the machinery of constitutional government quickly succumbed to dictatorship, generally military. In country after country, generals, admirals,

Postcolonial Africa faced numerous challenges at the end of the twentieth century, including the spread of the AIDS pandemic and the need to produce more food. These men in Botswana are thrashing a harvest of sorghum, a grain that has become one of the key agricultural products in the commodity-based economies of most African nations.
(Peter Essick/Aurora Photos)

colonels, majors, and officers of lesser rank pushed aside the civilian rulers. The warrior caste, often a law unto themselves, became the accomplices and tools of the new rulers, tyrannizing the population. Nigeria, which at least made sporadic efforts to preserve constitutional government (and its federal system for the multiethnic state), counted six military coups in the years from 1966 to 1985. Of over 150 African heads of state in the first three decades of independence, only six voluntarily relinquished their offices, and most presided over governments that were repressive, corrupt, and tyrannical. Until the late 1980s there were few examples of free elections, multiparty systems, political pluralism, orderly changes of government, or freedom from censorship.

But in the late 1980s and in the 1990s the spread of democracy worldwide caught up in Africa as well. By 1999, 32 of 53 African states had free or partly free elections of some credibility, and this trend continued into the

Spread of democracy

new century. The orderly election and presidency in South Africa of Nelson Mandela and the transition to his successor provided reassurances of South Africa's democratic progress. Nigeria ended years of repressive and corrupt military rule when the country was restored to civilian rule. A new generation of leaders paid increasing attention to health care, education, and women's needs and rights. In the 1990s more than 30 sub-Saharan countries adopted economic reforms liberalizing trade and investment, stabilizing currencies, and privatizing cumbersome and wasteful state enterprises. A small group of states showed economic growth rates of over 6 percent. The Organization of African Unity pledged to punish with economic sanctions any African government that came to power by military coup.

Yet talk of an African renaissance could not ignore the continent's continuing social and economic crises. In the early twenty-first century sub-Saharan countries still filled all the bottom ranks in global tables of economic growth. Fewer than half of young Africans were attending schools, and the economic gap between Africa and the rest of the world was widening.

No single theory could explain African problems. Some pointed to nineteenth-century European imperialist rule and exploitation as the root cause. Colonial rule lasted only a few generations but perhaps long enough

Africa's problems

to undermine African societies and institutions or to hinder the development of autonomous new ways of life. Above all, it had undeniably eroded African confidence and experience in self-governing institutions. On the other hand, postcolonial failure seemed to be largely a failure of political leadership. When the European colonial rulers departed, they left highly centralized authoritarian states in the hands of small elite groups with little political experience. Europeans had established colonies like the Belgian Congo to be exploited for profit, and their postcolonial African successors often followed in the same path. The new rulers transformed the national independence party into the sole or dominant government party. Although ostensibly opposed to ethnic separatism, the political leaders often manipulated ethnic rivalries to enhance their own power. The Cold War also contributed to the setback of democracy in that the Western-Soviet competition for client states led to the support of dictators. American policy was designed to win and retain reliable allies in the fight against communism, and the Americans applied no litmus tests of democracy before giving financial aid. In the 1980s, for example, the four largest African recipients of American economic aid were the rightist dictators in Liberia, Somalia, and Zaire, and the anti-Communist rebel leader in Angola.

The key question for much of the African continent was how to anticipate and prevent crises leading to war, a goal that required institutional safeguards to ensure that the military remained subordinate and accountable to civilian authority. For the outside world the question was how to provide economic assistance that would be used constructively and improve the quality of life for all.

Some Africans argued that to counter separatist ethnic and regional forces, cope with economic underdevelopment, and provide the cohesion necessary for national unity, strong, single-party governments were more effective than multiparty democratic systems. President Museveni, who had accomplished so much in Uganda to overcome the chaos and torment of the early years of independence, put his concept of a "no-party democracy" to a referendum in 2000, and voters accepted his recommendation that what he called "the Movement" be the sole governing party. Western-style democracy was still difficult to nurture in societies with high rates of illiteracy or disease, a small middle class, and cultural traditions of lifetime tenure for chiefs and kings. But other Africans rejected such arguments and maintained that they should choose and control their rulers, and the governments they lived under, and one day would do so.

"No-party democracy"

Many of the African states for a time were professedly Marxist. They spoke of "African socialism" and styled their regimes "people's democratic republics." In Mozambique the main avenues were named for Lenin and Mao Zedong; the flag of the People's Republic of the Congo (in colonial times the French Congo) flying in Brazzaville displayed a hammer and sickle. Such regimes turned away from free enterprise, which they identified with the profit-making, exploitation, and racial humiliation of Western colonialism. They looked to government, public ownership, and centralized planning to oversee new economic structures that would hasten development and provide a more egalitarian society. They nationalized their industries and collectivized agriculture. In the years of the Cold War many of these countries received technical and material assistance from the U.S.S.R., the Soviet bloc, and the People's Republic of China. But rigid state control and overly centralized planning (as in the Communist countries themselves) led to economic stagnation and corruption.

African socialism

Once self-sufficient in food, Africa after 1964 became an importer of food. Wars and preparations for wars were costly, so that expenditures on arms often exceeded the international financial assistance received for economic development. Yet in spite of the painfully slow progress in improving the quality of life, Africans in the first generations of independence felt a new sense of control over their own destiny. They were not eager to cast them-

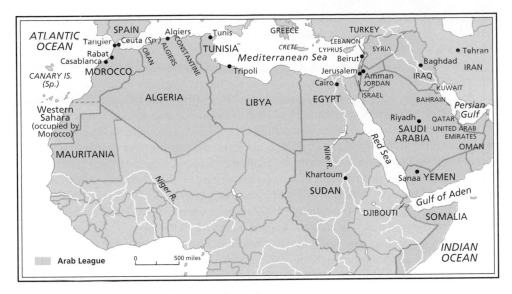

THE MODERN ARAB WORLD

The Arabic language zone is one of the most extensive in the world, reaching from the Atlantic Ocean to the Persian Gulf. In 1945 the Arab states formed a League, which came to have 22 members. The League proved to be rather loose and its members often disagreed, but after 1948 all Arab nations expressed varying levels of suspicion and hostility toward the Israeli state in the midst of an otherwise predominantly Arab world.

selves in the Western democratic image or simply to follow Western economic models, although globalization might well limit or preclude other options. Economic growth was nevertheless a prerequisite to survival and to the improvement of human lives, as were political stability and peace. African nations were still moving toward these often elusive goals almost a half-century after independence.

118.   FERMENT IN THE MIDDLE EAST

The Islamic and the Arab World

In the Islamic, or Muslim, world, the age of colonial domination also ended, and a powerful renewed sense of identity emerged. Much of the Islamic world was determined to share in modernization and material advances, but many Muslims wanted to develop or reform their societies

Islamic identity

without assimilating Western cultural patterns. Religious and cultural traditions slowed the pace of modernization or influenced emerging new institutions. An elitist organization of society, traditional obstacles to full equality for women, and widespread illiteracy presented powerful obstacles to social change. The 40 or so identifiable Islamic countries, Arab and non-Arab, differed vastly from each other so that the Islamic world had no single sense of identity; Sunni and Shiite Muslims were often in conflict and sometimes in violent confrontation with each other. Although the pace of transformation was uneven, older life styles were being undermined everywhere. In many cases strong tensions developed as Islamic traditionalists resisted secular changes. Turkey made a concerted effort to protect the secular society decreed by its founder, Kemal Atatürk; but elsewhere, in Saudi Arabia, Iran, Afghanistan, Sudan, and other countries, Islamic fundamentalism created virtual theocracies.

The heartland of Islam was the Arab world and the Arabian peninsula, where the Muslim religion was founded by Muhammad in the seventh century, but under the caliphs who succeeded Muhammad and who commanded both religious and secular authority, Islam had swept from the Arabian peninsula into non-Arab lands. Turks and other non-Arab peoples who were converted to Islam continued the expansion. The Ottoman Empire, founded by the Ottoman Turks, ruled at its height in the sixteenth century over Arab and non-Arab peoples and included Palestine, with sites holy to Judaism, Christianity, and Islam. When the empire gradually disintegrated in the modern centuries, the Europeans expanded their economic and political influence in the Middle East. From the Ottoman Empire emerged many of the states of the contemporary Muslim world, Arab and non-Arab, at first as international trusteeships and mandates and then as independent nations.

The Middle East

The term "Middle East" itself is imprecise but widely used. For the Europeans who coined the term it meant the geographic area midway between Europe and East Asia, but "Middle East" is used now to designate that part of the world that is predominantly Islamic in religion and culture stretching from the states of North Africa to Western Asia. The major non-Arab Muslim states include Indonesia (with the world's largest Islamic population), Malaysia, Pakistan, Bangladesh, Afghanistan, and Iran (the only country where the Shiite rather than the Sunni branch of Islam prevails).[2] The Islamic world also includes a half-dozen states in central Asia in the former Soviet Union. Millions of Muslims, non-Arab and Arab, also live in India, in Africa, in the Balkans, and increasingly in western Europe and the United States. At the opening of the twenty-first century there were about 1.1 billion Muslims, or close to one-fifth the world's population, second in numbers only to Christianity in all its branches.

About one-fifth of the world's Muslims, or some 200 million, are Arabs, that is, people whose primary language is Arabic. Because the language of the Qur'an (or Koran), used in the religious practices of Muslims worldwide, is Arabic, it is in a sense the second language of non-Arab Muslims as well. The Arab states stretch from the Atlantic coast of North Africa to the Persian Gulf, from Morocco to Iraq.[3] In that part of the Middle East lies a large part of the world's petroleum reserves on which the economic activity of the industrial world depends, and the region has been one of the modern world's most troubled areas.

The Arab states

The Arab states that emerged from the collapse of the Ottoman Empire at the end of the First World War became League of Nations mandates under British or French administration, with the expectation of one day receiving independence. Egypt became nominally independent in 1922 and Iraq, in 1932, although the

---

[2]The schism originated in an armed struggle over the succession to Muhammad after the prophet's death in 632, in which the Shiite faction supported Ali, Muhammad's son-in-law, and the Sunni favored another line of succession. The schism became permanent. There are also differences in doctrine and ritual between the two important divisions. The Shiite form of Islam became the state religion in Persia (Iran) in the sixteenth century and has remained dominant in Iran, but there are important Shiite communities in Iraq, Pakistan, Yemen, and elsewhere.

[3]The principal Arab states are Morocco, Algeria, Tunisia, Egypt, and Libya, in North Africa; Lebanon, Syria, Jordan, and Iraq (Israel's neighbors), close to the eastern Mediterranean; and Saudi Arabia, Yemen, Oman, the United Arab Emirates, Qatar, Bahrain, and Kuwait, in the Arabian peninsula.

British retained treaty rights in each until after 1945. The other Arab states became independent during or after the Second World War, when the British and French ended their mandates. In 1945 Egypt, Iraq, Lebanon, Saudi Arabia, Syria, and Jordan formed the influential League of Arab States, or Arab League. Libya, after gaining independence in 1951, also became a member. In the decades that followed, newly independent Arab states as well as the Palestinian National Authority joined so that it grew to have 22 members by the end of the twentieth century.

The unity of the Arab world is more fragile than often thought. Divisive rivalries persist. The pan-Arabism advocated by Egypt's Colonel Nasser in the 1950s and Libya's Colonel Qaddafi in the 1980s failed to rally lasting support. A United Arab Republic joining Egypt and Syria in 1958 was short-lived. After the Second World War, however, the Arab states found common cause in their opposition to the state of Israel, which itself had emerged as a new sovereign state in the Middle East in 1948. The Arab states viewed Israel as a Western-backed intrusion into their land, and the result was a series of continuing tensions and conflicts that frequently brought wider international forces into play.

Arab rivalries

The Emergence of Israel

Zionism, evolving in the late nineteenth century as a response to European anti-Semitism, became a movement to establish (or reestablish) a Jewish homeland in Palestine, then part of the Ottoman Empire. A small number of Jewish pioneers from Russia and eastern Europe made their way to Palestine before 1914. During the First World War, while at war with the Ottoman Empire, the British by the Balfour Declaration of 1917 voiced support for "a Jewish homeland in Palestine" but in other ways supported emergent Arab nationalism. In 1923, after the demise of the Ottoman Empire, the British received a League of Nations mandate for Palestine, and a growing number of Jewish settlers arrived in the 1920s and 1930s.

The whole question of Palestine poignantly reemerged at the end of the Second World War when the homeless survivors of the Nazi Holocaust, which had all but wiped out central and eastern Europe's Jews, sought out Palestine as a place of refuge. But in deference to Arab protests the British limited immigration and turned away whole shiploads of refugees. The Jewish leaders pressed their cause with the United Nations and sympathetic American political circles and contested the British restrictions, at times resorting even to terrorist activities directed against the British. In 1947 the United Nations in a vote supported by both the United States and the Soviet Union recommended partition of Palestine into two parts: a Jewish sector and an Arab sector, with the area around Jerusalem under international control.

The question of Palestine

The Arabs, who had boycotted the UN committee hearings, rejected the partition, complaining that they were being asked to make sacrifices for Europe's persecution of the Jews. Both sides prepared for conflict. On May 14, 1948, when the Zionist leaders proclaimed the Republic of Israel, Israel's five Arab neighbors—Syria, Lebanon, Jordan, Egypt, and Iraq—refused recognition and invaded the new state. The Israelis (as the citizens of the new republic called themselves) not only defended themselves but also counterattacked. In the course of the fighting at least 600,000 Palestinian Arabs fled, or were forced by the Israelis to flee, to Jordan, Lebanon, Syria, and other Arab states. During the war Jordan took over the West Bank of the Jordan River, and part of Jerusalem and Egypt took the Gaza Strip, but elsewhere Israel gained territory.

The creation of the State of Israel in 1948 marked the triumphant culmination of a long-developing campaign to establish an independent Jewish state in the Middle East. The first prime minister of Israel, David Ben-Gurion, is pictured here, signing the proclamation that established the new Israeli state, opened an important new era in Jewish history, and led to a long conflict with the surrounding Arab nations.

(Associated Press, AP)

By the end of hostilities and the armistice of 1949 Israel had increased its originally allotted land by about half. Jerusalem came under divided control. The plan for international control was abandoned. Jordan now governed East Jerusalem, but Israel retained control of West Jerusalem. The Arab states, unwilling to negotiate peace or even recognize the existence of Israel as a sovereign state, made little effort to absorb the Palestinian refugees who had fled to the Arab states and who continued to live in overcrowded, squalid refugee camps for decades to come.

The New State of Israel

A Jewish homeland

The Israelis saw themselves as creating a Jewish homeland after the Holocaust, so that persecuted Jews would never again be without a refuge. Under a Law of Return Jewish immigrants from anywhere in the diaspora were automatically entitled to citizenship. Secular-minded founders of the state like David Ben-Gurion did not define the role of religion too closely. Freedom of religion and freedom of conscience were equally to be protected, but rabbinical authorities were to control such matters as marriage and divorce, definitions of Jewishness, and observance of the Sabbath. Ultra-Orthodox Jews eventually came to exert influence out of proportion to their numbers and to create a larger political voice for themselves than originally envisaged.

After independence Israel over the years built a modern, Western-style, urban, industrial society with a democratically elected parliament, the Knesset, and a lively political culture. For many years the moderately socialist Labor party governed. The country provided a large role for labor unions and agricultural cooperatives (famous as *kibbutzim*), extensive health and educational services, and support for scientific and technological research. About half the economy was government-controlled until a later shift to privatization.

Economic growth

Economic development took off swiftly. Through ingeniously engineered irrigation schemes the Israelis reclaimed vast stretches of the Negev desert. The amount of land under cultivation more than doubled. In 1948 Israel produced only one-third of its food; by the early 1970s it was producing enough to meet almost all of its domestic needs and began to export. Industry expanded. Before long the Israelis exported electronic products, precision instruments, and military hardware. Extensive for-

The creation of Israel and the subsequent Arab-Israeli war of 1948–1949 drove some 600,000 Palestinian Arabs into neighboring countries and refugee camps. These Palestinians were living in 1956 at a camp on the West Bank of the Jordan River—an area that came under Israeli control after the Six Day War in 1967 and remained a source of conflict as the Palestinians later sought to establish an independent state in this territory.
(Getty Images)

eign investment, especially from the United States, further stimulated economic development. Living standards exceeded those of other countries in the Middle East and compared favorably to those of western Europe.

Over 2 million immigrants arrived in the decades after 1948. Many Jews arrived from the Arab states in North Africa and from Arab and non-Arab Muslim states in Asia, forced to abandon established communities where their families had lived for centuries but where Jews were now persecuted. From 1989 to 1992 about 400,000 Soviet Jews, finally permitted by the Soviet government to migrate, reached Israel. The population of 870,000 in 1948 reached about 5,750,000 by the opening of the twenty-first century. In the 1990s problems of unemployment, housing shortages, and a lack of skilled jobs surfaced, especially for the former Soviet Jews. At great financial strain, but benefiting from American foreign aid, the Israelis also developed powerful modern military forces and air power. They built nuclear reactors for the production of electric power and quietly created a nuclear military capacity.

The Arab-Israeli Wars after Independence

Four more Arab-Israeli wars were fought after 1948–1949, one in each of the next four decades, in 1956, 1967, 1973, and 1982. Israel, with Britain and France as allies, went to war with Egypt in 1956 when Egypt nationalized the Suez Canal and attempted to bar Israeli shipping. In 1967 Israel waged the Six-Day War against Egypt, Syria, and Jordan, when Egypt moved to close the Gulf of Aqaba

Territorial struggles

to Israel, which would have strangled the Israeli economy. The outcome of the brief fighting in 1967 was momentous. After defeating the three Arab armies, Israel took from Jordan the West Bank of the Jordan River and East Jerusalem; from Syria, the Golan Heights (from which the Syrians had been able to shell Israeli settlements); and from Egypt, the Sinai Peninsula and Gaza Strip. Israel emerged with territory four times its original size; a rapidly growing population of over 1 million additional Arabs came under Israeli rule. The Israeli occupation of Palestinian towns and the later development of Israeli settlements in the occupied territories provoked the further development of Palestinian nationalism, new demands for an independent Palestinian state, and the emergence of radical Palestinian groups that began to launch terrorist attacks against Israel.

The next war broke out in 1973 when Egyptian and Syrian forces attacked the Israelis on the Jewish holy day Yom Kippur. Israel recovered from the surprise attack, defeated the Syrian army, and trapped the Egyptian forces in the Sinai Peninsula. With the Israelis near victory and in control of additional Arab territory, the League of Arab States suddenly introduced a new strategic weapon in support of Egypt and Syria, an embargo on oil shipments. Although the embargo was lifted a few months later, early in 1974, the oil-producing nations had quadrupled the price of oil, with global economic consequences far beyond the conflict in the Middle East. Meanwhile, the war ended with an American-mediated settlement. Israel withdrew from the west bank of the Suez Canal, but continued to occupy most of the Sinai Peninsula.

In 1982 Israel invaded war-torn Lebanon, where a divisive civil war had created virtual anarchy in Lebanese society. Israel had become the target of repeated raids from Lebanese territory organized by the Palestine Liberation Organization (PLO) and by guerrilla forces of Islamic sects armed by Islamic states, including Syria, Iraq, and Iran. Israeli forces pushed as far north as Beirut, forced the expulsion of the PLO, and then withdrew, although continuing for many years to hold a narrow security zone in southern Lebanon. No brief summary of these wars can convey the grief and suffering that each brought to the Israelis, the Palestinians, and the people in neighboring Arab states.

Middle East and the Cold War

The Middle East became a theater of Cold War rivalries as well. The United States had disapproved of the British-French-Israeli Suez Canal intervention in 1956, but after that crisis it generally supported Israel and also provided extensive economic assistance. France, originally a staunch Israeli ally, for a time turned against Israel when de Gaulle in the 1960s decided he needed to help restore a balance of power in the region by supporting the Arab states. The U.S.S.R., one of the original backers of the Jewish state, reversed itself and sent arms to Egypt and other Arab states. The United States, following its Cold War strategy of containment, remained determined to prevent Soviet influence from expanding in the Middle East. The Eisenhower Doctrine, which pledged American support to countries in the Middle East resisting communism, was welcomed by Israel, while many of the Arab states resented it and looked to the Soviets for support—though they did not favor Communism within their own nations.

The PLO

The Palestinian Arabs grew steadily more militant, conducting guerrilla warfare against Israel and engaging in terrorist activities within Israel and in other parts of the world. Under the leadership of Yasir Arafat, the PLO became a full member of the Arab League in 1964 and received recognition in many quarters as a government-in-exile for the Palestinian Arabs. The PLO professed to speak for all Palestinians, not only the 1.5 million under Israeli occupation but also those who had fled as refugees and who by this time numbered as many as 3 million. The PLO demanded the evacuation of all territories occupied by Israel after 1967 and

In one of the recurring cycles of Middle Eastern violence, Israel responded to attacks from guerrilla bases in Lebanon by sending its army as far north as Beirut in 1982. These Israeli troops were patrolling streets in the Muslim sector of the Lebanese capital during the military operation that drove the Palestine Liberation Organization out of Beirut. Although the Israeli army soon withdrew to southern Lebanon, Israel retained control over a small "security zone" within Lebanese territory until 2000.

(Nackstrand/Sipa Press)

ISRAEL AND ADJOINING REGIONS

"Palestine" is the term by which Europeans long designated a small region of predominantly Arab population on the east coast of the Mediterranean. The area belonged to the Ottoman Empire until the end of the First World War. In 1922 the League of Nations made the territory a mandate of Great Britain, which soon responded to Arab dissatisfactions by placing restrictions on the migration of European Jews, who had been moving into Palestine since the rise of Zionism in the late nineteenth century. After the deaths of millions of Jews in the Holocaust during the Second World War, the Zionist aspiration for an independent Jewish state won new international support. In 1947 the United Nations proposed a partition of Palestinian lands to create a new Jewish state and a division of the city of Jerusalem into separate zones. The Arabs

rejected this plan, but in the Arab-Israeli war of 1948 the Israelis won control of wider bound-aries than those first proposed. The Arab states still refused to recognize Israel. In the Six-Day War of 1967 the Israelis occupied additional territory, as shown in the fourth panel, labeled AFTER 1967. In 1973, in the Yom Kippur War, Egypt and Syria attacked to regain their lost lands, but Israel defeated them and continued to occupy the Sinai Peninsula and other territo-ries, although Egypt eventually won control of the east bank of the Suez Canal. Under a peace treaty that Israel and Egypt negotiated in 1979, Israel returned the Sinai to Egypt, but retained the small area known as the Gaza Strip. In 1993 Israel agreed to begin withdrawing from some areas of the occupied territories and allow the first steps toward self-government for the Pales-tinians. A new Palestinian Authority emerged to govern the autonomous Palestinian communi-ties, but a long series of later conflicts and negotiations had still not led to a final peace settlement or an independent Palestinian state in the early twenty-first century. In 2005, how-ever, Israel removed all Jewish settlements and its military forces from the Gaza Strip.

called for the establishment of a sovereign independent Palestinian state in the West Bank of the Jordan River and the Gaza Strip, but the Israelis continued their occupation.

The Arab states meanwhile rejected proposals for a comprehensive peace agreement, condemning the post-1967 Israeli military occupation and even refusing to recognize Israel's right to exist as a nation. In 1975 the Arab states persuaded the UN General Assem-bly, where the former colonial states of Asia and Africa now held a majority, to adopt a res-olution condemning Zionism as a form of racism, even though Zionism had originated as a defense against anti-Semitism and Israel had been established, in part, as a response to the Nazi Holocaust. The resolution remained in effect until it was repealed in 1992.

Palestinian terrorist attacks within Israel and elsewhere altered the political scene in Israel itself. In 1977 Labor for the first time lost control of the government to a conservative, nationalist party of the center-right, Likud, founded by religious groups. Likud could govern only through coalitions, but it retained its parliamentary majority by receiving the sup-port of the religious parties. The Israeli posture toward the Palestinians became more

Israelis vs. Palestinians

intransigent. Menachem Begin as Likud prime minister encouraged Israelis to make permanent settlements in the occupied West Bank of the Jordan River (for which he even used the Biblical names of Judea and Samaria) and the Gaza Strip, and he rejected negotiations with the PLO. In 1980 the government unified the Israeli capital by unilaterally annexing East Jerusalem, which it had occupied since 1967.

Without a settlement new and even deadlier conflicts threatened to break out. At issue were the disposition of the territories occupied by Israel since 1967, the demand of the Palestinian Arabs for an independent national state, assistance to the Palestinian Arab refugees, and the recognition and guarantee of Israel's legitimacy and security. The Egyptian president Anwar al-Sadat, recognizing the impasse and eager to recover lost Egyptian territory, broke the united Arab front against Israel when in 1978 he visited Israel and addressed the Knesset in Jerusalem. In 1979, with the United States acting as mediator, Sadat and Begin signed a peace treaty in Washington in the presence of President Carter. Israel agreed to withdraw from the Sinai Peninsula except for the Gaza Strip and was guaranteed the free use of the Suez Canal. Outraged at Sadat's recognition of Israel's legitimacy as a sovereign state, the other Arab states expelled Egypt from the Arab League. Sadat himself was later assassinated by Islamic extremists in his own army. His successor, President Mubarak, remained cautiously friendly to Israel, as did King Hussein of Jordan. Syria, Libya, and Iraq assumed the lead in rejecting any wider settlement. To thwart Iraq's threatened nuclear capacity Israel in 1982 took the bold step of bombing a nuclear facility near Baghdad but meanwhile continued to build up its own unannounced nuclear capacity.

Israel, the Occupied Territories, and Peace Negotiations

In the 1980s over 1.5 million Palestinian Arabs lived in the West Bank and Gaza Strip, occupied by Israel since the 1967 war. At the end of 1987 nationalist agitation by young Palestinians flared up into a sustained uprising, the *intifada*, as it was called in Arabic. The Israeli military met the stone-throwing, fire-bombing, and civil disobedience with armed force, and casualties mounted. The suppression of the rebellion polarized Israel politically, hurt its economy, and threatened to undermine its democracy. The PLO exploited the popular uprising to press for recognition of an independent Palestinian state.

The intifada

As the Cold War wound down in the late 1980s, the Arab states could no longer be certain of Soviet support, and the United States continued to encourage negotiations. Any genuine settlement would have to revolve around the formula "land for peace": Israel to give up some or all of the territory occupied since 1967 in return for Arab recognition of Israel's legitimacy and existence. The status of the Palestinians would have to be resolved in favor of some form of self-government or statehood. Israel's continuing insecurity lay rooted in the fact that its small population lived in a hostile Middle East. A politically divided Israel, still haunted by Holocaust memories, feared for the nation's security and the safety of its citizens. For some, territorial expansion was one answer. Begin's successors continued the Likud party's support for increased Jewish settlement in the occupied territories. Many other Israelis recognized the legitimate grievances of the Palestinian Arabs, accepting the fact that Jews and Arabs had to find ways to live together in the small land.

"Land for peace"

In 1992 the possibilities of peace negotiations with the Arabs revived when a Labor coalition formed a new government headed by Yitzhak Rabin and Shimon Peres. Rabin halted additional settlements in the West Bank and reopened peace talks. Although official

Israeli Prime Minister Yitzhak Rabin and PLO Chairman Yasir Arafat signed the Oslo accords in Washington in September 1993. This diplomatic event marked the first official agreement between Israel and the Palestinians, and it set the agenda for later, inconclusive negotiations throughout the 1990s. Radicals on both sides condemned the terms of the Oslo agreement, however, and they soon turned to violence. Rabin became one of the victims when he was assassinated by a Jewish extremist in 1995. In this picture, Chairman Arafat is standing next to President Clinton as they both observe the Israeli prime minister signing the accords.
(Time Life Pictures/Getty Images)

negotiations continued, it was secret talks carried on between Israelis and Palestinians in Oslo, Norway, outside regular diplomatic channels, that led in 1993 to an extraordinary agreement between Prime Minister Yitzhak Rabin and Yasir Arafat, which was signed in Washington at a ceremonial event with President Bill Clinton. Under the Oslo accords Israel recognized the Palestine Liberation Organization as the representative of the Palestinian people and agreed to initial steps for Palestinian self-government, including its own security forces. The PLO in turn recognized Israel's legitimate existence as a sovereign state and agreed to abjure acts of violence. Despite many unresolved issues, Arab-Israeli relations seemed to be moving toward a settlement with the PLO, in which other Arab states might eventually join. In accordance with the agreement Israel withdrew its armed forces from most of the Gaza Strip and from Jericho in the West Bank and took steps to allow Palestinian self-rule under a "Palestinian National Authority" in the West Bank and in Gaza.

But intransigent groups on both sides began to derail the fragile agreement. Violence erupted again, and in 1995 a fanatical Jewish extremist assassinated Prime Minister Rabin. In 1996 Peres and the Labor coalition lost the elections to the hard-line Likud leader Benjamin Netanyahu, who immediately relaxed the freeze on new Jewish settlements in the West Bank and Gaza Strip. Even so, Netanyahu, yielding to pressure from the United States, met with Arafat in 1998 and agreed to carry out the Oslo agreement calling for surrender in stages of the occupied West Bank. Even these moderate concessions cost Netanyahu conservative and rightist support. Ehud Barak, a military man and former Israeli chief of staff, representing Labor, centrist, and some religious parties, campaigned on a pledge to move forward with peace negotiations and defeated Netanyahu in new elections. Under continuing American brokering, negotiations resumed. Israel began its withdrawal from the West Bank, and Barak, as he had promised, withdrew Israeli armed forces from its southern Lebanon security zone.

A fragile agreement derailed

Barak also made overtures to Syria over the return of all or part of the Israeli-held Golan Heights. His concessions alarmed many Israelis and he lost his majority in the Knesset. Still determined to represent what he considered the popular will for peace, he nonetheless met once again with Arafat in Washington in July 2000, but the new talks foundered, principally over the status of Jerusalem. Despite all that had been offered him, Arafat insisted on his obligation to the entire Arab and Muslim world to claim sovereignty over East Jerusalem and its Muslim holy places and make it the capital of the Palestinian state. Violence erupted again. Arafat, the Israelis protested, seemed unable to control his people. A second *intifada* broke out in the streets of Jerusalem and rapidly spread, provoked initially by an unannounced visit to Muslim sites in East Jerusalem by the hard-line Ariel Sharon, a former top military commander in earlier wars, a determined opponent of Barak's concessions, and now seeking to replace him. As Palestinian violence escalated, public opinion turned against Barak, and in early 2001 Sharon became prime minister by a sweeping popular vote. Many Israelis remained troubled. Some were willing to support the surrender of the occupied territories to the Palestinian Arabs and to work out compromises on the Israeli settlements and other issues. But many more believed that the concessions had gone too far. They too wanted peace but with firmer guarantees of security.

A new intifada

The opportunity for a peace settlement on the basis of the Oslo accords seemed to slip away, and the troubled region plunged into a new cycle of terrorist attacks, Israeli reprisals, and mounting casualties on both sides. The Israeli and Palestinian leaders, Sharon and Arafat, remained intransigent, but the impasse began to break after Arafat's death in 2004. The Palestinian National Authority chose a more moderate president, Mahmoud Abbas, and progress seemed possible. The United States took a more active part in furthering a "road map" to peace; and Sharon removed Israeli settlers and troops from the Gaza Strip, ending the 38-year occupation of that small, crowded territory. At the same time, however, Sharon's government built a controversial new wall along the border between Israeli and Palestinian lands (incorporating some formerly Palestinian land) and continued to support the extensive network of Jewish settlements that was interspersed among the territories of the Palestinian National Authority on the West Bank. The new Palestinian president was meanwhile unable to control the radical Hamas party (which won Palestinian parliamentary elections in 2006), and terrorist attacks by Palestinian extremists continued to cause death and disruption within Israel. The idea of exchanging "land for peace" had still not produced a general peace agreement, and Palestinian aspirations for a fully independent, stable nation-state had not yet become a political reality. Although the extremists on both sides were unwilling to compromise, most Israelis and Palestinians favored some kind of peaceful resolution to a conflict that had taken countless lives, disrupted economic life, and distorted political cultures in the entire region for more than five decades. Despite all the setbacks and the continuing violence, new political alignments in Israel offered a new promise of progress toward peace; but the "road map" did not lead directly or quickly to a comprehensive peace plan that the two sides would accept and implement.

Libya and Syria

Libya and Syria both added to the explosiveness in the Middle East. The discovery of oil in Libya in 1959 transformed a country of 4 million people into a leading petroleum producer. In 1969 Colonel Muhammar al-Qaddafi ousted the existing monarchy, established a personal dictatorship, and agi-

Mubammar al-Qaddafi

tated for an extremist Arab nationalism. Using his country's oil wealth for political purposes, he projected himself as a spokesman for pan-Arabism and aspired to a leadership role in African affairs as well. Libya became headquarters for terrorist activities in Europe and elsewhere. Neither economic sanctions nor even military reprisals deterred Qaddafi. In 1997 the United States officially included Libya on its short list of states actively sponsoring international terrorism. Qaddafi continued to hold dictatorial power into the twenty-first century, but he moved away from his earlier nationalist radicalism, renounced international terrorism, and abandoned efforts to develop and stockpile chemical weapons.

The early years of the Syrian Arab Republic were marked by extreme political instability and a succession of military coups. In 1963 one such coup brought the pan-Arab Baath party to power and led to a new one-party government. In 1971, in the tenth coup of its kind, Hafez al-Assad, a former defense minister, took power and ruled dictatorially for close to 30 years until his death in 2000. Assad ruthlessly suppressed all opposition, including an insurrection of the Muslim Brotherhood in 1982, in which his air force killed tens of thousands.

Hafez al-Assad

Assad remained one of the most resolute enemies of Israel, intent on recovering all the Arab territory lost since 1967, especially Syria's strategic Golan Heights. In the chaotic civil war in Lebanon he had supported radical Arab militant sects and sent some 35,000 troops as a "peacekeeping force." In the end, to the resentment of many Lebanese, he was virtually in control of Lebanon. At his death Assad's son was quickly named the new president in a carefully prearranged succession. The new president, Bashar al-Assad, continued most of his father's policies, but bowing to a popular uprising and international pressure he eventually withdrew Syrian troops from Lebanon. The Baath party meanwhile clung to power in Syria, even as war in neighboring Iraq threatened to spill over the Syrian border in the years after 2003.

119. REVOLUTION AND WAR IN THE PERSIAN GULF

The Revolution in Iran

Where change occurred rapidly in the Middle East, it was clear that traditionalists often resented the Westernizing influence of modern economic and cultural forces. They opposed secularism and the disruption of older religious and cultural institutions as a Western subversion. Yet the outside world was not prepared for the fierce anti-Westernism of the Islamic revolution that erupted in 1979, not in an Arab state, but in Iran, where the principal language was Persian (or Farsi). Iran was a Shiite state, whereas nine-tenths of the Islamic world adhered to the Sunni branch of Islam, but the Shiite revolutionary leaders in Iran helped to foment a new religious revivalism everywhere in the Muslim world.

Over the centuries Persia (or Iran, as it was known after 1935) had a long history of foreign domination. At the opening of the twentieth century, as we have seen, Britain and Russia, coveting its newly discovered oil resources, divided it into spheres of influence. After the First World War the British had tried to retain control, but in 1921 an army officer, Reza Khan, seized power, assumed the title of shah, or hereditary ruler, in 1925, and embarked on a program of modernization. During the Second World War, however, in 1941, when some of his machinations brought him threateningly close to the Axis, the British and Russians occupied the country and forced him to abdicate in favor of his son, Muhammad Reza. The young shah identified with the West.

Foreign domination

After the war American influence became dominant. When Prime Minister Mossadegh and a leftist parliament moved to nationalize and control the oil industry in the early 1950s, the shah, with clandestine support from the American CIA, ousted him and blocked the attempt. With oil wealth and extensive American military and economic aid, the shah embarked upon an ambitious development program. He broke up estates controlled by feudal landowners and the Islamic clergy, reorganized the armed forces, and sent students in large numbers to study abroad. The pace and breadth of secularization and modernizing reforms pleased urban business and professional interests but alienated others, especially in the countryside. Moreover the shah presided over an increasingly authoritarian regime, crushing opposition and dissent with his secret police. His huge personal wealth also did not go unnoticed. The United States, pleased with the modernization of its anti-Soviet ally in a strategic part of the world, ignored the swelling internal restlessness. In 1978 religious-inspired protests and strikes and riots broke out as the opposition coalesced. A tidal wave of demonstrations forced the shah to flee the country in January 1979.

In February the aged leader of the religious community, Ayatollah Ruhollah Khomeini (ayatollah is the highest rank in the Shiite religious hierarchy), returned from exile in

Ayatollah Khomeini's "Islamic republic"

Paris, where for the past 15 years he had been denouncing the shah's pro-Western, anticlerical, and irreligious regime. He quickly assumed leadership of the revolution and proclaimed an "Islamic republic." His newly formed revolutionary guards routed the shah's troops. Supreme control rested with the ayatollah and his council of religious guardians, appointed to guarantee the new regime's strict commitment to Islam and to ensure control of the revolution through a network of mosques.

The revolutionary authorities forcefully restored traditional Islamic ways of life. Women were ordered to wear the chador, the traditional long black dress covering them from head to toe. The necktie was outlawed for men, who were also encouraged to grow beards. The authorities banned Western music, classical and popular, from radio and television and enforced the Islamic prohibition on alcohol. Islamic law, to be interpreted by the clerics, took precedence over secular law. Soon revolutionary justice, in the form of drumhead trials and public execution for religious, moral, or political offenses, cost the lives of thousands. The ayatollah's theocracy pushed aside moderate leaders, even those who had welcomed the overthrow of the shah. The first president was forced to flee into exile; the foreign minister was executed. The new regime imposed tight state control over the economy and nationalized many industries. In the chaos, oil production and revenues fell.

"The great Satan"

Militants, many of them university students, aroused to frenzied heights by the ayatollah's fervid denunciations of the United States as "the great Satan," took action on their own. Reacting to the admission of the ailing shah to the United States in the autumn of 1979, revolutionary guards and students seized the American embassy in Tehran in retaliation and held 50 American hostages for close to 15 months, demanding the return of the shah and his wealth to Iran. The hostage crisis weakened the administration of President Carter, and the failure of an ill-conceived rescue mission added to American humiliation.

The War between Iran and Iraq

Iran made no secret of its desire to establish a position of leadership in the Muslim world and to project its Shiite theocracy as a model for others. In 1980 war broke out when Iraq,

The revolution in Iran brought on a wave of militant, anti-Western demonstrations. These Iranian women, wearing the chador to assert their strong Islamic values, showed their determined support for Islamic religious traditions and the new political order by wielding powerful, modern weapons.
(Christine Spengler/Sygma/Corbis)

its Arab neighbor to the west, launched an attack on Iranian territory. Iraq, rich in oil, was an aggressively nationalistic Arab state under a secular military regime headed by Saddam Hussein, who ruled as a dictator. His party, the Arab Baath party, was dedicated to Arab revival. A competing branch of the movement ruled in Syria. But ideology was less important to Hussein than the concentration of political power at home and the use of military power for national ends abroad.

The Ayatollah Khomeini had denounced Iraq both for persecuting its large Shiite community and for abandoning Islamic principles. The Shiites comprised a large majority of the Iraqi population, but the Sunni minority dominated the dictatorship and the Baath party. Both the Shiites and a sizable ethnic group, the Kurds, suffered brutal oppression and severe mistreatment under the Iraqi regime. The war itself erupted over a long-smoldering border dispute between the two states concerning a waterway that served as a vital outlet for Iraq to the Persian Gulf. Although awarded to Iraq by an international commission, it had fallen under Iran's control. Iraq, seizing an opportunity to exploit the revolutionary turmoil in Iran and gambling on a quick victory, bombed Iranian oil fields in 1980, invaded Iran, and occupied the disputed territory. Iran rallied after the initial invasion, expelled the Iraqi forces from its borders in 1982, and pushed deep into Iraq, hoping to overthrow Hussein and his regime. When Iraq stiffened its defenses, Iran dispatched assault waves of young conscripts, reminiscent of warfare during the First World War. In one of the rare instances

Long-smoldering border dispute

since that war, both sides also used poison gas on the battlefield. Iraq used it as well against its Kurdish minority, which it accused of collaborating with Iran.

As the war dragged on, it assumed a larger international dimension. The land war became a tanker war in the Persian Gulf, involving Saudi Arabia, Kuwait, and other Arab Gulf states dependent on trade with the West and unsympathetic to Iran's Shiite fundamentalism. Both Iran and Iraq attacked neutral shipping in the Persian Gulf to prevent arms deliveries. When the attacks threatened the flow of oil, the United States, supported by the British and French, stepped up its naval presence. The Western navies kept oil shipments flowing and reinforced what had become the continuing strategic objective of preserving Western influence in the Gulf.

Cease-fire

By 1987 the Iranian counteroffensive had failed. In August 1988 Iran accepted a cease-fire. The eight-year war had cost tens of thousands of lives on both sides. The Iranian economy was in shambles; its armed forces were exhausted and depleted. The ayatollah's appeal for a holy war had gone unheeded by other Muslim nations and had alienated the Arab Gulf states. But he retained a dedicated following in Iran and still sought to assert his authority in the Islamic world. His call to the Islamic faithful for the assassination of the novelist Salman Rushdie for allegedly blaspheming Muhammad in one of his books shocked the international community. After Khomeini's death in 1989 moderate and pragmatic elements within the Islamic government urged economic reconstruction and the reestablishment of the country's ties to the outside world. In 1992 a new president with moderate economic and foreign policies won a parliamentary majority. President Rafsanjani was able to restrain the most radical excesses of the revolution, but the nation now had a new spiritual leader, Ayatollah Ali Khameini, who retained paramount power.

Changing Iran

Iran in the 1990s became a land of continuing paradoxes and contradictions. A dual power structure existed and the country was no longer a completely closed society or theocracy as in the revolutionary decade. The middle classes assumed an active economic life. There was outspoken criticism of clerical power. In 1997, when the religious authorities gave voters an even freer choice of presidential candidates, 70 percent of the voters (the voting age was 15) chose an even more reform-minded president, Muhammed Khatami. He was a cleric himself and a descendant of religious leaders, but he had a broad intellectual outlook and had studied and written on Western political philosophy. Khatami committed himself to political and economic reform, a civil society, the rule of law, and a freer atmosphere, including a free press. He and others like him believed that Islam and democracy were not incompatible. Yet he had to work within the religious system established by the revolution. The religious authorities controlled the military, the police, the courts, and much of the media, and even held a veto power over the eligibility of candidates for office. While the president called for dialogue with the outside world, the religious leaders kept up their denunciations of the West, America, and Israel. The president moved and spoke cautiously.

A new generation

Meanwhile a new generation of liberal-minded clerics loosened their stranglehold. The stringent dress and behavior codes were relaxed. Globalization had its effect. Western consumer products were in demand, alcohol became available, and music from the outside world could now be heard. Women dressed as they wished in private circles even if they still wore head scarves and cloaks in public. President Khatami and his program received wide support, and he easily won election to a second term in 2001. Many Iranians, especially young people, recognized that without change the country faced economic stagnation and political isolation, and they resented the social and moral straitjacket in which they found themselves. Iranian theologians were

CHRONOLOGY OF NOTABLE EVENTS, 1948–2005

1948	Republic of Israel is established; Arab states go to war against Israel
1948	Afrikaner Nationalist Party expands rigid racial segregation in South Africa through *apartheid* laws
1954–1962	Algerian nationalists wage war for independence from France
1956	Britain, France, and Israel attack Egypt after it nationalizes Suez Canal
1957	Ghana is the first British colony in Africa to win independence
June 1967	Six-Day War leads to Israel's military occupation of Palestinian lands on West Bank of Jordan River and the Gaza Strip
1967–1970	In Nigeria Ibo secession movement in Biafra is suppressed
1971–1972	Idi Amin takes power in Uganda and begins expulsion of Asians
1973	Yom Kippur War: Egypt and Syria fight a new war with Israel; conflict leads to Arab oil embargo as a strategic geopolitical weapon
1979	Ayatollah Khomeini leads Islamic Revolution in Iran
1982	Israel invades Lebanon to suppress Palestinian guerrilla groups
1993	Oslo agreement between Palestinians and Israelis; recognizes Israel's right to exist and a new Palestinian National Authority
1991	American military campaign drives Iraq's Saddam Hussein from Kuwait
1994	First nonracial, democratic elections in South Africa; Nelson Mandela is elected president
1994	Hutus attack Tutsi communities in Rwanda, killing over 500,000 people
2000–2001	Palestinian uprising *(intifada)* erupts after breakdown of Israeli-Palestinian peace negotiations
2004–2005	Death of Palestinian leader Yasir Arafat; Israel withdraws from Gaza Strip

themselves arguing that believers in Islam had to be free in their private lives from outside coercion and pressure.

Despite the growing support for a more liberal interpretation of Islam, Iran's conservative clerics still retained a strong following in the country and exercised great political power, including control over candidates in elections. Many wanted to reimpose the Islamic orthodoxy of the revolutionary decade. President Khatami seemed more and more powerless. When he denounced the American intervention in Iraq, however, he expressed a sentiment in Iran that transcended all ideological lines. The Iranian presidential elections in 2005 did not offer voters a wide choice, yet the results of the elections were somewhat unexpected. The more moderate candidate lost decisively to the conservative young mayor of Tehran, Mahmoud Ahmadinejad, who won support for his populist economic program but was also known for his strict adherence to conservative clerical values and for keeping faith with the Islamic revolution of 1979. Popular support for the conservatives seemed to grow stronger after the American-led invasion of Iraq in 2003 and after the United States led the international opposition to Iran's development of nuclear capacities. Ironically, the American war in Iraq meanwhile accomplished two of Iran's long-sought international objectives—the overthrow of Saddam Hussein and the political ascendancy of Iraq's Shiite majority.

The Iranian population at large, envious of the economic growth and prosperity of the outside world, had increasingly supported the relaxed political order during the 1990s. Education, available only for the urban rich before 1979, was now widespread and included wide opportunities for women. In the 1990s the number of young women entering universities and training themselves for modern skills tripled. With government encouragement, the population grew from 34 million in 1976 to over 68 million in 2005.

Traditional vs. modern

The Iranian revolution raised the larger question of whether traditional Islamic values, rigidly enforced as they were in the revolutionary decade, could accommodate modernization, democracy, and a pluralist society. The revolution in Iran had unsettled the entire Islamic world, but if Iran were to succeed in following a more moderate course, it could perhaps temper Islamic extremism in other Muslim countries too. The new president, however, could set the clock back and revert to tightened clerical control over Iranian society. He was vehement in insisting on Iran's nuclear rights and denouncing the Americans who had taken the lead in opposing them.

Iraq and the Persian Gulf War of 1990–1991

Iraq, for its part, emerged from the war with Iran with battle-seasoned armed forces but without real victory and with a troubled economy. Saddam Hussein was resolved to recoup his country's economic fortunes. Unable to persuade the other oil-producing states, particularly Kuwait, to curb production and raise oil prices, he denounced his small Arab neighbor to the south, pressed vague territorial claims (going back to the Ottoman Empire and the British protectorate), and in August 1990 invaded and annexed Kuwait. Many in the West feared that he might move next against Saudi Arabia, expand his influence over the Persian Gulf, and acquire a stranglehold over the world's oil resources.

President George Bush took the lead in winning support from the international community, including several Arab nations, and from the UN Security Council for economic sanctions against Iraq and for military measures if necessary. Over the next few months the United States with the support of a multinational Western and Arab coalition pursued a massive buildup in the deserts of Saudi Arabia. When Iraq refused to withdraw from Kuwait, the Americans and their allies unleashed in early 1991 a crushing air attack and followed with a ground assault, which quickly forced Iraq's withdrawal.

Operation Desert Storm

Operation Desert Storm was remarkably successful, but no effort was made to continue on to Baghdad to dislodge Hussein from power. In defiance of the cease-fire terms, Iraq over the next several years appeared to challenge the UN-imposed ban on the manufacture of nuclear, chemical, and other weapons of mass destruction and obstructed international inspection. Western governments believed at the time that Iraq was developing such weapons and could one day deploy them.

The maintenance of stability in this vital area of the Middle East with its many rivalries and competing interests remained critical not only for the states of the Persian Gulf, the Arab nations, and Israel but also for the international community as well. The installation of American military forces in Saudi Arabia after the Gulf War of 1991 contributed to the emergence of a new radical Islamic terrorist group called Al-Qaida. It was led by a wealthy Saudi exile, Osama bin Laden, who set up his secret headquarters first in Sudan and then in the mountains of Afghanistan. Al-Qaida proclaimed its violent intention to drive the United States from the "holy lands" of Islam, where Mecca and other Muslim holy places were located. The region thus remained a highly unsettled site of both religious and political tensions, and the new terrorist organization extended its reach to other parts of the world. Meanwhile some in the West called for Saddam Hussein's removal from power in Iraq, while others worried that his removal could create a power vacuum and generate further instability. Sanctions were imposed on Iraq after the war in order to restrain Hussein's military ambitions, but the economic restrictions brought more hardship to the Iraqi people than to the dictator. A later momentous American decision to overthrow the Iraqi regime would lead to a new war that would open in 2003—a conflict to which we shall return in Chapter 27.

Changes in the Middle East

The Islamic world in the Middle East was therefore in the midst of flux and ferment, caught between traditional social and religious beliefs and modern economic and cultural changes. Beginning with the Iranian revolution of 1979, a wave of religious radicalism had accelerated across the region. Islamic fundamentalists rejected such ideas as separation of religion and state and challenged secular tenets. Many sought Islamic theocracies. Women were often the chief targets. Ostensibly to protect them from the dangers of the modern world, religious radicals demanded their segregation and deprived them of educational and vocational opportunities. During the 1990s, for example, Afghanistan fell victim to the extremist Taliban movement, which had emerged in control of the country after a long war, supported by the United States, against the Soviet Union. The Taliban government imposed the strictest forms of repression, refusing women the right to attend schools or work outside the home and enforcing rigid dress codes. For the population as a whole, they wished to mete out punishments in accordance with the sharia, the centuries-old Islamic legal code. Although it was shunned by virtually all other nations and government leaders, the Taliban-controlled Afghan society became an important meeting place for Islamic radicals who sought to introduce strict Islamic laws in their own countries.

Islam in flux and ferment

In Egypt the government responded to religious extremism by outlawing the Muslim Brotherhood, which it held responsible for assassinations and other acts of violence. Yet Islamic leaders could rally thousands of young people in Cairo to force the secular government to drop the sponsorship of books considered blasphemous to Islam. In Turkey the army, guardians of the Turkish secular state, took measures against attempts to undermine its secular tradition. In Algeria, as we have seen, the military's nullification of the Islamic party's victory at the polls in 1991 led to the formation of armed militant groups that fell upon parts of the population with wholesale massacres. In Sudan the Islamic regime in the north continued its military campaign to enforce Islam on the entire country.

But cultural changes were also transforming many Islamic nations, as in Iran. Many Muslims favored an Islamic framework for society, but not a rigid Islamic state. Sentiment grew for more flexible interpretations of ancient Koranic law. In Saudi Arabia, where women could not drive cars or dine unaccompanied in public in the presence of men and where the authorities decreed ancient punishments like amputation for theft and beheading for more serious crimes, a new generation urged the modification of such practices. Egypt saw a remarkable breakthrough for women in 2000, when it enacted one of the Muslim world's most far-reaching reforms of family law. Under the new law in Egypt a woman was henceforth free to divorce a husband with or without his consent. Reformers successfully argued that such

Cultural changes

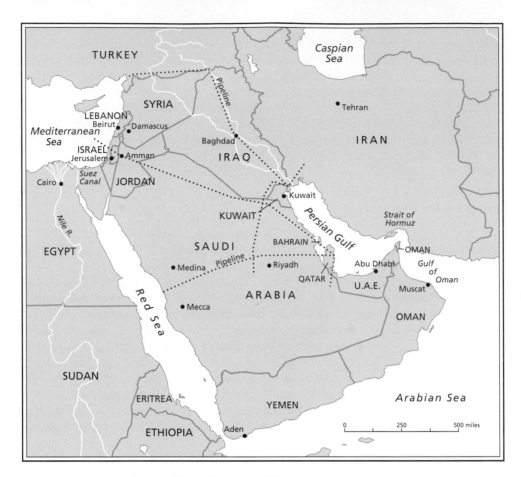

THE PERSIAN GULF AND THE MIDDLE EAST

The map shows important pipelines that move oil across this strategically important region of the world. The oil is exported both by sea from the Persian Gulf and by pipelines that connect the oil-producing centers to the Mediterranean and to the Red Sea. To protect the flow of this vital commodity, the Western oil-consuming countries sent naval forces to the Gulf during the Iran-Iraq war of 1980–1988 and reacted to a later Iraqi assault on its neighbors by driving Iraq's army out of Kuwait in 1991.

reforms should be viewed as a modern updating of the equal rights accorded women by the Qur'an. When in Kuwait the emir decreed that women were eligible to vote and compete in elections, the courts and the legislature at first blocked the decree, but the Kuwaiti parliament eventually changed course and voted in 2005 to give political rights to women. Many of the cultural changes in law and social patterns were taking place in smaller Arab states like Kuwait.

The nations of the Middle East often lacked independent political parties and credible parliaments, and the region remained a stronghold of authoritarianism. Although elections were held, their outcomes were generally predictable. What did make a social and political difference, however, was the greater access to the outside world. Satellite television, the Internet, electronic

Impact of the outside world

The city of Jiddah, a thriving port on the Red Sea, is one of the rapidly growing urban centers in contemporary Saudi Arabia. These men have stopped along one of the city's busy streets to engage in one of the daily prayers prescribed by Islam. Surrounded by high-rise apartments, automobiles, and modern traffic problems, they show how people in Islamic societies are blending important religious traditions into the patterns of contemporary social life.

(Liaison Agency)

communications, and close commercial interactions with the rest of the world had a powerful impact. The new era of globalization was opening horizons, and the world of Islam, from its heartland in the Arab countries to the far reaches of Africa and Asia was steadily evolving in new and diverse directions.

120. THE DEVELOPING WORLD

At the beginning of the twentieth century, or even in 1945, the sweeping nature and extent of the anticolonial revolution was unanticipated. At best the Western leaders of the colonial empires expected their colonies to evolve slowly toward self-government. The rapid and complete dissolution of the colonial systems was therefore astounding. The age of imperialism had been accompanied by exploitation, brutality, and degradation; and it left an enduring scar on subject peoples all over the globe. Yet paradoxically Western imperialism was also the instrument whereby many of the scientific, material, intellectual, and humanitarian achievements of the West spread to the rest of the world. The West no longer dominated these areas politically; but its culture, technology, and institutions carried a lasting impact. Industry, science, secularization, social mobility, the rule of law, the idea of individual freedom, and other new values or institutions created dislocations and tensions throughout much of the decolonized world. In some instances, as in Iran's Islamic revolution and in radical Islamic or religious movements elsewhere, resentments at the Western intrusion exploded, but mostly there was hope that some amalgam could be forged of modernization and traditional values.

In few parts of the formerly colonial world did Western-style liberal and democratic institutions prevail during the early years of national independence. Economically, neither the newly independent nations nor the international assistance programs were able to raise per capita levels of agricultural and industrial production significantly. Illiteracy and disease persisted, and living standards still lagged behind those of the industrialized nations. Independence brought a new sense of dignity, but it did not automatically bring freedom, self-government, human rights, and the improvement of the human condition. In many parts of the world the campaign for political and economic liberalization did not begin to show results until the 1980s.

The Development Experience

The United States took the lead after 1945 in assisting the developing countries with money and technical aid, but other industrial countries, as they recovered from the Second World War, also committed growing shares of their annual gross national product (GNP) to development assistance. (By the early twenty-first century, the top ten nations making grants of international aid—ranked by gifts as a percentage of GNP—were all in Europe; the United States still gave the most money but its percentage of GNP ranked twentieth). International agencies provided additional funding and expertise. With modern science, technology, and financial assistance, it was believed that the developing countries could look forward to modernization, economic growth, and social progress. Many of the new leaders of the postcolonial nations, however, believed that central planning, nationalized economies, and government controls would accomplish these ends more rapidly. Nehru's moderate socialism and economic planning in India provided one model. Others turned to the Communist models of the Soviet Union or China. Still others followed the Japanese example of private capitalism in partnership with government. South Korea, Taiwan, Singapore, and Hong Kong in Asia, adopting the Japanese pattern, industrialized and created remarkably successful export economies with high living standards for their people.

In the postwar decades international agencies helped finance projects for agriculture, industry, health, and education. The 1960s were the "development decade." President Kennedy spoke of raising the "banner of hope" for the poor and hungry. Dams and wells, irrigation schemes, hydroelectric projects, factories and processing mills, and education at all levels became part of the program. Industrialization, it was believed, could end or reduce excessive dependence on imports. In agriculture a "Green Revolution" pioneered by agricultural scientists in the United States, involving the use of chemical fertilizers, new high-yield hybrids, and modern planting and harvesting techniques, enabled farmers to increase productivity. The initial results were promising. Many of the developing countries experienced significant progress, achieving targets of 5 to 6 percent growth annually; per capita income rose; infant mortality rates fell. In the 1960s it seemed possible to speak of "a revolution of rising expectations."

The development decade

But advances in the poorer nations did not bring much change in their relative global economic position. They still did not share proportionately in the industrial world's spectacular postwar economic expansion, in the course of which per capita income in the wealthier nations tripled. The gap between richer and poorer nations widened rather than narrowed. Using the United Nations and other organizations as a forum, the developing nations in the late 1960s argued for a reshaping of the international economy—a "new international economic order"—to offer them greater access to the investment funds, technology, and markets of the West and to shift international financing from Western-dominated agencies like the World Bank to wider international control.

In the tensions of the Cold War the developing nations had formed a bloc of neutralist, nonaligned states. Beginning with 25 states in 1961, the Third World bloc steadily increased in numbers, and although it was nonaligned, it was always more critical of the wealthier West than of the Soviet Union. Because the states were situated mainly in the southern parts of the two hemispheres, their challenges to the wealthiest nations also assumed the configuration of a "north-south" contest.

The "nonaligned states"

The recession that began in 1974 brought a decline in international trade and a shrinkage of international assistance funds. In the 1980s, the developing countries staggered under heavy debts incurred during the earlier optimistic years. Oil-producing countries, particularly, had overcommitted themselves because they calculated on a continuing rise in oil prices, but oil prices either dropped or remained stagnant during most of the 1980s. Debt, principally to private commercial banks, soared, one-third of it owed by the four Latin American countries, Argentina, Brazil, Mexico, and Venezuela.

After five decades of the development experience, per capita income in the poorest countries had scarcely risen. Almost everywhere the agricultural sector had received a lower priority than the industrial. Agricultural production, even when it increased, often failed to keep up with explosive population growth. To earn the foreign exchange needed to finance the development of an industrial infrastructure, governments encouraged export crops and neglected the production of food for their own people—an agricultural economy was considered a sign of inferiority. Although the developing countries began building their own industries, many of their products failed to compete successfully either at home or in the world market. Much of the economic aid and foreign investment had been channeled to industrial projects in the capitals or other large cities, sometimes to nonproductive and extravagant showpieces.

Development's impact

In the rush for development, government control frequently led to clumsy bureaucracies, extravagance, and corruption. Many governments used development funds to boost national prestige and pride rather than to improve the economic conditions of their people. Inadequate assistance failed to help the rural poor, who sank into deeper poverty. Millions meanwhile fled the countryside for the presumed attractions of city life, only to face joblessness, live in congested shantytowns or slums, and breathe polluted air. Some industrial projects in the Third World were undertaken at enormous cost to the environment.

Changing Worlds and Persistent Problems

In the 1980s economic growth regressed. Forty-three developing countries finished the decade with a decline in per capita real income. The percentage of the world's population living in poverty, slowly shrinking in earlier decades, rose again. Because of population growth, the numbers of the impoverished were far larger than before. As the twentieth century drew to a close well over one billion human beings lived in poverty, mainly in sub-Saharan Africa, Asia, Latin America, and the Middle East. Hundreds of millions suffered from disease and malnutrition.

One billion impoverished

The developing countries, of course, were far from homogeneous. The People's Republic of China (generally not included as part of the Third World but occupying a separate and unique category of its own) continued to industrialize and modernize in its own way. The "little tigers" in East Asia built powerful

The developing countries in Asia, Africa, and Latin America had all entered the global economy by the early twenty-first century, but they continued to struggle with unemployment, rapid population growth, congested cities, and environmental problems. This traffic jam in Bandung, Indonesia, exemplifies the stream of people and vehicles that now flows through crowded city streets in every nation of the developing world.
(Joanna B. Pinneo/Aurora Photos)

export economies and raised living standards. In South Korea per capita income rose spectacularly in the years 1970 to 1990 from $270 to $5,400. India, Indonesia, Malaysia, and Thailand as well as Argentina, Brazil, Chile, and Mexico were all industrializing and modernizing. These nations, or at least large numbers of people within these nations, were leaving the Third World behind and forming an intermediate category of their own as "newly industrialized countries." The oil-rich states of the Middle East and elsewhere had the potential, if they chose to do so, to turn their national wealth into the further modernization of their economies and societies. Meanwhile at the very bottom of the economic performance scale were the "least developed countries," among them a number of sub-Saharan African states; Bangladesh in South Asia; and Haiti in the Western Hemisphere. Together they formed a kind of "Fourth World," an impoverished group of hundreds of millions of people lacking bare necessities.

Market economies and the state

The countries with the greatest success in development had progressed within a framework of market economies, but the debate continued over the role of government in stimulating economic development. Even in the successful market economies, governments played a significant supporting role; and government support for schools, transportation, and infrastructure remained essential for all developing economies. In many of the poorer developing countries, however, the overriding presence of the state, government ownership and controls, bureaucratic interference, and imprudent fiscal policies had choked off growth and progress.

The maldistribution of wealth was particularly acute in nations where there were fewer goods and services to distribute and where they were often distributed with gross inequity between the elite who cultivated ever higher standards of luxury and the impoverished masses. Despite some success stories, the rising expectations and hopeful visions of the early postwar decades often turned into ever deeper frustrations for many of the world's peoples. In point of fact at the opening of the twenty-first century there was no Third World. There were only two worlds, one relatively rich, one poor. And the relations between these worlds remained critically important in the evolving global economy.

Reappraising Development

In the closing years of the twentieth century a spirited debate emerged in development circles and international donor agencies about the nature and direction of development assistance. The discussions and criticisms attracted broad public attention and at times ignited confrontational street demonstrations. The major international lending agencies admitted the disappointing progress in reducing poverty and accepted their share in the blame. The number of people living in extreme poverty in the world, that is, surviving on $1 a day, fell only slightly, from 1.3 billion in 1990 to 1.2 billion at the end of the decade. In sub-Saharan Africa it had barely changed.

The two major international agencies, the World Bank and the International Monetary Fund (IMF), both under new leadership, acknowledged a need to shift from "growth and development" to a more explicit commitment to "poverty reduction." Over the years the World Bank had generously financed the building of roads, dams, bridges, and power plants, judging their success solely in quantitative terms, asking only, to cite one example, how much new electricity a project *Reduction of poverty* had generated but failing to ask how it had improved lives, reduced poverty, or affected local cultures. The catalogue of inappropriate projects was long and sometimes bizarre. Electrical equipment arrived in villages where no electricity was available, recycled clothing was sent to areas where it hurt local weavers, and grain shipments were sent to countries where they adversely affected local growers. Historically, foreign aid had gone to central governments, but it was now apparent that local governments and communities would have to play a larger role than in the past. Human development indexes were to be prepared, focusing not on per capita income alone but on literacy, life expectancy, health, nutrition, and the status of women and children. Donor governments meanwhile agreed to cancel the debt of many of the world's poorest countries in Africa, Asia, and Latin America and to help Third World countries gain freer access to the markets of the industrial world.

The IMF came under heavy criticism. It had intervened in many currency crises over the years, generally pressuring governments to reduce spending and imposing overly rigid austerity measures that ignored the nation's social needs. Exceeding its original mission, it had reoriented development policies in directions it considered economically desirable but with little recognition of the social or political consequences. Agreement emerged that the IMF should restrict itself to resolving currency and other short-time financial crises, no small task in itself, and leave development policies to the World Bank.

Another large and contentious issue was the impact of the global economic integration. Its most extreme critics argued that global trading systems and financial markets increased poverty, sharpened social divisions, *Impact of global integration*

Postcolonial nations in Africa and Asia have sought to develop the new technologies and communication systems that are essential for contemporary economic and cultural life, in part because a growing "digital divide" threatens to widen other economic differences between wealthy and poor nations. These young men were working on computer problems at Ibadan University in Nigeria during the early years of computer technology, but their concentration and perplexity reflect the universal effort to comprehend and manage new information technologies in modern societies around the world.
(Marc & Evelyne Bernheim/Woodfin Camp & Associates)

hurt the environment, exploited local working people, used child labor shamelessly, and shifted control over people's lives to multinational corporations and the pursuit of profit. Although economic evidence did suggest that globalization had accomplished far less to relieve poverty and inequality than originally predicted, others maintained that free trade and information technology stimulated economic growth and would help the poor to improve their lives in the coming decades of the twenty-first century.

The vigorous debates on development policies may have shaped new priorities for future governmental and international development aid. A related debate explored the extent to which the developing countries might be left behind by the new information technology. The world of computers and the Internet, like other technological innovations, further widened the economic gap between rich and poor nations and raised new questions about how best to reduce the growing digital divide. All such debates about the development experience reflected the linkage between the historical legacy of the former colonial empires, the rapid process of decolonization, the expansion of the global economy, and the emergence in the second half of the twentieth century of the largest number of independent nation-states that the world had ever seen.

For interactive exercises, glossary, chronologies, and more, go to the *Online Learning Center* at **www.mhhe.com/palmer10.**

Chapter 25

COEXISTENCE, CONFRONTATION, AND THE NEW GLOBAL ECONOMY

We must turn from our account of the new and emerging nations of the world, which at times has carried us into the twenty-first century, to the international political tensions and the vicissitudes of the global economy in the decades following the early postwar era. By the late 1950s western Europe and Japan had drawn on American aid and their own technical expertise to rebuild their war-damaged cities and factories. Responding to the new challenges of a bipolar world and the global ambitions of two competing superpowers, western Europe had joined more closely together economically in the evolving European Community and buried many of its old antagonisms. Regions of the world that formerly were part of European colonial empires were everywhere asserting their independence. China was positioning itself as another major Communist power. The global economy grew increasingly interdependent and the vicissitudes of economic expansion and contraction reverberated worldwide. Older distinctions became blurred. The emergence of Japan made it impossible to identify industrial and financial might with the West, and even the Soviet bloc expanded its trade and financial exchanges with non-communist countries.

Yet the Cold War continued to manifest itself in an escalating nuclear arms race and in the worldwide confrontation of the two superpowers, each of which attempted to prevent the other from gaining the ascendancy. The stockpiling of nuclear arms and the development of sophisticated long-range delivery systems led to the accumulation of unparalleled destructive power. The nuclear missiles supposedly were built for deterrence and not for use, and a new kind of balance of power emerged that preserved the peace. The world nonetheless lived under the threat of a possible nuclear catastrophe, and neither economic nor intellectual life could fully escape from the global shadow of the Cold War.

As time passed, the phenomenon of "bipolarity," or the predominance of the two superpowers, the United States and the Soviet Union, gradually gave way to new global

Chapter emblem: Chinese pro-democracy crowds surround a statue of the "Goddess of Liberty" in Beijing's Tiananmen Square in the spring of 1989. (Peter Turnley/Corbis)

configurations. But while the charged atmosphere lasted, despite periods of détente, the world was forced to live with repeated crises. As late as 1985 no one could foresee how or when the Cold War would end.

✑ 121.   CONFRONTATION AND DÉTENTE, 1955–1975

The Soviet leaders who succeeded Stalin after 1953 seemed at times more conciliatory and willing to acknowledge the need for arms control and cooperation in the nuclear age. An alternative of peaceful coexistence and competing world systems promised to open up,

Periods of détente

and there were even recognizable periods of détente, or formal relaxation of tensions. But dangerous confrontations recurred, the nuclear arms buildup assumed unprecedented forms and dimensions, and relations seesawed over the next several decades between conciliation and crisis.

By 1955 the Cold War had stabilized. In Asia the Korean War was over. In Europe the North Atlantic Treaty Organization (NATO), strengthened by the West German armed forces, faced the Warsaw Pact nations. The iron curtain still divided Europe, but the threat of direct military confrontation receded. The Western powers and the Soviet Union were even able to agree in 1955 on a treaty with Austria, ending the joint Allied occupation and leaving Austria independent and neutral.

We have seen how Khrushchev had emerged as the dominant Soviet leader. Sharp-tongued, volatile, boastful, he announced that the Soviets would abandon their revolutionary principles only "when shrimp learn to whistle" and pledged that the Soviets would "bury" Western capitalism. Nonetheless he rejected the inevitability of war and empha-

Pressures for coexistence

sized the "possibility and necessity of peaceful coexistence." President Eisenhower, in office from 1953 to 1961, continued the policy of containment and the American military buildup. Eisenhower's secretary of state, John Foster Dulles, who saw the Cold War in almost apocalyptic terms as a Manichean contest between good and evil, at one point urged a "rollback"

of Soviet power. Despite his rhetoric, and despite active American military support for anti-Communist forces in Central America, Asia, Africa, and elsewhere, American policy remained limited to containment. Both superpowers recognized the need for coexistence in the nuclear age.

In 1955 President Eisenhower, along with the British and French, met at Geneva with Soviet leaders in a friendlier atmosphere than any since the Second World War. Although they reached no new agreements, the American president could speak of "a new spirit of conciliation and cooperation." But tensions mounted over Berlin. The Soviets, incensed that East Germans were fleeing in large numbers to West Berlin and then to the Federal Republic of Germany, demanded that the Western powers end their occupation of West Berlin, but Eisenhower forcefully rejected the ultimatum, and the crisis passed. In 1959, when Khrushchev visited President Eisenhower at his weekend retreat in Camp David, they spoke of peaceful coexistence and even of mutual disarmament.

At a second summit conference in Paris, the superpowers continued to recognize their common interests in preserving stability and peace. But by then Khrushchev, under criticism at home and from Mao in China for being too conciliatory toward the West, produced

Cooperation fades

irrefutable evidence of American reconnaissance flights over Soviet territory and broke up the conference. By the summer of 1960 the "spirit of Geneva" and the "spirit of Camp David" had faded. When Khrushchev spoke before the United Nations, he boasted of Soviet arms production and denounced the United States. Crises over Berlin and elsewhere were far from settled.

The United States, unwavering in its resolve to maintain the defense of western Europe, accepted Soviet hegemony east of the iron curtain. The Americans protested but did not intervene when in 1953 the Soviets put down antigovernment riots in East Berlin, or when in 1956 the Soviets exerted pressure on Poland to curb its reform movement, or when the Soviets, even more dramatically, sent troops and tanks that year to crush the Hungarian revolt, or later, in 1968, the Czech uprising. The United States offered little more than moral encouragement to dissident groups in all of these eastern European states.

At the same time one part of the world after another was being brought into the American strategic defense system. In the Suez crisis in 1956 (which broke out simultaneously with the troubles in Hungary) the United States deterred Britain, France, and Israel from pressing military action against Egypt, at least in part because it might have encouraged Soviet intervention. The three countries were frustrated, but the Soviets were kept out. The "Eisenhower Doctrine" asserted American primacy in the defense of the Middle East and pledged protection to any government in that region against "international Communism." Under that policy, Eisenhower dispatched marines to Jordan and Lebanon in 1958 when their pro-Western governments were threatened. In the Western Hemisphere the United States rallied the Latin American republics to resist domination or control of any American state by the "international Communist movement." American foreign policy in the Cold War remained based on the premise that unrest on every continent was Soviet-inspired. That premise sometimes prevented Americans from understanding the complex local causes of regional conflicts around the world.

American Cold War policy

The nuclear arms race continued. In October 1957 the Soviets, to the world's astonishment, demonstrated their prowess in the new era of rocket technology when they successfully launched *Sputnik,* the first artificial satellite to orbit in outer space. A few months later the United States launched its own space satellite, *Explorer I.* The space age had opened, and the military implications of space rocketry quickly became apparent. The same principles of propulsion could launch both satellites and armed missiles over long distances. In 1958 the Soviets developed the first intercontinental ballistic missile (or ICBM) capable of delivering nuclear warheads to North America and elsewhere thousands of miles away. The United States in turn developed its own intercontinental ballistic missiles and proceeded to build an arsenal of nuclear weapons far larger than that of the Soviets.

A new kind of arms race, based on "mutual deterrence," emerged; it was useless to speak of "massive retaliation." Now that American cities were vulnerable to nuclear destruction, anxiety spread in western Europe that the United States might not so readily defend it. De Gaulle, the French president, voiced these and other misgivings in the 1960s and called for a more independent role for the West Europeans. Rejecting the rigid bipolar patterns of the Cold War and viewing postwar international relations as a traditional struggle between great powers rather than as a conflict of ideologies, he called for a return to a more open recognition of spheres of national interest and for Europe's reunification—"from the Atlantic to the Urals." He declined to follow the American lead in foreign policy in Europe or elsewhere. Although he kept France in the Atlantic alliance, in a gesture of independence he withdrew France from the integrated NATO military command in 1966 and pressured NATO into moving its headquarters from French soil. His aspirations for a

A new kind of arms race

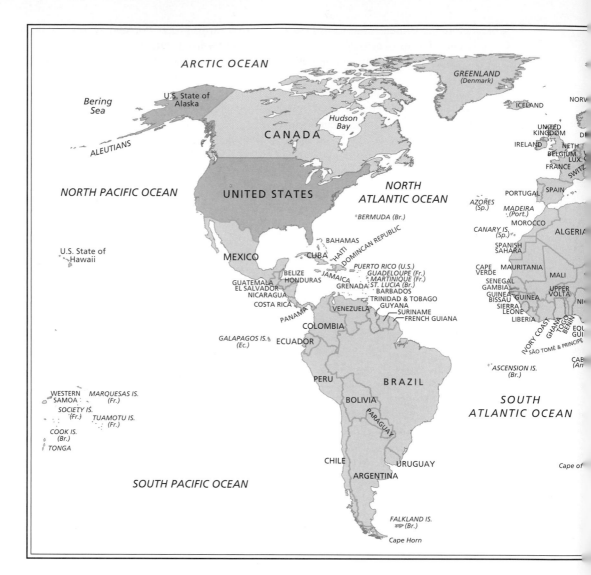

THE WORLD ABOUT 1970

This political map of the world about 1970 shows a number of important changes after the end of the Second World War: the breakup of the European colonial empires in Asia and Africa, the emergence of some 50 independent republics in Africa and of several new states in Asia, the emergence of the People's Republic of China, and the peripheral expansion of the Soviet Union.

leadership role on the international scene troubled many Europeans, but he nevertheless articulated European uneasiness with American hegemony over the West in world affairs.

The Kennedy Years, 1961–1963

The gravest direct Soviet-American confrontations came during the Kennedy presidency. President John F. Kennedy heightened the rhetoric of the Cold War, proclaiming that the United States "had to pay any price, bear any burden, meet any hardship, support any

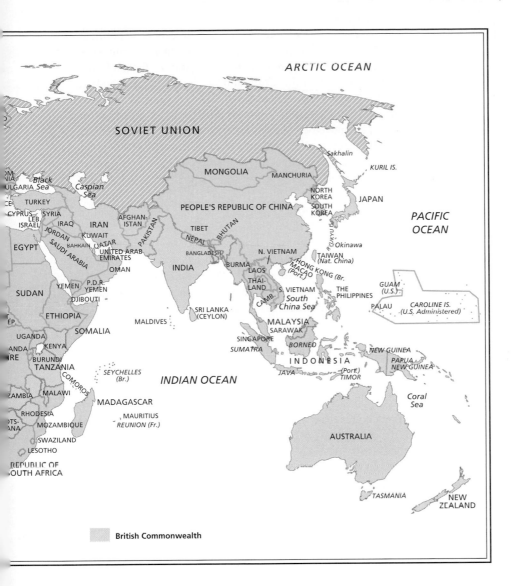

ARCTIC OCEAN

SOVIET UNION

MONGOLIA   MANCHURIA

Sakhalin

KURIL IS.

PEOPLE'S REPUBLIC OF CHINA

NORTH KOREA
SOUTH KOREA

JAPAN

PACIFIC OCEAN

Black Sea   Caspian Sea

BULGARIA

TURKEY

CYPRUS SYRIA
LEB.
ISRAEL   IRAQ   IRAN   AFGHAN-ISTAN
JORDAN KUWAIT   PAKISTAN
EGYPT   SAUDI ARABIA
BAHRAIN QATAR
UNITED ARAB EMIRATES
OMAN

NEPAL BHUTAN

TIBET

BANGLADESH

N. VIETNAM

INDIA   BURMA   LAOS
THAI-LAND

Okinawa

TAIWAN
(Nat. China)

HONG KONG (Br.)
MACAO
(Port.)

GUAM
(U.S.)

CAROLINE IS.
(U.S. Administered)

PALAU

SUDAN

YEMEN   P.D.R. YEMEN
DJIBOUTI

ETHIOPIA

SRI LANKA
(CEYLON)

MALDIVES

S. VIETNAM
CAMB.
South China Sea

THE PHILIPPINES

UGANDA   KENYA

SOMALIA

MALAYSIA
SARAWAK

SINGAPORE

SUMATRA

BORNEO

NEW GUINEA

PAPUA
NEW GUINEA

BURUNDI
TANZANIA

SEYCHELLES
(Br.)

INDIAN OCEAN

COMOROS

INDONESIA

JAVA   (Port.)
TIMOR

Coral Sea

ZAMBIA   MALAWI

RHODESIA

MOZAMBIQUE

MADAGASCAR

MAURITIUS
REUNION (Fr.)

AUSTRALIA

SWAZILAND
LESOTHO

REPUBLIC OF SOUTH AFRICA

TASMANIA

NEW ZEALAND

British Commonwealth

friend or oppose any foe in order to assure the success and survival of liberty." He took steps to close what was termed the "missile gap." Alarmed by Soviet successes in space, he pledged that the Americans would reach the moon before the end of the decade and encouraged large expenditures for space exploration. At the same time Kennedy increased foreign aid to the developing countries and sponsored the Peace Corps, which took young Americans to Latin America, Asia, and Africa to aid in social and economic development programs designed to improve life and reduce the attractions of communism. For Latin America, which resented the large sums that had gone to Europe, he organized the Alliance for Progress to encourage investment and growth.

In Cuba, Kennedy inherited an explosive situation. Many in the United States and elsewhere had initially regarded Fidel Castro as a progressive leader favorably disposed to democracy and committed to much needed change in a country where a dictatorship had long kept the population impoverished and repressed. But Castro, no simple reformer, inaugurated a sweeping agrarian program,

Kennedy and Cuba

expropriated large American corporate holdings, and imprisoned or executed political opponents. Thousands of Cubans fled to the United States, settling in large numbers around Miami. Although Castro originally kept his movement aloof from the Cuban Communist party, he now openly joined ranks with the Communists. President Eisenhower, who dealt with Castro's leftist regime before Kennedy came to office, became alarmed by the threat of communism in the Western Hemisphere and imposed a strict embargo on imports from Cuba. Castro for his part moved closer to the Soviet Union. Within a short time, four-fifths of Cuban trade was with the Soviets and eastern Europe. The United States broke off diplomatic relations, and the CIA secretly trained a small group of Cuban refugees for an armed invasion of the island.

Kennedy inherited the plans for the invasion and, without seriously reassessing the situation resolved to go forward with it to end the Communist menace 90 miles from the American mainland. The invasion at the Bay of Pigs in April 1961, without adequate air protection, turned into a failure; most of the 1,500 invaders were captured. Castro now inflated his revolutionary rhetoric, openly projected himself as a Marxist-Leninist, affirmed the country's ties with the Soviet Union, and championed the cause of international revolution throughout Latin America and elsewhere. The United States tightened its embargo.

The Bay of Pigs

At a meeting with Kennedy in Vienna that year, Khrushchev, the Soviet leader, delivered a new ultimatum for the Western powers to leave Berlin. Kennedy, smarting over the Bay of Pigs defeat, reaffirmed the Western resolve to remain in Berlin. He asked Congress to expand American military forces, inaugurated a civil defense program, and made plans for fall-out shelters in the event of nuclear war. The Atlantic alliance backed him. The immediate crisis passed. But in the summer of 1961 the Soviets, exasperated at the continuing exodus from East Berlin (over 3 million East Germans had already fled), constructed the Berlin Wall, a 28-mile rampart of concrete and barbed wire, with armed sentry stations. The Wall stood as a grim physical reminder of the Cold War; hundreds of East Germans who attempted to cross the barrier met their deaths. The Soviet Union also ended a three-year moratorium on nuclear testing; both countries resumed tests underground and in the atmosphere.

The Berlin Wall

The Cuban Missile Crisis of 1962

The most dangerous Western-Soviet confrontation occurred not in Berlin but in Cuba, where in the fall of 1962 Khrushchev showed an unanticipated recklessness. Announcing his intention to defend Cuba against a second American invasion (plans for which existed), he dispatched Soviet soldiers and technicians to the island to construct missile sites that would have brought the American mainland within target range. For the United States this Soviet intrusion on America's own doorstep was unthinkable and could even inalterably change the nuclear balance between the two superpowers.

During 13 tense days in October President Kennedy and his advisers resolved not to take any hasty military action but to stand firm against the Soviet military presence in Cuba, fully aware that the showdown could lead to nuclear war. Kennedy imposed a blockade (or quarantine) of the island, forbidding further deliveries of arms and supplies. The launching of any nuclear missile from Cuba, he made clear, would lead to a "full retaliatory response upon the Soviet Union." At the height of the emergency American planes carrying nuclear bombs were airborne. Although Khrushchev blustered that

The bleak, concrete Berlin Wall became both a physical and symbolic expression of the bitter divisions in Europe during the Cold War. This picture, which shows a section of the newly constructed Wall near the famous Brandenburg Gate, illustrates the stark separation between East and West Berlin that the Soviets sought to establish when they built the Wall in 1961. Although the Wall accomplished the Soviets' short-term political objective by stopping the exodus of East Germans, it also confirmed the repressive character of Soviet-controlled states in eastern Europe.
(Sipa Press)

the blockade was illegal, he backed down; on October 24 two Soviet ships and their submarine escort turned back. In one note Khrushchev agreed to remove the missile sites in return for an American pledge not to invade Cuba. In a second note, more aggressive in tone, he demanded the removal of American missile sites in Turkey. Kennedy replied only to the first message, but privately let it be known that the United States would

An eyeball-to-eyeball confrontation eventually remove its missiles in Turkey. By October 28 the most ominous crisis of the Cold War, an "eyeball-to-eyeball" confrontation, as the American Secretary of State Dean Rusk described it, was over.

Khrushchev had lost face; he was weakened still further at home, and in 1964, for this and for other reasons, he was ousted from power. The People's Republic of China, which was assuming the role of spokesman for the Third World, ridiculed his capitulation in the Cuban missile confrontation. Even though tensions once again eased, and the Soviet leaders would never again show such recklessness, the Cuban crisis had a direct effect on the arms race. Both the Soviet Union and the United States moved to expand their nuclear arsenals, and the Soviets under Khrushchev's successors were determined to achieve nuclear parity.

The United States and the Vietnam War

The resolve to contain Communist expansion entangled the United States in deepening hostilities in Southeast Asia. In Vietnam, as we have seen, the Communist leader Ho Chi Minh had led an anticolonial war against the French that lasted over eight years, from 1946 to 1954. After France acknowledged its military defeat, an international conference at Geneva in 1954 formally recognized the independence of Vietnam (temporarily dividing it into a northern and southern sector), as well as the independence of Laos and Cambodia, all part of former French Indochina.

Vietnam divided

But in Vietnam Communists and anti-Communists now confronted each other in a divided country. In the north Ho Chi Minh consolidated his Communist regime, its capital at Hanoi. A Western-backed regime under Ngo Dinh Diem governed the south, its capital in Saigon. Neither regime wanted a divided country, but the Geneva conference had partitioned Vietnam at the 17th parallel until general elections for a unified country could be held in 1956. In the interval the armies of the rival regimes were to withdraw behind the stipulated boundary, across which there was to be free movement of peoples. In the months that followed, close to 1 million Vietnamese fled southward. In South Vietnam a referendum in 1955 established an independent republic.

The government in South Vietnam, already aware that the Communists had acquired a large popular following in the wars against the Japanese and French, refused to participate in the scheduled countrywide elections. Communist guerrilla forces, known as the Viet Cong, who had stayed behind when the main army withdrew under the 1954 Geneva agreement, began a campaign to undermine the South Vietnamese government. The National Liberation Front emerged as a rival civil authority. Skilled in insurgent warfare, the Viet Cong won popular support by distributing land and by denouncing South Vietnam as a puppet of the West. Regular army units from North Vietnam soon reinforced the Communist guerrilla units in the south. Ho Chi Minh, while never sacrificing his political independence, received generous aid for his regime from the U.S.S.R. and from the People's Republic of China. South Vietnam, hard-pressed despite technical advice and assistance from the United States, appealed for more and more American aid.

"Like a tumbling row of dominoes"

The United States, from President Eisenhower on, saw a need to fill the vacuum created by the French withdrawal and to check Communist expansion in Indochina. To prevent the other states in Southeast Asia from toppling one by one—"like a tumbling row of dominoes," in his phrase—Eisenhower sent some limited aid and military advisers, but Kennedy further bolstered the Diem regime with additional military advisers, financial backing, and arms. The United States acted on the premise that this was not a civil war among the Vietnamese but a war between two independent states, one anti-Communist and therefore to be supported, and the other Communist, receiving aid and support from the Soviet Union and Communist China. Vietnam was seen as part of the global struggle between communism and democracy. While the repressive character of the regime in the north was apparent, the southern regime's authoritarian practices, ineptitude, corruption, and acts of coercion, especially against its large Buddhist population, became increasingly embarrassing to its American sponsors.

American involvement deepened and spanned the administrations of five presidents, Eisenhower, Kennedy, Johnson, Nixon, and Ford. Under Eisenhower a few hundred military advisers were present, and military and economic aid began; as early as 1959 two American military advisers were killed in an attack north of Saigon. In 1961, under Kennedy, additional military advisers and American support troops arrived; a year later 4,000 military personnel were on hand, and the first battle deaths were reported. The Kennedy administration, through the CIA, intervened in South Vietnamese politics; the Americans first propped up and then in 1963 helped to overthrow the increasingly repressive government of Diem, in the course of which Diem and his brother were murdered.

After Kennedy's assassination in November 1963, and the succession of Lyndon B. Johnson to the presidency, American military intervention in Vietnam gained added momentum. In 1964, on the alleged ground that North Vietnamese torpedo boats in the Gulf of Tonkin had attacked United States destroyers, an allegation that later proved unfounded, Johnson ordered immediate air strikes against North Vietnam and secured support for a joint congressional resolution empowering him to take "all necessary measures" to defend the United States and its ally. The Gulf of Tonkin resolution was the only explicit congressional sanction for the deepening American involvement. In 1965 American marines arrived. After 1965 heavy air raids on supply bases in the north and on Communist-controlled areas in the south became an almost daily occurrence. American bombers attacked as far north as Hanoi.

Gulf of Tonkin resolution

To root out the elusive Viet Cong in the countryside, American soldiers conducted "search and destroy" missions among the villagers, and American planes dropped incendiary materials and chemicals, burning whole villages, defoliating hundreds of thousands of acres of land, and turning the survivors into homeless refugees. The bombing raids, the commitment of American ground troops, and the casualties mounted. In 1966 there were close to 200,000 American troops in Vietnam; by 1969 at their maximum there were close to 550,000. In the massive bombings from 1965 to 1969 the Americans dropped more tons of explosives than against the Axis powers in the Second World War.

The large-scale American military intervention was unable to overcome the persistence of the North Vietnamese, aided by the Soviet Union, which never directly intervened with combat troops but lent assistance of other kinds. American military reports about the "pacification" of the countryside and about the number of enemy casualties (or "body counts") were confounded by the Communists' Tet, or New Year's, offensive at the opening of 1968. Although unsuccessful, the scale of the Communist offensive shook American complacency about the outcome of the war. To many it became clear that a negotiated settlement would be necessary.

The Tet offensive

VIETNAM AND ITS NEIGHBORS ABOUT 1970

The French built up their colonial empire in Indochina during the 60 years before the Second World War, controlling the old Asian territories of Cambodia, Laos, and Vietnam. Shaken by Japanese occupation of the region during the Second World War, the French were unable to defeat a postwar Vietnamese movement for independence that drew strength also from Communist affiliations. When the French withdrew in 1954, the Geneva Accords provided for partition of Vietnam until national elections could take place and unity could be restored, but the elections never took place. Since the north was now Communist, the United States provided economic and military support for an anti-Communist regime in South Vietnam. This involvement grew in the 1960s as the conflict between North and South Vietnam developed into a large-scale war. The United States intervened with over 500,000 troops and heavy air bombardments, but the American forces (like the French before them) could not defeat the Vietnamese Communists. American troops were gradually withdrawn in the early 1970s, and North Vietnam eventually won the war. Hostilities ended in 1975 with Communist regimes in control of a unified Vietnam and of Laos and Cambodia.

America's allies in western Europe were critical of the deepening American involvement. De Gaulle, a moralizer when it suited his purposes, called it "detestable" for "a great nation to ravage a small one." In the United States the war became a root cause of disorders and protests on college campuses and in the cities. Criticism of American policy added fuel to the worldwide student demonstrations of 1968. A wide array of public opinion turned against the war. Some opponents raised larger issues. They questioned whether the United

Critics of American involvement

States, despite its enormous strength, should assume the responsibility, or even had the capability, to police the world against Communist aggression; whether the American presence in Vietnam was an unwanted foreign intervention reminiscent of Western intrusion in the age of imperialism; whether the South Vietnamese regime could be stabilized and democratized to make the sacrifices worthwhile; and whether the air raids and continued hostilities might not end in the tragic devastation of the unfortunate country. Some critics with a knowledge of Asian history argued that the Vietnamese had a long record of independence and that even a Vietnam united under the Communists would not lead to subordination to the Soviets, or to China, with which Vietnam historically had had many differences.

The need to win the war became an obsession with President Johnson. Like his predecessors, he was convinced that it was in America's vital interest to contain communism in Southeast Asia; otherwise the Communists would be "in Hawaii and next they will be in San Francisco." Like his predecessors, he too refused to repeat what he took to be the lessons of appeasement of the 1930s. Above all, he could not see himself presiding over the first war lost by the United States, even when the war jeopardized his unquestionably important domestic reform program. But with victory remote, and with resentment against the war rising, he decided not to seek reelection in 1968 and announced a halt to the bombing in the north so that peace negotiations could go forward. By November 1968 all bombing ceased—for a time.

Peace talks opened in Paris even though the fighting went on. Johnson's successor, President Nixon, pledged an early end to the war, promised "Vietnamization," that is, to shift to South Vietnam the major responsibility for its own defense, so that American troops could begin to withdraw. Yet the United *Vietnamization* States in the next three years in some ways became even more deeply involved. In response to stalemated peace talks and continuing Communist advances, Nixon and his national security adviser and later secretary of state, Henry Kissinger, called for the resumption of heavy air attacks and widened the war by invading Cambodia to cut off North Vietnamese supply lines. The war spread to Laos as well.

Demonstrations mounted in the United States at the widening of the unpopular war. Meanwhile Kissinger opened up secret talks with North Vietnam representatives and finally brought about a cease-fire agreement in January 1973. The agreement ended direct military involvement for the United States and concluded the longest war—like the Korean, an undeclared one—the country had ever fought. Over eight years elapsed from the arrival of the first Marine contingent in 1965 to the with- *U.S. withdrawal* drawal of the last troops at the end of March 1973, or 12 years, if the involvement is dated from 1961.

Following the withdrawal of American troops, hostilities between North and South Vietnam continued as each sought additional territory before a final settlement was reached. Both sides violated the cease-fire, and fighting resumed on a major scale in 1973. Although the administration remained committed to the defense of South Vietnam, Congress refused additional expenditures for military aid. Corruption and demoralization in South Vietnam grew worse; army desertions mounted. The end, nevertheless, came as a surprise. At the close of 1974, the North Vietnamese captured key cities in the southern provinces. The government of South Vietnam lost heart and ordered withdrawal to the coast; a planned retreat degenerated into rout. North Vietnam, with victory in its grasp, poured thousands of troops south across the demilitarized zone. Swarms of refugees fleeing south added to the confusion. By April 1975 North Vietnam's armies controlled three-fourths of South Vietnam, and Saigon fell.

North Vietnamese troops entered Saigon and renamed the capital Ho Chi Minh City in honor of the Communist leader who had meanwhile died in 1969. After more than 30 years of almost continuous fighting—against the Japanese, against the French, and in the civil war between north and south in which the United States had massively intervened—

Peace and Communist victory

peace had finally come to the country, and with it Communist victory. Reunification and reorganization of the country proceeded quickly. The new regime launched a "political reeducation" campaign, nationalized property, and forcibly moved large numbers of the population from the cities to the countryside. Thousands, mostly ethnic Chinese, tried to flee in makeshift, overcrowded boats, many perishing in the attempt or discovering that the countries which they reached would not offer them a haven.

In the wake of North Vietnam's victory, Cambodia and Laos also fell under Communist control. Thirty years after the end of the Second World War, all of former French Indochina was in Communist hands, and a reunified Vietnam emerged as a new military power in Southeast Asia.

The costs of war

The Vietnam War was extremely costly for the Vietnamese people; 1.3 million Vietnamese died in the fighting and bombings. For the United States the war was a searing experience. Battle and battle-related deaths exceeded 58,000, higher than in the Korean War. The domestic impact of the military expenditures was heightened by the failure to place taxes on a wartime basis, contributing to inflationary pressures. The political and moral costs were enormous. The war created a mistrust of presidential power in the United States—of an "imperial presidency." In 1973 Congress adopted legislation to curb presidential initiatives that could lead to future episodes like the war in Vietnam. The war had left Americans with a disturbing series of painful images and memories: the deadly bombings, the gruesome battle scenes visible in the first war reported in detail on television, the revelation of atrocities and war crimes committed by American troops (as at My Lai in 1968, first covered up and then made the subject of a public inquiry and trial), and the demoralization of veterans, who were convinced that their sacrifices in the unpopular war had brought them little recognition. America's giant industrial and military power had failed to bring victory. Technological superiority in armaments and air power proved inadequate against an enemy skilled in insurgent warfare and imbued with a revolutionary zeal.

The travail of Southeast Asia did not end. During the war North Vietnam had infiltrated border areas of Cambodia and helped arm Communist insurgents, the Khmer Rouge, which, after a lengthy civil war, overthrew the Cambodian government. In 1975 the leader of the Cambodian Communists, the ruthless Pol Pot, subjected Cambodia to brutal dictatorship and grisly terror; an unknown number, but over 2 million people, died in the small Buddhist country from 1975 to 1978 as a result of mass executions, forced labor, and famine.

The Khmer Rouge turned out to be more pro-Chinese than suited Vietnam or the Soviet Union. In 1979 Vietnam invaded Cambodia and overthrew the Pol Pot regime: China took retaliatory steps, but could not force Vietnam to withdraw from Cambodia until the Soviets themselves encouraged the Vietnamese withdrawal in the late 1980s. Ancient rivalries between China and Vietnam and between Vietnam and Cambodia, as well as tensions between the Soviet Union and China, prolonged the agonies of South-

Communism and nationalism

east Asia. There was no monolithic communism in this part of the globe, where nationalism was as important as Communism in shaping the violent conflicts of the postcolonial era.

This photograph of terrified children fleeing from the bombing of their village in South Vietnam suggests how the disturbing pictures and television images of the Vietnam War raised painful moral questions and contributed to the development of a strong antiwar movement in the United States.
(Associated Press, AP)

Brezhnev: The "Prague Spring"

Leonid I. Brezhnev, who emerged as the dominant Soviet leader after Khrushchev's fall from power in 1964 and came to head both party and state, was intent, with reckless disregard for the costs to the economy, on building the country's military and naval strength to compete with the United States. Yet he avoided direct confrontation and saw political and economic advantages in a relaxation of tensions and arms negotiations. The open rift with Communist China made détente with the West even more important. But the two superpowers continued to vie with each other for influence in the Middle East, Africa, and other strategic areas of the world; and the Soviets consolidated their hold on eastern Europe.

Despite the failure of the Hungarian uprising in 1956, the longing for freedom and independence in eastern Europe could not be suppressed. When in 1968 the reforms of Alexander Dubček threatened the one-party state in Czechoslovakia, Brezhnev and the party leadership ruthlessly crushed the "Prague spring." They dispatched 250,000 troops, including token Polish, Hungarian, and East German contingents, to suppress the incipient revolution and remove Dubček and his reformist allies from power. The

The citizens of Prague responded angrily to the Soviet military forces in their city in August 1968, but they could do little against the 250,000 well-armed troops. These young people cele- brated the destruction of a Soviet tank; elsewhere in the city, however, the Soviets were destroying the reformist government of Alexander Dubček and suppressing the movement that had attempted to create a more democratic political system in Czechoslovakia.
(Getty Images)

The Brezhnev Doctrine

"Brezhnev Doctrine" that year proclaimed the Soviet right to intervene in the name of "proletarian internationalism" in any Communist country to protect "socialism" against "internal or external forces" and prevent the "restoration of a capitalist regime." It was in its own way a kind of mirror image of the Truman Doctrine. Czechoslovakia returned to a tight dictatorship ruled by party bosses with close ties to Moscow. The United States did no more than protest the armed intervention in Czechoslovakia, demonstrating once again that it would not openly challenge Soviet control over eastern Europe in what was tacitly accepted as a sphere of Soviet influence. But the invasion of Czechoslovakia, like the suppression of the 1956 Hungarian uprising, alienated the Communist faithful in many parts of the world and undermined the Soviet leadership of Western Communist parties, which strongly denounced the military intervention.

Brezhnev and Nixon

Although President Nixon, who took office in 1969, continued and even intensified the war in Vietnam, he introduced greater flexibility into the American policy of containment and pursued a policy of systematic détente in the Cold War. With Kissinger (and somewhat like de Gaulle) he believed in the balance of power diplomacy of an earlier age, and he assumed that each country's long-range

Nixon and détente

national self-interest and geopolitical concerns should count more than ideology. The growing importance of the People's Republic of China had to be recognized. The United States would be unable to curb Soviet expansion altogether, but it could offer economic concessions and other inducements for cooperation and peace.

Under the Nixon-Kissinger policy the United States linked Western technology, trade, and investment to Soviet cooperation in international affairs. The economic inducements were important because the Soviet Union's economic difficulties were aggravated by its growing arms burden. Khrushchev's earlier boast of surpassing the West economically had proved hollow. The Soviets badly needed Western technology, Western investment credits, and, because of their persistent agricultural crises, Western grain. In the new atmosphere American and West European private bankers made large loans to the East European nations, which benefited even more than the Soviets from détente. The two Germanys moved closer together in economic relations, recognized each other diplomatically, and were admitted to the United Nations in 1973 as two separate sovereign states.

The Nixon-Kissinger policies developed out of a reassessment of global realities. Unlike the bipolar situation in 1945 when there were only two superpowers, there were now other emergent power centers, and the most important of them was the People's Republic of China. In 1971 the United States withdrew its objections to the entry of the People's Republic of China into the United Nations as a replacement for Taiwan, although it would still recognize "two Chinas" *The opening to China* and work toward their peaceful reunification one day as "one country, two systems." Then in an unannounced move in 1972, after careful secret preparations, Nixon, who had built his domestic political career on anticommunism, took the dramatic step of visiting Mao in Beijing to initiate diplomatic and economic relations with China.

The American opening to China increased pressure on the Soviets to pursue détente. The Soviet arms buildup under Brezhnev signified that the Soviets were approaching nuclear parity, and both the United States and the Soviet Union found it to their advantage to negotiate arms reduction. The Strategic Arms Limitation (or SALT) talks begun under President Johnson were resumed. In 1972 *SALT I* Nixon and the Soviet leaders reaffirmed the goal of "peaceful coexistence" and signed the SALT I treaty. Each nation agreed to reduce its antimissile defense system to make it possible to work toward equality in offensive weapons. They agreed also to hold offensive weapons to a fixed number for a period of five years. The treaty did not halt the arms race, but it reduced fears on both sides of a preemptive strike and promised continued negotiations. After Nixon resigned from the presidency in 1974 following the Watergate scandal, détente continued under his successor, President Gerald Ford.

Détente offered an opportunity to settle or phase out some unresolved issues of the Second World War. In 1975, in what resembled a peace conference for Europe, three decades after the Second World War had ended, 35 nations—the 16 members of NATO, the 7 Warsaw Pact states, and 12 European countries not formally members of either alliance—met at Helsinki over a period of two years in a Conference on Security and Cooperation in Europe. They pledged to work for *The Helsinki accords* peace, economic and cultural cooperation, and the protection of human rights. The Helsinki accords, although not a formal treaty, ratified the European territorial boundaries established after the Second World War and set up "Helsinki watch committees" for the surveillance of human rights in nations that signed the agreements. The U.S.S.R. considered the commitment to human rights a small price to pay in exchange for the economic and other benefits of détente. It still expected to keep strict limits on dissent within its own country and in its East European satellites, but it failed to see how much the Helsinki accords would encourage dissenters to defy repression. The Helsinki conference was the high point of Cold War détente; not long thereafter, in 1979, Soviet-Western relations took another downward turn. But we must first turn to the changing world economy, to which the Soviet Union and the Eastern bloc were now more closely tied than ever before.

122. COLLAPSE AND RECOVERY OF THE GLOBAL ECONOMY: THE 1970s AND 1980s

Interdependence is a form of dependency, and the expansion of the global economy after the Second World War made each country more vulnerable to events in distant places. In 1974, after two and a half decades of spectacular growth, the Western economic boom came to an abrupt end. Signs of economic slowdown and inflationary pressures were already visible in the late 1960s, and recession might have occurred in any event, but it was the oil embargo growing out of the Arab-Israeli war in the autumn of 1973 that precipitated the crisis.

Oil had replaced coal as a major source of energy. Readily available at low prices, it came primarily from the vast reserves of the Middle East and was transported easily and economically by tanker through the Persian Gulf and Suez Canal. The major international oil companies, mostly American, for a long time controlled prices and production, and purchasers paid for the oil in dollars. The Western economies, the Japanese, and others in Asia had come to depend on cheap oil. In 1960, 14 of the oil-exporting countries in the

OPEC

Middle East, Africa, and Latin America formed the Organization of Petroleum Exporting Countries (or OPEC) to curb the monopoly concessions enjoyed by foreign companies and to assume a larger share of authority over production and prices.

Within OPEC the Arab states of the Middle East were the most assertive. The oil issue turned intensely political during the Arab-Israeli war of October 1973 when the Arab oil-producing states embargoed the shipment of oil to states accused of supporting Israel. The OPEC cartel cut back production and quadrupled oil prices. Apprehension spread in western Europe and Japan, and in the United States, which needed foreign oil to supplement its domestic resources. Never had an essential commodity risen in price so rapidly; the entire global industrial complex seemed vulnerable. The oil shortage and the price escalation, coming on the heels of the international monetary difficulties and devaluations of the dollar in 1971–1973, sharply increased the balance of payment deficits for all oil-importing countries, undermined currencies, accelerated an inflationary spiral already underway, and seriously interrupted the spectacular growth of the West European economies.

Dependence on oil

The immediate panic caused by the oil embargo passed, but prices remained at a much higher level. Later in the decade, in 1979, a second oil crisis occurred when Iran, in the midst of its revolution, halted oil exports and the OPEC cartel again doubled prices. In the 1980s the Iran-Iraq War once more reduced global oil supplies and threatened the free movement of tankers through the Persian Gulf, prompting the United States and other Western countries to take naval action. Eventually, however, the oil cartel proved less cohesive and intimidating than originally feared. Additional energy resources became available. After the discovery of oil in the North Sea, Britain and Norway became exporters of oil. The Netherlands and other countries turned to natural gas; France, to nuclear energy. Many countries initiated energy conservation measures. When prices declined in the 1980s as a result of falling demand, oil-producing countries like Nigeria and Mexico found themselves deeply in debt because they had geared their economies and government expenditures to the sale of high-priced oil. The decline in oil revenues led to restlessness in the Arab states, and later events in the Middle East showed the critical role that oil and oil prices continued to play in international affairs.

The Recession: Stagnation and Inflation

The recession that began in 1974 was severe, although it never approximated the depths of the Great Depression. What set it apart from previous economic declines was the accompanying inflation, which raced on in major industrial countries at double-digit annual figures.

In some European countries the annual rate of inflation rose to over 20 percent; it reached 27 percent in Britain in 1975. In the United States prices doubled over the course of the decade. For a time economic growth ground to a standstill in western Europe. By the late 1970s the recession was worldwide. Bankruptcies shook several countries; production declined; economic growth slowed or even halted. Over 10 percent of the American and West European labor force were unemployed. From a low point of 3.4 percent in 1969 unemployment in the United States rose to 10.8 percent in 1982. American factories operated at two-thirds their capacity. Unemployment once more became the bane of industrial capitalism.

The bane of industrial capitalism

The economic troubles were somewhat cushioned for the unemployed in industrial countries. Labor unions were still active, although declining in membership and influence, and welfare benefits were more advanced than they had been in the 1930s. Workers in Essen, Turin, Liverpool, or Detroit could count on severance pay, trade union benefits, and government unemployment compensation far beyond the welfare payments and dole of earlier generations. These benefits reduced human suffering and also limited the decline in consumer purchasing power. The recession, however, aggravated the problem of "structural unemployment." Because of automation, high technology, and the dwindling importance of older, less-efficient sectors (such as coal mining, shipbuilding, and other so-called smokestack industries), many workers would never return to their old jobs or use their old skills again.

Structural unemployment

The combination of stagnation and inflation (dubbed "stagflation" by journalists) created unprecedented problems for governments. Keynesian theory, which had gained a wide following after 1945, called for government spending and deficit financing in slow times to buoy demand and keep employment stable. With inflation rampant, such measures became questionable. The dilemma centered on whether curbing inflation or reducing unemployment should claim the highest priority. Efforts to fight inflation by tight money and high interest rates would discourage investment, aggravate the business slowdown, and swell the ranks of the unemployed. Government spending to prime the pump or reducing interest rates to facilitate private borrowing could feed inflation.

Stagflation

With the American economy troubled, the Western industrial countries looked to the Federal Republic of Germany and its powerful economy and trade surpluses to take the lead in expanding investment and production. Germany, however, mindful of the hyperinflation of the 1920s, set its highest priority on controlling inflation; it kept interest rates high and rejected expansionist policies. Other countries followed the same track. By the early 1980s inflation was brought under control in the United States and in western Europe, but in Europe unemployment continued at levels unheard of in the early postwar decades. The high unemployment put new pressures on government budgets, which had risen steadily in all the "welfare state" societies of the industrial world.

From 1950 to the mid-1970s the percentage of gross national product spent on social measures in the industrial countries had more than doubled, creating a pattern of rising taxes and government expenditures that came to be criticized as an obstacle to economic growth.

Faith in Keynes shaken

The established tenets of Keynesian economics were now challenged as never before. The British Conservative party leader Margaret Thatcher, who became prime minister in 1979, led the campaign against the welfare state and was soon joined by Ronald Reagan, the American Republican president from 1981 to 1989. Both leaders attacked the welfare state as costly, wasteful, paternalistic, and bureaucratic and blamed it for eroding individual initiative and responsibility. Nationalized industries, where they existed, also came under criticism.

Although conservative governments continued heavy expenditures for national defense, they curbed government spending on social measures. Meanwhile to stimulate production they offered numerous incentives to private enterprise, including tax reductions, deregulation, and restraints on unions that interfered with technological innovation. "Supply side" economics, as these ideas were labeled, emphasized increased production rather than the hitherto prevailing notion of increased consumer demand as most important for economic growth. The results were then expected to "trickle down" for everyone's benefit, with a safety net in place for the truly disadvantaged.

Supply side economics

The gradual return of prosperity, especially in the United States from about 1982 on, reinforced faith in the free-market economy, despite uneasiness about the continuing vicissitudes of the business cycle. Conservative economic theories and policies appeared to be confirmed by a worldwide movement toward market economies and away from centralized planning, which in its rigidly Marxist form had manifestly failed in the Soviet Union and eastern Europe. Defenders of the welfare state, however, continued to stress the importance of supplementing market economies with direct action by governments to meet individual and social needs. The welfare, or interventionist, state still served important social needs and seemed destined to survive, even if in modified form. A new generation of liberal, labor, and socialist leaders came to preach the virtues of a "new middle way" that leaned heavily on market economies as the key to economic growth but without surrendering the prerogatives of government in confronting the social and economic problems of modern societies.

Economic and Political Change in Western Europe

Britain was especially hard hit by the recession of the 1970s. Of all the industrial nations, it suffered the highest rate of inflation. Unemployment climbed, and the pound dropped to a new low in global financial markets. The trade unions refused to accept the sacrifices that even their own Labour party believed necessary to revive the economy, and disruptive strikes in coal and transportation exasperated much of the country. Radical factions in the

Conservatives sought to dismantle or reduce the social programs of the modern welfare state after they won control of the national governments in Great Britain and the United States during the 1980s. Prime Minister Margaret Thatcher and President Ronald Reagan, shown here at a meeting of Western government leaders in 1984, became close political allies and friends in these years. They both promoted conservative policies by reducing the government's participation in domestic economic life, though they increased national spending for military forces and believed that their governments should play a strong, activist role in international affairs.
(Getty Images)

Labour party pressed for increased nationalization of industry and for nonalignment in the Cold War. Alienated by the economic confusion and collapse of moral authority, which they blamed on Labour governments that had been in power since 1974, the voters in 1979 turned to the Conservatives.

Margaret Thatcher

Margaret Thatcher, the first woman prime minister in any major Western country, headed a Conservative government resolved to change matters. She immediately and decisively cut government expenditures, reduced imports, and resisted trade union wage demands. The focus shifted to investment, productivity, and economic growth. Inflation was curbed, but unemployment rose. The Thatcher government in its early years seemed headed for political trouble, but in 1982 Thatcher stirred old patriotic and imperial memories by dispatching a small armada 8,000 miles to the coast of South America, thwarting the attempted takeover of the Falkland (or Malvina) Islands by Argentina. The Conservatives won a sweeping parliamentary majority the following year.

For a time in the 1980s the Thatcher policies were successful. The government curtailed the power of the unions, returned over one-third of the nationalized industries to private enterprise, and made credit more readily available for business and for home buyers. Britain could soon point to the highest economic growth rate of all the European countries, rising productivity, low inflation, a stronger pound, a higher standard of living for most people, widened home ownership, and buoyant self-confidence. Unemployment, however, remained high; fiscal retrenchment hurt education, especially the universities; and pockets of deep depression persisted, especially in the north of England and in Scotland and Wales where traditional industries such as coal mining and shipbuilding faced difficulties competing in the new global economy. The south and southeast enjoyed a bustling prosperity, especially in the high-technology industries around London and Cambridge. Meanwhile London reinforced its position as a world financial center, and the United Kingdom became once again a leading creditor nation. Decades of economic decline and demoralization seemed to have been reversed. The opposition was disunited and in disarray. In the elections of 1987, Labour's popular vote dropped to its lowest point in decades, and union membership declined.

But when economic growth slowed after the stimulus of privatization and deregulation wore off, Thatcher introduced a number of fiscal measures that led to her fall in 1990. Her successor as prime minister, John Major, had to cope with a new recession that set in after 1990, a weakened pound, and unemployment. Labour, meanwhile, under new leadership that abandoned older ideas of class struggle and attracted a broad range of middle-class support, continued to challenge the Conservatives, arguing that the Thatcher era had

New Labour

favored the rich and fostered a less equitable society. Finally, under the moderate "New Labour" leadership of Tony Blair, the Labour party won the parliamentary elections in 1997 and regained control of the government for the first time since 1979. Blair and the increasingly moderate Labour party would remain in power on into the opening decade of the twenty-first century, winning a third consecutive electoral victory in 2005.

In France, politics in the 1980s veered toward the Left. An austerity program adopted in the 1970s by the conservative parties to combat inflation was unpopular, and the government's aloofness, elitism, and seeming unconcern with social issues under de Gaulle's successors helped the Socialist-led opposition grow in strength. In 1981 François Mitterrand achieved the goal he had set for himself and the Socialist party. He himself had had a varied career, some aspects of which were unknown until the last years of his life, including his association with right-wing causes in the early 1930s and his wartime service to the Vichy government before joining the Resistance movement. He was known as a moderate Socialist, whose socialism owed more to liberal idealism than to Marxism. A consummate politician, he revitalized the Socialist party and reached out to many who chafed at the social insensitivities of the Gaullists and Conservatives. "Changer la vie"—change life for everyone—was his campaign slogan. Not only did he win the presidency, but his Socialist party triumphantly gained an absolute majority in the National Assembly.

Mitterrand and "Changer la vie"

Labor reforms were immediately introduced. The workweek was reduced from 40 to 39 hours and a fifth week of annual paid vacation was added. Following up on the nationalizations of 1945, Mitterrand nationalized the remaining large banks as well as several leading industrial corporations. One of the few European leaders still faithful to Keynesian precepts in the 1980s, he expected government pump priming and labor reforms to raise purchasing power, stimulate the economy, and thus absorb the costs of the expanded welfare state. But increased labor costs reduced French competitiveness abroad, and private investment also dried up. The immediate consequences were slow economic growth, trade deficits, inflation, unemployment, and a weakening franc. Within two years Mitterrand abruptly changed course. He halted further nationalization and other reforms, insisted on retrenchment and austerity to cope with inflation, and placed a strong emphasis on modernization. Cutting off subsidies to decaying industries, he shifted government support to high technology. The new policies encouraged economic growth but contributed little to reducing unemployment. His Socialist followers were disenchanted and frustrated. Others in the country, however, were relieved to see him concentrate on strengthening the nation's economy rather than on sectarian politics.

Renewed economic problems, however, cost the Socialist party popular support. It lost its parliamentary majority in 1986 and Mitterrand was forced to govern with a Conservative prime minister. The term "cohabitation" entered the political language to signify a popularly elected president of one party governing with a prime minister who represented the opposing parliamentary majority. It was a precedent that de Gaulle never foresaw. But as an established practice

"Cohabitation"

that was repeated over the years to come, it became a legacy of Mitterrand that demonstrated the resiliency of the Fifth Republic. In the Gaullist tradition, however, the president continued to determine defense and foreign policy.

When in 1988 Mitterrand was reelected president, the Socialists regained a small plurality in the National Assembly. But unemployment, scandals involving Socialist ministers, and inroads by environmental and other groups led to a socialist rout in 1993 and the return of a large conservative majority. Cohabitation resumed under the conservative Gaullist Prime Minister Jacques Chirac, who was then elected to the presidency in the elections of 1995 and 2002, and the seesaw pattern of French politics continued in his administration. While the French economy strengthened impressively in the 1990s, unemployment remained a persistent problem, especially for young people. One measure, adopted by the Socialist prime minister, Lionel Jospin, reduced the workweek from 39 to 35 hours to create new jobs, but met with strong opposition from most employers. During these years women played a much larger role in French government and public institutions than ever before, occupying key ministries and high-level posts in business and professional life. A new law, to be implemented in stages, provided that women were to be candidates in elections for representative bodies in equal numbers with men. A few women writers and scholars were even admitted to the French Academy, a male bastion since 1635.

French workers, like workers in all the major industrial countries of Europe, were increasingly drawn from the immigrant communities that grew rapidly during the later decades of the twentieth century. These workers, who were protesting working conditions at a French automobile factory in 1982, represent some of the diverse ethnic and cultural origins of the contemporary French workforce.

(Richard Melloul/Sygma/Corbis)

*West European
Socialists*

Socialists and Social Democrats holding office in western Europe in these years championed modernization, market economies, and economic growth as the path to the good society; and their policies won broad support. Moderation and pragmatism succeeded in overshadowing if not entirely replacing older ideologies. Helmut Schmidt, the Social Democratic chancellor in West Germany from 1974 to 1982, was one leading exemplar. In Italy, Bettino Craxi and a Socialist coalition in 1983 ended the long tenure of the Christian Democrats, who had formed 40 consecutive cabinets since 1945. The Italian Socialists governed for an unprecedented four years but were barely distinguishable in policies and practices from the long-entrenched Christian Democratic establishment. In Spain the popular Socialist party leader, Felipe Gonzalez, in 1982 headed the first Left government since the Spanish Civil War of the 1930s and governed on into the mid-1990s. In Portugal, after the revolutionary turbulence of 1974, a Socialist and a Social Democratic party competed with each other on moderate platforms.

In West Germany Helmut Schmidt's Social Democratic government moved to control inflation through policies of retrenchment and fiscal conservatism, but the industrial slow-down of the late 1970s brought unemployment to a country which for years had known only labor scarcity. Even after recovery, unemployment persisted at about eight percent. The doors once open to guest workers began to close; bonuses were offered to those who would return home; activist reactionary groups (as in Britain, France, and Austria) alarmingly exploited antiimmigrant and antiforeign sentiment. In 1982 the Christian Democrats were returned to office with Helmut Kohl as chancellor, who would remain in office for the next 16 years. Economic growth resumed, although at more modest rates, and the mark maintained itself as one of the world's strongest currencies. The German Federal Republic remained the most productive nation in western Europe, accounting for a third of the combined output of the European Community. But heavy labor costs, resulting from high wages and generous social benefits, burdened the economy and reduced its competitiveness in world markets. Meanwhile the prospects in the 1980s for reunification of the two Germanys still seemed remote—Germany would apparently remain "one nation and two states," in Willy Brandt's phrase.

"One nation and two states"

The American Economy

The United States recovered from the post-1974 recession sooner and more completely than the Europeans. The American economy suffered business slowdowns and serious inflation from 1974 to 1982; but once inflation was brought under control, the economy began to grow in the 1980s. Deregulation of industry, encouraged under the Reagan and George H. W. Bush presidencies, and corporate streamlining or restructuring (often called downsizing) produced greater profits and stimulated economic growth, as did the beginnings of the computer revolution. Continuing interventions by the Federal Reserve Board, which raised or lowered interest rates, helped to protect against inflation. The stock market began to rise, as did real estate values. In the 1980s unemployment dropped below 6 percent, and the labor force grew at a time when unemployment was still a persistent problem in Europe, though many of the newly employed in the United States were entering lower-paying service industries. There were setbacks, including a dramatic but temporary fall in stock prices in 1987 and a failure of savings and loans banks, which had overextended their credit. A more general economic slowdown again set in after 1989, and unemployment rose to 7.8 percent. Campaigning on the poor performance of the economy, the Democratic candidate Bill Clinton was able to defeat President Bush in the election of 1992. At the time few recognized that by the spring of 1991 the economy was already embarking on an extraordinary expansion that would continue throughout the decade and into the opening of the new century.

There were still many areas of economic concern in the 1980s. The trading strength of the United States accentuated some of its economic problems. The oil crisis of the 1970s had ultimately reinforced the dollar (oil profits were invested in dollars), and the dollar's value rose steadily in the early 1980s, raising the cost of American goods in global markets. American exports also faced strong competition from western Europe and Japan, and from the newly industrialized small states in Asia, where labor costs were low and newer highly mechanized plants provided a competitive edge. The strong dollar made it difficult for the United States to sell its products and aggravated its already heavy trade deficit. The United States therefore sought to bring down the high value of the dollar by 1985. Over the next three years the dollar lost almost 50 percent of its value in relation to foreign currencies, declining to its lowest level since 1945 and creating a new challenge for the American economy. Japanese, West Europeans, Canadians, Arabs, and others seized the opportunity to buy into American corporations, banks, brokerage houses, and real estate. By the late 1980s foreign holdings of American assets totaled $1 trillion.

Economic concerns

Meanwhile the Japanese economy reached such giant dimensions that corporations like the Fujita Bank and the Toyota Corporation were valued at five to ten times the market value of the largest American companies. The Nomura Securities Corporation of Tokyo became at the time the largest brokerage firm in the world. Not one of the world's ten largest banks in the 1980s was American. From 1985 on, for the first time since 1914, the United States was a debtor nation. Foreign interests owned more assets in the United States than Americans owned abroad, which meant a steady outflow of interest, dividends, and rents. Even when American exports expanded, imports continued to grow and the trade balance remained unfavorable. The annual budget deficit mounted and the national debt soared from less than $1 trillion in 1981 to well over $4 trillion by 1990. Foreign capital financed the American debt and profited from the interest on American bonds.

Concern mounted, even as the American economy was recovering, over the weakness in exports, the balance-of-payments deficits, the burden of defense expenditures, the growing national debt, the large annual budget deficits, and the foreign acquisition of American assets. Analysts pointed to inadequate American savings and investment, a relative slowdown in productivity gains since the 1960s, a lag in industrial research and development, and shortcomings in American education for an increasingly competitive world. The American economy was still the largest in the world; in the early 1990s its gross domestic product exceeded $5 trillion, far ahead of Japan and Germany. But it had shown a relative decline in growth in relation to the other major industrial nations. Deep pockets of poverty and racial tensions persisted within the country. It was debated at the time whether the United States, still the premier political, economic, and military power, might lose its primacy because of economic weaknesses—as Spain, the Netherlands, France, and Britain had in earlier centuries.

Relative decline in growth

The prospects that opened up in the late 1980s of winding down the Cold War and of a measure of relief from the burden of arms expenditures brought some reassurances. Meanwhile, the Japanese economy, which had become increasingly based on an overinflated stock market and real estate values, entered in 1989 on a long period of difficulties that persisted throughout and beyond the following decade. Before long, American productivity, economic growth, technological innovation, and international competitiveness in the 1990s made most of the earlier jeremiads seem hollow or short-sighted.

The Financial World

The world's largest stock exchanges and financial markets were centered in New York City. Deregulation in the 1980s brought with it a sharp increase in financial acquisitions and mergers. New forms of trading in options and futures and widening participation by small investors contributed to the stock market's growth and volatility. Once again, as in the 1920s, the lines between speculation and investment became blurred. In October 1987, a tremor ran through the United States and world markets when stocks on the New York Stock Exchange in one day lost close to one-fourth their value, conjuring up memories of the October 1929 crash and the ensuing Great Depression. But the market recovered, and in the following decade it went on to reach new heights—and to experience also new periods of extreme volatility. The 1987 episode clearly demonstrated the interdependence of the world's financial markets. Reverberations of the 1987 shock in New York were felt instantly in London, Frankfurt, Tokyo, Hong Kong, Singapore, Taipei, Sydney, and elsewhere. The financial markets, like the currency markets, were decentralized but were more interwoven than ever before. With new systems of telecommunications and other advanced computer technology, a single financial market operated around the world and around the clock.

Speculation and investment

The sense of mutual interdependence in the global economy came to be widely shared. The United States, western Europe, and Japan recognized that the prosperity of each depended on the smooth functioning of the world economy. The heads of state of the seven largest industrial powers with market economies (the "Group of Seven"—the United States, Britain, France, the Federal Republic of Germany, Italy, Canada, and Japan) met from the 1970s on in annual economic summits to consult on the state of the economy. The leading central banks made efforts to stabilize interest and exchange rates. The Organization for Economic Cooperation and Development (OECD) brought together the 24 leading industrial nations of the world, and GATT continued its "rounds" of negotiations to reduce tariffs. The integration of the Soviet Union and eastern Europe into the global economy, initiated in the 1970s in the first period of détente, and the rapid political changes taking place there after the late 1980s provided further opportunities for international cooperation. The developing nations, however, remained somewhat on the economic periphery, their heavy debt and slow economic growth intensifying their dependence on the industrial world. They remained critical of a globalization that seemed to ignore or pay inadequate attention to their needs.

Mutual interdependence

The Enlarged European Community: Problems and Opportunities

After de Gaulle passed from the political scene in 1969, the way had opened for enlarging the six-nation European Community (EC). In 1973 Britain, Denmark, and Ireland were admitted; the 6 became 9. In the next decade, with the admission of Greece in 1981 and Spain and Portugal in 1986, the 9 became 12. In 1995, with the admission of Austria, Finland, and Sweden, the numbers grew to 15. The largest expansion made possible by momentous changes in Eastern Europe after 1989 and by the collapse of Soviet communism, would take place at the beginning of the twenty-first century, in 2004, when ten more nations from eastern and southern Europe (from Estonia to Malta) joined what had come to be known as the European Union.[1]

Enlargement brought new difficulties, aggravated by the economic slowdown of the 1970s and then by the wage differentials between richer and poorer countries. A food importer, Britain objected to the "common agricultural policy" agreed upon in 1968, whereby countries such as France and Italy received large subsidies for their farmers, whose products were withheld from the open market and stored at great expense to keep prices artificially high. The admission of the less industrially advanced southern Mediterranean states in the 1980s (and of eastern nations in the early twenty-first century) introduced serious regional differences. Despite the original promise and accomplishments of the Community as a whole, the free trading area remained far from complete. Countries still placed quotas on agricultural imports; France kept out Italian wines. Burdensome administrative regulations at the borders persisted.

Growing pains

Except for a limited circle of Europeanists, the enthusiasm for close political integration seemed to have dimmed. With enlargement and greater diversity, the Community became even more intergovernmental and less supranational. Britain was always reluctant

---

[1]By 2005 the European Union member states were Austria, Belgium, Cyprus, Czech Republic, Denmark, Estonia, Finland, France, Germany, Greece, Hungary, Ireland, Italy, Latvia, Lithuania, Luxembourg, Malta, Netherlands, Poland, Portugal, Slovakia, Slovenia, Spain, Sweden, and the United Kingdom. There was also a growing debate over the question of whether Turkey should become the next member of the EU.

Japan's financial markets developed into an important component of the international economy, attracting investments from all parts of the world. These traders at the Tokyo Stock Exchange in the early 1990s use advanced technologies to manage the sale of stocks and to keep track of the information that flows constantly through such markets and the international economic networks that they support.
(Sipa Press)

to support additional supranational authority for the Community. In periods of economic slowdown and monetary instability the national governments themselves had to cope with the problems. In 1973 the heads of government leaders began meeting as a council on a regular basis, the presidency rotating among the member states. The first elections to the European Parliament in 1979 were more symbolic than substantial, and the Parliament's role as a legislature failed to grow significantly. While the more ambitious dream of a United States of Europe went unrealized, the Community, for all its problems, remained an important institution, poised for further growth.

Toward a "Single Europe": the European Union

Even during the prosperous 1960s, the European economy did not maintain its growth in all areas. But in the 1970s the world itself was entering a new phase of industrialism, a "third industrial revolution," marked by the introduction of automation, computers, and other forms of advanced technology. Progress would no longer be measured in coal and steel or in ships and textiles but in nuclear reactors, microelectronics, telecommunications, computers, robotics, and space technology. In the "postindustrial" age data processing, information storage and retrieval, and more and more sophisticated communications capabilities were the keys to competitive success. In 1977 the first personal computer was produced for what would become a mass market, with rapid improvements to follow in speed and capacity. More workers

The postindustrial age

were employed in the service sector than in the older basic industries, and the service economy was growing faster than either agriculture or industry. It was widely noted that the global economy was eroding the economic and political autonomy of the nation-state. Using new technologies, the multinational corporations of the industrial world invested capital and set up shop across the globe, independent of all national boundaries.

In the new forms of technology, the Europeans found themselves for a time outdistanced by the Americans and the Japanese. American multinational corporations controlled most of the high-technology industries in Europe—before the Japanese arrived to compete. Trade competition from Japan and the rapidly developing industrial countries of the Pacific Rim grew. The post-1974 recession made it difficult for the Europeans to promote research and development. Western Europe lagged behind other parts of the world in recovering economically after 1974 or in coping with unemployment.

The European Community set about to reinvigorate itself in the 1980s. Although internal tariffs had disappeared, nontariff obstacles still impeded the flow of trade. Nationally dictated, and therefore varying, standards of production and quality prevailed. In 1987, by the "Single European Act" the 12 member-nations agreed to establish common production standards, remove impediments to the flow of capital, seek uniform tax rates, recognize each other's professional and commercial licensing, and honor a common charter of labor *The Single European Act* rights. They would create an integrated "single Europe," a "Europe without borders." A unified European currency and central banking system were projected for the end of the 1990s, and even a common defense and foreign policy were envisaged for the future. These arrangements were confirmed in a Treaty of European Union signed at Maastricht in the Netherlands at the close of 1991, and ratified after protracted debate by the parliaments or electorates of the member states by the end of 1992. Opponents in several countries raised objections to the loss of national control in so many areas, but the treaty was adopted. The European Community became the European Union (EU). The way was open to closer integration.

The European Union represented a domestic market of 345 million people (one-third larger than that of the United States) and by the early 1990s was the largest trading bloc in the global economy, accounting for 40 percent of all international trade. With the new steps toward integration and the later expansion of EU membership, Europeans hoped to enlarge investment, develop high technology, stimulate productivity, end the lagging rate of economic growth, and reduce an unemployment rate that was still distressingly high. For the world as a whole, a return to protectionism was always a lurking danger. Advocates of tariffs on imported goods could be *Dangers of protectionism* found in most industrial nations, and the industrial nations might divide into large regional trading blocs. New competitive barriers could interfere with the free trade that had contributed so much to post-1945 prosperity.

123.   THE COLD WAR REKINDLED

We must go back in time to pick up the flow of international affairs. In the summer of 1974 President Nixon resigned his office to avoid impeachment over his role in the Watergate scandal. His vice president, Gerald Ford, succeeded him. But in the next election the Democratic candidate Jimmy Carter won and took office in 1977. President Carter sought to infuse American foreign policy with moral idealism. Human rights, he declared, must be "the soul of our foreign policy." Détente with the Soviet *Human rights* Union was now more closely linked than before to respect for human rights; economic aid would be forthcoming only if the Soviets permitted freedom to dissenters, the right of emigration for Soviet Jews and others, and an end to the coercion of Poland. The Soviets did not take kindly to these public pressures. Both sides meanwhile reinforced their military and nuclear strength.

On the other hand both countries continued strategic arms talks and after tortuous negotiations signed a second strategic arms treaty in January 1979. They agreed to parity in strategic, or long-range, nuclear missiles. Although the number of powerful missiles remained high and nothing prevented the development of new sophisticated weapons, the agreement might have been an important breakthrough in arms control. But before it could

Soviet invasion of Afghanistan

be ratified by the Senate, the Soviet Union moved troops into the neighboring state of Afghanistan to bolster a weak pro-Soviet leftist regime. It was the first Soviet military intervention of that kind outside eastern Europe.

Carter denounced the invasion as a new phase of expansion by the Soviets threatening the entire Middle East—"a stepping stone in their possible control over much of the world's oil supplies." He warned that an attempt by any outside force to gain control of that region would be regarded as "an assault on the vital interests of the United States" and would be repulsed "by any means necessary, including military force." He withdrew the arms treaty from the Senate, embargoed sales of grain and high technology to the Soviets, took measures to increase the military budget, and set up procedures at home for a renewal of the draft.

The invasion of Afghanistan, Carter informed the U.S.S.R., was the most serious threat to world peace since 1945. The European allies were not as convinced. Some argued that the Afghanistan episode was a regional matter, that the Soviet Union was acting to prevent instability on its borders, and that détente should continue. Unwilling to disturb commercial relations with the Soviets and eastern Europe, they refused to support the economic embargo which, among other consequences, would have interfered with the completion of a Soviet natural gas pipeline to western Europe. As it developed, Afghanistan turned out to be the U.S.S.R.'s Vietnam. Some 100,000 troops fought for over 8½ years before withdrawing ignominiously in 1989. Like the Americans in Vietnam, the Soviets were unable to use their overwhelming military power to defeat the Muslim guerrillas who, armed with American weapons and supported by Pakistan, fought stubbornly from their Afghan mountain strongholds.

Hostages in Iran

At the very time of the Soviet intervention in Afghanistan, the United States had become preoccupied with the Iran hostage crisis, the seizing of American hostages by Iranian revolutionary militants in Tehran. It was a heavy blow to American prestige, compounded by the failure of an ill-fated rescue attempt. To add to Carter's humiliation, the American hostages were freed on the day that his Republican successor, Ronald Reagan, took office in January 1981.

The Reagan Years: From Revived Cold War to New Détente

There was no doubt of the new president's commitment to a hard line in the Cold War. The Soviet Union, Reagan asserted in 1983, represented "the focus of evil in the modern world." It was "an evil empire" with "dark purposes." Despite the strain on its economy, the Soviet Union during the 1970s had built up its military strength, modernized its conventional fighting forces, created a powerful navy, and achieved nuclear

Reagan and the "evil empire"

parity. With congressional support Reagan substantially increased defense appropriations, sponsored the largest peacetime military spending in the nation's history, and took a confrontational stand against communism

CHRONOLOGY OF NOTABLE EVENTS, 1957–1995

1957	Soviet Union launches first satellite into outer space
1961	Soviet Union constructs the Berlin wall to stop exodus from East Germany
1962	United States compels the withdrawal of Soviet missiles from Cuba
1965	United States begins more intensive military buildup and large-scale bombing in Vietnam
1968	Soviet troops enter Czechoslovakia to crush reform movement in Prague
1972	United States withdraws its last troops from Vietnam
1974	High oil prices and inflation contribute to global economic recession
1975	Communist forces in Vietnam take control of the country; Saigon becomes Ho Chi Minh City
1978	Deng Xiaoping, successor to Mao, launches sweeping economic reforms in China
1979	Margaret Thatcher becomes prime minister in England
1979	Soviet Union invades Afghanistan to protect left-wing regime
1980	Ronald Reagan is elected president of the United States
1981	François Mitterrand is elected president of France
1982	Helmut Kohl becomes chancellor of West Germany
1989	Democracy movement is suppressed in China
1992	Treaty of Maastricht establishes the European Union
1995	European Union membership expands to include 15 nations; in 2004 it expands to 25 nations

everywhere. He stepped up arms shipments to the Muslim guerrillas in Afghanistan and sent aid to Pakistan, which was backing the Afghan rebels. Against the Communist government in Poland he applied economic sanctions when, under pressure from the Soviets, it imposed martial law in 1981 to suppress the Solidarity trade union movement. He reinforced the embargo on the sale of high technology to the Soviets and to eastern Europe, but the embargo on grain sales was dropped because of opposition from American farmers.

In Central America and the Caribbean, Reagan accused the Soviets of using Castro's Cuba and the leftist Sandinista regime in Nicaragua as proxies to spread communism in the Western Hemisphere. The United States armed anti-Communist opponents of the regime in Nicaragua and reinforced dictatorial anti-Communist regimes in neighboring states and other parts of Latin America. In 1983 American forces invaded the small Caribbean island of Grenada to overthrow a leftist government that was permitting the Cubans to build an airport of potential military use.

Even more than his predecessors, Reagan and his foreign policy advisers supported repressive authoritarian regimes so long as they were anti-Communist, on the theory that one day such regimes might be liberalized; Communist governments, they believed, transformed their societies irreversibly. Critics, on the other hand, argued that revolutionary movements in Latin America and elsewhere sprang not from the Cold War but from protests against systems of privilege and exploitation; they opposed military solutions and support to repressive regimes as inappropriate responses.

Military actions

In Libya, the administration demonstrated the American willingness to take unilateral military action. American planes bombed military installations in retaliation for what it was convinced were Libyan-sponsored terrorist activities. In Lebanon, in the throes of civil war, the United States organized a multinational peacekeeping force in 1982. The American fleet landed marines, and Islamist terrorists retaliated by blowing up the American embassy and the American and French command centers, killing hundreds of American marines and French soldiers. The peacekeeping force withdrew.

In the war between Iran and Iraq that broke out in 1980, when attacks on tankers in the Persian Gulf threatened the flow of oil from the Arab Gulf states, the United States escorted a selected number of tankers under the protection of the American flag. The United States was intent on asserting American leadership in world affairs and on keeping the Soviets, insofar as possible, out of the Middle East.

Asserting American leadership

Nuclear Arms Control

The ultimate threat

No nuclear weapons were used in any conflict in the years after 1945, yet over every crisis hung the ultimate threat of a nuclear clash. We have seen how the earliest negotiations on nuclear disarmament, at a time when the United States alone possessed the atomic bomb, were broken off in 1947; how in 1949 the Soviets successfully tested their first atomic bomb, ending the American monopoly; and how the United States in 1952 and the Soviet Union shortly thereafter developed the hydrogen or thermonuclear bomb, which by its chain reaction had vastly more destructive capacity than the mere 20,000 tons of TNT of the Hiroshima bomb. By the 1960s both superpowers were building strategic long-range missiles, that is, intercontinental ballistic missiles, capable of delivering their nuclear warheads accurately and swiftly to targets in each other's homeland. They could be launched from land (from either stationary or mobile sites), from sea (from ships or submarines), or from bombers in the air. Guided missiles were the key strategic weapons of the modern age. Because of their immense destructive power, the nuclear weapons could not be used without unleashing unspeakable damage; they were different and distinct, it was agreed, from conventional weapons. The arms experts insisted that nuclear arms were built not for use but for deterrence.

Because nuclear testing threatened to poison the earth's atmosphere, and perhaps even damage the genetic endowment of present and future generations, controls were imperative. In 1963, despite Cold War tensions, the United States and the U.S.S.R. initiated a partial test-ban treaty, which banned testing in the atmosphere and permitted only underground testing. Concern over the spread of nuclear weapons prompted the two superpowers to propose a nonproliferation treaty, which was endorsed by the UN General Assembly in 1968 and eventually signed by over 130 states. It lacked binding force, however, and was ignored by those countries bent on developing nuclear power.

The United States had led the way in the development of nuclear weapons, with Britain also participating from the beginning. The Soviet Union had then followed; France in 1960 became a fourth nuclear power. The People's Republic of China in 1964 became a fifth; India in 1974, a sixth. By the early twenty-first century the list of countries that had achieved a nuclear capacity included Israel, Pakistan, and perhaps North Korea; and others such as Iran were suspected of seeking to develop nuclear weapons.

The fear that states that had demonstrated a flagrant disregard for international law or that terrorist organizations might come to possess nuclear materials prompted even greater concerns.

So long as the peaceful use of nuclear energy was encouraged, it was difficult to prevent proliferation. Nations purchasing nuclear power plants from industrial countries, ostensibly for peaceful purposes, could reprocess the plutonium from the spent fuel and build nuclear bombs, as India did. The search for alternative energy sources to replace oil stimulated many nations to build nuclear power plants that could be transformed for nonpeaceful purposes. Accidents at nuclear power plants, the most notorious of which were at Three Mile Island, Pennsylvania, in 1979 and, even more serious, at Chernobyl in Ukraine in 1986, did not deter the building of nuclear power plants but underscored the need for safer construction. From Chernobyl radioactive materials in the atmosphere traveled as far as western Europe.

Concerns about nuclear proliferation

From the 1960s on debate continued in the United States about the missile gap, about the comparative numbers of the American and Soviet missile systems deployed on land and sea and in the air, and about the vulnerability of the American land-based missile systems. Following the Soviet missile buildup after the Cuban crisis of 1962, the two superpowers had achieved a rough parity by the 1970s. Although both recognized superiority as an elusive goal, nothing restrained them from adding more and more strategic arms. Strategists on each side supported the buildup. Using advanced computer programs, they calculated the potential casualties in a nuclear exchange between the superpowers in millions of deaths (or "megadeaths") and evaluated the effects of deterrents and counterdeterrents and of "first strikes" and "counterstrikes" on each nation's ability to wage and survive nuclear war. The balance of power was spoken of as a "balance of terror"; experts referred to "mutually assured destruction" (the acronym for which, ironically, was MAD). Deterrence was the accepted formula.

MAD: mutually assured destruction

Each side amassed huge stockpiles of arms, capable of destroying each other many times over, in what was described as "overkill." The two superpowers were also under continuing pressure to modernize their systems competitively—at exorbitant cost. When the Soviets developed defense systems, that is, antiballistic missiles, which undermined deterrence, the American response was to build its own defense systems and more powerful offensive weapons—such as the MIRV (a "multiple independently targeted reentry vehicle"), a delivery system carrying up to ten nuclear warheads, each independently guided to separate targets, each warhead many times more powerful than the Hiroshima bomb. The Russians developed their own multiwarhead systems—all leading to an even higher level of armaments and greater uncertainty. Both sides had satellite reconnaissance systems, but for a time neither could determine the number of warheads on the other side and hence know with accuracy the other's capability. After the first SALT (or strategic arms limitation) treaty, signed in 1972, each side developed new weapons outside the classes that were limited. The United States developed cruise missiles, designed to fly low to the ground and hence protected from defense systems; the Soviets, supersonic bombers. A second arms treaty, signed in 1979 but not ratified until later, produced tentative agreement on equality in the total number of strategic long-range weapons, but protracted discussions continued.

Overkill

At the close of the 1980s each superpower possessed about 25,000 nuclear weapons, of which about 12,000 on each side were strategic, that is, long-range, or intercontinental. Together the two arsenals exceeded 500,000 megatons (millions of tons) of explosive

The rapid development of intercontinental missile systems in the 1960s led finally to a "balance of terror" or system of deterrence called "mutually assured destruction." According to this theory, all nations would be deterred from launching nuclear assaults because they could expect a retaliatory attack that would destroy their own cities and people. This is the prototype of a Titan Intercontinental Ballistic Missile (ICBM), which the United States began to store in underground silos during the Cold War arms race. Since the 1960s missiles with nuclear weapons have been kept ready for immediate launching as part of the strategic deterrence plan.
(Getty Images)

power, dwarfing the total explosive power used in all previous wars. If only a small number of these nuclear arms reached their targets, the two countries could destroy each other's major cities and countryside and kill millions in the attack and in the radioactive after-effects, which would spread to neighboring areas. In the "nuclear winter" that might follow, human survival itself was at risk. There was always the dread possibility of accident, miscalculation, or failure of communication. So deliberately suspended over the human race was the nuclear sword of Damocles that a direct communication link, or "hot line," was installed between the Kremlin and the White House in 1963, soon after the Cuban missile crisis; and in the following decades it was modernized and improved. It was designed to prevent the accidental outbreak of a nuclear war because of political misunderstanding, human error, or mechanical slipup; direct communication between the tribal chieftains was necessary in the nuclear age. No more than a 20-minute warning might be available.

The debate over security in the Cold War went beyond that of the defense strategists. Many pointed to the danger, the paradox, and even the immorality of building vast nuclear arsenals to prevent nuclear war; some (in the West) even urged unilateral disarmament. Others argued that without a high level of armaments a nation could be subject to nuclear blackmail. They maintained that the nuclear balance between the two opposing camps and the principle of deterrence had protected the peace. Everyone, to be sure, affirmed the need to reduce the political tensions and insecurity that fed the arms competition. Yet in the rekindled Cold War tensions of the early 1980s there seemed to be no solution to the impasse. Reluctantly, the world reconciled itself to the existing "balance of terror," except for piecemeal negotiations on arms limitations. It was only the unanticipated changes in the Soviet Union, its breakup, and the ending of the Cold War that brought unprecedented opportunities for nuclear arms reduction. But the altered situation would raise different dangers, leave proliferation a continuing threat, and still require constant reassessments of global safety.

Security debates

124. CHINA AFTER MAO

After Mao died in 1976, moderates and radicals competed for leadership. Mao's widow Jiang Qing, one of the firebrands of the Cultural Revolution, together with a small group of Maoist radicals, sought to win control and purge the moderates, but the attempt failed and she and her three associates—the so-called "gang of four"—were arrested and imprisoned. From behind the scenes Deng Xiaoping, the leader of the moderates, emerged by 1977 to become the most powerful figure in the country. Deng was a veteran party leader who had fallen out of favor with Mao in 1956–1957, was purged and humiliated in 1967 during the Cultural Revolution for having taken the "capitalist road," and purged for a third time in 1976 by the Maoist radicals. To counteract the Maoist cult of personality Deng over the years declined to accept the leading post in either government or party and instead placed his protégés in top positions, but everyone knew who was in command.

Deng's Reforms

By late 1978 Deng won the party over to a sweeping reform program designed to curb the radical and utopian phases of the revolution, deemphasize Marxist ideology and class struggle, and focus on economic growth and modernization. Deng proposed to transform the central economic planning, nationalized industry, and collectivized agriculture inherited from Mao—and indirectly from the Soviet Union. Without abandoning socialism as the eventual goal, he sanctioned numerous capitalist practices; he encouraged private enterprise, production for profit, and a competitive marketplace, at first in limited areas of the country and then more extensively. For state-owned industries he demanded profitability and accountability. The new system would be "a marriage," he said, "between a planned and a market economy." Dismantling the collectivized farms and communes, which had proved disastrous for agriculture, he allowed cultivation of the land by individual farmers and their families. He opened the country to foreign investment and welcomed Western

Both a planned and a market economy

science, technology, and management techniques. Although heavy industry was not neglected, Deng placed a new emphasis on consumer goods; factories that once manufactured military hardware began to produce refrigerators, washing machines, bicycles, and motorcycles.

China transformed

Deng's reforms transformed Chinese society. Their most striking success was in the countryside, where farmers sold a significant portion of their product on the open market. Within a decade output doubled; more food became available for the cities, and even for export. In other parts of the economy retail outlets, repair shops, and other small businesses were in private hands. Special economic enclaves were established along the southern coast to encourage foreign enterprise and investment, much of it from Hong Kong. Foreign capital flowed in; a stock exchange was introduced. Gross domestic product, which had never risen by more than 2 or 3 percent annually under Mao, grew at an average 9 percent annually in the 1980s and then at even higher rates. By the calculations of some international agencies China's economic output was the third largest in the world. Many of the new entrepreneurs (and some farmers) became wealthy. The big cities took on aspects of a consumer society. Temporary joblessness was tempered by a state network of social services—an "iron rice bowl." The country enjoyed an unprecedented rise in living standards. The People's Liberation Army was reduced in size, but was modernized and made more professional, and the government bureaucracy was trimmed down. State-owned industries still accounted for a major share of production, but the growing private sector, flourishing in the coastal regions, represented the most vigorous part of the economy.

Even if China remained a one-party state, a "people's democratic dictatorship" in one of the official phrases, and individual human rights (especially freedom of religion) were frequently violated, a more open and relaxed cultural and intellectual atmosphere prevailed. People tuned in on radio and television programs from the outside world. Students traveled and studied abroad. Many Western books were translated into Chinese. At no time since the Communist triumph in 1949 were the people so free to absorb ideas from the outside world. Foreign tourists visited in large numbers to see the new China. What earlier patriots and reformers like Sun Yat-sen had dreamed of, and Mao had failed to achieve because of his revolutionary excesses, Deng seemed to be accomplishing. Ideology was edged out by material advance, by the idea of a "rich and strong China."

Deng wished to provide an orderly succession. He therefore dislodged veterans of the older generation (many, like him, survivors of the Long March of 1934–1935) who had clung to older Maoist ways, resisted Western political and economic ideas, and tried to block reform. The old guard retained a network of influence, and the country deferred to Deng as a central authority figure, but younger leaders began to emerge.

Economic difficulties

As the decade progressed, Deng's reform program, for all its accomplishments, showed serious imperfections. The rapid economic growth fueled inflation (a 20 to 30 percent annual rate in the late 1980s). The emphasis on rising levels of consumption strained resources. Despite its avowals, the government did not liquidate its unprofitable state-owned industries, one-fifth of which operated at a loss. An erratic system of price controls encouraged a black market. Even agricultural production slowed down. The consumer society bred extravagance, conspicuous consumption, and wastefulness. Corruption, endemic in China, became widespread because government and party leaders were closely tied to business enterprises, government and private. Idealistic critics voiced dissatisfaction with the corruption and with growing inequities in a socialist society. In

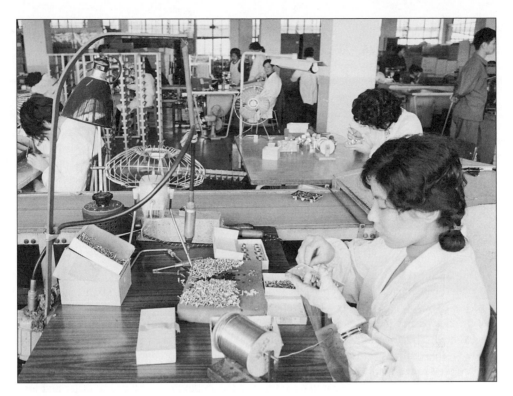

Economic reforms in the People's Republic of China after Mao's death in 1976 stimulated rapid expansion in the nation's economic output and gave China's low-wage industries a steadily growing role in global trade. These workers at a factory in Shanghai in the early 1980s were assembling components for televisions, which became one of the many products that China exported to consumer markets around the world.

(Richard Melloul/Sygma/Corbis)

response to these cumulative problems Deng in 1988 called for retrenchment and a pause in further reform.

With time and vigilance the economic difficulties in the transitional economy might have been overcome. What interrupted Deng's memorable decade of reform was the refusal to permit political reform and democratization to accompany the economic changes. Deng and others in the party believed that the country, for all its social advances, was unprepared for political democracy, which in their opinion would only breed chaos and confusion, as it had in the Cultural Revolution, and interfere with the order and stability necessary for economic growth and modernization. Further, nothing could be permitted to weaken the stewardship of the party, the heir to the old imperial dynasties, over the country's destiny.

Rejection of democracy

Yet in the freer atmosphere that Deng had encouraged, many of the country's intellectual leaders and younger people destined to be its future leaders pressed for a loosening of the party's political controls, a freer press, and the right to criticize the corruption and other shortcomings of the system. Political liberalization and democratic advances elsewhere in the world in the 1980s reinforced the restlessness in China.

The "Democracy Movement"

When at the end of 1986, Hu Yaobang, general secretary of the party and at the time the 82-year-old Deng's designated successor, encouraged the belief that greater political freedom might be permitted, students took to the streets to show their support. Hu vacillated in suppressing the demonstrations and the party summarily replaced him. Two years later the democratic ferment came to a head. Hu's death in April 1989 set off a series of student demonstrations in the huge central square in Beijing–Tiananmen Square, or Gate of Heavenly Peace. The demonstrators demanded democratization. Students from other parts of the country arrived to join what came to be called the "democracy movement," and ordinary citizens lent their support. The demonstrations mounted in intensity. At one point a statue of the Goddess of Liberty (its name and Phrygian cap recalling both the American and French revolutions) appeared. For seven weeks the demonstrators brought the capital and other parts of the country to a standstill. At the height of the ferment as many as a million people were massed in and around Tiananmen Square.

Tiananmen Square

For a time the party seemed likely to accede to some demands. Zhao Ziyang, who had succeeded Hu as party leader, pressed for conciliation. But Deng, who took the side of the hard-liners, would not tolerate a recurrence of anarchy and turmoil as in the Cultural Revolution, nor permit the continuing embarrassment and humiliation of the party, army, and government. The government imposed martial law. Although their numbers had somewhat declined, the students refused to abandon the square. In the predawn hours of June 4, the army moved in with tanks, trucks, and armored cars and opened fire, with hundreds of victims. Perhaps no government could have tolerated such defiance of law and order and loss of prestige; but even modest concessions, patience, or the exhaustion of the demonstrators might have brought the demonstrations to a peaceful end. The army and the Deng regime now had the people's blood on their hands. Deng's enormous popularity plummeted.

A "Western-inspired conspiracy"

In the repressive atmosphere that followed, Deng and the party attributed the "counterrevolutionary" rebellion to a "Western-inspired conspiracy." For his conciliatory stance Zhao was dismissed from his posts. The new party and government leaders, echoing Deng, alleged that counterrevolutionaries "had attempted to install capitalism in China and make it dependent on certain foreign countries." While the nation still urgently needed Western technology and foreign investment and wished to continue with its "socialist market economy," the party vowed to supervise the private sector closely, reinforce Marxist ideology and political education, and determine the pace and timetable of change. Thousands remained political prisoners, and the government resisted and resented all international pressures for their release.

In the distant past Confucian scholars, trained to enter the emperor's service, accepted the right of the emperor to rule autocratically but reserved the right to criticize harsh or incompetent rule. A ruler governed not by force alone but by moral example, virtue, and rectitude—or risked losing the "mandate of Heaven." The democracy movement brought into question the right of the party to rule in the old way, especially when authoritarianism was itself in decline in other parts of the world. The democracy movement demonstrated how deeply liberal values—"bourgeois liberalism," as it was denounced—had penetrated China and how powerful were the pressures for political change. Continuing economic modernization, even under authoritarian control, could still lead to political liberalization. Fortunes were fickle in China, as Deng's own career demonstrated; moderate leaders might

Pressures for political change

Enormous crowds gathered in Beijing's Tiananmen Square in the spring of 1989 to demand democratic reforms in the Chinese political system. The "democracy movement" drew students and others from many parts of the country. It also generated new political publications and popular symbols, including this statue of a Goddess of Liberty. The statue evoked memories of earlier political revolutions and became a prominent image of the democracy movement. The Chinese government ultimately suppressed the demonstrations by imposing martial law and dispersing the protestors, many of whom were killed or injured when the army opened fire.

(Peter Turnley/Corbis)

reemerge. After the passing of Deng and his aged contemporaries, a new generation was preparing to come to power.

Deng, a shadow of his former self, died in 1997, or as he had said earlier, he "went to meet Marx." His successor Jiang Zemin in some ways proved surprisingly moderate. He had been mayor of Shanghai and hence could distance himself from the events of 1989. He pursued Deng's goals of modernization even more vigorously and sought reconciliation with the West and closer integration into the global economy. Jiang remained the leader of the Communist party until 2002, seeking constantly to develop the Chinese economy and to strengthen China's growing influence as an international trading party. China was admitted to membership in the World Trade Organization in 2001, and Jiang gave Chinese business leaders an increasingly prominent role in the Communist party. Chinese factories (using the comparative advantage of low-wage labor) became leading global exporters of clothing, high-technology equipment, machinery, furniture, and many other products for the international consumer society; and an energetic entrepreneurial class emerged in the prosperous, expanding Chinese cities.

Jiang's economic policies were carried forward by Hu Jintao after he became party leader and in 2003 President of China. The country's dynamic economic development and huge population gave China an increasingly pivotal role in the international economy and political order of the twenty-first century, but the Chinese government was still criticized for human rights abuses, its belligerent stance on reunification with Taiwan, and its failure to develop a more open and democratic political system.

Population Growth in China

On a less dramatic front (beneath the surface of mere "events") the pressure of the expanding population on the economy remained serious. Not irrelevantly, the character for "population" in the Chinese language depicts a mouth. Of all the larger developing countries, however, China was the most successful in coping with population growth.

Population policies

Through a system of central and local control, including forms of outright coercion that Western societies would find difficult to accept, a one-child-per-family rule, massive education programs, and social pressures, the birth rate declined significantly. In the years of relative prosperity under Deng and his successors the government found it difficult to enforce the one-child rule because affluent families, both in the city and countryside, were willing to risk fines for having more than one child. Nor were contraceptive devices always the most modern or most efficient. Yet on balance the program was effective.

In 1982 the Chinese population passed the 1 billion mark, and it was still growing at the rate of 15 million annually in the early twenty-first century, reaching 1.3 billion by 2005. The need to feed, clothe, and house this immense population at rising consumption levels made enormous demands on the economy, no matter how modernized, and on the country's natural resources.

The dramatic growth in China's international trade and economic production demonstrated that international rivalries and conflicts had moved beyond the bipolar divisions that had shaped global politics as well as the global economy in the decades after 1945. Meanwhile, the Cold War threat of communist expansion, which had so preoccupied Western governments from the 1940s to the 1980s, rapidly disappeared in a series of revolutionary changes that swept through Eastern Europe in 1989—creating an unexpected upheaval that foreshadowed the collapse of the Soviet Union itself.

For interactive exercises, glossary, chronologies, and more, go to the *Online Learning Center* at **www.mhhe.com/palmer10.**

Chapter *26*

THE INTERNATIONAL REVOLT AGAINST SOVIET COMMUNISM

The world was astonished in the mid-1980s to see some of the basic structures of Soviet communism, as they had evolved since the Russian Revolution of 1917, begin to come apart. It was equally surprised by a series of extraordinary events in 1989 in central and eastern Europe, where the existing Communist regimes collapsed one by one and were replaced with virtually no violence. In an even more epochal event in 1991, the Communist regime of the Soviet Union itself, in power for 74 years, ended; and the U.S.S.R. disintegrated into Russia and its other component republics.

In a strict sense there was no actual revolution in 1989–1991, and indeed it was a source of wonder and satisfaction that such sweeping change could occur without armed struggle. The older regimes disappeared less by explosion than by implosion—a breakup from within. The "revolution" could remain peaceful because it faced no strong internal resistance or threat of foreign intervention. Yet the upheavals were revolutionary in that they demolished existing repressive authorities and brought abrupt, radical change. They reasserted ideals that were revolutionary when proclaimed in America in 1776, in France in 1789, throughout Europe in 1848, and in the West in 1919 and 1945 and were now called human rights and civil society. These ideals had been incorporated into the American Declaration of Independence and the French Declaration of the Rights of Man, and they had become the guiding ideals for democracies in most of the modern world. Democracy meant representative and constitutional government and freely contested elections; and freedom and independence meant guarantees against repression by one's own government or dictatorial foreign rule. Such ideas were now invoked again to support the new political revolutions of 1989.

With the Revolution of 1989 the people of central and eastern Europe could decide their own destiny. With the collapse of the U.S.S.R. one of the two superpowers that had dominated international affairs since 1945 disappeared. The Cold War, as the world had known it, came to an end, even if Russia remained a large and important power. A new

Chapter emblem: Germans destroying the Berlin Wall in November 1989. (Getty Images)

global political era opened, understandably with new challenges and frustrations, but also with expectations for a more peaceful international order.

125. THE CRISIS IN THE SOVIET UNION

Neither the transformation of central and eastern Europe nor of the Soviet Union could have taken place as they did without the changes in the U.S.S.R. that began in 1985. It is not easy to explain how the reformist Soviet leader Mikhail S. Gorbachev could have risen to supreme power from within the Soviet system except that the country was in dire straits and the party leadership itself was desperate. As a young man Gorbachev studied at the university in Moscow and at the agricultural institute in Stavropol, his home city in south-western Russia. After working as an agricultural researcher, he received a full-time party assignment in the region and came to the attention of Yuri V. Andropov (soon to be the party general secretary) and other party leaders in Moscow. His appointment to the party secretariat in Moscow in 1978, with special responsibility for agriculture, afforded him a privileged view of the country's deep economic troubles. By 1980 he was a member of the Politburo, and by 1984 he was being groomed by Andropov for top party leadership. After the frustrating experience of an incapacitated Brezhnev clinging to power and of Andropov and Konstantin U. Chernenko, his two successors, dying in office after only brief terms, the Politburo in March 1985 decided that it was time for a more forceful, younger leader. At 54, Gorbachev was by far its youngest member. Andrei Gromyko, for many years foreign minister of the U.S.S.R., ultimately endorsed Gorbachev and is said to have reassured those with doubts: "He has a nice smile but he has iron teeth."

Gorbachev at once demonstrated a dynamism and vigor that had been absent from recent Soviet leadership. His first task was to convince the party and country of the need

Perestroika

for fundamental economic restructuring if economic stagnation was to be overcome—*perestroika* he called it. By *perestroika* he meant a drastic modification of the centrally planned command economy inherited from Stalin and carried forward with only minor changes since. However well the older system had served the industrialization of the country, the test of the Second World War, and postwar reconstruction, it was ill-suited for the contemporary industrial world. Industry and agriculture urgently needed freedom from restraints to release creative energies, provide incentives for productivity, raise quality levels, and satisfy consumer needs. Gorbachev's proposed remedies were decentralization; self-management for industry and agriculture; an end to the rigidity imposed by the party and government bureaucracy; and incentives for productivity. He moved cautiously, believing that exhortation and a sense of urgency would bring results, but his appeals and initial moderate reforms quickly clashed with the vested interests of the entrenched bureaucrats.

For his economic restructuring to succeed, Gorbachev had to have the support of the

Glasnost

country, which he hoped to win through political change. Thus he also called for *glasnost,* or "openness," which he closely linked to economic reform. By *glasnost* he meant the right to voice the need for change, the freedom to criticize the existing system, and the willingness even to reexamine past mistakes and wrongdoings. Even if it originally had a more limited objective, *glasnost* soon took on a dynamic of its own. It led to an unprecedented liberalization of Soviet society, a freer press, and an end to the decades of totalitarian control over political, cultural, and intellectual life. The ferment choked off after Khrushchev's "thaw" was reborn. Newspapers, theater, the arts, and political discourse opened up as at no time before. Books and plays written in the 1960s or earlier but never permitted publication or performance made their appearance, including Pasternak's *Dr. Zhivago* and eventually even Solzhenitsyn's *Gulag Archipelago,* the novel that gave the outside world the name for Stalin's network of forced labor camps. Gorbachev permitted the physicist Andrei Sakharov, a leading dissenter and committed opponent of the regime, to return to Moscow from exile and take an active part in political life. Soviet Jews, who had earlier been refused permission to leave the country, were allowed to emigrate in larger numbers. The atmosphere changed visibly. People became freer and less fearful. The legal codes were revised to encompass a measure of civil liberties, allow freedom of expression, and reduce police abuses. The KGB itself came under public and legislative scrutiny. Gorbachev even spoke of freedom of conscience and tolerance for religion, negotiating a rapprochement with the Orthodox church.

In 1987, on the very occasion of the 70th anniversary of the Bolshevik Revolution, Gorbachev spoke openly of "Stalin's enormous and unforgivable crimes." A monument to Stalin's victims was planned, while the press openly discussed their total number, clearly in the tens of millions. New history textbooks were prepared, as well as a revised history of the party. Gorbachev told the country that there should be "no forgotten names or blanks in history or literature."

Although Gorbachev did not challenge the role of the Communist party as the directing agent of Soviet society, he was clearly introducing changes that would curb its monopoly on power. Remembering how Khrushchev had been dislodged after only a few years, he set out to mobilize a wide popular base for himself. Reform could not simply be imposed from above. The people, he said, needed more than a "good tsar." Constitutional reforms in 1988 created a new national legislature, and multicandidate elections were to replace the traditional one-party slate of nominees. What began as a technocratic vision of a more efficient economy was moving the country to a sweeping transformation of Soviet life and society.

Gorbachev's constitutional reforms

In the freer atmosphere the government released long-suppressed information about poor grain harvests, inefficient state enterprises, and nuclear accidents before the disaster at Chernobyl in 1986. At party meetings and at the new Congress of People's Deputies the public heard for the first time outspoken critiques of Soviet society: descriptions of poverty, corruption, crime, alcoholism, and drugs; of serious shortcomings in medicine, health, and housing; of environmental decay. Tens of millions, perhaps one-fifth the population, lived in poverty.

Gorbachev soon recognized that the country's economic problems were more intractable than he had thought, but he persisted with his gradualist reform program. Private enterprise and state industries were one day to be integrated into a market-based economy, linked to the outside world. Foreign capital for trade and investment and joint ventures with foreign firms were to be welcomed. Soviet managers were encouraged to travel abroad to learn advanced (sometimes elementary) business and accounting practices. But many of these reforms remained paper decrees only; party officials and government bureaucrats helped checkmate others. The older economic system remained virtually unchanged. Gorbachev shrank from moving more rapidly to a market-oriented competitive economy. His concerns about painful short-term dislocations and political unrest reinforced his commitment to reform rather than abandon the older system in its entirety.

Limited economic reforms

Gorbachev's reforms in agriculture also fell far short of what was needed. Accepting the existing structure of state and collective farms, he did little more than allow them greater managerial autonomy. Production did not rise. Belatedly, he launched a more extensive agrarian policy. Farmers and farm families would be permitted to work with state and collective farms on a share-crop basis, or farm their own land. They could lease land for their lifetime and even bequeath this right to their children. But the state remained the legal owner of the land—not as in China, where Deng had at the very beginning of his reforms dismantled the collective farms, returned the land outright to the farmers, and reaped the benefit in increased production. Despite Gorbachev's overtures to small independent farmers, little more than one percent of the land shifted to private hands.

The party's grip loosened

But the constitutional and political changes he had initiated significantly loosened the monopoly grip of the party. In March 1989 openly contested, multicandidate elections were held, the first since 1917, though well over half the seats were reserved for the party and various state-sponsored associations. Voters elected a Congress of People's Deputies, which in turn chose a smaller standing legislative body to meet more frequently. Both were empowered to initiate legislation and freely debate issues. In 1990, under another constitutional reform, the Congress of People's Deputies created a presidency with broad executive powers modeled on the American and French examples. The Congress elected Gorbachev president.

Criticisms of Gorbachev

Gorbachev brought about stunning political changes, unprecedented in the years since the revolution. Western political leaders in the era of the Great Depression had sought to save capitalism by reforming it. Gorbachev was likewise bent on saving the Communist system by reform. Yet the country remained divided and disoriented. It was torn between the old guard, who resisted the Gorbachev changes, and a growing group of democratic reformers in the central legislature and in the newly elected parliaments of the restless component republics who believed that Gorbachev had not gone far enough in either political or economic matters. As time went by, praise for his policies gave way to criticism for the continuing dismal economic record; his indecisive, sometimes contradictory, steps in shaping a market economy; and his reluctance to revamp the collectivized agricultural system. He also seemed determined to repress ethnic unrest and was rejecting the demands of the constituent republics for greater freedom from central control. The military, the industrial bureaucrats, and the party were still in command.

The loosening of totalitarian controls unleashed long-suppressed ethnic tensions in the country. Azerbaijan and Armenia fought over a disputed enclave within Azerbaijan, where the majority of the inhabitants were Armenian; violence also flared up in Georgia and elsewhere. Every one of the 15 federated constituent republics of the Soviet Union began to raise demands for independence. Secessionist pressures understandably went furthest in the three Baltic republics. People in Latvia, Lithuania, and Estonia remembered their 20 years of independence between the two world wars; how they had fallen victim to the Nazi-Soviet pact of 1939; and how one-third of their population had been killed, deported, or driven into exile in the war and postwar years. In the freer atmosphere of *glasnost,* the constituent republics, which had come to consider themselves trapped within the Soviet empire, were able to denounce Soviet control. For his part Gorbachev was willing to create a federation council to advise on matters relating to the republics but would not risk the wrath of the old guard by going beyond that.

Mikhail Gorbachev advocated economic and cultural reforms that came to be known in general terms as the call for *glasnost*, or "openness," and *perestroika*, or "structural reforms." Gorbachev expected the reforms to benefit agriculture as well as the industrial sector of the Soviet economy, and he campaigned for his program among both farmers and workers. He is shown here (smiling, on the left) during a meeting with potato farmers near Moscow in 1987. Such contacts with people in the countryside affirmed the spirit of *glasnost*, but the reforms on state-owned farms did not go far enough to bring about a rise in agricultural production. (TASS/SOVFOTO)

Gorbachev and the West

As the new era evolved, Communist ideology and the view of world affairs that had helped to create and prolong the Cold War were also transformed. Gorbachev repudiated ideological struggle. He cited the progress of science and technology as requiring "a different road to the future." In an interdependent globe besieged by nuclear, ecological, and economic dangers, the highest concern must be "universal human interests" and the "universal human idea." Since Marx and Lenin had taught their followers to reject "universal" ideals as a smoke screen for class rule and oppression, the turnabout was startling.

Gorbachev changed the image of the Soviet Union as a military threat and promoter of world revolution. He became a familiar and popular figure in Western capitals as a negotiator, diplomat, and often Western-style politician. He followed his conciliatory words with deeds. He removed troops and weapons from eastern Europe, negotiated nuclear arms reduction agreements with the United States, ended the war in Afghanistan, and helped to resolve Cold War regional conflicts. And he accepted, even encouraged, reforms in eastern Europe,

Encouraging détente

probably not foreseeing how far they would go. He spoke up for human rights, paid tribute to the standards embodied in the Helsinki accords, and called for a "common European home" for western and eastern Europe. The Cold War of the post-1945 years, which had been brought on, or intensified, by Soviet revolutionary ideology and expansionism—which in turn had led to the American containment policy and countercrusade—gave promise of ending. For Gorbachev, as a matter of policy, détente and arms reduction were essential to relieve the intolerable military burden on the Soviet economy; détente went hand in hand with domestic reform. From their low point in the early 1980s Soviet–United States relations abruptly changed after 1985. A new and more genuine spirit of détente emerged, holding out higher expectations for peace and disarmament than at any time since 1945.

Early in the Reagan administration, in 1981, Soviet-American discussions had resumed on strategic arms limitations, but in an atmosphere of mistrust, suspicion, and continuing arms buildup. Especially disturbing was the deployment in eastern Europe in the late 1970s of new Soviet intermediate-range nuclear missiles capable of reaching targets within a radius of 600 to 1,500 miles. Together with its European allies the United States had reinforced existing defenses in western Europe with equally modern American nuclear missiles while simultaneously pressing the Soviets to reduce or remove theirs. The construction of the American missile sites touched off mass popular protest demonstrations in western Europe, but the West European governments remained firm in their support. In Reagan's first term of office he had not met with the incapacitated Brezhnev or with either of the two ailing Soviet leaders who in quick succession followed him. But in 1985, after the emergence of Gorbachev, the possibilities for arms limitation opened up. Unlike his predecessors, Gorbachev seemed to view détente as a means to help the ailing Soviet economy and as an essential diplomatic process for avoiding catastrophe in the nuclear age. For his part, Reagan, confident that the United States had rebuilt its own military strength, held four summit meetings with Gorbachev over the next two and a half years.

End of the Cold War

At their third meeting, in Washington in December 1987, the two presidents made a remarkable breakthrough by consenting to remove the intermediate-range missiles each had installed in Europe. Gorbachev agreed also to reduce the number of short-range nuclear missiles. The Soviets were willing to destroy over four times as many missiles as the United States. Even more unprecedented was the Soviet willingness to permit the United States to verify the destruction of the weapons—the on-site verification which had long been a stumbling block to arms reduction. Finally, the two leaders agreed to continue negotiations on the reduction of strategic, or long-range, nuclear weapons.

In summit meetings in Washington and Moscow, the two presidents had closer contact with each other's people than ever before. Gorbachev mingled with throngs in crowded Washington streets. Reagan, in the shadow of Lenin's tomb in Moscow, spoke openly about the Soviet repression of dissidents, the refusal to permit Jews to emigrate, religious persecution, and the ongoing war in Afghanistan. Gorbachev in turn committed his country to the withdrawal of Soviet troops from Afghanistan—a "bleeding wound" he called it. Meanwhile Gorbachev lent encouragement to the vast changes taking place in eastern Europe. In 1990 Gorbachev and President George H. W. Bush, Reagan's successor, could jointly hail the end of the Cold War. In 1991 they signed a strategic arms treaty pledging each nation to scale down by about a third its arsenal of long-range nuclear missiles.

126. THE COLLAPSE OF COMMUNISM IN CENTRAL AND EASTERN EUROPE

Meanwhile in the mid-1980s central and eastern Europe remained under Stalinist-type party bosses, some in office for over 30 years, impervious to pressure for reform. But cracks and fissures were apparent even before Gorbachev's reforms in the Soviet Union. The years of détente had already opened up the East European states to Western loans and investments and to closer contacts with the West. Dissidents called for a recognition of the human rights guaranteed by the Helsinki accords in 1975, to which the Soviet Union and the East European bloc had subscribed. They wrote about ending party-state dictatorships and the restoration one day of a "civil society," in which people could live their lives free from the dictates of the state.

As in the Soviet Union itself, East Europeans discussed the short-comings of their centrally planned economies, which had stagnated since the 1970s. Initiative and productivity were stifled, and large subsidies propped up inefficient state-run monopolies unchallenged by competi-
Economic stagnation

tion. The older plants and industrial infrastructure were decaying; the environment was deteriorating. A scarcity of investment capital prevented the growth of new industries. Only in Hungary had decentralizing reforms and tentative steps toward a market economy been adopted. In East Germany, the showcase for achievements under central planning, economic growth had slowed and consumer goods were scarce. Even if state-run planned economies were to continue, many argued for new market competition, incentives for entrepreneurs and workers, and encouragement of joint ventures with the outside capitalist world.

Poland: The Solidarity Movement

In the 1970s and 1980s demands for economic reform and political liberalization surfaced almost everywhere, but nowhere so forcefully as in Poland. Gomulka, who governed Poland for 14 years after 1956, disappointed the reformers. He used troops to put down strikes, persecuted church leaders, and in 1968 permitted an anti-Semitic campaign against the small number of Jews still living in Poland. In 1970, after riots over food prices, the party replaced him with the reform-minded Edmund Gierek, who embarked on an ambitious economic development program, financed by heavy borrowing from the West. The initial results were promising, but to meet its rising debt obligations, the country expanded exports at the expense of domestic consumption. Economic conditions steadily deteriorated.

In 1980 the rise in food prices led to widespread strikes, which began in the Lenin shipyards in Gdansk and spread rapidly. A somewhat freer political atmosphere made it possible for workers to create an aggressive independent trade union federation, Solidarity, the first of its kind in any Communist country. It found a militant leader and national symbol of protest in Lech Walesa. Before long Solidarity claimed a national membership of 10 million industrial and agricultural workers.
Lech Walesa

With church backing, its leaders called for free elections and a role for Solidarity in government. The Soviets, then still in the Brezhnev era, once again saw a socialist regime threatened. They put heavy pressure on the Polish government and party to curb Solidarity, oust Gierek, and install the dependable and steely General Jaruzelski as party head and premier. When strikes and demonstrations continued, raising the threat of Soviet military intervention, Jaruzelski in 1981 imposed martial law, banned Solidarity, and arrested its leaders.

But once the power of Solidarity was curbed and the Soviet threat of intervention passed, Jaruzelski himself took a different tack. To placate labor he lifted martial law and initiated a reform program of his own. International pressure also contributed to liberalization. John Paul II, the first Polish pope to head the Roman Catholic church, inspired huge demonstrations for freedom during visits to Poland after his elevation to the papacy in 1978; and Lech Walesa was honored with a Nobel Peace Prize in 1983.

Jaruzelski's efforts at economic reform failed to improve the economy or mollify widespread resentments. Meanwhile, in the later 1980s, Gorbachev's liberalizing reforms in the Soviet Union encouraged further reforms in Poland and suggested that the Soviets would not intervene to check liberalization in eastern Europe. The growing recognition that the "Brezhnev Doctrine" was dead even encouraged a movement for reform within the Polish Communist party itself.

In 1989 Jaruzelski and the party leadership permitted parliamentary elections, in which Solidarity and other groups were free to put forward candidates, although the Communist party was guaranteed a fixed number of seats. The first open elections in Poland in over 40 years gave Solidarity a landslide victory in all contested seats. A Solidarity-led coalition cabinet was formed in which the Communists were a minority. The party took steps to transform itself into a Western-type socialist party, but many of its members drifted away. The party-state dictatorship ended without bloodshed. The dike in eastern Europe was breached.

Reforms within the party

The new government moved at once to restructure the economy along free-market lines. Sharp differences emerged between Lech Walesa, elected president in 1990, and his one-time political allies; and former Communists soon returned to the political scene, but Poland was henceforth in charge of its own destiny.

Hungary: Reform into Revolution

In Hungary the attempt at reform in 1956, initiated by the Communist party leadership itself, had been brusquely interrupted when the Soviets intervened with troops and tanks to suppress the "counterrevolution." Imre Nagy, the party leader, and other leaders of the revolt were hanged. For the next 32 years, hard-liner János Kádár ran the country. But even under Kádár the party, without relinquishing its monopoly on political control, moved away from an inflexible centrally planned economy, encouraged a degree of private enterprise, and turned to the West for capital investment. For a time the economy expanded and standards of living rose, but the limited reforms accomplished no fundamental change. After 1985, in the wake of Gorbachev's reforms in the Soviet Union, some of which were modeled on the Hungarian example itself, a new drive for political and social change began to develop.

In 1988 the party, eager to encourage change and still maintain power, eased Kádár out of office. The new leadership opened the way to opposition parties and multiparty elections and began to dismantle the older party-state apparatus. It dissolved the Communist party, reconstituting it along socialist and social–democratic lines, and a wide range of independent political groups came forward. Reform, initiated by the party itself, had turned into revolution, and without bloodshed. The new leaders reclaimed the 1956 uprising as a progressive movement and for-

Party initiatives

The independent Polish trade union movement, Solidarity, gained the support of millions of workers in the early 1980s. Solidarity organized strikes and demonstrations, demanding better wages for workers and major reforms in the Communist political system. These demonstrators gathered to support Solidarity at a rally outside the court buildings in Warsaw in November 1980. The Solidarity movement was suppressed after martial law was imposed the following year, but the Polish Communist party could never destroy the movement's popular appeal. Solidarity eventually won control of Poland's first new government in free elections that took place at the end of the decade.
(Getty Images)

mally condemned those who had invited Soviet intervention. Nagy's body was exhumed from a mass grave and given a hero's reburial. By sweeping aside the humiliation of 1956, the country reasserted its national independence, restored self-government and civic freedom, and opened the way to a market-oriented economy and a pluralist democracy.

The developments in Hungary precipitated even more dramatic events. The new Hungary, looking westward, symbolically demolished a portion of the barbed-wire barrier on its Austrian border. A few months later, in September 1989, when large numbers of East Germans vacationing in Hungary sought to emigrate to the West, Hungary opened its border with Austria and allowed the Germans to exit. For the first time since 1961 East Germans found a safe way to leave their country.

The German Democratic Republic: Revolution and Reunification

Given Gorbachev's positive attitude toward reform, it was understandable that the pace of change in eastern Europe would accelerate, but neither he nor anyone else could have anticipated its full dimensions. In the four hard-line dictatorships—the German Democratic Republic, Czechoslovakia, Bulgaria, and Romania—there still appeared to be little chance for a Communist sharing of power in the spring of 1989, let alone a revolutionary transformation. Yet by the end of that year the Communist regimes had fallen in all of these countries.

In the German Democratic Republic Erich Honecker, in power since 1961, stubbornly held the line against reform. Although the country boasted the strongest economy and highest per capita income in eastern Europe, its citizens enjoyed far fewer amenities than the West Germans. The Berlin Wall built in 1961 still barred their exodus to the West. Even though Honecker had agreed after 1970 to the closer economic and political relations with West Germany initiated by Willy Brandt's *Ostpolitik* in 1969, he refused to relax controls at home. But the East Germans excitedly watched the Gorbachev changes in the Soviet Union and the rush of events in Poland and Hungary. When in the autumn of 1989 Hungary opened the way for them to leave, thousands seized the opportunity. The trickle soon became a flood. The East Germans, many of them skilled workers and professionals, fled the repression and drabness of the German Democratic Republic for the Federal Republic of Germany, where as Germans they were entitled by law to receive citizenship and assistance in finding homes and jobs. By the end of 1989, 350,000 of East Germany's population of 17 million had left, and many more emigrated in the early months of 1990.

Flight from Honecker's rule

When demonstrations against the East German government mounted, Gorbachev clearly signaled that Honecker could not expect the Soviet troops stationed in East Germany to save the regime, and he even warned against the use of force to prevent reform. In Leipzig, over 100,000 demonstrators, assembling in churches, marched in solemn procession with lighted candles, calling for the resignation of party and government leaders and for an end to the police state. The party forced Honecker to resign.

The new leadership promised elections and confirmed the right of free and unrestricted travel. On November 9, 1989, when the government opened up the hated symbol of confinement itself, the Berlin Wall, excited Berliners on both sides of the barrier tore it down. The exodus to West Germany continued. By now even the new freedom of movement, the end of censorship, the new parliamentary supervision over the state security police, and the pledge of free elections did not suffice. Many East Germans were infuriated by public disclosure of the corruption and luxurious living that Honecker and the party elite had enjoyed while ordinary people suffered over the years. The entire party structure now came crashing down. The Politburo and Central Committee resigned. Honecker and other leaders were arrested on charges of corruption and embezzlement, and younger reformers assumed control. Delegates from a wide variety of opposition groups, exultant over their "gentle" revolution, met with reform-minded representatives of the former Communist party to oversee the transition to a new constitutional regime, which many still envisaged as a socialist but democratic society.

Corruption within the party

Once the German Democratic Republic was no longer Communist, however, pressure for reunification began to build. Helmut Kohl, the Christian Democratic chancellor in West Germany, took the initiative to reunite the two Germanys. For many of the wartime Allies the prospect of a reunified Germany of close to 80 million people, possessing one of the world's most powerful economies, stirred grim ghosts of the past. The "German question" resurfaced. The entire postwar settlement stood at issue. Since no final peace treaty had ever been signed, reunification required the approval of the four major Allied powers of the Second World War. There was hesitation, especially in France and Britain, but it was difficult, as the Americans argued, to deny the German people the right of self-determination 45 years after the end of the war. Moreover, the Federal Republic of Germany had demonstrated its commitment to democracy. There was confidence that a reunified Germany could integrate East Germany and remain part of democratic western Europe and the European Community. Despite the unspeakable crimes of the Nazi era, it seemed unreasonable to insist upon unalterable traits of national character or to punish future generations for atrocities of the past.

The "German question" revived

Reunification moved forward swiftly. The four Allied powers, including the U.S.S.R., gave their approval and relinquished their occupation rights. Germany confirmed the earlier cession of territories in the east to the U.S.S.R. and Poland and pledged the inviolability of the German-Polish border. The two German states merged their economies and the West German mark became the common currency. On October 3, 1990, the two states formally united to become an enlarged Federal Republic of Germany, its capital to be reestablished within a few years in Berlin. In the first nationwide elections, Chancellor Kohl and his Christian Democrats, who played a key role in the reunification, won a sweeping victory. Although the postelection exhilaration was soon tempered by the gigantic problems of modernizing and absorbing the thoroughly decayed East German economy, Germany had been reunited under democratic auspices.

Czechoslovakia: "'89 is '68 Upside Down"

In Czechoslovakia the ruling hard-liners who took power after Soviet military forces had ruthlessly crushed the "Prague spring" in 1968 disapproved of Gorbachev's reforms in the Soviet Union and stifled dissent at home. But the dissidents quietly grew in numbers and influence. Charter '77, an organization of intellectuals formed after the Helsinki accords of 1975, became a rallying point for the struggle against the dictatorship. The Czech public followed with intense interest the disintegration of Communist power in Poland, Hungary, and East Germany. When demonstrations broke out in the autumn of 1989, the government arrested the dissident leaders, but thousands of demonstrators in Prague called for the release of the imprisoned dissidents and for the government's resignation. Reformers came together in a loose coalition and found inspiring leadership in the dissident writer Vaclav Havel, an outspoken opponent of the regime who had repeatedly suffered persecution and imprisonment for his views.

The demonstrations grew in intensity. When 350,000 demonstrators in Prague on November 24 furiously demanded an end to the party-state dictatorship and a general strike threatened to bring the country to a standstill, the government and party leaders all at once resigned. Alexander Dubček, the hero of 1968, dramatically appeared on a balcony alongside a new reform-minded Communist prime minister, who appointed opposition leaders to his cabinet, pledged a free press and free elections, dissolved the secret police, and abolished the compulsory teaching of Marxism-Leninism in the universities.

The destruction of the Berlin Wall in November 1989 provided dramatic physical and symbolic evidence of the collapse of Communist regimes in eastern Europe. Young people shattered the Wall in a great celebration that released long-suppressed political anger and marked the culmination of a nonviolent revolution in East Germany. Within a year, the two postwar German states were united in a new, enlarged Federal Republic of Germany, which faced the social and economic challenges of bringing two different societies into an integrated national political system.
(Robert Wallis/Sipa Press)

The party's 41-year monopoly on power ended. Havel became provisional president and led a new cabinet in which the Communists were a minority. Gorbachev took steps to withdraw the 75,000 Soviet troops stationed in the country since 1968. In the excitement someone exultantly observed: "'89 is '68 upside down." The people had wrested control without bloodshed in a "velvet" revolution that liberated the country.

A "velvet revolution"

Of all the nations in the Eastern bloc Czechoslovakia had the strongest democratic tradition. Despite long-standing ethnic tensions, it had developed a genuine parliamentary democracy in the interwar years and was the last of the East European states to fall under Communist dictatorship after the Second World War. Even though its economy was one of the strongest of the Eastern bloc, it lagged far behind the West and required large infusions of capital to modernize its older technology. It moved rapidly toward a market-oriented economy and a pluralist democracy—the civil society that Havel, now elected president of the republic, and others had sought. But an unexpected political sequel followed within three years. The country came apart when Slovak political leaders pressed for an independent Slovakia, which some had wanted since 1918. A negotiated settlement arranged for the peaceful division of the country in January 1993 into two independent and sovereign nations—the Czech Republic and Slovakia.

Bulgaria's Palace Revolution, Bloodshed in Romania

Even Bulgaria, considered the most docile of the Soviet client states, succumbed to the new revolutionary contagion. Mass demonstrations in Sofia demanded an end to the Communist dictatorship, and pressure from within the party forced the resignation of the party chief who had run the country for 35 years. His foreign minister, who replaced him, pledged parliamentary elections, economic reforms, and an end to the party's absolute control of power. New political groups emerged, fragmented yet strong enough to press for reform.

The revolution in Bulgaria was essentially a palace coup within the party, but it, too, arose in response to deep mass resentments. In a country that had known little freedom even in the pre-Communist years, the question was whether the reform-minded former Communists who, like many others elsewhere, renamed themselves Socialists, could work together with the new opposition to create a true democracy.

Only in Romania did events take a violent turn in 1989. It seemed at first as though the revolution would not even reach Bucharest. Since 1965, the dictator Nicolae Ceausescu had firmly controlled party and government, ruling with the help of his wife and family and building a cult of personality around himself. He remained isolated in a rigid autocracy with a large private security force, which he favored over the regular army. His Stalin-like ambition was to transform a backward agrarian society into a modern industrial society regardless of the human cost. For his modernization program he borrowed heavily from the West, but to remain independent of the outside world he insisted that the country regularly pay the burdensome interest on its debt. He used state resources to build an enormous presidential palace. All dissent was kept under tight surveillance and control. What was distinctive about Ceausescu was his break from Moscow and his independent position in foreign and military affairs. Unlike the other members of the Warsaw Pact, he had supported Israel in the Arab-Israeli wars and had refused to join the invasion of Czechoslovakia in 1968.

The Ceausescu regime

Throughout the revolutionary autumn of 1989 Ceausescu ignored the upheavals in central and eastern Europe. But in December protest riots broke out in Timisoara, a key provincial capital. The military refused to fire on the demonstrators, but the dictator's security forces took over, killing hundreds. Word of the brutality spread, sparking new protests. When the security forces attempted to suppress demonstrators in Bucharest, angry crowds forced the dictator to flee the capital.

Ceausescu's security forces

For days a battle raged between the security forces and regular army units supporting the revolutionists until the security forces were routed. Ceausescu and his wife were apprehended in the provinces and executed by a firing squad. A National Salvation Front, consisting of former officials of the Ceausescu regime and emergent opposition leaders, took control. Although former Communists dominated the new regime and the strength of the democratic forces remained limited, the party's authority ended and the most repressive dictatorship of the Eastern bloc came to an ignominious end.

The Revolutions of 1989 in Central and Eastern Europe

Except in Romania, the revolution was carried out everywhere by placards and candles, not by rifles. Solidarity's early struggle in Poland and Gorbachev's liberalization in the Soviet Union made it possible for revolutionary changes in central and eastern Europe to take place as they did. With a suddenness that took even the closest observers by surprise, smoldering discontents flared up all at once. Gorbachev, committed to curtailing economic and military obligations for the sake of the Soviet economy, accepted the end of the Communist regimes imposed by Stalin after the Second World War.

The groundwork for change had been prepared by the growing economic ties and contacts with the West during the years of détente, the Helsinki accords, the stubborn challenge of Solidarity, and the courage of the dissidents. But it was Gorbachev's clear signal that the Soviets would not intervene outside their own borders that made the stupendous chain of revolutionary events possible, toppling one regime after another. The dramatic flight of the East Germans symbolized the desire of all eastern Europe to escape from behind the iron curtain. The revolutionists, armed only with a moral cause, would have found it difficult to prevail if any of their own governments had chosen to use the full power of the army and police. The repression at Tiananmen Square in China in June 1989 might have been repeated in eastern Europe. But the ruling elites, without Soviet support to bolster them, yielded; they simply lacked the will to govern under a system that had lost legitimacy and credibility, even among those who controlled it.

Gorbachev's decisive role

127.   THE COLLAPSE OF THE SOVIET UNION

Before the stunning developments in eastern Europe could be fully absorbed, an even more epochal event occurred. An all but bloodless revolution brought the collapse of communism in 1991 in the very epicenter of world communism, undoing the Russian Revolution of 1917 and ending three-quarters of a century of Communist party rule. The Union of Soviet Socialist Republics, heir to the one-time tsarist empire, dissolved into its component republics. Russia reemerged.

How did this collapse of a seemingly impregnable regime with a heavy apparatus of military and police security occur? We have already seen how Gorbachev in the years after 1985 opened up Soviet society to revitalize the system but avoided the more decisive measures that might have ended the hegemony of the Communist party. Gorbachev vacillated between the reformers and the hard-line conservatives. A superb political tactician—no one could have brought the party and the system as far as he had—he nonetheless gave the impression that he did not know how thorough a transformation he would ultimately permit. The old guard became further embittered as they witnessed the loss of Soviet control over eastern Europe. Meanwhile the economy worsened, and by 1990 production was in steep decline. Gorbachev tried plan after plan, but the economic structure remained virtually unchanged. In addition, not only the Baltic republics, as might have been expected, but the Russian republic itself and all the other component republics of the U.S.S.R. were pressing for sovereignty—self-government and control over their political and economic fortunes.

The "Creeping Coup d'État"

In the autumn of 1990 Gorbachev again was maneuvering. He replaced reform-minded ministers and other key officials with old-guard appointees unsympathetic to his reform program. He summarily abandoned an important "500-Day" economic plan that would have freed prices and moved more swiftly to a market economy. The plan would also have curtailed the military budget and given broad economic powers to the republics. It now appeared that military force was to be deployed against the secessionist Baltic republics, which earlier, in the spring of 1990, had proclaimed their independence. In January 1991 Soviet troops, apparently taking matters into their own hands without Gorbachev's prior approval, used military force against demonstrators in Lithuania, with a loss of lives; and there was anxiety about where the military might move next.

The democratic reformers grew alarmed by the turn of events. Some spoke of "six wasted years of reform communism" and of a "creeping coup d'état." They had concluded that the country's economic problems could not be resolved short of demolishing the entire central planning structure, and also that each republic must be allowed to work out its own destiny. To the reformers Gorbachev seemed a barrier to further change, and he in turn grew increasingly hostile to them, convinced that he alone knew the proper pace of reform.

Uneasiness of reformers

The democratic reformers turned to a political figure who on the surface seemed an unlikely choice as their leader. Boris N. Yeltsin was blunt and outspoken, not by any definition an intellectual. His personal style made a striking contrast to the suave, smooth, and urbane Gorbachev, but Yeltsin knew the Communist party well, and all its secrets. He had been party boss in Moscow and a member of the Politburo. When in 1987 he openly attacked the privileges, perquisites, and downright incompetence of the party officials, he had been dismissed from his posts, vilified in the press, and sent off into the political wilderness. Humiliated by Gorbachev and the party, he found allies among the democratic reformers, who saw in him a populist figure around whom they could rally public support. They helped polish some of his rough edges, undertook his political reeducation, and converted him into an opposition leader of stature.

Elected to the Soviet legislature in March 1989, he played a key role in the opposition. With the encouragement of his political allies, however, he turned to a new, and seemingly unpromising, power base, the Russian legislature, that is, the legislature of the Russian constituent republic. Elected to it in 1990, he became chairman and used his position to step up his attacks on Gorbachev, the party, and the central government. Then, benefiting from a Gorbachev concession permitting the constituent republics to choose their presidents in direct popular elections, he won election in June 1991 as president of the Russian republic in an overwhelming victory over his Communist opponents—the first president in Russian history to be elected by popular vote. It was a distinction that Gorbachev, elected president of the U.S.S.R. solely by the Soviet Congress, could not claim. (It was at the time of Yeltsin's election that Russia's second largest city voted to change its name from Leningrad back to St. Petersburg, as it had been called before 1914.) From his new position of strength Yeltsin demanded immediate independence for the three Baltic states and self-government for Russia and the other Soviet constituent republics.

Yeltsin becomes opposition leader

Gorbachev, intent on keeping the country and the union intact, began negotiations with the presidents of the republics. He agreed to surrender considerably more autonomy to the 15 republics, including substantial control over the economic and financial resources that Moscow had always tightly guarded. The three Baltic republics, insisting on full independence, refused to participate in the negotiations, as did Georgia, now embroiled in its own internal turmoil. But in August 1991 the Russian republic and eight other constituent republics agreed to sign Gorbachev's "union treaty," which created a framework for the republics to share power within a new political federation.

The Failed August Coup

For the old-guard hard-liners in the party, the military, and the secret police the treaty was the final straw—the end of the union as originally created by Lenin in 1922 after the Bolshevik Revolution of 1917 and the ensuing civil wars. Despite lip service to the sovereignty of the republics and the federal structure set forth in the Soviet constitution, the Soviet Union was from the beginning, and increasingly under Stalin, a Russian-dominated centralized nation, virtually the successor to the empire of the tsars. To abandon the union was more than many of the old guard could tolerate. The day before the treaty was to be signed, a small coterie of eight hard-liners acted to seize power. They included high-ranking party and government functionaries, among them, the head of the KGB and the commander of the Soviet land forces. All key figures were Gorbachev appointees. Several of the plotters, including the chief of Gorbachev's personal cabinet, arrived at Gorbachev's summer home in the Crimea, possibly hoping to win him to their side. When under forced detention he refused to cooperate or yield to pressure, they proclaimed a Committee of State Emergency to replace him.

The *Putschists* expected the coup to be a simple operation. Resistance in the country, they were convinced, could be overcome by a simple show of military strength. But they miscalculated, underestimating the new political forces alive in the country. Gorbachev disavowed the plotters. In Moscow Yeltsin gained additional stature when he rallied the Russian legislature in defense of Gorbachev, warned that anyone supporting the coup would be subject to grave criminal charges, and appealed for popular support against any military show of force. But the assault never came. At least one KGB unit disobeyed orders to attack; other tank units advanced only half-heartedly. There was some sporadic street fighting, and three civilian deaths. The coup failed within four days. The plotters turned out to be feckless and irresolute bunglers. The Central Committee of the party did not speak out during these events, but its silence seemed to sanction the attempted coup.

The failed coup

Gorbachev, his ordeal over, returned to Moscow. He had demonstrated with courage that he was not the prisoner of the old guard and now went further. Because of the party's complicity in the affair, he resigned as general secretary. Yet he still failed to comprehend how far matters had gone. He believed it sufficient only to replace the traitors and "return to the business of reform." Once again he defended "socialism" as "the choice made in 1917" and stressed the need to preserve the unity of the U.S.S.R. so that the country would not fall apart.

Yeltsin dissolves the regime

Yeltsin acted immediately and decisively on an entirely different agenda. As president of the Russian republic, he issued a series of decrees, describing the Communist party as "not a political party but an unlawful apparatus that took over the Soviet state" and denouncing it as "one of the principal villains" in the attempted coup. Suspending its activities throughout the Russian republic, he transferred to the state the party's vast property, along with its files and archives. The Soviet Congress of People's Deputies meeting in Moscow soon validated the decrees for the entire country before voting itself out of existence. In many ways what happened in the aftermath of the failed coup was the culmination of the Gorbachev six-year reform era. But the dissolution of the party-state regime, at Yeltsin's hands, was the revolution.

All that remained of the earlier framework was a federation council consisting of the presidents of the constituent republics, over which Gorbachev continued to preside. It immediately recognized the independence of the three Baltic republics. For the country as a whole Gorbachev still hoped to salvage his older idea, a "union of sovereign states," which, while granting self-government to the republics, would retain a central authority. But the republics pressed for full independence; hostility toward central authority had intensified after the bungled coup. The very party leaders, as in the Ukrainian S.S.R., who themselves once suppressed separatist movements, had by now taken over the leadership of nationalist independence movements.

The Ukrainian S.S.R. proclaimed itself independent as Ukraine (no longer to be referred to as *the* Ukraine) immediately after the August coup. In December, Yeltsin announced that Russia would not remain in the union without Ukraine. Thereupon the three Slavic states—Russia, Ukraine, and Belarus (the new name for Byelorussia), the states that had originally created the Union of Soviet Socialist Republics in December 1922—dissolved it. Gorbachev resigned as president. Yeltsin at once occupied his office in the Kremlin.

The U.S.S.R. dissolves

The other republics of the Soviet Union also agreed to its dissolution. A loose organization called the Commonwealth of Independent States (CIS) consisting of Russia and ten other republics came into existence.[1] The Baltic states had already gone their separate ways. Georgia, still in turmoil, did not join until a few years later. The Union of Soviet Socialist Republics, for close to seven decades the world's largest multinational state, stretching over one-sixth the earth's surface and 11 time zones, with close to 300 million people, one of the world's two superpowers for over 40 years after the Second World War, simply disappeared as a geographic entity. Russia, still the world's largest nation in area and itself a mixture of many peoples, succeeded to the Soviet Union's permanent seat on the UN Security Council.

Gorbachev returned to private life, declaring "the main task" of his life to have been accomplished. He has to be counted as one of the great reformers in history. The "Gorbachev factor," as it has been called, made an immeasurable difference. His tragedy was that he failed to build a new system to replace the communism that he had undermined. He unleashed powerful winds of change that ultimately he could not direct or control. He drastically altered a totalitarian system yet refused to recognize that the demolition of the entire structure was necessary. Eventually he became a danger to the old order and an impediment to the new. Yeltsin, who took undisguised satisfaction in the fall of his once all-powerful rival, said of him:

Gorbachev's legacy

---

[1]The 11 republics affiliating themselves with the Commonwealth of Independent States, created December 25, 1991, as successor to the U.S.S.R. in order of population (with their capitals in parentheses) were as follows: Russian Federation (Moscow), Ukraine (Kiev), Uzbekistan (Tashkent), Kazakhstan (Alma-Ata), Belarus (Minsk), Azerbaijan (Baku), Tajikistan (Dushanbe), Moldova (Chisinau), Kyrgyzstan (Bishkek), Turkmenistan (Ashkhabad), and Armenia (Yerevan). Georgia (Tbilisi) joined in 1993. Former Communist leaders retained control of most of the new governments until the early twenty-first century, when revolutionary, democratizing changes took place in several of the republics.

Boris Yeltsin's firm resistance to an attempted coup against the government of Mikhail Gorbachev by old-guard Communists in August 1991 confirmed Yeltsin's stature as the most popular political figure at the time. He is shown here waving to the huge crowd that gathered outside the Parliament building to show its support for the political reforms that were transforming the Soviet Union. Yeltsin was the first popularly elected president of Russia when it was still part of the U.S.S.R., a position he continued to occupy after the formal dissolution of the Soviet Union in December 1991.
(Reuters/CORBIS)

"We, like the world, respect him for what he did, especially in the first years of *perestroika* beginning with 1985 and 1986." After that, he said, the "errors" began. Russia, predicted George Kennan, one of America's preeminent diplomat-historians and Russian specialists, would eventually regard Gorbachev as the "person who led it out of bondage" even if "he was unable to reach the Promised Land." But it was not yet time to render final historical judgments. For the vast lands and peoples that had once been the Soviet Union, and for Russia and Yeltsin himself in 1991, the future held many uncertainties, a future in which the entire world had an enormous stake.

128.   AFTER COMMUNISM

Marxist-Leninist ideology as the undergirding for one-party dictatorship still persisted at the opening of the twenty-first century in the People's Republic of China, the world's most populous country, and in the smaller states of North Korea, Vietnam, and Cuba. Albania, the last of the Communist regimes in Europe, and the most impoverished, threw off Communist rule in 1991. Yugoslavia's disintegration after the end of communism, as we shall see, unfolded separately. In western Europe, most notably in France, Italy, Spain, and Portugal, once strong Communist parties reexamined their beliefs, at times abandoned the party name, and adapted to changed circumstances. Marxism, born in the mid-nineteenth century in response to the instability and inequities of industrial capitalism, would survive as a scholarly, analytical tool; but it held little or no popular appeal as a political philosophy and program of political action. Proletarian internationalism likewise lost much of its appeal because it had been used to support an ill-concealed Soviet hegemony.

The revolutions of the late twentieth century in the Soviet Union and central and eastern Europe seemed to herald the international triumph of the historic political liberalism of Western societies. The democratic reformers sought free elections, political and civil rights, and respect for human dignity. Their people had too long been the pawns of totalitarian party-state regimes which self-righteously demanded sacrifice and subservience in the name of an ultimate utopia. The reformers objected to the centrally planned bureaucratic command economies, which had deprived almost everyone of decent living standards. They envied the immeasurably more prosperous economies of the United States, western Europe, and elsewhere, even if they, too, had their share of inequalities, economic insecurity, and social and ethnic problems. The official formula that all citizens enjoyed the rights and privileges of an egalitarian "socialist" society had only concealed political repression, economic stagnation, and social immobility. For many, the public revelation of the Communist party elite's special privileges and luxuries proved the final shock.

Triumph of liberalism

The revolutionary changes made possible, but did not guarantee, democratic and pluralist societies in which the citizens themselves through responsible government could shape their political and economic future. The road to democracy and free economies was not an easy one. If democratic governments failed to take root, new authoritarian political parties and repressive governments could reemerge. The revolutionary changes released many ugly currents, ominous for the future—anti-Semitism, xenophobia, chauvinistic nationalism, irredentism—all easily mobilized when discontented people seek scapegoats for their frustrations.

Russia, the other former Soviet republics, and the countries of central and eastern Europe entered a period of difficult transition. In principle, they were transforming their political systems into representative democracies and their centrally planned economies into competitive market economies. But bureaucrats and managers of the old order often remained in control under new labels. Many, especially in Russia, used the knowledge and networks of privileged positions in the older regimes to benefit financially from the newly privatized enterprises. Despite infusions of international aid, the new regimes struggled to cope with the disorienting challenges of a free market, capitalist economy, new technologies, and a global financial system.

Difficult economic and political transitions

The market economy could take many forms. The state had always played a large role in central and eastern Europe. It was unlikely that the new regimes would turn to a pure laissez-faire model of private enterprise, which did not actually exist in even the most capitalist Western economies. Governments would remain actively engaged, seeking to ensure a protective network of social services. As for socialism, marginal as it was in American life, democratic socialism and social democracy still had considerable appeal in Europe.

The Soviet experience had tarnished, even poisoned, the image of socialism; but its egalitarian message retained an attraction when linked to respect for democracy and individual rights as propounded by various European Socialist and Social Democratic parties. Meanwhile all countries with capitalist market economies and democratic political systems, in the West and elsewhere, were challenged to create societies that could overcome economic instability, individual insecurity, unemployment, and gross social and economic injustices. Democracies and market economies offered a means toward desired ends, not final goals in themselves. It was now generally assumed, however, that prosperity and productivity could do far more to overcome social inequities than would-be utopias.

Russia after 1991

At the close of 1991 the Russian flag replaced the Soviet hammer and sickle over the Kremlin. As of January 1, 1992, the Union of Soviet Socialist Republics ceased to exist. The 15 Soviet republics were independent states. Officially, the Russia that emerged from the Soviet Union was the Russian Federation, with 21 "federated republics" of its own and with numerous additional ethnic-based territorial units. With almost twice the land area of the United States and a population of almost 150 million, Russia, even if in desperate economic straits, was still a significant world power.

The most pressing international concern was the nuclear weaponry of the former U.S.S.R. Yeltsin had worked out an agreement with the other former Soviet republics whereby Russia alone was to retain nuclear weapons. Although four-fifths of the nuclear weapons were located on Russian soil, nuclear arms were positioned in Ukraine, Kazakhstan, and Belarus. The United States mediated an agreement under which the three republics consented to dismantle their weapons in return for generous financial reimbursement. Russia for its part soon began the initial stage of dismantling its vast arsenal of strategic weapons in accordance with the arms reduction treaty that had been signed with the United States in 1991.

Nuclear arms

The new Russia, like the Soviet Union in its final stages, faced separatist threats. Several of its "federated republics" adopted their own constitutions, flags, and anthems and before long enjoyed considerable de facto independence from Moscow. Only in the southern Chechen Republic did the secessionist threat become reality, and before long Russia was involved in a brutal, draining war to prevent secession by Chechnya. Meanwhile 25 million Russians who had long made their home in other parts of the former Soviet Union came to be regarded in those places as foreigners and in some instances were treated with hostility.

Separatist pressures

In domestic affairs Yeltsin faced severe economic problems. He and his succession of prime ministers met with little success in making the transition to a market economy. In the first four years of Yeltsin's presidency production declined, the ruble fell in value, and standards of living sank. Life at times seemed more trying for the average citizen than before the collapse of communism. The regional and local governments tended to ignore Moscow and even withheld tax collections. The erosion of government authority contributed to widening corruption and crime throughout the country.

Despite large infusions of capital from the United States and international lending agencies, the Russian economy and financial institutions remained in deep disorder. After temporizing at first, Yeltsin turned to a Western-oriented economist as his key adviser and economics minister in the belief that a swift transition to a market economy would be the least painful course. From late 1991, a flood of decrees deregulated prices, ended or cut subsidies to state-owned industries, and moved forward with privatization. But most Russians suffered a serious decline in living standards by the spring of 1992 while privatization enriched others who bought into former state industries at bargain prices. An industrial and financial oligarchy of "robber barons" developed a system of crony capitalism; and a shadow economy run by mafia-type gangsters appeared on the borderlines of the legal system.

The failure of the economic program intensified Yeltsin's struggle with the legislature, where a mixed group of Communists and nationalists rejected the austerity program and attacked the "elite theorists" who had allowed prices to rise. In the spring of 1993 a frustrated Yeltsin appealed to the country to support a new constitution that would provide for "a strong presidential republic." That September Yeltsin dissolved the legislature and called for new elections as well as for a referendum on his proposed constitution. For two weeks the lawmakers, denouncing the dissolution as "a coup d'État," refused to leave the parliament building. Demonstrators, incited by the legislative leaders, threatened insurrection. Yeltsin felt bound to act. On October 4 tanks fired on the building and set it ablaze. The legislators were evacuated and the leaders were arrested. Over 100 persons died in the confrontation and many more were injured. In point of fact, both sides shared in the blame for the conflict, but the violence showed that Russia was still going through its revolution.

Yeltsin's new constitution

The new constitution, approved in December 1993, gave broad political authority to the president, including the right to dissolve the legislature. A popularly elected lower house, the State Duma, the old name deliberately chosen because of its pre-Soviet roots, replaced the former Congress of People's Deputies. The elections to the new Duma proved a setback for the candidates of the reform parties, who had underestimated popular discontent. The Communist party and its political allies won a good share of the seats. The top popular vote winner, an ultranationalist, Vladimir Zhirinovsky by name, spoke openly in inflammatory rhetoric of reuniting the old Russian empire and reviving Russia's military might.

In a stinging rebuke to Yeltsin, the new Duma in one of its first acts voted amnesty to the legislative leaders arrested in October—and to the hard-line old-guard plotters against Gorbachev in the failed coup of August 1991. Lacking the necessary political support, Yeltsin's ministers abandoned many of the economic reforms and restored government controls on wages, prices, and profits. Yeltsin himself as president now possessed greatly expanded executive powers but diminishing authority. He was showing physical and emotional strain. Erratic and impulsive, with worsening health problems and given to excessive drinking, he was frequently absent from his Kremlin office over the remaining years of his presidency, and at times vanished from public view.

Yeltsin's problems

Meanwhile, Yeltsin's political troubles continued in the Chechen Republic. Chechnya, in the oil-rich Caucasus, its population mostly Islamic, had a long tradition of rebellion and stubborn resistance to Russian domination. In 1991, as the Soviet Union was collapsing, the Chechens had demanded independence, or at least equal partnership with Russia. Militant guerrilla forces now proclaimed independence, but Russia was intent on retaining control of its southern borderlands and the links to central Asia as well as strategic oil resources and pipelines. The threat of a secessionist precedent for other federal republics was also an ongoing concern.

RUSSIAN FEDERATION IN 2000

The map shows the territories of the Russian Federation, the largest and most important of the republics to emerge from the breakup of the former Soviet Union (U.S.S.R.) in 1991. The hatched lines indicate the lands of the other former Soviet republics, which are clustered to the south and west of the Russian Federation. The Federation itself consists of some 21 "federated units," including Chechnya, where the Russians have waged a military campaign to suppress a Chechen independence movement. The vast lands of the Russian Federation make it territorially the largest nation in the world. Much of this land is sparsely populated, however, and Russia's population has been declining. The Federation's 144 million people ranked eighth on the list of the world's most populous nations in 2005.

For three years Yeltsin did nothing except to support covert efforts to overthrow the rebel regime. Suddenly, toward the end of 1994, at the urging of his entourage who saw an opportunity to make political capital out of a quick victory, Yeltsin gave orders to invade Chechnya. In a grievous failure of military intelligence the invasion led to disastrous results. For close to two years the Russian army sank into a frustrating guerrilla war for which its poorly trained conscript army was ill-prepared and ill-equipped. When the army failed to take the capital city of Grozny, the military resorted to air bombing and rockets, killing thousands of civilians. In April 1996 Yeltsin, admitting that the military action in Chechnya was "the greatest mistake" of his first four years as president, withdrew the army. Chechen cities, towns, and villages had been destroyed and some 20,000 to 40,000 of Russia's Chechen citizens had

Chechnya invaded

The Russian military campaign to suppress a secessionist movement in the Republic of Chechnya during the 1990s led to a difficult war against Chechen guerilla forces. The Russian army eventually regained control of Chechen towns and the capital city of Grozny, but only after bombardments had killed thousands of civilians and forced people such as this woman in Grozny to flee from their homes and bombed-out neighborhoods.
(Thomas Dworzak/Magnum Photos)

been killed. The war was widely criticized at home and abroad, and the Chechen independence struggle was not yet over.

In the presidential elections of June 1996 Yeltsin, agile politician that he was, won reelection but only after he was forced into a run-off with the Communist party's candidate. The Chechen war cost Yeltsin some support, but the weak state of the economy was his most serious handicap. The economic stagnation and draining budgetary deficits continued well into Yeltsin's second term. In March 1998 Yeltsin appointed a cabinet of young reformers who in turn met with opposition. Economic difficulties assumed enormous proportions: a deep slide in the ruble, currency devaluation, and default in payments on the country's foreign debt. The International Monetary Fund (IMF) and Western banks stepped in to prevent utter bankruptcy.

The deteriorating economy brought further political instability. Yeltsin made a whole series of short-lived cabinet appointments and changed his prime minister five times in 18 months. Finally, in August 1999, he appointed as his prime minister Vladimir V. Putin, a former intelligence operative who had been stationed in East Germany and then served as head of the domestic security agency, the reorganized KGB. It was transparent that Yeltsin was choosing his successor to run in the presidential elections in 2000.

Putin chosen as successor

Suddenly trouble broke out anew in Chechnya. Chechen guerrillas crossed over into the neighboring republic of Dagestan in an unsuccessful effort to agitate for support. In the fall of 1999 mysterious explosions in Moscow and nearby cities took the lives of some 300 civilians. Prime Minister Putin at once blamed the explosions on Chechen terrorists and the government proceeded to take drastic military measures. Intent on avoiding the costly Russian mistakes of the earlier war, the army launched large-scale air and artillery attacks on the Chechen cities and countryside. The results for the Chechen population were deadly, with a minimal loss of Russian troops. Over 4,000 deaths were reported and over 200,000 refugees were forced to flee their homes. The Chechen capital was destroyed. The United States and its allies condemned the Russian response, but the government's aggressive action was popular in Russia and Putin's decisiveness enhanced his political stature.

On the last day of December 1999 Yeltsin dramatically announced his resignation and, in accordance with the constitution, appointed Putin acting president. The date of the presidential elections was advanced by three months. Yeltsin had found his successor. In the elections that followed in the spring of 2000 Putin readily won election.

Yeltsin left a mixed record. He had not been a pioneering champion of reform in the U.S.S.R. as Gorbachev had been in 1985, but once ousted from the inner circles of the party he allied himself with the reformers. He was the first democratically elected president of the Russian republic while it was still part of the U.S.S.R., and he supported the independence movements of the other Soviet republics. He rallied the population to reject the hard-liners' coup against Gorbachev and became a chief architect of the Soviet Union's dissolution. His efforts to introduce Western-style market reforms met with only limited success. He had supported the disastrous intervention in Chechnya in 1994–1996, which exposed the incompetence of the army and alienated international opinion, and the renewed assault on Chechnya a few years later. In his second term it seemed possible that reforms might turn the economy around, but within two years his economic program was in shambles. Yeltsin enjoyed the trappings of power, but he was uninterested in the details of government. Power in the country had shifted to a group of industrial tycoons allied with a coterie of Kremlin insiders. His two terms as president disappointed his Western sympathizers and democratic reformers within Russia as well. Yet he left the country with a constitutional system intact, and the way was still open for democracy to take root.

An ambiguous legacy

Yeltsin's historical legacy would depend in part on the policies and democratic commitments of his successor. Putin's newfound reputation was based largely on his vigorous prosecution of the war in Chechnya. Yet he knew how to pledge commitment to democracy, pay his respect to the reformers of the 1980s, and hail the protection of private property as one of the "hallmarks of civilization." To some, however, his proclaimed dedication to a "strong state" aroused concerns, and Putin's governing methods seemed to become more authoritarian over the course of his first term and after he won reelection to the presidency in 2004. Responding in part to the continuing problem of Chechen terrorism (which included shocking terrorist attacks on a large Moscow theater and a public school in a small town), Putin promoted the centralization of state power and suppressed his opponents in the government, in the media, and in elite business circles. In international affairs, Putin sought to shape a more independent and assertive Russian foreign policy, openly opposing American military intervention in Iraq in 2003 and steadily improving relations with China. A gradually strengthening Russian economy enabled Putin to develop a more forceful assertion of Russia's international interests, but the nation's future role in the evolving global economy and international political order remained uncertain.

Almost two decades after the collapse of the Soviet Union, the old Leninist-Stalinist communism was gone. No one expected Russia to return to a command economy and the

CHRONOLOGY OF NOTABLE EVENTS, 1980–2001

1980–1981	"Solidarity" labor movement leads campaign for reform in Poland
1985	Mikhail Gorbachev assumes leadership of the Soviet Union
1986	Nuclear accident at Chernobyl releases dangerous radioactivity in Ukraine
1987	The United States and Soviet Union agree to remove intermediate-range missiles from Europe
1989	Soviet Union withdraws its military forces from Afghanistan
1989	Berlin Wall is dismantled; Communist regime collapses in East Germany
1989	Communist regimes are dissolved in Poland, Czechoslovakia, Bulgaria, Hungary, and Romania
1990	German reunification creates an enlarged Federal Republic of Germany
1991	Boris Yeltsin is elected President of Russia and leads resistance to attempted coup by antireform faction of Communist party
1991–1996	Yugoslavia breaks apart; Serbian and Croatian forces pursue "ethnic cleansings" in Bosnia and Croatia
1992	The Union of Soviet Socialist Republics is officially dissolved
1994–1996	Russia wages military campaign against secessionist movement in Chechnya
1999	NATO forces launch air attacks on Serbia to stop Serbian assaults on Muslims in the province of Kosovo
2000	Vladimir Putin succeeds Yeltsin as President of the Russian Federation
2000–2001	Slobodan Milosevic is forced out of power in Serbia and sent to stand trial at the war crimes tribunal in the Hague

rigidities of central planning or to put together the pieces of the old Russian empire of the tsars or the Soviets. Although Putin's critics complained about growing threats to democratic political institutions, Russia had a constitution, civil rights, freedom of religion, and free, contested elections. That more was not accomplished in Russian economic and political life after the disappearance of the Soviet Union had to be balanced against the seven decades of twentieth-century dictatorship.

The Resurgence of Nationalism: the Breakup of Yugoslavia

Of all the explosive issues that confronted Europe after the downfall of communism in 1989, ethnic nationalism proved the most intractable. Nationalist passions resurfaced after a long period of political suppression during the decades of Communist rule. Czechoslovakia, as we have seen, divided peacefully in 1993 in response to Slovak pressures. But in Yugoslavia, the large multiethnic, multinational federation that had been created at Versailles in 1919, politically ambitious leaders stirred up old national and even religious tensions which tore the state apart and confronted Europe and the international community with violence, armed combat, atrocities, floods of refugees, and civilian suffering not seen in Europe since the Second World War.

What happened in Yugoslavia was deeply rooted in historical animosities that were awakened and exploited for selfish political purposes by nationalist political leaders in the wake of communism's collapse in eastern Europe. To go back in time, the Balkan peninsula had been conquered by the Ottoman Turks in the fourteenth century. Serbia, once a powerful medieval kingdom attached to the Eastern Orthodox church, fell under Ottoman rule in 1389 and remained under Turkish rule for close to 500 years. In 1878 it broke away from the decaying Ottoman Empire and with the backing of the European Great Powers regained its status as an independent kingdom. Its neighbors Croatia and Slovenia had also been ruled by the Ottomans, but Croatia and Slovenia rejoined the Austrian Habsburg empire in the late seventeenth century and reaffirmed their ties with Roman Catholicism and central Europe. Bosnia (more precisely Bosnia and Herzegovina) long had a mixed population of Serbs, Croats, and Muslims; many Bosnians of Slavic blood in the long years of Turkish rule had adopted Islam. It too was freed from Ottoman rule in 1878 but was taken over by the Habsburg empire.

Political leaders and historical animosities

When both the Austrian and Ottoman empires collapsed at the end of the First World War, Serbia together with other South Slav nationalists in 1918 proclaimed a "Kingdom of the Serbs, Croats, and Slovenes." At the Paris Peace Conference in 1919 it was permitted also to annex Bosnia, Montenegro (also ethnically Serb), and other formerly Ottoman territories. All were now joined together under the Serb monarchy in a large multinational federation. For many years the nationalities held together in a somewhat uneasy alliance under a kind of royal dictatorship. In 1929 King Alexander in a symbolic effort at achieving greater unity changed the country's name to Yugoslavia (or South Slav state). Croat separatism remained alive and a Croat nationalist assassinated King Alexander in 1934. Yet many people spoke of themselves as Yugoslavs and regarded Belgrade as their capital, and the outside world accepted a Yugoslav national identity.

During the Second World War, after the Nazis invaded Yugoslavia in 1941, the internal tensions in the Serb-dominated country reemerged. Croatia proclaimed its independence and for a time was governed as a separate Nazi puppet state. A Croat fascist organization, the Ustachi, collaborated with the Nazis in rounding up and brutally mistreating Serbs, Jews, and others. For the country as a whole the Yugoslav military resistance to Hitler turned divisive and eventually evolved into a civil war between the royalist (mostly Serb) army and guerrilla forces (mainly non-Serb) led by the prewar Communist leader Marshal Tito. By his greater effectiveness against the Nazis, Tito won the support of Churchill and Roosevelt and then triumphed in the civil war.

After its wartime ordeal, with some 2 million of its people dead, Yugoslavia emerged in the postwar years under a Communist regime headed by Tito, who soon broke with Moscow. In 1946 he set up a federal republic with six component "republics" (Serbia, Croatia, Slovenia, Bosnia, Montenegro, and Macedonia), along with two "autonomous provinces," one of which was Kosovo. Although himself a Croat, he suppressed all separatist movements with an iron hand, but allowed each of the republics a degree of autonomy. In Bosnia he recognized the Bosnian Muslims as a distinct "national group" and gave them equal status with the Serbs and Croats. So long as Tito lived, Yugoslavia retained its national unity and identity. It was when he died in 1980 that latent separatist movements reemerged. His successors in the next several years, who had to struggle with a troubled economy also, tried various solutions, including a rotating federal presidency, but with little success. When in

Marshal Tito

NATIONALITIES IN CENTRAL AND EASTERN EUROPE

The map shows national boundaries and the location of various peoples at the end of the twentieth century. East Germany has been reunited with the rest of Germany. Czechoslovakia has broken into the Czech Republic and Slovakia. The state of Yugoslavia has lost control over Slovenia, Croatia, Bosnia, and Macedonia, all of which are now independent nations. Yugoslavia consists now of only Serbia and Montenegro. A numerous Serbian population remains in Bosnian territory, along with Croats and a large number of Slavic-speaking Muslims. The population in Macedonia includes many Albanians. The region of Kosovo, though officially part of Serbia, has a preponderantly Albanian Muslim population; it remained under the control of NATO military forces after the Balkan war in 1999. There are many Hungarians in the countries that surround Hungary, and about 1 million Turks live in Bulgaria. Moldova has been an independent nation since 1991 (it was part of the Soviet Union from 1940 to 1991), but much of its population speaks Romanian. Although the region's diverse ethnic groups have often lived together peacefully for long periods of their history, the modern nationalist emphasis on cultural differences and identities, at times inflamed by political leaders, has produced strong ethnic hostilities and recurring cycles of violence.

After the breakup of Yugoslavia in 1991, Serbs and Croats sought to create their own national enclaves in Bosnia by driving Bosnian Muslims from territories where they had lived for centuries. This violent process of "ethnic cleansing" led to Serbian massacres of Muslims in cities such as Srebenica and Sarajevo, where these people were marking the graves of victims in a Muslim cemetery.
(Abbas/Magnum Photos)

1989 communism collapsed all over eastern Europe, the regime in Yugoslavia collapsed as well. Yugoslavia's reform Communists (now calling themselves Socialists) relaxed the party's authoritarian grip on the country, faced up to its nationalities problem, and held open elections on the country's future. Only Serbia and Montenegro (the two Serb states were always closely allied) voted to maintain the federal republic. Croatia, Slovenia, Macedonia, and Bosnia all voted for parties committed to independence.

Former Communist leaders, like Slobodan Milosevic in Serbia and Franjo Tudjman in Croatia, seeing power slip away, placed themselves at the head of nationalist cru-

Nationalist secessions

sades. Milosevic, the Serbian president, rallied Serbs in Bosnia, Croatia, and Slovenia to fight to remain under Serb control whenever secession took place. His fiery speeches and tactics backfired. Alarmed by Serb militancy, Croatia and Slovenia each held a referendum and in 1991 proclaimed its independence. They received immediate recognition from the international community, which was persuaded that prompt recognition would forestall Serb military action.

In Bosnia, the situation was even more complicated. The Serbs and Croats together comprised over half the population, but the Muslims, as the largest single national group, dominated the government; over the opposition of the Serb and Croat representatives, the Muslim nationalist leaders declared Bosnia's independence. The secession of Croatia, Slovenia, and Bosnia and their immediate international recognition infuriated Milosevic, who now governed the former Yugoslavia as a rump state consisting of only Serbia and Montenegro.

Open warfare broke out in mid-1991. Local Serb paramilitary forces, reinforced by army units from Belgrade, proceeded to carve out enclaves in the secessionist states, where Serbs lived in significant numbers, and to drive out non-Serbs. In the fighting in Croatia and Slovenia Serb forces continued to seize territory until a temporary cease-fire was arranged.

Tudjman meanwhile goaded the Croat nationalists into action. The worst violence occurred when both Serbs and Croats attempted to create enclaves for themselves in Bosnia. For years the mixed population there, despite ethnic and religious differences, had lived peacefully side by side and had even intermarried. In the war that ensued, the Serb military forces brutalized the Muslim population. The barbaric deeds, labeled "ethnic cleansing," included large-scale expulsions, wholesale civilian slaughter, pillage, and rape. A prolonged siege of Sarajevo took place. At Srebenica in eastern Bosnia Serb militia executed some 8,000 Muslim men and buried them in mass graves. A shocked world could scarcely believe such events were occurring in civilized Europe in the closing decade of the twentieth century.

But the international community could not agree on measures to cope with the situation. United Nations contingents were unable even to deliver food and medical supplies. Given the historical complexity of the Balkans and the memories of earlier ferocious conflicts, neither the European powers, which might have been expected to take the lead, nor the United States would intervene with any meaningful show of force. The Security Council, however, imposed economic sanctions against the former Yugoslavia (which, as we have seen, consisted now of only Serbia and its historical ally, Montenegro), embargoed the shipment of arms, and made plans for war crimes trials at The Hague.

In 1994, to end the siege of Sarajevo, the United Nations, the United States, and the North Atlantic Treaty Organization (NATO) mediated a cease-fire and threatened air strikes if it were violated. For Bosnia a partial diplomatic settlement was negotiated. Croats and Muslims agreed to create a Croat-Muslim federation in what remained of Bosnian territory after the Serb conquests. The Serbs now occupied two-thirds of Bosnia and one-third of *UN and U.S. mediation* Croatia, with no intention of surrendering their gains. By 1994, 200,000 people were dead or missing, mostly in the fighting in Bosnia since 1991; there were about 4.4 million displaced persons. And still the fighting went on. In 1995 the Croatian army repulsed the Serb military and recovered most of the territory it had lost to the Serbs four years earlier. The Croats undertook their own "ethnic cleansing" program, expelling over 200,000 Serbs. In Bosnia the Serb offensive failed as well. Finally, in 1996, Serbia agreed to terms mediated by the United States at a meeting in Dayton, Ohio, accepting the new boundaries of Croatia and Bosnia and agreeing that UN peacekeepers would supervise the settlement in Bosnia.

An additional source of trouble soon developed, this time within Serbia itself in its province of Kosovo, where a growing separatist movement alarmed the Serbs. As early as 1989 Milosevic, as part of his initial pro-Serb agitation throughout Yugoslavia, had rescinded the province's autonomy. Ethnic Albanians, Muslim in religion, had long lived in Kosovo; through immigration from Albania and with large families, they had grown in such numbers that they now made up 90 percent of the population of two million. The Kosovars, as they were known, considered themselves related in religion, language, and culture to fellow Albanians in Albania. The Serbs were especially concerned because they themselves viewed Kosovo as a kind of holy land, where their ancestors had fought and lost the famous battle of Kosovo in 1389 to the Ottoman Turks.

The separatist movement grew at first under moderate leadership, but the Kosovars soon turned to their small but militant liberation army. In 1998 Milosevic launched a military offensive aimed at wiping out the Kosovar forces. Serb military and police units blasted villages and towns to root out the rebels, killing civilian men, women, and children as well. International efforts to mediate failed. In 1998 the United States and NATO, acting not only because of the egregious human rights violations but because of the threat to the stability of the wider Balkan region, warned Milosevic that it would not allow the Serbs to do in Kosovo what they done in Bosnia a few years earlier. Milosevic nonetheless continued the wholesale Serb offensive, with mandates for "ethnic cleansing" that seemed intended to destroy the Kosovars or drive them into exile. By that time over 800,000 Kosovars had been forced to flee; at least 10,000 were dead.

Kosovar separatism repressed

In March 1999 NATO, for the first time in its 50-year history, undertook a military offensive, launching large-scale air attacks against Serbia. The bombing, led by the United States, continued for 78 days with severe damage in Belgrade and elsewhere before Milosevic yielded. It was, to be sure, an attack upon a sovereign European state not charged with external aggression, and it seemed to violate a fundamental principle of national sovereignty. But the egregious abuses by Serbia and the violations of human rights against its own citizens were viewed as illegal, murderous actions that required and justified what President Clinton described as "humanitarian intervention." New international law was being made. The United States and its European allies were compensating for the failure of the international community to act against the mass killings in Bosnia (and in Rwanda) a few years earlier.

The NATO air offensive

The refusal of the American leadership in the bombing offensive to commit ground troops, as some of its NATO allies urged, or even to announce it as an option, may have prolonged the bombing, but made it easier for the American president to retain political support at home. In the end Milosevic had to yield, but a Russian-backed UN Security Council resolution confirmed Yugoslav sovereignty over Kosovo even if Milosevic had to accept 50,000 armed NATO troops as peacekeepers there.

That summer Kosovars returned under international protection. The UN forces faced the difficult task of relief and reconstruction and of providing security for both Kosovars and Serbs. The indictment of Milosevic as a war criminal by the international court at The Hague and his international isolation added to his unpopularity, but he did not give up power until he unexpectedly lost an election in the fall of 2000 and was forced to resign after massive demonstrations demanded the recognition of his opponent, a respected law professor who had kept aloof from the regime. Vojslav Kostunica took office with broad popular and international support, but he faced enormous economic problems as well as the unsettled future of Kosovo. Under international pressure, Milosevic was handed over in 2001 to the war crimes tribunal to face trial at The Hague, where his trial did not begin until 2005. Meanwhile, the Serbian political situation remained unsettled as die-hard nationalists continued to oppose those who favored closer economic and political relations with western Europe. The twentieth-century name, Yugoslavia, was no longer used after Serbia and Montenegro created a new federation in 2003; and by 2005 a new president was struggling to introduce reforms in the country's economic and political institutions. Tensions continued in Kosovo, which remained under UN administration.

Milosevic ousted

Economic sanctions, military setbacks, and Serbia's isolation from other European societies helped fuel the growing opposition to Serbian president Slobodan Milosevic. This crowd in the streets of Belgrade was part of a massive protest movement that demanded Milosevic's resignation after he lost an election in the fall of 2000. The protests forced Milosovic to accept the electoral victory of his opponent, Vojslav Kostunica, thus demonstrating again the important influence of popular mobilization in the former Communist states of central and eastern Europe.
(Spasa Dakic/Sipa Press)

Central and Eastern Europe after 1989

But we must return to central and eastern Europe, where developments took place more peacefully than in Yugoslavia. Following the revolutionary changes of 1989, Europe was no longer divided into East and West. The former Communist nations were moving toward democracy, the rule of law, and a free economy. But as in Russia, law and government had fallen into disrepute during the more than four decades of Soviet control; crime, corruption, and cynicism toward authority had become a method of survival. The success in open elections of former Communists, who had helped reconstruct their parties under various names and with varying degrees of reform, resulted from the hard times associated with the traumas of transition; but the new reform Communists, it must be said, learned to live and work with the democratic parties. Virtually every country in the former Soviet bloc for a time had either a head of state or head of government who had once been a Communist political leader. Poland in 1993 had its first ex-Communist prime minister and in 1995 an ex-Communist president. Many of the post-Communist societies experienced a repetition of the greed and rapaciousness of early Western capitalism. As in Russia, the former ruling and managerial elites profited personally from the newly privatized state industries, accumulating economic power and wealth.

The 1989 revolution assessed

Some observers judged the "revolution" of 1989 harshly, arguing that despite its significance in overthrowing a failed system and casting off foreign domination, the new regimes were bent mainly on emulating the material successes of the West. The goal of a democratic, civil society to supplement the organized state seemed to have faded. Party politics and party maneuvering became the rule. Because the revolution was peaceful, some speculated, a revolutionary catharsis may have been missing.

Confronting the past

Yet there was a partial effort to reckon with the past. The former German Democratic Republic conducted trials and purges and opened the files of the East German secret security police (the Stasi), dramatically revealing wide networks of informers. The Czechs tried to ban men and women accused of serving as informers or collaborators from participation in political life for stipulated time periods, but that led to abuses and was abandoned. The Poles at first sought to draw a "thick line," as they described it, between past and present, but then they too conducted purges and opened police files. Some said the Europeans might have benefited from "truth commissions," as in Latin America or South Africa before which past offenders against human rights could come forward to admit their misdeeds without necessarily expecting forgiveness.

Poland, Hungary, and the Czech Republic took the lead in the transition to democratic freedoms, market economies, the rule of law, and pluralist societies, closely followed by the three Baltic states, Estonia, Latvia, and Lithuania. They all looked forward to admission to the European Union, which would eventually take place in 2004. From 1995 on economies in central and eastern Europe were growing. The most prosperous countries were those that adopted the most drastic economic measures, even though the initial social consequences at the time were painful. Poland was the best example of a country that benefited from such "shock therapy" and from the mid-1990s enjoyed a vigorous expanding economy. Despite persistent problems, the overall economic balance sheets showed progress throughout central and eastern Europe. The revolutionary upheavals of 1989 and their aftermath would long be remembered as the final events in the Cold War of the second half of the twentieth century, which now gave way to the conflicts of a new era.

For interactive exercises, glossary, chronologies, and more, go to the *Online Learning Center* at **www.mhhe.com/palmer10.**

Chapter 27

THE CHANGING MODERN WORLD

The demise of Soviet-style Communist regimes in Europe after 1989–1991 suggested to some observers that the history of the modern world would henceforth evolve in only one direction. All modern societies, according to such theorists, were in fact already moving on their own erratic paths toward a universal system of liberal democracies and free market economies. But it soon became evident that this imagined "end of history" was by no means the only direction in which history could evolve. New movements arose to challenge the global capitalist economy, the ascendancy of Western political theories, the secularism of modern cultures, and the powerful influence of the United States—which had emerged from the Cold War as the world's sole superpower.

There were new and continuing conflicts among competing religious or ethnic groups and among nations that competed for power and commercial advantages in the global economy. Warfare itself changed when militant, extremist groups increasingly dramatized their grievances or waged violent political campaigns through the indiscriminate tactics of terrorist bombings. Facing such opponents, the most powerful national governments found that traditional methods of international warfare—invasions, the surrender of enemy governments, military occupations—could no longer achieve the decisive political and military closure that modern nation-states expected to reach at the end of their wars.

No sooner had the Cold War receded into historical memory than global struggles over natural resources, economic interests, and cultural values began to shape a new series of international conflicts and wars. By the early twenty-first century, the United States and some other Western nations had become deeply involved in the long-simmering conflicts of the Middle East, preoccupied by the dangers of terrorism, and entangled in protracted military campaigns against Islamic groups in Afghanistan and Iraq. The much-anticipated

Chapter emblem: View of the planet Earth, photographed from Apollo 17 in December 1972. (NASA)

post–Cold War "peace dividend" disappeared almost immediately in a new cycle of military interventions, shadowy intelligence operations, and deadly terrorist attacks.

Amid these cycles of violence and conflict, however, the deeper historical patterns of human migration, global economic exchange, technological innovation, transnational cultural interaction, and changing social mores continued to appear in all regions of the world. Computer technologies and communications systems now moved information around the globe with instantaneous speed; a global "culture industry" spread the same music, films, foods, and fashions throughout the world; evolving conceptions of knowledge and scientific research reshaped intellectual debates as well as artistic creativity; and new opportunities for the education, professional careers, and social and political rights of women continued to expand in almost every modern nation. The pace of change seemed to be increasing in all spheres of modern life, creating a "global village" that was both united and divided by the processes of contemporary globalization.

129. WESTERN EUROPE AFTER THE COLD WAR

Economic and Political Uncertainties in the New International Context

It was generally expected that the nations of central and eastern Europe would at first suffer in the post-Communist transition to democracies and market economies. What was unanticipated was the burden of economic and political troubles that western Europe found itself confronting. Buoyant and self-confident because of continuing prosperity during the 1950s and 1960s, the people of western Europe were first jolted by the recession of the 1970s that combined economic stagnation with inflation. By the mid-1980s the European democracies had recovered, although with lower growth rates than in the past and with discomfiting levels of unemployment.

Costs of German reunification

In Germany the economic situation after 1989 was complicated by the reunification with East Germany. The steep costs of absorbing East Germany's decayed economy and the decision to convert the East German mark on an equal basis with the West German made inflation a threat. To combat it the German Bundesbank kept interest rates high. But tight money choked off credit and investment when downturns occurred as in the early 1990s, delaying economic recovery for itself and its European neighbors and leading to currency devaluations and instability. The German economy remained sluggish long after political unification was completed.

Despite recovery, many West Europeans had remained unemployed. By the early 1990s unemployment rose to postwar highs. For the members of the European Union the unemployment figure approached 19 million, or more than 12 percent of the workforce. Long-term unemployment became a recognized phenomenon, as well as the disconcerting corollary that many workers would never again be employed at their old skills. Young people especially were hurt by shrinking job prospects.

Persistent unemployment

The Europeans slowly came to realize what had only been suspected in the earlier recession, that the problem of unemployment was not temporary, limited to the business cycle, but was deep-seated and structural. High labor costs that included generous welfare-state benefits for unemployment, disability, retirement, and extended paid vacations undercut western Europe's ability to compete globally. Many corporations, like their American counterparts, began to restructure, sharply reducing employment rolls and introducing other economies. American and European multinational corporations shifted manufacturing operations to developing countries in Asia and other parts of the world where labor costs and benefits were lower. For the first time in the years since 1945 the West European nations, echoing the British example under the Thatcher government, took steps to roll back the welfare state as it had evolved by consensus since the end of the Second World War.

Western Europe: Political Crises and Discontents

There was widespread dissatisfaction with the governing political parties of the center and center-left, which were judged to have held office too long and seemed incapable of providing fresh vision for the future. Shocking revelations of scandal and corruption tarnished the Christian Democratic and Socialist parties in several major countries.

The rising dissatisfaction with European political cultures could perhaps be seen most clearly in Italy, where anger against the governing elite became symptomatic of the wider European response to political cronyism. For years the Christian Democrats had dominated the political scene, forming successive coalition governments, with the Right in the 1950s and with the Socialists and other parties in the 1960s. By the 1970s in the midst of economic setbacks their popular support shrank rapidly. In the 1980s the Socialists replaced them, heading a cabinet for a record four years. Meanwhile the country's second strongest party, the Italian Communist party, which had earlier demonstrated its independence from Moscow, was excluded from government at the national level but won numerous mayoralties and control of municipal councils. In 1989, with the collapse of communism and end of the Cold War, the party renamed itself the Democratic Party of the Left and began a new quest for participation in the national government.

Italy's Christian Democrats

Over the years the Christian Democrats had kept a tight grip on power and patronage and maintained close ties both to state-owned enterprises and private business. In good part because the Christian Democrats projected themselves as Italy's defenders against communism they were shielded from scrutiny or criticism. But in the early 1990s evidence surfaced of bribes, kickbacks, and payoffs for government contracts up to the highest political levels. There had been illegal payments to the political parties and even widespread collusion with organized crime. Former prime ministers, cabinet ministers, and parliamentary deputies of all political parties as well as top business executives were implicated. So tainted was the Christian Democratic party that it returned to an earlier name for itself, the Popular Party. The aroused electorate in 1993 approved a new electoral system, one feature of which was to abandon proportional representation.

In the elections in 1994 both the former Christian Democratic party and the Socialist party were routed. Three new parties won and formed a Center-Right coalition. But the new parties inspired little confidence and their political leaders were unable to provide stability or serve as civic models. All the governments inherited public deficits, economic slowdown, unemployment, social tensions, and the continuing corruption inquiries. In 1998 the Popular Party joined with the Democratic Party of the Left to form a cabinet, and Massimo d'Alema, the head of the former Communist party, became prime minister. The reconstructed Communists were committed to financial stability, private enterprise, and economic growth as the best means of advancing social needs. But this cabinet lasted only briefly. In 2001 the conservative media magnate Silvio Berlusconi headed a coalition that won the elections; its Center-Right majority promised stability but also aroused misgivings about the ambitious

New parties

The populations of all modern nations have become increasingly diverse as immigrants and mobile workers stream across national borders in search of better jobs, education, cultural freedom, and basic human rights. These children at a primary school in contemporary London exemplify the diverse racial, ethnic, and cultural backgrounds of the people who now live in contemporary multicultural nations. Immigration is constantly changing the workforce, schools, food, music, and neighborhoods of modern cities; it also at times provokes anti-immigrant political movements and affects the political culture of every nation.
(© Christine Osborne/Corbis)

prime minister and his assertive *Forza Italia* party (the name itself derived from the championship soccer team that he owned). Berlusconi nevertheless remained in office longer than most of his predecessors. Fending off charges of corruption and criticism of his support for the U.S.-led invasion of Iraq, he overcame losses in a number of elections and managed to retain power in the face of mounting domestic opposition. In 2005 he reintroduced proportional representation in order to divide his opponents.

Europe's Immigrants and Refugees

We have already seen how the influx of millions of immigrants and refugees since the 1960s was altering the nature of European societies. In the 12 years from 1980 to 1992, 15 million new immigrants arrived to make their home in western Europe. Some sought political asylum, but mainly they came in search of wider economic opportunities than could be found in their own impoverished countries. They were usually willing to fill the lower-paid, less-desirable jobs that the Europeans did not want. When the Cold War ended and Communist barriers came down, a flood of refugees left eastern Europe, and additional refugees streamed in from war-torn Yugoslavia.

The steady flow of immigrants visibly changed the ethnic composition of Europe. In Germany Turkish workers settled in with their families as permanent residents; many reared their children as Muslims. In France in a population of 57 million in the mid-1990s, 4 million, or 7 percent, were foreign-born—mainly Arabs from North Africa and immigrants from other former French African colonies but also Vietnamese from Southeast Asia. In Britain, with a population of 56 million, at least 2.5 million could be counted as "ethnic minorities," mainly from various parts of Asia, Africa, and the Caribbean. Nations that had long sent emigrants to all parts of the world now found themselves absorbing large new populations from abroad.

Shifts in Europe's ethnic composition

The xenophobic hostility which had manifested itself earlier in western Europe again flared up. In Germany there were physical assaults on Turks, firebombings, and other acts of violence. Neo-Nazis in Germany, "skinheads" in Britain (who dated from the 1950s), neo-Fascists in Italy, and followers in France of Jean-Marie Le Pen's National Front agitated the immigrant issue and even resorted to racist violence. Governments adopted laws to reduce or eliminate further immigration. Germany in 1993 repealed a constitutional provision that had offered asylum to "all persecuted on political grounds," but it became virtually impossible to distinguish between political and economic refugees. France moved toward "near-zero" immigration and abandoned a tradition going back to the Revolution of granting citizenship to any child born on French soil. Unemployment and troubled economies made the social tensions potentially explosive and fed prejudices of all kinds, including anti-Semitism. But western Europe was only one outpost of a global crisis of refugees and migrants on the move.

Western Europe seemed to be settling into an era of persistent gloom, pessimism, and political frustration during the early 1990s. The end of the Cold War had not automatically ushered in peace, prosperity, and harmony. Unemployment, especially for the young, marred the economic scene. In the euphoria following the collapse of communism, few had anticipated the resurgence of the explosive nationalism that brought bloodshed to the Balkans. Western Europe, for all its announced commitment to democratic institutions and for all its military strength, feared the entanglements of intervention so much that until the American-led air offensive in Kosovo it refrained from decisive action. On the political scene conservative and centrist political leaders offered few new initiatives, and the Left seemed in disarray. On the other hand, many still believed, or hoped, that western Europe would reach out to central and eastern Europe, continue to work toward a united Europe, and reassume a central role in the world's economy and international affairs. But even the most optimistic Europeans increasingly recognized that the pursuit of such goals would require bold new economic or political initiatives.

Post-Cold War gloom

130. NATION-STATES AND ECONOMIES IN THE AGE OF GLOBALIZATION

Economic Recovery and a "Third Way" in Politics

In the 1990s the American President Bill Clinton set the tone for a new type of democratic politics. Taking his lead from Republican pro-business policies, Clinton promoted a program that favored economic growth and productivity but combined it with such social issues as health care and education and concern for the disadvantaged and minorities. He was favored by an upturn in the business cycle. In 1992, the American economy began to embark on a peacetime expansion that exceeded the previous nine-year record of the 1960s. Unemployment dropped to an all-time low, trade and production expanded, the stock market rose to unprecedented heights. The economy benefited from earlier corporate cost-cutting and restructuring as well as from the emergence and growth of the revolutionary new computer industries and information economy. Before long the global economy, buoyed by American prosperity, followed suit despite financial crises in Asia, Latin America, and elsewhere. Clinton also pursued an activist foreign policy, especially in the Arab-Israeli conflict in the Middle East. His second term as president was marred, however, when his denial of sexual indiscretions with a young woman intern led to a vote of impeachment by the House of Representatives; the Senate after a trial came short of the two-thirds vote needed for his removal from office.

Clinton found a kindred political spirit in the buoyant British Labour Party leader Tony Blair, who also adopted many conservative pro-business policies.

Clinton and Blair

Blair persuaded his party to abandon what still remained of its earlier socialist and welfare-state platform. Neutralizing the party's older trade union and left-wing bastions, he projected an image of the party as "New Labour." The best prescription for prosperity was to encourage economic growth and industry but without satisfying "pure selfish individualism" or neglecting social needs, which he accused Thatcher and the Conservative party of doing. A market economy and private enterprise would unleash productive forces that would benefit everyone. After four Conservative electoral victories since 1979 and 18 years of Conservative leadership, the country gave the Labour Party in 1997 its largest margin of victory since 1945.

As in the United States, the economy turned upward in Britain. Blair's political strength and popularity also enabled him to institute a number of constitutional changes. The United Kingdom had long had a highly centralized government, with all power emanating from the Westminster Parliament in London. The Labour party with its large majority in the House of Commons took unprecedented steps toward a devolution of power to a new parliament in Scotland, where the reform was intended to defuse a strong separatist movement, and to a new legislative assembly in Wales. Each gained broad jurisdiction over its internal affairs. Voters in Scotland for the first time since the Act of Union of 1707 went to the polls to elect their own parliament, and in Wales voters elected an assembly for the first time ever. Critics saw the devolution of authority as the "undoing of Britain" and an erosion of parliamentary sovereignty. Others recognized that stability did not necessarily mean resistance to change. No one wished to repeat the mistakes of earlier years when Britain's resistance to home rule for Ireland had led to continuing violence, partition, and prolonged strife.

In Northern Ireland matters seemed to be taking a more peaceful turn.

The settlement in Northern Ireland

The Protestant and Catholic parties reached an agreement in 1998, moving to end a violent conflict that over the past 30 years had cost the lives of over 3,000 people. The new arrangements authorized a legislative council of representatives from Britain, Northern Ireland, and the Republic of Ireland, and a sharing of power in a joint cabinet. Northern Ireland thus gained a new opportunity for self-government, but the introduction of the new self-governing institutions was delayed when the Irish Republican Army (IRA) and other paramilitary groups resisted calls for complete disarmament. By 2005, however, the IRA had in fact given up its weapons, and there was reason to believe that the long, violent conflict between Catholics and Protestants might finally be giving way to a more peaceful era in Northern Ireland's politics and society.

In another momentous break with tradition a reform bill in 1998 stripped the hereditary peers in the House of Lords of their parliamentary seats. The hereditary seats, it was widely recognized, represented a political anachronism, untenable in a contemporary democracy. A reorganized House of Lords would consist only of lifetime peers. Many in Britain were opposed, but others placed the reform in the established tradition of broadening the suffrage and other democratic innovations.

In Germany and in France political leaders also represented the new politics of the Left and Left-Center. In Germany the Social Democratic Chancellor, Gerhard Schröder, replaced Helmut Kohl in 1998 after the Christian Democratic chancellor's 16 years in office. Schröder, whose party's moderate wing had triumphed over its more radical elements, was committed to curbing the generous provisions of the postwar welfare state, which had driven up labor costs and made it difficult to hire new workers. He too spoke of his program as a "middle way," and—despite the problem of chronic unemployment—the Social Democrats held on to power in the elections of 2002. Subsequent elections in 2005, however, failed to produce a clear majority for either of the major German parties, and a coalition government emerged after extended negotiations. Angela Merkel, the leader of the Christian Democrats, became not only Germany's first woman chancellor but also the first chancellor to reach that office from the former East Germany. Half of the cabinet ministries went to Social Democrats, however, creating an unusual Left-Right collaboration.

Schröder

In France Daniel Jospin, a long-time moderate Socialist leader who hoped to continue President Mitterrand's reformist policies, became prime minister in 1997. Two years earlier he had lost the presidential elections to his conservative Gaullist opponent Jacques Chirac, but the Socialists soon won a majority in the legislature; under the now established practice of "cohabitation" the president appointed Jospin prime minister. Jospin, though still resolutely committed to a large role for government on social issues, believed in moderation and pragmatism, favored a market economy and moved forward with the privatization of state-owned industries. The constitution meanwhile was amended to curtail the powerful role of the Gaullist-inspired French presidency by reducing the term of office from seven to five years. The Socialist party was now so fragmented, because of its dissatisfaction with Jospin, that in the 2002 presidential election it could not muster enough votes for Jospin even to remain a candidate in the second round of the election. It was the extremist right-wing candidate Jean–Marie Le Pen who faced Chirac. Leftist and other voters, to their consternation, had to rally to Chirac, who easily won reelection.

Jospin

Despite such setbacks in various national elections, the political leaders who advocated a "middle" or "third" way between conservatism and welfare-state socialism continued to promote a moderate reform agenda in the early twenty-first century. Although they insisted that governments should play an active role in dealing with social and economic problems, they also called for reduced public spending, budget balancing, limits on regulation, and a climate of opportunity for business enterprise. Pragmatism and moderation seemed to be triumphant over older socialist views and the welfare-state ideology that had prevailed in the years after the Second World War.

Japan in the 1990s

The 1990s were an economic and political watershed for Japan. Its economy had expanded almost uninterruptedly since the postwar years. In the 1970s and 1980s capital investment in industry, and especially in advanced technology, grew at times at twice the rate of American and West European investment. But in the summer of 1991 Japan suffered a severe financial crisis and sank into a deep and stubborn recession.

The downturn signaled a problem that was more than a swing in the business cycle. The country was paying the price for years of uncontrolled speculation at home and abroad. Investors, including the largely unregulated banks, had made risky forays into real estate and financial markets. Government control over monetary policy had been lax. A very rapid rise in the price of stocks and real estate had created a "bubble economy," not unlike the economy of the 1920s in the United States that had led to the Great Depression. When the price bubble burst in 1991, Japan suffered bank failures and bankruptcies, and as the downturn continued, the government unsuccessfully tried to revive the economy with belated and ineffective fiscal and monetary policies. Japan's export economy added to its difficulties. Over the years the country had exported freely while sharply restricting imports, and other nations finally rebelled. New low-cost competition was now invading Japan's own markets. Japan also was forced to deal with social pressures. Although wages, educational opportunities, and living standards remained high, housing was scarce and expensive and the country's infrastructure suffered from neglect.

The price of speculation

In the midst of its economic troubles a political crisis, unprecedented in the years since the Second World War, shook the country. Cumulative evidence mounted of bribery, corruption, and ties to organized crime among high-ranking political and business leaders. In 1993 the Liberal Democratic party, which had dominated political life and served as the political pillar of Japan's prosperity and stability, for the first time lost its parliamentary majority in the Diet and fell from office. New faces and new parties emerged to replace the old guard, even though the country's bureaucracy remained entrenched. The recession dragged on and currency and financial crises in much of Asia in 1998 set recovery back, but the economy showed signs of renewed growth by the middle of the following decade. Unemployment began to decline, stock prices rose again, and industrial investments steadily increased. The crisis and prolonged recession had transformed the country, but Japan was not to be counted out as one of the world's leading political and economic powers. Efforts at political reform stimulated a reexamination of the past and aroused hopes for a revived economy, a more democratic future, and a more flexible society. But in the early twenty-first century Japan had somewhat faded as the model of postwar industrial and financial success and served instead as a cautionary example of a "bubble economy" that had burst.

The European Union: Widening and Deepening

By the opening of the twenty-first century European integration had made remarkable progress since six West-European nations had created the Common Market in the 1950s. The European Economic Community, established in 1957, became the European Community in 1965, and it in turn became the European Union (EU) under the Treaty of Maastricht signed in 1991. Having grown to 25 member nations after 2004 (with more countries seeking to join), the EU was an economic superpower. It had become the world's largest single economic market with over 440 million people, closely bound together in noneconomic ways as well.

As agreed under the Maastricht treaty, the EU embarked in the 1990s on one of its most ambitious enterprises, the voluntary adoption of a common currency. Twelve EU nations began to use the new "euro" in 2002 for financial transactions and the cash payments of daily life, replacing such historic national currencies as the franc, the mark, and the lira. The euro's value fluctuated in

A common currency

global financial markets, but it quickly became a major international currency and competed strongly against the American dollar. Three EU members—Britain, Sweden, and Denmark—chose not to adopt the euro, and the ten new states that joined the EU in 2004 remained outside the euro currency zone, pending further internal economic reforms. In another unprecedented step a European Central Bank was established in Frankfurt with the authority to set monetary policy for the member countries. The effects of this monetary policy on each country's social and economic policies became a new controversial issue in European politics as the various national economies came under a more centralized system of monetary management.

Meanwhile the requirements for admission to the European Union remained firmly attached to liberal political and economic models. An applicant nation had to demonstrate its commitment to "liberty, democracy, respect for human rights and fundamental freedoms, and the rule of law." A functioning free market economy was also required. In contrast to its slow expansion earlier, the EU now welcomed all European nations meeting its specifications, and it was also considering the possible admission of Turkey.

The EU was also "deepening" in additional ways. The Maastricht treaty had called for the continued development of common foreign and defense policies. The failure of the Europeans to prevent or halt the bloody events in Bosnia or in Rwanda in the early 1990s and the later failure to thwart Serbia's assault on Kosovo had embarrassed the Europeans. In June 1999 the EU foreign ministers resolved to develop a capacity for collective military action of their *Common foreign and defense policies* own. The EU began to move toward creating an armed force supplementary to but not supplanting NATO. The Atlantic alliance would remain firm, but a new "European Defense Agency" came into full operation after 2005. The new military cooperation signaled Europe's intention to end its long-term dependence on the United States and to reject the status of "an American protectorate." These developments both pleased and disturbed American policy makers who wanted Europe to play an independent role, especially in European matters, but did not wish to see resources drained off from NATO.

The EU political and bureaucratic structures did not change as rapidly as the evolving economic or defense policies. The European Commission, with an extensive civil service bureaucracy in Brussels, served as its executive and administrative branch and had the right to initiate proposals for legislation. The European Parliament, elected by a European-wide electorate, supervised the budget and debated Commission proposals. This representative body never aroused much enthusiasm, and voter turnout in the member nations at election time remained low. Although the heads of government held regularly scheduled meetings, the foreign ministers of the member-nations meeting as a council convened frequently to discuss and vote on matters of common interest. The meetings of this council provided an opportunity for the EU to take positions on international issues that extended well beyond Europe itself. It had not been anticipated that the ministers would evolve into the chief policy-making body, but in some ways it tied the EU to democratic support in a way that the European Commission had failed to do.

The early impetus for supranationalism in the Union faded, but what remained was the close cooperation of the ministers representing the member-states, discussing and making decisions on the basis of a half-*Cooperation or supranationalism?* century of common values and experience and a large body of jurisprudence and legal principles under the jurisdiction of the Union's Court of Justice. Each nation saw its stability, prosperity, and security enhanced by membership in the Union and recognized that the loss of sovereignty had been less than feared.

Opposition to EU
Constitution

But there was strong opposition to a proposed EU constitution that would have created the framework for a more coherent, integrated political union. Although some countries supported the proposed constitution, voters in France and the Netherlands rejected the proposal in 2005, throwing open the whole question of how the EU might proceed with further integration. Many Europeans favored the proposed constitution, particularly for its broad guarantees of social and economic rights and entitlements, but many others expressed concern about perceived threats to European living standards and social values or to specific national interests — especially after the major expansion of the EU membership in 2004. The European Union was therefore not likely to develop in the near future as its more visionary advocates had anticipated, even if in its present form it had become an unprecedented example of economic and political cooperation that fundamentally altered Europe. After centuries of European warfare, the continent had reached a historical turning point in which war between the leading European powers seemed unimaginable.

French-German cooperation, which had been the original driving force behind the success of European integration, still remained crucial. Many people in both countries looked forward to an even closer French-German alliance, partly to give leadership to the newer EU members from Eastern Europe and partly to offset British influence. No one could predict, however, the future evolution of an enlarged and still growing European Union that could be seen as a potential alternative or even rival to the global political and economic power of the United States. In Europe the older strategic threat from the Soviet Union was gone, but many

Uneasiness over
American-led
globalization

Europeans now saw a threat to the European way of life in American-led "globalization," which Europeans criticized as a worship of mass consumerism and a materialistic abandonment of social and cultural values. To Europeans, even among admirers of American accomplishments, the EU provided an essential balance to American hegemony in world affairs.

The "New Economy": The 1990s and Beyond

The global economy that reemerged after the Second World War seemed to enter a new phase in the 1990s. Globalization was the key word. It meant the more rapid and efficient movement of capital and technology worldwide across all geographical and political boundaries. The United States took the lead in globalization and in the development of what came to be known as the "new economy," but large multinational corporations of other nations also had operations in all regions of the world.

An information
economy

The new economy was an information economy. At its base was the computer revolution and the Internet, a word scarcely known at the decade's beginning. By the late 1990s it was in everyone's vocabulary, and at the disposal of tens of millions in offices and homes worldwide. It provided instant access to information of all kinds. It was as if a new industrial revolution was setting in and at an accelerated speed exceeding all previous industrial changes. Trade expanded. The flow of private investment capital from the industrial nations to the developing countries quickened. Living standards in many parts of the world rose, all tied to growing trade and investment. Globalization, driven by the profit motive, arguably held greater potential for Third World countries than foreign aid or loans from governments and international agencies.

The United States was the driving force in the new global economy. The American economy began an initial period of quiet growth and expansion in 1982. The inflation of

The European Union fostered political cooperation as well as close economic collaboration among its member nations. This picture shows the president of the European Commission addressing members of the European Parliament in Brussels—the city that served as headquarters for the European Commission's civil service bureaucracy and as the site for regular meetings of the European Union's foreign ministers. (Associated Press, AP)

This office of International Business Machines stands near a mosque in Istanbul, Turkey, suggesting a cultural and economic juxtaposition of the new and the old that also often appears beside Gothic cathedrals in Europe and Buddhist temples in Thailand—wherever modern technologies enter into long-established societies. The international economy now depends upon computers and digital information systems that link East and West as well as the newest and oldest forms of human cultural expression. (Courtesty of IBM Archives, Somers, New York)

the 1970s had been brought under control by high interest rates imposed by the Federal Reserve Board, the nation's politically independent central bank, which continued its periodic interventions to adjust to economic changes. There were setbacks and brief recessions, but by 1992 the economy began a period of uninterrupted growth. Unemployment declined to 4 percent, the lowest since the 1960s. Government revenues were available for many purposes, and some were used to reduce the national debt. American productivity, aided by computer technology, rose. Inflation with respect to consumer prices, although not for equities and real estate values, was kept in check. Consumer confidence and purchases, buoyed by the rising values of stocks and homes and the availability of credit, remained high. The long boom finally stalled in the early years of the new century when both the stock market and the rate of economic growth began to decline. By that time, however, the country had experienced the longest period of uninterrupted economic expansion in its history.

But there were troubled areas elsewhere in the industrial world. Japan, still suffering from a long severe recession after its financial collapse in 1989, only began to recover at the end of the 1990s; and there were continuing crises in Russia's unsettled economy, including the drastic devaluation of the ruble in 1998. Especially serious were currency and financial crises in 1997–1998 in several of the hitherto golden economies of Asia. The troubles there began with a loss of confidence and collapse of the currency in Thailand and led to a withdrawal of foreign investment that sent currencies tumbling in Malaysia, South Korea, Indonesia, Hong Kong, and Singapore—the very countries that had helped create the "Asian miracle." Speculation in real estate and equities in these countries had gone wild. Imprudent business practices came home to roost.

Troubled areas

Responding to Asia's economic problems, the IMF made multibillion-dollar loans but imposed austerity measures that brought social hardships and contributed to new tensions and difficult adjustments within various Asian nations. Many workers feared that the economic opportunities of globalization would be offset by the continuing quest for cheap labor or by a breakdown in the services or assistance available for the poorest social classes. To enhance competitive power in the global marketplace large corporations in the United States, Europe, and Asia were turning to low-wage labor in poorer countries and buying other companies to become even larger, within and across national lines. Multinational corporations grew in numbers and size everywhere, and there seemed to be little concern over foreign companies' taking over domestic corporations. London regained much of its financial prestige and strength as the financial center for European mergers and amalgamations, which accelerated as never before.

Japan's difficulties

As the American stock market boomed in the 1990s and new computer technology companies soared in value, some observers recalled the prosperity and speculative excesses of the 1920s and the American stock market crash in October 1929. Despite warnings from some quarters against "irrational exuberance," stock values kept climbing. Some also saw warnings in the collapse of the Japanese bubble after 1989. Still others recalled past speculative fever and manias in history: tulips in the seventeenth century; colonization schemes in the eighteenth; canals, railroads, gold, and silver in the nineteenth.

The computer technology revolution

The computer revolution and the emergence of the new computer technology companies created a new economy in many ways. They helped the economy to grow through greater productivity and helped fuel the rising prices in global stock markets. Computer wizards as well as brokers, financial executives, and entrepreneurs of all kinds became wealthy, often at an early age. Inventions in makeshift garage workplaces by hitherto obscure individuals, backed by venture capital, led to the establishment of multibillion-dollar corporations. The president of Microsoft, Bill Gates, became the richest man in the world, counting a fortune in the billions.

The new global economy generated unprecedented wealth, but the vast system of industrial production and financial exchange was also vulnerable to regional economic crises or political upheavals, all of which could now affect economies around the world. Optimistic economists responded to the Cassandras who worried about a future financial "crash" by arguing that this was a "new economy" and that market prices would be sustained on a new high plateau. But some economists had made somewhat similar predictions in 1929. There were indeed grounds for believing that the market did reflect profound changes in the American and global economy closely related to increased productivity, but there were warning signs in the early years of the new century that speculative fever had gone too far. Shock waves reverberated throughout the economy when high-technology computer stocks, which had risen in price all out of proportion to their earnings, lost much of their value in the early years of the new century, and real estate values began to soften.

The two most important developments in the computer revolution of the 1990s were the Internet and the World Wide Web. The Internet began from modest beginnings in the late 1960s in the United States as a government-sponsored project to enhance communications. Computer scientists

The Internet

around the world enlarged its scope and made it easier for individuals and companies to utilize in their daily work. The World Wide Web was first developed in 1980 at a nuclear physics research center near Geneva when the young English physicist Tim Berners-Lee developed a program to process information through electronic associations and linkages. For a time it remained neglected, but by 1990 he and others had revived and perfected it. By means of the Internet, the World Wide Web became a mass medium navigated by hundreds of millions around the world every day, and its users continued to multiply. It revolutionized communications; people could send electronic mail to each other, negotiate financial transactions, make purchases, tap all kinds of sources for information and education, and use the Web for entertainment as well. Many compared the significance of the new computer technology to the invention of the printing press in the fifteenth century. So rapidly was the new technology developing in speed, efficiency, and versatility that new, more powerful computer models became available almost immediately after earlier ones had first come into use.

Nearly half of the world's Internet users at the beginning of the new century were to be found in the United States, and English became the dominant language of the Internet. Some Europeans and Asians expressed concern that the Internet represented not only an immense step toward globalization but also toward Americanization. However, global competition continued. A Finnish company held the lead in the cellular phone market, computer specialists developed innovative software programs in India, and companies in Taiwan manufactured many of the most advanced computer chips. But a serious gap opened up meanwhile between those who had the opportunity and means to avail themselves of the new computer technology and those who did not. A "digital divide" emerged both within countries and between the wealthy and poorer countries of the world.

Many raised questions about the spectacular American economy of the 1990s and its impact on American society. The economic boom seemed to have left those at the bottom

The computer revolution of the 1990s transformed modern culture and education as well as the management of government and economic institutions. These students at a university computer center were working in what had become a "virtual library" for the distribution of knowledge, information, opinion and entertainment in the contemporary world.
(Bill Bachmann/Photoedit)

Gap between rich and poor

of the economic ladder falling behind. The gap between rich and poor was widening. In the years from 1988 to 1998 the income of the wealthiest fifth of American families rose by 15 percent as against less than 1 percent for the poorest fifth. The incomes of the poor and of many working-class and middle-class families fell or stagnated even when entire families worked. The gap grew wider between those who could save, invest, and build more wealth and those who could not. More Americans were living below the poverty line in 1999 than in 1969, and the economic gap between the rich and poor continued to grow in the first decade of the new century. Lack of opportunity for education and training in the new skills presented a new kind of challenge for the poor and for workers whose jobs disappeared in the global quest for lower-cost labor.

The worldwide faith in the market and market forces presented other challenges as well. Faith in a kind of oversimplified laissez-faire market economy spread globally, a kind of "market fundamentalism," not unlike a religious faith. The invisible hand would make it all right for everyone in the end, its supporters said, and a rising tide would lift all boats. Globalization and the world's market economy, its advocates claimed, made intervention by governments unnecessary. The argument found critics everywhere. In France, where unemployment was high, some argued that it was immoral for corporations to earn large profits while at the same time laying off workers in what were described as "abusive job cuts."

Meanwhile the growth in world commerce led to the creation in 1994 of a more formal World Trade Organization (WTO) to replace the General Agreement on Tariffs and Trade (GATT) in effect since 1948. GATT had been immensely successful in lowering tariffs and enlarging world trade through informal bargaining procedures and agreements. By 1986 it had grown to include 92 nations. In 1995 the United States succeeded in creating a permanent, more formal organization. The WTO was authorized to draw up and oversee agreements, enforce trade rules, and settle disputes. It grew to 150 participants by 2005 but at its first new-style open bargaining sessions in Seattle, it met with opposition and demonstrations in the streets, as would soon become the pattern at subsequent meetings elsewhere. The negotiated free trade agreements, the critics protested, paid little attention to environmental and labor conditions, or even to the widespread exploitation of child labor in large parts of the developing world. The developing nations, for their part, saw themselves at risk of losing out on cheaper labor costs, one of their chief competitive advantages; and they pointedly underscored the large share of ecological damage for which the industrial nations were responsible. Subsidies to agriculture in wealthier countries placed the less industrial nations, dependent on either the export or import of food, at a disadvantage. Critics of the new international trade system rejected arguments for free trade as a means of enhancing living standards for all. The violence of the popular protests offended many, but they aroused new sensitivities to social issues worldwide.

The founding of the WTO

Globalization, already visible in earlier periods of the world's history, and especially so in the nineteenth and twentieth centuries, seemed to be the defining social and economic theme for the new century. National boundaries, though not disappearing, were increasingly transcended by cross-boundary transactions and global exchanges in the world of communications, industry, culture, travel, food, popular entertainment, even apparel. To some, globalization was still thought of as "Westernization" or "Americanization." By the early twenty-first century, however, it defined only the latest phase of modernization, shared by many more of the world's people than ever before. The giant multinational corporations, no longer exclusively European or American but home-based in nations all over the world, depended as never before on the movement of capital, goods, trained personnel, technology, and ideas that flowed across traditional national boundaries.

Critics of globalization

131. INTELLECTUAL AND SOCIAL TRANSITIONS IN MODERN CULTURES

Intellectual and cultural life does not usually evolve through the dramatic public events or conflicts that reshape politics or economic relations. Yet the transitions in modern intellectual life and social mores have transformed modern history during all the years of international conflict and revolutionary change that we have discussed. People define themselves and their cultures in activities that go far beyond politics and economics. They constantly develop new forms of knowledge, philosophy, religious belief, creative art, and social life, all of which both influence and respond to the transformations of the modern world. Although much of twentieth-century culture had its origins in the years 1871 to 1914, science, philosophy, the arts, and religion crossed new frontiers or took new directions over the course of the twentieth century and set the stage for the new century. Even to single out a few of these developments will suggest the vast changes of the contemporary era.

One sign of globalization—or what some critics have called "Westernization"—is the growing popularity of similar foods and consumer products in different societies and national cultures. This Chinese child is enjoying a famous American beverage as he sits on the Great Wall of China. Most of the present wall dates from the seventeenth century, but some parts were built 2,000 years ago to protect Chinese culture from the foreign intrusions of that day. Although such walls no longer impede the flow of cultures, fashions, or products across national borders, different societies still find distinctive ways to use the consumer goods and ideas that reach them through the global economy.

(Andanson James/Corbis Sygma)

The Advance of Science and Technology

Science and technology expanded rapidly in the half-century before the First World War, but the pace quickened in the following years. Scientific discovery advanced more rapidly in the years after 1919 than in all previous human history. For one thing, more scientists were at work. At the opening of the twentieth century, about 15,000 scientists were exploring scientific problems; in the latter half of the century, over a half-million scientists were engaged in research, more than in all previous centuries combined. Over 85 percent of all scientists who have ever lived are at work in our own age.

Medicine and public health

The average person experienced the triumphs of science most dramatically in medicine and public health. Nothing in previous medical discovery could equal the contributions of sulfa drugs, antibiotics, cortisone, and other substances used to combat formerly crippling or deadly diseases, including pneumonia and tuberculosis; hormones, adrenaline, and insulin were also available to promote health or relieve suffering. Vaccines combated a number of dread diseases, including, after 1955, poliomyelitis; by 1975 smallpox had been all but eradicated worldwide. Remarkable accomplishments in surgery included the transplanting of vital organs. Apart from the advances in medical science, people benefited from modern technology in almost every aspect of their daily lives. For entertainment, radio and the motion picture were available and, after the Second World War, television. Washing machines, freezers, frozen foods, and microwave ovens lightened household duties. After 1947 airplanes could fly faster than the speed of sound; giant aircraft could traverse huge distances in a few hours; tourist travel to distant parts of the earth became commonplace. A world of electronics, robotics, rocketry, and space technology opened. Many people came to believe that technological solutions could be found for every problem.

It was therefore a shattering experience when the fatal disease AIDS (Acquired Immuno-Deficiency Syndrome) appeared in the early 1980s and by the 1990s was assuming global epidemic proportions. The first case was reported in the United States in mid-1981, but the disease seems to have originated earlier and elsewhere. Deaths from the disease mounted, and it was estimated that tens of millions had the disease or were infected with HIV, the human immunodeficiency virus that caused it. While medical scientists worked in the early twenty-first century to devise a preventive vaccine or to prolong the lives of its victims, educational efforts to stop its spread focused on sexual practices, intravenous drug use, and the protection of blood supplies. Uncertainty and anguish increased as time went by without a cure for what loomed as the greatest threat since the Black Death of the fourteenth century. Meanwhile, the threat of other pandemics also emerged in the new century, including a new avian or "bird" flu that began to spread in Asia and appeared to resemble the flu virus that had caused the deadly worldwide pandemic of 1918.

Nuclear Physics

In pure, or theoretical, science the transformation of physics in the twentieth century could be compared only to the scientific revolution of the sixteenth and seventeenth centuries. Early in the twentieth century scientists had discovered the natural radioactivity of certain elements, physicists like Max Planck and Albert Einstein had developed quantum physics and relativity theory, and Einstein had propounded his now famous formula for the conversion of mass into energy ($e = mc^2$). After 1919 a series of discoveries led to a deeper understanding of the atom. The cyclotron, developed by British scientists in 1932 at Cambridge University, made it possible to penetrate or "bombard" the nucleus of the atom at high speed. The nucleus, scientists learned, consisted not only of protons but of other particles like neutrons as well. In 1938 the German chemist Otto Hahn discovered that when he bombarded the atomic nucleus of the heavy radioactive element uranium with neutrons, it became unstable and split into two, which meant that energy trapped within the atom could be released. Additional scientists, including Lise Meitner, a German-Jewish scientist who had been forced to flee Nazi Germany, helped to expand upon these findings. In 1939 Nils Bohr, a Danish physicist, brought word of these developments to American scientists.

The implications of this breakthrough in theoretical science were clear. If the atoms in a large amount of uranium were split in a chain reaction, enormous amounts of energy would be released. In the troubled atmosphere of 1939 the possibility arose of its use for military purposes. When the war came, scientists in the United States, including Einstein, who had fled the Nazis in 1934, prevailed upon the American government to explore its military use before the Germans succeeded in doing so. In 1942 American and British scientists and European refugee scientists like the Italian Enrico Fermi brought about the first sustained nuclear chain reaction. This in turn led to the secret preparation of the atomic bomb at Los

The first atomic bomb

Alamos, New Mexico and to its use by the United States against Japan at Hiroshima and Nagasaki in August 1945.

After the war even more staggering technical developments followed. The hydrogen or thermonuclear bomb was built independently by the Americans and by the Soviets in 1952–1953; it involved nuclear fusion, or the joining together of hydrogen and other elements at great heat, using the atomic or fission bomb as a detonator with a stupendous chain reaction. Such thermonuclear fusion is responsible for the energy of the sun itself.

The first use of nuclear energy was therefore for military purposes, but it held constructive peacetime potential; a tiny grain of uranium (or plutonium, another radioactive element) could produce power equal to almost three tons of coal. By the 1990s over 15 percent of the world's electricity was generated by nuclear power plants; in France, over 65 percent. At the same time the awesome explosive powers unleashed by the scientists and the dangers of radioactivity were alarming. Accidents in nuclear power plants threatened the surrounding population and environs with the release of radioactive gases; nor could nuclear meltdowns be ruled out. Popular opposition to the building of nuclear power plants grew, as did concern over their proper design and the disposition of nuclear waste.

The nuclear danger

In military affairs a true nuclear clash of arms could mean apocalypse. Scientists such as Robert Oppenheimer who had helped to develop the first atomic bomb believed it to be so awesome a weapon as to make its future use unthinkable and in that way bar future major wars. In part they were correct; a balance of terror emerged so that over the years since August 1945 no nuclear weapon has been used in warfare. But nuclear bombs became part of the world's arsenal, an ever-present threat to human life and to the planet itself.

In later years scientists used linear accelerators like the cyclotron and even more powerful colliders and supercolliders as atom smashers to explore the nature of the atom and the behavior of its subatomic particles. Theoretical physicists continued to advance complex new concepts such as string theory and thus persisted in their search for an overarching theory that would explain the interrelationship of gravity, electromagnetism, and nuclear force, all of which were to be found in the subatomic world and in the cosmos as a whole.

Social Implications of Science and Technology

As in the case of nuclear physics, science in the contemporary age was closely allied with technology and the organized effort to exploit new scientific findings. Government and industry subsidized most scientific research. Laboratory equipment was expensive, and complex investigation required large-scale collaborative efforts; the solitary scientific investigator virtually disappeared. The subsidization of research for national purposes raised fears that scientific discoveries might serve political goals rather than meet pressing social or human needs.

Science had always affected the way people thought about themselves and their universe. The Copernican revolution had removed the earth from its central position in the scheme of things; Darwinian evolution had demonstrated that *Homo sapiens* was biologically a species that had evolved and survived. The philosophical implications of contemporary physics were only vaguely understood, yet they reinforced theories of relativism in all spheres. Ironically, at the very time that the average person was awed by the capabilities of science, scientists themselves recognized that they did not possess a magic key to the nature of things. Generally they claimed no more than the ability to determine, or guess at, relationships, which in the world of the atom (as in the cosmos itself) remained mysterious and uncertain.

Some thoughtful persons questioned scientific and technological advance and asked whether modern technology had grown beyond human control. Ecologists pointed to the wastage and despoliation of natural resources and the threat to the environment. In another way the life-preserving features of medicine and public health could result in overpopulation and in perhaps unmanageable pressure upon the limited resources of the globe. The techniques developed to save or prolong human life also raised ethical and legal issues, including new definitions of life and death, and the rights in such matters of patients, families, hospitals, and physicians. Questions arose over test-tube fertilization and other forms of artificial conception made possible in the late 1970s, and later over stem-cell research using human embryos. Those who condemned modern technology extolled the virtues of a prescientific and preindustrial age; others called for sharper awareness of how scientific advances posed new dangers or new ethical dilemmas. In an age of destructive weaponry and threats to the environment, no longer was the advance of science and technology unequivocally equated with the idea of progress.

Questioning scientific advances

Meanwhile, in the quest to understand nature the old divisions between the sciences broke down and new sciences appeared. Biochemistry, cell and molecular biology, biophysics, astrophysics, geophysics, and other subdisciplines arose; and all made intensive use of mathematics. In biology genetics made striking advances. While physicists discovered new atomic particles, biochemists isolated the organic substance found in the genes of all living cells, the chemical carriers of all hereditary characteristics. When scientists deciphered the genetic "code" and synthesized the basic substance of heredity (DNA), it became possible by splicing genes to alter the characteristics of plant and animal species and to clone or reproduce in the laboratory an animal such as a frog or a sheep with desired hereditary characteristics. The implications for the possibility of even human cloning at some future date were staggering. Meanwhile biotechnologists were revolutionizing food production by genetically engineering new varieties of crops, which provoked strong objections in various quarters. Medical scientists could also hope to conquer inherited diseases, a goal that moved closer to reality when researchers announced in 2000 that they had decoded the human genome—the more than 3 billion chemical units of DNA that control the human body and also contribute to genetic-based illnesses.

The other life sciences and social sciences also grew in importance. Psychological exploration of human behavior, as well as the treatment of mental and emotional disorders through psychiatry and psychoanalysis, expanded rapidly. Freud, who had first developed his theories of psychoanalysis before 1914, became more widely known in the 1920s. His emphasis on the human sex drive and sexual repression was later much modified. Many students of human behavior argued that his contributions were not universally or scientifically valid but reflected the values of pre-1914, middle-class, male-dominated Viennese society. A variety of schools emerged with different interpretations and techniques, and drugs were developed to treat psychological depression and other mental illnesses. But the search, initiated by Freud, for the unconscious sources of individual and collective human conduct remained a hallmark of contemporary thought and culture.

Impact of Freud

Anthropologists and other social scientists increasingly stressed the relativism of all culture. They denied notions of cultural superiority or hierarchies of cultural values, or even that there were objective criteria of historical progress. If Western society, they noted, made notable progress in science and technology, other cultures accomplished more in self-discipline, individual integrity, and human happiness. The adjective "primitive," as opposed to "civilized," tended to disappear, and a cultural humanism emerged that recognized and esteemed values distinct from the Western tradition.

Space Exploration

Among the most dramatic developments in science and technology in the second half of the twentieth century was space exploration. In the 1950s the Soviets and the Americans competed with each other as part of the Cold War; each made important advances in rocket research. Both the U.S. and the U.S.S.R. mastered multistage rocket launching. The Soviets opened the space age when in 1957 they launched *Sputnik,* the world's first artificial satellite; in 1961 they sent the first human, Yuri A. Gagarin, in orbital flight around the earth. The Americans sent their own astronauts into space in 1961 and 1962. In the 1960s both countries launched unmanned automated spaceships to probe and explore the moon and then the planets of the solar system and their satellites. Early in the 1960s President Kennedy pledged that Americans would land on the moon before the end of the decade. In 1969 three American astronauts, as planned in Project Apollo, made the quarter-million-mile journey to the moon, and millions of viewers around the globe watched on television as Neil Armstrong took his first steps on the moon. The Americans made five additional trips to the moon over the next three years. Automated robot spaceships were launched in the 1960s and later on long journeys to explore the planets of the solar system. The American spaceships approached or orbited the planets and soft-landed instrument packages, which over a period of years sent back a rich harvest of data, providing more knowledge than ever before possessed about the nature and origins of the planets and the earth itself. The later space probes explored the more distant planets. *Voyager 2,* launched in 1977, traveling close to 4.5 billion miles over 12 years' time, reached the outermost planets before flying into interstellar space. In 1990 the United States placed in orbit the Hubble space telescope, capable of seeing light years away into distant galaxies and reporting back its findings.

U.S.-Soviet competition

The Soviets also conducted impressive space probes to the moon, to Mars, and to Halley's comet, whose behavior had been predicted in the seventeenth century and which once again returned close enough for observation in 1986. The Soviets also built a permanent space station and set records in testing human endurance in weightless space.

As time went on, Cold War rivalries played less of a role in space exploration, but military objectives were never completely absent. The U.S. and U.S.S.R., and later other countries, launched spy satellites for reconnaissance and information gathering. The United States initiated research in the 1980s into an enormously costly strategic defense initiative that would deploy laserlike weapons in outer space (hence called "Star Wars") as a defensive shield against nuclear missile attacks. The project was abandoned in 1990 but was revived again in the following decade, with ardent champions and equally vehement critics.

International cooperation

In the 1980s space enterprise showed promise of international cooperation and was no longer confined to the military superpowers. France, Japan, China, and other countries became spacefaring nations, planning and launching satellites and space probes of their own. The European Space Agency carried out its own operations. A multinational human expedition to Mars sometime in the

Exploration of outer space marked an important new phase in the modern search for knowledge about the Earth and other planets of the solar system. In contrast to earlier explorations such as the European voyages to the New World, millions of people were watching on television when the first human beings walked on the surface of the moon. The American astronaut Neil Armstrong took this picture of Edward E. Aldrin, Jr., as the two men made one of their "moonwalks" in July 1969. Although this dramatic event was a famous milestone in the history of human exploration, later space programs focused principally on unmanned space exploration and on orbiting space stations.
(NASA)

twenty-first century was discussed. After the Cold War the Americans and the Russians began to cooperate in space, most notably in the development and joint use of a Russian-built space station. On the other hand, the need for human expeditions came under serious scrutiny. Dismayed by the human cost of deadly accidents (including the disintegration of the American space shuttle *Columbia* as it reentered the earth's atmosphere after a flight in 2003), some critics contended that unmanned space flights might accomplish more, at less cost, and at less risk to human life. Many objected to the enormous expense of space exploration when acute social needs at home remained unfulfilled. But its champions defended it as part of the continuing human effort to cross new frontiers, expand horizons, and explore the unknown. The twentieth century may ultimately be remembered, apart from the destructiveness of its terrible wars, as the century in which humans first set foot on the moon, and with robot spaceships devised and guided by human intelligence, began to explore the universe.

Philosophy: Existentialism in the Postwar Years

In the early years after the Second World War, a new group of philosophers in Europe and North America developed a loosely organized body of ideas called "existentialism." The existentialists formed no one school of thought and held no coherent body of principles. There were religious and atheist existentialists. Yet all held some beliefs and attitudes in common. All reflected a troubled civilization, a world disturbed by war and oppression, a civilization of material progress and moral uncertainty in which the individual could be crushed by the very triumphs of science and technology, and in which human life itself seemed to have lost higher purpose or inherent meaning.

Existentialist thought owed a debt to Pascal, Nietzsche, and others who had underscored the tragic element in human existence and the limitations on the power of human reason. More directly it owed a debt to Søren Kierkegaard, the nineteenth-century Danish religious philosopher. But it was French writers, and especially Jean-Paul Sartre, who after the Second World War developed existentialist thought in literature and philosophy in a form that for a time gave it a wide popular following. In a hostile world, the existentialists contended, human beings had to make choices and commitments on their own. They were "condemned to be free" and were alone responsible for the choices and actions that defined their very existence; for most existentialists, the nature of a human being's existence was defined by what he or she did rather than by some deeper spiritual essence. Authentic existentialists therefore had to move beyond philosophical contemplation and take action in the world, even though they were aware that human action might fail to change the world. Albert Camus, influenced by the existentialists, drew upon the myth of Sisyphus, who was condemned continuously to roll his stone uphill, though it always rolled back down again. The very humanity of Sisyphus grew out of courage and perseverance at a hopeless and absurd task. Existentialism emphasized the anguish of human existence, the frailty of human reason, the fragility of human institutions, and the need to reassert and redefine human freedom. Although its popular following waned and Sartre himself was dislodged from his earlier lofty eminence, existentialism never completely disappeared from contemporary philosophy or religion.

Jean-Paul Sartre

Philosophy: Logic and Language; Literary Criticism; History

Professional philosophy in the twentieth century seemed to contribute less to an understanding of contemporary problems than in the past. Always concerned with the origins and nature of knowledge, it had also shared an interest in metaphysics and ethics. In the early twentieth century it became highly analytical, focusing especially on the limits and criteria of knowledge. In the formal study of logic, mathematical symbols replaced the use of traditional language. On the eve of the First World War Bertrand Russell and Alfred North Whitehead had explored logic and mathematics in their monumental *Principia Mathematica*. In the 1920s an influential group of philosophers and mathematicians in Vienna, among them Ludwig Wittgenstein, sought to introduce the methodology and precision of mathematics into the study of philosophy as a whole, in what they called logical positivism. They rejected the ambiguities of language used in traditional speculation on morals and values, turning away from the nondemonstrable—that is, "God, death, what is higher," in Wittgenstein's phrase. The Vienna group disintegrated in the 1930s, but logical positivism remained influential. Most professional philosophers continued to emphasize scientific rigor and linguistic analysis. A smaller but growing number, responsive to contemporary ethical concerns, devoted themselves to unresolved human and social dilemmas.

New studies in philosophy, linguistic analysis, and semiotics (that is, the study of signs and symbols in communication) drew attention to the complex relation between language and reality. Philosophers also challenged many of the dualisms taken for granted in Western thought. In literary studies "deconstruction" theory emerged after the 1960s to offer new methods of analysis and criticism. Its

Deconstruction

proponents sought to analyze, or "deconstruct," a body of writing or "text" (which could be a painting or other kind of cultural object as well) to examine its implicit cultural assumptions and its indebtedness to its cultural traditions. No single valid meaning was to be attached to any individual work. According to its advocates, deconstruction made it possible to reveal the philosophical, class, racial, ethnocentric, or sexual assumptions hidden in the language of a work. It also contested older hierarchical standards of literary quality, blurred distinctions between elite and popular culture, made less of a dichotomy between fact and fiction (and other dualisms), and broadened the existing canon of writings studied in literature, history, law, religion, and other disciplines.

The work of the critic was said to be as much a creative enterprise as literary or artistic creation itself. Propounded originally in the late 1960s in broad philosophical terms by the French philosopher Jacques Derrida, and developed further by other writers and scholars of various disciplines and nationalities, deconstruction won its largest following in the United States. Its opponents viewed it as abandoning traditional literary history and rejecting rational, critical standards that had shaped modern thought since the Enlightenment.

The writing of history also underwent a profound change. A group of French historical scholars (called the *Annales* school, from a journal with which they were associated) gained wide influence after the Second World War. They focused on long-term elements in historical change such as population, economy, climate, and natural resources; relegated politics to a lesser role; and avoided the traditional narrative of "events." They studied also the lives of ordinary people in the past and tried to reconstruct the collective outlook of social classes. The newer social history in France, England, and the United States also paid special attention to the inarticulate and illiterate and to all those with strong oral traditions, such as the American slaves in the antebellum South, the English working classes, and the peoples of Africa, reconstructing their culture and lives despite scarce written sources. Another new emphasis greatly expanded the historical study of women from antiquity to the present, leading, among other results, to cultural and social reassessments of entire historical eras. A variety of social themes also received new historical attention: marriage, divorce, the family, childhood, sexuality, even insanity and death through the ages. For their part, many traditional historians who had not been wholly insensitive to these concerns widened their own narratives to include such social and cultural themes.

New interests among historians

The Creative Arts

The revolution against older traditions in the creative arts assumed new dimensions. Ever since the Renaissance visual artists had followed certain norms of representation and space perspective. But much of twentieth-century art prided itself on being nonobjective; it rejected the idea of imitating or reconstructing nature, or mirroring it with realism or photographic fidelity. The artistic revolution inaugurated in France before 1914 accelerated in the interwar years and after 1945. It seemed to mirror the political turbulence of the times and the disillusionment with rationalism and optimism. It reflected the influence of Freudian and other schools of psychology and the emphasis on the unconscious and irrational, as well as the relativity of the new physics and its uncertainties about the nature of matter, space, and time.

Artists in the contemporary era continued the pre-1914 experimentation in color, form, and use of materials, but went well beyond, seeing the world around them in new

INVASION OF THE NIGHT

By Roberto Sebastian Matta Echaurren (Chilean, lived in France, United States, Italy, 1911–2002)

This work is an example of the modern trend toward abstract art, though it also shows the influence of European surrealism. Painted in New York in 1941 by a Chilean artist who worked in Europe during the 1930s and later lived mostly in Italy, this picture suggests the sense of dread or dislocation that creative artists often expressed during and after the Second World War. The figures in this painting cannot be identified, but the artist uses forms, colors, and shapes to convey the chaos and disorder of a world that is falling into darkness. Matta's artistic abstractions as well as his migratory life on three continents represent recurring tendencies in both the work and personal experiences of many twentieth-century artists.

(San Francisco Museum of Modern Art, Bequest of Jacqueline Marie Onslow-Ford (82.50). Photography by Ben Blackwell.)

Seeing the world in new ways

ways. The innovative work of earlier artists such as Picasso—whose cubist paintings had systematically distorted and deformed material objects or human figures—was followed by increasingly abstract artistic experiments during the later twentieth century, as may be seen by comparing Picasso's *Les Demoiselles d'Avignon* on p. 619 with Matta Echaurren's *Invasion of the Night* at the top of this page. Some artists expressed themselves through geometric form; others left reality behind and tried to represent their own unconscious fears or

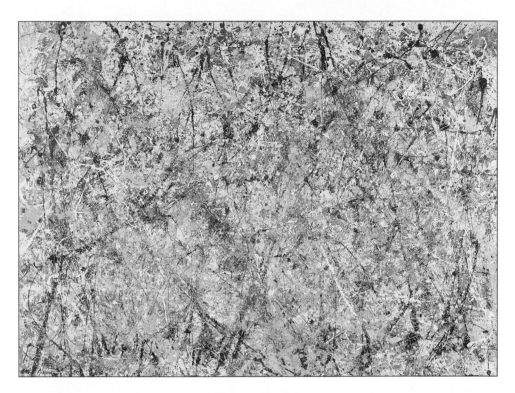

The movement toward abstract art culminated in paintings such as Jackson Pollock's *Number 1, 1950, Lavender Mist*. Using patterns and colors rather than images of people or natural objects, Pollock sought to convey an atmosphere or sensibility that could be at once baffling and fascinating. Pollock and other artists working in New York helped to make the United States a leading center of modern art after the Second World War.
(Jackson Pollock (1912–56), *Lavender Mist: Number 1, 1950*. National Gallery of Art, Washington, DC/Bridgeman Art Library © 2007 Artists Rights Society (ARS), New York)

desires. The results were fascinating but frequently baffling, as in the painting by Jackson Pollock, *Number 1, 1950, Lavender Mist,* which appears above. After the Second World War, the United States took over from Europe the leadership role in the visual arts and evolved new forms of abstract art.

Contemporary art resulted in original and striking expressions of form and color, but the conscious subjectivism widened still further the gap between artist and public. The artist, painter, and sculptor (and the poet, musician, playwright, and novelist, who were also rejecting the older conventions) were conveying their own visions of the world, not an objective reality that could easily be understood by others. Perhaps the greatest innovation was that the public, baffled as it was by much of contemporary art, came to accept the avant-garde as normal, even if on occasion it rebelled against it. Democratic societies accepted the need for artistic experimentation and innovation, which had been frowned upon or banned as degenerate or socially dangerous in totalitarian societies like Nazi Germany and the Soviet Union. Representational art, of course, never completely disappeared anywhere, and many artists reaffirmed it, contributing to a growing pluralism in contemporary art.

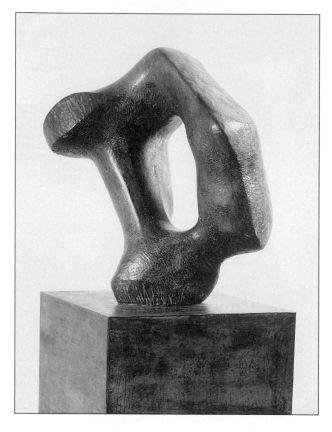

Non-representational art became as common in sculpture as it was in twentieth-century painting. This work by the influential English sculptor Henry Moore, *Mother and Child* (1959), shows how the modern representation of classical artistic themes radically altered Western sculptural traditions that went back to the Renaissance and even to antiquity.
(Scala/Art Resource, NY © The Henry Moore Foundation.)

Subjectivism and the unconscious in literature

The focus on subjectivism and the unconscious was reflected in literature too. The reconstruction of lost time and the unfolding of the individual's innermost experience through a stream of consciousness and flood of memories, which had appeared first in the work of Marcel Proust and James Joyce before and shortly after the First World War, remained important for a new generation of novelists and playwrights after 1945. Not only writers but also cinematographers experimented with probing the unconscious in evocative but mystifying ways. All of this cultural experimentation contrasted with the popular entertainment provided through the mass media, especially movies and daily diets of television "soap operas" and "sit-coms."

Postmodernism

Sometime in the early 1970s the phenomenon of postmodernism emerged in architecture, literature, and other art forms. In all areas the postmodernists borrowed from the past and mixed the old and new, and the popular and elite, to suit their tastes. Unlike modernists from the late nineteenth century on, the postmodernists did not reject the commercialization and materialism of contemporary culture but embraced it and incorporated it in new ways, often with humor. The American architect Robert Venturi and his collaborators wrote a book called *Learning from Las Vegas* (1972). Composers introduced street noises (and silences) into their music. Repetition, as in the commercial world of packaging, marketing, and television advertising, was adopted as an artistic technique. The artist Andy Warhol painted serial pictures of Coca-Cola bottles and of the film star Marilyn Monroe. In fiction the postmoderns mingled actual events and fantasy. A play by Harold Pinter, winner of the Nobel Prize for literature in 2005, Samuel Beckett, or Eugène Ionesco challenged traditional theatrical conventions. Indeed, a Pinter play such as *The Homecoming* or a Beckett play such as *Waiting for Godot* could be as baffling as a work of postmodernist art; and it was very different from a play by Shakespeare, Molière, Ibsen, or Shaw. The postmoderns also rejected traditional ideas of structure, seeing no need in literature or art for a beginning, a middle, and an end. Postmodernism was both a phase of the modernist rebellion against traditionalism and a fragmented sequel to it with new messages. Where modernism typically sought to convey an artist's unique personal vision, postmodernists insisted that writers inevitably expressed the language and values of their culture rather than a distinctive individual consciousness. Because the writer's life and personal experience were now deemed less important for the study of literature, it was possible to speak metaphorically of the "death of the author."

Religion in the Modern World

Religion was in flux in the modern world. With the continuing inroads of secularism, the challenges of science, and the post-1945 advances of communism in eastern Europe, China, and elsewhere, organized religion encountered many obstacles. But the churches survived Marxist regimes and retained their vitality. Statistics on religious affiliation are never exact, but some figures on the religions with the largest number of adherents in the opening years of the twenty-first century were clear. Islam, with well over 1 billion adherents, was the fastest-growing faith; it made large inroads in postcolonial Africa. There were close to 800 million Hindus and 350 million Buddhists in the world. Christianity, if all branches are added together, remained the largest religion, counting close to 2 billion adherents, of which more than half were Roman Catholic, a fourth were Protestant, and a fourth were Eastern Orthodox.

The ecumenical movement in Christianity, that is, the organized effort to unite the many branches of Protestantism, and eventually all Christianity, which began in the nineteenth century, made headway throughout the half-century after the Second World War. A World Council of Churches was *The ecumenical movement* founded in 1948. In historic breakthroughs toward the end of the century Lutheran churches announced a reconciliation and alliance with the Episcopalian churches, and Lutherans and Calvinists resolved theological differences over Luther's definition of salvation, "justification by faith." When in the 1960s the Roman Catholic church abandoned its insistence on a privileged position within Christianity, it too encouraged ecumenicism. All Christian churches moved toward a closer dialogue with non-Christian world faiths as well.

As in the late nineteenth century, tensions between modernism (in its religious sense) and fundamentalism continued. Many of the Protestant *Religious tensions* churches in the twentieth century for the most part reconciled their traditional teachings with science and Biblical scholarship, minimized the supernatural and dogmatic aspects of their faith, and sought to adapt the teachings of the gospel to the social needs of the contemporary world. But the two world wars and other social and cultural upheavals dealt a blow to theological modernism and to the inherent optimism of the social gospel. In the 1920s, not only did fundamentalism revive but an intellectual reaction also set in among Protestant theologians who emphasized revealed religion and elements of faith. The Swiss theologian Karl Barth in his writings from 1919 to the 1960s endeavored to lead Protestantism back to the root principles of the Reformation. There was much interest in Kierkegaard who, like Luther, had resolved his own deep anguish by a personal commitment to religious experience. After the Second World War, as a result of the work of Barth, Paul Tillich, and others, a powerful movement in Protestantism reasserted its dependence on revealed religion and denied that human reason could ever properly judge divine revelation. Some church writers, unable to explain the wrenching experience of the Second World War and the Holocaust, spoke of "post-Auschwitz theology" and of "God's removal from history." Evangelical Protestantism, with its literal adherence to the gospel, spellbinding preachers, and revivalist emotional appeal also flourished, especially in the United States, and conducted a continuing crusade against the teaching of Darwin and evolution in the schools. But other Protestants generally accepted religious scholarship and the intellectual validity of modern scientific knowledge.

The Roman Catholic church was passing through one of its great historic phases beginning in the second half of the century. Although the church no longer actively suppressed all forms of modernism, the Vatican in the early postwar years reaffirmed dogmatic training in the seminaries. In 1950 Pius XII (1939–1958), who headed the church during the Second World War (and was criticized in some quarters for insufficiently opposing the terrible Nazi atrocities against the Jews), proclaimed the Assumption, the literal, or bodily ascent of the Virgin Mary into heaven, the only new Roman Catholic dogma to be promulgated in the entire twentieth century.

Pius XII was succeeded in 1959 by John XXIII. Although elected at the age of 77, and reigning for only four years until his death in 1963, John proved to be one of the most innovative popes of modern times, working to bring the church and its teachings into greater harmony with the contemporary world. His powerful encyclicals gave a global emphasis to the older social teachings of the church and called upon the wealthier nations to share their resources with the less favored. The first encyclical ever addressed to Catholics and non-Catholics alike, *Pacem in Terris* (1963), appealed for peace and human rights. A champion of ecumenicism, he opened dialogues with other faiths. In 1962, against the advice of his own theologians, he convened the Second Vatican Council, the first such council since 1870, and as it turned out, the most important since the sixteenth-century Council of Trent. Vatican II, as it came to be called, reshaped contemporary Catholicism.

Vatican II

John did not live to see the Council's labors completed, but was the principal inspiration for its reforms. His successor Paul VI (1963–1978) shared John's social concerns and encouraged ecumenicism, but was more conservative in other ways. The Council completed its work in 1965. Accepting the principle of religious pluralism, it abandoned the older insistence on a Catholic monopoly on religious truth. It affirmed the principle of collegiality, which had gone into eclipse in the modern centuries, the view that the pope must share his authority with the prelates of the church, thus strengthening the authority of the national churches on substantive matters. It revised the liturgy and various church practices. The Mass, henceforth, would be conducted in vernacular tongues instead of in Latin, which had been the rule for centuries. The Council relaxed restrictions on dress for priests and nuns. In one historic declaration, the Council explicitly absolved the Jewish people from the charge of deicide that had fed and inflamed anti-Semitism over the ages. John XXIII's goal—the revitalization and updating of church teachings and practices—was amply fulfilled by the Council. There were limits to the changes, to be sure. The Council reaffirmed celibacy for the clergy and refused to sanction the ordination of women as priests. Paul VI, meanwhile, upheld papal supremacy and took

Pope John Paul II combined his defense of the traditional values of Roman Catholic Christianity with a reliance on the most advanced forms of travel and communications. He is shown here on an airplane during the early years of his pontificate. Traveling more widely than any of his predecessors, John Paul II contributed to the growth and visibility of the Roman Catholic church throughout the world. The rapidly growing number of Roman Catholics in Asia, Africa, and Latin America (along with the many adherents in Europe and North America) gave the Roman Catholic church and its pope a wider global presence than at any time in history. (Getty Images)

a firm conservative stance on moral issues, especially against all artificial means of birth control.

After Paul VI's death in 1978 (and when a successor, John Paul I, died after only 34 days in office), John Paul II, the archbishop of Cracow, became the new head of the church, the first Polish pope ever elected, and *John Paul II* the first non-Italian pontiff in over 450 years. Robust, earthy, energetic, versatile in languages, and with a keen sense of pageantry and papal majesty, he brought an added dynamism to the church. Not only did he encourage the Christian ecumenical movement, but he also reached out to non-Christians as well, traveling widely in Asia, Africa, and Latin America. During the Cold War years he entered into diplomatic negotiations with the Soviet Union and the Communist countries of eastern Europe to improve the status of the church and contributed much to the revolutionary transformation of his own country and eastern Europe in the 1980s.

In his indefatigable global travels John Paul presided over Mass for millions of Roman Catholics, and he offered apologies for past wrongs going back to the Crusades and including the abuses of the Inquisition, whose archives he opened to historians. He apologized for the Inquisition's condemnation of scientists like Galileo. In formal statements and documents he offered specific apologies to the Jews for abuses they had suffered over the centuries and especially for the ordeal of the Holocaust, and in a historic visit to Jerusalem he prayed at the Western Wall.

Although on global, social, and economic issues John Paul held progressive views and was sharply critical of unbridled capitalism and irresponsible materialism, in matters of church doctrine and governance he favored orthodoxy and papal supremacy. He appointed conservative archbishops, bishops, and cardinals, silenced dissenting theologians, and curbed the growing assertiveness of national churches. He would not countenance marriage for the clergy, the ordination of women as priests (an innovation accepted by the Church of England in 1994), rights of divorce (or of remarriage for the divorced), or homosexuality.

Objections to Vatican centralism

John Paul's stance on many issues engendered protest against the "new Roman centralism," the failure to modernize the church more thoroughly, and the unwillingness to respect the spirit of shared authority promised by the Council. His defenders argued that in upholding tradition he was restoring a balance upset by overly rapid changes in the church introduced by Vatican II. Although weakened by declining health in his later years, John Paul remained active in setting church policies and in defending his theological principles until the last days of his life in 2005. The church cardinals quickly chose a 78-year-old German theologian who had been a close aide of John Paul to serve as the next pope. Entering office as a well-known spokesman for his predecessor's policies, the new pope, Benedict XVI, undertook to defend the ideas and administrative system that the Vatican had promoted during the long and momentous pontificate of John Paul II.

Judaism

Judaism was haunted in the years after 1945 by the traumatic experience of the Holocaust. At the beginning of the twenty-first century there were about 14 million Jews in the world, including 5.8 million in the United States, 4.6 million in Israel, and 2.4 million in Europe. The earlier trend to secularism persisted, but more striking was the vitality of all its branches, Orthodox, Conservative, and Reform. Jews everywhere, and especially in the United States, many not Zionists, lent moral and financial support to the state of Israel, although many were troubled by Israeli militancy and intransigence and by the role in domestic politics of ultraorthodox religious groups that refused to accept a secular state. Anti-Zionism, not only in the Arab world but elsewhere as well, at times served as a thin screen for anti-Semitism. In the former Soviet Union (as in several Islamic states in the Middle East), Jews had met harassment and persecution and, when permitted, emigrated in large numbers. The collapse of communism reignited older currents of anti-Semitism in eastern Europe.

The major non-Western religions, Islam, Hinduism, and Buddhism, also made efforts to adjust millennia-old doctrines to the secular tendencies of the contemporary age; but in some instances such changes were adamantly rejected. Eastern religions attracted new adherents in the West: Islam drew many new believers in the multicultural cities of Europe and North America; Buddhist meditative teachings and practices gained new followings among Western students, intellectuals, and others. The large numbers of African and Asian immigrants to western Europe, and of Asian and Hispanic immigrants to the United States, brought their religious faiths with them, transforming both religious and cultural life in the increasingly diverse nations of the modern world.

Spread of fundamentalism

The latter part of the twentieth century also saw the rise and spread of militant religious reform movements (often called "fundamentalist" by outsiders), especially in the Islamic world. All such movements rejected modern secularism and turned to the literal reading of ancient texts for their own guidance and to impose rules of conduct on others. Nowhere did popular frenzy and the adulation of a religious leader reach such heights as in Iran in 1979; but Muslim activists were also at work in Egypt, Algeria, Nigeria, and elsewhere seeking to subvert secular regimes, impose theocracies, and use state power to enforce religious views. Iran after its revolution in 1979 and Afghanistan under the Taliban regime were among the most extreme examples of countries where Islamic law, or sharia, took precedence over all other law. In several states, as in Sudan, militant regimes also attempted to impose Islamic law on nonbelievers.

The fundamentalists in all societies typically demanded an unswerving adherence to the sacred texts regardless of changing times and circumstances; an identification of religion with political and moral values; and a strict moral code extending to diet, dress, and the relationship of the sexes—all interpreted and enforced by messianic religious leaders who mobilized mass followings to accomplish these ends. Muslim fundamentalism had a counterpart in an extremist Hindu movement in India, which unleashed violence against the Muslims in the country and threatened the secular state.

Fundamentalism could be found in evangelical Christian sects and in extremist Orthodox Jewish quarters as well. It easily bred intolerance and separatism, and ran counter to the blending of cultures in the contemporary world. In the West the separation of political and religious authority had become so widely accepted that it often became difficult to understand the strength and appeal of the new religious ferment.

Activism: The Youth Rebellion of the 1960s

In the second half of the twentieth century young people acquired a collective cultural and generational identity that young people seemed not to have possessed in earlier historical periods. It was now possible to speak of a youth market, a youth culture, youth movements. In part the phenomenon was demographic in origin, the result of the extraordinary number of births in the decade and a half after the Second World War—the "baby boom." A large cohort grew up in a rapidly changing world, and they developed a generational identity through a new popular culture that appeared in music, fashion, films, and advertising. Youth culture became a key component of modern global culture.

In the 1960s a youth political activism made a startling appearance, marked by a widespread student rebellion. A generation came to college age and attended institutions of higher learning in larger numbers than ever

Youth activism

before. It was a generation that grew up in an era of global change and scientific breakthroughs, to which their elders were not dependable guides. They took for granted the scientific, technological, and other accomplishments of their world and concentrated on its deficiencies   the flagrant contradictions of wealth and poverty within and among nations, racial injustice, discrimination, colonialism, the impersonal quality of mechanized society and bureaucratized institutions (including colleges and universities), the violence that destroyed human beings in continuing wars, and always the threat of nuclear destruction. The rebelliousness extended beyond the traditional generation gap; it was directed at all established society and reiterated romantic or utopian themes that had influenced social criticism since the beginnings of modern history.

The revolt burst forth in the late 1960s in widely separate parts of the world. The cultural revolution in China, although in an entirely different context, was not unrelated and indirectly inspired it. At the peak of the movement in 1967–1968 students demonstrated and rioted on campuses and battled police all over the world; American, Canadian, Mexican, West German, French, Italian, and Spanish universities were heavily involved.

1968

France was one center of the storm. Demonstrations there reached near-revolutionary dimensions in the spring of 1968 and threatened to overthrow the regime when 10 million workers also went out on strike, partly in sympathy with students and partly for their own grievances. But the government eventually restored order, and many of the initial grievances in the overcrowded, impersonal universities were almost forgotten in the wider, but quickly passing, French upheaval.

A global youth culture emerged in the 1960s and 1970s, creating distinctive styles of dress and an international market for new forms of popular music. Rock musicians such as this English band, The Rolling Stones, toured the world and wrote songs that helped to shape a generational identity spanning nations and cultures. The band's lead singer Mick Jagger is seen here with guitarist Keith Richards at a concert in Los Angeles in 1973.
(Neal Preston/Corbis)

Some of the earliest and largest political demonstrations took place in the United States, sparked by the African-American struggle for civil rights and heightened by resistance to American involvement in the unpopular Vietnam War. The assassinations in 1968 of the dedicated black leader of the civil rights movement, Martin Luther King, Jr., and of Robert Kennedy, brother of the slain president, fueled further anger in the ranks of the young.

The rebelling students often defined their collective identities through rock music, unconventional styles of dress, and a language of their own. Some activists also made icons out of controversial revolutionary leaders who symbolized opposition to the established Western political order: Fidel Castro and his martyred Lieutenant Che Guevara, Ho Chi Minh, Mao Zedong, militant American black leaders like Malcolm X, the heralds of the colonial revolution such as Frantz Fanon (the West Indian author of *The Wretched of the Earth*), and others. They read the neo-Marxist philosopher Herbert Marcuse, who warned that the very tolerance of bourgeois society was a trap to prevent true protest against injustice; they learned from him that the industrial working class, co-opted by the existing system, was no longer a revolutionary force. A "New Left" dismissed older revolutionaries in the Soviet Union as stodgy bureaucrats and affirmed that revolutionary leadership would come from Maoist China or other places in the Third World. They attacked materialism, affluence, and conformity, and the power structure of contemporary society. Many believed in militant confrontations that recalled an older anarchism and nihilism. They called on each other to transform or destroy various social, political, and cultural traditions, assuming that their generation could overcome the social hierarchies and injustices in modern democratic societies.

Emergence of the New Left

The rebellion in its mass phase faded by the early 1970s. In the United States it helped bring the Vietnam War to an end. Only a small number of extremists carried on a kind of urban guerrilla war through underground terrorist organizations—the Bader–Meinhof gang in Germany, the Red Brigades in Italy, the Weathermen in the United States. Mostly, the rebels of 1968 moved on to places in established society. While many people shuddered at the attack on traditional institutions and orderly processes, others were shaken out of their complacency about social or racial inequities. Efforts were made to reform university administration and to provide more adequate teaching facilities. The youth movement, even after its political radicalism subsided, had a continuing effect on all age groups in loosening older standards of language, dress, and sexual mores.

The Women's Liberation Movement

The feminist, or women's liberation, movement was another, but more enduring, manifestation of twentieth-century and contemporary social ferment. From the time of the French Revolution, as noted earlier, a few thinkers in France and England had raised the question of equal rights for women, and a women's political movement had also developed in the United States by the mid-nineteenth century. Elizabeth Cady Stanton and a small group of associates in 1848, inspired in part by revolutionary developments in Europe that year, had proclaimed a declaration of independence for women, demanding the right to vote, equal compensation for work, legal equality in property and other matters, and expanded educational opportunities. In Britain, later in the century, the suffragettes raised similar demands in their militant campaign for the vote. Women won the right to vote before the First World War in a few American states and in a few of the smaller countries; after 1918, in many more nations, including the United States and Britain; and after 1945, in almost all other countries. But other objectives went unrealized.

The militant twentieth-century phase of the women's movement began in the United States in the mid-1960s, partly as a parallel to the civil rights movement of the African-American population. The women's liberation movement, inspired by such books as Simone de Beauvoir's *The Second Sex,* published in France in 1949, and Betty Friedan's *The Feminine Mystique,* which appeared in the United States in 1963, contended that women, half or more of the human race, had always been and continued to be oppressed by a male-dominated society and that women were systematically denied access to positions of authority, leadership, property, and power. Although the more blatant forms of legal discrimination, in such matters as property rights for example, had been or were being removed, twentieth-century feminists demanded an end to all barriers to equal participation in the economy and society. Betty Friedan's influential book appealed to women to give up traditional lives devoted mainly to the home and family and utilize their education, skills, and abilities in the outside world as well. Large numbers of women entered the job market for the first time in the 1970s. Between 1970 and 1990 the ratio of women to men working in the economy in the United States or actively seeking employment rose from 37 women per 100 men to 62 per 100 men. The new role for women required adjustments in family responsibilities, which were not always easily arranged or accepted.

Inspirations and demands

The campaign for equal rights called upon a different agenda in the poorer, less developed countries of the world, where women generally had to overcome centuries-old patterns of repression, abuse, and disregard of the most elementary human rights. The United Nations from the time of its founding had committed itself to equal political, economic, and educational rights for women. But in many parts of Africa, Asia, and Latin America adult illiteracy rates were still significantly higher for women and were declining more slowly. In 2000 it was estimated that of 110 million children worldwide not attending

The French writer Simone de Beauvoir, shown here in 1947, wrote about the social position of women in her widely read book *The Second Sex* (1949). Beauvoir analyzed the constraints and myths that affected women in what she described as patriarchal societies and called for the independence or liberation of women in contemporary social and political life. Her work became an influential statement of themes and ideas that helped shape a new international women's movement in the 1960s and 1970s.
(Hulton-Deutsch Collection/Corbis)

schools two-thirds were female. Yet in the developing world, where a majority of the world's women lived, opportunities for women, especially in education, could help accelerate social advances for the entire population.

At UN-sponsored international conferences government delegates and representatives from nongovernmental organizations affirmed the "universal rights of women" and insisted on their right to decide freely on matters relating to all aspects of their lives free from "coercion, discrimination, or violence." Discrimination, it turned out, was not confined to capitalist societies. Despite Communist verbal promises, the advance to equality, or even to equality of opportunity, in the former Soviet Union and in the People's Republic of China did not match the official rhetoric.

UN support for women

Some women, more so than in the past (when only a few reigning women sovereigns were able to exercise political power), came to hold positions of the highest authority in their countries in the years after 1945. Among them were Indira Gandhi in India, Golda Meir in Israel, Corazón Aquino in the Philippines, Benazir Bhutto in Pakistan, Margaret Thatcher in Britain, and a growing list of other women presidents or prime ministers in such widely differing countries as Sri Lanka, Portugal, Norway, Iceland, Nicaragua, Ireland, Bangladesh, France, Poland, Turkey, Finland, Canada, Indonesia, Germany, Liberia and Chile. Women were thus entering widely into modern political life, but it was also true, as feminists and others continued to stress, that men still dominated legislative assemblies and governments in general in most countries of the world at the beginning of the twenty-first century.

Meanwhile the development of advanced contraceptive technology, especially of the birth control pill in the early 1960s, and the legalization and greater access to safer abortion procedures in a growing number of modern societies, provided a new biological freedom and autonomy for women. Changing social patterns tolerating sexual freedom and new and more equal forms of relationships between the sexes in marriage also contributed to social liberation. In the first decade of the twenty-first century women were filling a larger share of places in higher education and in professional schools than ever before. In the United States women students made up more than half the number of undergraduate students in colleges and universities and were close to that ratio in law and medical schools. As more women became part of the labor force at all levels, the demand arose not only for equal compensation for equal work, still far from realized, but also for better pay for jobs that were poorly compensated because they had been traditionally filled by women. Although there were disagreements within and outside the women's liberation movement on the methods and tempo of change, wide agreement existed on the need to utilize fully all of society's human resources in every part of the globe. If that could be accomplished, it would count among the most memorable of the revolutionary changes of the contemporary era.

132. INTERNATIONAL CONFLICT IN THE TWENTY-FIRST CENTURY

The end of the Cold War and the demise of the U.S.S.R. in 1991 transformed the foundations on which international relations had rested since 1945. The Western campaign to contain communism, for which there had been a broad consensus in American public opinion, was over. The United States was now the sole superpower, the leading economic and military power of the globe. The key question was whether it could handle this power with restraint and with consideration for its allies and other nations. International stability in good part depended on how it conceived of its responsibilities in world affairs and how it shaped its relationships with the UN, its European allies, Russia, China, and the developing world. A new configuration of world affairs began to emerge, but its outlines and the American role were only roughly apparent. Peace and security remained the world's most pressing problems. Two new challenges appeared: the eruption of conflicts more frequently within nations than between nations and the danger of terrorism, which spread into almost every region of the world.

The twentieth century, heralded in its opening years for its promise of peace and progress, had seen more than 200 million people perish as victims of wars and brutal regimes. Five million deaths resulted directly or indirectly from armed conflict in the last decade alone. It was clear that the end of the Cold War had not brought peace to the world, but the older patterns of warfare between nation-states seemed to be breaking down by the early twenty-first century. The new wars tended to be conflicts between religious or ethnic groups within a national territory or between guerrilla forces and high-tech national armies that sought to suppress them. These new wars could last for years, in part because they were no longer waged by opposing national governments that were able to negotiate a truce or a peace settlement.

Some close analysts of international affairs maintained that the new world order might best be understood in the context of rivalries and conflicts between religion-based civilizations, not between nation-states. There was already some evidence of this. The Russian offensive against Chechnya had anti-Islamic overtones, as did the Serb and Croat attacks on Muslims in Bosnia and the Serb war against the Albanian Muslims in Kosovo. In turn, Orthodox Christian church leaders in Russia and Greece condemned the Western air offensive against Serbia. India, once intended as a haven for a tolerant secularism, was now increasingly Hindu-oriented, and its clashes with Islamic Pakistan over Kashmir and other matters were sharpened by religious tensions. The conflicts between Israel and its Arab neighbors in the Middle East had distinctive religious over-

Religious divisions could shape conflicts

tones. The extremist Muslim Taliban rulers in Afghanistan willfully destroyed ancient Buddhist sculptures as offensive to their faith. Chinese communism displayed something of the older Confucian and imperial tra-
ditions hostile to the outside world and was intolerant of religious threats to its rule. The wars launched by the United States against the Muslim countries of Afghanistan and Iraq in the early twenty-first century also took on religious meaning because some saw these conflicts as a battle between different religious and cultural traditions and values, or even as a revival of the medieval Crusades.

But nonreligious factors remained preponderant in international affairs, and even in religion-based civilizations there was marked diversity. A common faith in Islam did not prevent Iran and Iraq from their bloody war in 1980–1988 or protect Kuwait from invasion by Iraq in 1990. The world's religions were far from homogeneous, and all had been touched to some degree by secularism and globalization. There were enduring conflicts between branches of the major religions—Catholics and Protestants in Northern Ireland, for example, and Shiites and Sunnis in the many parts of the Middle East. The two great wars of the twentieth century had originated in conflicts between nations in the Christian West itself.

Recognizing global diversity

It was nevertheless important to call attention to the global diversity of traditions, cultures, and religions if only to shed any illusions in the West that it was destined to spread its ideas and values across the world unchallenged. Western civilization, with its Judeo-Christian heritage, had been enriched by interaction with other civilizations. By the twenty-first century its global influ-
ence was undeniable, but people in the West needed to recognize the existence of deep-seated cultural allegiances in every part of the world and to understand the enduring importance of cultural differences in diplomatic affairs, economic exchanges, and political conflicts.

The United Nations

The much-used term "international community" was indispensable but defied precise def-
inition. The closest approximation to it was the United Nations. Here the Security Council was the dominant institution. The original roster of five permanent members of the Council, the victors in the Second World War, had been modified only in 1971 when the Peo-
ple's Republic of China replaced Nationalist China and in 1991 when Russia succeeded to the seat of the dissolved U.S.S.R. The political and economic changes in the world spurred proposals for giving other large powers permanent seats, so that they might exercise inter-

UN membership expands

national responsibilities commensurate with their economic and military resources. Even the veto power of the five permanent powers came into question.

The United Nations counted over 190 member nations by the first decade of the twenty-first century, and even the smallest new nations were permitted to join. The 80 smallest members of the UN, it turned out, represented less than ten percent of the world's population.

It was in the General Assembly that the new states mainly exercised their authority. Regardless of size, each member deliberated and voted in full equality. As we have seen,

CHRONOLOGY OF NOTABLE EVENTS, 1949–2004

1949	Simone de Beauvoir's publication of *The Second Sex* helps to launch a new international campaign for women's rights
1968	Youth movements in many nations press for political and social change
1969	American astronauts land on the surface of the moon
1978	John Paul II becomes Pope—the first Pole ever elected to the papacy
1991	Treaty of Maastricht establishes the new European Union
1994	World Trade Organization is established to mediate international trade
1997	Financial crises disrupt the economies of east and southeast Asia
1997	Labour Party wins elections in Great Britain; Tony Blair becomes Prime Minister
1998	Political agreement in Northern Ireland offers plan to end violence between Protestants and Catholics
1998	Social Democrats win elections in Germany; Gerhard Schröder becomes Chancellor
2001	Al-Qaeda terrorist attacks on New York and Washington; United States and its allies overthrow Taliban regime in Afghanistan
2002	The "euro" becomes the common currency of 12 European nations
2003	American and British forces invade Iraq and overthrow the regime of Saddam Hussein, but face prolonged war against "insurgents"
2004	European Union membership grows to 25 nations

the General Assembly frequently served as a forum for the grievances of the developing nations against the wealthier industrial world. Several of the UN's agencies played significant roles in dealing with population, health, social welfare, and humanitarian issues. After the Cold War, the developing nations somewhat tempered their anti-Westernism, but they continued to demand a high priority for their enormous economic needs, including debt relief.

Debate went on in the United Nations, the European Union, and elsewhere over the interpretation of human rights. The Universal Declaration of Human Rights, adopted by the UN in 1948, had focused on political and civil rights, emphasizing protection from arbitrary arrest, imprisonment, and torture. Pressure later mounted to broaden the largely political definition to include economic rights, the necessity of meeting human needs within each country, and the right to international development assistance for those purposes.

Defining human rights

An even more complex issue troubled the United States, the UN, and the broader international community: The developing nations at times contended that even the political and civil rights generally described as universal were really Western and should be modified to fit the culture, history, and religions of other parts of the world. Equality for women or the rights of children, in this interpretation, could have different meanings in countries whose cultural traditions differed from those of the West. But many across the globe maintained that human rights, no matter how difficult to define, of Western origin or not, represented a common core of values that should protect every individual human being against enslavement, violation, or discrimination. Respect for cultural pluralism or local traditions should not cover or excuse any form of human indignity.

Implications of Western definitions

The practical implications of such debates were significant. In many Islamic countries there were fewer opportunities for women to attend school, work outside the home, drive cars, or vote. The governing regime in Sudan was still sanctioning slavery and forcibly converting its non-Islamic population to Islam. Polygamy was still widely practiced and sanctioned by some religions and cultures. Some African peoples still practiced female genital mutilation. In many parts of the world young children, boys and girls, were forced to serve in combat by guerrilla military units. To abolish cruel and unusual punishments many nations would have to ban flogging, mutilation, and maiming as punishments. The United States itself had a large prison population and retained capital punishment, the latter now banned in the European Union. There was little desire to meddle in the internal affairs of other peoples, but it was difficult to ignore egregious violations of human rights or to accept the argument that Western values were being imposed on others.

Politically, the explosion of virulent ethnic and religious-based nationalism after the end of the Cold War confronted the UN with new issues of humanitarian assistance and intervention. UN peacekeeping came to include help in the reconstruction of devastated countries and peoples as well as a protective military presence. Supporters of the UN's expanding role urged advanced planning for troubled areas to prevent the escalation of conflict. They projected rapid deployment forces, as once envisaged, with contingents drawn from the member states. Much depended on the support of the United States, which maintained its leadership role in the Security Council but refused to place any of its own troops in UN-controlled peacekeeping forces, criticized the UN's large bureaucracy, and demanded reforms in the administration and financial management of UN activities.

Although the UN was often criticized for its inability to prevent wars or act decisively on global social problems, its broad goals remained as formulated in 1945: to control and reduce the scourge of war, advance human rights, promote equality, protect the independence of nations, encourage social progress, raise living standards, and work for peace and security. But the world's nations, large and small, were not ready to subordinate their national interests or sovereignty to any international organization. Without armed power of its own, the United Nations could not prevent powerful sovereign nations from going to war or stop such wars or civil wars after they began.

U.S. leadership in international affairs

The United States, as the sole superpower after 1991, exercised the leading role in international affairs, even if in concert with its European allies and other major powers. At times, however, it took initiatives that made it difficult to distinguish between American unilateralism and international action. The Security Council in 1990 condemned Iraq's aggression against Kuwait, but it was the United States that assembled a formidable multinational military force, including over a half-million American troops, and in 1991 forced the Iraqi withdrawal from Kuwait.

In 1992, toward the close of the first President Bush's administration, American troops were used for the first time to reinforce UN peacekeeping forces in Somalia, in northeast Africa, where warring militias had made it impossible to deliver food and other supplies to the starving population. President Clinton in the next administration continued the policy, calling for an "assertive multilateralism." But peace had not yet been achieved and more than peacekeeping was required. In a failed military mission in October 1993, American military units under American command were attacked by Somali paramilitary groups and 18 American soldiers were killed. Publicly televised scenes of corpses dragged

WHEEL MAN
By Ernest Trova (American, 1927–)

Trova has created a dehumanized, life-size bronze figure of no particular sex, age, race, culture, or environment. Compressed between the two wheels, it seems to present humanity as the victim of its own complicated inventions. The wheels may also symbolize the rolling vicissitudes of human fortune. The date 1965 is inscribed on the base, and the whole faceless assemblage suggests that the wheels of human progress and civilization have not exactly carried human beings to the happy condition that an earlier, more optimistic age had expected.

(Solomon R. Guggenheim Museum, New York, Gift of John G. Powers Fund, 1965 (65.1777) Photograph by David Heald © Solomon R. Guggenheim Foundation, New York)

through the streets incited Congress to sweep away "assertive multilateralism" and for a time restrict similar intervention.

Recommendations to enlarge the authority and functions of the UN lost support and even seemed to threaten the peacekeeping role that the UN had successfully pursued for some 40 years in places like Zaire (now Congo), southern Lebanon, Cyprus, Cambodia, Angola, and elsewhere. In part the new attitude explained the failure of the UN or the United States and its allies to act in Bosnia in 1992–1993, when outside intervention might have stopped the terrible atrocities against Bosnia's Muslim population. The same misgivings were behind the failure to take timely action to prevent the massacre of the Tutsi people in 1994 in Rwanda, in which some 800,000 Tutsi were killed and hundreds of thousands were driven into exile; and there was little concerted action to stop the atrocities sanctioned by the Islamic government in Sudan against the non-Islamic black peoples in Darfur.

In some later crises, however, the international community did take action. As we have noted earlier, the massive American-led air offensive by NATO against the former Yugoslavia in 1999 set a precedent for multinational "humanitarian intervention" within a sovereign state, although no ground troops were used. The UN did not join the war, but played a major role in postwar peacekeeping in Kosovo. International war crimes trials were held for political and military leaders charged with war crimes and crimes against humanity in Rwanda and in the former Yugoslavia. An international force also intervened to protect the people of East Timor after they voted in a UN-sponsored referendum for independence from Indonesia and then faced virtual butchery by Indonesian paramilitary forces.

Multinational humanitarian intervention

It was a formidable challenge to decide on the legitimate use of international force against sovereign nations to protect threatened or abused populations. As President Clinton noted, the UN's mission from the time of its charter was to protect the world from the scourge of war. "If so," he announced in 2000 to a special planning and celebratory millennium meeting of the United Nations, "we must respect sovereignty and territorial integrity but still find a way to protect people as well as borders." UN Secretary General Kofi Annan strongly endorsed his plea.

NATO, Russia and the New International Cooperation

Many in the United States favored military intervention when American national interests were involved, and many supported the American role in mediation as pursued by successive administrations in troubled areas, such as the Middle East. The new American president, elected in late 2000, George W. Bush, son of the former President Bush, reassessed the concept of "humanitarian intervention," but soon initiated other military actions when he decided that American interests were at risk. Meanwhile the Europeans took steps to strengthen the independent military and defense role for the European Union. The French, following the precedent of de Gaulle in the Cold War years, called for recognition of a "multipolar world," in which the EU would be a more equal partner, and they objected, if only in rhetoric, to the hegemony of the "American hyperpower."

Russia's role undefined

The role of Russia in the new world order was critical but not yet precisely defined. That it was still a major power and not ready to abandon aspirations to an important role in world affairs was evident in its pro-Serb stance in the Balkans. How to deal with an assertive Russia still armed with thousands of nuclear weapons was a major challenge. NATO, meanwhile, at American initiative, admitted Hungary, Poland, and the Czech Republic as full members in 1999; and seven other countries of formerly Soviet-controlled central and eastern Europe joined in 2004. The Central and East European nations not only wished to be full partners in Europe but also saw their membership in NATO as the best guarantee of their future security. The admission of several states on the very borders of Russia, however, was regarded by many Russians as a provocation. On the other hand, Russia's president became a member of what was now the Group of 8, the heads of government of the major industrial democracies; and there were regular consultations with NATO through a council established in 2002 to facilitate cooperation on various international issues.

Nuclear disarmament loomed as another key issue in the post–Cold War international order. The collapse of the U.S.S.R. promised to end the "balance of terror" that had resulted from the nuclear buildup of the two superpowers. Despite some initial obstacles, the United States and Russia agreed on the voluntary reduction of nuclear arms. The number of nuclear warheads in the world, of which the largest number were held by the United States and the U.S.S.R., was reduced in the 15 years between the mid-1980s and 2000. Nonetheless the head of the UN's nuclear monitoring agency reported at the close of 2005 that there were still 27,000 nuclear warheads in various parts of the world, which, he said, could mean "the destruction of entire nations in a matter of minutes."

The threat of nuclear proliferation persisted, keeping the issue high on the international agenda. By the end of the twentieth century 187 nations had signed the 1968 Non-Proliferation Treaty. At one of the periodic meetings held to review the status of the treaty, in May 2000, the five major nuclear powers—the United States, Russia, Britain, France, and China—in the first such declaration ever made pledged themselves "unequivocally" to the eventual elimination of all nuclear weapons. There was satisfaction and reassurance also that since August 1945 no nuclear bomb had been exploded in warfare. That additional nations such as North Korea and Iran might be developing nuclear arms nevertheless gave cause for continuing concern. A major setback to the progress of nuclear arms control was the refusal of the United States Senate in late 1999 to ratify the Comprehensive Nuclear Test Ban Treaty because the U.S. insisted that the nation's security and the security of other states required periodic testing of the American nuclear arsenal. Almost all other countries ratified this treaty, which would have prohibited all nuclear weapons testing. In addition, President George W. Bush's proposals to resume work on a missile defense shield and to pursue the development of smaller bombs called "nuclear earth penetrators" threatened to upset existing arms control policy, which since the Antiballistic Missile Treaty of 1972 had focused on the reduction of offensive weapons and banned the building of defensive ones.

If relations with Russia were important, so also were Western relations with the People's Republic of China. Some saw engagement with Communist China through trade and other forms of peaceful interchange as the path to take. Others insisted that the West could not keep silent in the face of human rights violations, the suppression of religious groups, and the mistreatment of Tibet. The United States was committed to a two-China policy that recognized the continuing existence of a non-Communist Taiwan until peaceful union could take place, but there were alarming Chinese threats of forcible annexation. China could be expected to make its considerable weight felt in world affairs and to oppose future international intervention for human rights abuses.

Relations with the People's Republic of China

Meanwhile the world's attention turned to the pressing problems of international terrorism and to new wars in Afghanistan and Iraq.

Terrorism and War after September 11, 2001

We have seen how the United States became steadily more involved in the Middle East during the latter part of the twentieth century—in the Iran-Iraq War of the 1980s, in the Persian Gulf War of 1991, and in other episodes; but American involvement entered a new phase of extended military conflict in the new century, when on September 11, 2001, radical Islamic terrorists carried out a surprise attack against the United States. Dispatched to America by the extremist Islamic organization known as al-Qaeda, committed terrorists from the Middle East set out on a carefully prepared suicide mission. Fifteen of the 19 terrorists were from Saudi Arabia. They had spent considerable time in the United States, where several had even undergone flight training. The terrorists hijacked four large American commercial airliners, each loaded with passengers, and crashed two of the planes into the towers of the World Trade Center in New York; the third plane crashed into the Pentagon in northern Virginia; the fourth crashed to the ground in rural Pennsylvania without reaching its intended target.

September 11, 2001

The hijackers managed to accomplish their mission on a busy weekday morning, causing complete destruction of the World Trade Center, crowded with people at work, and significant damage to one side of the vast Pentagon complex. There were 3,000 deaths. No one was prepared for such an attack. There had never been a terrorist attack of this kind and on this scale in the history of the United States or indeed in the whole deadly history of terrorism throughout the world. The closest parallel in the American experience was the

Terrorists linked to the extremist Islamic organization al-Qaeda crashed hijacked commercial airplanes into the World Trade Center in New York City and the Pentagon in northern Virginia on September 11, 2001. This picture shows the World Trade Towers just after the crash of a second aircraft. The United States responded to these devastating attacks by launching a global "war on terror" that would include American-led military campaigns to overthrow hostile regimes in Afghanistan and Iraq.
(Reuters/Corbis)

Japanese attack on Pearl Harbor in 1941, but that had not taken place in the continental United States and was directed against military targets. Many saw the terrorist attack in September 2001 as a turning point in modern American history, in part because it destroyed the long-held assumption that wide oceans protected the United States from foreign enemies.

President George W. Bush received authorization from the American Congress for the use of all necessary resources to mount a counter-attack against enemies who, he said, "hate our freedom of religion, our freedom of speech, our freedom to vote. . . ." The "war on terror," which began in September 2001, was defined in terms that in some ways evoked the language of the Cold War against the Soviet Union. Under new legislation called the "Patriot Act," the president also acquired wide executive powers to deal with terrorist threats within the United States. There was, however, no national enemy that loomed like the Soviet Union as the obvious military opponent in a new global conflict. American intelligence agencies had been tracking the al-Qaeda organization, and there was some later evidence that an intimation of such an impending attack had become available, but little of this was known to the public at the time.

War on terror

The al-Qaeda leader, Osama bin Laden, had found welcome support from the radical Islamic Taliban regime in Afghanistan, yet he controlled no government or armies or industrial infrastructure that might be attacked in conventional military operations. From time to time he delivered fiery speeches about his self-appointed mission. The al-Qaeda organization had emerged in the aftermath of the first Gulf War against Iraq, when American forces came to be permanently stationed in Saudi Arabia and when the Saudi monarchy entered into a new close alliance with the United States. The "founding statement" of al-Qaeda accused the United States of "occupying the lands of Islam in the holiest of places, the Arabian peninsula, plundering its riches, dictating to its rulers, humiliating its people, . . . and turning its bases . . . into a spearhead through which to fight the neighboring Muslim peoples." Al-Qaeda called on its followers to launch attacks against America, which had begun in the 1990s with the bombing of American embassies in Africa, continued with a destructive assault on an American naval ship near the Arabian peninsula in 2000, and then escalated in the devastating attack of September 11, 2001.

al-Qaeda

American forces, with the backing of a strong coalition of NATO allies, at once mounted a large-scale air assault on Afghanistan and, with the aid of Afghan forces opposed to the Taliban, quickly brought about the overthrow of the regime in Kabul. A large number of al-Qaeda militants were captured or killed, but bin Laden himself escaped and remained at large years after the campaign ended. A new Afghan government under President Hamid Karzai, with the help of American and other financial aid, began to rebuild the country, while a continuing but more limited American war against guerrilla forces continued in the mountainous border areas. There was reason to believe that a stable regime in Kabul, together with the support of the neighboring government in Pakistan under President Musharraf, could block the further operations of Islamic radicals and the still active guerrilla forces in Afghanistan.

War in Afghanistan

Although the attempt to capture bin Laden and permanently crush al-Qaeda had proved unsuccessful in the Afghan campaign, the Bush administration decided that the dictatorial Iraqi regime of Saddam Hussein posed an equally serious threat to the United States. Iraq was an oil-rich nation of strategic importance for the entire Middle East, and it now stood accused of stockpiling chemical, biological, and nuclear weapons of mass destruction. The Bush administration had become persuaded that the United States had a mission after the end of the Cold War to curb dictatorships and help spread democracy, even unilaterally if necessary; and it seemed to have harbored for some time a desire to overthrow Saddam Hussein's regime in Iraq. The war on terror was thus expanded to include plans for a preemptive assault on Iraq, although no imminent threat from that country seemed to be present. To be sure, American and British intelligence reports indicated that Iraq was developing weapons of mass destruction, but other sources were less confident. The Bush administration also linked Iraq to the threats from Islamic terrorism, but there seemed to be no hard evidence of such links. Although some critics decried the impending action against Iraq as a diversion from the true war on terror, the American Congress in October 2002 authorized President Bush to use all necessary force to defend the United States and to compel Iraqi compliance with weapons inspections.

American view of Iraq

Responding to American concerns, the UN Security Council passed a resolution demanding that teams of UN-appointed weapons inspectors be allowed to enter Iraq and search for the weapons of mass destruction that Saddam Hussein was allegedly hiding. The inspectors were unable to find such weapons, but the American and British governments insisted that the Iraqis were concealing evidence and that the UN should sanction military action to enforce compliance with UN resolutions that Iraq had apparently refused to accept. Britain was the only permanent member of the Security Council to support the

United States. When France, Germany, and Russia refused to support the resolution that would have authorized an invasion of Iraq, President Bush and Prime Minister Blair resolved to go to war without the authorization of a UN resolution. A small group of other nations also agreed to provide limited assistance so that it became possible to speak of a coalition force.

War in Iraq

The American invasion began in March 2003. Powerful American forces, with the support of Britain and a few small contingents from the coalition, quickly swept north from bases in Kuwait to overthrow Saddam Hussein's government in Baghdad. Armed resistance melted away, and Saddam Hussein himself fled. Despite massive looting and a general breakdown of law and order, which the strategists of the invasion had failed to foresee, major combat operations appeared to be over. In May 2003 President Bush announced that the mission had been accomplished, and optimistic American planners expected Iraqi oil revenues to finance much of the nation's reconstruction. But a violent insurgency soon erupted, especially in the Sunni Arab region to the north and west of Baghdad, where much of the population feared the political ascendancy of Iraq's Shiite majority. The Americans had not fully taken into account the country's sharp ethnic and religious divisions, which Saddam had kept under tight control. Under Saddam's officially secular regime and Baathist party dictatorship, the minority of Sunni Arabs, about one fifth of the nation's 27 million people, had brutally victimized the Shiites, who comprised about three fifths of the population, as well as the Kurds, who were not Arabs but were Muslims, and made up the remaining fifth.

Insurgent forces in Iraq

The insurgency had not been expected. Most American strategists had counted on Iraqis to accept the Americans as liberators, not as invaders or occupiers. Within weeks the Americans appointed a "Coalition Provisional Authority" to manage the occupation. It seemed logical for the Americans and the provisional authority they had set up to disband the Iraqi army and police forces and to prevent former Baathists from assuming any new role in the country. But many of the disaffected Sunnis and former Baathists joined the insurgent forces that now sprang up across Iraq. Although the Sunnis, resenting the loss of their former power, were the most active participants in the insurgency, many Iraqis of all backgrounds seemed arrayed against the invasion by the American and Western "infidels." The insurgents were reinforced by militant Islamic sympathizers who infiltrated from Syria and other Islamic states. The Kurds meanwhile preserved order in their northern region of the country through their own paramilitary forces.

Campaigns against insurgents

The growing violence seriously disrupted the plans for reconstructing Iraq's oil industry and technological infrastructure. Electric power and other necessities became scarce, and living conditions were difficult for most Iraqis. In the meantime, a comprehensive American search of the entire country found no weapons of mass destruction—whose alleged existence had been the principal and urgent rationale for the invasion. American forces responded to the new violence by waging campaigns against insurgents in the countryside and major cities, imprisoning large numbers of suspects, and capturing Saddam Hussein and many of his former officials. They undertook to train Iraqis for service in the country's new security and police forces, many of whom soon became victims themselves of insurgent violence. American casualties also steadily mounted. Roadside bombs destroyed trucks and tanks, and suicide bombers killed or maimed both American soldiers and thousands of Iraqi civilians.

On the political front the Americans took steps toward creating a more independent Iraqi government. In 2004 the Coalition Provisional Authority was dissolved and political authority was transferred to an interim Iraqi government. Three successive elections in the following year brought Iraqis to the polls in large numbers. The first election, in January 2005, chose a transitional parliament whose main task was to write a new Iraqi constitution, but most Sunni Arabs boycotted the election and thereby lost the opportunity to participate in the drafting of the constitution. The constitution was subsequently adopted in a second, nationwide vote in October, and the Sunni Arabs again for the most part refused to participate.

Elections in Iraq

The new constitution generally satisfied the Shiites and the Kurds because it gave virtual autonomy to a large Shiite region in the south and to the Kurds in the north, each with control over the oil resources and revenues in those regions. The Sunnis were frustrated by this political decentralization and by the growing influence of Shiite religious authorities in the new government. With American prodding, it was agreed that the next parliament would take steps to amend the constitution and submit the changes to another national referendum. When the third Iraqi election was held in December 2005, this time for a parliament of 275 seats elected for a four-year term, there was wide participation by all of the nation's ethnic and religious groups, including the Sunnis, and by a coalition of secular parties. The major Shiite religious parties won the largest number of seats in the new parliament, the Kurds won the expected majorities in their northern region, and the Sunnis gained some seats by winning in the Sunni-dominated provinces and in parts of Baghdad. Both the Sunni and secular political parties, however, charged their opponents with electoral fraud, and a new wave of violence spread across the country. The political situation thus remained unsettled and deeply affected by sectarian and ethnic conflicts, despite the impressive, courageous turnout of Iraqi voters and the widespread desire for a stable, effective, and more democratic government.

Results of Iraqi elections

The Bush administration refused to set a timetable for the departure of American troops. As the number of American deaths and casualties mounted into the thousands (and Iraqi deaths and casualties increased into the tens of thousands), support for the war declined in the United States, in Britain, and in much of the rest of the world, where public opinion had never really favored the American invasion from the beginning. Criticism grew even sharper when the elections seemed unlikely to produce the stable democratic political culture that had been anticipated and when the results raised fears that militant Shiites might try to establish an Islamic theocracy on the Iranian model. There was also concern that the American departure, whenever it came, would leave divisive ethnic and religious tensions that could lead to a prolonged civil war.

Declining support for war

The war caused additional dismay in the United States and elsewhere when news reports accompanied by shocking photographs revealed that American soldiers had humiliated and tortured Iraqi prisoners. Some of the abuses resembled brutal methods that had been common under the dictatorial regime of Saddam Hussein. Although they may have been encouraged by loosely veiled instructions from their superiors who sought information from suspected insurgents, only a few low-rank soldiers were tried and punished. Large numbers of suspects were also imprisoned and apparently tortured by the new Iraqi police. Amid reports of such practices in Iraq and of abusive interrogation techniques at secret American detention centers in other

Abuse of prisoners

locations, the United States Senate voted overwhelmingly in 2005 to adopt a resolution banning the use of torture by Americans.

Terrorism continues

Meanwhile, terrorist attacks by al-Qaeda and its sympathizers continued to kill people around the world—from resort hotels in Indonesia to the trains and subways in Spain and Britain. There was growing anxiety that the United States had entered another Vietnam-style "quagmire," that the war in Iraq had distracted from the wider war on terrorism, and that military action alone would never eliminate the Islamic terrorist threats. Others worried that the war was creating new hostility for America and the West, driving more disaffected and enraged young Muslims into extremist terrorist camps.

President Bush, who won election to a second term in 2004, stressed that the war on terror was strengthening America and its allies. He pointed to the political progress in Afghanistan and Iraq, where millions had turned out to vote, as evidence of a new democratic culture in the Middle East. Much of the American public, however, became skeptical about the president's defense of the war and his expansion of presidential powers, which included the wire-tapping of American citizens without following established legal procedures. Yet he had pledged to be a "war president," and he repeatedly reminded the country that the terrorist threat had not passed.

Conflict in twenty-first century

How events might evolve or what might happen in neighboring countries remained unclear. It was certain, however, that the long-anticipated end to the Cold War had not brought the "end of history" or the end of human conflict. In the opening years of the twenty-first century the world was enmeshed in conflicts that reflected the deep-seated forces of contemporary nationalism, global economic competition, and militant ethnic or cultural identities; and such conflicts gained intensity everywhere from deeply held religious beliefs and long historical memories.

 133. SOCIAL CHALLENGES IN THE TWENTY-FIRST CENTURY

The Population Explosion

Of all the social developments in the second half of the twentieth century one of the most spectacular was the growth of the world's population. From about 1950, as a result of medical discoveries, improved health and sanitation measures, declining infant mortality, and more efficient food production and distribution, death rates declined dramatically while birth rates rose. In India, for example, the death rate in 2000 was half the 1950 figure and its population rose from 350 million in 1950 to over to 1 billion at the beginning of the twenty-first century. Globally, the number of human beings grew so rapidly that demographers spoke of a population explosion. In 1950, when the contemporary takeoff began, world population totaled 2.5 billion; at the end of the century it exceeded 6 billion. Never before had human beings lived through a doubling of the world's population in their own lifetime.

Growth in the late twentieth century

It took the world millions of years for its human population to reach the quarter-billion mark some 2,000 years ago. Not until about 1650 did the population double to a half-billion. It then doubled in less than two centuries to reach its first billion about 1830. By about 1930, in only one century, it again doubled to reach 2 billion. By 1960, in a little over 30 years, it grew to 3 billion; 14 years later, in 1974, to 4 billion; 13 years later, by 1988, to 5 billion; and in 1999 after only 11 years, it passed the 6 billion mark. The time required to add a billion people to the world's population, and for the population to double in size, had grown shorter than ever before in history. The annual growth rate for much of this time, close to 2 percent, meant the addition of well over 80 million people annually.

Although predictions were never certain, demographers began to find indications of a slowdown in the rate of growth. Sometime between 1965 and 1970 the global annual growth rate seems to have peaked at about 2 percent and then began to decline, unevenly and irregularly, to about 1.5 percent. Nonetheless, because of the huge population base demographers still pushed well into the future the time and estimated figure at which stabilization might be achieved. Even with a reduced growth rate, the world population figure was projected for 2050 at a range of from 8 to 12.5 billion, with some thought that it could peak at just over 11 billion. A debate continued over the "carrying capacity" of the earth, the maximum number of humans that the earth's resources could sustain.

The population growth rate after about 1965 was showing signs of decline because of declining birth rates, a pattern manifesting itself not only in the industrial world but in the developing world as well. The population increase in the second half of the twentieth century, it will be recalled, was largely a phenomenon of the developing world in Asia, Africa, and Latin America, where three-fourths of the world lived and where birth rates were highest. By contrast, in North America and in Europe birth rates were already lower. Industrialization, urban life, education, and social pressures for smaller families had begun to reduce birth rates ever since the late nineteenth century. In many industrially developed countries in Western Europe as well as in Japan, Canada, Australia, and elsewhere growth rates were now below the population replacement rate of 2.1 children. Italy and Spain had the lowest rates with an average of 1.2 children per woman of child-bearing age, and Italy was expected to decline from a population of 57 million to 51 million in the next 25 years unless considerable immigration took place. In the United States the population was still growing, in good part because of immigration and immigrant families. Measured against the dramatic rise in global figures and in the developing world, Europe and North America were experiencing a shrinking share of world population.

A new social factor was that after earlier resistance to Western calls for control over family size, the developing countries were now accepting the need to limit population growth. In 1970 women in the less developed countries were having an average of six children, but by the opening of the twenty-first century, only 30 years later, women in these countries were having an average of four children. Whether the decline was due to voluntary control over family size, the availability of family planning counseling, or a greater empowerment of women over their lives and access to education and employment was still under discussion.

Changing birth rates

Although fertility rates began to decline in the developing countries, population growth still threatened to cancel economic advances. Even with lower birth rates the total number of births annually would not decline sharply because of the large population base. Contraceptive technology, with its many advances, was increasingly accessible but still not available to everyone. The number of couples in the developing world with access to family planning is judged to have grown from 10 percent to 60 percent in recent decades. But at least 100 million women of child-bearing age, it has been estimated, still lacked access to fertility control. Several of the world's major religions continued to forbid artificial birth control measures, numerous societies restricted educational and vocational opportunities for

Population and economic growth

women, and traditional patterns of life in many parts of the world, especially the poorest, encouraged large families for the sustenance and support of the elderly. The impact of the global population explosion in the second half of the twentieth century would be felt far into the future.

The Environment

As serious a threat as growing numbers posed for the world's resources, the planet also faced other dangers. From 1950 to 2000 world industrial production grew more than fivefold, burning coal, oil, and natural gas, and consuming a variety of synthetic chemicals, all of which emitted heat-trapping gases into the atmosphere. Although the full implications remained controversial, many scientists and aroused citizens were convinced that these emissions were eroding the protective upper ozone layer in the atmosphere that shields the earth from excessive solar heat and harmful radiation, and that the resulting global warming of the climate would have serious consequences. One troubling sign was that the decade of the 1990s was the warmest globally in 600 years, and the warming trend continued in the new century. The ongoing debate prompted governments worldwide to convene periodic conferences to try to agree on regulatory measures.

Environmental pollution and damage

Industrial pollution also caused the acid rain that laid waste to many forests, lakes, and rivers in the industrial nations. Severe environmental damage in the former Soviet Union, the Soviet-bloc nations, and the People's Republic of China confirmed that pollution was not confined to any single economic system; central planners had pressed development with little regard for the ecological consequences. Developing nations also paid little attention to their environment. Under the pressure of expanding population and rapid urbanization, they permitted the slashing and burning of tropical forests for ranching, timber exports, and resettlement. Arable acreage declined; pasture land turned into desert. From 1950 to 2000 the world lost over one-fifth of its topsoil and one-fifth of its tropical rain forests. Plant and animal species were endangered. Nowhere was this more striking than in Latin America and Africa. The partial loss of the Amazon Forest in Brazil before preventive measures were taken dramatized the extent of the damage.

From the 1970s on a newly sensitized world began to speak of sustainable growth rates, growth that could be maintained without the destruction of humanity's natural habitat. Alternative forms of energy, some as old as the sun and the wind, others new, like nuclear energy (with proper safeguards, to be sure) were proposed. Emissions from industrial factories and from vehicles came under stricter controls. The United States Environmental Protection Agency came into existence in 1970. In 1973 representatives of 80 nations signed an agreement to protect endangered species. In 1989 a number of industrial nations agreed to stop production of chlorofluorocarbons, which released dangerous amounts of chlorine into the upper atmosphere and were widely used in air-conditioning and in aerosol propellants. Other meetings and treaties followed. In 1992, at the first "Earth Summit" meeting in Rio de Janeiro, representatives of 178 countries pledged to protect plant and animal species and to take steps in a "climate treaty" to halt global warming. In 1997 representatives from 150 countries met at Kyoto, where they agreed to reduce the emission of so-called greenhouse gases by 50 percent by 2010.

Sustainable economic growth

As awareness of ecological dangers grew, grass-roots environmental organizations multiplied, and in several countries emerged as "Green" political parties. Despite the

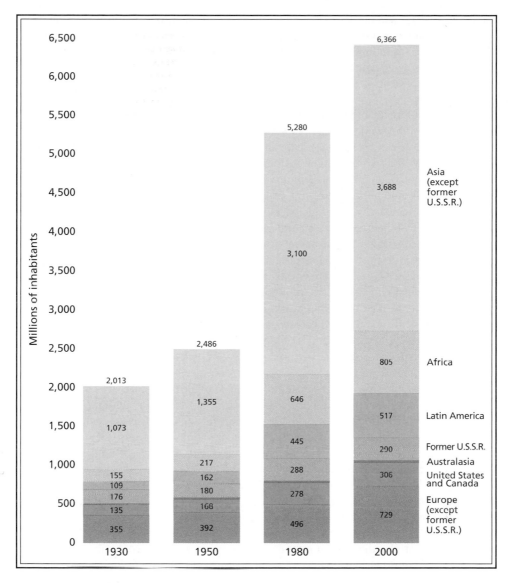

THE POPULATION EXPLOSION

The world's population has more than tripled in size since 1930, but the growth has been most rapid over the last five decades, especially in Latin America, Africa, and Asia. Before the twentieth century, world population had never before doubled in any half-century, so the recent increase can truly be called an "explosion." The world's population passed the 6 billion mark in 1999. Although wealthy societies have lower growth rates than most poor nations, the wealthy societies consume the largest portion of the world's resources. Future population growth is expected to occur mainly in the less industrialized regions of the globe, but demands on the earth's limited resources will continue to grow in both the wealthy and poor nations. The question is whether the growth of population and the growing demand for resources can be slowed in ways that will protect the earth's increasingly overstrained environment.

(United Nations Demographic Yearbook)

numerous pledges and measures to counter the threat of environmental deterioration, there was opposition to strict environmental regulations in some poor countries and in industrialized countries, including China, India, Australia, and the United States (which withdrew from the Kyoto agreement in 2001). Meanwhile, the developing nations slowed the adoption and enforcement of environmental laws that were viewed as impediments to economic progress.

Population growth and the threat to the environment added to the world's concerns at the beginning of the twenty-first century and the new millennium. Many of the most pressing concerns, however, were not new: the implications for society of contemporary science and technology, the sovereignty of nations, peace among nations, and the quest within nations for freedom, dignity, and economic well-being. All were aspects of one overriding problem. How could human beings in each generation on earth, regardless of sex, color, creed, religion, nationality, or ethnic background—beings said by some to be made in the image of God, by others to have a natural right to life, liberty and happiness, by still others to have the freedom to create meaning in a meaningless universe—live out their lives in peace, fulfill their destiny, and pass on their heritage to future generations?

The constant changes and upheavals in contemporary human history might be compared to cataclysms in the natural world. A cataclysm is not a time of downfall only. Mountains crumble, but others are thrust up. Lands vanish, but others rise from the sea. So it is with the political and social cataclysm of our times. Old landmarks are worn down. Empires pass away; new nations arise in their place. Subjugated peoples regain independence; rigid ideologies collapse. The ascendancy of Europe, the West, and the European nations closes; they learn to negotiate with others, not to rule them. There is a greater fluidity in social relationships. Women and minorities struggle for equal places in society. But social justice and peace remain elusive goals. The gap between rich and poor among nations, and within nations, is not easily overcome. Old and new diseases, natural catastrophes, and armed conflicts exact their toll. Resurgent nationalism feeds on intolerance and hatred. Never has war been so potentially destructive; the menace of a nuclear war that would blight much of civilization wanes but does not disappear. Uncontrolled economic development threatens the environment, and population growth presses on natural resources. International cooperation and intervention are needed to protect human rights, end or prevent wars, and sustain the earth's billions.

But there is a growing global recognition of all these concerns. To close this long history on a note of placidity would indeed be inappropriate, but it would also be wrong to close on a note of doom. The history of the modern world shows the astonishing range of human imagination and ingenuity, and there are good historical reasons to believe that people will continue to confront future problems and challenges with determination and creativity.

For interactive exercises, glossary, chronologies, and more, go to the *Online Learning Center* at **www.mhhe.com/palmer10.**

APPENDIX,
SUGGESTIONS FOR
FURTHER READING,
INDEX

RULERS AND REGIMES
In Principal European Countries since 1500

HOLY ROMAN EMPIRE

Habsburg Line

Maximilian I, 1493–1519

Charles V, 1519–1556

Ferdinand I, 1556–1564

Maximilian II, 1564–1576

Rudolph II, 1576–1612

Matthias, 1612–1619

Ferdinand II, 1619–1637

Ferdinand III, 1637–1657

Leopold I, 1658–1705

Joseph I, 1705–1711

Charles VI, 1711–1740

Charles VI was succeeded by a daughter, Maria Theresa, who as a woman could not be elected Holy Roman Emperor. French influence in 1742 secured the election of

Bavarian Line

Charles VII, 1742–1745

On Charles VII's death the Habsburg control of the emperorship was resumed.

Lorraine Line

Francis I, 1745–1765 (husband of Maria Theresa)

Habsburg-Lorraine Line

Joseph II, 1765–1790 (son of Francis I and Maria Theresa)

Leopold II, 1790–1792

Francis II, 1792–1806

The Holy Roman Empire became extinct in 1806.

AUSTRIAN DOMINIONS

The rulers of Austria from 1438 to 1740, and at least titular kings of Hungary from 1526 to 1740, were the same as the Holy Roman Emperors. After 1740:

Habsburg Line (through female heir)

Maria Theresa, 1740–1780

Joseph II, 1780–1790

Leopold II, 1790–1792

Francis II, 1792–1835

In 1804 Francis II took the title of Emperor, as Francis I of the Austrian Empire. Austria was declared an "empire" because Napoleon proclaimed France an empire in that year, and because the demise of the Holy Roman Empire could be foreseen.

Ferdinand I, 1835–1848

Francis Joseph, 1848–1916

Charles I, 1916–1918

The Austrian Empire became extinct in 1918.

BRITISH ISLES

Tudor Line

Kings of England and Ireland

Henry VII, 1485–1509

Henry VIII, 1509–1547

Edward VI, 1547–1553

Mary I, 1553–1558

Elizabeth I, 1558–1603

In 1603 James VI of Scotland, a great-great-grandson of Henry VII, succeeded to the English throne.

Stuart Line

Kings of England and Ireland, and of Scotland

James I, 1603–1625
Charles I, 1625–1649

Republican Interregnum

The Commonwealth, 1649–1653
The Protectorate
Oliver Cromwell, 1653–1658, Lord Protector
Richard Cromwell, 1658–1660

Restored Stuart Line

Charles II, 1660–1685
James II, 1685–1688

In 1688 James II was forced out of the country, but Parliament kept the crown in a female branch of the Stuart family, calling in Mary, the daughter of James II, and her husband William III of the Netherlands. Mary died in 1694.

William III and Mary II, 1689–1702/1694
Anne, 1702–1714

In 1707, through the Union of England and Scotland, the royal title became King (or Queen) of Great Britain and Ireland. The Stuart family having no direct Protestant heirs, the throne passed in 1714 to the German George I, Elector of Hanover, a great-grandson of James I.

Hanoverian Line

Kings of Great Britain and Ireland

George I, 1714–1727
George II, 1727–1760
George III, 1760–1820
George IV, 1820–1830
William IV, 1830–1837

William IV having no heirs, the British throne passed in 1837 to Victoria, a granddaughter of George III. Though the British family has continued in direct descent from George I, it has dropped the Hanoverian designation and is now known as the House of Windsor. From 1877 to 1947 the British rulers bore the additional title of Emperor (or Empress) of India.

Victoria, 1837–1901
Edward VII, 1901–1910
George V, 1910–1936
Edward VIII, 1936
George VI, 1936–1952
Elizabeth II, 1952–

FRANCE

Valois Line

Louis XI, 1461–1483
Charles VIII, 1483–1498
Louis XII, 1498–1515
Francis I, 1515–1547
Henry II, 1547–1559
Francis II, 1559–1560
Charles IX, 1560–1574
Henry III, 1574–1589

In 1589 the Valois line became extinct, and the throne passed to Henry of Bourbon, a remote descendant of French kings of the fourteenth century.

Bourbon Line

Henry IV, 1589–1610
Louis XIII, 1610–1643
Louis XIV, 1643–1715
Louis XV, 1715–1774
Louis XVI, 1774–1792

The Republic

Convention, 1792–1795
Directory, 1795–1799
Consulate, 1799–1804

The Empire

Napoleon I, 1804–1814, Emperor of the French and King of Italy

Restored Bourbon Line

Louis XVIII, 1814–1824

(Royalists count a Louis XVII, 1793–1795, and date the reign of Louis XVIII from 1795.)

Charles X, 1824–1830

The Revolution of 1830 gave the throne to the Duke of Orleans, descendant of Louis XIII.

Orleans Line

Louis-Philippe, 1830–1848

Second Republic

1848–1852

Second Empire

Napoleon III, 1852–1870, Emperor of the French

Third Republic

1870–1940

Vichy Regime

1940–1944

Provisional Government

1944–1946

Fourth Republic

1946–1958

Fifth Republic

1958–

PRUSSIA (AND GERMANY)

A continuous Hohenzollern line ruled until 1918.

Electors of Brandenburg and Dukes of Prussia

George William, 1619–1640

Frederick William, 1640–1688, the "Great Elector"

Frederick III, 1688–1713

In 1701 Frederick III was permitted by the Holy Roman Emperor to entitle himself King in Prussia, as Frederick I.

Kings of Prussia

Frederick I, 1701–1713

Frederick William I, 1713–1740

Frederick II, the "Great," 1740–1786

Frederick William II, 1786–1797

Frederick William III, 1797–1840

Frederick William IV, 1840–1861

William I, 1861–1888

In 1871 William I took the title of German Emperor.

German Emperors

William I, 1871–1888

Frederick III, 1888

William II, 1888–1918

The German Empire became extinct in 1918. It was succeeded by the

Weimar Republic

1919–1933

(The Weimar Republic is an unofficial title for what was still called the Deutsches Reich, a phrase not easy to translate accurately.)

The Third Reich

1933–1945

(The Third Reich is an unofficial title for the Deutsches Reich under Adolf Hitler.)
Allied Military Government in 1945 was followed by

German Federal Republic (West Germany)

1949–1990

German Democratic Republic (East Germany)

1949–1990

The two Germanys were united in 1990.

German Federal Republic

1990–

SARDINIA (AND ITALY)

In 1720 Victor Amadeus II, Duke of Savoy, took the title of King of Sardinia, having acquired the island of that name. The kingdom was often called Piedmont because of the king's older mainland domain.

Kings of Sardinia

Victor Amadeus II, 1720–1730

Charles Emmanuel III, 1730–1773

Victor Amadeus III, 1773–1796

Charles Emmanuel IV, 1796–1802

Victor Emmanuel I, 1802–1821

Charles Felix, 1821–1831

Charles Albert, 1831–1849

Victor Emmanuel II, 1849–1878

In 1861 Victor Emmanuel II took the title of King of Italy.

Kings of Italy

Victor Emmanuel II, 1861–1878

Humbert I, 1878–1900

Victor Emmanuel III, 1900–1946

Humbert II, 1946

In 1946 the Kingdom of Italy became extinct and was succeeded by the

Italian Republic

1946–

SPAIN

Ferdinand and Isabella, 1479–1504/1516

Isabella died in 1504, but Ferdinand lived until 1516, whereupon the Spanish thrones were inherited by their grandson Charles, who became Charles V of the Holy Roman Empire, but was known in Spain as Charles I.

Habsburg Line

Charles I, 1516–1556

Philip II, 1556–1598

Philip III, 1598–1621

Philip IV, 1621–1665

Charles II, 1665–1700

With Charles II the Spanish Habsburg line became extinct, and the throne passed to the French Bourbon grandson of Louis XIV of France and great-grandson of Philip IV of Spain.

Bourbon Line

Philip V, 1700–1746

Ferdinand VI, 1746–1759

Charles III, 1759–1788

Charles IV, 1788–1808

Bonaparte Line

Joseph, 1808–1813 (brother of Napoleon)

Restored Bourbon Line

Ferdinand VII, 1813–1833

Isabella II, 1833–1868

In 1868 Isabella abdicated; after a regency, and a brief reign by Amadeus I (Savoy), 1871–1873, there was a short-lived First Republic, 1873–1874, succeeded by

Alfonso XII, 1874–1885

Alfonso XIII, 1885–1931

In 1931 a republican revolution unseated Alfonso XIII.

Second Spanish Republic

1931–1936

Spanish Civil War

1936–1939

Regime of General Francisco Franco

1939–1975

Upon the death of Franco the Bourbon family was restored.

Juan Carlos I, 1975–

RUSSIA (AND U.S.S.R.)

Grand Dukes of Moscow

Ivan III, the "Great," 1462–1505

Basil III, 1505–1533

Ivan IV, the "Terrible," 1533–1584

In 1547 Ivan IV took the title of Tsar of Russia.

Tsars of Russia

Ivan IV, the "Terrible," 1547–1584

Theodore I, 1584–1598

Boris Godunov, 1598–1605

Time of Troubles

1604–1613

Romanov Line

Michael, 1613–1645

Alexis, 1645–1676

Theodore II, 1676–1682

Ivan V and Peter I, 1682–1689

Peter I, the "Great," 1689–1725

Catherine I, 1725–1727

Peter II, 1727–1730

Anna, 1730–1740

Ivan VI, 1740–1741

Elizabeth, 1741–1762

Peter III, 1762

Catherine II, the "Great," 1762–1796

Paul, 1796–1801

Alexander I, 1801–1825

Nicholas I, 1825–1855

Alexander II, 1855–1881

Alexander III, 1881–1894

Nicholas II, 1894–1917

In 1917 the tsardom became extinct.

Provisional Government
1917

Communist Revolution
1917

Union of Soviet Socialist Republics
1922–1991

In 1991 the Communist regime ended and the U.S.S.R. dissolved into its component republics (Russia, Ukraine, Belarus, etc.), loosely associated with each other in a Commonwealth of Independent States.

Russian Federation
1991–

Suggestions for Further Reading

The following bibliographical guide is intended for the convenience of students, teachers, and general readers. Although professional students of history may also find it useful, no attempt has been made to provide comprehensive coverage of special areas or topics or to include specialized monographs. Although many older volumes have been included, the aim throughout has been to call attention to recent historical works to which the reader may turn for additional bibliographical guidance. Classification follows the plan of chapters in the present book. For reasons of space, untranslated works in foreign languages have been excluded, as have been general textbooks, articles in periodicals, and (with a few exceptions) primary source materials. When a second date of publication for a book is given without further specification, it is generally the date of the most recent reprinting or reissue. We have also included up-to-date information on useful Web sites that may be consulted for additional information or sources on the themes of each chapter. Such sites often change and evolve, but the Web addresses were all "active" when this book went to press.

Many of the book titles are available in paperback; up-to-date listings may be found in *Books in Print* and in the *Paperback Book Guide for Colleges*.

INTRODUCTION
Guides, Reference Works, and Special Topics
An invaluable bibliographical tool for historical works published prior to 1992 is the American Historical Association's *Guide to Historical Literature* (3rd ed., 2 vols., 1995). Much expanded since its second edition in 1961, the *Guide* consists of 48 sections organized into regional, national, chronological, and topical categories, with coverage from prehistory to the present. It provides annotated entries for thousands of books and articles as well as an introductory essay for each section, all carefully indexed. The *Guide*'s first section, "Theory and Practice in Historical Study," provides a convenient introduction to historical method, historiography, philosophy of history, demography, the many varieties of history, and other important subjects. To keep up with the outpouring of historical books, however, it is important to read the book reviews and listings of new books in the *American Historical Review*, the *Journal of Modern History*, *The Journal of World History*, the (London) *Times Literary Supplement*, the *New York Review of Books*, and other periodicals, and the book reviews in the daily and weekend press. A valuable source of information on relevant articles is *Historical Abstracts*, which is also available in an electronic database. Many historical resources are now accessible on the Internet, though readers must use such materials with careful assessments of their reliability. For a helpful guide to history on the Internet, organized by thematic categories, readers may consult D. A. Trinkle and S. A. Merriman (eds.), *The History Highway: A 21st-Century Guide to Internet Resources* (rev. 2006).

Brief descriptions of major events and historical figures as well as a chronology of world history may be found in the *Oxford Encyclopedia of World History* (1998); there are also useful chronologies in J. Paxton and E. W. Knappman (eds.), *The Wilson Calendar of World History* (1999), and in P. N. Stearns (ed.), *Encyclopedia of World History: Ancient, Medieval, and Modern* (2001), the most recent edition of an invaluable reference for chronology. Of the many multivolume encyclopedias, the *Encyclopedia Britannica* (rev. 2005, with CD-ROM) remains the most valuable, and articles may also be found electronically at www.britannica.com. Convenient one-volume reference tools are the *Cambridge Encyclopedia* (rev. 2000), and the *Columbia Encyclopedia* (6th ed., 2000), which is now updated regularly in an electronic edition.

Several encyclopedias provide excellent up-to-date articles on themes and events in both world history and European history. See, for example, W. H. McNeill, et al. (eds.), *Berkshire Encyclopedia of World History* (5 vols., 2005), and J. Dewald (ed.), *Europe, 1450–1789: Encyclopedia of the Early Modern World* (6 vols., 2004).

Among historical atlases that place European history in its world setting, G. Parker (ed.), the (London) *Times Atlas of World History* (rev. 1993) and N. Grove (ed.), *National Geographic Society Atlas of World History* (1997) are impressive. Also useful, and periodically updated, are the *Rand McNally Atlas of World History*, Hammond's *Historical Atlas of the World*, and the Penguin Historical Atlas series. Of many geographical atlases one of the best is the *National Geographic Atlas of the World* (8th ed., 2005).

Of multivolume historical series, the New *Cambridge Modern History* (14 vols., 1957–1979) remains useful, though it is no longer "new." The volumes, which will be referred to in the chapters below, contain outstanding contributions by specialists from all over the world. There are other series, to which reference will be made below, under the auspices of various publishers.

Geographical influences on European history are discussed in N. J. G. Pounds, *An Historical Geography of Europe* (3 vols., 1973– 1985) and in the essays in E. Genovese and L. Hochberg (eds.), *Geographic Perspectives in History* (1989). The case for new conceptualizations in geography is made in M. W. Lewis and K. E. Wigen, The *Myth of Continents: A Critique of Metageography* (1997). I. G. Simmons, *Changing the Face of the Earth: Culture, Environment, and History* (rev. 1996) traces the human impact on the planet over the centuries; E. Le Roy Ladurie examines an important subject in *Times of Feast, Times of Famine: A History of Climate since the Year 1000* (trans. 1971).

For the impact of famine, disease, and the movement of peoples, one may read W. H. McNeill, *Plagues and Peoples* (1976) and *The Global Condition: Conquerors, Catastrophes, and Community* (1992); T. McKeown, *The Origins of Human Disease* (1988); A. Crosby, *Germs, Seeds and Animals: Studies in Ecological History* (1994); and K. F. Kiple (ed.), *The Cambridge World History of Human Disease* (1993), a valuable reference work. On cultural advantages and disadvantages in the encounters between peoples, J. Diamond, *Guns, Germs, and Steel: The Fate of Human Societies* (rev. 2005), is rewarding; the same author examines various cultural responses to changing environmental conditions in *Collapse: How Societies Choose to Fail or Succeed* (2005).

Of the many books on military history treating war as a social and human phenomenon, three outstanding studies ranging from earliest times to the present are A. Jones, *The Art of War in the Western World* (1989); R. L. O'Connell, *Of Arms and Men: A History of War, Weapons, and Aggression* (1990); and J. Keegan, *A History of Warfare* (1993); the latter, like others of Keegan's books, is especially noteworthy. Of interest in a related category is M. Walzer, *Just and Unjust Wars* (rev. 1992). The importance of technology is stressed in B. Brodie and F. Brodie, *From Crossbow to H-Bomb* (rev. 1973); W. H. McNeill, *The Pursuit of Power: Technology, Armed Force, and Society since A.D. 1000* (1982); and M. van Creveld, *Technology and War: From 2000 B.C. to the Present* (1988).

A few books of special interest deserve mention here: W. H. McNeill, *The Rise of the West: A History of the Human Community* (rev. 1991), a notable effort to recount the human experience in a global setting,

which has been continued in J. R. McNeill and W. H. McNeill, *The Human Web: A Bird's-eye View of Human History* (2003); E. R. Wolf, *Europe and the People without History* (1982), by an anthropologist, which portrays Western history as seen by non-Western societies in Asia, Africa, and the Americas; P. Kennedy, *The Rise and Fall of the Great Powers: Economic Change and Military Conflict from 1500 to 2000* (1987), which examines the political and economic fortunes of the European nations that successively played the leading role in world affairs in the modern centuries; and J. Barzun, *From Dawn to Decadence: 500 Years of Cultural Life, 1500 to the Present* (2000), a provocative study of Western thought since the sixteenth century. Two wide-ranging efforts at a synthesis of European history are N. Davies, *Europe: A History* (1996), a highly idiosyncratic but challenging work; and J. M. Roberts, *A History of Europe* (1996), a more conventional, thoughtful account. F. Fernández-Armesto, *Millennium: A History of the Last Thousand Years* (1995), is an ambitious attempt at global history. K. A. Appiah and H. L. Gates, Jr., *The Dictionary of Global Culture* (1998) is a pioneer effort to integrate the contributions of Western and non-Western cultures.

Changing Directions in Historical Writings

For a sampling of insights into contemporary trends in historical writing, one may turn to M. Kammen (ed.), The *Past before Us: Contemporary Historical Writing in the United States* (1980); T. K. Rabb and R. I. Rotberg (eds.), *The New History: The 1980s and Beyond* (1982); P. Burke (ed.), *New Perspectives on Historical Writing* (rev. 2001); J. Appleby, L. Hunt, and M. Jacob, *Telling the Truth about History* (1994); G. Iggers, *Historiography in the Twentieth Century: From Scientific Objectivity to the Postmodern Challenge* (1997); L. Kramer and S. Maza, *A Companion to Western Historical Thought* (2002); M. T. Gilderhus, *History and Historians: A Historiographical Introduction* (rev. 2003); and two challenging books by B. Southgate, *History: What and Why? Ancient, Modern, and Postmodern Perspectives* (rev. 2001), and *What Is History For?* (2005).

One of the major contemporary interests of historians has been social history. Stimulated by the *Annales* school of historical writing in France (the name derived from the French periodical *Annales: économies, sociétés, civilisations,* which in 1994 was renamed *Annales: histoire, sciences sociales*), and by newer kinds of working-class history in England, in which E. P. Thompson, *The Making of the English Working Class* (1963), was a pioneer, historians have concerned themselves with a social history distinct from traditional interests in social classes and labor and laboring conditions. They have been examining such subjects as the history of the family, women, sexuality, marriage, the everyday lives and outlook (or *mentalité*) of the urban and rural poor, and popular culture—all studied as history "from the bottom up." Many such works are listed below in the appropriate chapters. An introduction to the newer social history and to popular culture is provided in O. Zung (ed.), *Reliving the Past: The Worlds of Social History* (1985); P. Burke, *Popular Culture in Early Modern Europe* (rev. 1994); C. Mukerjee and M. Schudson (eds.), *Rethinking Popular Culture* (1990); and L. Berlanstein (ed.), *Rethinking Labor History: Essays on Discourse and Class Analysis* (1993). A useful collection of recent contributions to the newer social history is available in R. M. Goldin (ed.), *The Social Dimension of Western Civilization* (4th ed., 1999).

Although the *Annales* historians have contributed a good deal to the newer social history, they have also been important for their emphasis, often quantitative and interdisciplinary, on long-term factors that influence the course of historical change, such as geography, environment, resources, climate, population, diet, and disease, which in their view often merit closer attention than "events." Here F. Braudel, *The Mediterranean and the Mediterranean World in the Age of Philip II* (2 vols., 1949; trans. 1974; rev. and abridged 1 vol. ed., 1992), was a pioneering work; his other books are described in the chapters below.

There has been much attention in recent decades to the history of women. Many of the writings call for reassessments of various historical eras from the viewpoint of women's status in the era and for the fuller integration of the history of women into general history. Contributions to the history of women in Europe and the West may be sampled in R. Bridenthal, S. Stuard, and M. Wiesner (eds.), *Becoming Visible: Women in European History* (rev. 1998), with essays covering ancient times to the twentieth century; M. J. Boxer and J. H. Quataert (eds.), *Connecting Spheres: European Women in a Globalizing World, 1500 to the Present* (rev. 2000), case studies with informative overview chapters; B. S. Anderson and J. P. Zinsser, *A History of Their Own: Women in Europe from Prehistory to the Present* (2 vols.; rev. 2000), thematically organized; and B. G. Smith, *Changing Lives: Women in European History since 1700* (1989), a helpful narrative account. G. Duby and M. Perrot (gen. eds.), *A History of Women in the West* (trans. 1992–1994), is a multivolume history from ancient times to the present. Important theoretical perspectives on the role of gender in historical understanding can be found in *Women, History and Theory: The Essays of Joan Kelly* (1984); J. W. Scott, *Gender and the Politics of History* (rev. 1999); and B. G. Smith, *The Gender of History: Men, Women, and Historical Practice* (1998). The role of gender in both ancient and modern global history is examined in B. G. Smith (ed.), *Women's History in Global Perspective* (2004). G. Lerner provides many insights into women and history in *The Creation of Patriarchy* (1986) and *The Creation of Feminist Con-*

sciousness: From the Middle Ages to 1870 (1993). Diverse collections of documents on women's history can be found in J. C. Fout and E. Reimer (eds.), *European Women: A Documentary History, 1789–1945* (1980); J. O'Faolain and L. Martines (eds.), *Not in God's Image: Women in History from the Greeks to the Victorians* (1973); E. O. Hillerstein, L. P. Hume, and K. M. Offen (eds.), *Victorian Women: Women's Lives in England, France, and the United States* (1981); and S. G. Bell and K. M. Offen (eds.), *Women, the Family, and Freedom: The Debate in Documents* (2 vols.; 1983).

Psychological approaches to the writing of history are explored in S. Friedländer, *History and Psychoanalysis* (trans. 1978); P. Loewenberg, *Decoding the Past: The Psychohistorical Approach* (1982); P. Gay, *Freud for Historians* (1985); and the more theoretical work of D. LaCapra, *History in Transit: Experience, Identity, Critical Theory* (2004). For an introduction to the quantitative analysis of historical data, one may turn to K. H. Jarausch and K. A. Hardy, *Quantitative Methods for Historians: A Guide to Research, Data, and Statistics* (1991). Two useful introductions to a crucial component of contemporary historical work are J. L. Reiff, *Structuring the Past: The Use of Computers in History* (1991) and D. I. Greenstein, *A Historian's Guide to Computing* (1994). There is much practical information on historical research and writing in J. Barzun and H. F. Graff, *The Modern Researcher* (rev. 2004).

The tapping of neglected sources through the methods of oral history is examined in P. Thompson, *The Voice of the Past: Oral History* (1978); D. Henige, *Oral Historiography* (1982); D. K. Dunaway and W. K. Baum (eds.), *Oral History: An Interdisciplinary Anthology* (1984); and K. Howarth, *Oral History* (1999). A contemporary medium is explored in J. E. O'Connor (ed.), *Image as Artifact: The Historical Analysis of Film and Television* (1990); R. Rosenstone (ed.), *Revisioning History: Film and the Construction of a New Past* (1995) and *Visions of the Past: The Challenge of Film to Our Idea of History* (1995).

Changing assessments of cultural and intellectual history, borrowing from philosophy, linguistics, anthropology, and literary criticism, which may remain elusive for many readers, may be sampled in L. Hunt (ed.), *The New Cultural History* (1989); V. E. Bonnell and L. Hunt (eds.), *Beyond the Cultural Turn: New Directions in the Study of Society and Culture* (1999); D. LaCapra, *Rethinking Intellectual History: Texts, Contexts, Language* (1983); C. Ginzburg, *Clues, Myths, and the Historical Method* (trans. 1992); D. R. Kelley, *The Descent of Ideas: The History of Intellectual History* (2002); and two helpful books by P. Burke, *Varieties of Cultural History* (1997) and *What Is Cultural History?* (2004).

Some books critical of the trends in historical writing that have emerged since the 1970s include

J. Barzun, *Clio and the Doctors: Psychohistory, Quantohistory, and History* (1974); J. H. Hexter, *On Historians: Some of the Makers of Modern History* (1979); T. S. Hamerow, *Reflections on History and Historians* (1987); G. R. Elton, *Return to Essentials: Some Reflections on the Present State of Historical Study* (1993); G. Himmelfarb, *The New History and the Old* (1987) and *On Looking into the Abyss: Untimely Thoughts on Culture and Society* (1994); and E. Fox-Genovese and E. Lasch-Quinn (eds.), *Reconstructing History: The Emergence of a New Historical Society* (1999). Two probing accounts of the historical profession in the United States, with insights into past and present historiographical debates, are J. Higham, *History: Professional Scholarship in America* (rev. 1989); and P. Novick, *That Noble Dream: The "Objectivity Question" and the American Historical Profession* (1988).

On the relationship of history to other disciplines and its own distinctive role, one may turn to such varied explorations as E. H. Carr, *What Is History?* (1962); P. Gay, *Style in History* (1974); L. Gottschalk, *Understanding History* (rev. 1969); A. Marwick, *The Nature of History* (rev. 1989); L. Gossman, *Between History and Literature* (1990); D. LaCapra, *History and Criticism* (1985); and H. V. White, *Metahistory: The Historical Imagination in Nineteenth-Century Europe* (1973). Of special interest for the relationship of the discipline to the social sciences are P. Burke, *History and Social Theory* (1993); T. J. McDonald (ed.), *The Historic Turn in the Human Sciences* (1996); J. Elster, *The Cement of Society: A Study of Social Order* (1991) and *Nuts and Bolts from the Social Sciences* (1991); and J. Gaddis, *The Landscape of History: How Historians Map the Past* (2002).

Among thoughtful reflections by historians who have themselves made notable contributions to the writing of history, the following may be suggested: F. Gilbert, *History: Choice and Commitment* (1977); W. H. McNeill, *Mythistory and Other Essays* (1986); C. Vann Woodward, *Thinking Back: The Perils of Writing History* (1986) and *The Future of the Past* (1989); L. Stone, *The Past and the Present Revisited* (1987); D. Cannadine, *The Pleasures of the Past* (1989); W. J. Bouwsma, *A Usable Past* (1990); M. Beloff, *An Historian in the Twentieth Century* (1992); G. Lerner, *Why History Matters: Life and Thought* (1997); C. E. Schorske, *Thinking with History* (1998); and E. J. Hobsbawm, *Interesting Times: A Twentieth-Century Life* (2002). An insightful study of how historians write about themselves can be found in J. D. Popkin, *History, Historians, and Autobiography* (2005). Other interesting historical reflections appear in two collections of interviews with contemporary historians: H. Abelove (ed.), *Visions of History* (1984), and R. Adelson (ed.), *Speaking of History: Conversations with Historians* (1997).

Useful Web Sites

For interactive historical maps, readers might consult *Mapping History: The Darkwing Atlas Project* at http://darkwing.uoregon.edu/~atlas/, a well-designed site that includes maps and images of Europe, the Americas, and global history. Useful chronological information can be found at the *WebChron Project*, http://campus.northpark.edu/history/WebChron/, and at *World History: Hyper History*, www.hyperhistory .com/online_n2/History_n2/a.html. An accessible, general introduction to historical timelines, maps, and images is also available through the site of the *History Channel* at www.historychannel.com/. Readers might also visit the site of the *American Historical Association* for reports on developments in contemporary historical scholarship and teaching, www.historians.org.

1. THE RISE OF EUROPE
Prehistoric and Ancient Times

For prehistory, the reader may wish to consult B. Fagan, *People of the Earth: An Introduction to World Prehistory* (rev. 2004); P. Phillips, *The Prehistory of Europe* (1980); T. Champion et al., *Prehistoric Europe* (1984); and B. Cunliffe (ed.), *The Oxford Illustrated Prehistory of Europe* (1994). Of special interest are M. R. Ehrenberg, *Women in Prehistory* (1989) and W. W. Barber, *Women's Work: The First 20,000 Years: Women, Cloth, and Society in Early Times* (1994).

Informative accounts for the ancient world include T. B. Jones, From *the Tigris to the Tiber* (rev. 1983); C. G. Starr, *A History of the Ancient World* (rev. 1991); and H. Howe and R. T. Howe, *The Ancient World* (1987). For Mesopotamia and Egypt one may read J. Hawkes, *The First Great Civilizations* (1973); H. Saggs, *The Greatness That Was Babylon* (1991); M. A. Murray, *The Splendor That Was Egypt* (rev. 2004); and C. Freeman, *Egypt, Greece, and Rome: Civilizations of the Ancient Mediterranean* (1999).

Excellent summaries of Greek and Roman antiquity, from the eighth century B.C. through the second century A.D., are found in J. Boardman, J. Griffin, and O. Murray (eds.), *The Oxford History of the Classical World* (1986); other valuable accounts of the ancient world include L. de Blois and R. J. van der Spek, *An Introduction to the Ancient World* (1997) and M. Grant, *The Founders of the Western World: A History of Greece and Rome* (1991). There are rewarding insights in M. I. Finley's many writings on Greece and Rome, among them *The Legacy of Greece: A New Appraisal* (1981) and *Politics in the Ancient World* (1983). An outstanding study of women in Greece and Rome is S. B. Pomeroy, *Goddesses, Whores, Wives, and Slaves: Women in Classical Antiquity* (1975, 1995); one may also read S. Blundell, *Women in Ancient Greece* (1995).

In addition to numerous surveys of classical Greece, the reader will profit from S. B. Pomeroy et al., *Ancient Greece: A Political, Social, and Cultural History* (1999). For Alexander the Great, one should read P. Green, *Alexander of Macedon, 356–323 B.C.* (1974, 1991). On the rise and fall of the Hellenistic civilization that Alexander helped create, one may read E. S. Gruen, *The Hellenistic World and the Coming of Rome* (2 vols., 1984); P. Green's critical *Alexander to Actium: The Historical Evolution of the Hellenistic Age* (1991); and G. W. Bowersock, *Hellenism in Late Antiquity* (1990), a more sympathetic brief assessment.

Among many surveys of Rome and Roman civilization, one may suggest H. H. Scullard, *A History of the Roman World, 753–146 B.C.* (rev. 2002); and for all aspects of Roman society, see K. Christ, *The Romans: An Introduction to Their History and Civilization* (trans. 1984) and M. T. Boatwright, D. J. Gargola, and R. J. A. Talbert, *The Romans: From Village to Empire* (2004). Earlier Roman history is examined in H. MacDonald, *Republican Rome* (1966) and C. Nicolet, *The World of the Citizen in Republican Rome* (trans. 1980). Books on the Empire include P. Garnsey and R. Saller, *The Roman Empire: Economy, Society and Culture* (1987) and C. M. Wells, *The Roman Empire* (rev. 1992). There is also an important account of Rome's relations with other ancient cultures in P. Wells, *The Barbarians Speak: How the Conquered Peoples Shaped Roman Europe* (1999).

For the coming of Christianity, comprehensive introductions may be found in W. H. C. Frend, *The Rise of Christianity* (1984) and in R. A. Fletcher, *The Barbarian Conversion: From Paganism to Christianity* (1998). Early Christianity's interaction with both the politics and philosophy of the ancient world is examined in C. Freeman, *The Closing of the Western Mind: The Rise of Faith and the Fall of Reason* (2002). The many efforts to reconstruct the historical Jesus include A. N. Wilson, *Jesus* (1992) and J. D. Crossan, *Jesus: A Revolutionary Biography* (1994). On St. Augustine and his times, there is a sensitive account by P. Brown, *Augustine of Hippo* (rev. 2000) and a lively appraisal by G. Wills, *Saint Augustine* (1999). For all aspects of theology there is the magisterial work of J. Pelikan, *The Christian Tradition* (5 vols., 1971–1989), the first three volumes of which relate to the Middle Ages.

The Middle Ages: The Formation of Europe

Among many surveys of the medieval era as a whole, B. Tierney and S. Painter, *Western Europe in the Middle Ages, 300–1475* (rev. 1999); and C. W. Hollister and J. M. Bennett, *Medieval Europe: A Short History* (rev. 2006) are excellent. A successful effort emphasizing social history is E. Peters, *Europe and The Middle Ages* (rev. 1997). G. Holmes (ed.), *The Oxford Illustrated History of Medieval Europe* (1988), available also in abridged form (1992), is a collaborative work of distinction and J. Le Goff, *Medieval Civiliza-*

tion, 400–1500 (trans. 1988), is a remarkable synthesis by a leading French historian of the *Annales* school. Historians who have reshaped our understanding of the medieval era are examined in N. Cantor, *Reinventing the Middle Ages* (1992).

Fundamental to the reassessment of Europe's emergence in the early medieval centuries is R. W. Southern, *The Making of the Middle Ages* (1953, 1993). Another important work of synthesis is P. Brown, *The Rise of Western Christendom: Triumph and Diversity, A.D. 200–1000* (rev. 2003), building on the author's numerous other works on late antiquity. Also available are D. Hay, *Europe: The Emergence of an Idea* (rev. 1968); G. Barraclough, *The Crucible of Europe: The Ninth and Tenth Centuries in European History* (1976); C. Brooks, *Europe in the Central Middle Ages, 916–1154* (rev. 2000); and G. Duby, *The Making of the Christian West, 980–1140* (trans. 1968). For the era of Charlemagne one may read P. Geary, *Before France and Germany: The Creation and Transformation of the Merovingian Empire* (1988); R. Collins, *Charlemagne* (1998); M. Becher, *Charlemagne* (trans. 2003); and P. Riché, *Daily Life in the World of Charlemagne* (trans. 1978).

The Byzantine Empire and the Islamic World

There are many books on the two civilizations in the Middle East that flourished while Europe in the early medieval centuries was in the so-called Dark Ages. For the Byzantine, or Eastern Roman, Empire, one may read the comprehensive, scholarly account by W. Treadgold, *A History of the Byzantine State and Society* (1998), and a shorter work by the same author, *A Concise History of Byzantium* (2001); T. E. Gregory, *A History of Byzantium* (2005); and J. J. Norwich, *A Short History of Byzantium* (1997). The essence of Byzantine culture is captured in H. C. Evans (ed.), *The Glory of Byzantine Art and Culture of the Byzantine Medieval Era, A.D. 893–1261* (1997). The end of the empire is graphically described in S. Runciman, *The Fall of Constantinople, 1453* (1965). Valuable for all aspects of Byzantine civilization is A. P. Kazhdan (ed.), *The Oxford Dictionary of Byzantium* (3 vols., 1991).

Good starting points for the study of Islam include B. Lewis, *Islam in History: Ideas, People and Events in the Middle East* (rev. 1993), *Islam and the West* (1993), and his many other writings; W. M. Watt, *The Majesty That Was Islam: The Islamic World, 661–1100* (rev. 1990); and M. G. S. Hodgson, *The Venture of Islam: Conscience and History in a World Civilization* (3 vols., 1974), from the beginnings to the mid-twentieth century. Accounts of the founder of Islam include T. W. M. Watt, *Muhammad: Prophet and Statesman* (1961), a condensation of a detailed two-volume study; M. H. Haykal, *The Life of Muhammad* (trans. 1976); M. Rodinson, *Muhammad* (trans.

1971, 2002); and K. Armstrong, *Muhammad: A Biography of the Prophet* (1993). The historical legacy of early Islam is examined in R. Asian, *No God but God: The Evolution of Islam* (2005). The best introduction to Arab history is A. Hourani, *A History of the Arab Peoples* (rev. 2002); other informative accounts include B. Lewis, *The Arabs in History* (rev. 1993); P. Mansfield, *The Arabs* (rev. 1985); and M. Rodinson, *The Arabs* (1981). There are many interesting cultural insights in R. Bulliett, *The Camel and the Wheel* (1975), while S. N. Fisher and W. Ochsenwal, *The Middle East: A History* (rev. 1997) studies the region from pre-Islamic times on. D. J. Geanakoplos focuses on the interrelationships of the three civilizations in *Medieval Western Civilization and the Byzantine and Islamic Worlds: Interaction of Three Cultures* (1979), while M. L. Colish, *Medieval Foundations of the Western Intellectual Tradition, 400–1400* (1998), provides a valuable comparative survey of the three cultures.

Readers can find contrasting accounts of European views of Islamic societies in E. Said, *Orientalism* (1978, 1995), and M. Rodinson, *Europe and the Mystique of Islam* (trans. 1987); and a helpful, brief overview is available in R. M. Easton, *Islamic History as Global History* (1990).

The Middle Ages: Economy, Politics, Society

For economic development, the pioneering books by H. Pirenne on the origins of the cities, revival of trade, and other social and economic developments still merit reading, but they have been superseded by more recent research. Among useful histories are R. S. Lopez, *The Commercial Revolution of the Middle Ages, 950–1350* (rev. 1976); G. Duby, *The Growth of the European Economy* (1974); and J. L. Bolton, *The Medieval Economy, 1150–1500* (1980). Also informative are N. J. G. Pounds, *An Economic History of Medieval Europe* (rev. 1994); C. M. Cipolla, *Before the Industrial Revolution: European Society and Economy, 1000–1700* (rev. 1980); and J. Day, *Medieval Market Economy* (1987). The volumes in the collaborative *Cambridge Economic History of Europe* (1941 ff.) provide authoritative but highly specialized accounts. The second volume, M. M. Postan and E. Miller (eds.), *Trade and Industry in the Middle Ages* (1952, 1987), was thoroughly revised for its new edition. L. White, Jr., *Medieval Technology and Social Change* (1962) and *Medieval Religion and Technology* (1978) illustrate some of the scholarship which has dispelled the image of the early medieval years as technologically stagnant.

E. Ennen, *The Medieval Town* (trans. 1979), incorporates the considerable research since Pirenne, but it may be supplemented by D. Nichols, *The Growth of the Medieval City* (1997); and K. D. Lilley, *Urban Life in the Middle Ages, 1000–1450* (2002). On feudalism and manorialism, useful introductions are available in F. L. Ganshof, *Feudalism* (rev. 1964), and J. S. Critch-ley, *Feudalism* (1978). An imaginative effort at comparing ideal models and material realities is G. Duby, *The Three Orders: Feudal Society Imagined* (trans. 1980). M. Bloch's classic contributions include *Feudal Society* (1938–40; trans. 1961) and *Slavery and Serfdom in the Middle Ages* (trans. 1975).

Studies of the emergent monarchical states include B. Guenée, *States and Rulers in Later Medieval Europe* (trans. 1985), and S. Reynolds, *Kingdoms and Communities in Western Europe, 900–1300* (rev. 1997), which stresses cultural bonds. An important collaborative work is C. Tilley (ed.), *The Formation of National States in Western Europe* (1975). Of the many books available for the national formations the following are a sampling. For Germany: G. Barraclough, *Origins of Modern Germany* (rev. 1984); and T. Reuter, *Germany in the Early Middle Ages, c. 800–1056* (1991); For England: M. T. Clanchy, *England and Its Rulers, 1066–1272* (rev. 1998); and T. Rowley, *The High Middle Ages, 1200–1540* (1986) in the *Making of Britain* series. For Spain: A. MacKay, *Spain in the Middle Ages: From Frontier to Empire 100–1500* (1989); and there is valuable information in L. P. Harvey, *Islamic Spain, 1250 to 1500* (1990). For France: J. Dunbabin, *France in the Making, 843–1180* (rev. 2000); E. M. Hallam, *Capetian France, 987–1328* (1983); and E. James, *The Origins of France: From Clovis to the Capetians, 500–1000* (1980). For the Italian city-states one may read D. Waley, *The Italian City Republics* (rev. 1988) and P. J. Jones, *The Italian City-State: From Commune to Signoria* (1997).

Social History

The first two volumes of *A History of Private Life*, P. Veyne (ed.), *From Pagan Rome to Byzantium* (1987) and G. Duby (ed.), *Revelations of the Medieval World* (1988), explore aspects of social history, as do R. Fossier, *Peasant Life in the Medieval West* (trans. 1988) and H. W. Goetz, *Life in the Middle Ages: From the Seventh to the Thirteenth Century* (1993). For women in the Middle Ages, their constraints and opportunities, one may read A. Lucas, *Women in the Middle Ages: Religion, Marriage, and Letters* (1984); S. Shahar, *The Fourth Estate: A History of Women in the Middle Ages* (1984); D. Herlihy, *Opera Muliebria: Women at Work in Medieval Europe* (1990); E. Ennen, *The Medieval Woman* (1990); and a useful, concise summary by J. M. Bennett, *Medieval Women in Modern Perspective* (2000). Informative collections of essays include J. M. Bennett et al. (eds.), *Sisters and Workers in the Middle Ages* (1989); M. Erler and M. Kowaleski (eds.), *Women and Power in the Middle Ages* (1988); M. Erler and M. Kowaleski (eds.), *Gendering the Master Narrative: Women and Power in the Middle Ages* (2003); and J. M. Bennett and A. M. Froide (eds.), *Single Women in the European Past* (1999). The transformation of the household is masterfully explored in D. Herlihy, *Medieval Households* (1985), which may be supplemented by the important works of B. A. Hanawalt, *The Ties That Bound: Peasant Families in Medieval England* (1986) and *Of Good and Ill Repute: Gender and Social Control in Medieval England* (1998). Special subjects are explored in C. Brooke, *The Medieval Idea of Marriage* (1989), in J. A. Brundage, *Law, Sex, and Christian Society in Medieval Europe* (1990), and in N. Orme, *Medieval Children* (2001).

The Middle Ages: Intellect and Piety

Intellectual developments and scholasticism are discussed in many of the books already cited but are also examined with insight in R. C. Dales, *The Intellectual Life of Western Europe* (rev. 1992); B. B. Price, *Medieval Thought: An Introduction* (1992); M. L. Colish, *Medieval Foundations of the Western Intellectual Tradition, 400–1400* (1997); and J. Pelikan, *The Growth of Medieval Theology, 600–1300* (1981), Vol. III of his *The Christian Tradition* referred to earlier. For political thought and philosophy one may also turn to J. B. Morrall, *Political Thought in Medieval Times* (rev. 1980); and W. Ullman, *A History of Political Thought in the Middle Ages* (1965).

For the universities one may read C. H. Haskins, The *Rise of the Universities* (1923, 1979); H. Rashdall's monumental *The Universities of Europe in the Middle Ages* (3 vols., 1895; revised and reissued 1936, 1987); and H. de Ridder-Symoens (ed.), *Universities in the Middle Ages* (1992). For ancient and medieval scientific activities as background to the emergence of modern science, an excellent synthesis is D. C. Lindberg, *The Beginnings of Western Science. The European Scientific Tradition in Philosophical, Religious, and Institutional Context, 600 B.C. to A.D. 1450* (1992).

Valuable introductions to the church as an institution are M. Deanesley, *A History of the Medieval Church, 590–1500* (rev. 1969); C. Morris, *The Papal Monarchy: The Western Church from 1050 to 1250* (1989); J. Lynch. *The Medieval Church: A Brief History* (1992); and I. W. Frank, *A History of the Medieval Church* (trans. 1995). For the popes from the earliest times on, a wealth of information is available in J. N. D. Kelly (ed.), *The Oxford Dictionary of Popes* (1986); and in E. Duffy, *Saints and Sinners: A History of the Popes* (rev. 2002); and for all aspects of church history one may turn to J. McManners, *The Oxford Illustrated History of Christianity* (1990). Of special interest is J. Sayers, *Innocent III: Leader of Europe, 1198–1216* (1994).

For the lives of the saints and the society in which they lived, one may read D. Weinstein and R. M. Bell, *Saints and Society: The Two Worlds of Western Christendom, 1000–1700* (1983). Other insights into religious life may be obtained from C. Brooke, *The Monastic World, 1000–1300* (1974), and C. H. Laurence, *Medieval Monasticism* (1989).

For the treatment of heresy in medieval society one may read E. Le Roy Ladurie, *Montaillou: The Promised Land of Error* (trans. 1978); and E. Peters, *Inquisition* (1988). Peters has also written a broad study, *Torture* (rev. 1996), which includes its incorporation into medieval law and practice. A sweeping indictment of medieval intolerance toward "outside" groups is presented in R. I. Moore, *The Formation of a Persecuting Society: Power and Deviance in Western Europe, 950–1250* (1987), while scholarly explorations of medieval attitudes toward such groups can be found in J. Boswell, *Christianity, Sexual Tolerance, and Homosexuality: Gay People in Western Europe from the Beginning of the Christian Era to the Fourteenth Century* (1980). On medieval Jewry one may turn to K. R. Stow, *Alienated Minority: The Jews of Medieval Latin Europe* (1992); L. B. Glick, *Abraham's Heirs: Jews and Christians in Medieval Europe* (1999); and R. Chazan, *Fashioning Jewish Identity in Medieval Western Christendom* (2004). The roots of anti-Semitism are explored in R. S. Wistrich, *Anti-Semitism: The Longest Hatred* (1992).

The Crusades

The expansion and conquests of medieval Europeans are described in J. R. S. Phillips, *The Medieval Expansion of Europe* (rev. 1998), and in R. Bartlett, *The Making of Europe: Conquest, Colonization, and Cultural Change, 950–1350* (1993), an important synthesis. The Crusades may be approached through J. R. Smith, *The Crusades: A Short History* (1987); T. F. Madden, *The New Concise History of the Crusades* (rev. 2005); T. Ashridge, *The First Crusade: A New History: The Roots of Conflict between Christianity and Islam* (2005); the detailed, colorful S. Runciman, *A History of the Crusades* (3 vols., 1951–54, 1987); H. E. Mayer, *The Crusades* (rev. and trans. 1988); and the collaborative multivolume K. M. Setton (ed.), *History of the Crusades* (6 vols., 1955–90). The assault on Jewish communities in the Rhineland as a consequence of the First Crusade is carefully examined in R. Chazan, *European Jewry and the First Crusade* (1987), while the twelfth-century Muslim foe of the Crusaders is studied in A. S. Ehrenkrentz, *Saladin* (1978).

Useful Web Sites

A vast range of documents and modern scholarly works on the ancient and medieval world can be found at numerous university-sponsored Web sites; see, for example, the *Ancient World Mapping Center* at the University of North Carolina, www.unc.edu/awmc/; the *Perseus Digital Library* at Tufts University, www.perseus.tufts.edu/cache/perscoll_Greco-Roman.html; and the *Internet Ancient History Sourcebook* at Fordham University, www.fordham.edu/halsall/ancient/asbook2.html, where readers will also find an excellent *Internet Medieval Sourcebook*, www.fordham.edu/

halsall/sbook.html. Other comphrehensive sites focusing on the medieval era include *The Labyrinth* at Georgetown University, http://labyrinth.georgetown .edu/, which provides helpful information on Islam and Byzantium as well as every aspect of medieval Europe; and valuable resources on medieval women are available at the Haverford College library site, *Feminae: Medieval Women and Gender Index*, www .haverford.edu/library/reference/mshcaus/mfi/mfi.html.

2. THE UPHEAVAL IN WESTERN CHRISTENDOM, 1300–1560

Two books by J. R. Hale, *The Civilization of Europe in the Renaissance* (1993) and *Renaissance Europe, 1480–1520* (rev. 2000), are outstanding. Other helpful overviews for these years encompassing the later Middle Ages, the Renaissance, and the Reformation include S. E. Ozment, *The Age of Reform, 1250–1550: An Intellectual and Religious History of Late Medieval and Reformation Europe* (1980); H. F. Koenigsberger, *Early Modern Europe, 1500–1789* (1987); E. F. Rice, Jr., and A. Grafton, *The Foundations of Early Modern Europe* (rev. 1993); and D. Nicholas, *The Transformation of Europe, 1300–1600* (1999). There are informative chapters in G. R. Potter (ed.), *The Renaissance, 1493–1520* (rev. 1991) and G. R. Elton (ed.), *The Reformation, 1520–1599* (rev. 1990), Vols. I and II of the *New Cambridge Modern History*. T. K. Rabb, *Renaissance Lives: Portraits of an Age* (rev. 2001) provides vivid accounts of notable figures. War and diplomacy are explored in G. Mattingly, *Renaissance Diplomacy* (1971); M. S. Anderson, *The Rise of Modern Diplomacy,* 1450–1919 (1993); and J. R. Hale, *War and Society in Renaissance Europe, 1450–1620* (1985, 1998); while E. L. Eisenstein explores the printing press as a direct and indirect agent of cultural change in *The Printing Revolution in Early Modern Europe* (1984).

Much newer social history has centered on the early modern centuries. Here P. Burke, *Popular Culture in Early Modern Europe* (rev. 1994), ranging in time from 1500 to 1800, is a fundamental analysis. C. Ginzburg, *The Cheese and the Worms: The Cosmos of a Sixteenth-Century Miller* (trans. 1980) reconstructs the mentality of an obscure Italian miller of the age. N. Z. Davis, *Society and Culture in Early Modern France* (1975) illuminates the religious and other beliefs of nonliterate peasants and *The Return of Martin Guerre* (1983) recounts a fascinating episode in village life. R. Chartier (ed.), *Passions of the Renaissance* (1988), the third volume of the *History of Private Life* series, opens the door to aspects of life among all classes in this era. G. Huppert, *After the Black Death: A Social History of Early Modern Europe* (rev. 1998) is a valuable study. Other aspects of social history are examined in K. von Greyerz (ed.), *Religion and Society in Early Modern Europe,*

1500–1800 (1984) and in R. Jütte, *Poverty and Deviance in Early Modern Europe* (1994), a volume in the *New Approaches to European History* series. The ambivalent position of women in the Renaissance is ably conveyed in M. L. King, *Women of the Renaissance* (1991), an outstanding study; I. Maclean, *The Renaissance Notion of Women* (1980); O. Hufton, *The Prospect Before Her: A History of Women in Western Europe, 1500–1800* (1995), and M. E. Wiesner, *Women and Gender in Early Modern Europe* (rev. 2000), also a volume in the *New Approaches to European History* series.

Disasters of the Fourteenth Century

Two brief surveys of the era are R. E. Lerner, The *Age of Adversity: The Fourteenth Century* (1968) and M. McKisack, *The Fourteenth Century, 1307–1399* (1959, 1991). B. W. Tuchman, *A Distant Mirror: The Calamitous Fourteenth Century* (1978) is a vivid account of war, disease, and religious schism written for the general reader. G. Leff, *The Dissolution of the Medieval Outlook: An Essay on Intellectual Change in the Fourteenth Century* (1976), despite the title, stresses the continuity of medieval thought. J. Kaye, *Economy and Nature in the Fourteenth Century: Money, Market Exchange, and the Emergence of Scientific Thought* (1998) explores the influence of economic life on early scientific thought. The growing restlessness within the church before the Reformation is described in F. Oakley, *The Western Church in the Later Middle Ages* (1979) and R. N. Swanson, *Church and Society in Late Medieval England* (1989). Heresies of the period may be examined in H. Kaminsky, *A History of the Hussite Revolution* (1967); in R. Rex, *The Lollards* (2002); and in M. Lambert, *Medieval Heresy: Popular Movements From the Gregorian Reform to the Reformation* (rev. 2002).

The devastating fourteenth-century plague that swept Europe and other parts of the globe from 1347 to 1351 is examined in W. H. McNeill, *Plagues and Peoples* (1976), cited earlier; R. S. Gottfried, *The Black Death: Natural and Human Disaster in Medieval Europe* (1983); D. Herlihy, *The Black Death and the Transformation of the West* (1997); N. F. Cantor, *In the Wake of the Plague* (2001); J. Kelley, *The Great Mortality: An Intimate History of the Black Death* (2005); and S. K. Cohn, *The Black Death Transformed: Disease and Culture in Early Renaissance Europe* (2002), which challenges the usual physiological explanations for the plague. A useful work, which includes documents from the era, is J. Alberth, *The Black Death: The Great Mortality of 1348–1350: A Brief History with Documents* (2005). The long war between France and England over the years 1337 to 1453 may be studied in A. Curry, *The Hundred Years War* (rev. 2003). The works by D. Seward, *The Hundred Years War: The English in France, 1337–1453* (rev. 1999) and C. Allmand, *The Hundred Years' War: England and France at War, c. 1300–c. 1450* (1988) explore the war's impact on both countries. Of the large literature on the "Maid of Orléans" a recent brief account with fresh interpretations is M. Gordon, *Joan of Arc* (2000) in the *Penguin Lives* series.

For the *jacqueries* and other popular revolts one may read M. Mollat and P. Wolff, *The Popular Revolutions of the Late Middle Ages* (trans. 1972) and G. Fourquin, *The Anatomy of Popular Rebellion in the Middle Ages* (trans. 1978).

The phenomenon of witchcraft in the early modern centuries between 1450 and 1750 has understandably attracted a good deal of attention. During those years more than 100,000 people, mainly but not exclusively women, were prosecuted in secular and ecclesiastical courts, and many were put to death. To understand the phenomenon, K. Thomas, *Religion and the Decline of Magic* (1971) is of fundamental importance, but one may also turn to J. Klaits, *Servants of Satan: The Age of the Witch Hunts* (1985); C. Larner, *Witchcraft and Religion: The Politics of Popular Belief* (1985); C. Ginzburg, *Ecstasies: Deciphering the Witches' Sabbath* (1991); and B. P. Levack, *The Witch-Hunt in Early Modern Europe* (rev. 1995), which synthesizes the literature. Available also are M. D. Bailey, *Battling Demons: Witchcraft, Heresy, and Reform in the Later Middle Ages* (2003); G. K. Waite, *Heresy, Magic, and Witchcraft in Early Modern Europe* (2003); W. Behringer, *Witches and Witch-Hunts: A Global History* (2004); and R. Briggs, *Witches and Neighbors: The Social and Cultural Context of European Witchcraft* (1997), based on a wide range of materials from all parts of Europe.

The Renaissance in Italy

In addition to the general accounts already cited, one may turn for all aspects of the Renaissance to the now-classic study by M. P. Gilmore, *The World of Humanism, 1453–1517* (1952, 1983). The concept of the "Renaissance" itself, which is still debated, was skillfully explored in classic works by J. Burckhardt, *The Civilization of the Renaissance in Italy* (1860, 1990) and W. K. Ferguson, *The Renaissance in Historical Thought: Five Centuries of Interpretation* (1948). Readers will also find important interpretations of Renaissance culture and its enduring influence in W. J. Bouwsma, *The Waning of the Renaissance* (2000). For the quickening of activities in the Italian city-states one turns to D. Hay and J. Law, *Italy in the Age of the Renaissance, 1380–1530* (1989); P. Burke, *The Italian Renaissance: Culture and Society in Italy* (rev. 1999); F. Braudel, *Out of Italy, 1450–1650* (trans. 1992), by the *Annales* historian; J. Najemy (ed.), *Italy in the Renaissance, 1300–1550* (2004); E. Welch, *Art and Society in Italy, 1350–1500* (1997); and I. Rowland, *From Heaven to Arcadia: The Sacred and the Profane in the Renaissance* (2004). The revived interest in the classics is examined in R. Weiss, *The Renaissance Discov-*

ery of Classical Antiquity (1969, 1988), and the philosophical debates of the time are examined in B. P. Copenhaver and C. B. Schmitt, *Renaissance Philosophy* (1992), and in A. Levi, *Renaissance and Reformation: The Intellectual Genesis* (2002). Some additional insights into Renaissance culture are offered in L. Jardine, *Worldly Goods: A New History of the Renaissance* (1997). The fusion of politics and humanism (or "civic humanism") is traced in a pioneering work by H. Baron, *The Crisis of the Early Italian Renaissance: Civic Humanism and Republican Liberty in an Age of Classicism and Tyranny* (1955, 1966). The relationship of politics and cultural life is also graphically portrayed in L. Martines, *Power and Imagination: City States in Renaissance Italy* (1979); and the interaction between commercial and intellectual life is explored in T. Parks, *Medici Money: Banking, Metaphysics, and Art in Fifteenth-Century Florence* (2005). A famous Renaissance prelate is portrayed in C. Shaw, *Julius II: The Warrior Pope* (1993).

Of the large literature on Machiavelli, there is a brief, insightful study by J. R. Hale, *Machiavelli and Renaissance Italy* (1960) and a more recent study by the intellectual historian Q. Skinner, *Machiavelli: A Very Short Introduction* (2000); S. de Grazia, *Machiavelli in Hell* (1989), an intriguing intellectual biography; A. J. Parel, *The Machiavellian Cosmos* (1992); and M. Viroli, *Machiavelli* (1998). A provocative study of political thought and discourse as influenced by the Renaissance from the fifteenth to the eighteenth centuries is J. G. A. Pocock, *The Machiavellian Moment: Florentine Political Thought and the Atlantic Republican Tradition* (rev. 2003). J. R. Hale (ed.), *A Concise Encyclopedia of the Italian Renaissance* (1981) is a convenient reference tool.

Numerous studies focusing on each of the Italian city-states have helped illuminate the world of humanism, of which only a few titles can be cited here. Much of the focus has been on Florence, for which G. Brucker, *Renaissance Florence* (rev. 1983) and G. Holmes, *The Florentine Enlightenment, 1400–50* (1992) are the most helpful. Other informative studies include J. R. Hale, *Florence and the Medici: The Pattern of Control* (1978), an especially insightful account; R. A. Goldthwaite, *The Building of Renaissance Florence: An Economic and Social History* (1980); M. Becker, *Florence in Transition* (2 vols., 1967–69); D. Weinstein, *Savanorola and Florence* (1970); and C. Fusero, *The Borgias* (trans. 1973). A colorful popular account is C. Hibbert, *Florence: The Biography of a City* (1993).

Outstanding studies of Venice with varying perspectives include F. C. Lane, *Venice: A Maritime Republic* (1973); W. H. McNeill, *Venice, The Hinge of Europe, 1081–1797* (1974); R. Finlay, *Politics in Renaissance Venice* (1980); and E. Muir, *Civic Ritual in Renaissance Venice* (1981). Valuable studies in social and cultural history include the books by G. Ruggiero,

The Boundaries of Eros: Sex Crime, and Sexuality in Renaissance Venice (1985); S. Chojnacki, *Women and Men in Renaissance Venice* (2000); and P. F. Brown, *Private Lives in Renaissance Venice: Art, Architecture, and the Family* (2004). For Rome one may read P. Partner, *Renaissance Rome, 1500–1559: A Portrait of a Society* (1976) and C. L. Stinger, *The Renaissance in Rome* (reissued 1998).

The Renaissance outside Italy

One of the best introductions to the northern Renaissance can still be found in the classic work by J. Huizinga, *The Autumn of the Middle Ages* (1924; new trans., 1996); one should also read the same author's *Erasmus and the Age of Reformation* (1924,1984). For the Dutch humanist one may also read R. M. Bainton, *Erasmus of Christendom* (1969, 1988); E. Rummel, *Erasmus* (2004); J. McConica, *Erasmus* (1991); and L. Halkin, *Erasmus: A Critical Biography* (trans. 1993). For Christian humanism in general and its contribution to the religious changes of the age, one turns to J. H. Overfield, *Humanism and Scholasticism in Late Medieval Germany* (1984).

The New Monarchies

A good overview is provided in R. Bonney, *The European Dynastic States, 1494–1660* (1991). For England, J. Youings, *Sixteenth-Century England* (1984) examines all aspects of the age. J. R. Lander, *Government and Community: England, 1450–1509* (1980) describes in detail the curbing of feudal power and the evolution of the modern state. Also helpful for England are E. F. Jacob, *The Fifteenth Century* (1961, 1993) and A. Goodman, *The New Monarchy: England, 1471–1534* (1988). For France several books are illuminating: L. Febvre, *Life in Renaissance France* (trans. 1977); and H. A. Lloyd, *The State, France, and the Sixteenth Century* (1983). Two good biographies of "new monarchs" are J. M. Tyrell, *Louis XI* (1980) and R. J. Knecht, *Renaissance Warrior and Patron: The Reign of Francis I* (1982, rev. 1994), the latter a biography of distinction.

General Works on the Reformation

Syntheses of the sixteenth-century upheaval in church and society may be found in L. W. Spitz, *The Protestant Reformation, 1517–1559* (1985) and in M. Gray, *The Protestant Reformation: Belief, Practice, and Tradition* (2003). Other informative accounts are available in E. Cameron, *The European Reformation* (1991); D. MacCulloch, *The Reformation: A History* (2004); and P. Collinson, *The Reformation: A History* (2004).

For political and social background one may turn to H. Holborn, *A History of Modern Germany: The Reformation* (1959), the first volume of his three-volume history of Germany; R. P. Hsia (ed.), *The German People and the Reformation* (1988); and R. W. Scribner, *Popular Culture and Popular Movements in Reformation Germany* (1987). Recent accounts of the leading ruler of the age are available in W. S. Maltby, *The Reign of Charles V* (2002) and H. Kleinschmidt, *Charles V: The World Emperor* (2004).

Biographical accounts of Luther include R. H. Bainton, *Here I Stand: A Life of Martin Luther* (1950, 1994); H. Oberman, *Luther: Man Between God and the Devil* (trans. 1990); M. Brecht, *Martin Luther* (2 vols., trans. 1985, 1990); and M. Marty, *Martin Luther* (2004), an interesting analysis by a noted American historian of religion. E. H. Erikson offers psychoanalytic insights into the religious leader's identity crisis in *Young Man Luther: A Study in Psychoanalysis and History* (1962). Among other studies are H. G. Haile, *Luther: An Experiment in Biography* (1980); M. U. Edwards, Jr., *Luther's Last Battles: Politics and Polemics, 1531–1546* (1983); and G. Brendler, *Martin Luther: Theology and Revolution* (1989). The appeal of Lutheran ideas is skillfully analyzed in R. W. Scribner, *For the Sake of Simple Folk: Popular Propaganda in the German Reformation* (1981); in P. Blickle, *The Revolution of 1525: The German Peasants' War from a New Perspective* (trans. 1981); and in B. Scribner and G. Benecke (eds.), *The German Peasant War, 1525: New Viewpoints* (1979).

An admirable biography of Calvin, capturing the spirit of the man and his times, is W. J. Bouwsma, *John Calvin: A Sixteenth Century Portrait* (1987). Studies of the reformer's thought and influence include F. Wendel, *Calvin: The Origins and Development of His Religious Thought* (trans. 1963, reissued 1987) and P. Helm, *John Calvin's Ideas* (2004). The wider development of the Calvinist movement is examined in P. Benedict, *Christ's Churches Purely Reformed: A Social History of Calvinism* (2002). An outstanding biography of another reformer is G. R. Potter, *Zwingli* (1977), on whom W. P. Stephens has also written *Zwingli: An Introduction to His Thought* (1992). R. H. Bainton, *Hunted Heretic: The Life and Death of Michael Servetus* (1960) may be compared with J. Friedman, *Michael Servetus: A Case Study in Total Heresy* (1978). Studies of another important religious reformer can be found in W. S. Reid, *Trumpeter of God: A Biography of John Knox* (1975) and R. K. Marshall, *John Knox* (2000).

The cities in which the major events of the Reformation occurred are examined in W. Monter, *Calvin's Geneva* (1967) and S. E. Ozment, *The Reformation in the Cities: The Appeal of Protestantism to Sixteenth Century Germany and Switzerland* (1975). S. E. Ozment, *When Fathers Ruled: Family Life in Reformation Europe* (1983) describes the patriarchal household as less tyrannical than traditionally portrayed. R. H. Bainton, *Women of the Reformation* (3 vols., 1971–77) studies the contributions of women to the religious changes of the era; and S. Marshall (ed.), *Women in Reformation and Counter-Reformation Europe: Public and Private Worlds* (1989) provides informative essays on women of the time in various social contexts.

The Reformation in England

The course of the Reformation in England may be approached through a number of helpful syntheses: A. G. Dickens, *The English Reformation* (rev. 1989); J. J. Scarisbrick, *The Reformation and the English People* (1986); and R. Rex, *Henry VIII and the English Reformation* (1993). Recent scholarship is also communicated in P. Marshall and A. Ryrie (eds.), *The Beginnings of English Protestantism* (2002); in W. I. P. Hazlett, *The Reformation in Britain and Ireland: An Introduction* (2003); and in S. Doran and C. Durston, *Princes, Pastors, and People: The Church and Religion in England, 1529–1689* (rev. 2003).

The influential English scholar, statesman, and martyr is studied in R. Marius, *Thomas More: A Biography* (1985), a somewhat critical and unsympathetic account; while P. Ackroyd, *The Life of Thomas More* (1998) and J. A. Guy, *Thomas More* (2000) create a more balanced appraisal of a complex personality. Also available is L. L. Martz, *Thomas More: The Search for the Inner Man* (1990). The conflicts between English Catholics and Protestants are examined in E. Duffy, *The Stripping of the Altars* (rev. 2005) and in A. F. Marotti, *Religious Ideology and Cultural Fantasy: Catholic and Anti-Catholic Discourses in Early Modern England* (2005).

Three older but still provocative books dealing with the social and economic implications of the Reformation for the future course of England are R. H. Tawney, *Religion and the Rise of Capitalism* (1926, 1962), insightful even if modified by later research; C. Hill, *Reformation to Industrial Revolution: The Making of Modern English Society* (1967), also emphasizing class interests; and H. R. Trevor-Roper, *Religion, the Reformation, and Social Change* (rev. 1984), which is less persuaded by the connection between religion and class.

A distinguished biography focusing on the king as well as the events of his reign is J. J. Scarisbrick, *Henry VIII* (1968, 1986); also thoughtful is L. B. Smith, *Henry VIII: The Mask of Royalty* (1971), which may be supplemented by the more recent work of M. A. R. Graves, *Henry VIII, A Study in Kingship* (2000) and A. Weir, *Henry VIII: The King and His Court* (2001). On the history of Henry's wives, in addition to several individual biographies for each, one may read A. Fraser, *The Wives of Henry VIII* (1992); A. Weir, *Six Wives of Henry VIII* (1992); and D. Starkey, *Six Wives: The Queens of Henry VIII* (2003). Henry VIII's two immediate successors and their brief reigns are described in S. Alford, *Kingship and Politics in the Reign of Edward VI* (2002); D. M. Loades, *Mary Tudor* (1989); and C. Erickson, *Bloody Mary: The Life of Mary Tudor* (1993). Books on Elizabeth will be described in the next chapter, but for studies of religion in all or part of her reign one may turn to A. Morey, *The Catholic Subjects of Elizabeth I* (1978) and P. Collinson's two books, *The Elizabethan Puritan Movement* (1967, 1990) and *The Religion of Protestants: The Church in English Society, 1559–1625* (1983).

Other Reformation Themes

The various forms of Protestantism are placed in doctrinal perspective in B. M. G. Reardon, *Religious Thought in the Reformation* (rev. 1995) and A. McGrath, *Reformation Thought* (1988), while the radical movements of the era may be studied in G. H. Williams, *The Radical Reformation* (rev. 1992); N. Cohn, *The Pursuit of the Millennium: Revolutionary Messianism in Medieval and Reformation Europe* (rev. 1970); and M. A. Mullett, *Radical Religious Movements in Early Modern Europe* (1980). An important subject is explored in H. Kamen, *The Rise of Toleration* (1967).

On the relation between economic change and Protestant religious doctrine, especially Calvinism, a debate that was opened by Max Weber in *The Protestant Ethic and the Spirit of Capitalism* (1904, 1985) and further developed by R. H. Tawney in the 1920s, one may read G. Marshall, *In Search of the Spirit of Capitalism: An Essay on Max Weber's Protestant Ethic Thesis* (1982), a balanced review; and the essays in H. Lehmann and G. Roth (eds.), *Weber's Protestant Ethic* (1993) and in W. H. Swatos Jr. and L. Kaelber (eds.), *The Protestant Ethic Turns 100: Essays on the Centenary of the Weber Thesis* (2005), which add many new insights.

The Catholic response to the Reformation is studied in N. S. Davidson, *The Counter Reformation* (1987), which provides a brief overview, and in M. D. W. Jones, *The Counter Reformation: Religion and Society in Early Modern Europe* (1995). Important for the Catholic response and other matters is J. Pelikan, *Reformation of Church and Dogma, 1300–1700* (1983), Vol. IV of his *The Christian Tradition*. H. Jedin, *The Council of Trent* (2 vols., 1957–61) presents the fullest account of the important council and its reforms. Introductions to the literature on the Society of Jesus are provided in W. B. Bangert, *A History of the Society of Jesus* (1972) and J. P. Donnelly, *Ignatius of Loyola: Founder of the Jesuits* (2004). A masterful review of the early Jesuits is J. O'Malley, *The First Jesuits* (1999). There are also biographies of Loyola by P. Caramon (1990) and W. Meissner (1992), the latter a psychoanalytical study.

Useful Web Sites

Several Web sites provide access to information on the crisis of the later middle ages; see, for example, information about the plague in Britain at the useful site of the British radio network, *BBC-History*, www.bbc.co.uk/history/society_culture/welfare/black_01.shtml; the excellent *Internet Medieval Sourcebook* at

Fordham University, cited earlier, includes materials on the disasters of the fourteenth century at www .fordham.edu/halsall/sbook1w.html. For sources on the history of withcraft, one may visit *The Witch Hunts* at http://history.hanover.edu/early/wh.html. There are helpful links to diverse themes in the history of both the Renaissance and Reformation at the Web site of the *History Department, University of Colorado, Colorado Springs*, http://web.uccs.edu/ history/globalhistory/renaissance.htm. More links to the history of all European countries in the Renaissance era can be found at *Medieval and Renaissance Europe: Primary Historical Documents*, www.lib .byu.edu/~rdh/eurodocs/, where readers can also locate helpful material on the early monarchical states. The evolution of the French state is examined with useful documents and images at a Library of Congress site called *Creating French Culture*, which is available at www.loc.gov/exhibits/bnf/bnf0001.html. The Reformation can be explored through Fordham University's *Internet Modern History Sourcebook* at www.fordham.edu/halsall/mod/modsbook.html; and see also the excellent links at the Web site of *The Centre for Reformation and Renaissance Studies*, affiliated with the University of Toronto, at www.crrs .ca/library/webresources/webresources.htm.

3. ECONOMIC RENEWAL AND WARS OF RELIGION, 1560–1648

Of general treatments for these years, covering institutional and international developments, the best guides are G. Parker, *Europe in Crisis, 1598–1648* (rev. 2001); H. Kamen, *Early Modern European Society* (2000), which describes the evolving social history of the era; V. G. Kiernan, *State and Society in Europe, 1550–1650* (1987); and J. H. Elliott, *Europe Divided, 1559–1598* (rev. 2000). F. Braudel's magisterial work stressing broad geographic, demographic, and economic developments, *The Mediterranean and the Mediterranean World in the Age of Philip II* (rev. and abr. ed., 1992), has been cited in the introductory section.

Analytical treatments focusing on the concept of crisis in the seventeenth century (and useful for this and the following chapter) include T. Aston (ed.), *Crisis in Europe, 1560–1660: Essays from Past and Present* (1966); G. Parker and L. M. Smith, *The General Crisis of the Seventeenth Century* (1978); T. K. Rabb, *The Struggle for Stability in Early Modern Europe* (1976); and T. Munck, *Seventeenth-Century Europe: State, Conflict, and the Social Order in Europe, 1598–1700* (rev. 2005). Agrarian and urban unrest is studied in P. Zagorin, *Rebels and Rulers, 1500–1660* (2 vols., 1982); J. A. Goldstone's sociological study, *Revolution and Rebellion in the Early Modern World* (1991); and C. Tilly, *European Revolutions, 1492–*

1992 (1992). The impact on society of military change is examined in G. Parker, *The Military Revolution: Military Innovation and the Rise of the West, 1500–1800* (rev. 1996) and in J. Black, *A Military Revolution? Military Change and European Society, 1550–1800* (1991). B. M. Downing, *The Military Revolution and Political Change: The Origins of Democracy and Autocracy in Early Modern Europe* (1992) is intended to revise and supplement B. Moore, *The Social Origins of Dictatorship and Democracy: Lord and Peasant in the Making of the Modern World* (1966, reissued 1993).

The Opening of the Atlantic

Good introductions to European exploration and settlement, beginning in the pre-Columbian age, are F. Fernández-Armesto, *Before Columbus: Exploration and Colonization from the Mediterranean to the Atlantic, 1229–1492* (1987); J. H. Parry, *The Age of Reconnaissance: Discovery, Exploration, and Settlement, 1450–1650* (rev. 1981); and G. Scammell, *The First Imperial Age: European Overseas Expansion, 1400–1715* (1989). Still interesting is S. E. Morison, *The European Discovery of America* (2 vols., 1971–74, 1993), but a more analytical overview of European imperial expansion is available in D. B. Abernethy, *The Dynamics of Global Dominance: European Overseas Empires, 1415–1980* (2000); and there is a helpful survey of European expansion throughout the world in D. R. Ringrose, *Expansion and Global Interaction* (2001). C. M. Cipolla stresses the importance of technology for the European explorations in *Guns, Sails, and Empires: 1400–1700* (1965, reissued 1985), as does A. W. Crosby in a far-ranging study, *The Measure of Reality: Quantification and Western Society, 1250–1600* (1997). China's naval exploits in the early 15th century are described in L. E. Leviathes, *When China Ruled the Seas* (1994).

The 500th anniversary of Columbus's first voyage stimulated the appearance of numerous books, many vehemently critical of the European impact on the New World and seeing the voyages less as discovery than intrusion or conquest, or at best as an encounter between very different peoples and cultures. Three examples of this critical literature are K. Sale, *Christopher Columbus and the Conquest of Paradise* (rev. 2006); T. Todorov, *The Conquest of America: The Question of the Other* (trans. 1984, reissued 1999); and D. E. Stannard, *American Holocaust: Columbus and the Conquest of the New World* (1993). Two balanced accounts placing Columbus in the context of his time without overlooking the consequences of the European arrival are W. D. Phillips, Jr., and C. R. Phillips, *The Worlds of Christopher Columbus* (1991) and F. Fernández-Armesto, *Columbus* (1991); the latter author provides additional assessments in *Columbus and the Conquest of the Impossible* (rev. 2000), ambitious but not as satisfactory as some of his other books. Other scholarly efforts to examine much that remains obscure about the explorer are D. Heinge, *In Search of Columbus: The Sources for the First Voyage* (1991) and V. Flint, *The Imaginative Landscape of Christopher Columbus* (1992). P. K. Liss, *Isabel the Queen* (1992) is a thoughtful biography of his patron.

A splendidly illustrated catalog prepared for an exhibition to commemorate the quincentenary, J. A. Levenson (ed.), *Circa 1492: Art in the Age of Exploration* (1991), presents the impressive art and artifacts of people from all over the globe in this age, including the New World. In two thoughtful books A. W. Crosby demonstrates that European plants, animals, and diseases had as much to do with the success of European expansion and the consequent devastation of the indigenous peoples as military conquest: *The Columbian Exchange: Biological and Cultural Consequences of 1492* (rev. 2003) and *Ecological Imperialism: The Biological Expansion of Europe, 900–1900* (1986), a broader study. C. C. Mann describes the diversity of Native American societies before the arrival of Europeans in *1491: New Revelations of the Americas before Columbus* (2005). For the impact of the discoveries on European thought, one may turn to W. Brandon, *New Worlds for Old: Reports from the New World and Their Effect on the Development of Social Thought in Europe, 1500–1800* (1986); J. H. Elliott, *The Old World and the New, 1492–1650* (1970, 1992); and A. Pagden's two books, *European Encounters with the New World: From Renaissance to Romanticism* (1992) and *Lords of All the World: Ideologies of Empire in Spain, Britain, and France, c. 1500–c. 1850* (1995). The latter may be compared with the two works of P. Seed, *Ceremonies of Possession in Europe's Conquest of the New World, 1492–1640* (1995) and *American Pentimento: The Invention of Indians and the Pursuit of Riches* (2001). On European interactions with native peoples in the years after the initial explorations, see the important books of J. Axtell, *Beyond 1492: Encounters in Colonial North America* (1993) and *Natives and Newcomers: The Cultural Origins of North America* (2001).

Portugal and Spain in Europe and Overseas

The best introduction to the overseas exploits of both countries is L. N. McAlister, *Spain and Portugal in the New World, 1492–1700* (1983). Portuguese maritime and colonial enterprises are recounted in C. R. Boxer, *The Portuguese Seaborne Empire: 1415–1825* (rev. 1991); one may also read B. W. Diffie and G. D. Winius, *Foundations of the Portuguese Empire, 1415–1580* (1977). On Portugal, there are sound histories by J. M. Anderson, *The History of Portugal* (2000) and D. Birmingham, *A Concise History of Portugal* (rev. 2003); and on the Iberian peninsula as a whole, S. G. Payne, *A History of Spain and Portugal* (2 vols., 1973).

The best accounts for Spain in the early modern centuries are J. H. Elliott, *Imperial Spain, 1469–1714*

(1964, reissued, 2002), which may be supplemented by his *Spain and Its World, 1500–1700* (1986); J. Lynch, *Spain under the Habsburgs, 1516–1700* (2 vols.; rev. 1992); and H. Kamen, *Empire: How Spain Became a World Power, 1492–1763* (2003). Social trends in Spanish society are discussed in J. Casey, *Early Modern Spain: A Social History* (1999). For the Spanish monarch one may read P. Pierson, *Philip II of Spain* (1975) and G. Parker, *Philip II* (rev. 1995) and *The Grand Strategy of Philip II* (1998). H. Kamen, *Philip of Spain* (1997) is more sympathetic than other biographical accounts. On the Spanish arm of the Counter-Reformation H. Kamen, *The Spanish Inquisition: A Historical Revision* (1997) attempts to redress the balance in favor of a less harsh judgment, to which even his own earlier writings contributed. However, the works of B. Netanyahu, *The Origins of the Inquisition in Fifteenth-Century Spain* (rev. 2001) and J. Perez, *The Spanish Inquistion: A History* (trans. 2005) stress the human costs of religious persecutions.

Although G. Mattingly, *The Armada* (1959, 1989) remains the classic study of this dramatic episode in its diplomatic and ideological setting, readers will wish to turn also to C. Martin and G. Parker, *The Spanish Armada* (rev. 1999); F. Fernández-Armesto, *The Spanish Armada: The Experience of War in 1588* (1989); and the more recent works of J. McDermott, *England and the Spanish Armada: The Necessary Quarrel* (2005) and N. Hanson, *The Confident Hope of A Miracle: The True History of the Spanish Armada* (2005).

Books examining Spain after the age of Philip II include R. A. Stradling, *Philip IV and the Government of Spain, 1621–1665* (1988) and two outstanding studies by J. H. Elliott: *The Revolt of the Catalans: A Study in the Decline of Spain, 1598–1640* (1963, 1984) and *The Count-Duke of Olivares: The Statesman in an Age of Decline* (1986), on Philip IV's principal adviser from 1621 to 1643.

For the Spanish empire in the new world one may read C. Gibson, *Spain in America* (1966, 1990); J. H. Parry, *The Spanish Seaborne Empire* (1966); S. J. Stein and B. H. Stein, *Silver, Trade, and War: Spain and America in the Making of Early Modern Europe* (2000); D. J. Weber, *The Spanish Frontier in North America* (1995); and C. M. MacLachlan, *Spain's Empire in the New World: The Role of Ideas in Institutional and Social Change* (1988). A pioneer inquiry into the impact of the discovery of silver upon economic changes in Europe was E. J. Hamilton, *American Treasure and the Price Revolution in Spain, 1501–1650* (1934, 1965), although some of its conclusions have been modified. The subject is also examined in P. Vila, *A History of Gold and Money, 1450–1920* (trans. 1976) and in J. N. Ball, *Merchants and Merchandise: The Expansion of Trade in Europe, 1500–1630* (1977). For the Spanish conquest, readers may turn to M. Wood, *Conquistadors* (2000), the work of a writer who has also produced a documentary film on the subject. Modern historical scholarship is reflected in R. L. Marks, *Cortés: The Great Adventurer and the Fate of Aztec Mexico* (1993) and in H. Thomas, *Conquest: Montezuma, Cortés, and the Fall of Old Mexico* (1994). On attempts by the church and others to mitigate the evils of the conquest one still turns to L. Hanke, *The Spanish Struggle for Justice in the Conquest of America* (1949, reissued 2002). The best scholarly accounts of the enforced labor and demographic consequences of the conquest may be found in the chapters contributed to L. Bethell (ed.), *The Cambridge History of Latin America,* Vols. I and II: *Colonial Latin America* (1988). An informative survey for all aspects of Latin America in the colonial era is M. A. Burkholder and L. L. Johnson, *Colonial Latin America* (rev. 2003).

The Atlantic slave trade and slavery, which launched the massive migrations of people that historians now call the African Diaspora, can be studied in numerous important historical works. Among the most informative are H. S. Klein, *African Slavery in Latin America and the Caribbean* (1987); V. B. Thompson, *The Making of the African Diaspora in the Americas, 1441–1900* (1988); R. Blackburn, *The Making of New World Slavery* (1997); D. Eltis, *The Rise of African Slavery in the Americas* (2000); and W. Klooster and A. Padula (eds.), *The Atlantic World: Essays on Slavery, Migration, and Imagination* (2005). The writings of D. B. Davis, *Slavery and Human Progress* (1984) and *The Problem of Slavery in Western Culture* (1988), as well as his other volumes cited in later chapters, offer penetrating insights, as do O. Patterson's books *Slavery and Social Death: A Comparative Study* (1982) and *Freedom in the Making of Western Culture* (1991). The historical background is presented in W. D. Phillips, *Slavery from Roman Times to the Early Transatlantic Trade* (1985), carrying the story to 1650, and in B. Lewis, *Race and Slavery in the Middle East* (1990). E. Williams, *Capitalism and Slavery* (1944, reissued 1994) early emphasized that the emerging Atlantic economy was supported by African slavery, a theme on which there are informative essays in B. L. Solow (ed.), *Slavery and the Rise of the Atlantic System* (1991). The grim story of the slave trade is recounted in many books, among them J. Pope-Hennessy, *Sins of the Fathers: A Study of the Atlantic Slave Traders 1441–1807* (1968); P. D. Curtin, *The Atlantic Slave Trade* (1969); H. S. Klein, *The Middle Passage* (1978); J. A. Rawley, *The Transatlantic Slave Trade* (1981); and C. A. Palmer, *Human Cargoes: The British Slave Trade to Spanish America, 1700–1739* (1981). H. Thomas, *The Slave Trade: The Story of the Atlantic Slave Trade, 1440–1870* (1997) graphically conveys its multinational character. A case study of slavery on a Caribbean plantation is available in T. Burnard, *Mastery, Tyranny, and Desire: Thomas Thistlewood and His Slaves in the Anglo-Jamaican World* (2004). Two valuable syntheses of historical writings on slavery in its North American setting are P. Kolchin, *American Slavery, 1619–1877* (1993) and I. Berlin, *Many Thousands Gone: The First Two Centuries of Slavery in North America* (1998).

Changing Social Structures, Early Capitalism, Mercantilism

A key study of early economic history is J. De Vries, *The Economy of Europe in an Age of Crisis, 1600–1750* (1976). One will wish to consult also R. Davis, *The Rise of the Atlantic Economies* (1973); C. M. Cipolla, *Before the Industrial Revolution: European Society and Economy, 1000–1700* (rev. 1994); P. Kriedte, *Peasants, Landlords, and Merchant Capitalists: Europe and the World Economy 1500–1800* (1983); and A. K. Smith, *Creating a World Economy: Merchant Capital, Colonialism, and World Trade, 1400–1825* (1991). The reasons why rapid economic change took place in western Europe rather than elsewhere are explored in E. L. Jones, *The European Miracle: Environments, Economics, and Geopolitics in the History of Europe and Asia* (rev. 2003) and in J. Baechler et al. (eds.), *Europe and the Rise of Capitalism* (1988).

A remarkable though often impressionistic account of social and economic change in the early modern centuries is the three-volume work of F. Braudel, *Civilization and Capitalism, 15th–18th Century* (trans. 1981–84; reissued 1992): Vol. I, *The Structures of Everyday Life;* Vol. II, *The Wheels of Commerce;* and Vol. III, *The Perspective of the World.* The broad themes of the work are summarized in *Afterthoughts on Material Civilization and Capitalism* (trans. 1977). Another large-scale study, reflecting the influence of Braudel and focusing on the shifting of economic power is I. Wallerstein, *The Modern World-System* (3 vols. 1974), analyzing the origins of the world economy, mercantilism, and the expansion of the global economy from 1730 to the 1840s. The development of a capitalist economy is also traced in W. N. Parker, *Europe, America, and the Wider World: Essays on the Economic History of Western Capitalism* (2 vols., 1984, 1991); and important intercultural dimensions are added in P. D. Curtin, *Cross-Cultural Trade in World History* (1984).

Much of the debate on the early modern centuries focuses on the continuity of European economic history since the Middle Ages and on early industrialization. The debate on "protoindustrialization" is examined in P. Kriedte (ed.), *Industrialization before Industrialization: Rural Industry and the Genesis of Capitalism* (1981) and in M. P. Gutmann, *Toward the Modern Economy: Early Industry in Europe, 1500–1800* (1988).

For demography one may turn to M. W. Flynn, *The European Demographic System, 1500–1820*

(1981); and for the growth of cities one may consult P. M. Hohenberg and L. H. Lees, *The Making of Urban Europe, 1000–1994* (rev. 1995) and J. De Vries, *European Urbanization, 1500–1800* (1984). There are valuable chapters in C. M. Cipolla (ed.), *The Fontana Economic History of Europe: The Sixteenth and Seventeenth Centuries* (1974) and in E. E. Rich and C. H. Wilson (eds.), *Cambridge Economic History of Europe*, Vol. IV (1976) and Vol. V (1977).

Revolt of the Netherlands

G. Parker, *The Dutch Revolt* (1977), an admirable comprehensive study, may be compared with P. Geyl's masterful older account, *The Revolt of the Netherlands, 1555–1609* (1932; trans. 1958) and *The Netherlands in the Seventeenth Century, 1609–1715* (2 vols.; trans. 1961–64). Dutch political culture is examined in H. H. Rowen, *The Princes of Orange: the Stadholders in the Dutch Republic* (1988); and W. S. Maltby, *Alba: A Biography* (1983) studies the Duke of Alba, the Spanish governor sent to suppress the Dutch in the mid-sixteenth century and who thereby helped to create the Dutch nation.

The Tudor Age: Elizabethan England

The best syntheses for the Tudor monarchs are G. R. Elton, *England under the Tudors* (rev. 1991); and J. Guy, *Tudor England* (1988); a useful collection of articles is available in J. Guy (ed.), *The Tudor Monarchy* (1997). Informative for the Tudors and their successors are D. M. Loades, *Politics and Nation: England, 1450–1660* (rev. 1999) and J. Guy and J. Morrill, *The Tudors and Stuarts* (1993), a volume in the *Oxford History of Britain*.

For the Elizabethan era one may read W. T. MacCaffrey's trilogy of distinction—*The Shaping of the Elizabethan Regime* (1968), *Queen Elizabeth and the Making of Policy, 1572–1588* (1981), and *Elizabeth I: War and Politics, 1588–1603* (1992). For the religious question in these years one may turn to D. MacCulloch, *The Later Reformation in England, 1547–1603* (rev. 2001). A survey of foreign affairs is available in R. B. Wernham, *The Making of Elizabethan Foreign Policy* (1980). On the naval and imperial side one may also read D. B. Quinn and A. N. Ryan, *England's Sea Empire, 1550–1642* (1983) and K. R. Andrews, *Trade, Plunder, and Settlement: Maritime Enterprise and the Genesis of the British Empire, 1480–1630* (1985).

Of the numerous biographies of Elizabeth one may read A. Somerset, *Elizabeth I* (1992, 2003), a lively volume; S. Bassnett, *Elizabeth I: A Feminist Perspective* (1988); D. M. Loades, *Elizabeth I* (2003); and the concise account in S. Doran, *Queen Elizabeth I* (2003). There are other commendable studies by L. B. Smith (1976), E. Erickson (1983), A. Weir (1998), and C. Haigh (rev. 2001). A. Fraser, among her many notable volumes, has written *Mary Queen of Scots* (1969, 1993). On Elizabeth's devoted courtier,

H. Kelsey, *Sir Francis Drake: The Queen's Pirate* (1998) is a scholarly account.

An overview of society and economy is helpfully presented in D. M. Palliser, *The Age of Elizabeth: England under the Later Tudors, 1547–1603* (rev. 1992). Social and economic changes of the age, or that take their start in this age, are masterfully explored in L. Stone, *The Crisis of the Aristocracy, 1558–1641* (1965; abr. ed., 1967) and in L. Stone and J. C. Stone, *An Open Elite?: England, 1540–1880* (1984; abr. ed., 1986), which questions upward social mobility in England. Other important studies are G. E. Mingay, *The Gentry: The Rise and Fall of a Ruling Class* (1976); A. Macfarlane, *The Origins of English Individualism: The Family, Property, and Social Transition* (1978); and I. W. Archer, *The Pursuit of Stability: Social Relations in Elizabethan London* (1991).

Historical research to reconstruct the history of the family is brilliantly exemplified in L. Stone's several works: *The Family, Sex, and Marriage in England, 1500–1800* (1977; abr. ed., 1979), *Road to Divorce: England, 1530–1987* (1990), and in a volume of revealing case studies, *Uncertain Unions and Broken Lives: Marriage and Divorce in England, 1660–1857* (1995). Other recommended studies are R. A. Houlbrooke, *The English Family, 1450–1700* (1984); J. R. Gillis, *For Better, For Worse: British Marriages, 1600 to the Present* (1985); A. Macfarlane, *Marriage and Love in England: Modes of Reproduction, 1300–1840* (1987); and B. J. Harris, *English Aristocratic Women 1450–1550: Marriage and Family, Property and Careers* (2002). R. A. Houlbrooke's *Death, Religion, and the Family in England, 1480–1750* (1998) examines views of death in this era.

Two important books are P. Laslett, *The World We Have Lost: England before the Industrial Age* (1965, rev. 2004), a pioneering work that presents a somewhat overly stable picture of these years, and E. A. Wrigley and R. S. Schofield, *The Population History of England, 1541–1871* (1981), a model of demographic research.

Disintegration and Reconstruction of France

Informative introductions to the religious and dynastic turmoil in sixteenth-century France include R. Briggs, *Early Modern France, 1560–1715* (rev. 1998); H. A. Lloyd, *The State, France, and the Sixteenth Century* (1983); and R. J. Knecht, *French Renaissance Monarchy: Francis I and Henry II* (rev. 1996). J. H. M. Salmon's two books are of special value: *Society in Crisis: France in the Sixteenth Century* (rev. 1979) and *Renaissance and Revolt: Essays in the Intellectual and Social History of Early France* (1987). Major French works available in translation are R. Mandrou, *Introduction to Modern France, 1500–1640: An Essay in Historical Psychology* (trans. 1976); E. Le Roy Ladurie's two studies *The French Peasantry, 1450–1660* (rev. and trans. 1986) and *Early Modern*

France, 1460–1610 (trans. 1993); and R. Mousnier, *The Institutions of France under the Absolute Monarchy, 1598–1789* (2 vols., trans. 1979–84), an exhaustive study of society and the state.

The religious wars are also explored in N. M. Sutherland's *The Massacre of St. Bartholemew and the European Conflict, 1559–1572* (1973) and *The Huguenot Struggle for Recognition* (1980); B. B. Diefendorf, *Beneath the Cross: Catholics and Huguenots in Sixteenth-Century Paris* (1991); H. Heller, *Iron and Blood: Civil Wars in Sixteenth-Century France* (1991); M. P. Holt, *The French Wars of Religion, 1562–1629* (1996); and R. J. Knecht, *The French Civil Wars, 1562–1598* (2000). The intellectual dimension is examined in D. R. Kelley, *The Beginning of Ideology: Consciousness and Society in the French Reformation* (1981). An illuminating biography of the first Bourbon king, D. Buisseret, *Henri IV* (1984) may be supplemented by M. Greengrass, *France in the Age of Henri IV: The Struggle for Stability* (rev. 1995); R. S. Love, *Blood and Religion: The Conscience of Henry IV, 1553–1593* (2001); and the comprehensive work of N. M. Sutherland, *Henry IV of France and the Politics of Religion: 1572–1596* (2 vols., 2002)

Constitutional developments are comprehensively explored in J. R. Major, *Representative Government in Early Modern France* (1980), stressing the vitality of the early representative bodies; in P. Anderson, *Lineages of the Absolutist State* (1974); in H. H. Rowen, *The King's State: Proprietary Dynasticism in Early Modern France* (1980), examining the state as royal property; and in E. Le Roy Ladurie, *The Royal French State, 1460–1610* (trans. 1994), describing the changing public functions of the royal government. The cultural values of the early modern nobility are examined in E. Schalk, *From Valor to Pedigree: Ideas of Nobility in France in the Sixteenth and Seventeenth Centuries* (1986) and K. B. Neuschel, *Word of Honor: Interpreting Noble Culture in Sixteenth-Century France* (1989).

For the era of Louis XIII and the minister who overshadowed him one reads V. L. Tapié, *France in the Age of Louis XIII and Richelieu* (trans. 1974; reissued 1984). The king himself is studied in A. Lloyd Moote, *Louis XIII, The Just* (1989). The scholarship on Richelieu includes W. F. Church, *Richelieu and Reason of State* (1972); J. Bergin, *Cardinal Richelieu: Power and the Pursuit of Wealth* (1985) and *The Rise of Richelieu* (1991); R. J. Knecht, *Richelieu* (1991); D. Parrott, *Richelieu's Army: War, Government, and Society In France, 1624–1642* (2001); and A. Levi, *Cardinal Richelieu and the Making of France* (2000). The strengthening of royal power under Richelieu and his successor is examined in R. Bonney, *Society and Government in France under Richelieu and Mazarin, 1624–1661* (1988) and in J. Bergin and L. Brockless (eds.), *Richelieu and His Age* (1992). An important work by J. B. Collins, *The State in Early Modern France* (1995), stresses the close connection between the monarchy and social elites; and a penetrating comparative study of Richelieu and of his Spanish contemporary and rival, the Count-Duke of Olivares, can be found in J. H. Elliott, *Richelieu and Olivares* (1984).

The Thirty Years' War, 1618–1648

The most up-to-date authoritative account is G. Parker (ed.), *The Thirty Years' War* (rev. 1997), which includes chapters on all phases of the war. A useful, brief survey is available in P. Limm, *The Thirty Years' War* (1984). Other accounts include the classic work by C. V. Wedgwood (1938, reissued 2005), and other accounts by G. Pagès (trans. 1971), and J. V. Polisensky (trans. 1971). Biographical accounts of key leaders can be found in G. Mann, *Wallenstein: His Life Narrated* (trans. 1976) and M. Roberts, *Gustavus Adolphus* (1992). A detailed treatment of all aspects of Swedish history is to be found in the books of M. Roberts: *The Early Vasas: A History of Sweden, 1523–1611* (1968, 1986); *Gustavus Adolphus and the Rise of Sweden* (1973); *The Swedish Imperial Experience, 1560–1718* (1979); and *The Age of Liberty: Sweden, 1719–1772* (1986). The conversion to Catholicism of Gustavus Adolphus's daughter and her abdication is told in G. Masson, *Queen Christina* (1968) and in S. Svolpe, *Christina of Sweden* (trans. and abr. 1966), by a Swedish historian.

Useful Web Sites

Print and artistic resources on European exploration in the Atlantic world are available at an excellent Web site, *American Journeys,* at the Wisconsin Historical Society, www.americanjourneys.org. There are additional sources on the age of explorations at *European Voyages of Exploration,* which may be found at www.ucalgary.ca/applied_history/tutor/eurvoya/, and at a site maintained by the Library of Congress, *1492 Exhibit,* www.ibiblio.org/expo/1492.exhibit/intro.html. A helpful collection of links is available at the *African Diaspora in Latin America,* which is part of a comprehensive site on Latin American history at the University of Texas, http://lanic.utexas.edu/la/region/african/. For a well-organized site on all aspects of Tudor England, readers may visit *Tudor History* at http://tudorhistory.org/; and there is a useful Web site for current research on this era in French history at *Historians of Early Modern France,* www.history.emory.edu/BEIK/index.htm. Helpful material on an important conflict may be found at *The Thirty Years War,* www.pipeline.com/~cwa/tywhome.htm. Readers will also find numerous other sites on early modern European history by visiting *Best of History Web Sites* at www.besthistorysites.net/EarlyModernEurope.shtml.

4. THE GROWING POWER OF WESTERN EUROPE, 1640–1715

General accounts of the seventeenth century overlap with many of the books described in the preceding chapter. Informative general works include D. H. Pennington, *Europe in the Seventeenth Century* (rev. 1989) and J. Bergin (ed.) *The Seventeenth Century: Europe, 1598–1715* (2001). Two commendable general histories that begin with these years are W. Doyle, *The Old European Order, 1660–1800* (rev. 1992) and G. R. R. Treasure, *The Making of Modern Europe, 1648–1780* (1985). For international affairs, diplomacy, and war, two thoughtful accounts are D. McKay and H. M. Scott, *The Rise of the Great Powers, 1648–1815* (1983) and J. Black, *The Rise of the European Powers, 1679–1793* (1990). The diplomatic practices and institutions of the age are described in W. J. Roosen, *The Age of Louis XIV: The Rise of Modern Diplomacy* (1976), while the nature of warfare is examined in J. Childs, *Armies and Warfare in Europe, 1648–1789* (1982) and in M. S. Anderson, *War and Society in Europe of the Old Regime, 1618–1789* (rev. 1998).

The Dutch Republic

For the Netherlands in the seventeenth century one may read C. Wilson, *The Dutch Republic and the Civilization of the Seventeenth Century* (1968), an excellent brief introduction, and S. Schama, *The Embarrassment of Riches: An Interpretation of Dutch Culture in the Golden Age* (1988), an exemplary synthesis of art history and social history. Of special interest are three books by J. I. Israel: *The Dutch Republic: Its Rise, Greatness, and Fall, 1477–1806* (1995), *The Dutch Republic and the Hispanic World, 1606–1661* (1982), and *Dutch Primacy in World Trade, 1585–1740* (1989). Colonial expansion is described in C. R. Boxer, *The Dutch Seaborne Empire, 1600–1800* (1965); the Dutch economy is examined in J. A. van Houtte, *An Economic History of the Low Countries, 800–1800* (1977) and J. De Vries, *The Dutch Rural Economy in the Golden Age, 1500–1700* (1974).

For William of Orange, the best study is S. B. Baxter, *William III and the Defense of European Liberty, 1650–1702* (1966). A comprehensive biography of a leading Dutch statesman is H. H. Rowen, *Jan de Witt: Statesman of "True Freedom"* (1978; abr. 1986). Rowen also examines the later stadholders in a book that was noted earlier, *The Princes of Orange: The Stadholders in the Dutch Republic* (1988).

Seventeenth-Century England

Three judicious accounts of the seventeenth-century political and religious conflicts are D. Hirst, *Authority and Conflict: England, 1603–1658* (1986); D. Hirst, *England in Conflict, 1603–1660: Kingdom, Community, Commonwealth* (1999); and G. E. Aylmer, *Rebellion or Revolution?: England, 1640–1660* (1986). Other recommended general works include A. Stroud, *Stuart England* (1999); R. Lockyer, *The Early Stuarts: A Political History of England, 1603–1642* (rev. 1999) and, by the same author, *Tudor and Stuart Britain, 1485–1714* (rev. 2005); B. Coward, *The Stuart Age: England 1603–1714* (rev. 2003); and R. Bucholz and N. Key, *Early Modern England, 1485–1714* (2004).

For social and economic developments, illuminating studies include C. Wilson, *England's Apprenticeship, 1603–1763* (rev. 1984); K. Wrightson, *English Society, 1580–1680* (1982); and J. A. Sharpe, *Early Modern England: A Social History, 1550–1760* (rev. 1997). Books on the gentry and aristocracy have been cited in Chapter 3; to them should be added J. V. Beckett, *The Aristocracy in England, 1660–1914* (1988).

Few subjects have been as debated as the political and religious conflicts in seventeenth-century England. Some historians stress class and ideological conflict and interpret the events as the first modern European revolution. Others downplay what they see as anachronistic ideological interpretations, emphasize local rivalries, and insist on the importance of day-to-day contingencies. As an introduction to divergent interpretations one may compare L. Stone, *The Causes of the English Revolution, 1629–1642* (rev. 2002) and three books with much the same title by C. Russell (1990), A. Hughes (rev. 1998), and N. Carlin (1999).

For the general reader, the narrative excitement of the events is captured in C. V. Wedgwood's trilogy *The King's Peace, 1637–1641* (1955, reissued 1983), *The King's War, 1641–1647* (1959), and *A Coffin for King Charles: The Trial and Execution of Charles I* (1964), in which she demonstrates that the "why" (the analysis) must flow from the "how" (the narrative). A dramatic account, with considerable attention to military aspects, is C. Hibbert, *Cavaliers and Roundheads: The English Civil War, 1642–1649* (1993). For the opening episodes of these years A. Fletcher, *The Outbreak of the English Civil War* (1981) and K. Sharpe, *The Personal Rule of Charles I* (1992), both of which tend to minimize long-term social and economic causes, may be compared with L. J. Reeve, *Charles I and the Road to Personal Rule* (1989); R. Cust, *The Forced Loan and English Politics* (1986); and R. Brenner, *Merchants and Revolution* (1992). Of special interest also is C. Carlton, *Going to the Wars: The Experience of the British Civil Wars, 1638–1651* (1992).

Studies that downplay broader ideological interpretations but provide detailed narrative and analysis include C. Russell's books, *The Crisis of Parliaments* (1971), *Parliaments and English Politics, 1621–1629* (1979), and *The Fall of the British Monarchies, 1637–1742* (1991), which may be read along with J. Morrill, *The Revolt of the Provinces: Conservatism and Revolution in the English Civil War, 1630–1650* (1980) and *The Nature of the English Revolution* (1993), a collection of essays.

Studies of the first Stuart king in England include R. Lockyer, *James VI and I* (1998) and W. B. Patterson, *King James VI and I and the Reunion of Christendom* (1997). Assessments of his ill-fated successor appear in C. Carlton, *Charles I: The Personal*

Monarch (rev. 1995) and P. Gregg, *King Charles I* (1984). On the prelate who reinforced the king's persecution of the Puritans, H. R. Trevor-Roper's impressive *Archbishop Laud, 1573–1645* (rev. 1988) has not been superseded but should be read along with C. Carlton, *Archbishop William Laud* (1988).

For Cromwell many maintain that C. Firth, *Oliver Cromwell and the Rule of the Puritans in England* (1900; reissued many times) remains the best biographical account, but more recent studies include A. Fraser, *Cromwell, The Lord Protector* (1973); C. Hill, *God's Englishman* (1972); J. Morrill, *Oliver Cromwell and the English Revolution* (1990), generally unsympathetic; B. Coward, *Oliver Cromwell* (1991); and D. L. Smith, *Oliver Cromwell: Politics and Religion in the English Revolution, 1640–1658* (1991). Cromwell's military leadership is examined in A. Marshall, *Oliver Cromwell: Soldier: The Military Life of a Revolutionary at War* (2004), while an impressive study of Cromwell's army is available in I. Gentles, *The New Model Army in England, Ireland, and Scotland, 1645–1653* (1992). A good introduction to the Cromwellian era and the interregnum is R. Hutton, *The British Republic, 1649–1660* (1990), while a more detailed study is A. Woodrych, *Commonwealth to Protectorate* (1982).

Christopher Hill has done much to influence class and ideological interpretations of seventeenth-century events. His several Marxist-inspired but not dogmatic studies emphasize that the ideas of the age reflected economic class interests and that many contemporary political and social issues first emerged in the radicalism of the period. Among his books are *Puritanism and Revolution* (1958), *The Century of Revolution, 1603–1714* (1961, 1980), *Intellectual Origins of the English Revolution* (rev. 1997), *The World Turned Upside Down: Radical Ideas during the English Revolution* (1972), *Change and Continuity in Seventeenth-Century England* (rev. 1991), and *England's Turning Point: Essays on 17th-Century English History* (1998). Additional examples of inquiries into the radicalism of the age are M. Walzer, *The Revolution of the Saints: A Study in the Origins of Radical Politics* (1965); P. G. Rogers, *The Fifth Monarchy Men* (1966); G. E. Aylmer, *The Levelers in the English Revolution* (1975); and B. Manning, *The English People and the English Revolution, 1640–1649* (1976). An important assessment is J. O. Appleby, *Economic Thought and Ideology in Seventeenth Century England* (1978, reissued 2004), while an intriguing study in social history relating popular culture to the political ferment of the age is D. Underdown, *Revel, Riot, and Rebellion: Popular Politics and Culture in England, 1603–1660* (1985). The same author has also written *Pride's Purge: Politics and the Puritan Revolution* (1971, 1985), *Fire from Heaven: Life in an English Town in the Seventeenth Century* (1992), and *A Freeborn People: Politics and the Nation in Seventeenth-Century England* (1996).

Class and ideological interpretations may also be sampled in R. Cust and A. Hughes (eds.), *Conflict in Early Stuart England: Studies in Religion and Politics, 1603–1642* (1991); J. P. Somerville, *Politics and Ideology in England, 1603–1642* (1986); and T. Cogswell, *The Blessed Revolution: English Politics and the Coming of War, 1621–1624* (1989).

For Ireland good introductions beginning with this age are provided in J. C. Beckett, *The Making of Modern Ireland, 1603–1921* (rev. 1981) and R. F. Foster, *Modern Ireland, 1600–1972* (1988); for the Cromwellian years there are several important studies: P. B. Ellis, *Ireland, 1652–1660* (1975); T. C. Barnard, *Cromwellian Ireland: English Government and Reform in Ireland, 1649–1660* (1975); and J. S. Wheeler, *Cromwell in Ireland* (1999). Many other aspects of Irish history are explored in R. F. Foster (ed.), *The Oxford Illustrated History of Ireland* (1989).

The Restoration: Charles II; James II; The Revolution of 1688

Two of the best accounts of this and the age that followed are J. R. Jones, *Country and Court: England, 1658–1714* (1978) and G. Holmes, *The Making of a Great Power: Late Stuart and Early Georgian Britain, 1660–1722* (1993). For the end of the Protectorate and the restoration of the monarchy, one also turns to P. Seaward, *The Restoration, 1660–1688* (1991) and R. Hutton, *The Restoration: A Political and Religious History of England and Wales, 1658–1667* (1985, 1993). The king's abilities are assessed in A. Fraser, *Royal Charles: Charles II and the Restoration* (1971), perhaps the best of her many biographies; in J. R. Jones, *Charles II: Royal Politician* (1987); and in R. Hutton, *Charles II: King of England, Scotland, and Ireland* (1990). For his successor M. Ashley, *James II* (1977) is fair and factual, as is J. Miller, *James II: A Study of Kingship* (1977, 1989), which stresses the monarch's personal integrity but failure as a king.

For the background to the Revolution of 1688 and subsequent events one may read, among other accounts, D. Ogg, *England in the Reign of James II and William III* (1955, 1984); S. Prall, *The Bloodless Revolution: England, 1688* (1972); J. R. Jones, *The Revolution of 1688 in England* (1972); and J. Childs, *The Army, James II, and the Glorious Revolution* (1980). Brief surveys are available in J. Miller, *The Glorious Revolution* (rev. 1997) and in M. Mullett, *James II and English Politics, 1678–1688* (1994). A special subject is admirably studied in L. G. Schwoerer, *The Declaration of Rights, 1689* (1981). G. M. Trevelyan, *The English Revolution 1688–1989* (1939, 1965), a classic defense of the revolution, argues that the revolution strengthened conservatism for the eighteenth century but that the long-run consequences made it a turning point in history. The Whig historian is himself studied in D. Cannadine, *G. M. Trevelyan: A Life in History* (1993). Another assessment of the revolution, W. A.

Speck, *Reluctant Revolutionaries: Englishmen and the Revolution of 1688* (1988) sees the events as a decisive though not inevitable step toward parliamentary government. A more recent work by E. Cruickshanks, *The Glorious Revolution* (2000) challenges the Whig interpretation and portrays James II as an enlightened advocate of religious toleration. Evolving historical interpretations are discussed in J. I. Israel (ed.), *The Anglo-Dutch Movement: Essays on the Glorious Revolution and Its World Impact* (1991); in L. G. Schwoerer (ed.), *The Revolution of 1688–1689: Changing Perspectives* (1992); and in S. C. A. Pincus (ed.), *England's Glorious Revolution: A Brief History with Documents* (2005); and there are additional insights in H. R. Trevor-Roper's essays, *From Counter Reformation to Glorious Revolution* (1992).

For the role played in international affairs by William of Orange after he took the English throne in 1689, one may read D. W. Jones, *War and Economy in the Age of William III and Marlborough* (1988). Winston Churchill's detailed biography of John Churchill, the military commander who was his ancestor, is available as W. S. Churchill, *Marlborough: His Life and Times* (4 vols., 1933–38; abr. ed., 1968). G. M. Trevelyan, *England under Queen Anne* (3 vols., 1930–34) vividly portrays the succeeding age; and on the sovereign herself, E. Gregg, *Queen Anne* (1980) is excellent. The background to the Act of Union of 1707 joining England and Scotland is explored in B. P. Levack, *The Formation of the British State: England, Scotland, and the Union, 1603–1707* (1987).

For women in seventeenth-century England one may turn to A. Fraser, *The Weaker Vessel: Woman's Lot in Seventeenth Century England* (1985), a series of portraits, mostly of upper-class women. The scholarly essays in M. Prior (ed.), *Women in English Society, 1500–1800* (1985) relate to women of all classes. A pioneering work in social history of continuing value is A. Clark, *Working Life of Women in the Seventeenth Century* (1919, 1993), and R. Thompson, *Women in Stuart England and America* (1974) is a successful comparative study. More recent works, with an emphasis on social history, include S. D. Amussen, *An Ordered Society: Gender and Class in Early Modern England* (1988); A. Hughes, *English Revolution and Gender* (2006); and A. Lawrence, *Women in England, 1500–1760* (1994). L. G. Schwoerer illuminates the independent life of a seventeenth-century woman in *Lady Rachel Russell: "One of the Best of Women"* (1987), while S. Rowbotham ranges across a much wider historical era in *Hidden from History: Rediscovering Women in History, from the 17th Century to the Present* (1974, 1989).

The France of Louis XIV

Many of the general accounts cited at the beginning of this chapter focus on the French predominance in this age. In addition, the following books explore various aspects of Louis XIV and his reign: J. B. Wolf, *Louis XIV* (1968), a comprehensive biography, may be supplemented by T. Dunlap, *Louis XIV* (2000), and by A. Levi, *Louis XIV* (2004). Readers may also turn to A. Lossky, *Louis XIV and the French Monarchy* (1994); and F. Bluche, *Louis XIV* (1990), a detailed narrative. Available also are the essays in P. Sonnino et al. (eds.), *The Reign of Louis XIV* (1991), while P. Burke, *The Fabrication of Louis XIV* (1992) examines the molding of the king's image over his long reign. A broader study of the whole era can be found in W. Doyle (ed.), *Old Regime France, 1648–1789* (2001).

Other interpretive volumes include V. L. Tapié, *The Age of Grandeur* (rev. 1966), and O. Ranum, *Paris in the Age of Absolutism* (rev. 2002). Three studies by P. Goubert—*Louis XIV and Twenty Million Frenchmen* (trans. 1970), his more detailed *The Ancien Regime: French Society, 1600–1750* (trans. and abr. 1974), and *The French Peasantry in the Seventeenth Century* (trans. 1986)—are invaluable studies of French society and the people of the time. C. Tilly, *The Contentious French: Four Centuries of Popular Struggle* (1986), an incisive study of popular restlessness and collective action, begins with these years; and W. Beik, *Urban Protest in Seventeenth-Century France: The Culture of Retribution* (1997) examines popular resistance to authority. A comprehensive study of the mid-century challenge to royal authority is O. Ranum, *The Fronde: A French Revolution, 1648–1652* (1993).

Three books focusing on provincial institutions and other limitations of royal authority, and providing added insights into the methods by which Louis XIV ruled, are W. Beik, *Absolutism and Society in Seventeenth-Century France: State Power and Provincial Aristocracy in Languedoc* (1985); R. Mettam, *Power and Faction in Louis XIV's France* (1988); and S. Kettering, *Patrons, Brokers, and Clients in Seventeenth-Century France* (1986). J. M. Smith, *The Culture of Merit: Nobility, Royal Service, and the Making of Absolute Monarchy in France, 1600–1789* (1996) describes the king's response to noble aspirations for recognition and glory. Two older books that examine constraints on royal authority are A. L. Moote, *The Revolt of the Judges: The Parlement of Paris and the Fronde, 1643–1652* (1971) and L. Rothkrug, *Opposition to Louis XIV: The Political and Social Origins of the Enlightenment* (1965).

A biography of the French finance minister is available in A. Trout, *Jean-Baptiste Colbert* (1978). Financial matters are examined on a broad scale in J. Dent, *Crisis in France: Crown, Financiers, and Society in Seventeenth-Century France* (1973) and in R. Bonney, *The King's Debts: Finance and Politics in France, 1589–1661* (1981). The global expansion of French trade is discussed in C. J. Ames, *Colbert, Mercantilism, and the French Quest for Asian Trade* (1996).

Religious matters are explored in E. I. Perry, *From Theology to History: French Religious Controversy and the Revocation of the Edict of Nantes* (1973); A. Sedgwick, *Jansenism in Seventeenth-Century France* (1977); W. Doyle, *Jansenism: Catholic Resistance to Authority from the Reformation to the French Revolution* (2000); and in a special way in W. Scoville, *The Persecution of the Huguenots and French Economic Development, 1680–1720* (1960). On the colonial empire one may read W. J. Eccles, *The French in North America, 1500–1783* (rev. 1998); and various religious aspects of French expansion in the new world are examined in A. Greer, *Mohawk Saint: Catherine Tekakwitha and the Jesuits* (2005) and in N. Z. Davis, *Women on the Margins: Three Seventeenth-Century Lives* (1995).

C. C. Lougee, *Le Paradis des Femmes: Women, Salons, and Social Stratification in Seventeenth Century France* (1976) examines the evolving cultural influence of French women, a theme also explored in E. C. Goldsmith (ed.), *Going Public: Women and Publishing in Early Modern France* (1995); a more general work is W. Gibson, *Women in Seventeenth-Century France* (1989); and an outstanding woman of letters is studied in J. A. Ojala and W. T. Ojala, *Madame de Sévigné: A Seventeenth-Century Life* (1990). An important cultural theme is treated in J. DeJean, *Ancients Against Moderns: Culture Wars and the Making of a Fin de Siècle* (1997).

On Louis XIV's military policies one may read an excellent survey, J. A. Lynn, *The Wars of Louis XIV, 1667–1714* (1999). Other works on the subject include P. Sonnino, *Louis XIV and the Origins of the Dutch War* (1988) and H. Kamen, *The War of Succession in Spain, 1700–1715* (1969). Two books about the final stages of Habsburg rule in Spain are H. Kamen, *Spain in the Later Seventeenth Century, 1665–1700* (1980), in which he sees revival rather than decline on the eve of the French attack, and R. A. Stradling, *Europe and the Decline of Spain, 1580–1720* (1981). For Spain in the century after the Habsburgs, an outstanding account is J. Lynch, *Bourbon Spain, 1700–1808* (1989).

Useful Web Sites

For an introduction to the Dutch republic, one may visit *The Williamite Universe,* http://let.uu.nl/ogc/William/, a site that provides information on William III and other aspects of Dutch history. Readers will find useful information on Cromwell and the wider history of the English Civil wars by visiting *The Oliver Cromwell Website,* http://olivercromwell.org/index/htm; and *BBC-History* provides additional resources for research on all majors events of the seventeenth century through the links at www.bbc.co.uk/history/. *The Official Web Site of the British Monarchy* provides information about the history of every British king, including those who faced opposition in the seventeeth century at http://royal.gov.uk/output/page5

.asp. Valuable materials on France and wider European developments can be located through *The Society for Seventeenth Century French Studies* in Britain, at http://solinuxbrookes/ac.uk/mark/17/webres.html.

Interesting images and information about Louis XIV's great palace are available in English; see the *Chateau de Versailles,* www.chateauversailles.fr/en/index.php; and there are very helpful links to Web sites on the history of early modern European women at *Early Modern Resources,* www.earlymodernweb.org.uk/emr/index.php/category/themes/gender/.

5. THE TRANSFORMATION OF EASTERN EUROPE, 1648–1740

J. H. Shennan, *Liberty and Order in Early Modern Europe: The Subject and the State, 1650–1800* (1986), focusing on France and Russia, highlights differences in the development of western and eastern Europe. Informative books that explain the complexities of central and eastern Europe, carrying their accounts toward the present, are L. C. Tihany, *A History of Middle Europe: From the Earliest Times to the Age of the World Wars* (1976); P. Wandycz, *The Price of Freedom: A History of East Central Europe from the Middle Ages to the Present* (rev. 2001); P. D. Longworth, *The Making of Eastern Europe: From Prehistory to Postcommunism* (rev. 1997); R. Bideleux and Ian Jeffries, *A History of Eastern Europe: Crisis and Change* (1998); and E. Niederhauser, *A History of Eastern Europe Since the Middle Ages* (trans. 2003). P. R. Magocsi, *Historical Atlas of East Central Europe* (1993), Vol. I of the series *A History of Central Europe,* is an impressive work of reference. J. W. Sedlar, *East Central Europe in the Middle Ages, 1000–1500* (1994) synthesizes the medieval period, while A. Maczak et al., *East Central Europe in Transition* (1985) focuses on the fourteenth to the seventeenth centuries. For the Balkans, valuable studies are L. S. Stavrianos, *The Balkans since 1453* (1958, 2000); B. Jelavich and C. Jelavich, *The Balkans* (1965); R. Ristelheuber, *A History of the Balkan Peoples* (trans. 1971); and P. F. Sugar, *Southeastern Europe under Ottoman Rule, 1354–1804* (1977), in the series on Central Europe cited above.

The Ottoman Empire

Readers will find informative accounts of the Ottoman empire in a number of recent works, including J. McCarthy, *The Ottoman Turks: An Introductory History to 1923* (1997); C. Imber, *The Ottoman Empire, 1300–1650: The Structure of Power* (2002); and S. Turnbull, *The Ottoman Empire, 1326-1699* (2003), which is a concise survey. Important coverage of Ottoman history is also found in J. Goodwin, *Lords of the Horizon: A History of the Ottoman Empire* (1999); and in D. Quataert, *The Ottoman Empire, 1700–1922* (2000). The social foundations of Ottoman power are described in H. Inalcik and D. Quataert (eds.), *An Eco-*

nomic and Social History of the Ottoman Empire, 1300–1914 (1994), while L. P. Peirce, *The Imperial Harem: Women and Sovereignty in the Ottoman Empire* (1993) describes the political role and influence of women. Ottoman relations and interactions with Europe, which are currently attracting historical attention, are explored in K. M. Setton, *Venice, Austria, and the Turks in the Seventeenth Century* (1991); R. Schwoebel, *The Shadow of the Crescent: The Renaissance Image of the Turk, 1453–1517* (1967); N. Bisaha, *Creating East and West: Renaissance Humanists and the Ottoman Turks* (2004); and D. Goffman, *The Ottoman Empire and Early Modern Europe* (2002). C. E. Bosworth, *The New Islamic Dynasties: A Chronological and Genealogical Manual* (1996) is a useful reference tool.

Austria and the Habsburgs: To 1740

Basic for these years are R. A. Kann, *A History of the Habsburg Empire, 1526–1918* (1974); R. J. Evans, *The Making of the Habsburg Empire, 1550–1770* (1979); C. Ingrao, *The Habsburg Monarchy, 1618–1815* (rev. 2000); J. Bérenger, *The History of the Habsburg Empire, 1273–1700* (trans. 1994); and P. S. Fichtner, *The Habsburg Monarchy, 1490–1848: Attributes of Empire* (2003). A number of important essays on social and political history have been collected in C. Ingrao (ed.), *State and Society in Early Modern Austria* (1994). J. P. Spielman has written *Leopold I of Austria* (1977), a balanced treatment of the seventeenth-century emperor; and for Eugene of Savoy, an outstanding biography is D. McKay, *Prince Eugene of Savoy* (1977). A vivid account of the Turkish siege of 1683 is available in J. Stoye, *The Siege of Vienna* (rev. 2000).

The Holy Roman Empire:
The German States

A good introductory survey of German history is M. Fulbrook, *A Concise History of Germany* (rev. 2004). H. Holborn, in his *History of Modern Germany, Vol. II: 1648–1840* (1975), covers the fluid situation in the Holy Roman Empire after the Thirty Years' War, as does J. Gagliardo, *Germany under the Old Regime, 1600–1790* (1991). A useful, brief survey is P. H. Wilson, *The Holy Roman Empire, 1495–1806* (1999), which summarizes recent historical challenges to older assumptions about the Empire's flaws and failures. One will also wish to read E. Sagorra, *A Social History of Germany, 1648–1914* (1977), with many fascinating insights, and R. Vierhaus, *Germany in the Age of Absolutism* (1988), which studies the years 1618–1763. G. Benecke, *Society and Politics in Germany, 1500–1750* (1974) presents the case for the Empire as a viable constitutional entity, while two important contributions to understanding the formation of the German political tradition are F. L. Carsten, *Princes and Parliaments in Germany* (1959) and M. Walker, *German Home Towns: Community, State,*

and General Estate, 1648–1871 (1971). J. A. Vann thoroughly explores the evolving social structure and institutions of a key principality in *The Making of a State: Württemberg, 1593–1793* (1984).

For Prussia, convenient introductions are F. L. Carsten, *The Origins of Prussia* (1954) and H. W. Koch, *A History of Prussia* (1978). A thoughtful evocation of the state (dissolved after the Second World War) is T. von Thadden, *Prussia: The History of a Lost State* (1986). An invaluable study going well beyond the scope of this chapter is G. A. Craig, *The Politics of the Prussian Army, 1640–1945* (1956, 1964). Important also is H. Rosenberg, *Bureaucracy, Aristocracy, and Autocracy: The Prussian Experience, 1660–1815* (1958), which may be supplemented by the essays in P. G. Dwyer, *The Rise of Prussia, 1700–1830* (2002). On the early Hohenzollerns, one may read F. Schevill, *The Great Elector* (1974) and R. Ergang, *The Potsdam Führer: Frederick William I, Father of Prussian Militarism* (1941, 1972). Books on Frederick the Great are cited in Chapter 8.

Russia: To 1725

There are many excellent narrative accounts of Russian history with good coverage of the early years; for example, one may read N. V. Riasanovsky and M. D. Steinberg, *A History of Russia* (rev. 2004); R. Bartlett, *A History of Russia* (2005); and P. Dukes, *A History of Russia, c. 882–1996* (1998). For the early years and the expansion and transformation of Muscovy, one may turn to R. O. Crummey, *The Formation of Muscovy, 1304–1613* (1987), while P. Dukes, *The Making of Russian Absolutism, 1613–1801* (rev. 1990) traces the tsardom from the beginning of the Romanov dynasty over the next two centuries. The military side to Russian society and the "service state" are ably examined in J. L. H. Keep, *Soldiers of the Tsar: Army and Society in Russia, 1462–1874* (1985) and the rural scene is studied in J. Blum, *Lord and Peasant in Russia from the Ninth to the Nineteenth Century* (1961). P. Avrich examines social upheavals in *Russian Rebels, 1600–1800* (1972), while R. Mousnier treats agrarian unrest comparatively in *Peasant Uprisings in Seventeenth-Century France, Russia, and China* (trans. 1970).

The early rulers are studied in A. Pavlov and M. Perrie, *Ivan the Terrible* (2003); and in I. de Madariaga, *Ivan the Terrible: First Tsar of Russia* (2005), an outstanding study of the brutal ruler. W. B. Lincoln, *Autocrats of All the Russias* (1981) is a remarkable large-scale study of the Romanovs, the 15 tsars and 4 tsarinas who ruled Russia between 1613 and 1917. A more recent study of the changes in the early modern period can be found in S. Dixon, *The Modernisation of Russia, 1676–1825* (1999); and Russia's early imperial expansion is examined in the important work by J. P. LeDonne, *The Grand Strategy of the Russian Empire, 1650–1831* (2004). An absorbing impressionistic cultural history is J. H. Billington, *The*

Icon and the Axe: An Interpretive History of Russian Culture (1966), while a provocative reassessment of Russia's relationship to European intellectual and cultural history is M. Malia, *Russia under Western Eyes: From the Bronze Horseman to the Lenin Mausoleum* (1999).

On Peter and the reforms of his reign, an older outstanding biography, M. Klyuchevsky, *Peter the Great* (trans. 1958), may be compared with the briefer, more recent accounts by S. J. Lee, *Peter the Great* (1993); M. S. Anderson, *Peter the Great* (rev. 1995); and L Hughes, *Peter the Great, A Biography* (2002). Peter's interest in western Europe is discussed in L. Hughes (ed.), *Peter the Great and the West: New Perspectives* (2001). An excellent account of Russian society, culture, and government in this era appears in the comprehensive, insightful study by L. Hughes, *Russia in the Age of Peter the Great* (1998), in which she neglects no aspect of Peter's rule. R. K. Massie, *Peter the Great: His Life and World* (1980) is a long, vivid, and colorful popular account, less critical of Peter than other studies. N. V. Riasanovsky, *The Image of Peter the Great in Russian History and Thought* (1985) examines the ruler's long-range cultural impact, while one aspect of his cultural revolution is examined in J. Cracraft, *The Petrine Revolution in Russian Architecture* (1988). An admirable study in comparative cultural history is D. W. Treadgold, *The West in Russia and China: Religious and Secular Thought in Modern Times* (2 vols., 1973), the first volume of which covers Russia for the years 1472–1917. For Sweden, and for Peter's great Swedish rival, an outstanding biography is R. N. Hatton, *Charles XII of Sweden* (1969). A number of important studies by M. Roberts and others have been cited in Chapter 3; for these years M. Roberts, *The Swedish Imperial Experience, 1560–1718* (1979) deserves mention. The Baltic shore is explored in S. P. Oakley, *War and Peace in the Baltic, 1560–1790* (1992).

Useful Web Sites

Resources on Ottoman history can be found at *World Civilizations*, www.wsu.edu:8080/~dee/OTTOMAN/OTTOMAN1.HTM, which is part of an excellent Web site at Washington State University, and at *Internet Islamic History Sourcebook*, www.fordham.edu/halsall/islam/islamsbook.html, where readers may locate links to Ottoman materials from the outstanding internet resources at Fordham University. On the Habsburgs and the Austrian empire, readers will find useful resources at *The Imperial House of Hapsburg*, www.hapsburg.com/home.htm, and at the helpful links from this site. There is concise, well-organized information on early modern Prussia, Poland, Russia, and other European states at the wide-ranging British Web site, *History World*, www.historyworld.net/, where readers will find valuable timelines as well as other interactive materials. On Russian imperial history in the age of Peter the Great, one may consult the materials pertaining to the *History and Culture of Russia* at www.geographica.com/russia.rushis.01.htm; and readers will find excellent links to a wide range of resources on the early history of Russia at Bucknell University's *Russian Studies Program*, www.bucknell.edu/Russian.

6. THE SCIENTIFIC VIEW OF THE WORLD

Histories of Science

An outstanding, broad-ranging study is B. L. Silver, *The Ascent of Science* (1998). A valuable new series on the history of modern science is available in D. C. Lindberg and R. Numbers (eds.), *The Cambridge History of Science* (2003–06), a collaborative project that will eventually include eight volumes. An older, but still useful collaborative survey is L. P. Williams and H. J. Steffens (eds.), *The History of Science in Western Civilization* (3 vols., 1977–78), from antiquity to the twentieth century. Other excellent historical accounts include R. Olson, *Science Deified and Science Defied: The Historical Significance of Science in Western Culture* (2 vols., 1982–91), a far-reaching study ranging from prehistory to 1820. Ancient and medieval science is also explored in D. C. Lindberg, *The Beginnings of Western Science* (1992), cited in Chapter 2. Other important perspectives on the long history of science appear in M. Serres (ed.), *A History of Scientific Thought: Elements of a History of Thought* (trans. 1995) and in the comprehensive analysis of the historical study of science by H. F. Cohen, *The Scientific Revolution: A Historiographical Inquiry* (1994). For individual scientists one may consult the *Dictionary of Scientific Biography* (8 vols., 1970–80) and for new works in the history of science, the annual bibliographies published in *Isis*.

The Scientific Revolution

For the fundamental reorientation of thinking about nature and the universe in early modern times, three older but still valuable introductions are H. Butterfield, *The Origins of Modern Science* (rev. 1965); A. Koyré, *From the Closed World to the Infinite Universe* (1968); and A. R. Hall, *The Revolution in Science, 1500–1750: The Formation of the Modern Scientific Attitude* (rev. 1983). These works may now be supplemented by K. Park and L. Daston, *Early Modern Science* (2006), which is the third volume in *The Cambridge History of Science*. Other informative accounts include A. G. Debus, *Man and Nature in the Renaissance* (1978) and R. S. Westfall, *The Construction of Modern Science* (1971). Of special interest are I. B. Cohen's *The Newtonian Revolution* (1980) and *Revolution in Science* (1985), an encyclopedic study of the transformation of scientific ideas. Useful shorter surveys of this era may be found in J. R. Jacob, *The Scientific Revolution: Aspirations and Achievements, 1500–1700* (1998);

J. Henry, *The Scientific Revolution and the Origins of Modern Science* (rev. 2002); and S. Shapin, *The Scientific Revolution* (1996), which examines the cultural dimensions of scientific knowledge. On the nature of revolutionary breakthroughs in science a highly influential work has been T. S. Kuhn, *The Structure of Scientific Revolution* (1962, rev. 1970, reissued 1989), which challenges the belief in progressive, cumulative scientific advance and emphasizes the role of shifting cultural assumptions in the development of scientific knowledge. Kuhn has also written *The Copernican Revolution* (1957, 1985). Some historians of science have questioned traditional views of the scientific revolution, arguing that the changes in thought proceeded slowly and that most early modern scientists retained decidedly unmodern views of human knowledge. For discussion of these issues, readers may turn to M. J. Osler (ed.), *Rethinking the Scientific Revolution* (2000). P. B. Medawar, *Pluto's Republic* (1982), humorously entitled but a serious book, explores the persistence of pseudo- and quasi-scientific thinking from Bacon to the present.

For all aspects of technology and the practical application of science, one may consult C. Singer et al., *A History of Technology* (8 vols., 1954–84). Three related books are A. Pacey, *The Maze of Ingenuity* (1976); S. Shapin and S. Schaffer, *Leviathan and the Air Pump* (1985); and L. Jardine, *Ingenious Pursuits: Building the Scientific Revolution* (2000). Technology as a social force is explored in the classic study of L. Mumford, *Technics and Civilization* (1934, reissued 1963) and in O. Mayr, *Authority, Liberty, and Automatic Machinery in Early Modern Europe* (1986). A brief, informative survey appears in E. D. Brose, *Technology and Science in the Industrializing Nations, 1500–1914* (1998).

A number of provocative studies relate the scientific revolution to the political and social ferment and economic developments in seventeenth-century England and stress the practical implications for a commercial society. Here two pioneer studies were R. K. Merton, *Science, Technology, and Society in Seventeenth Century England* (1970) and C. Webster, *The Great Instauration: Science, Medicine, and Reform, 1626–1660* (1975). An admirable synthesis is M. C. Jacob, *The Cultural Meaning of the Scientific Revolution* (1988), a work that has been revised and expanded in *Scientific Culture and the Making of the Industrial West* (1997). The applications of Newtonian science are examined in M. C. Jacob and L. C. Stewart, *Practical Matter: Newton's Science in the Service of Industry and Empire, 1687–1851* (2004). Connections between early scientific writing and early modern literature are analyzed in E. Spiller, *Science, Reading, and Renaissance Literature: The Art of Making Knowledge, 1580–1670* (2004).

Biographically Oriented Accounts

The contributions of the pioneer astronomers are described in many of the books already cited and in

A. Armitage, *The World of Copernicus* (1972); J. M. Caspar, *Kepler* (reissued 1993); and K. Ferguson, *Tycho and Kepler: The Unlikely Partnership that Forever Changed Our Understanding of the Heavens* (2002), an accessible double biography of two major scientists and their times . For Galileo one may read A. Koyré, *Galileo Studies* (1978); while a study of his scientific activities is available in S. Drake, *Galileo at Work: His Scientific Biography* (1978), in which the author has reconstructed the scientist's instruments and examined his notebooks; the same author has written a concise biographical study, *Galileo* (2001). The condemnation that Galileo aroused from the Church and other authorities is described in J. J. Langford, *Galileo, Science, and the Church* (rev. 1992), while P. Redondi, *Galileo: Heretic* (trans. 1987) is a provocative, not entirely convincing, revisionist account. Galileo's links to the culture of patronage are examined in M. Biagioli, *Galileo, Courtier* (1993); and helpful accounts of the wider culture in which he worked can be found in J. Renn (ed.), *Galileo in Context* (2001). For Newton, R. S. Westfall, *Never at Rest: A Biography of Isaac Newton* (1982, 1993) is a biography of distinction; D. Berlinski, *Newton's Gift: How Sir Isaac Newton Unlocked the System of the World* (2000) is illuminating on the man and his accomplishments; and there are also notable biographies by G. E. Christianson (1984), A. R. Hall (1992), and J. Gleick (2003). Newton's fascination with other forms of thought is described in the influential revisionist work of B. J. T. Dobbs, *The Janus Face of Genius: The Role of Alchemy in Newton's Thought* (1991).

Science and Thought

Three informative studies of a key figure in the new science are P. Zagorin, *Francis Bacon* (1998), which is especially strong on Bacon's intellectual contributions; L. Jardine and A. Stewart, *Hostage to Fortune: The Troubled Life of Francis Bacon* (1998), which describes in detail all aspects of his complex career; and C. Whitney, *Francis Bacon and Modernity* (1986). B. H. G. Wormald, *Francis Bacon: History, Politics, and Science, 1561–1626* (1993) remains a major appraisal. Descartes and his influence are described in T. Sorell, *Descartes* (1987), and in P. A. Schouls, *Descartes and the Enlightenment* (1989). Readers may turn to H. M. Bracken, *Descartes* (2002) for a concise account of his life and ideas. The complexities of Cartesian thought are examined from new perspectives in S. Bordo (ed.), *Feminist Interpretations of René Descartes* (1999).

The role played by women in the scientific revolution is skillfully explored in L. Schiebinger, *The Mind Has No Sex? Women in the Origins of Modern Science* (1989), the title derived from Descartes. It may be read along with the same author's *Nature's Body: Gender in the Making of Modern Science* (1993, reissued 2004), focusing on eighteenth-century studies of plants and animals. An important book by

E. Harth, *Cartesian Women: Versions and Subversions of Rational Discourse in the Old Regime* (1992), compares the role of women intellectuals in the seventeenth and eighteenth centuries.

For Pascal one may read A. Krailsheimer, *Pascal* (1980); H. M. Davidson, *Blaise Pascal* (1983); and J. R. Cole, *Pascal: The Man and His Two Loves* (1995), which offers debatable psychological interpretations of the writer's life and work. There is a perceptive, brief study of Pierre Bayle by E. Labrousse, *Bayle* (trans. 1983). Skepticism is further explored in F. L. Baumer, *Religion and the Rise of Skepticism* (1960) and in R. H. Popkin, *The History of Skepticism from Savonarola to Spinoza* (rev. 2003); Montaigne, its sixteenth-century exemplar, is studied in excellent biographies by D. M. Frame (1965) and H. Friedrich (trans. 1991), which may be compared with G. Hoffmann, *Montaigne's Career* (1998). A judicious, balanced biography of the seventeeth-century Dutch philosopher is S. Nadler, *Spinoza: A Life* (1999). The cultural influence of Spinoza and other skeptical thinkers is analyzed in the wide-ranging work of J. I. Israel, *The Radical Enlightenment: Philosophy and the Making of Modernity 1650–1750* (2002). A provocative book exploring the relationship of rationalism to Western thought from the seventeenth century on is E. Gellner, *Reason and Rationalism* (1990).

For the political thought of the period an overview is provided in F. L. Baumer, *Modern European Thought: Continuity and Change in Ideas, 1600–1950* (1977). On Locke one may read J. Dunn, *The Political Thought of John Locke* (1969), and the same author's *Locke: A Very Short Introduction* (rev. 2003); R. Ashcraft, *Locke's Two Treatises of Government* (1986); and E. J. Lowe, *Locke* (2005). There are also useful accounts of Locke's life and work in W. M. Spellman, *John Locke* (1997) and in K. L. Cope, *John Locke Revisited* (1999). Hobbes is studied in two notable books by A. Martinich, *Hobbes, A Biography* (1999), and *Hobbes* (2005); in A. A. Rogow, *Thomas Hobbes: Radical in the Service of Reaction* (1986); and in R. Tuck, *Hobbes* (1989), a brief appraisal. Useful for French thinkers in these years is N. O. Koehane, *Philosophy and the State in France: The Renaissance to the Enlightenment* (1980). Two important studies of modern conceptions of individual identity also discuss the intellectual history of this era: C. Taylor, *Sources of the Self: The Making of the Modern Identity* (1989) and J. Seigel, *The Idea of the Self: Thought and Experience in Western Europe Since the Seventeenth Century* (2005).

Useful Web Sites

Resources on European science in the sixteenth and seventeenth centuries can be found at Rice University's *Galileo Project* at http://galileo.rice.edu/index.html, an excellent site that focuses on Galileo but includes many other valuable materials and links. Addi-

tional information on early astronomy and other sciences is available at *History of Astronomy*, www.astro.uni-bonn.de/%Epbrosche/astoria.html. There are useful materials and helpful links on seventeenth–century science at the Web site of the *Newton Project,* at Imperial College, London, http://newtonproject.ic.ac.uk/. The history of early modern philosophy, including bibliographic materials and links to sites on Bacon, Descartes, Spinoza, Bayle and others, can be explored through the excellent *Stanford Encyclopedia of Philosophy* at http://plato.stanford.edu/.

7. THE STRUGGLE FOR WEALTH AND EMPIRE

For the years covered in this chapter, helpful syntheses include T. C. W. Blanning (ed.), *The Eighteenth Century* (2000) and Blanning's more recent book, *The Culture of Power and the Power of Culture: Old Regime Europe, 1660–1789* (2002); I. Woloch, *Eighteenth Century Europe: Tradition and Progress, 1715–1798* (1982); M. S. Anderson, *Europe in the Eighteenth Century, 1713–1783* (rev. 2000); J. Black, *Eighteenth-Century Europe* (rev. 1999); and W. Doyle, *The Old European Order, 1660–1800* (rev. 1992). Europe's colonial empires and the new global trading system are examined in J. Black, *Europe and the World, 1650–1830* (2002). A useful reference work is J. Black and R. Porter (eds.), *A Dictionary of Eighteenth-Century World History* (1993).

Popular Culture and Everyday Life

The differences between elite and popular culture emerge from three books mentioned earlier: P. Burke, *Popular Culture in Early Modern Europe* (rev. 1994); K. Thomas, *Religion and the Decline of Magic* (1971); and F. Braudel, *The Structures of Everyday Life* (trans. 1981, 1991), the first volume of his three-volume study. They may be supplemented by the essays in A. Mitchell and I. Deák (eds.), *Everyman in Europe: Essays in Social History* (2 vols., rev. 1997). There are also studies of English social mores in K. Olsen, *Daily Life in 18th-Century England* (1999) and in P. Langford, *Englishness Identified: Manners and Character, 1650–1850* (2000). The role of language in shaping social identities is examined in an insightful work by P. Burke, *Languages and Communities in Early Modern Europe* (2004).

The Global Economy and the Colonial Empires

The final two volumes of Braudel's work, *The Wheels of Commerce* (trans. 1983) and *The Perspectives of the World* (both reissued in 1991), offer remarkable accounts of the global economy. A far-ranging study relevant for the years after 1650 is S. W. Mintz, *Sweetness and Power: The Place of Sugar in Modern History* (1985). The celebrated speculative ventures of the age are graphically described in J. Carswell, *The South Sea Bubble* (1960); in the relevant chapters of C. P. Kindleberger, *Manias, Panics, and Crashes: A History of Financial Crises* (1978); in J. K. Galbraith, *A Short History of Financial Euphoria: A Hymn of Caution* (1993); and in R. Dale, *The First Crash: Lessons from the South Sea Bubble* (2004).

Several books on European overseas expansion listed for Chapters 3 and 4 also discuss the eighteenth century. To these must be added H. Furber's excellent synthesis, *Rival Empires of Trade in the Orient, 1600–1800* (1976); J. H. Parry, *Trade and Dominion: The European Overseas Empires in the Eighteenth Century* (1971); two works by G. Williams, *The Expansion of Europe in the Eighteenth Century: Overseas Rivalry, Discovery, and Exploitation* (1966) and *The Great South Sea: English Voyages and Encounters, 1570–1750* (1997); P. K. Liss, *Atlantic Empires: The Network of Trade and Revolution, 1713–1826* (1983); P. D. Curtin, *Cross-Cultural Trade in World History* (1984), cited earlier; and A. K. Smith, *Creating a World Economy: Merchant Capital, Colonialism, and World Trade, 1400–1825* (1991). One may also read the relevant chapters of D. K. Fieldhouse, *The Colonial Empires: A Comparative Survey from the Eighteenth Century* (rev. 1982). A valuable, collaborative work under the general editorship of W. R. Louis, *The Oxford History of the British Empire* (5 vols., 1998–1999), offers up-to-date research by specialists and includes two volumes on the early era of global expansion: N. Canny (ed.), *British Overseas Enterprise to the Close of the Seventeenth Century* and P. J. Marshall (ed.), *The Eighteenth Century*.

The impact of Asia on Europe in the early modern centuries from the sixteenth century on is studied in great detail in D. F. Lach, *Asia in the Making of Europe* (3 vols., 1965–93), of which E. J. Van Kley is coauthor of volume 3. A useful collaborative work is A. T. Embree and C. Gluck (eds.), *Asia in Western and World History: A Guide for Teaching* (1997).

P. Lawson, *The East India Company: A History* (1993) describes its activities from its beginnings in 1603 to its demise in 1857; a wide-ranging collection of early and recent historical writings on the same subject has been brought together in P. Tuck, *The East India Company, 1600–1858* (6 vols., 1998). The eighteenth-century impact on India is further explored in P. Woodruff [Mason], *The Men Who Ruled India* (2 vols., 1954–57) and in P. J. Marshall, *The Making and Unmaking of Empires: Britian, India, and America, c. 1750–1783* (2005), which examines how Britain expanded its imperial role in India while it was losing imperial control of its American colonies. A recent study of the controversial British governor general is available in J. Bernstein, *Dawning of the Raj: The Life and Trials of Warren Hastings* (2000). For India itself the best introductions appear in P. Spear, *The Oxford History of Modern India, 1740–1975* (rev.

1978); S. Wolpert, *A New History of India* (rev. 2000); J. Keay, *India: A History* (2000); and H. Kulke and D. Rothermund, *A History of India* (rev. 2004), and P. Robb, *A History of India* (2002). J. E. Schwartzberg (ed.), *A Historical Atlas of South Asia* (rev. 1992) is a superb atlas.

For the French in North America one may read W. J. Eccles, *The French in North America, 1500–1783* (rev. 1998), cited earlier, and *The Canadian Frontier, 1534–1760* (1974); P. Boucher, *Les Nouvelles Frances: France in America, 1500–1815* (1989), a brief illustrated account; and D. H. Usner, Jr., *Indians, Settlers, & Slaves in a Frontier Exchange Economy: The Lower Mississippi Valley Before 1783* (1992). The importance of the West Indies for the Atlantic economy emerges from N. F. Crouse, *The French Struggle for the West Indies, 1665–1713* (1944); R. S. Dunn, *Sugar and Slaves* (1972); and S. W. Mintz's *Sweetness and Power* (1985), cited above.

British Politics and Society in the Eighteenth Century

Books on eighteenth-century France are listed below in Chapter 8, but two works should be mentioned here: C. Pevitt, *The Man Who Would be King: The Life of Philippe, Duc d'Orléans: Regent of France* (1998); and R. Butler, *Choiseul* (1980).

There is a growing literature on eighteenth-century British politics and society after the settlement of 1688–1689. L. B. Namier, who wrote with precision and depth but insisted on narrow political and parliamentary history, long had an enormous influence. His most important books were *The Structure of Politics at the Accession of George III* (2 vols., 1920; 1957) and *England in the Age of the American Revolution* (rev. 1961). He also launched a large-scale collaborative project in prosopography, or collective biography, seeking to reconstruct in minute detail the composition of the modern British parliaments. His approach, adopted by other historians, downplayed the importance of ideology in the seventeenth-century revolutions, as discussed in Chapter 4, and even the triumph of Parliament over crown in 1688. His continuing influence is demonstrated in J. P. Kenyon, *Revolution Principles: The Politics of Party, 1689–1720* (1977, 1990) as well as in J. C. D. Clark's two books: *English Society, 1688–1832* (1985) and *Revolution and Rebellion* (1986).

J. Brewer has widened the political arena in two innovative works, *Party Ideology and Popular Politics at the Accession of George III* (1976) and *The Sinews of Power: War, Money, and the English State, 1688–1783* (1989). At the same time E. P. Thompson's interest in social history has influenced eighteenth-century studies. Thompson's own work on this era includes *Whigs and Hunters: The Origin of the Black Act* (1976). For other books affording broad insights into eighteenth-century British politics and society one may turn to G. S. Holmes, *British Politics in the Age of Anne* (1967, 1987) and *The Age of Oligarchy: Pre-Industrial Britain, 1722–1783* (1993); N. Rogers, *Whigs and Cities: Popular Politics in the Age of Walpole and Pitt* (1989); W. A. Speck, *The Birth of Britain: A New Nation, 1700–1710* (1994) and *Stability and Strife: England, 1714–1760* (1977); and J. Black, *Eighteenth-Century Britain, 1688–1783* (2001).

For the economy and society one may read three informative accounts: N. McKendrick, J. Brewer, and J. H. Plumb, *The Birth of a Consumer Society: The Commercialization of Eighteenth-Century England* (1982); P. Langford, *A Polite and Commercial People: England, 1727–1783* (1989); and R. Porter, *English Society in the Eighteenth Century* (rev. 1990). One may also read P. Mathias, *The First Industrial Nation: An Economic History of Britain, 1700–1914* (rev. 1983); C. P. Hill, *British Economic and Social History, 1700–1982* (rev. 1985); and P. Langford and C. Harvie, *The Eighteenth Century and the Age of Industry* (1992), in the *Oxford History of Britain*. F. M. L. Thompson, *The Cambridge Social History of Britain, 1750–1950* (rev. 1993) begins with these years. For an excellent, wide-ranging study of the era's cultural history, one may turn to J. Brewer, *The Pleasures of the Imagination: English Culture in the Eighteenth Century* (1997).

Biographical accounts include R. N. Hatton, *George I, Elector and King* (1979); J. H. Plumb, *Sir Robert Walpole* (2 vols., 1951–56), a biography of distinction, and *The First Four Georges* (1956); H. T. Dickinson, *Walpole and the Whig Supremacy* (1973); and J. Black, *Robert Walpole and the Nature of Politics in Early Eighteenth-Century England* (1990). There are biographies of the elder Pitt by S. Ayling (1976), P. D. Brown (1978), and J. Black (rev. 1999). The Jacobite uprisings are discussed in books by B. Lenman (1995), P. K. Monod (1983), J. L. Roberts (2002), C. Duffy (2003), and F. McLynn (1981). McLynn has also written a biography of the Young Pretender, *Bonnie Prince Charlie: Charles Edward Stuart* (1991) as well as *Crime and Punishment in Eighteenth-Century England* (1989), which traces the prevailing insecurity to the Jacobite threat. The latter may be supplemented by P. Linebaugh, *The London Hanged: Crime and Punishment in the Eighteenth Century* (1992), an impressive study.

Especially insightful on the formation of the British national identity in these years is L. Colley, *Britons: Forging the Nation, 1707–1837* (1992), which may be supplemented by H. F. Kearney, *The British Isles: A History of Four Nations* (1989). W. A. Speck's informative survey, *A Concise History of Britain, 1707–1975* (1993) begins with these years.

The Great War of the Mid-Eighteenth Century, 1740–1763

R. Browning, *The War of the Austrian Succession* (1993) is an outstanding wide-ranging study of the first phase of the mid-eighteenth century conflict; and there is an excellent comprehensive account of the second important war in F. Anderson, *Crucible of War: The Seven Years' War and the Fate of Empire in British North America, 1754–1766* (2000); a briefer account is available from the same author in *The War that Made America: A Short History of the French and Indian War* (2005); and in D. Marston, *The Seven Years' War* (2001). The latter subject is studied also in J. Keegan in *Fields of Battle: The Wars for North America* (1996).

J. Brewer, *The Sinews of Power: War, Money, and the English State, 1688–1783* (1989), noted earlier, persuasively demonstrates that it was the fiscal strength and war-making capacities of the British parliamentary government after 1688 that made possible Britain's ascent as a global power. For the crisis created by the mid-century wars, in addition to the biographical accounts of Pitt already cited, one may read M. Peters, *Pitt and Popularity: The Patriot Minister and London Opinion during the Seven Years' War* (1980) and R. Middleton, *The Pitt-Newcastle Ministry and the Conduct of the Seven Years' War, 1757–1762* (1985).

C. Duffy, *The Army of Maria Theresa: The Armed Forces of Imperial Austria, 1740–1780* (1977) ably explores the nature of the Habsburg army, and the same author examines Frederick's skill in statecraft and military prowess in *Frederick the Great: A Military Life* (1985). Other aspects of Frederick's military and foreign policies are discussed with perceptive insights in T. Schieder, *Frederick the Great* (trans. 2000). Additional works on Frederick are listed below in Chapter 8.

Some Useful Web Sites

For information and links on the finanical panics of the era, see the *Bubble Project* at Dalhousie University, http://myweb.dal.ca/dmcneil/bubble.html. There are useful materials and links on the early British empire at *BBC-History*, hhtp.bbc.co.uk/history/state/empire. The history of France's role in early America can be explored through the links at the *Virtual Museum of New France*, http://www.vmnf.civilization.ca/vmnf/vmnf .asp. The Web site of *The Royal Historical Society*, at http://www.rhs/ac/uk/bibl/bibwel.asp, offers links to numerous resources on eighteenth-century history and culture. The themes of both early modern and modern global history are addressed regularly at *World History Connected*, http://worldhistoryconnected.press.uiuc .edu/, the site of an excellent "e-journal" that offers up-to-date information and analysis of the transnational exchanges in world history.

8. THE AGE OF ENLIGHTENMENT

For background, the eighteenth-century accounts listed at the beginning of Chapter 7 should be consulted and to them should be added A. Goodwin (ed.), *The American and French Revolutions, 1763–1793*

(1965), Vol. VIII of T*he New Cambridge Modern History*. There are helpful essays in D. E. D. Beales, *Enlightenment and Reform in Eighteenth-Century Europe* (2005) and a valuable overview in O. Hufton, *Europe: Privilege and Protest: 1730–1789* (rev. 2000). Readers will also find an intriguing, comprehensive account of the later eighteenth century in F. Venturi, *The End of the Old Regime in Europe, 1776–1789* (2 vols., trans. 1991).

Enlightenment Thought

The most wide-ranging survey of the thought of the era is P. Gay, *The Enlightenment: An Interpretation* (2 vols., 1966–69), a comprehensive work that praises the rationalist themes of many eighteenth-century writers; the author also explores some of his theses in *The Party of Humanity: Essays on the French Enlightenment* (1964). Other influential, older interpretations are to be found in E. Cassirer, *The Philosophy of the Enlightenment* (1932; trans. 1951); A Cobban, *In Search of Humanity: The Role of the Enlightenment in Modern History* (1960); N. Hampson, *A Cultural History of the Enlightenment* (1969); and I. O. Wade, *The Structure and Form of the French Enlightenment* (2 vols., 1977). An informative concise introduction is M. Cranston, *Philosophers and Pamphleteers: Political Theorists of the Enlightenment* (1986), while two useful, brief surveys entitled *The Enlightenment* are available by R. Porter (rev. 2001) and D. Outram (1995). G. Himmelfarb, *The Roads to Modernity: The British, French, and American Enlightenments* (2004) is provocative but not always convincing when it elevates British and American contributions above those of the French. Readers may also turn to M. C. Jacob (ed.), *The Enlightenment: A Brief History with Documents* (2001).

Many recent works on the Enlightenment stress the role of social and cultural institutions that promoted the circulation of ideas and new forms of intellectual debate. This approach to the Enlightenment has been influenced by the challenging work of J. Habermas, *The Structural Transformation of the Public Sphere* (trans. 1989). Among the many recent studies that examine institutions of the Enlightenment "public sphere," readers will find valuable insights in D. Goodman, *The Republic of Letters: A Cultural History of the French Enlightenment* (1994), which discusses the role of women in French salons; D. Gordon, *Citizens Without Sovereignty: Equality and Sociability in French Thought, 1670–1789* (1994); A. Goldgar, *Impolite Learning: Conduct and Community in the Republic of Letters* (1995); and T. Munck, *The Enlightenment: A Comparative Social History, 1721–1794* (2000), which argues that the new ideas spread widely beyond the elite centers of intellectual life. Other important books include U. Im Hof, *The Enlightenment* (trans. 1994) and D. Roche, *France in the Enlightenment* (1993, trans. 1998), a balanced, informative, and entertaining work by a leading French historian. Interesting work on more specific topics may be found in M. C. Jacob, *Living the Enlightenment: Freemasonary and Politics in Eighteenth-Century Europe* (1991) as well as in O. P. Grell and R. Porter (eds.), *Toleration in Enlightenment Europe* (2000). M. Vovelle (ed.), *Enlightenment Portraits* (1997) brings to life many of the people of the age; and D. M. McMahon examines the critics of Enlightenment thought in *Enemies of the Enlightenment: The French Counter-Enlightenment and the Making of Modernity* (2001).

On the theme of progress, readers may consult the classic work by J. B. Bury, *The Idea of Progress: An Inquiry into Its Origin and Growth* (1920, 1955) and R. Nisbet, *History of the Idea of Progress* (rev. 1994), which treats the concept on a broad time scale. The idea has also been examined in A. M. Melzer, J. Weinberger, and M. R. Zinman (eds.), *History and the Idea of Progress* (1995). On economic thought and the early advocates of free trade, there is E. Fox-Genovese, *The Origins of Physiocracy: Economic Revolution and Social Order in Eighteenth-Century France* (1976) and the important work of P. Groenwegen, *Eighteenth-Century Economics: Turgot, Beccaria and Smith and Their Contemporaries* (2002).

The Philosophes

There are numerous books on the leading thinkers of the Enlightenment. On Voltaire, P. Gay, *Voltaire's Politics: The Poet as Realist* (rev. 1988) reveals Voltaire's pragmatic reactions to the events of his day; H. Mason, *Voltaire: A Biography* (1981) is a concise authoritative account; J. Gray, *Voltaire* (1999) offers a brief introduction; and A. J. Ayer, *Voltaire* (1986) stresses Voltaire as crusader. More recent studies include R. Pearson, *Voltaire Almighty: A Life in Pursuit of Freedom* (2005) and I. Davidson, *Voltaire in Exile* (2005), which focuses on the philosophe's later life and career. For Montesquieu one may read an outstanding study by R. Shackleton, *Montesquieu: A Critical Biography* (1961) and an illuminating brief examination of his thought in J. N. Shklar, *Montesquieu* (1987). On Diderot, A. M. Wilson's biography (2 vols., 1957, 1972) is admirable and P. N. Furbank, *Diderot: A Critical Biography* (1992) is equally impressive and adds new materials.

For the elusive Rousseau, a comprehensive introduction is L. G. Crocker, *Jean-Jacques Rousseau* (2 vols., 1968), while E. Cassirer, *The Question of Jean-Jacques Rousseau* (trans. 1963) remains fundamental. In addition to many other studies, readers may turn to J. H. Huizinga, *Rousseau: The Self-Made Man* (1975); R. Grimsley, *Jean-Jacques Rousseau* (1983); and M. Cranston's important reassessment, *Jean-Jacques: The Early Life and Works of Jean-Jacques Rousseau, 1712–1754* (1982), with a sequel, *The Noble Savage: Jean-Jacques Rousseau, 1754–1762* (1991). Two challenging books are J. Miller, *Rousseau: Dreamer of Democracy* (1984) and J. N. Shklar, *Men and Citizens: A Study of Rousseau's Social Theory* (1985). The work of M. Hulliung, *The Autocritique of Enlightenment: Rousseau and the Philosophes* (1994), describes Rousseau's critical analysis of his own era's intellectual culture. Rousseau's life and thought are also examined in L. Damrosch, *Jean-Jacques Rousseau, Restless Genius* (2005), an excellent biography.

On Condorcet, K. M. Baker has written the exhaustive *Condorcet: From Natural Philosophy to Social Mathematics* (1975), while D. Williams, *Condorcet and Modernity* (2005) discusses both the ideas and political vision of a philosophe who also participated in the French Revolution. On the leading biologist or "natural historian" of the age, one may read J. Roger, *Buffon* (trans. 1998). On a lesser known philosophe sympathetic to the poorer classes, an excellent account is D. G. Levy, *The Ideas and Careers of Simon-Nicholas-Henri Linguet* (1980). H. G. Payne, *The Philosophes and the People* (1971) traces the divergent views of the famous writers toward the lower classes, as does H. Chisick, *The Limits of Reform in the Enlightenment* (1981).

For the connection between the ideas of the Enlightenment and the Revolution one still reads the classic work of D. Mornet, *Intellectual Origins of the French Revolution* (trans. 1933), which saw a more direct link than some contemporary scholars would concede. Three major reassessments are F. Furet, *Interpreting the French Revolution* (trans. 1981); K. M. Baker, *Inventing the French Revolution: Essays in the Political Culture of the Eighteenth Century* (1990); and R. Chartier, *The Cultural Origins of the French Revolution* (trans. 1991). Two books on the use and abuse of the ideas of the philosophes by the later revolutionaries are N. Hampson, *Will and Circumstance: Montesquieu, Rousseau, and the French Revolution* (1984) and C. Blum, *Rousseau and the Republic of Virtue: The Language of Politics in the French Revolution* (1986).

Intellectual ties between France and America are discussed in L. Gottschalk and D. F. Lach, *Toward the French Revolution: Europe and America in the Eighteenth-Century World* (1973) and in S. Schiff, *A Great Improvisation: Franklin, France, and the Birth of America* (2005). On Franklin one may also read C. A. Lopez, *Mon Cher Papa: Franklin and the Ladies of Paris* (rev. 1990) and two excellent biographies by E. S. Morgan (2002) and W. Isaacson (2005). Books that explore the significance of the Americas for European life and thought include A. Gerbi, *The Dispute of the New World, 1750–1900* (1973); S. Brandon, *New Worlds for Old* (1986), cited in Chapter 3; and C. Vann Woodward, *The Old World's New World* (1991), on changing European perceptions of America. An outstanding effort to explore the most important collaborative work of the French Enlightenment is R. Darnton, *The Business of Enlightenment: A Publishing History of the Encyclopédie, 1775–1800* (1979). The same author's other books, among them

Mesmerism and the End of the Enlightenment in France (1968), *The Literary Underground of the Old Regime* (1985), and *The Great Cat Massacre and Other Episodes in French Cultural History* (1984) help explain popular culture and radical political thought among ordinary men and women of the age. An engaging recent study of the philosophes' cultural and political ambitions is available in P. Blom, *Enlightening the World: Encyclopédie, the Book that Changed the Course of History* (2005). The growth of literacy is explored, especially for the years after 1680, in F. Furet and J. Ozouf, *Reading and Writing: Literacy in France from Calvin to Jules Ferry* (trans. 1983); the history of reading is also examined in R. Chartier, *The Cultural Uses of Print in Early Modern France* (trans. 1987). W. Roberts, *Morality and Social Class: Eighteenth-Century French Literature and Painting* (1974) links the creative arts to political and social life, as do A. Boime, *Art in an Age of Revolution, 1750–1800* (1987) and M. Craske, *Art in Europe, 1700–1830* (1997).

The Enlightenment:
Scotland, England, Italy, Germany

An informative introduction to Scotland in this age is D. Allan, *Scotland in the Eighteenth Century* (2001), and valuable assessments of the important Scottish thinkers are available in A. C. Chitnis, *The Scottish Enlightenment: A Social History* (1976) and in G. Davie, *The Scotch Metaphysics: A Century of Enlightenment in Scotland* (2001), which also describes the influence of Scottish philosophy in the nineteenth century. Other helpful books are K. Haakonssen, *The Science of a Legislator: The Natural Jurisprudence of David Hume and Adam Smith* (1981); D. Forbes, *Hume's Philosophical Politics* (1984); A. Fitzgibbons, *Adam Smith's System of Liberty, Wealth, and Virtue: the Moral and Political Foundations of the Wealth of Nations* (1995); and J. Dwyer, *The Age of the Passions: An Interpretation of Adam Smith and Scottish Enlightenment Culture* (1998). The essays in three collaborative volumes are rewarding: I. Hont and M. Ignatieff (eds.), *Wealth and Virtue in the Shaping of the Political Economy in the Scottish Enlightenment* (1984); D. Daiches et al. (eds.), *A Hotbed of Genius: The Scottish Enlightenment, 1730–1790* (1987); and J. Dwyer and R. B. Sher (eds.), *Sociability and Society in Eighteenth-Century Scotland* (1993).

For the Enlightenment in its British setting, one may read J. Redwood, *Reason, Ridicule, and Religion: The Age of Enlightenment in England, 1660–1750* (1976) and R. Porter, *The Creation of the Modern World: The Untold Story of the British Enlightenment* (2000), a wide-ranging work that stresses Britain's distinctive contributions to Enlightenment culture. The relation between religion and new democratic movements is examined in B. Semmel, *The Methodist Revolution* (1973), which sees Wesleyan evangelicalism as the English counterpart to democratic stirrings in Europe and America; and R. Hattersley, *A Brand from the Burning: The Life of John Wesley* (2002) examines a key leader. J. G. A. Pocock subtly reexamines a number of British thinkers, including Hume, Gibbon, and Burke, in *Virtue, Commerce, and History: Essays in Political Thought and History* (1985). For Gibbon the brief J. W. Burrow, *Gibbon* (1985) and P. B. Craddock's admirable two-volume biography (1982–88) are available, but readers should also turn to the monumental work of J. G. A. Pocock, *Barbarism and Religion* (4 vols., 1999–2005), which examines Gibbon's work and places it in a wider context of Enlightenment historical writing. For the German poet-philosopher Goethe, one may turn to N. Boyle, *Goethe: The Poet and the Age* (2 vols., 1991, 2000).

H. Maestro has written a comprehensive biography of the Italian jurist and reformer who served the Austrian state, *Cesare Beccaria and the Origins of Penal Reform* (1973). For the Italian city-states in this age there are available D. Carpanetto and G. Ricuperati, *Italy in the Age of Reason, 1685–1789* (1987) and F. Venturi, *Italy and the Enlightenment: Studies in a Cosmopolitan Century* (1972). The leading Italian philosopher of the Enlightenment, little known in his own time but increasingly influential in recent years, is studied in L. Pompa, *Vico: A Study of the "New Science"* (1975); P. Burke's brief *Vico* (1985); M. Lilla, *G. B. Vico: The Making of an Anti-Modern* (1993); G. Mazzotta, *The New Map of the World: The Poetic Philosophy of Giambattista Vico* (1999); and R. C. Miner, *Vico, Genealogist of Modernity* (2002).

Other Enlightenment Themes

Religion and related themes are examined in R. R. Palmer, *Catholics and Unbelievers in Eighteenth Century France* (1939); F. E. Manuel, *The Changing of the Gods* (1983); J. M. McManners, *Death and Enlightenment: Changing Attitudes to Death among Christians and Unbelievers in Eighteenth Century France* (1982); J. M. Byrne, *Religion and the Enlightenment: From Descartes to Kant* (1997); and the wide-ranging survey by W. R. Ward, *Christianity Under the Ancien Régime, 1648–1789* (1999). An important episode is studied in D. D. Bien, *The Calas Affair: Persecution, Toleration, and Heresy in Eighteenth Century Toulouse* (1960), while M. C. Jacob, *The Radical Enlightenment: Pantheists, Freemasons, and Republicans* (1981) explores radical ideas that flourished in Dutch literary circles. J. Riskin, *Science in the Age of Sensibility: The Sentimental Empiricists of the French Enlightenment* (2002) challenges older assumptions about the era's pervasive rationalism; and there is an intriguing study of the philosophes' conception of truth and falsehood in D. W. Bates, *Enlightenment Aberrations: Error and Revolution in France* (2002).

For an introduction to women in the Enlightenment, their accomplishments and the constraints upon them, one may turn to K. Rogers, *Feminism in Eighteenth-Century England* (1976); the essays in S. I. Spencer (ed.), *French Women and the Age of Enlightenment* (1985); the important work on the salons by D. Goodman (1994), cited earlier; N. R. Gelbart, *Feminine and Opposition Journalism in Old Regime France: Le Journal des dames* (1987); and S. C. Maza, *Private Lives and Public Affairs: The Causes Célèbres of Prerevolutionary France* (1993), which discusses the images of women in late eighteenth-century legal disputes. The life of the marquise who headed the best known of the many salons in France is recounted in B. Craveri, *Madame du Deffand and Her World* (trans. 1994).

On a special subject, A. Hertzberg, *The French Enlightenment and the Jews* (1968) contends that by downgrading all religions the philosophes (and especially Voltaire) contributed to anti-Semitism; also critical of the Enlightenment is J. Katz, *Out of the Ghetto: The Social Background of Jewish Emancipation, 1770–1870* (1973). But Jewish integration into European society in these years is explored in R. Mahler, *A History of Modern Jewry, 1780–1815* (1971); J. Israel, *European Jewry in the Age of Mercantilism, 1550–1750* (rev. 1998); and F. Malino and D. Sorkin (eds.), *From East to West: Jews in a Changing Europe* (1990), which focuses on the years 1750 to 1870. The views of eighteenth-century intellectuals are examined in excellent recent books by A. Sutcliffe, *Judaism and the Enlightenment* (2003) and J. M. Hess, *Germans, Jews, and the Claims of Modernity* (2002). H. Sachar, *A History of the Jews in the Modern World* (2005) provides a scholarly, highly readable account focusing on the years from the Enlightenment to the present.

France in the Old Regime

Several books on modern France examine developments in the eighteenth century; among them are C. Jones, *The Great Nation: France from Louis XV to Napoleon, 1715–99* (2002) and R. Price, *An Economic History of Modern France 1730–1914* (1981). Price has also written *A Concise History of France* (rev. 2005). A. Moulin, *Peasantry and Society in France since 1789* (1991) examines important social themes.

Books that study the era for its own sake and not merely as a prologue to the Revolution include P. R. Campbell, *The Ancien Regime in France* (1988) and E. Le Roy Ladurie, *The Ancien Regime: A History of France, 1610–1774* (trans. 1996). The financial crisis is explored in depth in J. F. Bosher, *French Finances, 1770–1795: From Business to Bureaucracy* (1970).

The changing role of the nobility may be studied in older works by F. L. Ford, *Robe and Sword: The Regrouping of the French Aristocracy after Louis XIV* (1953) and R. Forster, *The Nobility of Toulouse in the Eighteenth Century* (1960), as well as in Forster's other books. G. Chaussinand-Noguret, *The French Nobility in the Eighteenth Century* (1985) portrays the prerevolutionary nobility as socially productive; and J. M. Smith examines the nobility's contribution to conceptions of French nationhood in *Nobility Reimagined: The Patriotic Nation in Eighteenth-Century France* (2005). The response to problems of poverty and hunger in eighteenth-century France may be examined in O. Hufton, *The Poor of Eighteenth-Century France, 1750–1789* (1974); in S. L. Kaplan's detailed and impressive *Bread, Politics, and Political Economy in the Reign of Louis XV* (2 vols., 1976) and his two later volumes on related themes (1994, 1996); and in S. M. Adams, *Bureaucrats and Beggars: French Social Policy in the Age of Enlightenment* (1990). Parisian life at the time is graphically reconstructed in D. Roche, *The People of Paris* (trans. 1987). The status of domestic servants as a key to broader social relations is examined in S. C. Maza, *Servants and Masters in Eighteenth Century France: The Uses of Loyalty* (1983) and in C. Fairchilds, *Domestic Enemies: Servants and Their Masters in Old Regime France* (1984). Maza also discusses French conceptions of social class in *The Myth of the French Bourgeoise: An Essay on the Social Imaginary, 1750–1850* (2003), which argues that the bourgeoisie did not exist as the coherent social group that its critics imagined.

Enlightened Despotism in Europe

A thoughtful brief introduction is J. G. Gagliardo, *Enlightened Despotism* (1967), while L. Krieger, *An Essay on the Theory of Enlightenment and Despotism* (1975) is a difficult but rewarding analysis.

German political fragmentation and cultural stirrings are examined in J. G. Gagliardo's *Reich and Nation: The Holy Roman Empire as Idea and Reality, 1763–1806* (1980) and *Germany under the Old Regime, 1600–1790* (1991). R. Vierhaus, *Germany in the Age of Absolutism* (1988) is a brief survey, while J. J. Sheehan, *Germany, 1770–1866* (1989) is an outstanding larger history that begins with this period. For Prussia and Frederick the Great, one may turn to D. B. Horn, *Frederick the Great and the Rise of Prussia* (1969) and R. B. Asprey, *Frederick the Great: The Great Enigma* (1986) as well as to the recent biographies by G. MacDonogh, *Frederick the Great: A Life in Deed and Letters* (1999) and D. Fraser, *Frederick the Great* (2000). His bureaucracy is examined in H. C. Johnson, *Frederick the Great and His Officials* (1975).

A concise introduction to eighteenth-century Austria is E. Wangermann, *The Austrian Achievement, 1700–1800* (1973). D. F. Good, *The Economic Rise of the Habsburg Empire, 1750–1914* (1984) begins with these years, while P. G. M. Dickson, *Finance and Government under Maria Theresa, 1740–1780* (2 vols., 1988) is an in-depth economic study. The Habsburg empress may be studied in E. Crankshaw, *Maria Theresa* (1969); her son may be studied in P. P. Bernard, *Joseph II* (1968), a brief, balanced account;

in T. C. W. Blanning, *Joseph II* (1994); and in D. Beales, *Joseph II*, Vol. I: *In the Shadow of Maria Theresa, 1741–1780* (1987), which shows in detail how Joseph attempted to shape policy even before his own reign began in 1780.

Enlightened despotism in Russia is examined in a judicious large-scale study by I. de Madariaga, *Russia in the Age of Catherine the Great* (1981), available in abridged form as *Catherine the Great: A Short History* (1990), and in her *Politics and Culture in Eighteenth-Century Russia: Collected Essays* (1998). For a somewhat different appraisal, one may read J. T. Alexander, *Catherine the Great: Life and Legend* (1988). There are also biographies of Catherine by C. Erickson (1995) and S. Dixon (2001). Other valuable studies of eighteenth-century Russia include two works by M. Raeff, *Origins of the Russian Intelligentsia: The Eighteenth-Century Nobility* (1966) and *Political Ideas and Institutions in Imperial Russia* (1994), as well as D. Ransel, *The Politics of Catherinean Russia* (1975). Additional insights are provided in J. Burbank and D. L. Ransel (eds.), *Imperial Russia: New Histories for the Empire* (1998). Economic developments are traced in A. Kahan, *The Plow, the Hammer, and the Knout: An Economic History of Eighteenth-Century Russia* (1985), and revolts and social stirrings may be studied in P. Avrich, *Russian Rebels, 1600–1800* (1972), cited earlier, and in two books by J. T. Alexander on the Pugachev uprising: *Autocratic Politics in a National Crisis* (1969) and *Emperor of the Cossacks* (1973).

Poland: The Partitions

For Poland in these years one may turn to N. Davies, *A History of Poland: God's Playground* (2 vols., rev. 2005), Vol. I: *The Origins to 1795* and *Heart of Europe: A Short History of Poland* (1984) as well as the accounts in J. Lukowski and H. Zawadzki, *A Concise History of Poland* (2001) and A. J. Prazmowska, *A History of Poland* (2004). The quarrel over the succession to the Polish throne is recounted in J. L. Sutton, *The King's Honor and the King's Cardinal [Fleury]: The War of the Polish Succession* (1980). On the eighteenth-century partitions, J. Lukowski, *The Partitions of Poland, 1772, 1793, 1795* (1999) updates and expands upon older studies. For the years that followed the partitions, one turns to P. Wandycz, *The Lands of Partitioned Poland, 1795–1918* (1974), Vol. VII of *A History of East Central Europe*. A special subject is treated in B. D. Weinryb, *The Jews of Poland: A Social and Economic History of the Jewish Community in Poland from 1100 to 1800* (rev. 1976), and in the essays in C. Abramsky et al. (eds.), *The Jews in Poland* (1986). K. Friedrich, *The Other Prussia: Royal Prussia, Poland, and Liberty, 1569–1772* (2000) examines the history of Polish-Prussian relations.

The American Revolution and Britain

Major works by R. R. Palmer, J. Godechot, and others exploring the American and French Revolutions in a broader eighteenth-century revolutionary setting are described in the next chapter. H. F. May, *The Enlightenment in America* (1976) and H. S. Commager, *The Empire of Reason: How Europe Imagined and America Realized the Enlightenment* (1977) are both challenging books. For background to the revolution one should read B. Bailyn, *The Ideological Origins of the American Revolution* (1967; 1992). The link with events and ideas in seventeenth-century England is stressed in E. S. Morgan, *Inventing the People: The Rise of Popular Sovereignty in England and America* (1988); and the influence of Enlightenment ideas on American leaders is discussed in D. Staloff, *Hamilton, Adams, Jefferson: The Politics of Enlightenment and the American Founding* (2005).

For a sampling of interpretive studies one may turn to I. R. Christie and B. W. Labaree, *Empire or Independence, 1760–1776: A British-American Dialogue on the Coming of the American Revolution* (1976); B. Bailyn, *Faces of Revolution: Personalities and Themes in the Struggle for American Independence* (1990); J. P. Greene, *Understanding the American Revolution: Issues and Actors* (1995); and two books by G. S. Wood, *The Radicalism of the American Revolution* (1991) and *The American Revolution: A History* (2002). Important examples of the expanding research on the history of women in this era may be found in L. K. Kerber, *Women of the Republic: Intellect and Ideology in Revolutionary America* (1980); in M. B. Norton, *Liberty's Daughters: The Revolutionary Experience of American Women* (1980, 1996); and in C. Berkin, *Revolutionary Mothers: Women in the Struggle for America's Independence* (2005). British responses to the revolutionary events in America are discussed in K. Perry, *British Politics and the American Revolution* (1990); in H. T. Dickinson (ed.), *Britain and the American Revolution* (1998); and in S. Conway, *The British Isles and the War of American Independence* (2000).

For the military aspects of the war one may turn to J. Shy, *A People Numerous and Armed: Reflections on the Military Struggle for American Independence* (rev. 1990) and S. Conway, *The War of American Independence* (1995). The French contribution is examined in J. Dull, *The French Navy and American Independence* (1975); in L. Kennett, *The French Forces in America, 1780–1783* (1978); and in S. F. Scott, *From Yorktown to Valmy: The Transformation of the French Army in an Age of Revolution* (1998).

For diplomacy and international affairs there are F. W. Brecher, *Securing American Independence: John Jay and the French Alliance* (2003) and H. M. Scott, *British Foreign Policy in the Age of the American Revolution* (1991); and on the peace negotiations, R. B. Morris, *The Peacemakers: The Great Powers and American Independence* (1965) is an outstanding study.

For Britain in the eighteenth century one should also consult the books described in Chapter 7. In addition, on movements for parliamentary reform informative studies include J. R. Pole, *Political Representation in England and the Origins of the American Revolution* (1967); P. D. G. Thomas, *John Wilkes: A Friend to Liberty* (1996); M. Turner, *British Politics in an Age of Reform* (1999); and E. H. Gould, *The Persistence of Empire: British Political Culture in the Age of the American Revolution* (2000). Two books by I. R. Christie, *Wars and Revolutions: Britain, 1760–1815* (1982) and *Stress and Stability in Late Eighteenth-Century Britain: Reflections on the British Avoidance of Revolution* (1984) are rewarding.

Useful Web Sites

The *International Centre for Eighteenth-Century Studies* maintains a comprehensive Web site at www.c18.org, where readers will find links to diverse materials on all aspects of eighteenth-century history and culture; and there are more useful links at the *International Society for Eighteenth-Century Studies*, www.isecs.org. The *Voltaire Foundation*, www.voltaire.ox.ac.uk, is another good starting point for further research on the Enlightenment as well as the life and work of France's best-known philosophe. Two valuable sites for resources on early American history and the American Revolution are maintained by the *Gilder Lehrman Institute of American History* at www.gilderlehrman.org and by the *History Matters* project at George Mason University, www.historymatters.gmu.org, both of which have outstanding links to other materials. The collection of electronic sources at Fordham Univeristy, *Internet Modern History Sourcebook*, includes links to many valuable eighteenth-century materials at www.fordham.edu/halsall/mod/modsbook2.html.

9. THE FRENCH REVOLUTION

Still useful works on the revolutionary era include A. Goodwin (ed.), *The American and French Revolutions, 1763–1793* (1965), Vol. VIII of the *New Cambridge Modern History,* and its sequel volume, C. W. Crawley (ed.), *War and Peace in an Age of Upheaval, 1793–1830* (1965). Books encompassing the revolutionary era as a whole include E. J. Hobsbawm, *The Age of Revolution: Europe, 1789–1848* (1962, reissued 1996); N. Hampson, *The First European Revolution, 1776–1850* (1969); and C. Breunig and M. Levinger, *The Revolutionary Era, 1789–1850* (rev. 2002); of special value is G. Best, *War and Society in Revolutionary Europe, 1770–1870* (1982).

The French Revolution

As the bicentennial in 1989 of the French Revolution demonstrated, the French themselves are less divided than formerly over the legacy of 1789, but wide differences in scholarly interpretation, emphasis, and conceptualization persist. The reader may assess current scholarship through F. Furet and M. Ozouf (eds.), *A Critical Dictionary of the French Revolution* (trans. 1989), which consists of 99 encyclopedia-type articles covering events, institutions, persons, and ideas, as well as historians of the Revolution. Another informative compendium is S. F. Scott and B. Rothaus, *Historical Dictionary of the French Revolution, 1787–1799* (2 vols., 1985). Four impressive volumes incorporating the contributions of many international scholars have been published as *The French Revolution and the Creation of Modern Political Culture:* Vol. I, K. M. Baker (ed.), *The Political Culture of the Old Regime* (1987); Vol. II, C. Lucas (ed.), *The Political Culture of the French Revolution* (1989); Vol. III, F. Furet (ed.), *The Influence of the French Revolution on Nineteenth-Century Europe* (1989); and Vol. IV, K. M. Baker (ed.), *The Terror* (1994). The Revolution is viewed in thoughtful perspective for the general reader by eight scholars in G. Best (ed.), *The Permanent Revolution: The French Revolution and Its Legacy, 1789–1989* (1989); in depth by specialists in C. Lucas (ed.), *Rewriting the French Revolution* (1991); and in E. J. Hobsbawm, *Echoes from the Marseillaise: Two Centuries Look Back on the French Revolution* (1990), an insightful examination of liberal, Marxist, and revisionist interpretations.

Of narrative histories S. Schama, *Citizens: A Chronicle of the French Revolution* (1989), carrying the events to 1794, effectively captures their color and drama. Comprehensive political narratives are available in W. Doyle, *The Oxford History of the French Revolution* (rev. 2002); J. F. Bosher, *The French Revolution* (1988); D. G. M. Sutherland, *France, 1789–1815: Revolution and Counterrevolution* (1986), and by the same author, *The French Revolution and Empire, the Quest for a Civic Order* (2003) ; and A. Forrest, *The French Revolution* (1995). Other useful recent surveys include J. Popkin, *A Short History of the French Revolution* (rev. 2002); P. McPhee, *The French Revolution, 1789–1799* (2002); and D. Andress, *French Society in Revolution, 1789–1799* (1999). One still reads with profit the older work of C. Brinton, *A Decade of Revolution, 1789–1799* (1934, 1962); and the wider meaning of the Revolution is discussed in the influential work of F. Furet, *Revolutionary France, 1770–1880* (trans. 1992).

For special aspects the reader may turn to E. Kennedy, *A Cultural History of the French Revolution* (1989), which ably communicates the cultural effervescence of the age; F. Aftalion, *The French Revolution: An Economic Interpretation* (trans. 1990); and R. Cobb, *The French and Their Revolution* (1998), a collection of writings by an English historian interested in the history of the lower classes. The popular response to revolutionary events is examined in

D. Andress, *The French Revolution and the People* (2004); and D. Bell discusses the emergence of French nationalism before and during the Revolution in *The Cult of the Nation in France: Inventing Nationalism, 1680–1800* (2001). The art of the era comes alive in R. Paulson, *Representations of Revolution, 1750–1800* (1987), cited in the previous chapter, while architectural design is explored imaginatively in J. A. Leith, *Space and Revolution* (1991). In another area R. R. Palmer, *The Improvement of Humanity: Education and the French Revolution* (1985) examines the educational institutions which sought to disseminate revolutionary ideals.

There is a helpful introduction to the wide range of historical interpretations of the French Revolution in M. R. Cox (ed.), *The Place of the French Revolution in History* (1998). Recent debates among historians may be sampled in T. C. W. Blanning (ed.), *The Rise and Fall of the French Revolution* (1996) and in G. Kates (ed.), *The French Revolution: Recent Debates and New Controversies* (1998). A comprehensive summary of French views during the Revolution's bicentennial is available in S. L. Kaplan, *Farewell Revolution* (2 vols., 1995). There are numerous older volumes, now more important to historiography than to history, by writers of such vastly differing viewpoints as Jules Michelet, Jean Jaurès, Hippolyte Taine, Thomas Carlyle, Louis Madelin, Pierre Gaxotte, Alphonse Aulard, and Albert Mathiez.

Many twentieth-century scholars emphasized the class basis of the Revolution and saw political differences emerging from the economic self-interest of groups and factions. A classical synthesis of this approach, which nonetheless retains a judicious balance, is G. Lefebvre, *The French Revolution* (1951; 2 vols. in trans. 1962–64). A more extreme example, stressing class struggle, is A. Soboul, *The French Revolution, 1789–1799: From the Storming of the Bastille to Napoleon* (trans. 1977). The class struggle is also highlighted in G. Rudé, *The French Revolution* (1988). Two books by A. Cobban, *The Myth of the French Revolution* (1953) and *The Social Interpretation of The French Revolution* (1964), vigorously rejected the notion of a "bourgeois revolution."

New ways to study the Revolution as a cultural phenomenon rather than as a revolution of social classes are explored in F. Furet, *Interpreting the French Revolution* (1978; trans. 1981), cited earlier. The new methodology is exemplified in two books by L. Hunt: *Politics, Culture, and Class in the French Revolution* (1984) and *The Family Romance of the French Revolution* (1992), which approaches the questions of legitimacy and authority by examining the wide use of family metaphors during the Revolution. Cultural aspects of the Revolution are also explored in J. R. Censor and L. Hunt, *Liberty, Equality, Fraternity: Exploring the French Revolution* (2001), an innovative book that includes a CD-ROM disk with images and songs from the revolutionary era. The emphasis on symbolic meanings appears also in M. Ozouf, *Festivals and the French Revolution* (1988) and in H. J. Lesebrink, *The Bastille: A History of a Symbol of Despotism and Freedom* (trans. 1997).

The Events of the Revolution

For the immediate background of the Revolution, including the financial crisis, one may read M. Vovelle, *The Fall of the French Monarchy, 1787–1792* (trans. 1984); W. Doyle, *Origins of the French Revolution* (rev. 1999); J. Egret, *The French Pre-Revolution, 1787–1788* (trans. 1977); and the two older volumes by G. Lefebvre: *The Coming of the French Revolution* (trans. 1947) and *The Great Fear of 1789: Rural Panic in Revolutionary France* (trans. 1982). The final effort at financial reconstruction is recounted in R. D. Harris, *Necker: Reform Statesman of the Ancien Regime* (1979) and *Necker and the Revolution of 1789* (1988). J. Hardman's two books, *Louis XVI* (1992) and *Louis XVI: The Silent King* (2000), provide thoughtful accounts of the king and his reputation. The famous queen is described in E. Lever, *Marie Antoinette: The Last Queen of France* (trans. 2000) and in a biography by A. Fraser, *Marie Antoinette: The Journey* (2002). The fate of the royal family is also examined in M. Price, *Louis XVI, Marie Antoinette, and the Fall of the French Monarchy* (2004); and the king's attempted escape from France is the subject of an excellent book by T. Tackett, *When the King Took Flight* (2003).

The reform phase of the Revolution under the first two legislative bodies is studied in N. Hampson, *Prelude to Terror: The Constituent Assembly and the Failure of Consensus, 1789–1791* (1989) and C. J. Mitchell, *The French Legislative Assembly of 1791* (1988). The coming of the war in 1792 and the radicalization of the Revolution may be studied in M. Bouloiscau, *The Jacobin Republic, 1792– 1794* (trans. 1984), and in M. J. Sydenham, *The First French Republic 1792–1804* (1974). Other studies of the Jacobins and their ideas may be found in M. Kennedy, *The Jacobin Clubs in the French Revolution, 1793–1795* (2000) and in P. Higonnet, *Goodness Beyond Virtue: Jacobins during the French Revolution* (1998), which offers a more sympathetic view of the Jacobins than most recent works.

For the year of the Terror the reader may turn to A. Soboul, *The Parisian Sans-Culotte and the French Revolution, 1793–1794* (trans. 1964); R. R. Palmer, *Twelve Who Ruled: The Year of the Terror in the French Revolution* (1941; reissued 2005); C. Lucas, *The Structure of the Terror* (1973); and D. Andress, *The Terror: The Merciless War for Freedom in Revolutionary France* (2006). A dramatic episode foreshadowing the Terror is recounted in D. J. Jordan, *The King's Trial: Louis XVI vs. The French Revolution* (1979).

Different aspects of the Revolution are explored in M. Vovelle, *The Revolution Against the Church:* *From Reason to the Supreme Being* (trans. 1991); P. Jones, *The Peasantry in the French Revolution* (1988); and J. Markoff, *The Abolition of Feudalism: Peasants, Lords and Legislators in the French Revolution* (1996). A. Forrest, *The French Revolution and the Poor* (1981) examines the welfare legislation adopted in the revolutionary decade. Changes in family life and gender relations are discussed in S. Desan, *The Family on Trial in Revolutionary France* (2004). For a summary of how the revolutionaries conceived of human rights, one may turn to the analysis and documents in L. Hunt (ed.), *The French Revolution and Human Rights* (1996); and an important study of social changes across the entire revolutionary and Napoleonic era appears in I. Woloch, *The New Regime: Transformations of the French Civic Order: 1789–1820s* (1994).

The role of women in this era is explored in J. B. Landes, *Women and the Public Sphere in the Age of the French Revolution* (1988), which argues that the Revolution reduced the rights of women in France; L. Kelly, *Women of the French Revolution* (1989); S. E. Meltzerand and L. W. Rabine (eds.), *Rebel Daughters: Women and the French Revolution* (1992); and J. Heuer, *The Family and the Nation: Gender and Citizenship in Revolutionary France, 1789–1830* (2005). The essays in D. G. Levy and H. B. Applewhite (eds.), *Women and Politics in the Age of the Democratic Revolution* (1990) study women activists in revolutionary Europe and America; and the work by M. Yalom, *Blood Sisters: The French Revolution in Women's Memory* (1993) examines accounts by women who participated in the revolutionary events. The expansion of women's writing during the revolutionary decade is the subject of C. Hesse, *The Other Enlightenment: How French Women Became Modern* (2001); and the relation between gender and the new French nationalism is analyzed in J. B. Landes, *Visualizing the Nation: Gender, Representation, and Revolution in Eighteenth-Century France* (2001).

Among R. Cobb's illuminating books about the life and activism of the lower classes are *The Police and the People: French Popular Protest, 1789–1820* (1970); *Paris and Its Provinces, 1792–1802* (1975); and *The People's Armies* (1961, 1987), an impressive study of the armed groups that scoured the countryside for food and other military needs of the revolutionary government. For the counterrevolution one turns to the broader narratives cited above and to J. Godechot, *The Counter-Revolution* (trans. 1971); J. Roberts, *The Counter-Revolution in France, 1787–1830* (1990); C. Tilly, *The Vendée* (1964); and M. Hutt, *Chouannerie and the Counter-Revolution* (1984).

For the reaction after Robespierre's downfall and the regime that followed, one may turn to D. Woronoff, *The Thermidorean Regime and the Directory, 1794–1799* (trans. 1984) and to M. Lyons, *France under the Directory* (1975). The crushing of the Babeuf uprising is described in R. B. Rose, *Gracchus Babeuf: The First Revolutionary Communist* (1978); Babeuf's ideas are also discussed in I. H. Birchall, *The Spectre of Babeuf* (1997).

War and Diplomacy

On the coming of the war in 1792 and the first two coalitions one may read T. C. W. Blanning, *The Origins of the French Revolutionary Wars* (1989) and the same author's *The French Revolutionary Wars, 1781–1802* (1996); there is also a useful, brief account in G. Fremont-Barnes, *The French Revolutionary Wars* (2001). The French army that fought the war is described in impressive detail in J. P. Bertaud, *The Army of the French Revolution: From Citizen-Soldiers to Instrument of Power* (trans. 1988); it may be supplemented by A. Forrest, *Conscripts and Deserters: The Army and French Society during the Revolution and Empire* (1989). Military technologies are discussed in K. Alder, *Engineering the Revolution: Arms and Enlightenment in France, 1763–1815* (1997). On the emergence of Bonaparte one may turn to M. Crook, *Napoleon Comes to Power: Democracy and Dictatorship in Revolutionary France, 1795–1804* (1998). Additional books on Napoleon are listed in the following chapter.

Biographical Accounts

J. M. Thomson, *Leaders of the French Revolution* (1929, 1988), sketching 11 outstanding personalities, is a classic account that still merits reading. Specific biographical accounts include B. Luttrell, *Mirabeau* (1990); M. Forsyth, *Reason and Revolution: The Political Thought of the Abbé Sieyès* (1987); W. H. Sewell, *A Rhetoric of Revolution: The Abbé Sieyès and "What is the Third Estate?"* (1994); L. Gottschalk's two volumes on Lafayette in the French Revolution (1969, 1973); and C. D. Connor, *Jean Paul Marat: Scientist and Revolutionary* (1997), sympathetic to Marat's radicalism. N. Hampson has written the most fair-minded account of a controversial political leader in *Danton* (1978, 1988), while G. May, *Madame Roland and the Age of Revolution* (1970) sympathetically portrays a Girondist leader who fell victim to the Terror. A. G. Sepinwall examines the ideas and actions of another influential leader in *The Abbé Grégoire and the French Revolution: The Making of Modern Universalism* (2005).

A balanced biography of the most prominent figure on the Committee of Public Safety is J. M. Thompson, *Robespierre* (1935, 1988). One also may read M. Gallo, *Robespierre, the Incorruptible: A Psychobiography* (trans. 1971), provocative but not completely convincing; G. Rudé, *Robespierre: Portrait of a Revolutionary Democrat* (1975), which makes the best possible case for the Jacobin leader; N. Hampson, *The Life and Opinions of Maximilien Robespierre* (1974, 1988), which asks observers to react to the often contradictory evidence; D. P. Jordan, *The Revolutionary*

Career of Maximilien Robespierre (1985); and J. Hardman, *Robespierre* (1999). A useful collection of recent scholarship is available in C. Haydon and W. Doyle (eds.), *Robespierre* (1999). Robespierre's associates are studied in N. Hampson, *Saint-Just* (1991) and in L. Gershoy, *Bertrand Barère: A Reluctant Terrorist* (1962).

The Revolution outside France

For the view of the French Revolution as part of a broader European and Atlantic movement, one may turn to R. R. Palmer, *The Age of the Democratic Revolution: A Political History of Europe and America, 1760–1800* (2 vols., 1959–64); the first volume, *The Challenge*, carries the account to 1792 and the second, *The Struggle*, to 1800; see also by the same author *The World of the French Revolution* (1970). The conclusions of the French scholar J. Godechot are available in summary form as *France and the Atlantic Revolution, 1770–1799* (1975). Along related lines P. Higonnet traces the genesis of the republican idea in *Sister Republics: The Origins of French and American Republicanism* (1988), while M. Durey, *Transatlantic Radicals and the Early American Republic* (1997) looks at British political activists who migrated to America during the era of the French Revolution. There is a useful survey of the Revolution's enduring international influence in J. Klaits and M. H. Haltzel (eds.), *The Global Ramifications of the French Revolution* (1994). The German states are studied in T. C. W. Blanning, *The French Revolution in Germany: Occupation and Resistance in the Rhineland, 1792–1802* (1983); and in J. M. Diefendorf, *Businessmen and Politics in the Rhineland, 1789–1834* (1980).

Events in the Netherlands are examined in S. Schama, *Patriots and Liberators: Revolution and Government in the Netherlands, 1780–1813* (1977) and in northern Europe in H. A. Barton, *Scandinavia in the Revolutionary Era, 1760–1815* (1986). The Irish rebellion of 1798 is placed in its European setting in M. Elliott, *Partners in Revolution: The United Irishmen in France* (1982) and *Wolfe Tone: Prophet of Irish Independence* (1989); and in the wide-ranging work of R. B. McDowell, *Ireland in the Age of Imperialism and Revolution, 1760–1801* (1979).

For repercussions in Haiti and the African-American world, one may read the classic work of C. L. R. James, *The Black Jacobins: Toussaint L'Ouverture and the San Domingo Revolution* (1938, 1963), which should be supplemented by D. P. Geggus, *Slavery, War, and Revolution: The British Occupation of Saint Domingue, 1793–1798* (1982), and by the same author, *Haitian Revolutionary Studies* (2002); M. Duffy, *Soldiers, Sugar, and Seapower: The British Expeditions to the West Indies and the War against Revolutionary France* (1987); and L. Dubois, *Avengers of the New World: The Story of the Haitian Revolution* (2004), an excellent recent account. The struggle against slavery in Haiti and elsewhere is also the subject of A. Hochschild, *Bury the Chains: Prophets and Rebels in the Fight to Free an Empire's Slaves* (2005). There are helpful essays in D. B. Gaspar and D. P. Geggus (eds.), *A Turbulent Time: The French Revolution and the Greater Caribbean* (1997), and in D. P. Geggus (ed.), *The Impact of the Haitian Revolution in the Atlantic World* (2001).

An outstanding study of British reaction to the Revolution is A. Goodwin, *The Friends of Liberty: The English Democratic Movement in the Age of the French Revolution* (1979), while an informative brief essay is H. T. Dickinson, *British Radicalism and the French Revolution, 1789–1815* (1985). A more recent brief survey appears in C. Emsley, *Britain and the French Revolution* (2000); longer discussions of the era's political debates and conflicts can be found in M. Morris, *The British Monarchy and the French Revolution* (1998) and in J. Mori, *Britain in the Age of the French Revolution* (2000). An informative older book that focuses on popular unrest in both France and England is G. Rudé, *The Crowd in History: A Study of Popular Disturbances in France and England, 1730–1848* (1964).

The revolutionary career in England, America, and France of a leading revolutionist of the age is studied in J. Keane, *Tom Paine: A Political Life* (1995) and in E. Foner, *Tom Paine and Revolutionary America* (rev. 2005). Paine's political thought is examined in A. J. Ayer, *Thomas Paine* (1989) and in M. Philip, *Paine* (1989). For the thought and career of a leading Englishwoman of the age, a pioneer feminist sympathetic to the Revolution, one may read J. Todd, *Mary Wollstonecraft: A Revolutionary Life* (2000); C. Franklin, *Mary Wollstonecraft: A Literary Life* (2004); and L. Gordon, *Vindication: A Life of Mary Wollstonecraft* (2005).

In a comparative study C. B. A. Behrens, *Society, Government, and the Enlightenment: The Experiences of Eighteenth-Century France and Prussia* (1985) seeks to explain the different responses to the challenges of the age, while J. C. Lamberti, *Tocqueville and the Two Democracies* (trans. 1989) grapples with Tocqueville's explanations of why revolution led to an era of instability in France and to stable constitutional government in the United States.

Early efforts to study the phenomenon of revolution on a comparative basis include C. Brinton, *The Anatomy of Revolution* (1935, 1965) and H. Arendt, *On Revolution* (1963). J. Talmon in *The Origins of Totalitarian Democracy* (1952) and his other books saw the roots of twentieth-century dictatorship in the radical phase of the French Revolution—a controversial theme that has attracted strong criticism as well as some new support in recent scholarship. There is also a stimulating comparative analysis in A. J. Mayer, *The Furies: Violence and Terror in the French and Russian Revolutions* (2000).

Useful Web Sites
Readers will find an excellent collection of documents, images, and accounts of the French Revolution by visiting a Web site at George Mason University, *Liberty, Equality, Fraternity: Exploring the French Revolution*, which is located at http://chnm.gmu.edu/revolution/. There are additional sources to explore in the *Internet Modern History Sourcebook*, www.fordham.edu/halsall/mod/modsbook13.html, and there is a helpful site called *Links on the French Revolution* at the University of Portsmouth in Britain, http://userwww.port.ac.uk/andressd/frlinks.htm.

10. NAPOLEONIC EUROPE
Many of the books on the Revolution cited in the previous chapter continue on into the Napoleonic age. Informative surveys of Europe in the age of Napoleon are available in O. Connelly, *The French Revolution and Napoleonic Era* (rev.1991) and M. Broers, *Europe Under Napoleon, 1799–1815* (1996); and the latter author also examines Napoleon's imperial policies in *The Napoleonic Empire in Italy, 1796–1814: Cultural Imperialism in a European Context?* (2005). Other useful accounts include S. J. Woolf, *Napoleon's Integration of Europe* (1991); M. Lyons, *Napoleon Bonaparte and the Legacy of the French Revolution* (1994); O. Bernier, *The World in 1800* (2000); and A. Grab, *Napoleon and the Transformation of Europe* (2003). Two reference works for the age are O. Connelly et al. (eds.), *Historical Dictionary of Napoleonic France* (1985) and C. Emsley, *The Longman Companion to Napoleonic Europe* (1993).

Napoleon and Napoleonic France
For Napoleonic France a valuable synthesis of French society is L. Bergeron, *France under Napoleon* (trans. 1981), while R. Holtman, *The Napoleonic Revolution* (1967) is a brief judicious assessment. A more recent account may be found in A. Horne, *The Age of Napoleon* (2004). A. Boime continues his *Social History of Modern Art* with Vol. II: *Art in the Age of Bonapartism, 1800–1815* (1992).

Of the many biographies and biographically oriented studies of Napoleon, several may be singled out: J. M. Thompson, *Napoleon Bonaparte: His Rise and Fall* (1952); G. Lefebvre, *Napoleon* (2 vols., 1935; trans. 1969), a work of distinction; F. M. Markham, *Napoleon* (1964); and the comprehensive A. Schom, *Napoleon Bonaparte* (1997). Other accounts—all entitled *Napoleon*—by R. Dufraisse (trans. 1990), G. Ellis (1997), and R. S. Alexander (2001) may also be recommended. I. Woloch, *Napoleon and His Collaborators: The Making of a Dictatorship* (2001) shows how Napoleon rose to power and controlled his empire. The empire that Napoleon governed is studied in O. Connelly, *Napoleon's Satellite Kingdoms* (1965, 1990); G. Ellis, *The Napoleonic Empire* (rev. 2003); and C. Emsley, *Napoleonic Europe* (1993). Napoleon as a military leader is appraised in G. E. Rothenberg, *The Art of Warfare in the Age of Napoleon* (1978) and in the same author's *The Napoleonic Wars* (1999);

O. Connelly, *Blundering to Glory: Napoleon's Military Campaigns* (1987); and J. R. Elting, *Swords around a Throne: Napoleon's Grande Armée* (1988); D. Gates, *The Napoleonic Wars, 1803–1815* (1997); and A. Horne, *How Far from Austerlitz? Napoleon, 1805–1815* (1997).

The Continental blockade is studied in G. Ellis, *Napoleon's Continental Blockade* (1991). The Spanish military effort, along with popular resistance, is studied in books on the Peninsular War by D. Gates (1986) and C. J. Esdaile (1988). On the campaign in Russia, readers may consult N. Nicolson, *Napoleon: 1812* (1986). Britain's role in the later Napoleonic wars is described in R. Muir, *Britain and the Defeat of Napoleon, 1807–1815* (1996). On the final phase of the emperor's career one may read N. MacKenzie, *The Escape from Elba: The Fall and Flight of Napoleon, 1814–1815* (1982) and A. Schom, *One Hundred Days: Napoleon's Road to Waterloo* (1992).

The career of Napoleon's famous diplomat is examined in P. Dwyer, *Talleyrand* (2002). Studies of prominent women in this era include A Stuart, *The Rose of Martinique: A Life of Napoleon's Josephine* (2004); E. Bruce, *Napoleon and Josephine: The Improbable Marriage* (1995); J. C. Herold's older biography of Madame de Staël, *Mistress to an Age* (1958, 1979); R. Winegarten, *Mme de Staël* (1985); G. R. Besser, *Germaine de Staël Revisited* (1994); M. Fairweather, *Madame de Staël;* and M. Gutwirth et al. (eds.), *Germaine de Staël: Crossing the Borders* (1991). Napoleon's family is studied in F. Markham, *The Bonapartes* (1975).

Britain in the Time of Napoleon

The war era receives special attention in J. Ehrmann, *William Pitt the Younger* (2 vols., 1969–84) and in P. Mackesy, *War without Victory: The Downfall of Pitt, 1799–1802* (1984). There are biographies of Lord Nelson by B. Lavery (2003), and by R. Knight (2005), the latter providing perhaps the best scholarly study to date. Other accounts of the famous naval commander include the excellent works of J. Sugden, *Nelson: A Dream of Glory, 1758–1797* (2004) and J. S. A. Hayward, *For God and Glory: Lord Nelson and His Way of War* (2003). For Wellington one may turn to J. Strawson, *The Duke and the Emperor: Wellington and Napoleon* (1994) and R. Holmes, *Wellington: The Iron Duke* (2002). The impact of the war and other economic changes of the age are explored in C. Emsley, *British Society and the French Wars, 1973–1814* (1980) and in A. D. Harvey, *Britain in the Early Nineteenth Century* (1978). British expansion overseas is examined in C. A. Bayly, *Imperial Meridian: The British Empire and the World, 1780–1830* (1989). Important books on the slave trade in this era are D. B. Davis, *The Problem of Slavery in the Age of Revolution, 1770–1823* (1975, reissued 1999); J. Walvin, *Making the Black Atlantic: Britain and the African Diaspora* (2000); and R. Anstey, *The Atlantic Slave Trade and British Abolition, 1760–1810* (1975).

Other Countries in Napoleonic Times

For Anglo-American relations in the decades from 1795 to 1823, there are the three volumes of B. Perkins: *The First Rapprochement* (1955), *Prologue to War* (1961), and *Castlereagh and Adams* (1964). American developments during this era are examined in M. Smelser, *The Democratic Republic, 1801–1815* (1986) and in R. Horsman, *The New Republic: The United States of America 1789–1815* (2000). D. R. Hickey, *The War of 1812: A Forgotten Conflict* (1989) provides a useful description of the war; and a more recent military history is available in W. R. Borneman, *1812, The War that Forged a Nation* (2004).

For the German states, in addition to books cited in the two previous chapters, one may read H. Kohn, *Prelude to Nation-States: The French and German Experience, 1789–1815* (1967); H. Brunschwig, *Enlightenment and Romanticism in Eighteenth Century Prussia* (trans. 1974); and B. Giesen, *Intellectuals and the German Nation: Collective Identity in an Axial Age* (1998), a sociological account of German national identity in the Napoleonic era. For the reactions in Prussia there is the older, but still valuable, assessment of W. M. Simon, *The Failure of the Prussian Reform Movement, 1807–1819* (1955); one may also read W. O. Shanahan, *Prussian Military Reforms, 1786–1813* (1966). On the Prussian military theorist, P. Paret has written a comprehensive biography, *Clausewitz and the State* (1976, reissued 1985) and has edited the famous tract *On War* written in 1832 (ed. 1989).

For Russia in this era one may read the early sections of D. Saunders, *Russia in the Age of Reaction and Reform, 1801–1881* (1992); and for Alexander, one may consult A. McConnell, *Tsar Alexander I: Paternalistic Reformer* (1970); A. Palmer, *Alexander I, Tsar of War and Peace* (1975); and J. M. Hartley, *Alexander I* (1994).

The best account of Spain in the Napoleonic era is G. H. Lovett, *Napoleon and the Birth of Modern Spain* (2 vols., 1965), which may be supplemented by C. J. Esdaile, *Fighting Napoleon: Guerillas, Bandits and Adventurers in Spain, 1808–1814* (2004). The revolutionary events in the Western Hemisphere ignited by Napoleon's invasion of Spain are recounted in J. Lynch, *The Spanish American Revolutions, 1808–1820* (rev. 1986); in J. E. Rodríguez, *The Independence of Spanish America* (1998); in the wide-ranging, detailed account of L. D. Langley, *The Americas in the Age of Revolution 1750–1850* (1996); and in the relevant sections of L. Bethell (ed.), *The Cambridge History of Latin America, Vol. II: Colonial Latin America* (1988).

Wartime Diplomacy
and the Congress of Vienna

An informative study of the era's decisive diplomatic event can be found in T. Chapman, *The Congress of Vienna: Origins, Processes and Results* (1998). Detailed accounts of Metternich's role are available in E. E. Kraehe, *Metternich's German Policy, Vol. I: The Contest with Napoleon, 1799–1814* (1963) and Vol. II: *The Congress of Vienna, 1814–1815* (1983). H. Kissinger, *A World Restored: Metternich, Castlereagh and the Problem of Peace, 1812–1822* (1957, 1973) is a penetrating study by a scholar who later turned diplomat; it should now be supplemented with P. W. Schroeder, *The Transformation of European Politics, 1763–1848* (1994).

Useful Web Sites

A wide-ranging commercial site, *The Napoleonic Guide*, offers a valuable collection of sources, helpful links, and many other materials on the Napoleonic era at www.napoleonguide.com/. Readers will find other useful information at the site of *The Institute on Napoleon and the French Revolution*, www.fsu.edu/~napoleon/, which is maintained at Florida State University, and at the site of the *Napoleon Series*, www.napoleon-series.org, which is a comprehensive, well-maintained resource on all aspects of Napoleon's career and empire.

11. INDUSTRIES, IDEAS, AND THE STRUGGLE FOR REFORM, 1815–1848

The resettling of European institutions after the French Revolution and Napoleon in many ways marked the opening of a new historical era. There are thus numerous general, national, and topical histories that take their starting point around 1815.

Nineteenth-Century Europe

Helpful guides to all aspects of nineteenth-century history include M. S. Anderson, *The Ascendancy of Europe, 1815–1914* (rev. 2003); W. Simpson and M. Jones, *Europe, 1783–1914* (2000); and R. Gildea, *Barricades and Borders: Europe, 1800–1914* (rev. 2003). Useful discussion of European politics, society, and economic life is available in T. C. W. Blanning (ed.), *Short Oxford History of Europe: The Nineteenth Century* (2000); and the first half of the century may be surveyed in J. Sperber, *Revolutionary Europe, 1780–1850* (2000).

For a valuable work on the social history of the nineteenth century one may read M. Perrot (ed.), *From the French Revolution to the Great War* (1987), Vol. IV of the *History of Private Life*. Numerous other works on social and on women's history in these years are cited in chapter 15. For social classes one may turn to J. Kocka and A. Mitchell (eds.), *Bourgeois Society in Nineteenth-Century Europe* (1993); P. M. Pilbeam, *The Middle Classes in Europe, 1789–1914: France,* *Germany, Italy, and Russia* (1990); G. Crossick and H. G. Haupt, *The Petite Bourgeoisie in Europe, 1780–1914: Enterprise, Family and Independence* (1995); and for the upper classes, D. Lieven, *The Aristocracy in Europe, 1815–1914* (1992). For rural change in the late eighteenth and nineteenth centuries, there are J. Blum, *The End of the Old Order in Rural Europe* (1978) and A. Moulin, *Peasantry and Society in France since 1789* (trans. 1991). For religion one may read H. McLeod, *Religion and the People of Western Europe, 1789–1970* (1981); and O. Chadwick, *The Secularization of the European Mind in the Nineteenth Century* (1976). On women in the nineteenth century, in addition to general works already cited, useful books are P. Branca, *Women in Europe since 1750* (1978); S. Delamont and L. Duffin (eds.), *The Nineteenth-Century Woman: Her Cultural and Physical World* (1978); and P. S. Robertson, *An Experience of Women: Patterns and Change in Nineteenth-Century Europe* (1982). More recent works on women in this era include L. Abrams, *The Making of Modern Woman: Europe, 1789–1918* (2002); and R. G. Fuchs and V. E. Thompson, *Women in Nineteenth-Century Europe* (2005).

Europe, 1815–1848

General guides to the reorientation after 1815 may be found in W. L. Langer, *Political and Social Upheaval, 1832–1852* (1969); in J. Droz, *Europe Between Revolutions, 1815–1848* (trans. 1980); in Vol. IX of the *New Cambridge Modern History*, C. W. Crawley (ed.), *War and Peace in an Age of Upheaval, 1793–1830* (1965); and in Vol. X, of the same series, J. P. T. Bury (ed.), *The Zenith of European Power, 1830–1870* (1960). E. J. Hobsbawm has written one of his provocative interpretive histories on this era, *The Age of Revolution, 1789–1848* (1962, reissued 1996), the first volume of a trilogy on what he calls the "long nineteenth century," 1789–1914. Changes in art and culture are examined in A. Boime, *Art in An Age of Counterrevolution* (2004); and for the papacy in the revolutionary ferment of the age, one may read O. Chadwick, *The Popes and European Revolution* (1981).

Industrial Revolution

One of the best introductions to economic history during and since the Industrial Revolution is D. S. Landes, *The Unbound Prometheus: Technological Change and Industrial Development in Western Europe from 1750 to the Present* (1969). Other informative accounts are S. Pollard, *Peaceful Conquest: The Industrialization of Europe, 1760–1970* (1981); C. Trebilcock, *The Industrialization of the Continental Powers, 1780–1914* (1981); and T. Kemp, *Industrialization in Nineteenth Century Europe* (rev. 1985). There are thoughtful essays in R. Sylla and G. Toniolo (eds.), *Patterns of European Industrialization: The Nineteenth Century* (1991); in P. Mathias and J. A.

Davis (eds.), *The First Industrial Revolutions* (1990); and in M. Teich and R. Porter (eds.), *The Industrial Revolution in National Context: Europe and the USA* (1996). The social and political implications of an industrial civilization are examined in J. McManners, *European History: Men, Machines, and Freedom* (1967); and in E. A. Wrigley, *People, Cities, and Wealth: The Transformation of Traditional Society* (1987). S. M. Beaudoin (ed.), *Industrial Revolution* (2003) provides a summary and sampling of recent historical studies.

The complexities surrounding the emergence of industrialism in England are examined in numerous books. Brief informative accounts include a classic account by T. S. Ashton, *The Industrial Revolution, 1760–1830* (1948, reissued 1998); and other surveys by P. Deane, *The First Industrial Revolution* (rev. 1979); P. Mathias, *The First Industrial Nation: An Economic History of Britain, 1700–1914* (rev. 1983); and K. Morgan, *The Birth of Industrial Britain: Economic Change 1750–1850* (1999). Morgan has also written a companion volume, *The Birth of Industrial Britain: Social Change, 1750–1850* (2004). Additional interpretive accounts include M. Berg, *The Age of Manufactures, 1700–1820: Industry, Innovation, and Work in Britain* (1985); E. A. Wrigley, *Continuity, Chance, and Change: The Character of the Industrial Revolution in England* (1988); and P. Hudson, *The Industrial Revolution* (1992).

Insights into the nineteenth-century manufacturers are provided in A. Howe, *The Cotton Masters, 1830–1860* (1984); F. Crouzet, *The First Industrialists* (1985); L. Davidoff and C. Hall, *Family Fortunes: Men and Women of the English Middle Class, 1780–1850* (1987); and R. S. Fitton, *The Arkwrights: Spinners of Fortune* (1989). Changes in British agriculture may be studied in D. B. Grigg, *English Agriculture* (1989); K. D. M. Snell, *Annals of the Labouring Poor: Social Change and Agrarian England 1660–1900* (1985); and M. Overton, *Agricultural Revolution in England: The Transformation of the Agrarian Economy 1500–1850* (1996).

Social Consequences of Industrialism

There is a large and controversial literature on the effects of industrial change on the British working classes. F. Engels, *The Condition of the Working Class in England* [1844; reissued, D. McLellan (ed.), 1993] and A. Toynbee, *Lectures on the Industrial Revolution in England* (1884, 1969) were classic descriptions of such exploitation. Meanwhile J. L. Hammond and B. Hammond in several vehement books, such as The *Town Labourer, 1760–1832: The New Civilization* (1919) and *The Age of the Chartists* (1930), also stressed the economic abuse of the working classes. For somewhat modified views one may read M. I. Thomas, *Responses to Industrialization: The British Experience 1780–1850* (1976); and R. Gray, *The Factory Question and Industrial England, 1830–1860* (1996). P. Laslett, *The World We Have Lost: England before the Industrial Age* (rev. 1973) contrasts the new age with what he saw as the stability of the early modern centuries. The social experiences of workers are also discussed in H. J. Voth, *Time and Work in England 1750–1830* (2000). E. P. Thompson, *The Making of the English Working Class* (1963), in a highly influential book presents the picture of a militant working-class culture emerging to resist industrial society. For a helpful synthesis the reader may turn to two books by J. Rule: *The Experience of Labour in Eighteenth-Century English Industry* (1984) and *The Labouring Classes in Early Industrial England, 1750–1850* (1986). Agrarian labor is examined in R. Barry, *Rural England: Labouring Lives in the Nineteenth Century* (2004).

Working-class experiences are also depicted in D. Vincent, *Bread, Knowledge and Freedom: A Study of Nineteenth-Century Working Class Autobiography* (1981); I. Pinchbeck, *Women Workers and the Industrial Revolution, 1750–1850* (1930, reissued 1981); I. Pinchbeck and M. Hewitt, *Children in English Society* (2 vols., 1969–1973); and G. Holloway, *Women and Work in Britain since 1840* (2005). In a very different vein G. Himmelfarb, *The Idea of Poverty: England in the Early Industrial Age* (1984) and *Poverty and Compassion: The Moral Indignation of the Late Victorians* (1991) examine the writings of these years to demonstrate the complexities involved in defining poverty and social responsibilities.

For protest movements of the age D. G. Wright, *Popular Radicalism: The Working Class Experience, 1780–1880* (1988) is helpful as a summary; it may be supplemented by C. Tilley, *Popular Contention in Great Britain, 1758–1834* (1995, reissued 2005). Special studies include M. I. Thomas, *The Luddites: Machine-Breaking in Regency England* (1970); R. Reid, *The Peterloo Massacre* (1989); E. J. Hobsbawm and G. Rudé, *Captain Swing* (1969), a study of the rural poor and agrarian unrest; and J. Knott, *Popular Opposition to the 1834 Poor Law* (1986).

For the Chartists recommended books include T. Ward, *Chartism* (1973); D. Jones, *Chartism and the Chartists* (1975); D. Thompson, *The Chartists: Popular Politics in the Industrial Revolution* (1984); R. Brown, *Chartism* (1998); and J. K. Walton, *Chartism* (1999). The development of a political culture among British workers is described in J. Epstein, *In Practice: Studies in the Language and Culture of Popular Politics in Modern Britain* (2003). The creation in England and Ireland of a modern police system to suppress popular protest is studied in S. H. Palmer, *Police and Protest in England and Ireland, 1780–1850* (1988).

An overall view of social policy and reform is available in S. G. Checkland, *British Public Policy, 1776–1939* (1985). For the pressures to repeal the tariffs on grain, one may read P. A. Pickering and A. Tyrell, *The People's Bread: A History of the Anti-Corn Law League* (2000). On the Reform Bill of 1832, M. Brock, *The Great Reform Act* (1973) is an outstanding study; and N. D. LoPatin, *Political Unions, Popular Politics, and the Great Reform Act of 1832* (1999) discusses the mass political mobilizations of this period.

Several books study the antislavery movement as part of this age of protest. Slavery as an institution is masterfully explored in several books by D. B. Davis, including for these years, *The Problem of Slavery in the Age of Revolution, 1770–1823* (1975). The final phases of slavery in the Atlantic world are examined in R. Blackburn, *The Overthrow of Colonial Slavery* (1989); D. Eltis, *Economic Growth and the Ending of the Transatlantic Slave Trade* (1988); A. Hochschild, *Bury the Chains: Prophets and Rebels in the Fight to Free an Empire's Slaves* (2005), cited earlier; and S. Drescher's four books: *Econocide: British Slavery in the Era of Abolition* (1977), *Capitalism and Anti-Slavery: British Mobilization in Comparative Perspective* (1988), *From Slavery to Freedom: Comparative Studies in the Rise and Fall of Atlantic Slavery* (1999), and *The Mighty Experiment: Free Labor versus Slavery in British Emancipation* (2002). There are useful source materials on the abolitionist movement in the the third volume of K. Morgan (ed.), *The British Transatlantic Slave Trade* (4. vols. 2003). Other useful books on the antislavery movement include D. Turley, *The Culture of English Antislavery, 1780–1860* (1991) and J. Walvin, *Making the Black Atlantic: Britain and the African Diaspora* (2000), cited earlier, which provides a concise description of both the slave trade and the movement to abolish it.

For Britain after 1815 and the Victorian age that opened in 1837, readers may turn to W. A. Hay, *The Whig Revival, 1808–1830* (2005), and the older survey by N. Gash, *Aristocracy and People: Britain, 1815–1865* (1979). A. Briggs, *The Age of Improvement, 1783–1867* (rev. 2000) and his other books on social history are also useful. Of special importance are J. W. Osborne, *The Silent Revolution: The Industrial Revolution in England as a Source of Cultural Change* (1972); and H. Perkin, *The Origins of Modern English Society, 1780–1880* (1969, 1985).

Among the many biographies of the political leaders and reformers of the age, one may read F. A. Smith, *Lord Grey, 1764–1845* (1990); J. W. Derry, *Charles, Earl Grey: Aristocratic Reformer* (1992); N. Gash's outstanding study of Peel: *Mr. Secretary Peel and Sir Robert Peel* (2 vols.; rev. 1985); J. Pollock, *Wilberforce* (1978), and by the same author, *Shaftesbury, The Poor Man's Earl* (1985); J. Dyck, *William Cobbett and Rural Popular Protest* (1992); and N. C. Edsall, *Richard Cobden: Independent Radical* (1986). There are biographies of Robert Owen by G. D. H. Cole (rev. 1966) and M. I. Cole (1953, 1969);

and a more recent study by I. L. Donnachie, *Robert Owen: Owen of New Lanark and New Harmony* (2000). Radical social criticism is also studied in W. Stafford, *Socialism, Radicalism, and Nostalgia, 1775–1830* (1986). For women in the era one may turn to J. Perkin, *Victorian Women* (1993); K. Gleadle, *British Women in the Nineteenth Century* (2001); and two useful anthologies of writings by and about women: J. H. Murray, *Strongminded Women and Other Lost Voices from Nineteenth-Century England* (1982), and M. Sanders (ed.), *Women and Radicalism in the Nineteenth Century* (4 vols. 2001).

France, 1815–1848

Among general accounts that begin in this era are A. Jardin and A. J. Tudesq, *Restoration and Reaction, 1815–1848* (1973; trans. 1983); R. Magraw, *France, 1815–1914: The Bourgeois Century* (1983); J. P. T. Bury, *France, 1814–1940* (rev. 2003); R. Price, *A Social History of Nineteenth-Century France* (1988); W. Fortescue, *Revolution and Counter-Revolution in France, 1815–1852* (1988); and R. Tombs, *France, 1814–1914* (1996). A helpful work of reference is E. L. Newman (ed.), *Historical Dictionary of France from the 1815 Revolution to the Second Empire* (2 vols.; 1987). Of special interest is F. Furet, *Revolutionary France, 1770–1880* (trans. 1992), which describes the struggle in the nineteenth century to absorb the changes introduced by the Revolution. For economic developments one may turn to F. Caron, *An Economic History of Modern France* (trans. 1979) and R. Price, *An Economic History of Modern France, 1730–1914* (1981). An insightful monograph illuminating the sexual division of labor in French rural industry is G. L. Gullickson, *The Spinners and Weavers of Auffray* (1986). The essays in K. S. Vincent and A. Klairmont-Lingo (eds.), *The Human Tradition in Modern France* (2000), covering the years 1789 to the present, seek to restore the human and personal element in French historical writing for these years.

For the years 1815–1830 G. de Bertier de Sauvigny, *The Bourbon Restoration* (trans. 1966) remains valuable, while S. Mellon, *The Uses of History: A Study of Historians in the French Restoration* (1958) and A. B. Spitzer, *The French Generation of 1820* (1987) add special insights. The evolving liberal movements of this era are discussed in L. Kramer, *Lafayette in Two Worlds* (1996), which also describes the links between France and America; and the liberal opposition is further examined in R. S. Alexander, *Re-Writing the French Revolutionary Tradition: Liberal Opposition and the Fall of the Bourbon Monarchy* (2003). Conservative ideas and activities are analyzed in D. Porch, *Army and Revolution: France, 1815–1848* (1974); and R. Rémond, *The Right Wing in France: From 1815 to de Gaulle* (trans. 1966), useful for this period and for the twentieth century. An insightful study of an important conservative thinker is available in O. Bradley, *A Modern Maistre: The Social and Political Thought of Joseph de Maistre* (1999). For religion A. Dansette, *The Religious History of Modern France* (2 vols.; trans. 1961) may be supplemented by R. Gibson, *A Social History of French Catholicism, 1789–1914* (1989) and N. Ravitch, *The Catholic Church and the French Nation, 1685–1985* (1990).

The July Monarchy

For the revolutionary events of 1830 one may read D. H. Pinkney, *The French Revolution of 1830* (1972); P. Pilbeam, *The 1830 Revolution in France* (1991), an insightful analytical study rather than a narrative; and C. H. Church, *Europe in 1830: Revolution and Political Change* (1983), which places the revolution in its Europeanwide setting. Other aspects of the July Revolution, with attention to developments outside Paris, are examined in J. Popkin, *Press, Revolution, and Social Identities in France, 1830–1835* (2002). For Louis Philippe's reign one may read H. A. C. Collingham, *The July Monarchy* (1988), a detailed political account, and D. H. Pinkney, *Decisive Years in France, 1840–1847* (1986), which presents the years of the July Monarchy as a watershed in French social and economic development. Labor and popular stirrings are examined in R. J. Bezucha, *The Lyon Uprising of 1834* (1974) and E. Berenson, *Populist Religion and Left-Wing Politics in France, 1830–1852* (1984).

An impressive study in cultural and social history focusing on the importance of the Revolution in the political culture and lives of the people is M. Agulhon, *The Republic in the Village: The People of the Var from the French Revolution to the Second Republic* (1971; trans. 1982). Diverse approaches to social history are found also in W. H. Sewell, Jr., *The Language of Labor from the Old Regime to 1848* (1980) and two books by W. M. Reddy, *The Rise of Market Culture: The Textile Trade and French Society, 1750–1900* (1984) and *The Invisible Code: Honor and Sentiment in Postrevolutionary France, 1814–1848* (1997). P. N. Stearns explores class relationships in *Paths to Authority: The Middle Class and the Industrial Labor Force in France, 1820–1848* (1978). Studies in urban history include J. M. Merriman, *The Red City: Limoges and the French Nineteenth Century* (1985) and *The Margins of City Life: Explorations of the French Urban Frontier, 1815–1851* (1991); and W. H. Sewell, Jr., *Structure and Mobility: The Men and Women of Marseille, 1820–1870* (1985). L. Kramer, *Threshold of a New World: Intellectuals and the Exile Experience in Paris, 1830–1848* (1988) conveys the cultural vitality of the city as it appeared to exiles like Marx and others. An older study of importance is L. Chevalier, *Laboring Classes and Dangerous Classes in Paris during the First Half of the Nineteenth Century* (trans. 1973).

Biographical accounts of two historians who became important political leaders in these years are

J. P. T. Bury and R. P. Tombs, *Thiers, 1797–1877* (1986) and D. Johnson, *Guizot: Aspects of French History, 1787–1874* (1963, 1975). For the last Bourbon king one may read V. D. Beach, *Charles X of France* (1971); and for Louis Philippe, T. Howarth, *Citizen-King* (1961). Readers will find an excellent introduction to the lives of women in this era in J. B. Margadant (ed.), *The New Biography: Performing Femininity in Nineteenth-Century France* (2000).

Germany, 1815–1848

J. J. Sheehan, *German History, 1770–1866* (1990) is invaluable for these years. Also informative are D. Blackbourn, *History of Germany, 1780–1918: The Long Nineteenth Century* (rev. 2003); F. B. Tipton, *A History of Modern Germany Since 1815* (2003); W. Carr, *A History of Germany, 1815–1990* (1991); and H. James, *A German Identity, 1770–1990* (1990), perceptive on economic and other matters. Two important inquiries into the failure of German liberal democracy before 1914 are J. J. Sheehan, *German Liberalism in the Nineteenth Century* (1978) and J. L. Snell and H. A. Schmitt, *The Democratic Movement in Germany, 1789–1914* (1976). There are thoughtful essays in J. Breuilly (ed.), *19th-Century Germany: Politics, Culture, and Society 1780–1918* (2001); and in L. E. Jones and K. H. Jarausch (eds.), *In Search of a Liberal Germany: German Liberalism from 1789 to the Present* (1990).

Austria, Russia, Poland, Greece, Spain, Italy, and Other Countries

On the Habsburg monarchy after 1815, C. A. Macartney, *The Habsburg Empire, 1790–1918* (1969) is a masterful survey with full treatment of the nationalities. Recommended also are A. Sked, *The Decline and Fall of the Habsburg Empire 1815–1918* (rev. 2001); and R. Okey, *The Habsburg Monarchy, c. 1765–1918: From Enlightenment to Eclipse* (2000). Foreign affairs are emphasized in B. Jelavich, *The Habsburg Empire in European Affairs, 1814–1918* (1969) and F. R. Bridge, *The Habsburg Monarchy among the Great Powers, 1815–1918* (1991). All aspects of Austrian history on into the twentieth century are ably treated in B. Jelavich, *Modern Austria: Empire and Republic, 1815–1986* (1987).

For Europe from the Baltic to the Aegean, R. Okey, *Eastern Europe, 1740–1985* (rev. 1986) covers these years; and another well-informed, comparative study of the region may be found in T. I. Behrend, *History Derailed: Central and Eastern Europe in the Long Nineteenth Century* (2003). For Russia, two outstanding accounts are H. Seton-Watson, *The Russian Empire, 1801–1917* (1967) and D. Saunders, *Russia in the Age of Reaction and Reform, 1801–1881* (1993). On the life of the early nineteenth-century tsar, there is the work of J. M. Hartley, *Alexander I* (1994). A major study of Alexander's successor is W. B. Lincoln, *Nicholas I: Emperor and Autocrat of All the Russias*

(1978). For these years one may also read M. Zetling, *The Decembrists* (1985); M. Raeff, *The Decembrist Movement* (1966), a narrative with documents; and P. O'Meara, *The Decembrist Pavel Pestel: Russia's First Republican* (2003), which describes the life of a key participant. For Poland, one may turn to the second volume of N. Davies, *A History of Poland: God's Playground* (2 vols.; 1981); his briefer *Heart of Europe: A Short History of Poland* (1986); and P. Wandycz, *The Lands of Partitioned Poland 1795–1918* (1974).

For the Balkans in these years informative volumes are B. Jelavich, *History of the Balkans* (2 vols.; 1983); B. Jelavich and C. Jelavich, *The Establishment of the Balkan National States, 1804–1920* (1980); and S. Pavlowitch, *A History of the Balkans, 1804–1945* (1999). For Greece a balanced authoritative study is R. Clogg, *A Concise History of Greece* (rev. 2002). Stirrings in this period are described in C. M. Woodhouse, *The Greek War of Independence* (1952); D. Brewer, *The Greek War of Independence* (2003); and R. Clogg (ed.), *The Struggle for Greek Independence* (1973), a collection of essays.

For the initial phases of the ferment in Italy good introductions are D. Beales, *The Risorgimento and the Unification of Italy* (1971); H. Hearder, *Italy in the Age of the Risorgimento, 1790–1870* (1983); S. Woolf, *A History of Italy, 1700–1860* (1986); and C. M. Lovett, *The Democratic Movement in Italy, 1830–1876* (1982).

For Belgium and the Dutch Netherlands in these and subsequent years, a discerning account by an eminent Dutch historian is E. H. Kossman, *The Low Countries, 1780–1940* (1978). The emerging importance of Belgium in international affairs is traced in J. E. Helmreich, *Belgium and Europe: A Study of Small-Power Diplomacy* (1976). For Spain, a balanced, comprehensive account is R. Carr, *Spain, 1808–1975* (rev. 1982), which may be supplemented by the more recent accounts in C. J. Esdaile, *Spain in the Liberal Age: From Constitution to Civil War, 1808 1939* (2000); and in C. J. Ross, *Spain, 1812–1996* (2000).

Nineteenth-Century Thought

Two overall surveys carrying cultural and intellectual history forward to the twentieth century are G. L. Mosse, *The Culture of Western Europe: The Nineteenth and Twentieth Centuries* (rev. 1988) and R. N. Stromberg, *European Intellectual History since 1789* (rev. 1993). A special theme is skillfully explored in O. Chadwick, *The Secularization of the European Mind in the Nineteenth Century* (1976). Older general works include W. H. Coates, H. V. White, and J. S. Schapiro, *The Emergence of Liberal Humanism: An Intellectual History of Western Europe* (2 vols. 1966, 1970), which examines the nineteenth century in the second volume; M. Peckham, *Beyond the Tragic Vision: The Quest for Identity in the Nineteenth Century*

(1962); and M. Mandelbaum, *History, Man, and Reason: A Study in Nineteenth-Century Thought* (1971).

Among the many books on Hegel and Hegelian thought one may turn to L. Dickey, *Hegel: Religion, Economics, and the Politics of Spirit, 1770–1807* (1987); T. Pinkard, *Hegel: A Biography* (2000); F. C. Beiser, *Hegel* (2005); and J. E. Toews, *Hegelianism: The Path toward Dialectical Humanism 1805–1841* (1985), a difficult but rewarding book.

The "Isms"

On the nature of ideology, the best introduction is D. McLellan, *Ideology* (rev. 1995). Also helpful are D. Hawkes, *Ideology* (rev. 2003); and G. Rudé, *Ideology and Popular Protest* (1980); and for political alignments, D. Caute, *The Left in Europe since 1789* (1966); and H. Rogger and E. Weber (eds.), *The European Right: A Historical Profile* (1965).

The vast literature on nationalism, including many older studies by C. J. H. Hayes and H. Kohn, may be approached through P. Alter, *Nationalism* (rev. 1994); E. J. Hobsbawm, *Nations and Nationalism since 1780* (rev. 1992); E. Gellner, *Nations and Nationalism* (1983); several books by A. D. Smith, *The Ethnic Origins of Nations* (1986), *National Identity* (1991), and *Chosen Peoples* (2003); and L. Kramer, *Nationalism: Political Cultures in Europe and America, 1775–1865* (1998). A useful collection of essays is available in G. Eley and R. G. Suny (eds.), *Becoming National: A Reader* (1996). B. Anderson's book, *Imagined Communities: Reflections on the Origin and Spread of Nationalism* (rev. 1991), has contributed an influential conceptual framework for much of the recent scholarship on nationalist movements. An impressive comparative work on nationalism, studying England, the United States, France, Germany, and Russia, is L. Greenfeld, *Nationalism: Five Roads to Modernity* (1992); and her more recent critical analysis of nationalist thought is available in *Nationalism: A Critical Introduction* (2002).

Political and cultural meanings of romanticism are examined from diverse political perspectives in J. Barzun, *Classic, Romantic, and Modern* (rev. 1961, 1975) and *Berlioz and the Romantic Century* (1950, 1982); M. H. Abrams, *Natural Supernaturalism: Tradition and Revolution in Romantic Literature* (1971); J. McGann, *The Romantic Ideology: A Critical Investigation* (1983); N. Rosenblum, *Another Liberalism: Romanticism and the Reconstruction of Liberal Thought* (1987); N. V. Riasanovsky, *The Emergence of Romanticism* (1992); and M. Cranston, *The Romantic Movement* (1994).

For classical liberalism, a thoughtful introduction is J. Gray, *Liberalism* (rev. 1995), which may be read along with A. Arblaster, *The Rise and Decline of Western Liberalism* (1984); J. G. Merquior, *Liberalism, Old and New* (1991); P. Kelly, *Liberalism* (2005); and J. Rawls, *Political Liberalism* (rev. 2005), a searching philosophical inquiry. An influential earlier account was H. J. Laski, *The Rise of European Liberalism* (1936, reissued 1997). An insightful collection of essays by Isaiah Berlin, *The Crooked Timber of Humanity* (1990, 1998), stresses a liberal's suspicion of utopian schemes to change human beings in revolutionary ways. The interaction between liberal theory and political practice is examined in A. S. Kahan, *Liberalism in Nineteenth-Century Europe: The Political Culture of Limited Suffrage* (2003). Readers will find a useful anthology in D. Sidorsky (ed.), *The Liberal Tradition in European Thought* (1970).

Among books on the leading exemplar of classical liberalism, one may read, W. Stafford, *John Stuart Mill (1998)*, a concise introductory account; N. Capaldi, *John Stuart Mill: A Biography* (2004); G. Himmelfarb, *On Liberty and Liberalism: The Case of John Stuart Mill* (1974); B. Semmel, *John Stuart Mill and the Pursuit of Virtue* (1984); and the unsympathetic M. Cowling, *Mill and Liberalism* (rev. 1990). Diverse views of Mill's key themes may be found in J. Skorupski, (ed.), *The Cambridge Companion to Mill* (1998). In an area where Mill and Harriet Mill pioneered, A. Rossi has edited John Stuart Mill and Harriet Taylor Mill, *Essays on Sex Equality* (1970). Mill and others are studied in S. R. Letwin, *The Pursuit of Certainty: David Hume, Jeremy Bentham, John Stuart Mill, Beatrice Webb* (1963). Bentham is also studied in a biography by M. Mack (1963) and in brief appraisals by J. Dinwiddy (1989), and J. E. Crimmins (2003). For the French setting an admirable study is G. A. Kelly, *The Humane Comedy: Constant, Tocqueville, and French Liberalism* (1992), which may be supplemented by B. Fontana, *Benjamin Constant and the Post-Revolutionary Mind* (1991).

For the persistence of conservatism one may read P. Viereck, *Conservatism Revisited: The Revolt against Revolt, 1815–1949* (rev. 2005); J. Weiss, *Conservatism in Europe, 1770–1945* (1977); R. A. Nisbet, *Conservatism: Dream and Reality* (1986); T. Honderich, *Conservatism* (1991); and P. Suvanto, *Conservatism from the French Revolution to the 1990s* (trans. 1997). An influential analysis of conservative thought is available in A. O. Hirshman, *The Rhetoric of Reaction* (1991).

Good starting places for the study of the socialist and revolutionary tradition are F. E. Manuel, *The Prophets of Paris: Turgot, Condorcet, Saint-Simon, Fourier, Comte* (1962), which stresses the link between Enlightenment ideas and nineteenth-century social thought, and J. H. Billington, *Fire in the Minds of Men: Origins of the Revolutionary Faith* (1980), which focuses on the more conspiratorial revolutionaries. F. E. Manuel and F. P. Manuel masterfully trace an important theme in *Utopian Thought in the Western World* (1979), which may be supplemented with two books by K. Kumar, *Utopia and Anti-Utopia in Modern Times* (1987), and *Utopianism* (1991).

Books on Marx and Marxism will be cited in the following chapter. The best one-volume introduction to the origins and evolution of socialism is A. S. Lindemann, *A History of European Socialism* (1983). Informative also are L. Derfler, *Socialism since Marx: A Century of the European Left* (1973); W. Lerner, *A History of Socialism and Communism in Modern Times* (rev. 1994); and B. Crick, *Socialism* (1987). G. Lichtheim, *The Origins of Socialism* (1969), *A Short History of Socialism* (1970), and his other writings are especially valuable. Two large-scale comprehensive studies are G. D. H. Cole, *A History of Socialist Thought* (4 vols.; 1953–1956), covering the years 1789–1939; and C. Landauer and others, *European Socialism* (2 vols.; 1960), which covers about the same years. Utopian socialists are studied in two excellent books by J. F. Beecher: *Charles Fourier: The Visionary and His World* (1987) and *Victor Considérant and the Rise and Fall of French Romantic Socialism* (2001). Other early socialists are examined in F. E. Manuel, *The New World of Henri Saint-Simon* (1956); G. G. Iggers, *The Cult of Authority: The Political Cult of the Saint-Simonians* (rev. 1970); and R. B. Carlisle, *The Proffered Crown: Saint Simonianism and the Doctrine of Hope* (1987).

Early feminist thought is discussed in J. Rendall, *The Origins of Modern Feminism: Women in Britain, France and the United States, 1780–1860* (1985); M. LeGates, *In Their Time: A History of Feminism in Western Society* (2001); K. Offen, *European Feminisms, 1700–1950: A Political History* (2000); G. Bock, *Women in European History* (trans. 2002); S. K. Foley, *Women in France Since 1789* (2004); and C. G. Moses and L. W. Rabine, *Feminism, Socialism, and French Romanticism* (1993), a valuable book that includes excerpts from the texts of early feminist authors. Recent biographies on important women writers in this era include S. Grogan, *Flora Tristan* (1998); B. Jack, *George Sand* (2000); R. Bolster, *Marie d'Agoult: the Rebel Countess* (2001); and P. Stock-Morton, *The Life of Marie d'Agoult, alias Daniel Stern* (2001). The ideas of writers such as Sand and d'Agoult are also examined in W. Walton, *Eve's Proud Descendants: Four Women Writers and Republican Politics in Nineteenth-Century France* (2000).

On the link between socialism and women activists, one may read M. J. Boxer and J. H. Quataert (eds.), *Socialist Women: European Socialist Feminism in the Nineteenth and Early Twentieth Centuries* (1978) and other books to be cited in Chapter 15. A. Fried and R. Sanders, *Socialist Thought: A Documentary History* (rev. 1993) is a handy anthology.

Economic Thought

An innovative and rewarding book is M. Berg, *The Machinery Question and the Making of Political Economy, 1815–1848* (1980). There are valuable accounts of key thinkers in D. P. O'Brien, *The Classical Economists Revisited* (rev. 2004); in J. K. Galbraith, *The Age of Uncertainty* (1977), a sprightly series of essays on economic thinkers from Adam Smith to the present; and in R. Heilbroner, *The Worldly Philosophers* (rev. 1999), which is useful on the economic liberals. For Adam Smith's moral and economic ideas, an especially thoughtful overview is J. Z. Muller, *Adam Smith in His Time and Ours: Designing the Decent Society* (1992). Muller has expanded his history of economic ideas in *The Mind and the Market: Capitalism in Modern European Thought* (2002). Informative also are D. Winch, *Adam Smith's Politics* (1978); and P. H. Werhane, *Adam Smith and His Legacy for Modern Capitalism* (1991). For Malthus, a useful biographical account is P. James, *Population Malthus: His Life and Times* (1979), while S. Hollander, *The Economics of Thomas Robert Malthus* (1996) analyzes his ideas.

International Affairs after the Congress of Vienna

For diplomacy and international affairs, two valuable surveys are F. R. Bridge and R. Bullen, *The Great Powers and the European States System, 1851–1914* (rev. 2005) and N. Rich, *Great Power Diplomacy, 1815–1914* (1980). An important reevaluation is P. W. Schroeder, *The Transformation of European Politics, 1763–1848* (1994), which sees the era after 1815 not as a restoration but as a revolutionary transformation of international relations; Schroeder has also written *Metternich's Diplomacy at Its Zenith, 1820–1823* (1962). H. Kissinger, the former American Secretary of State, discusses the post-1815 years in *Diplomacy* (1994). In addition to older studies by C. K. Webster and other historians of the era of Castlereagh and Palmerston, one may turn to C. J. Bartlett, *Castlereagh* (1967); J. Derry, *Castlereagh* (1976); W. Hinde, *George Canning* (1989); K. Bourne, *Palmerston: The Early Years* (1982); and P. R. Ziegler, *Palmerston* (2003). American foreign policy in these years is assessed in B. Perkins, *The Creation of a Republican Empire, 1776–1865* (1993).

The involvement of the European powers and the United States in Latin America is studied in R. Miller, *Britain and Latin American in the Nineteenth and Twentieth Centuries* (1993); D. Perkins, *A History of the Monroe Doctrine* (1941, 1963); and E. R. May, *The Making of the Monroe Doctrine* (1975, reissued 1992). A special perspective is provided in J. J. Johnson, *A Hemisphere Apart: The Foundations of United States Policy toward Latin America* (1990), which focuses on the years 1815–1830. For all aspects of the colonial revolutions one may turn to J. Lynch, *The Spanish American Revolutions, 1808–1821* (rev. 1986); M. P. Costeloe, *Response to Revolution: Imperial Spain and the Spanish American Revolutions, 1810–1840* (1986); D. Bushnell and N. Macaulay, *The Emergence of Latin America in the Nineteenth Century* (rev. 1994); and the chapters in Vol. III of L. Bethell (ed.), *The Cambridge History of Latin America* (1988). Biographical studies are available in

D. Bushnell, *Simón Bolívar: Liberation and Disappointment* (2003); J. L. Salcedo-Bastardo, *Bolívar: A Continent and its Destiny* (trans. 1977); and J. Kinsbrunner, *Bernardo O'Higgins* (1968).

Useful Web Sites

Readers will find excellent sources for this era through the links in Fordham University's *Internet Modern History Sourcebook* at www.fordham.edu/halsall/mod/modsbook.html; this outstanding resource includes materials on the Industrial Revolution; "isms" such as socialism, romanticism, feminism, and nationalism; the history of major European nations; and the new nineteenth-century nations in the Americas. There are also valuable materials on nineteenth-century thought and the "isms" at *The Stanford Encyclopedia of Philosophy*, http://plato.stanford.edu/; other helpful sites include *The Nationalism Project* at www.nationalismproject.org; *Utilitarian Resources* at www.utilitarianism.com, with links to numerous works on this influential nineteenth-century intellectual and political movement; and *BBC History, Industrialisation* at www.bbc.co.uk/history/society_culture/industrialisation, which provides interesting material on the new industrial economy in Britain.

12. REVOLUTIONS AND THE REIMPOSITION OF ORDER, 1848–1870

An older but still useful synthesis for the revolutions of 1848 is W. L. Langer, *Political and Social Upheaval, 1832–1852* (1969). Other informative studies include P. N. Stearns, *1848: The Revolutionary Tide in Europe* (1974); P. Jones, *The 1848 Revolutions* (rev. 1991); J. Sperber, *The European Revolutions, 1848–1851* (rev. 2005); and the essays in R. J. W. Evans and H. P. Von Strandmann, *The Revolutions in Europe, 1848–1849* (2000). Of special interest is L. B. Namier, *1848: The Revolution of the Intellectuals* (1944, 1992), which sees the events in central and eastern Europe as ushering in an age of nationalism, not of liberalism. E. J. Hobsbawm continues his provocative triology for the years 1789–1914 with *The Age of Capital, 1848–1875* (1976). A. J. P. Taylor, *The Struggle for Mastery in Europe, 1848–1918* (1954, reissued 1971) remains unequalled as a study of international affairs for these years.

Revolutions in Various Countries

FRANCE. General histories include G. Duveau, *The Making of a Revolution* (trans. 1968); R. Price, *The French Second Republic: A Social History* (1972); and W. Fortescue, *France and 1848: The End of Monarchy* (2005). Informative also are the essays edited by R. Price, *Revolution and Reaction: 1848 and the Second French Republic* (1976), while M. Agulhon, *The Republican Experiment, 1848–1852* (1983) subtly examines republican and revolutionary symbolism.

Studies offering insights into popular militancy include P. H. Amann, *Revolutions and Mass Democracy: The Paris Club Movement in 1848* (1976); M. Traugott, *The Armies of the Poor* (rev. 2002); J. M. Merriman, *The Agony of the Republic: The Repression of the Left in Revolutionary France, 1848–1851* (1978); and T. W. Margadant, *French Peasants in Revolt: The Insurrection of 1851* (1979).

HABSBURG LANDS. For Austria there are several volumes on the Habsburg empire cited in Chapter 11, but for more specific studies of Francis Joseph and his long reign from 1848 to 1916 one may read A. Palmer, *Twilight of the Habsburgs: The Life and Times of Emperor Francis Joseph* (1995) and S. Beller, *Francis Joseph* (1996).

For the empire in revolt one may read R. J. Rath, *The Viennese Revolution of 1848* (1957); H. J. Hahns, *The 1848 Revolutions in German-Speaking Europe* (2001), which also discusses events in Germany; S. Z. Pech, *The Czech Revolution of 1848–1849* (1979); and I. Deák, *The Lawful Revolution: Louis Kossuth and the Hungarians, 1848–1849* (1979), a vivid account. The end of the revolution is described in A. Sked, *The Survival of the Habsburg Empire* (1979) and I. W. Roberts, *Nicholas I and the Russian Intervention in Hungary* (1991).

ITALY. Books on the beginnings of the Risorgimento have been cited in Chapter 11; others on unification will be described in the chapter that follows. Studies relevant to 1848 are G. M. Trevelyan's classic account, *Garibaldi's Defense of the Roman Republic, 1848–1849* (1907, reissued 1988) and P. Ginsborg, *Daniele Manin and the Venetian Revolution of 1848–49* (1979). There is also useful information on the people and events of this era in J. A. Davis (ed.), *Italy in the Nineteenth Century: 1796–1900* (2000). GERMANY AND THE FRANKFURT ASSEMBLY. In addition to L. B. Namier, *1848: The Revolution of the Intellectuals* (1946, 1992), cited earlier, which is sharply critical of the Frankfurt Assembly, informative studies include E. Eyck, *The Frankfurt Parliament, 1848–1849* (1968), a detailed account of the assembly itself; W. Siemann, *The German Revolution of 1848–49* (trans. 1998); and J. Sperber, *Rhineland Radicals: The Democratic Movement and the Revolution of 1848–1849* (1991), which focuses on the more radical elements in the revolution.

ENGLAND AND IRELAND. The confrontations with both Chartism and Irish nationalism are recounted in J. Saville, *1848: The British State and the Chartist Movement* (1987); other books on Chartism have been noted in Chapter 11. A special subject is graphically treated in C. B. Woodham-Smith, *The Great Hunger: Ireland 1845–1849* (1962), which may be supplemented by J. S. Donnelly, *The Great Irish Potato Famine* (2001).

Marx and Marxism

D. McLellan, *Karl Marx: A Biography* (rev. 1995) is an outstanding account of Marx's life and thought;

other insightful studies include J. Seigel, *Marx's Fate: The Shape of a Life* (1978, 1993); I. Berlin, *Karl Marx: His Life and Environment* (rev. 1996); S. K. Padover, *Karl Marx: An Intimate Biography* (1978); B. Mazlish, *The Meaning of Karl Marx* (1984); and A. W. Wood, *Karl Marx* (rev. 2004), a work that examines Marx's philosophy. An amusing but overly flippant account is F. Wheen, *Karl Marx: A Life* (2000). Helpful for the life and thought of Engels are studies by S. Marcus (1974); D. McLellan (1978); T. Carver (1990); J. D. Hunley (1990), and S. H. Rigby (1992).

On Marxism and the theoretical foundations of socialism, there is an enormous and controversial literature, to which the books cited for the beginnings of socialism in Chapter 11 and for the years after 1870 in Chapter 15 may offer some additional guidance. Recommended studies include J. Elster, *An Introduction to Karl Marx* (1986); R. N. Hunt, *The Political Ideas of Marx and Engels* (2 vols.; 1976–1984); R. Tucker, *The Marxian Revolutionary Idea* (1969) and *Philosophy and Myth in Karl Marx* (rev. 2001); G. Lichtheim, *Marxism: An Historical and Critical Study* (1961); and S. Avinieri, *The Social and Political Thought of Karl Marx* (1968, 1990). The intellectual context that shaped Marx's early work is examined in W. Breckman, *Marx, The Young Hegelians, and the Origins of Radical Social Theory* (1999).

E. Wilson's older book, *To the Finland Station: A Study in the Writing and Acting of History* (1940, reissued 1972), is an imaginative discussion of the use of history by socialists and non-socialists. Insights into the Marxist interpretation of history are provided in G. A. Cohen, *Karl Marx's Theory of History: A Defence* (rev. 2001), an especially cogent analysis; W. H. Shaw, *Marx's Theory of History* (1978); and M. Rader, *Marx's Interpretation of History* (1979). R. Williams, *Marxism and Literature* (1977) demonstrates one aspect of the wider applicability of Marx's theories.

For Auguste Comte and positivism there are available A. R. Standley, *Auguste Comte* (1981), the best brief introduction; M. Pickering, *Auguste Comte: An Intellectual Biography* (1992); W. M. Simon, *European Positivism in the Nineteenth Century* (1963); D. G. Charlton, *Positivist Thought in France during the Second Empire* (1959); and T. R. Wright, *The Religion of Humanity: The Impact of Comtean Positivism on Victorian Britain* (1986). G. Lenzer has edited *Auguste Comte and Positivism: The Essential Writings* (rev. 1998).

Napoleon III and Bonapartism

The best overviews are in A. Plessis, *The Rise and Fall of the Second Empire, 1852–1871* (trans. 1985) and in R. Price, *The French Second Empire: An Anatomy of Political Power* (2001). Other informative accounts are J. M. Thompson, *Louis Napoleon and the Second Empire* (1954, 1967); G. P. Gooch, *The Second Empire* (1960), a collection of judicious essays; J. P. T. Bury, *Napoleon III and the Second Empire* (1964); and

W. H. C. Smith, *Second Empire and Commune: France, 1848–1871* (rev. 1996), which emphasizes the regime's disastrous foreign policy and collapse. A useful reference tool is W. E. Echard (ed.), *Historical Dictionary of the French Second Empire* (1985).

Biographical treatments include T. A. B. Corley, *Democratic Despot: A Life of Napoleon III* (1961); W. H. C. Smith, *Napoleon III* (1973); J. F. McMillan, *Napoleon III* (1991); and F. Bresler, *Napoleon III* (1999). There are three evocative explorations of the age by R. L. Williams: *The World of Napoleon III* (1957), *The Mortal Napoleon III* (1971), and *Manners and Murders in the World of Louis Napoleon* (1975); and a study by D. Bagley, *Napoleon III and His Regime: An Extravaganza* (2000). On the reconstruction of Paris in these years, one may read D. H. Pinkney, *Napoleon III and the Rebuilding of Paris* (1958); D. P. Jordan, *Transforming Paris: The Life and Labors of Baron Haussmann* (1995); and N. Papayanis, *Planning Paris Before Haussmann* (2004), a study of the ideas that preceded and influenced Haussmann. A recent, sympathetic biography of the empress may be found in D. Seward, *Eugénie: The Empress and Her Empire* (2004). Tendencies in later years to praise Napoleon III for presiding over political stability are explored in S. L. Campbell, *The Second Empire Revisited: A Study in French Historiography* (1978).

Useful Web Sites

Readers will find an extensive collection of writings on all aspects of the revolutions by visiting the *Encyclopedia of Revolutions of 1848* at www.cats.ohiou.edu/~Chastain. There are useful materials on the history of Marxism, beginning with Marx but including many other writers and political activists at the *Marxists Internet Archive*, www.marxists.org; and additional information on the era of 1848 is available at the previously cited *Internet Modern History Sourcebook*, which is located at the Fordham University site, www.fordham.edu/halsall/mod/modsbook.html. Further information on Napoleon III may be found at Napoleon.Org, a site that includes images and other materials on the French Second Empire as well as the history of Napoleon I at www.napoleon.org.

13. THE GLOBAL CONSOLIDATION OF LARGE NATION-STATES, 1859–1871

J. P. T. Bury (ed.), *The Zenith of European Power, 1830–1871* (1966), cited in Chapter 11, offers many informative chapters; and N. Rich, *The Age of Nationalism and Reform, 1850–1890* (1970), provides a balanced synthesis. Analytical books on nationalism have been cited in Chapter 11.

The Crimean War

For the war itself and its complexities one may read A. Palmer, *The Banner of Battle, The Story of the Crimean War* (1987); T. Royle, *Crimea: The Great Crimean War, 1854–1856* (2001); and a concise account by J. Sweetman, *The Crimean War* (2001). The diplomatic aspects are studied in W. Baumgart, *The Peace of Paris, 1856* (1981); N. Rich, *Why the Crimean War? A Cautionary Tale* (1985); D. Wetzel, *The Crimean War: A Diplomatic History* (1985); and D. M. Goldfrank, *The Origins of the Crimean War* (1993). An impressive book rehabilitating Austrian policy is P. W. Schroeder, *Austria, Great Britain, and the Crimean War: The Destruction of the European Concert* (1972), while J. S. Curtiss, *Russia's Crimean War* (1979) sees the Western powers as more responsible than Russia for the outbreak. The famous "Charge of the Light Brigade" is skillfully recounted in C. B. Woodham-Smith, *The Reason Why* (1953); and the same author has written a biography of Florence Nightingale (1951, reissued 1983). For the founding spirit behind modern nursing two more recent biographies are available by H. Small (2000) and by B. Dossey (2001).

Unification of Italy

To the books on unification that have already been cited should be added F. J. Cappa, *The Origins of the Italian Wars of Independence* (1992); M. Clark, *The Italian Risorgimento* (1998); and the concise account by L. Riall, *The Italian Risorgimento* (1994). For the unification leaders, D. Mack Smith has written the most informative studies: *Cavour and Garbaldi in 1860* (1954, 1985); *Giuseppe Garibaldi* (1956); *Cavour* (1985), which is critical of the Piedmontese stateman's opportunism; and *Mazzini* (1994). One may also read C. Hibbert, *Garibaldi and His Enemies* (1966), a vivid popular account; and J. Ridley, *Garibaldi* (1975), a detailed, authoritative study. An outstanding history of Italy after unification is D. Mack Smith, *Modern Italy* (rev. 1997). The same author's *Italy and Its Monarchy* (1990) is an unflattering portrait of the House of Savoy.

Bismarck and the Founding of the Second Reich

G. A. Craig, *Germany, 1866–1945* (1978) is a masterful account covering the years from Bismarck to Hitler, with many insights into German society and culture; a companion volume, *The Germans* (1982), equally perceptive, is a series of thematic essays; and the same author's *The Politics of the Prussian Army, 1640–1945* (1956, 1964) is as useful for the nineteenth and twentieth centuries as for the earlier years.

For Bismarck two comprehensive accounts are O. Pflanze, *Bismarck and the Development of Germany* (3 vols.; 1990), demonstrating how Bismarck controlled the dynamic social and economic forces of his day; and L. Gall, *Bismarck: The White Revolutionary* (2 vols.; trans. 1986–1987). E. Eyck, *Bismarck and the German Empire* (1950, 1984) summarizes this German historian's larger critical work. Other biographical accounts include A. Palmer, *Bismarck* (1976), a judicious, well-balanced account; A. J. P. Taylor, *Bismarck: The Man and the Statesman* (1955, 1987), less judicious but provocative; J. E. Rose, *Bismarck* (1987); and E. Feuchtwanger, *Bismarck* (2002). D. G. Williamson, *Bismarck and Germany, 1862–1890* (rev. 1998) is a useful brief introduction; and B. Waller, *Bismarck* (rev. 1997) is an informative essay. G. O. Kent, *Bismarck and His Times* (1978) is especially useful for the historiographical debate on Bismarck.

Social and economic aspects of unification are studied in W. O. Henderson, *The Rise of German Industrial Power, 1834–1914* (1976) and T. S. Hamerow, *The Social Foundations of German Unification, 1858–1871* (2 vols.; 1969–1972). An interesting account of Bismarck's Jewish financial adviser, illuminating much of German history during these years, is F. Stern, *Gold and Iron: Bismarck, Bleichröder, and the Building of the German Empire* (1977). W. J. Mommsen, *Imperial Germany, 1867–1918* (trans. 1995) is a collection of essays by an influential German historian.

For the events of 1870–1871, recommended studies include W. Carr, *The Origins of the Wars of German Unification* (1991); M. Howard, *The Franco-Prussian War: The German Invasion of France, 1870–1871* (rev. 2001), a major study of the war and related events; and G. Wawro's two books for these years, *The Austro-Prussian War: Austria's War with Prussia and Italy in 1866* (1996), and *The Franco-Prussian War: The German Conquest of France in 1870–1871* (2003).

Austria-Hungary

For the Compromise of 1867 and the creation of the Dual Monarchy, the volumes by C. A. Macartney and other studies cited in Chapter 11 will be helpful. W. S. Johnston, *The Austrian Mind: An Intellectual and Social History* (1976) covers broad aspects of Austrian life, while Jewish contributions to Habsburg culture and society are sympathetically assessed in R. S. Wistrich, *The Jews of Vienna in the Age of Franz Joseph* (1989); S. Beller, *Vienna and the Jews* (1989); and W. O. McCagg, Jr., *A History of Habsburg Jews, 1670–1918* (1993). For the military, there are studies by G. E. Rothenberg, *The Army of Francis Joseph* (1976) and I. Deák, *Beyond Nationalism: A Social and Political History of the Habsburg Officer Corps, 1848–1918* (1990), which illuminates the Dual Monarchy in other ways. For Hungary, G. Szabod, *Hungarian Political Trends between the Revolution and the Compromise, 1849–1867* (1977) provides insights into Magyar politics and society, while the story is carried forward to a later era in J. K. Hoensch, *A History of Modern Hungary, 1867–1994* (1996), and in B. K. Kiraly, *Basic History of Modern Hungary: 1867–1999* (2001).

The Russia of Alexander II, 1855–1881

An authoritative treatment for these years is provided in D. Saunders, *Russia in the Age of Reaction and Reform, 1801–1881* (1992), cited in Chapter 11, and R. Pipes, *Russia under the Old Regime* (1974). On the reign of the last five rulers from Alexander I to Nicholas II, S. Harcave has written *Years of the Golden Cockerel: The Last Romanov Tsars, 1814–1917* (1968), a subject covered also in the latter portions of W. B. Lincoln, *The Romanovs: Autocrats of All the Russias* (1981). The Romanov exercise of power is described in the wide-ranging work of R. S. Wortman, *Scenarios of Power: Myth and Ceremony in Russian Monarchy* (2 vols. 1995, 2000).

On the reforms of Alexander II one may turn to D. Lieven, *Russia's Rulers Under the Old Regime* (1989), which describes Alexander's efficient bureaucracy, and to the recent account in E. Radzinsky, *Alexander II: The Last Great Tsar* (2005), informative for Russian society of the era and the man himself. The peasant emancipation may be studied in J. Blum, *The End of the Old Order in Rural Europe* (1978); G. T. Robinson, *Rural Russia under the Old Regime* (1930, 1980); T. Emmons, *The Russian Landed Gentry and the Peasant Emancipation of 1861* (1968); and D. Moon, *The Abolition of Serfdom in Russia, 1762–1907* (2001).

For the activist world of nineteenth-century Russia and the world of the Russian exiles, there is a helpful synthesis: F. Venturi, *A History of the Populist and Socialist Movements in Nineteenth-Century Russia* (trans. 1983); and many special studies, among them E. H. Carr, *The Romantic Exiles: A Nineteenth Century Portrait Gallery* (1933, 1949) and *Michael Bakunin* (1937, reissued 1975); M. A. Miller, *The Russian Revolutionary Emigrés 1825–1870* (1986); A. P. Mendel, *Michael Bakunin: Roots of Apocalypse* (1982); M. E. Malia, *Alexander Herzen and the Birth of Russian Socialism* (1961); V. Broido, *Apostles into Terrorists: Women and the Revolutionary Movement in the Russia of Alexander II* (1977); and I. Berlin, *Russian Thinkers* (1978), which is especially rewarding.

United States

The Civil War and Reconstruction have been the subject of many histories, but two books present each with remarkable narrative skill and analytical insight: J. M. McPherson, *Battle Cry of Freedom: The Civil War Era* (1988) and E. Foner, *Reconstruction: America's Unfinished Revolution, 1863–1877* (1988); the latter author has continued his analysis of this pivotal era in *Forever Free: The Story of Emancipation and Reconstruction* (2005). The essays in S. Forster and S. Nagler (eds.), *On the Road to Total War: The American Civil War and the German Wars of Unification, 1861–1871* (1997), model studies in comparative history, demonstrate the origins of twentieth-century warfare in these two conflicts.

Books by D. B. Davis and others on slavery and the slave trade as a Western institution have been cited earlier. To them may be added O. Patterson, *Slavery and Social Death: A Comparative Study* (1982), which examines the institution and practice in various cultures and eras. A large literature has developed on the slave experience in North America, which P. Kolchin, *American Slavery, 1619–1877* (1993), skillfully synthesizes; the same author has also written two outstanding comparative studies, *Unfree Labor: American Slavery and Russian Serfdom* (1987), and *A Sphinx on the American Land: The Nineteenth-Century South in Comparative Perspective* (2003). Two leading examples of the literature on American slavery are E. D. Genovese, *Roll, Jordan, Roll: The World the Slaves Made* (1974) and H. G. Gutman, *The Black Family in Slavery and Freedom, 1750–1925* (1976). Two valuable surveys of African-American history are J. H. Franklin and A. A. Moss, Jr., *From Slavery to Freedom: A History of African Americans* (rev. 2000) and M. F. Berry and J. Blassingame, *Long Memory: The Black Experience in America* (1982).

Canada, Australia, New Zealand

Informative introductions to the history of Canada include M. Conrad and A. Finkel, *Canada, A National History* (2003); J. M. Bumsted, *A History of the Canadian Peoples* (2003); G. Woodcock, *A Social History of Canada* (1988); J. L. Granatstein and others, *Nation: Canada since Confederation* (rev. 1991); and J. L. Finlay and D. N. Sprague, *The Structure of Canadian History* (2 vols.; 1992), which is especially insightful. The growth of Canadian self-government within an imperial framework is described in J. M. Ward, *Colonial Self-Government: The British Experience, 1759–1856* (1976); and the emergence of the dominion idea, beginning in these years, is comprehensively treated in W. D. McIntyre, *The Commonwealth of Nations: Origins and Impact, 1869–1971* (1977). *The Encyclopedia of Canada* (4 vols.; 1988) is a valuable reference tool. The Australian story is ably recounted in S. Macintyre, *A Concise History of Australia* (rev. 2004); G. Blainey, *A Shorter History of Australia* (1994); and J. Rickard, *Australia: A Cultural History* (rev. 1996). A valuable reference tool is J. Bassett, *The Oxford Illustrated Dictionary of Australian History* (1993). The wider regional history is discussed in D. Denoon, P. Mein-Smith, and M. Wyndham, *A History of Australia, New Zealand and the Pacific* (2000). An excellent introduction to New Zealand is G. W. Rice (ed.), *The Oxford History of New Zealand* (rev. 1992).

Japan and the West

Two books by C. Totman provide comprehensive overviews of Japan before and during the modern era: *Early Modern Japan* (1993) and *A History of Japan* (rev. 2005). Other informative histories include E. O. Reischauer, *Japan: The Story of a Nation* (rev. 1989); W. G. Beasley, *The Rise of Modern Japan: Political, Economic and Social Change Since 1850* (rev. 2000); and M. B. Jansen, *The Making of Modern Japan* (2000).

The best account of the Meiji era is W. G. Beasley's *The Meiji Restoration* (1972), but it may be supplemented by K. B. Pyle, *The Making of Modern Japan* (rev. 1996) and C. Gluck, *Japan's Modern Myths: Ideology in the Late Meiji Period* (1985). For the Japanese occupation of Korea, P. Duus, *The Abacus and the Sword: The Japanese Penetration of Korea, 1895–1900* (1998) is rewarding.

Useful Web Sites

Interesting visual materials and other sources on the Crimean war can be found in the collection of the Library of Congress, *Roger Fenton Crimean War Photographs*, which is at www.loc.gov/rr/print/coll/251_fen.html. A helpful site on the reform-minded Russian Tsar, *Alexander II and His Times*, is maintained at Eastern Michigan University, www.emich.edu/public/history/moss/; and readers will find useful information and links to other Web sites on modern Japan at Columbia University's *Asia for Educators*, http://afe.easia.columbia.edu/. Additional resources for examining the consolidation of nation states in Asia, Europe, and North America are at Fordham University's *Internet Modern History Sourcebook*, www.fordham.edu/halsall/mod/modsbook.html, which has been noted in previous chapters. For excellent links to materials pertaining to the era of the American Civil War and Reconstruction, one may also visit the previously noted *History Matters* at http://historymatters.gmu.edu/, a site maintained in conjunction with the American Social History Project/Center for Media & Learning at the City University of New York and the Center for History and New Media at George Mason University.

14. EUROPEAN CIVILIZATION, 1871–1914: ECONOMY AND POLITICS

Books on cultural and social history are mainly described in Chapter 15, but many titles overlap. Two older volumes that help to provide a still useful synthesis for these years are C. J. H. Hayes, *A Generation of Materialism, 1871–1900* (1941, 1983), portraying the dual nature of the age as climax of enlightenment and seedtime of future turmoil; and O. J. Hale, *The Great Illusion, 1900–1914* (1971), exploring the many accomplishments of the early twentieth-century years and the widespread belief in continuing peace and progress. E. J. Hobsbawm completes his books on the years 1789–1914 with *The Age of Empire, 1875–1914* (1988). The early chapters of J. Joll, *Europe Since 1870* (rev. 1990) are helpful for this period. G. Barraclough, *An Introduction to Contemporary History* (1964), a provocative essay, emphasizes the need for a global approach to the years since 1890, a theme developed at length in J. Romein, *The Watershed of Two Eras: Europe in 1900* (trans. 1978). Also of interest are N. Stone, *Europe Transformed, 1878–1919* (rev. 1999), and R. W. Winks and R. J. Q. Adams, *Europe, 1890–1945: Crisis and Conflict* (2003).

There are informative chapters in F. H. Hinsley (ed.), *Material Progress and Worldwide Problems, 1870–1898* (1962) and C. L. Mowat (ed.), *The Shifting Balance of World Forces, 1898–1945* (rev. 1968). C. Nicholls (ed.), *Power: A Political History of the Twentieth Century* (1990) and S. Pollard (ed.), *An Economic History of the Twentieth Century* (1990) begin with these years.

The European and World Economy

For Europe economic and social development is studied in F. B. Tipton and R. Aldrich, *An Economic and Social History of Europe, 1890–1939* (1987), with a sequel volume for later years. For industrial growth on the Continent, one may also turn to A. S. Milward and S. B. Saul, *The Development of the Economies of Continental Europe, 1850–1914* (1977); C. P. Kindleberger, *Economic Growth in France and Britain, 1851–1950* (1963); and W. O. Henderson, *The Rise of German Industrial Power, 1834–1914* (1976), cited earlier.

For the global economy during these years, W. W. Rostow, *The World Economy: History and Prospect* (1978) is an ambitious effort to study industrial growth from its origins in eighteenth-century Britain to its global diffusion. Other useful works include W. Ashworth, *A Short History of the International Economy since 1850* (rev. 1987); W. Woodruff, *The Impact of Western Man: A Study of Europe's Role in the World Economy, 1750–1960* (1966); and A. G. Kenwood and A. L. Longheed, *The Growth of the International Economy, 1820–2000* (rev. 2000). K. Pomeranz, *The Great Divergence: Europe, China, and the Making of the Modern World Economy* (2000) discusses European colonialism in a comparative study of the evolving world economic system.

International finance is examined in C. P. Kindleberger, *A Financial History of Western Europe* (rev. 1992), cited earlier; M. DeCecco, *The International Gold Standard: Money and Empire* (rev. 1984); R. S. Sayers, *The Bank of England, 1891–1944* (2 vols., 1985); and R. C. Michie, *Capitals of Finance: The London and New York Stock Exchanges, 1850–1914* (1987). The role of foreign capital in the economy of the United States is analyzed in M. Wilkins, *The History of Foreign Investment in the United States to 1914* (1989).

Demography and Migration

Several books on population growth, also useful here, have been cited earlier. C. M. Cipolla, *The Economic History of World Populations* (1962) and T. H. Hollingsworth, *Historical Demography* (1969) are good guides. Recommended studies include T. McKeown, *The Modern Rise of Population* (1977); D. Grigg, *Population Growth and Agrarian Change* (1980); C. Tilly (ed.), *Historical Studies of Changing Fertility* (1978); and two books by M. Livi Bacci, *The Population of Europe* (2000) and *A Concise History of World Population* (rev. 2001), which carries the story of population growth into the contemporary era.

For the movement of peoples, two collections of essays are helpful: W. H. McNeill and R. S. Adams (eds.), *Human Migration; Patterns and Politics* (1978) and I. Glazier and L. deRosa (eds.), *Migration across Time and Nations: Population Mobility in Historical Contexts* (1986). Additional informative works include P. Taylor, *The Distant Magnet: European Migration to the United States* (1971); L. P. Moch, *Moving Europeans: Migration in Western Europe since 1650* (rev. 2003); K. J. Bade, *Migration in European History* (2003); and T. J. Hatten and J. G. Williamson, *Global Migration and the World Economy* (2006). On the absorption of America's immigrants, S. Thernstrom and others (eds.), *Harvard Encyclopedia of American Ethnic Groups* (1980) is a valuable work of reference.

France, 1871–1914

For France in this era the reader may turn to J. M. Mayeur and M. Rebérioux, *The Third Republic from Its Origins to the Great War, 1871–1914* (trans. 1984) and M. Agulhon, *The French Republic, 1879–1992* (trans. 1993), a challenging interpretive study. Concise surveys are available in R. Gildea, *France, 1870–1914* (rev. 1996) and R. D. Anderson, *France, 1870–1914: Politics and Society* (1977). A provocative Marxist analysis is provided in S. Elwitt's two-volume study: *The Making of the Third Republic* (1975) and *The Third Republic Defended* (1988). Readers will also find a helpful analysis of this period in C. Sowerwine, *France Since 1870: Culture, Politics and Society* (2001). Recent treatments of the revolutionary uprising that ushered in the Third Republic include R. Tombs, *The Paris Commune, 1871* (1999) and D. Shafer, *The Paris Commune: French Culture, Politics, and Society at the Crossroads of the Revolutionary Tradition and Revolutionary Socialism* (2005).

A valuable guide to major themes in French history and to writings on France beginning with these years is J. F. McMillan, *Twentieth-Century France: Politics and Society in France, 1898–1991* (1992), while two works of reference are P. Hutton (ed.), *Encyclopedia of the French Third Republic* (2 vols.; 1986) and D. Bell and others (eds.), *A Biographical Dictionary of French Political Leaders since 1870* (1990).

Outstanding biographies include J. P. T. Bury's three-volume study (1936–1981) of Gambetta; D. R. Watson, *Georges Clemenceau* (1974), on the Radical parliamentarian and premier; and H. Goldberg, *The Life of Jean Jaurès* (1962), on the Socialist tribune. Informative studies of the Dreyfus affair may be found in D. Johnson, *France and the Dreyfus Affair* (1967); E. Cahm, *The Dreyfus Affair in French Society and Politics* (1996); M. P. Johnson, *The Dreyfus Affair* (1999); L. Derflur, *The Dreyfus Affair* (2002); and C. E. Forth, *The Dreyfus Affair and the Crisis of*

French Manhood (2004), which examines wider cultural responses to the Affair.

Great Britain, 1871–1914

E. J. Feuchtwanger, *Democracy and Empire: Britain, 1865–1914* (1985) places the period in broad context. Other useful surveys include N. McCord, *British History, 1815–1906* (1991); D. Read, *The Age of Urban Democracy: England, 1868–1914* (rev. 1994); and K. Robbins, *The British Isles, 1901–1951* (2003). The economy is studied in F. Crouzet, *The Victorian Economy* (trans. 1982); S. Pollard, *British Economy, 1870–1914* (1989); E. J. Hobsbawm, *Industry and Empire* (rev. 1999); and B. W. E. Alford, *Britain in the World Economy since 1880* (1996). Special insights are added in A. L. Friedberg, *The Weary Titan: Britain and the Experience of Relative Decline, 1895–1905* (1989) and B. Porter, *Britain, Europe, and the World, 1850–1986* (rev. 1987). Two valuable bibliographical guides are H. J. Hanham (ed.), *Bibliography of British History, 1851–1914* (1977) and A. F. Havighurst, *Modern England, 1901–1984* (rev. 1988).

The patterns of urban and rural life and the shift to an urban society are examined in two outstanding collaborative histories: H. J. Dyos and M. Wolff (eds.), *The Victorian City* (2 vols.; 1973) and G. E. Mingay (ed.), *The Victorian Countryside* (2 vols.; 1981); the shift to an urban society is examined in detail in G. E. Mingay, *The Transformation of Britain, 1830–1939* (1986). The changing fortunes of the landed aristocracy are studied in F. M. L. Thompson, *English Landed Society in the Nineteenth Century* (1989) and D. Cannadine, *The Decline and Fall of the British Aristocracy* (1990), which focuses with telling detail on the 1870s to the present.

In addition one may read G. M. Young, *Portrait of an Age: Victorian England* (2 vols.; 1934, 1977); three books by A. Briggs: *Victorian People* (1954), *Victorian Cities* (1963), and *Victorian Things* (1989); G. S. R. Kitson Clark, *The Making of Victorian England* (1967); and the descriptions of Victorian society in A. N. Wilson, *The Victorians* (2003). Of the many biographies of Victoria, one may still turn to E. Longford, *Queen Victoria* (1965), a sympathetic yet balanced account, and S. Weintraub's two books: *Victoria* (rev. 1996), a reappraisal with interesting insights, and *Uncrowned King: The Life of Prince Albert* (1997); a more recent analysis may be found in W. L. Arnstein, *Queen Victoria* (2003).

In addition to many older studies of Gladstone, there are useful biographies by E. J. Feuchtwanger (1975), P. Stansky (1979), and R. Jenkins (1997); there are also concise accounts by E. F. Biagini (2000) and M. Partridge (2003). For Disraeli, older biographies have been superseded by R. Blake, *Disraeli* (1967, 1998), a biography of distinction; there are other studies by G. Bradford (1983), J. Vincent (1990), S. Weintraub (1993), and E. J. Feuchtwanger (2000). One may also read R. Shannon, *The Age of Disraeli,*

1868–1881: The Rise of Tory Democracy (1992). In addition to older biographies, useful works on Joseph Chamberlain include R. Jay, *Joseph Chamberlain* (1981) and M. Balfour, *Britain and Joseph Chamberlain* (1985). There is a comprehensive four-volume biography of David Lloyd George by J. Grigg (1973–2002); briefer accounts are available by M. Pugh (1988), S. Constantine (1991), C. Wrigley (1992), and I. Packer (1998). For Asquith one may read R. Jenkins, *Asquith* (rev. 1986); and for Balfour, R. F. Mackay, *Balfour: Intellectual Statesman* (1985).

On the extension of the suffrage in 1867 one may read M. Cowling, *1867: Disraeli, Gladstone, and Revolution: The Passing of the Second Reform Bill* (1967) and F. B. Smith, *The Making of the Second Reform Bill* (1966). The transformation of the Liberals in the early twentieth century is studied in G. L. Bernstein, *Liberalism and Liberal Politics in Edwardian England* (1986) and D. Powell, *The Edwardian Crisis: Britain, 1910–1914* (1996). An important account of a critical event is B. K. Murray, *The People's Budget, 1909–1910: Lloyd George and Liberal Politics* (1980). The emergence of the "new liberalism" in the early twentieth century is clarified in D. Roberts, *Origins of the British Welfare State* (1960); P. Clarke, *Liberals and Social Democrats* (1978); M. Freeden, *The New Liberalism: An Ideology of Social Reform* (1978); and J. Brown, *The Welfare State in Britain* (1993). J. Gray, *Isaiah Berlin* (1996), and Berlin's own writings exemplify the later evolution of twentieth-century liberalism.

The Irish question is discussed in J. C. Beckett, *The Making of Modern Ireland* (rev. 1981), cited earlier; K. T. Hoppen, *Ireland since 1800: Conflict and Conformity* (rev. 1999); O. Walsh, *Ireland's Independence* (2002); and in two books by D. G. Boyce: *Ireland, 1828–1923* (1992) and *Nationalism in Ireland* (rev. 1995). There is a remarkable study focusing on the years 1912–1921 by G. Dangerfield, *The Damnable Question: A Study of Anglo-Irish Relations* (1976). The same author's *The Strange Death of Liberal England* (1935, 1997) remains provocative as a searching study of the tensions in English society between 1910 and 1914. For informative essays on Britain's global influence in this era, one may turn to Vols. 3 and 4 of *The Oxford History of the British Empire*: A. Porter (ed.), *The Nineteenth Century* (1999) and J. M. Brown and W. R. Louis (eds.), *The Twentieth Century* (1999).

The German Empire, Italy

To books for Germany in the nineteenth century already cited may be added: H. U. Wehler, *The German Empire, 1871–1918* (1973; trans. 1985), reflecting the thinking of an influential generation of German historians; V. R. Berghahn, *Imperial Germany, 1871–1918* (rev. 2005) and *Modern Germany: Society, Economy, and Politics in the Twentieth Century* (rev. 1987); the concise surveys by M. Sturmer, *The German Empire,*

1870–1918 (2000), and by M. S Seligmann and R. R. McLean, *Germany from Reich to Republic, 1871–1918* (2000); and the important comprehensive study by M. L. Anderson, *Practicing Democracy: Elections and Political Culture in Imperial Germany* (2000).

Other stimulating, interpretive works on imperial Germany and class relationships include D. Blackbourn and G. Eley, *The Peculiarities of German History: Bourgeois Society and Politics in Nineteenth-Century German History* (1984); G. Eley, *From Unification to Nazism: Reinterpreting the German Past* (1986); D. Blackbourn, *Populists and Patricians: Essays in Modern German History* (1987); R. J. Evans, *Rethinking German History: Nineteenth Century Germany and the Origins of the Third Reich* (1990); and the essays in two useful collections: J. C. Fout (ed.), *Politics, Parties, and the Authoritarian State: Imperial Germany, 1871–1918* (2 vols.; 1986), and G. Eley (ed.), *Society, Culture, and the State in Germany, 1870–1930* (1996).

For developments in the immediate post-Bismarckian years one may read J. C. G. Röhl, *Germany without Bismarck: The Crisis of Government in the Second Reich, 1890–1900* (1968). Two outstanding biographies of William II are M. Balfour, *The Kaiser and His Times* (1964) and L. Cecil's two-volume work: *William II: Prince and Emperor, 1859–1900* (1989) and *Emperor and Exile, 1900–1941* (1996). T. A. Kohut, *Wilhelm II and the Germans* (1991) is an insightful study, as is J. C. G. Röhl, *The Kaiser and His Court: Wilhelm II and the Government of Germany* (1996). The universities in this era are examined in K. H. Jarausch, *Students, Society, and Politics in Imperial Germany: The Rise of Academic Liberalism* (1982); and the same author has also written an illuminating biographical study of Bethmann-Hollweg (1973). Of special interest for pre-1914 German society are R. Gay, *The Jews of Germany* (1992) and F. Stern, *Einstein's German World* (1999).

The best narrative accounts of Italy since unification are D. Mack Smith, *Modern Italy* (rev. 1997), cited earlier, and M. Clark, *Modern Italy, 1871–1995* (rev. 1996). For the years after unification, an illuminating account is C. Seton-Watson, *Italy from Liberalism to Fascism, 1870–1925* (1967), which may be supplemented by J. A. Thayer, *Italy and the Great War: Politics and Culture, 1870–1915* (1964); S. Saladino, *Italy from Unification to 1919* (1970); and R. A. Webster, *Industrial Imperialism in Italy, 1908–1915* (1976).

Useful Web Sites

Useful materials on economic history are available through the Web site of Binghamton University's *Fernand Braudel Center for the Study of Economies, Historical Systems, and Civilizations* at http://fbc .binghamton.edu/, where historians stress the development of global economic exchanges. Readers will also find links to helpful resources at Leiden University's *History of International Migration*, www.let .leidenuniv.nl/history/migration/, a site that includes information on migration patterns over several centuries. There is an excellent collection of French images and sources on the Paris commune at Northwestern University's site, *The Siege and Commune of Paris*, www.library.northwestern.edu/spec/ siege/. Accessible historical overviews and other materials on Britian have been collected at www.bbc .co.uk/history/timelines/britain/o_early_20cent.shtml, which is a component of the informative *BBC-History* Web site.

15. EUROPEAN CIVILIZATION, 1871–1914: SOCIETY AND CULTURE

Many books on the social, cultural, and intellectual history of the nineteenth century have been listed in earlier chapters, beginning with Chapter 11.

Labor, Social Democracy, Socialism

Overall introductions include H. Mitchell and P. N. Stearns, *Workers and Protest: The European Labor Movement, the Working Classes, and the Origins of Social Democracy, 1890–1914* (1971); A. Przeworski, *Capitalism and Social Democracy* (1985); D. Sassoon, *One Hundred Years of Socialism: The West European Left in the Twentieth Century* (1996), taking its start in 1889; and G. Eley, *Forging Democracy: the History of the Left in Europe, 1850–2000* (2002).

There are many specific studies of Socialist parties in each country. For Germany, informative books include C. E. Schorske, *German Social Democracy, 1905–1917* (1955); P. Gay, *The Dilemma of Democratic Socialism: Eduard Bernstein's Challenge to Marx* (rev. 1962); M. B. Steger, *The Quest for Evolutionary Socialism: Eduard Bernstein and Social Democracy* (1997); S. Pierson, *Marxist Intellectuals and the Working Class Mentality in Germany, 1887–1912* (1993); W. M. Maehl, *August Bebel: Shadow Emperor of the German Workers* (1980); S. Berger, *Social Democracy and the Working Class in Nineteenth and Twentieth Century Germany* (2000); and V. L. Lidtke, *The Outlawed Party: Social Democracy in Germany, 1878–1890* (1966). Lidtke has also written an outstanding study of the working-class culture that developed around the German Socialist movement: *The Alternative Culture: Socialist Labor in Imperial Germany* (1985).

For Britain N. MacKenzie and J. MacKenzie, *The Fabians* (1977) skillfully combines biography and social and intellectual history, while two leading Fabians, Sidney and Beatrice Webb, are studied in R. J. Harrison, *The Life and Times of Sidney and Beatrice Webb* (2000) and P. Beilharz and C. Nyland (eds.), *The Webbs, Fabianism, and Feminism* (1998). Informative works on George Bernard Shaw include biographies by M. Holroyd (1998), which condenses a comprehensive, multivolume study, and L. Hugo (1999). The origins of British socialism are probed in S. Pierson, *Marxism and the Origins of British Socialism* (1973) and *British Socialists: The Journey from Fantasy to Politics* (1979); and a related subject is studied in R. Moore, *The Emergence of the Labour Party, 1880–1924* (1978), a thoughtful synthesis. The role of women in early British socialism is examined in J. Hannam and K. Hunt, *Socialist Women: Britain, 1880s to 1920s* (2002).

For France, for an overall view with many interesting insights, one may read T. Judt, *Marxism and the French Left: Studies in Labour and Politics in France, 1830–1981* (1986); R. Magraw, *A History of the French Working Class* (2 vols.; 1992), the first volume studying the years 1815–1870; the second, 1871–1939; P. M. Pilbeam, *French Socialists Before Marx: Workers, Women and the Social Question in France* (2000); and R. Stuart, *Marxism at Work: Ideology, Class, and French Socialism during the Third Republic* (1992). There are informative biographical studies of Socialist leaders; among them H. Goldberg on Jean Jaurès (1962), cited earlier; L. Derfler (1977) and M. M. Farrar (1991) on Alexandre Millerand; L. Derfler on Paul Lafargue (2 vols.; 1991, 1998); and K. S. Vincent on Pierre-Joseph Proudhon (1985) and Benoît Malon (1992).

On the Socialist international organization, J. Joll, *The Second International, 1889–1914* (rev. 1974) is a concise survey; and J. Braunthal, *History of the International* (3 vols.; trans. 1961–1980) is a detailed study. The breakup of the International is described in G. Haupt, *Socialism and the Great War: The Collapse of the Second International* (1972). The most comprehensive introduction to anarchism is G. Woodcock, *Anarchism: A History of Libertarian Ideas and Movements* (1962), but also useful are J. Joll, *The Anarchists* (rev. 1981); R. D. Sonn, *Anarchism* (1992); and C. Ward, *Anarchism: A Very Short Introduction* (2004).

Labor History in Cultural Context

Recent labor history has attempted to convey the experiences of laboring men and women apart from organized labor movements and to integrate labor protest into a broader cultural context. Here E. P. Thompson's works have been cited earlier. Another exemplar, E. J. Hobsbawm, has written, among other books, *Primitive Rebels* (rev. 1971), *Labouring Men* (1964), and *Workers: Worlds of Labour* (1985). A successful study of the English experience in these years is S. Meacham, *A Life Apart: The English Working Class, 1890–1914* (1977). Other interesting works for British labor are J. Benson, *The Working Class in Britain, 1850–1939* (1989); D. M. MacRaild and D. E. Martin, *Labour in British Society, 1830–1914* (2000); J. Bourke, *Working-Class Cultures in Britain, 1890–1960: Gen-*

der, Class, and Ethnicity (1994); and A. McIvor, *A History of Work in Britain, 1880–1950* (2001).

For France examples of labor history include J. W. Scott, *The Glassmakers of Carmaux: French Craftsmen and Political Action in a Nineteenth-Century City* (1974); B. H. Moss, *The Origins of the French Labor Movement, 1830–1914: The Socialism of Skilled Workers* (1976); L. R. Berlanstein, *The Working People of Paris, 1871–1914* (1984); M. P. Hanagan, *The Logic of Solidarity: Artisans and Workers in Three French Towns, 1871–1914* (1980); D. Reid, *The Miners of Decazeville* (1986) and *Paris Sewers and Sewermen* (1991); J. G. Coffin, *The Politics of Women's Work: The Paris Garment Trades, 1750–1915* (1996); and N. L. Green, *Ready-to-Wear and Ready-to-Work: A Century of Industry and Immigrants in Paris and New York* (1997), an excellent study of twentieth-century labor that exemplifies the cross-cultural themes of comparative social history. A comprehensive study is G. Noiriel, *Workers in French Society in the 19th and 20th Centuries* (trans. 1990); and the strike as a social phenomenon in these years is studied in M. Perrot, *Workers on Strike: France, 1871–1890* (trans. 1987). The importance of syndicalism is examined in several older books and in S. Milner, *French Syndicalism and the International Labor Movement, 1900–1914* (1990).

For Germany books providing broad insights into politics, society, and class include D. Crew, *Town in the Ruhr: A Social History of Bochum, 1860–1914* (1979); D. Blackbourn, *Class, Religion, and Local Politics in Wilhelmine Germany* (1980); M. Nolan, *Social Democracy and Society: Working Class Radicalism in Düsseldorf, 1890–1920* (1980); and S. H. F. Hickey, *Workers in Imperial Germany: The Miners of the Ruhr* (1985).

Women's History, Women's Rights, Feminism

Books on recent themes in women's history have been cited in the introductory section and in earlier chapters. For the background to women's history in modern Europe, one may turn to K. Offen, *European Feminisms, 1700–1950: A Political History* (2000); P. Branca, *Women in Europe since 1750* (1978); S. Delamont and L. Duffin (eds.), *The Nineteenth-Century Woman: Her Cultural and Physical World* (1978); P. S. Robertson, *An Experience of Women: Patterns and Change in Nineteenth-Century Europe* (1982); and I. Bloom, K. Hagemann, and C. Hall (eds.), *Gendered Nations: Nationalisms and Gender Order in the Long Nineteenth Century* (2000), which examines conceptions of manhood and womanhood in this era. Women's lives and activities are documented in E. O. Hellerstein, L. P. Hume, and K. M. Offen (eds.), *Victorian Women: A Documentary Account of Women's Lives in Nineteenth-Century England, France, and the United States* (1981). S. Rowbotham, *A Century of Women: The History of Women in Britain and the*

United States (1997) begins with chapters on the era before The First World War.

For Britain in this era a sampling of the many studies that examine the status and role of women of various backgrounds would include M. Vicinus, *Suffer and Be Still: Women in the Victorian Age* (1973), and the volume she has edited, *A Widening Sphere: Changing Roles of Victorian Women* (1977); P. Branca, *Silent Sisterhood: Middle Class Women in the Victorian Home* (1975); E. Longworth, *Eminent Victorian Women* (1981); and B. Caine, *Victorian Feminists* (1982). J. Giles, *Women, Identity and Private Life in Britain, 1900–50* (1995) describes the experiences of women in the early twentieth century.

Working-class women are studied in N. C. Solden, *Women in British Trade Unions, 1874–1976* (1978) and E. Roberts, *A Woman's Place: An Oral History of Working Class Women* (1985). A key social problem is thoughtfully examined in J. R. Walkowitz, *Prostitution and Victorian Society: Women, Class, and the State* (1980); the same author has also written *City of Dreadful Delight: Narratives of Sexual Danger in Late-Victorian London* (1992). One may also read P. McHugh, *Prostitution and Victorian Social Reform* (1980).

The struggle for women's suffrage is studied in C. Rover, *Women's Suffrage and Party Politics in Britain, 1866–1914* (1967); D. Morgan, *Suffragists and Liberals: the Politics of Woman Suffrage in England* (1975); A. Rosen, *Rise Up Women!: The Women's Social and Political Union, 1903–1914* (1974); C. Law, *Suffrage and Power: The Women's Movement, 1918–1928* (1997); and J. Liddington and J. Norris, *One Hand Tied Behind Us: The Rise of the Women's Suffrage Movement* (rev. 2000). D. Mitchell's popular account, *The Fighting Pankhursts: A Study in Tenacity* (1967), may be supplemented by P. W. Romero, *E. Sylvia Pankhurst: Portrait of a Radical* (1987); and B. Winslow, *Sylvia Pankhurst: Sexual Politics and Political Activism* (1996). In addition, S. S. Holton, *Feminism and Democracy: Women's Suffrage and Reform Politics in Britain, 1900–1918* (1986) focuses on less known provincial suffragists, and S. K. Kent, *Sex and Suffrage in Britain, 1860–1914* (1990) sees the suffrage campaign as part of a broader movement for a reformed society.

The history of women in the Third French Republic is examined in J. F. McMillan, *Housewife or Harlot: The Place of Women in French Society, 1870–1940* (1981), the title derived from a remark by Proudhon, and in the same author's excellent *France and Women, 1789–1914: Gender, Society, and Politics* (2000). S. C. Hause with A. R. Kenney, *Women's Suffrage and Social Politics in the French Third Republic* (1984) explores the failed movement in these years to extend the suffrage to women.

Other works on French women in this age include B. G. Smith, *Ladies of the Leisure Class: The Bourgeoises of Northern France in the Nineteenth Century* (1982); C. G. Moses, *French Feminism in the Nineteenth Century* (1984); J. W. Scott, *Only Paradoxes to Offer: French Feminists and the Rights of Man* (1996); M. L. Roberts, *Disruptive Acts: The New Woman in Fin-de-Siècle France* (2002); and E. A. Accampo and others, *Gender and the Politics of Social Reform in France, 1870–1914* (1995). An informative comparative study is T. McBride, *The Domestic Revolution: The Modernization of Household Service in England and France, 1820–1920* (1976). The essays in J. B. Margadant (ed.), *The New Biography: Performing Femininity in Nineteenth-Century France* (2000) have been cited earlier.

On the activist role of women in the Socialist movement one may turn to R. J. Evans, *Comrades and Sisters: Feminism, Socialism, and Pacifism in Europe, 1870–1945* (1987); and M. J. Boxer and J. H. Quataert (eds.), *Socialist Women: European Socialist Feminism in the Nineteenth and Early Twentieth Centuries* (1978), cited earlier. For the German Socialists there is J. H. Quataert, *Reluctant Feminists in German Social Democracy, 1865–1917* (1979); and for the French, C. Sowerwine, *Sisters or Citizens: Women and Socialism in France since 1876* (1982); and P. Hilden, *Working Class Women and Socialist Politics in France: A Regional Study, 1880–1914* (1986). For Rosa Luxemburg and her contributions to German and international socialism, J. P. Nettl, *Rosa Luxemburg* (2 vols., 1966; abridged 1 vol., 1969) is an admirable biography. Other studies include books by N. Geras (1976), E. Eltinger (1987), R. Abraham (1989), S. E. Bronner (1990), D. E. Shepardson (1996), and J. Mathilde (trans. 2000).

The role of women in German society is examined in R. F. B. Joeres and M. J. Maynes (eds.), *German Women in the Eighteenth and Nineteenth Centuries* (1986); J. C. Fout (ed.), *German Women in the Nineteenth Century: A Social History* (1984); and U. Frevert, *Women in German History: From Bourgeois Emancipation to Sexual Liberation* (1989).

R. J. Evans provides a comparative study in *The Feminists: Women's Emancipation Movements in Europe, America, and Australia, 1840–1920* (1977) and focuses on a single country in *The Feminist Movement in Germany, 1894–1933* (1976). On the transatlantic and international campaign in the nineteenth century, one may turn to B. S. Anderson, *Joyous Greetings: The First International Women's Movement, 1830–1860* (2000). The scene in Russia is studied in R. Stites, *The Women's Liberation Movement in Russia: Feminism, Nihilism, and Bolshevism, 1860–1930* (rev. 1991). On the two pioneer women leaders of emancipation in the United States, one may read G. C. Ward, *Not for Ourselves Alone: The Story of Elizabeth Cady Stanton and Susan B. Anthony* (1999).

Cultural and Intellectual History

Helpful surveys of cultural and intellectual history are available in G. L. Mosse, *The Culture of Western Eu-*

rope: The Nineteenth and Twentieth Centuries (rev. 1988) and R. N. Stromberg, European Intellectual History Since 1789 (rev. 1994), both cited earlier; and the more recent work by J. Winders, European Culture Since 1848 (2001). A few special books on this period also deserve mention. R. Wohl, The Generation of 1914 (1979) relates the restlessness of the postwar generation to the prewar ferment; B. W. Tuchman, The Proud Tower: A Portrait of the World before the War, 1890–1914 (1966) is an older, popular account with colorful vignettes; and E. R. Tannenbaum, 1900: The Generation Before the Great War (1976) offers a potpourri of insights into the social history of the times. A. J. Mayer, The Persistence of the Old Regime: Europe to the Great War (1981) contends that aristocratic values dominated European society and culture down to 1914. A positive assessment of the closing years of the nineteenth century emerges from the essays in M. Teich and R. Porter (eds.), Fin de Siècle and Its Legacy (1990). Changing conceptions of European selfhood and individual experience are explored in three notable works of European intellectual history, J. Seigel, The Idea of the Self: Thought and Experience in Western Europe Since the Seventeenth Century (2005); J. E. Goldstein, The Post-Revolutionary Self: Politics and Psyche in France, 1750–1850 (2005); and M. Jay, Songs of Experience: Modern American and European Variations on a Universal Theme (2005).

In a special category and a major contribution to social and cultural history of this era is P. Gay, The Bourgeois Experience: Victoria to Freud (5 vols.; 1984–1998); the five volumes illuminate in fascinating detail how Victorian men and women in their emotional life were not inhibited by social restraints. One should also read D. Newcome, The Victorian World Picture (1997), on how the world perceived the Victorians and how they perceived themselves. The cultural history of homosexuality in this era is examined in a wide-ranging account by G. Robb, Strangers: Homosexual Love in the 19th Century (2004).

For France an unconventional social history with absorbing details and insights is T. Zeldin, France, 1848–1945 (2 vols.; 1973–1977, 1992): Vol. I, Ambition, Love and Politics, and Vol. II, Intellect, Taste and Anxiety. Other aspects of French social and cultural history are studied in E. Weber, France, Fin de Siècle (1986), which offers vignettes and anecdotal insights into French society and life; the same author demonstrates that French national unity was accomplished only belatedly by such agencies as the schools and army in Peasants into Frenchmen: The Modernization of Rural France, 1870–1914 (1976). The arts and cultural life are examined in R. Shattuck, The Banquet Years: The Arts in France, 1885–1918 (1958); T. J. Clark, Image of the People (1973) and The Painting of Modern Life: Paris in the Art of Monet and His Followers (1984, 1999); and J. Seigel, Bohemian Paris: Culture, Politics, and the Boundaries of Bourgeois

Life, 1830–1930 (1986). J. H. Rubin, Impressionism (1999) offers a useful introduction to this influential group of artists.

Three introductions to the origins of modern art in France and subsequent developments are H. H. Arnason, History of Modern Art (rev. 2004); S. Pendergast and T. Pendergast (eds.), Contemporary Artists (rev. 2002); and R. R. Brettell, Modern Art, 1851–1929: Capitalism and Representation (1999), which relates the major avant-garde innovations to the rapid social, economic, and political changes of the age. S. Kern, The Culture of Time and Space, 1880–1918 (1983) also stresses the cultural responses to changing modern technologies.

C. E. Schorske, Fin de Siècle Vienna: Politics and Culture (1979) is a remarkable study of political, artistic, and intellectual responses to the failures of late-nineteenth-century liberalism in central Europe. Important also is A. Janik and S. Toulmin, Wittgenstein's Vienna (1973), while an evocative portrait of life and creativity in the second city of the empire is J. Lukacs, Budapest 1900 (1989).

New Movements in Science

A general introduction to science in the nineteenth and early twentieth centuries is available in D. Knight, The Age of Science (1986). On biology, evolution, and Darwinism there is a considerable literature, much of it published in recent years. One may turn to A. Desmond, The Politics of Evolution (1989); A. Desmond and J. Moore, Darwin (1991); D. I. Hull, Darwin and His Critics (1993); and a two-volume study by J. Browne, Charles Darwin: Voyaging (1995) and Charles Darwin: The Power of Place (2002). Desmond has also written an extraordinary biography of Darwin's forceful champion, Huxley: From Devil's Disciple to Evolution's High Priest (1997). The ongoing debate about Darwin's theories may be sampled in N. Eldridge, Reinventing Darwin (1995); the same author's The Triumph of Evolution and the Failures of Creationism (2000); and D. J. Depew and B. H. Weber, Darwinism Evolving (1995). S. Jones, Darwin's Ghost: "The Origins of the Species" Updated (2000) is a remarkable rewriting of Darwin in light of the evolutionary biology that has developed since his day. Other books on evolution written by P. J. Bowler (1990), J. Bowlby (1991), and D. Young (1993) also merit attention.

Brief biographical accounts of two other key biologists of this era are L. J. Jordanova, Lamarck (1985) and V. Orel, Mendel (1985). The breakthrough in geology and its cultural impact may be studied in C. C. Gillispie, Genesis and Geology (1951); R. Porter, The Making of Geology (1977); D. R. Dean, James Hutton and the History of Geology (1992); and S. J. Gould, Time's Arrow, Time's Cycle: Myth and Metaphor in the Discovery of Geological Time (1987).

For the impact of these scientific developments on religion, informative studies include W. Irvine,

Apes, Angels, and Victorians (1955, 1983); J. R. Moore, *The Post-Darwinian Controversies* (1979); D. C. Lindberg and R. L. Numbers (eds.), *Historical Essays on the Encounter between Christianity and Science* (1986); and H. J. Brooke, *Science and Religion: Some Historical Perspectives* (1991). On the famous Scopes trial of 1925 in the United States, an even-handed scholarly account is E. J. Larson, *Summer for the Gods: The Scopes Trial and America's Continuing Debate over Science and Religion* (1998).

Debates on the nature of scientific discovery still refer often to the influential work of T. S. Kuhn, *The Structure of Scientific Revolutions* (1962, 1989). On the emergence of modern physics and the transformation of Newtonian concepts one may turn to V. F. Weisskopf, *Physics in the Twentieth Century* (1972) and B. L. Cline, *Men Who Made a New Physics* (1965, 1987). Einstein may be approached through two major biographies: A. Pais, *"Subtle is the Lord" The Science and the Life of Albert Einstein* (1982), and A. Folsing, *Albert Einstein* (1993, trans. 1997), excellent both for Einstein's science and his personal life. There are informative accounts also by R. W. Clark (1971), J. Bernstein (1973), M. White and J. Gribbon (1994), D. Brian (1996), and P. D. Smith (2003). Recommended biographies of two other contributors to the new physics are S. Quinn, *Marie Curie* (1995) and R. L. Sime, *Lise Meitner: A Life in Physics* (1997).

For Freud there is an older biography by E. Jones, an English co-worker (1 vol. abridged; 1974), and many other studies including the thoughtful work by P. Gay, *Freud: A Life for Our Time* (1988). A. Storr, *Freud* (1989) is a good brief assessment; and J. Lear, *Freud* (2005) examines his contributions to modern thought. To sample the large literature critical of Freud one may read A. Esterson, *Seductive Mirage: An Exploration of the Work of Sigmund Freud* (1993) and the essays in M. S. Roth (ed.), *Freud: Conflict and Culture* (1998).

Social Thought

Outstanding works are H. S. Hughes, *Consciousness and Society: The Reorientation of European Social Thought, 1890–1930* (1958); G. Masur, *Prophets of Yesterday: Studies in European Culture, 1890–1914* (1961); M. Biddis, *Age of the Masses: Ideas and Society Since 1870* (1977); W. R. Everdell, *The First Moderns: Profiles in the Origins of Twentieth-Century Thought* (1997); and J. W. Burrow, *The Crisis of Reason: European Thought, 1848–1914* (2000). Virtually a history of thought from Herbert Spencer to the recent past is W. W. Wagar, *Good Tidings: The Belief in Progress from Darwin to Marcuse* (1972); on that theme one may also read R. Nisbet, *History of the Idea of Progress* (1980, reissued 1994), and a thoughtful collaborative volume, G. Almond and others (eds.), *Progress and Its Discontents* (1982).

The best studies of Nietzsche are W. A. Kaufmann, *Nietzsche: Philosopher, Psychologist, An-*

tichrist (rev. 1974); R. Hayman, *Nietzsche: A Critical Life* (1980); R. J. Hollingdale, *Nietzsche: The Man and His Philosophy* (rev. 1999); and T. B. Strong, *Friedrich Nietzsche and the Politics of Transfiguration* (rev. 2000). There are other biographical and analytical studies by C. Brinton (1941, 1965), J. P. Stern (1979), R. Schacht (1983), G. Clive (1984), and R. Wicks (2002). Useful anthologies for these years include R. N. Stromberg (ed.), *Realism, Naturalism, and Symbolism: Modes of Thought and Expression in Europe, 1848–1914* (1968); E. Weber (ed.), *Movements, Currents, Trends: Aspects of European Thought in the Nineteenth and Twentieth Centuries* (1991); and A. Fried and R. Sanders, *Socialist Thought: A Documentary History* (rev. 1993).

Religion since 1871

The relationship between secularized European civilization and its Christian origins is ably treated in O. Chadwick, *The Secularization of the European Mind in the Nineteenth Century* (1976), cited in Chapter 11, and H. McLeod, *Religion and the People of Western Europe, 1789–1989* (rev. 1997). For religious thought J. Pelikan, *Christian Doctrine and Modern Culture: Since 1700* (1990), the final volume of his comprehensive *The Christian Tradition*, may be read along with C. Welch, *Protestant Thought in the Nineteenth Century* (2 vols.; 1985), the second volume studying the years 1870–1914. For the Roman Catholic reactions to the changes in science and religious scholarship, one may read T. M. Loome, *Liberal Catholicism, Reform Catholicism, and Modernism* (1979) and L. R. Kurtz, *The Politics of Heresy: The Modernist Crisis in Roman Catholicism* (1986).

For Judaism H. M. Sachar, *The Course of Modern Jewish History* (rev. 1990) and *A History of Israel: From the Rise of Zionism to Our Time* (rev. 1996) relate the nineteenth-century background; the same author has written the comprehensive survey, *A History of Jews in the Modern World* (2005), cited earlier. The fullest account of Zionism's emergence as an ideology is the impressive three-volume study by D. Vital: *The Origins of Zionism* (1975); *Zionism: The Formative Years* (1982); and *Zionism: The Crucial Phase* (1987), which carries the story to 1919. A more concise account may be found in M. Brenner, *Zionism: A Brief History* (trans. 2003); and another insightful work is S. Avinieri, *The Making of Modern Zionism: The Intellectual Origins of the Jewish State* (1981).

The Assault on Liberalism: Racism, the Cult of Violence

Many of the books cited earlier in this chapter under Social Thought examine the undermining of liberal values in the late nineteenth century, with implications for the years that followed. Two classic studies are H. Arendt, *The Origins of Totalitarianism* (rev. 1973), an influential, far-reaching work; and J. Barzun, *Darwin, Marx, Wagner: Critique of a Heritage* (rev.

1981), which stresses similarities as the author sees them in the way each of these figures undermined classical liberalism. These books may be supplemented by J. W. Burrow, *The Crisis of Reason: European Thought, 1848–1914* (2000), cited earlier.

For racism and anti-Semitism in these years one may read P. Pulzer, *The Rise of Political Anti-Semitism in Germany and Austria* (rev. 1988); L. Poliakov, *The Aryan Myth: A History of Racist and Nationalist Ideas in Europe* (trans. 1974); J. Katz, *From Prejudice to Destruction: Anti-Semitism, 1700–1933* (1980); G. L. Mosse, *Toward the Final Solution: A History of European Racism* (1978); and two books by P. L. Rose, *Revolutionary Anti-Semitism in Germany from Kant to Wagner* (1991) and *Wagner: Race and Revolution* (1992). Anti-Semitism is placed in broad historical perspective in R. S. Wistrich, *Anti-Semitism: The Longest Hatred* (1992), a remarkable account ranging from pre-Christian times through the twentieth century; G. I. Langmuir, *History, Religion, and Anti-Semitism* (1990) and *Toward a Definition of Anti-Semitism* (1991); and two works by A. S. Lindemann, *Esau's Tears: Modern Anti-Semitism and the Rise of the Jews* (1997) and *Anti-Semitism before the Holocaust* (2000). European racial ideologies during these years are also examined in P. Brantlinger, *Dark Vanishings: Discourses on the Extinction of Primitive Races, 1800–1930* (2003).

Books on anti-Semitism in France relating to the Dreyfus Affair include S. Wilson, *Ideology and Experience: Anti-Semitism in Modern France at the Time of the Dreyfus Affair* (1982), which is especially insightful; books on the affair itself have already been cited. A. S. Lindemann, *The Jew Accused: Three Anti-Semitic Affairs: Dreyfus, Beilis, Frank, 1894–1915* (1991) skillfully compares the French affair with episodes in tsarist Russia and the United States. For comparative insights in other frameworks, one may read G. Fredrickson, *The Comparative Imagination: On the History of Racism, Nationalism, and Social Movements* (1998). J. J. Roth, *The Cult of Violence: Sorel and the Sorelians* (1980) is illuminating on the inspiration behind syndicalism. The origins of twentieth-century fascist ideology are studied in Z. Sternhell, *Neither Right Nor Left: Fascist Ideology in France* (1986) and, in collaboration with others, *The Birth of Fascist Ideology: From Cultural Rebellion to Political Revolution* (trans. 1994); these two much debated, controversial books find the roots of fascist thought in the ideas and ideology of the Left. A precursor of fascism is studied in C. S. Doty, *From Cultural Rebellion to Counterrevolution: The Politics of Maurice Barrès* (1976) and R. Soucy, *Fascism in France: The Case of Maurice Barrès* (1972).

Useful Web Sites

There are links to all aspects of the modern history of labor and workers at *WWW Virtual Library Labour History*, which is maintained at the International Institute of Social History in Amsterdam at www.iisg .nl/~w3vl/. Readers will also find links from this site to materials on the history of socialism, and the same Dutch Institute maintains *WWW Virtual Library Women's History* at www.iisg.nl/w3vlwomenshistory/, an excellent resource in English. Documents expressing the ideas of the new labor and women's movements as well as the themes of new intellectual trends such as Darwinism and Freudianism are available at Fordham University's *Internet Modern History Sourcebook*, www.fordham.edu/halsall/mod/modsbook.html, which has been cited in earlier chapters. There are excellent examples of Impressionism and other late nineteenth-century art at the site of the French *Musée d'Orsay*, www.musee-orsay.fr, which may be searched in English, and at *The Art Institute of Chicago*, www.artic.edu. Information and valuable links to other materials on Einstein and the science of his era may be found at the *Albert Einstein Archives*, /www.albert-einstein.org/, a site based at The Hebrew University of Jerusalem. There are links to multiple sites on modern religious thought at the *Virtual Religion Index*, http://virtualreligion.net/vri/, a useful gateway to diverse materials on the history of all the world's major religions.

16. EUROPE'S WORLD SUPREMACY, 1871–1914

Many of the general accounts for the years 1871–1914 cited in the two previous chapters will also be helpful here. Informative introductions, some moving on into the twentieth century, include W. D. Smith, *European Imperialism in the Nineteenth and Twentieth Centuries* (1982); V. G. Kiernan, *From Conquest to Collapse: European Empires from 1815 to 1960* (1982); J. N. Pieterse, *Empire and Emancipation* (1980); and H. L. Wesseling, *The European Colonial Empires, 1815–1919* (trans. 2004). W. L. Langer, *The Diplomacy of Imperialism, 1890–1902* (2 vols.; 1935, 1951, 1965) remains valuable. The connections between imperialism and European political cultures are discussed in J. Pitts, *A Turn to Empire: The Rise of Imperial Liberalism in Britain and France* (2005); and the role played by Western technology in European expansion is examined in D. R. Headrick, *The Tools of Empire* (1981) and *The Tentacles of Progress* (1988). Similar themes are addressed in M. Adas, *Machines as the Measure of Men: Science, Technology, and Ideologies of Western Dominance* (1989). The role played by disease is examined in S. Watts, *Epidemics and History: Disease, Power, and Imperialism* (2000). A long-range view of European imperialism is provided in D. B. Abernathy, *The Dynamics of Global Dominance: European Overseas Empires, 1415–1980* (2001).

Imperialism in General

Debate about the nature of imperialism has in part been stimulated by the seminal study of R. Robinson and J. Gallagher, *Africa and the Victorians: The Official Mind of Imperialism* (1961, 1981), comparing political and economic motives; the debate is summarized in W. R. Louis (ed.), *Imperialism: The Robinson-Gallagher Controversy* (1976). Informative studies include D. Fieldhouse's two books, *Economics and Empire, 1830–1914* (1973) and *Colonialism, 1870–1945* (1981); and P. J. Cain and A. G. Hopkins, *British Imperialism: Innovation and Expansion, 1688–1914* (2 vols.; 1993). French imperial ideas and practices are examined in A. L. Conklin, *A Mission to Civilize: The Republican Idea of Empire in France and West Africa, 1895–1930* (1997). Motives and justifications for nineteenth-century imperialism are also analyzed in C. Reynolds, *Modes of Imperialism* (1981); T. Smith, *The Pattern of Imperialism* (1982); W. J. Mommsen, *Theories of Imperialism* (trans. 1980); and A. L. Conklin and I. C. Fletcher (eds.), *European Imperialism, 1830–1930: Climax and Contradiction* (1999). For the earlier phase of European imperialist expansion and cultural interaction in Egypt and India, see the colorful account in M. Jasanoff, *Edge of Empire: Lives, Culture, and Conquest in the East, 1750–1850* (2005).

Provocative discussions of the confrontation between Europeans and non-Europeans include R Maunier, *The Sociology of Colonies: An Introduction to the Study of Race Contact* (2 vols.; 1949); D. Mannoni, *Prospero and Caliban: The Psychology of Colonization* (1956), which stresses the psychological impact on both rulers and the governed; T. Geiger, *The Conflicted Relationship: The West and the Transformation of Asia, Africa, and Latin America* (1967); G. W. Goug, *The Standards of "Civilization" in International Society* (1984); V. G. Kiernan, *The Lords of Human Kind: Black Man, Yellow Man, and White Man in the Age of Empire* (1987); and P. D. Curtin, *The World and the West: The European Challenge and the Overseas Response in the Age of Empire* (2000). European views of other cultures are also examined in M. L. Pratt, *Imperial Eyes: Travel Writing and Transculturation* (1992). E. Said, in an influential book, *Culture and Imperialism* (1994), explains how imperialism affected European culture itself. The issue of gender in European empires is examined in N. Chaudhuri and M. Strobel (eds.), *Western Women and Imperialism: Complicity and Resistance* (1992); and P. Levine (ed.), *Gender and Empire* (2004), which focuses on the British Empire.

British and Other European Imperialisms

Recommended studies for British imperialism include B. Porter, *The Lion's Share: A Short History of British Imperialism, 1850–2004* (rev. 2004), a lively and informative account; R. Hyam, *Britain's Imperial Century, 1815–1914* (1976); and C. A. Bayly, *The Imperial Meridian: The British Empire and the World, 1780–1830* (1989). Domestic responses to imperialism are examined in B. Porter, *The Absent-Minded Imperialists: Empire, Society, and Culture in Britain* (2004); and the opponents of imperialism are discussed in the same author's *Critics of Empire: British Radical Attitudes to Colonialism in Africa, 1895–1914* (1968). Excellent discussions of British colonial expansion may be found in W. R. Louis (ed.), *The Oxford History of the British Empire* (5 vols.; 1998–1999), of which the relevant volumes for this period are A. Porter (ed.), *The Nineteenth Century* (1999) and J. M. Brown (ed.), *The Twentieth Century* (1999). Accounts of people living within the empire may be found in P. D. Morgan and S. Hawkins (eds.), *Black Experience and the Empire* (2004).

The imperial activities of the other European powers are described in W. D. Smith, *The German Colonial Empire* (1978); H. Brunschwig, *French Colonialism, 1871–1914* (1960; trans. 1966); B. Singer and J. Landgon, *Cultured Force: Makers and Defenders of the French Colonial Empire* (2004); and M. Kuietenbrouwer, *The Netherlands and the Rise of Modern Imperialism* (trans. 1991). On both the theory and practice of imperialism an important comparative study is W. Baumgart, *Imperialism: The Idea and Reality of British and French Colonial Expansion, 1880–1914* (trans. 1982). Cross-cultural and interracial interactions are studied in J. Clancy-Smith and F. Gouda (eds.), *Domesticating the Empire: Race, Gender, and Family Life in French and Dutch Colonialism* (1998).

The Americas

For all aspects of relationships with Latin America, the essays in the first five volumes of L. Bethell (ed.), *The Cambridge History of Latin America* (1988) are valuable: Vols. I and II, *Colonial Latin America;* Vol. III, *From Independence to c. 1870;* and Vols. IV and V, *From 1870 to 1930.* D. Bushnell and N. Macaulay, *The Emergence of Latin America in the Nineteenth Century* (rev. 1994) is a helpful survey; it may be supplemented by E. B. Burns, *The Poverty of Progress: Latin America in the Nineteenth Century* (1980) and by chapters on this period in J. Chasteen, *Born in Blood and Fire: A Concise History of Latin America* (rev. 2006).

The background to Napoleon III's fiasco in Mexico and the French intervention during the 1860s is discussed in N. N. Baker, *The French Experience in Mexico, 1821–1861* (1979) and M. Cunningham, *Mexico and the Foreign Policy of Napoleon III* (2001). Informative histories of Mexico are R. E. Ruiz, *Triumphs and Tragedy: A History of the Mexican People* (1992); E. Krauze, *Mexico, Biography of Power: A History of Modern Mexico, 1810–1996* (trans. 1997); and B. Hamnett, *A Concise History of Mexico* (1999). The nineteenth-century Mexican leader Benito Juárez is studied in B. Hamnett, *Juárez* (1994); and the Indian revolutionary leader Emiliano Zapata, in biographies by J. Womack (1968) and R. Parkinson (1980). The last Brazilian monarch and his attempts at modernization are studied in R. J. Barman, *Citizen-Emperor: Pedro I and the Making of Brazil, 1825–1891* (2000).

For the imperialist activities of the United States in these years, one may consult W. LaFeber, *The New Empire* (1963); F. Merk, *Manifest Destiny and Mission in American History* (1963); and J. Dobson, *America's Ascent: The United States Becomes a Great Power, 1880–1914* (1978). Interpretive studies include W. A. Williams, *The Tragedy of American Diplomacy* (rev. 1988), highly critical of American imperialism; and E. R. May, *Imperial Democracy* (1961, reissued 1973) and *American Imperialism: A Speculative Essay* (1968), which are balanced assessments of American motives.

For the Spanish-American War one may read D. F. Trask, *The War with Spain in 1898* (1981); I. Musicant, *Empire by Default: The Spanish American War and the Dawn of the American Century* (1998); and the provocative analysis by L. Perez, Jr., *The War of 1898: The United States and Cuba in History and Historiography* (1998). Other studies of American expansion include S. Karnow, *In Our Image: America's Empire in the Philippines* (1989); B. M. Linn, *The Philippine War, 1899–1902* (2000); M. Tate, *The United States and the Hawaiian Kingdom* (1965); D. McCullough, *The Path between the Seas: The Creation of the Panama Canal, 1870–1914* (1977); and W. LaFeber, *The Panama Canal* (rev. 1989).

The Ottoman Empire, the Middle East, and the Balkans

An informative synthesis for the years since the founding of Islam is S. N. Fisher and W. Ochsenwald, *The Middle East: A History* (rev. 1997); the region's nineteenth-century history is examined in E. Karsh and I. Karsh, *Empires of the Sand: The Struggle for Mastery in the Middle East, 1789–1923* (1999). An excellent study of late Ottoman history is available in D. Quataert, *The Ottoman Empire, 1700–1922* (2000). For the role of the Ottoman Empire in European diplomacy and for national stirrings in the Empire, the books cited in Chapter 11 by M. S. Anderson (1966) and M. E. Yapp (1988) are instructive.

S. Deringil, *The Well-Protected Domains: Ideology and the Legitimation of Power in the Ottoman Empire, 1876–1909* (2001) describes the positive aspects of the often maligned Empire. J. Haslip, *The Sultan: The Life of Abdul Hamid II* (1958) is a vivid scholarly biography. The attempts at reform are discussed in D. Kushner, *The Rise of Turkish Nationalism, 1876–1908* (1977) and M. S. Hanioglu, *Preparation for a Revolution: The Young Turks, 1902–1908* (2001). For Egypt, there are available D. S. Landes, *Bankers and Pashas: International Finance and Economic Imperialism in Egypt* (1958); R. L. Tignor, *Modernization and British Colonial Rule in Egypt,*

1882–1914 (1966); and T. Mitchell, *Colonising Egypt* (1988), a cultural history of European attitudes and policies. Carrying the story toward the present is P. J. Valikiotis, *The History of Modern Egypt: From Muhammad Ali [Mehemet Ali] to Mubarek* (rev. 1991). The diplomacy surrounding the construction of the Suez Canal may be studied in J. Pudney, *Suez: De Lesseps' Canal* (1969); and Z. Karabel, *Parting the Desert: The Creation of the Suez Canal* (2003). The French experience in Lebanon is examined in J. F. Spagnolo, *French and Ottoman Lebanon, 1861–1914* (1977), and the Italian occupation of Libya is studied in C. G. Segrè, *Fourth Shore: The Italian Colonization of Libya* (1975).

For the rivalries in the Balkans and the emergent nationalist movements, in addition to books cited in Chapter 11, one may turn to B. H. Sumner, *Russia and the Balkans, 1870–1880* (1974) and B. Jelavich, *Russia's Balkan Entanglements, 1806–1914* (1991).

Africa

Excellent introductions to African history are R. Oliver, *The African Experience: From the Olduvai Gorge to the 21st Century* (2000); J. Iliffe, *Africans: The History of a Continent* (1995); J. Reader, *Africa: A Biography of the Continent* (1998); and J. D. Fage with W. Tordoff, *A History of Africa* (rev. 2002), with chapters on the colonial era. Other valuable introductions include B. Davidson, *Africa in History* (rev. 1991); R. W. July, *A History of the African People* (rev. 1998); and P. D. Curtin and others, *African History* (rev. 1995). African historians, including A. E. Afigbo, E. A. Ayandele, and others study the continent over the past two centuries in *The Making of Modern Africa* (2 vols.; rev. 1986). The years of colonial domination and the African response are also studied by African scholars in J. F. A. Ajayi (ed.), *Africa in the Nineteenth Century until the 1880s* (1989) and A. A. Boahen (ed.), *Africa under Colonial Domination, 1880–1935* (1985; abridged ed. 1990). The use of oral histories in the reconstruction of African history is elucidated in J. Vansina, *Oral Tradition as History* (1985) and is demonstrated by the same author in *Kingdoms of the Savanna* (1966).

P. Duignan and L. H. Gann, *Burden of Empire: An Appraisal of Western Colonialism South of the Sahara* (1967) and their other writings emphasize a "benevolent imperialism." In the same tradition, T. Pakenham has written a detailed narrative, *The Scramble for Africa: The White Man's Conquest of the Dark Continent from 1870 to 1912* (1992). These books may be compared with A. A. Boahen, *African Perspectives on Colonialism* (1989); F. McLynn, *Hearts of Darkness: The European Exploration of Africa* (1993); and M. E. Chamberlain, *The Scramble for Africa* (rev. 1999).

Available also are H. S. Wilson, *The Imperial Experience in Sub-Saharan Africa since 1870* (1977), a well-balanced synthesis; and for the French experience, W. B. Cohen, *Rulers of Empire: The French Colonial Service in Africa* (1971) and *The French Encounter with Africans: White Response to Blacks, 1530–1880* (1980). On the slave trade and its abolition, in addition to works cited in Chapters 3, 9, 10, and 11, one may read B. Davidson, *Black Mother: Africa and the Atlantic Slave Trade* (rev. 1980); and on the Brussels Conference of 1889, S. Miers, *Britain and the Ending of the Slave Trade* (1975).

There are biographical studies of Livingstone by, among others, O. Ransford (1978) and M. Buxton (2001). Other leading figures are examined in R. Hall, *Stanley: An Adventurer Explored* (1976), highly informative; F. J. McLynn, *Stanley* (2 vols.; 1989, 1991); J. Bierman, *Dark Safari: The Life Behind the Legend of Henry Morton Stanley* (1990); J. H. Waller, *Gordon of Khartoum* (1988); J. Pollock, *Gordon: The Man Behind the Legend* (1993); and M. F. Perham, *Lugard* (2 vols.; 1956, 1960), an impressive older work. J. Pollock, *Kitchener: Architect of Victory, Artisan of Peace* (2001) and P. Warner, *Kitchener: The Man behind the Legend* (1986), somewhat adulatory, may be compared with T. Royle, *The Kitchener Enigma* (1986), which is more critical. The brief biography of Cecil Rhodes by J. Flint (1976) merits reading, but R. I. Rotberg, *The Founder: Cecil Rhodes and the Pursuit of Power* (1988, 1990) is an outstanding study enriched by psychological insights. For a biography of the African leader who defeated the Italians at Adowa, one may read H. G. Marcus, *The Life and Times of Menelik II: Ethiopia, 1844–1913* (1975).

The best studies of the Belgian atrocities in the Congo are R. Slade, *King Leopold's Congo* (1962); R. Anstey, *King Leopold's Legacy* (1966); and the vivid A. Hochschild, *King Leopold's Ghost: A Story of Greed, Terror, and Heroism in Colonial Africa* (1998).

For the emergence of the Union of South Africa and later events, L. Thompson, *A History of South Africa* (rev. 2000), is a superb synthesis; also available is R. Ross, *A Concise History of South Africa* (1999). The South African War of 1899–1902 is recounted in B. Farwell, *The Great Boer War* (1999) and T. Pakenham, *The Boer War* (1979). A thoughtful biographical account relating to these years is K. Ingham, *Jan Christian Smuts: The Conscience of a South African* (1986).

Asia

Among informative general surveys of the European impact on Asia are the older works by K. M. Pannikar, *Asia and Western Dominance: The Vasco da Gama Epoch of Asian History, 1498–1945* (rev. 1959); E. S. Dodge, *Islands and Empires: Western Impact on the Pacific and East Asia* (1976); R. Murphey, *The Outsiders: The Western Experience in India and China* (1977); and later chapters in the same author's *East Asia: A New History* (rev. 2004). Case studies of European expansion in Asia are provided in I. Copeland, *The Burden of Empire: Perspectives on Imperialism and Colonialism* (1991). A number of more recent books have argued that the economic and social institutions of Asian societies should be studied for their own importance and should not be viewed simply as a response to the arrival of the Europeans. These arguments are developed in R. B. Wong, *China Transformed: Historical Change and the Limits of European Experience* (1997); A. G. Frank, *Reorient: Global Economy in the Asian Age* (1998); and K. Pomeranz, *The Great Divergence: Europe, China, and the Making of the Modern World Economy* (2000).

For India, one may read W. Golant, *The Long Afternoon: British India, 1601–1947* (1975); M. E. Chamberlain, *Britain and India: The Interactions of the Peoples* (1974); C. A. Bayly, *Indian Society and the Making of the British Empire* (1990); J. M. Brown, *Modern India: The Origins of an Asian Democracy* (rev. 1994); and L. James, *Raj: The Making and Unmaking of British India* (1999). The revolt of 1857 is studied in C. Hibbert, *The Great Mutiny: India, 1857* (1978); E. Stokes and C. A. Bayly, *The Peasant Armed: The Indian Rebellion of 1857* (1986); and T. R. Metcalf, *The Aftermath of Revolt: India, 1857–1870* (1964). The contest between Britain and Russia for remote parts of central Asia is recounted in K. E. Meyer and S. B. Brysac, *Tournament of Shadows: The Great Game and the Race for Empire in Central Asia* (2000).

One of the best introductions to East Asia is J. K. Fairbank, E. O. Reischauer, and A. M. Craig, *East Asia: Tradition and Transformation* (1989, with periodic revisions); and for China, J. K. Fairbank and M. Goldman, *China: A New History* (rev. 1998). Other overviews of China include J. A. G. Roberts, *A Concise History of China* (1999); and I. C. Y. Hsu, *The Rise of Modern China* (rev. 2000). J. E. Wills, Jr., *Mountain of Fame: Portraits in Chinese History* (1994) provides a valuable biographical approach to Chinese history. J. D. Spence, *The Search for Modern China* (rev. 1999) goes back over four centuries with perceptive insights into China's relations with the West. The same author's *The Gate of Heavenly Peace: The Chinese and Their Revolution, 1895–1980* (1981) links earlier history to twentieth-century revolutions, the subject also of J. K. Fairbank, *The Great Chinese Revolution, 1800–1985* (1986).

A detailed authoritative study of the mid-nineteenth century Taiping upheaval is Jen Yu-wen, *The Taiping Revolutionary Movement* (1973), but one may also read S. Y. Teng, *The Taiping Rebellion and the Western Powers* (rev. 1977); and on its self-professed Christian leader, J. D. Spence, *God's Chinese Son: The Taiping Heavenly Kingdom of Hong Xiuquan* (1996). The Opium Wars are studied in J. K. Fairbank, *Trade and Diplomacy on the China Coast: The Opening of the Treaty Ports, 1842–1854* (2 vols.; 1953); H. G. Gelber, *Opium, Soldiers and Evangeli-*

cals: Britain's 1840–42 War with China and its After-math (2004); and in books by P. W. Fay (1975, 1997) and B. Inglis (1976). The antiforeign upheaval of 1898–1900 is examined in J. W. Esherick, *The Origins of the Boxer Uprising* (1987); D. Preston, *Besieged In Peking: The Story of the 1900 Boxer Rising* (1999); L. Xiang, *The Origins of the Boxer War: A Multinational Study* (2003); and P. A. Cohen, *History in Three Keys: The Boxers as Event, Experience, and Myth* (1997), which describes both Chinese and European interpretations of the events at the time and in historical memory.

On the American role in the Far East and the Open Door policy one may read W. Cohen, *America's Response to China* (rev. 2000); J. C. Thomsen, Jr., P. W. Stanley, and J. C. Perry, *Sentimental Imperialists: The American Experience in East Asia* (1981); and A. Iriye, *Pacific Estrangement: Japanese and American Expansion, 1897–1911* (1972). The confrontation between Russia and Japan is studied in I. Nish, *The Origins of the Russo-Japanese War* (1985); and D. Walder, *The Short Victorious War: The Russo-Japanese Conflict, 1904–1905* (1975). The Japanese occupation of Korea is recounted in P. Duus, *The Abacus and the Sword: The Japanese Penetration of Korea* (1998).

Useful Web Sites

There are helpful sources and links on imperialism, Africa, South Asia, and East Asia at the extraordinary site created by Paul Halsall at Fordham University (and often cited in previous chapters). For imperialism in general, visit the *Internet Modern History Sourcebook*, www.forham.edu/halsall/mod/modsbook.html, which also includes materials on postcolonial Latin America; for Africa, there is the *Internet African History Sourcebook*, at www.fordham.edu/halsall/africa/africasbook.html; and for Asia, readers will find the *Internet Indian History Sourcebook*, www.fordham.edu/halsall/india/indiasbook.html; and the *Internet East Asian History Sourcebook*, www.fordham.edu/halsall/eastasia/eastasiasbook.html, which includes excellent materials on China and Japan as well as links to helpful sources on European imperialism. Valuable resources and links on the Ottoman Empire are included in the *Internet Islamic History Sourcebook*, www.fordham.edu/halsall/islam/islamsbook.html. An accessible introduction to the British Empire may be found at *BBC-History-Empire*, www.bbc.co.uk/history/state/empire.

17. THE FIRST WORLD WAR

Accounts of international relations emphasizing the shift in the twentieth century from a European to a global balance of power include G. Ross, *The Great Powers and the Decline of the European States System, 1914–1945* (1983); F. R. Bridge and R. Bullen, *The Great Powers and the European States System,* *1814–1914* (rev. 2005), which traces prewar international relations from the nineteenth century to the eve of the war; C. J. Bartlett, *The Global Conflict: The International Rivalry of the Great Powers, 1880–1990* (rev. 1994); and W. R. Keylor, *The Twentieth-Century World: An International History* (rev. 2001).

Diplomatic Background, Origins, Responsibilities

The most judicious account of the war's complex origins, assessing both the evidence and divergent interpretations, is J. Joll, *The Origins of the First World War* (rev. 1992), which may be supplemented by G. Martel, *The Origins of the First World War* (rev. 2003). Attempts to examine and synthesize the continuing debate over war responsibility are J. W. Langdon, *July 1914: The Long Debate: 1918–1990* (1991); R. J. W. Evans and H. P. Van Strandmann (eds.), *The Coming of the First World War* (1989); A. Mombauer, *The Origins of the First World War: Controversies and Consensus* (2002); and D. Fromkin, *Europe's Last Summer: Who Started the Great War in 1914?* (2004), which blames Germany for the outbreak of the war.

The controversy reopened after 1945 when the West German scholar Fritz Fischer, on the basis of new archival materials, argued the case for German culpability in *Germany's Aims in the First World War* (1961; trans. 1967) and in several later books. He argued that Germany had to grasp for "world power" or face decline and that elite groups in Germany pressed this objective to thwart democratization.

On diplomacy in the decades after 1870, there is a masterful diplomatic account in two volumes by G. F. Kennan: *The Decline of Bismarck's European Order: Franco-Russian Relations, 1875–1890* (1979) and *The Fateful Alliance: France, Russia, and the Coming of the First World War* (1984). A colorful reconstruction of the era for the general reader, focusing on monarchs, military leaders, and diplomats is available in R. K. Massie, *Dreadnought: Britain, Germany, and the Coming of the First World War* (1992). N. Ferguson, *The Pity of War* (1999), despite many striking insights into diplomatic and military matters, argues, not convincingly, that there was no compelling reason for the British to become involved and that the consequences were disastrous for Britain.

D. E. Lee's careful study, *Europe's Crucial Years: The Diplomatic Background of World War I, 1902–1914* (1974), reaffirms the argument that each state acted out of desperate concern for its own presumed interests. The influence of national elites is examined in R. F. Hamilton and H. H. Herwig, *Decisions for War, 1914–1917* (2004). Domestic and foreign considerations are linked in a British series of books that includes V. R. Berghahn, *Germany and the Approach of War in 1914* (rev. 1993); Z. S. Steiner, *Britain and the Origins of the First World War* (1977); R. J. B. Bosworth, *Italy, the Least of the Great Powers: Italian*

Foreign Policy before the First World War (1980); J. F. V. Keiger, *France and the Origins of the First World War* (1984); D. C. B. Lieven, *Russia and the Origins of the First World War* (1984); and S. R. Williamson, Jr., *Austria-Hungary and the Origins of the First World War* (1991).

For prewar diplomacy and strategic planning, readers will find especially useful three books by P. Kennedy: *The Rise of the Anglo-German Antagonism, 1860–1914* (1980), *Strategy and Diplomacy, 1870–1945* (1984), and a collaborative volume he has edited, *War Plans of the Great Powers, 1880–1914* (1979). The Balkan antecedents of the war are examined in R. C. Hall, *The Balkan Wars, 1912–1913: Prelude to the First World War* (2000).

The involvement of the United States in the war is studied in E. R. May, *The World War and American Isolation, 1914–1917* (1959), an outstanding study; R. Gregory, *The Origins of American Intervention in the First World War* (1971); R. H. Ferrell, *Woodrow Wilson and World War I* (1985); M. Harries and S. Harries, *The Last Days of Innocence: America at War, 1917–1918* (1997).

The War

For the war readers may turn to the comprehensive accounts in H. Strachan, *The First World War* (2004); D. Stevenson, *Cataclysm: The First World War as Political Tragedy* (2004); and M. S. Neiberg, *Fighting the Great War: A Global History* (2005). Other informative narratives appear in works by M. Gilbert (1995), J. Keegan (1999), and M. Howard (2002). Books focusing on the social impact of the war include M. Ferro, *The Great War, 1914–1918* (trans. 1973); K. Robbins, *The First World War* (1984); B. E. Schmitt and H. C. Vedeler, *The World in the Crucible, 1914–1919* (1984); and J. M. Winter, *The Experience of World War I* (1989).

Books that seek to convey the ordeal of trench warfare on the western front include E. J. Leed, *No Man's Land: Combat and Identity in World War I* (1979); T. Ashworth, *Trench Warfare, 1914–1918: The Live and Let-Live System* (1980); and J. Ellis, *Eye-Deep in Hell: Trench Warfare in World War I* (1989). J. Keegan, *The Face of Battle* (1976), in one memorable chapter evokes the horrors of the Somme. For the American military experience, one may read E. M. Coffman, *The War to End All Wars* (1968, 1998). The naval war is described in R. K. Massie, *Castles of Steel: Britain, Germany, and the Winning of the Great War at Sea* (2003).

The Home Front: Social, Economic, and Cultural Impact of the War

For the impact of war and of preparations for war on European society, one should read B. Bond, *War and Society in Europe, 1870–1970* (rev. 1998); A. Marwick, *War and Social Change in the Twentieth Cen-*

tury (1975), a comparative examination of five countries; and G. Hardach, *The First World War, 1914–1918* (1977), focusing on the economic aspects of the war and its consequences.

For the war on the home front one may turn to J. Williams, *The Other Battleground: The Home Fronts—Britain, France and Germany, 1914–1918* (1972); N. M. Heyman, *Daily Life During World War I* (2002); and the essays in R. Wall and J. Winter (eds.), *The Upheaval of War: Family, Work, and Welfare in Europe, 1914–1918* (1989). For Britain, one may read J. M. Winter, *The Great War and the British People* (1986), an outstanding volume; B. Waites, *A Class Society at War: England, 1914–1918* (1988); and J. Bourne, *Britain and the Great War, 1914–1918* (1989). For Germany: J. Kocka, *Facing Total War: German Society, 1914–1918* (trans. 1984); L. V. Meyer, *Victory Must Be Ours: Germany in the Great War, 1914–1918* (1995); and R. Chickering, *Imperial Germany and the Great War, 1914–1918* (1998). The dictatorial powers that the German generals preempted are examined with telling detail in M. Kitchen, *The Silent Dictatorship: The Politics of the German High Command under Hindenburg and Ludendorff, 1916–1918* (1976). For France: J. J. Becker, *The Great War and the French People* (trans. 1986); P. J. Flood, *France, 1914–1918: Public Opinion and the War Effort* (1989); and L. V. Smith, S Audoin-Rouzeau, and A. Becker, *France and the Great War, 1914–1918* (2003). For the United States D. M. Kennedy, *Over Here: The First World War and American Society* (1980, reissued 2004) is informative.

The contributions of women to the war effort are examined in S. R. Grayzel, *Women and the First World War* (2002); G Braybon, *Women Workers in the First World War: The British Experience* (1981); M. W. Greenwald, *Women, War, and Work: The Impact of World War I on Women Workers in the United States* (1980); and D. Schneider and C. Schneider, *Into the Breach: American Women Overseas in World War I* (1991).

The devastating worldwide influenza epidemic that doubled the combat toll is described in A. W. Crosby, *America's Forgotten Pandemic: The Influenza of 1918* (1976, 1990); G. Kolata, *The Story of the Great Influenza Pandemic of 1918* (2000); and J. M. Barry, *The Great Influenza: The Epic Story of the Deadliest Plague in History* (2004).

One of the tragedies of the war, the forced deportation of the Armenians by the Turkish authorities, and the ensuing mass deaths, is recounted in C. J. Walker, *Armenia: The Survival of a Nation* (rev. 1990); D. M. Lang, *The Armenians: A People in Exile* (1989); R. Melson, *Revolution and Genocide: On the Origins of the Armenian Genocide and the Holocaust* (1993), which sees the episode as the first chapter in twentieth-century ethnic destruction; and D. Bloxham, *The Great Game of Genocide: Imperialism, National-*

ism, and the Destruction of the Ottoman Armenians (2005), a well-researched study of the international context in which the assault on the Armenians took place.

The cultural meaning of the war is examined in P. Fussell, *The Great War and Modern Memory* (1975, 2000), a moving account of how the miseries of the war became part of contemporary literature and culture; S. Hynes, *A War Imagined: The First World War and English Culture* (1992); and G. Robb, *British Culture and the First World War* (2002). Other studies of the war's impact on intellectual life are R. Wohl, *The Generation of 1914* (1979); R. N. Stromberg, *Redemption by War: The Intellectuals and 1914* (1982); J. Cruickshank, *Variations on Catastrophe: Some French Responses to the Great War* (1982); F. Field, *British and French Writers of the First World War* (1991); A. Roshwald and R. Stites (eds.), *European Culture in the Great War: The Arts, Entertainment and Propaganda, 1914–1918* (1999); M. Ecksteins, *The Rites of Spring: The Great War and the Birth of the Modern Age* (1989, 2000), an inquiry into the shaping of a new cultural consciousness; and G. Mosse, *Sites of Mourning: The Great War in European Cultural History* (1996).

Wartime Diplomacy

For wartime diplomacy one profits from D. Stevenson, *The First World War and International Politics* (1988). Two provocative studies focusing on the diplomatic duel between the United States and Russia are V. S. Mamatey, *The United States and East Central Europe, 1914–1918* (1975) and A. J. Mayer, *Wilson vs. Lenin: The Political Origins of the New Diplomacy* (1959). The fate of the German colonial empire is explored in W. R. Louis, *Great Britain and Germany's Lost Colonies, 1914–1919* (1967).

For Allied activities in the Middle East, and on the revolt of the Arabs against the Turks, one may begin with T. E. Lawrence, *Seven Pillars of Wisdom* (1926, 1935), fascinating but to be read with caution, and J. Wilson, *Lawrence of Arabia: The Authorized Biography of T. E. Lawrence* (1989), the fullest account. Focusing on the Middle East and the end of the Ottoman Empire are C. E. Dawn, *From Ottomanism to Arabism* (1973); H. M. Sachar, *The Emergence of the Middle East, 1914–1924* (1969); P. C. Helmreich, *From Paris to Sèvres: The Partition of the Ottoman Empire at the Peace Conference of 1919–1920* (1974); D. Fromkin, *A Peace to End All Peace: Creating the Modern Middle East, 1914–1922* (1989), especially informative; and the previously cited work by E. Karsh and I. Karsh, *Empires of the Sand: The Struggle for Mastery in the Middle East, 1789–1923* (1999), providing the background to the postwar settlement.

The emergence of the British mandate for Palestine is studied in impressive detail in L. Stein, *The Balfour Declaration* (1961) and R. Sanders, *The High Walls of Jerusalem: A History of the Balfour Declaration and the Birth of the British Mandate* (1984).

The Peace

For the armistice, one may turn to S. Weintraub, *A Stillness Heard Round the World: The End of the Great War, November 1918* (1987), a colorful evocation of the war's end, and B. Lowry, *Armistice 1918* (1996), a thorough diplomatic analysis. The postwar revolutionary mood is described in G. Schulz, *Revolution and Peace Treaties, 1917–1920* (trans. 1972); and F. L. Carsten, *Revolution in Central Europe, 1918–1919* (1972). The end of the Dual Monarchy is studied in A. J. May, *The Passing of the Habsburg Monarchy, 1914–1918* (2 vols.; 1966) and Z. A. B. Zeman, *The Breakup of the Habsburg Empire, 1914–1918* (1961).

On the Paris peace conference, the best introductions are A. Sharp, *The Versailles Settlement: Peacemaking in Paris* (1991), and the more comprehensive M. MacMillan, *Paris 1919: Six Months that Changed the World* (2002). The decision-making process itself is studied in H. Elcock, *Portrait of a Decision: The Council of Four and the Treaty of Versailles* (1972). The debates are available in P. Mantoux (ed.), *The Paris Peace Conference, 1919: Proceedings of the Council of Four* (1955; trans. 1964).

On Wilson's role, the best study is A. Walworth, *Wilson and His Peacemakers: American Diplomacy at the Paris Peace Conference, 1919* (1987); also helpful are K. A. Clements, *The Presidency of Woodrow Wilson* (1992), a concise appraisal; A. Heckscher, *Woodrow Wilson* (1992), a detailed full-length biography; and insightful brief biographies by L. Auchincloss (2000) and H. W. Brands (2003). There are also two insightful studies by A. S. Link, the editor of Wilson's collected papers: *Wilson the Diplomatist* (1957) and *Woodrow Wilson: War, Revolution, and Peace* (1979). Biographies of Clemenceau by D. R. Watson (1974) and D. S. Newhall (1991), and of David Lloyd George by J. Grigg (1973–1985) and others have been cited in Chapter 14; to them should be added J. F. V. Keiger, *Raymond Poincaré* (1997).

A study arguing that the major preoccupation underlying decisions at Versailles was the threat of Bolshevism and domestic radicalism is A. J. Mayer, *Politics and Diplomacy of Peacemaking: Containment and Counter-Revolution at Versailles, 1918–1919* (1967); it may be compared with J. M. Thompson, *Russia, Bolshevism, and the Versailles Peace* (1966), which views the revolutionary threat as important but not dominating. Important balanced reappraisals, many based on new archival materials, may be found in the contributions to M. F. Boemeke, G. D. Feldman, and E. Glaser (eds.), *The Treaty of Versailles: A Reassessment After 75 Years* (1998). The emergence of new nations in central Europe is described in S. Bonsal, *Suitors and Suppliants: The Little Nations at Versailles* (1964), and the Polish question is carefully examined by a Danish historian, K. Lundrgreen-Nielsen, *The Polish Problem at the Paris Peace Conference* (trans. 1979). On the disputed issue of reparations, J. M. Keynes, *The Economic Consequences of the Peace* (1920), became the single most influential book, vehemently critical of the entire peace settlement. E. Mantoux, *The Carthaginian Peace—or the Economic Consequences of Mr. Keynes* (1946), provided a vigorous later reply to Keynes. The first volume of a valuable three-volume study, R. Skidelsky, *John Maynard Keynes: A Biography: Vol. 1, Hopes Betrayed, 1883–1920* (1986), carries Keynes through the peace conference; there is also a one-volume edition of Skidelsy's biographical study, *John Maynard Keyes, 1883–1946: Economist, Philosopher, Statesman* (2005).

Useful Web Sites

There are numerous links to both documents and images from the First World War at *The World War I Document Archive*, a site at the Brigham Young University Library, www.lib.byu.edu/~rdh/wwi/. Other resources may be found at *The Museum of the Great War*, a French museum that provides English-language materials at www.historial.org/; and there are materials focusing on Britain at *BBC-History-World War One*, www.bbc.co.uk/history/war/wwone/. Helpful materials on the postwar settlement are available at *Paris Peace Conference*, www.nv.cc.us/home/cevans/Versailles/Index.html.

18. THE RUSSIAN REVOLUTION AND THE SOVIET UNION

With the collapse of the Soviet Union in 1991 new archival materials have made it possible to confirm, modify, or refute earlier works and to rethink twentieth-century Russian history. Recent histories include O. Figes, *A People's Tragedy: A History of the Russian Revolution* (1997) and G. Hosking, *Russia and the Russians* (2001), an excellent one-volume narrative. The same author's *Russia: Empire and Nation* (1997) may be compared with D. Lieven, *The Russian Empire and Its Rivals* (2001). Other surveys include C. Evtuhov and R. Stites, *A History of Russia: Peoples, Legends, Events, Forces since 1800* (2004); and R. Service, *A History of Modern Russia: From Nicholas II to Putin* (2003), which begins with the pre-revolutionary era. M. E. Malia, *The Soviet Tragedy: A History of Socialism in Russia, 1917–1991* (1993) maintains that the Revolution's utopian goals were doomed from the beginning; the same author's *Russia Under Western Eyes: From the Bronze Horseman to the Lenin Mausoleum* (1999) argues that Russia at least since Peter the Great was always more Western-oriented than most observers believed. M. Lewin, *The Soviet Century* (2005) is an insightful assessment by a long-time student of the Soviet regime. Additional accounts will be listed in later chapters.

Russia before 1917: Late Tsarist Russia

A number of books on nineteenth-century Russia have been cited earlier. For late tsarist Russia one may read L. Kochan, *Russia in Revolution, 1890–1918* (1966) and H. Rogger, *Russia in the Age of Modernization and Revolution, 1881–1917* (1983).

Political thought and ferment may be studied in F. Venturi, *Roots of Revolution* (trans. 1983), cited earlier; A. Vucinich, *Social Thought in Tsarist Russia* (1976); and P. Pomper, *The Russian Revolutionary Intelligentsia* (rev. 1993). Two books stressing the non-revolutionary progressive views of many pre-1914 Russian intellectuals are I. Berlin, *Russian Thinkers* (1978), cited earlier, and A. H. Kelly, *Toward Another Shore: Russian Thinkers between Necessity and Choice* (1998). The world of labor is examined in V. E. Bonnell, *Roots of Rebellion: Workers' Politics and Organizations in St. Petersburg and Moscow, 1900–1914* (1983) and in the volume she has edited of workers' autobiographical accounts, *The Russian Worker: Life and Labor under the Tsarist Regime* (1983). Cultural life in this period is the subject of L. McReynolds, *Russia at Play: Leisure Activities at the End of the Tsarist Era* (2003).

An important political leader who served the tsar is described in R. Pipes, *Struve* (2 vols.; 1970–1980), informative on the fate of liberalism. Right-wing extremism linked to anti-Semitic pogroms is explored in W. Laqueur, *Black Hundred: The Rise of the Extreme Right in Russia* (1993). For the emergent revolutionary leaders one may read L. Haimson, *The Russian Marxists and the Origins of Bolshevism* (1955); I. Getzler, *Martov* (1967); S. H. Baron, *Plekhanov* (1963); and A. Ascher, *Pavel Axelrod and the Development of Menshevism* (1972). On the anarchists, there is P. Avrich, *The Russian Anarchists* (1967), and on a leading exemplar, M. A. Miller, *Kropotkin* (1976) and C. Cahm, *Peter Kropotkin and the Rise of Revolutionary Anarchism* (1989).

The events of 1905 are narrated and analyzed in a valuable two-volume account by A. Ascher: *The Revolution of 1905: Vol. I, Russia in Disarray* (1988) and Vol. II, *Authority Restored* (1992), carrying the story to 1907. Also informative is A. M. Verner, *The Crisis of Russian Autocracy: Nicholas II and the 1905 Revolution* (1990).

Explorations of the ill-fated effort to establish a constitutional monarchy after 1905 include A. E. Healy, *The Russian Autocracy in Crisis, 1905–1907* (1976); and G. Hosking, *The Russian Constitutional Experiment: Government and Duma, 1906–1914* (1973). The Russian wartime experience is vividly described in W. B. Lincoln, *In War's Dark Shadow* (1983) and *Passage through Armageddon* (1986). The confusion at the court graphically emerges from R. K. Massie's *Nicholas and Alexandra* (1967, 2000). For the last Romanoff one may also read M. Ferro, *Nicholas II: The Last of the Tsars* (1993) and R. D.

Warth, *Nicholas II: The Life and Reign of Russia's Last Monarch* (1998). E. Radzinsky, *The Last Tsar: The Life and Death of Nicholas II* (trans. 1992) reconstructs the execution of the royal family in 1918; the same author has also used a newly available dossier on Rasputin to write a vivid biography of the mad monk who became the royal family's close adviser, *The Rasputin File* (trans. 2000).

The Revolutions of 1917

The best account of the earlier revolution is T. Hasegawa, *The February Revolution: Petrograd, 1917* (1981); there are other informative studies by G. Katkov (1967), M. Ferro (1971), and E. N. Burdzhalov (1987). The ill-fated Kerensky is studied in R. Abraham, *Alexander Kerensky: The First Love of the Revolution* (1987).

For the fullest and most comprehensive account of the revolutionary years one turns to R. Pipes, *The Russian Revolution* (1990) and *Russia Under the Bolshevik Regime* (1994), the latter carrying the story through Lenin's death in 1924. Available also is C. Read, *From Tsar to Soviets: The Russian People and the Revolution, 1917–1921* (1996). Focusing on the social breadth and depth of the revolution are two books by M. Ferro: *The Fall of Tsarism and the Origins of Bolshevik Power* (trans. 1967) and *October 1917: A Social History of the Russian Revolution* (trans. 1980).

The best introductions to the civil war, the formation of the Soviet state, and foreign intervention are E. Mawdsley, *The Russian Civil War* (1987); W. B. Lincoln, *Red Victory: A History of the Russian Civil War* (1990); V. N. Brovkin, *Behind the Front Lines of the Civil War: Political Parties and Social Movements in Russia, 1918–1922* (1994); and D. J. Raleigh, *Experiencing Russia's Civil War: Politics, Society, and Revolutionary Culture in Saratov, 1917–1922* (2002). For the withdrawal from the war and the subsequent Allied intervention, one may turn to G. F. Kennan, *Soviet-American Relations, 1917–1920* (2 vols.; 1956–1958) and R. H. Ullman, *Anglo-Soviet Relations, 1917–1921* (3 vols.; 1961–1972). The peace imposed by Germany is described in an older work by J. W. Wheeler-Bennett, *The Forgotten Peace: Brest-Litovsk, March 1918* (1939, 1966); the stormy relations of the Soviet Union with newly independent Poland are described in P. S. Wandycz, *Soviet-Polish Relations, 1917–1921* (1969). A helpful reference guide for all these events is H. Shukman (ed.), *The Blackwell Encyclopedia of the Russian Revolution* (rev. 1994).

The U.S.S.R.

For the early years one should read R. Pipes, *Russia Under the Bolshevik Regime* (1994), cited earlier, which examines in detail the consolidation of the dictatorial regime by 1924. P. Avrich, *Kronstadt, 1921* (1970, 1991), describes the leftist uprising and its suppression. An institution that was destined to endure is

studied in L. D. Gerson, *The Secret Police in Lenin's Russia* (1976) and G. Leggett, *The Cheka: Lenin's Political Police* (1981).

For the years under Lenin and the early years of Stalin's rule one may consult E. H. Carr's synthesis of his massive 14-volume study (1950–1979), *The Russian Revolution: From Lenin to Stalin* (1979, reissued 2004), in which Carr seeks to make the best possible case for the reconstruction of Soviet society in the years 1917–1929. Focusing on sociological and cultural aspects of this period are R. Stites, *Revolutionary Dreams: Utopian Vision and Experimental Life in the Russian Revolution* (1988); V. Brovkin, *Russia after Lenin: Politics, Culture and Society, 1921–1929* (1998); G. Hosking, *The First Socialist Society: A History of the Soviet Union from Within* (rev. 1990), which carries a comprehensive social history through to the end of the Soviet experiment; and S. Fitzpatrick's three books: *The Russian Revolution, 1917–1932* (1982), *The Cultural Front: Power and Culture in Revolutionary Russia* (1992), and *Everyday Stalinism: Ordinary Life in Extraordinary Times* (1999). For all aspects of economic developments from 1917 on, one may turn to A. Nove, *An Economic History of the U.S.S.R.* (rev. 1992). A good general account of the years from the Revolution to Stalin's death is H. Carrère d'Encausse, *A History of the Soviet Union, 1917–1953* (2 vols.; trans. 1982).

Stalin's collectivization of agriculture may be studied in M. Lewin, *Russian Peasants and Soviet Power* (trans. 1975) and R. Conquest, *The Harvest of Sorrow: Soviet Collectivization and the Terror-Famine* (1986), which graphically reconstructs the ruthlessness of collectivization and the accompanying famine of 1932.

For the political terror in the Stalin era the most revealing studies are R. Medvedev, *Let History Judge: The Origins and Consequences of Stalinism* (trans. 1989), by a Soviet dissident historian; and for the party purges and terror of 1936–1938, stressing the enormity of the now officially conceded blood bath, R. Conquest, *The Great Terror: A Reassessment* (1968, 1990). Some of the corroborative new evidence surfacing in the years after 1985 is discussed in R. Pipes, *The Unknown Lenin: From the Soviet Archives* (1997); W. Laqueur, *Stalin: The Glasnost Revelations* (1990); and A. Applebaum, *Gulag: A History* (2003). The origins of the party purges are examined in R. Conquest, *Stalin and the Kirov Murder* (1989), and from a different perspective in the controversial J. A. Getty, *Origins of the Great Purges: The Soviet Communist Party Reconsidered, 1933–1938* (1986). Stalin's tyrannical repression of the Communist inner circle is described in S. S. Montefiore, *Stalin: The Court of the Red Tsar* (2003).

Biographical Accounts

Among older biographical accounts for these years are B. D. Wolfe, *Three Who Made a Revolution: A Biographical History* [Lenin, Trotsky, Stalin] (1948,

1964); H. Shukman, *Lenin and the Russian Revolution* (1987); and A. B. Ulam, *Lenin and the Bolsheviks* (1965, 1969). There are also lives of Lenin by D. Shub (1948, 1966), R. Conquest (1972), R. H. W. Theen (1973), and M. Lewin (1978); and a more recent work by R. Service, *Lenin—A Biography* (2000), a well-researched study. Lenin's wife and her fate in the Stalin years are ably studied in R. H. McNeal, *Bride of the Revolution: Krupskaya and Lenin* (1972).

I. Deutscher's overly sympathetic three-volume *Life of Trotsky* (1954–1963), and R. Segal, *Leon Trotsky* (1979), also sympathetic, may be compared with the more balanced appraisals by R. S. Wistrich, *Trotsky: Fate of a Revolutionary* (1979); I. Howe, *Leon Trotsky* (1979); and I. D Thatcher (2003). S. F. Cohen, *Bukharin and the Bolshevik Revolution: A Political Biography, 1888–1938* (1973, 1980) is an outstanding study of a leading Old Bolshevik who helped shape Lenin's New Economic Policy and, had he prevailed, who might have averted Stalin's dictatorship.

For an outstanding study of Stalin in the years before the Second World War one may read R. C. Tucker, *Stalin as Revolutionary, 1879–1929* (1973) and *Stalin in Power: The Revolution from Above, 1928–1941* (1990). Other biographical accounts are A. B. Ulam, *Stalin: The Man and His Era* (1973); the imaginative but uncritical I. Deutscher, *Stalin: A Political Biography* (1967); R. H. McNeal, *Stalin: Man and Ruler* (1988); and R. Service, *Stalin: A Biography* (2005), which examines both public policies and Stalin's private life.

In a special category, a series of biographies by D. Volkogonov has appeared in English translation. Volkogonov was for many years a top-ranking Soviet military intelligence official with unique access to key archival sources, and his books provide indispensable special information. Among them are *Stalin: Triumph and Tragedy* (trans. 1992), *Lenin: A New Biography* (trans. 1994), *Trotsky: The Eternal Revolutionary* (trans. 1996), and for his overall review of Soviet history, *Autopsy for an Empire: The Seven Leaders Who Built the Soviet Regime* [Lenin to Gorbachev] (trans. 1998).

Among thoughtful earlier efforts to assess the Russian experience from the revolution on into the interwar years and beyond are T. H. Von Laue, *Why Lenin? Why Stalin? A Reappraisal of the Russian Revolution, 1900–1930* (rev. 1993); E. Acton, *Rethinking the Russian Revolution* (1990); S. F. Cohen, *Rethinking the Soviet Experience: Politics and History since 1917* (1985); and two books by M. Lewin: *The Making of the Soviet System: Essays in the Social History of Interwar Russia* (1985) and *The Gorbachev Phenomenon: A Historical Interpretation* (rev. 1991). Books on the last years of the Soviet regime and on its collapse in 1991 will be described in Chapter 26.

Other Themes and Institutions

On other subjects and institutions one may read R. Kolkowitz, *The Soviet Military and the Communist Party* (1967); L. R. Graham, *Science and Philosophy in the Soviet Union* (1972) and his other writings; and C. V. James, *Soviet Socialist Realism* (1973), on the arts and literature. For Soviet policies toward various nationalities, one may turn to T. Martin, *The Affirmative Action Empire: Nations and Nationalism in the Soviet Union, 1923–1939* (2001). Accounts of Soviet religious policies are available in S. P. Ramet (ed.), *Religious Policy in the Soviet Union* (1992) and N. Davis, *A Long Walk to Church: A Contemporary History of Russian Orthodoxy* (1995). The Jewish question is thoughtfully explored in Z. Gitelman, *The Jews of Russia and the Soviet Union* (1988); A. Vaksberg, *Stalin Against the Jews* (1994); G. Kostyrchenko, *Out of the Red Shadows: Anti-Semitism in Stalin's Russia* (1996); and J. Brent and V. Naumov, *Stalin's Last Crime: The Plot Against the Jewish Doctors, 1948–1953* (2003).

The role of women in the prerevolutionary and postrevolutionary years may be studied in R. Stites, *The Women's Liberation Movement in Russia: Feminism, Nihilism, and Bolshevism, 1860–1930* (rev. 1991); L. Engelstein, *The Keys to Happiness: Sex and the Search for Modernity in Fin-de-Siècle Russia* (1992), on the late nineteenth century; G. W. Lapidus, *Women in Soviet Society: Equality, Development, and Social Change* (1978); B. E. Clements and others (eds.), *Russia's Women: Accommodation, Resistance, Transformation* (1990); L. Edmondson (ed.), *Women and Society in Russia and the Soviet Union* (1992); and S. Fitzpatrick and Y. Slezkine (eds.), *In The Shadow of Revolution: Life Stories of Russian Women from 1917 to the Second World War* (2000).

Soviet Foreign Relations and World Communism

Still useful for Soviet foreign policy are A. B. Ulam, *Expansion and Coexistence: The History of Soviet Foreign Policy, 1917–1973* (rev. 1974) and his other writings; and the volumes by L. F. Fischer: *The Soviets in World Affairs, 1917–1929* (rev. 1960) and *Russia's Road from Peace to War: Soviet Foreign Relations, 1917–1941* (1969).

On the Comintern, one may turn to K. E. McKenzie, *Comintern and World Revolution, 1928–1943* (1964); K. McDermott and J. Agnew, *The Comintern: A History of International Communism from Lenin to Stalin* (1997); and the essays in T. Rees and A. Thorpe (eds.), *International Communism and the Communist International, 1919–43* (1998). The clash of Bolshevism with French, Italian, and German socialism is ably explored in A. S. Lindemann, *The "Red Years": European Socialism vs. Bolshevism, 1918–1920* (1974), while R. Wohl examines the French experience with insight and depth in *French Communism in the Making, 1919–1924* (1966).

Useful Web Sites

The *Internet Modern History Sourcebook* includes linked documents on the Russian Revolution at www.fordham.edu/halsall/mod/modsbook39.html; and there are links to additional resources on early twentieth-century Russia at the previously cited *Russian Studies at Bucknell University*, www.departments.bucknell.edu/russian/. Readers will also find excellent materials on the revolutionary era and later periods of Russian history at the Web sites of the *School of Slavonic and East European Studies* in London, www.ssees.ac.uk/index/htm; the University of Pittsburgh's *Russian and East European Studies Virtual Library*, www.ucis.pitt.eud/reesweb/; and the *Russian and East European Network Information Center* at the University of Texas, http://reenic.utexas.edu/eenic/index.html. These sites provide up-to-date links to other sites with documents, images, biographical narratives, and historical information on Russia and other republics that were part of the U.S.S.R.

19. DEMOCRACY, ANTI-IMPERIALISM, AND THE ECONOMIC CRISIS AFTER THE FIRST WORLD WAR

A number of general histories of the twentieth century begin with the First World War and the revolutionary changes that accompanied it. Among these are E. J. Hobsbawm, *The Age of Extremes: A History of the World, 1914–1991* (1994), an insightful book on the years between the First World War and the collapse of the Soviet Union, which he calls the "short twentieth century"; J. A. S. Grenville, *A History of the World from the 20th to the 21st Century* (rev. 2005), a detailed narrative; and H. Evans and others, *The American Century* (1998), an interpretive account of major developments and issues. Informative also are the essays in R. W. Bulliet (ed.), *The Columbia History of the Twentieth Century* (1998) and M. Howard and R. Louis (eds.), *The Oxford History of the Twentieth Century* (1998, 2000). A useful reference book for twentieth-century world history is C. Cook and J. Stevenson, *The Routledge Companion to World History since 1914* (2005).

For Europe in the twentieth century one may read S. M. Di Scala, *Twentieth Century Europe: Politics, Society, Culture* (2004); R. O. Paxton, *Europe in the Twentieth Century* (rev. 2004), especially informative; H. James, *Europe Reborn: A History, 1914–2000* (2003); and M. Mazower, *Dark Continent: Europe's Twentieth Century* (1999), a thoughtful book which sees more negative than positive features in Europe's history during these years.

The attempt in the interwar years to put together a shattered polity in Europe is described in M. Kitchen, *Europe Between the Wars* (1988) and Z. Steiner, *The Lights that Failed: European International History, 1919–1933* (2005), an insightful account that stresses the constructive efforts to rebuild postwar European societies and diplomacy. Two efforts to examine the pattern of reconstruction in Europe after the war are C. S. Maier, *Recasting Bourgeois Europe: Stabilization in France, Germany and Italy in the Decade after World War I* (1975), stressing the link between interest groups and conservative governments, and D. P. Silverman, *Reconstructing Europe after the Great War* (1982). Additional books for the interwar years, including works on the new states of central and eastern Europe, are described in the chapter that follows.

International Relations in the 1920s

Introductions to international affairs in this era are P. Renouvin, *War and Aftermath, 1914–1929* (1968); S. Marks, *The Illusion of Peace: International Relations in Europe, 1918–1933* (1976); and A. P. Adamthwaite, *The Lost Peace: International Relations in Europe, 1918–1939* (1981). The high point of reconciliation with Germany is ably treated in J. Jacobson, *Locarno Diplomacy: Germany and the West, 1925–1929* (1972). For American foreign policy encompassing the interwar years and the two world wars, A. Iriye, *The Globalizing of America, 1913–1945* (1993) is illuminating.

B. Kent, *The Spoils of War: The Politics, Economics, and Diplomacy of Reparations, 1918–1932* (1989) synthesizes the considerable literature on the complex reparations question, on which related studies include M. Trachetenberg, *Reparations in World Politics: France and European Economic Diplomacy, 1916–1923* (1980); S. A. Schuker, *The End of French Predominance in Europe* (1976); B. F. Martin, *France and the Après Guerre, 1918–1924* (1999); and A. P. Adamthwaite, *Grandeur and Misery: France's Bid for Power in Europe, 1914–1940* (1995), which describes French objectives in this period. The American role in these years is studied in M. P. Leffler, *The Elusive Quest: America's Pursuit of European Stability and French Security* (1979), and on a broader scale in F. Costigliola, *Awkward Dominion: American Political, Economic, and Cultural Relations with Europe, 1919–1933* (1984). America's growing economic and cultural influence is examined in V. de Grazia, *Irresistible Empire: America's Advance Through Twentieth-Century Europe* (2005). On the British role one may read A. Orde, *British Policy and European Reconstruction after the First World War* (1990). The response of the United States and Britain to the revolutionary events of the era, and not only to the revolution in Russia, is examined critically in L. C. Gardner, *Safe for Democracy: The Anglo-American Response to Revolution, 1913–1923* (1984).

The cooperation between the Soviet Union and Weimar Germany is studied in K. Rosenbaum, *Community of Fate: German-Soviet Diplomatic Relations, 1922–1928* (1965); and H. L. Dyck, *Weimar Germany and Soviet Russia, 1926–1933* (1966). The wider diplomatic context is the subject of S. Salzmann,

Great Britain, Germany, and the Soviet Union: Rapollo and After, 1922–1934 (2003); and Germany's leading diplomat is described in J. R. C. Wright, Gustav Stresemann: Weimar's Greatest Statesman (2002).

For the League of Nations one may read F. S. Northedge, The League of Nations: Its Life and Times, 1920–1946 (1986), which notes that despite its shortcomings it helped to transform the older diplomacy; and E. Goldstein, The First World War Peace Settlements, 1919–1925 (2002), which includes the early history of the League. A special problem in which the League played an important role is discussed in a wide-ranging study, M. R. Marrus, The Unwanted: European Refugees in the Twentieth Century (1985). Books on efforts at disarmament include R. Dingman, Power in the Pacific: The Origins of Naval Arms Limitation, 1914–1922 (1976) and E. W. Bennett, German Rearmament and the West, 1932–1933 (1979).

Anticolonialism in Asia: East Asia

For China in the early part of the twentieth century, in addition to books cited in Chapter 16, there are informative introductions in F. Wakeman, The Fall of Imperial China (1975); and in the essays in F. Wakeman and R. L. Edmonds (eds.), Reappraising Republican China (2000). The story of the last Manchu (or Qing) ruler (later appointed by the Japanese to rule in conquered Manchuria) is recounted in B. Power, The Puppet Emperor: The Life of Pu Yi, Last Emperor of China (1986).

Biographical studies for Sun include C. M. Wilbur, Sun Yat-sen: Frustrated Patriot (1976) and M. C. Bergère, Sun Yat-Sen (trans. 1998). On the resentments stirred by the Chinese treatment at Versailles, one should read V. Schwarcz, The Chinese Enlightenment: Intellectuals and the Legacy of the May Fourth Movement of 1919 (1986). The era of Chiang Kai-shek and Guomindang rule is studied in L. Eastman, The Abortive Revolution: China under Nationalist Rule, 1927–1937 (1974, 1990); J. C. Strauss, Strong Institutions in Weak Polities: State Building in Republican China, 1927–1940 (1998) and in the comprehensive biographical study by J. Fenby, Chiang Kai Shek (2004). On the emergent Communist movement one may read A. Dirlik, The Origins of Chinese Communism (1988), and the accounts of the Long March of 1934–1935 by D. Wilson (1972), H. Salisbury (1984), and B. Yang (1990).

General books on Japan have been cited in Chapter 13. On the rise of militarism in Japan one should read J. B. Crowley, Japan's Quest for Autonomy: National Security and Foreign Policy, 1930–1938 (1966). Japanese-American relations and the failure to arrive at an international settlement in East Asia is traced in A. Iriye: Pacific Estrangement: Japanese and American Expansion, 1897–1911 (1972, 1994) and After Imperialism: The Search for New Order in the Far East, 1921–1931 (1965, 1990). M. Harries and S. Harries,

Soldiers of the Sun: The Rise and Fall of the Japanese Imperial Army (1992) carries its subject from 1904 to military collapse in 1945.

Accounts of the Japanese intervention in China during the 1930s are available in M. Dryburgh, North China and Japanese Expansion, 1933–1937 (2000), and in P. Duara, Sovereignty and Authenticity: Manchuko and the East Asian Modern (2003). The brutal Japanese assault on Nanjing in 1937 is described in I. Chang, The Rape of Nanking (1997) and H. Katsuichi, The Nanjing Massacre (trans. 1999); its continuing effects on national memories in China and Japan are analyzed in J. A. Fogel (ed.), The Nanjing Massacre in History and Historiography (2000) and F. F. Lei, R. Sabella, and D. Liu (eds.), Nanking 1937: Memory and Healing (2002).

Anticolonialism in Asia: The Middle East and South Asia

An older study of the nationalist ferment is provided in J. Romein and J. E. Romein, The Asian Century: A History of Modern Nationalism in Asia (trans. 1962), which may be supplemented by H. Grimal, Decolonization: The British, French, Dutch, and Belgian Empires, 1919–1963 (1978) and the essays in P. Duara (ed.), Decolonization: Perspectives from Now and Then (2003). In addition to books cited in Chapters 16 and 17, introductions to the Middle East and the continuing importance of the "Eastern question" include P. Mansfield, The Ottoman Empire and Its Successors (1973); W. L. Cleveland, A History of the Modern Middle East (2004); J. L. Gelvin, The Modern Middle East: A History (2005), which includes analysis of both the Ottoman Empire and modern Arab nationalism; E. Monroe, Britain's Moment in the Middle East, 1914–1971 (rev. 1981); and M. E. Yapp, The Near East since the First World War (rev. 1996). French imperial policies during this period are examined in M. Thomas, The French Empire Between the Wars: Imperialism, Politics, and Society (2005).

For the Turkish Revolution, B. Lewis, The Emergence of Modern Turkey (rev. 2002) remains the best introduction. Among other useful studies are E. J. Zürcher, Turkey: A Modern History (rev. 2004); W. F. Weiker, The Modernization of Turkey (1981); and F. Ahmad, The Making of Modern Turkey (1993). Biographical accounts of the Turkish statesman-reformer include J. P. D. Balfour [P. Kinross], Atatürk: A Biography of Mustafa Kemal (1965, 1992) and A. Mango, Atatürk: The Biography of the Founder of Modern Turkey (2001), a balanced, comprehensive account that distributes both praise and criticism. An insightful book carrying the story to the end of the century is N. Pope and H. Pope, Turkey Unveiled: A History of Modern Turkey (1999).

Arab stirrings in the Middle East in these years are discussed in Z. B. Zeine, Struggle for Arab Independence (1977); J. E. Kedouri, Islam and the Modern

World (1980); two notable books by J. L. Gelvin, *Divided Loyalties: Nationalism and Mass Politics in Syria at the Close of the Empire* (1999), and *The Israel-Palestine Conflict: One Hundred Years of War* (2005); J. Jankowski and I. Gershoni (eds.), *Rethinking Nationalism in the Arab Middle East* (1997); and B. M. Nafi, *Arabism, Islamism and the Palestine Question, 1908–1941* (1998). The response of the European powers is described in A. Williams, *Britain and France in the Middle East and North Africa, 1914–1967* (1969).

For the Indian subcontinent, two histories that try to understand developments in Indian terms and not as reactions to the West are P. Spear, *The Oxford History of Modern India* (rev. 1979) and S. Wolpert, *A New History of India* (rev. 2004). Recommended also is S. Sarkar, *Modern India, 1885–1947* (rev. 1989). The origins of Indian nationalism are discussed in A. Seal, *The Emergence of Indian Nationalism* (1968); Ian Talbot, *India and Pakistan* (2000), which describes the development of both Hindu and Muslim national identities; and W. Gould, *Hindu Nationalism and the Language of Politics in Late Colonial India* (2004).

Of many existing studies of Gandhi one may turn to J. M. Brown's impressive trilogy: *Gandhi's Rise to Power in Indian Politics* (1972); *Gandhi and Civil Disobedience* (1977), carrying the story to 1934; and *Gandhi: Prisoner of Hope* (1990). Informative also are S. Wolpert, *Gandhi's Passion: The Life and Legacy of Mahatma Gandhi* (2001); A. Copley, *Gandhi* (1987), a good brief account; D. Arnold, *Gandhi* (2001); and M. B. Steger, *Gandhi's Dilemma: Nonviolent Principles and Nationalist Power* (2000), which thoughtfully examines Gandhi's complex ideas. For Nehru, among many studies there are S. Gopal, *Jawaharlal Nehru: A Biography* (1 vol. abridged ed.; 1993); S. Wolpert, *Nehru: A Tryst with Destiny* (1996); and J. M. Brown, *Nehru* (1999). Nehru's autobiography, *Toward Freedom* (1941), and his other writings provide insights into the anticolonial mind. For the career and life of Nehru's daughter, his successor in office, one may read K. Frank, *The Life of Indira Nehru Gandhi* (2001).

The Depression:
Collapse of the World Economy

Books on the impact of the depression on politics and society in various countries will appear in the following chapter.

The economy of the post-1919 world may be studied in D. N. Aldcroft, *From Versailles to Wall Street: The International Economy in the 1920s* (1977) and G. Ziebura, *World Economy and World Politics* (trans. 1990). For the stock market collapse, J. K. Galbraith, *The Great Crash, 1929* (1955, 1988) is a vivid account, while a comprehensive analysis of the worldwide depression is C. P. Kindleberger, *The World in Depression, 1929–1939* (rev. 1986). Informative too are P. Fearon, *The Origins and Nature of the Great Slump, 1929–1932* (1979); M. Klein, *Rainbow's End: The Crash of 1929* (2001), focusing on the United States; and D. Rothermund, *The Global Impact of the Great Depression, 1929–1939* (1996), which describes the economic crisis in all parts of the world.

There are helpful essays in W. Laqueur and G. L. Mosse (eds.), *The Great Depression* (1970) and K. Brunner (ed.), *The Great Depression Revisited* (1981). An often neglected subject is examined in A. J. H. Latham, *The Depression and the Developing World, 1914–1939* (1981). Two informative international studies are E. W. Bennett, *Germany and the Diplomacy of the Financial Crisis, 1931* (1962) and A. Schubert, *The Credit-Anstalt Crisis of 1931* (1992), on the Austrian bank failure.

For Keynes, there is the illuminating second volume of the three-volume biography by R. Skidelsky, *John Maynard Keynes: The Economist as Saviour, 1920–1937* (1993). There are also biographical accounts by D. E. Moggridge (1992), the editor of Keynes's papers, and by C. Hession (1989). One may also read P. Clarke, *The Keynesian Revolution in the Making, 1924–1936* (1989).

There are useful descriptions of modernist literature in R. J. Quinones, *Mapping Literary Modernism* (1985) and M. Levenson (ed.), *The Cambridge Companion to Modernism* (1999). For examples of the social themes in interwar literature, readers may turn to the relevant chapters of W. B. Rideout, *The Radical Novel in the United States, 1900–1954: Some Interrelations of Literature and Society* (1956, 1992); and L. Browder, *Rousing the Nation: Radical Culture in Depression America* (1998).

Useful Web Sites

Excellent materials and links to numerous other sites on diplomacy and the League of Nations may be found in the *Research Guide to League of Nations Documents and Publications*, at the library of Northwestern University, www.library.northwestern.edu/govpub/collections/league/background.html. There are also links and readings on modern international relations and anticolonial movements at *Resources for the Study of International Relations and Foreign Policy*, a Web site of V. Ferraro in the International Relations Program at Mount Holyoke College, www.mtholyoke.edu/acad/intrel/feros-pg.htm. Useful materials on Asia, the Middle East, and decolonization are available at the indispensable *Internet Modern History Sourcebook*, www.Fordham.edu/halsall/mod.modsbook.html. Documents, images, and other materials on the leader of India's national independence movement may be found at *The Complete Site on Mahatma Gandhi*, www.mkgandhi.org/.

20. DEMOCRACY AND DICTATORSHIP IN THE 1930s

Some general accounts for the interwar years and the Great Depression have been described in the previous chapter, and books on the international crisis of the 1930s will appear in the chapter that follows. Helpful introductions to the democracies and dictatorships in this era are P. Brendon, *The Dark Valley: A Panorama of the 1930s* (2000); R. W. Winks and R. J. Q. Adams, *Europe, 1890–1945: Crisis and Conflict* (2003), cited earlier; D. C. Large, *Between Two Fires: Europe's Path in the 1930s* (1990); and J. Jackson (ed.), *Europe, 1900–1945* (2002).

The United States and the New Deal

The interwar years, the impact of the depression, and the New Deal may best be approached through W. E. Leuchtenburg, *The Perils of Prosperity, 1914–1932* (rev. 1993) and *Franklin D. Roosevelt and the New Deal, 1932–1940* (1963); T. H. Watkins, *The Great Depression: America in the 1930s* (1993); and a more recent, impressive account, D. M. Kennedy, *Freedom from Fear: The American People in Depression and War, 1929–1945* (1999).

Several biographical accounts of Roosevelt offer insights into his presidency and the bold but pragmatic efforts to cope with the Great Depression. Among the most illuminating are A. M. Schlesinger, Jr., *The Age of Roosevelt* (3 vols.; 1956–1960); J. M. Burns, *Roosevelt: The Lion and the Fox* (1956); the more recent, concise study by R. Jenkins, *Franklin Delano Roosevelt* (2003); and A. L. Hamby, *For the Survival of Democracy: Franklin Roosevelt and the World Crisis of the 1930s* (2004), a well-balanced analysis. The effect on those who lived through the economic crisis is vividly portrayed in C. Bird, *The Invisible Scar* (1966); S. Terkel, *Hard Times: An Oral History of the Great Depression* (1970, 1986); and R. S. McElvaine (ed.), *Down and Out in the Great Depression* (1983). The growth of the labor movement in these years may be studied in I. Bernstein, *The Turbulent Years* (1970), and the impact on women in W. D. Wandersee, *Women's Work and Family Values, 1920–1940* (1981). Two informative comparative studies are S. Salter and J. Stevenson, *The Working Class and Politics in Europe and America, 1929–1945* (1989) and J. A. Garraty, *The Great Depression* (1986), which examines diverse national responses to the crisis in the United States and Europe.

Britain between the Wars

General accounts for Britain, some extending beyond the interwar years, are A. J. P. Taylor, *English History, 1914–1945* (1965), written with the author's usual verve; A. Marwick, *A History of the Modern British Isles, 1914–1999* (2000); and M. Beloff, *Wars and Welfare: Britain, 1914–1945* (1984). An overview of the British economic scene is provided in S. Pollard, *The Development of the British Economy, 1914–1990* (rev. 1992).

An outstanding account of changes in British life is provided in J. Stevenson, *British Society, 1914–1945* (1984). Other suggested studies include S. Glynn and J. Oxborrow, *Interwar Britain: Social and Economic History* (1976); J. Stevenson and C. Cook, *The Slump: Society and Politics during the Depression* (1978); S. Hynes, *The Auden Generation: Literature and Politics in the 1930s* (1977); R. Blythe, *The Age of Illusion: Some Glimpses of Britain between the Wars, 1919–1940* (rev. 1984); and R. McKibben, *Classes and Cultures: England 1918–1951* (1998). The postwar lot of the British wartime women workers is portrayed in D. Beddoe, *Back to Home and Duty: Women between the Wars, 1919–1939* (1989), and women activists are described in B. Harrison, *Prudent Revolutionaries: Portraits of British Feminists between the Wars* (1987). The campaign for women's rights is also examined in M. Pugh, *Women and the Women's Movement in Britain, 1914–1999* (2000).

On the decline of the Liberal party and the rise of Labour, one may read M. Freeden, *Liberalism Divided: British Political Thought, 1914–1938* (1986). For the general strike of 1926 and the cabinet crisis of 1929, the best synthesis is P. Williamson, *National Crisis and National Government: British Politics, the Economy, and the Empire, 1926–1932* (1992); and the new role of the Labour party is examined in D. Howell, *MacDonald's Party: Labour Identities and Crisis, 1922–1931* (2002). Among many biographies, there are studies of Ramsay MacDonald by D. Marquand (1977) and by A. Morgan (1987); and of his rival conservative leader by R. Jenkins, *Baldwin* (1987). K. Rose, *King George V* (1984) is a scholarly biography of the monarch.

On British relations with the empire and dominions one may turn to D. Kennedy, *Britain and Empire, 1880–1945* (2002); N. Mansergh, *The Commonwealth Experience* (rev. 1982); and M. Kitchen, *The British Empire and Commonwealth: A Short History* (1996). An outstanding study of Ireland in this era is J. M. Curran, *The Birth of the Irish Free State, 1921–1923* (1980) and on a broader time scale, J. J. Lee, *Ireland, 1912–1985: Politics and Society* (1990). The thorny issue of Northern Ireland is examined in N. Mansergh, *The Unresolved Question: The Anglo-Irish Settlement and Its Undoing, 1912–1972* (1991) and M. Mulholland, *The Longest War: Northern Ireland's Troubled History* (2002).

France between the Wars

General accounts for these years are P. Bernard and H. Dubief, *The Decline of the Third Republic, 1914–1938* (trans. 1985); J. P. Azéma, *From Munich to the Liberation, 1938–1944* (trans. 1985), somewhat more probing; and W. Fortescue, *The Third Republic in France, 1870–1940: Conflicts and Continuities*

(2000), which provides excellent source materials. There are incisive essays in S. Hoffmann and others, *In Search of France: The Economy, Society, and Political System in the Twentieth Century* (1963). An illuminating study of government planning, which was less successful in the interwar years than later, is R. F. Kuisel, *Capitalism and the State in Modern France: Renovation and Economic Management in the Twentieth Century* (1981). The political and social divisions within France are colorfully conveyed in E. Weber, *The Hollow Years: France in the 1930s* (1994).

The response to the depression and the threat to the Third Republic are explored in two books by J. Jackson: *The Politics of Depression in France, 1932–1936* (1985) and *The Popular Front in France: Defending Democracy, 1934–1938* (1988). For the Socialist leader of the Popular Front one may read J. Colton, *Léon Blum: Humanist in Politics* (1966, 1987) and J. Lacouture, *Léon Blum* (1977; trans. 1982). Other studies of the political left in the Popular Front era include N. Greene, *Crisis and Decline: The French Socialist Party in the Popular Front Era* (1969); D. Caute, *Communism and the French Intellectuals, 1914–1960* (1965); and D. R. Brower, *The New Jacobins: The French Communist Party and the Popular Front* (1968). For right-wing and fascist-type movements, in addition to books cited in Chapter 15, one may read R. Soucy, *French Fascism: The First Wave, 1924–1933* (1985) and *French Fascism: The Second Wave, 1933–1939* (1995). French national identity is examined in H. Lebovics, *True France: The Wars over Cultural Identity, 1900–1945* (1992). Studies of the countryside include G. Wright, *Rural Revolution in France: The Peasantry in the Twentieth Century* (1964) and R. O. Paxton, *French Peasant Fascism: Henry Dorgères' Greenshirts and the Crisis of French Agriculture, 1929* (1997). French responses to the rise of Nazism are examined in several useful recent books: R. Davis, *Anglo-French Relations before the Second World War: Appeasement and Crisis* (2001); B. F. Martin, *France in 1938* (2005); and J. B. Duroselle, *France and the Nazi Threat: The Collapse of French Diplomacy, 1932–1939* (trans. 2004).

Italy: The Fascist Experience

A helpful introduction to the general development of modern Italy may be found in S. M. Di Scala, *Italy: From Revolution to Republic, 1700 to the Present* (rev. 2004). The rise of Italian Fascism is examined in E. Wiskemann, *Fascism in Italy* (1969) and in F. Chabod, *A History of Italian Fascism* (1963), concise but perceptive. There is also an impressive account of the early years, A. Lyttelton, *The Seizure of Power: Fascism in Italy, 1919–1929* (1973), and a concise survey of the entire Fascist era in P. Morgan, *Italian Fascism, 1915–1945* (2004). Mussolini's flamboyant precursor is studied in J. Woodhouse, *Gabriele d'Annunzio: Defiant Archangel* (1998).

The Fascist state is examined in R. Sarti, *Fascism and the Industrial Leadership in Italy, 1919–1940* (1971) and M. Gallo, *Mussolini's Italy: Twenty Years of the Fascist Era* (1973). The Fascist impact on Italian society is comprehensively examined in E. R. Tannenbaum, *The Fascist Experience: Italian Society and Culture, 1922–1945* (1972); V. de Grazia, *The Culture of Consent: Mass Organization of Leisure in Fascist Italy* (1981) and *How Fascism Ruled Women: Italy, 1922–1945* (1991); and E. Gentile, *The Socialization of Politics in Fascist Italy* (1994), portraying fascism as a civic and political religion.

The compromise with the church is explored in J. F. Pollard, *The Vatican and Italian Fascism, 1920–1932* (1985). Mussolini's racial policy, moving on into the war years, is studied in M. Michaelis, *Mussolini and the Jews: German-Italian Relations and the Jewish Question in Italy, 1922–1945* (1978); S. Zuccotti, *The Italians and the Holocaust: Persecution, Rescue, and Survival* (1988); and A. Stille, *Benevolence and Betrayal: Five Italian Jewish Families under Fascism* (1993), a poignant portrayal.

On Il Duce, the best studies are by D. Mack Smith, *Mussolini* (1982), straightforward and comprehensive, and the more recent biography by R. J. B. Bosworth, *Mussolini* (2002); the latter is now complemented by his valuable *Mussolini's Italy* (2006), which examines the impact of fascism on Italian society. There are also informative biographies by I. Kirkpatrick, *Mussolini: Study of a Demagogue* (1964); J. Ridley, *Mussolini* (1997); M. Clark, *Mussolini* (2005); and A. L. Cardoza, *Benito Mussolini: The First Fascist* (2006). Other useful studies include A. J. Gregor, *Young Mussolini and the Intellectual Origins of Fascism* (1979) and Z. Sternhell, *The Birth of Fascist Ideology: From Cultural Rebellion to Political Revolution* (1993), a controversial but outstanding study cited earlier.

Foreign and colonial policy is examined in G. Barclay, *The Rise and Fall of the New Roman Empire: Italy's Bid for World Power, 1890–1943* (1973) and D. Mack Smith, *Mussolini's Roman Empire* (1976). The last phase of the dictator's career is narrated in detail in F. W. Deakin, *The Brutal Friendship: Mussolini, Hitler, and the Fall of Italian Fascism* (1962), the final chapters of which are available as *The Six Hundred Days of Mussolini* (1966).

Germany, 1919–1933: The Weimar Republic

For the collapse of the Weimar Republic and the emergence of Hitler, several of the longer-range histories of Germany by G. A. Craig and others, cited in Chapters 13 and 14, will also be helpful. For accounts of Weimar one may turn to A. J. Nicholls, *Weimar and the Rise of Hitler* (rev. 2000); S. Taylor, *Revolution and Counter-Revolution in Germany 1918–1933* (1984); E. Kolb, *The Weimar Republic* (trans. 1988); H. Heiber, *The Weimar Republic: Germany, 1918–1933* (1986); H. Mommsen, *The Rise and Fall of*

Weimar Democracy (trans. 1996); and R. J. Evans, *The Coming of the Third Reich* (2003), the first volume of his projected trilogy.

The most informed inquiry into German efforts to cope with the depression is H. James, *The German Slump: Politics and Economics, 1924–1936* (1986). The inability of the political parties and diverse interest groups to cooperate is examined in L. E. Jones, *German Liberalism and the Dissolution of the Weimar Party System, 1918–1933* (1989). W. L. Guttman, *The German Social Democratic Party, 1875–1933* (1981) examines a major party of the Left. The resort to extraparliamentary tactics receives attention in J. M. Riehl, *Paramilitary Politics in Weimar Germany* (1977); P. Fritzsche, *Rehearsals for Fascism: Populism and Political Mobilization in Weimar Germany* (1990); and E. Rosenhaft, *Beating the Fascists? The German Communists and Political Violence, 1929–1933* (1984). The question of army loyalties is examined in depth in F. L. Carsten, *The Reichswehr and Politics, 1918 to 1933* (trans. 1966); J. W. Wheeler-Bennett, *The Nemesis of Power: The German Army in Politics, 1918–1945* (rev. 1964); and G. A. Craig, *The Politics of the Prussian Army, 1640–1945* (1956, 1964), cited earlier.

Among thoughtful efforts to explore the ideological roots of Weimar's failure are F. Stern, *The Politics of Cultural Despair: A Study in the Use of the Germanic Ideology* (1961) and G. L. Mosse, *The Crisis of German Ideology: Intellectual Origins of the Third Reich* (1964). Cultural history in these years is examined in P. Gay, *Weimar Culture: The Outsider as Insider* (1968, 2001); W. Laqueur, *Weimar: A Cultural History, 1918–1933* (1974); and D. J. K. Peukert, *The Weimar Republic: The Crisis of Classical Modernity* (trans. 1992). A helpful discussion of key political figures is available in P. Stachura, *Political Leaders in Weimar Germany: A Biographical Study* (1993).

Germany, 1933–1945: The Third Reich

A valuable introduction to the vast literature on the Third Reich is I. Kershaw, *The Nazi Dictatorship: Problems and Perspectives of Interpretation* (rev. 2000), while P. Ayçoberry, *The Nazi Question: An Essay on the Interpretation of National Socialism, 1922–1975* (trans. 1981) and J. Lukacs, *The Hitler of History* (1997) are helpful historiographical studies. Two successful recent efforts to provide a thoughtful overview of the Nazi era are K. P. Fischer, *Nazi Germany* (1995) and M. Burleigh, *The Third Reich* (2000); there is also an excellent account of the Nazi regime in R. J. Evans, *The Third Reich in Power, 1933–1939* (2005), the second volume of his projected trilogy, informative on the lives of people as well as the politics and ideology of the regime.

On the coming to power of the Nazis one may first turn to M. Broszat, *Hitler and the Collapse of Weimar Germany* (trans. 1987), focusing on the years 1929–1933. An informative study is H. A. Turner, *German Big Business and the Rise of Hitler* (1985), which may be supplemented by his *Hitler's Thirty Days to Power: January 1933* (1997). Two studies illuminate the Nazi appeal to diverse segments of the population: W. S. Allen, *The Nazi Seizure of Power: The Experience of a Single German Town, 1922–1945* (rev. 1989) and J. H. Grill, *The Nazi Movement in Baden, 1920–1945* (1984). Two efforts to assess the Nazi appeal at the polls are R. F. Hamilton, *Who Voted for Hitler?* (1982) and T. Childers, *The Nazi Voter: The Social Foundations of Fascism in Germany, 1919–1933* (1983), which both tend to confirm that Nazi support came from all segments of the population, not only from the lower-middle class. How the movement's "populist nationalism" rallied wide support is recounted in P. Fritzsche, *Germans Into Nazis* (1998).

M. H. Kater, *The Nazi Party: A Social Profile of Members and Leaders, 1919–1945* (1983) is an exhaustive sociological analysis of those who joined and led the party, while D. Orlow, *The History of the Nazi Party* (2 vols.; 1969–1973) is a comprehensive organizational history. There are many studies of such key Nazi institutions as the SS, the Gestapo, and the courts, too numerous to cite here. For the military one may read O. Bartov, *Hitler's Army: Soldiers, Nazis, and War in the Third Reich* (1991).

Religion and related matters are examined in E. C. Helmreich, *The German Churches under Hitler* (1979); D. Bergen, *Twisted Cross: The German Christian Movement in the Third Reich* (1996); G. Lewy, *The Catholic Church and Nazi Germany* (1964); and S. Friedländer, *Pius XII and the Third Reich* (1966). Books on Hitler's persecution of the Jews, and on the death camps and the Holocaust, will be described in the next chapter, but one should mention here L. S. Dawidowicz, *The War against the Jews, 1933–1945* (1976); S. Gordon, *Hitler, Germans, and the Jewish Question* (1984); and S. Friedländer, *Nazi Germany and the Jews: The Years of Persecution, 1933–1939* (1997).

On the Nazi state four outstanding analyses are K. D. Bracher, *The German Dictatorship* (trans. 1970); M. Broszat, *The Hitler State* (trans. (1981); K. Hildebrand, *The Third Reich* (1984); and M. Burleigh and W. Wippermann, *The Racial State: Germany, 1933–1945* (1992). D. Schoenbaum, *Hitler's Social Revolution: Class and Status in Nazi Germany, 1933–1939* (1966) sees a leveling effect not accomplished by earlier German regimes. Studies exploring new avenues to understanding popular responses include I. Kershaw, *The "Hitler Myth": Image and Reality in the Third Reich* (1987); D. J. K. Peukert, *Inside Nazi Germany: Conformity, Opposition, and Racism in Everyday Life* (trans. 1987); P. Ayçoberry, *The Social History of the Third Reich* (trans. 2000); and C. Koonz, *The Nazi Conscience* (2003), which argues that the Nazis gained support by claiming to represent the virtues of the German people. There are also perceptive insights into life under the Nazis in R. Bessel (ed.), *Life in the Third Reich* (1987) and G. L. Mosse, *Nazi Culture: Intellectual, Cultural, and Social Life in the Third Reich* (1966).

The best study of women in the Third Reich, with special attention to those who supported and those who resisted the regime, is C. Koonz, *Mothers in the Fatherland: Women, the Family, and Nazi Politics* (1987). It may be supplemented by J. Stephenson, *Women in Nazi Society* (1976) and *The Nazi Organization of Women* (1981); E. Heineman, *What Difference Does a Husband Make: Women and Marital Status in Nazi and Postwar Germany* (1999); and the essays in R. Bridenthal and others, *When Biology Became Destiny: Women in Weimar and Nazi Germany* (1989).

That there was no mass resistance but opposition only from resolute individuals and small groups emerges from two comprehensive accounts: P. Hoffmann, *German Resistance to Hitler* (rev. 1988) and M. Balfour, *Withstanding Hitler in Germany 1933–1945* (1989). These accounts may be supplemented by J. Fest, *Plotting Hitler's Death* (trans. 1997). One may also consult D. C. Lodge (ed.), *Contending with Hitler: Varieties of German Resistance in the Third Reich* (1992) and on the Resistance legacy, M. Geyer and J. W. Boyer (eds.), *Resistance Against the Third Reich, 1933–1990* (1994).

Of the many biographies of Hitler the two volumes of I. Kershaw are undoubtedly now the most authoritative: *Hitler, 1889–1936: Hubris* (1998) and *Hitler, 1936–1945: Nemesis* (1999), a remarkable study explaining how Germans identified with Hitler and how his arrogance and pride brought him initial success and then disaster. Two earlier biographies are outstanding: A. Bullock, *Hitler: A Study in Tyranny* (1952, 1964), and J. C. Fest, *Hitler* (trans. 1975). Bullock has also written a remarkable in-depth comparative study, *Hitler and Stalin: Parallel Lives* (1992). Hitler's early years in Vienna have been reexamined in B. Hamann, *Hitler's Vienna: A Dictator's Apprenticeship* (1999). R. Binion, *Hitler among the Germans* (1976) uses psychoanalytical methods to explain the inner wellsprings of the obsessed leader, while R. L. Waite, *The Psychopathic God: Adolf Hitler* (1977) effectively combines psychoanalytical and more conventional techniques. Two interpretive essays that raise pertinent questions are S. Haffner, *The Meaning of Hitler* (trans. 1980) and W. Carr, *Hitler: A Study in Personality and Politics* (1979). The end of the leader and his regime is vividly recounted in H. R. Trevor-Roper, *The Last Days of Hitler* (rev. 1966).

Some of Hitler's associates are studied in J. C. Fest, *The Face of the Third Reich: Portraits of the Nazi Leadership* (trans. 1977); B. F. Smith, *Heinrich Himmler: A Nazi in the Making, 1900–1926* (1971); R. Smelser, *Robert Ley: Hitler's Labor Front Leader*

(1989); and R. G. Reuth, *Goebbels* (trans. 1994). Hitler's foreign minister is studied in M. Bloch, *Ribbentrop* (1993), a detailed diplomatic account, and J. Weitz, *Hitler's Diplomat: The Life and Times of Joachim Ribbentrop* (1992). G. Serenz, *Albert Speer: His Battle with Truth* (1995) is highly critical of Hitler's wartime economic planner. Two convenient handbooks on the institutions and personalities of the regime are R. S. Wistrich, *Who's Who in Nazi Germany* (rev. 1995) and C. Zentner and F. Bedürftig, *The Encyclopedia of the Third Reich* (2 vols.; 1991).

Defining Totalitarianism and Fascism

The origins and nature of twentieth-century ideologies are explored in many books, notably in K. D. Bracher's comprehensive *A History of Political Thought in the Twentieth Century* (trans. 1984). Among efforts to examine totalitarianism, Left and Right, are C. J. Friedrich and Z. K. Brzezinski, *Totalitarian Dictatorship and Autocracy* (rev. 1965); H. Arendt, *Origins of Totalitarianism* (rev. 1966), cited in Chapter 15; H. Bucheim, *Totalitarian Rule* (trans. 1967); and S. P. Soper, *Totalitarianism: A Conceptual Approach* (1985). An important comparative study is the collection of essays in I. Kershaw and M. Levin (eds.), *Stalinism and Nazism: Dictatorships in Comparison* (1997). R. O. Paxton, *The Anatomy of Fascism* (2004) is the best recent effort to arrive at a general definition of fascist ideas and political movements.

For other insightful studies of fascism as a phenomenon of the interwar years, one must turn to S. G. Payne, *A History of Fascism, 1914–1945* (1995); F. L. Carsten, *The Rise of Fascism* (rev. 1980); H. R. Kedward, *Fascism in Western Europe, 1900–1945* (1969); R. De Felice, *Fascism* (1976), by the Italian biographer of Mussolini; and W. Laqueur, *Fascism: Past, Present, Future* (1996). Readers will find E. Nolte, *Three Faces of Fascism: Action Française, Italian Fascism, National Socialism* (trans. 1966), provocative but difficult.

Other European Developments in the Interwar Years

Spain and the Spanish Civil War are discussed in the following chapter. The most informative volumes on central and eastern Europe are J. Rothschild, *East Central Europe between the Two World Wars* (1975); A. Palmer, *The Lands Between: A History of East-Central Europe since the Congress of Vienna* (1970); and I. T. Berend, *Decades of Crisis: Central and Eastern Europe Before World War II* (1998). A special subject is ably explored in E. Mendelsohn, *The Jews of East Central Europe between the World Wars* (1983).

A few titles may be suggested for some of the successor states. For Austria: C. E. Edmondson, *The Heimwehr and Austrian Politics, 1918–1936* (1978); M. Kitchen, *The Coming of Austrian Fascism* (1980); F. L. Carsten, *Fascist Movements in Austria: From*

Schönerer to Hitler (1977); B. F. Pauley, *Hitler and the Forgotten Nazis: A History of Austrian National Socialism* (1981) and *From Prejudice to Persecution: A History of Austrian Anti-Semitism* (1998). For Hungary: C. A. Macartney, *October Fifteenth: A History of Modern Hungary, 1929–1945* (2 vols.; rev. 1962); R. L. Tönes, *Bela Kun and the Hungarian Soviet Republic* (1967), on the short-lived Communist regime of 1919; and T. Sakmyster, *Hungary's Admiral on Horseback: Miklós Horthy, 1918–1944* (1999). For Czechoslovakia: J. Kolvoda, *The Genesis of Czechoslovakia* (1985); Z. A. B. Zeman, *The Masaryks: The Making of Czechoslovakia* (1976, 1991); E. Wiskemann, *Czechs and Germans* (rev. 1967); V. Olivova, *The Doomed Democracy: Czechoslovakia in a Disrupted Europe, 1918–1938* (1972); and C. S. Leff, *National Conflict in Czechoslovakia: The Making and Remaking of a State, 1918–1987* (1988), which carries the story toward the present. For Yugoslavia: I. Banac, *The National Question in Yugoslavia* (1985), an informative inquiry into the genesis of the multiethnic state, for which other books will be cited in Chapter 26; F. Singleton, *A Short History of the Yugoslav Peoples* (1985); and R. West, *Black Lamb and Grey Falcon* (1941, 1992), a gifted journalist's older insightful account. For Poland: M. K. Dziewanowski, *Poland in the Twentieth Century* (1977); A. Polonsky, *Politics in Independent Poland, 1921–1939* (1972); and the volumes of N. Davies cited in Chapter 11. For Finland and the Baltic states: J. H. Wuorinen, *A History of Finland* (1965); D. G. Kirby, *Finland in the Twentieth Century* (1979); and G. von Rauch, *The Baltic States—Estonia, Latvia, and Lithuania: The Years of Independence, 1917–1940* (trans. 1974, 1995).

Useful Web Sites

There are excellent links to documents, images, and other materials on America in the 1930s at the *New Deal Network*, a site maintained by the Franklin and Eleanor Roosevelt Institute, http://newdeal.feri.org/. Readers will find links to information and resources on all aspects of European society and politics in the 1930s (and other eras too) at the helpful British site, *Spartacus Educational*, which provides a convenient student-level guide to information on key events and influential historical figures at www.spartacus.schoolnet.co.uk/.

21. THE SECOND WORLD WAR
Spain and the Spanish Civil War

The most comprehensive narrative account of the Spanish conflict, including the international ramifications, is H. Thomas, *The Spanish Civil War* (rev. 2001), in which Franco's skill as a manipulator and survivor clearly emerges. But other recommended accounts are G. Jackson, *The Spanish Republic and the Civil War, 1931–1939* (1965; abridged ed., 1974); B. Bolloten, *The Spanish Civil War: Revolution and Counterrevolution* (1991); P. Broué and E. Témime, *The Revolution and the Civil War in Spain* (trans. 1972); A. Beevor, *The Spanish Civil War* (1982, 2001); and H. Browne, *Spain's Civil War* (rev. 1996). Brief overviews are available in F. Ribeiro de Meneses, *Franco and the Spanish Civil War* (2001), and F. Lannon, *The Spanish Civil War* (2002). G. Esenwein and A. Shubert, *Spain at War: The Spanish Civil War in Context, 1931–1939* (1995), and R. Carr, *The Spanish Tragedy: The Civil War in Perspective* (1977, 2000), add broader analytical insights.

The American response to the war is examined in A. Guttman, *The Wound in the Heart: America and the Spanish Civil War* (1962) and R. P. Traina, *American Diplomacy and the Spanish Civil War* (1968). The emotions stirred by the events are evoked by S. Weintraub, *The Last Great Cause: The Intellectuals and the Spanish Civil War* (1968). The volunteers who fought for the Republic are studied in C. Geiser, *Prisoners of the Good Fight: The Spanish Civil War, 1936–1938* (1994); M. Jackson, *The International Brigades in the Spanish Civil War, 1936–1938* (1994); and P. N. Carroll, *The Odyssey of the Abraham Lincoln Brigade: Americans in the Spanish Civil War* (1994). A large-scale critical study of Franco is P. Preston, *Franco: A Biography* (1995); but one may also read S. Ellwood, *Franco* (1994) and G. A Hodges, *Franco: A Concise Biography* (2000), which offers a psychological interpretation of Franco's actions. S. G. Payne has written a comprehensive study, *Fascism in Spain, 1923–1977* (1999); an earlier study on Franco's years in power, *The Franco Regime, 1936–1975* (1987); and an account of the Soviet role in the war, *The Spanish Civil War, the Soviet Union, and Communism* (2004).

Background to the Second World War

Although there is no one comprehensive treatment taking into account all the sources now available for the diplomacy of the interwar years and the background to the Second World War, there are a number of important books on the subject. Among the most informative general inquiries into the coming of the war are P. Renouvin, *World War II and Its Origins: International Relations 1929–1945* (trans. 1969); M. Baumont, *The Origins of the Second World War* (trans. 1978); P. M. H. Bell, *The Origins of the Second World War in Europe* (rev. 1997); R. Overy with A. Wheatcroft, *The Road to War* (1999); and A. J. Crozier, *The Causes of the Second World War* (1997).

On the 11 months between Munich and the outbreak of the war, D. C. Watt, *How War Came: The Immediate Origins of the Second World War, 1938–1939* (1989) is a masterful study. One may also read S. Aster, *1939: The Making of the Second World War* (1973) and M. J. Carley, *The Alliance That Never Was and the Coming of World War II* (1999) on the failure to create a Western-Soviet alliance at the time. A. J. P. Taylor's *The Origins of the Second World War* (1961) depicts Hitler as one who did not desire war but took advantage of his opponents' uncertainty. On the Taylor thesis one may read the evaluations in G. Martel (ed.), *"The Origins of the Second World War" Reconsidered: The A.J.P. Taylor Debate after Twenty-Five Years* (1986) and R. Boyce and E. M. Robertson (eds.), *Paths to War: New Essays on the Origins of the Second World War* (1989).

A major study of German foreign policy based on exhaustive use of the documents and strongly emphasizing Hitler's responsibilities and initiatives is G. L. Weinberg, *Hitler's Foreign Policy: The Road to World War II, 1933–1939* (1970, 2005). A second study with similar conclusions is N. Rich, *Hitler's War Aims* (2 vols.; 1973–1974). For assessments of German foreign policy one may also read K. Hildebrand, *The Foreign Policy of the Third Reich* (1974); J. Hiden, *Germany and Europe, 1919–1939* (rev. 1993); E. Jäckel, *Hitler's World View* (1981); and the essays in V. R. Berghahn and M. Kitchen (eds.), *Germany and the Age of Total War* (1981).

British policy in the 1930s, including the economic and political constraints on a more assertive policy, is examined in M. Cowling, *The Impact of Hitler: British Politics and British Policy, 1933–1940* (1975); R. P. Shay, Jr., *British Rearmament in the Thirties: Politics and Profits* (1977); G. C. Peden, *British Rearmament and the Treasury, 1932–1939* (1979); and F. McDonough, *Neville Chamberlain, Appeasement, and the British Road to War* (1998), which shows the links between domestic and foreign policies. The opposition to appeasement is examined in W. R. Rock, *Appeasement on Trial: British Foreign Policy and Its Critics, 1938–1939* (1966); N. Thompson, *The Anti-Appeasers* (1971); and two books by R. A. C. Parker, *Chamberlain and Appeasement* (1993) and *Churchill and Appeasement* (2000). K. Robbins, *Appeasement* (rev. 1997) provides a brief overview of the debate.

For the 1930s Winston Churchill's *The Gathering Storm* (1948), covering his years in the opposition, the first volume of his indispensable six-volume history, described below, offers valuable perspectives. Biographical studies focusing on British foreign policy include two studies of Anthony Eden, one highly critical, by D. Carlton (1981); the second more defensive, by R. Rhodes James (1987); and a study of Sir Samuel Hoare by J. A. Cross (1977). For Neville Chamberlain there is a study by J. Charmley (1990), somewhat defensive, and a balanced assessment by W. R. Rock (1969).

Among the several impressive studies that examine British foreign policy in long-range perspective are F. S. Northedge, *The Troubled Giant: Britain among the Great Powers, 1916–1939* (1966); P. Kennedy, *The Realities behind Diplomacy: Background Influences on British External Policy, 1865–1980* (1983); and C. J. Bartlett, *British Foreign Policy in the Twentieth Century* (1989).

For French foreign policy in these years the fullest accounts are by A. P. Adamthwaite, *France and the Coming of the Second World War, 1936–1939* (1977) and *Grandeur and Misery: France's Bid for Power in Europe, 1914–1940* (1995), cited earlier. They may be supplemented by R. J. Young, *France and the Origins of the Second World War* (1996). The limited options of the Popular Front are carefully examined in N. Jordan, *The Popular Front and Central Europe: The Dilemmas of French Impotence, 1918–1940* (1992).

There are many books on specific episodes and subjects. The German militarization of the Rhineland is examined in J. T. Emerson, *The Rhineland Crisis, 7 March 1936* (1977). On the annexation of Austria, one may read J. Gehl, *Austria, Germany and the Anschluss, 1931–1938* (1963) and D. Wagner and G. Tomkowitz, *Anschluss: The Week Hitler Seized Vienna* (1971). For Munich the best detailed account is T. Taylor, *Munich: The Price of Peace* (1978), but there are informative essays in I. Lukes and E. Goldstein (eds.), *The Munich Crisis, 1938: Prelude to World War II* (1999); and the Soviet response is examined in H. Ragsdale, *The Soviets, the Munich Crisis, and the Coming of World War II* (2004). G. A. Craig and F. Gilbert (eds.), *The Diplomats, 1919–1938* (1953, 1994) includes valuable chapters on the individuals who helped make foreign policy in the era.

Studies focusing on eastern Europe include A. Cienciala, *Poland and the Western Powers, 1938–1939* (1968); S. Newman, *March 1939: The British Guarantee to Poland* (1976); and A. J. Prazmowska, *Britain, Poland, and the Eastern Front, 1939* (1987). The origins and subsequent history of the German-Soviet Pact of August 23, 1939, are recounted in A. Read and D. Fisher, *The Deadly Embrace: Hitler, Stalin and the Nazi Soviet Pact, 1939–1941* (1989).

The role of the United States in these years is traced in two comprehensive volumes by W. L. Langer and S. E. Gleason, *The Challenge to Isolation, 1937–1940* (1952, 1964) and *The Undeclared War, 1940–1941* (1953, 1968). Other important studies include C. A. MacDonald, *The United States, Britain, and Appeasement, 1930–1939* (1981); D. Reynolds, *The Creation of the Anglo-American Alliance, 1937–1941* (1982); and W. R. Rock, *Chamberlain and Roosevelt: British Foreign Policy and the United States, 1937–1940* (1989). The most informative study of Roosevelt's foreign policy, sympathetic yet critical, is R. Dallek, *Franklin D. Roosevelt and American Foreign Policy, 1932–1945* (1979, 1995). For the war years it may be supplemented by J. M. Burns, *Roosevelt: The Soldier of Freedom* (1970); F. Marks, *Wind over Sand: The Diplomacy of Franklin Roosevelt* (1988); and W. F. Kimball, *The Juggler: Franklin Roosevelt as Wartime Statesman* (1991) and *Roosevelt, Churchill, and the Second World War* (1997).

For the widening of the Japanese invasion of China in 1937 and the later expansion of the European conflict into a global war, one may read A. Iriye, *The Origins of the Second World War in Asia and the Pacific* (1987); and W. Carr, *Poland to Pearl Harbor* (1985). The attack of December 7, 1941, is studied in R. Wohlstetter, *Pearl Harbor: Warning and Decision* (1962); G. W. Prange, *At Dawn We Slept: The Untold Story of Pearl Harbor* (1981); and H. C. Clausen and B. Lee, *Pearl Harbor: Final Judgment* (1992), an updating of an official inquiry first published in 1946.

The War: Military Aspects

Of the numerous narrative histories of the war, the most comprehensive and up-to-date syntheses are J. Keegan, *The Second World War* (1989, 2005) and G. L. Weinberg, *A World at Arms: A Global History of World War II* (rev. 2005). Also available are M. Gilbert, *The Second World War* (rev. 1991); H. P. Willmott, *The Great Crusade* (1990); P. Calvacoressi, G. Wint, and J. Pritchard, *Total War: Causes and Courses of the Second World War* (rev. 1989); R. A. C. Parker, *The Second World War: A Short History* (rev. 1997); A. W. Purdue, *The Second World War* (1999), a concise overview of the main events; S. Tucker, *The Second World War* (2004); and M. Hastings, *Armageddon: The Battle for Germany, 1944–1945* (2004), which focuses on the war's final military campaigns. *The Oxford Companion to World War II* (1995) helps provide encyclopedic coverage of all aspects of the war, and D. Flower and J. Reeves, *The War, 1939–1945: A Documentary History* (1960, 1997) is a helpful anthology. J. Keegan has edited the superb *Times Atlas of the Second World War* (1989), and he analyzes historical and other writings on the war, including the myths and controversies surrounding it, in *The Battle for History: Re-fighting World War II* (1996). W. S. Churchill, *The Second World War* (6 vols.; 1948–1953; 1 vol. abridged, 1959), already mentioned, is a valuable, full-dress history by the historian-statesman written in the grand style, but it should be read in conjunction with other studies now available. M. Gilbert, *Churchill: A Life* (1992) synthesizes Gilbert's monumental official biography (8 vols.; 1966–1989). Of many other biographies K. Robbins, *Churchill* (1992) and J. Keegan, *Winston Churchill* (2002) provide balanced brief studies; J. Lukes, *Churchill: Visionary, Statesman, Historian* (2002) examines Churchill's strategic ideas; and I. S. Wood, *Churchill* (2000) surveys the historical literature on the British prime minister. Churchill's view of the war is also examined in G. Weinberg, *Visions of Victory: The Hopes of Eight World War II Leaders* (2005), an important work that includes analysis of other key figures such as Hitler, Stalin, and Roosevelt.

Many volumes of the detailed official histories of the United Kingdom, Canada, and the United States appeared in the decades after the war. Of special note is S. E. Morison, *The Two-Ocean War* (1963), which summarizes the multivolume U.S. Navy official history. On naval warfare, R. Hough, *The Longest Battle: The War at Sea, 1939–1945* (1986) is also available. Another important aspect is examined in R. J. Overy, *The Air War, 1939–1945* (1980), and the greatest air battle is described in R. Hough and D. Richards, *The Battle of Britain* (1989). C. K. Webster and N. N. Frankland, *Strategic Air Offensive against Germany, 1939–1945* (1961) demonstrates that Allied strategic bombing was less effective than thought at the time.

The Allied penetration and use of the highest secret German military code in Operation Ultra is recounted in F. Winterbotham, *The Ultra Secret* (1974) and R. Lewin, *Ultra Goes to War* (1979). A comprehensive account of cryptography covering all theaters of the war is S. Budiansky, *Battle of Wits: The Complete Story of Codebreaking in World War II* (2000).

The military aspects of France's defeat in 1940 may be approached through A. Horne, *To Lose a Battle: France, 1940* (1969); G. Chapman, *Why France Fell: The Defeat of the French Army in 1940* (1969); A. Beaufre, *1940: The Fall of France* (trans. 1968); A. Shennan, *The Fall of France, 1940* (2000); J. Jackson, *The Fall of France: The Nazi Invasion of 1940* (2003); and E. R. May, *Strange Victory: Hitler's Conquest of France* (2001), a provocative in-depth study, which concludes that the German victory was far from inevitable. The background to the defeat is explored in R. F. Young, *In Command of France: French Foreign Policy and Military Planning, 1933–1940* (1978) and M. S. Alexander, *The Republic in Danger: General Maurice Gamelin and the Politics of French Defence, 1938–1940* (1993). The relationship with Britain is studied in E. M. Gates, *End of the Affair: The Collapse of the Anglo-French Alliance, 1939–1940* (1981). W. L. Shirer, *The Collapse of the Third Republic: An Inquiry into the Fall of France in 1940* (1969) is a thoughtful older account by a reflective journalist; and M. Bloch, *Strange Defeat* (1940) is an incisive memoir by the eminent medievalist later executed as a member of the Resistance. J. Blatt (ed.), *The French Defeat of 1940: Reassessments* (1997) is a valuable set of essays.

The Russo-Finnish conflict of 1939–1940 is narrated in R. W. Condon, *The Winter War* (1972); F. Chew, *The White Death* (1971); and W. Trotter, *A Frozen Hell: The Russo-Finnish Winter War of 1939–1940* (1991, 2000). For the war in eastern Europe after the German invasion one may read A. Clark, *Barbarossa: The Russian-German Conflict, 1941–1945* (1965, 1996); two works by A. Seaton, *The Russo-German War* (1971, 1993), and *Stalin as Military Commander* (1976); and two works by J. Erickson, *The Road to Stalingrad* (1975, 1999) and *The Road to Berlin* (1984, 1999). A. Paul, *Katyn: The Untold Story of Stalin's Polish Massacre* (1991), and G. Stanford, *Katyn and the Soviet Massacre of 1940* (2005) describe the early episode of the war in which over 4,000 Polish officers and soldiers captured in 1939 were executed at Stalin's orders, as confirmed by recently opened archives.

The war in the Pacific is ably presented in C. Bateson, *The War with Japan* (1968); S. Ienaga, *The Pacific War: World War II and the Japanese, 1931–1945* (trans. 1978), by a distinguished Japanese historian; and A. Iriye, *Power and Culture: The Japanese-American War, 1941–1945* (1981), offering important insights. M. Harries and S. Harries, *Soldiers of the Sun* (1992), cited earlier, recounts the story of the imperial army in conquest and collapse, while H. T. Cooke and T. F. Cooke, *Japan at War: An Oral History* (1992) provides unusual eyewitness testimony to Japanese military conduct. A far-reaching study examining the impact of the war on Asia is C. Thorne, *The Far Eastern War: States and Societies, 1941–1945* (1985, 1988). On the last phase in the Pacific, W. Craig, *The Fall of Japan* (1968) helps illuminate debates over how inevitable or imminent Japan's surrender was. This issue is also addressed in the controversial work of T. Hasegawa, *Racing the Enemy: Stalin, Truman, and the Surrender of Japan* (2005), which argues that the Soviet Union's entry into the war against Japan was the key factor in the Japanese decision to surrender.

On the development of the atomic bomb and its first use one may read R. Rhodes, *The Making of the Atomic Bomb* (1986), a remarkably comprehensive account, which may be supplemented by J. S. Walker, *Prompt and Utter Destruction: Truman and the Use of Atomic Bombs against Japan* (rev. 2004). M. Walker, *German National Socialism and the Quest for Nuclear Power, 1939–1949* (1990) describes the German effort to create an atomic bomb.

The War: Social and Economic Impact

For the social and economic impact of the war the best one-volume synthesis is A. S. Milward, *War, Economy, and Society, 1939–1945* (1977). For the British wartime scene, A. Calder, *The People's War: Britain, 1939–1945* (1969) is highly informative, while A. Marwick, *The Home Front: The British and the Second World War* (1977) is a graphic documentary and photographic account. E. S. Beck, *The European Home Fronts, 1939–1945* (1993) is a useful brief synthesis. The wartime Soviet scene is studied in detail in J. Barber and M. Harrison, *The Soviet Home Front, 1941–1945* (1992). Various phases of the American domestic scene are treated in D. M. Kennedy, *Freedom from Fear* (1999), already cited; R. J. Maddox, *The United States and World War II* (1992); and A. M. Winkler, *Home Front U.S.A.* (1986). A spirited treatment of the GI's, civilians-turned-soldiers, appears in various books by S. E. Ambrose, which are synthesized in *The Victors: Eisenhower and His Boys, the Men of World War II* (1998). The American troops stationed in Britain are studied with good humor in D. Reynolds, *The American Occupation of Britain,*

1942–1945 (1995). On the other hand W. L. O'Neill, *America's Fight at Home and Abroad in World War II* (1993), M. C. C. Adams, *The Best War Ever: America and World War II* (1994), and P. Fussell, *Wartime: Understanding and Behavior in the Second World War* (1989) deflate military and civilian leadership.

The entry of women into the wartime labor force is examined in K. Anderson, *Wartime Women: Sex Roles, Family Relations, and the Status of Women during World War II* (1981); L. J. Rupp, *Mobilizing Women for War: German and American Propaganda, 1939–1945* (1978); and the essays in M. R. Higonnet and others, *Behind the Lines: Gender and the Two World Wars* (1987). Women's wartime experiences are also described in N. A. Dombrowski (ed.), *Women and War in the Twentieth Century* (1999); H. Diamond, *Women and the Second World War in France, 1939–1948* (1999); E. Yellin, *Our Mothers' War: American Women at Home and at the Front during World War II* (2004); and J. B. Litoff and D. C. Smith (eds.), *American Women in a World at War* (1997), which includes writings by women who served in the military or worked in war industries.

Many aspects of the home front in Germany are covered in books cited in the previous chapter. That Hitler did not prepare for war in depth because he expected a quick victory emerges from B. A. Carroll, *Design for Total War: Arms and Economics in the Third Reich* (1968) and A. S. Milward, *The German Economy at War* (1965). R. J. Overy, *War and Economy in the Third Reich* (1995), by contrast, argues that the German economy was well prepared for prolonged military production.

Hitler's New Order:
Collaboration and Resistance

The first attempt to study the German occupation of Europe as a whole appeared in A. Toynbee and V. Toynbee (eds.), *Hitler's Europe* (1954). Numerous studies have since appeared on individual countries, many on the French experience.

Among the most informative books on the French responses to the Nazi occupation are J. Jackson, *France: The Dark Years, 1940–1944* (2001), a comprehensive analysis; P. Burrin, *France Under the Germans: Collaboration and Compromise* (trans. 1997); I. Ousby, *Occupation: The Ordeal of France* (1997); and R. Gildea, *Marianne in Chains: Daily Life in the Heart of France during the German Occupation* (2002). A concise overview is available in P. Davies, *France and the Second World War: Occupation, Collaboration and Resistance* (2001). R. O. Paxton, *Vichy France: Old Guard and New Order, 1940–1944* (1972) examines the ideology and policies of the Vichy regime. Paxton and M. R. Marrus, *Vichy France and the Jews* (1981, 1995) demonstrates the French initiative for many actions against the Jews, on which one should also read S. Zucotti, *The Holocaust, the*

French, and the Jews (1993). J. F. Sweets, *Choices in Vichy France: The French under Nazi Occupation* (1986) poignantly demonstrates the complexities of collaboration and resistance in an industrial city. A. S. Milward, *The New Order and the French Economy* (1970) surveys the economic aspects of the regime, while cultural aspects may be approached through A. Kaplan, *Fascism, Literature, and French Intellectual Life* (1986); G. Hirshfeld and P. Marsh (eds.), *Collaboration in France: Politics and Culture during the Nazi Occupation, 1940–1944* (1989); and M. C. Cone, *Artists under Vichy* (1992). For the French postwar struggle to face up to the Vichy trauma one should read H. Rousso, *The Vichy Syndrome: History and Memory in France since 1944* (trans. 1991); E. Conan and H. Rousso, *Vichy: The Ever-Present Past* (trans. 1998); and R. J. Golsan, *Vichy's Afterlife: History and Counterhistory in Postwar France* (2000).

The Resistance in France may be studied in D. Schoenbrun, *Soldiers of the Night: The Story of the French Resistance* (1980); J. F. Sweets, *The Politics of Resistance in France, 1940–1944* (1976); H. R. Kedward, *Resistance in Vichy France* (1978) and *In Search of the Maquis* (1993); and M. L. Rossiter, *Women in the Resistance* (1985). The liberation is dramatically described in R. Aron, *France Reborn* (trans. 1964); related events, in P. Novick, *The Resistance versus Vichy: The Purge of Collaborators in Liberated France* (1969) and H. R. Lottman, *The Purge* (1986). The divisions in France over the purge are studied in M. Koreman, *The Expectation of Justice: France, 1944–1946* (1999). On the trials of collaborators, some of them years later, one may read R. J. Golsan (ed.), *Memory, the Holocaust, and French Justice: The Bousquet and Touvier Affairs* (1996) and A. Kaplan, *The Collaborator: The Trial and Execution of Robert Brassillach* (2000). For the years from the 1930s to liberation, Charles de Gaulle's *War Memoirs* (3 vols.; trans. 1958–1960) are indispensable. De Gaulle's wartime difficulties with London and Washington are described in F. Kersaudy, *Churchill and de Gaulle* (1982) and R. Aglion, *Roosevelt and de Gaulle: Allies in Conflict* (trans. 1988), by one of de Gaulle's diplomats. For de Gaulle, J. Lacouture's biography (2 vols.; trans. 1992) is the outstanding account: Vol. I, *The Rebel, 1890–1944,* and Vol. II, *The Ruler, 1945–1970;* there is a more recent brief account in J. Jackson, *Charles de Gaulle* (2003).

A sampling of studies of other countries under the German occupation include W. Warmbrunn, *The Dutch under German Occupation, 1940–1945* (1963); G. Hirschfeld, *Nazi Rule and Dutch Collaboration, 1940–1945* (trans. 1988); A. S. Milward, *The Fascist Economy in Norway* (1972); R. L. Braham, *The Hungarian Labor Service System, 1939–1945* (1977); J. Gillingham, *Belgian Business and the Nazi New Order* (1977); and M. Mazower, *Inside Hitler's Greece: The Experience of Occupation, 1941–1944*

(1993). The Polish experience is recounted in J. T. Gross, *Polish Society under German Occupation* (1979) and R. C. Lukas, *The Forgotten Holocaust: The Poles under German Occupation, 1939–1944* (1986). N. Davies, *Rising '44: "The Battle for Warsaw"* (2003) recounts the Polish uprising against the Germans, which was crushed in 1944. In its Norwegian setting, collaborationism is illustrated in detail in O. K. Hoidal, *Quisling: A Study in Treason* (1989). The Nazi purloining of Europe's art treasures is described in L. H. Nicholas, *The Rape of Europa: The Fate of Europe's Treasures in the Third Reich and the Second World War* (1994). The role of the Swiss banks in concealing the looted gold used for the Nazi war effort is disclosed in I. Vincent, *Silent Partners: Swiss Bankers, Nazi Gold, and the Pursuit of Justice* (1998).

For the Europewide Resistance there is the informative study by H. Michel, *The Shadow War: The European Resistance, 1939–1945* (trans. 1972); the useful M. R. D. Foot, *Resistance: European Resistance to Nazism, 1940–1945* (1977); and J. Haestrup, *European Resistance Movements, 1939–1945* (rev. 1981), a comprehensive account. The renovative spirit of the Resistance and its message for the postwar world are captured in J. D. Wilkinson, *The Intellectual Resistance in Europe* (1981). The ethical aspects of collaboration and resistance are explored in R. Bennett, *Under the Shadow of the Swastika: The Moral Dilemmas of Resistance and Collaboration in Hitler's Europe* (1999). Books on the German Resistance have been cited in Chapter 20.

The Holocaust

There is a large literature on the grim subject of the Nazis' systematic, willful, mass slaughter of the European Jews during the war years. The most informative and comprehensive study is R. Hilberg, *The Destruction of the European Jews* (3 vols.; rev. 2003), which may be supplemented by the same author's *Perpetrators, Victims, Bystanders: The Jewish Catastrophe, 1933–1945* (1992). The early organization of the Nazi system of mass murder is described in C. R. Browning, *The Origins of the Final Solution: The Evolution of Nazi Jewish policy, September 1939–March 1942* (2004), an outstanding, carefully researched study. Other important studies are M. Gilbert, *The Holocaust: The History of the Jews of Europe during the Second World War* (1986); L. S. Dawidowicz, *The War against the Jews, 1933–1945* (1976), cited earlier; Y. Bauer, *A History of the Holocaust* (1982) and *Rethinking the Holocaust* (2001); and L. Yahil, *The Holocaust: The Fate of European Jewry, 1932–1945* (trans. 1990). A provocative interpretive account is A. J. Mayer, *Why Did the Heavens Not Darken? The "Final Solution" in History* (1989), which sees the root cause in earlier twentieth-century destructiveness. An exhaustive reference work, with contributions by many scholars and with bibliographies in many languages, is I. Gutman (ed.), *Encyclopedia of the Holocaust* (4 vols.; 1990), while the best one-volume coverage is in W. Laqueur (ed.), *The Holocaust Encyclopedia* (2001). M. Gilbert has edited an *Atlas of the Holocaust* (1993).

H. Fein, *Accounting for Genocide: National Responses and Jewish Victimization during the Holocaust* (1979) examines the diversity of the experience in different countries, while R. L. Braham, *The Politics of Genocide: The Holocaust in Hungary* (2 vols.; 1981) is an outstanding study of one country. A key episode of Jewish resistance is recounted in I. Gutman, *The Jews of Warsaw, 1939–1943: Ghetto, Underground, Revolt* (trans. 1982).

Among many studies of the concentration and death camps one should read Primo Levi's moving accounts of his experience, *Survival in Auschwitz* (trans. 1947; 1958) and *The Drowned and the Saved* (trans. 1986). One may also read E. Kogon, *The Theory and Practice of Hell* (1950); T. Des Pres, *The Survivor: An Anatomy of a Life in the Death Camps* (1976); T. Segev, *Soldiers of Evil: The Commandants of the Nazi Concentration Camps* (trans. 1989); and W. Sofsky, *The Order of Terror: The Concentration Camp* (trans. 1997). On the link between the medical profession and the killings R. J. Lifton, *The Death Doctors: Medical Killing and the Psychology of Genocide* (1987) may be read along with H. Friedlander, *The Origins of Nazi Genocide* (1995), focusing on its prewar program of euthanasia for the sick and the handicapped.

For the debate over the origin of the Holocaust, that is, between "intentionalists," who see the genocidal destruction as motivated from the beginning by Hitler and his ideology, and "functionalists," who see it as developing incrementally once the Nazis controlled eastern Europe, the best synthesis is C. Browning, *The Path to Genocide: Essays on Launching the Final Solution* (1992). Hitler's fundamental responsibility is described in G. Fleming, *Hitler and the Final Solution* (1984) and R. Breitman, *The Architect of Genocide: The Final Solution* (1991).

The subject of much discussion and controversy, D. Goldhagen, *Hitler's Willing Executioners: Ordinary Germans and the Holocaust* (1996) argues that ordinary Germans, not only Nazi extremists, participated in the brutal killings because they shared a German legacy of "eliminationist anti-Semitism." On the other hand, C. Browning, *Ordinary Men: Reserve Police Battalion 101 and the Final Solution in Poland* (1992, 1999) demonstrates that peer pressures on the German participants seemed to be more important than any historical legacy of anti-Semitism.

How historians have written about the subject is explored in L. S. Dawidowicz, *The Holocaust and the Historians* (1981); M. R. Marrus, *The Holocaust in History* (1987); and D. Cesarani (ed.), *After Eichman: Collective Memory and the Holocaust since 1961*

(2005). A much discussed essay on the question of responsibility and guilt is H. Arendt, *Eichmann in Jerusalem: A Report on the Banality of Evil* (1963, 1994), written at the time of the trial of the high-ranking bureaucrat who carried out much of the operation. Y. Bauer, *The Holocaust in Historical Perspective* (1978) argues the uniqueness of the episode and disputes later misuses of the word "genocide"; on that issue, one may also read L. Kuper, *Genocide: Its Political Use in the Twentieth Century* (1982).

The acrimonious debate among German historians in the mid-1980s, in which E. Nolte and others sought to mitigate the evils of the Holocaust by comparing it to other twentieth-century atrocities such as those of Stalin, is thoughtfully explored in C. S. Maier, *The Unmasterable Past: History, Holocaust, and German National Identity* (1988) and R. J. Evans, *In Hitler's Shadow: West German Historians and the Attempt to Escape from the Nazi Past* (1989). On a related subject one may read J. Kramer, *The Politics of Memory: Looking for Germany in the New Germany* (1996). Broader efforts to deny or minimize the Holocaust are critically scrutinized in two persuasive books: D. E. Lipstadt, *The Growing Assault on Truth and Memory* (1993) and P. Vidal-Naquet, *Assassins of Memory: Essays on the Denial of the Holocaust* (trans. 1992).

There is a large literature on the failure of the authorities in the United States, Britain, and the Vatican to rescue the doomed European Jews; among the more searching inquiries are B. Wasserstein, *Britain and the Jews of Europe, 1939–1945* (1979); M. Gilbert, *Auschwitz and the Allies* (1981); and R. Breitman, *Official Secrets: What the Nazis Planned, What the British and Americans Knew* (1998). On the role of the Vatican in these years one may read J. F. Morley, *Vatican Diplomacy and the Jews during the Holocaust, 1939–1945* (1980) and M. Phayer, *The Catholic Church and the Holocaust, 1930–1965* (2000), a comprehensive account. Two studies indicting the wartime pope for failure to take more decisive action are J. Cornwell, *Hitler's Pope: The Secret History of Pius XII* (1999) and S. Zucotti, *Under the Very Windows: The Vatican and the Holocaust in Italy* (2001).

For the Nazi atrocities against other ethnic groups in Europe, including Russians, Poles, Gypsies, and others, one may read B. Wytwycky, *The Other Holocaust: Many Circles of Hell* (1986), a brief introduction and the essays in M. Berenbaum (ed.), *A Mosaic of Victims: Non-Jews Persecuted and Murdered by the Nazis* (1992). For the fate of the Gypsies, or Roma, one may read I. Fonseca, *Bury Me Standing: The Gypsies and Their Journey* (1995).

The proceedings of the Nuremberg trials were published by the postwar International Military Tribunal as *Trial of the Major War Criminals before the International Military Tribunal, 1945–1946* (42 vols.; 1947–1949) and *Nazi Conspiracy and Aggression* (8 vols., 2 supplements; 1946–1958). B. F. Smith's two books, *Reaching Judgment at Nuremberg* (1977) and *The Road to Nuremberg* (1981) argue that the trials prevented an anarchic bloodbath and should not be dismissed as merely "victor's justice." Other thoughtful discussions are found in E. Davidson, *The Trial of the Germans: Nuremberg, 1945–1946* (1966); W. Maser, *Nuremberg: A Nation on Trial* (1979); R. E. Conot, *Justice at Nuremberg* (1983); J. E. Persica, *Nuremberg: Infamy on Trial* (1995); and T. Taylor, *The Anatomy of the Nuremberg Trials* (1993), by a chief prosecutor who analyzes deficiencies in the procedures and questions the effectiveness of the trials as a deterrent to later wrongdoing. M. R. Marrus, *The Nuremberg War Crimes Trial, 1945–46: A Documentary History* (1997) provides a concise analysis as well as excerpts from key documents. The trials of the Japanese war leaders are critically analyzed in R. Minear, *Victor's Justice: The Tokyo War Crimes Trial* (1979), which should be supplemented by P. R. Piccigallo, *The Japanese on Trial: Allied War Crimes Operations, in the East, 1945–1951* (1979) and A. C. Brackman, *The Other Nuremberg: The Untold Story of the Tokyo War Crimes Trials* (1987). On national responses in later years to these events one may read an insightful study by I. Buruma, *The Wages of Guilt: Memories of War in Germany and Japan* (1994).

Wartime Diplomacy and Origins of the Cold War

A large literature has emerged stressing the origins of the Cold War in Soviet-American wartime relations. The volumes of H. Feis, sympathetic to the Western leaders, are indispensable as an introduction: *Churchill, Roosevelt, Stalin: The War They Waged and the Peace They Sought* (1957), covering the years from 1941 to the collapse of Germany; *Between War and Peace: The Potsdam Conference* (1960); and on the last phase, *The Atomic Bomb and the End of the War in the Pacific* (1961, 1966). Of special value are G. Smith, *American Diplomacy during the Second World War, 1941–1945* (rev. 1985); J. L. Gaddis, *The United States and the Origins of the Cold War, 1941–1947* (rev. 2000); and the early chapters of the same author's *The Cold War: A New History* (2005); V. Mastny, *Russia's Road to the Cold War* (1979); and R. V. Daniels, *Russia: The Roots of Confrontation* (1985).

On the American use of the atomic bomb one may read M. J. Sherwin, *A World Destroyed: The Atomic Bomb and the Grand Alliance* (1975), an impressive, balanced study, and G. Herken, *The Winning Weapon: The Atomic Bomb in the Cold War, 1945–1950* (1980, 1988). For the debate over the dropping of the bomb, a debate that was renewed on its 50th anniversary, one may read G. Alperowitz and others, *The Decision to Use the Atomic Bomb and the Architecture of an American Myth* (1995), highly critical; while R. V. Maddox, *The Hiroshima Decision Fifty Years Later* (1995) defends the use of the bomb. The continuing moral dilemma is ably presented in R. J. Lifton and G. Mitchell, *Hiroshima in America: Fifty Years of Denial* (1995). The use of the bomb is critically assessed in G. Alperowitz, *Atomic Diplomacy: Hiroshima and Potsdam* (rev. 1994).

On population movements during and following the war there are available J. B. Schechtman, *European Population Transfer, 1939–1945* (1946); E. M. Kulischer, *Europeans on the Move: War and Population Changes, 1917–1947* (1948); M. J. Proudfoot, *European Refugees, 1939–1952* (1957); M. R. Marrus, *The Unwanted: European Refugees in the Twentieth Century* (1985, 2002), cited earlier; and M. Wyman, *DP: Europe's Displaced Persons, 1945–1951* (1989, 1998).

Useful Web Sites

A comprehensive, well-organized listing of Web sites on every aspect of the Second World War may be found at *World War II Links on the Internet*, http://history.acusd.edu/gen/ww2.links.html., which was compiled by S. Schoenherr at the University of San Diego. Additional materials on the war, focusing somewhat on Great Britain, are available at *BBC-History-World War Two*, at www.bbc.co.uk/history/war/wwwtwo/, a component of the informative BBC historical site; and other resources may be consulted at the Belgian-based *Centre for Historical Research and Documentation on War and Contemporary Society*, at www.cegesoma.be/. Readers will find helpful links to diverse sources on France during the war and the Nazi occupation at *Vichy Web*, http://artsweb.gham.ac.uk/vichy/, an excellent site maintained in Great Britain by S. Kitson at the University of Birmingham. The best starting point for Web-based materials on the Holocaust is the *The United States Holocaust Memorial Museum*, at www.ushmm.org/.

22. COLD WAR AND RECONSTRUCTION AFTER THE SECOND WOLRD WAR
The Cold War

Informative narratives for the global history of the post-1945 years include P. Calvacoressi, *World Politics, 1945–2000* (rev. 2001) and D. Reynolds, *One World Divisible: A Global History since 1945* (2000); and for the twentieth century as a whole, J. M. Roberts, *Twentieth Century: The History of the World, 1901 to 2000* (2000); C. Pointing, *The Twentieth Century: A World History* (1999); E. J. Hobsbawm, *The Age of Extremes, 1914–1991* (1994), cited earlier; and W. R. Keylor, *The Twentieth-Century World and Beyond: An International History Since 1900* (rev. 2006). Studies examining the Cold War with new historical perspectives after the collapse of the Soviet Union include M. Walker, *The Cold War: A History* (1994); R. Crockett, *The Fifty Years' War: The United States and the Soviet Union in World Politics, 1941–1991* (1995); S. J. Ball, *The Cold War: An International History, 1947–1991* (1998), and J. L. Gaddis, *The Cold War: A New History* (2005). In addition to other books on the wartime origins of the Cold War, cited in the previous chapter, thoughtful works include D. Sharnik, *Inside the Cold War* (1987); W. LaFeber, *America, Russia, and the Cold War, 1945–2000* (rev. 2002); W. I. Cohen, *America in the Age of Soviet Power, 1945–1991* (1993); and F. J. Harbutt, *The Cold War Era* (2002). J. L. Gaddis has helped to evaluate interpretations of the Cold War on the basis of archival evidence now available from the Soviet files in *We Now Know: Rethinking Cold War History* (1997), much of which confirms many earlier interpretations. For a judicious assessment of the Cold War compromises in Europe one may read M. Trachtenberg, *A Constructed Peace: The Making of the European Settlement, 1945–1963* (1999).

Two early efforts to examine the tensions in broader historical perspective, going back to 1917, are L. Halle, *The Cold War as History* (1967) and A. Fontaine, *History of the Cold War* (2 vols.; trans. 1968–1969). A large revisionist literature blamed American postwar political and economic ambitions or miscalculations for the Cold War. One of the most cogent of such interpretations is W. A. Williams, *The Tragedy of American Diplomacy* (rev. 1988), cited earlier. For guidance to the literature as a whole, including the revisionist accounts, one may turn to J. L. Black, *Origins, Evolution and Nature of the Cold War: An Annotated Bibliography* (1986) and J. W. Young, *The Longman Companion to America, Russia, and the Cold War, 1941–1998* (rev. 1999). E. H. Judge and J. W. Langdon (eds.), *The Cold War: A History through Documents* (1999) provides a helpful selection of key documents.

The transition from the Second World War to the postwar years is explored in R. Douglas, *From War to Cold War, 1942–1948* (1981); J. L. Gormly, *The Collapse of the Grand Alliance, 1945–1948* (1987); H. Thomas, *Armed Truce: The Beginnings of the Cold War, 1945–1946* (1986); and F. J. Harbutt, *The Iron Curtain: Churchill, America, and the Origins of the Cold War* (1986). D. McCullough, *Truman* (1992), is a colorful, carefully researched biography; Secretary of State Dean Acheson is studied in biographies by D. Brinkley, *Dean Acheson: The Cold War Years, 1953–1971* (1992) and J. Chace, *Acheson* (1998), a detached and comprehensive treatment. On the diplomat who helped shape the American containment policy and later regretted the heavy emphasis on military force that it came to assume, one should read G. F. Kennan, *American Diplomacy* (rev. 1984), among his several other books. Kennan, Acheson, and other key American foreign policy figures are studied in W. Isaacson and E. Thomas, *The Wise Men* (1986). On the "Munich syndrome," the

resolve by Truman and others not to repeat the appeasement of the 1930s, one may read G. Rystad, *Prisoners of the Past* (1982), E. R. May, *The Lessons of the Past: The Use and Misuse of History in American Foreign Policy* (1973); and D. Halberstam, *The Best and the Brightest* (1972), principally on the war in Vietnam.

Two informative volumes on the nuclear dangers confronting the postwar world are D. Holloway, *Stalin and the Bomb: The Soviet Union and Atomic Energy, 1939–1956* (1994) and R. Rhodes, *Dark Sun: The Making of the Hydrogen Bomb* (1995), a sequel to his book on the atomic bomb cited in the previous chapter. The revolutionary implications of nuclear weapons for the post-1945 world are discussed in M. Mandelbaum, *The United States and Nuclear Weapons, 1946–1976* (1979) and *The Nuclear Revolution: International Politics before and after Hiroshima* (1981). Additional books on nuclear arms and disarmament will be suggested in later chapters.

The origins, founding, and subsequent history of the United Nations are studied in T. Hoopes and D. Brinkley, *FDR and the Creation of the UN* (1998); S. Meisler, *United Nations: The First Fifty Years* (1998); and S. C. Schlesinger, *Act of Creation: The Founding of the United Nations* (2003). The limitations of international cooperation are astutely assessed in T. M. Franck, *Nation against Nation* (1985) and A. Roberts, *United Nations, Divided World* (1988).

Economic Reconstruction and the Reshaping of the World Economy

Informative studies of postwar economic reconstruction and of the economic growth that followed for close to three decades are H. van der Wee, *Prosperity and Upheaval: The World Economy, 1945–1980* (1986) and P. Armstrong, A. Glyn, and J. Harrison, *Capitalism since World War II: The Making and Breakup of the Great Boom* (1984). They may be supplemented by the analysis of European developments in D. H. Aldcroft, *The European Economy, 1914–2000* (rev. 2001) and by the essays in S. A. Marglin and J. B. Schor (eds.), *The Golden Age of Capitalism: Reinterpreting the Postwar Experience* (1990).

The Bretton Woods monetary arrangements and their evolution are examined in R. Solomon, *The International Monetary System, 1945–1981* (1982) and, in a sequel volume, *Money on the Move: The Revolution in International Finance since 1980* (1999). More general studies, which include valuable information on the postwar era, include S. Pollard, *The International Economy since 1945* (1997); J. Mills, *Managing the World Economy* (2000), a useful survey of the twentieth century as a whole; and R. K. Schaeffer, *Understanding Globalization* (rev. 2005).

Thoughtful surveys of Europe for the first several decades of the postwar era include C. E. Black and others, *Rebirth: A Political History of Europe since World*

War II (rev. 1999); D. Urwin, *A Political History of Europe since 1945* (rev. 1997); P. Thody, *Europe Since 1945* (2000); M. Fulbrook (ed.), *Europe since 1945* (2001), which includes helpful essays on politics, social history, economic changes, and culture; and T. Judt, *Postwar: A History of Europe Since 1945* (2005), an excellent, wide-ranging survey and analysis.

For the American role in reconstruction M. J. Hogan, *The Marshall Plan: America, Britain, and the Reconstruction of Western Europe, 1947–1952* (1987) is outstanding. Other books that merit attention are A. S. Milward, *The Reconstruction of Western Europe, 1945–1951* (1984), which credits European initiative and skills as much as American aid; C. L. Mee, *The Marshall Plan and the Launching of the Pax Americana* (1980); D. W. Ellwood, *Rebuilding Europe: Western Europe, America, and Postwar Reconstruction, 1945–1955* (1992); and the essays in M. Schain (ed.), *The Marshall Plan: Fifty Years After* (2001). An impressive synthesis on postwar reconstruction in all aspects is P. Duignan and L. H. Gann, *The Rebirth of the West: The Americanization of the Democratic World, 1945–1958* (1992). The same authors have extended their analysis of transatlantic relations in *The USA and the New Europe, 1945–1993* (1994).

Some of the social consequences of the economic changes in Europe are also explored in S. Rothman, *European Society and Politics: Britain, France, and Germany* (1976) and G. Therborn, *European Modernity and Beyond* (1995). An important social issue receives attention in three books by S. Castles: *Here for Good: Western Europe's New Ethnic Minorities* (1984); *Migrant Workers in European Societies* (1989); and, with M. J. Miller, *The Age of Migration: International Population Movements in the Modern World* (rev. 2003). Other works on the growing multiculturalism of European societies include G. Dale and M. Cole (eds.), *The European Union and Migrant Labour* (1999) and S. Castles and A. Davidson, *Citizenship and Migration: Globalization and the Politics of Belonging* (2000).

The postwar welfare state is examined in D. E. Ashford, *The Emergence of the Welfare States* (1987). On Keynes and Keynesianism, influential in the managed economies of the early postwar decades, one may read R. Lekachman, *The Age of Keynes* (1966) and books on Keynes cited in Chapter 20. R. Skidelsky, *John Maynard Keynes: Fighting for Britain, 1937–1946* (2000) concludes his three-volume biography, which is also available in a concise one-volume edition (2005). On the postwar role of governments one may also read S. Lieberman, *The Growth of the European Mixed Economies, 1945–1970* (1977) and the essays in A. Graham with A. Seldon (eds.), *Government and Economies in the Postwar World* (1990).

On western European economic integration, A. S. Milward, *The European Rescue of the Nation-State* (rev. 2000) is an outstanding study that explores and interprets the origins of the European Community, while J. Lukacs, *Decline and Rise of Europe* (1965, 1976) provides additional historical background. Informative also for these years are J. Gillingham, *Coal, Steel, and the Rebirth of Europe, 1945–1955: The Germans and the French from Ruhr Conflict to Economic Community* (1991) and D. W. Urwin, *The Community of Europe: A History of European Integration since 1945* (rev. 1995). A good brief introduction is F. Lewis, *Europe: Road to Unity* (1992). For a key architect of European unity, one may turn to M. Bromberger and S. Bromberger, *Jean Monnet and the United States of Europe* (trans. 1969) and D. Brinkley and C. Hacket (eds.), *Jean Monnet: The Path to European Unity* (1991). Additional books on European integration will be cited in Chapter 27.

The Western Countries and Japan after 1945

BRITAIN. K. O. Morgan, *British History since 1945: The People's Peace* (rev. 2001) and D. Childs, *Britain since 1945: A Political History* (rev. 2001) provide good overviews. Britain's loss of primacy and world power is discussed in M. W. Kirby, *The Decline of British Economic Power since 1870* (1981); R. Blake, *The Decline of Power, 1915–1964* (1985); B. Porter, *Britain, Europe, and the World, 1850–1986: Delusions of Grandeur* (1987); and in two incisive analyses by C. Barnett: *The Collapse of British Power* (1986) and *The Pride and the Fall: The Dream and Illusion of Britain as a Great Nation* (1987). That the reasons for decline remained controversial, however, emerges from the debate and discussion in A. Sked, *Britain's Decline: Problems and Perspectives* (1987) and from the essays in B. Collins and K. Robbins (eds.), *British Culture and Economic Decline* (1990).

The best account of the postwar Labour governments and the emergence of the welfare state is K. O. Morgan, *Labour in Power, 1945–1951* (1984), a balanced study with in-depth portraits of Clement Attlee and other key figures; informative also is H. Pelling, *The Labour Governments, 1945–1951* (1984). The creation and consolidation of the welfare state is studied in P. Gregg, *The Welfare State* (1969); and T. O. Lloyd, *Empire, Welfare State, Europe: History of the United Kingdom, 1906–2001* (rev. 2002). For the social impact one may read A. Marwick, *British Society since 1945* (rev. 2003) and A. Sampson, *The Changing Anatomy of Britain* (rev. 1983). Special subjects are explored in two books by Z. A. Layton-Henry: *The Politics of Race in Britain* (1984) and *The Politics of Immigration: "Race" and "Race" Relations in Postwar Britain* (1992).

FRANCE. Fourth and Fifth Republics. A concise survey is available in R. Gildea, *France since 1945* (rev. 2002); and a useful reference tool is W. Northcutt (ed.), *Historical Dictionary of the French Fourth and Fifth Republics, 1946–1991* (1991). The best syntheses for the short-lived Fourth Republic are J. P. Rioux,

The Fourth Republic, 1944–1958 (trans. 1987) and F. Giles, *The Locust Years: The Story of the French Fourth Republic, 1946–1958* (1996). I. M. Wall's two books, *The United States and the Making of Postwar France, 1945–1954* (1991) and *France, The United States, and the Algerian War* (2001), and R. Kuisel, *Seducing the French: The Dilemma of Americanization* (1993) are insightful on American political and cultural influences. Kuisel's *Capitalism and the State in Modern France* (1981), cited in Chapter 20, places government direction of the postwar economy in historical perspective. The reform minister Mendès-France's reform efforts in the early 1950s are sympathetically portrayed in J. Lacouture, *Pierre Mendès-France* (trans. 1984). Incisive on the cultural and political scene are T. Judt, *Past Imperfect: French Intellectuals, 1944–1956* (1992), a critique of the political influence of Sartre and other intellectuals in the early postwar years, and *The Burden of Responsibility: Blum, Camus, Aron and the French Twentieth Century* (1998), on three influential figures who he believes made more positive contributions.

Of the colonial wars that helped bring down the Fourth Republic, the war in Indochina is graphically portrayed in B. B. Fall, *Street without Joy: Indochina at War, 1946–1954* (rev. 1964) and *Hell in a Very Small Place: The Siege of Dien Bien Phu* (1967); and in M. Woodrow, *The Last Valley: Dien Bien Phu and the French Defeat in Vietnam* (2004). Other books on Vietnam and Indochina will be cited in Chapter 25. The ill-fated effort to retain Algeria is described in A. Horne, *A Savage War of Peace: Algeria, 1954–1962* (rev. 1987), a comprehensive account and J. Talbott, *The War without a Name: France in Algeria, 1954–1962* (1980). Subsequent relationships with Algeria are traced in J. Reudy, *Modern Algeria: The Origins and Development of a Nation* (rev. 2005). For the Fifth Republic there are available S. Berstein, *The Republic of de Gaulle, 1958–1969* (trans. 1993), an excellent synthesis; S. Hoffmann's informative *Decline or Renewal? France since the Popular Front: Government and People, 1936–1986* (1988), and M. Larkin, *France since the Popular Front: Government and People, 1936–1996* (rev. 1997). J. Lacouture's authoritative biography of de Gaulle (2 vols.; trans. 1992) has been mentioned in Chapter 21; there are also biographical accounts by B. Ledwidge (1983), D. Cook (1984), A. Shennan (1993), C. Williams (1997), and J. Jackson (2003).

GERMANY. For West Germany during the years of partition an impressive comprehensive narrative is D. L. Bark and D. R. Gress, *A History of West Germany* (2 vols.; rev. 1993). A briefer account is M. Balfour, *West Germany: A Contemporary History* (rev. 1982). For the West German "economic miracle" one may read J. C. Van Hook, *Rebuilding Germany: The Creation of the Social Market Economy, 1945–1957* (2004) and A. Kramer, *The West German Economy, 1945–1955*

(1991); and for the powerful economy that emerged, E. Hartrich, *The Fourth and Richest Reich* (1980). Of special interest is V. R. Berghahn, *The Americanization of West German Industry, 1945–1973* (1986). Konrad Adenauer's accomplishments are assessed in biographical studies by R. Irving, *Adenauer* (2002) and C. Williams, *Adenauer: The Father of the New Germany* (2000); and the career of another important German leader is examined in B. Marshall, *Willy Brandt* (1990).

For West and East Germany, including the relationship of the two states over the four postwar decades of partition, two informative accounts are H. A. Turner, Jr., *Germany from Partition to Reunification* (rev. 1992) and M. Fulbrook, *History of Germany, 1918–2000: The Divided Nation* (rev. 2002). T. Garton Ash, *In Europe's Name: Germany and the Divided Continent* (1993) incisively reassesses Willy Brandt's efforts to improve East-West relations. For the formation and early years of the German Democratic Republic, one should read N. M. Naimark, *The Russians in Germany* (1995). The East German Communist state is examined in P. Major and J. Osmond (eds.), *The Workers' and Peasants' State: Communism and Society in East Germany under Ulbricht* (2002); and the history of Berlin and the Berlin Wall is the subject of A. Tusa, *The Last Division: A History of Berlin, 1945–1989* (1997).

There are provocative insights into the German search for self-understanding in R. Dahrendorf, *Society and Democracy in Germany* (1967); F. Stern, *Dreams and Delusions: The Drama of German History* (1987, 1999); and two books cited earlier: G. A. Craig, *The Germans* (1982) and H. James, *A German Identity, 1770–1990* (1990).

ITALY AND SPAIN. Three insightful studies of Italian political life are F. Spotts and T. Wieser, *Italy: A Difficult Democracy* (1986); J. LaPalombara, *Democracy, Italian Style* (1987); and R. Putman, *Making Democracy Work: Civic Traditions in Modern Italy* (1993). All three describe the paradox whereby the country has known remarkable social and economic progress despite political difficulties. For the postwar years one may also read D. W. Ellwood, *Italy, 1943–1945* (1985); N. Kogan, *A Political History of Postwar Italy* (2 vols.; 1966–1981); P. Ginsborg, *A History of Contemporary Italy: Society and Politics, 1943–1988* (1990, 2003); and the essays in P. McCarthy, *Italy since 1945* (2000). The American role in the early years is assessed in J. L. Harper, *America and the Reconstruction of Italy, 1945–1948* (1986). The special role of the Italian Communist party from liberation to the mid-1980s is examined in J. B. Urban, *Moscow and the Italian Communist Party: From Togliatti to Berlinguer* (1986) and A. De Grand, *The Italian Left in the Twentieth Century: A History of the Socialist and Communist Parties* (1989).

For Spain changes under Franco are well conveyed in J. Grugel and T. Rees, *Franco's Spain* (1997);

the transition to a modern democracy after Franco is described in K. Maxwell and S. Spiegel, *The New Spain: From Isolation to Influence* (1994) and V. Pérez-Diaz, *Spain at the Crossroads* (1999).

JAPAN. One of the best introductions to contemporary Japan is E. O. Reischauer and M. B. Jansen, *The Japanese Today: Change and Continuity* (rev. 1995). Books that analyze Japanese changes after the wartime defeat and occupation include J. W. Dower, *Embracing Defeat: Japan in the Wake of World War II* (1999), an insightful account of the American occupation, and *Japan in War and Peace* (1993); D. Irokawa, *The Age of Hirohito: In Search of Modern Japan* (1998), for the years 1926–1989, a remarkable social history of transition from an agrarian to an industrial society; P. Smith, *Japan: A Reinterpretation* (1997); and H. P. Bix, *Hirohito and the Making of Modern Japan* (2001). For the postwar years one may also turn to P. J. Bailey, *Postwar Japan, 1945 to the Present* (1996), an excellent, brief narrative account. Of special interest are C. Johnson, *MITI and the Japanese Miracle: The Growth of Industrial Policy, 1925–1974* (1982), on the government research and development agency and W. W. Lockwood, *State and Economic Enterprise in Japan* (1986). A critical assessment of the troubled Japanese economy in the 1990s is C. Wood, *The Bubble Economy* (1992).

The Soviet Union: From Stalin to Brezhnev

Of the many volumes for the Stalin years listed in Chapter 18, one of the best assessments is A. B. Ulam, *Stalin: The Man and His Era* (1987). The postwar years and the evolution of the Soviet system after Stalin are explored in A. Nove, *Stalinism and After: The Road to Gorbachev* (rev. 1989); S. Bialer, *Stalin's Successors: Leadership, Stability, and Change in the Soviet Union* (1980) and *The Soviet Paradox: External Expansion, Internal Decline* (1986); and A. Nove, *An Economic History of the USSR, 1917–1991* (rev. 1992). Foreign policy is studied in R. Edmonds, *Soviet Foreign Policy: The Brezhnev Years* (1983) and V. Mastny, *The Cold War and Soviet Insecurity* (1996); and the origins and nature of the Soviet involvement in Afghanistan are studied in M. Urban, *The War in Afghanistan* (rev. 1990).

For the Soviet dissenters one may turn to R. Conquest, *The Politics of Ideas in the USSR* (1967); P. Reddaway, *Russia's Underground Intellectuals* (1970); A. Rothberg, *The Heirs of Stalin: Dissidence and the Soviet Regime, 1953–1970* (1972); and R. T. Tökes (ed.), *Dissent in the U.S.S.R.: Politics, Ideology, and People* (1975). M. Scammell, *Solzhenitsyn* (1984) provides a balanced assessment of the controversial novelist. A. Knight, *The KGB: Police and Politics in the Soviet Union* (rev. 1990) carries the story of the secret police to the mid-1980s. Anti-Semitism in these years may be studied in L. Rapoport, *Stalin's War against the Jews: The Doctors' Plot and the Soviet So-*

lution (1990); B. Pinkus, *The Soviet Government and the Jews, 1948–1967* (1985), cited earlier; and R. O. Freedman (ed.), *Soviet Jewry in the Decisive Decade, 1971–1980* (1987). For the international Communist movement in the postwar years, A. Westoby, *Communism since World War II* (rev. 1989) provides in-depth coverage. An initial effort to assess Soviet archival material is V. Zubak and C. Pleshakov, *Inside the Kremlin's Cold War: From Stalin to Khruschev* (1996).

Eastern Europe under Soviet Domination

How communism was imposed on eastern Europe was explored in an early work by H. Seton-Watson, *The East European Revolution* (rev. 1956). The years of Communist domination and the mounting restiveness in eastern Europe are studied in J. Rothschild and N. M. Wingfield, *Return to Diversity: A Political History of East Central Europe since World War II* (rev. 2000) and G. Schöpflin, *Politics in Eastern Europe, 1945–1992* (1993).

For Hungary and the uprising of 1956 one may read P. C. Zinner, *Revolution in Hungary* (1962); B. Kovrig, *Communism in Hungary from Kun to Kádár* (1979); and C. Gati, *Hungary and the Soviet Bloc* (1988). Czechoslovakia as victim, first of Hitler, then of Stalin, is examined in E. Toborsky, *President Eduard Benes: Between East and West, 1938–1948* (1981). The crisis of 1968 is studied in G. Golan, *The Czechoslovak Reform Movement: Communism in Crisis, 1962–1968* (1971); K. N. Skoug, Jr., *Czechoslovakia's Lost Fight For Freedom, 1967–1969* (1999), by a former American diplomat who was in Prague at the time; and books by V. Kusin (1971), Z. A. B. Zeman (1969), and K. Dawisha (1984).

For the emergence of communism in Yugoslavia, A. Djilas, *The Contested Country: Yugoslav Unity and Communist Revolution, 1919–1953* (1991) is an outstanding study. Informative on Tito's efforts to govern the multinational state are D. Rusinow, *The Yugoslav Experiment, 1948–1974* (1977); D. Wilson, *Tito's Yugoslavia* (1979); H. Lydall, *Yugoslavia in Crisis* (1989); and J. Ridley, *Tito* (1994). Additional books for the former Yugoslavia and for other East European countries after communism will be described in Chapter 26.

China under Mao

As background to the emergence of communism, and for a sense of the continuing revolution in China in modern times, books cited in Chapters 16 and 19 will also be helpful. One of the best overall histories is J. K. Fairbank and M. Goldman, *China: A New History* (rev. 1998), cited earlier. For the years after 1949 informative overviews are M. Meisner, *Mao's China and After* (rev. 1999) and L. Ditmer, *China's Continuous Revolution: The Post-Liberation Era, 1949–1981* (1987). There are authoritative chapters in the collaborative *Cambridge History of China*, R. MacFarquhar and J. K. Fairbank (eds.), Vol. 15: *The People's Repub-*

lic, published in two parts for the years 1949–1982 (1987, 1992). J. Becker, *Hungry Ghosts: Mao's Secret Famine* (1996) carefully reconstructs the three terrible years of famine 1959–1961 precipitated by Mao's Great Leap Forward. For the upheaval of 1966–1969, R. MacFarquhar, *The Origins of the Cultural Revolution* (3 vols., 1974–1997) is indispensable. Two biographies of Mao are rewarding: P. Short, *Mao: A Life* (2000), detailed, colorful, and comprehensive; and J. D. Spence, *Mao Zedong* (1999), a concise, insightful account. They may be supplemented by Mao's personal physician's revealing memoir, Li Zhisui, *The Private Life of Chairman Mao* (trans. 1994) and by J. Chang and J. Halliday, *Mao: The Unknown Story* (2005), which describes Mao as an exceptionally cruel, ruthless, and personally ambitious figure.

The Korean War

For background J. Matray, *The Reluctant Crusade: American Foreign Policy in Korea, 1941–1950* (1985) is helpful. The fullest inquiry into the origins of the Korean War, openly revisionist, is B. Cumings, *The Origins of the Korean War* (2 vols.; 1981–1990); it may be compared with P. Lowe, *The Origins of the Korean War* (rev. 1997). There are concise narratives of the war in P. Lowe, *The Korean War* (2000) and S. H. Lee, *The Korean War* (2001). The war's strategic significance is examined in W. Stueck, *Rethinking the Korean War: A New Diplomatic and Strategic History* (2004). The Chinese role is studied in S. G. Zhang, *Mao's Military Romanticism: China and the Korean War, 1950–1953* (1995). The military aspects are emphasized in A. Bevin, *Korea* (1987) and J. B. Toland, *In Mortal Combat: Korea, 1950–1953* (1992). An interesting biographical study is D. S. Suh, *Kim Il Sung: The North Korean Leader* (1988). For the two Koreas after the war one may read B. Cumings, *Korea's Place in the Sun* (1997), critical of both Koreas, and D. Oberdorfer, *The Two Koreas: A Contemporary History* (rev. 2001).

Useful Web Sites

Helpful resources for the international history of the postwar era are available at *Cold War Policies*, which, like a previously noted site on the Second World War, is maintained by S. Shoenherr at the University of San Diego, http://history.acusd.edu/gen/20th/coldwar0 .html; this may be supplemented with materials compiled by V. Ferraro at *Documents Relating to American Foreign Policy, The Cold War*, www.mtholyoke .edu/acad/intrel/coldwar.htm, a valuable collection at Mount Holyoke College cited in Chapter 19, and by the useful information at the *Cold War International History Project*, which is one of the numerous programs at the Woodrow Wilson International Center for Scholars, www.wilsoncenter.org/. There are also informative interviews, images, and other sources at *CNN-Cold War*, which was created in conjunction with a documentary series and may be visited at www

.cnn.com/specials/cold.war/. The best gateway to materials on the Soviet Union and all of eastern Europe in this period is the University of Pittsburgh's *Russian and East European Studies Virtual Library*, www.ucis.pitt.eud/reesweb/, which was cited in Chapter 18. Numerous documents and other materials on the postwar history of all the larger European and Asian nations are available at the *Internet Modern History Sourcebook*, www.fordham.edu/halsall/mod/ modsbook.html.

23. POSTCOLONIAL NATIONS IN ASIA AND LATIN AMERICA
Anticolonial Movements and the Breakup of European Empires

Many of the books mentioned in Chapters 16 and 19 should also be consulted for the background to the anticolonial revolutions after 1945. There are useful introductions in two works by R. F. Betts, *Uncertain Dimensions: Western Overseas Empires in the Twentieth Century* (1985) and *Decolonization* (rev. 2004), and in an older work by R. Emerson, *From Empire to Nation: The Rise to Self-Assertion of Asian and African Peoples* (1960). The end of colonial rule is comprehensively treated in F. Ansprenger, *The Dissolution of Colonial Empires* (1989), while informative briefer accounts are available in M. E. Chamberlain, *Decolonization: The Fall of the European Empires* (rev. 1999) and J. Springhall, *Decolonization since 1945* (2001). There is a useful collection of essays by historians in James D. Le Sueur (ed.), *The Decolonization Reader* (2003) and excerpts from the writings of theorists who opposed colonialism in P. Williams and L. Chrisman (eds.), *Colonial Discourse and Post-Colonial Theory* (1994). Books that examine colonial administration in the final phases before independence include M. Perham, *Colonial Sequence, 1930–1949* (1976); R. F. Holland, *European Decolonization, 1918–1981* (1985); F. Furedi, *Colonial Wars and the Politics of Third World Nationalism* (1994); and H. Spruyt, *Ending Empire: Contested Sovereignty and Territorial Partition* (2005). American responses to the breakup of empires are examined in D. Ryan and V. Pungong (eds.), *The United States and Decolonization* (2000) and D. D. Newsom, *The Imperial Mantle: The United States, Decolonization, and the Third World* (2001), which argues that the United States came to be viewed as an imperial nation as the European empires receded. There are vignettes of selected Asian and African nationalist leaders in H. Tinker, *Men Who Overturned Empires: Fighters, Dreamers, and Schemers* (1987). A widely read, impassioned brief for anticolonialism was F. Fanon, *The Wretched of the Earth* (trans. 1963), by a French West Indian physician and political activist.

On nationalism and the emergent nations, many of the books cited in Chapter 11 on the older nationalism should also be consulted. To them should be added

E. Kedourie (ed.), *Nationalism in Asia and Africa* (1971); A. D. Smith: *Nationalism in the Twentieth Century* (1979), *The Ethnic Origins of Nations* (1986), *Nations and Nationalism in a Global Era* (1995), and *Nationalism: Theory, Ideology, History* (2001); and B. Anderson, *Imagined Communities: Reflections on the Origin and Spread of Nationalism* (rev. 1991), cited earlier. A challenging work by D. Chakrabarty, *Provincializing Europe: Postcolonial Thought and Historical Difference* (2000), examines postcolonial efforts to define national cultures in opposition to European cultural traditions.

End of European Empires in Asia

The disintegration of the British empire is studied in J. Darwin, *Britain and Decolonization: The Retreat from Empire in the Post-War World* (1988) and his briefer accounts, *End of Empire* (1991), and *The End of the British Empire: The Historical Debate* (1991); D. A. Low, *Eclipse of Empire* (1991); D. W. McIntyre, *British Decolonization, 1946–1997* (1998); D. Judd, *Empire: The British Imperial Experience from 1765 to the Present* (1996); and J. Lawrence, *The Rise and Fall of the British Empire* (1996). There are valuable essays in Vol. 5 of the *Oxford History of the British Empire*: J. M. Brown (ed.), *The Twentieth Century* (1999). Wartime controversies between Churchill and Roosevelt are skillfully analyzed in W. R. Louis, *Imperialism at Bay: The United States and the Decolonization of the British Empire 1941–1945* (1978). Of special interest for Britain's continuing global role are P. J. Cain and A. G. Hopkins, *British Imperialism: Crisis and Deconstruction, 1914–1990* (1993) and J. G. A. Pocock, *The Discovery of Islands: Essays in British History* (2005), which analyzes Britain's enduring global influence. British and French reactions to the loss of empire are compared in M. Kahler, *Decolonization in Britain and France* (1984).

The Indian nationalist struggle, the British withdrawal from the Indian subcontinent, and the early years of independence are examined in S. Sarkar, *Modern India, 1885–1947* (rev. 1989); H. V. Hodson, *The Great Divide: Britain-India-Pakistan* (rev. 1985, 1997); J. M. Brown, *Modern India: The Origins of an Asian Democracy* (rev. 1994); and A. Read and D. Fisher, *The Proudest Day: India's Long Road to Independence* (1998). For India, and the politics and culture of South Asia in general, one may turn for guidance to S. Wolpert, *A New History of India* (rev. 2004). Biographies of Gandhi and Nehru have been cited in Chapter 19. For the years of independence after August 15, 1947, one may turn to P. Brass, *The Politics of India since Independence* (rev. 1994); S. Tharoor, *India from Midnight to the Millennium* (1997); and G. Das, *India Unbound: The Social and Economic Revolution from Independence to the Global Information Age* (2000). Among the thoughtful assessments of contemporary India are A. T. Embree,

Utopias in Conflict: Religion and Nationalism in Modern India (1990); B. Crossette, *India: Facing the Twenty-First Century* (1993); and S. Khilnani, *The Idea of India* (1998). The resurgence of Hindu nationalism is studied in P. Van der Veer, *Religious Nationalism: Hindus and Muslims in India* (1994); C. Jaffrelot, *The Hindu Nationalist Movement in India* (1997); T. B. Hansen, *The Saffron Wave: Democracy and Hindu Nationalism in Modern India* (1999); and C. Bhatt, *Hindu Nationalism: Origins, Ideologies and Modern Myths* (2001). For an introduction to cultural debates in which Indian theorists have had an important global influence, readers may turn to B. Moore-Gilbert, *Postcolonial Theory: Contexts, Practices, Politics* (1997).

For Pakistan and its founder informative studies are A. Jalal, *The Sole Spokesman: Jinnah, the Muslim League, and the Demand for Pakistan* (1985); S. Wolpert, *Jinnah of Pakistan* (1984); and A. S. Ahmed, *Jinnah, Pakistan, and Islamic Identity* (1997). The failure to integrate East Pakistan with the new state and the secession of Bangladesh are studied in R. Jakan, *Pakistan: Failure in National Integration* (1972). Informative for India, Pakistan, and South Asia in general is S. Bose and A. Jalal, *Modern South Asia: History, Culture, Political Economy* (rev. 2004).

For all East Asia the best introduction is J. K. Fairbank, E. M. Reischauer, and A. M. Craig, *East Asia: Tradition and Transformation* (rev. 1989). For developments in Southeast Asia, the best introduction is D. R. SarDesai, *Southeast Asia, Past and Present* (rev. 2003). A brief thematic survey of culture and politics in the region may be found in M. S. Heidhues, *Southeast Asia, A Concise History* (2000). The war fought by the British in the Malay peninsula is described in R. Jackson, *The Malayan Emergency: The Commonwealth Wars, 1948–1966* (1990). For the British success in attracting the newly independent states to membership in the transformed Commonwealth of Nations, one may read R. J. Moore, *Making the New Commonwealth* (1987).

The French response to anticolonial movements is examined in R. F. Betts, *France and Decolonization* (1991); A. Clayton, *The Wars of French Decolonization* (1994); and E. T. Jennings, *Vichy in the Tropics: Petain's National Revolution in Madagascar, Guadeloupe, and Indochina, 1940–44* (2004). The struggle against the Dutch in Indonesia and the years of independence may be approached through L. De Jong, *The Collapse of a Colonial Society: The Dutch in Indonesia During the Second World War* (2002); A. Vickers, *A History of Modern Indonesia* (2005); and two biographical accounts: J. D. Legge, *Sukarno: A Political Biography* (rev. 2003) and R. E. Elson, *Suharto: A Political Biography* (2001). The American colonial system in Asia is described in S. Karnow, *In Our Image: America's Empire in the Philippines* (1989).

Changing Latin America

Changes in Latin America are examined in T. E. Skidmore and P. H. Smith, *Modern Latin America* (rev. 2005); L. Bethell (ed.), *Latin America since 1930* (1994); and R. Thorp, *Progress, Poverty, and Exclusion: An Economic History of Latin America in the Twentieth Century* (1998). An especially rewarding book is P. H. Smith, *Democracy in Latin America: Political Change in Comparative Perspective* (2005). A helpful reference work is S. Collier and others, *The Cambridge Encyclopedia of Latin America and the Caribbean* (rev. 1992).

The vicissitudes of American policies toward Latin America are explored in L. Langley, *America and the Americas* (1989); R. A. Pastor, *Whirlpool: United States Foreign Policy toward Latin America and the Caribbean* (1992); and W. LaFeber, *Inevitable Revolutions: The United States in Central America* (rev. 1993). Readers will find helpful accounts of the largest nations in R. M. Levine, *The History of Brazil* (1999), B. Fausto, *A Concise History of Brazil* (1999), K. Burton, *The History of Mexico* (2000), and B. R. Hamnett, *A Concise History of Mexico* (1999). An excellent guide, including cultural interactions, is R. H. Holden and E. Zolov (eds.), *Latin America and the United States: A Documentary History* (2000).

Useful Web Sites

A useful Web site on South Asia is *Manas: History and Politics of India*, www.sscnet.ucla/edu/southasia/history/mainhist.html, which is at UCLA. Readers will also find excellent materials on modern India and Pakistan at the *Internet Indian History Sourcebook*, www.fordham.edu/halsall/india/indiasbook.html, a component of the comprehensive Internet site on historical sources at Fordham University. Helpful gateways to materials on modern southeast Asia are available at *Southeast Asia Web*, www.gunung.com/seasiaweb/; and at *East and Southeast Asia: An Annotated Directory of Internet Resources*, http://newton.uor.edu/Departments&Programs/AsianStudiesDept/, a site maintained by R. Y. Eng at the University of Redlands. The best links on modern Latin American history will be found at the *Latin American Network Information Center* (LANIC) at the University of Texas, http://lanic.utexas.edu/, where one finds material on the history and culture of every Latin American country.

24. EMPIRES INTO NATIONS: AFRICA AND THE MIDDLE EAST AFTER THE SECOND WORLD WAR

Readers will find valuable discussions of modern Africa and the Middle East in many of the general books on European empires, anticolonial movements, and postcolonial nationalisms that were cited in Chapter 23. The following works therefore focus on more specific regional and national themes.

A New Africa

To the histories of Africa cited in Chapter 16 should be added the informative J. Iliffe, *Africans: The History of a Continent* (1996). The two best recent surveys of modern African history are F. Cooper, *Africa Since 1940: The Past of the Present* (2002) and P. Nugent, *Africa Since Independence: A Comparative History* (2004). For decolonization two indispensable volumes are P. Gifford and W. R. Louis (eds.), *The Transfer of Power in Africa: Decolonization, 1940–1960* (1982) and *Decolonization and African Independence: The Transfer of Power, 1960–1980* (1988). Good overviews are provided in J. D. Hargeaves, *Decolonization in Africa* (rev. 1996) and H. S. Wilson, *African Decolonization* (1994). An insightful survey for the years 1914 to the present is available in B. Davidson, *Modern Africa: A Social and Political History* (rev. 1994). There is a comprehensive analysis of social changes in F. Cooper, *Decolonization and African Society: The Labor Question in French and British Africa* (1996); and the same historian has examined the legacy of imperial systems in *Colonialism in Question: Theory, Knowledge, History* (2005). Important additional perspectives by African historians are provided in A. A. Mazrui (ed.), *Africa since 1935* (1993). Assessments of the years of independence include B. Davidson, *The Black Man's Burden: Africa and the Curse of the Nation-State* (1992), which sees the Western model of the nation-state as an artificial importation into the continent; C. Young, *The African Colonial State in Comparative Perspective* (1994), stressing the harmful legacy bequeathed by colonialism; G. B. N. Agittey, *Africa in Chaos* (1998), an angry critique of African governments and economic policies by a writer from Ghana; and M. Meredith, *The Fate of Africa: From the Hopes of Freedom to the Heart of Despair* (2005), a wide-ranging survey of postcolonial history. The obstacles to democracy are examined in L. A. Villalón and P. VonDoepp (eds.), *The Fate of Africa's Democratic Experiments: Elites and Institutions* (2005). Francophone Africa is studied in E. Mortimer, *France and the Africans, 1944–1960* (1969) and J. F. Clark and D. E. Gardinier (eds.), *Political Reform in Francophone Africa* (1997). The career of the poet-statesman of Senegal is portrayed in J. G. Vaillant, *Black, French, and African: A Life of Léopold Sédar Senghor* (1990).

The best historical account of South Africa and its peoples is L. Thompson, *A History of South Africa* (rev. 2000), cited in Chapter 16, while a good brief introduction is N. Worden, *The Making of Modern South Africa* (rev. 2000). One may also read F. Welsh, *South Africa: A Narrative History* (1998), informative but somewhat Eurocentric, and R. Ross, *A Concise History of South Africa* (1999). Thoughtful accounts of two brutal episodes are R. R. Lemarchand, *Burundi: Ethnic Conflict and Genocide* (1996); G. Prunier, *The Rwanda Crisis: History of a Genocide* (1996); and M. Mamdani, *When Victims Become Killers: Colonialism, Nativism, and the Genocide in Rwanda* (2001). On Darfur one may read J. Flint and A. de Waal, *A Short History of a Long War* (2006) and G. Prunier, *Darfur: The Ambiguous Genocide* (2005). Among the many studies of the struggle against apartheid are D. Ottoway, *Chained Together* (1992); M. Meredith, *In the Name of Apartheid: South Africa in the Postwar Period* (1989); and three works by A. Sparks, *The Mind of South Africa* (1990), *Tomorrow Is Another Country: The Inside Story of South Africa's Road to Change* (1995), and *Beyond the Miracle: Inside the New South Africa* (2003). A. Sampson, *Mandela: The Authorized Biography* (2000) also merits reading.

The Middle East

Good introductions to the modern history of this complex region of the world include M. Kammrava, *The Modern Middle East: A Political History Since the First World War* (2005); I. Pappé, *The Modern Middle East* (2005), stressing the region's social history; and two previously cited works by J. L. Gelvin, *The Modern Middle East: A History* (2004) and W. L. Cleveland, *A History of the Modern Middle East* (2004). There is also a useful collection of essays in A. H. Hourani, P. Khoury, and M. Wilson (eds.), *The Modern Middle East* (rev. 2004).

Books that examine the variety and complexity of Islam and its political manifestations include H. Munson, Jr., *Islam and Revolution in the Middle East* (1988); E. Swan, *Radical Islam: Medieval Theology and Modern Politics* (rev. 1990); B. Lewis, *The Political Language of Islam* (1988) and *Islam and the West* (1993); J. I. Esposito, *The Islamic Threat: Myth or Reality?* (1992); B. B. Lawrence, *Shattering the Myth: Islam Beyond Violence* (1998); F. Halliday, *Islam and the Myth of Confrontation: Religion and Politics in the Middle East* (2003); and L. Diamond, M. F. Plattner, and D. Brumbert (eds.), *Islam and Democracy in the Middle East* (2003). Two books that examine the ideologies of contemporary religious movements are B. Tibi, *The Challenge of Fundamentalism: Political Islam and the New World Disorder* (rev. 2002) and R. S. Appleby (ed.), *Spokesmen for the Despised: Fundamentalist Leaders of the Middle East* (1997).

For Iraq informative studies include W. R. Polk, *Understanding Iraq* (2005), with informative historical background material; P. Marr, *The Modern History of Iraq* (rev. 2004); M. F. and P. Sluglett, *Iraq since 1958: From Revolution to Dictatorship* (rev. 2001); and S. Khalil [K. Makiya], *Republic of Fear: The Politics of Modern Iraq* (rev. 1998). The Iraqi dictator and the Baath party dictatorship are also studied in E. Karsh and I. Rautsi, *Saddam Hussein: A Political Biography* (rev. 2002).

Three introductions to the history of modern Israel are H. M. Sachar, *A History of Israel* (2 vols.; rev. 1996); M. Gilbert, *Israel A History* (1998); and A. Bregman, *A History of Israel* (2003). Two biographies that help explain the early idealism of Zionism are J. Reinharz, *Chaim Weizmann* (2 vols.; 1985–1993), and S. Teveth, *Ben-Gurion: The Burning Ground, 1866–1948* (1987); there are studies also of Golda Meir by E. Ayres (1969) and P. Mann (rev. 1973). Two books that examine conflicting ideals of labor Zionism, nationalism, and religious conservatism are M. Cohen, *Zion and State: Nation, Class, and the Shaping of Modern Israel* (1987) and Z. Sternhell, *The Founding Myths of Israel: Nationalism, Socialism, and the Making of the Jewish State* (trans. 1998). Insights into ultra-Orthodox pressures are provided in D. Landau, *Piety and Power: The World of Jewish Fundamentalism* (1993).

The Arab-Israeli wars from 1948 to 1973 are traced in R. Ovendale, *The Origins of the Arab-Israeli Wars* (rev. 1999); A. Bregman, *Israel's Wars: A History since 1947* (2002); and in a concise survey by T. G. Fraser, *The Arab-Israeli Conflict* (rev. 2004). Two moving accounts of Israeli-Palestinian tensions are T. L. Friedman, *From Beirut to Jerusalem* (rev. 1991) and D. K. Shipler, *Arab and Jew: Wounded Spirits in a Promised Land* (rev. 2002). Thoughtful studies focusing on the Palestinians are B. Kimmerling and J. S. Migdal, *Palestinians: The Making of a People* (1993); C. P. Smith, *Palestine and the Arab-Israeli Conflict* (rev. 2001); J. L. Gelvin, *The Israel-Palestine Conflict: One Hundred Years of War* (2005), cited in Chapter 19; and two books by Israeli revisionist historians: A. Shlaim, *The Iron Wall: Israel and the Arab World since 1948* (2000) and B. Morris, *A History of the Zionist-Arab Conflict, 1881–1999* (1999), synthesizing his earlier books on Arab-Israeli relations and the Palestinian refugees.

The Revolution in Iran

The revolutionary events in Iran may be studied in N. R. Keddie, *Modern Iran: Roots and Results of Revolution* (rev. 2003); D. Wilber, *Iran Past and Present: From Monarchy to Islamic Republic* (rev. 1981); S. Bakhash, *The Reign of the Ayotollahs: Iran and the Islamic Revolution* (rev. 1990); M. M. Milani, *The Making of Iran's Islamic Revolution* (rev. 1994); and R. Mottahedeh, *The Mantle of the Prophet: Religion and Politics in Iran* (1985, 2000). R. Wright's three books carry the story toward the present: *In the Name of God: The Khomeini Decade* (1989), *Sacred Rage: The Wrath of Militant Islam* (1989), and *The Last Great Revolution: Turmoil and Transformation in Iran* (2000). An informative biography is B. Moine, *Khomeini: Life of the Ayotollah* (2000). For the American involvement one may read J. A. Bill, *The Eagle and the Lion: The Tragedy of American-Iranian Relations* (1988) and K. M. Pollack, *The Persian Puzzle: The Conflict Between Iran and America* (2004), informative for the historical background on Iran and on the years since 1979. The eight-year war between Iran and Iraq is described in D. Hiro, *The Longest War: The Iran-Iraq Military Conflict* (1991) and E. Karsh (ed.), *Iran-Iraq War: Impact and Implications* (1990).

Modernization and Development in the Third World

The impact of modernization is examined historically and comparatively in works that show a growing skepticism about earlier views of how modernity would develop around the world. Examples of this debate appear in I. R. Sinai, *The Challenge of Modernisation* (1964) and *In Search of the Modern World* (1968); L. S. Stavrianos, *Global Rift: The Third World Comes of Age* (1981); T. H. Von Laue, *The World Revolution of Westernization: The Twentieth Century in Global Perspective* (1987), which stresses the destabilizing effects of modernization; A. Y. So, *Social Change and Development: Modernization: Dependency and World System Theories* (1990), which examines three influential views of economic development; and D. K. Fieldhouse, *The West and the Third World: Trade, Colonialism, Dependence, and Development* (1999). J. D. Sachs, *The End of Poverty: Economic Possibilities for Our Time* (2005) is an especially thoughtful book. On the world refugee crisis of the era one may read S. Ogato, *The Turbulent Decade: Confronting the Refugee Crisis of the 1990s* (2005) by the UN High Commissioner at the time.

For development models followed in the post-1945 years, one may also read A. Bagchi, *The Political Economy of Underdevelopment* (1982), an important study; H. W. Arndt, *Economic Development: The History of an Idea* (1987); W. W. Rostow, *Theorists of Economic Growth from David Hume to the Present* (1990); B. L. Billet, *Modernization Theory and Economic Development: Discontent in the Developing World* (1993); M. Wolfe, *Elusive Development* (1996); B. Hettne, *Development Theory and the Three Worlds* (rev. 1995); L. E. Harrison, *Underdevelopment Is a State of Mind* (rev. 2000); R. D. Stone, *The Nature of Development* (1992); and A. Sen, *Development as Freedom* (2000). Many of these are critical of efforts to introduce Western-style development in different cultural contexts or without adequate preparation.

For the development experience in Africa one may turn to R. Dumont, *False Start in Africa* (1966); C. Young, *Ideology and Development in Africa* (1982); D. K. Fieldhouse, *Black Africa, 1945–1980: Economic Decolonization and Arrested Development* (1986), which studies both British and French former colonies; L. Cockcroft, *Africa's Way: A Journey from the Past* (1990); and J. Iliffe, *The African Poor: A History* (1987).

For Asia one may read R. A. Scalapini, *The Politics of Development: Perspectives on Twentieth-Century Asia* (1989), an insightful small book, and A. Richards and J. Waterbury, *A Political Economy of the Middle East* (rev. 1996). Available also are J. Mayall and A. Payne (eds.), *The Fallacies of Hope: The Post-Colonial Record of the Commonwealth Third World* (1991) and T. Kemp, *Industrialization in the Non-Western World* (rev. 1989).

An important, early introduction to the North-South debate over a new international economic order was the report by the Independent Commission on International Development chaired by Willy Brandt: *North-South: A Program for Survival* (1980). It may be supplemented by W. A. Lewis, *The Evolution of the International Economic Order* (1978); A. Fishlow and others, *Rich and Poor Nations in the World Economy* (1978); B. Nossiter, *The Global Struggle for More: Third World Conflicts with the Rich Nations* (1986); and J. W. Warnock, *Politics of Hunger: The Global Food System* (1987). Other themes of the debate emerge in C. Thomas and P. Wilkin (eds.), *Globalization and the South* (1997), which argues that new global economic patterns are adding to global social inequalities; and in two concise, balanced surveys by M. Waters, *Globalization* (rev. 2001); and M. B. Steger, *Globalization: A Very Short Introduction* (2003).

Useful Web Sites

Readers will find useful materials on African and Middle Eastern History at the *Internet African History Sourcebook*, the *Internet Islamic History Sourcebook*; and the *Internet Jewish History Sourcebook*, all of which are available as links at Fordham University's *Internet Modern History Sourcebook*, www.fordham .edu/halsall/mod/modsbook.html. There are also excellent sources and images at the *African Online Digital Library*, www.africandl.org/; and other useful links may be found through the Web sites of Michigan State University's *African Studies Center*, http://africa.msu .edu/, and Stanford University's *Africa South of the Sahara* at www.sul.stanford.edu/depts/ssrg/africa/ guide.html. Links to diverse sources of information on the modern history of all Middle Eastern nations and societies are maintained at *The Middle East Network Information Center*, http://menic.utexas/edu/menic/, a site at the University of Texas.

25. COEXISTENCE, CONFRONTATION AND THE NEW GLOBAL ECONOMY
International Relations: Confrontation and Détente

To the books described in Chapters 21 and 22 that focus on the postwar decades of Soviet-American relations may be added R. Levering, *The Cold War* (1994); S. Brown, *The Faces of Power: United States Foreign Policy from Truman to Clinton* (rev. 1994); and G. A. Craig and F. Loewenheim (eds.), *The Diplomats, 1939–1979* (1994), a valuable set of essays.

How the developing world became involved in the Soviet-Western confrontation is explored in R. J. Barnet, *Intervention and Revolution: The United*

States in the Third World (1968); G. Kolko, *Confronting the Third World: U.S. Foreign Policy, 1945–1980* (1988), critical of U.S. policies; B. D. Porter, *The U.S.S.R. in Third World Conflicts: Soviet Arms and Diplomacy in Local Wars, 1945–1980* (1984); and G. Lundestad, *East, West, North, South: Major Developments in International Politics since 1945* (rev. 2005), by a Norwegian historian.

For the background and nature of Castro's revolution in Cuba one may read L. A. Perez, Jr., *Cuba: Between Reform and Revolution* (rev. 2006); J. M. del Aquila, *Cuba: Dilemmas of a Revolution* (rev. 1994), which includes an account of Castro's military activities in Africa; and M. Merez-Stable, *The Cuban Revolution: Origins, Course, Legacy* (1993). R. E. Quirk, *Fidel Castro* (1993) is a critical biographical assessment. Other biographies by T. Szulc (1986), T. M. Leonard (2004), and B. Skierka (2004) also analyze Castro's life and career. There are good biographies of Che Guevara by L. L. Anderson (1997) and J. Castañeda (1997).

The best introduction to the Kennedy years is M. R. Beschloss, *The Crisis Years: Kennedy and Khrushchev, 1960–1963* (1991). The Bay of Pigs episode is described in T. Higgins, *The Perfect Failure* (1987) and the essays in J. G. Blight and P. Kornbluh (eds.), *The Politics of Illusion: The Bay of Pigs Invasion Reexamined* (1998). The missile crisis of 1962 is studied in L. Brune, *The Missile Crisis* (rev. 1996); G. T. Allison and P. D. Zelikow, *Essence of Decision: Explaining the Cuban Missile Crisis* (rev. 1999); A. L. George, *Awaiting Armageddon: How Americans Faced the Cuban Missile Crisis* (2003); S. M. Stern, *The Week the World Stood Still: Inside the Secret Cuban Missile Crisis* (2005); and A. Fursenko and T. Naftali, *"One Hell of a Gamble": Khrushchev, Castro, and Kennedy, 1958–1964* (1997), by a Russian and an American scholar with access to Khrushchev's papers. The deliberations of Kennedy and his advisers are available in E. R. May and P. D. Zelikow, *The Kennedy Tapes: Inside the White House during the Cuban Missile Crisis* (1998).

On the American relationship with its NATO allies in the Cold War years, one may read R. J. Barnet, *The Alliance* (1983); D. P. Calleo, *Beyond American Hegemony* (1987); and L. S. Kaplan, *NATO and the United States* (rev. 1994).

The Vietnam War

Two studies that place post-1945 events in Vietnam in historical perspective are A. B. Woodside, *Community and Revolution in Modern Vietnam* (1976) and W. J. Duiker, *The Rise of Nationalism in Vietnam, 1900–1941* (1976). The struggle for independence is recounted in J. P. Harrison, *The Endless War: Vietnam's Struggle for Independence* (1989); A. Short, *The Origins of the Vietnam War* (1989); D. R. SarDesai, *Vietnam: The Struggle for National Identity* (rev.

1992); M. B. Young, *The Vietnam Wars, 1945–1990* (1991), a valuable synthesis; and W. J. Duiker, *The Communist Road to Power in Vietnam* (rev. 1996). Duiker has also written a scholarly biographical account of the Vietnamese leader, *Ho Chi Minh* (2000).

The American involvement is skillfully explored in G. McT. Kahin, *Intervention: How America Became Involved in Vietnam* (1986), which perceives the United States as ignoring the nationalist aspects of the war and seeing it as Communist aggression only. American miscalculations are heavily emphasized in D. Halberstam, *The Best and the Brightest* (1972), cited in Chapter 22; L. Berman, *Lyndon Johnson's War* (1989); and D. Kaiser, *American Tragedy: Kennedy, Johnson, and the Origins of the Vietnam War* (2000). R. S. McNamara, *In Retrospect: The Tragedy and Lessons of Vietnam* (1995) looks back with regret on his role as defense secretary from 1961 to his resignation in 1968. A defense of the American involvement as essential to its global containment policy is M. Lind, *Vietnam: The Necessary War: A Reinterpretation of America's Most Disastrous Conflict* (1999).

American military actions are studied in S. Karnow, *Vietnam: A History* (rev. 1994, 1997); R. D. Schulzinger, *A Time for War: The United States and Vietnam, 1941–1975* (1997); L. H. Addington, *America's War in Vietnam* (2000), a concise, informative narrative; and D. L. Anderson, *The Vietnam War* (2005). On the extension of the war under Nixon and Kissinger one may read W. Shawcross, *Kissinger, Nixon, and the Destruction of Cambodia* (1979) and S. Hersh, *The Price of Power* (1983). For Cambodia there are three valuable studies by D. P. Chandler: *The Tragedy of Cambodian History: Power, War, and Revolution since 1945* (1991), *A History of Cambodia* (rev. 2000), and *Brother Number One: Pol Pot* (rev. 1999). An especially insightful book examining Cambodian cultural traditions is A. L. Hinton, *Why Did They Kill? Cambodia in the Shadow of Genocide* (2005). M. van Creveld, *The Transformation of War* (1991) is a searching reassessment of guerrilla warfare and other patterns of modern conflict.

The Nuclear Arms Buildup

There are numerous books on the nuclear arms buildup, the apocalyptic dangers the world has learned to live with, and the contributions of strategic deterrence to the armed peace in the Cold War years. An outstanding exhaustive study is McG. Bundy, *Danger and Survival: Choices about the Bomb in the First Fifty Years* (1988); only gradually, he notes, was it recognized that the bomb could not be thought of as an instrument of war like other weapons. Other counsels on strategy, accepting deterrence but calling for continuing efforts at nuclear arms control, are G. F. Kennan, *The Nuclear Delusion: Soviet-American Relations in the Atomic Age* (1983); S. Zuckerman, *Nuclear Illusion and Reality* (1982); G. Gasteyer,

Searching for World Security (1987); M. Mandelbaum, *The Fate of Nations: The Search for National Security in the Nineteenth and Twentieth Centuries* (1988); and J. Newhouse, *War and Peace in the Nuclear Age* (1989). Another kind of literature has called for a fundamental rethinking about nuclear arms. Representative are J. Schell's two books, *The Fate of the Earth* (1982) and *The Abolition* (1984), both now available in a one-volume edition (2000); the same author's *The Gift of Time: The Case for Abolishing Nuclear Weapons Now* (1998); and F. Dyson, *Weapons and Hope* (1984), by an eminent physicist. A thoughtful contribution to the discussion is J. Finnis, J. M. Boyle, Jr., and G. Grisez, *Nuclear Deterrence, Morality, and Realism* (1987). The worldwide movement for nuclear disarmament is examined in A. Carter, *Peace Movements: International Protest and World Politics since 1945* (1992).

Books that illuminate the successes and failures of détente include R. L. Garthoff, *Détente and Confrontation* (rev. 1994); R. W. Stevenson, *The Rise and Fall of Détente* (1985); and W. Bundy, *A Tangled Web: The Making of Foreign Policy in the Nixon Presidency* (1998), an in-depth critical assessment. Also available are R. D. Schulzinger, *Henry Kissinger: Doctor of Diplomacy* (1989); W. Isaacson, *Kissinger: A Biography* (1992); R. C. Thornton, *The Carter Years: Toward a New Global Order* (1991); and T. G. Patterson, *Meeting the Communist Threat: Truman to Reagan* (1989). For assessments of American foreign policy and the search for security in the perspective of over four decades one should read the important works of J. L. Gaddis, *The Long Peace: Inquiries into the History of the Cold War* (1987), *We Now Know: Rethinking Cold War History* (1997), and *Strategies of Containment: A Critical Appraisal of American National Security During the Cold War* (rev. 2005). T. J. McCormick, *America's Half-Century: United States Foreign Policy in the Cold War and After* (rev. 1995); and N. Friedman, *The Fifty Years' War: Conflict and Strategy in the Cold War* (2000). The collapse of the Soviet Union in 1991 and the altered international scene have brought additional books, cited in Chapter 26.

The World Economy: Global Recession

To books on the global economy as it developed in the first four decades after 1945 may be added W. M. Scammell, *The International Economy since 1945* (rev. 1983); A. G. Kenwood and A. I. Lougheed, *The Growth of the International Economy, 1820–1980* (1983); and S. Pollard, *The International Economy since 1945* (1997). For the multinational corporations as they evolved in this era one may turn to R. Vernon, *Storm over the Multinationals* (1977); and R. J. Barnet and J. Cavanagh, *Global Dreams: Imperial Corporations and the New World Order* (1994). The role of oil in the economy and in global politics is admirably described in D. Yergin, *The Prize: The Epic Quest for Oil, Money, and Power* (1991) and P. R. Odell, *Oil and World Power* (rev. 1986).

The historic link between economic strength and political and military hegemony is traced masterfully in P. Kennedy, *The Rise and Fall of the Great Powers: Economic Change and Military Conflict from 1500 to 2000* (1987), cited earlier; it may be read along with M. Olson, *The Rise and Decline of Nations* (1982). Kennedy's volume and other books in the 1970s and 1980s raised the question of America's relative decline in economic leadership. The Japanese challenge, in particular, was described in C. V. Prestowitz, Jr., *Trading Places: How We Allowed Japan to Take the Lead* (1988). On the challenge from more than one source one may read L. Thurow, *Head to Head: The Coming Economic Battle among Japan, Europe, and America* (1992), which describes the "geo-economic" struggle. The phenomenal economic growth of Hong Kong, Taiwan, Singapore, and South Korea is described in E. F. Vogel, *The Four Little Dragons* (1991); and the role of governments in such economies is examined in R. Wade, *Governing the Market: Economic Theory and the Role of Government in East Asian Industrialization* (rev. 2004). The decline of older American industry is examined in B. Bluestone and B. Harrison, *The Deindustrialization of America* (1982), but the continuing importance of the American economy is emphasized in M. Feldstein (ed.), *The United States in the World Economy* (1988); H. R. Nye, *The Myth of American Decline* (1990); and two books by J. S. Nye, *Bound to Lead: The Changing Nature of American Power* (1990) and *Power in the Global Information Age* (2004).

The impact of the global recession that began in 1974 and the dilemmas it posed for policymakers are studied in several of the books on the global economy cited in Chapter 22; to them should be added L. Anel, *Recession, the Western Economies, and the Changing World Order* (1981); E. S. Einhorn and J. Logue, *Welfare States in Hard Times* (1982); and R. Skidelsky (ed.), *The End of the Keynesian Era* (1977).

In addition to books cited in Chapter 22, the operations, accomplishments, and problems of the European Community may be studied in D. Swann, *The Economics of the Common Market* (rev. 1988) and *European Economic Integration* (1996) and H. Brugmans (ed.), *Europe: Dream, Adventure, Reality* (1987), assessing the first 30 years of West European integration. On progress toward closer unity and the transformation of the European Community (EC) into the European Union (EU) under the Maastricht treaty, good guides are available in two books by J. Pinder, *European Community: The Building of a Union* (rev. 1995) and *The European Union: A Very Short Introduction* (2001); and in T. Bainbridge and A. Teasdale, *The Penguin Companion to European Union* (rev. 2004).

Western Europe:
Politics and Society since 1974

For Britain, Margaret Thatcher's conservative leadership and the changes in Britain in the decade after 1979 are assessed in P. Jenkins, *Mrs. Thatcher's Revolution: The Ending of the Socialist Era* (1988); P. Riddell, *The Thatcher Era and Its Legacy* (rev. 1991); H. Young, *The Iron Lady: A Biography of Margaret Thatcher* (1989); and A. Seldon and D. Collings, *Britain Under Thatcher* (2000). The historical legacy of Conservative rule is examined in E. A. Reitan, *The Thatcher Revolution: Margaret Thatcher, John Major, and Tony Blair, 1979–2001* (2003). Two comparative studies of the conservative efforts in the United States and Britain in the 1980s to curb the welfare state, encourage entrepreneurial spirit, and revive national pride are J. Krieger, *Reagan, Thatcher, and the Politics of Decline* (1986); A. Gamble, *The Free Economy and the Strong State* (rev. 1994); and P. Pierson, *Dismantling the Welfare State? Reagan, Thatcher, and the Politics of Retrenchment* (1994).

For France, Mitterrand's leadership of the Socialist party and his presidency are assessed in J. W. Friend, *Seven Years in France: François Mitterrand and the Unintended Revolution, 1981–1988* (1989) and *The Long Presidency: France in the Mitterrand Years, 1981–1995* (1998); in M. Mclean (ed.), *The Mitterrand Years: Legacy and Evaluation* (1998); and in D. S. Bell, *François Mitterrand: A Political Biography* (2005).

For the evolution of socialism one may read M. Harrington, *Socialism: Past and Future* (1989); S. Padgett and W. Patterson, *A History of Social Democracy in Postwar Europe* (1991); and D. Sasson, *One Hundred Years of Socialism: The West European Left in the Twentieth Century* (1997), cited earlier; and G. Eley, *Forging Democracy: The History of the Left in Europe, 1850–2000* (2002).

On developments in Spain one may read R. Carr and J. P. Fusi-Azpurúa, *Spain: Dictatorship to Democracy* (rev. 1981); P. Preston, *The Triumph of Democracy in Spain* (1986); and K. Maxwell and S. Spiegel, *The New Spain: From Isolation to Influence* (1994). F. J. R. Salvadó, *Twentieth-Century Spain* (1999) places recent events in a wider historical context. For Portugal, the revolution of 1974 and the gradual emergence of political stability are studied in H. G. Ferreira and M. W. Marshall, *Portugal's Revolution: Ten Years On* (1986); T. Gallagher, *Portugal: A Twentieth Century Interpretation* (1983); and the later chapters of D. Birmingham, *A Concise History of Portugal* (rev. 2003).

The Communist World: China after Mao

Several of the volumes cited for the Mao era also describe Deng's program of modernization and liberalization. To these may be added H. E. Salisbury, *The New Emperors: China in the Era of Mao and Deng* (1992), by an insightful journalist; R. Evans, *Deng Xiaoping and the Making of Modern China* (rev. 1997); M. Goldman, *Sowing the Seeds of Democracy: Political Reform in the Deng Xiaoping Era* (1994); and J. Gittings, *The Changing Face of China: From Mao to Market* (2005).

Assessments providing balanced judgments on Deng's reforms, the post-Deng years, and the prospects for democratization since the setbacks at Tiananmen Square are J. B. Starr, *Understanding China: A Guide to China's Economy, History, and Political Structure* (1997); J. Miles, *The Legacy of Tiananmen: China in Disarray* (1997); C. J. Calhoun, *Neither Gods nor Emperors: Students and the Struggle for Democracy in China* (1994); A. J. Nathan, *China's Transition* (1998); B. Gilley, *Tiger on the Brink: Jiang Zemin and China's New Elite* (1999); and R. L. Kuhn, *The Man Who Changed China: The Life and Legacy of Jiang Zemin* (2004). Informative also are the essays in R. MacFarquhar (ed.), *The Politics of China: The Eras of Mao and Deng* (1997) and D. Shambaugh (ed.), *Deng Xiaoping: Portrait of a Chinese Statesman* (1997). One of the most detailed accounts of the setback to democracy at Tiananmen Square in 1989 is J. Wong's colorfully entitled *Red China Blues: My Long March from Mao to Now* (1996). O. Schell and D. Shambaugh (eds.), *The China Reader: The Reform Era* (1999) is an excellent collection of documents and commentaries on recent Chinese politics, society, and economic change.

Useful Web Sites

The *Woodrow Wilson International Centre for Scholars* provides a helpful Web site with materials on all regions of the contemporary world and on themes such as international security and the global economy, accessible through a link to "programs" at www.wilsoncenter.org/. A well-organized Web site, *The Wars for Vietnam*, edited by R. Brigham at Vassar College, http://vietnam.vassar.edu/, offers a concise narrative of major events and links to documents; other materials may be found at *Vietnam Online*, www.pbs.org/wgbh/amex/vietnam/, a Web site created to accompany an excellent documentary film for the Public Broadcasting Service. Current debates on international conflicts and security issues may be explored through the Web site of Stanford University's *Center for International Security and Cooperation*, at http://cisac.stanford.edu/. There are helpful links to resources on the global economy at *Understanding the Face of Globalization: Internet Resource Guide*, www.uwm.edu/Dept/CIE/Resources/globalization/, a site developed by A. Dye at the University of Wisconsin, Milwaukee. Readers will find current information on the European Union and other aspects of contemporary Europe at the *UCLA Center for European and Eurasian Studies*, www.international.ucla.edu/euro/; and additional information is available at the EU Web site, *Europa—The European Union On-Line*, http://europa.eu.int/. There are useful links to materials on contemporary China at the University of Hawaii's *Center for Chinese Studies*, www.chinesestudies hawaii edu/

26. THE INTERNATIONAL REVOLT AGAINST SOVIET COMMUNISM

It is difficult to assess the durable value of the literature dealing with the events and developments of recent years. For new books the reviews and bibliographies published in the periodical and daily press and in the professional journals should be consulted.

The Soviet Union: Crisis, Reform, and Collapse

Efforts to assess the Gorbachev reforms in their historical context include A. Nove, *Glasnost in Action: Cultural Renaissance in Russia* (1989); A. Aslund, *Gorbachev's Struggle for Economic Reform* (rev. 1991); B. Kerblay, *Gorbachev's Russia* (1989); G. Hosking, *The Awakening of the Soviet Union* (1991); A. Brown, *The Gorbachev Factor* (1996), a convincing assessment; and G. W. Breslauer, *Gorbachev and Yeltsin as Leaders* (2002). The final phase of the Cold War is examined in J. F. Matlock, *Reagan and Gorbachev: How the Cold War Ended* (2004), an important work by a former American diplomat. Especially valuable also is J. B. Dunlop, *The Rise of Russia and the Fall of the Soviet Empire* (1993), while M. E. Malia, *The Soviet Tragedy: A History of Socialism in Russia, 1917–1991* (1994), cited earlier, critically evaluates the more than seven decades. F. Furet, *The Passing of an Illusion* (trans. 1999), by a distinguished French historian, assesses the ending of an era in which many in the West and elsewhere were attracted to communism.

The Collapse of Communism and the Dissolution of the Soviet Union

For the events of 1991 and the dissolution of the U.S.S.R., one may turn to D. Remnick, *Lenin's Tomb: The Last Days of the Soviet Empire* (1993), by a perceptive journalist-observer; J. F. Matlock, Jr., *Autopsy on an Empire* (1995), a compelling contribution by the American ambassador at the time; and R. V. Daniels, *The End of the Communist Revolution* (1993). On the ethnic and national tensions that led to the dissolution of the union one may read H. Carrère d'Encausse, *The End of the Soviet Empire: The Triumph of the Nations* (trans. 1993); G. I. Mirsky, *On Ruins of Empire: Ethnicity and Nationalism in the Former Soviet Union* (1997); and R. G. Suny, *The Soviet Experiment: Russia, the U.S.S.R., and the Successor States* (1998).

Assessments of the Yeltsin presidency and efforts at economic reform may be found in R. W. Davies, *Soviet History in the Yeltsin Era* (1997); D. Remnick, *Resurrection: The Struggle for a New Russia* (1997); T. Gustafson, *Capitalism Russian Style* (1997), especially informative for the economy; and A. Shleifer and D. Treisman, *Without a Map: Political Tactics and Economic Reform in Russia* (2000). The suppression of the Chechen rebellion is studied in J. Dunlop, *Russia Confronts Chechnya* (1998) and in M. Evangelista, *The Chechen Wars* (2002).

The Transformation of Central and Eastern Europe, 1989

Several books have already been cited in Chapter 22 for central and eastern Europe in the post-1945 years. The growing restiveness under Soviet domination also emerges from M. Charlton, *The Eagle and the Small Birds: Crisis in the Soviet Union from Yalta to Solidarity* (1984) and G. Schöpflin and N. Woods (eds.), *In Search of Central Europe* (1989); the opposition to the Soviets is also described in M. Pittaway, *Eastern Europe, 1939–2000* (2004).

T. Garton Ash, a British journalist-historian, vividly describes the collapse of the Communist regimes in central and eastern Europe in 1989 as he witnessed and reflected on these events in *The Uses of Adversity: Essays on the Fate of Central Europe* (1989) and *The Magic Lantern: The Revolution of '89 Witnessed in Warsaw, Budapest, Berlin, and Prague* (1990). Other informative studies include Z. A. B. Zeman, *The Making and Breaking of Communist Europe* (1991); the essays in I. Banac (ed.), *Eastern Europe in Revolution* (1992); G. Stokes, *The Walls Came Tumbling Down: The Collapse of Communism in Eastern Europe* (1993); and V. Bunce, *Subversive Institutions: The Design and the Destruction of Socialism and the State* (1999). Of special interest is J. Lévesque, *The Enigma of 1989; the U.S.S.R. and the Liberation of Eastern Europe* (1997), an effort to assess the Soviet Union's reactions.

Careful assessments of the events leading to German reunification are T. Garton Ash, *In Europe's Name: Germany and the Divided Continent* (1993), cited in Chapter 22; K. H. Jarausch, *The Rush to German Unity* (1994); E. Pond, *Beyond the Wall: German's Road to Unification* (1993); C. S. Maier, *The Crisis of Communism and the End of East Germany* (1997), with special insights into the decayed East German economy; and P. Zelikow and C. Rice, *Germany Unified and Europe Transformed: A Study in Statecraft* (1997), with early access to key documents.

A few additional books on the Revolution of 1989 in the central and eastern European countries merit citing. For Poland one may read A. Kemp-Welch, *The Birth of Solidarity* (1991) and J. Harrison, *The Solidarity Decade: Poland, 1980–1991* (1993). For Czechoslovakia there are available B. Wheaton and Z. Kavan, *The Velvet Revolution* (1992); two biographical accounts of its leader, communicating the playwright-statesman's thought and influence: E. Kriscova, *Vaclav Havel: The Authorized Biography* (1993), somewhat uncritical; J. Keane, *Vaclav Havel* (2000), exploring in depth his political career both as dissident activist and as president. An informative survey of Czech history carrying the story toward the present is D. Sayer, *The Coasts of Bohemia: A Czech History* (1999), while E. Stein, *Czecho/Slovakia: Ethnic Conflict, Constitutional Fissure, Negotiated Breakup* (1997) helps explain the peaceful separation of the Czech Republic and Slovakia in 1993. For the revolt against the Romanian dictator one may read N. Ratesh, *Romania: The Entangled Revolution* (1992), an informative brief account, and P. Siani-Davies, *The Romanian Revolution of December 1989* (2005), the best comprehensive study.

The Baltic states, where the independence movements helped catalyze the dissolution of the U.S.S.R., are studied in A. Lieven, *The Baltic Revolution: Estonia, Latvia, Lithuania and the Path to Independence* (1993) and R. J. Misiunas and R. Taagepera, *The Baltic States: Years of Dependence, 1940–1990* (1993), a detailed account of the years under Soviet rule.

The Disintegration of Yugoslavia

To books cited earlier on Balkan history one should add M. Glenny, *The Balkans: Nationalism, War, and the Great Powers, 1804–1999* (2000) and M. Mazour, *The Balkans: A Short History* (2000), an insightful distillation of the complex story. For the background and nature of the Tito years one should read A. Djilas, *The Contested Country: Yugoslav Unity and Communist Revolution, 1919–1953* (1991), cited earlier; R. West, *Tito and the Rise and Fall of Yugoslavia* (1995); and J. R. Lampe, *Yugoslavia as History: Twice There Was a Country* (1996), focusing on the years 1918–1941, the Second World War, and the years 1945–1991.

The events of the 1990s may be followed in T. Judah, *The Serbs: History, Myth and the Destruction of Yugoslavia* (2000), which graphically demonstrates that the breakup was the consequence of demagogic incitement of ethnic animosities, not the ethnic differences themselves; L. Silber and A. Little, *Yugoslavia: Death of a Nation* (1999); and M. Glenny, *The Fall of Yugoslavia: The Third Balkan War* (rev. 1996). The Serb dictator and his regime are studied in R. Thomas, *Serbia Under Milosevic: Politics in the 1990s* (1999), and in D. Bujosevic and I. Radovanovic, *The Fall of Milosevic: The October 5th Revolution* (2003). Additional biographical details are provided in D. Dodier and L. Branson, *Milosevic: Portrait of a Tyrant* (2000); and in A. Lebor, *Milosevic: A Biography* (2002). Secession and the wars that followed are studied in M. Tanner, *Croatia: A Nation Forged in War* (rev. 2001) and N. Malcolm, *Bosnia: A Short History* (rev. 1996).

For the international reactions to the ethnic warfare one may turn to J. Gow, *Triumph of the Lack of Will: International Diplomacy and the Yugoslav War* (1997); W. Bert, *The Reluctant Superpower: United States Policy in Bosnia, 1991–1995* (1997); D. Rohde, *Endgame: The Betrayal and Fall of Srebrenica: Europe's Worst Massacre since World War II* (1997), on the mass slaying of Bosnian Muslims; and R. Holbrooke, *To End a War* (1998), by the American diplomat who helped negotiate the Dayton accords. M. Ignatieff, *The Warrior's Honor: Ethnic War and the Modern Conscience* (1998) reflects on the moral dilemmas the events posed to the international community; and S. J. Kaufman, *Modern Hatreds: The Symbolic Politics of Ethnic War* (2001) and V. R. Gagnon, *The Myth of Ethnic War* (2004) provide additional insights on eastern Europe.

For the suppression of the rebellion in Kosovo one may read N. Malcolm, *Kosovo: A Short History* (1998) and M. Vickers, *Between Serb and Albanian: A History of Kosovo* (1998); and for the American-led NATO air offensive against Serbia, M. Ignatieff, *Virtual War: Kosovo and Beyond* (2000) and T. Judah, *Kosovo: War and Revenge* (2000).

After Communism: Central and Eastern Europe

Insightful books include R. Dahrendorf, *Reflections on the Revolution in Europe* (1991); T. Rosenberg, *The Haunted Land: Facing Europe's Ghosts after Communism* (1995); and R. Skidelsky, *The Road from Serfdom: The Economic and Political Consequences of the End of Communism* (1996). There are also well-informed analyses of central European societies in T. Garton Ash, *History of the Present: Essays, Sketches, and Dispatches from Europe in the 1990s* (1999). The efforts to establish stable democracies are assessed in R. Rose and others, *Democracy and Its Alternatives: Understanding Post-Communist Societies* (1998); P. Juviler, *Freedom's Ordeal: The Struggle for Human Rights and Democracy in Post-Soviet States* (1997); and V. Tismaneanu, *Fantasies of Salvation: Democracy, Nationalism and Myth in Post-Communist Europe* (1998). Some unsavory aspects of the postliberation era are described in P. Hockenos, *Free to Hate: The Rise of the Right in Post-Communist Eastern Europe* (1993).

Useful Web Sites

There are useful links to diverse resources on the recent history of central and eastern Europe and the countries of the former Soviet Union at *REENIC: Russian and East European Network Information Center*, a site at the University of Texas, http://reenic .utexas.edu/reenic/; at the *East Central European Center* of Columbia University, www.columbia.edu/cu/ sipa/REGIONAL/ECE/homepage.html; and at the University of Pittsburgh's *Russian and East European Studies Virtual Library*, www.ucis.pitt.edu/reesweb/, an excellent starting point for links to materials on both the fall of Soviet communism and the later history of the former communist nations in central Europe.

27. THE CHANGING MODERN WORLD
Europe since the 1990s

Books that examine the new configuration of European relationships and the evolving European Union include A. E. Stent, *Russia and Germany Reborn: Unification, the Soviet Collapse, and the New Europe* (1999); E. Pond, *The Rebirth of Europe* (rev. 2002); M. Keens-Soper, *Europe in the World: The Persistence of Power Politics* (1999); and M. Emerson, *Redrawing the Map of Europe* (1999). There are helpful accounts of international cooperation in E. Bomberg and A. Stubb (eds.), *The European Union—How Does it Work*; and D. Dinan, *Europe Recast: A History of the European Union* (2004). T. Judt, *A Grand Illusion? An Essay on Europe* (1996) expresses pessimism on the future of European unity, but he has provided further analysis of this process in his comprehensive *Postwar: A History of Europe since 1945* (2005), cited earlier. The most optimistic view on this subject is the stimulating if not entirely convincing M. Leonard, *Why Europe Will Run the 21st Century* (2005). A fresh overview of Britain in the postwar half-century is presented in H. Young, *This Blessed Plot: Britain and Europe from Churchill to Blair* (1999); and Tony Blair's "new Labour" program is examined in A. Giddens, *The Third Way: The Renewal of Social Democracy* (1998); and M. A. Sully, *The New Politics of Tony Blair* (2000). For Italy three books that examine the unseating of the Christian Democrats in the 1990s and the attempts to deal with the corruption that tarnished the regime include A. Stille, *Excellent Cadavers: The Mafia and the Death of the Italian Republic* (1995); M. Frei, *Italy: The Unfinished Revolution* (1996); and P. McCarthy, *The Crisis of the Italian State* (1995).

Culture, Science, and Thought

Many of the books described in Chapter 15 should be consulted, including H. S. Hughes, *Consciousness and Society: The Reorientation of European Social Thought, 1890–1930* (1958), which examines post-Enlightenment ways of looking at science and the social sciences, and G. L. Mosse, *The Culture of Western Europe* (rev. 1988). An informative survey, focusing especially on the twentieth century, is J. Winders, *European Culture since 1848* (2001).

For distinctions between "modernism" and "postmodernism" in various contexts, one may read S. Toulmin, *Cosmopolis: The Hidden Agenda of Modernity* (1989); Z. Bauman, *Legislators and Interpreters: On Modernity, Post-Modernity, and Intellectuals* (1987); J. McGowan, *Postmodernism and Its Critics* (1991); M. Sarup, *An Introductory Guide to Poststructuralism and Postmodernism* (rev. 1993); and E. Heartney, *Postmodernism* (2001). Newer trends in historical writing are assessed in J. Appleby, L. Hunt, and M. Jacob, *Telling the Truth about History* (1994), cited in the Introduction, and W. Thompson, *What Happened to History?* (2000). There are provocative insights in W. H. McNeill, *The Pursuit of Truth: A Historian's Memoir* (2005). Two helpful surveys are available in C. Butler, *Postmodernism: A Very Short Introduction* (2002); and C. Belsey, *Poststruc-*

turalism: A Very Short Introduction (2002). A postmodern critique of historical studies is developed in K. Jenkins, *Why History?* (1999); while K. Windschuttle, *The Killing of History* (1998) strongly objects to the assault by literary critics, social theorists, and others on more traditional conceptions of historical knowledge. Other works on modern historical thought are cited in the Introduction.

A helpful survey of intellectual trends after the Second World War is R. N. Stromberg, *After Everything: Western Intellectual History since 1945* (1975); the same author has written *Makers of Modern Culture: Five Twentieth-Century Thinkers* (1991), exploring Freud, Einstein, Wittgenstein, Joyce, and Sartre. N. E. Cantor, *The American Century: Varieties of Culture in Modern Times* (1997) is vehemently critical of contemporary cultural trends. A very different critical view appears in the Marxist analysis in F. Jameson, *Postmodernism, or the Cultural Logic of Late Capitalism* (1991) and T. Eagleton, *The Idea of Culture* (2000).

Useful introductions to the professional philosophers are available in J. Passmore, *Recent Philosophers* (rev. 1985) and A. J. Ayer, *Philosophy in the Twentieth Century* (1982). Two recommended biographical accounts of twentieth-century philosophers are C. Moorehead, *Bertrand Russell: A Life* (1993) and R. Monk, *Ludwig Wittgenstein: The Duty of Genius* (1990). Of special interest is J. Maritain, *On the Use of Philosophy* (1961), by an influential Roman Catholic philosopher. The origins and nature of existentialism may be studied in R. C. Solomon, *From Rationalism to Existentialism: The Existentialists and Their Nineteenth-Century Backgrounds* (1972, 2001); R. Aronson, *Camus and Sartre* (2004); A. Cohen-Salal, *Sartre* (trans. 1987); and T. R. Koenig, *Existentialism and Human Existence* (1992). For Michel Foucault, several of whose influential historical works have been cited in the Introduction, an unflattering personal portrait emerges from D. Eribon, *Michel Foucault* (trans. 1991) and J. Miller, *The Passion of Michel Foucault* (1993); his ideas are examined in S. Mills, *Michel Foucault* (2003). Another influential French thinker is described in N. Royle, *Jacques Derrida* (2003). L. E. Cahoone (ed.), *From Modernism to Postmodernism: An Anthology* (rev. 2003), provides a useful collection of readings from key figures in modern and contemporary cultural and intellectual movements The debate on Freud, referred to in Chapter 15, continues with numerous books, among them P. Robinson, *Freud and His Critics* (1993), which defends Freud but explores the challenges to his influence.

Introductions to the complexities of contemporary art are provided in A. Neumeyer, *The Search for Meaning in Modern Art* (trans. 1964); L. Parmesani, *Art of the Twentieth Century: Movements, Theories, Schools, and Trends 1900–2000* (2000); and S. Hunter and J. Jacobus, *Modern Art: Painting, Sculpture, Architecture* (rev. 1985). A. Appel, Jr., *The Art of Celebration: Twentieth-Century Painting, Literature, Sculpture, Photography, and Jazz* (1992), stresses the vitality of contemporary culture, including popular culture; while R. Templin (ed.), *The Arts: A History of Expression in the Twentieth Century* (1991), is informative on both the visual arts and literature.

Western religious thought is explored in J. Macquarrie, *Twentieth-Century Religious Thought* (rev. 2002), and J. C. Livingston, *Modern Christian Thought: From the Enlightenment to Vatican II* (1971). R. N. Bellah, *Beyond Belief: Essays on Religion in a Post-Traditional World* (1970, 1991) explores the major world religions in diverse cultural contexts. The rise and growing strength of religious fundamentalist movements in Judaism, Christianity, and Islam is studied in K. Armstrong, *The Battle for God* (2000); and M. E. Marty, *When Faiths Collide* (2005), examines conflicts among religions in the contemporary world.

The continuing debate between science and religion is studied in S. L. Jaki, *The Road of Science and the Ways to God* (1978); J. H. Brooke, *Science and Religion: Some Historical Perspectives* (1991); and M. H. Barnes, *The Co-Evolution of Religious Thought and Science* (2000). For the profound doctrinal and social changes in contemporary Roman Catholicism one may turn to J. D. Holmes, *The Papacy in the Modern World, 1914–1978* (1981); and E. O. Hanson, *The Catholic Church in World Politics* (1987). For the recent popes there are biographies of John XXIII by M. Trevor (1967) and L. Elliott (1973); of Paul VI by P. Hebblethwaite (1993), a detailed and documented account; and valuable assessments of John Paul II in J. Kwitny, *Man of the Century: The Life and Times of John Paul II* (1998), and in G. O'Connor, *Universal Father: A Life of Pope John Paul II* (2005).

Books on Einstein and early twentieth-century physics have been cited in Chapter 15. Two good introductions are B. L. Cline, *Men Who Made a New Physics* (1965, 1987), cited earlier, and B. Greene, *The Elegant Universe* (1999). A. Pais has followed up his biography of Einstein (1982) with *Niels Bohr's Times: In Physics, Philosophy, and Polity* (1992). For contemporary physics one may turn also to H. C. Von Baeyer, *The Taming of the Atom: The Emergence of the Visible Microworld* (1992) and J. Bernstein, *Quantum Profiles* (1991) and *Cranks, Quarks, and the Cosmos* (1993). A remarkable biographical account of the leading architect of the first atomic bomb is K. Bird and M. J. Sherwin, *American Prometheus: The Triumph and Tragedy of J. Robert Oppenheimer* (2005). Of special interest to the general reader will be L. M. Krauss, *Fear of Physics: A Guide for the Perplexed* (1993).

On the biological revolution, an excellent introduction is S. Jones, *The Language of the Genes: Biology, History and the Evolutionary Future* (1994), while E. F. Keller, *The Century of the Gene* (2000), is informative but somewhat technical. One may also read R. Olby, *The Path to the Double Helix* (1974); H. F. Judson, *The Eighth Day of Creation: The Makers of Revolution in Biology* (1979); and B. Wallace, *The Search for the Gene* (1993). In J. Watson, *The Double Helix: A Personal Account of the Discovery of the Structure of DNA* (rev. 1980), a scientist describes himself and other biologists at work. On the need for communication between scientists and nonscientists, an indispensable book remains C. P. Snow, *The Two Cultures and the Scientific Revolution* (1959; new critical ed., with introduction by S. Collini, 1993). It may be supplemented by B. Appleyard, *Understanding the Present* (1993), on the links of science, philosophy, and society; and F. J. Dyson, *The Sun, the Genome, and the Internet* (1999), by a renowned physicist.

To study modern medicine in perspective one should turn to R. Porter, *The Greatest Benefit to Mankind: A Medical History of Humanity* (1998). The setback to medical science and the challenges to society posed by the appearance of AIDs are studied in M. D. Grmek, *History of AIDs: Emergence and Origin of a Modern Pandemic* (trans. 1990); E. Fee and D. Fox (eds.), *AIDS: The Making of a Chronic Disease* (1991); V. Berridge and P. Strong (eds.), *AIDS and Contemporary History* (1993, 2002); and K. R. Hope, Sr. (ed.), *AIDS and Dvelopment in Africa* (1999), which examines the pandemic's social effects on the continent that has been most affected by the disease. Of special interest for health matters is L. Garrett, *Betrayal of Trust: The Collapse of Global Public Health* (2000).

For space exploration in all its aspects, one should read W. A. McDougall, *The Heavens and the Earth: A Political History of the Space Age* (1985); W. J. Walter, *Space Age* (1992); and W. E. Burrows, *This New Ocean: The Story of the Space Age* (1998), a comprehensive survey. Special dimensions are added in J. S. Lewis and R. A. Lewis, *Space Resources: Breaking the Bonds of Earth* (1987).

Activist Movements: 1968 and Its Legacy

A comprehensive account of the student upheaval of 1968 as a worldwide phenomenon is D. Caute, *The Year of the Barricades: A Journey through 1968* (1988); it may be supplemented by G. Katsiafacis, *The Imagination of the New Left: A Global Analysis of 1968* (1987); T. Gitlin, *The Sixties* (1987); A Marwick, *The Sixties: Cultural Revolution in Britain, France, Italy, and the United States* (1998); M. Kurlansky, *1968: The Year that Rocked the World* (2004); and the essays in C. Fink and others (eds.), *1968: The World Transformed* (1999). The turbulent French scene in 1968 is studied in R. Aron, *The Elusive Revolution* (trans. 1969); A. Touraine, *The May Movement: Revolt and Reform* (trans. 1979); and M. Seidman, *The Imaginary Revolution: Parisian Students and Workers in*

1968 (2004). K. Reader, *The May 1968 Events in France* (1993) includes documents from the period as well as a wide range of historical interpretations. P. Berman, *Power and the Idealists* (2005) sympathetically explores the legacy of 1968 through the career of Joachim Fischer, youthful activist at the time and later German foreign minister.

The Women's Liberation Movement

For the background to the women's liberation movement, the books on the history of women described in the Introduction and in Chapter 15 will also serve as a guide. A thoughtful survey is O. Banks, *Faces of Feminism: A Study of Feminism as a Social Movement* (1981, 1986); J. S. Chafetz and A. G. Dworkin, *Female Revolt: The Rise of Women's Movements in World and Historical Perspective* (1986); and D. Dahlerup (ed.), *The New Women's Movement* (1986). I. Whelehan, *Modern Feminist Thought: From the Second Wave to "Post-Feminism"* (1995) describes the historical development of feminist theories that shaped the modern women's movement; and M. Schneir, *Feminism in Our Time: The Essential Writings: World War II to the Present* (1994), provides a useful collection of influential writings. The links in the United States between feminism and the civil rights movement and the changing status of American women are studied in W. R. Chafe, *The Paradox of Change: American Women in the 20th Century* (rev. 1992). For the European context, good introductions are J. Lovenduski, *Women and European Politics: Contemporary Feminism and Public Policy* (1986) and G. Kaplan, *Contemporary Western European Feminism* (1992); while J. Gelb, *Feminism and Politics* (1990) compares American and European experiences. The British scene is studied in S. Rowbotham, *The Past Is Before Us: Feminism in Action since the 1960s* (1989) and in her impressive comparative study, *A Century of Women: The History of Women in Britain and the United States* (1997). For the United States a recent synthesis with helpful bibliographical guidance is R. Rosen, *The World Split Open: How the Modern Women's Movement Changed America* (2000). For France one may turn to C. Duchen, *Feminism in France: From May '68 to Mitterrand* (1986) and *Women's Rights and Women's Lives in France, 1944–1968* (1994); D. M. Stetson, *Women's Rights in France* (1987); J. W. Scott, *Parité: Sexual Equality and the Crisis of French Universalism* (2005); and a selection of readings in E. Marks and I. De Courtivron (eds.), *New French Feminisms: An Anthology* (1980). A convenient anthology for the German scene is H. Altbach and others (eds.), *German Feminism: Readings in Politics and Literature* (1984); for Italy one may read L. C. Birnbaum, *Liberazione della Donna: Feminism in Italy* (1986).

On women's changing role in various settings and cultures a sampling of additional books would include C. Coquery-Vidrovitch, *African Women: A Modern History* (trans. 1997); N. R. Keddie and B. Baron (eds.), *Women in Middle Eastern History: Shifting Boundaries in Sex and Gender* (1991); M. L. Meriwether and J. E. Tucker (eds.), *Social History of Women and Gender in the Modern Middle East* (1999); L. A. Brand, *Women, the State, and Political Liberalization: Middle Eastern and North African Experiences* (1998); J. Nash and H. I. Safa (eds.), *Women and Change in Latin America* (1986); and F. Miller, *Latin America: Women and the Search for Social Justice* (1991), an impressive study. Valuable comparative assessments are I. Tinker (ed.), *Persistent Inequalities: Women and World Development* (1990) and the insightful A. Sen, *Inequality Reexamined* (1996), by a leading development economist and social philosopher. The failure to achieve promised equality in socialist societies is examined in books on the Soviet Union cited in Chapter 18; to them may be added F. du P. Gray, *Soviet Women: Walking the Tight Rope* (1990). For China one may read J. Stacey, *Patriarchy and Socialist Revolution in China* (1983); the essays in T. E. Barlow (ed.), *Gender Politics in Modern China* (1994), and C. K. Gilmartin (ed.), *Engendering China: Women, Culture and the State* (1994); E. R. Judd, *The Chinese Women's Movement Between State and Market* (2002); and P. Ngai, *Made in China: Women Factory Workers in a Global Marketplace* (2005).

Population, Resources, Environment

One of the best introductions to the global demographic explosion of our times and the pressure on natural resources is J. E. Cohen, *How Many People Can the Earth Support?* (1997), a provocative demographic analysis relating population numbers to living standards; and L. R. Brown, *Outgrowing the Earth: The Food Security Challenge in an Age of Falling Water Tables and Rising Temperatures* (2005) examines the environmental problem of water supplies and global warming. The "fertility collapse" in the West and its social and political implications are studied in M. S. Teitelbaum and J. M. Winter, *A Question of Numbers: High Migration, Low Fertility, and the Politics of National Identity* (1998). The growing proportions of the elderly in the population, especially in industrial countries, is the subject of P. G. Peterson, *Gray Dawn: How the Coming Age Wave Will Transform America—and the World* (1999). The Chinese dilemma is analyzed in E. C. Economy, *The River Runs Black: The Environmental Challenge to China's Future* (2005).

Good introductions to environmental issues are D. Worster (ed.), *The Ends of the Earth: Perspectives on Modern Environmental History* (1988); A. Gore, *Earth in the Balance: Ecology and the Human Spirit* (1992); J. R. McNeill, *Something New Under the Sun: An Environmental History of the Twentieth-Century World* (2000); and J. Hughes, *An Environmental History of the World: Humankind's Changing Role in the*

Community of Life (2001), which describes both the premodern and modern history of human interaction with the environment. Environmentalism is also examined in C. O. Paepke, *The Evolution of Progress: The End of Economic Growth and the Beginning of Human Transformation* (1993); C. Ponting, *A Green History of the World: The Environment and the Collapse of Great Civilizations* (1991); and J. Diamond, *Collapse: How Societies Choose to Fail or Succeed* (2005).

International Conflicts After the Cold War

The end of the Cold War brought a number of thoughtful studies on the changing international scene, among them W. G. Hyland, *The Cold War Is Over* (1991); J. L. Gaddis, *The United States and the End of the Cold War* (1992); *We Now Know: Rethinking Cold War History* (1997); and *The Cold War: A New History* (2005), all cited earlier; and J. Chace, *The Consequences of the Peace: The New Internationalism and American Foreign Policy* (1992). Additional insightful studies include M. Mandelbaum, *The Dawn of Peace in Europe* (1996), and his other books; S. Hoffmann, *World Disorder: Troubled Peace in the Post–Cold War Era* (1999) and *The Ethics and Politics of Humanitarian Intervention* (1996); and M. Howard, *The Invention of Peace: Reflections on War and International Order* (2001). H. Kissinger, *Diplomacy* (1994), and in his three volumes of memoirs, offers historical and other perspectives on international relations from the viewpoint of an influential policymaker.

For the United States the tensions between American national interests and the assumption of international leadership in the contemporary era emerge from these books and from G. Bush and B. Scowcroft, *A World Transformed* (1998), by the former president and his national security adviser. These themes are explored for the Clinton administration in R. W. Haass, *The Reluctant Sheriff: The United States after the Cold War* (1998), and D. Callahan, *Unwinnable Wars: American Power and Ethnic Conflict* (1998). A. J. Bacevich, *American Empire: The Realities and Consequences of U.S. Diplomacy* (2002), describes America's international role as a new form of imperial ascendancy; and Bacevich, a former American military officer, further examines the global political situation in a collection of essays by experts in international relations, Bacevich (ed.), *The Imperial Tense: Prospects and Problems of American Empire* (2003).

China's role in the new era is studied in C. Patten, *East and West: China, Power, and the Future of Asia* (1998), written by the last British governor of Hong Kong, while American relationships with China are studied in J. H. Mann, *About Face: A History of America's Curious Relationship with China, from Nixon to Clinton* (1999).

The continuing nuclear threat is explored in McG. Bundy, W. J. Crowe, Jr., and S. D. Drell, *Reduc-*

ing Nuclear Danger: The Road Away from the Brink (1993); M. van Crevel, *Nuclear Proliferation and the Future of Conflict* (1993); and W. E. Burrows and R. Windrem, *The Dangerous Race for Superweapons in a Fragmenting World* (1994). For terrorism and its implications for contemporary society one may turn to R. E. Rubinstein, *Alchemists of Revolution: Terrorism in the Modern World* (1987); P. Wilkinson, *Terrorism in the Modern World* (1987); B. Hoffman, *Inside Terrorism* (1998), a concise but comprehensive, historically informed account; and C. Townshend, *Terrorism: A Very Short Introduction* (2002). There are insightful essays in W. Gutteridge (ed.), *The New Terrorism* (1986) and W. Reich (ed.), *Origins of Terrorism: Psychologies, Ideologies, Theologies, States of Mind* (1990). American vulnerability is studied in R. A. Falkenrath and others, *America's Achilles Heel* (1998), examining nuclear, biological, and chemical threats. M. Juergensmeyer, *Terror in the Mind of God: The Global Rise of Religious Violence* (rev. 2003) and J. Burke, *Al-Qaeda: The True Story of Radical Islam* (rev. 2004) describe the history of a now well-known religious-based terrorism.

For the Persian Gulf War of 1990–1991 one may read D. Hiro, *Desert Shield to Desert Storm: The Second Gulf War* (1992), excellent on the military aspects; L. Freedman and E. Karsh, *The Gulf Conflict, 1900–1991: Diplomacy and War in the New World Order* (1993), a comprehensive account; and a briefer study in A. Finlan, *The Gulf War 1991* (2003). The dictator's continued hold on power is examined in A. Cockburn and P. Cockburn, *Out of the Ashes: The Resurrection of Saddam Hussein* (1994).

The terrorist attack on America in 2001 is analyzed by F. Halliday in *Two Hours that Shook the World: September 11, 2001: Causes and Consequences* (2002); M. Ruthven, *A Fury for God: The Islamist Attack on America* (2002); M. L. Dudziak (ed.), *September 11 in History: A Watershed Moment?* (2003); and J. Randal, *Osama: The Making of a Terrorist* (2004) describes the Al-Qaeda leader whose terrorist group organized the attack. There is much valuable information in *The 9/11 Commission Report: Final Report of the National Commission on the Terrorist Attacks Upon the United States* (2004), both literate and probing; B. Lawrence has compiled a collection of bin Laden's speeches in *Messages to the World: The Statements of Osama bin Laden* (2005). Books on the Iraq War include G. Packer, *The Assassins' Gate: America in Iraq* (2005); A. Shadid, *Night Draws Near: Iraq's People in the Shadow of America's War* (2005), by a journalist who was in Baghdad in the months after the American invasion; and L. Diamond, *Squandered Victory: The American Occupation and the Bungled Effort to Bring Democracy to Iraq* (2005), by a former advisor to the Coalition Provisional Authority in Iraq. C. Hitchens, *A Long Short War: The Postponed Liberation of Iraq* (2003) describes the war as a much-needed American intervention to depose a brutal dictator, which may be compared with N. Soderberg, *The Superpower Myth: The Use and Misuse of American Might* (2005).

The explosive ethnic tensions in the contemporary world are thoughtfully examined in D. P. Moynihan, *Pandemonium: Ethnicity in International Politics* (1993); W. Pfaff, *The Wrath of Nations: Civilization and the Furies of Nationalism* (1993); and A. D. Smith, *Myths and Memories of the Nation* (2000). Of interest also are M. Juergensmeyer, *The New Cold War? Religious Nationalism Confronts the Secular State* (1993); M. Ignatieff, *Blood and Belonging: Journeys into the New Nationalism* (1994); and M. J. Esman, *An Introduction to Ethnic Conflict* (2004).

A much-discussed, controversial book, S. P. Huntington, *The Clash of Civilization and the Remaking of World Order* (1996), sees future conflicts among civilizations shaped by the world's major historic religions and warns against Western "universalist" missions in international affairs. The complex historical nature of Western culture as opposed to simplistic notions of democracy and market capitalism is well conveyed in D. Gress, *From Plato to NATO: The Ideas of the West and Its Opponents* (1998). Two books exposing the failures of twentieth-century regimes that sought to reshape human society are R. Conquest, *Reflections on a Ravaged Century* (1999), describing the human costs of war and totalitarianism, and J. C. Scott, *Seeing Like a State: How Certain Schemes to Improve the Human Condition Have Failed* (1998). Both may be read in conjunction with Isaiah Berlin's rejection of utopianism and social engineering in *The Crooked Timber of Humanity* (1990, 1998), cited earlier, and his other writings in defense of pluralist liberalism.

Human Rights

On the increasing importance of human rights issues in international affairs readers may find informative historical studies in P. G. Lauren, *The Evolution of Human Rights: Visions Seen* (1999); J. Morsink, *The Universal Declaration of Human Rights: Origins, Drafting, and Intent* (1999); and the essays in Y. Danieli and others (eds.), *The Universal Declaration of Human Rights: Fifty Years and Beyond* (1999). An eloquent statement by a Roman Catholic philosopher is J. Maritain, *The Rights of Man and Natural Law* (1986), cited earlier. W. T. de Bary, *Asian Values and Human Rights* (1998) makes clear that cultural relativism should not affect universal human rights.

A key study examining past and present efforts to judge and punish crimes against humanity and human rights abuses is Y. Beigbeder, *Judging War Criminals: The Politics of International Justice* (1999); other informative books, inspired by events in Bosnia, Rwanda, and elsewhere, include W. Shawcross, *Deliver Us from Evil: Peacekeepers, Warlords, and a World of Endless Conflict* (2000); A. Neier, *War Crimes: Brutality, Genocide, Terror, and the Struggle for Justice* (1999), strongly supportive of international jurisdictions; and M. Minow, *Between Vengeance and Forgiveness: Facing History after Genocide and Mass Violence* (1999), less convinced of the efficacy of international tribunals.

On the question of political justice and retribution by postdictatorial regimes in Europe and elsewhere, a large-scale study is available in N. J. Kritz (ed.), *How Emerging Democracies Reckon with Former Regimes* (3 vols.; 1995). For Europe, informative books on the subject are J. McAdams, *Judging the Past in Unified Germany* (2000); J. Borneman, *Settling Accounts: Violence, Justice, and Accountability in Postsocialist Europe* (1997); and the essays in I. Deák, J. T. Gross, and T. Judt (eds.), *The Politics of Retribution in Europe: World War II and Its Aftermath* (2000).

Modern Society, Information Technology, Globalization

The present and future impact of information technology on contemporary society may be studied in M. Dertouzos, *What Will Be: How the New World of Information Will Change Our Lives* (1997); and F. Cairncross, *The Death of Distance: How the Communications Revolution Is Changing Our Lives* (rev. 2001), an updated edition to keep pace with technological changes.

On the much discussed issue of globalization helpful introductions include T. L. Friedman, *The Lexus and the Olive Tree* (1999), on the gap between modernization and traditional values as well as on attempts to narrow the gap by such instruments as the Internet; and by the same author, *The World Is Flat: A Brief History of the Twenty-First Century* (2005), which describes the contemporary processes of global economic exchange. The debate on globalization continues in P. Kennedy, *Preparing for the Twenty-First Century* (1993); J. N. Rosenau, *Along the Domestic-Foreign Frontier: Exploring Governance in a Turbulent World* (1997), touching on such questions as the erosion of sovereignty; R. Gilpin, *The Challenge of Global Capitalism* (2000), an especially helpful, balanced study; and R. Heilbroner, *Twenty-First Century Capitalism* (1999). Highly critical of efforts to remake the world on Western economic models are W. Greider, *One World, Ready or Not: The Manic Logic of Global Capitalism* (1997); J. Gray, *The Delusions of Global Capitalism* (1999); and E. Luttwak, *Turbo-Capitalism: Winners and Losers in the Global Economy* (1999), the title referring to unregulated market economies. Other illuminating books include D. Yergin, *The Commanding Heights: The Battle Between Government and the Marketplace That Is Reshaping the Modern World* (1998); J. H. Mittleman, *The Globalization Syndrome: Transformation and Resistance* (2000), informative on the opposition to international lending agencies and the World Trade Organization; J. Micklethwaite and A. Wooldridge, *A Future Perfect: The Essentials of Globalization* (2000), which sees the benefits of present trends outweighing the disadvantages; and J. Bhagaviti, *In Defense of Globalization* (2004). In G. Soros, *The Crises of Global Capitalism* (1998) an investment banker–philanthropist argues that the emphasis on free markets has overshadowed social responsibilities.

On the related question of the role played by cultural values in economic development thoughtful analyses include H. De Soto, *The Mystery of Capital: Why Capitalism Triumphs in the West and Fails Everywhere Else* (2000); D. S. Landes, *The Wealth and Poverty of Nations* (1998), an important book cited earlier; and the essays in L. E. Harrison and S. P. Huntington (eds.), *Culture Matters: How Values Shape Human Progress* (2000). The lessons of financial history from the seventeenth century to the present are ably conveyed in E. Chancellor, *Death Take the Hindmost: A History of Financial Speculation* (1999), while financial markets in the United States and elsewhere at the turn of the twenty-first century are shrewdly scrutinized in R. J. Shiller, *Irrational Exuberance* (2000). Studying the financial crises of the 1990s in various parts of the world and the prolonged recession in Japan, P. R. Krugman in *The Accidental Theorist: And Other Dispatches from the Dismal Science* (1998) and *The Return of Depression Economics* (1999) argues for neo-Keynesian expansionist government policies. One of the most discussed books in recent years, F. Fukuyama, *The End of History and the Last Man* (1992), perceptive in some ways, proved to be overly optimistic about the triumph of liberal democracy after the fall of Soviet communism. On predictions in general, R. Heilbroner, *Visions of the Future: The Distant Past, Yesterday, Today, Tomorrow* (1995) explores the expectations of earlier generations about their future and the fate of those expectations. R. D. Germain (ed.), *Globalization and Its Critics* (2000) provides useful writings by economists on recent debates about the international economy.

Useful Web Sites

Useful sites for materials on eastern and western Europe have been noted in earlier chapters, but readers should also visit Brigham Young University's *Center for the Study of Europe*, http://kennedy.byu.edu/partners/CSE/, which provides excellent links to diverse materials on contemporary European history. This site may be supplemented by the resources at *Europa—The European Union On-Line*, http://europa.eu.int/. For the history of women in all parts of the world, the best place to begin is *H-Women Internet Links*, at www.h-net.org/~women/links/. There is helpful information on global population trends, economic development, environmental changes, human rights, and other issues at the Web site of the *United Nations*, www.un.org. Valuable, updated materials on the economic, political, and cultural components of globalization are available at the *Yale Center for the Study of Globalization*, www.ycsg.yale.edu/center/, where readers will also find resources on subjects such as terrorism, international conflicts, health care, and the environment. The Yale Center's Internet publication, *YaleGlobal Online*, http://yaleglobal.yale.edu/, provides current, well-informed perspectives on events and conflicts in all regions of the world.

Dates given after names of rulers and popes are the years of reigns or pontificates; those given for all others are the years of birth and death.

Pronunciation is indicated where it is not obvious. With foreign words the purpose is not to show their exact pronunciation in their own language but to suggest how they may be acceptably pronounced in English. Fully Anglicized pronunciations are indicated by the abbreviation *Angl.* Pronunciation is shown by respelling, not by symbols, except that the following symbols are used for vowel sounds not found in English:

ø   indicates the sound of ö as in Göttingen. To form this sound, purse the lips as if to say *o,* and then say *ay* as in *ate.*

U   indicates the sound of the French *u,* or of German *ü.* To form this sound, purse the lips as if to say *oo,* and then say *ee* as in *eat.*

aN, oN, uN, iN indicate the sounds of the French nasal vowels. Once learned, these are easily pronounced, roughly as follows: For aN, begin to pronounce the English word *on,* but avoid saying the consonant *n* and "nasalize" the *ah* sound instead. For oN do the same with the English *own;* for uN, with the English prefix *un-;* for iN, with the English word *an.*

The sound of *s* as in the word *treasure* is indicated by *zh.* This sound is common in English, though never found at the beginning or end of a word. *igh* always indicates the so-called long *i* as in *high.* The vowel sound of *hoot* is indicated by *oo,* that of *hood* by *ŏo.*

Compared with English, the European languages are highly regular in their spelling, in that the same letters or combinations of letters are generally pronounced in the same way.

Index